# CRITICAL SURVEY OF
# Poetry

## *Fourth Edition*

# British, Irish, and Commonwealth Poets

# CRITICAL SURVEY OF
# Poetry
## *Fourth Edition*

## British, Irish, and Commonwealth Poets

## Volume 1
### Dannie Abse—Sir George Etherege

*Editor, Fourth Edition*
## Rosemary M. Canfield Reisman
*Charleston Southern University*

SALEM PRESS
Pasadena, California
Hackensack, New Jersey

*Editor in Chief:* Dawn P. Dawson

*Editorial Director:* Christina J. Moose    *Research Supervisor:* Jeffry Jensen

*Development Editor:* Tracy Irons-Georges    *Research Assistant:* Keli Trousdale

*Project Editor:* Rowena Wildin    *Production Editor:* Andrea E. Miller

*Manuscript Editor:* Desiree Dreeuws    *Page Desion:* James Hutson

*Acquisitions Editor:* Mark Rehn    *Layout:* Mary Overell

*Editorial Assistant:* Brett S. Weisberg    *Photo Editor:* Cynthia Breslin Beres

*Cover photo:* Margaret Atwood (Bernd Thissen/dpa/LANDOV)

Some of the essays in this work, which have been updated, originally appeared in the following Salem Press publications, *Critical Survey of Poetry, English Language Series* (1983), *Critical Survey of Poetry: Foreign Language Series* (1984), *Critical Survey of Poetry, Supplement* (1987), *Critical Survey of Poetry, English Language Series, Revised Edition*, (1992; preceding volumes edited by Frank N. Magill), *Critical Survey of Poetry, Second Revised Edition* (2003; edited by Philip K. Jason).

∞ The paper used in these volumes conforms to the American National Standard for Permanence of Paper for Printed Library Materials, X39.48-1992 (R1997).

**Library of Congress Cataloging-in-Publication Data**

Critical survey of poetry. — 4th ed. / editor, Rosemary M. Canfield Reisman.

     v. cm.

Includes bibliographical references and index.

   ISBN 978-1-58765-582-1 (set : alk. paper) — ISBN 978-1-58765-588-3 (set : Brit., Irish, Comm. poets : alk. paper) — ISBN 978-1-58765-589-0 (v. 1 : Brit., Irish, Comm. poets : alk. paper) — ISBN 978-1-58765-590-6 (v. 2 : Brit., Irish, Comm. poets : alk. paper) — ISBN 978-1-58765-591-3 (v. 3 : Brit., Irish, Comm. poets : alk. paper)

1. Poetry—History and criticism—Dictionaries. 2. Poetry—Bio-bibliography. 3. Poets—Biography—Dictionaries. I. Reisman, Rosemary M. Canfield.

   PN1021.C7 2011

   809.1'003 — dc22

2010045095

First Printing

PRINTED IN THE UNITED STATES OF AMERICA

# PUBLISHER'S NOTE

*British, Irish, and Commonwealth Poets* is part of Salem Press's greatly expanded and redesigned *Critical Survey of Poetry* Series. The *Critical Survey of Poetry, Fourth Edition*, presents profiles of major poets, with sections on other literary forms, achievements, biography, general analysis, and analysis of the poet's most important poems or collections. Although the profiled authors may have written in other genres as well, sometimes to great acclaim, the focus of this set is on their most important works of poetry.

The *Critical Survey of Poetry* was originally published in 1983 and 1984 in separate English- and foreign-language series, a supplement in 1987, a revised English-language series in 1992, and a combined revised series in 2003. The *Fourth Edition* includes all poets from the previous edition and adds 145 new ones, covering 843 writers in total. The poets covered in this set represent more than 40 countries and their poetry dates from the eighth century B.C.E. to the present. The set also offers 72 informative overviews; 20 of these essays were added for this edition, including all the literary movement essays. In addition, 7 resources are provided, 2 of them new. More than 500 photographs and portraits of poets have been included.

For the first time, the material in the *Critical Survey of Poetry* has been organized into five subsets by geography and essay type: a 4-volume subset on *American Poets*, a 3-volume subset on *British, Irish, and Commonwealth Poets*, a 3-volume subset on *European Poets*, a 1-volume subset on *World Poets*, and a 2-volume subset of *Topical Essays*. Each poet appears in only one subset. *Topical Essays* is organized under the categories "Poetry Around the World," "Literary Movements," and "Criticism and Theory." A *Cumulative Indexes* volume covering all five subsets is free with purchase of more than one subset.

## BRITISH, IRISH, AND COMMONWEALTH POETS

The 3-volume *British, Irish, and Commonwealth Poets* contains 196 poet profiles, arranged alphabetically. For this edition, 13 new essays have been added,

and 9 have been significantly updated with analysis of recently published books or poems.

Each volume begins with a list of Contents for that volume, a Complete List of Contents covering the entire subset, and a Pronunciation Key. The poet essays follow in alphabetical order, divided among the three volumes. The third volume contains the Resources section, which features three tools for interpreting and understanding poetry: "Explicating Poetry," "Language and Linguistics," and "Glossary of Poetical Terms." The "Bibliography," "Guide to Online Resources," "Time Line," "Major Awards," and "Chronological List of Poets" provide guides for further research and additional information on British, Irish, and Commonwealth poets; comprehensive versions appear in *Topical Essays* and *Cumulative Indexes*. The "Guide to Online Resources" and "Time Line" were created for this edition.

*British, Irish, and Commonwealth Poets* contains a Geographical Index of Poets; a Categorized Index of Poets, in which poets are grouped by culture or group identity, literary movement, historical period, and poetic forms and themes; and a Subject Index. The *Critical Survey of Poetry* Series: Master List of Contents identifies poets profiled in *British, Irish, and Commonwealth Poets* as well as poets profiled in other *Critical Survey of Poetry* subsets. The *Cumulative Indexes* contains comprehensive versions of the categorized, geographical, and subject index.

## UPDATING THE ESSAYS

All parts of the essays in the previous edition were scrutinized for currency and accuracy: The authors' latest works of poetry were added to front-matter listings, other significant publications were added to back-matter listings, new translations were added to listings for foreign-language authors, and deceased authors' listings were rechecked for accuracy and currency. All essays' bibliographies—lists of sources for further consultation—were revised to provide readers with the latest information.

The 9 original poet essays in *British, Irish, and Com-*

*monwealth Poets* that required updating by academic experts received similar and even fuller attention: All new publications were added to listings, then each section of text was reviewed to ensure that recently received major awards are noted, that new biographical details are incorporated for still-living authors, and that analysis of works includes recently published books or poems. The updating experts' names were added to essays. Those original articles identified by the editor, Rosemary M. Canfield Reisman, as not needing substantial updating were nevertheless reedited by Salem Press editors and checked for accuracy.

## ONLINE ACCESS

Salem Press provides access to its award-winning content both in traditional, printed form and online. Any school or library that purchases *British, Irish, and Commonwealth Poets* is entitled to free, complimentary access to Salem's fully supported online version of the content. Features include a simple intuitive interface, user profile areas for students and patrons, sophisticated search functionality, and complete context, including appendixes. Access is available through a code printed on the inside cover of the first volume, and that access is unlimited and immediate. Our online customer service representatives, at (800) 221-1592, are happy to help with any questions. E-books are also available.

## ORGANIZATION OF POET ESSAYS

The poet essays in *British, Irish, and Commonwealth Poets* vary in length, with none shorter than 2,000 words and most significantly longer. Poet essays are arranged alphabetically, under the name by which the poet is best known. The format of the essays is standardized to allow predictable and easy access to the types of information of interest to a variety of users. Each poet essay contains ready-reference top matter, including full birth and (where applicable) death data, any alternate names used by the poet, and a list of Principal Poetry, followed by the main text, which is divided into Other Literary Forms, Achievements, Biography, and Analysis. A list of Other Major Works, a Bibliography, and bylines complete the essay.

- *Principal poetry* lists the titles of the author's major collections of poetry in chronological order, by date of original appearance. If an author has published works in another language and the works have been translated into English, the titles and dates of the first translations are provided.

- *Other literary forms* describes the author's work in other genres and notes whether the author is known primarily as a poet or has achieved equal or greater fame in another genre. If the poet's last name is unlikely to be familiar to most users, phonetic pronunciation is provided in parentheses after his or her name. A Pronunciation Key appears at the beginning of all volumes.

- *Achievements* lists honors, awards, and other tangible recognitions, as well as a summation of the writer's influence and contributions to poetry and literature, where appropriate.

- *Biography* provides a condensed biographical sketch with vital information from birth through (if applicable) death or the author's latest activities.

- *Analysis* presents an overview of the poet's themes, techniques, style, and development, leading into subsections on major poetry collections, poems, or aspects of the person's work as a poet. Although the majority of poets in *British, Irish, and Commonwealth Poets* wrote in English only, some of the profiled poets have written works in other languages. As an aid to students, those foreign-language titles that have not yet appeared in translation are followed by a "literal translation" in roman and lowercase letters when these titles are mentioned in the text. If a title has been published in English, the English-language title is used in the text.

- *Other major works* contains the poet's principal works in other genres, listed by genre and by year of publication within each genre. If applicable, the dates and titles of English translations of foreign-language works are listed.

- *Bibliography* lists secondary print sources for further study, annotated to assist users in evaluating focus and usefulness.

- *Byline* notes the original contributor of the essay. If the essay was updated, the name of the most recent updater appears in a separate line and previous updaters appear with the name of the original contributor.

## APPENDIXES

The "Resources" section in volume 3 provides tools for further research and points of access to the wealth of information contained in *British, Irish, and Commonwealth Poets*.

- *Explicating Poetry* identifies the basics of versification, from meter to rhyme, in an attempt to demonstrate how sound, rhythm, and image fuse to support meaning.
- *Language and Linguistics* looks at the origins of language and at linguistics as a discipline, as well as how the features of a particular language affect the type of poetry created.
- *Glossary of Poetical Terms* is a lexicon of more than 150 literary terms pertinent to the study of poetry.
- *Bibliography* identifies general reference works and other secondary sources that pertain to British, Irish, and Commonwealth poets.
- *Guide to Online Resources*, new to this edition, provides Web sites pertaining to poetry and British, Irish, and Commonwealth poets.
- *Time Line*, new to this edition, lists major milestones and events in poetry and literature in Great Britain, Ireland, and the Commonwealth nations in the order in which they occurred.
- *Major Awards* lists the recipients of major poetry-specific awards in Great Britain, Ireland, and the Commonwealth nations and general awards where applicable to poets or poetry, from inception of the award to the present day.
- *Chronological List of Poets* lists all 196 poets covered in *British, Irish, and Commonwealth Poets* by year of birth, in chronological order.

## INDEXES

The Geographical Index of Poets lists all poets covered in *British, Irish, and Commonwealth Poets* by country or region. The Categorized Index of Poets lists the poets profiled in *British, Irish, and Commonwealth Poets* by culture or group identity (such as Jewish culture, gay and lesbian culture, and women poets), literary movements, schools, and historical periods (such as Cavalier poets, Elizabethan Age, Irish Literary Revival, Graveyard School, and Modernism), and poetic forms and themes (such as political poets, war poets, ekphrastic poetry, prose poetry, nature poetry, and sonnets). The *Critical Survey of Poetry* Series: Master List of Contents lists not only the poets profiled in *British, Irish, and Commonwealth Poets* but also those in other subsets, allowing users to find any poet covered in the complete series. The Subject Index lists all titles, authors, subgenres, and literary movements or terms that receive substantial discussion in *British, Irish, and Commonwealth Poets*. Listings for profiled poets are in bold face.

## ACKNOWLEDGMENTS

Salem Press is grateful for the efforts of the original contributors of these essays and those of the outstanding academicians who took on the task of updating or writing new material for the set. Their names and affiliations are listed in the "Contributors" section that follows. Finally, we are indebted to our editor, Professor Rosemary M. Canfield Reisman of Charleston Southern University, for her development of the table of contents for the *Critical Survey of Poetry, Fourth Edition* and her advice on updating the original articles to make this comprehensive and thorough revised edition an indispensable tool for students, teachers, and general readers alike.

# CONTRIBUTORS

Paul Acker
*Brown University*

James Lovic Allen
*University of Hawaii at Hilo*

Phillip B. Anderson
*University of Central Arkansas*

Andrew J. Angyal
*Elon University*

Stanley Archer
*Texas A&M University*

Rosemary Ascherl
*Colchester, Connecticut*

James R. Aubrey
*United States Air Force Academy*

Linda C. Badley
*Middle Tennessee State
    University*

William Baker
*Northern Illinois University*

David Barratt
*Montreat College*

Larry David Barton
*Bemidgi, Minnesota*

Walton Beacham
*Beacham Publishing Corp.*

Kirk H. Beetz
*Davis, California*

Elizabeth J. Bellamy
*Winthrop College*

Todd K. Bender
*University of Wisconsin-Madison*

Donna Berliner
*University of Texas at Dallas*

Richard Bizot
*University of North Florida*

Robert G. Blake
*Elon University*

Robert E. Boenig
*Texas A&M University*

Allyson Booth
*United States Naval Academy*

Neal Bowers
*Iowa State University*

Harold Branam
*Savannah State University*

Jeanie R. Brink
*Arizona State University*

Mitzi M. Brunsdale
*Mayville State College*

Ann M. Cameron
*Indiana University, Kokomo*

Edmund J. Campion
*University of Tennessee*

Michael Case
*Arizona State University*

G. A. Cevasco
*St. John's University*

Diana Arlene Chlebek
*The University of Akron Libraries*

John R. Clark
*University of South Florida*

David W. Cole
*University of Wisconsin Colleges*

Caroline Collins
*Quincy University*

Richard Collins
*Xavier University of Louisiana*

John J. Conlon
*University of South Florida,
    St. Petersburg*

John W. Crawford
*Henderson State University*

Galbraith M. Crump
*Kenyon College*

Diane D'Amico
*Allegheny College*

Dennis R. Dean
*University of Wisconsin-Parkside*

Paul J. deGrategno
*Wesleyan College*

Mary De Jong
*Pennsylvania State University*

Bill Delaney
*San Diego, California*

Desiree Dreeuws
*Sunland, California*

Robert Eddy
*Fayetteville State University*

Robert P. Ellis
*Worcester State College*

Richard Kenneth Emmerson
*Walla Walla College*

Ann Willardson Engar
*University of Utah*

Thomas L. Erskine
*Salisbury University*

Sarah Fedirka
*Arizona State University*

Thomas C. Foster
*University of Michigan-Flint*

Kenneth Friedenreich
*Dana Point, California*

Edward V. Geist
*Forest Hills, New York*

Jay A. Gertzman
*Mansfield University*

Richard F. Giles
*Wilfrid Laurier University*

Ronald K. Giles
*East Tennessee State University*

C. Herbert Gilliland
*United States Naval Academy*

Dennis Goldsberry
*College of Charleston*

Lois Gordon
*Fairleigh Dickinson University*

Sidney Gottlieb
*Sacred Heart University*

Robert Edward Graalman, Jr.
*Oklahoma State University*

John R. Griffin
*University of Southern Colorado*

Stephen I. Gurney
*Bemidji State University*

R. S. Gwynn
*Lamar University*

Katherine Hanley
*St. Bernard's Institute*

Maryhelen Cleverly Harmon
*University of South Florida*

John Harty III
*University of Florida*

Robert W. Haynes
*Texas A&M University*

William J. Heim
*University of South Florida*

Michael Hennessy
*Southwest Texas State University*

Sarah Hilbert
*Pasadena, California*

Donald D. Hook
*Trinity College*

Wm. Dennis Horn
*Clarkson University*

Earl G. Ingersoll
*SUNY College at Brockport*

Tracy Irons-Georges
*Glendale, California*

Miglena Ivanova
*Coastal Carolina University*

Maura Ives
*Texas A&M University*

Philip K. Jason
*United States Naval Academy*

Ed Jewinski
*Wilfrid Laurier University*

Christopher D. Johnson
*Francis Marion University*

Leslie Ellen Jones
*Pasadena, California*

Paul Kane
*Vassar College*

Arthur Kincaid
*Glenn Mills, Pennsylvania*

Frederick Kirchhoff
*Fort Wayne, Indiana*

B. G. Knepper
*Sioux City, Iowa*

Philip Krummrich
*University of Georgia*

Rebecca Kuzins
*Pasadena, California*

Michael M. Levy
*University of Wisconsin-Stout*

Leon Lewis
*Appalachian State University*

James Livingston
*Northern Michigan University*

Archie K. Loss
*Pennsylvania State University, Erie*

John F. McDiarmid
*New College of Florida*

Gina Macdonald
*Nicholls State University*

Richard D. McGhee
*Arkansas State University*

Arthur E. McGuinness
*University of California, Davis*

Kevin McNeilly
*University of British Columbia*

Bruce K. Martin
*Drake University*

Richard E. Matlak
*College of the Holy Cross*

Laurence W. Mazzeno
*Alvernia College*

Richard E. Meyer
*Western Oregon State College*

Michael R. Meyers
*Pfeiffer University*

Edmund Miller
*Long Island University*

Mark Minor
*Westmar College*

Thomas Moisan
*Saint Louis University*

Gene M. Moore
*Virginia Commonwealth University*

Michael D. Moore
*Wilfrid Laurier University*

Christina J. Moose
*Pasadena, California*

Gerald W. Morton
*Auburn University-Montgomery*

Carole Moses
*Lycoming College*

Joseph Natoli
*Irvine, California*

Emma Coburn Norris
*Troy State University*

Leslie Norris
*Brigham Young University*

George O'Brien
*Georgetown University*

Elizabeth Spalding Otten
*Manchester, New Hampshire*

Robert M. Otten
*Marymount University*

Cóilín Owens
*George Mason University*

Richard J. Panofsky
*Las Vegas, Nevada*

Michael P. Parker
*United States Naval Academy*

Janet Polansky
*University of Wisconsin*

Norman Prinsky
*Augusta State University*

Charles H. Pullen
*Queen's University*

Mark Rich
*Cashton, Wisconsin*

Richard E. Rogal
*Illinois State University*

Samuel J. Rogal
*Illinois State University*

Jill Rollins
*Trafalgar School*

Joseph Rosenblum
*Greensboro, North Carolina*

Diane M. Ross
*Lake Forest College*

Jay Ruud
*Northern State University*

Gregory M. Sadlek
*University of Nebraska-Omaha*

Ruth Salvaggio
*Virginia Tech*

John F. Schell
*University of Arkansas at
    Little Rock*

Katherine Snipes
*Eastern Washington University*

Robert Lance Snyder
*Georgia Institute of Technology*

Charlotte Spivack
*University of Massachusetts,
    Amherst*

Vivien Stableford
*Reading, United Kingdom*

L. Robert Stevens
*North Texas State University*

Eve Walsh Stoddard
*St. Lawrence University*

Gerald H. Strauss
*Bloomsburg University*

Alan Sullivan
*Fargo, North Dakota*

Christopher J. Thaiss
*George Mason University*

John Thomson
*United States Air Force Academy*

Andy K. Trevathan
*University of Arkansas*

Gary F. Waller
*Wilfrid Laurier University*

Marie Michelle Walsh
*College of Notre Dame of
    Maryland*

Shawncey Webb
*Taylor University*

Thomas Willard
*University of Arizona*

Eugene P. Wright
*North Texas State University*

Gay Pitman Zieger
*Santa Fe College*

# CONTENTS

# COMPLETE LIST OF CONTENTS

## Volume 1

# VOLUME 2

# VOLUME 3

# PRONUNCIATION KEY

To help users of the *Critical Survey of Poetry* pronounce unfamiliar names of profiled poets correctly, phonetic spellings using the character symbols listed below appear in parentheses immediately after the first mention of the poet's name in the narrative text. Stressed syllables are indicated in capital letters, and syllables are separated by hyphens.

## VOWEL SOUNDS

| *Symbol* | *Spelled (Pronounced)* |
|---|---|
| a | answer (AN-suhr), laugh (laf), sample (SAM-puhl), that (that) |
| ah | father (FAH-thur), hospital (HAHS-pih-tuhl) |
| aw | awful (AW-fuhl), caught (kawt) |
| ay | blaze (blayz), fade (fayd), waiter (WAYT-ur), weigh (way) |
| eh | bed (behd), head (hehd), said (sehd) |
| ee | believe (bee-LEEV), cedar (SEE-dur), leader (LEED-ur), liter (LEE-tur) |
| ew | boot (bewt), lose (lewz) |
| i | buy (bi), height (hit), lie (li), surprise (sur-PRIZ) |
| ih | bitter (BIH-tur), pill (pihl) |
| o | cotton (KO-tuhn), hot (hot) |
| oh | below (bee-LOH), coat (koht), note (noht), wholesome (HOHL-suhm) |
| oo | good (good), look (look) |
| ow | couch (kowch), how (how) |
| oy | boy (boy), coin (koyn) |
| uh | about (uh-BOWT), butter (BUH-tuhr), enough (ee-NUHF), other (UH-thur) |

## CONSONANT SOUNDS

| *Symbol* | *Spelled (Pronounced)* |
|---|---|
| ch | beach (beech), chimp (chihmp) |
| g | beg (behg), disguise (dihs-GIZ), get (geht) |
| j | digit (DIH-juht), edge (ehj), jet (jeht) |
| k | cat (kat), kitten (KIH-tuhn), hex (hehks) |
| s | cellar (SEHL-ur), save (sayv), scent (sehnt) |
| sh | champagne (sham-PAYN), issue (IH-shew), shop (shop) |
| ur | birth (burth), disturb (dihs-TURB), earth (urth), letter (LEH-tur) |
| y | useful (YEWS-fuhl), young (yuhng) |
| z | business (BIHZ-nehs), zest (zehst) |
| zh | vision (VIH-zhuhn) |

# CRITICAL SURVEY OF
# Poetry
## *Fourth Edition*

# British, Irish, and Commonwealth Poets

# A

## DANNIE ABSE

**Born:** Cardiff, Wales; September 22, 1923

PRINCIPAL POETRY

*After Every Green Thing*, 1949

*Walking Under Water*, 1952

*Tenants of the House: Poems, 1951-1956*, 1957

*Poems, Golders Green*, 1962

*A Small Desperation*, 1968

*Demo*, 1969

*Selected Poems*, 1970

*Funland, and Other Poems*, 1973

*Collected Poems, 1948-1976*, 1977

*Way Out in the Centre*, 1981 (in United States as *One-Legged on Ice*, 1983)

*Ask the Bloody Horse*, 1986

*White Coat, Purple Coat: Collected Poems, 1948-1988*, 1989

*Remembrance of Crimes Past: Poems, 1986-1989*, 1990

*On the Evening Road*, 1994

*Selected Poems*, 1994

*Welsh Retrospective*, 1997

*Arcadia, One Mile*, 1998

*Be Seated, Thou: Poems, 1989-1998*, 2000

*New and Collected Poems*, 2003

*Yellow Bird*, 2004

*Running Late*, 2006

*New Selected Poems*, 2009

*Two for Joy: Scenes from Married Life*, 2010

OTHER LITERARY FORMS

Dannie Abse (abs) has always been a prolific writer, not only contributing poems to many journals, including *American Review*, *The Times Literary Supplement*, *Encounter*, *Jewish Quarterly*, and *Jewish Chronicle Literary Supplement*, but also producing a volume of semi-autobiographical prose (sometimes called a novel), *Ash on a Young Man's Sleeve* (1954), and the novels *Some Corner of an English Field* (1956) and *O. Jones, O. Jones* (1970). In 1974, he published his autobiography, *A Poet in the Family*. Another collection of autobiographical pieces and reflections on the writing of poetry and autobiography, *A Strong Dose of Myself* (1983), was followed by *Journals from the Ant Heap* (1986) and *Intermittent Journals* (1994), sets of musings on various public and personal events, and by *Goodbye, Twentieth Century: The Autobiography of Dannie Abse* (2001). In 2007, Abse published *The Presence*, a very powerful meditation following the death of his wife, Joan, in an automobile accident in June, 2005. The book is the result of a diary he started after his wife's death in an attempt to come to terms with his grief, sadness, and loss, and to document their more than fifty years of marriage. He has also written several plays, among them *House of Cowards* (pr. 1960), *The Dogs of Pavlov* (pr. 1969), *Pythagoras* (pr. 1976), and *Gone in January* (pr. 1978).

ACHIEVEMENTS

Dannie Abse's literary achievement is all the more remarkable considering that he was a practicing physician. He became head of the chest clinic at the Central Medical Establishment in London in 1954 and retired from medicine in 1989. His literary interests extend naturally into the field of medicine, as may be seen in *Medicine on Trial* (1967).

Abse's literary honors span several decades. He won the Charles Henry Foyle Trust Award for *House of Cowards* in 1960, the Welsh Arts Council Literature Awards for *Selected Poems* in 1970 and for *Pythagoras* in 1979, and the Jewish Chronicle Book Award for *Selected Poems* in 1970. He held a visiting fellowship of the humanities at Princeton University in 1973-1974 and became a fellow of the Royal Society of Literature in 1983. Abse received the Cholmondeley Award for distinction in poetry in 1985, the Roland Mathias Poetry Prize for *Running Late* in 2007, the Arts Council of Wales Book of the Year Award for *The Presence* in 2008, and the Wilfred Owen Poetry Award in 2009. He was awarded an honorary doctorate from the University of Wales in 1989 and one from the University of Glamorgan in 1997.

BIOGRAPHY

Daniel Abse was born in 1923 in South Wales, the youngest of four children. Two of his brothers were influential in his education. Wilfred (the oldest), who became a psychoanalyst, introduced him to Sigmund Freud and guided him toward medicine as a profession. His brother Leo was instrumental in his becoming interested in politics, as Leo was Member of Parliament for Pontypoll—a Welsh Labour constituency—for many years and was a vocal and dynamic Labour figure. Dannie Abse has retained these interests in medicine and politics throughout his life, and they have had a pronounced effect on his writing.

Abse became interested in poetry during the Spanish Civil War (1936-1939) and began writing during his last year at school. In the Royal Air Force during World War II, he served in the Mass Radiography Section in London; it was during this period that he became acquainted with art historian Joan Mercer, who would become his wife. His first book of poems was accepted for publication in 1946, and in 1947, as he relates in his essay "My Medical School," he returned to Cardiff, having decided that he no longer wished to be a physician. At the urging of his family, however, he returned to London, where he was qualified as a physician in 1950. He served in the Royal Air Force from 1951 to 1955, an experience on which he drew for the background of his second novel *Some Corner of an English Field*, and thereafter, Abse simultaneously pursued his medical and artistic careers, with considerable success in both.

Between 1949 and 1954, Abse and some friends edited a poetry magazine called *Poetry and Poverty*, which led to the anthology *Mavericks* (1957), edited by Abse and Howard Sergeant. This collection was intended to rival the fashionable *New Lines* anthology published in 1956, which featured the work of such poets as Philip Larkin, John Wain, and Kingsley Amis. In his autobiography, Abse explains his editorial policy in producing *Mavericks*, comparing it to A. Alvarez's *The New Poetry* (1962). He concedes that *Mavericks* was not a success, attributing its failure to the fact that not enough of the poems lived up to his editorial ideal "of being written out of the heat of personal predicament and therefore imbued with a strong current of feeling."

Abse was married to Mercer in 1951, and she and his family became an important stimulus to his writing. In fact, it might be said that Abse was essentially a family man, for parents, brothers, wife, and children, as well as his Jewish heritage—and since the publication of *A Small Desperation* in 1968, his medical profession as well—have all influenced his writing. Hutchinson published Abse's first collection *After Every Green Thing* in 1949. Anthony Whittome, Abse's editor at Hutchinson since the early 1970's, in his "Foreword" to *New Selected Poems*, echoes the words of the poet Elaine Feinstein in stating that Abse is "one of our few great poets of married love."

ANALYSIS

Poetically, Dannie Abse owes allegiance to no particular school. A humanist, his tendency is to explore complex philosophical themes through things visible and comprehensible in daily existence. At the beginning of his career, he was strongly influenced by the work of Dylan Thomas. Later, however, he moved away from the mode of adjectival and rhetorical excess that was Thomas's hallmark to a quieter, more questioning style of writing. Drawing on his professional life for incident metaphor, he acquired his own poetic style, easily recognized by the student of modern poetry. His voice is gentle, never strident; the personality that emerges from the writing is endearing, not irritating. He expresses ideas that occur to all but not everyone has the ability to voice.

In the "Introductory Note" to *Collected Poems, 1948-1976*, Abse briefly outlines some of the impulses that motivate his writing and makes it clear that one of his strongest motivations is his desire to share the wealth of his experiences with the reader. There is a strand of humanism in his work, reinforced by his obvious belief that in communication lies humankind's hope of salvation. Over and over again, his poetry stresses all people's common humanity and the vulnerability of each person without the support and understanding of his or her fellows. Paradoxically, however, Abse also states that one of his ambitions is "to write poems which appear translucent but are in fact deceptions. I would have the reader enter them, be deceived he could see through them like sea-water, and be puzzled when he cannot quite touch the bottom." Here, he seems to be balancing a wish to communicate with an artist's prerogative to retain some of his work for himself.

### EARLY POEMS

In his early work (perhaps surprisingly, considering the fact that many of his most impressionable early years were overshadowed by World War II), neither Abse's Jewishness nor his role as a physician is particularly noticeable, although the scientific (if not always specifically medical) cast of his mind is ever present in his analytical, questioning style. He is capable of seeing at least two sides to every question and, apparently, believes that nothing is as it seems, that all is deception and ambiguity. When he speaks of attempting to achieve a "translucence" in his writing, what he seems to mean is poetry of infinite possibility, an effect produced by infinite ambiguity.

His ability to see two sides of every question is clearly illustrated in such poems as "Duality" and "Odd." In later works, he writes less fancifully and rhetorically, having taken very much to heart the aphorisms that he quotes at the beginning of his *Collected Poems, 1948-1976:* William Carlos Williams's "No ideas but in things," and Alfred North Whitehead's "Truth adds to interest."

In his early writing, Abse is concerned with religion in an abstract rather than a personal sense, as though his emotions become engaged in the question only after he has first thought the matter through. His feelings of paranoia are much more noticeable in the early work, combined with an uncertainty of identity and expressions of anger and alarm, directed against those impersonal forces that may shape the ultimate destiny of humanity. Questions of faith come to interest him only later in his writing. For example, in "Verses at Night" and "New Babylons," he expresses his anxiety, both about the possibility of the Holocaust and the intolerable social pressures that human beings exert on one another.

These themes appear repeatedly in Abse's work, sometimes expressed rather enigmatically. For example, in "The Uninvited," Abse reflects on the effect of the unforeseen and unexpected events in his life, those occasional moments when he may feel that one of life's

overwhelming questions may be about to be answered. In this poem, the moment of revelation passes, leaving the speaker changed by disappointment and very much aware of his own isolation. There is often an almost mystical strain in Abse's early work that seems to have diminished as he has matured.

A related preoccupation is how people react to the unexpected and to change. In *A Poet in the Family*, Abse relates that even moving from one street to another nearby in the same city caused him considerable distress as a child, and this awareness of and sensitivity to change has remained with him throughout his life. The related questions of change and humankind's search for identity appear in "Duality," "The Trial," "The Magician," and, in modified form, in "The Second Coming," among other poems.

### WALES AND DYLAN THOMAS

Less elusive than some of his other themes, Abse's sense of nationality permeates his writing, especially in such poems as "Leaving Cardiff," "The Game," and "Return to Cardiff," as well as in his more colloquial poems relating to childhood figures and incidents. Especially in these latter poems, which are worlds away from his usual abstract, questioning style, the influence of Thomas is apparent. It must be pointed out that Thomas almost inevitably influenced most writers of this generation, especially Welsh writers. In Abse's case, it is possible to see an awareness of Thomas's work in "Epithalamion," "The Meeting," "The Mountaineers," and, more appropriately, in "Elegy for Dylan Thomas." He then seems to shake himself free of Thomas's ghost until much later in his poetic career, when his character sketches begin to emerge.

### CRISES OF IDENTITY

Abse has gradually shaped his own voice. In *A Poet in the Family*, he relates the tale of his visit to the United States under the aegis of John Malcolm Brinnin, where he followed in Thomas's footsteps, watched hopefully but apprehensively by an audience that seemed constantly to be waiting for him to give evidence of being a wild Welsh bard. "I, at once," says Abse, "became nicer than myself, more polite, better behaved." Perhaps this ever-present reminder of a very different artistic persona serves to underline Abse's preoccupation with crises of identity: in his own case, as a Welshman, a Jew, and a physician. The importance of his Jewish heritage and his family can be seen in the 1981 collection *Way Out in the Centre*, in which he also explores his two roles as poet and physician. In fact, until the 1960's, Abse grappled with his difficulty in acknowledging his medical life in his poems. Critic Sergeant noted a turning point in Abse's poetry when, with the publication in 1968 of *A Small Desperation*, Abse began to write "as a whole man" and incorporate the "complexity of his experience" into his work.

### "FUNLAND"

The essence of Abse's poetry is to be found in his longest and perhaps most impressive poem, "Funland," from the collection of the same name and also reprinted in *New Selected Poems*. The poem was read on British Broadcasting Corporation Radio 3 in 1971, and in his introductory remarks, Abse made this observation about the poem's origin: "Many years ago in conversation, the novelist, Elias Canetti, said to me, 'The man suffering from paranoia is correct. Someone *is* standing behind that door pumping invisible gas through the keyhole. For we are dying, right now, a little every minute.'" Abse believes that a kind of paranoia is natural to human beings. (Perhaps this stems from the fact that he is himself a member of three minority groups, two ethnic and one professional.)

Abse's roles as Welshman, Jew, and practicing physician are significant in this work. Speaking of "Funland," he has said that "the earth is no ordinary 'hospital' but a lunatic asylum whose inmates live out suffering lives of black comedy." In "Funland," he combines elements of the surreal with images of deception and illusion, using his knowledge of psychoanalysis as well as a more elementary overview of human motivations to produce what is one of the cornerstones of his poetic achievement. Magicians, illusion, and the difficulties human beings create for themselves in society are major themes in "Funland."

In the poem's introduction, Abse refers to the contrast between the modern white lab coat, the "disguise" of modern medicine, and the purple cloak of an old-style charismatic magician, as if recognizing that faith and illusion play an important part in the work of the modern physician, just as they did to healers in more primitive times. Here is found a half-expressed ten-dency toward mysticism, which provides continual tension in Abse's writing. Along with apparently believing that humankind as a whole is involved in a collective crisis of identity, Abse seems to think that those foolish enough to take life at face value deserve to be deceived by it. This is all a part of his attempt to imbue his work with "translucence."

### ARCADIA, ONE MILE

*Arcadia, One Mile* (a volume commemorating the fiftieth anniversary of Abse's first volume of poetry published by Hutchinson) appeared as the poet turned seventy-five years old, and it marks his mature development and the integration of many of his themes. One poem, "O Taste and See," is a celebration of all that is temporary; another, "The Maestro," focuses on the role of music in Abse's poetic. Several are grounded in Welsh lore; others, such as "Alzheimer's," reflect Abse's experience as a physician. Even stories of the Bible are retold here. Above all, however, Abse contemplates life and its inevitable definer, death, from the vantage of a cultured, wise, and erudite person well positioned to contemplate his own mortality and also the meaning of life to a secular Jew and scientist who seeks that meaning, that immortality, in ongoing life—whether contemplating a newborn in "New Granddaughter" or the memory of a dead friend in "An Interrupted Letter."

There is also a sense of history, dominated not surprisingly by the Holocaust, as Abse looks back at the twentieth century and gratefully, without bitterness, acknowledges both the century's brutality and his fortune in having lived a good life in a world where life justifies itself merely by its own survival.

### RUNNING LATE

*Running Late*, dedicated in memory of Abse's wife, appeared in 2006. It contains thirty-nine poems, none of which had appeared previously in book form. The subjects reflect preoccupations. For instance, his Jewish inheritance is seen in the eight verses of four lines each of "Gershom's Daughter." There are poems having Ogmore, Abse's coastal retreat near Cardiff, as their foundation, including "The Dog at Ogmore-by-Sea," "At the Concert," "That Unseasonable July in Ogmore," and "On the Coastal Road," which evokes memories of his father fishing from the rocks. In "The

Dog at Ogmore-by-Sea," the poet conveys the isolation and loneliness of the seaside resort once the weekend visitors have left: Only a dog remains. Memories of the past pervade "At the Concert," a poem using Abse's familiar quatrain form. An argument with his wife, the carcass of a bird devoured by a worm, and images of loneliness without his wife dominate the moving "That Unseasonable July in Ogmore."

Many of the finest poems in the collection concern the poet's wife, Joan. For instance, "The Malham Bird" is dedicated to her and dated 2004, the final year of her life. The poet recalls their initial secret holiday on the Welsh coast, their swimming naked together, and the gull that swooped down near them. Many years later, the poet thinks of a black-feathered bird, the malham of Eden, from the perspective of a man with three grandchildren. The world of the past becomes a prelapsarian one.

The final poem of the collection, "Lachrymae," also to be found in *New Selected Poems*, is divided into three parts. The first two have three stanzas; the third part, two stanzas. In the first part, the initial three-line verse simply but movingly and sparingly states the fact that the poet attended the funeral: His wife, Joan, is not named, transformed into the impersonal "she." The poet returns home to a home no longer a home. In the second six-line verse, Joan's spiritual presence is all pervasive and diminishes the survivor, the poet. The final six-line verse of the first section speaks of the letters received by Abse that make him weep. Unable to sleep, he awaits the disappearance of his memory. The second section, with its three stanzas of five lines each, recalls their love, the present, and recent memories of her accompanying him in bed. The final two stanzas of six lines each move from recent memories to those of the present placed amongst the stark background of Hampstead, its pond and now—places he used to go to with his wife. "Lachrymae" is a superb poem of lament, interweaving the past, the present, memory, and the bleakness of the here and now.

### NEW SELECTED POEMS

Surprising omissions from *New Selected Poems* include many of Abse's poems remembering figures from his Cardiff past, such as "Uncle Isidore," and "Tales of Shatz," the somewhat lengthy poem celebrat-

ing a rabbi from Abse's youth, both of which appeared in *Collected Poems, 1948-1976*. However, "Cousin Sidney," a moving five-verse, six-line lament for the poet's cousin killed in World War II, is included. Other reprinted poems include "White Coat, Purple Coat" and "The Stethoscope," which draw on the poet's medical expertise, depicting his relationships with patients and people's mortality. It is hardly surprising that the distinguished critic M. L. Rosenthal writes that Abse "is a lyric poet of death, whose imaginative reach can be both adventurous and demanding."

*New Selected Poems* is divided into three parts. The first part, "Earlier Poems," contains twenty poems, including Abse's "Elegy for Dylan Thomas," "Return to Cardiff," "A Night Out," and "Not Adlestrop," four of his most anthologized poems. "Return to Cardiff," first published in *Poems, Golders Green*, has a nostalgic, evocative quality prevalent in Abse's best poems. "A Night Out," one of his most powerful poems, also initially appeared in *Poems, Golders Green*. In this poem, a husband and wife are spending an evening in the West End at a fashionable art cinema watching a film on the concentration camps. In the film, they see children of the same age as their own walking into the gas chambers as if they were departing on a day trip. The husband and wife return home to their comfortable London suburban home, put their children to bed and sleep, all safely watched over by a German au pair. The normal routines of postwar London life are juxtaposed with screen images that haunt the husband. As Rosenthal observes in Joseph Cohen's *The Poetry of Dannie Abse* (1983), "The sense of being merely actors ourselves in some sort of irreversibly progressing film makes the sexual act at the end" of the poem "an embodiment of the elegiac, a possible contribution to the Auschwitz of the future, and a betrayal of grief."

"Welsh Valley Cinema 1930's," previously published in *Arcadia, One Mile*, a three-verse poem of ten lines, appears in the third section, "Later Poems." In this poem, the poet retreats to the past, to the traumatic 1930's, a period of economic unemployment in his native Wales, and to his perennial theme of the juxtaposition between reality and illusion.

Abse's lyrical voice has continued to flow undiminished in spite of personal tragedy and aging. Abse's dualities are identified by Daniel Hoffman, in his contribution to Cohen's volume, as fivefold: "British/Jewish, English/Welsh, seeker/skeptic, bourgeois/bohemian, poet/doctor." His later love poems, which are laments for the loss of his beloved wife, place his work among the poetic constellations of post-World War II and late twentieth century poetry in English.

OTHER MAJOR WORKS

LONG FICTION: *Some Corner of an English Field*, 1956; *O. Jones, O. Jones*, 1970; *There Was a Young Man from Cardiff*, 1991; *The Strange Case of Dr. Simmonds and Dr. Glas*, 2002.

PLAYS: *Fire in Heaven*, pr. 1948 (also known as *In the Cage*, pb. 1967); *Hands Around the Wall*, pr. 1950; *House of Cowards*, pr. 1960; *The Eccentric*, pr. 1961; *Gone*, pr. 1962; *The Joker*, pr. 1962; *Three Questor Plays*, 1967 (includes *In the Cage, House of Cowards*, and *Gone*); *The Dogs of Pavlov*, pr. 1969; *Pythagoras*, pr. 1976; *Gone in January*, pr. 1978; *The View from Row G: Three Plays*, 1990 (includes *House of Cowards, The Dogs of Pavlov*, and *Pythagoras*).

NONFICTION: "My Medical School," 1947; *Ash on a Young Man's Sleeve*, 1954; *Medicine on Trial*, 1967; *A Poet in the Family*, 1974; *Miscellany One*, 1981; *A Strong Dose of Myself*, 1983; *Journals from the Ant Heap*, 1986; *Intermittent Journals*, 1994; *Goodbye, Twentieth Century: The Autobiography of Dannie Abse*, 2001; *The Two Roads Taken: A Prose Miscellany*, 2003; *The Presence*, 2007.

EDITED TEXTS: *Mavericks*, 1957 (with Howard Sergeant); *European Verse*, 1964; *Modern Poets in Focus*, 1971-1973 (numbers 1, 3, 5); *Thirteen Poets*, 1972; *My Medical School*, 1978; *Wales in Verse*, 1983; *Doctors and Patients*, 1984; *Voices in the Gallery: Poems and Pictures Chosen by Dannie and Joan Abse*, 1986; *The Music Lover's Literary Companion*, 1988 (with Joan Abse); *The Hutchinson Book of Postwar British Poets*, 1989; *Twentieth Century Anglo-Welsh Poetry*, 1997; *One Hundred Great Poems of Love and Lust*, 2006.

BIBLIOGRAPHY

Abse, Dannie. "Interview: Dannie Abse." Interview by J. P. Ward. *New Welsh Review* 2 (Autumn, 1989): 8-12. Abse reveals his poetic goal: to illuminate allegory with human experience. He describes how his work as a medical doctor informs his poetry. An interesting article for both undergraduates and advanced students.

Baker, William, and Tabachnick, Stephen. "Reflections on Anglo-Jewish Poetry." *Jewish Quarterly* 26, no. 3-4 (1978-1979): 73-84. Includes an analysis of Abse's poetry.

Cohen, Joseph, ed. *The Poetry of Dannie Abse: Critical Essays and Reminiscences*. London: Robson Books, 1983. Authors of the appreciations collected here are mostly fellow poets; they include Donald Davie, D. J. Enright, Theodore Weiss, Vernon Scannell, and Daniel Hoffman. John Ormond contributes "An ABC of Dannie Abse," cataloging numerous recurring images in the poetry. Abse's musicality, his treatment of Jewish identity, and other important themes in the poetry and plays are examined as well. Includes an interview with Abse and a selected bibliography.

Curtis, Tony. *Dannie Abse*. Cardiff: University of Wales Press/Welsh Arts Council, 1985. An artfully made book that reviews Abse's life and works chronologically. Curtis examines influences on the poet; his study is more thematic than technical, calling attention to Abse's views of religion, the practice of medicine, and love. Provides a bibliography.

Davies, Daniel. "Not Mourning, but Waving." Review of *Arcadia, One Mile*. *The Lancet*, October 24, 1998, 70. Surveys this late collection as a reflection of Abse's themes as a whole.

Hoffman, Daniel. "Dannie Abse." In *Poets of Great Britain and Ireland, 1945-1960*, edited by Vincent B. Sherry, Jr. Vol. 27 in *Dictionary of Literary Biography*. Detroit: Gale Research, 1984. A detailed assessment of Abse's poetic achievement.

_____. "Doctor and Magus in the Work of Dannie Abse." *Literature and Medicine* 3 (1984): 21-31. In modern culture, scientists have replaced priests in the role of wise men, according to Hoffman. He sees Abse as being like a sorcerer, or a magus, for he blends his real-life role as a man of science into his poetry, thus melding art and science.

Lawson, Peter, ed. *Passionate Renewal: Jewish Poetry in Britain Since 1945—An Anthology*. Nottingham,

England: Five Leaves, 2001. Lawson's introduction contains a useful discussion of Abse's poetic work, and the collection reprints twenty Abse poems.

Walters, Michael. Review of *Remembrance of Crimes Past*. *The Times Literary Supplement*, November 2-8, 1990, 1184. A rather uncomplimentary review of Abse's 1990 collection. Walters faults "hackneyed writing" that at times is "too comfortably nonchalant" and at other times manifests "overexertion." However, he also says that "two or three poems . . . recall how fine a craftsman Abse can be."

Whittome, Anthony. Foreword to *New Selected Poems*, by Dannie Abse. London: Hutchinson, 2009. Whittome was Abse's editor at Hutchinson from the early 1970's. His "Foreword" makes judicious observations on Abse's poetry.

*Vivien Stableford; Christina J. Moose; Sarah Hilbert*
*Updated by William Baker*

---

# JOSEPH ADDISON

**Born:** Milston, Wiltshire, England; May 1, 1672
**Died:** London, England; June 17, 1719
**Also known as:** Marmaduke Myrtle

PRINCIPAL POETRY
"To Mr. Dryden," 1693
*A Poem to His Majesty*, 1695
*Praelum Inter Pygmaeos et Grues Commisum*, 1699
"A Letter from Italy," 1703
*The Campaign*, 1705
"To Her Royal Highness," 1716
"To Sir Godfrey Kneller on His Portrait of the King," 1716

OTHER LITERARY FORMS

Joseph Addison wrote in almost every genre common in British literature during the reigns of William III and Queen Anne. Besides poetry in Latin and English, Addison composed an opera, a tragedy, a comedy, a travel book, a scholarly account of ancient Roman coins, political pamphlets, and hundreds of essays

contributed to *The Tatler* (1709-1711), *The Spectator* (1711-1712, 1714), and other periodicals. The variety of works he attempted is a reflection of the active literary culture of the time, a reflection of Addison's wide learning, and the story of a writer in search of his proper niche. The numbers show that he found it in periodical journalism.

Because of Addison's varied canon, there has yet to be a satisfactory complete edition. The first collection, edited by Thomas Tickell in 1721, omitted some embarrassing early works and many of the periodical essays. A new collected edition a century later restored some early works and offered a fuller selection of essays. Two good modern critical editions cover most of Addison's corpus: *The Miscellaneous Works* (1914) includes everything but the essays, and Donald Bond's *The Spectator* (1965) covers the most famous periodical to which Addison contributed. The other papers for which he wrote await modern editions. *The Letters of Joseph Addison*, an unrevealing collection, was published in 1941.

ACHIEVEMENTS

Joseph Addison's literary reputation has risen and fallen periodically, for reasons which have had little to do with his artistic achievement. His contemporaries and the next generation praised Addison highly for expressing not only Whig political principles but also classical qualities that gave English literature a dignity it had previously lacked. Readers and writers in the Romantic Age, however, found Addison unoriginal and conventional. The Victorians restored Addison to his pedestal because he spoke well of virtue and painted the picture of the Christian gentleman. Twentieth century critics often assail his work as only a historical reflection of growing bourgeois society; many personally dislike the man for accommodating himself to the class structure of eighteenth century England.

Although such judgments affect how often Addison is reprinted and how much he is read, his place in literary history rests firmly on two achievements: his role in the development of the periodical essay and his prose style. Through his collaboration with Sir Richard Steele on *The Tatler*, *The Spectator*, and *The Guardian* (1713), Addison helped establish the periodical essay as a permanent part of literature. These periodicals

*Joseph Addison* (Library of Congress)

made the twin activities of reading and thinking about literary topics part of an educated person's daily life. Although ostensibly essays, Addison's and Steele's works really constitute a fascinating variety of stories, sketches, sermons, and lectures. What won readers to the periodical essay was its resourcefulness and flexibility in both form and content.

Addison's second lasting achievement was his prose style, seemingly informal and natural yet rhetorical and artistic, capable of handling a wide range of topics. Addison was one of several writers (including John Dryden and Jonathan Swift) whose innovations enabled prose to rival poetry as a fit medium for literary expression. For the next two centuries, writers literally went to school with Addison; stylists as diverse as Benjamin Franklin and Thomas Hardy began by imitating Addison. Samuel Johnson defined Addison's achievement in an immortal assessment: "Whoever wishes to attain an English style, familiar but not coarse, and elegant but not ostentatious, must give his days and nights to the volumes of Addison."

## BIOGRAPHY

Joseph Addison might easily have followed in his father's footsteps: attending Oxford University, becoming a minister of the Anglican Church, pursuing a series of increasingly important ecclesiastical posts, and supporting the divine right of the Stuart kings. However, Addison, like many other sons, took a different path.

Two revolutionary currents swept up Addison while he was at Oxford. The first was an enthusiasm for the "New Philosophy," the scientific method that was challenging the supremacy of classical learning. The second was the Glorious Revolution of 1688, which brought William III to the throne in place of James II and established the principle that Parliament's choice of a king weighed equally with God's anointing of his earthly representative. Addison followed the traditional classical curriculum at Oxford (so well that he achieved repute for his Latin poetry), but with the idea of supporting a new English culture and political order. Modeled on the Roman concept of an educated citizenry, this new order would be the greatest civilization England had ever known: A literate and cultivated populace would sensibly cooperate in their own governance with an eye toward developing a thriving commercial economy at home and leadership among European nations.

While at Oxford, Addison expressed his enthusiasm for this new concept of civilization in poems that brought him to the attention of leading Whig politicians. In 1699, Lord Somers and Lord Halifax secured for Addison a grant from William III allowing him to travel throughout the Continent and to prepare for government service. Addison remained abroad until late 1703, when the death of William ended his pension. He did little for a year until, at the request of two of Queen Anne's ministers, Halifax and Sidney Godolphin, he wrote *The Campaign* to celebrate the military victories of the duke of Marlborough against the French. This successful poem won for him a position as a commissioner of appeals.

Addison now moved in a circle of Whig politicians and writers called the Kit-Kat Club. The politicians, when in power, supported the writers by patronage; the writers helped the politicians gain or keep power by writing public relations puffs and pamphlets. Addison's new position and circle of contacts paved the way for a series of increasingly important appointments within the government. His contacts with other writers introduced him to new literary endeavors, some of which were taken up to support the government and some for their own sake.

In the next decade, from 1707 to 1717, Addison worked his way to prestigious positions in both the political and the literary worlds. His governmental progress was not even, for ministers came and went rapidly under Queen Anne, and Addison's party was sometimes out of favor. Addison was elected to Parliament in 1708, served as secretary to the council that oversaw the accession of George I in 1714, and became secretary of state in 1717. His literary progress was likewise by fits and starts. His first try at the theater, an opera, *Rosamond* (1707), was a failure. His joint ventures into periodical journalism with Sir Richard Steele (1709-1712) were spectacularly successful. His writing for *The Tatler* and *The Spectator*, along with his dramatic success *Cato* (1713), enabled Addison to create his own literary circle, "The Little Senate," which met at Button's Coffeehouse and continued the traditions of the Kit-Kat Club.

His pen was at his party's call. When George I's accession in 1714 brought a military challenge from the Stuart "Pretender," Addison's literary skills came to the Hanovers' support. In poems such as "To Sir Godfrey Kneller on His Portrait of the King" and in the periodical *The Freeholder: Or, Political Essays* (1715-1716) Addison argued that the nation was better off with a king who supported the reforms of 1688 than one who promised a return to Stuart absolutism.

Political and literary success had substantial rewards. Addison bought the pleasant estate of Bilton Hall, married the widowed countess of Warwick, and fathered a daughter, Charlotte. In 1718, however, illness forced him to resign the post of secretary of state, and the last months of his life were marred by a public fight with his former partner Steele over the Peerage Bill. On his deathbed, legend holds, Addison summoned his dissolute stepson to witness "how a Christian can die." Addison never lacked confidence in his religious, political, or literary convictions.

## ANALYSIS

Joseph Addison wished to incorporate the style and qualities of classical Greek and Roman poetry, with appropriate adjustments, into English. The adaptation met with some success: His poetry brought him literary recognition and political favor, but—unlike his prose—it has not endured. The reasons are clear: His ideas about poetry were limited, his comic talent found better expression in other genres, and popular taste turned away from classicizing when it grew sated. Addison's ideas about poetry were simple ones and commonplace in his time. He defined poetry as ornamented thought, as a truth, which the poet wished to teach, made pleasant to the mind by the images created through elegant language. He judged the most important kind of poetry to be public poetry that treated moral and heroic topics.

These criteria were derived from classical Roman poetry, which Addison praised highly in his youthful essays for its power to raise "in our minds a pleasing variety of scenes and landscapes, whilst it teaches us." Addison especially admired the concept of the poet as a teacher who expressed to his society its highest ideals and principles. He wished England to have its Vergils and Horaces who would be the familiar acquaintances of the nation's leaders and would sing the glory of their country. Finally, Addison found in the classical Roman poets an urbane and cultured tone that stressed simplicity and civility. To a nation that had undergone a political revolution in 1688 and would experience two decades of intense Whig and Tory rivalry for office, such virtues seemed appropriate for the whole society as well as for individuals.

### LATIN VERSE

Addison first published in Latin and first achieved note among his contemporaries for a series of Latin poems written in the 1690's and issued collectively in *Musarum Anglicanarum Analecta* (1699). Two are complimentary odes to Oxford professors, two are descriptions (of an altar and a barometer), three are comic verses (on a puppet show, on a bowling match, and on an imaginary war), and one is a celebration of peace with France. They are, for the most part, elegant pieces designed to show off the author's stylistic ability to ornament mundane as well as special topics.

The best of these Latin poems is the *Praelum Inter Pygmaeos et Grues Commisum* (the war between the pygmies and the cranes), a mock-heroic poem whose humor derives from applying the conventions of epic poetry to the strife between foot-and-a-half-tall men and a flock of birds. Filled with descriptions of the combatants, landscapes, and fighting, the poem nevertheless hinges on the reader's appreciation of the incongruity between epic conventions and unheroic matter, and Addison wisely does not prolong the narration; the tale comprises one hundred fifty-nine lines.

### ENGLISH VERSE

Latin verse, however, could please only an academic audience. If Addison wished to reach a wider audience, he would have to try his hand at English verse. His success in Latin verse won for him a chance to translate passages of Vergil and Ovid for an anthology. While keeping the original stories intact, Addison did not hesitate to add running explanations to his translations or to substitute familiar allusions for unfamiliar ones. In these poems and in subsequent translations, Addison strove to make classical literature accessible to an audience whose knowledge of the originals was often perfunctory and polite.

### POETRY OF PERSONAL COMPLIMENT

One classical poetic form that Addison imitated in English was the poem of personal compliment to an important person. Most of his major poems are in this mode: "To Mr. Dryden," "To the King," "A Letter from Italy," "To Her Royal Highness," and "To Sir Godfrey Kneller on His Portrait of the King." Each addresses some personage at a crucial moment in that personage's or the nation's life. Each expresses the writer's admiration for the subject with the implication that the writer speaks on behalf of the larger public. Because the occasion is noteworthy, the writer achieves dignity by finding an appropriate classical parallel.

Holding these works together as dignified statements is the poetic line. Addison's consistent verse form is the iambic (a pair of ten-syllable, rhyming lines), which he writes almost prosaically. His couplets have been called "correct" or "polite" because they are obviously arranged and proceed logically. They are not difficult to follow, either alone or in groups; single couplets seldom invert word order, and pairs or triplets tend to restate central themes or images. Addison's poetry requires little effort from reader or listener; rather, it suggests authoritative and declarative statements that are already within the reader awaiting expression.

### "A LETTER FROM ITALY"

Addison's use of ornamental but subdued poetic structures reflects his belief that on important public occasions, "Poetry in higher thoughts is lost." Clear expression of important ideas outweighs virtuoso technique. In each of his compliment poems, Addison mixes personal admiration, classical ornament, and public sentiment. The best of them is "A Letter from Italy," which Addison addresses, while on his European tour, to his patron Charles Montagu, who helped secure the pension that allowed him to travel. The poem was highly regarded in the eighteenth century because of its easy mixing of personal experience and political themes.

The first forty lines report the pleasure of the Latin scholar looking for the first time at the actual landscape depicted in the poems he knows so well: "I seem to tread on Classic ground." The poet realizes that the landscape, while attractive, does not possess in reality the greatness which the ancient poets attributed to it in their verse. Their words have worked on the reader's imagination, revealing an importance or meaning in the landscape undetected by the senses.

The next section applies this insight to Charles Montagu, who himself had written a poem praising King William's victory over James II in the Battle of the Boyne. Montagu's verse brings out the significance of a clash that in numbers appears minor but in meaning is crucial. The battle reminds all Englishmen that they are the maintainers of European liberty against the French and their Stuart lackeys.

The rest of the poem contrasts the warm climate and natural fertility of Italy with the cool climate and rocky soil of England. The former appears more fortunate but suffers under the oppression of French occupation, while the latter is happily free under a brave king and wise statesmen. The most vigorous lines in the poem are those describing the political liberty that Englishmen enjoy. When Addison wrote the poem, his patron had just been removed from the ministry, and the traveler must have wondered whether his tour of the Continent would ever lead to a government position. "A Letter from Italy" offers the consolation that both poet and patron, exiles of different sorts, are suffering for a good cause.

### THE CAMPAIGN

Addison tried his hand once at an epic poem, *The Campaign*, written to celebrate the duke of Marlborough's victories over the French army in the summer of 1704. The poem was popular on publication, gained Addison a government post, and remained in circulation for most of the century, but a growing sense that it was little more than "a gazette in rhyme," to use Joseph Warton's famous phrase, gradually eliminated it from the ranks of great English poems. It is not, however, a mean performance; it demonstrates how Addison applied classical poetic conventions and values to English material. Of many poems written about Marlborough's victory, only *The Campaign* comes close to being remembered. Although modern readers seldom appreciate poems that make warfare seem gallant—especially if that gallantry is expressed in polite couplets—this poem is an accurate and just celebration of one of England's most extraordinary generals, John Churchill.

Addison might have written a great poem because the situation boasted "a theme so new" that it could have revolutionized heroic poetry. Churchill was not a typical epic hero; he was a commoner whose father's loyalty to Charles II and whose own military prowess had brought him into aristocratic rank. Addison intends to praise a man who achieves princely honors more on "the firm basis of desert" than by birth.

Unfortunately, despite this new theme, Addison had difficult material with which to work. Churchill had indeed won two crucial and bloody battles over the French in that summer of 1704, but important to his success was the skillful way he had marched his troops into enemy territory and seized tactical advantages in the field. Marching and maneuvering are not the stuff of great epic poetry, yet Addison could hardly omit them, because his readers knew all the details from newspaper accounts.

Addison is therefore restricted to obvious sequences of march, fight, march, fight, march. Classical conventions help elevate this mundane structure: The marches rise in dramatic intensity by epic similes of the hunt as Marlborough's army stalks the French. The battles are similarly pictured in heroic metaphors that describe them as clashes of elemental powers in nature. Around and in between these sections, Addison recounts the context of the battles of Blenheim and Schellenberg: England's struggle against France for European leadership. As does any epic hero, Marlborough fights (as England does) with divine sanction. In the style of his complimentary poems, Addison finds a classical parallel for the new kind of hero: the Roman general Flavius Stilicho who, although not a patrician, won honor by marching from frontier to frontier to protect the empire against barbarian invasion.

*The Campaign* may be likened to a series of tableaux that verbally depict the crucial episodes of that summer; to make sure that no observer misses the importance of the occasion, Addison arrays all the mighty personages there, and the hero is dressed resplendently. Such dignified and static description is not to modern taste, but in his time Addison's adaptation of classical trappings to English materials was fresh and novel.

### HYMNS

Ironically, Addison's most lasting poems are those least concerned with public statements. In the late summer and early fall of 1712, Addison published, as part of five *Spectator* essays, five original hymns. Each hymn appeared as an illustration of the essay's thesis. For example, the topic of *Spectator* 444 is the vulnerability of human beings to unexpected catastrophes that can be countered only by humankind's reliance on God's supporting grace. As a model of reliance, Addison offers a rendering of the Twenty-third Psalm, in which David trusts the Lord, his shepherd.

Addison's hymns have none of the drama of the religious poetry of John Milton or John Donne, but they offer common Christian attitudes in beautifully simple language. They were frequently anthologized in hymnals after their publication. The hymn of *Spectator* 465, "The Spacious Firmament on High," expresses what might be called Addison's "classical Christianity," that rational piety that found its motive for faith in the magnificence of the world instead of in the preachings of churchmen:

The spacious firmament on high
With all the blue ethereal sky,
And spangled heavens, a shining frame,
Their great original proclaim. . . .

Such hymns have neither the insight nor the form to capture the drama of spiritual struggle, but there are many occasions on which a community prefers to celebrate its faith rather than express its doubts or review its struggles. For those occasions Addison's hymns are just right.

OTHER MAJOR WORKS

PLAYS: *Rosamond*, pr., pb. 1707 (libretto; music by Thomas Clayton); *Cato*, pr., pb. 1713; *The Drummer: Or, The Haunted House*, pr., pb. 1716.

NONFICTION: *Remarks upon Italy*, 1705; *The Tatler*, 1709-1711 (with Richard Steele); *The Whig Examiner*, 1710; *The Spectator*, 1711-1712, 1714 (with Steele; also known as *The Sir Roger de Coverly Papers*); *The Guardian*, 1713 (with Steele); *The Lover*, 1714 (with Steele; as Marmaduke Myrtle, Gent.); *The Reader*, 1714 (with Steele); *The Freeholder: Or, Political Essays*, 1715-1716; *The Old Whig*, 1719; *Dialogues upon the Usefulness of Ancient Medals*, 1721; *The Letters of Joseph Addison*, 1941 (Walter Graham, editor); *The Spectator*, 1965 (Donald Bond, editor).

TRANSLATION: *Fourth Georgic*, 1694 (of Vergil's *Georgics*).

EDITED TEXT: *Musarum Anglicanarum Analecta*, 1699.

MISCELLANEOUS: *The Miscellaneous Works*, 1914 (A. C. Guthkelch, editor).

BIBLIOGRAPHY

Addison, Joseph. *The Letters of Joseph Addison*. Edited by Walter Graham. 1941. Reprint. St. Clair Shores, Mich.: Scholarly Press, 1976. About seven hundred of Addison's letters are represented here, covering a twenty-year period from 1699 to 1719. Among the addressees are William Congreve, Jonathan Swift, and the philosopher Gottfried Wilhelm Leibniz. Forty letters to Addison are included.

Bloom, Edward A., and Lillian D. Bloom. *Addison and Steele: The Critical Heritage*. Boston: Routledge and Kegan Paul, 1980. This invaluable collection reprints critical estimates of the authors and their journals from the early 1700's onward. It contains many of the famous as well as hard-to-find evaluations by eighteenth century commentators. These entries help the student trace the rise and fall of Addison and Steele's reputation.

_____. *Joseph Addison's Sociable Animal: In the Market Place, on the Hustings, in the Pulpit*. Providence, R.I.: Brown University Press, 1971. The lengthiest study of Addison's contribution to the worldview of the emerging British middle class. By connecting ideas scattered throughout the periodical essays, the Blooms systematize Addison's economic, political, and religious thinking.

Carritt, E. F. "Addison, Kant, and Wordsworth." *Essays and Studies* 22 (1937): 26-36. This landmark study reveals Addison's anticipation of the succeeding era of poets. Shows how Immanuel Kant, often connected with the first Romantic generation in England, was influenced by Addison and how Samuel Taylor Coleridge was the catalyst between Kant and William Wordsworth.

Ellison, Julie. *Cato's Tears and the Making of Anglo-American Emotion*. Chicago: University of Chicago Press, 1999. Taking issue with what Ellison sees as a dominantly Americanist criticism that has studied sentiment as a female, and specifically domestic, possession, Ellison instead theorizes sentiment as a widely circulating and historically contingent discourse in canonical and lesser-known Anglo-American literature of the eighteenth century. Such a critical position produces an intense discursive exploration of the changing literary trope of the sentimental man.

Haan, Estelle. *Vergilius Redivivus: Studies in Joseph Addison's Latin Poetry*. Philadelphia: American Philosophical Society, 2005. Latin poetry scholar Haan looks at Addison's Latin poetry and how Latin poetry influenced English poetry.

Johnson, Samuel. "Addison." In *Lives of the English Poets*, edited by George Birkbeck Hill. Vol. 2. 1905. Reprint. Hildesheim, Germany: Georg Olms, 1968. This fine edition is replete with helpful notes. Johnson's praise is high: "Whoever wishes to attain an English style, familiar but not coarse, and elegant but not ostentatious, must give his days and nights to the volumes of Addison."

Knight, Charles A. *Joseph Addison and Richard Steele: A Reference Guide, 1730-1991*. New York: G. K. Hall, 1994. Contains history, criticism, and bibliographies for the two writers.

Otten, Robert M. *Joseph Addison*. Boston: Twayne, 1982. This study appreciates Addison's achievement as a writer who constantly adapted to the changing demands of audience and circumstance. It discusses Addison's inventiveness in approaching familiar topics or repeated themes through a variety of techniques and perspectives.

Smithers, Peter. *The Life of Joseph Addison*. 2d ed. Oxford, England: Clarendon Press, 1968. Smithers is Addison's most comprehensive, sympathetic, and judicious biographer. He appreciates that Addison's vision of citizenship underlies both his own career and his effort to bring "Philosophy into Clubs and Assemblies." The book is especially good at placing Addison's literary works in their historical context.

*Robert M. Otten*

---

# Æ

## George William Russell

**Born:** Lurgan, County Armagh, Ireland; April 10, 1867

**Died:** Bournemouth, England; July 17, 1935

### Principal poetry

*Homeward: Songs by the Way*, 1894
*The Earth Breath, and Other Poems*, 1897
*The Divine Vision, and Other Poems*, 1903
*The Nuts of Knowledge: Lyrical Poems Old and New*, 1903
*By Still Waters: Lyrical Poems Old and New*, 906
*Collected Poems*, 1913, 1919, 1926, 1935
*Gods of War with Other Poems*, 1915

*Voices of the Stones*, 1925
*Midsummer Eve*, 1928
*Dark Weeping*, 1929
*Enchantment, and Other Poems*, 1930
*Vale, and Other Poems*, 1931
*The House of the Titans, and Other Poems*, 1934
*Selected Poems*, 1935

### Other literary forms

In addition to his enormous amount of poetry, Æ (AY-ee) wrote pungent essays in almost every imaginable field, from literary criticism to politics, economics, and agriculture. These essays are collected in such volumes as *Some Irish Essays* (1906) and *The Living Torch* (1937). His interest in that department of letters would eventually lead him to become editor of *The Irish Homestead*, and later *The Irish Statesman*. He also tried his hand at fiction with *The Mask of Apollo, and Other Stories* (1904), ranging from the Asian-tinged "The Cave of Lillith" and "The Meditation of Ananda" to the Celtic-influenced "A Dream of Angus Oge," in which Æ characteristically blends East and West.

He also attempted drama with *Deirdre* (1902), the first important play to be performed by the company that was later to become the Irish National Theatre. Æ compiled his own spiritual autobiography, *The Candle of Vision* (1918), and in both it and *Song and Its Fountains* (1932), he attempted to explain his mysticism and poetic theory, which for him were one and the same. In *The National Being* (1916), Æ combines history with prophecy. *The Interpreters* (1922) consists of a dialogue among several characters typifying various positions in the Irish revolutionary movement—the heretic, the poet, the socialist, the historian, the aesthete, and the industrialist. In *The Avatars* (1933), Æ created a "futurist fantasy" in which mythical heroes, or avatars, appear and spread joy wherever they go. They are removed by the authorities, but their cult grows through legends and artistic records.

In addition to his literary and journalistic work, Æ maintained an extensive correspondence, a part of which has been published in *Some Passages from the Letters of Æ to W. B. Yeats* (1936), *Æ's Letters to Mínánlabáin* (1937), and *Letters from Æ* (1961).

ACHIEVEMENTS

Æ's greatest contribution to Irish literature came from neither his artistic endeavors nor his journalistic and political involvement but rather from his unceasing kindness to younger writers. Frank O'Connor has said that Æ was the father of three generations of Irish poets. Among his discoveries were James Joyce, Padraic Colum, James Stephens, Frank O'Connor, Austin Clarke, and Patrick Kavanagh. As a poet, Æ is less known today for his own work, most of which is now out of print, than for his enormous influence on the younger generation, including William Butler Yeats. Although earlier critics grouped Æ with Yeats and John Millington Synge as one of the three major figures in the Irish Literary Revival, later criticism, such as Richard Finneran's *Anglo-Irish Literature* (1976), generally considers Æ among the lesser revival figures such as Lady Augusta Gregory, Oliver St. John Gogarty, and James Stephens.

It is difficult to select one artistic achievement for which Æ is remembered today, because so much of his work was indirect, involving the support of other artists, ideas, revivals, friendship, political expression, agriculture, economics, nationalism, mysticism, the Abbey Theatre, and art in general. Yeats's wife may have best summarized Æ's achievements when she told her husband that he was a better poet but that Æ was a saint.

BIOGRAPHY

The events of Æ's early years are somewhat obscure. He was born George William Russell into the Northern Irish Protestant family of Thomas Elias Russell and Mary Anne (Armstrong) Russell. When he was eleven, his family moved to Dublin, and Æ was educated at the Rathmines School. From 1880 to 1900, he attended the Dublin School of Art for a few months each year, where he met Yeats, a fellow student. Their long friendship was a troubled one, since Yeats felt that Æ never fulfilled his artistic potential.

Æ's first employment may have been as a clerk in a Guinness brewery, a job he soon quit. Painting was Æ's natural activity, but this was sacrificed because his family could not afford such luxuries, and he turned to literature. From 1890 to 1897, he worked in a warehouse twelve hours a day; in the evenings, he served as librarian of the Dublin Lodge of the Theosophical Society, where he lived. In the midst of all this, he still found time to publish his first two volumes of poetry, *Homeward* and *The Earth Breath, and Other Poems*.

The most important event in Æ's life occurred in 1887 when he discovered Theosophy. He had been a mystic from childhood, and becoming an ardent adherent, he utilized the principles of Theosophy. It was only after the death of Madame Blavatsky, the founder of the Theosophical Society, that he severed his official connection with Theosophy.

The mystic Æ later evolved into a philosopher and a political sage respected on both sides of the Atlantic. For his entire adult life, he was active in the cooperative agricultural movement of Sir Horace Plunkett's Irish Agricultural Organization Society and in the Home Rule movement.

Having achieved a certain security through his position as organizer in the Irish villages for Horace Plunkett, the agrarian reformer, Æ married Violet North. They had two sons, one of whom became an

Æ (©CORBIS)

American citizen. Æ was never a domestic man because his variety of interests kept him busy and often away from home. When his health showed signs of deteriorating, Plunkett made him editor of the cooperative journal *The Irish Homestead*. In 1923, the journal merged with *The Irish Statesman*, with Æ again as editor; in 1930, however, the paper failed because of enormous legal expenses. Æ remained in Ireland until late in his life, when he toured the United States, and after the death of his wife, he spent most of his time abroad.

Æ was nearly six feet tall and became corpulent in old age. He had a russet beard, "mousecolored" hair, and blue-gray eyes covered by spectacles; he wore shabby clothes and was a perpetual pipe smoker. Æ looked like what he was—a thinker somewhere between a farmer and a mystical poet. In accord with Irish tradition, he was a great talker and an inspired speaker. His voice was mellow, with a strong north Irish accent. He painted all his life but never exhibited or sold his paintings, preferring instead to give them to his friends. Æ was intensely involved in the arts, but he always felt that people were more important, and he worked throughout his life for the welfare of humankind.

His pen name Æ (or A. E.) grew out of this tradition. It was originally Æon but a proofreader let it appear as Æ. Russell accepted the change and used it from that point on. Why Æon? John Eglinton recounted that Æ once made a drawing of the apparition in the Divine Mind of the idea of Heavenly Man. Unable to sleep one night, a voice gave him a title for his work, "Call it the Birth of Æon." His eye was caught by a passage in August Neander's *Allgemeine Geschichte der christlichen Religion und Kirche* (1825-1852; *General History of the Christian Religion and Church*, 1847-1855), on the doctrine of the Aeons. In a letter, he described the following elements of the word: *A*, the sound for God; *Æ*, the first divergence from *A; Au*, the sound continuity for a time; and *N*, change. Thus, Æon represents revolt from God, the soul's passage through its successive incarnations in humankind homeward to God, and finally God's amplification.

In 1935, Æ died from cancer at Bournemouth, England, his home after the death of his wife. Some years earlier he had written that the dead are happier than the living and that he did not fear death for himself or for others.

## ANALYSIS

In his excellent introduction to *The Living Torch*, Monk Gibbon remarks that Æ's poetry began as that of a mystic and remained so to the end. Æ saw the poet not as an artisan of beauty but rather as a seer and prophet who derived a special authority from communion with the esoteric wisdom of the past. As Gibbon points out, Æ's poetry contains a beauty of thought and a sincerity of utterance, but in some poems, the form seems inadequate and the imagery vague.

Like other poets in the Irish Renaissance, Æ attempted to define Irishness in terms of the mysticism, reverie, and wavering rhythms of the Celtic Twilight, but his poetic voice remained a faint one. Some of Æ's best poetry is contained in his first two books: *Homeward* and *The Earth Breath, and Other Poems*. Some of his late work is also very good, but it is marred by a tendency to philosophize.

Æ will continue to have a place in literary history, but his prose and poetry are comparable only to the best imaginative work of the secondary figures of his day. Æ survives not as a painter or poet but as an exemplar of his age.

## HOMEWARD

Æ's philosophy includes a pantheistic adoration of nature, and he argues that the important thing about Ireland is the primitiveness of the country and its people. The very title of *Homeward* indicates the author's attitude toward life. Ernest Boyd in his *Appreciations and Depreciations: Irish Literary Studies* (1918) has stated that "home" for Æ signifies the return of the soul to the oversoul, the spirit's absorption into the universal spirit—a doctrine that reflects his interest in Ralph Waldo Emerson, Henry David Thoreau, and Walt Whitman.

*Homeward* is a narrative of Æ's spiritual adventures, a record of the soul's search for the Infinite. Æ's poems are songs with sensuous, unearthly notes, records of the inner music of his life. They do not speak of humankind's mundane experiences but rather of those moments of divine vision and intuition when humankind's being dissolves into communion with the eternal. In that moment when the seer has come to his spiritual vision, he is truly at home.

Alone with nature, Æ beholds in his poetry the beauties of the phenomenal world, and through this experience, the poet is lifted toward participation in the eternal. The conditions that usually produce an exalted mood are those associated with morning or evening twilight, the quietude of the hills, and the silent, lonely countryside; such scenes are typical of both his poetry and his paintings. On innumerable occasions, the poet seeks the soft dusk of the mountains for meditation. Often his verses suggest the coming of daylight and the initial glories of sunlight as the seer pays homage to the light after a night of rapture on the mountainside.

However, solitude is not the sine qua non for Æ's visions. In "The City," his mood is unaltered by the change of setting. The poet's immortal eyes transfigure the mortal things of the city. The reader is reminded of another Metaphysical poet, T. S. Eliot, as Æ paints the gloom of the metropolis while managing to retain bright glimmers of hope.

Wayne Hall in his *Shadowy Heroes* (1980) has pointed out that, in recording his most intense experiences (his ecstatic visions), Æ produced his most notable work. The most successful poems in *Homeward* are "By the Margin of the Great Deep," "The Great Breath," and the sequence "Dusk," "Night," "Dawn," and "Day." "Dusk" begins at sunset, that special moment for poetic visions. At this early point in the volume, the vision of the speaker draws him away from domestic life and human contact toward "primeval being." Sunset also introduces "The Great Breath." The fading sky of this poem seems to suggest both a cosmic flower and an awareness that the death of beauty occasions its most complete fulfillment. This unstable insight, Hall points out, as with the paradox of spiritual union through physical separation in "By the Margin of the Great Deep," becomes more nearly resolved in the four-poem sequence. In "By the Margin of the Great Deep," rather than a sunset, chimney fires of the village mingle in the sky, signifying the merging of humanity within the vastness of God.

For Æ, night usually brings despair and the loss of vision, as in "The Dawn of Darkness." In "Waiting" the speaker can only hope that dawn will reawaken human-

ity to its former joy. In the poem "Night," however, Æ changes directions as night brings on a rebirth of spirit and beauty, a complete union of souls, while "Dawn" initiates a fragmentation of unity. In the light of common day, vision is lost but not entirely forgotten.

The sequence of poems from "Dusk" to "Day" succeeds far better than Æ's other attempts to link mortal pain with immortal vision. For Æ, to have a human spirit, a person must know sorrow. The path to wisdom is a road paved with the burdens of the world. Too often, however, he fails to integrate one world into the other, beyond the level of unconvincing abstraction.

OTHER MAJOR WORKS

LONG FICTION: *The Avatars*, 1933.

SHORT FICTION: *The Mask of Apollo, and Other Stories*, 1904.

PLAY: *Deirdre*, pr. 1902.

NONFICTION: *Some Irish Essays*, 1906; *The National Being*, 1916; *The Candle of Vision*, 1918; *The Interpreters*, 1922; *Song and Its Fountains*, 1932; *Some Passages from the Letters of Æ to W. B. Yeats*, 1936; *Æ's Letters to Mínánlabáin*, 1937; *The Living Torch*, 1937 (Monk Gibbon, editor); *Letters from Æ*, 1961.

MISCELLANEOUS: *The Descent of the Gods: Comprising the Mystical Writings of G. W. Russell "A.E.,"* 1988 (Raghavan Narasimhan Iyer and Nandini Iyer, editors).

BIBLIOGRAPHY

Allen, Nicholas. *George Russell (Æ) and the New Ireland, 1905-1930*. Portland, Oreg.: Four Courts Press, 2003. Looks at Æ and his relationship with Ireland as an artist and man.

Davis, Robert Bernard. *George William Russell ("Æ")*. Boston: Twayne, 1977. The first chapter sketches the external events of Æ. His varied interests are elaborated in six succeeding chapters, with focuses on the mystic, the poet, his drama and fiction, the economist, the statesman, and the critic. A brief conclusion assesses Æ's contributions. Provides a chronology, notes, an index, and an annotated, select bibliography.

Figgis, Darrell. *Æ, George W. Russell: A Study of a Man and a Nation*. San Rafael, Calif.: Coracle

Press, 2008. A biography of Æ that looks at his poetic works and his contributions to Ireland.

Kain, Richard M., and James H. O'Brien. *George Russell (Æ)*. Lewisburg, Pa.: Bucknell University Press, 1976. The first three chapters, by Kain, present a biography of Æ by examining his personality, his early success, and his decline. The last two chapters, by O'Brien, examine Æ's interests in Theosophy and his work as a poet. Contains a chronology and a select bibliography.

Kuch, Peter. *Yeats and Æ: The Antagonism That Unites Dear Friends*. Totowa, N.J.: Barnes & Noble, 1986. This work examines the relationship between William Butler Yeats and George William Russell from their first meeting in art class to their split in 1908. Kuch provides excellent background on the inner workings of the London-Dublin esoteric worlds that shaped both men. Especially valuable is his ability to sort through the many branches of the esoteric tradition.

Loftus, Richard J. *Nationalism in Modern Anglo-Irish Poetry*. Madison: University of Wisconsin Press, 1964. Chapter 5, "The Land of Promise," is a substantial examination of Æ's attitudes toward Irish nationalism. His optimism turned to anger, then to disillusionment. Rarely did he include his private political feelings in his public verse. *The House of the Titans, and Other Poems* is analyzed for nationalistic implications. Supplemented by notes, a bibliography, and an index.

Mercier, Vivian. "Victorian Evangelicalism and the Anglo-Irish Literary Revival." In *Literature and the Changing Ireland*, edited by Peter Connolly. Totowa, N.J.: Barnes & Noble, 1982. Evangelicalism is examined as the background to Æ's career. His father made Æ aware of the power of conversion, which occurred away from evangelicalism to Theosophy for him. He helped to establish Theosophy as a sect similar in status to that of a Protestant evangelical group. Includes notes and an index.

Summerfield, Henry. *That Myriad-Minded Man: A Biography of George William Russell, "A. E.," 1867-1935*. Gerrards Cross, Ireland: Colin Smythe, 1975. Chapter 1 explains Russell's mysticism. His nationalism is then examined. Chapter 4 focuses on farm interests, and the following chapter describes his journalism from 1905 to 1914. Russell's pacifism is then posed against the violence of war in two chapters, and a final chapter covers his last years. Complemented by illustrations, notes, and an index.

*John Harty, III*

---

# RICHARD ALDINGTON

**Born:** Portsmouth, Hampshire, England; July 8, 1892
**Died:** Sury-en-Vaux, France; July 27, 1962

PRINCIPAL POETRY

*Images, 1910-1915*, 1915 (enlarged 1919)
*The Love of Myrrhine and Konallis, and Other Prose Poems*, 1917
*Reverie: A Little Book of Poems for H. D.*, 1917
*Images of Desire*, 1919
*Images of War: A Book of Poems*, 1919
*War and Love, 1915-1918*, 1919
*The Berkshire Kennet*, 1923
*Collected Poems, 1915-1923*, 1923
*Exile, and Other Poems*, 1923
*A Fool i' the Forest: A Phantasmagoria*, 1924
*Hark the Herald*, 1928
*Collected Poems*, 1929
*The Eaten Heart*, 1929
*A Dream in the Luxembourg*, 1930
*Movietones*, 1932
*The Poems of Richard Aldington*, 1934
*Life Quest*, 1935
*The Crystal World*, 1937
*The Complete Poems of Richard Aldington*, 1948

OTHER LITERARY FORMS

Richard Aldington established himself in the literary world of London as a youthful poet, but later in life he increasingly devoted his attention to prose fiction, translation, biography, and criticism. His first novel, *Death of a Hero* (1929), drew favorable attention, and it was followed in 1930 by *Roads to Glory*, a collection of thirteen short stories. Aldington continued to publish fiction until 1946, when his last novel, *The Romance of Casanova*, appeared.

From early in his career, Aldington was highly regarded as a translator. He translated *Remy de Gourmont: Selections from All His Works* (1929; 2 volumes) from French, *The Decameron of Giovanni Boccaccio* (1930) from Italian, *Alcestis* (1930) from classical Greek, and other works from Latin and Provençal.

Aldington wrote biographies of the duke of Wellington (1943) and of Robert Louis Stevenson (1957), along with *Voltaire* (1925), *D. H. Lawrence: Portrait of a Genius But . . .* (1950), and *Lawrence of Arabia: A Biographical Enquiry* (1955), along with a substantial body of critical essays.

Other miscellaneous works include *Life for Life's Sake: A Book of Reminiscences* (1941) and *Pinorman: Personal Recollections of Norman Douglas, Pino Orioli, and Charles Prentice* (1954). Aldington also edited *The Viking Book of Poetry of the English-Speaking World* (1941).

## ACHIEVEMENTS

Despite Richard Aldington's extensive publications in criticism and in a variety of literary genres, he remains inextricably associated with the movement known as Imagism, of which he was certainly a founding member, along with the American poets H. D. (Hilda Doolittle) and Ezra Pound.

Although only twenty years old when Imagism was conceived in 1912, Aldington found himself part of a minirevolution against wordiness and imprecision in poetry, a revolution formulated in terms of advocacy of effective images and cogent free verse.

Aldington's later poems, though eliciting occasional praise from distinguished critics, actually did little to enhance the reputation he had earned as an Imagist. In 1947, Aldington was awarded the James Tait Black Memorial Prize for his biography of Wellington, and shortly before his death he was invited to Moscow, where his achievements were celebrated by the Soviet Writers' Union.

## BIOGRAPHY

Richard Aldington was born Edward Godfree Aldington in Portsmouth, England, but spent most of his youth in Dover before enrolling at University College in London in 1910. A year later, his family having suffered from a financial reverse, Aldington left the college and went to work for a newspaper. He had already developed a keen interest in poetry and soon met others who shared his enthusiasm, including the Americans H. D. and Ezra Pound. Pound urged that the three promulgate their poetic affinities for precision, economy of language, striking images, and free verse, and Aldington and H. D. agreed, thus creating the literary movement known as Imagism.

Pound encouraged Harriet Monroe, editor of *Poetry*, a new literary magazine, to publish Imagist verse, and in 1912, three poems by Aldington appeared, earning their author forty dollars and publicly establishing the twenty-year-old poet as a representative of the new movement. In London, Aldington met William Butler Yeats and other luminaries. He visited Paris and Italy and, in 1914, having married H. D. in the previous year, became assistant editor of a journal named *The Egoist*, which developed into a significant outlet for Imagist productions. In the same year, ten of Aldington's poems were published in *Des Imagistes*, an anthology edited by Pound that also included poems by H. D., James Joyce, Ford Madox Ford, Amy Lowell, and William Carlos Williams, among others.

Aldington's first collection of his own work was *Images, 1910-1915*, which came out in 1915, by which time he had also embarked on his long career of literary translation, publishing *The Poems of Anyte of Tegea* and *Latin Poems of the Renaissance* that year. In 1916, he volunteered for military service and saw action on the front until the end of the war. He was eventually discharged from service with the rank of captain. His experiences of the horrors of combat sent him back to England a changed man, and his marriage to H. D.— which had already suffered from their prolonged separation—proved unable to survive the challenge of their collective trauma. Though not officially divorced until 1938, Aldington and H. D. actually ended their marriage shortly after World War I.

Returning to London's literary life, Aldington resumed his career as poet and critic, accepting a position writing for the *Times Literary Supplement* and continuing to publish poems, translations, and criticism. He eventually decided, however, to move to the country, where he hoped to be able to work without distraction. This move was successful, and Aldington read, wrote, and translated diligently in his rural environment for several years, visiting Italy in 1922 and in 1926. In 1924, he published his first long poem, *A Fool i' the Forest*, which may be retrospectively regarded as a final departure from the Imagist lyrics of his youth. By 1927, Aldington was spending time in Paris, where he met Ernest Hemingway and Hart Crane, and in 1928, he decided to leave England for good.

In 1929, Aldington published the novel *Death of a Hero*, which was based on his own experiences during World War I. This year also saw the appearance of another long poem, *The Eaten Heart*. Aldington remained in Italy and France during most of the next several years, with trips to Africa, Spain, and Portugal, and, as always, he worked steadily wherever he was. By the time European totalitarianism drove him from the Continent in 1935, Aldington had three more novels, another long poem, and a book of short stories in print, along with more translations.

With Benito Mussolini dominating Italy, Francisco Franco holding sway in Spain, and Adolf Hitler ruling Germany, Aldington, whose attitude toward Britain had not changed since 1928, looked westward. He crossed the Atlantic in 1935 and lived for several months in Tobago before moving to the United States, where he eventually took up residence in Connecticut. He had published *Life Quest*, a long poem, in 1935, and in 1937 he published a novel titled *Very Heaven* and his last long poem, *The Crystal World*.

Despite his initial enthusiasm for the United States, Aldington gradually became disenchanted with American life. In 1943 he published *The Duke, Being an Account of the Life and Achievements of Arthur Wellesley, First Duke of Wellington*, the Wellington biography that would later win Aldington the James Tait Black Memorial Prize. In 1944, he spent some time as a Hollywood film writer, but, shortly after the war, he returned to France. In 1946, *The Romance of Casanova*, a novel, marked the end of Aldington's publication of fiction. From this point onward, though he remained industrious, his output was restricted to criticism and biography.

Aldington had been a personal friend of D. H. Law-

*Richard Aldington* (Library of Congress)

rence and had always admired Lawrence's work, and in 1950 he issued *D. H. Lawrence: Portrait of a Genius But . . .* , a work that was followed by two publications that would damage Aldington's reputation and income for the rest of his life. *Pinorman*, a memoir focused on Aldington's old acquaintance Norman Douglas, aroused resentment among Douglas's friends and adherents, who regarded it as a betrayal on Aldington's part. Still more controversial was *Lawrence of Arabia* (1955), which attacked the putative heroism, modesty, and truthfulness of a revered hero of World War I. Lawrence's admirers exerted some remarkable efforts to prevent the publication of this book, and when it at length appeared, many of them engaged in vehement personal attacks on Aldington. These attacks caused a serious reduction in Aldington's royalties, as booksellers and publishers refused to handle his works, and he remained on the defensive and in financial difficulties for the rest of his life.

Aldington went on to publish *Introduction to Mistral* (1956), *Frauds* (1957), and *Portrait of a Rebel: The Life and Work of Robert Louis Stevenson* (1957). In 1962, he went to the Soviet Union at the invitation of the Soviet Writers' Union and was honored there for his contributions to literature. He died on July 27, 1962, near Sury-en-Vaux, France.

ANALYSIS

Richard Aldington's reputation as poet has been unduly shaped by the circumstances under which he published his early works. As one of the three original Imagists (along with Ezra Pound and H. D.), he at twenty was several years younger than his literary partners. Pound, already rather famous and something of a swashbuckler, aggressively cultivated the reputation of a trendsetter, and H. D.'s lyric gifts must have been enhanced in Aldington's eyes by her beauty. Pound and H. D. had already been friends for years, so the young Aldington must have felt privileged to have been admitted to their circle and to have his work appreciated by them.

IMAGISM

It is clear that the famous principles of Imagism—directness, economy, and musical phrasing—are as frequently absent from Imagist poetry as they are present, and one must suspect the dogmatic hand of Pound in their formulation. Aldington's very early "Choricos" already suggests divergence from the movement's program:

> Brushing the fields with red-shod feet,
> With purple robe
> Searing the grass as with a sudden flame,
> Death,
> Thou hast come upon us.

Here there are colors ("red," "purple"), powerful verbs ("Brushing," "Searing"), alliteration, and assonance, but there is conspicuously no concrete image, and the absence of such an image works effectively to represent the mystery of death, whose certainty is more evident in inevitability than in visibility. However, some conscious efforts were made by Aldington to focus on clear, arresting images. In "Round-Pond," he wrote:

> Water ruffled and speckled by galloping wind
> Which puffs and spurts it into tiny pashing breakers
> Dashed with lemon-yellow afternoon sunlight.
> The shining of the sun upon the water
> Is like a scattering of gold crocus petals
> In a long wavering irregular flight.

As pleasant and as exuberant as these lines are, they prepare no modernist jolt, for some lines later the poem concludes, "Even the cold wind is seeking a new mistress." This conclusion deflates the gentle pretensions of the preceding lines and seemingly defies the rigid seriousness of the announced program of Imagism.

Although Aldington's youthful work betrays influences that do not appear to have been fully integrated in his vision, his erudition and his sensitive ear for the music of language often helped him create his own voice. The Imagists' passion for classical poetry, tempered as it was by their experiments with English versions of Japanese poetry, combined in Aldington's case with his reading of Walt Whitman and Algernon Charles Swinburne to produce insights that were first to be subjected to the psychological stress of front-line combat and later to the implications of Aldington's long recuperation from his wartime experiences. In 1915, Aldington was able to express emotional simplicity with his understated lines from "Epigrams": "She has new leaves/ After her dead flowers,/ Like the little almond tree/ Which the frost hurt." In the same collection, however, his rage about the pain of his childhood is elaborated at Whitmanesque length in a performance in which outrage consistently outdistances art:

> The bitterness, the misery, the wretchedness
>   of childhood
> Put me out of love with God,
> I can't believe in God's goodness;
> I can believe
> In many avenging gods.

Though the doors to poetic recognition had been opened by his own talent as well as by the encouragement of his friends, Aldington was still developing a personal technique when the war came. World War I was a devastating experience for him, however. He wrote poems during and after the war in which some of his Imagist techniques are manifest, but it is in his collection *Exile, and Other Poems* that the effects of the trauma of war are revealed. Recalling his grim life in combat in the poem "Eumenides," Aldington mused about

> That boot I kicked
> (It had a mouldy foot in it)
> The night K's head was smashed
> Like a rotten pear by a mortar.

The title of the poem, of course, refers to the monstrous Furies of Greek mythology, and Aldington was not to conquer his personal Furies until, at the end of the decade, he put his war experiences into prose with *Death of a Hero* and *Roads to Glory*, a sequence of short stories. *Exile, and Other Poems*, in fact, marks the end of Aldington's effort to express himself artistically in short poems.

### THE LONG POEMS

Aldington's first long poem, *A Fool i' the Forest*, was published in 1924. Subtitled *A Phantasmagoria*, the work combines a variety of poetic forms with narrative free verse to represent the psychomachia of the modern individual in crisis, evoking echoes of the past (William Shakespeare) and responding to contemporary poetry, notably that of T. S. Eliot. The shifting setting of the poem takes its protagonist from Greece to the trenches of France and finally back to London, where, his hopes defeated, he subsides into a conventional existence.

*A Dream in the Luxembourg* was written in 1928 but not immediately published. It was inspired by a love affair commenced at the time by Aldington, though it is notably devoid of the techniques generally considered poetic. Aldington published another of his long poems, *The Eaten Heart*, in 1929, and this poem also shows its author's rejection of conventional poetics. It focuses, as had *A Fool i' the Forest*, upon the fragmentation of modern existence, the dehumanization resulting from the rise of technology, and human isolation.

*Life Quest*, like Joyce's *Ulysses* (1922), evokes Homer's *Odyssey* (c. 725 B.C.E.; English translation, 1614), but the journey here also partakes of the religious qualities of the medieval quest. Aldington's hero makes his way at the end of the poem to Gibraltar, perhaps suggesting the poet's own decision to go to the United States.

Aldington's last long poem and last published poem, *The Crystal World*, appeared in 1937. Divided into two main sections, each with subsections, this poem marks both a return to lyricism and Aldington's own farewell to the composition of poetry. The poem explores the mystery and the promise of love, its frustrations and consummations. Aldington, now a middle-aged man and a veteran of more than war, ended his poetic career writing of love.

### OTHER MAJOR WORKS

LONG FICTION: *Death of a Hero*, 1929; *The Colonel's Daughter*, 1931; *All Men Are Enemies*, 1933; *Women Must Work*, 1934; *Very Heaven*, 1937; *Seven Against Reeves*, 1938; *Rejected Guest*, 1939; *The Romance of Casanova*, 1946.

SHORT FICTION: *At All Costs*, 1930; *Last Straws*, 1930; *Roads to Glory*, 1930; *Two Stories: Deserter and The Lads of the Village*, 1930; *A War Story*, 1930; *Stepping Heavenward*, 1931; *Soft Answers*, 1932.

PLAY: *A Life of a Lady*, pb. 1936 (with Derek Patmore).

NONFICTION: *Literary Studies and Reviews*, 1924; *Voltaire*, 1925; *French Studies and Reviews*, 1926; *D. H. Lawrence: An Indiscretion*, 1927; *Remy de Gourmont: A Modern Man of Letters*, 1928; *Artifex: Sketches and Ideas*, 1935; *D. H. Lawrence: A Complete List of His Works, Together with a Critical Appreciation*, 1935; *W. Somerset Maugham: An Appreciation*, 1939; *Life for Life's Sake: A Book of Reminiscences*, 1941; *The Duke, Being an Account of the Life and Achievements of Arthur Wellesley, First Duke of Wellington*, 1943; *Four English Portraits, 1801-1851*, 1948; *Jane Austen*, 1948; *The Strange Life of Charles Waterton, 1782-1865*, 1949; *D. H. Lawrence: Portrait of a Genius But . . .*, 1950; *Ezra Pound and T. S. Eliot, a Lecture*, 1954; *Lawrence L'Imposteur: T. E. Lawrence, the Legend and the Man*, 1954; *Pinorman: Personal Recollections of Norman Douglas, Pino Orioli, and Charles Prentice*, 1954; *A. E. Housman and W. B. Yeats, Two Lectures*, 1955; *Lawrence of Arabia: A Biographical Inquiry*, 1955; *Introduction to Mistral*, 1956; *Frauds*, 1957; *Portrait of a Rebel: The Life and Work of Robert Louis Stevenson*, 1957; *Richard Aldington: Selected Critical Writings, 1928-1960*, 1970 (Alister Kershaw, editor); *A Passionate Prodigality*, 1975 (Alan Bird, editor); *Literary Lifelines*, 1981 (Lawrence Durrell, editor).

TRANSLATIONS: *Latin Poems of the Renaissance*, 1915; *The Poems of Anyte of Tegea*, 1915; *The Garland of Months*, 1917 (of Folgore Da San Gemignano); *Greek Songs in the Manner of Anacreon*, 1919; *The Poems of Mealeager of Gadara*, 1920; *The Good-Humoured Ladies*, 1922; *French Comedies of the XVIIIth Century*, 1923; *Voyages to the Moon and the Sun*, 1923 (of Cyrano de Bergerac); *A Book of "Characters" from Theophrastus*, 1924; *Dangerous Acquaintances*, 1924 (of Pierre Choderlos de Lacos' novel; *Les Liaisons dangereuses*); *Candide, and Other Romances*, 1927 (of Voltaire); *Fifty Romance Lyric Poems*, 1928; *The Great Betrayal*, 1928; *Remy de Gourmont, Selections from All His Works*, 1929; *Alcestis*, 1930 (of Euripides); *The Decameron of Giovanni Boccaccio*, 1930; *Great French Romances*, 1946.

EDITED TEXT: *The Viking Book of Poetry of the English-Speaking World*, 1941.

BIBLIOGRAPHY

Crawford, Fred D. *Richard Aldington and Lawrence of Arabia: A Cautionary Tale*. Carbondale: Southern Illinois University Press, 1998. A detailed description of the controversy arising from Aldington's biography of T. E. Lawrence. The frequent quotations from Aldington provide an excellent portrait of his character in middle age, and other material gives insights into his life as poet.

Doyle, Charles. *Richard Aldington: A Biography*. Carbondale: Southern Illinois University Press, 1989. This most comprehensive and up-to-date biography of Aldington does ample justice to his many-faceted gifts as a writer.

_____, ed. *Richard Aldington: Reappraisals*. Victoria, B.C.: University of Victoria Press, 1990. A collection of essays that reconsider Aldington's reputation as poet, novelist, and writer of nonfiction. The assumption behind this collection is that Aldington was unjustly blacklisted as a result of his frank treatment of T. E. Lawrence.

Gates, Norman T. *The Poetry of Richard Aldington: A Critical Evaluation and an Anthology of Uncollected Poems*. University Park: Pennsylvania State University Press, 1974. A thorough study that reviews the criticism of Aldington's poetry from 1910 to the early 1970's and assesses his position as a poet and speaker of his time. This scholarly and appreciative work has located 129 uncollected poems in newspapers, periodicals, and unpublished manuscripts, as well as early books of his poetry omitted from *The Complete Poems*. Includes a valuable bibliography of primary and secondary sources.

_____, ed. *Richard Aldington: An Autobiography in Letters*. University Park: Pennsylvania State University Press, 1992. An effort to display Aldington's temperament and experiences by means of selections from his correspondence.

Kempton, Daniel, and H. R. Stoneback, eds. *Writers in Provence: Proceedings of the First and Second International Richard Aldington Conferences*. New Paltz, N.Y.: Gregau Press and the International Richard Aldington Society, 2003. These essays on Aldington presented at an international conference shed light on his works and life.

Kershaw, Alister, and Frédéric-Jacques Temple, eds. *Richard Aldington: An Intimate Portrait*. Carbondale: Southern Illinois University Press, 1965. An anthology of favorable comments on Aldington from various distinguished persons, including T. S. Eliot, Lawrence Durrell, Sir Herbert Read, and C. P. Snow. Also contains an excellent bibliography of Aldington's writings.

McGreevy, Thomas. *Richard Aldington: An Englishman*. 1931. Reprint. New York: Haskell House, 1974. An earlier, full-length study of Aldington, with critical commentary of his works only up to 1931. An appreciative study, it covers Aldington's novels and poems, with emphasis on *Death of a Hero*.

Smith, Richard Eugene. *Richard Aldington*. Boston: Twayne, 1977. A comprehensive survey of Aldington's work, noting that his leadership in the Imagist movement during the 1920's was but a small part of his varied and productive literary career. Includes criticism of Aldington's major novels as well as his work as a biographer, translator, and critic. A selected bibliography is provided.

Zilboorg, Caroline, ed. *Richard Aldington and H. D.: Their Lives in Letters, 1918-1961*. New York: Palgrave, 2003. A collection of letters between two Imagist poets who were husband and wife, with a commentary and introduction that sheds light on their poetry.

*Robert W. Haynes*

# WILLIAM ALLINGHAM

**Born:** Ballyshannon, Ireland; March 19, 1824
**Died:** London, England; November 18, 1889

PRINCIPAL POETRY

*Poems*, 1850 (enlarged 1861)
*Day and Night Songs*, 1854 (revised and enlarged 1855 as *The Music Master, a Love Story, and Two Series of Day and Night Songs*)
*Laurence Bloomfield in Ireland*, 1864
*Fifty Modern Poems*, 1865
*Songs, Ballads, and Stories*, 1877
*Evil May-Day*, 1882
*Blackberries Picked Off Many Bushes*, 1884
*Irish Songs and Poems*, 1887
*Rhymes for the Young Folk*, 1887 (also known as *Robin Redbreast, and Other Verses*, 1930)
*Flower Pieces, and Other Poems*, 1888
*Life and Phantasy*, 1889
*By the Way: Verses, Fragments, and Notes*, 1912
*The Poems of William Allingham*, 1967 (John Hewitt, editor)

OTHER LITERARY FORMS

Although known primarily as a poet of light lyrics, William Allingham also wrote prose pieces and a diary. Few would deny that *William Allingham: A Diary* (1907) is one of the best literary diaries of the Victorian period. Primarily a product of his English years, it records conversations and encounters with an impressive array of eminent Victorian personalities. Alfred, Lord Tennyson, and Thomas Carlyle were intimates, and there is much about Robert Browning and Dante Ga-

briel Rossetti. Allingham's formal prose turns out to be surprisingly substantial. Starting in 1867, he wrote more than twenty travelogues for *Fraser's Magazine*. Narrated under the pseudonym Patricius Walker, the travelogues are notable for their expository emphasis. The traveler will sometimes pass opinion on what he has seen in his wanderings (Wales, Scotland, provincial England, parts of the Continent), but for the most part, he concentrates on describing scenery and reporting local customs and historical tidbits about the area. A selection of these pieces was later issued as *Rambles* (1873), while most of them were collected in the first two volumes of a posthumously published edition of his prose. The third volume of this work, *Varieties in Prose* (1893), contains Irish sketches and literary criticism.

ACHIEVEMENTS

William Allingham deserves the elusive label "Anglo-Irish." His reputation as a minor Victorian poet is largely the result of the popularity of a few frequently anthologized poems of Irish inspiration, subject matter, and sentiment. Like so many other "minor" literary figures, however, his historical significance goes beyond his accomplishment in any single genre. His foremost achievement is in lyric poetry. He had a knack for spinning songs and ballads. The most famous of these is "The Fairies," a delightful children's rhyme about the elvish world, which inevitably appears in anthologies of Irish verse. Also frequently anthologized is "The Winding Banks of Erne," a tender farewell to Ireland from an emigrant as he sets sail for the New World. Over the years, these two favorites have been included in most of the standard collections of Irish verse: Stopford A. Brooke and T. W. Rolleston's (1900), Padraic Colum's (1922), Lennox Robinson and Donagh MacDonagh's (1958), and Devin Garrity's (1965), among others. To complete their selection from Allingham's work, editors often include lyrics such as "A Dream" and "Four Ducks on a Pond," and ballads such as "Abbey Asaroe" and "The Maids of Elfin Mere."

A dozen or so preservable short poems from a canon of several hundred does not seem to be a very significant achievement. The quality of these poems is sufficiently high, however, to secure at least a minor position in Irish poetry, and, when he is considered in the light of Irish literary history, Allingham's stature grows substantially. As Ernest Boyd points out in *Ireland's Literary Renaissance* (1916), the third quarter of the nineteenth century was a transitional period in Irish literature, sandwiched between an earlier period of predominantly political verse and the later full renaissance led by William Butler Yeats and his circle. During this transitional period, there appeared a few poets who, though not of the first rank, were nevertheless serious, competent artists who celebrated Irish themes without lapsing into propaganda. Allingham was one of these, ranking alongside Aubry de Vere and just below Samuel Ferguson in importance. A country seeking to establish its cultural identity cannot afford to overlook the literary accomplishments of any of its native citizens. Allingham helped to set the stage for the later flowering of Irish verse, and his historical importance was recognized by poets of the Irish Renaissance, particularly Katherine Tynan, Yeats, Lionel Johnson, and Colum.

Yeats above all is responsible for securing Allingham's modest niche in literary history. In an article entitled "A Poet We Have Neglected," Yeats gave an appreciation of Allingham's Irish songs and ballads, noting the poet's facility at capturing ephemeral moods and moments. "It is time," he declared, "for us over here to claim him as our own, and give him his due place among our sacred poets; to range his books beside Davis, Mangum, and Ferguson." Four years later he was writing to Tynan that "you, Ferguson and Allingham are, I think, the Irish poets who have done the largest quantity of fine work." In 1905, he put together and published a small selection of Allingham's best poems (*Sixteen Poems by William Allingham*). More important than Yeats's service to Allingham's reputation, however, is Allingham's influence on Yeats's own poetry. In 1904, Yeats wrote to Mrs. Allingham, "I am sometimes inclined to believe that he was my own master in verse, starting me in the way I have gone whether for good or evil." Allingham's success with ballads and songs encouraged Yeats to explore those genres during the early part of his career, and specific borrowings have been noticed by critics.

Allingham's short verse deserves wider recognition than its slight representation in anthologies seems to warrant. It is true that an enormous amount of inferior work must be waded through, but a reading of his entire canon reveals several dozen poems worth keeping in addition to the well-known ones. There is, for example, an interesting series of poems all entitled "Aeolian Harp." Although these poems are inspired more by English poetic convention than by "Irish scenes and Irish faces" (Yeats's phrase), they are nevertheless fairly successful imitations of the type of reflective poem for which Samuel Taylor Coleridge is known. Some of the sonnets, such as "Autumnal Sonnet" and "Winter Cloud," are very expressive, and there is even a sparkling translation of "The Cicada" from the *Greek Anthology* (first century C.E.). The most judicious twentieth century selection of Allingham's poetry is found in Geoffrey Taylor's anthology *Irish Poets of the Nineteenth Century* (1951), which contains about fifty pages of his shorter poetry. A selection that appeared in 1967 (*The Poems of William Allingham*, edited by John Hewitt) contains about twenty shorter poems, plus excerpts from longer ones.

Allingham's second major achievement was *Laurence Bloomfield in Ireland*, a long narrative in verse about Irish tenant-landlord relations in the midnineteenth century. Many later critics, including Taylor and Alan Warner, place *Laurence Bloomfield in Ireland* first on the list of Allingham's achievements. Yeats castigated it, as he did all of Allingham's longer poetry, but William Gladstone praised it and even quoted from it in the House of Commons. After reading it, Ivan Turgenev told a mutual friend, "I never understood Ireland before!" Allingham himself considered *Laurence Bloomfield in Ireland* his best work. The poem's modest popularity was partly owing to its contemporary subject matter and partly to its artistic strengths. It ran through several editions during Allingham's lifetime.

His third major area of achievement is his prose, including travelogues, occasional pieces, and a diary. Critic Sean McMahon labels Allingham's posthumously published *William Allingham* his "greatest" work, ranking it above *Laurence Bloomfield in Ireland* and the lyrics.

BIOGRAPHY

William Allingham can be considered more quintessentially Anglo-Irish than other representatives of that breed because he was truly poised between the two spheres. In his first thirty-nine years, Ireland was his home; the last twenty-six were spent almost exclusively in England. Allingham's final visit to Ireland occurred as early as 1866, on the occasion of his father's funeral. The demarcation between the two lives, however, is not as clear as the mere circumstance of residence would seem to indicate. During the Irish years (1824-1863), he often visited England, where most of his friends and correspondents were. During the English years (1863-1889), his mind constantly returned to Ireland, as is evidenced in his writing and conversation.

Allingham was born in the western Ireland port town of Ballyshannon, County Donegal, situated at the mouth of the River Erne. Ballyshannon and vicinity would provide the setting for most of his well-known ballads and lyrics. His family was Protestant, having migrated from Hampshire more than two hundred years earlier. *William Allingham: A Diary* reports that his parents, William and Elizabeth, were both "undemonstrative," and his mother's early death in 1833 probably contributed to a curious personality trait observable in Allingham throughout his life—a simultaneous love of solitude and desire for companionship. "Has anyone walked alone as much as I?" he asked in his diary in 1865, and then immediately gave the counterpoint: "And who fonder of congenial company?"

His father, formerly a merchant, removed his son from a local boarding school at the age of thirteen and installed him as a clerk in the branch bank that he had managed for several years. Thenceforth Allingham educated himself at home during his spare time, no mean feat in the light of his later scholarship. When he was twenty-two, he secured a position in the Customs Service at eighty pounds a year, serving in Ballyshannon and other Ulster towns, and even for a short time on the Isle of Man. He assayed cargoes, visited shipwrecks, audited crew pay-

rolls, no doubt did reams of paperwork, and, significantly, inspected fittings and provisions on immigrant ships heading for the United States. During those years he produced his first three volumes of poetry—*Poems*, *Day and Night Songs*, and *The Music Master, a Love Story, and Two Series of Day and Night Songs*—which, together, contain the core of his best ballads and lyrics.

Allingham's Irish period ended in 1863 when he transferred to the English port of Lymington, on the southern coast opposite the Isle of Wight. Long before this, however, he had become acquainted with England. Starting in 1847, he had made annual visits to London, eventually breaking into several different circles of artists. Through Leigh Hunt, Allingham met Carlyle; Coventry Patmore introduced him to Rossetti and the Pre-Raphaelites, as well as to Tennyson. During the early 1850's, he was especially intimate with Rossetti, "whose friendship," he wrote in a dedication to one volume of his collected works, "brightened many years of my life, and whom I never can forget."

*William Allingham* (Getty Images)

Rossetti's letters to Allingham are numerous, interesting, and accessible (*The Letters of Rossetti to Allingham*, 1897, G. B. Hill, editor). The intimacy with Tennyson and with Carlyle deepened after Allingham's transfer to England. In 1864, he published *Laurence Bloomfield in Ireland*, much revised from its original form in *Fraser's Magazine*, and in 1865, *Fifty Modern Poems*. The latter must be considered more a product of his Irish period.

In 1870, acting on Carlyle's advice, Allingham retired from the civil service to become subeditor of *Fraser's Magazine*, under J. A. Froude, whom he succeeded as editor in 1874. The same year he married Helen Paterson, an established watercolorist only half his age. They had three children. In 1879, Allingham retired permanently, moving to Witley, Surrey, in 1881, then to Hampstead in 1888, his final home. He had been awarded an annual civil pension of sixty pounds in 1864; it was increased to one hundred pounds in 1870. The last twenty years witnessed a decline in poetic output. *Songs, Ballads, and Stories* contains mostly work from previous volumes, though as a collection it may be the best single repository of Allingham's poetry. *Evil May-Day* will remain his least successful volume, mainly because of the heavy didactic nature of the title piece, which whines and frets in blank verse for some eight hundred lines. Ironically, the book also contains his most succinct lyric, the gemlike "Four Ducks on a Pond." His last major original production was *Blackberries Picked Off Many Bushes*, composed entirely of short aphoristic verse.

## ANALYSIS

As a poet, William Allingham will remain known primarily for his lyrics and for *Laurence Bloomfield in Ireland*. He had a lyric voice of unusual charm. He had an eye alert to local beauty. He had a heart sensitive to those passing emotions and thoughts, which, in the aggregate, form the very fabric of human experience. The voices that moved his voice to sing were principally Irish, though not exclusively so. He chose to live the latter third of his life in England; his temperament was largely English; he derived his sense of literary community and artistic purpose from English sources. What poetic strengths he did have are a product of his love for England and Ireland. Those strengths should not be underrated. "I am genuine though not great," he once wrote to a friend, adding "and my time will come."

The chief strengths of Allingham's best lyrics and songs are their simplicity and musicality. His themes are the universal ones: the joys and frustrations of romantic love, the many faces of nature, the quality of country life, humankind's ultimate relation to an indecipherable universe, memories of happier times, the supernatural, and death. His simplicity of style is typified by the following stanza from "The Lighthouse":

> The plunging storm flies fierce against the pane,
> And thrills our cottage with redoubled shocks:
> The chimney mutters and the rafters strain;
> Without, the breakers roar along the rocks.

As he does here, Allingham commonly uses familiar rhyme schemes, keeps syntax straight, and restrains metaphor to an unusual degree. His syntactical purity is such that the only departures from normal word order permitted are entirely conventional poetic inversions ("Many fine things had I glimpse of"). Even then he manages to avoid the grosser sort of inversion, as when the main verb is delayed until the end of the line for mere rhyme's sake ("Loud larks in ether sing"). Implicitly in several poems, explicitly in personal conversations, Allingham criticized the convoluted style of Robert Browning's poetry, friend though he was. Instead, in poetry (see "The Lyric Muse") and prose (*Rambles*, "To Dean Prior"), he holds up Robert Herrick as a model of lyricism. Not too much should be made of that, however, since the serious Allingham would never imitate the cavalier element in Herrick's verse, although he did approve of its "elegant naivete." One might discern an elegance, certainly a gracefulness, in the naïve treatment of idyllic love in the opening lines of this untitled poem:

> Oh! were my Love a country lass,
> That I might see her every day,
> And sit with her on hedgerow grass
> Beneath a bough of may.

Here as elsewhere in his most successful lyrics, Allingham keeps diction simple. Surely the freshness of lines such as these has some value today.

## WILLIAM ALLINGHAM

The musical element is so omnipresent in Allingham's poetry that the distinction between song, lyric, and ballad is sometimes obscured. Many of his enduring poems tend toward song. The musical element adds sweetness, or in some instances liveliness, to the simplicity of his poetry. *William Allingham* records a conversation with William Makepeace Thackeray, in which Allingham wholeheartedly agrees with the novelist's dictum, "I want poetry to be musical, to run sweetly." It is not always easy, however, to determine whether the musical charm of a particular song derives from meter, rhyme, phonetic effects, or from a combination of the three. From *William Allingham* and other prose writings it is apparent that Allingham considered meter to be the very soul of poetry. In fact, some of the most significant entries in his diary include those in which Tennyson and his Irish devotee discuss the technicalities of metrical effects. Lines such as "The pulse in his pillowed ear beat thick" ("The Goblin Child of Ballyshannon") echo Tennyson both metrically and phonetically. Repetition of the haunting place-name "Asaroe" in "Abbey Asaroe" shows that Allingham could choose a word for its rhythm and sound; its precise placement in each stanza shows a talent for emphasis. On the other hand, rhyme is a prominent feature of Allingham's verse. Triplets, internal rhyme, and refrains are not uncommon.

### FAIRY POEMS

Sprightly music, such as that which makes children laugh and sing, contributes in part to the popularity of Allingham's beloved fairy poems. Justly most famous of these is "The Fairies," with its traditional opening:

> Up the airy mountain,
> Down the rushy glen,
> We daren't go a-hunting
> For fear of little men.

Others, however, are almost as highly cherished. "Prince Brightkin," a rather long narrative, has some brilliant touches of whimsicality. In "The Lepruchan," the wee shoemaker escapes his captors by blowing snuff in their faces. In "The Fairy Dialogue," mischievous sprites confound housewives attempting to do their daily chores. It should be noted, however, that much of Allingham's verse contains an opposite charm, that of sweet sadness. Many of his descriptive poems, as well as many of the romantic lyrics, are tinged with a sense of regret, of longing for something unattainable. Allingham could sing in a minor key. This tendency derives partly from personal temperament, partly from the fashion of the times, partly from literary imitation of the Graveyard school or even the Spasmodic school of poetry. He might be said to have anticipated the tone of voice adopted by writers of the Celtic Twilight. For example, one, "Aeolian Harp," opens and closes with the question, "O what is gone from us, we fancied ours?" Yeats so appreciated the way the poem enshrouds its *sic transit* theme with a meditative plaintiveness that he included it in his selection of Allingham's verse.

### INFLUENCE OF BALLADS

Allingham wrote only a handful of ballads, but his work was sufficiently crucial to establish him as a modern pioneer in this form. During his Irish period, study of the local folk ballad became a sort of hobby. He listened to balladeers at country market fairs, transcribed lyrics and melodies, and collected anonymous broadsheet ballads sold by hawkers. Next, he produced his own ballads, printed and circulated them as anonymous ha'penny broadsheets (a few of which have survived), and had the pleasure of hearing them sung in the streets and cottages of Ireland. Later, Yeats, Colum, and other poets of the Irish Renaissance took up the genre. Five of Allingham's broadsheet ballads were collected in the volume of 1855, which also has a preface describing the difficulties of adapting peasant Anglo-Irish idiom to verse. The best of these are "Lovely Mary Donnelly" and "The Girl's Lamentation." There is in the former poem a blind fiddler who, although sad because he could not see the pretty lass, "blessed himself he wasn't deaf" on hearing her winsome voice. The girl's lament is for the perfidy of her lover and also for her own loss of chastity, since "a maid again I can never be/ Till the red rose blooms on the willow tree." A third broadside ballad, "Kate O' Ballyshanny," belongs with these two in quality. Allingham also wrote a few literary ballads, perhaps imitating Rossetti or the Romantic poets. The best of these are "The Maids of Elfinmere," "The Abbot of Innisfallen," "Squire Curtis," and "St. Margaret's Eve."

*Critical Survey of Poetry*

## POETIC DETRACTIONS

Allingham liked Herrick's lyrics for their simplicity "without flatness." The problem with his own verse is that most of it is both simple and flat. His failings as a poet, which, in Sean McMahon's phrase, keep him entrenched "on the foothills of Parnassus," are largely ones common to his period. Victorian oppressive seriousness, mediocrity of thought, and gushy sentimentality too often invade his poetry. At times the effusion of emotion becomes embarrassingly urgent:

> Mine—Mine
> O Heart, it is thine—
> A look, a look of love!
> O wonder! O magical charm!
> Thou summer-night, silent and warm!

One is reminded of Percy Bysshe Shelley's "Indian Serenade." This tendency toward triteness extends past content into the realm of technique. For instance, eighteenth century poetic diction is resurrected and put to facile uses, so that one finds the earth to be "the whirling sphere," the night sky "the starry dome," and a field of wildflowers "the daisied lea."

Allingham's typical faults are magnified in his longer poems. "Evil May-Day" suffers especially from high seriousness. It is a philosophical discussion about the impact of science on traditional morality. The crisis of doubt, of the disorientation caused by a widespread questioning of creeds outworn, was a legitimate concern to Victorians, but Allingham's handling of it becomes painfully didactic. He treated the same issues more palatably in prose (see *Rambles*, "At Exeter," and "At Torquay"). "The Music Master," a tale about the tragic effects of prematurely severed love, suffers somewhat from sentimentality, but more so from lack of dramatic incident. Dante Gabriel Rossetti, who often asked Allingham for advice about his own poetry, wrote that "'The Music Master' is full of beauty and nobility, but I'm not sure it is not TOO noble or too resolutely healthy."

## LAURENCE BLOOMFIELD IN IRELAND

The exception to this general awkwardness in the longer forms is *Laurence Bloomfield in Ireland*, which runs to nearly five thousand lines. Its fictionalized account of tenant-landlord relations provides a valuable sketch of economic and class struggles in rural Ireland a decade before the Land League and just before the first heated period of Fenian activity. The extreme right and extreme left are staked out by the reactionary landlords and the incendiary Ribbonmen respectively; the sensible, humane middle is occupied by Bloomfield (the ideal landlord) and the Dorans (the ideal peasant family). In outline form, the plot seems unpromisingly thin. Bloomfield, who has recently assumed control of his estate, is feeling his way cautiously into landlordism. He objects to the bigoted, self-servicing attitudes of the other landlords in the district, but as yet lacks the confidence to challenge the status quo. In addition, the secret societies are active in the district. Their activities, usually directed against the ruling class, range from the merely disruptive to the criminally violent. Neal Doran, a good lad, son of an aging tenant farmer, is drawn into the fringes of the insurgent movements. When he is arrested for fighting at a market fair, Pigot, the hardhearted agent for Bloomfield and other landlords, moves to evict the Dorans from the farm they had worked so hard to establish. It is then that Bloomfield acts decisively. Moved by the sight of the old man's grief, he dismisses Pigot, who is assassinated on his way home, and releases Doran. Time is telescoped in the latter section of the narrative: In the years to come, Bloomfield works hard at being the ideal landlord. He institutes revolutionary reforms, such as allowing tenants to buy their farms, and in general plays the enlightened, paternal ruler.

The poem's flaws are readily apparent. The lengthy coda, consisting of two whole books, seems tacked on, and occasionally a digression unnecessarily interrupts the flow of narrative. The poem was originally written under the pressure of monthly serial publication, which probably accounts for some of the structural flaws. After receiving proofs of book 12 from *Fraser's Magazine*, Allingham confided in *William Allingham*, "It's not properly compacted to plan, and never will be now." Another flaw is that Bloomfield, the central figure, is weakly drawn. The same might be said for the Dorans. Both are too pure to be believable. Nevertheless, a more pervasive and damaging problem is inconsistency in the quality of the verse.

The poem's strengths, however, far outweigh its

weaknesses. In fact, virtually every modern critic writing on Allingham has given it high praise, particularly for its portraiture of Irish types and its many fine character sketches. The satiric portraits of the landlords in book 2 are worthy of Alexander Pope. A wide spectrum of types is surveyed, from the haughty aristocrat to the licentious absentee to the clever usurer who hides his exploitation behind a surface of unctuous piety. Less barbed but equally effective are the portraits of clergymen, especially Father John Adair. The poem is also strong in its close observation of Irish life. Depicting "every-day Irish affairs" was a "ticklish literary experiment" (preface, 1864 edition), but Allingham seems to have captured the essential fabric of life in his native Ballyshannon. To John Drinkwater, the poem is "second to none in the language as a description of peasant life and peasant nature" ("The Poetry of William Allingham," *New Ireland Review*, February, 1909). In this regard *Laurence Bloomfield in Ireland* is often compared to Oliver Goldsmith's "Deserted Village" and George Crabbe's "Borough." Allingham goes among the people, even into the most wretched hovel, showing their virtues and their vices. The description of the harvest fair in book 9 is alive with sights and sounds—the throngs of people, traders' disputes, beggars' blessings, the flourish of Her Majesty's recruiting party—a sort of poetic Irish version of William Powell Frith's *Derby Day* (1858).

Dealing with potentially flammable political material, Allingham strives for a precarious neutrality. Actually, however, this noncommittal position is a fusion of conservative and liberal elements. Allingham was not an advocate of home rule. He felt that Ireland did not yet have the political experience or the administrative skills to assume such responsibility. However, his advocacy of peasant proprietorship of land (or at least increased security of tenancy) puts him firmly in the liberal camp.

### BLACKBERRIES PICKED OFF MANY BUSHES

After *Laurence Bloomfield in Ireland* and *Fifty Modern Poems*, the quality and quantity of Allingham's verse fall off sharply. Yeats and others have seen this atrophy as evidence that his Muse was essentially Irish. Undeniably, the only substantial, entirely new poetic work of the English period was *Blackberries*

*Picked off Many Bushes*. Many of its aphorisms and short satiric rhymes are very good, but as a whole they lack brilliance, and it is likely that his reliance on abbreviated modes indicates a faltering confidence in the ability to create more ambitious poetry.

### OTHER MAJOR WORKS

PLAY: *Ashby Manor*, pb. 1883.
NONFICTION: *Rambles*, 1873; *Varieties in Prose*, 1893 (3 volumes); *William Allingham: A Diary*, 1907.

### BIBLIOGRAPHY

Cronin, Anthony. *Heritage Now: Irish Literature in the English Language*. New York: St. Martin's Press, 1983. An excellent, concise review of Allingham's life, work, and importance in the poetic canon. The significance of Allingham's Irish heritage and his love of London are well explained and vividly rendered. Cronin also includes assessments of Allingham's poetry by his contemporaries.

Howe, M. L. "Notes on the Allingham Canon." *Philological Quarterly* 12 (July, 1933): 290-297. Howe offers a distinctly personal critique of Allingham's work. He defends "The Fairies" from critics who labeled it hastily written, reveals the history behind "The Maids of Elfinmere," and untangles the relationships between Allingham, Dante Gabriel Rossetti, and William Morris. Howe also effectively argues the importance and grace of Allingham's overlooked dramas, essays, and short poems.

Hughes, Linda K. "The Poetics of Empire and Resistance: William Allingham's *Lawrence Bloomfield in Ireland*." *Victorian Poetry* 28, no. 2 (Summer, 1990): 103. Allingham's long narrative poem is discussed and analyzed in relation to the history of the English and the Irish peasants.

Husni, Samira Aghacy. "Incorrect References to William Allingham." *Notes and Queries* 30 (August, 1983): 296-298. An essential document for all Allingham scholars and students. Husni sets the record straight regarding common mistakes related to Allingham. These errors range from incorrect dates and titles of poems and books to generalizations about his poetry and relationships with contemporaries. Among those he finds guilty of errors are critics Katherine Tynan, Ifor Evans, and M. L. Howe.

Kavanagh, P. J. "Somewhat Surprising, Somewhat Surprised." *The Spectator* 283, no. 8941 (December 18, 1999): 71-72. A review of *William Allingham* with some biographical information about Allingham's relationship with Thomas Carlyle and Alfred, Lord Tennyson.

Quinn, Justin. *The Cambridge Introduction to Modern Irish Poetry, 1800-2000.* New York: Cambridge University Press, 2008. Provides an overview of the history and development of poetry in Ireland. Contains a chapter on Allingham, James Henry, and Samuel Ferguson.

Samuels Lasner, Mark. *William Allingham: A Biographical Study.* Philadelphia: Holmes, 1993. Samuels Lasner approaches Allingham by providing essential information with exceptionally rich notes on the production histories of the books, yet all this is presented in a humane style that serves as an excellent model of how to make an author bibliography both technically satisfactory and readable.

Warner, Allan. *William Allingham.* Lewisburg, Pa.: Bucknell University Press, 1975. Warner devotes his study to three aspects of Allingham: first, his narrative poem "Laurence Bloomfield in Ireland," second, his achievements as a lyric poet and writer of ballads and songs, and third, his prose as exemplified in *William Allingham.* In each of these areas, Warner illustrates Allingham's real powers of observation, imagination, and reflection.

Welch, Robert. *Irish Poetry from Moore to Yeats.* Totowa, N.J.: Barnes & Noble, 1980. Welch examines Allingham in the context of his contemporaries—such as Thomas Moore, Jeremiah Joseph Callanan, and James Clarence Mangan—and the Irish poetic tradition. He skillfully guides the reader toward an appreciation of Allingham's objectivity, love of common life, political common sense, appreciation of nature, and, most important to Welch, his warmth and humanity.

*Michael Case*

# MATTHEW ARNOLD

**Born:** Laleham, England; December 24, 1822
**Died:** Dingle Bank, Liverpool, England; April 15, 1888

## PRINCIPAL POETRY

*The Strayed Reveller, and Other Poems*, 1849
*Empedocles on Etna, and Other Poems*, 1852
*Poems*, 1853
*Poems, Second Series*, 1855
*New Poems*, 1867
*Poems, Collected Edition*, 1869
*Poetical Works of Matthew Arnold*, 1890

## OTHER LITERARY FORMS

Throughout his life Matthew Arnold wrote critical works on literature, culture, religion, and education that made him the foremost man of letters in Victorian England. This large body of prose is available in a standard edition: *The Complete Prose Works of Matthew Arnold* (1960-1976, Robert Henry Super, editor), with textual notes and commentary. Essays important to an understanding of Arnold's contribution to the discipline of literary criticism include *Preface to Poems* (1853), "Wordsworth," "The Study of Poetry," and "Literature and Science." "Culture and Anarchy" explains the philosophical positions and biases from which Arnold criticized literature and society. Also available are editions containing his letters and notebooks.

## ACHIEVEMENTS

In 1840, while he was a student at Rugby, Matthew Arnold won the Poetry Prize for "Alaric at Rome," and three years later, then at Oxford University, he won the Newdigate Poetry Prize for "Cromwell." From this official recognition of his poetic gift, Arnold began a career that produced what T. S. Eliot calls in *The Use of Poetry and the Use of Criticism* (1933), "academic poetry in the best sense; the best fruit which can issue from the promise shown by the prize-poem." However, Arnold wrote many poems that rise far above the merely academic, though popular interest in his poetry never approached the following of his more technically and expressively gifted contemporaries, Alfred, Lord Tennyson, and Robert Browning. Admittedly, Arnold's poems lack the polished texture that characterizes the great Victorian poetry; critics often complain about Arnold's lack of "ear." The novelist George Eliot, however, early recognized, in the *Westminster Review* (July, 1855), what has been increasingly the accepted opinion: "But when . . . we linger over a poem which contains some deep and fresh thought, we begin to perceive poetic beauties—felicities of expression and description, which are too quiet and subdued to be seized at the first glance." Whatever his prosodic deficiencies, Arnold still composed several lyric and narrative poems which take their place with the best that the age produced.

In a century notable for elegies, "Thyrsis," for Arnold's friend Arthur Hugh Clough, ranks with Percy Bysshe Shelley's *Adonais* (1821), Walt Whitman's "When Lilacs Last in the Dooryard Bloom'd" (1865), and Tennyson's *In Memoriam* (1850) as distinguished additions to the genre. "The Scholar-Gipsy" and "Dover Beach" contain the lyric energy and power that justify both their numerous anthology appearances and a body of criticism that places them among the most frequently explicated poems in the language.

In 1857, Arnold won election as Professor of Poetry at Oxford and, in 1862, was reelected to another five-year term. Receiving permission to abandon the customary Latin, Arnold delivered his lectures in English and invigorated the professorship with lectures ranging from the individual (Homer, Dante) to the topical ("The Literary Influence of Academies") to the broadly critical (*On the Study of Celtic Literature*, 1867). Though his critical writings on English culture, literature, and religion made him a controversial figure, Arnold gained respect in his post as inspector of schools, serving twice as assistant commissioner on official committees dispatched to study European schools, and eventually becoming a senior inspector in 1870, the same year in which Oxford conferred on him an honorary D.C.L. degree. In 1883, he visited the United States on a lecture tour that, though not triumphal, was at least a measure of his commanding stature as a critic and poet.

## BIOGRAPHY

Matthew Arnold, born on Christmas Eve, 1822, at Laleham, England, was the second child and eldest son of five boys and four girls in the family of Thomas Arnold and Mary Penrose Arnold. At the time of the poet's birth, his father, a graduate of Oxford, was performing his duties as master at the school in Laleham, preparing himself intellectually and professionally for his appointment in 1828 as headmaster of Rugby, where he set about reforming the narrowly classical curriculum to include emphasis on language, history, and mathematics and to reflect his "broad church" liberalism, while insisting that his students maintain his own high standards of discipline and moral conduct. Though his reformist views on both church and school invited attack from traditional quarters, the elder Arnold exerted over his students, family, and English education a lingering influence after his premature death at the age of forty-seven.

Although there was an undoubtedly tense relationship between headmaster father and poetically inclined son (who, at times, neglected his studies and sported the dress and talk of a dandy), Arnold's elegiac tribute to his father in "Rugby Chapel" confirms his mature appreciation for his father's magisterial qualities of

*Matthew Arnold* (Library of Congress)

mind and conduct. Likewise, Arnold took a distinct pride in the Cornish ancestry of his mother, whose father was a clergyman named John Penrose and whose mother's maiden name was Trevenen. Arnold's interest in Celtic literature derived from this ancestral connection, received further stimulation from a trip to Brittany in 1859 to visit the schools, and finally resulted in the lectures *On the Study of Celtic Literature*. Whatever the exact influence of his parents, Arnold certainly felt the familial strains which, on the one side, tended toward the moral and intellectual honesty and practicality of the headmaster and, on the other, toward the imaginative and expressive charm of the Celtic mother.

Arnold married Frances Lucy Wightman in 1851 after his celebrated infatuation, rendered in the "Switzerland" poems, for the beautiful "Marguerite," a woman now identified by Park Honan in *Matthew Arnold: A Life* (1981) as Mary Claude, "a descendant of French Protestant exiles" who came to live near the Arnold family home at Fox How. Matthew and Frances Lucy had six children, two daughters and four sons, in a happy marriage three times saddened by the early deaths of Basil at two, Thomas at sixteen, and William at eighteen.

Two years after his retirement from the wearying post of school inspector, Arnold entered in his diary, under the date of April 15, 1888, "Weep bitterly over the dead." That day, at Liverpool awaiting the arrival of his daughter and granddaughter from the United States, he collapsed from a heart attack and died.

ANALYSIS

A commonplace beginning for criticism of Matthew Arnold's poetry is one or another of his many well-known critical statements that provide a basis for showing how well or how poorly the critic's precept corresponds with the poet's practice. One must remember, however, that most of Arnold's best work as a poet preceded his finest work as a critic and that his letters reveal dissatisfaction with his poetic "fragments," as he called them. He did believe that his poems would have their "turn," just as Tennyson's and Browning's had, because they followed closely the trend of modern thinking. Indeed, Arnold's modernity—his sense of

alienation, moral complexity, and humanistic values—makes his work, both critical and creative, a continuing presence in the literary world.

The sense of alienation that carries so much thematic weight in Arnold's poetry reaches back into his childhood. As a child, he wore a brace for a slightly bent leg. This had an isolating, restricting effect on a boy who enjoyed running and climbing. Also, he early realized the irony of numbers, because, as the second born, he found that his parents' time and attention did not easily spread over nine children, and, at fourteen, he spent what surely seemed like a year in exile at Winchester School. The need for attention influenced his pose as a dandy, and he probably enjoyed his reputation as an idler, especially in his circle of family and friends who upheld and practiced the Victorian principles of work and duty.

Of course, the religious and social atmosphere in which Arnold approached adulthood conditioned his perception of the alienating forces at work in England: He entered Oxford during the Tractarian controversy that divided conservative and liberal elements in the Church of England, and he knew about the general economic and social discontent that separated the working class from the wealthy. With such factious elements at work—including the dispute between religion and science on the origin of earth and humankind—Arnold, facing his own lover's estrangement in "To Marguerite—Continued," could write with justifiable irony that "We mortal millions live alone." With good reason, then, Arnold formed his ideas on the wholesome effect of order and authority, of education and culture recommended in his prose—evident alike in that quest for unity, wholeness, and joy which, in the poems, his lyric and narrative speakers find so elusive.

In addition to the poems discussed below, the following poems are considered among Arnold's best work: "The Forsaken Merman," "The Strayed Reveller," "Palladium," "The Future," "A Dream," and "A Summer Night." Although Arnold's work has been very influential, even at its best it contains elements which can bother the modern reader, such as the over-reliance on interrogative and exclamatory sentences, giving to his ideas in the former case a weighty, rhetorical cast and, in the latter, an artificial rather than a natural emphasis. There is, however, a consistency in the melancholy, elegiac tone and in the modern concern with humankind's moral condition in a world where living a meaningful life has become increasingly difficult that makes Arnold's poetry rewarding reading.

### "TO A FRIEND"

In the early sonnet "To a Friend," Arnold praises Sophocles, in one of his memorable lines, because he "saw life steadily, and saw it whole." "Wholeness" was the controlling thought behind the poet's vision: "an Idea of the world in order not be prevailed over by the world's multitudinousness," he tells Clough in a letter critical of the "episodes and ornamental work" that distract both poet and reader from a sense of unity. This unity of idea, in perception and execution, is necessary for poetry "to utter the truth," as Arnold says in his essay on William Wordsworth, because "poetry is at bottom a criticism of life . . . the greatness of a poet lies in his powerful and beautiful application of ideas to life,—to the question: How to live." For Arnold, this question is itself "a moral idea."

If Sophocles saw life "whole," he also, according to Arnold, saw it "steadily." For Arnold, Sophoclean steadiness implies two distinct but complementary processes. First, as physical steadiness, *seeing* is the broad sensory reaction to the range of stimuli associated with the poet's "Idea of the world." One may note, for example, the last six lines of "Mycerinus" with their heavy emphasis on auditory imagery—"mirth waxed loudest," "echoes came," "dull sound"—which perfectly conclude the preceding philosophical implications of six long years of reveling by King Mycerinus. These implications appear in a series of "it may be" possibilities, and the imagery underscores the essential uncertainty of the auditors ("wondering people") because the sounds are really once-removed "echoes," partly "Mix'd with the murmur of the moving Nile." There is an attempt to match appropriately the sensations with the subject.

The second point, related to physical steadiness, implies a type of mental fixity on the part of the observer, a disciplined exercise of consciousness operating throughout the temporal context of creative urge and eventual artistic fulfillment. Explaining the difficulty of this exercise for his own poetic practice, Ar-

nold writes to Clough that "I can go thro: the imaginary process of mastering myself and the whole affair as it would then stand, but at the critical point I am too apt to hoist up the mainsail to the wind and let her drive." In short, Arnold recognizes a lack of mental fixity to accompany the poetic inspiration; he can, imaginatively, see the "whole," but, at the critical point of artistic execution, he lets go, becoming, at the expense of the whole, too insistent or expansive in one thematic or descriptive part. The lyric "Despondency" addresses this problem in the typically elegiac tone of Arnold's poetic voice. The lyric speaker says that "The thoughts that rain their steady glow/ Like stars on life's cold sea" have "never shone" for him. He has seen the thoughts which "light, like gleams, my spirit's sky," but they appear "once . . . hurry by/ And never come again." He laments the absence of that conscious persistence that preserves the "steady glow" of thought bearing directly on the moral vastness of "life's cold sea."

In a more general way, seeing life steadily allies itself to the "spontaneity of consciousness" for which Arnold praises Hellenism in *Culture and Anarchy* (1869). This spontaneity suggests a physical and mental alertness which instantly responds to "life as it is," a consciousness prone to thinking but unencumbered by the predisposition to action that describes the force of "conduct and obedience" behind Hebraism, the other major tradition in Western civilization. Sophocles, the model Hellenist, possesses the "even-balanced soul" that holds in steady counterpoise the old dichotomy of thought and feeling, a pre-Christian possibility coming before the "triumph of Hebraism and humankind's moral impulses." Thus, as a letter to Clough shows, Arnold appreciates the burden of seeing steadily and whole for the modern poet whose subject matter is perforce a criticism of life, a burden compounded because "the poet's matter being the hitherto experience of the world, and his own, increases with every century." This "hitherto experience," both Hellenic and Hebraic, overlaying Arnold's own, accounts for his interest in remote, historical subjects such as "Mycerinus," "Empedocles on Etna," "Tristram and Iseult," "Sohrab and Rustum," and "Balder Dead"—which nevertheless contain critical implications for living morally, even joyfully, in the incipiently modern world of Victorian England.

## POETIC DUALITIES

This "then and now" conception of the human experience has its analogues in the dualities that, as critics often note, Arnold's poems constantly explore: the moral and the amoral, the mind and the body, thought and feeling, the contemplative life and the active life, or, as scholar Douglas Bush labels them in *Matthew Arnold* (1971), the "Apollonian-Dionysian antinomy" of Arnold's ideas. Here again the dynamics for seeing steadily emerge because the poet must look simultaneously in polar directions, resisting all the while the temptation to "hoist up the mainsail to the wind and let her drive."

In his best poems, Arnold seeks the vantage point—call it a poetic situation—from which he can see steadily the dualities that, in the poem's thematic reconciliation, coalesce in the wholeness of the "Idea." Arnold warns, however, in the "Preface to Poems," against the poetic situations "from the representation of which, though accurate, no poetical enjoyment can be derived . . . those in which the suffering finds no vent in action . . . in which there is everything to be endured, nothing to be done." For Arnold, the problem of poetic situation means finding "a vent in action" which does not overwhelm the speculative nature of the idea, and the solution often comes in the form of the "quest," the symbolically active.

## "THE SCHOLAR-GIPSY" AND "THYRSIS"

"The Scholar-Gipsy" is on a quest, "waiting for the spark from heaven to fall." When the spark falls, he can share with the world the secret art, learned from the "gipsy-crew," of ruling "the workings of men's brains." Until then, he wanders mysteriously from Berkshire Moors to Cumner Hills, pensively cast in an ageless "solitude," exempt from the "repeated shocks" and "strange disease of modern life." The shepherd who lyrically tells the scholar-gipsy's story speaks for the Victorians who also "await" the spark from heaven, but, with "heads o'ertax'd" and "palsied hearts," cannot acquire the immortalizing agency of a quest with "one aim, one business, one desire." The antithesis is clear: "Arnold's Gipsy," as Honan says, "represents stability in a world of flux and change, creative inwardness in a world of lassitude, stagnation, frustration, and dividedness." The shepherd, a part of the modern world but temporarily secluded in the imaginative distance of "this high field's dark corner," discovers the physical and mental steadiness to tell the story, to see concurrently the past and present, and to indict his society through the quest of the mythic wanderer.

"Thyrsis," a monody for Clough, follows the same stanza form and rhyme scheme of "The Scholar-Gipsy," continuing too the unifying strategy of the quest, this time for the "signal elm-tree," which has itself become a symbol for the perpetual existence of "our friend, the Gipsy-Scholar." In this way, Arnold aligns Clough with the legendary rover; Clough, however, unlike the Gipsy, "could not wait" the passing of the "storms that rage" in their fragmented society. With night descending, Corydon (Arnold's persona) sees, but does not achieve, the object of his quest; but he cries "Hear it, O Thyrsis, still our tree is there!" So lives the Gipsy-Scholar, so remains, in the symbolic activity of the quest, the idea of hope: Corydon will "not despair." As in "The Scholar-Gipsy," Arnold turns the old genre of pastoral elegy to topical account, and the poem achieves a balanced steadiness, as much about Corydon as about Thyrsis, as much about hope as about despair, as much about life as about death.

The idea of the quest—or the hunt, or the journey—recurs again and again in Arnold's poetry, providing the "vent in action" required by the expanding idea. The journey may be inward, as in "The Buried Life," in which Arnold says that humankind's impulse to know the "mystery" of its heart sends it delving into its "own breast." Here the poet tries to reconcile the dualities of outward "strife" (in "the world's most crowded streets") and inner "striving" (toward "the unregarded river of our life"). This self-questing journey, however, ironically needs the impetus of "a beloved hand laid in ours," "another's eyes read clear," and then, in the respite of love, one "becomes aware of his life's flow." There is, though faint, an optimistic strain rising through the modern sense of isolation, even permitting the poet, in "Resignation," to make a virtue of necessity by accepting "his sad lucidity of soul."

For Arnold, though, isolation and solitude are not similar; they represent yet another set of opposites: isolation, a state of rejection and loneliness, is to be shunned, while solitude, a state of reflection and inspiration, is to be sought. Away from the "sick hurry" of modern life, the poet in solitude achieves the steadiness of feeling and perception required for the aesthetic fulfillment of his or her idea. Arnold's lyric speakers enjoy solitude: The shepherd in "The Scholar-Gipsy" and "Thyrsis," or the lounger in Kensington Gardens who finds "peace for ever new" in the "lone, open glade," is analogous, in the "Austerity of Poetry," to the "hidden ground/ Of thought" within the Muse herself. However, there is always the ironic danger: Empedocles, on the verge of suicide, drops his laurel bough because he is "weary of the solitude/ Where he who bears thee must abide." Arnold needs the creative succor of a solitude that carries over, as he says in "Quiet Work," into a life "Of toil unsever'd from tranquillity," a life that, even as Empedocles admits, still "leaves human effort scope." This "human effort" becomes the dynamics behind Arnold's own quest to focus and balance the idea with the action, to elevate and juxtapose the moral propositions of antagonistic extremes: life and death, love and hate, alliance and alienation.

### "STANZAS FROM THE GRANDE CHARTREUSE"

"Stanzas from the Grande Chartreuse" follows the typically Arnoldian pattern. The first sixty-five lines witness the sensory perception and steadiness of the speaker, his spontaneity of consciousness comprising a mixture of imagery—visual ("spectral vapours white"), auditory ("strangled sound"), tactile ("forms brush by"). There is the anticipatory journey or quest: "The bridge is cross'd, and slow we ride/ Through forest up the mountainside." Then, at line sixty-six, there is the idea, framed in the rhetorical question: "And what am I, that I am here?" The speaker admits that the object of his ultimate quest is really elsewhere, for the "rigorous teachers" of his youth "Show'd me the high, white star of Truth,/ There bade me gaze, and there aspire." That abstract quest, though, must temporarily defer to this cold physical journey to the Grande Chartreuse, a monastery in the French Alps, where the troubled speaker can shed his melancholy tears in the presence of a profound religious faith. No longer young and feeling caught in the forlorn void between the faiths of a past and future time, he is "wandering between two worlds, one dead,/ The other powerless to be born." The past age of faith, still ascetically practiced in the Carthusian monastery,

and a desirable future age "which without hardness will be sage,/ And gay without frivolity" bracket a divisively inert time in which the sciolists talk, but, with their fathers' history of pain and grief as justification, "The Kings of modern thought are dumb."

Fraser Neiman, in *Matthew Arnold* (1968), summarizes the common emotional ground of the anchorite and Arnold: They both "turn to a quest for inward peace," but Arnold must find his in solitude, in the buried life, in quiet work, in, as Neiman says, "a profound inwardness . . . not incompatible with the world of activity." The poem concludes with images of "action and pleasure"—the "troops," the "hunters," the "gay dames" passing below the monastery—representing a life again rejected by the Carthusians but, as the reader infers, accepted by the speaker, who has had, at least, the catharsis of his tears. The emphasis, though, is on the idea, an idea that Arnold tries to see steadily and whole through the confrontation of opposites: the ascetic, contemplative life of the anchorite, "Obermann," and the past at the top of the Etna-like mountain (where, one gathers, the "suffering finds no vent in action"), versus the secular, restless life of "Laughter and cries" at the bottom of the mountain where "Years hence, perhaps, may dawn an age,/ More fortunate." "Stanzas from the Grande Chartreuse" renders in setting, mood, and idea the predicament of the poet, expressed in Arnold's earlier poem, "Stanza in Memory of the Author of 'Obermann'":

> Ah! two desires toss about
> The poet's feverish blood.
> One drives him to the world without,
> And one to solitude.

### "DOVER BEACH"

"Dover Beach" fits into the same structural pattern of imagery, idea, and resolution. The opening of the poem establishes the physical and mental awareness of the speaker, a person attuned to the sensory stimuli of the scene before him. The counterpointed imagery of sight and sound in the first verse paragraph divides as naturally as a Petrarchan sonnet: The visual imagery of the first eight lines suggests peace and serenity ("the moon lies fair," "the tranquil bay"), but the auditory imagery of the next six lines, signaled by the turn of the imperative "Listen!," introduces the "grating roar/ Of pebbles" which, in the climax of the paragraph, "Begin, and cease, and then again begin,/ With tremulous cadence slow, and bring/ The eternal note of sadness in." The imagistic division, the modulated caesura, and the irregular pattern of end and internal rhymes provide the lyric energy leading up to the emotional dimension of sadness which the second verse paragraph quickly converts to the mental dimension of thought. In a transitional effect, the auditory imagery surrounding the "note of sadness" connects with the image of Sophocles who "long ago/ Heard it on the Aegaean," bringing "Into his mind the turbid ebb and flow/ Of human misery." Critics sometimes object to the shift in imagery from full to ebb tide, but the crucial thematic point lies not so much in the maintenance of parallel imagery as in the formulation of idea: "we/ Find also in the sound a thought/ Hearing it by this distant northern sea." Thus, the perception of dualities—full and ebb tide, present and past time, physical and metaphorical seas—prepares for the "then and now" structure of the third verse paragraph: the "Sea of Faith" was once full, like the tide at Dover, but the lyric speaker can "only hear/ Its melancholy, long, withdrawing roar."

The sociological interpretation, to select just one critical approach, maintains that the disillusioned speaker refers to the debate between religion and science then dominating the intellectual effort of so many Victorians. If the "Sea of Faith" came to full tide with the "triumph of Hebraism and humankind's moral impulses," the preceding image of Sophocles adds poignance to the speaker's resignation in the face of the constant factor of "human misery." Whereas Sophocles could, in an ancient world, see life steadily and see it whole in its tragic but nevertheless human consequences, the speaker enjoys no such certainty. The retreating Sea of Faith takes with it the moral and spiritual basis for "joy" and "love" and "peace." The speaker's own attempt to see modern life steadily and to see it whole, successful or not, leads to the resolution of the lyric cry: "Ah, love, let us be true/ To one another!" The world may no longer offer the comfort of "joy" and "certitude" and "help for pain," but the lovers may create their own interpersonal world where such pleasures presumably exist.

Some critics fault the ending of "Dover Beach," which imaginatively transports the couple to "a darkling plain," leaving behind the sea imagery that guides the speaker's emotional and mental state throughout the poem. The ending, however, maintains the consistency of auditory imagery ("confused alarms," "armies clash") that concludes each of the preceding verse paragraphs, and the "struggle and flight" of the "ignorant armies" echo, in appropriately harsher terms, the "retreating" roar of the Sea of Faith. Furthermore, the principle of duality, carefully set up in the poem, works at the end: Physically, the lovers are still by the quiet, beautiful cliffs of Dover, but figuratively, at an opposite extreme, they find themselves "as on a darkling plain."

OTHER MAJOR WORKS

PLAY: *Merope: A Tragedy*, pb. 1858.

NONFICTION: *Preface to Poems*, 1853; *On Translating Homer*, 1861; *Essays in Criticism*, 1865; *On the Study of Celtic Literature*, 1867; *Culture and Anarchy*, 1869; *St. Paul and Protestantism, with an Introduction on Puritanism and the Church of England*, 1870; *Friendship's Garland*, 1871; *Literature and Dogma*, 1873; *God and the Bible*, 1875; *Last Essays on Church and Religion*, 1877; *Discourses in America*, 1885; *Civilization in the United States*, 1888; *Essays in Criticism, Second Series*, 1888; *The Complete Prose Works of Matthew Arnold*, 1960-1976 (Robert Henry Super, editor).

MISCELLANEOUS: *The Works of Matthew Arnold*, 1903-1904 (15 volumes).

BIBLIOGRAPHY

Bush, Douglas. *Matthew Arnold: A Survey of His Poetry and Prose*. New York: Macmillan, 1971. A very good introduction to Arnold's life and works.

Collini, Stefan. *Matthew Arnold: A Critical Portrait*. Oxford, England: Clarendon Press, 2008. A biography and critical examination of the life and works of Arnold.

D'Agnillo, Renzo. *The Poetry of Matthew Arnold*. Rome: Aracne, 2005. A study of the poetry of Arnold. Contains a chapter analyzing "Empedocles on Etna." Looks at the theme of loss and redemption.

Dawson, Carl, ed. *Matthew Arnold, the Poetry: The Critical Heritage.* London: Routledge & Kegan Paul, 1973. Collects more than sixty reviews and essays written between 1849 and 1898. Gives a fascinating view of how Arnold was received and understood by his contemporaries. Presents some of the contexts to which his writing was responding. Contains an extensive bibliography and index.

Hamilton, Ian. *A Gift Imprisoned: The Poetic Life of Matthew Arnold.* New York: Basic Books, 1999. The simple, fablelike structure of this account relies on the notion that Arnold wrote almost all his best poems before he wrote his best prose—an assumption that is a matter of scholarly dispute. Hamilton's achievement in this book is to have shifted attention away from Arnold's prose and back to his poetry.

Honan, Park. *Matthew Arnold: A Life.* New York: McGraw-Hill, 1981. A definitive biography of Arnold, accessible to the general reader and illuminating to the scholar. Most of this biographical information had never before appeared in print. The biography is lively as well as thoroughly researched and documented. Includes a generous index.

Machann, Clinton. *Matthew Arnold: A Literary Life.* New York. St. Martin's Press, 1998. This study is a succinct and well-articulated exposition of Arnold's intellectual and literary concerns, spanning his career in chronological chapters. Emphasizes Arnold's achievement as an essayist: His ethical, interpretive, and instructional concerns are given full play, and due allowance is made for both the scope and limitations of his vision.

Mazzeno, Laurence W. *Matthew Arnold: The Critical Legacy.* Rochester, N.Y.: Camden House, 1999. Mazzeno surveys the critical response to Arnold. Resembling an annotated bibliography in that it treats its material item by item, this is a book for those interested in the scholarship on Arnold.

Murray, Nicholas. *A Life of Matthew Arnold.* New York: St. Martin's Press, 1997. A biographical study that critically examines Arnold's work.

Neiman, Fraser. *Matthew Arnold.* New York: Twayne, 1968. This fine introduction to Arnold's wide-ranging work presents only enough biographical information to give shape and meaning to the analysis of Arnold's writing. Presents the study of Arnold's thought as a way into the study of mid-Victorian thought. Includes a chronology and a brief annotated bibliography.

*Ronald K. Giles*

# MARGARET ATWOOD

**Born:** Ottawa, Ontario, Canada; November 18, 1939

PRINCIPAL POETRY
*Double Persephone*, 1961
*The Circle Game*, 1964 (single poem), 1966 (collection)
*Kaleidoscopes Baroque: A Poem*, 1965
*Talismans for Children*, 1965
*Expeditions*, 1966
*Speeches for Dr. Frankenstein*, 1966
*The Animals in That Country*, 1968
*What Was in the Garden*, 1969
*The Journals of Susanna Moodie*, 1970
*Procedures for Underground*, 1970
*Power Politics*, 1971
*You Are Happy*, 1974
*Selected Poems*, 1976
*Two-Headed Poems*, 1978
*True Stories*, 1981
*Snake Poems*, 1983
*Interlunar*, 1984
*Selected Poems II: Poems Selected and New, 1976-1986*, 1987
*Selected Poems, 1966-1984*, 1990
*Poems, 1965-1975*, 1991
*Poems, 1976-1989*, 1992
*Morning in the Burned House*, 1995
*Eating Fire: Selected Poems, 1965-1995*, 1998
*The Door*, 2007

OTHER LITERARY FORMS
Margaret Atwood's publishing history is a testimonial to her remarkable productivity and versatility as a

writer. As well as a poet, she is a novelist, a short-fiction writer, a children's author, an editor, and an essayist. *The Edible Woman* (1969), Atwood's first novel, defined the focus of her fiction: mainly satirical explorations of sexual politics, where self-deprecating female protagonists defend themselves against men, chiefly with the weapon of language. Other novels include *Surfacing* (1972), *Lady Oracle* (1976), *Life Before Man* (1979), *Bodily Harm* (1981), *Cat's Eye* (1988), *The Robber Bride* (1993), *Alias Grace* (1996), *The Blind Assassin* (2000), *Oryx and Crake* (2003), *The Penelopiad: The Myth of Penelope and Odysseus* (2005), and *The Year of the Flood* (2009). *The Handmaid's Tale* (1985), a dystopian novel set in a post-nuclear, monotheocratic Boston, where life is restricted by censorship and state control of reproduction, is the best known of Atwood's novels and was made into a commercial film of the same title, directed by Volker Schlöndorff.

*Dancing Girls, and Other Stories* (1977) and *Blue-beard's Egg* (1983) are books of short fiction, as are

*Margaret Atwood* (Courtesy, Vancouver International Writers Festival)

*Wilderness Tips* (1991), *Good Bones* (1992), and *Moral Disorder* (2006). Atwood has written children's books: *Up in the Tree* (1978), which she also illustrated, *Anna's Pet* (1980, with Joyce Barkhouse), *For the Birds* (1990), *Princess Prunella and the Purple Peanut* (1995), *Rude Ramsay and the Roaring Radishes* (2003), and *Bashful Bob and Doleful Dorinda* (2004). A nonfiction book for young readers is *Days of the Rebels: 1815-1840* (1977).

Atwood's contributions to literary theory and criticism have also been significant. Her idiosyncratic, controversial, but well-researched *Survival: A Thematic Guide to Canadian Literature* (1972) is essential for the student interested in Atwood's version of the themes that have shaped Canadian creative writing over a century. Her *Second Words: Selected Critical Prose* (1982) is one of the first works of the feminist criticism that has flourished in Canada. She also produced *Strange Things: The Malevolent North in Canadian Literature* (1995). A related title is *Negotiating with the Dead: A Writer on Writing* (2002).

ACHIEVEMENTS

Critical success and national and international acclaim have greeted Margaret Atwood's work since her first major publication, the poetry collection *The Circle Game*. Poems from that collection were awarded the 1965 President's Medal for Poetry by the University of Western Ontario in 1966, and after commercial publication, the collection won for Atwood the prestigious Governor-General's Award for poetry in 1967. In that same year, Atwood's *The Animals in That Country* was awarded first prize in Canada's Centennial Commission Poetry Competition. The Chicago periodical *Poetry* awarded Atwood the Union League Civic and Arts Poetry Prize in 1969 and the Bess Hokin Prize in 1974. Since that time, Atwood's numerous awards and distinctions have been more for her work in fiction, nonfiction, and humanitarian affairs. She has received several honorary doctorates and many prestigious prizes, among them the Toronto Arts Award (1986), *Ms.* magazine's Woman of the Year for 1986, the Ida Nudel Humanitarian Award from the Canadian Jewish Congress, and the American Humanist of the Year Award for 1987. In fact, at one time or another, Atwood has won just about every literary award for Canadian writers. In 2000, Atwood won the Booker Prize for the best novel by a citizen of the United Kingdom or British Commonwealth.

BIOGRAPHY

Margaret Eleanor Atwood was born into a family that encouraged inquiry and discovery. An important stimulus to her intellectual curiosity was certainly the family's yearly sojourns in the remote bush of northern Ontario and Quebec, where Atwood's father, an entomologist, carried out much of his study and research. It is likely that this environment shaped Atwood's ironic vision and her imagery. Atwood's writing, especially her poetry and her second novel, *Surfacing*, are permeated with her intimate knowledge of natural history and with her perception of the casual brutality with which the weak are sacrificed for the survival of the strong.

Studying between 1957 and 1961 for her undergraduate degree in English at Victoria College, University of Toronto, Atwood came under the influence of Canadian poet Jay MacPherson and especially of Northrop Frye, one of the twentieth century's preeminent critical theorists. They encouraged Atwood's early poetry and directed her toward biblical and mythological symbol and archetype, still strong forces in her writing.

Between 1961 and 1963, Atwood pursued graduate studies in English at Harvard University, receiving her M.A. in 1962. In 1963, she met fellow graduate student James Polk, whom she married in 1967, when after a period of working, writing, and teaching, Atwood returned to Harvard to pursue a Ph.D. (beginning thesis work on the English metaphysical romance). In Canada, however, her burgeoning success as a writer and her involvement as a university teacher of creative writing soon superseded her formal studies.

In the early 1970's, Atwood traveled in Europe and then returned to Canada to continue writing and teaching. She became an editor at House of Anansi Press, one of the many Canadian publishing houses that sprang up in the fertile late 1960's to encourage young and sometimes experimental writers. She also met novelist Graeme Gibson, who may have influenced her own foray into experimental fiction, *Surfacing*. After

her divorce from Polk in 1973, Atwood moved with Gibson to rural Alliston, Ontario, where their daughter Jess was born in 1976.

Throughout the 1980's and 1990's, Atwood's overall output was steady, though she did not continue to produce very much new poetry. In the latter 1980's, Atwood made successful forays into the field of screenwriting for film and the musical theater. Her increased involvement with world social and political issues is evident in her vice-chairmanship of the Writers' Union of Canada and her presidency of PEN International, where she has waged a vigorous battle against literary censorship. Her association with Amnesty International has prompted an increasingly strong expression of her moral vision. She has continued to publish regularly in Canadian, American, and European media and has received worldwide recognition as a major contemporary writer.

ANALYSIS

Margaret Atwood's poetry deals essentially with paradox and struggle in both art and life. Her first (and now generally inaccessible) chapbook of poetry, *Double Persephone*, contains the components of her vision, which she elucidates in her next nine poetry collections with more depth, conviction, and stylistic maturity, but whose elements she changes little. An overview of Atwood's poetry reveals patterns expressed through mythological and biblical allusion and recurring imagery relating to mutability, metamorphosis, near annihilation, and, ultimately, adaptation and definition. References to eyes, water, mirrors, glass, photographs, maps, and charts abound. The archetypal journey/quest motif is a vital component of Atwood's vision. It is worked out metaphorically in the historical context of European exploration and settlement of the Canadian wilderness, the pioneer's battle with alienation, loneliness, and the struggle to articulate a new self in a new world. If the pioneer masters the new "language," he or she will survive; his or her divided self will become whole. This life-and-death struggle is also carried out in the psychological arena of sexual politics. Much of Atwood's poetry (especially *Procedures for Underground* and *Power Politics*) explores—at first with anger, later with resignation, always with irony—the damage that men and women inflict on one another despite their interdependence. In Atwood's poetry, chaos is perceived as the center of things; it is the individual's quest, as both artist and natural being, to define order, meaning, and purpose—to survive.

### THE CIRCLE GAME

*The Circle Game*, Atwood's first major poetry collection, represents the outset of an artistic and personal journey. The artist-poet (whose voice is personal, ironic, and female) struggles to shape chaos into order through language, whose enigmatic symbols she must master and control. Language is a set of tools, the key component of the poet's bag of tricks, packed for the (metaphoric) journey undertaken, for example, in *The Circle Game*'s "Evening Trainstation Before Departure":

> Here I am in
> a pause in space
> hunched on the edge
> of a tense suitcase.

Language, however, is duplicitous; it is a weapon that can rebound against the poet herself. She is engaged in a constant struggle to interpret and communicate without being subsumed, as suggested in "The Sybil": "she calls to me with the many/ voices of the children/ not I want to die/ but You must die."

In life, chaos comprises process, flux, and the temporal; the struggle for the individual is both to understand his or her own nature and to reconcile himself or herself to the processes of nature, history, and culture. The external, natural world mirrors the self; it speaks the siren language of the primitive and lies in wait to ambush with casual cruelty human beings' fragile civility. Through recognition, struggle, and reconciliation, the individual can transcend his or her destructive self, mirrored in the natural world. Throughout *The Circle Game*, the self, both artistic and psychological, struggles to be born. The creative impulse is strong, the instinct for survival great, but *The Circle Game*'s "Journey to the Interior" says that the individual does not yet understand the ambiguous messages of either art or life and is in danger: "and words here are as pointless/ as calling in a vacant/ wilderness."

The opening poem, "This Is a Photograph of Me,"

presents a paradox. In the photograph, the speaker's image is barely discernible, suspended as if in a watery grave, yet awaiting redefinition, new birth: "I am in the lake, in the center/ of the picture, just under the surface." In "Camera," the artist is reviled for the impulse to capture life in a static form when the impulse to the kinesis, the process of life, is so compelling: "Camera man/ how can I love your glass eye? . . . that small black speck/ travelling towards the horizon/ at almost the speed of life/ is me." Who is "me"? It is the androgynous, divided self, defined metaphorically in the powerful poem "After the Flood, We." "We" are Deucalion and Phyrra, in Greek mythology the sole male and female survivors of the mythic flood, suspended over the misty shapelessness of the drowned old world, designated by Zeus as the only humans deserving of survival. The female speaker differentiates between "I" and "you," "you" being an intimate who is here (as elsewhere throughout Atwood's poetry) the male. These two are charged with creating a new world. The self-absorbed male is a casual progenitor, "tossing small pebbles/ at random over your shoulder," but the female persona perceives horror, a Frankenstein's monster rising up to overwhelm "the beauty of the morning." The threat to process and growth, both artistic and personal, is the strongest of perceived evils. A sense that the artist-speaker is not yet equal to the task, has not yet found the appropriate language, is particularly strong in "The Messenger," where "a random face/ revolving outside the window" fades into oblivion because, the poem's ironic tone implies, the message is brought to the inappropriate recipient; the messenger shouts "desperate messages with his/ obliterated mouth/ in a silent language."

In *The Circle Game*, a game motif is evident in the titles and metaphoric significance of several poems ("Playing Cards," "An Attempted Solution for Chess Problems," and the collection's title poem). Intelligence, even cunning, is required. Knowing the divided self is the key to becoming the artist fit to pass on the message vital for survival. The collection's final poem, "The Settlers," suggests that perhaps success will come in laying the foundation for future understanding. The poet-narrator optimistically envisions a transformation through natural evolution into messages for the future, though understanding is still in doubt: "children run, with green/ smiles (not knowing/ where)." As yet the tools, the language, are lacking. The simple innocence of a children's circle game becomes weighted with foreboding; critic Rosemary Sullivan observes, "The narcissism of the circle game claims the narrator, and confines Atwood herself in its prisoning rhythms. We have yet to see the circle effectively broken."

### THE ANIMALS IN THAT COUNTRY

The journey of discovery continues in *The Animals in That Country* and is undertaken in several metaphorical arenas: the natural, the historical, the cultural, and, above all, the arena of the self. Again, the artist-self is found wanting. Several poems such as "Provisions" and "The Surveyors" suggest that the pioneer brings the wrong equipment to the new world because he or she has a faulty concept of the terrain and its natural inhabitants. Later generations distance themselves as soon as possible from the natural interrelationship of human and animals, the hunt being transformed into a ritualized game and then an irrelevance, as the collection's title poem points out.

Self-definition in a modern cultural setting also eludes the speaker in this collection's poems. At its writing, Atwood was on the second of her two sojourns at Harvard. Her own dislocation in American society and her distaste (expressed in letters to friends and colleagues in Canada) for American materialism and the accelerating Vietnam War are expressed in poems such as "The Landlady" and "It Is Dangerous to Read Newspapers." Her sense of alienation, from both place and people, is sadly noted in "Roominghouse, Winter": "Tomorrow, when you come to dinner/ They will tell you I never lived here." An ironic view emerges in an encounter with a relief map of Canada in the poem "At the Tourist Centre in Boston." An increasingly irate narrator asks first herself and then the receptionist, "Do you see nothing/ watching you from under the water?// Was the sky ever that blue?// Who really lives there?" That series of ominous questions signals a return journey to the interior of both Canada and the still unmapped and undefined self.

The definitive exploration of people's relationship to the natural world, to history, and to their own warring selves takes place in two of the collection's most powerful poems, "A Night in the Royal Ontario Museum" and "Progressive Insanities of a Pioneer." In the former, the speaker is inadvertently locked in the museum, "this crazed man-made/ stone brain," and is compelled to undergo a metaphoric journey to the beginnings of natural and human history. The worst horror to contemplate is preexistence, nondefinition: "I am dragged to the mind's/ deadend, . . . lost/ among the mastodons." In "Progressive Insanities of a Pioneer," this struggle to redefine the self out of chaos is explored in a metaphorical battle between a pioneer and the wilderness. In seven sections, or chapters, the story of the pioneer's failure unfolds relentlessly, the poem's flat and terse diction underscoring the horror of his descent into insanity and death. Seeking to impose order on the perceived chaos of his surroundings, the pioneer fails to acknowledge the necessity of adapting to the wilderness rather than subjugating it. He does not learn the language; instead, he makes a futile effort to structure, to classify. He is doomed to failure and annihilation, drowning in a metaphorical flux of Leviathan proportions.

### THE JOURNALS OF SUSANNA MOODIE

Success in these parallel journeys both into the physical wilderness and into the self is achieved, however, by the persona who informs and narrates Atwood's next collection of poems, *The Journals of Susanna Moodie*. J. W. Dunbar Moodie and his wife, Susanna, were impoverished English gentry who emigrated to Canada in 1832 and took up a land grant in the bush near what is now Peterborough, Ontario. Their seven-year sojourn in the bush before they settled in the town of Belleville was a searing experience for Susanna. Steeped in nineteenth century Romanticism and possessing to no small degree the arrogance of her class, Susanna arrived in Canada with the rosy expectations of vulnerable people unscrupulously lured from home by the promise of bountiful land, a temperate climate, congenial neighbors, and best of all, freedom from taxation. The harsh reality of life in the wilderness destroyed many; Susanna, though, was able to draw on a previously untapped toughness of spirit that eventually turned her from a homesick gentlewoman into a self-sufficient, grudgingly loyal Canadian who contributed much to a fledgling Canadian culture. She recorded her experiences in a pair of accounts entitled *Roughing It in the Bush: Or, Forest Life in Canada* (1852) and *Life in the Clearings Versus the Bush* (1853). In them, readers detect a duality of her attitude and personality that Atwood exploits to advantage in *The Journals of Susanna Moodie*. In her contemplation of the physical and spiritual wildernesses that confront her, Susanna's fear and despair is evident but so, increasingly, is a testy strength and a reluctant love for her new country.

The collection is divided into three sections that treat respectively Susanna's immigration, her sojourn in the bush, and her later years in Belleville and Toronto. Metaphorically, the "journals" chronicle the passages of Susanna's life: the rebirth and redefinition of the self that beginning in a new land requires; the trial by fire (in Susanna's case, literal) of life in the hostile wilderness; finally, reconciliation and death, where physical burial marks a spiritual intermingling with the new land, ironically becoming alien again through twentieth century urbanization.

In "Journal 1," Susanna repeatedly expresses the realization of her need for a new identity; familiar psychological landmarks are now irrelevant. In "Further Arrivals" she observes, "We left behind . . . our civilized/ distinctions// and entered a large darkness." At first, she is threatened at every level, perceiving her husband as "the wereman," her "first neighbours" as "speaking a twisted dialect," and the wilderness as consciously malicious. Despite the familiar human instinct to order, catalog, and impose, Susanna recognizes the need for compromise: "Resolve: to be both tentative and hard to startle/ . . . in this area where my damaged knowing of the language means/ prediction is forever impossible." Susanna survives seven years of loneliness and physical hardship that transform her. She departs for Belleville with a sense that she does not yet fully understand her relationship with the wilderness. In "Departure from the Bush," she observes, "In time the animals/ arrived to inhabit me./ . . . There was something they almost taught me/ I came away not having learned." From the relatively civilized perspective of Belleville, Susanna contemplates the relationship between pioneer and wilderness with a mixture of bitterness and resignation. In the three "dream" poems of the

"Journal 2" section, she recognizes in the natural cycle the inexorable interrelationship of life and death (often violent) of which humankind is an integral part. Her own ambivalence is expressed in "The Double Voice": "Two voices/ took turns using my eyes"; while one saw "the rituals of seasons and rivers," the other pointed out "a dead dog/ jubilant with maggots." In "Journal 3," Susanna's reconciliation with her new self and with her harsh new land is completed; after her death, her defiant voice can still be heard over the roar of the twentieth century Toronto built over her bones. As Atwood says in the afterword to this collection, "Susanna Moodie has finally turned herself inside out, and has become the spirit of the land she once hated."

### PROCEDURES FOR UNDERGROUND

Having left Susanna Moodie speaking prophetically from her underground grave, Atwood made the underground the shaping metaphor of her next poetry collection, *Procedures for Underground*. She returns to a theme that dominated *The Circle Game*: the power of the artist to shape and articulate both internal and external experience. Critic Jerome Rosenberg reminds readers of Atwood's observation that artists who experience the creative process make "a descent to the underworld"; the artist's role is a mystical and powerful one (and perhaps subversive, the collection's title suggests). The artist persona is set apart from ordinary human relationships, as a seer is, by the ability to interpret experience outside the literal. In the title poem, the expectations of the artist blessed (or cursed) with second sight are grimly described: "Few will seek your help/ with love, none without fear."

The artist's compulsion to define, shape, interpret, and preserve permeates the collection's imagery. In "Three Desk Objects," the writer's tools are transformed by this purpose: "My cool machines/ . . . I am afraid to touch you/ I think you will cry out in pain// I think you will be warm, like skin." Many of the poems describe the capturing of images, meanings, and moments through a variety of artistic media. "Woman Skating" ends with "Over all I place/ a glass bell"; "Younger Sister, Going Swimming" has her dive recorded on the poet's paper; "Girl and Horse, 1928" and "Projected Slide of an Unknown Soldier" explore time and history through the "freeze-frame" of photography. However, the artist fails to capture or interpret the "underground" aspect of the person. Human nature remains impenetrable, a language unlearned, a primeval mystery unsolved, as the poem "A Soul, Geologically" says. "Where do the words go/ when we have said them?" is the plaintive question in "A Small Cabin."

The most ominous note in the collection is struck by a poem that returns to the game motif of *The Circle Game* and makes a sad commentary on the passage from innocence to experience. In "Game After Supper," a memory of a happy children's game of twilight hide-and-seek turns macabre when the reader understands that the small child plays with spectral cousins long dead of diphtheria and that the seeker is a threatening, anonymous male figure. "He will be an uncle,/ if we are lucky," comments the speaker wryly, but the sexual threat is clear, and the stage is set for the largely sexual struggle that provides the primary focus in Atwood's next collection. From here onward, her concern is more with external relationships; it is probably fair to say that this shift in focus marks the end of her most powerful work as a poet.

### POWER POLITICS

*Power Politics*, written when Atwood's first marriage was breaking up, focuses primarily on human relationships, though Atwood's parallel concerns with humans in natural and social history and with interpreting the dual self are also strongly present. Specifically, *Power Politics* chronicles the destructive love-hate relationship that can exist between incompatible men and women. In this pessimistic collection, signals are missed, messages are misinterpreted, and the battle is mutually lost. The menacing, shadowy "tall man" of "Game After Supper" resolves into an aggrieved male partner; the anguished female speaker explores their inability to fulfill each other sexually, intellectually, or spiritually. The inevitable failure of the relationship is evident from the collection's terse, vicious (and gratuitous) opening epigram: "you fit into me/ like a hook into an eye// a fish hook/ an open eye." The poems' titles provide an inexorable chronology of descent from love through suspicion, mutual betrayal, and accusation to sad resignation and parting. Much of the imagery is of battle; in the central, seven-section poem "They Are Hostile Nations," battle lines are drawn de-

spite a perceived mutual need: "Instead we are opposite, we/ touch as though attacking." Ultimately, the speaker blames herself for bringing to bear the weight of her expectations, emotional and artistic, on a partner unable to carry them. In "Hesitation Outside the Door," she addresses him sadly: "Get out while it is/ open, while you still can." However, in the final poem, "He Is Last Seen," the speaker mourns her partner's seeming escape "towards firm ground and safety" and away from the still-unresolved conflict underlying all Atwood's poetry thus far: that of the divided, unreconciled self.

### YOU ARE HAPPY

In *You Are Happy*, progress is made toward the resolution of this conflict. The ironic, pessimistic tone of *Power Politics* continues in the opening section. Human relationships fail once again for both emotional and artistic reasons; they cannot withstand the double assault of misunderstanding and misinterpretation. Imagery of water, ice, mirrors, eyes, and particularly cameras still prevails, as "Newsreel: Man and Firing Squad" shows: "No more of these closeups, this agony/ taken just for the record anyway." In the collection's middle sections, "Songs of the Transformed" and "Circe/Mud Poems," the poet confronts the limitations of art in controlling and interpreting human nature and behavior. Through the voice of the sorceress Circe, a compelling character in Homer's *Odyssey* (c. 725 B.C.E.; English translation, 1614) who transformed men into swine, Atwood acknowledges the limitations of mythmaking and the attraction of accepting life as it is, with its ambivalence and vitality: "I search instead for the others,/ the ones left over,/ the ones who have escaped from these/ mythologies with barely their lives." This positive realization is reiterated in the collection's last section. In "Late August," a new mood of voluptuous acceptance and fruitfulness is evident: "The air is still/ warm, flesh moves over/ flesh, there is no// hurry."

In this collection, Atwood's poetic skills show new direction. She intersperses her familiar spare, short poetic forms with more fluid prose poems. Indeed, the early 1970's marked the beginning of Atwood's shift away from poetry toward prose writing; the themes and imagery in many poems are explored more fully in novels from the same periods. There was a hiatus of four years until *Two-Headed Poems* appeared.

### Two-Headed Poems

Interestingly, much of *Two-Headed Poems* relates closely in tone, theme, and imagery to *The Journals of Susanna Moodie*, but where the voice in the latter was objectified and dramatized as Moodie's, the voice in *Two-Headed Poems* is subjective and intimate. This relationship can perhaps be partly explained by the fact that Atwood gave birth to her daughter Jess in 1976, and her experience of motherhood is strongly reflected in this first collection of poems since her daughter's birth. There is a subtle softening of the irony of tone and vision and of terse diction, a perceptible turn toward acceptance rather than rejection. The poems in this work suggest that Atwood has experienced not only artistically, but also personally, Moodie's sense of purpose and place in human history; Atwood too belongs to "the procession/ of old leathery mothers// passing the work from hand to hand,/ mother to daughter,// a long thread of red blood, not yet broken" ("A Red Shirt"). Poems such as "You Begin" reflect a renewed emotional and artistic purpose; "All Bread," with its motifs of sacrifice, sacrament, and Communion, expresses on one level acknowledgment of the rhythms of life and death inherent in nature, and on a parallel level the interdependence of the sexes, which marriage sanctifies. The poet has reconciled herself to the sometimes violent paradoxes that define life: natural, human, and artistic.

### True Stories

That emerging attitude of acceptance is put to the test in *True Stories*. This collection is Atwood's poetic response to her increasing political commitment; its focus is even more external and marks a renewed emphasis on social themes less markedly evident in earlier collections such as *The Animals in That Country*. The generalized setting of many of the poems is the dusty, brutal, and brutalized countries of the Caribbean and Central America. The central group of poems in *True Stories* deals with political torture: The description of actual tortures is graphic and horrifying, emphasized rather than undercut by the spare, brutal, direct diction and imagery of Atwood's poetic style. Whether the original accounts themselves are true is a question with which Atwood grapples. In the three groups of poems

in the collection (including a group of prose poems, "A True Romance"), she examines the role of artist as witness-bearer, and the ironies inherent in the examination of truth and reality through art. As in *Two-Headed Poems*, there is a final expression of a tentative faith in and acceptance of life, for all its paradoxes. "Last Day" declares, "This egg/ in my hand is our last meal,/ you break it open and the sky/ turns orange again and the sun rises/ again and this is the last day again." The collection's final allusion, then, is to the egg, universal symbol of immortality and hope.

### Interlunar

*Interlunar* returns to the strongly mythological themes, characters, and imagery of Atwood's first collections of poems. From the first, the components of Atwood's complex vision have been clear; reading her poetry in chronological order is an odyssey through the maturing and honing of her artistic skills rather than through a definition and articulation of vision.

The mysticism suggested in *Interlunar*'s title is confirmed in the poems themselves. They are arranged in subtitled groups, a favorite device of Atwood; the most fascinating is "Snake Poems," which explores the symbolism of snakes throughout human cultural and religious history. This includes their association with darkness, evil, destructiveness, and the male principle, as well as with wisdom, knowledge, creativity, and the female principle. Above all, their association with resurrection (for their ability to shed their skins) is explored and viewed (especially in "Metempsychosis") with Atwood's customary ambivalence. Resurrection is also a central theme of the title group of poems, "Interlunar." Intimations of mortality are seen to be on the poet's mind in such poems as "Bedside," "Anchorage," and "Heart Test with an Echo Chamber"; the doubtful comfort of resurrection is ironically considered in a set of poems titled for and concerned with the mythological figures of Orpheus, Eurydice, and Persephone. In this way, Atwood's poems and vision come full circle to her earliest poetic works, *Double Persephone* and *The Circle Game*.

The tone of the collection's title poem, "Interlunar," is uncharacteristically comforting and serene, the statement of a mature artist who recognizes that her odyssey toward understanding in art and life must be without end but need not be frightening: "Trust me. This darkness/ is a place you can enter and be/ as safe in as you are anywhere."

## MORNING IN THE BURNED HOUSE

*Morning in the Burned House* is Atwood's first collection of new poems in a decade. It shows no falling off of skill or intensity and a continuation of all her familiar themes. The poems in this volume tend to a darker lyricism, a sharper awareness of mortality. Although it is difficult to separate the personal from the political in Atwood's vision, the strongest newer poems seem to be those that are most intensely personal, such as the series on the death of her father. In other poems, the satiric, sardonic, and sometimes outrageously feminist Atwood is very much in evidence.

## THE DOOR

*The Door* is Atwood's first book of new poems in twelve years, although before and after the publication of *Morning in the Burned House*, she published collections of selected poems from her earlier career—before other genres, especially the novel, began to compete so strongly for her attention. Like Thomas Hardy, Atwood may be returning to poetry now that she is a comfortably independent writer. Additionally, novels require a huge investment of time and energy, and following her "big novel" *The Blind Assassin*, she may have turned to writing poems, which produces the satisfaction of completion more quickly than other forms.

Concerns of time and energy are central to *The Door*, since a number of these poems deal with aging—no surprise coming from a poet born in 1939. The dust jacket says it all: The photograph on the front is of Atwood as a young girl, standing at her front door, while the publicity photograph of the author on the back flap reveals a woman approaching seventy. Thus, the photographs are graphic emblems of *The Door* and serve as an entry to the title poem. Throughout the persona's lifetime, ironically represented in everyday language and images, the door swings open, offering glimpses of darkness within before it closes. In the end, the persona steps in, and the door closes behind her, suggesting her death.

The earlier poems in *The Door* often range between memories of childhood and concerns of the present. For example, the opening poem of the first section,

"Gasoline," seems to grow out of a sensory experience, allowing entry to the poet's childhood. Among the poet's more recent concerns are the advanced age of her parents, whose deaths will also move her toward the precipice. "My mother dwindles . . ." strikes a chord in all who have dealt with a parent's failing body and mind.

Another section of poems focuses on being a poet, especially an older poet. The tone is often unsentimental to the point of cynicism. In one poem, "The poet has come back . . ." from years of virtue to be a poet again. In another, "Owl and Pussycat, some years later," Pussycat reminds Owl of how they have achieved major reputations—won the prizes and written flattering blurbs about each other's work—but wonders what this "moulting owl" and "arthritic pussycat" have actually accomplished.

These are tough poems, not in their obscurity, but in their strong impulse toward the kind of realism readers more often expect in fiction than in poetry. "Nobody cares who wins"—wars, that is—although winning is better than losing. "Saint Joan of Arc on a postcard" looks like "a boned rolled leg of lamb." The opening line of the poem "The hurt child" ends with "will bite you." The persona here is reminiscent of Iris, the narrator of *The Blind Assassin*, or Penelope, the narrator of *The Penelopiad*—old and experienced enough to have lost the pleasures of sentimentalism, avoided the traps of self-delusion, and decided it is too late to do anything but tell the truth.

## OTHER MAJOR WORKS

LONG FICTION: *The Edible Woman*, 1969; *Surfacing*, 1972; *Lady Oracle*, 1976; *Life Before Man*, 1979; *Bodily Harm*, 1981; *The Handmaid's Tale*, 1985; *Cat's Eye*, 1988; *The Robber Bride*, 1993; *Alias Grace*, 1996; *The Blind Assassin*, 2000; *Oryx and Crake*, 2003; *The Penelopiad: The Myth of Penelope and Odysseus*, 2005; *The Year of the Flood*, 2009.

SHORT FICTION: *Dancing Girls, and Other Stories*, 1977; *Bluebeard's Egg*, 1983; *Murder in the Dark: Short Fictions and Prose Poems*, 1983; *Wilderness Tips*, 1991; *Good Bones*, 1992 (pb. in U.S. as *Good Bones and Simple Murders*, 1994); *Moral Disorder*, 2006.

NONFICTION: *Survival: A Thematic Guide to Canadian Literature*, 1972; *Days of the Rebels: 1815-1840*, 1977; *Second Words: Selected Critical Prose*, 1982; *Margaret Atwood: Conversations*, 1990 (Earl G. Ingersoll, editor); *Strange Things. The Malevolent North in Canadian Literature*, 1995; *Deux sollicitudes: Entretiens*, 1996 (with Victor-Lévy Beaulieu; *Two Solicitudes: Conversations*, 1998); *Negotiating with the Dead: A Writer on Writing*, 2002; *Moving Targets: Writing with Intent, 1982-2004*, 2004 (pb. in U.S. as *Writing with Intent: Essays, Reviews, Personal Prose, 1983-2005*, 2005); *Waltzing Again: New and Selected Conversations with Margaret Atwood*, 2006 (with others; Ingersoll, editor).

CHILDREN'S LITERATURE: *Up in the Tree*, 1978; *Anna's Pet*, 1980 (with Joyce Barkhouse); *For the Birds*, 1990; *Princess Prunella and the Purple Peanut*, 1995 (illustrated by Maryann Kowalski); *Bashful Bob and Doleful Dorinda*, 2004 (illustrated by Dušan Petričić); *Rude Ramsay and the Roaring Radishes*, 2004 (illustrated by Petričić).

EDITED TEXTS: *The New Oxford Book of Canadian Verse in English*, 1982; *The CanLit Foodbook: From Pen to Palate, a Collection of Tasty Literary Fare*, 1987 (compiled and illustrated by Atwood).

MISCELLANEOUS: *The Tent*, 2006.

BIBLIOGRAPHY

Appleton, Sarah A., ed. *Once Upon a Time: Myth, Fairy Tales and Legends in Margaret Atwood's Writings*. Newcastle, England: Cambridge Scholars, 2008. Examines Atwood's use of myth and fairy tales in her fiction and poetry.

Atwood, Margaret. *Margaret Atwood: Conversations*. Edited by Earl G. Ingersoll. Princeton, N.J.: Ontario Review Press, 1990. Atwood discusses many aspects of her writing and life with various interviewers.

_____. *Waltzing Again: New and Selected Conversations with Margaret Atwood*. Edited by Earl G. Ingersoll. Princeton, N.J.: Ontario Review Press, 2006. Atwood discusses writing in interviews conducted after 1987.

Bloom, Harold, ed. *Margaret Atwood*. New York: Bloom's Literary Criticism, 2009. This volume in-cludes an introduction by Bloom and provides critical analysis of Atwood's fiction and poetry.

Hengen, Shannon, and Ashley Thomson. *Margaret Atwood: A Reference Guide, 1988-2005*. Lanham, Md.: Scarecrow, 2007. Atwood's writings from 1988 to 2005 are covered in this resource, which in-cludes listings of citations, reviews, quotations, and interviews. Also contains a guide to Atwood resources on the Internet and a chronology of her publishing career.

Howells, Coral Ann. *Margaret Atwood*. 2d ed. New York: Palgrave Macmillan, 2006. In this lively critical and biographical study, Howells elucidates issues that have energized all of Atwood's work: feminist issues, literary genres, and her own identity as a Canadian, a woman, and a writer. Focuses on the fiction.

_____, ed. *The Cambridge Companion to Margaret Atwood*. New York: Cambridge University Press, 2006. Contains an essay on Atwood's poetry and poetics as well as on her major themes.

McCombs, Judith, ed. *Critical Essays on Margaret Atwood*. Boston: G. K. Hall, 1988. This indispensable volume contains thirty-two articles and essays, including assessments of patterns and themes in her poetry and prose. The entries are arranged in the chronological order of Atwood's primary works, beginning with *The Circle Game* and ending with *The Handmaid's Tale*. It includes a primary bibliography to 1986 and a thorough index.

Nischik, Reingard M., ed. *Margaret Atwood: Works and Impact*. Reprint. Rochester, N.Y.: Camden House, 2002. This sturdy gathering of original (not reprinted) criticism includes Lothar Hönnighausen's comprehensive "Margaret Atwood's Poetry 1966-1995" as well as Ronald B. Hatch's "Margaret Atwood, the Land, and Ecology," which draws heavily on Atwood's poetry to make its case.

Wilson, Sharon Rose, ed. *Margaret Atwood's Textual Assassinations: Recent Poetry and Fiction*. Columbus: Ohio State University Press, 2003. This collection of essays examines Atwood's poetry, including *Morning in the Burned House*, as well as her fiction.

*Jill Rollins; Philip K. Jason*
*Updated by Earl G. Ingersoll*

# W. H. AUDEN

**Born:** York, England; February 21, 1907
**Died:** Vienna, Austria; September 29, 1973

PRINCIPAL POETRY

*Poems*, 1930
*The Orators*, 1932
*Look, Stranger!*, 1936 (also known as *On This Island*, 1937)
*Letters from Iceland*, 1937 (with Louis MacNeice; poetry and prose)
*Spain*, 1937
*Journey to a War*, 1939 (with Christopher Isherwood; poetry and prose)
*Another Time*, 1940
*The Double Man*, 1941 (also known as *New Year Letter*)
*For the Time Being*, 1944
*The Sea and the Mirror*, 1944
*The Collected Poetry*, 1945
*The Age of Anxiety: A Baroque Eclogue*, 1947
*Collected Shorter Poems, 1930-1944*, 1950
*Nones*, 1951
*The Shield of Achilles*, 1955
*Homage to Clio*, 1960
*About the House*, 1965
*Collected Shorter Poems, 1927-1957*, 1966
*Collected Longer Poems*, 1968
*City Without Walls, and Other Poems*, 1969
*Epistle to a Godson, and Other Poems*, 1972
*Thank You, Fog*, 1974
*Collected Poems*, 1976 (Edward Mendelson, editor)
*Sue*, 1977
*Selected Poems*, 1979 (Mendelson, editor)
*Juvenilia: Poems, 1922-1928*, 1994 (Katherine Bucknell, editor)

OTHER LITERARY FORMS

Though known primarily as a poet, W. H. Auden (AWD-ehn) worked in a number of other forms, making him one of the most prolific and versatile poets of his generation. During the 1930's he wrote one play on his own—*The Dance of Death* (pb. 1933)—and collab-

orated on three others with his friend Christopher Isherwood. These retain their interest today both as period pieces and, to a lesser degree, as experimental stage dramas. The best of the plays, *The Dog Beneath the Skin: Or, Where Is Francis?* (pb. 1935), is an exuberant, wide-ranging work containing some of Auden's finest stage verse and illustrating many of his early intellectual preoccupations, including his interest in post-Freudian psychology. The other plays, *The Ascent of F6* (pb. 1936) and *On the Frontier* (pr., pb. 1938), are of less interest, especially the latter, which is largely an antifascist propaganda piece. After the 1930's, Auden turned his dramatic interests toward the opera, writing his first libretto, *Paul Bunyan*, in 1941 for Benjamin Britten. (The work was not published until 1976, three years after Auden's death.) His better-known librettos, written in collaboration with Chester Kallman, are *The Rake's Progress* (pr., pb. 1951), *Elegy for Young Lovers* (pr., pb. 1961), *The Bassarids* (pr., pb. 1966), and *Love's Labour's Lost* (pb. 1972). Little assessment has been made of his librettos and their relationship to his poetry. Auden's prose writing, by contrast, has been quickly and widely recognized for its range, liveliness, and intelligence. His work includes dozens of essays, reviews, introductions, and lectures written over the span of his career. Many of his best pieces are gathered in *The Dyer's Hand, and Other Essays* (1962) and *Forewords and Afterwords* (1973); other prose includes *The Enchafed Flood* (1950) and *Secondary Worlds* (1969). In addition to his plays, librettos, and prose, Auden wrote for film and radio and worked extensively as an editor and translator. *Plays and Other Dramatic Writings by W. H. Auden, 1928-1938*, edited by Edward Mendelson, was published by Princeton University Press in 1988. It includes Auden's collaborations with Christopher Isherwood and works by Auden alone.

ACHIEVEMENTS

At a time when poets no longer enjoyed the wide readership they once did, W. H. Auden achieved a considerable popular success, his books selling well throughout his lifetime. He was also fortunate in having several sympathetic, intelligent critics to analyze and assess his work. It is true that Auden had his share of detractors, beginning, for example, in the 1930's with the negative response to his work in the influential journal *Scrutiny*, and, later, in two essays by Randall Jarrell taking him to task for his various ideological changes. Even today some argue that Auden's work is uneven or that his later poetry represents a serious decline from the brilliance he demonstrated in the 1930's. In a sense, his reputation has been granted grudgingly and, by some, with reservations. Despite all this, however, Auden is generally regarded today as one of the major poets of the twentieth century. Several of his lyrics are well established as standard anthology pieces—"Lullaby," "As I Walked Out One Evening," "In Memory of W. B. Yeats," "Musée des Beaux Arts,"—but his larger reputation may well rest not on the strength of individual poems but on the impressive range of thought and technical virtuosity found in his work as a whole.

Auden's poetry is quintessentially the work of a restless, probing intelligence committed to the idea that poise and clearheadedness are possible, indeed necessary, in a world beset by economic, social, and political chaos. Auden possessed, in the words of Chad Walsh, an "analytic power," an "ability to break a question down into its elements, to find new ways of putting familiar things together." "There is hardly an Auden poem," Walsh concludes, "that does not bespeak, and speak to, the brain at work." Auden's intelligence, however, is rarely ponderous or pedantic, and part of his lasting achievement may be the blending of playfulness and seriousness that he managed to sustain in much of his best work.

Although some may doubt the profundity of Auden's thinking, few question his technical virtuosity. No poet in recent times can match the range of traditional forms he used and often revitalized in his work— oratorio, eclogue, sestina, sonnet, villanelle, closet drama, verse epistle, and ode. Auden often boasted, perhaps with justification, that he had written successfully in every known meter. Perhaps even more than for his use of traditional literary forms, however, Auden is admired for his songs, which Monroe Spears sees as "his most distinctive accomplishment and his most popular." Auden borrowed from an array of musical forms, using irony and parody to transcend the limits of the genre in which he was working. His ballads are es-

pecially well regarded, as are many of the lyrics he wrote for the stage.

Over the course of his career, Auden received numerous literary honors, beginning in 1937 with the King's Gold Medal for poetry. His other awards include Guggenheim Fellowships in 1942 and 1945, the Award of Merit Medal from the American Academy of Arts and Letters in 1945, the Pulitzer Prize in 1948, the Bollingen Prize in 1954, the National Book Award in 1956, the Austrian State Prize for European literature in 1966, and the Gold Medal in poetry from the American Academy of Arts and Letters in 1968. He became a member of the American Academy of Arts and Letters in 1948 and served as chancellor for the Academy of American Poets from 1954 to 1973. From 1956 to 1960, Auden held the honorary position of Professor of Poetry at Oxford.

## BIOGRAPHY

Wystan Hugh Auden was born in York, England, in 1907, the third and youngest son of George and Constance Auden. Before his youngest son was two years old, George Auden gave up a private medical practice in York and moved his family south to Birmingham, where he worked as the city's school medical officer. W. H. Auden's devout, middle-class family (both his parents were the children of clergymen) gave him a strong sense of traditional religious values and encouraged his early intellectual bent. His mother, Auden frequently said, was the strongest presence in his early years. He was particularly close to her and believed throughout his life that her influence was largely responsible for shaping his adult character.

Auden's father, a widely educated man in both the humanities and sciences, acquainted the young Auden at an early age with classical literature and Nordic myths, and encouraged his reading in poetry and fiction as well as scientific subjects, including medicine, geology, and mining. This early reading was supported by a close familiarity with nature, and Auden as a child developed a fascination for the landscape of limestone caves and abandoned mines that is recalled in several of his poems. Auden's first inclinations were, in fact, toward the scientific and natural rather than literary, and as a young boy he fancied himself a mining engineer.

His interest in science continued throughout his life and is reflected in the frequent use of scientific ideas and images in his poetry, and accounts, perhaps, for the stance of clinical detachment found in his early work.

In 1915, Auden was sent as a boarder to St. Edmund's school in Surrey, and, after completing his studies there in 1920, attended Gresham's School, an institution known for its excellence in the sciences. While at Gresham's, Auden gradually came to acknowledge his homosexuality and to question many of his middle-class values and religious beliefs; by the time he left Gresham's, he had abandoned his faith. It was also during this period that Auden, at the suggestion of Robert Medley, began to write his first poems.

In 1925, Auden enrolled at Christ Church, Oxford, where he discovered a congenial social atmosphere far different from the repressive climate at Gresham's. He found in the young don Nevill Coghill a sympathetic, stimulating tutor who was soon informed of Auden's intentions to become a "great poet." After a year of reading in the sciences, Auden turned his interests to English studies and soon developed an enthusiasm for the then unfashionable poetry of the Anglo-Saxon period. This confirmed his preference for the Nordic-Germanic rather than Continental romance tradition, a bias evident in much of his early poetry and, later, in *The Age of Anxiety*, with its close imitation of Old English metric and alliterative patterns.

During the Oxford years and in the decade that followed, Auden was the central figure of a group of writers, including Cecil Day Lewis and Stephen Spender, who shared his liberal political leanings. The 1930's became a sort of golden decade for Auden, a time of intellectual excitement and artistic vitality. With various friends he traveled widely—to Iceland with Louis MacNeice, and to China with Christopher Isherwood. Both visits resulted in collaborative books containing poetry by Auden. In 1937, Auden went to Spain where he worked for the Loyalist cause in the Spanish Civil War, which had become a rallying cause for intellectuals of the time. His experience led to the writing of *Spain*, the celebrated political poem that Auden later rejected because of the "wicked doctrine" of its concluding lines; he purged the poem from most subsequent collections of his work. During the 1930's Auden

was also active in his home country: He taught school from 1930 to 1935, helped found the Group Theatre in 1932, and published two volumes of poetry that secured for him a reputation as one of the most promising young poets of his generation. In 1935 he married Erika Mann, daughter of the German novelist Thomas Mann, to provide her with a British passport.

Auden's writing during the 1930's—both his poetry and the plays written in collaboration with Isherwood—largely constitutes a diagnosis of industrial English society in the midst of economic and moral decay. The diagnosis is made from the perspective of various ideologies that Auden adopted or toyed with during the late 1920's and 1930's—Freudian and post-Freudian psychology, Marxism, and liberal socialism.

In 1939, at the end of a full and brilliant decade, Auden and Isherwood decided to leave England permanently and move to the United States, which they had visited in the preceding year on their return trip from China. Auden's move to New York marked a major turning point in his life and career, for during this period he was gradually shifting away from many of his earlier intellectual convictions and moving toward a re-

*W. H. Auden* (©Jill Krementz)

affirmation of his childhood faith; in October, 1940 he returned to the Anglican communion. Many of his poems in the 1940's record the gradual move toward Christianity, including, most explicitly, his Christmas oratorio, *For the Time Being*. Auden's concern for the ills of modern society did not end, however, with his affirmation of faith, for he pursued this concern in various ways in his poetry, most notably in *The Age of Anxiety*, whose title became a catch phrase for the war-torn decade in which it was written. During the 1940's Auden held teaching posts at several American colleges but continued to write prolifically, working chiefly on his ambitious longer poems.

Auden's life after the 1940's fell into a somewhat more staid routine. In the 1950's he began writing libretti with Chester Kallman, whom he had met shortly after his arrival in the United States; he and Kallman remained companions and collaborators until the end of Auden's life. From 1948 to 1957, Auden spent each spring and summer on the island of Ischia in the Tyrrhenian Sea, prompting some to suggest that he had entered a post-American phase in his career. Then, beginning in 1957 and for the remainder of his life, he stayed half of each year in New York and half in a converted farmhouse that he and Kallman purchased in the village of Kirchstetten, Austria. In a poem written at the time, Auden saw his departure from Ischia as a reaffirmation of his essential northernness. In Kirchstetten, he settled into the happy domesticity celebrated in his *About the House* volume.

In 1972, his health failing, Auden decided to leave New York permanently and spend his winter season each year in a "grace and favour" cottage offered to him by the governing board of his old college, Christ Church, Oxford. As usual, he stayed the following spring and summer in Kirchstetten, and, on his way back to Oxford that fall, died of a heart attack in Vienna. He was buried, as he had wished, in Kirchstetten.

ANALYSIS

Read chronologically, W. H. Auden's poetry moves from alienation to integration; his work is a quest for wholeness, an escape from the isolated self, "where dwell/ Our howling appetites," into a community where the essential goodness of life is acknowledged despite the presence of sin. Over the course of his career, Auden's quest takes many forms, but his goal never varies; from beginning to end, he seeks to discover how love, in all its manifestations, can fulfill humankind's social and personal needs.

Auden began in the 1930's as a critic of his society, an outsider looking in and finding little to admire in what he saw. His early work is essentially a record of social ills; love is sought but rarely found. As he matures, however, Auden gradually becomes less of a diagnostician and more of a healer; he arrives eventually at a vision of love informed by human sympathy and, later, by religious belief. Once this vision is affirmed in his poetry, Auden again shifts direction, becoming more fully than before a comic poet, intent on celebrating the redemptive power of love and acknowledging the essential blessedness of life. These shifts in Auden's work are, of course, gradual and subtle rather than abrupt, but the division of his career into three phases provides a way to bring some sense of order to a body of work remarkable, above all else, for its diversity.

The early Auden is very much a poet of the 1930's— a time of economic depression and fascism, war and rumors of war. Faced with such a world, he adopts the pose of a clinical diagnostician anatomizing a troubled society. He sees the social and spiritual malaise of his time as a failure of communication; individuals are trapped inside themselves, unable to escape the forces of psychological and social repression that block the possibility of love.

**"CONSIDER"**

The poems that record Auden's diagnosis of his society are still considered by some to be his best. Although they are often bewildering to readers, they are admired for their energy and intensity, their brilliant, elusive surfaces. One of the most highly regarded of these early poems is "Consider," which illustrates Auden's early technical skill as well as his characteristic themes. The poem is divided into three verse paragraphs, each addressed to a different auditor by a speaker whose heightened theatrical language gives him an aloofness of tone which matches his arrogant message. Auden's voice in "Consider" typifies the detachment and impersonality of the early poems.

The first verse paragraph addresses the reader directly, asking that he "consider" a symbolic modern landscape "As the hawk sees it or the helmeted airman." From this great height, with the objective eye of the hawk, the speaker observes images of society on the verge of collapse: a cigarette end smoldering at the edge of a garden party; decadent vacationers at a winter resort, surrounded by signs of an impending war; and farmers "sitting in kitchens in the stormy fens." The vacationers, incapable of emotion, are "supplied with feelings by an efficient band," while the farmers, separated from them by physical distance and class barriers, yet equally lonely, listen to the same music on the wireless. Though explicitly social and political, the poem is also developed in personal and psychological terms; like the landscape, the individuals in the poem are "diseased," unable to establish genuine personal contacts.

Having drawn this grim picture of "our time," the speaker turns in the second verse paragraph to elucidate the psychological foundation of social ills, addressing, in the process, a "supreme Antagonist," who, according to Edward Mendelson, is the "*inner* enemy" that "personifies the fears and repressions that oppose love." The Antagonist finds an ample number of victims in the decadent society and spreads its evil, "scattering the people" and seizing them with "immeasurable neurotic dread." In this section, the poem's intense language and deliberate rhetorical excess are beautifully modulated, making the speaker aloof and detached yet with an edge of hysteria in his voice.

The final verse paragraph is addressed to the banker, the don, and the clergyman (representatives of the social elite), along with all others who seek happiness by following the "convolutions" of the distorted ego. The poem ends by warning the selfish and the elite of the inescapable psychological diseases that the Antagonist holds in store for them, diseases that will further destroy the possibility for love.

Auden's adaptation of various psychological theories in "Consider" is typical of his method in the 1930's, as is the detached clinical posture of the speaker and the explicit social and political concern voiced in the poem. Auden characteristically offers little hope and, given the extent of the ills he describes, his doing so might well have seemed facile. Auden's earliest poetry sometimes offers an idealized, vague notion of love as a healing force capable of breaking down repression and restoring social and personal relationships to their proper order. Usually, though, this message is faint and clearly secondary to the diagnostic aim of the poems.

### "LULLABY" AND "AS I WALKED OUT ONE EVENING"

In two love poems written somewhat later than "Consider," Auden approaches more explicitly the view of love hinted at in the earliest poems. "Lullaby," his best-known lyric, ends with the speaker's hope that his beloved may be "watched by every human love." The poem's emphasis, however, rests on the transience of "human love": The arm on which the sleeping lover rests is "faithless"; love is at best a temporary stay against loneliness. Likewise, in "As I Walked Out One Evening," Auden stresses the limitations of romantic and erotic love. "Time" lurks in the shadows and coughs when the lovers "would kiss," deflating the romantic delusions satirized at the beginning of the poem. Later, though, near the end, the chiming clocks of the city offer an injunction that suggests a new direction: "You shall love your crooked neighbor/ With your crooked heart." Though undercut by a number of ironies, the love described here moves tentatively toward the vision of the 1940's. Even so, the "human love" that Auden evokes in the 1930's seems insufficient to resolve the social and personal ills diagnosed by his poetry.

During the 1930's, Auden gradually left behind the various ideologies he had seriously (and, perhaps, half-seriously) adopted during the decade. Humphrey Carpenter, Auden's biographer, suggests that these ideologies—Marxism, post-Freudianism, liberal humanism—all had in common a fundamental belief in the natural goodness of man. Near the end of the decade, Auden began to question his liberal humanism, partly because of its inability to offer, as he put it, "some reason why [Adolf Hitler] was utterly wrong." The reason he sought turned out to be in Christianity, particularly the doctrine of humankind's sinful nature and its need, because of that nature, for forgiveness and redemption. The quest for love that began in the early poetry thus grows in the 1940's into a quest for Christian love.

There is, of course, no sudden shift in Auden's poetry as a result of the new direction in his thinking. Rather, at the end of the 1930's, he begins gradually to formulate this vision of *agape*; in a sense, he was already doing so in the two love poems examined above.

### "HERMAN MELVILLE"

The poem "Herman Melville," though written a year before Auden "officially" rejoined the Church in 1940, demonstrates his thinking at this crucial period, a time that coincided with his arrival in the United States. The poem also suggests something of Auden's more relaxed, lucid style, a shift that began in the mid-1930's away from the verbal glitter and rhetorical intensity of poems such as "Consider." "Herman Melville" is thus a good example of Auden's thematic and stylistic direction in the shorter poems published during the 1940's.

In the poem Auden describes Melville's life and literary career as a metaphorical "gale" that had blown the novelist "Past the Cape Horn of sensible success" and "deafened him with thunder." Near the end of his life, after Melville had exorcised his demons, he "sailed into an extraordinary mildness," entering a domestic contentment where he discovered "new knowledge"—that "Evil is unspectacular and always human" (Auden develops a similar idea in "Musée des Beaux Arts") and "that we are introduced to Goodness every day." What Melville found, in essence, is what Auden himself was in the process of accepting—the universality of humankind's sinfulness and the possibility that goodness (that is, grace and redemption) can, in an unspectacular fashion, transform the corrupt present, enabling humans to transcend their sinfulness.

At the end of the poem Auden describes Melville's exultation and surrender at his discovery of the transforming power of *agape*. The poem, while not autobiographical, certainly seems to be Auden's testing ground, his rehearsal of an idea that had been forming in his mind. Melville's discovery that his love had been "selfish" suggests perhaps that Auden has come full circle from his early poems, now denying completely the efficacy of eros, sexual-romantic love. Auden himself suggests, however, that this is not the case; writing for *Theology* in 1950, he argues that "agape is the fulfillment of eros, not its contradiction." Perhaps "Herman Melville" contains an early formulation of a position whose full complexity Auden had not yet resolved.

### THE AGE OF ANXIETY

If "Herman Melville" records Auden's initial approach to Christianity, then *The Age of Anxiety* shows his response to a modern society at odds with the directives of *agape*. The poem is the longest of the four extended works Auden wrote in the 1940's. The bulk of his energy during the decade went into these poems, which were ambitious undertakings in an age when the long poem had all but died out. *The Age of Anxiety* is a baroque eclogue, a pastoral form entirely incongruous with the poem's urban setting (New York) and its subject matter (four modern-day city dwellers during World War II). Auden also achieves irony with his imitation of Old English metric patterns. The contrast between an epic measure and the pettiness of modern life creates a mock-heroic tone.

The poem begins in a Third Avenue bar where four customers—Quant, Malin, Emble, and Rosetta—drink and discuss their lives. The conversation of these four representatives of modern humanity becomes an effort to find order in an age of chaos and disbelief. At the outset the characters drink in private corners of the bar, each dreaming (as Monroe Spears puts it) "of his own way of escape, but aware . . . of no recourse beyond the human level." Rosetta, for example, has "a favourite day-dream" of "lovely innocent countrysides," while the youthful Emble dreams of success achieved only in a hollow "succession of sexual triumphs." The four dreamers eventually move out of their private corners and begin to discuss the war. As they grow more and more drunk their discussion turns, in the second part of the poem ("The Seven Ages"), to the human, "the traveller through time . . . As he bumbles by from birth to death." Their analysis constitutes a psychological study of the maturation process of the individual and leads them to recognize their own failure in coming to terms with life. Their recognition is, however, only momentary, for in the poem's third section ("The Seven Stages") the four figures lapse into a drunken state of unconsciousness and travel over an allegorical dream landscape searching again for a solution of their own, and hence humankind's, dilemma.

The journey, however, is doomed to fail, for the four

seek not spiritual enlightenment but a way of escaping it. The first six stages of their vision carry them through (and they believe away from) the anxiety and suffering of the world, but they are merely led deeper into themselves. The truth revealed in the dream is that the world and its anxieties—which they can only see in distortion—are unbearable for modern human beings. The egotism of the dreamer will not allow them salvation.

The first six stages of the dream explore every possible path of escape. In the seventh stage, however, all hope is lost. They are now, as Emble says, "miles" from any "workable world." The quest has taken them into a landscape of "ravenous unreals." As the chaos closes in on them they turn away from it, refusing to attempt the only true quest—the seeking of spiritual knowledge not in their own illusions but in the redemption of the present moment through a religious commitment. At the end of the poem, Malin recognizes the failure of their journey. The moment is not redeemed, but the resolution of the poem defines their failure in Christian terms. In his final speech Malin describes modern humankind's unwillingness "to say Yes" to "That-Always-Opposite" who "Condescended to exist and to suffer death/ And, scorned on a scaffold, ensconced in His life/ The human household."

Thus the poem ends with humankind's refusal of *agape*, its resignation to loneliness, and its unwillingness to forgo egotism and accept the world as redeemed through the Incarnation. *The Age of Anxiety* takes up two main strands in Auden's work—the diagnosis of social and personal ills and the possibility of *agape* as a release from isolation. The four characters in this poem fail to achieve that release.

### LATER YEARS

*The Age of Anxiety* brings to an end what some have called Auden's American period. From 1948 to the end of his life, he spent half of each year abroad, and many of the poems of this time reflect the change of landscape. There is also a change in perspective, certainly not as radical as some of the earlier changes but a change nevertheless. Justin Replogle suggests that after 1950 Auden becomes an essentially comic poet whose emphasis shifts away from poetry as a repository for ideas. His work, says Replogle, "begins less to proclaim a belief than to celebrate one." The later po-

etry, then, is generally lighter in tone and technique than his earlier work, and Replogle's word "celebrate" is especially apt, for there are a variety of celebrations going on in the later work: of the natural world ("Bucolics"), of the five senses ("Precious Five"), of friends ("For Friends Only"), of the ordinary and domestic ("Thanksgiving for a Habitat"), and of earthly happiness ("In Praise of Limestone"). All these celebrations are enacted in *About the House*, a collection that typifies Auden's later style. The book celebrates the rooms of his converted farmhouse in Kirchstetten, Austria, becoming a sort of homage to domesticity.

### ABOUT THE HOUSE

*About the House* is the work of a poet who, in a sense, has arrived. Auden's quest for love as a cure for humankind's ills took him in the 1930's to a landscape of desperation, isolation, and decay. Gradually he discovered a basis on which, in the 1940's, he could build a vision of *agape*, a knowledge that, despite its sinfulness and guilt, humankind could be forgiven through grace; love was possible. In *About the House*, nearly forty years after his first poems appeared, the "cure" of love is still at the center of Auden's work; in his later work, however, the possibility of love is not so much proclaimed as celebrated.

"Tonight at Seven-Thirty," the dining-room poem in *About the House*, discusses with wit and charm the place where humans enact a ritual of celebration (the dinner party) that is nearly religious or mythical in its implications—the breaking of bread with friends. If many of Auden's poems call on humankind to love (often with didactic urgency), then the dining-room poem, like all of *About the House*, is informed by a gentle spirit of love. In one sense, the volume is a celebration of friendship; all the poems are dedicated to close friends, and several of them are addressed to people Auden loved. The *agape* proclaimed earlier now unobtrusively informs every poem as each room of the house becomes a celebration of some ordinary human activity—eating, sleeping, conversing, working.

"Tonight at Seven-Thirty" opens with a clever comparison of the eating habits of several species: plants ("one solitary continuous meal"), predators ("none of them play host"), and humans (who alone can "do the honors of a feast"). This definition is designed, first of all, to amuse; it nevertheless makes a serious point in asserting that only humans—"Dame Kind's thoroughbred lunatic"—can invite a stranger to the table and serve him first. Auden celebrates humankind's capacity for kindness, ritual, and even good manners—another recurrent motif in the later poems.

OTHER MAJOR WORKS

PLAYS: *Paid on Both Sides: A Charade*, pb. 1930; *The Dance of Death*, pb. 1933; *The Dog Beneath the Skin: Or, Where Is Francis?*, pb. 1935 (with Christopher Isherwood); *The Ascent of F6*, pb. 1936 (with Isherwood); *On the Frontier*, pr., pb. 1938 (with Isherwood); *Paul Bunyan*, pr. 1941 (libretto; music by Benjamin Britten); *For the Time Being*, pb. 1944 (oratorio; musical setting by Martin David Levy); *The Rake's Progress*, pr., pb. 1951 (libretto; with Chester Kallman; music by Igor Stravinsky); *Delia: Or, A Masque of Night*, pb. 1953 (libretto; with Kallman; not set to music); *Elegy for Young Lovers*, pr., pb. 1961 (libretto; with Kallman; music by Hans Werner Henze); *The Bassarids*, pr., pb. 1966 (libretto; with Kallman; music by Henze); *Love's Labour's Lost*, pb. 1972 (libretto; with Kallman; music by Nicolas Nabokov; adaptation of William Shakespeare's play); *The Entertainment of the Senses*, pr. 1974 (libretto; with Kallman; music by John Gardiner); *Plays and Other Dramatic Writings by W. H. Auden, 1928-1938*, 1988; *W. H. Auden and Chester Kallman: Libretti and Other Dramatic Writings by W. H. Auden, 1939-1973*, 1993.

NONFICTION: *The Enchafèd Flood*, 1950; *The Dyer's Hand, and Other Essays*, 1962; *Selected Essays*, 1964; *Secondary Worlds*, 1969; *A Certain World*, 1970; *Forewords and Afterwords*, 1973; *Prose and Travel Books in Prose and Verse: Volume I, 1926-1938*, 1996 (Edward Mendelson, editor); *Lectures on Shakespeare*, 2000 (Arthur Kirsch, editor); *Prose and Travel Books in Prose and Verse: Volume II, 1939-1948*, 2002 (Mendelson, editor); *The Complete Works of W. H. Auden: Prose, Volume III, 1949-1955*, 2007 (Mendelson, editor).

EDITED TEXTS: *The Oxford Book of Light Verse*, 1938; *The Portable Greek Reader*, 1948; *Poets of the English Language*, 1950 (5 volumes; with Norman Holmes Pearson); *The Faber Book of Modern American Verse*, 1956; *Selected Poems of Louis MacNeice*, 1964; *Nineteenth Century British Minor Poets*, 1966; *A Choice of Dryden's Verse*, 1973.

MISCELLANEOUS: *The English Auden: Poems, Essays, and Dramatic Writings, 1927-1939*, 1977 (Mendelson, editor).

BIBLIOGRAPHY

Arana, R. Victoria. *W. H. Auden's Poetry: Mythos, Theory, and Practice*. Amherst, N.Y.: Cambria Press, 2009. A critical examination of the poetry of Auden, examining his style, diction, and the limitary poems.

Carpenter, Humphrey. *W. H. Auden: A Biography*. Boston: Houghton Mifflin, 1981. Carpenter had access to private and unpublished material in crafting this comprehensive and compelling critical biography of the poet. It is the key source to biographical detail with which an Auden researcher should begin to situate Auden's poetry within his world and worldview.

Davenport-Hines, Richard. *Auden*. New York: Pantheon, 1996. This biography of Auden is also a history of some of the pressing and largely unresolved human and literary problems Auden faced in this lifetime.

Fuller, John. *W. H. Auden: A Commentary*. Princeton, N.J.: Princeton University Press, 1998. Brings to bear a great deal of erudition, along with meticulous critical attention, and covers the plays and libretti as well as the poetry. In this sense, it is indispensable for those readers who want to take Auden seriously, and at his word, on the concern for "truth" in writing.

Hecht, Anthony. *The Hidden Law: The Poetry of W. H. Auden*. Cambridge, Mass.: Harvard University Press, 1993. A close examination of the poetry of Auden.

Mendelson, Edward. *Early Auden*. New York: Viking Press, 1981. A brilliant synthesis of Auden's intellectual development and emotional history to 1939. Traces themes back to childhood fantasies, which are the substance of Auden's poetic self-analysis as symbols for public conditions in his time. The main movement of his art was from a private to a public language. Includes notes and index.

_____. *Later Auden*. New York: Farrar, Straus and Giroux, 1999. In discussing the verse, Mendelson covers both major works and less well known, later poems. This is a major study of a poet whose cries against social injustice resound far beyond his time and place.

Page, Norman. *Auden and Isherwood: The Berlin Years*. New York: St. Martin's Press, 1998. Examines the relationship between Auden and Christopher Isherwood, looking also at their friends and associates. Bibliography and index.

Sharpe, Tony. *W. H. Auden*. New York: Routledge, 2007. A biography of Auden that examines his life from literary, historical, and personal perspectives; analyzes his books of poetry and individual poems, and provides general criticism.

Smith, Stan, ed. *The Cambridge Companion to W. H. Auden*. New York: Cambridge University Press, 2004. Replete with tools for further research, this is an excellent aid to any study of Auden's life and work.

*Michael Hennessy*

# *B*

## THOMAS LOVELL BEDDOES

**Born:** Clifton, England; June 30, 1803
**Died:** Basel, Switzerland; January 26, 1849

PRINCIPAL POETRY

*The Improvisatore*, 1821
*The Poems, Posthumous and Collected, of Thomas Lovell Beddoes*, 1851
*The Poetical Works of Thomas Lovell Beddoes*, 1890
*The Poems of Thomas Lovell Beddoes*, 1907
*Selected Poems*, 1976

OTHER LITERARY FORMS

During his lifetime, Thomas Lovell Beddoes (BEHD-ohz) published only one volume of poetry, one play, scattered incidental poems, and a few newspaper articles written in German. His most substantial publications, *The Improvisatore* and the play *The Bride's Tragedy* (pr., pb. 1822), appeared when he was very young. The poems were published at Oxford; the play appeared on the London stage.

ACHIEVEMENTS

Thomas Lovell Beddoes was recognized during his lifetime as a promising young lyrical dramatist who never fulfilled the early expectations he raised. The one volume of poems and the single play—virtually all his work to be published during his lifetime—appeared while he was an undergraduate. They attracted sufficient attention to earn him the acquaintance and support of a small circle of London literary figures including Mary Shelley and William Godwin. Throughout the remainder of his life, however, Beddoes became increasingly aloof from literary "insiders." He gained a modest notoriety on the Continent for the fiery radicalism which caused him repeated conflicts with the authorities.

In the twentieth century, a number of scholars returned to Beddoes's work (most of it unpublished before his death, much of it never finished) with a new seriousness which gave him a firm though not exalted reputation among late Romantic (or early Victorian) writers. Beddoes is no longer seen as a mere anachronism, writing Elizabethan plays out of their time. Rather, he is seen as a man of deeply romantic temperament who tried to ground his commitment to the imagination in a rigorously scientific account of the human faculties. His failure to integrate these opposing tendencies resulted in strong tensions which generated a few powerful poetic characters and a poignant imagery in his work. The same tensions perhaps also contributed to the mood of despair which ended in his suicide.

BIOGRAPHY

Born at Clifton, England, Thomas Lovell Beddoes grew up under the shadow of a distinguished father (usually referred to as Dr. Beddoes to avoid confusion with the poet). Dr. Beddoes had been the friend of Erasmus Darwin, Samuel Taylor Coleridge, and other celebrated figures. The poet also grew up in the reflected fame of his aunt—the novelist Maria Edgeworth.

As a schoolboy at Charterhouse, Beddoes was a precocious student of the classics. There he wrote a juvenile short story, "Scaroni: Or, The Mysterious Cave" and also, apparently, some plays no longer extant. At Pembroke College, Oxford, Beddoes distinguished himself both as a student and as a writer. The success of *The Improvisatore* and *The Bride's Tragedy* led him to believe that he might expect a future in letters. He did not then know that he had already published the last significant work he would ever see in print. In 1825, after taking his degree in classics, Beddoes went abroad to improve his German and to scoop the cream of German learning at a time when both letters and the sciences were enjoying a burst of brilliance in Germany. In fact, however, Beddoes was never to return to England except for short interludes.

At Göttingen University, he polished the manuscripts of *Torrismond* (1851) and *The Second Brother* (1851) and tried to complete the project that was to occupy him for the rest of his life: *Death's Jest-Book: Or, The Fool's Tragedy* (pb. 1850). Failing in his attempt to complete these projects, Beddoes attempted suicide in 1829. In the same year, he was expelled by the university court on charges of drunken and disorderly behavior. His fortunes grew still more turbulent after he had transferred to the University of Würzburg: desultory composition, occasional political articles for the *Volksblatt*, a revolutionary speech at Gaibach, deportation from Munich, imprisonment for debt at Würzburg, a move to Zurich. In Switzerland, he found a temporarily safe haven and entered the University at Zurich in 1833, remaining there until 1837.

During the period of his German studies, Beddoes had become increasingly absorbed by a scientific interest that finally led to a degree in physiology. Thus, he can be seen as an interesting case of the nineteenth century polymath, trying fiercely to hold the humane and scientific cultures together in his own mind, on the eve of Matthew Arnold's and T. H. Huxley's open acknowledgment that classical and scientific education had become adversarial. Beddoes himself seems to have practiced his dissections in the futile hope of finding some undiscovered organ which could authenticate the arguments for human immortality, thus grounding metaphysics in physics.

Beddoes continued to create social difficulties for himself through both his political radicalism and his casual disregard for bourgeois conventions. In 1839, he experienced a continuing conflict with the Zurich police over his lack of a residence permit. In 1840, he moved to Berlin and attended the university. Back in Zurich in 1845, he was fined for disturbing the peace. He traveled to Frankfurt, where he suffered a long illness brought on by an infection he incurred while dissecting. After a brief trip to England, he went to Basel, Switzerland. On the morning following his arrival there, Beddoes deliberately opened an artery in his left leg. Six months later, after recuperating from the second attempt on his own life, Beddoes died—most likely a suicide—on January 26, 1849—too early in the year to enjoy the fall of Metternich and the broad victory of radicals throughout Europe. He was forty-five years old.

The fate of Beddoes's manuscripts is one of the most curious in literary history. Hours before his death, he bequeathed all his papers to his English friend T. F. Kelsall. Kelsall, in turn, left the extensive collection of largely unpublished Beddoes manuscripts to Robert Browning; Browning showed them to Edmund Gosse and Dykes Campbell, both of whom laid the foundation for modern critical studies by transcribing extensively from what they saw. At his own death, Browning left the black box containing the Beddoes materials to his son, Robert Waring "Pen" Browning. At the subsequent sale of Pen Browning's estate, the "Browning Box" of Beddoes papers did not appear. Its fate is still a mystery.

ANALYSIS

Thomas Lovell Beddoes's poetry (including his verse drama) focuses on three subjects: love, death, and madness. There is a constant theme: Love offers an entrance to the charmed world where spirit and nature are one; yet, just when love asserts its claims and some ideal of joy seems realizable, either madness or death intrudes with an ironic laugh to snatch away that love— the best hope that human beings have for something approximating transcendence. The reader is left with an ironic ambivalence toward the expectations of the spirit. Those expectations are linked ever more tightly, as Beddoes's poetry unfolds, with the mocking ironies (death and madness) which give the lie to dreams of love, immortality, and transcendence. Beddoes's ambivalence toward his own dream of immortality is partly a result of his progressively deeper commitment to scientific inquiry, with its rigorous rules of evidence. It is also in part a reflection of the ambivalence of the whole age. John Herschel, William Whewell, and Augustus De Morgan were all Victorian scientists, for example, who wrote highly romantic poetry. Charles Darwin enjoyed a wide reading in imaginative literature. However, it was becoming progressively clear that the specializations of scientific thought would soon put an end to the ideal fusion of science and the humanities which Beddoes sought.

The main body of Beddoes's work shows the ambivalence which he felt about all the great themes of literature: love, the meaning of suffering, the significance of everyday life, the possibilities for some sort of redemptive experience, and the hope for immortality. The fragmentation of his work, his desultory efforts to polish and finish it, his inability to commit himself to a dramatic poem with sufficient force to work it through, all suggest Beddoes's dilemma. He was a man whose learning and instincts were grounded in the classical past, a man who loved the great sureties of the great poets. In his own age, however, and in his own mind, those sureties were being eroded by a secular skepticism which denied him the assurance and joy of the old world, yet revealed no credible options for a man of the spirit living in an empirical and pragmatic age. Before Arnold, Beddoes was "caught between two worlds,/ One dead, the other powerless to be born." Before Franz Kafka, he sensed the abyss that underlies everyday experience. Biographies can never, of course, reconstruct all the sorrows and the intense impressions of a private person who lived long ago. It is clear enough from his work itself, however, that Beddoes believed that the illusions of a sacred and mythopoeic world were breaking up, that the losses to be suffered would throw enormous stress on the devices of sanity, and that in the end, death would mock the illusions, the losses, and even the madness itself by keeping its eternal secret.

### THE IMPROVISATORE

Such ambivalence appears as early as *The Improvisatore* and grows progressively more profound and ironic all the way through his work, culminating in *Death's Jest-Book*. *The Improvisatore* is a series of three ballad-like tales that suffer from a trite and overheated romanticism. These tales were published when Beddoes was eighteen years old, and they reflect his early quest for a lyrical style that would give voice to his yearnings for a mythopoeic, spiritual world. His images, however, are often clichés: "'Twas as though Flora had been sporting there,/ And dropped some jewels from her loosened hair." Sometimes the images are absurd conceits, similar to those of the Metaphysical poets two centuries earlier: "Her mouth!—Oh pardon me, thou coral cave,/ Prison of fluttering sighs . . . if I fail to tell/ The Beauty and the grace, that in thee dwell."

These early tales share in common the themes listed above: love, madness, and death. In each ballad, youthful or infant love loses its object—a sweetheart, a parent. This loss starkly transforms the protagonist. The youthful sense of a charmed and summertime reality gives way to a madness expressed in images of a horrific supernaturalism. The only escape from that madness is into death.

### THE BRIDE'S TRAGEDY AND THE SECOND BROTHER

*The Bride's Tragedy* and *The Second Brother* are more accomplished than *The Improvisatore*. There are fewer clichés. Still, these plays too might be thought melodramatic except that the romanticism is less feverish, and Beddoes's ability to control his lyricism, his characterizations, and his plot construction have clearly matured. In *The Bride's Tragedy*, Hesperus is secretly married to Floribel. Orlando, son of the duke, also loves Floribel but knows nothing of the marriage. He imprisons Hesperus's father and offers Hesperus his (Orlando's) sister in order to have Floribel for himself. Trapped (and jealous), Hesperus murders his secret wife. What enables this play to transcend such a melodramatic plot is a more mature lyricism, as in the song "Poor Old Pilgrim Misery," where the strong feelings of Hesperus are not merely enunciated (as Beddoes had enunciated emotions in *The Improvisatore*) but suggested through controlled images: "Beneath the silent moon he sits,/ a listening to the screech owl's cry,/ and the cold wind's goblin prate."

In 1825, Beddoes published his translation of some of J. C. F. Schiller's philosophic letters (their first translation into English) in *Oxford Quarterly Magazine*. His preface reveals the depth of the bifurcation of his own mind. "We seldom attain truth otherwise than by extremes; we must first exhaust error, and often madness before we end our toil at the far goal of calm wisdom." By this time his enthusiasms—poetry and science— have been polarized into a rigorous dialectic. His effort to integrate them is failing. His extremes are tending toward madness. He further claims that "scepticism and free-thinking are the feverish paroxysm of the human spirit, and must, by the very . . . concussion which they cause . . . help to confirm the health [of the soul]." His assurance on this point seems a romantic's whistling in the dark of rationalist doubt. Consider, for example, his translation of Schiller's first letter, Julius to Raphael: "There is nothing holy but truth. What reason acknowledges is truth . . . I have sacrificed all my opinions. . . .

My reason is now my all; my only security for diversity, virtue, immortality." Beddoes has set himself on an irreversible track. During the whole course of his writing he will find, like Julius, no earnest for love, wholeness, nor peace.

Beddoes's lyrical poems may be grouped under the headings Juvenilia (1818-1821), Outidana (1821-1825), The Ivory Gate (1830-1839), German Poems (1837-1845), and Lost Poems (1843-1848). These headings are used in H. W. Donner's definitive one-volume edition of Beddoes's complete works. Although the topics are various, a selected list of titles suggests how closely the lyrical poems are tied to the major themes already identified: "Threnody," "Fragments of a Dirge," "Epitaph," "The Tree of Life," "Dirge and Hymeneal," "Lament of Thanatos," "Thanatos to Kenelm," "The Last Judgment," "The Phantom-Wooer," and others of the same sort.

## DEATH'S JEST-BOOK

The poem "Dream Pedlary," written for inclusion in *Death's Jest-Book*, is typical of the mature Beddoes. It consists of five stanzas, the first of ten lines, rhyming *ababccaaab*, and the remaining four of nine lines each, rhyming *ababccaab*. Because some of the rhyming words are carried from one stanza to the next, a spare economy of form emerges which is well-suited to the stark theme of the poem. The poem begins with a question: "If there were dreams to sell,/ What would you buy?" Beddoes then offers images of various dreams for sale. In the first stanza, these dreams are described as "merry and sad," but in the second stanza the image chosen is a sad one, "a cottage lone and still." In the next stanza, the dream for sale is a "spell to call the buried," which gives way in the fourth stanza to the dream that "there are no ghosts to raise./ Out of death lead no ways." The last stanza expresses a death wish ("lie as I will do/ And breathe thy last") because the fear that death is a void at least validates the claim that "all dreams are made true"; that is, all dreams are only dreams and therefore truly dreams. The images have progressed from merry and sad dreams, through solitude (the lone cottage), to the dream of ghosts, to the dream of a nihilistic void where there are no ghosts. This terrible finality is so unthinkable to Beddoes that it draws and fascinates him.

No other work of Beddoes has achieved as high a standing with critics as *Death's Jest-Book*. He worked on this poetic drama for more than twenty years, and it was still unpublished at his death. This macabre play provides a historical link between the revenge tragedy of the Renaissance and the tale of terror in modern times. It strings together a powerful series of images: the court jester (Isbrand) in cap and bells who is driven by the wish for revenge to try to usurp the throne of Münsterberg; a conjuration scene in which the duke opens the tomb of his wife only to find there the ghost of a man he has murdered; and a dance of death consisting of painted figures who actually descend from the wall to act out a grotesque masque.

The play has the eloquence, the ghosts, and the strong-willed characters of an Elizabethan swashbuckler, but it also hints at the nihilism of a modern tale of terror. It is this latter fact that sets it apart from contemporaneous gothic tales such as those of Ann Radcliffe. The macabre events of *Death's Jest-Book*, such as the conjuration scene in a derelict Gothic cathedral, suggest the possibility that behind the terrors there lies no supernatural law of justice or piety, but rather a lawless abyss just a finger reach beyond everyday normalcy. The critic John Agar believes that Isbrand's tragedy is that he aspires to be a hero, not a villain (his motive, after all, was to avenge the deaths of his father and brother), but—lacking an adequate sense of his own limits—he becomes as evil as he had hoped to be good. Good intentions, it might be observed, do not save humans in a naturalistic world where there is no omnipotent judge to weigh those intentions.

Although the images of horror in the play are fairly conventional—a ghost (Wolfram, Isbrand's murdered brother), the skeletal *danse macabre*—nevertheless Beddoes's keenly spiritual sensibility, faced with the persuasions of a rigorous skepticism, suffers much as Kafka suffered from a tormenting recognition that life, love, kingdoms, even efforts at revenge, may be nothing but a macabre joke—death's jest. The characters in Beddoes's play sustain the conventional hope that death is only a mask for immortality: "Death is old and half worn out: Are there no chinks in it?" However, death keeps its mocking secret as these stage directions show: "The Deaths . . . come out of the walls, and dance fantastically to a rattling music . . . ; some seat themselves at the table and drink with mocking gestures." Later, as Isbrand dies, having briefly occupied the usurped throne, the ghost of his brother places the cap and bells upon his head again. All are absurd fools in *Death's Jest-Book*.

### OTHER MAJOR WORKS

PLAYS: *The Bride's Tragedy*, pr., pb. 1822; *Death's Jest-Book: Or, The Fool's Tragedy*, pb. 1850.

NONFICTION: *The Letters of Thomas Lovell Beddoes*, 1894.

MISCELLANEOUS: *The Complete Works of Thomas Lovell Beddoes*, 1928; *The Works of Thomas Lovell Beddoes*, 1935 (H. W. Donner, editor).

### BIBLIOGRAPHY

Baker, John Haydn. "'Toms Lacoon': A Newly Discovered Poem by Thomas Lovell Beddoes." *Victorian Poetry* 40, no. 3 (Fall, 2002): 261. Discusses a newly discovered poem that has Beddoes's characteristically ghoulish depictions of death.

Berns, Ute, and Michael Bradshaw, eds. *The Ashgate Research Companion to Thomas Lovell Beddoes*. Burlington, Vt.: Ashgate, 2007. Contains many essays on Beddoes and his works, with several on *Death's Jest-Book* and *The Bride's Tragedy*.

Bradshaw, Michael. *Resurrection Songs: The Poetry of Thomas Lovell Beddoes*. Burlington, Vt.: Ashgate, 2001. A critical analysis and interpretation of the poetry of Beddoes, looking at the poet's obsession with immortality and the fragmentation that characterizes his work.

Donner, H. W. *The Browning Box: Or, The Life and Works of Thomas Lovell Beddoes*. London: Oxford University Press, 1935. A collection of letters about Beddoes's life and poetry, by friends and admirers. The odd title refers to the box of materials given to Robert Browning after Beddoes's death.

_____. *Thomas Lovell Beddoes: The Making of a Poet*. 1935. Reprint. Folcroft, Pa.: Folcroft Library Editions, 1970. This comprehensive study of Beddoes's life and times balances biography with literary interpretation. Contains an informative introduction on nineteenth century theater and the influence of Elizabethan drama on Romantic poetry. A conclusion summarizes Beddoes's aesthetics. Illustrated.

Snow, Royall H. *Thomas Lovell Beddoes: Eccentric and Poet*. 1928. Reprint. Folcroft, Pa.: Folcroft Library Editions, 1970. This early biographical study concentrates on the poet's morbidity as his defining characteristic. Somewhat dated, especially in the ways it deals with the literature. Contains an annotated bibliography of Beddoes's books and periodical publications.

Thompson, James R. *Thomas Lovell Beddoes*. Boston: Twayne, 1985. A useful critical introduction to Beddoes. Includes a brief biography, a chronology, and a selected bibliography. Follows Beddoes's career from the early poems of Shelleyan and gothic derivation, through his growing interest in Jacobean drama and his satiric verse dramas, to his mature work obsessed with death.

*L. Robert Stevens*

---

# PATRICIA BEER

**Born:** Exmouth, Devon, England; November 4, 1924
**Died:** Honiton, England; August 15, 1999

### PRINCIPAL POETRY

*Loss of the Magyar, and Other Poems*, 1959
*The Survivors*, 1963
*Just Like the Resurrection*, 1967
*The Estuary*, 1971
*Driving West*, 1975
*Selected Poems*, 1979
*The Lie of the Land*, 1983
*Collected Poems*, 1988
*Friend of Heraclitus*, 1993
*Autumn*, 1997

### OTHER LITERARY FORMS

Aside from her poetry, Patricia Beer published two books of criticism, *An Introduction to the Metaphysical Poets* (1972) and *Reader, I Married Him* (1974), the latter being a study of the female characters in the works of Jane Austen, Charlotte Brontë, Elizabeth Gaskell, and George Eliot. She also published a book of fiction, *Moon's Ottery* (1978), and a nonfictional account of her childhood, *Mrs. Beer's House* (1968). The latter provides insights into the poet's development and serves as a gloss for much of her poetry, particularly that which is rooted in her childhood experiences. Although her publications reveal a variety of interests and a willingness to work in various literary forms, Beer's most significant writing and the principal focus of her energies was her poetry.

ACHIEVEMENTS

Patricia Beer won few formal honors in her lifetime. In 1958, she won second prize in the Cheltenham Festival of Art and Literature for *Loss of the Magyar, and Other Poems*. She was also a fellow of the Royal Society of Literature. Although she is not as widely known in the United States as some of her British contemporaries, she achieved a solid reputation in her native England as a deft craftsperson and a poet of genuine perception. Her accomplishments become even more significant when one considers how few of her fellow poets in the British Isles are women. Certainly, the poets with the widest reputations—Philip Larkin, Ted Hughes, and Dannie Abse, to name only a few—are all men. In this context, Beer occupied a position of considerable importance.

BIOGRAPHY

Patricia Beer was born November 4, 1924, in Exmouth, Devon, England, and is a member of the first generation in England to have ready access to higher education through the state school system. Coming from a working-class background, she made her way through the state schools by excelling at her studies. As a native of Devon with a pronounced Devonian accent, she remembered being drilled by elocutionists who were determined to teach her "proper" speech. She resisted the instruction and retained the accent that no doubt exerted an influence, however subtle, on her poetry. She left home to study at Exeter University but graduated with a bachelor's degree from the University of London and received another bachelor's degree

from St. Hugh's College at Oxford University. After graduation she embarked on a teaching career and was a lecturer in English at the University of Padua in Italy, where she stayed from 1946 to 1948 before moving on to the British Institute and then the Ministero Aeronautica, both in Rome. By 1953, Beer had moved back to England, and she began writing in earnest. She supported herself in a series of odd jobs through the 1950's, but in 1962, she went back to teaching at the University of London. She lectured there for several years. Her marriage to the writer P. N. Furbank had ended in divorce, and she married her second husband, John Damien Parsons, in 1964. In 1968, she chose to make writing her full-time profession. By that time, she had already seen several of her books published, including *Loss of the Magyar, and Other Poems*.

She would eventually divide her time between homes in Hampstead Heath (London) and Devon, considering her continued connection with the place of her birth an element essential to her creativity. She continued to write poetry and literary criticism in the years leading to her death and in the late 1990's contributed to the *London Review of Books*. She died in 1999 from a stroke.

ANALYSIS

As a child, Patricia Beer was strongly influenced by the Plymouth Brethren Church, a loosely structured, fundamentalist sect that flourished amid the working and lower-middle classes. Its principal theology was a strict moral code and a dependence on literal interpretation of the Bible. Beer recalled vividly the extemporaneous hellfire sermons and the hymns offering salvation, and these bits of childhood found their way into her poetry. In a larger context, the pervasive sense of death that she experienced regularly at the church services may well have afforded the main impetus for her poetry. In much of her work, she was preoccupied with death, and she frequently commented that she wrote poems against death. The relationship between her religious upbringing and her craft was a complex one, but there is little doubt that Beer's fundamentalist training helped form her as a poet.

Beer's childhood in Devon and her experiences in the Plymouth Brethren Church afforded her abundant material for poetry and a unique point of view. Just as her semirural Devonian background accounts for the rustic quality of much of her work, her childhood among the Plymouth Brethren, as well as the death of her mother when Beer was fourteen, helps to explain her ambivalent attitude toward death, a mixture of fascination and fear. It is this subtle but fundamental tension that underlies some of her most successful poems.

Although Beer explored feminist themes in her work, her tone was without rancor and she was rarely polemical. Rather, she typically presented her poems in a calm and understated voice. She was also not a single-issue poet and so did not feel bound to champion a feminist cause in every line of every poem, thereby avoiding the trap into which politically minded poets have frequently fallen. Beer commented that she wanted equality, not superiority, and that such a position precludes any kind of attack on the male establishment.

It would be a mistake, however, to view Beer only in the role of feminist poet; she transcended any such narrow category in both her aspirations and her accomplishments. Her voice was as distinct and genuine as that of Hughes or Larkin, and her carefully crafted poems are an important contribution to contemporary British poetry. At her best, she invited comparison with Elizabeth Bishop, for she has the same perceptive eye, the same gift for the exact image. A poem such as "Spanish Balcony," with its moon suspended "uselessly, in the smooth sky/ White and rumpled like a vaccination mark," is as precise and evocative as Bishop's celebrated description of the rainbow trout in "The Fish." The controlling mind behind the poem is sure and accurate.

### SELECTED POEMS

The publication of *Selected Poems* in 1979 marked an important milestone in Beer's career. In addition to winning for her the kind of recognition she had long deserved, it provided her with the opportunity to assess her own development and to select from twenty years of writing the poetry that she most wanted to preserve. Significantly, she included only eight poems from her first two books, *Loss of the Magyar, and Other Poems* and *The Survivors*. Although she was in her thirties

when those books were published, she later regarded them as juvenilia. In Beer's assessment, those early books lack conviction and an authentic voice. Beer's major development as a writer involved a movement toward the more personal and autobiographical. Along the way, she abandoned her reliance on mythology and consciously tried to pare down her style, seeking simplicity and directness.

Ironically, Beer grew distrustful of the spareness that characterized her writing and turned to a language that she regarded as more heightened. She did not, however, regard this as a return to her earlier style but rather as a progression into a kind of language that would have a more immediate impact on the reader. It seems that, during the middle part of her career, Beer was trying to find some point of balance between her initial work and her subsequent reaction to it. She later began to seek a marriage of technique and inspiration, and the fifteen "New Poems" that constitute the final section of *Selected Poems* suggest that she found it.

### DEATH

It has often been remarked that the two most common themes in poetry are the possibility of love and the inevitability of death, so it is perhaps unremarkable to find a poet dealing with either of these matters. Even so, Beer's preoccupation with death was noteworthy because she succeeded in capturing so much of the ambivalence that most people have toward it—the attraction and repulsion of the unknown. This viewpoint is effectively communicated in a short poem titled "Dilemma," in which Beer projected two possible role models for herself. The first is a Buddhist monk who screams so loudly when seven brigands approach to murder him that businessmen in Peking can hear him twenty miles away. The second is "the Queen in corny historical plays," who fixes her hair, forgives everybody, and moves to the executioner's block "With only a sidelong glance/ At the man with the axe." The monk and the queen represent two attitudes toward death—resistance and acquiescence—and Beer is free to choose the one she wishes to adopt. Thus, the poem's final line is a question: "Which ought I to be?" On the surface, this poem appears to be very simple, but it compresses a great deal of thought and attempts to bridge a gap as wide as the one between William Cullen Bryant's advice in "Thanatopsis" to embrace death gently like a sleeper and Dylan Thomas's exhortation to his father not to go "gentle into that good night."

### "THE CLOCK"

A variation on this theme is found in "The Clock," an excellent example of Beer's mastery of syllabics and her skillful employment of sounds, particularly assonance. She was most adept at using and then defusing the irresistible iambic trimeter in her six-syllable lines, as in the following pair: "Where once a pendulum/ Thudded like a cart-horse." The regularity of meter is effectively broken by an abundance of stresses, as though the thudding horse himself had broken in, and the entire poem is carried forward by the subtle suggestion of rhyme as exemplified by the four end-words in the fourth stanza: "this," "is," "death," "stairs." It is no accident that "death" stands out so starkly among the off-rhymes, because that is where Beer wished to put the stress, on obtrusive death itself. In this fashion, she made form and content work together in a most remarkable way. The focus of the poem is an old clock that stops every few days when its weights catch on the case. The old saying that "A stopped clock foretells death" leads Beer to speculate about the symbolic meaning of the event and she finds a lesson of her own in such folklore: "Obviously/ Death cannot come each time/ The clock stops. It may be/ Good practice to think so." The malfunctioning clock, then, becomes an important element in a rehearsal for death. As in "Dilemma," where Beer tried to decide how she will face death when it finally arrives, she is preparing herself for the inevitable, for the moment when time will truly stop for her. In a very real sense, Beer's poetry in general is a kind of rehearsal for death. She herself acknowledged that the impetus behind her decision to write poetry was her fear of dying.

### "THE EYES OF THE WORLD"

Initially, Beer's horror of death was somewhat mitigated by a fantasy of becoming famous and having thousands of people mourn her passing. The vehicle for her fame, decided on when she was only eight years old, was to be poetry. She "Turned poet for a lying-in-state/ As though comfort came from cut flowers," a decision that she examined at length in "The Eyes of the World." Somehow, to her child's mind, having the

world take note of her death would make the event less terrifying: "Something like this I felt might make it/ Tolerable: if everyone would stare/ At my last breaths and speak about them." She envied the fame of kings, of men on the moon, of Leda and Mary and the martyrs Latimer and Ridley, all seared into the consciousness of millions and thus given a kind of immortality.

The fantasy passed, however, when she matured and began to view the world more cynically, suspecting that the watchers were more likely to notice flaws and weaknesses than accomplishments. Further, she suspected that "The audience shut their eyes before we/ Shut ours," insensitive to another person's death or unable to see the process through to completion. The poem ends with the following reflection on the eyes of the world: "I cannot imagine now/ Why I believed they were the answer." As Beer discovered, the true answer to her fear of death was not to become famous but to learn to write about her fears. She found that she could not chase them away in the glare of public recognition but could embrace them privately and learn to live with them. Poems such as "Concert at Long Melford Church" and "After Death" show her bravely coming to terms with what she most feared. If the truce is shaky and the question of how to face death when it arrives remains unresolved, Beer nevertheless expanded her personal and poetic boundaries by confronting head-on what she most wished to flee.

### "CALLED HOME"

Related to the poems about death are Beer's poems about religion, particularly so because the religious group on which she focused is the death-obsessed Plymouth Brethren of her childhood. In "Called Home," the title recalls something that "the Plymouth Brethren used to say/ When someone died." The phrase creates a picture of "eternal domesticity," which was intended to be comforting, assuring the congregation that families would be reunited after death, as in the hymns "Shall We Gather at the River?" and "In the Sweet By-and-By." Having lost her ability to accept this simple picture of life after death, Beer claimed that "Loving an atheist is my hope currently." She wanted an "Ally who will keep non-company/ With me in a non-life, a fellow tombstone." The rejection of her previous belief and the adoption of a nihilistic view of life and death were integral to Beer's struggle. To come to terms with death, she imagined it at its most horrible, and this necessitated relinquishing the convenient crutches offered by the church and courageously confronting nothingness in its plainest form, not draped in domestic imagery.

### "ARMS"

The loss of faith is also treated in "Arms," but without the cynical, intellectual toughness that characterizes "Called Home." Indeed, "Arms" is poignant precisely because Beer gave in somewhat to her emotions and looked back on the lost faith of her childhood with sorrow and regret. She recalled that her innocent reliance on the "Everlasting Arms" gradually gave way to nightmare visions of drowned animals "Holding each other like bars" and then remembered her grandfather sinking with his brig in the North Sea, his arms around his son, "Protector, up to his knees/ In death, and that was the last/ That anyone saw of him." The poem progresses from a child's concern with the mortality of animals to an understanding that humans, even her grandfather, share in that mortality, and the immortal arms of her childhood belief become the ineffectual arms of her grandfather, disappearing forever beneath the waves.

### AUTOBIOGRAPHY

Beer's poems of death have immediacy because of their autobiographical nature, because the poet was willing to expose herself. The details of poems such as "The Clock," "The Eyes of the World," and "Arms" are factually accurate. The clock that stops every few days did exist; Beer did decide to become a poet when she was eight years old because she thought fame would help her accept death; and her grandfather went down with his brig, the *Magyar*, and was last seen by the only survivor with his arms around his son and the water rising.

Getting the facts down, however, was not Beer's final objective. She was after the truth behind the facts, and it is that truth that produces a response in the reader. Beer was, in the best sense of the term, a confessional poet, because her view always penetrated through the self to the larger background. Her movement as a poet was steadily away from the detached, manufactured poem toward the autobiographical, and as the poetry became more sharply focused on the immediate self

rather than on the self's past, Beer was likely to draw nearer to the confessional vein. Instinctively wary of the confessional poem, Beer's progress toward it was slow. There were, after all, the dangers of becoming too self-involved, too obscure, and Beer resisted the mode because of these potential hazards. Nevertheless, she seemed irresistibly led to write more and more about her immediate life. She thoroughly explored and exploited the material of her childhood, and so it is only natural that she turned her attention to her present self. Her best poems are those that risk an intense look at the self.

### THE ESTUARY

In the title poem of her fourth book, *The Estuary*, Beer looked intensely at herself and effectively brought together past and present as she reflected on the body of water that separated the two towns of her childhood—Exmouth, her father's home, and Torquay, her mother's place of origin. She found in the division a symbol not only of the distance between her mother and father in terms of their personalities but also of her own character, which was a combination of attributes inherited from both parents. On one side "stiff fields of corn grow/ To the hilltop, are draped over/ It surrealistically." On the other side, small white boats lean sideways twice a day as the tide goes out and comes in and "the sea pulls away their prop." One side is covered with lush and vigorous growth, while the other is represented by fragile boats that seem as susceptible to the intermittent tides as people are to fate or chance.

A reader does not need to know a great deal about Beer's background to appreciate the geographical metaphor, though some knowledge of her childhood may enhance one's understanding of the poem. It is clear from the poem itself that Beer was forced by circumstances to move from a normal life on one side of the river to "a house where all was not well" on the other. The poem does not indicate, however, just what the circumstances were nor why things were not well on the other side, focusing on effect and leaving the cause unspecified. There is no exposition to reveal that the move was precipitated by the death of Beer's mother when Beer was fourteen and that she crossed the river to live with relatives because her father seemed unable to manage his children alone.

With this information in hand, a reader may better understand the source of the poem, but the significant details of the poem itself operate independent of any such biographical footnotes. By dealing with the effects of the move rather than its causes, Beer was able to take a highly personal experience and give it a more general significance. The estuary, rather than remaining a simple fact of Beer's childhood, became a symbolic boundary that everyone must cross, and the move was not simply from Exmouth to Torquay but from childhood to adulthood, from the dreamlike growth on one side to a more conscious life on the tides of the other. The opposing banks are innocence and experience, and the move from one to the other is archetypal. Underscoring this symbolism is the estuary itself, the meeting place of fresh and salt water. The flow of the individual river into the sea parallels the movement of the child from her small, self-involved world into the larger community of responsibility.

### "SELF-HELP"

Beer used essentially the same technique in "Self-Help," employing her personal experiences as a telescope through which the larger world can be viewed. Meditating on the fact that she "was brought up on notions of self-help," she realized that she got where she is because she believed "that if/ You didn't help yourself in worldly matters/ Nobody else was at all likely to." She struggled alone and enjoyed her success alone, sitting on her sofa in Hampstead Village listening to the threatening noises of all those on the streets outside who wanted desperately to help themselves as well. She separated herself from the "Cockney accents" and "bathless flats," virtually becoming a living example of the model described in books on self-help, "Practising lawful self-advancement, preaching/ It, enjoying its rewards." Behind her smugness and her sense of separation, however, she feels a bond with all those who have not succeeded in helping themselves. She sees that "through/ The white comfortable mist a wind blows holes/ Lays bare the quagmire reaching for us all./ Whispers how soon we could be shouting 'Help.'" What she sensed is the common link of death, and she realized that despite her accomplishments she could never raise herself beyond the quagmire that reaches out for everyone. If there was truth in this perception,

there is also humility, for Beer put her successes into context and implicitly understood how small they look in terms of the ultimate struggle. In the final sense, she was alone, and yet, paradoxically, she was united with everyone. Death is the great separator, but it is also the great leveler, mindless of class distinctions and accomplishments.

Although Beer herself rejected the confessional label, poems such as "The Estuary" and "Self-Help" work as the best confessional poems have always worked, by using the personal details of the poet's life to discover larger meanings. Beer preferred to call her poems in this vein autobiographical, perhaps because the term "confessional" has come to connote obscurity and tedious self-involvement. Whatever label the poems are given, they unquestionably transcend the limitations of the purely personal, for Beer masterfully used her experiences and emotions as a bridge to the common ground shared by her and the reader. The personal is always a means to an end and never an end in itself. In fact, Beer's strengths as a poet seem to increase in direct proportion to her willingness to exploit her personal life for poetic material.

### "FEMALE, EXTINCT" AND "HOME"

Beer knew, too, how to approach sensitive topics, not by taking a position and arguing directly but by presenting a point of view obliquely, subtly. Her skills in this area were clearly on display in "Female, Extinct." The female of the title is never identified by species, and her wired-together rib cage and "bony gloves" with no marrow in them could belong to any vertebrate animal. The reference to "her sons, little dragons" suggests something reptilian, but the term "little dragons" is appositional and may be meant figuratively rather than literally. Now on display in the museum, the female once "Stood up with hundreds/ As if to bellow/ The Hallelujah Chorus." As a reconstructed artifact she seems to be saying something else: "Her passionate jaws/ Shout 'Give me time.'" This may well be a poem about the primordial struggle to survive, but it may just as well be about the more contemporary efforts of women to overcome their symbolic extinction. Beer created the possibility of the latter reading by leaving the type of female unspecified. Quite probably, she intended the poem to function on both levels of meaning, for the real point of the poem is the implied connection between the two kinds of females.

Equally subtle and effective is the short poem "Home." Here, the speaker, presumably a woman, looks out from her house, "as warm/ And secure as bathwater." Curiously, her sense of responsibility begins with a rejection of that responsibility. She discovers that she cannot remove herself from the world of human suffering, and she is beginning to understand that home has a larger significance than the safe house in which she would prefer to seal herself.

Both "Female, Extinct" and "Home" may be regarded as feminist poems because both address issues of great concern to women. The first may be taken as an implied warning of a present danger and the second as a charge to move beyond the walls of home into the surrounding world. Because Beer did not argue a position, she avoids the didactic and the abrasive, and her point of view seeps slowly into the reader's receptive consciousness.

Indeed, perhaps the best word to describe Beer's poetry in general is "understated." Whether writing about death, her childhood, or topics of a political nature, Beer's characteristic voice is one of composure. This is not to say that her poems are lacking in vitality; quite the opposite, for she has learned that the disparity between her calm perceptions and the themes derived from them creates a great deal of energy. One often has the sense that in Beer's poetry things have been defused, only to find on reflection that a small explosion has occurred in the mind.

OTHER MAJOR WORKS

LONG FICTION: *Moon's Ottery*, 1978; *The Star Cross Ferry*, 1991.

NONFICTION: *Mrs. Beer's House*, 1968; *An Introduction to the Metaphysical Poets*, 1972; *Reader, I Married Him*, 1974; *As I Was Saying Yesterday: Selected Essays and Reviews*, 2002.

BIBLIOGRAPHY

Beer, Patricia. *Mrs. Beer's House*. London: Macmillan, 1968. This is Beer's autobiography, the main source of public information about her life. Easy to read and an essential source for any student of the poet.

Montefiore, Janet. "Autumn." *The Times Literary Supplement*, October 9, 1998, p. 37. A critical review of Beer's *Autumn*.

Mullen, John. "Obituary: Patricia Beer, Poet with a Wry Line on Dissenters and Devon." *The Guardian*, August 19, 1999, p. 18. An obituary that describes Beer's life and parentage, focusing on her themes of death and religion.

Ravo, Nick. "Patricia Beer, Seventy-nine, Poet Who Explored Religion." *The New York Times*, August 23, 1999, p. 9. An obituary with brief biographical information.

Skelton, Robin. "Leaders and Others: Some New British Poetry." *Kenyon Review* 30, no. 5 (1968): 689-696. Skelton reviews Beer's volume *Just Like the Resurrection* and discusses it in comparison with the work of Ted Hughes and Thom Gunn, two other British poets who also published collections at that time. Interesting in that it offers a rare look at how Beer's contemporaries perceived her at that point in her career.

*Neal Bowers*

# APHRA BEHN

**Born:** Kent, England; July (?), 1640
**Died:** London, England; April 16, 1689
**Also known as:** Aphara Amis; Aphra Bayn; Aphra Johnson; Astrea

PRINCIPAL POETRY

*Poems upon Several Occasions, with "A Voyage to the Island of Love,"* 1684 (including adaptation of Abbé Paul Tallemant's *Le Voyage de l'isle d'amour*)
*Miscellany: Being a Collection of Poems by Several Hands*, 1685 (includes works by others)
*Selected Poems*, 1993
*The Poems of Aphra Behn: A Selection*, 1994

OTHER LITERARY FORMS

Although Aphra Behn (bayn) wrote more than a dozen separate pieces of fiction that critics of her day called novels, only a portion may legitimately be labeled as such. Principal among these is her most noted work of fiction, *Oroonoko: Or, The Royal Slave, a True History* (1688); others worthy of consideration are *Agnes de Castro* (1688), *The Fair Jilt: Or, The History of Prince Tarquin and Miranda* (1688), *The History of the Nun: Or, The Fair Vow-Breaker* (1689), and *The Nun: Or, The Perjured Beauty* (1697). During her lifetime, Behn established her literary reputation by writing for the London stage, creating more than fifteen plays.

## ACHIEVEMENTS

Critics may defend Aphra Behn's talent for drama and prose fiction as worthy of recognition beside that of her male contemporaries. As a writer of verse, however, she cannot claim a place among the poets of the first rank. This does not mean that her poetry has no value for the critic, the literary historian, or the general reader; on the contrary, her occasional verse is no worse than the political pieces of her colleagues (with the exception of John Dryden), while the songs and poems from her plays reflect her ability to manipulate verse as reinforcement for dramatic theme and setting.

In the nineteenth century, such poet-essayists as Leigh Hunt, Edmund Gosse, and Algernon Charles Swinburne recoiled initially from what they saw in Behn's occasional verse as indelicate and indecent language. They recovered sufficiently to find some merit in her songs. Hunt bemoaned her association with the rakes of the age, yet praised the songs as "natural and cordial, written in a masculine style, yet womanly withal." Gosse dubbed her "the George Sand of the Restoration"—an obvious reference that had nothing whatsoever to do with her literary abilities—although "she possessed an indisputable touch of lyric genius." Swinburne looked hard at a single poem, "Love in fantastic triumph sate," and concluded that "the virtuous Aphra towers above her sex in the passionate grace and splendid elegance of that melodious and magnificent song. . . ." The most attractive quality of her lyrical pieces is their spontaneity, demonstrating to the reader (or the theatergoer) that the best poetry need not be anchored to learning but can succeed because the lines are memorable, singable, and direct.

In her public verse, Behn had to compete with a large number of poets who tended to be more skilled mechanics and versifiers than she, and all of whom sought the same limited patronage and political favors as she. She found herself at a disadvantage because of her gender, which meant, simply, that her occasional verse did not always reach the widest possible audience. For example, such pieces as "A Pindarick on the Death of Charles II" (1685) and "A Congratulatory Poem to Her Most Sacred Majesty" (1688) may appear stiff and lacking in sincerity, but certainly no more so than the verses on the same subjects written by her contemporaries.

Behn's elegy on the death of Edmund Waller and her other contributions to a volume in memory of the departed poet in 1688 do, however, reflect a deep feeling of sorrow because of the occasion; these poems serve as a transition to her private verse, representing perhaps the highest level of Behn's poetic achievement. In "The Disappointment," for example, she reveals herself as a woman whose real desires have been obscured by frivolity and professionalism and who realizes that her laborious life is drawing to a close. The importance of such poems is that they provide the deepest insight into Behn; they draw a picture of the poet far more honestly and realistically than do the rumors, allusions, and innuendos set forth in countless biographical sketches and critical commentaries.

## BIOGRAPHY

Although the details surrounding the life of Aphra Behn have at least become stabilized, they have not always been clear. Her earliest biographer, the poet Charles Gildon (1665-1724), maintained that she was born at Canterbury, in Kent, the daughter of a man named Johnson. In 1884, however, Edmund Gosse discovered a marginal note in a manuscript belonging to the poet Anne Finch, countess of Winchelsea (1661-1720), revealing that Behn had been born at Wye, near Canterbury, the daughter of a barber—which John Johnson certainly was not. The countess's note receives support from an entry in the parish register of the Saints Gregory and Martin Church, Wye, to the effect that Ayfara Amis, daughter of John and Amy Amis, was baptized there on July 10, 1640. Apparently John-

*Aphra Behn* (Library of Congress)

son, related to Lord Francis Willoughby of Parham, adopted the girl, although no one seems certain of the exact year. Nevertheless, Ayfara Amis accompanied her stepparents on a journey to Surinam (later Dutch Guiana) in 1658, Lord Willoughby having appointed Johnson to serve as deputy governor of his extensive holdings there. Unfortunately, the new deputy died on the voyage; his widow and children proceeded to Surinam and took up residence at St. John's, one of Willoughby's plantations. The exact length of their stay has yet to be determined; later biographers, though, have settled upon the summer of 1663 as the most probable date of return. The family's tenure at St. John's forms the background of Behn's most celebrated production, her novel *Oroonoko*.

By 1665, the young woman was established in London, married to a wealthy Dutch merchant (or at least a merchant of Dutch ancestry) who may well have had connections in or around the court of Charles II. In 1665 came the Great Plague and the death of Behn's husband; his death proved disastrous for Behn. For un-

known reasons, the Dutch merchant left her nothing of substance—with the possible exception of his connections at court. Charles II, in the midst of his first war against the Dutch, hired Behn as a secret agent to spy against Holland; for that purpose, she proceeded to Antwerp. There she contacted another agent, William Scott, from whom she received various pieces of military information for forwarding to London. Although her work earned her little acknowledgment and even less money, Behn did conceive of the pseudonym Astrea, the name under which she published most of her poetry. Essentially, the venture into foreign intrigue proved a dismal failure for her; she had to borrow money and pawn her few valuables to pay her debts and provide passage back to England.

Once home, early in 1667, Behn found no relief from her desperate financial situation. Her creditors threatened prison, and the government ministers who had employed her refused any payment for espionage service rendered. Prison followed, most probably at Caronne House, South Lambeth, although again the specifics of time and length of term are lacking. Behn's later biographers speculate that she may have been aided in her release by John Hoyle (died 1692)—a lawyer of Gray's Inn, a wit, an intellectual, and bisexual, the principal subject and reason for Behn's sonnets, and the man with whom the writer carried on a long romance. In fact, Hoyle, to whom she refers often in her poems, is the only one of Behn's supposed lovers who can be identified with any certainty. When she finally gained her release from prison, she determined to dedicate the rest of her life to pleasure and to letters and to trust her own devices rather than to rely upon others whom she could not trust.

Behn launched her career as a dramatist in late December, 1670, at the New Duke's Theatre in Little Lincoln's Inn Fields, London. Her tragicomedy, *The Forced Marriage: Or, The Jealous Bridegroom* (pr. 1670), ran for six nights and included in the cast nineteen-year-old Thomas Otway, the playwright-to-be only recently in London from Christ Church, Oxford. The neophyte bungled his lines, and with that, his acting career came to a quick halt. Because of the length of the run, however, Behn, as was the practice, received the entire profit from the third performance; she could now begin to function as an independent artist. She followed her first effort in the spring of 1671 with a comedy, *The Amorous Prince: Or, The Curious Husband*, again at the New Duke's; another comedy, *The Dutch Lover*, came to Drury Lane in February, 1673, and by the time of her anonymous comedy, *The Rover: Or, The Banished Cavaliers, Part I*, in 1677, she had secured her reputation. Now she mixed easily with the likes of Thomas Killigrew, Edward Ravenscroft, John Wilmot, earl of Rochester, Edmund Waller, and the poet laureate, John Dryden—who would publish her rough translations from Ovid in 1683. With the reputation came offers for witty prologues and epilogues for others' plays, as well as what she desired more than anything—money. A confrontation, however, with the earl of Shaftesbury and the newly formed Whigs during the religiopolitical controversies of 1678, when she offended the opponents of Charles II in a satirical prologue to an anonymous play, *Romulus and Hersilia*, brought her once again to the brink of economic hardship; for the next five years, she was forced to abandon writing for the stage.

Fortunately, Behn could find other outlets for her art in popular fiction and occasional verse, although neither proved as profitable as the stage. Her series of *Love Letters Between a Nobleman and His Sister* (1683-1687) and *Poems upon Several Occasions* were well received, but the meager financial returns could not keep pace with her social expenses. When she did return to the stage in 1686 with a comedy, *The Lucky Chance: Or, An Alderman's Bargain*, she met with only moderate success and much public abuse. *The Emperor of the Moon*, produced the following year, fared somewhat better, although the London audience had seemingly lost its stomach for a woman playwright with Tory sympathies.

Behn continued to write fiction and verse, but sickness and the death of her one true artistic friend, Edmund Waller, both occurring in October, 1688, did little to inspire confidence in her attitudes toward life or art. Five days following the coronation of William III and Mary, on April 16, 1689, Behn died, the result, according to Gildon, of incompetent surgery. Nevertheless, she had risen high enough to merit burial in Westminster Abbey; in fact, her memorial, interestingly

enough, lies near that of the famous actor Anne Bracegirdle (died 1748), whose acting skills prolonged Behn's popularity well after the playwright's death. The fitting epitaph to Behn was provided by her lover, John Hoyle, who declared, "Here lies proof that wit can never be/ Defense against mortality."

ANALYSIS

The history of English poetry during the Restoration of Charles II and the reign of James II seems to have no room for Aphra Behn. The reasons, all having little or nothing to do with her true poetic abilities, are fairly obvious. To form a composite of the Restoration poet, one must begin with an outline of a gentleman who wrote verse for other gentlemen and a few literate ladies, who directed his efforts to a select group of coffeehouse and drawing-room wits, who wrote about politics, religion, scientific achievement, or war. He wrote poetry to amuse and to entertain, and even, on occasion, to instruct. He also wrote verse to attack or to appease his audience, those very persons who served as his readers and his critics. Thus, the Restoration poet vied with his colleagues for recognition and patronage—even for political position, favor, and prestige. He hurled epithets and obscenities at his rivals, and they quickly retorted. Of course, that was all done in public view, upon the pages of broadsheets and miscellanies.

Reflect, for a moment, upon the career of Dryden, who dominated the London literary scene during the last quarter of the seventeenth century. He stood far above his contemporaries and fulfilled the practical function of the Restoration man of letters: the poet, dramatist, and essayist who focused upon whatever subject or form happened to be current at a particular moment. Dryden succeeded because he understood his art, the demands of the times upon that art, and the arena in which he (as artist and man) had to compete. Around 1662 to 1663, he married Lady Elizabeth Howard, daughter of the earl of Berkshire and sister of Sir Robert Howard. Sir Robert introduced the poet to the reestablished nobility, soon to become his readers and his patrons. In 1662, Dryden joined the Royal Society, mainly to study philosophy, mathematics, and reason, in order "to be a complete and excellent poet." One result, in 1663, was a poem in honor of Walter Charleton, physician to Charles II; the poet praised the new scientific spirit brought on by the new age and lauded the efforts of the Royal Society and its support of such geniuses as Robert Boyle and Sir Isaac Newton. In February, 1663, *The Wild Gallant*, the first of Dryden's twenty-eight plays, appeared on the stage; although the comedy was essentially a failure, it marked the beginning of an extremely successful career, for Dryden quickly recognized the Restoration theater as the most immediate outlet for his art.

Certainly Dryden became involved in the major religious and political controversies of his day, both personally and poetically, and his fortunes fluctuated as a result. His reputation, however—as critic, dramatist, and poet laureate of England—had been secured, and he remained England's most outstanding, most complete writer. As a poet, he headed a diverse group of artists who, although not consistently his equals, could compete with him in limited areas: the classicists of the Restoration, carryovers from an earlier age—Edmund Waller and Abraham Cowley; the satirists—Samuel Butler, John Oldham, Sir Charles Sedley, the earls of Rochester and Dorset; the dramatists—William Wycherley, Sir George Etherege, Nathaniel Lee, Thomas Otway, William Congreve, George Farquhar, and Behn.

The point to be made is that unlike Dryden and his male counterparts, Behn had little time and even less opportunity to develop as a poet. Sexism prevented her from fitting the prototype of the Restoration poet; she lacked access to the spheres of social and political influence, mastery of classical languages and their related disciplines, and the luxury of writing when and what she pleased. The need for money loomed large as her primary motive, and as had Dryden, she looked to the London stage for revenue and reputation. She certainly viewed herself as a poet, but her best poetry seems to exist within the context of her plays.

One problem in discussing Behn's poetry is that one cannot always catalog with confidence those pieces attributed to her and written by others. Also, there is confusion regarding those pieces actually written by her but attributed to others. For example, as late as 1926, and again in 1933, two different editors of quite distinct editions of the earl of Rochester's poetry erroneously assigned three of Behn's poems to Rochester, and that error remained uncorrected until 1939. Textual matters aside, however, Behn's poetry still provides substantive issues for critical discussion. Commentators have traditionally favored the songs from her plays, maintaining that the grace and spontaneity of these pieces rise above the artificiality of the longer verses—the latter weighed down by convention and lack of inspiration. True, her major poem (at least in terms of its length) of two thousand lines, *A Voyage to the Island of Love*, while carrying the romantic allegory to extremes, does succeed in its purpose: a poetic paraphrase of the French original, and nothing more. Indeed, Behn, as a playwright, no doubt viewed poetry as a diversion and exercise; she considered both activities useful and important, and both provided added dimensions to her art. She was certainly not a great poet; but few during her time were. Her poetic success, then, must be measured in terms of her competence, for which she may, in all honesty, receive high marks and be entitled to a permanent place on the roster of poets.

### ABDELAZAR

At the head of the list are two songs from the play *Abdelazar: Or, The Moor's Revenge* (pr. 1676), the first a sixteen-line lyric known by its opening, "Love in fantastic triumph sate." Despite the trite (even by Restoration standards) dramatic setting—the usurper who murders his trusting sovereign and puts to death all who block his path to the throne—the poem reflects pure, personal feeling, as the poet laments over the misery of unrequited love. Behn depicts Love as a "strange tyrannic power" that dominates the amorous world; there is nothing terribly complicated, in either the sound or the sense of the language, for she relies upon simple sighs, tears, pride, cruelty, and fear. In the end, the poem succeeds because it goes directly to the central issue of the poet's personal unhappiness. "But my poor heart alone is harmed,/ Whilst thine the victor is, and free." The other song from *Abdelazar* is a dialogue between a nymph and her swain. The young lady, cognizant of the brevity of "a lover's day," begs her lover to make haste; the swain, in company with shepherds, shepherdesses, and pipes, quickly responds. He bears a stray lamb of hers, which he has caught so that she may chastise the creature ("with one angry look from thy fair eyes") for having wandered from the flock. The analogy between man and beast is obvious and nothing more need be said; the swain begs her to hurry, for "how very short a lover's day!"

### SONGS AND ELEGIES

There are other songs of equal or slightly less merit, and they all seem to contain variations on the same themes. In one, "'Tis not your saying that you love," the speaker urges her lover to cease his talk of love and, simply, love her; otherwise, she will no longer be able to live. Another, a song from Lycidus beginning "A thousand martyrs I have made," mocks "the fools that whine for love" and unmasks the fashion of those who, on the surface, appear deeply wounded by the torments of love when they actually seek nothing from love but its shallow pleasures. In a third song, "When Jemmy first began to love," Behn returns to the shepherd and his flock motif. On this occasion, the nymph, overpowered by Jemmy's songs, kisses, and general air of happiness, gives herself completely to him. Then the call to arms beckons; Jemmy exchanges his sheep hooks for a sword, his pipes for warlike sounds, and, perhaps, his bracelets for wounds. At the end, the poor nymph must mourn, but for whom it is not certain: for the departed Jemmy or for herself, who must endure without him? Finally, in one of the longest of her songs, a 140-line narrative titled "The Disappointment," Behn introduces some of the indelicacies and indiscretions of which Victorian critics and biographers accused her. By late seventeenth century standards, the piece is indeed graphic (although certainly not vulgar or even indecent); but it nevertheless succeeds in demonstrating how excessive pleasure can easily turn to pain.

Although Behn, whether by choice or situation, kept outside the arena of poetic competition of the sort engaged in by Dryden and his rivals, she managed to establish personal relationships with the major figures of her age. Dryden always treated her with civility and even kindness, and there are those who maintain that a piece often attributed to Behn—"On Mr. Dryden, Renegade," and beginning "Scorning religion all thy lifetime past,/ And now embracing popery at last"—was not of her making. In addition, she remained on friendly terms with Thomas Otway, Edward Ravenscroft, Edmund Waller, and the earl of Rochester.

### "ON THE DEATH OF THE LATE EARL OF ROCHESTER"

Behn wrote elegies for Waller and Rochester, and both poems are well suited to their occasion; yet they are two distinctly different poems. "On the Death of the Late Earl of Rochester" (1685) is an appeal to the world to mourn the loss of a great and multifaceted personality: The muses must mourn the passing of a wit, youths must mourn the end of a "dear instructing rage" against foolishness, maidens the loss of a heaven-sent lover, the little gods of love the loss of a divine lover, and the unhappy world the passage of a great man. Draped in its pastoral and classical mantles, the poem glorifies a subject not entirely worthy of glorification; yet, if the reader can momentarily forget about Rochester, the piece is not entirely without merit. After all, the poet did demonstrate that she knew how to write a competent elegy.

### "ON THE DEATH OF EDMUND WALLER"

More than seven years later, on October 21, 1687, the aged poet Edmund Waller died, and again Behn penned an elegiac response, "On the Death of Edmund Waller." Her circumstances, however, had changed considerably since the passing of Rochester in July, 1680. Her health was poor, her finances low, her literary reputation not very secure. Apparently she had to write the piece in some haste, specifically for a collection of poems dedicated to Waller and written by his friends. Finally, Behn was deeply affected by Waller's death and chose the opportunity to associate that event with her own situation—that of the struggling, ailing, and aging (although she was then only forty-seven) artist. Thus, she sets the melancholy tone at the outset by identifying herself as "I, who by toils of sickness, am become/ Almost as near as thou art to a tomb." Throughout, she inserts references to an untuned and ignorant world, the muses' dark land, the low ebb of sense, the scanty gratitude and fickle love of the unthinking crowd—all of which seem more appropriate to her private and professional life than to Waller's. Still, the poem is not an unusual example of the elegy; Behn was not the first poet to announce her own personal problems while calling upon the world to mourn the loss of a notable person.

Midway through the elegy to Waller, Behn provides

a clue that may well reveal her purpose as a poet and, further, may help to establish her legitimacy within the genre. She writes of a pre-Wallerian world of meaningless learning, wherein dull and obscure declamations prevented the blossoming of sensitive poets and true poetry and produced nothing that was "great and gay." During those barren years, she laments, there existed only thoughtless labor, devoid of instruction, pleasure, and (most important) passion. In a word, "the poets knew not Love." Such expressions and sentiments may appear, on the surface, as attempts to elevate the memory of her subject; in reality, they serve well to underline her own concerns for poetry as a means of bringing harmony to disorder, comfort to discord, and love to insensitivity. As a woman, she looked upon a poetic field dominated by masculine activity and masculine expression, by masculine attitudes and masculine ideals. Where, she must certainly have asked herself, could one find the appropriate context in which to convey to an audience composed of both males and females those passions peculiar to her sex and to her person?

Whether she actually found the form in which to house that passion—or whether she even possessed the craft and the intellect to express it—is difficult to determine. One problem, of course, is that Behn did not write a sufficient quantity of poetry beyond her plays and novels to allow for a reasonable judgment. Nevertheless, she never ceased trying to pour forth the pain and the love that dominated her emotions. She wrote (as in "'Tis not your saying that you love") that actions, not words, must reinforce declarations of love, for only love itself can sustain life. Without love, there is no life. Throughout her poems, that conclusion reverberates from line to line: Love is a triumph, a lover's day is short, the death of one partner means the spiritual (and automatic) death of the one remaining; a lover's soul is made of love, while the completion of an empty (and thus meaningless) act of love leaves a lover "half dead and breathless."

### EXOTIC SETTINGS

Perhaps the most interesting aspect of Behn's poetry is her taste for exotic settings. These backdrops appear to contradict her very way of life. Behn was a woman of the city, of the urban social and intellectual center of a nation that had only recently undergone po-

litical trauma and change. She belonged to the theater, the drawing room, the coffeehouse, the palace—even to the boudoir. Not many of those settings, however, found their way into her poetry. Instead, she selected for her poetic environments a composite that she called the "amorous world" ("Love in fantastic triumph sate"), complete with listening birds, feeding flocks, the aromatic boughs and fruit of a juniper tree, trembling limbs, yielding grass, crystal dew, a lone thicket made for love, and flowers bathed in the morning dew.

Even the obviously human subjects, both alive and dead, rarely walk the streets of the town or meditate in the quiet of their own earthly gardens. Thus, Dryden, in the midst of religious disorientation, wanders about upon the wings of his own shame, in search of "Moses' God"; Rochester flies, quick as departing light, upon the fragrance of softly falling roses; and Waller, a heaven-born genius, is described as having rescued the chosen tribe of poetry from the Egyptian night. Of course, in the last two instances, Behn wrote elegies, which naturally allowed her departed subjects greater room for celestial meanderings. Love, however, had to be relieved from its earthly, banal confines. Love was very much Behn's real subject as a poet, but she was never prepared to discuss it within the context of the harsh and often ugly realities of her own time and place.

### OTHER MAJOR WORKS

LONG FICTION: *Love Letters Between a Nobleman and His Sister*, 1683-1687 (3 volumes); *Agnes de Castro*, 1688; *The Fair Jilt: Or, The History of Prince Tarquin and Miranda*, 1688; *Oroonoko: Or, The Royal Slave, a True History*, 1688; *The History of the Nun: Or, The Fair Vow-Breaker*, 1689; *The Lucky Mistake*, 1689; *The Nun: Or, The Perjured Beauty*, 1697; *The Adventure of the Black Lady*, 1698; *The Wandering Beauty*, 1698.

PLAYS: *The Forced Marriage: Or, The Jealous Bridegroom*, pr. 1670; *The Amorous Prince: Or, The Curious Husband*, pr., pb. 1671; *The Dutch Lover*, pr., pb. 1673; *Abdelazer: Or, The Moor's Revenge*, pr. 1676; *The Town Fop: Or, Sir Timothy Tawdry*, pr. 1676; *The Rover: Or, The Banished Cavaliers, Part I*, pr., pb. 1677 (*Part II*, pr., pb. 1681); *Sir Patient Fancy*, pr., pb. 1678; *The Feigned Courtesans: Or, A Night's*

*Intrigue*, pr., pb. 1679; *The Young King: Or, The Mistake*, pr. 1679; *The Roundheads: Or, The Good Old Cause*, pr. 1681; *The City Heiress: Or, Sir Timothy Treat-All*, pr., pb. 1682; *The Lucky Chance: Or, An Alderman's Bargain*, pr. 1686; *The Emperor of the Moon*, pr., pb. 1687; *The Widow Ranter: Or, The History of Bacon of Virginia*, pr. 1689; *The Younger Brother: Or, The Amorous Jilt*, pr., pb. 1696.

TRANSLATIONS: *Aesop's Fables*, 1687 (with Francis Barlow); *Of Trees*, 1689 (of book 6 of Abraham Cowley's *Sex libri plantarum*).

MISCELLANEOUS: *The Case for the Watch*, 1686 (prose and poetry); *La Montre: Or, The Lover's Watch*, 1686 (prose and poetry); *Lycidus: Or, The Lover in Fashion*, 1688 (prose and poetry; includes works by others); *The Lady's Looking-Glass, to Dress Herself By: Or, The Art of Charming*, 1697 (prose and poetry); *The Works of Aphra Behn*, 1915, 1967 (6 volumes; Montague Summers, editor); *The Works of Aphra Behn*, 1992-1996 (7 volumes; Janet Todd, editor).

BIBLIOGRAPHY

Altaba-Artal, Dolors. *Aphra Behn's English Feminism: Wit and Satire*. Cranbury, N.J.: Associated University Presses, 1999. An examination of Behn's writings from the perspective of feminism. Bibliography and index.

Hughes, Derek, and Janet Todd, eds. *The Cambridge Companion to Aphra Behn*. New York: Cambridge University Press, 2004. Replete with tools for further research, this is an excellent aid to any study of Behn's life and work.

O'Donnell, Mary Ann. *Aphra Behn: An Annotated Bibliography of Primary and Secondary Sources*. 2d ed. Burlington, Vt.: Ashgate, 2003. Contains a detailed description of more than one thousand primary works and more than six hundred books, articles, essays, and dissertations written about Behn after 1666. These works are listed chronologically. Indexed.

Spencer, Jane. *Aphra Behn's Afterlife*. New York: Oxford University Press, 2000. An examination of Behn's works with emphasis on her influence. Bibliography and index.

Stapleton, M. L. *Admired and Understood: The Poetry of Aphra Behn*. Newark: University of Delaware Press, 2004. This study of Behn's poetry examines, among other works, *A Voyage to the Island of Love*.

Todd, Janet. *The Critical Fortunes of Aphra Behn*. Columbia, S.C.: Camden House, 1998. This work focuses on the critical reception of Behn after her death.

_____. *The Secret Life of Aphra Behn*. New Brunswick, N.J.: Rutgers University Press, 1996. The introduction summarizes efforts to study Behn's work and life, her place in literature, her ability to write in all the genres (except the sermon), and the biographer's efforts to overcome the paucity of biographical facts. Includes a bibliography of works written before 1800 and a bibliography of work published after 1800.

_____, ed. *Aphra Behn Studies*. New York: Cambridge University Press, 1996. Part 1 concentrates on Behn's plays, part 2 on her poetry, part 3 on her fiction, and part 4 on her biography. Includes an introduction outlining Behn's career and the essays in the volume and an index.

Wiseman, Susan. *Aphra Behn*. 2d ed. Tavistock, England: Northcote House/British Council, 2007. A biography of Behn that examines her life and work. Bibliography and index.

*Samuel J. Rogal*

# HILAIRE BELLOC

**Born:** La Celle-Saint-Cloud, France; July 27, 1870
**Died:** Guildford, England; July 16, 1953

PRINCIPAL POETRY

*The Bad Child's Book of Beasts*, 1896
*Verses and Sonnets*, 1896
*More Beasts for Worse Children*, 1897
*The Modern Traveller*, 1898
*A Moral Alphabet*, 1899
*Cautionary Tales for Children*, 1907
*Verses*, 1910
*More Peers*, 1911

*Sonnets and Verse*, 1923, 1938
*New Cautionary Tales*, 1930
*Sonnets and Verse*, 1954 (Reginald Jebb, editor)
*The Verse*, 1954 (W. N. Roughead, editor)

## OTHER LITERARY FORMS

Hilaire Belloc (BEHL-ahk) was a prolific and popular writer of prose. He is identified primarily as a historian and defender of the Roman Catholic religion, but he wrote history, biography, travel, literary criticism, church history and religious doctrine, political theory, and translation, as well as some autobiographical travel books which are difficult to categorize. In all, he wrote more than 150 books, as well as many book reviews and magazine articles. His prose and poetry both show a wide range of themes and forms.

Belloc was one of a number of Catholic writers of the period, including Francis Thompson, Gerard Manley Hopkins, Alice Meynell, and G. K. Chesterton. He wrote rebuttals to views of his Church held by the historians Edward Gibbon, H. G. Wells, and George Coulton, but he could also see its imperfections, remarking to a friend that such an institution could not have lasted a fortnight if it had not been divine.

## ACHIEVEMENTS

Although he was a man of letters in many genres, Hilaire Belloc often said in later years that he hoped to be remembered for his poetry. He wrote more than 170 poems in all and was a writer of both light and serious verse. Much of the former was intended for children, but it appealed to adults as well. The first edition of *The Bad Child's Book of Beasts* sold out in four days, and four thousand copies were sold in three months. This was followed by other nonsense books which were much praised. *The Spectator* ranked his satirical and comic verse with that of Edward Lear, and Sir Arthur Quiller-Couch commended it.

A volume of Belloc's serious poetry also appeared in 1896, and it increased in size in succeeding editions. Belloc was said by Desmond McCarthy to be the most underrated of poets. At a dinner in his honor on his sixtieth birthday, Chesterton said that such a ceremony "might have been fitting thousands of years ago at the festival of a great Greek poet," and that "Belloc's son-

nets and strong verse would remain like the cups and carved epics of the Greeks."

In later years, his poetry has been generally neglected, although the serious poems include many beautiful works. This neglect is probably the result of three circumstances. First, his themes and forms were traditional and classical rather than avant-garde. Second, his reputation as a prose writer made his poems seem secondary. Third, some of his best poems were not published in his collections of poetry until 1938. This was true of many of his epigrams and of the Juliet poems, which had been privately printed. His "Heroic Poem in Praise of Wine" probably has been his most admired work.

## BIOGRAPHY

Joseph Hilaire Pierre René Belloc was born in 1870 in La Celle-Saint-Cloud, near Paris, of a French father and an English mother. He was called Hilaire after his grandfather, a celebrated painter. His father died when he was a baby. When he was eight years old, his mother suffered financial reverses, and they moved to England. His home in Sussex would become a major influence in his life. He wrote his first poem when he was eight years old. In 1882, he was sent to the Oratory School at Edgbaston, a boarding school. While he did not like school, he nevertheless learned the classics, took parts in Latin plays, and won a prize in his last year. After leaving school, he considered joining the French navy, since he loved sailing, but he studied for only a term at the Collège Stanislas at Paris before finding it too restrictive. He was then apprenticed to a farmer to learn to be a land agent, but that did not work out either. He then turned to journalism and edited a weekly paper called *The Lamp*, in which some of his early poems appeared. Other early poems appeared in *The Irish Monthly* and *Merrie England*.

In 1889, he fell in love with Elodie Hogan, an Irish American visiting Europe with her family and whom he met at his mother's house. Belloc wanted to marry her, but she returned to California. He followed her to the United States in 1890 and made his way westward laboriously, often on foot, selling sketches to pay his way. Elodie's mother did not favor the marriage, and Elodie considered becoming a nun. The young woman persuaded Belloc to take the military training required of all French citizens. When he returned east, she sent him a letter refusing his proposal. He did join the Battery of the Eighth Regiment of Artillery at Toul, serving from November, 1891, to August, 1892, and very much enjoyed military life.

Although Catholics were not yet formally permitted to attend Oxford or Cambridge, Belloc became a student at Balliol College, Oxford, helped financially by his sister and her husband-to-be. In October, 1892, he received a history scholarship. During his three years at Oxford, he received the Brackenbury Prize for history, took a brilliant first, became president of the Union, and walked from Oxford to London in record time. He was deeply disappointed, however, that he did not receive a history fellowship, especially since it was awarded to another Catholic for the first time since the Reformation.

Elodie entered a convent but soon left, suffering from physical and nervous disorders. In 1896, Belloc went again to California, where they were married on June 16 despite Elodie's mother's objections; Belloc also did some lecturing while he was in the United States. The couple then lived in Oxford, where Belloc published his first collection of poems. He earned money by tutoring, giving University Extension lectures, and writing books, including *The Bad Child's Book of Beasts*. He wrote political articles and gave speeches for Liberal candidates. He wanted to apply for the professorship of history at Glasgow University, but that university did not favor a Catholic and prevailed upon Elodie to discourage him from applying.

In 1902, Belloc became an English citizen, and in 1906, he entered Parliament as the Liberal member from South Salford. Although he saw the House of Commons as a place of corruption and hypocrisy, he was reelected as an Independent.

He founded a weekly review, *The Eye Witness*. He moved from Oxford to Cheyne Walk and then in 1906 to King's Land, a house in Sussex near Horsham, where he enjoyed his four children and his many friends, including the Chesterton brothers. His wife, whose literary judgment he greatly respected, died at age forty-three in 1914, and ever after he dressed in

black and used black-bordered stationery. He traveled frequently to the Continent to study the scenes of his historical works. Unable to get an active appointment in World War I, he spent some time writing articles concerning the war.

He became ill in 1941 after his youngest son died in military service, and he had a stroke at the beginning of the next year, from which he recovered slowly. He died on July 16, 1953, just short of his eighty-third year.

## ANALYSIS

Hilaire Belloc enjoyed playing with various forms of verse while adhering to the ideals of the classics. His range was unusual: He could write, with almost equal facility, a heroic poem or an epigram, a sonnet or a ballade, a satire or a piece of nonsense verse.

What Belloc praised in others' verse he tried to achieve in his own. He said, in a preface to Ruth Pitter's poetry, that the classical spirit, which involved "rhythmic effect without emphatic lilt," subtlety without obvious complexity, and artistry without artifice, was al-

*Hilaire Belloc* (Time & Life Pictures/Getty Images)

most unknown in his time. In his preface to D. B. Wyndham Lewis's book on François Villon, he remarked that the clarity, relief, and vigor mentioned by Lewis were qualities of "hardness," explaining that the marks of hardness were inevitability, the sense that to change a line would be to destroy it; a sense of sequence, of smooth linking; and economy of speech. Belloc's most successful poems, particularly his epigrams, have this intensity.

### "Heroic Poem in Praise of Wine"

Belloc was classical in his ideals but innovative in his practice. His classicism bore poetic fruit in his "Heroic Poem in Praise of Wine," probably his best-known poem. The work (which was influenced by the French writer Clément Marot's vineyard song) was finished in 1928, although fragments of it had appeared earlier. Although it is a poem of praise treating a subject in an exalted way, Belloc the classicist is careful to refer to it as a heroic poem rather than an ode, for it is written in neither the Pindaric nor the Horatian form. The poem changes direction several times and ranges from heroic to mock-heroic.

The first stanza begins in the classical convoluted manner with infinitives of purpose, followed by several lines giving appositives for wine, and finally, five lines below the infinitives, the material to which they refer, an admonition to the Ausonian Muse. The stanza thus incorporates the classical statement of theme with the invocation of the Muse. The invocation to the Ausonian Muse, however, is amusing, since there was no Muse of lower Italy, thus making the reader suspect a partly humorous purpose in the elaborate beginning. The poet personifies wine as a mysterious friend of humanity, begetter of the arts and avenger of wrongs, and he calls upon the Muse to praise and enthrone it.

In the second stanza, the poet requests the Muse to sing of how the Charioteer from Asia with his panthers and the thyrsus twirling came to Greece. The wine of the first stanza has become Dionysus the god. Belloc achieves a sense of anticipation in his description of the ill-at-ease sea, the sudden glory of the mountain, the luminous sky, and the wind with the wonderful word that goes before the pageantlike progress. The group becomes a "something" or a shining cloud as it passes over the land; but everywhere it goes there is the mira-cle of the creation of vines, exuberantly portrayed with a double exclamation. The god is not named here; he is only alluded to by his characteristics. The next stanza shows the vines spreading everywhere, even as far as Africa, but also covering human habitations, thus being both wide and deep, exotic and domestic. In the next section, the day ends with Dionysus completing his journey, going from Spain to Ocean, where Hercules adores him. The author alludes to Hercules, expecting that his readers will have read of the Pillars of Hercules. The next section consists of only a single line, set off for emphasis, stating that the wine is better than riches or power.

The poet then seems to see people who breathe foul air from a well that is oozing slime along the floor of Hell and asks a rhetorical question concerning their identification—rhetorical because he answers it himself. They are the brood of sin, the cursed water-drinkers, and he says with ironic humor that their mothers must have been gin-sodden. This section is mock-heroic and satirical; Belloc attempts to guess their genealogy in the classical manner, calling them white slugs, an apt use of insect imagery to indicate their lack of vitality and character. Those who drink water instead of wine must, by implication, disapprove of it. Thus he uses the explosive "What!" to show indignation that the human race that was exiled from Paradise should have to suffer an evil (these people) with every good (the wine). In the next stanza, he says that even these filthy creatures were permitted to exist in the shadow of the bright Lord, an ambiguous term probably meaning Christ or Dionysus. Like John Milton, Belloc blends classical motifs with such Christian ones as Paradise. Whoever is contaminated by these creatures is condemned to drink the beverage of beasts. In the next section, the poet declares that the grapes are raised in vain for such as these in the various wine-growing regions to which he refers and, again proceeding in the negative, says that it is not for them "the mighty task/ Of bottling God the Father in a flask." The imagery is once more ambiguous, ostensibly Christian but possibly classical. He compares the dull, lifeless behavior of the water-drinkers with the inspired creativity of the wine-drinkers, who have companions in their sleep, as Dionysus had Ariadne. He exhorts the reader to forget the water-drinkers, to form the Dionysian ring and let Io sing. The inclusion of Io in the poem is appropriate since her frenzied condition produced by the gadfly sent by Hera was akin to the divine frenzy of the followers of Dionysus; furthermore, Io was an ancestor of Semele, the mother of Dionysus.

In the next stanza, Belloc addresses Dionysus directly as "Father Linaean" and entreats him not to abandon ruined humanity, as the other gods have done, attributing both architectural elements and rhyme to the god. The following stanza praises the god in three lines stating his powers of enlightening seers, making statues live, and making the grapes swell. In a pastoral strain, he wishes a peaceful life for a farmer; but, knowing that this is not possible, he remembers that all must face their passion (a Christian concept) and gives examples of ironic unsung tragedies.

The last stanza dramatizes old age and death in a series of images. He, too, having wasted long labor, will leave the sun and walk with the shadows, will look at the plain, not at the mountain, and will be alone with nothingness before him. The image of God becomes a military one, understandable in Belloc, who loved the military life: His Comrade-Commander (Christ) will drink with him in His Father's Kingdom. When the hour of death comes, Belloc says, let his youth appear with a chalice bearing an engraved blessing for his dying lips. His youth is here personified to provide a contrast to his age, but the image of a youth with a chalice also suggests Dionysus, who was portrayed as a youth in later representations, one of whose attributes was the *kantharos*, a large two-handled goblet. Dionysus was associated with death and the afterlife through the story of his descent into the underworld to rescue his mother and, in Thrace and in Orphic mythology, his death and resurrection. The ending of the poem would seem to be Christian in its references to wine as sacramental, although the image of wine as his last companion and of wine as raising the divine is not necessarily so. Belloc skillfully blended Christian and classical references in this unusual poem. His sonnet XXXVI, in praise of wine, ascribed its creation to the Christian God, who made people vintners as well as bakers so that they could have the sacraments. Belloc, it may be added, also wrote several drinking songs.

## "ON A DEAD HOSTESS"

The epigram is another classical form employed by Belloc, possessing that element of hardness that he so much admired. He achieved great economy in his use of comparisons. "On a Dead Hostess" begins with an explicit comparison of the subject to other people in this "bad" world by stating two superlatives. The hostess is lovelier than all others and better than everyone else; she has smilingly bid her guests goodnight and gone to her rest, a metaphor for her quiet death, mentioned only in the title. Belloc achieved delicacy here by implying rather than stating. In some of his epigrams suitable for inscriptions on sundials, the shadow represents death, as in one which says that "Loss and Possession, Death and Life are one,/ There falls no shadow where there falls no sun." In a few words, he conveys the idea of the positive inherent in the negative, the theme of John Keats's "Ode on Melancholy." In some of his humorous sundial epigrams, the sundials identify themselves as such and make some wry comment, such as that it makes a "botch/ Of what is done far better by a watch," and "I am a sundial/ Ordinary words/ Cannot express my thoughts on birds."

## EPIGRAMS

The epigrams were generally published for the first time in the collected poems of 1938, while the epigrammatic Juliet poems were privately printed in 1920 and 1934. Thus, some of these poems have not been as accessible as some of his lesser efforts. Many of the Juliet poems are compliments, some of them making use of classical allusions. In "The little owl that Juliet loved is dead," he explains that Pallas Athene took him, since "Aphrodite should not keep her bird," thus identifying Juliet with Aphrodite. In "On a Sleeping Friend," he declares that when she awakens, Dawn shall break over Lethe, the river of forgetfulness.

Belloc experimented with French forms, particularly the ballade and triolet. The triolet, which rhymes *abaaabab*, lines 1, 4, and 7 being identical, is appropriate for playful praise, but Belloc used it for more serious themes. The triolet beginning "The young, the lovely and the wise" says that they are intent on their going and do not seem to notice him. This makes him wonder about "my losing and my owing," presumably the things he has lost and the things he intended. In addition to the repetition of line 1 in lines 4 and 7, line 2 is repeated as line 8, thus giving the poem a strong echoic quality. Delicacy is also achieved by ambiguity; the reader is not exactly sure what is meant by the young's "going." It may be their going out into the world, being on their own. The young people are certain that they know where they are going, paying no attention to others. On the other hand, their "going" may be their death, to which the young are indifferent but about which older people are very much concerned.

### "YOUR LIFE IS LIKE A LITTLE WINTER'S DAY"

Belloc considered the sonnet to be the "prime test of a poet," as he said in his book *Milton* (1935). The sonnet "Your life is like a little winter's day" has a delicacy comparable to "The young, the lovely and the wise," and again an ambiguity contributes to the delicacy. It speaks directly to the reader, using "you" throughout, giving unusual immediacy to the subject of death. In the first line, the poet compares "your" life to a "little" day in winter, while the second line elaborates with a mention of a "sad" Sun rising late and setting early; thus life seems sad and wintry. The third line questions your going away, since you have just come; and the fourth line elaborates, saying that your going makes evening instead of noon. The reader is thus likened to the winter Sun, and the theme of departure is introduced. The next quatrain compares life to something else that is "little," a flute lamenting far away, beyond the willows. Willow trees are associated with sorrow and death. "A long way off" at the beginning of line 6 is repeated at the beginning of line 7, and because the music is far away, only its memory is left in the breeze. The poet implies that life is faintly heard, like the flute. The octave is Shakespearean in form, but the sestet reverses the usual rhyming couplet at the end, placing it at the beginning of the sestet. The sestet's rhyme scheme is *eefggf*, enabling another rhyming couplet, *gg*, to appear where it is hardly expected, before the last line. The sense of reversal and paradox of the rhyme scheme conveys the ironic nature of the subject matter. The third comparison here is that life is like a pitiful farewell that is wept in a dream, with only shadows present. Belloc's ending is couched in religious terms; he calls the farewell a benediction that has no fruit except a consecrated silence. The benediction or farewell is whis-

pered and comes too late, so that there is no response to it. The three comparisons, a little day in winter, a flute playing at a great distance, and a farewell made too late in a dream, all contribute to the sense of being incomplete. Life is unfulfilled, fleeting, and inconsequential, and the reference is not only to life in general but also to "your" life. This discrepancy between expectation and actuality is reinforced by the unexpected rhyme scheme.

### "THE END OF THE ROAD" AND "TO DIVES"

Belloc also experimented by trying to make the rhythm of a poem simulate the action. "The End of the Road" is a poem about the successful completion of Belloc's difficult journey to Rome and is reminiscent of the Carmina Burana of the Middle Ages. He manages to portray a rollicking hike by using many variations of the word "walked," by inverting the subject, and by making trochaic lines with a tripping meter: "Walked I, went I, paced I, tripped I." He goes on in that way for eleven lines, changes to Latin, then back again to English, calling on the major, doubtful, and minor prophets, among others. Another poem in which he tries to imitate motion by meter is his "Tarantella," in which he simulates the beat of the dance with short lines and internal rhymes.

Belloc's inventiveness extended to his satirical poems. "To Dives," the name meaning "rich man" in Latin, was inspired by Belloc's indignation at instances of unjust social and financial influence; it was written a week after Sir Henry Colville, commander of the Ninth Division in South Africa, was dismissed without court martial or public investigation. In "To Dives," Belloc adopts the manner of Horatian rather than Juvenalian satire, avoiding the fiery directness of some of his other satirical poems, including the sonnet "Almighty God, whose justice like a sun," which speaks indignantly of the plight of the poor. Belloc satirizes himself as well as his subject, saying to Dives that when they both go to Hell, Dives will stagger under his pack. Charon the ferryman will tell Dives that his baggage must go overboard.

There are many humorous touches here, including the formal address and the many possessions, including the fifteen kinds of boots for town, and the gifts for those already there, such as the working model of a burning farm to give to the little Belials, as well as the three biscuits for Cerberus. Dives assures Belloc that he will not burn with him, though he will have to leave his possessions behind and enter Hell as tattered and bare as his father was when he pushed a wheelbarrow (Belloc's smirk at the nouveau riche). When Charon sees how lightly the poet is provided with such things as honor, laughter, debts, and trust in God, he lets him pass, having tried to write poetry himself.

The poem ends with the rhetorical question to Dives as to who will look foolish, Dives, Belloc, or Charon. The answer is uncertain because "They order things so damnably in hell." Here Belloc has placed a contemporary rich man in the classical underworld and contrasted him with a poet; yet he represents himself as going there as well.

OTHER MAJOR WORKS

NONFICTION: *Paris*, 1900; *Robespierre*, 1901; *The Path to Rome*, 1902; *Avril*, 1904; *The Catholic Church and Historical Truth*, 1908; *Marie Antoinette*, 1909; *The Pyrenees*, 1909; *The French Revolution*, 1911; *The Four Men*, 1912; *The Servile State*, 1912; *The Cruise of the "Nona,"* 1925; *A History of England*, 1925-1941; *The Catholic Church and History*, 1926; *Milton*, 1935; *On the Place of Gilbert Chesterton in English Letters*, 1940.

BIBLIOGRAPHY

Corrin, Jay P. *G. K. Chesterton and Hilaire Belloc: The Battle Against Modernity*. Athens: Ohio University Press, 1981. Two champions of "democratic anarchy" are juxtaposed as writers and polemicists in an exploration that illuminates both of their careers. Corrin ably demonstrates the near inseparability of intellect and theological commitment of the two allies, while offering good expositions of the histories, fiction, and poetry of the lesser-known Belloc.

Lothian, James R. *The Making and Unmaking of the English Catholic Intellectual Community, 1910-1950*. Notre Dame, Ind.: University of Notre Dame Press, 2009. Examines Belloc's role in helping shape the English Catholic intellectual community and his lasting influence.

McCarthy, John Patrick. *Hilaire Belloc: Edwardian Radical*. Indianapolis, Ind.: Liberty Press, 1978. McCarthy's concern is to elucidate Belloc's career as a political conservative who opposes statism and the growing intervention of government in the private lives of individuals. This resourceful volume explains the relationship between Belloc's politics and economics, and his poetics, while offering an apologia for reading Belloc in the present.

Markel, Michael H. *Hilaire Belloc*. Boston: Twayne, 1982. Markel provides a sympathetic overview of Belloc's life and a mostly thorough exposition of his major and minor works. This source is the best starting place for gaining a sense of the breadth of Belloc's writing career and political commitments. Markel's bibliography of primary and secondary sources is succinct, but valuable.

Pearce, Joseph. *Literary Giants, Literary Catholics*. San Francisco: Ignatius Press, 2005. G. K. Chesterton and Hilaire Belloc are treated in the first part of this work on Catholic writers in England.

_____. *Old Thunder: A Life of Hilaire Belloc*. San Francisco: Ignatius Press, 2002. A biography of Belloc, nicknamed Old Thunder by his mother at birth, that describes a complicated individual. Pearce used previously unavailable manuscripts and photographs in the making of this work and had the help of Belloc's grandchildren.

Wilson, A. N. *Hilaire Belloc*. New York: Atheneum, 1984. A renowned novelist and biographer, Wilson provides researchers with an impeccable source of critical biographical material. Using previously unavailable Belloc letters and manuscripts, Wilson places Belloc and his writing within his historical milieu with affection and candor, refusing to ignore the darker side of Belloc's sympathies with the anti-Semitism of the 1930's and 1940's.

*Rosemary Ascherl*

# JOHN BETJEMAN

**Born:** London, England; August 28, 1906
**Died:** Trebetherick, Cornwall, England; May 19, 1984

PRINCIPAL POETRY

*Mount Zion: Or, In Touch with the Infinite*, 1931
*Continual Dew: A Little Book of Bourgeois Verse*, 1937
*Old Lights for New Chancels: Verses Topographical and Amatory*, 1940
*New Bats in Old Belfries*, 1945
*Slick but Not Streamlined*, 1947 (W. H. Auden, editor)
*Selected Poems*, 1948 (John Sparrow, editor)
*A Few Late Chrysanthemums*, 1954
*Poems in the Porch*, 1954
*Collected Poems*, 1958 (third edition as *John Betjeman's Collected Poems*, 1970)
*Summoned by Bells*, 1960
*High and Low*, 1966
*A Nip in the Air*, 1975
*Ten Late Chrysanthemums*, 1975
*Uncollected Poems*, 1982
*Faith and Doubt of John Betjeman: An Anthology of Betjeman's Religious Verse*, 2005
*Collected Poems*, 2006

OTHER LITERARY FORMS

The lifelong commitment to poetry on the part of John Betjeman (BEH-chuh-muhn) was matched by an equal dedication to the preservation of the best of English architecture, particularly that of the nineteenth century. Throughout his life, he was intent on opening the eyes of the public to the glories of Victorian architecture, and he and his friends John Piper (the painter) and Osbert Lancaster (the cartoonist) pursued this cause with such dedication and enthusiasm that they have probably done more to influence public taste in this area than anyone since John Ruskin. Such overriding interest in the quality of modern urban life, and, more specifically, its aesthetic excellence or excesses, is to be seen again and again in Betjeman's prose.

In 1933, soon after publication of his first volume of verse, he published *Ghastly Good Taste: Or, A Depressing Story of the Rise and Fall of English Architecture*. This work was followed in 1944 by *John Piper*, and then, in the 1950's and early 1960's, a spate of books on landscape and architecture as well as various Shell Guides: *First and Last Loves* (1952), *The English Town in the Last Hundred Years* (1956), *Collins' Guide to English Parish Churches* (1958), and *English Churches* (1964, with B. F. L. Clarke). *Betjeman's Cornwall* was published in 1984. He also edited a number of anthologies that illustrate his interests, including *English, Scottish, and Welsh Landscape* (1944), a collection of poetry edited with Geoffrey Taylor; he also collaborated with Taylor in editing *English Love Poems* (1957). In 1959, *Altar and Pew: Church of England Verses*, edited by Betjeman, was published, and in 1963 *A Wealth of Poetry*, edited with Winifred Hudley, was issued.

Betjeman was also an accomplished and sometimes inspired broadcaster, whether reading his own poems or describing and discussing architecture, and, for the most part, he wrote his own scripts. Unfortunately, none of his broadcasts has been published in book form, although such a book would probably prove to be as popular as his poetry and essays.

ACHIEVEMENTS

John Betjeman's most notable though least tangible achievement was to make poetry accessible once more to the reading public. He received the Russell Loines Award in 1956 from the American Academy of Arts and Letters, but until the publication of his *Collected Poems* in 1958, he was largely unknown. The publication of this volume by John Murray proved to be something of a literary phenomenon. Compiled and with an introduction by the earl of Birkenhead, it sold so quickly that it had to be reprinted three times within the month. It has been said that in the history of the John Murray publishing firm, nothing like it had been known since the first publication of Lord Byron's *Childe Harold's Pilgrimage* in 1812, when copies were sold to a clamoring crowd through the windows of the publisher's house on Albemarle Street. The most recent poetic success of unparalleled magnitude was that of

Alfred, Lord Tennyson in the mid-nineteenth century. So far-reaching was the effect of the publication of this volume that in 1959, when applicants interviewed for entry into an English school at a modern university were asked to name a modern poet, it is said that they would automatically answer "Betjeman." Before this, the most popular answer had been "T. S. Eliot."

It is impossible to explain fully the wide appeal of Betjeman's poetry. At the time it came to the fore, the Movement poets (Philip Larkin, John Wain, Kingsley Amis, and others, to be found in D. J. Enright's 1955 anthology *Poets of the 1950's*) were engaged in a philosophical reaction against the neo-Romanticism of the 1940's, typified by the vogue for the work of Edith Sitwell and the Dylan Thomas cult that emerged after that gifted writer's death in the United States in 1953.

It must have been extremely galling for these poets, engaged in stringent academic opposition to the tyranny of iambic pentameter and attempting to purge poetry of the lush metaphor and hyperbole of neo-Romanticism, to witness the meteoric rise to fame of a poet such as Betjeman. It is still true that a taste for Betjeman's poetry is regarded with suspicion in some academic and intellectual circles. John Wain, for example, gave voice to a ponderous and unfavorable judgment of Betjeman's verse autobiography *Summoned by Bells* when it was published in 1960, and when Philip Larkin, perhaps the best known of the Movement poets, expressed his own admiration for Betjeman's poetry, he too was greeted with disapprobation. Nevertheless, Betjeman's poetry continued to outsell that of others.

It may be that Betjeman's poetic contemporaries have regarded Betjeman with suspicion and dislike because of the force of an argument advanced by Robert Graves in his idiosyncratic but fascinating book *The Crowning Privilege* (1955)—that is, that poetry is not in itself commercial, so that poetry books that sell do not truly contain poetry. It may also be that the overwhelming success of a poet with an instantly recognizable poetic voice, who lauds and celebrates the mores of a way of life that has virtually vanished in the face of the inexorable march of progress, is not thought to be seemly by more stringent and muscular writers.

Whatever the reasons for Betjeman's success and

*John Betjeman* (Time & Life Pictures/Getty Images)

the scant respect with which his work is sometimes treated by more "serious" poets, there is no doubt that he was extensively honored, not only by the literary establishment but also by the country's ruling elite, by professional and academic bodies, and by an abiding public recognition and popularity.

Betjemen's *Selected Poems* won the Heinemann Award; he also won the Foyle Poetry Prize twice, the Duff Cooper Prize, and the Queen's Gold Medal for Poetry. He was a member of the Royal Commission on Historical Monuments in England from 1970 until 1976. He was made an honorary fellow of Keble College, Oxford, in 1972, and of Magdalen College, Oxford, in 1975. He was also awarded an honorary doctor of law from the University of Aberdeen, an honorary doctor of letters from the Universities of Oxford, Reading, Birmingham, Exeter, Liverpool, Hull, and of City University, and was made an honorary associate of the Royal Institute of British Architects (ARIBA).

In 1960, Betjemen was awarded a Commander of

the Order of the British Empire (CBE), followed by a Companion of Literature from the Royal Society of Literature in 1968; in 1969, he was knighted; and in 1972, he became poet laureate, that is, official court poet, responsible for writing poems for state occasions such as the investiture of the prince of Wales and the marriage of the prince of Wales to the Lady Diana Spencer. As poet laureate, he followed such distinguished practitioners of the art as William Wordsworth, Alfred, Lord Tennyson, and John Masefield.

Betjeman restored the status of poetry to a level where people who would never normally consider opening a book of verse were actually prevailed on to pay for the privilege of reading his work. When William Wordsworth (with Samuel Taylor Coleridge) published *Lyrical Ballads* in 1798, his expressed intention was to restore the status of the poet to that of "a man speaking to men," as well as to "exalt and transfigure the natural and the common." More than a hundred years later, with no publicity and no stated poetic philosophy, Betjeman succeeded in both of those aims— perhaps unconsciously, but undeniably.

## BIOGRAPHY

John Betjeman was one of those poets who are profoundly affected by their childhood environment. He was born in London in the early years of the twentieth century, into a class-ridden society, where even small differences in income were important in measuring a family's neighborhood status. This would probably have passed unnoticed had Betjeman been a less observant and sensitive child. As it is, although it is obvious from his poetry that none of the finer nuances of middle-class snobbishness escaped his eye, it is unclear whether these small cruelties were profoundly hurtful or whether the objectivity of the artist was already sufficiently developed to protect him. Certainly there is no bitterness in his poetry, so probably the latter explanation is the correct one. He recounts many of the events of his early life in *Summoned by Bells*, transporting the reader back in time to an England reminiscent of the world depicted by Arthur Conan Doyle, Edith Nesbit, and John Galsworthy.

After leaving Oxford without attaining a degree, Betjeman supported himself by teaching, while contin-

uing to write both poetry and topographical essays. In *Summoned by Bells*, he states quite clearly that as soon as he could read and write, he knew that he must strive to become a poet. Despite the disappointment that he caused his father by refusing to take his place in the family business, he was always true to that early ambition.

He married in 1933 and had a son and a daughter, although domestic considerations are not of primary importance in his work. His sense of place and his eye for the eccentricities of the English character were far more important to him.

Betjeman was named poet laureate in 1972. Although the post is bestowed as an accolade, it was probably a strain for a craftsman-poet such as Betjeman to have been expected to produce odes and hymns to order. He never found inspiration in the machinations of the higher echelons of humankind, but rather in the idiosyncrasies of its middle ranks. When he entered his seventies and was afflicted by ill health, he was no longer able to write as freely as he once had. Betjeman died in Trebetherick, Cornwall, in 1984. It is to be hoped that his later work, which cannot be judged as anywhere near his best, is not allowed to obscure the very real value and artistic achievement of his most productive middle years.

## ANALYSIS

It is somehow appropriate that the first item in the 1958 volume of John Betjeman's *Collected Poems* should be "Death in Leamington," for this poem touches on many of the themes that preoccupied him. Although he has been sometimes accused of facility, both because of the traditional rhyme and rhythms of his work and because of his tendency to stress the light-hearted and humorous, it soon becomes obvious to the reader that he was as aware of "the skull beneath the skin" as any apparently more serious writer.

### DEATH THEME

"Death in Leamington" deals with the death of an elderly person in the subdued atmosphere of an unfashionable English spa town, at a time when the town is almost as dead as the ostensible subject of the poem. The title is ambiguous, as is much of Betjeman's work. He equates the death of a person, and even of a generation, with the death and decay of the person's surroundings and traditions, and it is clear that he laments the passing of both.

For a poet who is often referred to as "lighthearted" and "humorous," he is surprisingly often to be found writing on the subject of death. Indeed, in his introduction to Betjeman's *Collected Poems*, the earl of Birkenhead compares him in this respect with Samuel Johnson. "On a Portrait of a Deaf Man," "Before the Anaesthetic: Or, A Real Fright," "Exeter," "Inevitable," "N. W. 5 & N. 6," and "Saint Cadoc" are only a few of the other poems in which he touches on various aspects of people's attitude toward their own mortality.

A particularly striking poem on this theme is "The Heart of Thomas Hardy," which is written with a degree of bathos and black humor. It describes the heart of Thomas Hardy as "a little thumping fig," a flight of poetic fancy that in itself should serve to ensure Betjeman's literary immortality. He goes on to describe the Mayor of Casterbridge, Jude the Obscure, Tess of the D'Urbervilles, and other products of Hardy's imagination coming to life and leaving their graves to confront their creator in the chancel of Stinsford Church. The poem is something of a literary joke, but it also illustrates Betjeman's interest in the supernatural. There are several other ghosts and eerie incidents described in his poetry, notably in "A Lincolnshire Tale" and the "Sir John Piers" poem sequence, the latter being among the finest in Betjeman's canon.

It would be wholly wrong to place too much emphasis on this darker side of Betjeman's work—indeed, many critics deal with it by the simple expedient of ignoring it; thus they feel justified in dismissing Betjeman as a nostalgic, sentimental apologist for a vanished empire-building middle class. To achieve a balanced view of his work, however, it is necessary to explore all his primary themes, and it is undeniable that there is a somber thread in the fabric of his work.

### A LIGHTHEARTED ATTRACTION TO WOMEN

It would be equally wrong to ignore the lighter side of Betjeman's poetry, especially when that is probably what initially attracts the casual reader to his writing. The most frequently anthologized of his poems are those that describe his attraction toward "large," athletic women—Miss Joan Hunter Dunn (in "A Subal-

tern's Love-Song"), Pam (in "Pot Pourri from a Surrey Garden"), and Myfanwy (in "Myfanwy" and "Myfanwy at Oxford"). These ideal women and his attitude toward them come together in "The Olympic Girl," where, after eulogizing at some length this perfect and unattainable young woman, he concludes sadly: "Little, alas, to you I mean,/ For I am bald and old and green." This sentiment, in various forms, appears ever more often in Betjeman's work and strikes a distinctly Prufrockian note. At first glance, T. S. Eliot and Betjeman seem to have little in common; in the early Betjeman, however, it is possible to detect an awareness of Eliot; for example, "Clash Went the Billiard Balls" is very reminiscent of the concluding section of "A Game of Chess" from *The Waste Land* (1922), and Betjeman's personae frequently recall "The Love Song of J. Alfred Prufrock."

### CHARACTERS OF EXPERIENCE

Eliot's smoky, desolate urban landscapes are not so far removed from Betjeman's "Slough," or even from his "Middlesex." Nor are Betjeman's delicately observed characters so far removed from Eliot's less personal portraits. The difference is, perhaps, that Eliot's characters are observed, while Betjeman's are experienced. It certainly takes much more intellectual effort to come to terms with Eliot, and perhaps this effort exerts a distancing effect on the reader, maintaining a welcome emotional detachment. It is much more difficult to maintain detachment from Betjeman's work. He was not a poet much given to analysis and metaphysical themes. Perhaps that is why he is often ignored by critics; they may admit to enjoying his poetry but are unprepared to acknowledge that in writing poetry that is comprehensible, and also of consistently high quality, he has achieved anything worthwhile.

### NATURE POEMS

Because Betjeman was often to be heard giving broadcasts and lectures on architecture and aspects of the British countryside that were especially dear to him, he is perhaps most commonly thought of as a "nature," or, more specifically, a "landscape" poet. However, he was not a nature poet in the Wordsworthian sense. Where he excelled was in his ability to express his delight in a particular area and a particular type of scenery, and to convey that delight to the reader. "Ireland with Emily" is an excellent example of this strain in his work; it is a poem that evokes country life in southern Ireland brilliantly, as, in a different mood, does "A Lament for Moira McCavendish." "Matlock Bath," from the collection *High and Low*, is another such poem, describing life in the nonconformist industrial Midlands of England. In other poems, he describes the Cornish coast and various parts of London, especially those areas near Highgate, where he spent his childhood and about which he writes at length in his verse autobiography, *Summoned by Bells*.

### HUMOR AS SATIRE

It is impossible to discuss the work of Betjeman fully without reference to his humor, yet a laborious treatment of this topic is the easiest way of rendering the humor itself ineffective and unfunny. Suffice to say that much of Betjeman's poetry has a considerable element of humor, but that it would be wrong to regard him as merely a funny writer. His humor always has a purpose, and often, as in "A Lincolnshire Tale," he uses humor for special effect, combining it with a degree of the macabre to make the reader chuckle and then shudder.

His best-known and most anthologized poems, such as "Hunter Trials" and "How to Get on in Society," are those that satirize various easily recognizable aspects of English middle-class life. "How to Get on in Society" covers much the same ground as Nancy Mitford does in *Noblesse Oblige* (1956)—that is, the distinction between "U" (university) and "non-U." The speaker in the poem is distinctly "non-U," but with "U" aspirations. Betjeman cleverly picks up all the social and linguistic pointers and strings them together to create a picture of a type of person in a social milieu recognizable to the English reader; yet he does so through only a few simple lines of conversation. Of course the poem is very much of its time; language change constantly, and such a poem written today would obviously have very different nuances. The same is not true of "Hunter Trials," which applies as much to horse-mad little girls now as it did when it was written.

### SEX AND LOVE

Betjeman was always interested in social distinctions—"Group Life: Letchworth" is an earlier example of his keen eye for the extreme and the ridiculous. It concludes with a reference to the cult of free love that flourished in some sections of English society, apparently in the wake of D. H. Lawrence. It has been suggested that Betjeman had a very ambivalent attitude toward sex, being able to deal with it effectively in his work only by making it funny. Leaving aside the thought that often the antics of human beings in love are very amusing to the detached observer, it seems unfair to dismiss Betjeman's subtleties so lightly. In "Group Life: Letchworth," he satirizes one aspect of the English attitude toward sexuality. In "Indoor Games near Newbury," he deals with a quite different, presexual love, and in "Beside the Seaside," the agony of adolescent love. Later, in such poems as "Senex" and "Late Flowering Lust," he takes an ironic, sometimes metaphysical look at the immutability of emotions as the flesh ages. He touches the same topic in "Sun and Fun," and it is part of his strength that he maintains his integrity of tone whether writing about a view he admires or a state of affairs that he obviously deplores. This is possibly why some critics seem to disapprove when he strays from the more familiar descriptive and social poetry to write about emotions. Critics are as likely to be alarmed by change as anyone else, but there is no need to think that change is necessarily always for the worse. In Betjeman's case, he merely showed that he could write about most things with skill, insight, and sympathy.

### LEGACY

It is difficult to assess the achievement of Betjeman, who had great public success yet remained outside the mainstream of English poetry. Unlike Eliot or Dylan Thomas, Betjeman inspired no school of poets who either imitate or react unfavorably to him, but he is widely read and admired, both by the general public (many of whom would never consider reading poetry if it were not for Betjeman) and by other poets. What is certain is that Betjeman's was a strong and individual poetic voice, whose influence, by virtue of his very popularity, has been far-reaching. Reading his work must make readers aware of both the beauties that surround them and the influences that conspire to threaten those beauties. To speak of the morality of art is to venture onto dangerous ground, yet in writing skillfully in a way that encourages readers to view humankind with tolerance and understanding, and the environment with respect, Betjeman must be thought of as a good poet in both senses of the word.

## OTHER MAJOR WORKS

NONFICTION: *Ghastly Good Taste: Or, A Depressing Story of the Rise and Fall of English Architecture*, 1933; *An Oxford University Chest*, 1938; *Antiquarian Prejudice*, 1939; *Vintage London*, 1942; *English Cities and Small Towns*, 1943; *John Piper*, 1944; *First and Last Loves*, 1952; *The English Town in the Last Hundred Years*, 1956; *Collins' Guide to English Parish Churches*, 1958; *English Churches*, 1964 (with B. F. L. Clarke); *Betjeman's Cornwall*, 1984; *John Betjeman Letters*, 1994-1995 (2 volumes); *John Betjeman: Coming Home*, 1997; *Trains and Buttered Toast: Selected Radio Talks*, 2006; *Sweet Songs of Zion: Selected Radio Talks*, 2007; *Betjeman's England*, 2009.

EDITED TEXTS: *English, Scottish, and Welsh Landscape*, 1944 (with Geoffrey Taylor); *English Love Poems*, 1957 (with Taylor); *Altar and Pew: Church of England Verses*, 1959; *A Wealth of Poetry*, 1963 (with Winifred Hudley).

MISCELLANEOUS: *Tennis Whites and Teacakes*, 2007.

## BIBLIOGRAPHY

Betjeman, John. *Letters*. Edited by Candida Lycett Green. 2 vols. London: Methuen, 1994. This comprehensive collection reveals many intimate details about the life of Betjeman, including the depth of his affection for his friends, his religious sentiment, and his relationships with his wife and with longtime mistress Elizabeth Cavendish. Covers letters written between 1926 and 1984.

Delany, Frank. *Betjeman Country*. London: John Murray, 1983. This remarkable travel book combines biographical commentary on Betjeman with excerpts from the poet's poems and numerous photographs of the places connected with the poems of Betjeman. Includes a primary bibliography.

Hamilton, Ian. *Against Oblivion: Some Lives of the Twentieth-Century Poets*. London: Viking, 2002. Contains a biography on the poet Betjeman.

Harvey, Geoffrey. "John Betjeman: An Odeon Flashes Fire." In *The Romantic Tradition in Modern British Poetry*. New York: St. Martin's Press, 1986. This provocative, informative study rejects the assessment of Betjeman as a minor establishment poet. Harvey views him as a "consistently subversive force in modern verse"—a committed writer mindful of a real audience.

McDermott, John V. "Betjeman's 'The Arrest of Oscar Wilde at the Cadogan Hotel.'" *Explicator* 57, no. 3 (Spring, 1999): 165-166. McDermott argues that Betjeman's poem, which seems at first to be a singular assault on the character of Oscar Wilde, proceeds, by subtle implication, to condemn the society that held Wilde up to scorn.

Morse, Greg. *John Betjeman: Reading the Victorians*. Portland, Oreg.: Sussex Academic Press, 2008. An examination of Betjeman's poetry in the context of the Victorian era.

Peterson, William S. *John Betjeman: A Bibliography*. New York: Oxford University Press, 2006. Peterson gives a thorough account of all of Betjeman's works, both published and unpublished, including contributions to periodicals, lectures, musical settings, recordings, radio and television broadcasts, and dramatic adaptations of his poetry. There are seventeen sections, providing thorough discussions about each work, including information about contents and publication histories. This biography provides a wealth of information and contains an index complete with annotations.

Taylor-Martin, Patrick. *John Betjeman: His Life and Work*. London: Allen Lane, 1983. This excellent study of Betjeman is a useful balance of critical commentary and biography. Taylor-Martin views Betjeman as a serious writer, not a light versifier. The text is supplemented by a select bibliography—primary texts, secondary books, and articles—and a list of his recordings.

Vestey, Michael. "Betjeman Recalled." *The Spectator* 278, no. 8793 (February 8, 1997): 52-53. Vestey reminisces about an interview with Betjeman that took place in the 1970's. The article follows on the heels of a Radio Two program *Softly Croons the Radiogram*, in which Betjeman's collaboration with composer Jim Parker to set his poetry to music was discussed.

Wilson, A. N. *Betjeman: A Life*. New York: Farrar, Straus and Giroux, 2006. This biography takes a close look at the private life of Betjeman, painting a portrait of his lifestyle, interests, and idiosyncrasies. Wilson draws on correspondence between Betjeman and his wife to shed light on their relationship and to give readers an accurate picture of his personality.

*Vivien Stableford*

# EARLE BIRNEY

**Born:** Calgary, Alberta, Canada; May 13, 1904
**Died:** Toronto, Ontario, Canada; September 3, 1995

PRINCIPAL POETRY

*David, and Other Poems*, 1942
*Now Is Time*, 1945
*The Strait of Anian*, 1948
*Trial of a City, and Other Verse*, 1952
*Ice Cod Bell or Stone*, 1962
*Near False Creek Mouth*, 1964
*Selected Poems 1940-1966*, 1966
*The Poems of Earle Birney*, 1969
*Pnomes, Jukollages, and Other Stunzas*, 1969
*Rag and Bone Shop*, 1971
*The Bear on the Delhi Road*, 1973
*What's So Big About Green?*, 1973
*The Collected Poems of Earle Birney*, 1975
*The Rugged and the Moving Times*, 1976
*Ghost in the Wheels: Selected Poems, 1920-1976*, 1977
*Fall by Fury*, 1978
*The Mammoth Corridors*, 1980
*Copernican Fix*, 1985
*Last Makings*, 1991
*One Muddy Hand: Selected Poems*, 2006

OTHER LITERARY FORMS

Earle Birney (BUR-nee), like many contemporary Canadian poets, both created and explicated the tradition of his country's writings. He wrote or edited more than two dozen volumes, including poetry, fiction, drama, criticism, and anthologies, as well as nearly a hundred short stories, pamphlets, essays, reviews, and articles. The novels *Turvey* (1949), which won the Stephen Leacock medal for humor, and *Down the Long Table* (1955) are well worth reading for an appreciation of Birney's sense of style. Of his critical articles and books, *The Creative Writer* (1966), *The Cow Jumped over the Moon: The Writing and Reading of Poetry* (1972), and *Spreading Time* (1980) are the most notable collections, for they offer invaluable insights into Birney's poetry.

ACHIEVEMENTS

Earle Birney's career has been laced with numerous honors. He won the Governor-General's Medal for poetry in 1942 for *David, and Other Poems* and in 1945 for *Now Is Time*, the Stephen Leacock Medal for Humour in 1949 for *Turvey*, the Borestone Mountain prize in 1951, a Canadian government fellowship to France in 1953, the Lorne Pierce Gold Medal from the Royal Society of Canada in 1953, and the President's Medal for Poetry from the University of Western Ontario in 1954. He was given a Nuffield Fellowship in 1958-1959 and Canada Council traveling fellowships throughout the 1960's and 1970's to most of the world regions, including Latin America, Australia, West and East Africa, Europe, and South Asia. Additionally, he won the Canada Council Medal for services to arts in 1968 and a Canada Council Senior Arts Fellowship from 1978 to 1980. He was named officer of the Order of Canada in 1981 and received an honorary degree from University of British Columbia in 1987.

BIOGRAPHY

Alfred Earle Birney was born on May 13, 1904, in Calgary, Alberta, which was then a part of the Northwest Territories. He spent his youth in Calgary, Banff, and Creston, British Columbia; graduated from Creston High School in 1920; and then worked at a variety of jobs to earn money for university study. By 1926, he had graduated from the University of British Columbia with first-class honors in English literature, and that autumn he entered the University of Toronto as a Leonard Graduate Fellow. During the next year, he concentrated on Old and Middle English, and his studies led to his later imitations of the Anglo-Saxon line in "Anglo-Saxon Street" and "Mappemounde." He graduated with an M.A. in 1927 and was married the same year.

From 1927 to 1934, he studied at the University of California, Berkeley, as well as in Toronto. Two years later, he completed his Ph.D. thesis, "Chaucer's Irony," and received his degree from the University of Toronto. From 1936 to 1940, Birney acted as the literary editor of *The Canadian Forum*, writing numerous articles for this journal. When World War II began, Birney served overseas in the Canadian armed forces as a personnel officer. He would later use this experience as the basis for his comic war novel *Turvey*.

In 1945, at the end of the war, he was appointed professor of English at the University of British Columbia (UBC). While at UBC, he was instrumental in establishing the first department of creative writing at a Canadian university. Once the program was set up, he invited American poets such as Charles Olson, Robert Creeley, and Robert Duncan to teach there. To some extent, these writers would greatly affect Birney's view of poetics; in particular, they expounded theories about spacing, breath, and projective verse that led Birney to revise many of his own ideas about these matters. Birney followed their direction, although he did not become a disciple of the Black Mountain movement. By 1963, Birney had become the chair of the Department of Creative Writing and also editor of *Prism International*. In 1964, Birney left UBC to become writer-in-residence at such institutions across Canada as the universities of Toronto, Waterloo, and Western Ontario. In 1968, as a Canada Council Fellow, he traveled to Australia, New Zealand, and other parts of the world; some of his best poetry deals with these experiences.

After 1969, Birney devoted his time primarily to his writing, leaving his career as an educator behind him. In the middle and late 1970's, he concentrated most of his energy on recording the developments in Canadian writing that he witnessed during his lifetime. In March of 1987, he suffered a serious heart attack and had an almost fatal stroke two months later. He decreased his writing considerably, although he continued to serve as a contributor of plays, talks, and readings to CBC Trans-

Canada radio programs—which he had been doing since 1945—until his death in 1995 and made frequent appearances on CBC television panels during this span of time as well.

ANALYSIS

Earle Birney's poetry reflects and summarizes the ambiguities, inconsistencies, and changes in direction in Canadian writing during the second half of the twentieth century. His central achievement was simple: He brought Canadian poetry from traditional conservatism through modernism and, finally, to postmodernism. As a result, his mere presence on the Canadian literary scene generated everything from respect to contempt. No writer in Canada stirred as much controversy about the nature, direction, and accomplishment of Canadian poetry; Birney will always be remembered and acknowledged. Literary nationalism had been the catchphrase of Canadian writing, but when it arrived in the form of Birney, Canadians discovered a contentious, outspoken gentleman who shocked the literary establishment.

The most distinguishing characteristic of Birney's poetry is its diversity. Birney cannot be associated with any single place, with any single movement (either political, social, or poetic), or with any single theme—he wrote about everything that interested him at the moment it interested him. The result may be a solitary poem quickly forgotten or an entire book of experiments immediately abandoned after publication. Birney's chameleon-like nature forced commentators to discuss his work in large, broad generalizations, but Birney's achievement does have a center, and that center rested in his belief that the future was always open and that nothing was ever quite finished or complete or final.

Permanence, for Birney, was an illusion; only death had finality. The recurring images of death, loss, and failure, suggested particularly in the autumnal imagery of his early and middle poetry, are present to emphasize that only one force defeats, or at least temporarily overcomes, death: the creative power inherent in the individual. In conjunction with his firm belief in the inward potential of the individual's creative energy, Birney maintained that art, like anything else, must be the expression of creative change. For these reasons, he would revise, alter, and completely transform an earlier poem to accommodate and reflect the changes he sensed in his world.

A volume of Birney's poems might include forms as diverse as pastiche, allegory, Anglo-Saxon forms, narrative and reflective poems, lyrics, limericks, found poems, and concrete or "shapomes" (poems that rely, almost wholly, on their visual, rather than verbal, effect). No single volume amassing all the various forms Birney used would be satisfactory, for Birney often not only changed and revised poems for later editions but entirely transformed their format and design, as well. A linear poem in one edition may appear in the next as a "shapome." In his *Selected Poems, 1940-1966*, Birney added dates after each poem to indicate the impermanence of his own "final" selection. "North of Superior," for example, is followed by the dates 1926-1945. Which is the "real" version? The poem of 1926 (or was this merely the first draft?) or the poem of 1945? Such questions can hardly be answered when the reader thinks of the poem "Mammorial Stunzas for Aimee Simple McFarcin," dated "Toronto 1932-San Francisco 1934" but first printed in 1959, then reprinted in a wholly transformed shape in 1966. The only possible complete and satisfactory edition of Birney's work would include all the versions of the revised and restructured poems, introduced by the following heading: The "final" version of any poem in this edition rests in the invisible creative energy suggested by every visible act of imagination (that is, every altered poem) included here.

### "DAVID"

Analysis of Birney's work inevitably begins with his first major poem, "David," a narrative that records the last day of "youth" in the mountains. Although the poem is entitled "David," it is centrally about Bobby, the narrator. Bobby possesses a naïve and sentimental view of nature, and David attempts to teach his younger friend the necessity of living in a world where beauty and magnificence have value only when death is recognized as both necessary and inevitable. The lyricism and descriptive detail in the poem move the reader most forcefully at the moments when death and beauty are inextricably entwined in the passages of description.

The climax of the poem is reached when David falls to a ledge far below. Bobby's error has caused the mishap, although David, now crippled, does not press the blame on his friend. Instead, David asks Bobby to demonstrate that he has grasped the principle of necessary death by pushing him off the ledge so that he will not have to live as an invalid. Bobby finally responds to David's requests. The conclusion of the poem focuses on Bobby's need to reorient and reevaluate his own outlook and attitudes, which he cannot do. For Bobby, nature is now frightening, horrific, and repugnant. Ironically, David has died for nothing; Bobby's idealism has simply turned to blind pessimism. The poem, however, forcefully depicts humans' need to incorporate not only new values but also values that may initially seem incomprehensible and alien. Bobby may fail, but the reader clearly sees that Birney favored David's vision of life, for it allows for both beauty and death without fear.

The initial publication of the poem created a shock, and for years Birney was inundated by letters asking him if he had once pushed a friend off a cliff. The confusion between literature and reality may seem humorous to the more experienced reader, but the fact that such letters were written and sent testifies to the impact of the poem. The same narrative, in later years, however, stirred an even greater debate. Birney suddenly modernized it. He stripped the poem of punctuation and inserted spaces for commas, semicolons, and periods. The argument about the purpose and significance of the changes continues even now: Can a traditional poem be "modernized" by simply omitting punctuation? Such a process, for the modern purist, defies any sense of organic form or poetic necessity. For many, Birney's revision was superficial tinkering.

The attacks on the so-called facile alterations of the poem are valid if one accepts the notion that poems of the past must remain in the past, but Birney would not accept that notion. He boldly challenged his detractors to explain their principles, even if they did not have the patience to listen to his reasoning. For Birney, no poem could be imprisoned in the abstraction called "the past": Every poem is read in the present; it is experienced in the present, and the sensibility of the present is attuned to verse without punctuation. Neither the sensibility that was at work in the "older" version nor the audience for whom it was intended still exists. The old must be pushed over the cliff to its death; the new must be incorporated.

Birney did not receive acceptance on this point, but, whatever a reader's attitude, an understanding of the poet's principles clarifies why Birney so markedly shifted and shifted again, even in experimental forms. In "Anglo-Saxon Street," for example, he created his best-known satire by using Old English stress and modern "kennings." In "Billboards Build Freedom of Choice," he used a variation of Olson's projective verse but, at the same time, sported with the ambiguities inherent in the slang of the 1950's and early 1960's. In "There Are Delicacies," he created a concrete poem that resembles a timepiece to remind a woman that there is only so much time for love. In a book called *What's So Big About Green?*, the poet had the words themselves printed in green ink to accompany his theme in visual form: Everything is capable of greenness, freshness, vitality, and rebirth. Birney's constant insistence on the dynamics of change was not an idle or frivolous gesture; the philosophy gave direction and unity to all he wrote.

### "TRIAL OF A CITY"

The philosophy of change, or the all too common lack of it, often led Birney to lash out with forceful and even vitriolic satires and parodies. Even in these works, Birney's central vision is not lost to anger or outrage. The work "Trial of a City: A Public Hearing into the Proposed Damnation of Vancouver" excellently illustrates the point. The work is a madcap fantasy of the future, the setting a kangaroo court wherein the sentence has already been pronounced, although the case is tried afterward. The powers that be can see no reason for halting the annihilation of the city until a common homemaker enters. She stands for the forces of creation and meaning and love. For her, there is neither causality nor inevitable end. Creative response to the moment, her presence insists, allows for life, passion, and continuance. For her, all human "freedom is renewable each moment," but only if the individual exercises his creative energy to embrace and accept.

The theme of "Trial of a City," then, despite its harsh attack on the stultified values of society (repre-

sented by the traditionalist, Mr. Legion), was typical of Birney's larger concerns. In form, the work also bore the marks of Birney's experimentalism, including everything from typographical idiosyncrasies in the manner of E. E. Cummings to the use of diction and thought echoing W. H. Auden.

Through the years, Birney gradually incorporated into his own work all the various developments in poetry since the 1930's and 1940's. His rhetoric based on image shifted to a rhetoric of voice, and from there to a rhetoric of visual design. At times, the ability to accommodate such disparate poetic modes resulted in profoundly moving verse dealing with humanity's place in a hostile world, as in "Mappemounde," and in delightful typographical humor, as in "Appeal to a Lady with a Diaper." Often, however, the all too predictable pursuit of novelty wears thin, and Birney's work becomes tiresome.

The tiresome poems cannot be reread, and therein lies their greatest weakness. On first reading, the timepiece design of the poem "There Are Delicacies" enchants; on the second reading, it bores. The language, the essence of the poetic craft, has been treated too lightly; the reverberations have been too easily lost. One can admire Birney's effort to be consistent, one can sympathize with his healthy and reinvigorating outlook, one can admire the notion that creative acts are always required and always possible, but one cannot always summon the energy to rejoice at poems that seem flat and stale once the novelty has worn off.

In the poems that can be reread, Birney's theme, form, language, typography, and verse form (be they traditional or modern) create fulfilling, enriching experiences. Anyone interested in poetry can read them, for the literary devices enhance the texture of the poems rather than point to themselves as being present and active (thereby inadvertently drawing the reader's eye from the true center of the poem—the content). The most important poems in this category may be loosely called Birney's "travel poems"; they deserve special attention.

### TRAVEL POEMS

Birney was not a regional poet. This point is significant, for the term "travel poem" is used here to encompass all poems wherein Birney's speaker is on the road, in a train, or in a new city, be that city in Canada or Japan. The poems have great force because usually, although not always, the reader, by the end of the poem, knows more than the person who did the traveling. Since the reader can measure both the speaker and what he thinks, as well as the atmosphere and history of the place visited, that reader is often in a privileged position to judge and evaluate both the ridiculous and the redeeming in human nature. This striking effect in the travel poems was the consequence of Birney's masterful control of both his speaker and his setting. Some of the best of the travel poems are "For George Lamming," "Arrivals," "The Bear on the Delhi Road," "Cartagena de Indias," "El Greco," "November Walk Near False Creek Mouth," and "A Walk in Kyoto." In these and the other travel poems, Birney concentrated on his favorite topic, the moment of needed creative impulse, and the speaker usually discovers his creative force as he reflects on his experience.

### "FOR GEORGE LAMMING"

"For George Lamming" best illustrates how Birney concentrated on the moment of change. The free-verse poem, lacking punctuation, suggests fluidity and freedom from beginning to end. It deals with the speaker's sudden insight into an experience he had in Kingston, Jamaica, where, invited to a party, he found himself totally in harmony with all who were there. More than "rum happy," he did not even recognize his joy until he looked in the mirror; then his face "assaulted" him. He was the only white among five or six black couples, and despite the color barrier, the history of black tensions, and the racial prejudice of the ages, these people had allowed him to share "unchallenged" their friendship and intimacy. The speaker will always feel "grateful" for having been allowed, even temporarily, to escape the prison of his own skin and his own prejudices (although he had not recognized them until that moment).

This summary of the poem slips over the numerous subtleties of the "master" and "slave" imagery used throughout (for language itself requires one to "risk words," although they are such "dull/ servants") to make a central point about Birney's artistry at its best: Creative insight, for Birney, represented the moment of transcendence of the narrow self. Imagination, in its largest sense, was, for Birney, an act or ability that is

not confined to poets or to poetry; it was the act of sympathetic insight and understanding available to all people at all times, provided they transcend themselves. If Birney, at times, insisted too loudly, if he pressed his experiments too often, if he revised and altered and again altered too persistently—these were merely the signs of his sincerity and consistency. Every altered and modified poem Birney presented can be, and probably should be, read as his unaltering embrace of constant change through individual creative gestures. As such, the poetry of Birney is a testament of one man's unshakable conviction that human growth, development, and perfection are possible.

### OTHER MAJOR WORKS

LONG FICTION: *Turvey*, 1949; *Down the Long Table*, 1955.

SHORT FICTION: *Big Bird in the Bush*, 1978.

PLAY: *The Damnation of Vancouver: A Comedy in Seven Episodes*, pb. 1952.

RADIO PLAY: *Words on Waves*, 1985.

NONFICTION: *The Creative Writer*, 1966; *The Cow Jumped over the Moon: The Writing and Reading of Poetry*, 1972; *Spreading Time*, 1980; *Essays on Chaucerian Irony*, 1985.

EDITED TEXTS: *Twentieth Century Canadian Poetry*, 1953; *New Voices*, 1956; *Selected Poems of Malcolm Lowry*, 1962.

### BIBLIOGRAPHY

Adams, Ian. "Marginality and Tradition: Earle Birney and Wilson Harris." *Journal of Commonwealth Literature* 24, no. 1 (1989): 88. Several works from Birney and Guyanese poet Wilson Harris are discussed. Both writers are generally credited with a major role in the establishment of a modern literature authentic of their region, and both view themselves as doing so out of a position of cultural marginality.

Aichinger, Peter. *Earle Birney*. Boston: Twayne, 1979. This introductory study looks at Birney's criticisms of capitalism, modern culture, and militarism. Divided thematically with chapters on biographical background, satire, love and death, myth, nature, poetic technique, and politics, the book concentrates on Birney's poetry over his criticism and prose fiction. The cynicism, raunchiness, and invective in Birney's later work are considered in a negative light.

_____. "Earle Birney." In *Canadian Writers and Their Works: Poetry Series*, edited by Robert Lecker, Jack David, and Ellen Quigley. Vol. 5. Downsview, Ont.: ECW Press, 1985. Contains a short introduction to Birney's life, his traditions and worldview, and a critical overview. Looks specifically at the alliterative verse, lyric poetry, experimental verse, and the narrative poems.

Cameron, Elspeth. *Earle Birney: A Life*. Toronto, Ont.: Viking, 1996. Shows Birney as a poet, novelist, soldier, journalist, academic, and world traveler. Cameron also covers his romantic life. In so doing, she calls on the copious materials (including hundreds of letters) archived at the University of Toronto.

Fink, Howard, et al. *Perspectives on Earle Birney*. Downsview, Ont.: ECW Press, 1981. A reassessment of Birney by eminent critics and authors, this collection was originally published as a special issue on Birney in *Essays on Canadian Writing* 21 (Spring, 1981). Pieces of Birney's poetry are interspersed with observations on his radio drama, Chaucerian scholarship, and political prose.

Latham, David. "From the Hazel Bough of Yeats: Birney's Masterpiece." *Canadian Poetry: Studies, Documents, Reviews* 21 (Fall/Winter, 1987): 52-58. Latham traces the influence of William Butler Yeats's "Song of the Wandering Aengus" on Birney's "From the Hazel Bough," a poem Birney considered his masterpiece.

Nesbitt, Bruce, ed. *Earle Birney: Critical Views on Canadian Writers*. New York: McGraw-Hill, 1974. Contains both positive and negative reviews and critical essays on Birney's craft and creativity mixed with a number of his prose pieces. The useful introduction gives an overview and appreciation, while in an epilogue, Birney himself reflects on his career and responds to some of the critical appraisals.

Noel-Bentley, Peter. "Earle Birney: An Annotated Bibliography." In *The Annotated Bibliography of Canada's Major Authors*, edited by Robert Lecker and

Jack David. Vol. 4. Downsview, Ont.: ECW Press, 1983. The standard bibliography of Birney's works.

St. Pierre, Paul Matthew. "Earle Birney." In *Canadian Writers, 1920-1959, Second Series*, edited by W. H. New. Vol. 88 in *Dictionary of Literary Biography*. Detroit: Gale Research, 1989. A helpful overview of Birney's life and career.

*Ed Jewinski*

# WILLIAM BLAKE

**Born:** London, England; November 28, 1757
**Died:** London, England; August 12, 1827

PRINCIPAL POETRY
*Poetical Sketches*, 1783
*All Religions Are One*, 1788
*There Is No Natural Religion*, 1788
*The Book of Thel*, 1789
*Songs of Innocence*, 1789
*The Marriage of Heaven and Hell*, 1790
*America: A Prophecy*, 1793
*Visions of the Daughters of Albion*, 1793
*Europe: A Prophecy*, 1794
*The [First] Book of Urizen*, 1794
*Songs of Innocence and of Experience*, 1794
*The Book of Ahania*, 1795
*The Book of Los*, 1795
*The Song of Los*, 1795
*Milton: A Poem*, 1804-1808
*Jerusalem: The Emanation of the Giant Albion*, 1804-1820
*The French Revolution*, 1913 (wr. 1791)
*Vala: Or, The Four Zoas*, 1963 (wr. 1795-1804; best known as *The Four Zoas*)
*The Poems of William Blake*, 1971

OTHER LITERARY FORMS
William Blake's prose includes *An Island in the Moon* (1987), *To the Public: Prospectus* (1793), *A Descriptive Catalogue* (1809), marginalia, and letters. It is almost a given with Blake scholarship and criticism

that the interrelation of poetry and design is vital. David V. Erdman's *The Illuminated Blake* (1975) includes all of Blake's illuminated works, text, and design, with a plate-by-plate commentary.

### ACHIEVEMENTS

William Blake's reputation during his lifetime was not a fraction of what it is today. He worked hard at his trade, that of engraving, but his style was not in fashion, and his commissions were few. His poverty and the laborious process of producing his own illuminated books for sale prevented him from producing more than two hundred copies of his own work in his lifetime. Even the *Songs of Innocence and of Experience*, which he sold sporadically throughout his career, remained virtually unnoticed by his contemporaries. What little reputation he had among his contemporaries was as an artist, ingenious but no doubt mad.

In 1863, Alexander Gilchrist's biography of Blake did much to establish Blake's reputation as an artist and a poet. The Yeats-Ellis edition of Blake (1893) further enhanced his fame, not as a forgotten painter and poet, but as a purveyor of esoteric lore. Accurate transcription of Blake's texts began only in the twentieth century with the work of Geoffrey Keynes. Modern critical work was pioneered by S. Foster Damon in 1924, but it was not until Northrop Frye's *Fearful Symmetry* in 1947 that Blake's work was treated as a comprehensible, symmetrical whole.

A poet-artist who imaginatively remolds his own age and its traditions and then produces poetry, engravings, and paintings within that re-created world is a poet-artist who will attract a wide variety of readers. Blake's profound understanding of the ways in which humans deal with the warring contraries within their minds has become a fertile source for modern psychology. Carl Jung referred to Blake as a visionary poet who had achieved contact with the potent wellspring of the unconscious. Blake's devotion to a humanistic apocalypse created through the display of exuberant energies and expanded imaginative perceptions has been an inspiration to two generations of twentieth century writers: first D. H. Lawrence, E. M. Forster, William Butler Yeats, and Aldous Huxley, and later, Norman O. Brown, Allen Ginsberg, Theodore Roszak, Colin Wilson, and John Gardner, among others. If a poet can be judged by the quality and quantity of the attention he receives, Blake certainly rose in the twentieth century from a vague precursor of Romanticism to one of the six major English Romantic poets.

### BIOGRAPHY

William Blake was born in Carnaby Market, London, on November 28, 1757. By the age of four, he was having visions: God put his head through the window to look at him, angels walked among the haymakers, and a tree was starred with angels. The visionary child was spared the rigors of formal schooling and learned to read and write at home. He attended a drawing school for four years and in 1772 began a seven-year apprenticeship to James Basire, engraver. He had already begun three years before to write the lyrics that were later printed in *Poetical Sketches*. It was not as a poet, however, that he would make his living but as an engraver who also could do original designs. The Gothic style of engraving that he learned from Basire was unfortunately somewhat passé. In later years,

*William Blake* (Library of Congress)

Blake had to sit back and watch other engravers receive commissions to execute his own designs.

At the age of twenty-two, Blake became a student of the Royal Academy, which meant that he could draw from models, living and antique, and attend lectures and exhibitions for six years. The politics of the day, as well as a spreading evangelical fervor, infused his life as an artist-poet. Blake was part of the 1780 Gordon Riots and was present at the burning of Newgate Prison. He was a vehement supporter of the French Revolution and attended radical gatherings that included William Godwin, Thomas Paine, Mary Wollstonecraft Shelley, and Joseph Priestley. Through John Flaxman, Blake developed an interest in Swedenborgianism. The doctrines of Emanuel Swedenborg seemed both to attract and to repel Blake. *The Marriage of Heaven and Hell* launched an attack on this movement.

In 1782, Blake married Catherine Boucher, whose life apparently became one with his. He tried his hand at running a print shop, but in 1785 it failed. He continued to make a meager living on commissions for designs and engravings, but these were the works of others. In 1800, he moved to Felpham near Chichester at the invitation of William Hayley, a minor poet, who attempted for the next three years to guide Blake's life into a financially lucrative mold. Blake returned as impoverished as ever to London in 1803, never to leave it again. In 1804, he was tried for sedition and was acquitted. It is ironic that Blake was not being tried for his pervasive iconoclasm, thoughts expressed in his unpublished work that would have set the eighteenth century on its head, but because a drunk had falsely accused him. In 1809, he had his one and only exhibition of sixteen paintings, an exhibition ignored by everyone except one reviewer, who attacked it viciously.

If the political and religious spirit of this period inspired Blake, it also worked against his prosperity as an engraver. Few in England during the Napoleonic wars could afford the luxury of commissioning the work of an engraver. In the last ten years of his life, Blake attracted the attention of a group of young painters whose admiration doubtless enriched this period of increasing poverty. On August 12, 1827, Blake died singing of the glories he saw in heaven.

ANALYSIS

William Blake's focus is primarily on inner states; the drama of the later books has been called a *psychomachia*, a drama of the divided psyche. In Blake's world, humankind was once integrated but suffered a Fall when reason sought to dominate the other faculties. The disequilibrium of the psyche, its reduced perception, is the creator of the natural world as it is now known.

**CONTRARIES**

The notion of "contraries" as defined and developed in *The Marriage of Heaven and Hell* provides a dialectical basis for the regeneration of this psyche. Contraries are to be understood as psychic or mental opposites that exist in a regenerated state, a redeemed paradisiacal state of unlimited energy and unbounded perception. Blake has in his total work depicted the progress to regeneration based on a conflict between contraries. Once contraries are accepted, energy is created, progress is inevitable, and reintegration occurs.

Blake's paradisiacal man differs from fallen man only in that he is aware of his divinity. Paradisiacal man perceives the majesty of the imagination, the passions, the reason, and the senses. The imagination in the redeemed state is called Urthona, and after the Fall, Los. Urthona represents that fourfold, unbounded vision that is the normal attribute of the redeemed man. Such vision is not bound by the particulars it produces through contraction, nor is it bound by the unity it perceives when it expands. Blake, in the imagination's true and saving role as poet, envisions the external world with a fourfold vision. Luvah, the passions or love, is represented after the Fall by Jesus, who puts on the robes of love to preserve some hint of divine love in the fallen world. Urizen, the zoa of reason, is the necessary boundary of energy, the wisdom that supplied form to the energies released by the other contraries. In the fallen world, he is the primary usurper of the dominion of other faculties. Tharmas, the zoa of the senses, has, in his paradisiacal form, unrestrained capacity to expand or contract his senses. In the fallen state, these senses remain but in an enervated condition. Sexuality, the sense of touch shared by two, is a means by which fallen man can regain his paradisiacal stature, but it is unfortunately a suppressed sense. The Blakean Fall that all the personified contraries suffer is a Fall from the divine state to the blind state, to the state in which none of their powers are free to express themselves beyond the severe limitations of excessive reason. Each of the contraries has his allotted place in the Fall; each sins either through commission or omission.

Contraries remain a concern of Blake from *The Marriage of Heaven and Hell* to the later prophecies: *The Four Zoas*, *Milton*, and *Jerusalem*. The metaphysic of contraries, the theoretical doctrine, is never denied. The opposition of energy to reason, however, dramatized in the Orc cycle, is no longer Blake's "main act" in the later books. From Night IX in *The Four Zoas* onward, Los, who embodies something akin to the Romantic concept of the sympathetic imagination, becomes the agent of regeneration. It is he who can project himself into the existence of his polar opposite and can accept the existence of that contrary in the act of self-annihilation and consequently forgive. Thus, the theory of contraries has not altered; any contrary can assume a selfhood in conflict with dialectic progression itself. Los preserves the dialectic while Orc maintains a hierarchy.

### INNOCENCE AND EXPERIENCE

Blake's concern with the earthly states of Innocence and Experience, with a fallen body and its contraries, has been associated with religious apocalypse. Blake's apocalypse involves a progression from Innocence to Experience and an acceptance of the contraries in those states. An acceptance of contraries would lead to the destruction of false perception and disequilibrium and eventually to a complete resurrection of the fallen body. Humanity would again possess divine proportions through a progressive development of its own nature rather than through obedience to the supposed laws of an external deity. Through the faculty of imagination, Blake intuits the divinity of humankind, the falseness of society, and the falseness of laws based on societal behavior. He perceives the spiritual essence of humans, displaying therefore a spiritual rather than a rational brand of humanism. Blake's assumption that the human is a fallen god makes his psychology more than a psychology; and it makes his humanism an apocalyptic humanism. His diagnosis of the divided psyche becomes a revelation, and his therapy, an apocalypse. Blake himself dons the mantle of a prophet.

Able to see God and his angels at the age of four, Blake gave precedence in his life to vision over the natural world. He would continue to see through and not with the eye, and what he saw he would draw in bold outline as ineluctable truth. Ultimately, even the heterodoxy of Swedenborgianism was an encroachment on the supremacy of his own contact with the spiritual world. Early inspired by the revolutionary spirit of the times, he continued throughout his life to advocate a psychic revolution within each person that would lead to regeneration.

### ARCHETYPAL THEMES

Blake's mission throughout his work is always apocalyptic, although he creates a political terrain in the Lambeth books (*The [First] Book of Urizen*, *The Book of Ahania*, *The Book of Los*, and *The Song of Los*) and a psychological one in his later prophecies (*The Four Zoas*, *Milton*, and *Jerusalem*). His focus moves from a political-societal revolution of apocalyptic proportions to a psychic, perceptual regeneration of each individual person. It is the regenerated person who can perceive both a unity beyond all diversity and a diversity within that unity.

*Songs of Innocence and of Experience* demonstrates Blake's concern for individual human life, in particular its course from innocence to experience. What are the destructive forces operating early on humans, on their childhoods, which ultimately imprison them and lead to "mind-forged manacles"? In *Songs of Innocence*, a glimpse of energies is uncircumscribed, of what humans were and again could be if they rightly freed themselves from a limited perception and repressed energies.

The later poems, *The Four Zoas*, *Milton*, and *Jerusalem*, are large-scale epics whose focus is a particularly Romantic one—epistemological and ontological transformation. Los, hero of the imagination, is not a hero who affirms the values of a culture, nor are his strengths and virtues uniformly admired by that culture. Like traditional epics, Blake's epics begin in medias res, but because the natural world is usually seen unclearly, it is worthless to speak of its beginning, middle, or end. The reader who enters the world of Blake's epics enters a psychic world, becomes a "mental traveller," and in his purest states reaches heights traditionally reserved for deity in the Judeo-Christian tradition and deities in the epics of Homer and Vergil.

Blake's work is not unconnected with the natural world, but he attempts to bracket out all but the irreducible elements of the archetypal, individual human life. Paradoxically, Blake's work is characterized by less structural context than that of any poet of whom one could readily think; yet that work is such a dramatic reaction to the eighteenth century and such a dramatic revelation of the new Romanticism that it is unrivaled as an intense portrait of both sensibilities.

### HUMANS IMAGINING

In reaction to John Locke's view that the perceiver is separated from the world because of his (or her) incapacity to do more than apprehend the secondary qualities of objects, Blake asserted the supremacy of individual perception. A human perceiving is a human imagining, an act that encompasses the totality of an individual's energies and personality. What is perceived depends on the imaginative act. The world can be construed only imaginatively. Humanity, Blake held, can apprehend the infinity within only through imagination. The London of Blake's poem of that name is a pitiable place because human imagination, human poetic genius, is repressed. London is at every moment available for imaginative transformation; so is every object in the natural world. In this view of imagination, Blake foreshadows Samuel Taylor Coleridge and especially Percy Bysshe Shelley and attacks the rationalism of the eighteenth century. The metaphysics of Francis Bacon, Isaac Newton, and Locke were despicable because they elevated rationality and denied imagination, thus standing in the way of regeneration.

Besides disagreeing with the philosophy and psychology of his own day, Blake criticized traditional religious and aesthetic views. Humanity's fallen perception created the world, not in seven days, but in what became a moment in time. Jesus was a man of revitalized perceptions, and he was fully conscious of his unlimited energies. Jesus was thus a supranatural man, one who had achieved the kind of regeneration that Blake felt it was in every person's power to achieve. In art, Blake applauded the firm outline of Michelangelo and Raphael and despised the indeterminacy of Rubens

and Titian. The artist who apprehended with strong imagination drew boldly because the truth was clearly perceived. Socially and politically, Blake, unlike Coleridge and William Wordsworth, remained unreconciled to the status quo. Blake's revolutionary zeal, most pronounced in the Lambeth books, remained undiminished, urging him to portray error so that it could be cast out. Only Shelley equals Blake's faith in poetic genius to transform the very nature of humanity and thus the very nature of the world humans perceive.

### SONGS OF INNOCENCE AND OF EXPERIENCE

*Songs of Innocence and of Experience* shows "the two contrary states of the human soul." The contraries cited in *The Marriage of Heaven and Hell* are "Attraction and Repulsion, Reason and Energy, Love and Hate. . . ." However, because these songs are not sung outside either Innocence or Experience but from within those states, the contraries are not fully presented in their ideal forms. The songs are from corrupted states and portray disproportionate contraries. Theoretically, each contrary state acts as a corrective to the other, and contraries in the *Songs of Innocence and of Experience* are suggested either in the text of the poem or in the accompanying design.

The introduction song to *Songs of Innocence and of Experience* is a good example not only of Blake's view of the role of Innocence and Experience in regeneration but also of the complexity of these seemingly simple songs. This song manages in its twenty lines to present a transition from absolute sensuous Innocence to a recognition of Experience and finally a transition to a higher state. The first stanza presents an almost complete picture of absolute carefree innocence. The adjective "wild" may imply a condemnation of an aspect of absolute Innocence. Because Blake believed that Experience brings an indispensable consciousness of one's actions so that choice becomes possible, the essential flaw in the state of Innocence is that it does not provide the child with alternatives.

The second stanza of this lyric presents the image of the lamb, a symbol of Christ. The lamb, while creating the image of the Innocence of Christ, also exhibits the equally true image of Christ crucified. It is this symbol of Experience that brings tears to the child, and on a psychological level, the child is emerging from a "wild" unconscious realm to a realm of consciousness, of Experience.

The third stanza presents two interesting additions: The pipe is replaced by human song and the child weeps with joy. The pipe had first produced laughter and then tears, but it is the human voice that elicits the oxymoronic reaction of joyful weeping. It is only in the human form that the attributes of the two contrary states of Innocence and Experience can exist harmoniously. "Piping down the valley wild" had brought unconstrained laughter, while the figure of the Christ-lamb had brought a more tearful vision of Experience; yet in stanza 3, such contrary reactions exist, unresolved but coexistent, as do the contrary states that foster them.

The fourth stanza alludes to the loss of childhood through the disappearance of the child of the poem and implies that the elemental properties of Innocence remain after the departure of the physical state of childhood. By plucking the hollow reed, Blake, the piper and singer, reveals a move toward creation that is fully realized in the last stanza. From the vision of Experience of stanza 2, and the acceptance of the necessary contrary states of Innocence and Experience through their inherent qualities, laughter and tears, presented in stanza 3, Blake has reached the higher plateau of conscious selflessness described in stanzas four and five. Through the act of creation, the conscious selfless act, which intends to give joy to every child, the conscious selflessness of Blake's paradisiacal reintegrated state is achieved.

### THE BOOK OF THEL

In *The Book of Thel*, a young girl in Innocence named Thel is fearful of advancing to a state of Experience. Lily, Cloud, Clay, and Worm, symbols of innocence and experience, try to allay her fears. Experience may contain key contraries in extreme form; it may be the wrath of the father and the restraint of morality and the curtailment of vision, but it is a state that provides Thel her only opportunity of advancement, of completion and eventual salvation. Experience is a necessary step to the "peace and raptures holy" described by the Cloud. Thel, however, surveys the traditional misfortune of Experience—mortality. She finds no meaningful comfort in the Lily's belief that from Experience, from death, one flourishes "in eternal vales." Thel laments the consciousness that is hers when she takes a

trial step into Experience. She finds morality, which represses sexual energy, unbearable. Thus, in spite of the eventual "peace and raptures holy" that Thel can proceed to from a state of Experience, her first look at that state proves too much for her. She flees Experience and consciousness to the vales of Har, the land of superannuated children, described in the poem *Tiriel*; it is a land of unfulfilled innocents who have refused to graduate into the world of Experience. A *Songs of Innocence* poem, "The Lamb," and a *Songs of Experience* poem, "The Tyger," depict the nature of perception in those states and the contraries that abide in each state. The poems may be viewed as "contrary poems."

The questions of the child in "The Lamb" are not the reason's questions but imagination's—questions he can answer because he has perceived the identity of himself, the lamb, and God. The equation is formed thus: The lamb is Christ the lamb; the child is Christ as a child; and the lamb and child are therefore joined by their mutual identity with Christ. In Innocence, all life is perceived as one and holy. Because there are two contrary states of the human soul and "The Lamb" is a product of only one, Innocence, it is not possible to conclude that this poem depicts Blake's paradisiacal state. The vines in the design are twisting about the sapling on both sides of the engraving, indicating in traditional symbolism the importance of going beyond childhood into Experience. If the child-speaker can see all life as one, can imaginatively perceive the whole, he cannot perceive the particularity, the diversity, which makes up that unity, which Experience's reason so meticulously numbers and analyzes. Even as the adult speaker of "The Tyger" can see only a fragmented world that his imagination is too weak to unify, so the child-speaker cannot see the fragments that comprise the world.

The spontaneity and carefree abandon of the lamb in Innocence can in Experience no longer be perceived in the form of a lamb. The perceiver in Experience fears the energy of Innocence and therefore shapes it into a form that his reason has deemed frightening—that of a tiger. This form that the tiger of the poem "The Tyger" possesses is symmetrical, its symmetry lying in its perfect relationship with the energy it contains. It is a "fearful symmetry" only to the perceiver in Experience, who is riddled with the prejudices of Experience, prejudices regarding what is good and what is evil, what is rational and what is irrational, or wild. The moral hierarchy of Experience—good is good and evil is evil—does not permit the perceiver in Experience to perceive a Keatsian "fineness" in the tiger, a marvelous interrelationship of form and energy.

The reader goes back and forth in this poem from a vision of the energies of the unconscious mind to a perception of the boundaries of those energies. It is the mixture of energy and boundary that the speaker-perceiver finds disturbing. The tiger in the first stanza is seen as a burning figure in the night, perhaps symbolizing the burning vibrant passions repressed in the darkened areas of the mind. The tiger perceived by the speaker can live only in the dark because both reason and moral hierarchy have relegated it to that realm. The tiger is, in its energies, in its fire, too great for the conscious mind to accept; yet, like a recurrent nightmare, the tiger burns brightly and cannot be altogether denied. The tiger cannot be quietly integrated into the personality of the speaker-perceiver without doing severe damage to the structure of self carefully fabricated by reason and moral hierarchy. Rather than transform himself, question himself, the speaker-perceiver questions the tiger's creator. What creator could possibly give form to such uncontrollable energy? How can such energy be satisfactorily bounded? The perceiver in Experience assumes that such energy as the tiger represents can be denied only through repression. It cannot be given necessary form; it must be perceived as having a fearful rather than a fine form. This speaker turns questioner and by his questioning reveals his subservience to analytical reason.

The questioner proceeds under the assumption that no creation can be greater than its creator, that in some way the dangerous, fearful energies of the tiger are amenable to that creator, are somehow part of that creator. Where is such a creator to be found? More specifically, where are those burning energies to be found in the spiritual realm? The questioner is already convinced that the creation of the tiger is a presumptuous act and he therefore concludes that Satan is the great presumer. This tiger is, therefore, in the questioner-perceiver's mind, Satan's work, a hellish creation

forged in the fires not of Blake's Hell but of a traditional Hell.

The final questions to be asked are merely rhetorical. The questioner has decided that his creator could never have created the tiger. The creator involved here has dared to create the tiger. There exists here a Manichaean split, a desperate attempt to answer the problem of the existence of evil. Part of humanity has been made by God and that part is good, while Satan has made the evil part of humanity, the part symbolized by the tiger. The only symbol of energy that the questioner-perceiver is prepared to face is that of the lamb. However, while the lamb sufficed in Innocence as representative of certain energies, it is no longer indicative of the growth of energy that is a mature person's in Experience. The tiger of Experience expresses the symbolic balance of energy and reason, fire and form; however, only a perceiver whose energies are brought from Innocence and matured in Experience under the guidance of reason in necessary proportions can perceive that balance. This uncorrupted perceiver can see the child lying down with the tiger, as in "A Little Girl Found." That tiger is the perfect symbol of the balance of contraries and is perceived as such; the tiger of "The Tyger" is also a perfect symbol but improperly perceived.

## THE MARRIAGE OF HEAVEN AND HELL

The raison d'être of the incorporation of all contraries as they are perceived in the two contrary states, Innocence and Experience, is provided in *The Marriage of Heaven and Hell*. It fulfills more than a mere metaphysical role. It is the foundation of Blake's prophecy, the basis not of extended system but of vision. *The Marriage of Heaven and Hell* preserves the whole body of contraries by a relentless attack on all divisive factors. Dualism in all areas is negated and the suppressed half of the fallen body, represented by the suppressed division of contraries, is supported and affirmed in opposition to the deadening voices of the "Angels."

The framework of *The Marriage of Heaven and Hell* is traditional Judeo-Christian religion and morality. Blake completely alters and destroys this traditional structure and replaces it with an equal acceptance of the two contrary states of the human soul and their inherent contraries. Energies that are indigenous to childhood must take their place alongside the necessary contraries of Experience—reason, repulsion, and hate. The traditional moral hierarchy of good over evil allows one state and its contraries to have ascendancy over the other. Blake boldly adopts the standard nomenclature and marries good and evil as true opposites, essential contraries. Both the passive and active traits of humankind's nature are assumed. Rather than an exclusive emphasis on good, as in the Judeo-Christian ethic, or evil, as in sadism, Blake seeks the reintegration of the unity of humans through the opposition of these strategic contraries. Once Blake's doctrine of contraries as presented in *The Marriage of Heaven and Hell* is understood, it becomes clearer what *Songs of Innocence and of Experience* is describing, what the basis of Orc's battle on behalf of energy in the Lambeth books is, and in what way Los preserves the contraries in the later books.

*The Marriage of Heaven and Hell* is a theoretical base for Blake's vision; however, the form of the work is by no means expository. It presents a dialectic of contraries in dialectical form. Blake's dialectic is not a system of reason in the Hegelian sense, not a system leading to an external synthesis and to the creation of new contraries. Blake's dialectic is composed of contraries immanent in the human personality, contraries that do not change but that generate increasing energy.

In the "Argument" section, "keeping the perilous path" refers to primal unity, Blakean primal unity, and means maintaining all contraries. The man in the vale maintains the dialectic between the conscious and unconscious mind. In Blake's view, once the "path is planted," once the Fall has occurred, man must journey forward, through Innocence and Experience to reintegration.

In Plate 3, Blake declares the immanence of contraries within the human personality and denies the moral dualism of the Judeo-Christian ethic. These contraries are not illusory; their opposition is real, but one contrary does not subsume or upset another. No hierarchy is imposed. The energies that are traditionally classified as "good" are not superior to the energies traditionally classified as "evil." Neither is the reverse true, because Blake is no disciple of the Marquis de Sade. In Blake's view, the hierarchy of morality is particularly insidious because it prevents man from espousing contraries and achieving the progression resulting from that act.

In Plate 4, Blake indicates that the contraries transcend the dualism of body and soul. It is the Devil who proclaims the body as the only portion of the soul, and thus Blake's Devil is his hero, his spokesman. This identification of the soul with the observable, physical body, when combined with Blake's notion of progression based on a dialectic of contraries, implies that although the body is a mere portion of the soul, its most debased portion, it is the only medium available to man by which an amplified body, a spiritual body or soul, can be reached. Contraries existing within the body that are perceived in this fallen world are accepted in pursuit of "ideal" or amplified contraries. In Blake's view, the body and its contraries are sacred.

In Plates 5 and 6, Blake's Devil says that energies are too often repressed. The person who represses his energies in turn suppresses the energies of others. Plate 5 begins the "Proverbs of Hell" section. The proverbs are designed to strengthen the imagination of the reader so that the dynamic of contraries is perceived. Once the reader perceives imaginatively the reality of this dynamic, the dynamic is maintained and energy ensues. Ever-increasing energy leads to ever-expanding perception, and perception, for Blake, ultimately determines ontology. The Proverbs of Hell are pithy "consciousness raisers," each demonstrating the dynamic or dialectic of contraries in both content and form.

Plate 11 continues Blake's assault on the priesthood. In Plates 12 and 13, Blake allies himself with the prophets, Isaiah and Ezekiel—voices of "firm persuasion" and "honest indignation." In Plates 14 and 15, Blake describes the creative process that produced *The Marriage of Heaven and Hell*. He further defines the psychic terrain in Plate 16 by presenting two groups, "Prolific" and "Devourer," that can be seen as personified categories incorporating all dichotomies previously discussed in *The Marriage of Heaven and Hell*; Devil-Evil-Energy-Hell are subsumed by the Prolific, and Angel-Good-Reason-Heaven are subsumed by the Devourer. Plates 17 to 20 contain Blake's "fantastic" satirical drama between an Angel and Blake, as Devil. Limited or bounded perception creates a world and an end for itself that a liberated, diabolical perception can alter in the twinkling of an eye. The Angel perceives such a world of error because he has no sense of the dynamic interplay of contraries, no idea that "Opposition is true Friendship."

### THE FRENCH REVOLUTION

Some of the political implications of Blake's doctrines in *The Marriage of Heaven and Hell* are evident in *The French Revolution*. This poem of twenty pages, posthumously published, has no accompanying designs and was written for the radical publisher Joseph Johnson. It is conjectured that by 1791 it was dangerous for an Englishman to express a revolutionary enthusiasm inspired by the French Revolution. In this poem, Blake's own political radicalism is not couched in symbolic terms, and therefore, he may have had second thoughts about printing it and risking imprisonment. Blake chronicles, with ample poetic license, the period in France from June 19 to July 15, when the king's troops were dispersed. Louis XVI and his nobles debate their course of action in the light of the growing revolution outside, and they finally decide to remove the troops surrounding Paris. In Blake's telling, this decision represents a renewed perception on the part of the king and his nobles. The Bastille, a symbol of political repression, consequently falls. In actuality, the Bastille fell before the decision was made to remove the king's troops.

### AMERICA

There is more of what will become Blake's completed mythology in *America* than there is in *The French Revolution*. Besides historical characters such as George Washington, Benjamin Franklin, and Thomas Paine, Blake here introduces Orc and Urizen, personifications of revolutionary energy and reason. In a preludium or preface, Vala, the shadowy female who symbolizes North America, is in chains. Her liberation occurs through her sexual relations with the fiery Orc. To Blake, therefore, a successful American revolution is not only political but also sexual. George III is the Angel of Albion (England) who worships Urizen and Urizen's law of the Ten Commandments. These two attempt to saturate America with their own diseases by sending a plague across the Atlantic to America. However, the plague is countered by the revolutionary zeal of Orc, who replaces the oppressions of Urizen with genuine political and sexual freedom. All Europe is affected by this revolution, but England, seeking the protection of Urizen, hurries to rebuild the gates of repression, the gates of moral good and evil and a dominant rationality.

Blake's Orc, revolutionary energy, successfully counters Urizen ("your reason") just as the French Revolution countered the Ancient Regime. However, the French Revolution lost its revolutionary energy in the tyranny of Napoleonic France. It became obvious to Blake that historical, political solutions—revolutions—could not effect a break in the historical cycle, a break that would be an apocalypse. Thus, in *The Four Zoas*, Orc becomes a destructive force in nature, an opponent of reason totally oblivious to reason's importance on a regenerated scale. Orc becomes as tied to the natural, unregenerated cycle as Vala, the embodiment of the natural process itself.

Although Urizen is easily defeated by Orc in *America*, he remains an important character in Blake's myth. He is at once Nobodaddy, a comical, ridiculous father figure, and the Ancient of Days, depicted with grandeur in the frontispiece to *Europe: A Prophecy*. Urizen represents the urge to structure and systematize, to reduce all to rational terms. In the language of our own day, he recognizes only what can be quantified and, like a good logical positivist, seeks empirical referents to instill meaning in words.

### EUROPE

*Europe* can be viewed as a continuation of *America* in which revolutionary zeal has been replaced by a repressive conservatism that binds both energies and perceptions. The time is the birth of Jesus, a time of possible regeneration through his example. This possibility is not realized and the world falls into a long sleep, an eighteen-hundred-year sleep of Nature. Los, the poetic genius, naïvely rejoices in a promise of peace while Urizen is attempting to rule outside his own domain; and Los's female counterpart, Enitharmon, is a victim of Urizen's dominion and seeks to bind sexual love with moral law. Urizen solidifies his rule, his brazen book of law that ignores imagination, forgiveness, and the necessity of self-annihilation. Edmund Burke and William Pitt, represented by the characters Palamabron and Rintrah, are also under the dominion of Urizen and Enitharmon. The revolutionary spirit of the youth of England is doomed. Pitt-Rintrah three times attempts to lead England to war, into total devastation. In Blake's view, however, Sir Isaac Newton and his system are the real beginning of devastation in England. Newton's blast on the trumpet does not lead to glorious apocalypse but to death-in-life. Enitharmon wakes and calls her perverted children to her—materialism, delusion, hypocrisy, sensualism, and seduction. The poem ends with Orc inspiring the French Revolution, the spirit of which will be challenged by a Urizenic England. Los, the poetic genius, summons his sons to the coming strife, but it is as yet unclear what his precise role will be. That role is defined in *The Four Zoas*, *Milton*, and *Jerusalem*.

### THE [FIRST] BOOK OF URIZEN AND THE BOOK OF LOS

In *The [First] Book of Urizen* and *The Book of Los*, Blake does not present a cryptic intermingling of history and myth but rather a first attempt at describing his cosmogony and theogony. *The Book of Los* tells the story of the Fall from Los's point of view and *The [First] Book of Urizen* from Urizen's point of view. Thus, the texts interconnect and gloss each other. The Fall is a fall into creation, one precipitated by Urizen's desire for painless joy, for laws binding everything, for "One King, one God, one Law." Urizen's usurpation of power is clearly an act of the Selfhood, a condition in which the legitimacy and importance of other energies are not recognized.

Los, as imagination, is the epistemological faculty by which truth or error is perceived. Urizen's revolt on behalf of reason skews perception and plunges Los into the Fall. The world of time and space, the Natural World, is formed by Los, and both Los and Urizen, fallen, are bound to this Natural World. A fall into sexuality follows the fall into materiality. Sexuality is subject to moral constraints. Science is a woven "woof," which is created to hide the void. Orc is born but his youthful exuberance is bound by the perversions of the Net of Religion, a direct product of the perverted dream of Reason. Urizen explores the dens of the material world and observes the shrunken nature of a humanity that has completely forgotten its eternal life.

### THE SONG OF LOS

*The Song of Los* can be viewed as the mythological framework for *America* and *Europe*. The first part of Los's song, "Africa," recounts history leading up to George III Guardian Prince of Albion's war against the Americans, as depicted in *America*. What exists here is also a historical counterpart to the mythology presented in *The [First] Book of Urizen* and *The Book of Los*. Dark delusion was given Moses on Sinai; abstract law to Pythagoras, Socrates, and Plato; a wretched gospel to Jesus; and the reprehensible Philosophy of the Five Senses to Newton and Locke. The second section, "Asia," is a continuation of *Europe*; it does not speak of events but of the psychological-physiological consequences of Urizen's reign. King, Priest, and Counsellor can only restrain, dismay, and ruin humanity in the service of Urizen. Orc rages over France, but the earth seems too shrunken, humankind too imprisoned to heed. Again, Orc himself, as revolutionary energy, is a questionable savior as he is described as a serpent. The energy of the French Revolution had become debased, and although Blake hoped for a renewal of its original energies, he was already too skeptical of revolution to present Orc as a hero.

### THE BOOK OF AHANIA

*The Book of Ahania* takes its name from Urizen's female counterpart or emanation, who comes into existence when Fuzon, an Orc-like figure, battles Urizen. Urizen immediately calls Ahania sin, hides her, and suffers jealousy. Ahania becomes the "mother of Pestilence," the kind of pestilence that is a result of a sexuality restrained by the moral law. Urizen's mind, totally victimized by a repressive rationality and the resulting morality, breeds monsters. From the blood of one of these monsters, Urizen forms a bow and shoots a rock at Fuzon, killing him. Fuzon is pictured as a revolutionary who has assumed the seat of tyranny previously occupied by Urizen. Urizen nails Fuzon to a tree, an act that imitates the death of Christ, Christ as rebel. Fuzon dies because he has not broken the material cycle and is thus vulnerable to the repressive laws of the material world. In the same fashion, the creators of the French Revolution failed to achieve a significant ontological and epistemological revolution and therefore became ensnared once again in nets of mystery that led to the

Reign of Terror. Fuzon and the French Revolutionaries achieve no true revolution and fall victim to the "black rock" formed by a mind whose energies are repressed in the name of reason and its countless offshoots.

### VISIONS OF THE DAUGHTERS OF ALBION

One of the ways to Blakean regeneration is through sexuality, specifically through a reassimilation of the female emanation and the re-creation of the Edenic androgynous body. In *Visions of the Daughters of Albion*, Oothoon is a female emanation; Theotormon is her male counterpart and a victim of a repressive moral code; Bromion is a spokesman of that code. Sexually, Oothoon represents the Prolific; the Devourer equivalent, the opposing sexual nature, must be created in Experience. Jerusalem, in the poem *Jerusalem*, becomes that female emanation cognizant of the nature of the regenerated, androgynous body, and she has gained that knowledge in Experience.

Oothoon is raped by Bromion, and Theotormon treats her like a harlot because she has been raped. Oothoon's imagination gives her a vision of her intrinsic sexual nature. Her vision is of the body, the sexual body no less, a body that is not distinct from the soul. In her newfound identity, Oothoon tries to bring Theotormon to the same vision, tries to bring him beyond the moral categories; but Theotormon demands a rational proof for all living things. Why, he asks implicitly, should he believe Oothoon is pure when the moral code clearly states that she is not pure? Bromion declares that only what can be perceived by the five senses has merit. Oothoon attacks priests and their restraining moral ethic but finally gives up trying to win Theotormon to her newly liberated vision. Her comprehension of the warped picture of sexuality in Experience as demonstrated by Theotormon and Bromion causes her to conclude that Experience has nothing to offer. Although she is not blinded regarding her own sexual nature, she is unable to reunite with Theotormon, male sexuality, and is denied a vision of sexuality based on energies of both Innocence and Experience. Thus, sexual relations, androgyny, and regeneration are denied both Oothoon and Theotormon.

### THE FOUR ZOAS

*The Four Zoas* is an unengraved poem written in two overlapping stages. The main characters, Luvah, Urizen, Tharmas, and Urthona, are the "zoas" of the human personality, each representing an inherent, indivisible quality of the human personality. However, these characters are true characters and not mere allegorical representations. *The Four Zoas* is Blake's account of a split in the Edenic personality of Man, called Albion, of a Fall into the cycle of the natural world, and of the labors of Los, the imagination, to reunite and regenerate the four zoas. This poem is both a historical drama inevitably unfolded in time and space and a psychological drama, one in which time and space have no validity. As a historical drama, the poem lends itself to the kinds of historical connections made in *Europe* or *America*, but this is not a consistent base from which to read the poem, nor will expectations of a conventional narrative structure be at all fruitful.

The poem begins when Luvah and Vala rush from the loins and into the heart and on to the brain, where they replace Urizen's ordering of the body's life with their own cyclical, generative ordering. This sleeping man, Albion, who has within him the whole world—the powers to contract and expand—wakes up in Night VIII of the poem. Albion was asleep because he was in repose in Beulah, a state of threefold perception between Eden (fourfold perception) and Generation (twofold perception). To be in Beulah is to be at rest from the dynamic interplay of contraries of Eden, Blake's paradisiacal state. The aura of Eden pervades Beulah but the threat of the lower state, Generation, is always present. A fall into a reduced perception is always imminent. In *The Four Zoas*, that fall occurs. The fall into Generation is a fall into the natural world; it is Blake's version of the biblical Fall.

In the state of Generation, Urizen declares himself God; the "mundane shell," the material world, is built, and Jesus appears and is sacrificed so that regeneration can become possible. Jesus is identified with Luvah, love; with Orc, revolutionary energy battling Urizen in the Lambeth Books; and with Albion, Universal Man. Under Jesus's inspiration, Los perceives the errors of the Fall and begins to build Jerusalem, a spiritual freedom in which regeneration is possible. From Night IX in *The Four Zoas* onward into *Milton* and *Jerusalem*, Los, who embodies something akin to the Romantic concept of sympathetic imagination, becomes the agent of regeneration. It is Los who can project himself into the existence of his contrary, can accept the existence of that contrary in the act of "self-annihilation," and can consequently forgive. Thus, in the later books, the theory of contraries is not altered; any contrary can assume a selfhood in conflict with dialectical progression itself. Los preserves the dialectic, while Orc maintains a hierarchy—"saviour" and "villain."

### MILTON

The historical John Milton is revived in Blake's *Milton* so that he can experience a personal self-annihilation that leads to the incorporation of his Spectre, Satan. Blake's Milton is a Milton of energy and imagination, a Milton determined to correct his view (expressed in *Paradise Lost*, 1667, 1674) that love "hath his seat in Reason." Through self-annihilation, Blake's Milton acknowledges the validity of Reason, his Spectre. Once Milton is united with his Spectre, he can preach effectively to the public. The repression of the reasoning power is peculiar only to the Blakean "heroes," such as Blake's Milton. Outside this Blakean world, in the world of Innocence and Experience, the reasoning power is not repressed but assumes the role of usurper, a faculty of mind that has overridden the powers of all other faculties. Reason as Blake perceived it in the eighteenth century was in complete control. It is this unrepressed, dominant, reasoning power that Milton calls a "Negation." The reasoning power that Blake's Milton finally accepts is reason as Spectre, not as Negation, reason in its Edenic proportions.

An act of self-annihilation also precipitates the union of female emanation and the fallen male principle. Blake's Milton is reconciled with his emanation, Ololon. What Blake's Milton undergoes here becomes a precedent for what Los and other contraries will undergo. In annihilating his Selfhood, the Los-Blake-Devil Selfhood, Blake's Milton shows that reason is a necessary contrary, that man is not ruled by energies alone. The Spectre as reason has been accepted and Blake's Milton attains an expanded perception. His emanation perceives her power fade. In "delighting in his delight," they are again one in sexuality.

Blake's Milton enables the contraries to be saved, enables a dynamic interplay of contraries once again to take place. In contrast, Orc's obdurate maintenance of his own Selfhood and his denial of Urizen's reality in any proportions did not preserve Edenic contraries and could not therefore lead to regeneration. Blake's Milton achieves self-annihilation through forgiveness, itself based on the imagination. It is Los, the imagination, who perceives the dialectic of contraries and recognizes the message of continued forgiveness. It is Los, the imagination, who is employed by each contrary in recognition of its polar opposite.

### JERUSALEM

In *Jerusalem*, Los and the Spectre of Urthona take center stage. Los addresses his Spectre as "my Pride & Self-righteousness," indicating that the Spectre's presence tends to affirm Los's obdurate Selfhood. Throughout *Jerusalem*, the reader witnesses a "compensatory" relationship between the Spectre and Los, although the Spectre seems to be "watching his time with glowing eyes to leap upon his prey." In Chapter IV, Los ends this struggle with his Spectre by accepting it. Once Los, identified here with Blake, becomes one with his Spectre, he appears to Albion, fallen humankind, in the form of Jesus and preaches forgiveness based on imaginative identification and self-annihilation. Jesus-Los annihilates himself before Albion and thus points to the necessary destruction of the Selfhood. Overwhelmed by this act, imaginatively caught in Jesus-Los's sacrifice, the albatross drops from Albion's neck, and it is the Selfhood. This is the apocalyptic moment when Albion, like the phoenix, descends to the flames and rises anew. Regeneration is intimately connected with self-annihilation, as it was in *Milton*.

Albion's emanation, Jerusalem, is also spiritual freedom. A reassimilation of Jerusalem generates a climate of freedom in which contraries can interact. Jerusalem as an emanation is beyond morality. She represents the whole of life, but a fallen Albion applies "one law" to her. Because of this application of a rigid "one law," a rigid hierarchical ethic, Jerusalem is separated from Albion. A female emanation repressed becomes a tyrant. Blake gives readers a close view of this "proud Virgin-Harlot," whom he calls Vala. The Vala whom Blake presents is corrupt, since she stands for restraint in all areas, especially moral, as opposed to Jerusalem-as-liberty. The Vala figure, advocate of a repressive morality, both tempts and lures, and also upholds the sense of sin. She thus becomes woman-as-tyrant. She is the femme fatale who incites desire but never acts. Such a morality turns love into prostitution, the free lover into a prostitute.

Again, Los, the imagination, perceives the validity of Jesus's word to Jerusalem regarding forgiveness, annihilation, and regeneration. Los applies what he has learned, unites with his own Spectre, and sends him forth to preach the methods of regeneration—forgiveness and self-annihilation. Albion regains his Jerusalem; spiritual freedom once again exists; and England itself has apocalyptically become Jerusalem, the city of God.

### OTHER MAJOR WORKS

LONG FICTION: *To the Public: Prospectus*, 1793; *An Island in the Moon*, 1987 (wr. c. 1784).

NONFICTION: *A Descriptive Catalogue*, 1809.

ILLUSTRATIONS AND ENGRAVINGS: *The Complaint and the Consolation: Or, Night Thoughts, by Edward Young*, 1797; *Blair's Grave*, 1808; *The Prologue and Characters of Chaucer's Pilgrims*, 1812; *The Pastorals of Virgil*, 1821; *Illustrations of the Book of Job*, 1825; *Illustrations of Dante*, 1827.

### BIBLIOGRAPHY

Ackroyd, Peter. *Blake: A Biography*. New York: Alfred A. Knopf, 1996. A penetrating biography of the poet.

Beer, John. *William Blake: A Literary Life*. New York: Palgrave Macmillan, 2005. This biography traces Blake's life, offering commentary on his religious background and painting a clear picture of the complexity of his poetry as well as his visual artistry.

Bloom, Harold, ed. *William Blake*. New York: Chelsea House, 2008. A collection of essays on Blake that examine his poetry, including *Jerusalem*, *Milton*, and *The Four Zoas*.

Bruder, Helen P. *William Blake and the Daughters of Albion*. New York: St. Martin's Press, 1997. Bruder's overt concern is with issues of "women, sexuality, gender, and sexual difference," but her book is perhaps better regarded as a reassessment of Blake's relation to popular culture. Bruder presents a thorough and astute reception history. Includes a bibliography and an index.

_____, ed. *Women Reading William Blake*. New York: Palgrave Macmillan, 2007. A collection of critical essays analyzing Blake's poetry from a feminist criticism perspective.

Frye, Northrop. *Fearful Symmetry: A Study of William Blake*. Princeton, N.J.: Princeton University Press, 1947. Frye interprets Blake's myth in terms of archetypal symbolic structures, which he also finds underlying much Western literature and mythology. Almost all later writers have been indebted to Frye, although some contemporary Blake critics are wary of being too captured by his ideas.

Lindsay, David W. *Blake: Songs of Innocence and Experience*. London: Macmillan, 1989. A very informative, if brief, introduction that examines a range of critical approaches to *Songs of Innocence and of Experience*. Lindsay's impartial discussions of different interpretations of selected poems will be useful for readers who want a concise survey of the field. The second part of the book gives attention to eight *Songs of Experience* in the context of Blake's other works. Includes bibliography.

Percival, Milton O. *William Blake's Circle of Destiny*. 1938. Reprint. New York: Octagon Books, 1977. This introduction to Blake's prophetic books has stood the test of time. Percival demonstrates that Blake's myth was firmly rooted in a traditional body of thought that included Neoplatonism, Kabala, alchemy, Gnosticism, and individual thinkers such as Jakob Böhme, Paracelsus, Emanuel Swedenborg, and Plotinus.

Roberts, Jonathan. *William Blake's Poetry: A Reader's Guide*. New York: Continuum, 2007. Provides keys to understanding the meaning of Blake's poetry and the complex images therein.

*Joseph Natoli*

# EDMUND BLUNDEN

**Born:** London, England; November 1, 1896
**Died:** Long Melford, Suffolk, England; January 20, 1974

PRINCIPAL POETRY

*Poems*, 1914
*The Harbingers*, 1916
*Pastorals*, 1916
*The Waggoner, and Other Poems*, 1920
*The Shepherd, and Other Poems of Peace and War*, 1922
*To Nature: New Poems*, 1923
*English Poems*, 1925
*Masks of Time: A New Collection of Poems, Principally Meditative*, 1925
*Retreat*, 1928
*Undertones of War*, 1928 (poetry and prose)
*Near and Far: New Poems*, 1930
*The Poems of Edmund Blunden, 1914-1930*, 1930
*To Themis: Poems on Famous Trials, with Other Pieces*, 1931
*Halfway House: A Miscellany of New Poems*, 1932
*Choice or Chance: New Poems*, 1934
*An Elegy, and Other Poems*, 1937
*Poems, 1930-1940*, 1940
*Shells by a Stream: New Poems*, 1944
*After the Bombing, and Other Short Poems*, 1949
*Poems of Many Years*, 1957
*A Hong Kong House*, 1962
*Eleven Poems*, 1965
*Selected Poems*, 1982
*Overtones of War*, 1996

OTHER LITERARY FORMS

The reputation of Edmund Blunden as a major British poet is founded primarily, and perhaps unfairly, on the poems he wrote about his service in World War I. Similarly, his popular prose works were connected to his wartime experiences. His most famous prose work, *Undertones of War* (1928), which includes a section of poems at the end, is one of the least vituperative of postwar British memoirs. Blunden's wartime experiences also featured prominently in the novel *We'll Shift Our Ground: Or, Two on a Tour* (1933), written in collaboration with Sylva Norman, in which two central characters visit the former battlefields of Flanders.

In contrast to his poetry and popular prose, Blunden's scholarly writing consisted primarily of biographies of important British literary figures—including Percy Bysshe Shelley, Lord Byron, and Charles Lamb—and rather impressionistic literary criticism. His scholarly approach was to focus on an author's life to understand his or her writings. Toward this end, Blunden wrote studies of a wide variety of major English poets, including the seventeenth century poet Henry Vaughan (1927), the Romantic poets Leigh Hunt (1930) and Shelley (1946), the Romantic essayist Lamb (1933), the early modern poet and novelist Thomas Hardy (1942), and fellow World War I poet Wilfred Owen (1931).

ACHIEVEMENTS

Edmund Blunden's formal honors had little to do with his war poetry. In 1950, for example, Blunden was elected an honorary member of the Japan Academy, mainly for his educational work with the United Kingdom Liaison Mission in Tokyo after World War II. In 1963, the Japanese government awarded Blunden the Order of the Rising Sun, Third Class. Blunden's greatest honor had to do with his work in education and criticism: In 1966, he was elected Professor of Poetry at Oxford.

BIOGRAPHY

Although he was born in London, Edmund Charles Blunden's early years were spent in Yalding, a small English village, where his father was employed as a schoolmaster. For the next thirteen years, Blunden's experience of life was formed in Yalding, where the age-old rhythms of agriculture held sway. In 1909, Blunden entered Christ College, a public school in London. Already endowed with both scholarly interests and a desire to write, Blunden won the Senior Classics scholarship to Queen's College, Oxford, in 1914. As it did for many in his generation, World War I interrupted Blunden's further studies.

In 1915, Blunden earned a commission in the Royal Sussex Regiment and was in active service until 1917.

Although two books of his poetry were accepted for publication before enlisting—*The Harbingers* and *Pastorals*—Blunden developed his poetic voice during active service. After the war and a brief stint at Oxford, he soon joined the staff of the *Athenaeum*, a literary journal. For most of the next four decades, Blunden's work life oscillated between literary journalism and teaching. For instance, a teaching post at Merton College, Oxford, lasted from 1931 to 1941 and was immediately followed by a job with the *Times Literary Supplement*, from 1941 to 1947.

From 1947 until his retirement in 1964, Blunden lived in Asia, first working in Japan and later taking a professorship of English literature at the University of Hong Kong. In 1966, after returning to England, Blunden was elected Professor of Poetry at Oxford University, a post he almost rejected because of ill health. By the early 1970's, the long-term effects of his war wounds forced him to retire from active life. He died in Long Melford, Suffolk, England, on January 20, 1974.

ANALYSIS

In *Heroes' Twilight* (1965, 1996), a study of World War I literature, the critic Bernard Bergonzi emphasizes the literariness of the average British officer, who "had received a classical education and [was] very well read in English poetry, so that [William] Shakespeare and [John] Milton, [William] Wordsworth and [John] Keats would be constantly quoted or alluded to when they wrote about the war." However true this observation may be of others, it is perfectly suited to Edmund Blunden. Blunden was the epitome of the well-educated, humane, and literary-minded British officer of World War I. Support for this argument comes in Blunden's *Undertones of War* when Blunden's commanding officer summons him to headquarters to express his admiration on learning that a published author serves under him. The respect accorded poetry is almost unbelievable until one considers Bergonzi's further point about the value of poetry during the war. Poetry provided "a sense of identity and continuity, a means of accommodating to life in a bizarre world as well as a source of consolation." As a form of shared experience and as a form of therapy, poetry helped

many British soldiers endure the barbaric conditions they faced.

In the 1960's, Bergonzi pointed out that Blunden could be distinguished from his contemporaries by "the intensity of his absorption in the countryside." Blunden was almost always considered a nature poet; that is, his interest lay in representing the interconnection between humans and the natural world. The critical status of nature poetry varies greatly over time; correspondingly, Blunden's critical reputation also varied. During the late 1920's and early 1930's, he was compared unfavorably to more experimental poets like T. S. Eliot and Ezra Pound; in the mid-1960's, his poetry seemed hopelessly old-fashioned to many Oxford University undergraduates, who vocally opposed his candidacy for Professor of Poetry. It is questionable whether either set of critics truly understood the value of nature for Blunden. Nature was to Blunden a complex and compelling subject for poetry.

**NATURE AS THE ART OF GOD**

The strongest of Blunden's reasons for writing nature poetry was to convey his deep love for the English countryside. As Bergonzi points out, "He knows the country with a deep knowledge and a deep love and it pervades the whole structure of his mind and feelings." This sense of deep intermingling of nature and the human mind is central to Blunden's poetry. In another critical study of Blunden's work, Thomas Mallon makes the same point, writing, "Poetry's chief task in describing nature [is] to capture its spirit, to communicate those feelings it gave to man." In a public address, Blunden endorsed the belief that "Nature hath made one World, and Art another. In brief, all things are artificial; for Nature is the Art of God." Thus, through his poetry Blunden could posit himself within this process of creation and understand more deeply the proper relationship of human beings, nature, and God. Seen in this way, Blunden's poetry is classifiable in terms of a series of interpenetrations of human beings and nature: the effect of nature on the human being, the effects of war on nature, the effect of war on humanity, and, finally, the effect of humans on nature.

**POEMS, 1914-1930**

This collection of previously published works contains some of Blunden's earliest and most accessible poems. Blunden often offered a straightforward view of nature as therapy for suffering humanity, particularly those who are facing death during war. In "The Pagoda," the speaker dwells on the crumbled building and the animals that inhabit it:

> The small robin reconnoitres,
> Unabashed the woodmouse loiters:
> Brown owls hoot at shadow-fall
> And deathwatch ticks and beetles drone.

Apart from a few suggestive words such as "reconnoiters," there is little to suggest that the speaker is in active service during wartime. Blunden pointed out, however, that the poem was provoked by a visit to "some château in ruins" near the front. It is characteristic of much of his earlier poetry that war should be almost entirely absent; for nature to provide therapy, it must first allow the sufferer to distance himself or herself from the war.

As Blunden puts it in "Bleue Maison," the speaker longs to

> attune [his] dull soul, . . .
> To the contentment of this countryside
> Where man is not for ever killing man
> But quiet days like these calm waters glide.

This poetic landscape is described in blissful terms that become even more clear as the speaker continues:

> And I will praise the blue flax in the rye,
> And pathway bindweed's trumpet-like attire,
> Pink rest-harrow and curlock's glistening eye,
> And poppies flaring like St. Elmo's fire.

There is little sense in this poem that nature here has suffered from the war; in fact, the landscape of "Bleue Maison" is almost unaffected by the war.

A similar sense of nature as a place of spiritual healing is presented in "Mont de Cassel," although the frightful fact of the war does intrude on this speaker's consciousness:

> Here on the sunnier scarp of the hill let us rest,
> And hoard the hastening hour
> Find a mercy unexpressed
> In the chance wild flower.

The mercy that the speaker seeks is unexpressed, unvoiced, but still present. In fact, as the speaker later puts it, the merciful therapy provided by the flower and "other things so small and unregarded" reduces the war to "a leering ghost now shriven."

Blunden frequently returned to the concept of nature as a place of healing in his poetry, yet many of his later poems present a different sense of the interpenetration of the natural and the human worlds. In some of his later poems, particularly those written after World War I, Blunden describes nature as scarred and suffering. In this second sense of the overall theme, Blunden shows the effect of war on nature. By "nature," Blunden does not mean untamed wilderness, but rather landscape and the plants and creatures that cling to existence in the face of human destructiveness.

### THE SHEPHERD, AND OTHER POEMS OF PEACE AND WAR

In *The Shepherd, and Other Poems of Peace and War*, published in 1922, Blunden's emphasis on the effect of war on nature is stated both clearly and emphatically. For instance, in the short work "A Farm Near Zillebeke," a rural home becomes a casualty of the war:

> The Line is all hushed—on a sudden anon
> The fool bullets clack and guns mouth again.
> I stood in the yard of a house that must die,
> And still the black hame was stacked by the door,
> And harness still hung there, and the dray waited by.

The depersonalization of the soldiers, "The Line," contrasts with the humanized "house that must die." In a poetic gesture reaching back to the Romantic period, Blunden uses the landscape to underscore the emotional significance of the moment.

This technique, called the pathetic fallacy by Samuel Taylor Coleridge and others, appears in another poem from the same collection, "1916 Seen from 1921." This poem turns on a central irony: The speaker, who has survived the war, is hardly alive spiritually. It is strongly implied that the speaker suffers from a form of guilt that is common in people who have survived harrowing and deadly experiences. Those who survived the war often felt guilty for living and would fruitlessly wonder why they lived on while so many others died. In this poem, the speaker clearly manifests this guilt:

Dead as the men I loved, [I] wait while life drags

Its wounded length from those sad streets of war
Into green places here . . .

The speaker implies that he was most alive during active service. The intensity of life during wartime cannot be replicated in peacetime, and the speaker cannot find solace in nature. The green places once "were my own;/ But now what once was mine is mine no more." The sense of guilt shouts down the voice of nature: "the charred stub outspeaks the living tree."

### UNDERTONES OF WAR

At the end of his prose memoir of the war, *Undertones of War*, Blunden included a series of poems, most of which were published between 1918 and 1928. In them, Blunden clearly demonstrates the effect that war has had on human beings. As in "1916 Seen from 1921," survivor's guilt figures prominently in some poems, but not all. In poems like "II Peter ii 22," Blunden offers a thoroughly negative representation of the postwar world to the returning veteran. In this poem, the speaker castigates a society in which "slinking Slyness rules the roost/ And brags and pimps" and in which

Quarrel with her hissing tongue
And hen's eye gobbles gross along
    To snap that prey
    That marched away
To save her carcass, better hung.

To this observer, the postwar society is corrupt and little understands or appreciates the sacrifices that World War I demanded of the British soldier.

### "AT THE GREAT WALL OF CHINA"

If society ignores the sacrifice of the soldier, Blunden certainly did not. In the later poem "At the Great Wall of China," published in *Poems of Many Years* in 1927, the poet describes the wall clearly and concisely, pointing out its structure and fortifications, yet finds himself thinking more about the lonely sentry who stood guard long ago:

But I half know at this bleak turret here,
In snow-dimmed moonlight where sure answers quail,
This new-set sentry of a long-dead year,
This boy almost, trembling lest he may fail
To espy the ruseful raiders, and his mind
Torn with sharp love of the home left far behind.

Understanding Blunden's life, it is tempting to interpret this poem as a disguised representation of his own feelings while standing guard in the trenches of the western front. However, the import of this poem is more universal: Its overall sense is to convey the tragedy of war in compelling human terms and to offer nature as solace, victim, and alternative.

### OTHER MAJOR WORKS

LONG FICTION: *We'll Shift Our Ground: Or, Two on a Tour*, 1933 (with Sylvia Norman).

NONFICTION: *The Bonadventure: A Random Journal of an Atlantic Holiday*, 1922; *On the Poems of Henry Vaughan: Characteristics and Imitations*, 1927; *Undertones of War*, 1928 (poetry and prose); *Leigh Hunt and His Circle*, 1930; *Charles Lamb and His Contemporaries*, 1932; *Votive Tablets*, 1932; *The Mind's Eye*, 1934; *Edward Gibbon and His Age*, 1935; *English Villages*, 1941; *Shelley: A Life Story*, 1947.

EDITED TEXT: *The Poems of Wilfred Owen*, 1931.

### BIBLIOGRAPHY

Barlow, Adrian. *The Great War in British Literature.* New York: Cambridge University Press, 2000. Although intended more for the student reader, this short book does an effective job of covering the major issues faced by British writers like Vera Brittain, Robert Graves, Richard Aldington, and Blunden.

Bergonzi, Bernard. *Heroes' Twilight: A Study of the Literature of the Great War.* 1965. Reprint. Manchester, England: Carcanet Press, 1996. Bergonzi's book was one of the first critical studies of its subject written for the nonacademic. This work postulates that British writers represented the war in terms of a "complex fusion of tradition and unprecedented reality."

Cross, Tim, ed. *Lost Voices of World War I.* Iowa City: University of Iowa Press, 1990. A moving anthology of poetry and other short works by writers who were killed in the conflict. It includes a fine introduction by Robert Wohl, a leading scholar of modernism, who offers valuable insight into how Blunden's British contemporaries felt about literature and the role it plays in society.

Hibbard, Dominic. *The First World War.* London:

Macmillan, 1990. This work offers a chronological study of the war seen through the eyes of the writers who represented it at the time and much later. Generally, Hibbard does not focus much attention on Blunden, although he does point out that writers were far from univocal in their treatment of the war; responses ranged from the kind produced by Blunden to the gossipy cynicism and outrage of Robert Graves and Siegfried Sassoon.

McPhail, Helen, and Philip Guest. *Edmund Blunden.* Barnsley, South Yorkshire, England: Cooper, 1999. A biography of Blunden that examines his life and works, focusing on his war writings.

Mallon, Thomas. *Edmund Blunden.* Boston: Twayne, 1983. Like other works in the Twayne series, this study of Blunden is a fine starting point for general readers who are unfamiliar with the poet or his poetry.

Scupham, Peter. "Edmund Blunden." In *British Writers: Supplement XI*, edited by Jay Parini. New York: Charles Scribner's Sons, 2006. A basic biography and analysis of Blunden's works.

Webb, Barry. *Edmund Blunden: A Biography.* New Haven, Conn.: Yale University Press, 1990. This biography goes into great detail about the difficulties he faced in finding suitable work and domestic happiness. The general picture that emerges is of a thoroughly decent, kindly man who made the best of the worst possible experiences.

*Michael R. Meyers*

---

# EAVAN BOLAND

**Born:** Dublin, Ireland; September 24, 1944

PRINCIPAL POETRY

*Twenty-three Poems*, 1962
*New Territory*, 1967
*The War Horse*, 1975
*In Her Own Image*, 1980
*Introducing Eavan Boland*, 1981 (reprint of *The War Horse* and *In Her Own Image*)

*Night Feed*, 1982
*The Journey, and Other Poems*, 1983
*Selected Poems*, 1989
*Outside History: Selected Poems, 1980-1990*, 1990
*In a Time of Violence*, 1994
*Collected Poems*, 1995 (pb. in U.S. as *An Origin Like Water: Collected Poems, 1967-1987*, 1996)
*The Lost Land*, 1998
*Against Love Poetry*, 2001
*Code*, 2001
*Three Irish Poets*, 2003 (with Paula Meehan and Mary O'Malley; Boland, editor)
*New Collected Poems*, 2005
*Domestic Violence*, 2007
*New Collected Poems*, 2008

OTHER LITERARY FORMS

Eavan Boland (BOW-lahnd) collaborated with Micheál Mac Liammóir on the critical study *W. B. Yeats and His World* (1971). Boland has contributed essays in journals such as the *American Poetry Review*; she also has reviewed for the *Irish Times* and has published a volume of prose called *Object Lessons: The Life of the Woman and the Poet in Our Time* (1995). With Mark Strand, she prepared the anthology *The Making of a Poem: A Norton Anthology of Poetic Forms* (2000).

ACHIEVEMENTS

Ireland has produced a generation of distinguished poets since 1960, and the most celebrated of them have been men. Of this group of poets, Seamus Heaney is the best known to American audiences, but the reputations of Thomas Kinsella, Derek Mahon, Michael Longley, Paul Muldoon, and Tom Paulin continue to grow. Poetry by contemporary Irishwomen is also a significant part of the Irish literary scene. Eavan Boland is one of a group of notable women poets including Medbh Mc-Guckian, Eithne Strong, and Eiléan Ní Chuilleanáin. In an essay published in 1987, "The Woman Poet: Her Dilemma," Boland indicates her particular concern with the special problems of being a woman and a poet. Male stereotypes about the role of women in society continue to be very strong in Ireland and make Irish-women less confident about their creative abilities. Women also must contend with another potentially de-personalizing pressure, that of feminist ideology, which urges women toward another sort of conformity. Boland and the other female Irish poets previously mentioned have managed to overcome both obstacles and develop personal voices.

Boland has served as a member of the board of the Irish Arts Council and a member of the Irish Academy of Letters. Her honors and awards include the American Ireland Fund Literary Award (1994), the Lannan Literary Award for Poetry (1994), the Bucknell Medal of Distinction from Bucknell University (2000), the Smartt Family Foundation Prize for *Against Love Poetry*, the John Frederick Nims Memorial Prize from *Poetry* magazine (2002), the John William Corrington Award for Literary Excellence from Centenary College of Louisiana (2002-2003), and the James Boatwright III Prize for Poetry from *Shenandoah* (2006) for "Violence Against Women."

*Eavan Boland* (Allison Otto/Courtesy, Stanford Daily)

## BIOGRAPHY

Eavan Boland was born on September 24, 1944, in Dublin, Ireland. Her parents were Frederick Boland and Frances Kelly Boland. Her father was a distinguished Irish diplomat who served as Irish ambassador to Great Britain (1950-1956) and to the United States (1956-1964). Her mother was a painter who had studied in Paris in the 1930's. Boland's interest in painting as a subject for poetry can be traced to her mother's encouragement. Because of her father's diplomatic career, Boland was educated in Dublin, London, and New York. From 1962 to 1966, she attended Trinity College, Dublin; beginning in 1967, she taught at Trinity College for a year. In 1968, she received the Macauley Fellowship for poetry.

In the 1980's, Boland reviewed regularly for the arts section of the *Irish Times*. In 1987, she held a visiting fellowship at Bowdoin College. She married Kevin Casey, a novelist, with whom she had two children: Sarah, born in 1975, and Eavan, born in 1978.

Boland began writing poetry in Dublin in the early 1960's. She recalls this early period: ". . . scribbling poems in boarding school, reading [William Butler]

Yeats after lights out, revelling in the poetry on the course. . . . Dublin was a coherent space then, a small circumference in which to . . . become a poet. . . . The last European city. The last literary smallholding." After her marriage, Boland left the academic world and moved into the suburbs of Dublin to become "wife, mother, and housewife." *In Her Own Image* and *Night Feed* focus on Boland's domestic life in the suburbs and especially on her sense of womanhood. In the 1990's, Boland taught at several universities in the United States. In 1995, she became a professor at Stanford University, where she has served as Bella Mabury and Eloise Mabury Knapp Professor in the Humanities as well as the Melvin and Bill Lane Professor and chair of the creative writing program.

## ANALYSIS

Hearth and history provide a context for the poetry of Eavan Boland. She is inspired by both the domestic and the cultural. Her subjects are the alienating suburban places that encourage people to forget their cultural roots, her children with their typically Irish names, demystified horses in Dublin streets that can still evoke the old glories from time to time, and the old Irish stories themselves, which at times may be vivid and evocative and at others may be nostalgic in nature. Boland's distinctly female perspective is achieved in several poems about painting that note the dominance of male painters—such as Jan van Eyck, Edgar Degas, Jean Auguste Dominique Ingres, and Pierre-Auguste Renoir—in the history of art from the Renaissance to the Impressionists. Women were painted by these artists in traditional domestic or agrarian postures. Boland perceives women as far less sanitized and submissive. Her collection *In Her Own Image* introduces such taboo subjects as anorexia, mastectomy, masturbation, and menstruation.

### NIGHT FEED

Two of Boland's works, *In Her Own Image* and *Night Feed*, deal exclusively with the subject of women. *Night Feed* for the most part examines suburban women and positively chronicles the daily routine of a Dublin homemaker. The book has poems about diapers, washing machines, and feeding babies. The cover has an idyllic drawing of a mother feeding a child. However, *In Her Own Image*, published two years before *Night Feed*, seems written by a different person. Its candid and detailed treatment of taboo subjects contrasts sharply with the idyllic world of *Night Feed*. Boland's ability to present both worlds testifies to her poetic maturity.

The need for connection is a major theme in Boland's poetry. Aware of traditional connections in Irish and classical myths, she longs for an earlier period when such ties came instinctively. Her sense of loss with respect to these traditional connections extends beyond mythology to Irish history as well, even to Irish history in the twentieth century. Modern-day Dubliners have been cut off from the sustaining power of myth and history. Their lives, therefore, seem empty and superficial. Surrounded with the shards of a lost culture, they cannot piece these pieces together into a coherent system.

The alienation of modern urban Irish people from their cultural roots is the subject of Boland's "The New Pastoral" (from *Night Feed*). She considers alienation from a woman's perspective. Aware of the myths that have traditionally sustained males, Boland desires equivalent myths for females. She longs for a "new pastoral" that will celebrate women's ideals, but she finds none. She encounters many domestic "signs," but they do not "signify" for her. She has a vague sense of once having participated in a coherent ritual, of having "danced once/ on a frieze." Now, however, she has no access to the myth. Men seem to have easier access to their cultural roots than women do. The legends of the cavemen contain flint, fire, and wheel, which allowed man "to read his world." Later in history, men had pastoral poems to define and celebrate their place in the world. A woman has no similar defining and consoling rituals and possesses no equivalent cultural signs. She seems a "displaced person/ in a pastoral chaos," unable to create a "new pastoral." Surrounded by domestic signs, "lamb's knuckle," "the washer," "a stink/ of nappies," "the greasy/ bacon flitch," she still has no access to myth. Hints of connection do not provide a unified myth:

> I feel
> there was a past,
> there was a pastoral
> and these
> chance sights—
> what are they all
> but late amnesias
> of a rite
> I danced once
> on a frieze?

The final image of the dancer on the frieze echoes both John Keats's Grecian urn and William Butler Yeats's dancers and golden bird. The contemporary poet, however, has lost contact. Paradoxically, the poem constitutes the "new pastoral," which it claims is beyond its reach. The final allusion to the dancer on the frieze transforms the mundane objects of domestic life into something more significant, something sacred.

Boland seems in conflict over whether women should simply conform to male stereotypes for women or should resist these pressures to lead "lesser lives," to attend to "hearth not history." Many poems in *Night Feed* accept this "lesser" destiny, poems such as "Night

Feed," "Hymn," and "In the Garden." The several poems in this volume that deal with paintings, "Domestic Interior," "Fruit on a Straight-Sided Tray," "Degas's Laundresses," "Woman Posing (After Ingres)," "On Renoir's *The Grape-Pickers*," all deal with paintings by male painters that portray women in traditional domestic or rural roles. The women in these paintings appear content with their "lesser lives." Poems such as "It's a Woman's World" seem less accepting, however, more in the spirit of *In Her Own Image*, which vigorously rejects basing one's identity on male stereotypes. "It's a Woman's World" complements "The New Pastoral" in its desire for a balance between hearth and history.

> as far as history goes
> we were never
> on the scene of the crime. . . .
> And still no page
> scores the low music
> of our outrage.

Women have had no important roles in history, Boland asserts. They produce "low music," rather than heroic music. Nevertheless, women can have an intuitive connection with their own "starry mystery," their own cosmic identity. The women in those paintings, apparently pursuing their "lesser lives," may have a sense of "greater lives." The male world (including male artists) must be kept in the dark about this, must keep believing that nothing mythic is being experienced.

> That woman there,
> craned to the starry mystery
> is merely getting a breath
> of evening air,
> while this one here—
> her mouth
> a burning plume—
> she's no fire-eater,
> just my frosty neighbour
> coming home.

### IN HER OWN IMAGE

The "woman's world" and the "starry mysteries" are presented far less romantically in *In Her Own Image*. The poems in this volume refuse to conform to male stereotypes of woman as happy domestic partner.

They explore male-female conflicts in the deepest and most intimate psychic places. The title *In Her Own Image* indicates the volume's concern with the problem of identity. Boland wishes to be an individual, free to determine her own life, but other forces seek to control her, to make her conform to female stereotypes. A woman should be perfect, unchanging, youthful, pure—in short, she should be ideal. Male-dominated society does not wish women to explore their own deepest desires. Women transform these social messages into the voice of their own consciences, or, in Sigmund Freud's terms, their own superegos: "Thou shalt not get fat!" "Thou shalt not get old!" "Thou shalt not get curious."

These naysaying inner voices dominate the first three poems of *In Her Own Image*: "Tirade for the Mimic Muse," "In Her Own Image," and "In His Own Image." The "mimic muse" in the first poem urges the speaker to "make up," to conceal aging with cosmetics. The illustration for this poem shows a chubby and unkempt woman gazing into a mirror and seeing a perfect version of herself—thin, unwrinkled, and physically fit. The phrase "her own image" in the second poem refers to another idealization, the "image" of perfection that the speaker carries around inside herself. She finally frees herself from this psychic burden by planting the image outside in the garden. The illustration shows a naked woman bending over a small coffin.

The third poem, "In His Own Image," considers the pressures of a husband's expectations on a wife's sense of self. The speaker in this third poem does not try to reshape her features with makeup. She is battered into a new shape by a drunken husband. No illustration appears with this poem.

The speaker's "tirade" in "Tirade for the Mimic Muse" begins at once and establishes the intensely hostile tone of much of *In Her Own Image*: "I've caught you out. You slut. You fat trout." She despises the impulse in herself to conform to a stereotype, to disguise the physical signs of time passing: "the lizarding of eyelids," "the whiskering of nipples," and "the slow betrayals of our bedroom mirrors." In the final section of the poem, the authentic self has suppressed those conforming impulses: "I, who mazed my way to womanhood/ Through all your halls of mirrors, making faces."

Now the mirror's glass is cracked. The speaker promises a true vision of the world, but the vision will not be idyllic: "I will show you true reflections, terrors." Terrors preoccupy Boland for much of this book.

"In Her Own Image" and "In His Own Image" deal with different aspects of the "perfect woman." The first poem has a much less hostile tone than does "Tirade for the Mimic Muse." The speaker seems less threatened by the self-image from which she wishes to distance herself. Images of gold and amethyst and jasmine run through the poem. Despite the less hostile tone, Boland regards this "image" as a burdensome idealization that must be purged for psychic health: "She is not myself/ anymore." The speaker plants this "image" in the garden outside: "I will bed her,/ She will bloom there," safely removed from consciousness. The poem "In His Own Image" is full of anxiety. The speaker cannot find her center, her identity. Potential signs of identity lie all around her, but she cannot interpret them:

> Celery feathers, . . .
> bacon flitch, . . .
> kettle's paunch, . . .
> these were all I had to go on, . . .
> meagre proofs of myself.

A drunken husband responds to his wife's identity crisis by pounding her into his own desired "shape."

> He splits my lip with his fist,
> shadows my eye with a blow,
> knuckles my neck to its proper angle.
> What a perfectionist!
> His are a sculptor's hands:
> they summon
> form from the void,
> they bring
> me to myself again.
> I am a new woman.

How different are these two methods of coping with psychic conflict. In "In Her Own Image," the speaker plants her old self lovingly in the garden. In "In His Own Image," the drunken husband reshapes his wife's features with violent hands. The wife in the second poem says that she is now a "new woman." If one reads this volume as a single poem, as Boland evidently intends that one should (all the illustrations have the same

person as their subject), one understands that the desperate tone of other poems in the book derives from the suffering of this reshaped "new woman," a victim of male exploitation.

The next four poems of *In Her Own Image* deal with very private subjects familiar to women but not often treated in published poems: anorexia, mastectomy, masturbation, and menstruation. Both the poems and Constance Hart's drawings are startlingly frank. The poet wants readers to experience "woman" in a more complete way, to realize the dark side of being female. The poems further illustrate Boland's sense of alienation from cultural myths or myths of identity. She desires connections, but she knows that she is unlikely to have them. She is therefore left with images that signify chaos rather than coherence, absence rather than presence, emptiness rather than fullness.

Two of the four poems, "Anorexia" and "Mastectomy," read like field reports from the battle of the sexes. The other two poems, "Solitary" and "Menses," have a female perspective but are also full of conflict. In the illustrations for "Anorexia," a very determined and extremely thin naked woman, arms folded, looks disapprovingly at a fat woman lolling on a couch. An anorectic woman continues to believe that she is fat, despite being a virtual skeleton. Boland introduces a religious level in the first three lines: "Flesh is heretic./ My body is a witch./ I am burning it." The conviction that her body is a witch runs through the whole poem. Here, in an extreme form, is the traditional Roman Catholic view that soul and body are separate. The body must be punished because since the Fall, it has been the dwelling place of the devil. The soul must suppress the body in order for the soul to be saved. This tradition provides the anorectic with a religious reason for starving herself. In this poem, she revels in the opportunity to "torch" her body: "Now the bitch is burning." A presence even more disturbing than the witch is introduced in the second half of the poem, a ghostly male presence whom the anorectic speaker desires to please. To please this unnamed male presence, the speaker must become thin, so thin that she can somehow return to the womb imagined here paradoxically as male: "I will slip/ back into him again/ as if I had never been away." This return to the male womb will atone for the sin of being born a woman, with "hips and breasts/ and lips and heat/ and sweat and fat and greed."

In "Mastectomy," male-female conflict predominates. Male surgeons, envious of a woman's breasts (an effective transformation of the male-centered Freudian paradigm), cut off a breast and carry it away with them. The shocking drawing shows one gowned male surgeon passing the breast on a serving dish to another gowned male surgeon. The woman who has experienced this physical and psychological violation cries despairingly "I flatten to their looting." The sympathetic words of the surgeon before the operation belie the sinister act of removing the breast. It can now become part of male fantasy, as a symbol of primal nourishment and primal home:

> So they have taken off
> what slaked them first,
> what they have hated since:
> blue-veined
> white-domed
> home
> of wonder
> and the wetness
> of their dreams.

The next two poems, "Solitary" and "Menses," deal with equally private aspects of a woman's life, autoeroticism and menstruation. "Solitary" has a celebratory attitude toward self-arousal. The drawing shows a relaxed naked female figure lying on her stomach. Religious imagery is used in this poem as it is in "Anorexia," but here the body is worshiped rather than feared. The only negative aspect of "Solitary" is its solitude. The female speaker is unconnected with another person. Solitary pleasures are intense but less so than the pleasures of intercourse. The reader is taken on a journey from arousal to orgasm to postorgasmic tranquility. The religious language at first seems gratuitous but then perfectly appropriate. The speaker affirms the holiness of her body: "An oratory of dark,/ a chapel of unreason." She has a few moments of panic as the old words of warning flash into her mind: "You could die for this./ The gods could make you blind." These warnings do not deter her, however, from this sacred rite:

> how my cry
> blasphemes
> light and dark,
> screams
> land from sea,
> makes word flesh
> that now makes me
> animal.

During this period of arousal and climax, her "flesh summers," but then it returns again to winter: "I winter/ into sleep."

"Menses" deals with the private act of menstruation. A cosmic female voice addresses the speaker as menstruation begins, attempting to focus her attention solely on the natural powers working in her body. The speaker resists this effort. She feels simultaneously "sick of it" and drawn to this process. She struggles to retain her freedom. "Only my mind is free," she says. Her body is taken over by tidal forces. "I am bloated with her waters./ I am barren with her blood." At the end of the poem, the speaker seems more accepting of this natural cycle. She reflects on two other cycles that she has experienced, childbirth and intercourse. All three cycles, she begins to see, make her a new person: "I am bright and original."

The final three poems of *In Her Own Image*, "Witching," "Exhibitionist," and "Making-up," return to the theme that "Myths/ are made by men" (from "Making-up"). Much of a woman's life is spent reacting to male stereotypes. In "Witching," Boland further explores the idea of woman-as-witch, which was introduced in "Anorexia." Historically, women accused by men of being witches were doomed. The charges were usually either trumped-up or trivial. Boland's witch fantasizes about turning the table on her male persecutors and burning them first:

> I will
> reserve
> their arson,
> make
> a pyre
> of my haunch . . .
> the stench
> of my crotch

It is a grim but fitting fate for these male witch-burners.

Another male stereotype, woman-as-stripper, is treated in the poem "Exhibitionist." This poem has the last accompanying drawing, a vulnerable young woman pulling her dress up over her head and naked to those watching her, perhaps as Boland feels naked toward those who have read through this volume. The male observers in "Exhibitionist" have in mind only gratifying their lusts. The speaker detests this exploitation and hopes to have a deeper impact on these leering males, hopes to touch them spiritually with her shining flesh:

> my dark plan:
> Into the gutter
> of their lusts
> I burn
> the shine
> of my flesh.

The final poem, "Making-up," returns to the theme of "Tirade for the Mimic Muse," that women must alter their appearances to please men, but that men have no such demands placed on them. The poem rehearses a litany of transformations of the speaker's "naked face." "Myths/ are made by men," this poem asserts. The goddesses men imagine can never be completely captured by that "naked face." A woman's natural appearance inevitably has flaws. Women are encouraged by men to disguise these flaws to make themselves look perfect. From these "rouge pots," a goddess comes forth, at least in men's eyes. Women should really know better.

> Mine are the rouge pots,
> the hot pinks, . . .
> out of which
> I dawn.

Boland is determined to make poetry out of her domestic life. *In Her Own Image* and *Night Feed* indicate that she has turned to the very ordinary subjects of hearth, rather than to the larger subjects of history, which she explored in her earlier volumes *New Territory* and *The War Horse*. In "The Woman Poet: Her Dilemma," Boland admits to uncertainty about this new orientation. She is encouraged especially, however, by the example of French and Dutch genre painters, whose work she calls "unglamorous, workaday, authentic," possessing both ordinariness and vision: "The hare in its muslin bag, the crusty loaf, the women fixed between menial tasks and human dreams." In her own equally ordinary domestic life, she believes that she has found a personal voice.

### THE JOURNEY, AND OTHER POEMS

Boland's next major collection, *The Journey, and Other Poems*, explores more fully the poetic implications of this uncertainty. *In Her Own Image* and *Night Feed* offer opposed accounts of Boland's concerns as a woman and a writer, the former vehemently critical and openly outraged at sexual injustices, the latter more generously idyllic and positive about the domestic side of her femininity. In *The Journey, and Other Poems*, Boland incorporates this ambivalence into the fabric of her poems, channeling the tension between her contrary aspects into an antithetical lyric energy; each piece, that is, derives its form and force from a doubleness in the poet's mind, an impulse to be at once critical and affirmative. Instead of lamenting her inner confusions and contradictions, however, Boland builds a new sense of the lyric poem and engages with renewed vigor the vexed questions of gender, tradition, and myth that characterize her work.

The collection is divided into three sections, forming a triptych. In traditional religious painting, a triptych is composed of three canvases, side by side, the outer two either elaborating on or visually supporting the central portion, which usually contains the main subject of the work. In *The Journey, and Other Poems*, the first and third sections comment on, refocus, and expand the thematically dense matter of the central section, which contains "The Journey"—one of Boland's finest lyric achievements—and its "Envoi." Furthermore, Boland uses the structure of the triptych to underscore the ambivalence she feels. In the first section, the reader encounters memorial and idyll; in the third section, the reader finds the opposite, a vehement critique of inherited sexual mores and the patriarchal "tradition." Only in the central portion of the volume, "The Journey," does Boland take on both aspects at once and attempt, not to reconcile one to the other, but to reanimate and reenergize what she calls a dying, diminished poetic language.

The volume opens with "I Remember," a nostalgic tribute to the poet's mother. Boland recalls her mother's studio and her own almost irrepressible need, as a child exploring that room, "to touch, to handle, to dismantle it,/ the mystery." Boland longs for the mystery of innocence and the childlike wonder of a lost time—before the harsh realities of Irish economics and suburban alienation had taken root—when the world seemed balanced, "composed," and beautiful; but in the poem, that world is veiled and hidden from her, like the otherworldly elegance of her mother's "French Empire chairs" over which opaque cotton sheets have been draped. Similarly, in "The Oral Tradition," in which Boland overhears two women exchanging gossip—figures who, emblematically, "were standing in shadow"—she longs for "a musical sub-text," an "oral song" that seems only to express itself in "fragments and innuendoes," which nevertheless resonate with "a sense/ suddenly of truth." Boland wants to discover the archetypal "truth" buried under opaque surfaces, and, as she says in "Suburban Woman: A Detail," to find traces of the lost "goddess" within her instinctive, feminine memory. She expresses her need to be "healed into myth" through poetry and to recover the deeply ingrained, basic "patterns" of her womanhood.

The third section works negatively, upsetting traditional myths of the archetypal feminine. In "Listen. This Is the Noise of Myth," Boland starts to recount a "story" of a man and a woman setting the stage for a traditional version of domestic order, but she becomes self-conscious and critical, calling her own methods into question, making her characters—especially the woman—into "fugitives" from their traditional roles. Boland proposes to "set truth to rights," defiantly dismantling the old stories. She laments that even she must put "the same mirrors on the old magic" and return to the "old romances." Despite the sweet lure of storytelling, Boland wants to remake her own role as an author, and though she finds herself repeatedly thwarted by the "consolations of the craft," she struggles on.

Several poems in the third section echo Boland's other work. "Tirade for the Lyric Muse" recalls her "Tirade for the Mimic Muse," but here the subject is plastic surgery. The speaker addresses a sister "in the crime," an epithet that suggests a fellow poet, but one who, in Boland's view, has betrayed herself and her implicit commitment to "truth" by having the ordinary "surface" of her face altered to conform to a false notion of "skin deep" beauty. The true "music" of poetry, for Boland, cannot be captured by outward conformity to the "cruel" standards of a male world. Poems such as "Fond Memory" and "An Irish Childhood in England: 1951" respond to lyrics such as "I Remember" in the first section, rejecting nostalgia and finding in Boland's own indelible Irishness a sense of exile and insecurity. To be an English-speaking Irish native is to be a perpetual outcast. Irishness, for Boland, represents her own inability to settle on a given set of values or a certain appearance of "truth"; her nationality, paradoxically, undermines easy acceptance of the safe "myths" she craves.

If the first section works to rediscover the force of myth and the last section to dismantle the false safety net of traditional roles, the central portion—"The Journey"—springs directly from a double impulse. "The Journey" is a dream-vision, a description of a mental journey to the underworld undertaken in the poet's dreams. Many medieval poets, including Geoffrey Chaucer, wrote dream-visions. Like these poets, Boland depicts herself falling asleep over an open book of classical poetry. This connection to tradition, both medieval and ancient, is important to the poem, which describes a poetics, an account of how poems are or ought to be written. Boland searches for a new, vital form of writing. She begins by stating angrily that "there has never . . . been a poem to an antibiotic. . . ." She questions what is the proper subject for poetry, introducing antibiotics as something about which no one would bother to write. She espouses the ordinary and the domestic rather than the ethereal of the "unblemished" as a basis for poetry. To heal people and to repair their diminished relationship to "the language," poetry must look with renewed energy to the particulars of everyday life.

In her dream, Boland descends with Sappho—the greatest ancient female poet, whom she has been reading—to the land of the dead, where she meets the ghosts of mothers and housewives, women in whose experiences Boland has been trying to discover her mythical roots. Boland pleads with her mentor to let her "be their witnesses," but she is told that what she has seen is "beyond speech." She awakens, only to find "nothing was changed," despite her vision of "truth," and she weeps. This poetic "misery," taken up in the poem's "Envoi," comes from disappointment at being incapable of resuscitating the lost myths of womanhood, the anxiety of trying to bless "the ordinary" or to sanctify "the common" without the comfort of a traditionally sanctioned muse. Boland's work, to revive the feminine in poetry, results in a difficult mixture of discovery, desire, dissatisfaction, and rage. "The Journey" is a complex poem, and one of Boland's best works. It expresses both a naïve, dreamy faith in the power of myth and "truth" and a severe self-consciousness that calls the elements of her feminine identity into question. The ability to dwell poetically on such a problematic duplicity in a single poem truly indicates Boland's literary accomplishment.

### IN A TIME OF VIOLENCE AND THE LOST LAND

Similar concerns, sometimes more deeply and darkly wrought, sometimes inscribed with a tonic humor, permeate Boland's poems of the 1990's. *In a Time of Violence* uses unusual and risky strategies to clarify the personal/political weave in Boland's vision. All those who lack autonomy are ultimately susceptible to victimhood and violence. This equation pertains to gender, nationhood, and any other form of identification. In *The Lost Land*, she continues to explore the issues and emotions of those who are victims of exile and colonialism. These are especially the burdens of "Colony," a major poem that makes up the first half of the book. Colonization, Boland says, is not just an act of governments, but an act of individuals—any exercise of power and dominance at the expense of the independence of others. It even applies to the relationships of parents and children, husbands and wives. These echoes weave their way more noticeably through the shorter poems in the collection. Along with the losses of place that Boland records—"place" having political, cultural, and psychic significance—she expresses here the loss of motherhood—another "place" of position that vanishes with time. Boland's constantly growing artistry, her ability to fasten on the telling concrete detail, and her hard-won personal and public authority make this collection outstanding.

### AGAINST LOVE POETRY

*Against Love Poetry* deftly reconciles the sacrifice of freedom necessary for a lasting marriage with "the idea of women's freedom." If such a move seems unexpected or contradictory, it nonetheless arises from the same impulse as Boland's earlier work: the desire to delineate the true experience of women's lives. The book's first half, a section entitled "Marriage," clarifies the book's title. The sentimental ideal of romantic love, by now a well-known part of the poetic tradition, cannot begin to render adequately the truths of married life: "It is to mark the contradictions of a daily love that I have written this. Against love poetry." Throughout the volume, Boland draws on history, myths, folktales, and memory, continually subverting clichéd versions of romantic love in favor of a more complex, if often more stark, reality. For example, the poem "Quarantine," the fourth poem in the "Marriage" section, follows the route of a married couple walking during the Irish potato famine. Ultimately, after the man struggles unsuccessfully to keep his ill wife warm, both die "Of cold. Of hunger. Of the toxins of a whole history." Here the narrative shifts, echoing the book's title briefly to declare that "There is no place here for the inexact/ praise of the easy graces and sensuality of the body." What is important, the poem emphasizes, is the ordinary yet striking reality of what happens: "Their death together in the winter of 1847. Also what they suffered. How they lived./ And what there is between a man and a woman./ And in which darkness it can best be proved."

As in her earlier work, Boland continues to blend personal history, folktale, and classical myth to overturn past and present stereotypes of women's lives. "Called," an entry in the section half of the book, describes the author's unsuccessful search for the grave of her grandmother who died young. With Boland's resolve to "face this landscape/ and look at it as she was looked upon://  Unloved because unknown./ Unknown because unnamed," the familiar landmarks are stripped away, the earth returns to its essences, and the poet drives home as constellations appear, "some of them twisted into women." Even as Boland notes the vital role of women within the cosmos, those who "single-handedly holding high the dome/ and curve and horizon of today and tomorrow," she acknowledges the pain of being marginalized: "All the ships looking up to them./ All the compasses made true by them./ All the night skies named for their sorrow." Not surprisingly, in "Suburban Woman: Another Detail," she aptly describes her writing as the process of selecting words "from the earth,/ from the root, from the faraway/ oils and essence of elegy:/ Bitter. And close to the bone."

Interestingly, Boland extends her range of subjects to include poetry about the little-known accomplishments of historical women from the remote and recent past. The first poem in the "Marriage" section portrays Hester Bateman, a British silversmith who in the nineteenth century took on the trade of her husband, engraving marriage spoons for an Irish customer. In the book's second section, "Code," Boland directly addresses Grace Murray Hopper, who verified the computer language known as COBOL: "Let there be language—/ even if we use it differently:/ I never made it timeless as you have./ I never made it numerate as you did." In both poems, Boland identifies strongly with her protagonists, demonstrating the ability of the woman artist to create the future and to reconcile oppositions: "composing this/ to show you how the world begins again:/ One word at a time./ One woman to another" ("Code").

### DOMESTIC VIOLENCE

In *Domestic Violence*, the late-night quarrels of a neighbor couple, the sectarian strife that erupted in Ireland in the 1960's, the poet's personal history, and the plight of Irish women become inextricably entwined. The title poem recalls how Boland and her husband, then newly married, watched the civil unrest known as the Troubles unfold in the grainy images of a small black-and-white television set, "which gave them back as gray and grayer tears/ and killings, killings, killings,/ then moonlight-colored funerals." In the same section, another poem, "How It Was Once in Our Country," evokes Ireland's turbulent history from previous centuries, relating the story of a mermaid who, according to some storytellers, "must have witnessed deaths" and remained below the water "to escape the screams." As always, there is the note of exile: "What we know is this/ (and this is all we know): we are now/ and we will always be from now on—/ for all I know we have always been—// exiles in our own country."

In the book's second section, Boland explores both past and present as she considers "last things," pondering what she will bequeath to her daughters. "Inheritance" expresses the poet's regret that she never learned the crafts of her predecessors: "the lace bobbin with its braided mesh,/ its oat-straw pillow and the wheat-colored shawl/ knitted in one season/ to imitate another." She also recalls a long night of tending to her first child: "When dawn came I held my hand over the absence of fever,/ over skin which had stopped burning, as if I knew the secrets of health and air, as if I understood them// and listened to the silence/ and thought, I must have learned that somewhere." In the entries that conclude this section, the poet's voice becomes more strident. "Windfall," an imagined rendering of the funeral for the grandmother whose grave she could not locate, describes "the coffin of a young woman/ who has left five children behind. There will be no obituary." The tragedy resides not only in her ancestor's unrecorded death, but also the insidious ways that language can be appropriated to justify ignoring lives that a culture or a country may consider insignificant:

> We say *Mother Nature* when all we intend is
> a woman was let die, out of sight, in a fever ward.
>
> Now say *Mother Ireland* when all that you mean is
> there is no need to record this death in history.

In "Letters to the Dead," the "signs and marks" used to inscribe ancient Egyptian pottery laid at the entrance of tombs become the poet's telling metaphor for a similar communication with her own ancestors. Ultimately, however, Boland's frank question reaches deep into Irish history:

> How many daughters stood alone at a grave,
> and thought this of their mothers' lives?
> That they were young in a country that hated
>    a woman's body.
> That they grew old in a country that hated a
>    woman's body
>
> They asked for the counsel of the dead.
> They asked for the power of the dead.
> These are my letters to the dead.

In a similar poem, "Violence Against Women," Boland mourns the female casualties of the Industrial Revolution, "women who died here who never lived:// mindless, sexless, birthless, only sunned/ by shadows, only dressed in muslin." For the poet, they resemble "shepherdesses of the English pastoral" trapped in traditional poetry, "waiting for the return of an English April/ that never came and never will again." Boland's closure questions and indicts the cultural and historical institutions that so often connive in the fate of women like Boland's grandmother.

Like her fellow poet and countryman Heaney, Boland's poetry has become a search for the images, symbols, and language that could adequately, realistically portray the struggles of women throughout history and her own pain at feeling like an exile in her own country. Throughout a career of patiently and carefully crafting poems, Boland has achieved an eloquence that is truly superlative.

OTHER MAJOR WORKS

NONFICTION: *W. B. Yeats and His World*, 1971 (with Micheál Mac Liammóir); *Object Lessons: The Life of the Woman and the Poet in Our Time*, 1995.

TRANSLATION: *After Every War: Twentieth-century Women Poets*, 2004.

EDITED TEXT: *The Making of a Poem: A Norton Anthology of Poetic Forms*, 2000 (with Mark Strand).

BIBLIOGRAPHY

Boland, Eavan. Interview by Patty O'Connell. *Poets and Writers* 22 (November/December, 1995). A lengthy conversation that ranges through Irish and American poetry, Dublin as an image in Boland's work, her mother, and poetry workshops.

Collins, Floyd. "Auspicious Beginnings and Sure Arrivals: Beth Ann Fennelly and Eavan Boland." *West Branch* 52 (Spring, 2003): 108-123. Contains an excellent discussion of *Against Love Poetry* and a comparison of Boland and Beth Ann Fennelly.

Constantakis, Sara, ed. *Poetry for Students*. Vol. 31. Detroit: Thomson/Gale Group, 2010. Contains an analysis of Boland's "Outside History."

Gonzalez, Alexander G., ed. *Contemporary Irish Women Poets: Some Male Perspectives*. Westport, Conn.: Greenwood Press, 1999. Enthusiastic responses by male critics to a wide range of Irish women poets include two strong essays on Boland: Thomas C. Foster's "In from the Margin: Eavan Boland's 'Outside History' Sequence" and Peter Kupillas's "Bringing It All Back Home: Unity and Meaning in Eavan Boland's 'Domestic Interior' Sequence."

Haberstroh, Patricia Boyle. *Women Creating Women: Contemporary Irish Women Poets*. Syracuse, N.Y.: Syracuse University Press, 1996. Compares Boland, Eithne Strong, Eiléan Ní Chuilleanáin, Medbh McGuckian, and Nuala Ní Dhomhnaill.

Keen, Paul. "The Doubled Edge: Identity and Alterity in the Poetry of Eavan Boland and Nuala Ní Dhomhnaill." *Mosaic* 33, no. 3 (2000): 14-34. Setting his investigation within the political and cultural upheavals in contemporary Ireland, Keen attends to Boland's theoretical writings to approach her poems. He sees her as rewriting Irish myths about the country and women rather than subverting them. Several key poems are examined with clarity and compassionate care. The comparative approach is fruitful.

McElroy, James. "The Contemporary Fe/Male Poet: A Preliminary Reading." In *New Irish Writing*, edited by James Brophy and Eamon Grennan. Boston: Twayne, 1989. McElroy defends Boland against critical charges of "stridency" and overstatement, arguing that her recurrent confrontations with the Irish domestic woman constitute a crucial part of her poetics of recovery and renewal, and that her willful reiterations of "female miseries" form a powerful catalog of matters that must be treated emphatically if Irish poetry is to recover its potency.

Randolph, Jody Allen, ed. *Eavan Boland: A Critical Companion*. New York: Norton, 2008. This volume, one of the first book-length studies of Boland, includes poetry and prose by Boland, interviews with her, and criticism of her work.

Villar-Argáiz, Pilar. *Eavan Boland's Evolution as an Irish Woman Poet: An Outsider Within an Outsider's Culture*. Lewiston, N.Y.: Edwin Mellen Press, 2007. Focuses on Boland as a female poet, presenting analysis of male-female relationships in her poetry. Includes an analysis of "Anorexic."

_____. *The Poetry of Eavan Boland: A Postcolonial Reading*. Dublin: Maunsel, 2008. This volume places Boland squarely within the context of post-colonial literature.

*Kevin McNeilly; Arthur E. McGuinness;*
*Philip K. Jason*
*Updated by Caroline Collins*

# WILLIAM LISLE BOWLES

**Born:** Kings Sutton, Northamptonshire, England; September 24, 1762
**Died:** Salisbury, Wiltshire, England; April 7, 1850

PRINCIPAL POETRY

*Fourteen Sonnets*, 1789 (enlarged 1794, 1796, 1798)
*Verses to John Howard*, 1789
*The Grave of Howard*, 1790
*Verses on the Benevolent Institution of the Philanthropic Society, for Protecting and Educating the Children of Vagrants and Criminals*, 1790
*Elegy Written at the Hot-Wells, Bristol*, 1791
*Monody, Written at Matlock*, 1791
*A Poetical Address to the Right Honourable Edmund Burke*, 1791
*Elegiac Stanzas, Written During Sickness at Bath*, 1796
*Hope: An Allegorical Sketch*, 1796
*Coombe Ellen*, 1798
*St. Michael's Mount*, 1798
*Song of the Battle of the Nile*, 1799
*Poems*, 1801
*The Sorrows of Switzerland*, 1801
*The Picture*, 1803
*The Spirit of Discovery: Or, The Conquest of the Ocean*, 1804
*Bowden Hill*, 1806
*The Little Villager's Verse Book*, 1806, 1837 (juvenile)
*Poems*, 1809

*The Missionary*, 1813
*The Grave of the Last Saxon*, 1822
*Ellen Gray*, 1823
*Days Departed*, 1828
*St. John in Patmos*, 1832
*Scenes and Shadows*, 1835

OTHER LITERARY FORMS

Although best known as a poet, William Lisle Bowles (bohlz) also published an edition of Alexander Pope, pamphlets of literary criticism regarding Pope (in a famous controversy with Lord Byron and others), sermons, antiquarian works, and an autobiographical fragment. A number of his letters are also extant (see Garland Greever's edition of them), but he is more memorably preserved in the recollections of others, as Thomas Moore and Samuel Taylor Coleridge fondly described and preserved his eccentricities.

ACHIEVEMENTS

Few people today regard William Lisle Bowles as a major poet, and some would speak contemptuously of him, for all his enormous output. Sharply contrasting with a modern sophisticated dismissal of his work, however, was the immediate and forceful influence that Bowles exerted on the first generation of British Romantic poets, including William Wordsworth, Robert Southey, Charles Lamb, and above all Samuel Taylor Coleridge. For them he was the herald of a new sensibility, almost a Vergil to follow beyond the desiccated landscape of neoclassical detachment into a richer vale of fresh response and honest moralizing. Having been educated in part by the poets he inspired, modern readers find it hard to appreciate Bowles's originality. Largely because he was transitional to better poets than himself, Bowles now appears to be of historical interest only. He is frequently omitted from modern anthologies altogether and appears in some literary histories only as a footnote to Coleridge.

BIOGRAPHY

William Lisle Bowles was born on September 24, 1762, at Kings Sutton, Northamptonshire (his father's vicarage), the son and grandson of clergymen and the eldest of seven children. At the age of seven he moved with his parents to Uphill, Somerset; on the journey southward, young Bowles saw the Severn Valley and derived from it a lifelong association of poetry with picturesque scenery.

From 1775 to 1781, Bowles was educated at Winchester School under Joseph Warton, who had written an essay critical of Alexander Pope and was a pre-Romantic advocate of descriptive poetry. Warton's feeling for nature, dislike of neoclassical rules, and knowledge of Vergil impressed Bowles (see his "Monody on the Death of Dr. Warton," 1819), who thereafter followed and enlarged on Warton's precepts. In 1781, Bowles went on to Trinity College, Oxford, where his master, Thomas Warton, Joseph's brother, further reinforced Bowles's dislike of neoclassicism and preference for lyric poetry, the ode and sonnet in particular. Bowles wrote "On Leaving Winchester School," his first important poem, retrospectively in 1782.

His record at Oxford was that of an unusually able student. In 1782, for example, Bowles won a scholarship that sustained him for the next five years. In 1783, his "Calpe Obsessa" (on the Siege of Gibraltar) was the Latin prize poem. Three years later, however, in 1786, Bowles's father died, leaving the family in difficult financial straits. Though Bowles received his B.A. degree the next year, his engagement to a niece of Sir Samuel Romilly appeared imprudent to her parents and was summarily broken off. In his disappointment, Bowles elected to travel through northern England, Scotland, Belgium, Germany, and Switzerland. While thus relieved, he composed a series of sonnets; published in 1789 at Bath as *Fourteen Sonnets*, they quickly made him famous.

Wordsworth, on vacation from Cambridge, read Bowles's sonnets that Christmas in London, as he was walking the streets with his brother John, and (as Mary Moorman has it in her biography of Wordsworth), "their graceful melancholy, dwelling on the memories of beloved places, at once made a strong appeal." Bowles's influence on Wordsworth is traceable in the latter's work from *Descriptive Sketches* (1793) to "Lines Composed a Few Miles Above Tintern Abbey" (1798). The first edition of Bowles's sonnets that Wordsworth read, however, was a rarity, for only one hundred

copies were published. There soon followed a second edition (also 1789) containing twenty-one sonnets, which Coleridge read—he was then a seventeen-year-old schoolboy at Christ's Hospital—and transcribed endlessly for his literary friends. As J. Shawcross has remarked, "in Bowles's sonnets Coleridge found the first genuinely unconventional treatment of Nature, the first genuine stimulus to an understanding of her 'perpetual revelation'" (*Biographia Literaria*, 1817). One of those to whom Coleridge sent Bowles's sonnets was Robert Southey, who soon shared his enthusiasm for them. "Buy Bowles poems, and study them well," he advised a friend in 1794. "They will teach you to write better, and give you infinite pleasure." Bowles was a major influence on Coleridge and his circle from 1789 to 1797, and these years were also the Wiltshire parson's most prolific.

The *Fourteen Sonnets* proved to be a remarkable success. Following the first and second editions of 1789, there was a third in 1794 containing twenty-seven sonnets and thirteen other poems. The fourth edition of 1796 was little changed, but the fifth (1796; two new poems) and sixth (1798; thirty sonnets and sixteen other poems, including *Hope*) both contained additions and plates. Less significant, except as evidence of Bowles's continuing popularity, were editions seven (1800), eight (1801), nine (1805), and ten (1809). Coleridge followed the earlier editions as they appeared and even wrote Bowles (whom he visited in September, 1797) to comment on his various omissions and emendations.

Coleridge acknowledged his own profound indebtedness to Bowles in a sonnet of December, 1794, "To the Rev. W. L. Bowles," which was printed in the *Morning Chronicle*, a London newspaper, on the day after Christmas, together with a note from Coleridge praising Bowles's sonnets XIII ("At a Convent"), XIX, and XXV as "compositions of, perhaps, unrivalled merit." In *Poems on Various Subjects* (1796), Coleridge reprinted his Bowles sonnet in a revised form. That same year he also published *A Sheet of Sonnets*, twenty-eight in all, designed to be bound up with Bowles's own, which Coleridge praised effusively in his preface. By 1802, however, Coleridge was no longer satisfied with Bowles, who had "indeed the *sensi-*

*bility* of a poet," but "not the *Passion* of a great Poet" (*Collected Letters*, 1956-1959).

Having met with considerable success, Bowles published much during these years. Among the poems added to later editions of his sonnets, for example, were humanitarian verses on John Howard, slavery, and the American Indian. His *Verses on the Benevolent Institution of the Philanthropic Society* furnished the epigraph to Southey's "Botany Bay Eclogues" (written in 1794). Bowles's *Elegy Written at the Hot-Wells, Bristol* was translated into French by Madame de Staël, who also admired his sonnets and *The Spirit of Discovery*. Both *Elegy Written at the Hot-Wells, Bristol* and *Monody, Written at Matlock* continued the strain of poetic melancholy that Bowles inherited from Thomas Gray and then applied to Romantic settings. He also wrote elegiac tributes to fellow clergymen during these years, as well as melancholy reflections occasioned by his own serious illness in December, 1795, from which the allegorical poem called *Hope* resulted. Writing to John Thewall in November, 1796 (the poem had actually appeared a few weeks before the year of its imprint), Coleridge found *Hope* to be a poem "without plan or meaning, but the component parts are divine." In addition to Bowles's own sickness, there had been that of Harriet Wake, his fiancé, who died a year following their engagement, in 1793. In 1797, Bowles married Magdeline Wake, his dead fiancé's younger sister.

Though his influence on Coleridge's circle was now waning (Coleridge's visit that year had been disillusioning), Bowles came before the public as an established author, producing a series of longer poems: *Hope* in 1796; *Coombe Ellen* and *St. Michael's Mount* in 1798; *Song of the Battle of the Nile* in 1799; the seventh edition of his *Sonnets* (including *Hope* and a preface) in 1800; *The Sorrows of Switzerland* in 1801; *The Picture* in 1803; and *The Spirit of Discovery* in 1804. It was a remarkably prolific sequence of now-forgotten poems.

In 1804, Bowles was appointed vicar at Bremhill, Wiltshire, where he continued to live for most of his remaining years. He was also appointed prebendary of Salisbury Cathedral and spent some time there every year. Bowles's sonnets continued to be popular, and he published yet another long poem in an eighteenth century mode (*Bowden Hill*) but quickly gained a new and more controversial reputation with his ten-volume edition of Pope and his essay on Pope's "Poetical Character" in 1806. His views on Pope were criticized in the *Edinburgh Review* of January, 1808, and Byron (influenced by the review) satirized Bowles in the anonymous first edition of *English Bards, and Scotch Reviewers* (1809), though John Cam Hobhouse wrote the actual lines on Bowles. In the acknowledged second edition (1809), Byron substituted lines of his own on Bowles, castigating him for opposing Pope, ridiculing his long poems ("Stick to thy sonnets, man!—at least they sell"), and jibing erroneously at an episode from *The Spirit of Discovery*, a poem that Byron had not seen at firsthand, as he admitted to Bowles three years later. Relations after 1812 were cordial, and Bowles even proposed that Byron add some lines (he did not) to Bowles's forthcoming long poem *The Missionary*. This latest effort, though it had four editions, was dismissed by George Daniel in *The Modern Dunciad* (1814): "While Bowles exists," he asked, "can satire want a dunce?" Similarly, John Hamilton Reynolds characterized Bowles as a gabbling goose in *The Champion* of April 7, 1816, and Bowles's outraged reply of May 12 did nothing to improve his reputation. That same year, Coleridge visited Bowles at Bremhill and had the temerity to correct his poems, for which he was hardly forgiven. The public, it seemed, had tired of Bowles and his evangelistic inanities.

Nevertheless, it was Coleridge who paid Bowles the tribute that immortalized him in literary history. In chapter 1 of *Biographia Literaria*, Coleridge specifically recalled his first acquaintance with Bowles's sonnets in 1789 and how, with almost equal delight, he later read three or four more publications by the same author, including *Monody, Written at Matlock* and *Hope*. Bowles and William Cowper were, for Coleridge, "the first who combined natural thoughts with natural diction; the first who reconciled the heart with the head." Coleridge also stated that Bowles's works "were of great advantage in the formation and establishment of my taste and critical opinions." Thus was the Wiltshire poet defended against his critics. Though later ones have often found Coleridge's enthusiasm for

Bowles inexplicable, his words are clear enough. Perhaps some of Coleridge's generosity toward Bowles reflected the assistance that Bowles had given him (through Byron) toward the publication of *Sibylline Leaves* (1817).

After 1817, Bowles was closely associated with Thomas Moore, of Sloperton Cottage (a three-hour walk from Bremhill), who has left a fine record of Bowles's eccentricities. In February, 1818, for example, Moore and his wife spent three or four days with Bowles at Bremhill and observed, "What an odd fellow it is! and how narrowly, by being a *genius*, he has escaped being set down for a *fool*!" But, Moore went on, "he is an excellent creature notwithstanding." That September, Moore praised Bowles in his diary as a delightful "mixture of talent and simplicity," then repeated his earlier opinion about Bowles's poetry almost word for word. That October, as well, Bowles seemed to Moore "the most delightful of all existing parsons or poets," for all his genius and blundering alike. There are brief glimpses in Moore also of Louisa Stuart Costello (1799-1877), the artist and poet whom Bowles had taken as his protégé. She is best known in literary history for *Songs of a Stranger* (1825), which was dedicated to Bowles. Her *Specimens of the Early Poetry of France* (1835) was dedicated to Moore.

The controversy over Pope began in earnest in 1819, when Thomas Campbell's *Specimens of the English Poets* appeared, championing Pope. Bowles immediately replied with a pamphlet essay on "The Invariable Principles of Poetry" (1819) addressed specifically to Campbell, whose remarks on Pope had been excerpted by the *Morning Chronicle* as an answer to Bowles. Bowles's pamphlet, originally intended as a public letter to Moore, was supposedly dictated by its author to a waiter in the bar of the White Hart pub, Salisbury. In all, Bowles wrote six pamphlets pertaining to the Pope controversy, two of them in response to letters from Byron. J. J. Van Rennes has listed twenty-nine publications generated by the controversy as a whole.

In the thirty years remaining to him, Bowles published six more volumes of poetry, including *The Grave of the Last Saxon*, *Ellen Gray*, *Days Departed*, *St. John in Patmos*, *Scenes and Shadows* (with an auto-

biographical fragment), and, for children, *The Little Villager's Verse Book*; none, except perhaps the last, had enduring merit. His more important medium in his later years was prose, and his most characteristic product the sermon. However welcome they may have been as guidance, Bowles's sermons seem not to have had more than local impact. Bowles remained productive until 1844, when the death of his wife crushed him. In January, 1845, he resigned his vicarate at Bremhill and retired to Salisbury, where he endured five years of senile helplessness until his death on April 7, 1850.

ANALYSIS

William Lisle Bowles was, with Thomas Warton and Charlotte Smith, among those who in the late eighteenth century sought to revive the sonnet form. His own sonnets are particularly noteworthy for their responsiveness to landscape. Their diction was influential, though less original than one might think, as some investigation of late eighteenth century descriptive poetry and the picturesque travel effusions of William Gilpin (1724-1804) confirm. If Bowles borrowed from other writers, however, greater writers borrowed from him. Thus, "To the River Wensbeck" is echoed by Samuel Taylor Coleridge in "Kubla Khan" and "Dejection: An Ode" (line 96). Similarly, Bowles's sonnet "To the River Itchin" influenced Coleridge's "To the River Otter," and his poem "On Leaving Winchester School" probably inspired two similar poems, "Sonnet: On Quitting School for College" and "Absence. Farewell Ode on Quitting School for Jesus College, Cambridge," by the better poet. Though ostensibly dated 1788, Coleridge's "Sonnet: To the Autumnal Moon" is almost surely an imitation of Bowles, just as Coleridge's "Anthem for the Children of Christ's Hospital" is an adaptation of Bowles's "Verses on the Philanthropic Society." Coleridge's sonnet "Pain" should also be compared with Bowles's sonnet XI, "At Ostend," to which it is indebted. Coleridge was indebted to Bowles not only for imagery, phrases, and subjects, but for attitudes as well. Thus, Bowles's early poems are topographical and melancholic, with time his major theme. He then moved toward more outgoing, humanitarian utterances and eventually to public manifestos full of noble sentiments but of no other lasting interest.

In Bowles's later sonnets, written after 1789 (when John Milton's influence on him became more evident), the diction is less stilted and of some historical importance. Sonnets XXIII to XXVII, for example, probably influenced William Wordsworth's "Lines Composed a Few Miles Above Tintern Abbey," which specifically echoes XXVII ("On Revisiting Oxford"). Sonnets XX and XXII anticipate the imagery of Percy Bysshe Shelley. Bowles was among the first of the minor descriptive poets to abandon much of eighteenth century diction in favor of a fresher, more experiential imagery, even if his own was weak, occasionally trite, moralistic, and too often encumbered by personification. Granting that Bowles failed to achieve poetry of lasting distinction himself, his own work still pointed toward the heights that Wordsworth and Coleridge achieved. Although Wordsworth's pronouncements in his preface to *Lyrical Ballads* (2d ed., 1800) do not always reflect his own poetic practices, they are surprisingly like a pro-and-con discussion of Bowles.

### MONODY, WRITTEN AT MATLOCK

Unfortunately, Bowles failed to develop as a poet beyond the promise of his later sonnets. His longer and more pretentious poems attracted readers in their day but now seem disappointingly flat. Among the best of them is *Monody, Written at Matlock*, which was a favorite with Coleridge. In it, an eighteenth century mind saturated with the melancholy of Thomas Gray confronts the Romantic landscape of the peak. Though a monody is normally a lament or dirge, often about another poet's death, it is hard to see what Bowles had to be so gloomy about, as there seems to be little connection between the landscape and his reflections, which are the expected ones of a poet revisiting a scene of his youth. There is, however, no better poem to compare with Wordsworth's "Lines Composed a Few Miles Above Tintern Abbey" to help one see both the conventionality and the originality of Wordsworth's masterpiece.

### THE PICTURE

A second longer poem of interest is *The Picture*, which (like Wordsworth's "Elegiac Stanzas") is based on a painting owned by Sir George Beaumont—in this case, a landscape by Peter Paul Rubens. Compared with Bowles's sonnets, *The Picture* already seems heavy-handed and regressive. It is still an interesting attempt at landscape aesthetics, however, and gathers within a single poem many of Bowles's characteristic pieties. Finally, there are good things in both *Coombe Ellen* and *St. Michael's Mount*, though the poems are overly long, easily outrunning their inspiration. Even at this early date, Bowles had begun to display his characteristic faults of insipidity, loquaciousness, and unoriginality.

### THE SPIRIT OF DISCOVERY

Bowles's longest poem (in five books) is *The Spirit of Discovery*, which, beginning with Noah, moves from the Egyptians, the Phoenicians, the Babylonians, and the Greeks to the discoveries of Columbus and Captain Cook. An appended prose analysis sufficiently describes the poem, which is a curious mixture of heroic aspiration and credulity. Although several of the Romantic poets, including Southey and Rogers, were attracted to Columbus and the age of exploration, only Coleridge (who preceded all of them) created major poetry on the theme, with *The Rime of the Ancient Mariner* (1798). Bowles's *The Spirit of Discovery*, with all its length and notes, is a pretentious failure, as were his works that followed. The only other work requiring mention is *The Missionary*, a long poem in eight cantos about Spaniards and Indians in South America; showing the influence of Wordsworth, Southey, and Sir Walter Scott, it involved some new techniques and was popular for a time.

OTHER MAJOR WORKS

PLAY: *The Ark: A Dramatic Oratorio*, pb. 1824.

NONFICTION: Pamphlets on the Pope controversy, 1819-1826; *Illustrations of Those Stipendous Monuments of Celtic Antiquity Avebury and Silbury, and Their Mysterious Origin Traced*, 1827; *Hermes Baritannicus*, 1828; *The Parochial History of Bremhill*, 1828; *The Life of Thomas Ken, D.D.*, 1830; *Annals and Antiquities of Lacock Abbey*, 1835; Sermons and pamphlets on religious controversies, various dates, to 1838; *A Wiltshire Parson and His Friends: The Correspondence of William Lisle Bowles*, 1926 (Garland Greever, editor).

BIBLIOGRAPHY

Little, Geoffrey, and Elizabeth Hall. "Coleridge's 'To the Rev. W. L. Bowles': Another Version?" *Review of English Studies: A Quarterly Journal of English Literature and the English Language* 32 (May, 1981): 193-196. This fine assessment of Bowles's poetry offers an illuminating overview of his poetic development.

May, Tim. "Coleridge's Slave Trade Ode and Bowles's 'The African.'" *Notes and Queries* 54, no. 4 (December, 2007): 504-510. May notes the influence that Bowles had on Samuel Taylor Coleridge's writing, and in particular how Bowles's work influenced Coleridge's Greek ode.

Modiano, Raimonda. "Coleridge and Wordsworth: The Ethics of Gift Exchange and Literary Ownership." *Wordsworth Circle* 20 (Spring, 1989): 113-120. In this comprehensive essay, Modiano provides informative coverage of English literature from 1800 to 1899 and examines the views of Coleridge, Wordsworth, and Bowles.

Rennes, Jacob Johan van. *Bowles, Byron, and the Pope Controversy.* New York: Haskell House, 1966. Bowles, who is referred to here as a "sonneteer of no mean deserts," edited a volume of Alexander Pope's works. In his edition, Bowles criticized Pope. This volume chronicles the correspondence that surrounded this controversy and provides useful background of Bowles and his contemporaries.

Vinson, James, ed. *Great Writers of the English Language.* 3 vols. New York: St. Martin's Press, 1979. The entry on Bowles, by Tony Bareham, calls him a second-rank poet, without much individuality. Nevertheless, he acknowledges that Bowles was carefully competent with an eye for details, and notes the popularity of *Fourteen Sonnets*, which restored dignity to a verse form that had been "neglected for the last two generations."

Wu, Duncan. "Wordsworth's Readings of Bowles." *Notes and Queries* 36 (June, 1989): 166-167. A perceptive and thorough reading of Bowles's poetry makes this essay worth consulting. Central to an appreciation and understanding of Bowles's imagination.

*Dennis R. Dean*

# NICHOLAS BRETON

**Born:** London(?), England; c. 1545
**Died:** London, England; c. 1626

PRINCIPAL POETRY

*A Smale Handfull of Fragrant Flowers*, 1575
*A Floorish upon Fancie*, 1577
*The Workes of a Yonge Wyt Trust Up with a Fardell of Pretie Fancies*, 1577
*The Toyes of an Idle Head*, 1582
*A Handfull of Holesome Hearbes*, 1584
*Brittons Bowre of Delights*, 1591
*Pilgrimage to Paradise*, 1592
*The Phoenix Nest*, 1593
*A Solemne Passion of the Soules Love*, 1595
*The Arbor of Amorous Devices*, 1597
*England's Helicon*, 1600
*Melancholike Humours*, 1600
*Pasquils Fooles-Cappe*, 1600
*Pasquils Mad-Cappe, Throwne at the Corruptions of These Times*, 1600
*Pasquils Mistresse: Or, The Worthie and Unworthie Woman*, 1600
*Pasquils Passe and Passeth Not*, 1600
*The Longing of a Blessed Heart: Or, Breton's Longing*, 1601
*No Whippinge nor Trippinge, but a Kinde Friendly Snippinge*, 1601
*The Ravisht Soule, and the Blessed Weeper*, 1601
*The Soules Heavenly Exercise*, 1601
*The Mothers Blessing*, 1602
*Olde Mad-Cappes New Gally-mawfrey*, 1602
*The Soules Harmony*, 1602
*A True Description of Unthankfulnesse*, 1602
*The Passionate Shepheard*, 1604
*Honest Counsaile*, 1605
*The Honour of Valour*, 1605
*The Soules Immortal Crowne*, 1605
*The Uncasing of Machiavels Instructions*, 1613
*I Would, and Would Not*, 1614
*The Hate of Treason*, 1616
*The Countess of Pembroke's Passion*, 1853
*Poems*, 1952 (Jean Robertson, editor)

## OTHER LITERARY FORMS

After 1600, the attention of Nicholas Breton (BREHT-uhn) turned to prose essays, dialogues, and fiction, including proverb collections and character sketches. *Auspicante Jehova: Maries Exercise* (1597) and *Divine Considerations of the Soule* (1608) are devotional treatises; such works as *Wits Private Wealth* (1607) and *Crossing of Proverbs* (1616) collect proverbs and other practical advice; and *Wits Trenchmour: Or, A Conference Between a Scholler and Angler* (1597) and *The Figure of Foure* (1597) discourse on daily life, including angling and other country pleasures. Breton's dialogues of youth and age, country and city, traveler and stay-at-home include *A Dialogue Full of Pithe and Pleasure* (1603), *The Wil of Wit, Wits Will or Wils Wit* (1597), and *An Olde Mans Lesson and a Young Mans Love* (1605). The vogue for travelers' tales appears not only in the dialogues but also in prose tales such as *Wonders Worth the Hearing* (1602) and *A Mad World, My Masters* (1603), while contemporary events are addressed in *A Murmurer* (1607), on the occasion of the Gunpowder Plot. Breton's romantic fiction, *The Strange Fortune of Two Excellent Princes* (1600) and *Grimellos Fortunes* (1604), frequently contains lyrics within the narrative, including the frequently anthologized "I would thou wert not fair, or I were wise." Always highly popular in London's booming pamphlet market, Breton was particularly successful with the epistolary *A Poste with a Packet of Mad Letters*, a much-reprinted series begun around 1603. His modern reputation as a prose writer depends chiefly on his contributions to the prose character, as in his *Characters upon Essaies, Morall and Divine* (1615), *The Good and the Badde* (1616), and especially *Fantasticks* (1626), containing characterizations of love, money, the seasons, the holidays, the times of day, and the months of the year. Many of the aforementioned titles (those without dates) may be found in Alexander B. Grosart's informative volumes on *The Works in Verse and Prose of Nicholas Breton* (1879). Breton's prose works were immensely successful best sellers.

## ACHIEVEMENTS

One of the first English authors to earn a living entirely by writing, Nicholas Breton spent fifty years producing literary works that encompass the height of the Renaissance and the beginning of the Jacobean period. A transitional figure, he provides a link between two related but highly contradictory sensibilities. Working in the major poetic categories of moral allegory in the style of Edmund Spenser, of lyric and pastoral in the Arcadian mode, of devotional meditation akin to that of Robert Southwell, and of popular verse satire, Breton bridges the gap between traditional and progressive, literary and colloquial, in a controlled and assured presentation that appears almost classical in its decorum. He treats the major topics of human and divine love, moral virtue, holiness and spiritual experience, honor and humility, court and country, the real versus the ideal social world, and the emotions of exultation and melancholy, integration and alienation. His settings in the Arcadian bowers of Renaissance pastoral prefigure Marvellian gardens, while his perception of the freshness and vigor of rural life, coupled with the depth and complexity of urban experience, helps to form the modern apprehension of the change in cultural values characteristic of early commercial capitalism. His conception of contemporary psychology of humors and the melancholy stance connects classical and medieval typology to the humorous characters of Ben Jonson and the seventeenth century dramatists, embodying the tension between traditional humanism and the new commercial ethic.

Always a popular writer with a keen sense of self-presentation and audience awareness, Breton employed a Renaissance poetic that looks forward to Metaphysical paradox. With careful prosody, simple diction, clear thought, and accessible imagery, he writes a consistently craftsmanlike verse that, as C. S. Lewis has noted in his definitive *English Literature in the Sixteenth Century* (1944), escapes the confines of the drab, undergoing gradual "aurification" into the golden. As one of the first such poets, and one with so long and distinguished a record of successful publication, Breton helped establish the poetics of the high Renaissance. Perhaps because of a lingering bias against the "popular" writer, or perhaps simply because of the extreme rarity of his surviving books, Breton has not always been accorded the attention he merits in literary histories and anthologies, an omission that still waits to be remedied.

BIOGRAPHY

The Breton, or Britton, family traced its roots to the company of William the Conqueror and held ancestral lands in Lincolnshire and in Layer-Breton, Essex, where Sir John LeBretoune was a knight banneret at the time of Edward I. Nicholas Breton's father, William, sought his living in London trade, establishing a respectable fortune speculating in church properties that had been confiscated during the Reformation. By the time of Nicholas's birth around 1545, the family consisted of prosperous members of London's mercantile class, holding its "capitall mansion house," according to William Breton's will, in Redcrosse Street, maintaining its country seats as well.

Following their father's death, the Breton sons' financial situation underwent a significant change, one that dictated the need to pursue professional careers. The marriage of the young men's mother, Elizabeth Bacon Breton (through whom the family was remotely connected with Sir Francis Bacon's family), to the poet George Gascoigne drained William Breton's substantial legacy away from his sons in a series of complicated legal maneuvers. Nevertheless, Nicholas Breton's youth seems to have been comfortable and even advantageous, as he was a part of the cultured middle class that so enjoyed the widening horizons of the English Renaissance. Although he seems to have been destined for one of the professions, Breton spent only a short while at Oriel College and never attained an academic degree. Nevertheless, he was familiar with classical and contemporary authors (Ovid, Petrarch, Dante, Torquato Tasso, Ludovico Ariosto, and Pastor Fido became his literary models) and with the courtly arts, which were to play a prominent role in his career as a poet in search of a patron. Although not much is known about his domestic life other than that he frequently adopted the literary pose of paterfamilias, it is known that he married Ann Sutton around 1592, and the births of four of their children and the deaths of two appear in the parish register of St. Giles, Cripplegate. For the apocryphal tradition that Ann was an "unquiet wife," little evidence can be found.

Of greater relevance to his literary career was Breton's close association with the Sidney circle, in the aura of which most of his lyric and divine poems were written. Mary Sidney, countess of Pembroke, appears as the ideal lady, a paragon of wisdom; the record of Breton's largely unsuccessful pursuit of her favor appears in various of his tales.

Although his early canon is still uncertain, Breton's literary career seems to have begun around 1575; this rather late date suggests that his poems had been circulating in manuscript from some time before. In any case, *A Floorish upon Fancie* was published in 1577. In 1589, Breton was mentioned in George Puttenham's *Arte of English Poesy* (reprinted in 1970), and he had the dubious fortune to be mocked by Thomas Nashe in 1591. The 1590's saw the publication of his first mature works, lyric and devotional poems in the Arcadian or Spenserian manner. His first aesthetically successful poem, the *Pilgrimage to Paradise*, a moral allegory in the Spenserian style with lyrics in the pastoral mode of Arcadianism, signals his break with the older tradition of Gascoigne. Many of Breton's lyrics, some still unidentified, appeared in the popular anthologies of the period. That his reputation as a lyric poet was firmly established is evidenced by the publication of *Brittons Bowre of Delights* by Richard Jones in 1591, which capitalized on the poet's name even though only about half the verses in the volume are Breton's, including his rather pedestrian elegy on the death of Sir Philip Sidney, "Amoris Lachrimae." *The Arbor of Amorous Devices* contains what is possibly Breton's best-known lyric, "Phillida and Coridon," played as a morning song by three musicians in country garb for Queen Elizabeth's entertainment at Elvetham, Hampshire, in 1591.

At the end of the century, Breton's attention turned to meditative devotional poetry with an intensity that his appreciative nineteenth century editor, Alexander B. Grosart, attributes to a conversion experience. The devotional series, from *A Solemne Passion of the Soules Love* to *The Soules Harmony*, presents a search for repentance, absolution, and spiritual union with the transcendent in the Christian Platonist and progressive English Protestant tradition. Breton's religious thought, while intensely personal and meditative, is always staunchly orthodox and accessible, avoiding the religious syncretism and esoteric influences characteristic of some of his contemporaries; it is staunchly conservative in its condemnation of what was popularly conceived of as atheism, represented as Machiavellianism or Epicureanism.

Throughout this period at the turn of the century, Breton adopted with increasing regularity the mask of the melancholy poet. This mask was a product of the contemporary psychology of humors and very conventional in the pastoral lyric; easy to see in this stance, however, is the growing alienation of the artist, divorced from both courtly influence and the common life, and always uncertain of status, conscious of the division between the pamphleteer's market and the calling of the New Poet whose advent had been perceived by Spenser. In his immensely popular *Pasquil* series, entertaining and edifying verse satires in the colloquial vein, Breton plays upon the melancholy aspect of the satirist. After the death of Elizabeth in 1603, his energies turned away from divine poetry to conventional moralizing in the popular mode, especially in the role of a crusty old paternal type, and ultimately away from verse to prose, particularly in the form of the dialogue and the character. It is as a prose writer that he is primarily thought of in seventeenth century studies. No one is sure of the circumstances or even the date of his death, which, as is perhaps fitting for one who lived so entirely by his pen, is usually assumed to be 1626, the year his last printed work, *Fantasticks*, was published.

ANALYSIS

Nicholas Breton's earliest published works introduce the theme of love and its loss, a concern that perhaps dominates all his verse. In the role of a self-deprecating journeyman poet trying his wings in "small handfuls" of flowers or herbs, sentiments "trussed up," "floorishes," or "toyes," Breton addresses courtly— that is, fanciful—love in a landscape peppered with gardens, dream visions, and the familiar courtly personifications of desire versus disdain. Fancy, the spirit of courtly love, keeps a school and a fort manned with allegorical figures and rustic types, where the young poet-lover receives an education in the ways of the court and courtliness. Banished into rural obscurity, he must struggle for reinstatement, a trial by which he learns to distrust "fansy fonde," affected courtliness, and infatuation, and to practice the important Bretonian virtue of patience—the long suffering of undeserved

slights in an atmosphere of pervasive, although vague, dissatisfaction, at the close of which he abruptly rejects all and turns his thoughts to eschatology. Although slight in themselves, and hopelessly old-fashioned in the style of Gascoigne and the older generation, these early works do establish the persona of the speaker, the themes of love and the ethical-religious life, and the pastoral mode for the mature works to come.

LYRIC POETRY

Of these mature works, surely the best-known are Breton's many lyrics, published in the popular verse anthologies. These lyrics are in the Petrarchan vein and the pastoral mode; to them Breton owes his reputation as a poet of "sweetness and purity," of a great sensitivity for nature and rural life. The earliest lyrics in *Brittons Bowre of Delights*, although conventional in imagery and plodding in meter, still possess a simple, musical appeal, whether celebrating ideal courtly love or complaining against love and fortune. One of Breton's favorite devices is foretelling doomsday in a series of unlikely perfections never found in the world, such as when "Words shall be deeds, and men shall be divine." In these poems and those in *The Phoenix Nest*, Breton introduces his pastoral lady, Phyllis, or Phillida, and the "silly shepherd" poet, whose vulnerable expressiveness permits the restorative working of the idyll, as well as his familiar setting of the garden with its herbal and rustic lore, such as in "A Strange Description of a Rare Garden-plot," where all the herbs are "weeds of wo," allegorical flowers.

The well-known "Phillida and Coridon," or "In the merry moneth of May," shows the naïve pastoral ideal in its dialogue, which begins in courtly coquetry ("He would loue, and she would not") but quickly moves into a pastoral world of frankness and good nature, and thus to lovers' oaths, "with kisses sweet concluded." The poem ends with a pastoral apotheosis in which Phillida becomes "Lady of the May," the queen of love, and that emotion, so long "abused" and "deluded" by courtly affection, is set right. This ideal world is darkened in "A sweete Pastorall," or "Good Muse rock me asleepe," by loss of love, the wreck of the shepherd's flock, and the silencing of the birds. In *The Arbor of Amorous Devices*, the lady has become even more ideal, perhaps in keeping with the growing influence of

Mary Sidney, more wise and "rich" in accomplishments, and more associated with virtue (Phillis) as opposed to the erotic Venus, whose Amor she blinds in "A Pastoral" ("On a hill there grows a flower").

Ultimately human love is rejected in favor of the divine. In Sonnet 3 of *The Passionate Shepheard*, Breton celebrates the advent of "wise" over foolish love and castigates "Lust the excrement of love." For the shepherd Bonerto, ideal love becomes the means of restoring faith and reason to a world darkened by age, death, and care; he says to his Aglaia, "I hate the world, but for they [thy] love." In this late collection of perhaps earlier verses, the shepherd and his lady live in the country of Minerva, or wisdom. In simple Marvellian couplets, they celebrate the pastoral ideal, free from dissimulation and conflict, which is the blight of the urban world. Breton's pastoral lyric attempts to re-create the Elizabethan Arcadia in a context that looks forward to Augustan gardens.

Among all of Breton's lyrics, perhaps the single most perfect is "A Sweet Lullabie," a simple, expressive treatment of the Bretonian topics of faithlessness and patience in an abandoned woman's song to her child, "Thy fathers shame, thy mothers griefe." Although it is crying, the infant is mercifully unaware of life's more sorrowful realities and the difficulties ensured by its uncertain legitimacy. The "Poor soule that thinkes no creature harme" is an eloquent contrast to an unfeeling world. As the baby is comforted by the song, the mother begins to hope that the child's charms can restore innocence and rightness to the world, securing the grace of both God and its "father false." The poem ends with the mother's wish that upon her death the child may vindicate her reputation, "Tell how by love she purchast blame," and appeal to its father's "gentle heart"—for although "His sugred words that me betrayde," he is yet of a "noble mind." This leads to a reversed ending in which the child laughs while the mother weeps, asking that it be shielded from the world's cruel inconstancy, "thy fathers qualitie."

### MORAL ALLEGORY

Turning from the lyric to more serious moral allegory in the Spenserian mode, Breton's *Pilgrimage to Paradise* recounts a dream vision in which the poet-pilgrim journeys from the "vain conceits" of courtliness to heavenly delights. Passing through the wilderness of the world with its assorted mythical temptations and metamorphosed creatures, he confronts the seven-headed monster of vice, the familiar medieval specter of the deadly sins, which he overcomes with angelic assistance, after avoiding the twin pitfalls of melancholy on one hand and overweening ambition on the other. Joining medieval personification to heroic epic, Breton illustrates the virtue of patience—here, informed moral choice—by setting ethical extremes, wealth and wisdom, gold and grace, against one another. To cross a turbulent sea, the pilgrim joins forces with a stoic fisherman, who has fled the court for a life of stalwart independence, thus uniting the active and the contemplative. The two negotiate a number of nautical perils to enter the city of the world, leading to a favorite Bretonian portrayal of a variety of human types—courtiers, merchants, churchmen, and foolish lovers—creating the city as a center of discontent, "outwarde wealth so ful of inwarde wo." Next, they encounter a more positive image of Renaissance culture, the university, and then the idealized court of Elizabeth, the "princely Queen," followed immediately by its dark mirror-image, a bloody battlefield, one of the small Brueghelesque landscapes that constitute an interesting aspect of Breton's vision. Ultimately they arrive at the church "Not built of lime or stone," a royal garden, a vision of the eternal bucolic in which is neither weed nor worm. The second part of the Pilgrimage, the "Countesse of Pembrokes love," presents the Countess as "true loves saint," the Phoenix of an earthly paradise addressing divine love in a soliloquy overheard by the poet. Rejecting all worldly pleasures and comparing herself to Mary Magdalen, she longs to be united with Christ, the true Phoenix.

This early Breton poem shows his Christian Platonist view of *caritas*, divine love, the basis of Breton's poetry in the many "passions" that followed. An undated but probably contemporary poem, addressed to Mary Sidney and, possibly for that reason, sometimes ascribed to her, is *The Countess of Pembroke's Passion*—"passion" being a Bretonian term for an extended meditation delineating the speaker's religious emotions. Repenting his early "fruitless labours and ruthless love," the poet meditates on Christ's passion, especially the example it gives of patience. Compared with later meditative poetry in the Metaphysical tradition, Breton's poem might seem conventional, but it does contain an unaffected, calm piety, a simple conversational style, and plain diction and imagery, as well as a dynamic emotional tone cast in simple yet flowing sestinas rhyming *ababcc*.

Breton's devotional poetry connects earlier religious polemic with later meditative poetry by developing the themes of the moral allegory in an interior and contemplative vein, attempting—in the style of Southwell, but without his extravagance—to cast religious experience in lyrical imagery. *A Solemne Passion of the Soules Love*, perhaps the most consistently satisfying of these attempts, celebrates the creative relationship between divine love and the human world. Standard biblical images join the more Petrarchan Phoenix and sun to create a sense of the contradiction between human weakness and divine perfection—lowly pebble and "azurde ski"—to be resolved through meditation. This exploration of spiritual transcendence, from despondency to ecstasy, appears most plainly in a two-part divine poem, *The Ravisht Soule, and the Blessed Weeper*, which first explores the experience of spiritual enlightenment (ravishment), and then offers the example of Mary Magdalen, whose lament and consolation at Christ's tomb is overheard in the poet's dream vision. *The Longing of a Blessed Heart*, an extended definition of divine-Platonic love, illustrates the relationship between the divine and the human and the transformation of the natural world by love. The poem's definition distinguishes *caritas* from other kinds of love in a discursive, conversational style anticipating the mood of seventeenth century meditative poetry: "Some thinke it [love] is a babe of Beautie's getting,/ Nurst up by Nature, and Time's onely breeding;/ A pretty work to set the wits a wheeting."

In his successful *Pasquil* series, Breton extends the quality of love or charity to the social world in an attempt to correct the vices of an increasingly complex order, applying an essentially medieval form to the matter of emerging seventeenth century policy. Prefiguring Jonsonian comedy of humors, Breton's satirist is a humorist suffering from extreme feelings motivated by anger or sorrow to which he gives vent in impas-sioned speech. In *Pasquils Mad-Cappe, Throwne at the Corruptions of These Times*, the satirist inveighs against the abuse of wealth and power, the ascendance of illusion over reality, folly above reason, conditions motivated by "Pride, power, and pence." His multitude of wealthy rascals is set against the good poor man "free from Fancie's vanities," who goes begging among the rich asses and dunces. "It is money makes or mars the man," Pasquil says, offering instead a pastoral ideal where "Pride shall goe down, and virtue shall encrease." *Pasquils Fooles-Cappe* addresses those too obtuse to heed the first jeremiad to bring about a more "honest kindness," without swaggerers, spendthrifts, lazy wives, wandering husbands, absentminded professors, or unscrupulous satirists. In the later installments of the *Pasquil* series, the conditions of melancholy and ambivalence render all human choice valueless. In *I Would, and Would Not*, the poet first claims and then rejects the entire gamut of human enterprise, resolving finally to preserve his own identity as a "religious servant" of common sense and a corrector of folly. It is not difficult to see in these complaints the dissatisfaction connected with the poet's uncertain status, the dangers of dwelling continually in the "fancy," concerns that appear in "An Epigraph upon Poet Spencer" in the *Melancholike Humours*, where the Spenserian characters lament that their creator has been forgotten.

## PROVERBS AND APHORISMS

In a lighter, more familiar vein are the sententious proverbs and aphorisms so popular among London's common readers, sentiments for wall samplers such as the Polonius-like patter of *Honest Counsaile*: "Nor pull up Hearbes, and cherish Weedes,/ Nor tittle-tattle, more than needs," or the maternal pithiness of *The Mothers Blessing*, or a twist on the familiar in a Machiavellian father's ruthless counsel in *The Uncasing of Machiavels Instructions*, properly rejected by his pious son. In *Pasquils Mistresse* the satirist debates the opposing characters of the worthy woman, whose Platonic intellect is her glory, and her unworthy opposite, the victim of feeling and folly.

Especially after the accession of James, Breton's moral verse occupies a considerably less lofty plane. *The Soules Immortal Crowne*, a heroic encomium of the seven moral virtues dedicated to the king, is remarkable chiefly for the extent to which "vertue," a variation of Renaissance *virtú* implying will and strength, displaces patience. Other verses dwell on gratitude and its polar opposite, ingratitude, the most virulent extreme of which Breton saw in the Gunpowder Plot of 1607. The end of *The Hate of Treason*, written for that occasion, glorifies the Jacobean court, castigating the mad aspirations of the "rebellious beastly Rablement," as *The Honour of Valour* glorifies the marital virtues of Lord Mountjoy by contrasting his stalwart traditionalism with the "drosse" of the present court in a vision of the eternal heroic rising above the "Dunghill" of contemporary policy. Although a far cry from the vision of the earlier divine poetry, these heroic ventures show Breton's concern with the ability of the human to transcend its limitations.

Whereas Breton's lyrics and moral allegory had early undergone the Elizabethan transformation from drab to golden, his later divine poetry and verse satire connect that change to the emerging seventeenth century consciousness. Always decorous in tone and diction yet iconoclastic in its perception of audience and of the self, Breton's Renaissance verse, set squarely in the mainstream of the moral and intellectual currents of his time, looks forward to the Metaphysical and the neoclassical alike.

## OTHER MAJOR WORKS

LONG FICTION: *The Strange Fortune of Two Excellent Princes*, 1600; *Grimellos Fortunes*, 1604.

NONFICTION: *Auspicante Jehova: Maries Exercise*, 1597; *The Figure of Foure*, 1597; *The Wil of Wit, Wits Will or Wils Wit*, 1597; *Wits Trenchmour: Or, A Conference Between a Scholler and Angler*, 1597; *Wonders Worth the Hearing*, 1602; *A Dialogue Full of Pithe and Pleasure*, 1603; *A Mad World, My Masters*, 1603; *A Poste with a Packet of Mad Letters*, 1603; *An Olde Mans Lesson and a Young Mans Love*, 1605; *A Murmurer*, 1607; *Wits Private Wealth*, 1607; *Divine Considerations of the Soule*, 1608; *Crossing of Proverbs*, 1616; *The Court and Country*, 1618.

MISCELLANEOUS: *Characters upon Essaies, Morall and Divine*, 1615; *The Good and the Badde*, 1616; *Fantasticks*, 1626; *The Works of Nicholas Breton*, 1879 (2 volumes; Alexander B. Grosart, editor).

## BIBLIOGRAPHY

Atkinson, Colin B., and Jo B. Atkinson. "Four Prayer Books Addressed to Women During the Reign of Elizabeth I." *Huntington Library Quarterly* 60, no. 4 (1999): 407-423. Discusses the changes in the place of women in religious thought and practice throughout the sixteenth century. Examines Breton's *A Handfull of Holesome Hearbes* and *Auspicante Jehova*, as well as two other prayer books.

Bullen, Arthur Henry. *Elizabethans*. 1924. Reprint. Great Neck, N.Y.: Core Collection Books, 1978. Bullen sketches the life and work of ten English authors of the Elizabethan period. He repeats the sketchy details known about Breton's life, then shows how the prolific author fits into his historical context.

Garnett, Richard, and Edmund Grosse. *English Literature: An Illustrated Record*. 2d ed. 2 vols. New York: Macmillan, 1935. Garnett and Grosse include a substantial essay on Breton and place him in the context of English literary history. This is an older study but a valuable one. Suitable for all levels.

Kunitz, Stanley, and Howard Haycraft, eds. *British Authors Before 1800: A Biographical Dictionary*. New York: Wilson, 1952. Provides a short biographical entry that seems to be based on the information provided in Sir Sidney Lee's article. Points out that Breton's literary influences come from the medieval period and not from his English Renaissance contemporaries. Breton was thought to have been a little too prolific. His only works of any distinction are his pastoral poems.

Lee, Sidney. "Nicholas Breton." In *The Dictionary of National Biography*, edited by Leslie Stephen and Sidney Lee. Vol. 2. Reprint. London: Oxford University Press, 1921-1922. This essay is the most interesting and detailed article about the life of Breton. Lee describes why Breton's birth and death dates are in doubt and insinuates that the poet had an affair with his patroness, Mary Sidney, the countess of Pembroke. Provides a detailed primary biography along with the whereabouts of Breton's few remaining first editions.

Tannenbaum, Samuel Aaron, and Dorothy R. Tannenbaum. *Nicholas Breton: A Concise Bibliography*.

New York: S. A. Tannenbaum, 1947. Breton has been almost completely ignored by scholars over the last three centuries. The Tannenbaums have published one of the only sources of any kind available on this Elizabethan poet. It is immensely valuable for the serious Breton student.

*Janet Polansky*

# ROBERT BRIDGES

**Born:** Walmer, Kent, England; October 23, 1844
**Died:** Boar's Hill, near Oxford, England; April 21, 1930

PRINCIPAL POETRY

*Poems*, 1873
*The Growth of Love*, 1876, 1890
*Poems, Second Series*, 1879
*Poems, Third Series*, 1880
*Prometheus, the Firegiver*, 1884 (verse masque)
*Eros and Psyche*, 1885
*Nero Part I*, 1885 (verse drama)
*The Feast of Bacchus*, 1889 (verse drama)
*Achilles in Scyros*, 1890 (verse drama)
*The Christian Captives*, 1890 (verse drama)
*Palicio*, 1890 (verse drama)
*The Return of Ulysses*, 1890 (verse drama)
*Shorter Poems, Books I-IV*, 1890
*The Humours of the Court*, 1893 (verse drama)
*Shorter Poems, Book V*, 1893
*Nero Part II*, 1894 (verse drama)
*Poetical Works of Robert Bridges*, 1898-1905 (6 volumes)
*Demeter*, 1905 (verse masque)
*Poems Written in MCMXIII*, 1914
*October, and Other Poems*, 1920
*The Testament of Beauty*, 1927-1929, 1930
*Poems*, 1931 (M. M. Bridges, editor)

OTHER LITERARY FORMS

Although Robert Bridges wrote poetry extensively, he was also a prolific scholar. His monograph on *Mil-* *ton's Prosody: An Examination of the Rules of the Blank Verse in Milton's Later Poems with an Account of the Versification of "Samson Agonistes* (1893, 1901) is a model of research. His *Collected Essays, Papers, Etc.* have been published in thirty parts by Oxford University Press (1927-1936). Bridges is probably most known in modern times for his correspondence with Gerard Manley Hopkins. Hopkins's letters to Bridges have been published (Oxford University Press, 1935, 1955), but Bridges destroyed his letters to Hopkins. The *Correspondence of Robert Bridges and Henry Bradley, 1900-1923* has been published (1940), as well as his *Three Friends: Memoirs of Digby Mackworth Dolben, Richard Watson Dixon, and Henry Bradley* (1932). Bridges also wrote a few poems in Latin.

ACHIEVEMENTS

Robert Bridges was poet laureate of England from 1913 until his death in 1930. In the last years of his life, he was generally thought to be the leading lyric poet of his time. His restrained, classical style was opposed to the extremes of Ezra Pound and T. S. Eliot and the rising tide of modernism in literature. Since his death, Bridges has fallen into obscurity. His six volumes of collected poems and plays are seldom read, even by specialists. Even if Bridges is not rehabilitated as a poet, however, he will be remembered as a significant scholar and editor. Bridges saved the poems of his friend Gerard Manley Hopkins from obscurity by editing them in 1918; thus he gave the world one of the major precursors of modernism. Bridges's studies of language and metrics were pioneering work, and he was one of the first to carry out real literary research in the modern sense. Finally, he is an important innovator in poetic form, whose discoveries place him on a par with acknowledged revolutionaries such as Eliot, Pound, Hopkins, and Walt Whitman as a creator of new forms of expression in poetic language.

BIOGRAPHY

Robert Seymour Bridges explicitly requested that no biography or biographical study should ever be made of him. He destroyed many of his personal papers, and his heirs have respected his wishes. Although there is no formal biography, the outlines of his life are well known. Bridges was the next-to-last child in a family of nine, born to comfortable landed gentry. Bridges went to Eton in 1854, where he showed an inclination toward the Oxford Movement. He matriculated at Corpus Christi College, Oxford University, in 1863, where he was athletic and popular as an undergraduate. He rowed stroke in the Corpus Christi boat in 1867 but took only a gentleman's second class degree in *literae humaniores*, the study of classical languages and the literature and philosophy of ancient Greece and Rome. At Oxford, he became a close friend of the brilliant but somewhat eccentric Hopkins, who became one of the most important modernist poets in English. Bridges and Hopkins carried on an extensive correspondence after their undergraduate days; although Bridges destroyed his letters to Hopkins, Hopkins's letters to Bridges have been published and provide a fascinating glimpse into the poetic workshop of these two talented men and their complicated personal relationship. Although Bridges was independently wealthy, he entered medical studies after he had completed the work for his B.A. degree at Oxford and earned his degree in medicine in 1874. He practiced for some time in various hospitals in London, sometimes under grueling conditions. In 1877, he was appointed assistant physician in the Hospital for Sick Children, Great Ormond Street. In 1881, he suffered a severe illness, apparently pneumonia with complications, and retired from his medical career at the age of thirty-seven.

In 1882, Bridges moved to Manor House, Yattendon, Berkshire. Two years later, he married Monica Waterhouse, the daughter of a famous architect. There, too, he and Harry Ellis Wooldridge produced *The Yattendon Hymnal* (1895-1899). In 1907, he moved to his final residence, Chilswell House, at Boar's Hill near Oxford. After publishing his first collection, *Poems*, in 1873, Bridges had been steadily publishing lyric poetry and closet dramas. His fame as a poet and man of letters increased over the decades until he was appointed poet laureate of England to succeed Alfred Austin in 1913. That year, together with Henry Bradley, Logan Pearsall Smith, and Sir Walter Raleigh, he founded the Society for Pure English. In his final years, Bridges was an enormously influential figure in the literary world, editing the poems of his deceased friend, Gerard Manley

Hopkins, in 1918, and composing his long philosophical poem *The Testament of Beauty*. He was decorated with the Order of Merit in 1929 and received honorary degrees from Oxford, St. Andrews University, Harvard, and the University of Michigan. He died at Boar's Hill, near Oxford, on April 21, 1930.

ANALYSIS

In the first half of the twentieth century, a literary revolution occurred. Pound, Eliot, and their associates overpowered the previous genteel Victorian style of polite verse. To the advocates of this modernist revolution, the lyric poems of Robert Bridges seemed to represent everything corrupt in art: Bridges was traditional, a craftsman, controlled, impersonal, polished, moral, and optimistic. Although he had served as poet laureate from 1913 until 1930 and was a very influential and respected writer for the last forty years of his life, the use of modernism obliterated his fame within a few years after his death, so that he is virtually unknown by modern readers. This fall from favor is not justified, and probably Bridges will one day be restored to his rightful position as a counterweight to Eliot in the 1920's, a worthy opponent of the new wave.

Bridges wrote only a few significant poems as a schoolboy. His serious inspiration came rather late, so that the poems collected in his first book, *Poems*, appear to have been written mainly in the preceding year. The 1873 collection is uneven, sometimes unsophisticated, and Bridges later tried to buy and destroy all the copies printed. He rewrote, added some poems, and deleted others entirely for his second series (1879) and his third series (1880). The *Shorter Poems* in four books published in 1890 grew out of the earlier volumes and established him as one of the leading poets of his time.

**POEMS, THIRD SERIES**

The 1880 *Poems, Third Series*, contains the justly famous "London Snow." This poem, written in rhymed iambic pentameter, describes London under an unusually heavy snowfall. Characteristically, Bridges describes the scene with detachment and great attention to detail. He tries to be accurate and not to inject an "unreal" sentiment into the scene. He tries to avoid the "pathetic fallacy," or the projection of imagined feelings onto nature. "When men were all asleep the snow came flying,/ In large white flakes falling on the city brown." There is nothing supernatural in Bridges's scene, nor is there any extravagant emotion. The snow falls until the city is buried under a seven-inch, bright white coating. The citizens of London awake early because of the unaccustomed light reflected from the whiteness. The city is strangely hushed, as business has come to a halt. Schoolboys taste the pure snow and throw snowballs. The trees are decked with snowy robes. Only a few carts struggle through the nearly deserted streets, and the sun gleams on the dome of St. Paul's Cathedral. Then, "sombre men, past tale of number" go forth to battle against the snow, trampling dark paths as they clear the streets and break the charm of the scene.

This moving poem in the plain style contrasts with the dark life in the city and the momentary ability of nature to create a miraculous transformation in the very heart of the urban environment. It suggests the momentary, but muted, spark of recognition of the city workers that there is some power of nature above human control. Bridges never resorts to any word or image in his text that is not plausible, easily understood, and "realistic." Comparing his description of London to Eliot's urban scenes, the reader easily sees a contrast between the modernist vision and the calm, controlled, delicate feelings of the more traditional work of Bridges.

Another highly praised poem in the 1880 *Poems, Third Series* is "On a Dead Child." Bridges was for some years a terribly overworked young doctor in an urban hospital. He once calculated that he had less than two minutes to spend with each of his patients a day. There is no doubt that he saw much of death. Under the circumstances, it would be easy to become callous, to shut out feelings altogether. On the other hand, no topic is more likely to lead the artist into sentimentality than the death of a young child. Bridges's poem delicately employs understatement. The speaker is probably a physician whose very young patient has just died. The poem is written in seven stanzas each of four lines rhyming *abba*. The length of the lines varies, probably following in a muted way the practice of sprung rhythm that Hopkins and Bridges developed in some of their lyrics. In the first three stanzas, the speaker notes how beautiful the dead child is and how the hopes of its parents have been disappointed. Then, as the speaker per-

forms his last services to the corpse, it seems that the infant hand clasps and holds his fingers momentarily. He thinks then about the universality of death hanging over all people; "Little at best can all our hopes avail us/ To life this sorrow, or cheer us, when in the dark,/ Unwilling, alone we embark." Bridges typically recognizes the hardness of the human lot, born to pain and death. He states plainly and directly humanity's condition, then faces it without whining or screaming, but with optimistic courage. In the death of a child, he sees the death of all humankind. There is no use pretending that death is not fearful; still, the best course for humans is to face fate with whatever assistance reason can offer.

### "LOW BAROMETER"

The poem that best exemplifies Bridges's mind and art is "Low Barometer." Written in seven stanzas, each of four lines rhyming *abab*, the poem imitates the long measure of the hymnal or the four-stress ballad line. Romantic poets frequently wrote poems about storms; typically they would imagine themselves standing on a mountain peak in the middle of lightning and rain, calling for their spirits to match the wild frenzy of nature. Bridges's poem attacks such Romantic evocations. He does not want emotional storms; he prefers reason, control, and understatement. A low reading on the barometer signals a coming storm, and the first stanza describes such an impending gale. On such a night, when the storm beats against the house, supernatural fears arise in people, terrors of "god or ghost." When a man imagines weird presences, his "Reason kens he herits in/ A haunted house." Reason becomes aware of the feeling of guilt and fear normally suppressed in everyday life. This "Pollution and remorse of time" awakened by the storm is aroused in the depths of the mind, like some monster that, with "sightless footsteps," mounts the stair and bursts open the door. Some people try to control such horrible feelings by religion, but the monstrous images roam the earth until nature itself at dawn withdraws the storm and thrusts "the baleful phantoms underground" once more. Nature restores calm and order in the end.

### THE GROWTH OF LOVE

Many poets celebrate raw emotion: love, fear, or anger at its highest pitch. Bridges did not value emotion for its own sake. He felt that feeling should be restrained by reason, although reason itself knows that it is not sufficient to meet humanity's ultimate crises, such as death. Wise people seek control and balance; only the ignorant give themselves over to uncontrolled emotion. Bridges wrote a sonnet sequence, *The Growth of Love*, first published in 1876 in twenty-four sonnets but extensively revised in later versions. This work is modeled on the sonnet sequence of William Shakespeare, although the individual poems are written more in the style of John Milton. The traditional erotic sonnet sequence takes the form of the utterances of a lover; some of the poems in the sequence are addressed to the beloved lady praising her beauty, some are poems of seduction, and some are laments at her "cruelty." Frequently the sonnet sequence has an overall plot, involving a rival for the lady's affection, who receives the lover's scorn. Other poems address a faithless beloved, in which the lover is caught in a love-hate relationship with his lady. Usually the sequence traces the progress of a love affair as the lover approaches the lady, woos her, wins her, and rejoices in his victory, but sees her affections cool as another lover intrudes into his domain.

Bridges constructs *The Growth of Love* in the tradition of such a sequence, but typically he "tones down" the violence of emotion in each of the traditional postures. The reader expects the lover to be hot and passionate, but Bridges's speaker is calm and analytical as he examines his relationship. As a picture of human love, these poems are disconcertingly cool. It is frequently the case that erotic poetry is a vehicle for a religious or philosophical idea. For example, the biblical Song of Solomon appears to be spoken by a lover to his beloved, but an analogical reading of the text reveals that the song is about the love of man and God. Probably Bridges intended his erotic sonnet sequence to have a similar analogical meaning. If one understands the beloved to be not a woman, but rather the ideal moral perfection in life, the overall detachment in the work is understandable. The broad argument of *The Growth of Love* is reflected in Bridges's later long philosophical poem *The Testament of Beauty*.

### POETICAL WORKS OF ROBERT BRIDGES

The *Poetical Works of Robert Bridges* was published between 1898 and 1905 in six volumes. More than four of these volumes are composed of poetical dramas and masques. Obviously, Bridges spent much effort in writing dramatic poetry. Equally obviously, these plays are quite unsuitable for the stage, lacking action and sharp characterization. All the plays except *Nero Part I* were intended to be performed, but only the masques *Prometheus, the Firegiver* and *Demeter* and the play *The Humours of the Court* were actually produced—and these in amateur renditions only. It is difficult to see why Bridges expended so much energy on this kind of writing. In contrast, Robert Browning began his literary career with a series of more or less failed plays but went on to develop his dramatic monologues as a new and powerful form of poetry; one can see Browning building on his early failures. No such clear line of development, however, is discernible in Bridges. Most of his plays were written in the decade of the 1880's, and when his influential collected *Shorter Poems, Books I-IV* of 1890 appeared, his lyric poems were seen not to represent a logical progression from the dramatic works with which he had been occupied.

Bridges's best plays are historical: *Nero Part I* and *Nero Part II*. While this study of the decline of the Roman emperor Nero into madness and violence is a reasonable topic for a play, it is one unsuited to Bridges's talents. When the author of such work writes the speeches of a mad character, he must assume the mask and speak with a certain amount of sympathy for the eccentric point of view of a madman. In Bridges's best poetry, however, unlike Browning in his dramatic poems, he never plays the devil's advocate, but it is precisely this that is required for a satisfactory dramatic treatment of Nero, one of those figures who, like the fearful men in the storm in "Low Barometer," are swept up by the "unbodied presences" and "horrors of unhouseled crime." Bridges never puts himself inside such figures; he always stands outside them, describing them, judging them, evaluating them. While this is the strength of his poetry, it makes it nearly impossible for him to bring to life a character who is vicious or insane.

Bridges wrote four masques based on classical mythology; his model was probably Milton's *Comus* (1634). Albert Guérard, in *Robert Bridges: A Study of Traditionalism in Poetry* (1942), maintains that Bridges's earliest and most impressive masque, *Prometheus, the Firegiver*, "symbolizes the substitution of the God of

Love of the New Testament for the Angry God of the Old Testament; or, more generally, of modern Christianity for all less 'human' religions." Many readers, however, will agree with Bridges's friend and best critic, Gerard Manley Hopkins, who warned him that he should not try to write about the Greek gods in any case, because they were frigid and remote from modern experience.

## THE TESTAMENT OF BEAUTY

In his last years, Bridges wrote a long philosophical poem, *The Testament of Beauty*. The poem falls into four books: *Introduction*, *Selfhood*, *Breed*, and *Ethick*. The overall problem is to fit modern science into a meaningful framework: the relationship of Darwinian theories of evolution to the moral purpose behind death and suffering. *The Testament of Beauty* seems to move digressively, and its argument is not entirely clear. *Introduction* discusses at length the ramifications of evolution. The second book, *Selfhood*, studies egotism, self-preservation, and selfishness in their manifestations in the lowest forms of life up to their presence in humankind's highest artistic accomplishments and its darkest violence. The book discusses the carnage of World War I. Can all evolution be moving toward such pointless destruction? The third book, *Breed*, treats sexual instinct. It traces the growth of love from elementary sex to spiritual love. The fourth book, *Ethick*, explores the role of "reason" in conduct. As one would expect from Bridges's other works, "reason" is the key, the difference between humane, ethical behavior and mere brutality. Reason balances the instincts and the impulses of the human organism, molding evolutionary pressures into moral refinement.

## MILTON'S PROSODY

Bridges's study of the metrical form of Milton's poetry is one of the earliest examples of truly scientific observation applied to literary problems. *Milton's Prosody* was first published in 1893 and later republished in expanded form with the inclusion of a paper by Bridges's associate William Johnson Stone, "Classical Metres in English Verse," in 1901. Poetry differs from prose, Bridges contends, in that poetry maintains some controlled repetition or patterning in the language which is not found in normal, everyday speech. For Bridges, there were four types of meter in English

verse: accentual syllabic, accentual, syllabic, and quantitative. Each controls a different element of language so as to create a repetitive pattern. Accent involves the relative loudness with which a syllable is pronounced. Some poems, such as traditional ballads, seem to follow a pattern only in the number of loudly pronounced syllables in each line, no matter how many unstressed syllables occur. This is purely accentual verse. Other poems seem to have the same number of syllables in corresponding lines, but varying numbers of accents. This is syllabic verse. Classical poetry in Latin and Greek appeared to have been regulated by long and short vowel sounds, and it was traditionally thought that patterns of long and short syllables could be made up into "feet," or metrical units, based on the vowel quantity of each syllable. In Milton's *Paradise Lost* (1667, 1674), however, Bridges discerned an accentual-syllabic system that forms its patterns of repetition based on both the number of syllables in each line and the position of the more loudly pronounced syllables.

What is unusual about Bridges's study is his method of basing his generalizations on close scientific observation. Critics of his work might argue that when he deals with Milton's language, there is room for much misunderstanding. Is he talking about the production of sound by the human voice apparatus, or is he talking about the code of written speech, so many marks on a page? Is he perhaps talking about the way the human mind apprehends sound? Apparently he is governed by thinking of language as the production of sound. He says that language has stress, unwittingly referring perhaps to the stress felt when one pronounces a syllable more loudly than another by exercising the diaphragm muscles. So long as one grants that he is talking about the production of sound, his study seems well argued.

*Milton's Prosody* is subtitled *An Examination of the Rules of the Blank Verse in Milton's Later Poems with an Account of the Versification of "Samson Agonistes."* Typically the blank verse line has three characteristics: it has ten syllables, has five stresses, and is rising; the stresses are on the even-positioned syllables. Bridges first establishes that these characteristics occur in *Paradise Lost* and then examines cases which seem to deviate from the norm, trying for a generalization that can account for all exceptions, much as a law of physics is deemed "true" when it explains all occurrences. In separate chapters, he examines exceptions to the number of syllables being ten, the number of stresses being five, and the position of stresses being rising. These discussions are too detailed for summary here, but they should be examined by any serious student of English metrics. When Bridges turns to Milton's later poems, *Paradise Regained* and *Samson Agonistes* (both 1671), he finds that there is a much less rigid patterning, and he tries to account for the wider variations found in these poems.

The final section of Bridges's 1901 volume is taken up with Stone's "Classical Metres in English Verse: A History and Criticism of the Attempts Hitherto Made, Together with a Scheme for the Determination of the Quantity of English Syllables, Based on Their Actual Phonetic Condition." This essay is particularly important because it is the basis for Bridges's actual experiments in writing English poetry in the quantitative measures of Latin and Greek. Stone's study, however, contains many doubtful statements about the nature of classical languages. He believed that there was no difference between the classical long/short vowel quantity and modern spoken English vowels, and this assumption is improbable. Nevertheless, Stone proposes a method for determining the quantity of English vowels and for establishing in modern English a meter comparable to his understanding of Latin and Greek meters. Stone's death caused Bridges to feel obliged to justify or demonstrate Stone's theory in practice, and so Bridges attempted the metrical experiments published in his collected poems. Bridges also made a number of translations from classical languages into English in which he tried to preserve in English the metrical quantitative structure of the original language. Some of these translations are of extremely high artistic quality, such as the translation of Homer's *Iliad* (c. 750 B.C.E.; English translation, 1611), book 24.

### LATER YEARS

From about 1890 to 1930, Bridges was considered one of England's leading lyric poets. His fame was eclipsed at his death, but he has become established as an important, if minor, poet, part of the background against which the great modernists rebelled. His most important contribution to literature has not as yet been fully recognized: He was a pioneering scholar and experimentalist in metrics, and his greatest achievement was not (as he thought) his dramatic poems or his long philosophical verse but his experiments in quantitative meters.

### OTHER MAJOR WORKS

NONFICTION: *Milton's Prosody: An Examination of the Rules of the Blank Verse in Milton's Later Poems with an Account of the Versification of "Samson Agonistes,"* 1893, 1901; *John Keats*, 1895; *The Necessity of Poetry*, 1918; *Collected Essays, Papers, Etc.*, 1927-1936; *Three Friends: Memoirs of Digby Mackworth Dolben, Richard Watson Dixon, and Henry Bradley*, 1932; *Correspondence of Robert Bridges and Henry Bradley, 1900-1923*, 1940.

### BIBLIOGRAPHY

Guérard, Albert, Jr. *Robert Bridges: A Study of Traditionalism in Poetry*. 1942. Reprint. New York: Russell & Russell, 1965. This standard work on Bridges includes a comprehensive study of the lyric, dramatic, and philosophical poems. Guérard contends that Bridges is misunderstood if regarded only as a poet of happy emotions and that he is intensely serious, with a view of life that is far from completely rosy. The dramatic poems and plays form the bulk of Bridges's work, and their study has been neglected. This book, heavily influenced by the critic Yvor Winters, defends Bridges's traditionalism. Includes a conspectus of Bridges's sources and analogues.

Holmes, John. "The Growth of *The Growth of Love* Texts and Poems in Robert Bridges's Sonnet Sequence." *Review of English Studies* 55, no. 221 (September, 2004): 583-597. Article examines whether the different texts of *The Growth of Love* are different versions of the same poem or are actually different poems. Holmes looks at the publishing history of the poems, analyzes changes and revisions, and compares techniques.

Phillips, Catherine. *Robert Bridges*. New York: Oxford University Press, 1992. This biography discusses the ways in which Bridges reflected his Victorian background and examines his friendship with Gerard Manley Hopkins. Phillips demonstrates the ways in which Bridges, who lived until 1930, anticipated a number of modern advancements.

Ritz, Jean-Georges. *Robert Bridges and Gerard Hopkins, 1863-1889: A Literary Friendship*. New York: Oxford University Press, 1960. Bridges and the late Victorian poet Gerard Manley Hopkins were close friends from the days of their college years at Oxford. Ritz discusses Bridges's academic interests and friendships and analyzes in detail his correspondence with Hopkins. (Only Hopkins's letters to Bridges have survived.) Particularly valuable is the presentation of each poet's discussion of the verse of the other. Hopkins endeavored to give Bridges's poems more drama and a personal touch. Ritz is especially informative on the way in which Bridges's poetry reflects his character.

Smith, Nowell Charles. *Notes on "The Testament of Beauty."* London: Oxford University Press, 1931. Still a standard guidebook to Bridges's most famous poem. Smith begins with a brief discussion of its theme. The poem attempts to present the place of humankind in the universe, principally using Charles Darwin's theory of evolution as a background. It thus aims to sum up science and philosophy poetically. The bulk of the book consists of detailed notes on the poem. The author explains unusual words, paraphrases Bridges's meaning, and points out references to other poets such as John Milton and William Wordsworth.

Sparrow, John. *Robert Bridges*. London: Longmans, Green, 1962. Sparrow centers his study on Bridges's doctrine that poetry should express beauty, understood as a form of goodness. Bridges had the ability to vividly portray scenes from nature, a principal source of his poetic inspiration. His diction is carefully calibrated to evoke the moods he wishes to convey. He was particularly adept at using difficult meter as an instrument of emotional presentation. Although Sparrow devotes some attention to Bridges's failures, he rates him among the foremost English poets, as he was unsurpassed in the creation of beautiful poems.

Stanford, Donald E. *In the Classic Mode: The Achievement of Robert Bridges*. Newark: University of Del-aware Press, 1978. This book offers a detailed analysis of Bridges's experiments in meter: accentuated verse, quantitative meter, and neo-Miltonic syllabics. The work aims to give a full portrait of Bridges's literary corpus and includes the most detailed discussions of his plays in the secondary literature. Bridges's criticism also comes in for attention, particularly his study of John Keats. The discussion of George Santayana's influence on *The Testament of Beauty* is excellent.

*Todd K. Bender*

---

# EMILY BRONTË

**Born:** Thornton, Yorkshire, England; July 30, 1818
**Died:** Haworth, Yorkshire, England; December 19, 1848
**Also known as:** Ellis Bell

PRINCIPAL POETRY
*Poems by Currer, Ellis, and Acton Bell*, 1846 (with Charlotte and Anne Brontë)
*The Complete Poems of Emily Jane Brontë*, 1941 (C. W. Hatfield, editor)
*Gondal's Queen: A Novel in Verse by Emily Jane Brontë*, 1955 (Fannie E. Ratchford, editor)

OTHER LITERARY FORMS
Although Emily Brontë (BRAHNT-ee) published only one novel, *Wuthering Heights*, it is this work for which she is best known. When the novel was published in 1847, it won some praise for its originality and power, but in general, reviewers found its violence disturbing and its dominant character, Heathcliff, excessively brutal. *Wuthering Heights* did not offer the charm and optimism that many readers wanted to find in a work of fiction. As is often the case with original work, it took time for the world to appreciate it fully; today, however, *Wuthering Heights* is given a prominent place among the significant novels of the nineteenth century and is often discussed for its elaborate narrative structure, its intricate patterns of imag-

ery, and its powerful themes of the soul's anguish and longing.

By the time Brontë began *Wuthering Heights*, she had long been using her imagination to create stories full of passionate intrigue and romance. First, as a young child she participated in a series of family games called Young Men's Plays, tales of military and political adventures primarily directed and recorded by the older children, her sister Charlotte and her brother Branwell. After Charlotte left for school in 1831, Emily and her younger sister Anne began their own creation, a long saga of an island they called Gondal, placed in the north Pacific yet very much resembling their own Yorkshire environment. They peopled this island-world with strong, passionate characters. Unfortunately, nothing remains of their prose chronicle of Gondal. Two journal fragments and two of the birthday notes that she and Anne were in the habit of exchanging make mention of this land. These notes also offer some insight into the everyday world of the Brontë household and are of great interest for this reason. The only other extant prose, besides a few unrevealing letters, is a group of five essays which she wrote in French as homework assignments while a student in Brussels. This material has since been translated by Lorine White Nagel and published under the title *Five Essays Written in French* (1948). Some similarities can be seen between the destructive and powerful descriptions of nature and human character discussed in these essays and the world of Brontë's poetry and fiction.

ACHIEVEMENTS

Emily Brontë did not at first desire public recognition for her poetry. In fact, when her sister Charlotte accidentally discovered a notebook of her poems, it took time for Emily to accept this discovery, even though Charlotte found the poems impressive and uncommon. More time was required for Charlotte to persuade this very private poet to join with her and Anne in a small publishing venture. Once persuaded, Emily did contribute twenty-one of her poems to the slim, privately printed volume *Poems by Currer, Ellis, and Acton Bell*. To disguise her sex, each sister chose a pseudonym corresponding to the first letter of her name. This disguise also protected Emily's privacy, which she very much

desired to keep; she resented Charlotte's later unintentional disclosure of Ellis Bell's true identity. This disclosure occurred after the three sisters had all published novels under the name of Bell, arousing considerable curiosity in the literary world. Unfortunately, their collection of poems sold only two copies. Later, after Emily's death, Charlotte, convinced of her sister's talent, tried to keep her poetic reputation alive by including eighteen previously unpublished poems in a second edition of *Wuthering Heights* and Anne's first novel, *Agnes Grey* (1847); however, despite her efforts, it was not until the twentieth century that Emily Brontë's poems received any serious critical attention.

Interest in the poetry began as biographers sought to piece together the life of the Brontë family. It increased when the fantasyland of Gondal was discovered. Attempts were made to reconstruct the story from the poems, for it became clear that Emily had written many of her poems as part of that world of passion and guilt. Further attention was given to the poetry as *Wuthering Heights* gained in recognition, although readers were inclined to interpret the poems merely as an apprenticeship to a more masterful novel. Only since the mid-twentieth century has criticism begun to focus on the poems for their own sake.

Because of the seeming quietness of Brontë's life and because she was never part of a literary circle beyond that of her own home, there is a temptation to see her as an example of the isolated genius, sculpturing her forms in an instinctive style. On the contrary, Brontë was a skillful poet working within the traditions of her Romantic predecessors, handling standard poetic forms with subtle and effective variations. Although the dramatic extremes she found in the works of Sir Walter Scott and Lord Byron led her at times to employ conventional phrases and touches of melodrama, at her best she was able to embody in controlled verse an intensity of genuine feeling that sprang from a love of nature and a worship of the imagination. In her poems of the night winds and the whirling snowstorms of the moors, she distinguishes herself as a poet of nature's starkly vital powers. In her poems of the imagination, she places herself in the visionary company of William Wordsworth and William Blake. Throughout her poetry she expresses the desire of the soul to transcend the mortal limitations of time and space to merge with a larger presence, the source of all energy and life. She was an artist faithful to her visions, whose poems attest the strength of the individual soul.

## BIOGRAPHY

Emily Jane Brontë was one of six children, five girls and a boy, born to an Anglican clergyman of Irish descent, Patrick Brontë, and his Cornish wife, Maria Branwell. When Emily was two years old, the family moved to Haworth, where her father had accepted a permanent curacy. Haworth, a place now often associated with the Brontë name, is a village on the moors of West Riding, Yorkshire, in the north of England. In Emily's day, this rural spot was quite removed from the changing events of city life. The parsonage itself is an isolated building of gray stone near an old cemetery with its slanting worn tombstones. In this somber-looking house, in this quiet village, Emily spent most of her life.

The people filling this world were few in number. As a parson's children, Emily and her brother and sisters were not encouraged to associate with the village children, who were regarded as lower in social status. Their father seems to have valued his privacy, often keeping to himself, even dining alone, although there is no reason to doubt his affection for his children. As a result of these social limitations, the children provided their own entertainment, which often consisted of acting out imaginative games and later writing them down. Their education was in part provided by their aunt, Elizabeth Branwell, who came to care for them after their mother died in September, 1821, shortly after their arrival in Haworth. Tutors in art and music were occasionally hired for the children, and at least two libraries were available to them: their father's, and that of the Keighley Mechanics' Institute.

Emily left Haworth few times in her life. When she did, it was usually to continue her education or to gain employment. At the age of six, she and three of her sisters—Maria, Elizabeth, and Charlotte—were sent to the Clergyman Daughters' School at Cowan Bridge. Their stay was brief, for when the two older sisters, Maria and Elizabeth, were stricken with tuberculosis, from which they later died, their father had all his

daughters sent home. Several years later, in 1835, Emily attended school for a few months at Roe Head with Charlotte. Their plan was to prepare themselves better for one of the few occupations open to them, that of governess. While at Roe Head, Emily became extremely distressed with her situation. In later years, after her death, Charlotte indicated that she believed the cause to have been intense homesickness. Shortly after this rather unsuccessful venture from home, Emily did leave again, this time to take a position as a teacher at a large school near Halifax called Law Hill, but again her stay was brief. She returned home, obviously unhappy with her life as a teacher. One last trip from Haworth was taken in 1842, when she accompanied Charlotte to Brussels to attend Madame Héger's school. The sisters wanted to increase their knowledge of German and French to become better qualified to open their own school, a project that was to remain only in the dream-

*Emily Brontë* (Library of Congress)

ing and planning stages. While in Brussels it again became clear that Emily was not comfortable in an environment strange to her, and when the sisters returned home in November, 1842, for their aunt's funeral, Emily remained, seemingly content to do so. Thereafter, she stayed at the parsonage, helping with the household chores. Her family accepted this choice and considered her contribution to the running of the household a valuable one. In September, 1848, Emily caught a cold while attending her brother's funeral. It developed into an inflammation of the lungs from which she never recovered. Her death was perhaps hastened by her refusal to seek medical attention until the very end.

Much consideration has been given to Brontë's inability to adjust to life away from Haworth. Emphasis has been placed on her love of the moors, which was so intense that she could not long be away from the heather and open fields. It is true that her work indicates an abiding—at times compelling—love for their somber beauty; however, some attention should also be given to the fact that all these journeys from home required adjusting to a structured world, one perhaps hostile to the private world of her imagination. It is clear that the powers of the imagination played a dominant role in Brontë's emotional life from her childhood on. Apparently, at home in the parsonage, she found an environment that suited the needs of her imagination and its creative powers.

As the fame of the Brontë family increased, Emily Brontë herself became a figure of legend. She was described as a passionate genius of almost mythic proportions, possessing supreme will and strength. This interpretation was encouraged very early by Charlotte, whose respect for her sister increased greatly during the last months of her life: In Charlotte's eyes, her seemingly unobtrusive sister had become a solitary being, towering above others, heroically hastening her death. So long has this view been presented that it is now inextricably woven with Emily Brontë's name and image. She herself left so few biographical clues that perhaps the actual woman must always be seen from a distance; however, in her work there is indeed evidence of a poet of original, imaginative power, who, having chosen her God of Visions, was able to give poetic expression to the essential emotions of the human soul.

## ANALYSIS

When interpreting Emily Brontë's poetry, one must first confront the Gondal problem: What is the significance of that exotic world of emotional drama that so occupied her imagination? Some readers argue that this imaginary world of rebellion and punishment, death and lost love, permeated all her work; others maintain that her finer poems were composed outside its dramatic, at times melodramatic, influences. Brontë's own division of the poems into two notebooks, one titled "Gondal Poems," the other left untitled, would suggest a clear separation; yet a subjective lyrical voice can be heard in many of the Gondal poems, and echoes of the Gondal drama can be heard in non-Gondal material. Because the original prose saga has been lost, perhaps no completely satisfactory solution can be found; nevertheless, a thematic approach to Brontë's poetry does provide a unifying interpretation.

Many of her Gondal characters are isolated figures who yearn for a time of love or freedom now lost. In the non-Gondal poems, the same voice of longing can be heard: The speakers of such poems as "The Philosopher" and "To Imagination" desire a time of union and harmony, or, as in "O Thy Bright Eyes Must Answer Now," a time of freedom from the restraints of reason and earthly cares. The Gondal characters, with their exotic-sounding names (such as Augusta Geraldine Almeda and Julius Brenzaida), are not beings separate and distinct from the poet herself; they are masks through which Brontë speaks. Therefore, although Brontë often uses the dramatic forms of direct address, inquiry, and dialogue, none of her poems can be adequately analyzed as if it were a dramatic monologue prefiguring the work of Robert Browning. She does not attempt to delineate a character through the subtleties of his speech in a particular time and place. The desperate situations in which she places her dramatic figures merely provide appropriate circumstances in which to express the emotional and at times mystical experiences of her own private world. Continually, her poems emphasize the creative power of the individual spirit as it struggles to define itself in relation to the "Invisible," the unseen source of all existence. This struggle in all its intensity is the predominant theme of her poetry, whether it is set in a Gondal prison or on a Yorkshire moor.

Intensity is one of Brontë's distinguishing characteristics. Her poetry gives the impression of having been cut as close to the center of feeling as possible. The portrayal of such passionate intensity can easily lead to excessive exclamations in which meaning is scattered, if not lost; in Brontë's case, however, her skillful handling of form provides the needed restraint. She achieves this control over her subject through such structuring devices as simple metrical patterns (she was especially fond of tetrameter and trimeter), strong monosyllabic rhymes, parallel phrasing, repetition of key words, and appropriately placed pauses. Her use of these devices allows her to shape the intensity into ordered movements appropriate to the subject, whether it be a mournful one or one of joyous celebration.

## "ROSINA ALCONA TO JULIUS BRENZAIDA"

One of the best examples of Brontë's use of these structuring techniques to control feeling can be found in her best-known love poem, "Rosina Alcona to Julius Brenzaida," one of her Gondal poems often anthologized under the title "Remembrance." Rosina Alcona is addressing her lover Julius, now dead for fifteen years. She asks to be forgiven for going on with her own life after losing him. The anguish the speaker feels is captured in the wavelike rhythms established in the first stanza through the use of pauses and parallel phrasing: "Cold in the earth, and the deep snow piled above thee!/ Far, far removed, cold in the dreary grave!" Monosyllabic rhyme and the repetition of significant words also aid in embodying the emotional quality of a yearning that is held in check.

Brontë often achieves control through repetition of a key word, one that is repeated but with varying connotations. In the beginning lines of the poem, the word "cold" presents two aspects of the literal circumstances: The lover lies cold in the grave, and the coldness of winter is upon the land. As the poem progresses, "cold" evolves in meaning to encompass the life of the speaker as well. Without her lover, the warmth and light of her life are gone. He was both the sun and stars, and without him the heavens are now dark. Her life through the fifteen years following Julius's death has been winter, continually as barren as the snow-covered land, and to endure such barrenness, she herself has had to become "cold." She has had to "check the tears of

useless passion" and to chill the "burning wish" to follow him to the grave. Moreover, losing him to death has taught her one of the "cold" realities of life: "existence can be cherished" even after all love and joy are gone from one's own life.

This expanded definition of the word "cold" is underscored by Brontë's use of antithesis, another technique typical of her style. In stanza 3, Brontë juxtaposes the image of the lover lying cold and still in his grave and the wild movements of the weather that will ultimately lead to the warmth of spring. In the final stanza, she returns to the same pair of opposites: stillness and movement. The speaker refuses to indulge too much in "Memory's rapturous pain," her wild feelings of love and sorrow, for fear that she could not then face the "empty world again," the still frozen world of her own life. With this last description of the "empty world," Brontë returns to the image of coldness with which she began, and the tolling, elegiac poem is brought to rest, although with the phrase "rapturous pain" she points to the restless, unreconciled feelings of the speaker. These conflicting desires between the longing to remember lost love and the need to forget point in turn to the paradoxical nature of the whole poem: The speaker tells of the necessity of forgetting her lover, and yet the poem itself attests to her loving memory of him.

## "THE PHILOSOPHER"

In the non-Gondal poem "The Philosopher" there is a description of "warring gods" within the "little frame" of the speaker's physical self. This image could easily serve as a metaphor for much of Brontë's poetry: Within the confines of poetic structure, she attempts to hold conflicting forces and their related images. "Oh Thy Bright Eyes Must Answer Now" is a significant poem in the Brontë canon, for it clearly sets forth the dimensions of these conflicts. The first half of the poem presents the conflict between imagination and reason, between spiritual needs and earthly cares. The speaker turns to the "bright eyes" of the "radiant angel" of her vision, to summon it to speak and defend her choice to worship its power, rejecting the demands of Reason, who in "forms of gloom" with a "scornful brow" judges and mocks her "overthrow." By the world's standards, she has been overthrown, for she has failed to achieve wealth and glory. She has shunned the "common path" and chosen the "strange road."

The second half of the poem examines the inner conflict regarding her relationship to the overseeing "radiant angel" of this strange road. In stanza 5, she addresses this angel as "Thee, ever present, phantom thing—/ My slave, my comrade, and my King!" The speaker controls the influence, good or ill, of this angel. Consequently, he is her slave, and yet he is a comrade, an equal who is always with her, bringing her "intimate delight," and finally—seeming to contradict completely these two roles of slave and comrade—he is her King, directing and dictating. In these lines, Brontë is expressing the conflicting desires within the soul itself: a desire to remain free without being isolated, and a desire to maintain individual identity while simultaneously merging with a larger and more powerful being.

The last stanza of this poem points to the troublesome question underlying the complicated life of Brontë's visions: Is she wrong to choose a faith that allows her own soul to grant her prayers? In a very real way, her own imagination has conjured up the angel who will defeat Reason. It is characteristic of Brontë to place such emphasis on individual power and will. Although this emphasis prefigures the work of later writers in which the self creates its own reality and its own gods, the unorthodox road that Brontë chose to follow did not lead her to this extreme conclusion. The last two lines of "Oh Thy Bright Eyes Must Answer Now" return to her "God of Visions": He must "plead" for her. Her power was expressed in her choice to worship him, and now he must come to defend her.

### God of visions and nature

Throughout Brontë's work there remains an emphasis on an outside power that could and would exist whether she herself existed or not. One of the last written and most famous of her poems, "No Coward Soul Is Mine," is a ringing affirmation of her faith in her choice of visions. Her soul stands sure in its relationship to the "Being and Breath" that "can never be destroyed." When suns and universes are gone, it will still remain.

Many of Brontë's poems describing nature also concern this prevailing spirit, and occasionally they seem to present a pantheistic vision; however, although the natural world clearly had the power to stir and inspire her, nature and her God of Visions are not synonymous. Primarily, Brontë uses nature to parallel a state of mind or soul, as she does in "Remembrance," where the cold snow-covered hills objectify the restrained feelings of the speaker. Often the open moors and the movement of the winds are used to embody the wild, free feelings of the human soul. In "Aye, There It Is! It Wakes To-night," Brontë uses the powerful and violent images of the storm to describe a person being transformed into pure spirit as her soul awakens to knowledge of some supreme spiritual power. Like lightning, her "feeling's fires flash," her gaze is "kindled," a "glorious wind" sweeps all memory of this mortal world from her mind, and she becomes "the essence of the Tempest's roaring." The last stanza concludes that this visionary experience prefigures the life of the soul after death, when, free from the prison of the body, it shall rise: "The dungeon mingle with the mould—/ The captive with the skies." In these last two lines, Brontë plays on a rather conventional simile of the body as prisonhouse of the soul to create an original effect. First, she unexpectedly and suddenly introduces the word "mould" to represent the process of the body's decay and the dust to which it returns, and second, she compares the action of the soul after death to this process of decay: The body will "mingle" with the earth; the soul with the skies. There is in this last line a sense of triumphant release, effectively represented in the long vowel sound of "skies" that sharply contrasts with the earlier mournful sounds of "cold" and "mould." Throughout the poem, Brontë has again controlled an intensely emotional subject through antithesis, simple monosyllabic rhymes, and terse metrical patterns.

### "Julian M. to A. G. Rochelle"

Perhaps the most famous of Brontë's poems depicting this visionary experience is the lengthy fragment of the Gondal poem "Julian M. to A. G. Rochelle," which Brontë published under the title "The Prisoner." The fragment consists of lines 13-44 and lines 65-92 of the original with four new lines added at the end to provide an appropriate conclusion. This slightly revised excerpt, although beginning with the voice of Julian telling of his decision to wander rather casually through the family dungeons, primarily concerns the mystical experiences of one of the prisoners. When she speaks, she displays a spirit undefeated by her imprisonment. Her body is able to endure the chains, for her soul is open to a nightly "messenger" who offers her the hope of "eternal liberty." Her response to this messenger occurs in a series of stages. First, she experiences a mingling of pain and pleasure as visions rise before her. Then she loses all awareness of her earthly self; the world and the body are forgotten. She then is able to experience an "unuttered harmony." Her outward senses and conscious mind have become numb so that the "inward essence" can be released. In the final stage, this inward essence—in one burst of energy, as if leaping—attempts to merge with the "Invisible," the "Unseen," which she also describes as a "home" and a "harbour." At this point, because she cannot completely escape the body and still live, she suddenly and painfully returns to a knowledge of her earthly self and its prison, the literal prison in which she finds herself and the prison of her own body. Only after death can she finally and permanently join with the "Unseen," and so she looks forward to Death as heralding the complete and lasting union with the source of these nightly divine visions.

Brontë's decision to excerpt these particular stanzas from one of her Gondal poems, and the fact that once excerpted they still function as a unified whole, again suggest that Gondal merely provided the stage and the costumes for a drama that was actually taking place in Brontë's own self. In fact, in this case the poem benefits from the cutting of the frame stanzas that are full of conventional descriptions of stone dungeons and Lord Julian's somewhat expected romantic response to the fair prisoner. Obviously, Brontë's interest and poetic talent lay in examining and capturing the visionary experience.

## OTHER MAJOR WORKS

LONG FICTION: *Wuthering Heights*, 1847.
NONFICTION: *Five Essays Written in French*, 1948 (Lorine White Nagel, translator); *The Brontë Letters*, 1954 (Muriel Spark, editor).

## BIBLIOGRAPHY

Barnard, Robert. *Emily Brontë*. New York: Oxford University Press, 2000. An overview of Brontë's life and work. Bibliography, maps, illustrations (some in color), index.

Barnard, Robert, and Louise Barnard. *A Brontë Encyclopedia*. Malden, Mass.: Blackwell, 2007. An alphabetical treatment of the life and writings of the Brontë family.

Davies, Stevie. *Emily Brontë: Heretic*. London: Women's Press, 1994. Examination of the complex personality that produced *Wuthering Heights* and a collection of haunting Romantic poetry.

Frank, Katherine. *A Chainless Soul: A Life of Emily Brontë*. Boston: Houghton Mifflin, 1990. Biographical study demonstrating the complex relationships between Emily Brontë and her family members.

Gezari, Janet. *Last Things: Emily Brontë's Poems*. New York: Oxford University Press, 2007. Although most works on Emily Brontë focus on her novel, this one provides critical analysis of her poetry.

Miller, Lucasta. *The Brontë Myth*. London: Jonathan Cape, 2001. Biography of the Brontë sisters, explaining how previous biographers have shaped readers' understanding of the three novelists' major works.

Pykett, Lyn. *Emily Brontë*. Savage, Md.: Barnes & Noble, 1989. Feminist assessment of Brontë's work.

Rollyson, Carl, and Lisa Paddock. *The Brontës A to Z: The Essential Reference to Their Lives and Work*. New York: Facts On File, 2003. Takes an encyclopedic approach to the family, including ill-starred brother Branwell. Includes discussions of even many of the lesser known poems, as well as details of the lives of the authors.

Vine, Steve. *Emily Brontë*. New York: Twayne, 1998. Biography and critical analysis of *Wuthering Heights* and Brontë's poetry, intended as an introduction for general readers.

Winnifrith, Tom, and Edward Chitham. *Charlotte and Emily Brontë: Literary Lives*. New York: St. Martin's Press, 1989. Brief assessment of the impact the two sisters had on each other's writing.

*Diane D'Amico*

# RUPERT BROOKE

**Born:** Rugby, England; August 3, 1887
**Died:** Aboard a hospital ship on the Aegean Sea;
    April 23, 1915

PRINCIPAL POETRY

*Poems*, 1911
*Collected Poems*, 1915
*1914, and Other Poems*, 1915
*Complete Poems*, 1932
*The Poetical Works of Rupert Brooke*, 1946
    (Geoffrey Keynes, editor)

OTHER LITERARY FORMS

Rupert Brooke's lasting work is to be found exclusively in his poetry, but his work in several other literary forms at least deserves mention. Brooke was attracted to the theater, and two of his works, one as a critic and one as an artist, reflect this interest. *John Webster and the Elizabethan Drama* (1916) was written as his fellowship dissertation and later published; although much criticized for its lack of scholarly decorum, it reveals a lively style and an author fascinated with the remarkable developments in Elizabethan theater. His only play, a one-act tragedy titled *Lithuania* (pb. 1935), can be read with some satisfaction despite its bizarre plot and uncertain tone. As always with Brooke, his skill with language helps camouflage his errors and excesses. As a journalist, Brooke mixed with strong effect the lyricism of a poet with the enthusiastic observations of an excited traveler, most prominently in a series of articles that described his tour of the United States, Canada, and the South Seas, written for the *Westminster Gazette*. In these delightful pieces, he adeptly and wittily penetrates such subjects as the American personality, a baseball game at Harvard, and the grandeur of the Rocky Mountains. These display British wonder, sometimes dismay, at the "new world" but always stop short of tasteless condescension. Finally, Brooke was a masterful and enthusiastic correspondent; his letters contain enchanting representations of matters both personal and universal as he comments on a variety of subjects.

ACHIEVEMENTS

Any attempt to measure the achievement of Rupert Brooke as a poet must also account for the impact of Brooke as a dashing public figure in life, and as a hero and martyr in death. This is not to devalue the richness of his best verse, for his canon is mostly sound, and the tragedy of his early death is amplified by the tragedy of artistic potential cut short. Still, if ever a poet has been linked with an era, his physical presence and intellectual attributes defining the sentiments of a nation and its people, then that poet is Brooke. Any evaluation of his work is at once confused and enriched by the clamor that surrounded his life, art, and death. His life as student, citizen, and soldier reflects values prized by the British as they entered the twentieth century and endured World War I. His art is complex, but not in a metaphysical way. Rather, its mystery can be ascribed to the tension produced when the convictions of a traditionalist in matters of form and structure are linked with the passionate voice of an exuberant Romantic. Brooke's preference for sonneteering is well known. His topics and themes are more often quaint and predictable than unique and shocking (an effect he often desired to achieve). The poetry is classically graceful and romantically intense, always ultimately sustained by a gift for language. Finally, however, Brooke's death during World War I, the sometimes crude publicity that surrounded it and his memory, and the subsequent legendary status accorded him ensured for all time that critics would find it difficult to separate his life from his art, in an attempt to assess his legacy.

BIOGRAPHY

Rupert Chawner Brooke was born in Rugby, England, on August 3, 1887. His father, William Parker Brooke, was a Rugby schoolmaster, an undistinguished but competent classical scholar, a person perhaps most noticeable for his very lack of noticeable traits. Rupert's mother, Mary Ruth Cotterill, dominated the family and is often described as an organizer—energetic, efficient, strict, even domineering. One of Rupert's brothers, Dick, died after a short illness in 1907; another, Alfred, was killed in World War I three months after Rupert's death. Several commentators have made much of the death of a child who would have been Rupert's older sister, implying that somehow Rupert was always affected by the notion of being a disappointing replacement for an adored and much-lamented daughter.

Rupert Brooke realized many benefits from, but at the same time was assuredly strained by, his family's association with the British educational system. Although not unhealthy, neither was he robust, and he was heartily encouraged to develop his intellectual skills first and foremost. As a youth he exhibited a tendency to role-play, most often typified by world-weariness and grandiloquent language. His more engaging qualities included an active mind, interest if not excellence in some sports, and (to understate) a pleasing appearance that later became a significant part of his legend.

Brooke's life at Rugby was notable for the variety of his academic, social, and even athletic interests, and for his ability to develop close friendships with interesting people, a trait that stayed with Brooke always. Many of his friends were remarkable and passionately loyal to him; even mere acquaintances could not deny intense curiosity about him. As a poet, his early works show a young man enchanted with words and full of the impulse to parody the masters. He was more enthusiastic than polished, becoming increasingly so with each English poet whose secrets he discovered, digested, and imitated. Brooke adored writing contests and seemed to delight in shocking the sensibilities of his friends and family.

As a student at King's College, Cambridge, Brooke continued these activities, but now for the first time found real independence from his family in a stimulating and glamorous setting. In addition to his reading and writing, he now discovered the delights of political debate, the mysteries of such disciplines as psychology, and the pleasures of acting. He excitedly joined political discussions, joined the Cambridge Fabian Society, and worked diligently on its behalf. As an actor he exhibited no real talent, in spite of his ability to deliver poetic lines with great enthusiasm and a physical presence that, according to many, was spectacular. His career at Cambridge, undistinguished academically, was nevertheless solid.

He cultivated still more fascinating friends, showed a preference for "modern" works, and matured as a poet. At the same time, he confessed a weary tolerance for life, an attitude that his many activities would seem to contradict.

After his formal education and before World War I, Brooke found both peace and adventure. He spent some time reading and writing in a charming setting, Grantchester, and reveled in his surroundings and leisure, a welcome relief from his school years. For excitement, Brooke embarked in 1913 to explore the Americas and the South Seas, an excursion financed by the *Westminster Gazette*; the newspaper had commissioned him to send back impressions of his tour. He must have enjoyed himself; the pace was hectic, and he was greeted enthusiastically and with respect by his various hosts. His articles, often supremely "British" and critical of a general lack of culture in the Americas, are nevertheless important and enjoyable, suggesting increasing powers of observation and description.

Brooke's return to Britain was personally trium-

*Rupert Brooke* (Library of Congress)

phant and satisfying. He had confessed homesickness during his travels but was little prepared for his outright joy at once again reaching British soil. His friends greeted him exuberantly, and a series of social and artistic activities kept him busy. His future, as artist, as critic, even perhaps as politician, seemed assured.

Brooke's dreams were to be stalled, shattered, and canceled by World War I. It is a curious measure of the impact of Brooke's work and personality that he, with limited exposure to battle, eventually dying of blood poisoning, should ultimately be accorded the lavish praise of his countrymen, who saw him as the spokesperson for a generation of heroes. With many of his friends, he had expressed early disgust for the very notion of war, but he changed attitudes quickly, voicing the desire to find high adventure while ridding the world of the Prussian menace. He joined the Artists' Rifles, sought a commission, and eventually landed a post as a sublieutenant in the Royal Naval Division. His only significant action was to march with a brigade in relief of Antwerp, where he witnessed the realities of war. The column, however, retreated quickly after a few days of occupying trenches.

Later, Brooke's division received its orders for the Aegean and Gallipoli. En route, Brooke contracted dysentery; his condition weakened, he would fail and seem to rally from time to time. He lingered but finally died on April 23, 1915, at the age of twenty-seven, aboard a French hospital ship, in the company of a school friend. He was buried the same day on the nearby island of Skyros, where a memorial was later raised in his honor.

Brooke's memory, however, lived on, sometimes in ways that were flattering and meaningful, other times in ways that were distorted and tasteless. The poet who wrote with conviction about fair England and the soldier's duty and privilege to serve was mourned and eulogized by many, not the least of whom was Winston Churchill, who had recognized the value of Brooke's verse. Beyond his work, there were other matters, more difficult to pinpoint but significant nevertheless, that contributed to his fame. His background, his education, and even his dashing good looks (he was called the "fair-haired Apollo," to his embarrassment) represented what was best about "the Empire," and much of

the British approach to this war was intimately involved, of course, with "the Empire" and all it implied. It is too bad, in a way, that this fine poet and remarkable person has had to bear these burdens, for the excessive publicity obscures what is best about his work and life. Paul Fussell has rightly called World War I an "ironic" war; by that he means that the gestures and ideals of the participants appear almost ludicrous in the context of the brutal efficiency of the new century. There is much that is ironic about World War I's most famous poet, too, for today Brooke is often admired, often condemned, but in both cases, usually for the wrong reasons.

ANALYSIS

Anyone who wishes to be objective in his evaluation of Rupert Brooke's short poetic career must acknowledge Brooke's weaknesses as well as his strengths. There is the untempered voice of boyish spontaneity, the popularizer of mindless and almost laughable patriotic sentimentalism, the friendly versifier of late Georgian poetry that did little but describe nature redundantly. This Brooke penned such lines as "There was a damned successful Poet; There was a Woman like the Sun./ And they were dead. They did not know it" ("Dead Men's Love"); he probably deserves ridicule for having done so. On the other hand, fortunately, there is also the exuberant and mature voice of a craftsperson, the defender of the noble sentiments of a nation in crisis, and the innovative artist who sought freshness and vitality even as he worked within traditional forms. This Brooke deserves acclaim.

The best approaches to understanding and appreciating the poetry of Brooke are to reveal the themes of place and sentiment that dominate his works, and to recognize the fascinating way in which he blends structural integrity and fluency, which appears spontaneous, passionate, and bordering on the experimental.

"THE OLD VICARAGE, GRANTCHESTER"

Perhaps the work that most reveals these traits is "The Old Vicarage, Grantchester." Written in Berlin in 1912, this unusual poem, sometimes flippantly comic and other times grossly nostalgic, shows Brooke's tendency to idealize the past, or the "other place," wherever and whenever he was not. Written in octosyllabic couplets, it can be praised for the clarity and tension of its best lines; it can also be condemned for the immature slackness of its worst. A homesick traveler, Brooke sits at a café table in Berlin, conscious of the activity, much of it repulsive, about him. He begins with a graceful recounting of the natural splendor of Grantchester and its environs, but these pleasant thoughts are rudely interrupted by the guttural sound of the German language spoken around him—"*Du lieber Gott!*"—which sets up an immediate and abrupt passage in which the "here" and "there" are effectively juxtaposed.

The sudden introduction of a phrase, in Greek, which means "if only I were," is a nice touch (linking classical and British civilization), followed by repetition of his desire, to be "in Grantchester, in Grantchester." There is a long catalog of reasons why one would wish to be "in Grantchester," detailing the natural splendor of the place and much more. Among the many pleasures, the most notable are the educational tradition (especially a reverence for classics), familiar and comfortable personalities, and the respect for truth and decorous behavior that may be found there.

It is true that this poem is extended far too long and becomes tediously redundant; it is just as true that some of the lines cause the reader to cringe, often because Brooke seems not to have considered the veracity of his assertions ("And men and women with straight eyes,/ Lithe children lovelier than a dream"), at other times because his slickness is only cute ("Ah God! to see the branches stir/ Across the moon at Grantchester!"). Still, one finds "The Old Vicarage, Grantchester" to be solid and mostly complete, if slightly flawed. First, Brooke manages to describe Grantchester fully, with sufficient detail to make the reader understand why the poet is moved to such excess and to sympathize with him. This is not only a celebration of pastoral elegance but also a characterization of the people of Grantchester verging on a statement of values tending toward thematic richness. The vocabulary of fiction employed here is no accident, as the poem has many qualities of the introductory chapters of a novel, complete with protagonist and dramatic action. Second, there is an irony in some of the passages that establishes a tone distinctly superior to juvenile "romanticizing."

In short, "The Old Vicarage, Grantchester" repre-

sents the best and worst of Brooke; not surprisingly, it is the kind of poem that leads to conflicting and confusing evaluations of his work. Those who praise him for his sensitive descriptions of his homeland, those who see in the poem evidence of wit and sparkling phrasing, and those who cringe at his excessive sentimentality will all find here numerous examples to support their contentions.

## 1914, AND OTHER POEMS

Whereas "The Old Vicarage, Grantchester" is vintage Brooke, he is best known for his sonnets, particularly those he wrote during 1914, shortly before his death, which glamorized the fate of martyred soldiers. Brooke evidently found great satisfaction in the sonnet form, and obviously the long relationship was liberating rather than inhibiting, for he showed thematic and structural flexibility while remaining true to the principles of sonneteering. In addition to his evocation of place, Brooke treated in his sonnets such diverse subjects as death, memory, time, psychic phenomena, growing up, lust, and, of course, the pain and pleasure of idealized love as found in the grand traditions of the sonnet. He wrote in the Petrarchan manner, complete with the requisite imagery of the distant and taunting enamorata; he mastered the English form and the difficult closing couplet of the Shakespearean sonnet; and he exhibited the logical strength and confidence so apparent in the Miltonic brand. When bored, he tried variations, such as introducing a sonnet with the couplet (as in "Sonnet Reversed"); his experiments are never disruptive, but suggestive of the strength of the form, and anticipatory of later twentieth century inventions (E. E. Cummings, for example, might be mentioned here).

The five "1914" sonnets reflect Brooke's facility in the sonnet form, while at the same time incorporating sentiments that touched his countrymen profoundly. All deal with the transcending reward that awaits those who make the supreme sacrifice for home and country during the Great War. Again, depending on one's perspective, the sonnets are either inspiring and gallant calls to arms for a generation of martyrs, or naïve and morbid musings that typify the tragic waste of the conflict. The first, "Peace," alludes, ironically, to the new life evident in those whose existence had turned stale, who now benefit from clarity of purpose. Those who must die lose little except "body" and "breath," and are glad to escape their environment. The second sonnet in this sequence, "Safety," can be linked with "Peace," in that those who are sacrificed are referred to as "we." Again the comforting thought recurs that a soldier's death (what might be called a "good death") is to be embraced, not feared, for it presumes the existence of a condition beyond suffering and fear, beyond time, even.

The next two sonnets of 1914, "The Dead" (I) and "The Dead" (II), refer to the martyrs in the third person, but the philosophy remains much the same. In the first, the poet calls for public recognition of an honorable departure from life: "Blow out, you bugles, over the rich Dead!/ There's none of these so lonely and poor of old,/ But, dying, has made us rarer gifts than gold." Ancestral dignity is the rationale for these extreme sentiments; "holiness," "honor," and "nobleness" are evoked as those who pour out "the red sweet wine of youth" are finally able to realize their true "heritage." In the second sonnet of this pair, the celebration is of a pastoral bent, not only in the description of those youths who exist so intimately with the natural world (". . . Dawn was theirs,/ And the sunset, and the colours of the earth."), but also in the elegiac sestet, where the world of the dead is little changed in its excellence.

In "The Soldier," Brooke writes in the first person. Perhaps it is this immediacy ("If I should die, think only this of me") that made the sonnet so touching for his countrymen. More likely it is the sentiments expressed that captured the tragedy of a proud nation losing its best young men in war and somehow finding solace in the loss. Some might even call the poem overbearing, chauvinistic. In the opening lines, the poet asserts that mourning should be brief, for wherever he may lie, that spot becomes "for ever England," where the "rich earth" is more enriched by "a dust whom England bore, shaped, made aware." In the sestet, lest the reader think that only the physical is to be exalted, Brooke suggests that the English soul, "this heart," or "pulse in the eternal mind" will inhabit the universe, much to our advantage.

### GEORGIAN INFLUENCE

Brooke's poetry, then, is by turns admirable and condemnable. Another way to account for this baffling but intriguing trait is to place his work in relationship to what is called the Georgian Revolt. Brooke's role in this curious, little-understood era was a significant one: First, he was a close friend of Edward Marsh, whose Georgian anthologies set the tone for the period and who was eventually chosen to write Brooke's official biography; second, Brooke contributed to the anthologies and worked diligently to publicize the "Georgian" productions; third, the nature of Brooke's public and artistic reputation is as debatable as the confused reputation of "Georgian" poetry.

What "Georgian" has come to mean, of course, is the overly romantic, intellectually slack, structurally contrived efforts of a few "waspish" poets who refused to accept the birth of the twentieth century. The original plan of Marsh, Brooke, and others had been to provide a forum through which a new, energetic brand of modern poetry could transcend the stifling dominance of what was being called Edwardian poetry. The early volumes of Georgian work reveal this kind of energy, at least in comparison with later volumes after the war, when many of the best contributors had either died (Brooke and Isaac Rosenberg, among others), lost interest (Robert Graves, Siegfried Sassoon), or gone their own ways (Ezra Pound, D. H. Lawrence). Unfortunately, the later examples of Georgian poetry are frequently used by critics to describe the whole movement; for poets and critics of the late 1920's and 1930's, who demanded rock-hard language and precise imagery, there was nothing to do but to attack the Georgians with a vengeance.

### OTHER MAJOR WORKS

PLAY: *Lithuania*, pb. 1935 (one act).

NONFICTION: *John Webster and the Elizabethan Drama*, 1916; *Letters from America*, 1916; *The Prose of Rupert Brooke*, 1956; *The Letters of Rupert Brooke*, 1968; *Friends and Apostles: The Correspondence of Rupert Brooke and James Strachey, 1905-1915*, 1998 (Keith Hale, editor).

### BIBLIOGRAPHY

Delaney, Paul. *The Neo-Pagans: Rupert Brooke and the Ordeal of Youth*. New York: Free Press, 1987. In 1911, Virginia Woolf half-derisively gave Brooke and his carefree circle the label "neo-pagans." In this balanced appraisal, Delaney focuses on the flaws in the group's philosophies that undermined their optimism about the future, causing conflicts and fragmenting their relationships. Contains notes and references, a bibliography, and an index.

Hale, Keith, ed. *Friends and Apostles: The Correspondence of Rupert Brooke and James Strachey: 1905-1914*. New Haven, Conn.: Yale University Press, 1998. This collection of letters records the friendship and love shared by Brooke and Strachey, who first met at the age of ten. They were both eighteen and students at Cambridge University when they renewed their acquaintance, which marks the beginning of the collection.

Hamilton, Ian. *Against Oblivion: Some Lives of the Twentieth-Century Poets*. London: Viking, 2002. Contains an entry on Brooke, examining his life and works.

Jones, Nigel H. *Rupert Brooke: Life, Death, and Myth*. London: Richard Cohen Books, 1999. William Butler Yeats called Rupert Brooke "the most beautiful man in England." Jones draws on Brooke's previously unpublished letters to reveal what the publisher calls the "unsentimental truth." *The Times* of London comments, "Brooke is sharply perceived, his inner corrosion convincingly described and analyzed."

Lehmann, John. *The Strange Destiny of Rupert Brooke*. New York: Holt, Rinehart and Winston, 1981. In this highly praised combination of biography and literary criticism, Lehmann explores Brooke's psychological history and explains why Brooke's friends expressed conflicting judgments about his character and abilities. Contains an index and a brief biography.

Read, Mike. *Forever England*. Edinburgh: Mainstream, 1997. This biography allows Brooke to speak for himself through the inclusion of poems and other writings. The work also provides a well-rounded picture of prewar England, providing detailed background to various persons and places alluded to in the texts.

Rogers, Timothy. *Rupert Brooke: A Reappraisal and Selection from His Writings, Some Hitherto Unpublished*. London: Routledge & Kegan Paul, 1971.

Rogers says that Brooke has often been judged unfairly; the poetry has created the myth, and the myth has obscured the best in Brooke's work. Along with his collection of representative prose and verse, Rogers provides critical commentary, arguing persuasively that the charge of dullness frequently leveled at Brooke is unwarranted. A bibliography concludes this slight volume.

Turner, John Frayn. *The Life and Selected Works of Rupert Brooke*. Rev. ed. Barnsley, South Yorkshire, England: Pen & Sword Military, 2004. An updated biography of Brooke, a poet of World War I, that looks at his life and his works.

*Robert Edward Graalman, Jr.*

---

# ELIZABETH BARRETT BROWNING

**Born:** Coxhoe Hall, County Durham, England; March 6, 1806
**Died:** Florence, Italy; June 29, 1861

PRINCIPAL POETRY
*The Battle of Marathon*, 1820
*An Essay on Mind, with Other Poems*, 1826
*The Seraphim, and Other Poems*, 1838
*The Cry of the Children*, 1844
*Poems*, 1844
*Poems: New Edition*, 1850 (including *Sonnets from the Portuguese*)
*Casa Guidi Windows*, 1851
*Aurora Leigh*, 1856
*Poems Before Congress*, 1860
*Last Poems*, 1862

OTHER LITERARY FORMS
Elizabeth Barrett Browning was an accomplished Greek scholar, and from her translations she learned a great deal of her own prosody. In 1833, she published a weak translation of Aeschylus's *Prometheus Bound*. In 1850, she included in her collected poems an entirely new and substantially improved version of the same play. "The Daughters of Pandarus," a selection from

the *Odyssey* (c. 725 B.C.E.; English translation, 1614), was translated for Anna Jameson's *Memoirs and Essays Illustrative of Art, Literature, and Social Morals* in 1846. She modernized selections from *The Canterbury Tales* (1387-1400) for R. H. Horne's edition of Geoffrey Chaucer in 1841. She submitted occasional translations to periodicals, such as three hymns of Gregory Nazianzen, which appeared in the *Athenaeum*, January 8, 1842. Browning also published a modest amount of prose criticism. Four articles on Greek Christian poets appeared anonymously in the *Athenaeum* during 1842. For the same journal, she published five articles (all in 1842) reviewing an anthology of English verse titled *The Book of the Poets* (1842). Later in the same year, she reviewed a new edition of William Wordsworth. In 1843, she reviewed R. H. Horne's *Orion: An Epic Poem in Three Books* (1843) for the *Athenaeum*, and then she gave up literary criticism to devote more time to her poetry.

## ACHIEVEMENTS

Elizabeth Barrett Browning's principal biographer, Gardner Taplin, believes that "It is the quality of her life even more than her artistic achievements which will live" (*The Life of Elizabeth Barrett Browning*, 1957). The reasons for this fact, he believes, are to be found "in her fulfillment as [a woman], in her courageous and impassioned protests against injustice to individuals and subject peoples, and in her broad, generous, idealistic, Christian point of view." Literary critics since her time have insisted on thinking of Browning as a great woman poet, or as the Sappho of the age, or as the first woman to write a sustained sequence of sonnets. Her husband thought of her simply as having written the finest sonnets since William Shakespeare. The headnote to "Seraphim" indicates specifically that she invited comparison with Aeschylus. "A Drama of Exile" is a continuation of the Adamic drama just beyond the events described by John Milton and clearly invites comparison with him. Her sonnets can be compared with those of Petrarch, Shakespeare, Milton, and William Wordsworth. Whether she meets the measure of these models is problematical in some cases, doubtful in others. Still, her aim is consistently high and her achievement is historically substantial. She gave a strong voice

to the democratic revolution of the nineteenth century; she was a vigorous antagonist of those she thought were the enemies of children, of the world's dispossessed, and of popular government.

## BIOGRAPHY

In 1861, Elizabeth Barrett Browning died in her husband's arms in a rented apartment (unfurnished for the sake of economy). She had been born Elizabeth Barrett Moulton in one of the twenty marbled bedrooms of her father's estate, Coxhoe Hall. Her father had inherited a substantial fortune and the promise of remunerative properties from his family in Jamaica. When Elizabeth was three years old, the family moved to a still larger home, Hope End, in Herefordshire. This was to be her home until the abolition of slavery brought about sharp retrenchments in the Barrett family's affairs in 1832. After three years at Sidmouth, on the channel coasts, the family moved to London. Elizabeth was twenty-nine. Her family's congregational Protestantism and its strong support for the Reform Bill of 1832 had already helped to establish the intellectual landmarks of her poetry—Christian idealism and a sharp social conscience. In London, as her weak lungs became a source of chronic anxiety, the dark and reclusive habits that were to lend a fearful realism to her ideals became fixed in her mode of life.

Such anxiety found its consolations in a meditative piety that produced an increasingly intense inwardness in the poet. This fact partly explains why her poems are so commonly reflective, and so rarely narrative or dramatic. Eventually, she even gave up attending chapel services. In 1837, her lungs were racked by a persistent cough. In 1838, she left London for Torquay, hoping the sea air would afford her some relief. When her brother Edward ("Bro") had concluded his visit there and planned to return to London, Elizabeth pleaded with him to stay. He did so, but in the summer of 1840, as he was boating with friends, a sudden squall capsized the boat, and Bro was drowned. Elizabeth, who had been using laudanum fairly steadily since arriving in Torquay, almost lost her mind from guilt and distress. Macabre visions came to her and prompted in her a sharply balanced ambivalence between a wish to live and a wish to die.

Elizabeth returned to the family home at 50 Wimpole Street in London, more nervous and withdrawn than ever. She rarely descended the stairs and, in the darkened room, came to depend ever more heavily on the morphine, "my amreeta, my elixir," which dulled her physical and spiritual pains. She called her room a "hermitage," a "convent," and a "prison." The heavy curtains were always drawn. After her marriage, the images of her poems became less abstract and more concrete as she came to participate afresh in the parade of life's affairs. For readers of her poetry, the Casa Guidi windows of later years seem dramatically open as the colorful banners and the sounds of singing pass by.

In January of 1845, Robert Browning, then an obscure poet, wrote to thank Elizabeth for praising him in a poem she had recently published. She replied to the letter but was not eager to meet him. She had already declined twice to receive calls from the venerable Wordsworth, whom she had met earlier. She did receive Browning several months later, however, and their famous courtship began. Both parties claimed that they had never been in love before, yet Elizabeth did have a history of strong attachments to men. When she had lived at Hope End, her informal tutor in Greek, H. S. Boyd, had become so confidential with her that quarrels with his wife resulted over the time spent with Elizabeth. At Sidmouth, she had formed a friendship with George Hunter, a minister, whose wife was allegedly mad. Years later, during Browning's courtship, Hunter even followed him once to Elizabeth's room, where an unseemly encounter took place. Browning, on the other hand, characteristically formed strong attachments to women—the Flowers sisters, Fanny Haworth, Julia Wedgwood. Still, for these two idealists, love was something quite particular, not a vague sentiment, and their claim seems authentic enough.

The principal obstacle to their courtship was Elizabeth's father. Strong-willed, pietistic, and politically liberal, Edward Moulton Barrett saw Robert Browning as a footloose adventurer with a barely supportable claim to being a sometime-poet. Browning had no reliable means of support, and Elizabeth's father was certain that if the two were married, Browning would merely live off Elizabeth's ample but not boundless fortune.

*Elizabeth Barrett Browning* (Library of Congress)

On September 12, 1846, while her family was away, Elizabeth, nearly fainting with fear, made her way to Saint Marylebone Parish Church. Robert met her there, and they were married. It was the first time he had seen her away from Wimpole Street. She returned home for one week and then slipped out of the house to begin the long journey to Italy with her husband. She never saw her father again. He wrote her a cruelly condemnatory letter, disinherited her, and sent her books out of the house to be stored (the bills to go to Elizabeth). She was forty years old, a poet widely respected in England and the United States.

The Brownings' most enduring home in Italy was at Florence in the Casa Guidi, a fifteenth century palace located very near the palace of the grand duke of Tuscany. Although Elizabeth's health was a constant concern to the couple, it is nevertheless clear that in Italy she recovered something of the vitality of her youth. She lived quietly with her husband but enjoyed occasional walks to the bridges of the Arno and trips to the local churches, which were filled with incomparable treasures of art. She entertained guests more readily than she had in London and was able to accept the praise that great figures of the world brought to her doorstep in recognition of her growing fame.

In 1846, Cardinal Giovanni Masoni-Ferretti was elected Pope Pius IX. He immediately freed thousands of political prisoners, provoking the anger of the Austrian government. Disturbances broke out in Florence. The grand duke granted the people of Tuscany a constitution. The ecstatic populace of Florence marched to the ducal palace—right beneath the Casa Guidi windows. Later, however, when it appeared that Austria would intervene, the pope refused to sanction a war between two Catholic countries, and the hopes of Italian nationalists were curtailed. Riots broke out; the liberals saw their near goals slipping away—and, in 1851, Elizabeth published *Casa Guidi Windows*, a reflection on these events.

Browning's health was in fact sufficiently improved that on March 9, 1849, she was able to deliver a child—her only one—without the expected complications. Indeed, she became exhilarated and active just after the birth of her son, seeming much stronger than when she first married.

During the last ten years of her life, Browning traveled extensively between Venice, Paris, and England. She found England, however, a somewhat alien place, more unyielding in manner than the Continent. When she was in London, she wrote seeking a reconciliation with her father, asking him at least to see her child. In reply, she received two packets containing the letters she had written home in the years since her marriage—all unread.

At the close of 1856, back in Italy, Browning published a "novel in verse," *Aurora Leigh*. Critics gave the book a somewhat ungenerous reception, but the public bought out issue after issue. It was a genuine best seller. She was by now a true celebrity.

One volume of poems remained to her. In many ways, it was her most controversial. *Poems Before Congress* is hardly a book, more nearly a pamphlet of poems. In it she praises Louis Napoleon, who had raised the fears of England again—Napoleon *redivivus*. English friends alleged that Browning was politically unsophisticated for supporting the French. Browning replied, however, that this Napoleon would pry Italy loose from Austrian fingers; thus, her refrain is the

same—Italian nationalism. The freedom of her adopted land would not be abandoned just because it caused fears at home. In the same spirit with which she had opposed slavery when abolition meant the loss of her family's fortune, she now opposed colonialist friends. Some in her own day said that Browning was politically naïve; but no one has ever denied the magnanimity of her love for humankind.

As the Italian national movement gained strength, Giuseppe Mazzini, Giuseppe Garibaldi, and the Conte di Cavour all unified great territorial patches of the peninsula, but Browning's strength waned. She could no longer keep up with her husband's vitality. She languished under the long struggle with her weak lungs. On a June night in 1861, protesting the fuss made over her, she lay down to sleep. Later she roused and, struggling to cough, relaxed into death.

## ANALYSIS

Elizabeth Barrett Browning did not think it a kindness when critics praised her as a "woman poet." She would think it much closer to essentials if she were praised instead as a Christian poet. An evangelical of an old Victorian strain, she prized learning, cultivated Greek as the language of the Christian revelation, studied the work of the church fathers, and brought a fine intellectual vigor to the manifestly Christian ethos that shapes her work.

Like her husband, Browning suffered somewhat at the close of the nineteenth century from the uncritical applause of readers who praised the religious thought in her work merely as religious thought. A century after her death—and again like her husband—Browning began to enjoy the approbation of more vigorous critics who called attention to an element of intellectual toughness in her work that earlier critics had ignored. Now it is widely agreed that her poetry constitutes a coherent working out of evangelical principles into a set of conclusions that bear on the most pressing issues of modern times: the progress of liberal democracy, the role of militant nationalism, the ambivalence of the "woman question," and the task of the poet in a world without decisive voices.

In each case, the resolution she works toward is a further realization of the evangelical principle of the priesthood of persons. In many evangelical thinkers, a contradiction appears at this point: The antinomian doctrine of the depravity of humankind seems to contravene the doctrine of the high efficacy of individual thought; evangelicalism has, therefore, often encouraged a strong anti-intellectual bias among its followers. Because redemption is a matter of divine grace extended to childlike faith, there is no great need for secular learning. Browning, however, worked out a reconciliation of the dilemma: Fallen men can govern themselves well by a system of checks and balances that allows the many (because it is in their interest to do so) to restrain the venality of the powerful few. This reconciliation of the evangelical paradox allowed Browning not only to affirm the great egalitarian movements of her day, but also to believe that in them history was making "progress" on an enormous, though not continuous, scale. As a result, the poet is able to maintain a rather rigorous evangelicalism that is progressive, yet is not so facile and glibly optimistic as her early readers sometimes supposed. If it is her evangelicalism that endeared her to her own age, it is her wry, even grim sense of the role that personal failures must play in any realistic expectation of progress that has interested later critics.

## THE SERAPHIM, AND OTHER POEMS

The evolution of the ideas discussed above can be traced from Browning's first serious volume, *The Seraphim, and Other Poems*, to her *Last Poems*. The title poem of the first volume is an attempt to transform the story of Jesus's crucifixion into a classical tragedy. She had just finished translating Aeschylus's *Prometheus Bound* and was determined to make of Christ a hero equal in tragic significance to Prometheus. Two angels descend from heaven, attending the death of Christ. The entire perspective given to the reader is through the eyes of these two angels. The poem fails because readers never see its tragic hero; they only hear from afar three among Christ's last sayings. Thus, Jesus never appears in the poem as a dramatic figure. It is possible, of course, that Browning was reluctant to bring Christ on stage and put fictitious words in his mouth. It seems hopeless, then, to expect that the hero will evoke the tragic empathies that Prometheus does; thus, her poem is not a genuinely tragic drama.

## POEMS

In her second major volume, *Poems*, Browning makes two important advances. The first is that her leading poem, "A Drama of Exile," is no longer a mere account of events. Rather, there is more invention and conflict than in earlier poems: Outside the garden, surrounded by a sinister-seeming nature, Eve meets Lucifer for the first time since her fall. On this occasion she rejects him. Then, in a mystical vision, Adam and Eve see and hear the omnipotent Christ rebuking the taunting spirits of fallen nature and the pride of the triumphant Lucifer. Eve now forgives Lucifer, and Christ forgives Eve. Here, the poet ventures a dramatic representation of her views with a series of invented situations that constitute a small episode in her effort to build a poetically Christian mythology.

The second advance of this volume over her previous one is technical. It is at this point in her career that Browning begins to experiment with the sonnet. The volume contains twenty-eight sonnets on various subjects. All are Italian in form (divided between an octet and a sestet), and in all cases the first eight lines rhyme *abba abba*. In the last six lines, however, Mrs. Browning uses two different patterns. Some of the poems end with a *cdcdcd* pattern; others end *cdecde*. The profit to the poet is that her attempts with the sonnet force on her a verbal economy that is more rigorous than that in her earlier volumes. Petrarch, for example, brought this Italian form to its pitch of perfection, allowing himself the five rhyme values of *abcd* and *e* (two rhyme values fewer than William Shakespeare uses); Browning occasionally restricts herself to four rhyme values in a single sonnet—*abcd*. This practice imposes on her vocabulary even stricter limits than those imposed by either the Petrarchan or the Shakespearean form. Furthermore, the sonnets—some about grief, tears, and work, with two about George Sand—force her to be less diffuse. They force her to find the concrete image that will quickly communicate a complex feeling, rather than simply talking the feeling out as she does earlier: "Experience, like a pale musician, holds a dulcimer of patience in his hand. . . ." Her religious sentiments also are forced into sharper images: "pale-cheeked martyrs smiling to a sword."

It is also in *Poems* that she includes the romance

"Lady Geraldine's Courtship," which was to have significant repercussions for her. It is in this poem that she praises Robert Browning—eliciting his first letter to her—and it is here that she first attempts a theme that will not be fully realized until *Aurora Leigh*; that romance is plausible but handicapped in an unromantic (that is, an industrial, mercantile) age.

The last poem in the volume of 1844, though brief, is an important one in the poet's canon. "The Dead Pan" consists of thirty-nine stanzas, each containing six lines of iambic tetrameters (which do occasionally fall into an unheroic jog-trot), together with a seventh line of four syllables acting as a refrain. The poem produces just the image necessary to give Browning's religious thought the freshness, clarity, and invention necessary if she is to avoid mere clichés of faith in the search for an authenticating power in her poems. The subject of the poem is the ancient claim made by Plutarch (in *De defectu oraculorum* in *Ethika*, after c. 100; *Moralia*, 1603) that at the very hour of Christ's crucifixion, a supernatural cry went out across the sea, "Great Pan is dead," and that from that moment the pagan oracles lost their vision and power. In the poem, Browning utters a long roll call of the pagan deities and names them to witness that the prophetic power of an old world, mythopoeic and visionary, personified in the spirits of place—of forest, stream, and grotto—has been subsumed by a Christianity that is the new crown triumphant to a faded, classical past.

The poem is also a challenge to the skepticism and materialism of the poet's own age. The Christian religion has subsumed the ancient gifts of mystery and vision and has sanctified them by a revelation that marks them as being true, and by an ethic that adds to them the imperative to love. For Browning, the oracular voice of the modern world is heard in poetry. Some nineteenth century thinkers believed that, with the death of the mythopoeic consciousness, humankind had entered an age of rational secularism from which there could be no historical return. Matthew Arnold was such a thinker. For him, the loss of mythopoeic sensibility implied the loss of tragic sensibility. Against this sort of plaintive skepticism, Browning raised her protest. The Christian narrative constitutes the mythos of modern times, and the oracular voice of poetry constantly reinvigorates this mythology. The creativity and the virtuoso invention of Christian poets proves the vitality of the myths from which they draw, to which they add their stories and songs. Pan is dead, but the spirit—now illuminated by science—is as quick as ever.

### POEMS: NEW EDITION

Browning's next collection appeared six years later, after her famous elopement to Italy. *Poems* is marked by the distinction of containing *Sonnets from the Portuguese*, which previously had been available only in a small private edition. These forty-four sonnets had been completed in 1847. They are technically more sure-handed than the earlier ones. The same Italian octet is here *abba abba*, but Browning has decided unequivocally on a sestet that rhymes *cdcdcd*. The *e* rhyme has disappeared. She limits herself to four rhyme values in each sonnet. The effect is a tight, organically unified sequence of sonnets. This impression of technical unity is enhanced by the single-minded theme of the poems: "this very love which is my boast." The poet has nevertheless avoided sameness in the sonnets by avoiding clichés and by writing from her own varied experience of love. For her, love had been exhilarating and risky during the days of her engagement, it had cruelly forced on her the determination to defy her father, it had sorrowfully juxtaposed her frailty to Robert's vigor, and it had pitted her will to live against her expectation of an early death. These experiences provide the images that keep her poems from being merely conventional and confessional. Throughout them all, there is a grim sense of herself that tries to avoid melodramatic self-deprecation on one hand, while expressing an honest sense of her own limits on the other. This ironic view of herself gives the poems an underlying psychological realism that holds their Romanticism in check: "What can I give thee back, O liberal/ and princely giver" (Sonnet VIII); "Accuse me not, beseech thee, that I wear/ Too calm and sad a face" (Sonnet XV); "Unlike are we, unlike, O princely heart" (Sonnet III).

### CASA GUIDI WINDOWS

In 1851, Browning published her sustained political poem, *Casa Guidi Windows*. By this time, she had found a clear political expression for her evangelical ethic, "Manhood's right divine . . . to elect and legislate." The poem is written in iambic pentameter, which is well suited to protracted discourse. To avoid a too-liberal capitulation to prosaic looseness, however, the poet uses a generalized rhyme scheme, *ababab cdcdcd efefef*, through verse paragraphs of various lengths. The interlocking triple rhymes serve as a restraint on the rhetoric of the poem, but it is not a heavy-handed check. The incidents in the poem are few; thus, the burden of success is thrown on its ideas.

During 1847, the Brownings were living in apartments in the Guidi Palace overlooking the Piazza del Gran Duca, a public square in Florence. From her windows, Browning was witness to a number of enthusiastic demonstrations of popular support for an Italian nationalism aimed at severing Italy's dependence on the Austrian hierarchy—a dependence forced on the country in the post-Napoleonic European settlement engineered by Prince Metternich. This nationalism culminated in a revolt that failed in 1848. From her windows, Browning saw the joyful crowds agitating for national autonomy. Part I of her poem celebrates their libertarian hopes, "*O bella libertà*." The Florence of Dante, Petrarch, and Boccaccio is a political prisoner; its poets and artists are suppressed. Still, it is not merely for the sake of its heroic past that Italy deserves to be free. "We do not serve the dead—the past is past. God lives and lifts his glorious mornings up/ Before the eyes of men awake at last. . . ." It is God who has made men free. Piety is on the side of liberty. The first part of the poem is a rhetorical appeal to the grand duke of Florence, and especially to Pope Pius IX, to side with the people in this great controversy. The poet's evangelical suspicion of Church authority is laid aside in the hope that "authority" will do justice against Austria.

Part II of *Casa Guidi Windows* was written in 1851, after the failure of the revolution. Browning had seen somber faces of the defeated loitering in the square. The leaders, she believed, had failed the people. The duke had taken "the patriot's oath," but "Why swear at all," she asks, "thou false Duke Leopold." The pope has also vacillated: "Priests, priests—there's no such name," she protests. Her evangelical instinct was true; the pope has failed; "All Christians! Levi's (priestly) tribe is dispossest." Her grim disappointments at the failure of Italian nationalism in Part II are balanced against the exalted hopes of Part I and are resolved into a more subdued hopefulness for the future: "We will trust God. The blank interstices/ Men take for ruins, He will build into/ With pillared marbles. . . ." Popular sovereignty will win out.

### AURORA LEIGH

Browning's longest poem, *Aurora Leigh*, appeared at Christmas, 1856. It is a narrative poem fulfilling her earlier wish to set a romance in an unromantic age. The ironies of such a circumstance are resolved for her when it becomes manifest to the protagonists that love is not only a "romantic" experience but also a universal ethic. It therefore disarms the meanness of spirit, the poverty of values that the poet associated with the growing skepticism of a scientific and industrial age. The poem consists of nine books of approximately (but by no means uniformly) twelve hundred lines each, all in unrhymed iambic pentameter—blank verse. The poet had by then discovered from her own experience, as so many English-language poets have, the suitability of blank verse for high eloquence on serious subjects. Although this poem has a more detailed narrative framework than most of Browning's poems, it still is characterized by long reflective passages in which she devotes intense thought to the important ideas that arise from the narrative events. From the beginning, critics have observed that her characters are not persuasive, the incidents seem improbable, and the diction is uniformly stilted. The themes discussed, however, are confronted with a directness and boldness almost unequaled among Victorian poets.

Aurora Leigh is born in Italy of an English father and an Italian mother. Orphaned early, she travels to England to be reared by her father's sister. She becomes a retiring, moderately successful poet. Her cousin Romney, who has inherited the Leigh title and fortune, is a deeply compassionate Christian socialist with a strongly activist disposition. Aurora and Romney are drawn to each other, yet they so little understand each other that there is constant friction between them. This concatenation of events and characters allows Browning to bring together all the ideas she most cares about and to work them out in a single crowning achievement. The state-of-England question (the poor and the privileged), the Germanic North and the Latin South (England and Italy), the condition of women, the role of the artist in a socially conscious world, the nature of progress, nationalism, and the impact of science are among the issues finally woven into the poem. After years of circling about each other, proposed marriages to third parties, and the exhaustion of Romney's fortune on an ungrateful community of the poor, Aurora and Romney recognize that their ambivalence toward each other is actually a rigorous—that is, a not very sentimental—form of love.

The issues of the poem are resolved in the most comprehensive working out of these problems that Browning ever undertook. Romney acknowledges that his social activism has been too doctrinaire, too manipulative; it has ignored the practical realities of human experiences. Aurora acknowledges that the ferocity of her independence has masked a deep need for intimacy. Each finds that love—as both an ethic and a sentiment—gives complexity and vitality both to the social question (Romney's problem) and to individual identity (Aurora's problem). The poet believes that this kind of love is grounded in an eternal Divine and is therefore the key to resolving the antinomies in an age of conflict—nationalists against empires, poor against rich, men against women, and faith against doubt.

### CHRISTIANITY

According to Lionel Trilling, "Behind the [nineteenth century] struggle of romanticism and rationalism lies . . . the diminution of the power of Christianity" (*Matthew Arnold*, 1939). Browning was keenly interested in this issue, and her poetry, when viewed as an organic whole, is a substantial and single-minded effort to infuse fresh force into Christian thought by a poetic quickening of the Christian mythos, as many of her poetic fictions show. For example, in "A Drama of Exile," Christ appears to Adam and Eve in a vision, "in the midst of the Zodiac"; he rebukes the Earth Spirits who have been taunting the people for their sins. "This regent and sublime Humanity," he tells the spirits "Though fallen, exceeds you . . . by their liberty to fall."

The poet's effort to take the ancient images of Christendom and elaborate them by sheer poetic invention into a revivified myth gives her work its unity, but it also imposes on her poems certain inherent limita-tions. She never quite comes to grips with the possibility that if Pan is truly dead, then her own vision lacks oracular authenticity. In "The Seraph and the Poet," however, she presses her case that the modern visionary is the poet:

> Sing, seraph with the glory
> heaven is high;
> Sing, poet with the sorrow! earth is low: The
>     universe's inward voice cry "Amen" to either
>     song for joy and woe:
> Sing, seraph—poet,—sing on equally!

By imputing death to Pan, Browning has imputed death to other mythologies than her own. All mythologies, however, share a common epistemology, a common access to the morning-time sense of the world and to the tragic conception of human experience. Browning severs these ties that her mythology shares with the other great visionary images of the universe. This separation imposes on her conception of faith a somewhat sectarian and doctrinaire limit. It means that her themes tend to be stated as issues (nationalism, poverty) rather than ideas. In her poems, there is no rigorous testing of her own first principles. Still, she is one of the great libertarians of her age, and all the disinherited of the world—children, women, slaves, poets—and all who love freedom will find in her work a brave and unequivocal voice.

### OTHER MAJOR WORKS

NONFICTION: *The Letters of Elizabeth Barrett Browning*, 1897; *The Letters of Robert Browning and Elizabeth Barrett Barrett*, 1898; *Diary by E. B. B.: The Unpublished Diary of Elizabeth Barrett Browning, 1831-1832*, 1969 (Philip Kelly and Ronald Hudson, editors).

MISCELLANEOUS: *Prometheus Bound, Translated from the Greek of Aeschylus: And Miscellaneous Poems*, 1833.

### BIBLIOGRAPHY

Cooper, Helen. *Elizabeth Barrett Browning, Woman and Artist*. Chapel Hill: North Carolina University Press, 1988. Cooper discusses Browning's career as an extended effort to bring about a felicitous union of her femaleness with her art. The book deals cogently with all the major work.

Dally, Peter. *Elizabeth Barrett Browning: A Psychological Portrait*. London: Macmillan, 1989. Dally traces Browning's feelings about her fate, family, marriage, and literary life. Beginning with Browning's childhood regret that the family fortune grew from the slave trade, Dally records her emotional life through childhood, courtship, marriage, and life in Italy. Contains notes, a select bibliography, and an index.

Forster, Margaret. *Elizabeth Barrett Browning: A Biography*. London: Chatto & Windus, 1988. This full-length biography of Browning expands readers' understandings of her childhood years through hundreds of letters uncovered since the standard works of Dorothy Hewlett (1952) and Gardner Taplin (1957). Forster uses feminist critics in her interpretation of the long poem *Aurora Leigh*, which is now considered a major work. An essential chronological study. Supplemented by thirty-three illustrations, a chronology, notes, a bibliography, and an index.

Kizer, Carolyn. "Ms. Browning's Heavy Heart: Elizabeth Barrett Browning's Last Poems." *Paris Review* 42, no. 154 (Spring, 2000): 210-215. An insightful discussion of one of Browning's last poems, "My Heart and I." With reference to the early drafts of the poem, Kizer documents its progress line by line. Also discusses Robert Browning's role in the revival of these poems.

Leighton, Angela. *Elizabeth Barrett Browning*. Brighton, England: Harvester Press, 1986. This valuable study uses feminist theory to revisit the most frequently anthologized poems of Browning and to explore the less well known works. Topics include the influence of family, the male literary tradition, her sexual isolation, and political opinions. Complemented by notes, a bibliography, and an index.

Markus, Julia. *Dared and Done*. New York: Knopf, 1995. Markus, a novelist and literary historian, lifts the veil of misconception that has long concealed the truth about the love and marriage of Elizabeth Barrett and Robert Browning. As Markus chronicles the personal and artistic growth of this devoted couple, she insightfully analyzes their social and political milieu and how it shaped their lives and poetry.

Mermin, Dorothy. *Elizabeth Barrett Browning: The Origins of a New Poetry*. Chicago: University of Chicago Press, 1989. Part of a series titled Women in Culture and Society, this essential study brings Browning out of the sentimental arena and reveals her as a poet who negotiated her way through fierce gender and class barriers. Eight chapters arranged chronologically focus on her emotional and artistic development. Contains notes, a bibliography, and an index.

Stephenson, Glennis. *Elizabeth Barrett Browning and the Poetry of Love*. Ann Arbor: University of Michigan Research Institute, 1989. The linguistic and thematic problems of a woman poet writing about love in a male-dominated poetic tradition forced Browning to invent a feminine rhetoric. Women wrote about love from within a conventional mask. In this study, Browning is shown to have rejected the mask and dramatized new possibilities in her early ballads as well as in her sonnets and longer poetic works. Includes notes, a bibliography, and an index.

Taplin, Gardner. *The Life of Elizabeth Barrett Browning*. London: John Murray, 1957. Until Margaret Forster's 1988 biography, Taplin's was the standard work on Browning. It filled a major gap in Victorian studies with a comprehensive study of letters and other sources. It is still useful. Twenty chapters give a chronological picture of the poet's early family life of wealth and comfort, her decision to elope and live in Italy, and her literary success. Contains notes, a bibliography, an index, and ten plates.

Wallace, Jennifer. "Elizabeth Barrett Browning: Knowing Greek." *Essays in Criticism* 50, no. 4 (October, 2000): 329-353. Although Victorian women writers were expected to be emotional and sentimental rather than intellectual, Browning was one of the most scholarly woman poets of the nineteenth century. Wallace discusses the way in which Browning broke the stereotypes of women during her time, and the ways in which this affected her writing.

*L. Robert Stevens*

# ROBERT BROWNING

**Born:** Camberwell, London, England; May 7, 1812
**Died:** Venice, Italy; December 12, 1889

PRINCIPAL POETRY

*Pauline*, 1833

*Paracelsus*, 1835

*Sordello*, 1840

*Bells and Pomegranates*, 1841-1846 (published in eight parts and contains *Dramatic Lyrics*, 1842, and *Dramatic Romances and Lyrics*, 1845)

*Christmas Eve and Easter Day*, 1850

*Men and Women*, 1855 (2 volumes)

*Dramatis Personae*, 1864

*The Ring and the Book*, 1868-1869 (4 volumes)

*Balaustion's Adventure*, 1871

*Prince Hohenstiel-Schwangau: Saviour of Society*, 1871

*Fifine at the Fair*, 1872

*Red Cotton Nightcap Country: Or, Turf and Towers*, 1873

*Aristophanes' Apology*, 1875

*The Inn Album*, 1875

*Pacchiarotto and How He Worked in Distemper*, 1876

*The Agamemnon of Aeschylus*, 1877 (drama translation in verse)

*La Saisiaz, and The Two Poets of Croisac*, 1878

*Dramatic Idyls*, 1879-1880 (in two parts)

*Jocoseria*, 1883

*Ferishtah's Fancies*, 1884

*Parleyings with Certain People of Importance in Their Day*, 1887

*The Poetical Works of Robert Browning*, 1888-1894 (17 volumes)

*Asolando*, 1889

*Robert Browning: The Poems*, 1981 (2 volumes)

OTHER LITERARY FORMS

Robert Browning wrote letters copiously. Published volumes of his correspondence include *The Letters of Robert Browning and Elizabeth Barrett Barrett, 1845-1846* (1926, 2 volumes; Robert B. Browning, editor), as well as volumes of correspondence between Browning and Alfred Domett, Isa Blagden, and George Barrett. Baylor University holds extensive manuscript and document collections concerning Browning from which *Intimate Glimpses from Browning's Letter File: Selected from Letters in the Baylor University Browning Collection* was published in 1934. An additional collection of about four hundred *New Letters of Robert Browning* has also been published (1950; W. C. DeVane and Kenneth L. Knickerbocker, editors).

For a short time, Browning also attempted to write plays. Unfortunately, the impracticality of performing his particular dramas on stage doomed them to failure. The majority of these works can be found in the *Bells and Pomegranates* series, published between 1841 and 1846.

ACHIEVEMENTS

Robert Browning is, with Alfred, Lord Tennyson, one of the two leading Victorian poets. Although Browning did not invent the dramatic monologue, he expanded its possibilities for serious psychological and philosophical expression, and he will always be considered a master of the dramatic poem. Browning's best poetry appears in three volumes: *Men and Women*, *Dramatis Personae*, and *The Ring and the Book*. Browning typically writes as if the poem were an utterance of a dramatic character, either a creation of his own imagination or his re-creation of some historical personage. He speaks through a mask, or dramatic persona, so that his poems must be read as little plays, or as scenes or fragments of larger dramas. The dramatic mask allowed him to create in his audience a conflict between sympathy and judgment: As the reader often judges the dramatic speaker to be evil, he nevertheless sympathizes with his predicament. The dramatic monologue allows the author to explore the thoughts and feelings of deviant psychology to an extent seldom practiced before. On the other hand, when the author always speaks through a character, taking on the limitations and prejudices of a dramatic figure, he conceals his own feelings and ideas from his reader. His critics charge that he evaded the writer's most important duty by failing to pass judgment on his characters, and by presenting murderers, villains, and whores without a word of moral reprobation. He is accused of valuing passion for its own sake, failing to construct his own framework of values that would allow the reader to evaluate and judge the ethical position of his characters. Nevertheless, Browning deserves to be read as a serious innovator in poetic form; his conception of dramatic character influenced modern fiction as well as poetry.

BIOGRAPHY

Robert Browning was born in a London suburb, Camberwell, on May 7, 1812. His family could be characterized as comfortably middle class, politically liberal, and dissenting in religion. His father, a prosperous employee of the Bank of England, had collected a large private library. The family was dominated to some extent by the powerful personality of Browning's mother, the former Sarah Anna Wiedemann from Dundee, who was deeply committed to the Congregational religion. At a time when Oxford and Cambridge were religious institutions, admitting only Anglican students, Browning attended the newly instituted University of London for a short time in 1828, but he did not complete a coherent course of study. Browning was largely self-taught, and like many autodidacts, he had difficulty appreciating how deeply learned he was and judging what his more conventionally educated audience would be likely to know. His poetry bristles with allusions and historical references that require a specialist's explanation.

As a boy, Browning showed remarkable enthusiasm for the work of Percy Bysshe Shelley. Such an admiration is particularly surprising in the light of their divergent beliefs. Shelley was antireligious, especially in his youth, and was in fact expelled from his university for publishing a pamphlet on the necessity of atheism, while Browning's mother was firmly committed to a fundamentalist and emotional Christian belief. In any event, throughout his life, Browning depicted churchmen in an unfavorable light in his poems—a tendency that is perhaps understandable in a follower of Shelley, but one that suggests considerable tension between the mother and her son over religious matters. Shelley glorified the romantic rebel, as in his depiction of Prometheus, for example; Browning's father, on the other hand, was employed by the Bank of England, and

the family comfort depended on the stability and success of that existing order. Shelley's extremely liberal ideas about politics and personal relationships must have been difficult to fit harmoniously into the boy's comfortable, religious, suburban home life.

In 1852, when Browning was forty years old, a collection of letters supposed to have been written by Shelley was published, and Browning was engaged to write the preface. The letters were discovered later to be spurious and the volume was withdrawn from publication, but Browning's preface remains one of his most important explanations of his artistic theory. In the preface, Browning makes his famous distinction between "objective" and "subjective" writers, which can be imagined as the difference between the mirror and the lamp. An objective poet reflects or mirrors the outer world, making it clearer and easier to understand by writing about what takes place outside himself. The subjective poet, however, is like a lamp projecting from his inner flame a light by which the reader sees everything in a new way. Although the words "subjective" and "objective" seem to get hopelessly tangled as the argument proceeds, it appears that Browning views his dramatic characters as lamps, shedding their light on the world, allowing the reader to imagine the inner flame that produces such rays of fancy and imagination, shaping and distorting whatever they fall on.

At the age of twenty, Browning published *Pauline*, which was to be the first step in a massive work projected to be the utterances of a series of characters distinct from the author himself. The work is in the tradition of Romantic confessional writing. John Stuart Mill wrote an unpublished review of *Pauline*, which eventually came to Browning's attention, in which he accused the poet of having a more intense and morbid self-consciousness than he had ever before seen in a sane man. These cutting words are particularly ironic coming from the author of Mill's *Autobiography* (1873), a totally self-conscious production. Nevertheless, Browning was stung by the criticism and in the future tried to hide his own identity, his personal self, ever more cleverly behind the mask of dramatic speakers. *Pauline* was followed by *Paracelsus* and *Sordello*. These three works all treat the predicament of an artist or seer at odds with his environment and his historical age. The

*Robert Browning* (Library of Congress)

phenomenon of alienation, estrangement from one's own culture and time, is one of Browning's repeated topics, as is the role of the artist and the artist's relationship to society at large. Betty B. Miller in *Robert Browning: A Portrait* (1953) argues that there is a close identification between Browning and the central characters in these three works, so that Paracelsus is Browning, his garden at Wurzburg is identical to Browning's garden at the family home in Camberwell, and so on.

For about ten years, from 1837 to 1847, Browning devoted much of his energy to writing stage plays. These must be considered practical failures, although *Strafford* (pr., pb. 1837) ran for five performances on the professional stage with the famous tragedian William Charles Macready in the hero's role. Browning had difficulty in treating external action, which is necessary in a staged performance, and turned instead to internal conflicts that were invisible to his audience. Although the plays simply did not work on stage, they were the workshop for the great dramatic monologues in *Men and Women* and *Dramatis Personae*.

In 1845-1846 Browning courted the semi-invalid poet Elizabeth Barrett. They were married on September 12, 1846, and fled immediately to Italy. The popular imagination has clothed this romance in a gauze of sentimentality, so that Browning appears as a knight in shining armor rescuing his maiden from her ogre of a father. Even a cursory reading of the Browning-Barrett letters suggests that the romance was rather more complicated and contradictory. Miller's *Robert Browning* suggests that Browning had a need to be dominated by a woman. His mother supplied that role until her death in 1840, and then he found her surrogate in Elizabeth Barrett, who was a considerably more famous writer than he was at the time. Miller points to places where Elizabeth simply took the controlling hand in their relationship and points to the nine-year period of silence between *Men and Women* and *Dramatis Personae* as the consequence of Elizabeth's domination of Browning until her death on June 29, 1861. The truth is probably not so sinister as Miller thinks, nor so blissful as depicted in modern popular musicals such as Ron Grainer's *Robert and Elizabeth* (1964). There appear to have been areas of gross disagreement between Elizabeth and Robert that would have been difficult to reconcile in day-to-day life. For example, Elizabeth, like Browning's mother, believed in the spiritual world, while Browning distrusted those who made supernatural claims.

The publication of *The Ring and the Book*, along with the earlier *Men and Women* and *Dramatis Personae*, established Browning as one of the major writers of the nineteenth century. *The Ring and the Book* tells, from a number of sharply differing points of view, the story of a scandalous murder case. It resembles the plan of Browning's earliest work, *Pauline*, in that it represents the speech of "Brown, Smith, Jones, and Robinson," who are characters quite distinct from the author. It was a project of which Elizabeth had disapproved in her lifetime. Browning's later works became more and more cryptic and complex as he further pushed his ideas of dramatized poetry, but his fame grew rapidly, spurred by the formation of the Browning Society in London in 1881. Following his death in Venice, December 12, 1889, his body was moved to England and interred in Westminster Abbey.

ANALYSIS

Boyd Litzinger in *Time's Revenges: Browning's Reputation as a Thinker, 1889-1962* (1964) reviews the critical reception of Robert Browning's work during the decade after his death and finds that his immense popularity was based on three chief beliefs among his readers: Browning was a defender of Christianity, although his specific beliefs were subject to considerable doubt; he was admired for an optimistic worldview and his works were thought to urge humanity to higher and higher efforts to improve its condition; and he was considered to be a serious philosopher and man of ideas.

This analysis seems seriously misguided. Browning's religious teachings are contradictory at best. His frequent comic and hostile portraits of churchmen are hard to reconcile with conventional Christian belief. His alleged optimism does not account for the gray sadness of Andrea del Sarto's world or the bloody trial of Count Guido or even the dauntless but perhaps meaningless call of Childe Roland's horn in the face of the Dark Tower. As a "philosopher," Browning seems to have a taste more for questions than for answers, and although he expands certain ideas such as the conflict of social role versus private personality or the concept of magnificent failure, he does not develop a coherent system comparable to the philosophic poetry of John Milton.

From the perspective of the present, Browning claims a place of first importance as a protomodernist, a writer who anticipated some of the major developments in art and literature occurring at the beginning of the twentieth century. His use of the dramatic monologue anticipated and to a degree influenced the limited and unreliable narration of such masterpieces of modernism as Joseph Conrad's *Heart of Darkness* (1902) and Ford Madox Ford's *The Good Soldier* (1915). His conception of relativistic and fragmented worlds in which a character is not at home anticipated the vision of T. S. Eliot's *The Waste Land* (1922). His sense of character, defined by the conflict between social roles and internal impulses held in a sometimes unstable equilibrium, was confirmed by modern psychology. Browning is most interesting when seen not as a Victorian sage but as a forerunner of modernism.

## "PORPHYRIA'S LOVER"

"Porphyria's Lover," published along with "Johanes Agricola" under the caption "Madhouse Cells" in *Dramatic Lyrics*, exemplifies Browning's use of the dramatic monologue. Written in sixty lines of iambic quatrameter (rhymed *ababb*), the poem is spoken entirely by a dramatic character, much like the soliloquies in William Shakespeare's plays. Typically, the monologue can occur only at a moment of inaction, enabling the character to pause from whatever he has been doing and reflect for a moment. What he proceeds to say implies a larger framework of surrounding circumstances: the dramatic situation. Understanding the dramatic situation within a monologue necessitates reader participation to discover the circumstances that are only implied in the poem.

By looking closely at the text of "Porphyria's Lover," the reader learns that the speaker is a man who has just strangled his lover, Porphyria. The dead woman's head rests on his shoulder as he speaks, and he looks with approval on the murder he has committed. The speaker relates the events of the dark, stormy evening: Alone in a cottage, he waited for his beloved Porphyria to enter. Evidently, her absence had been the result of her attendance at a "gay feast," one of the "vainer ties" which Porphyria presumably cultivated. Left alone, the speaker had become obsessed by the need for Porphyria's presence, and when she finally entered the cottage, her lover could only think, "mine, mine, fair, perfectly pure and good." Strangling her in her own hair, he has propped her dead head on his shoulder, and so he sits as he speaks his monologue. Exultant that he has done the perfect thing, he ends his speech with the words, "And yet God has not said a word."

The dramatic monologue is always spoken by a dramatic character, creating a condition called limited narration. Everything that the reader hears is limited to what the speaker sees, thinks, and chooses to tell. Frequently, limited narration can be "unreliable," so that the reader has reason to believe that the speaker is mistaken or lying. In "Porphyria's Lover" the problem of unreliable narration occurs when the speaker says that the perfect thing to do in his situation was to strangle his beloved.

Some critics point to a poem such as this and assert that Browning's form of writing is vicious, that he evades his duty as a moral teacher by not passing judgment on his characters' actions. In reply, many scholars argue that Browning has indeed provided sufficient guidance for the reader to form a normative judgment, thus overriding the limited and defective judgment of the murderer. The careful reader of this poem will find much evidence to indict the speaker as a madman and criminal. His very mention of God in the closing line reveals an expectation of punishment. Such an expectation could result only from a subconscious admission of guilt. Thus, even the murderer in a deranged way has brought a moral judgment on himself. Browning has developed a situation that produces a conflict in the reader between sympathy for the character and judgment of him. The beauty rather than the fault of this poem is Browning's mastery at creating such a conflict and involving the reader in its solution.

### "My Last Duchess"

"My Last Duchess," another poem published in *Dramatic Lyrics*, exhibits many of the features discussed with reference to "Porphyria's Lover," while showing a considerable advance in artistic power and seriousness. Browning's dramatic poems fall into three categories: soliloquies, in which the persona speaks alone or *solus* on stage; monologues, in which a single speaker on stage addresses a defined dramatic audience, who must be imagined present; and epistles, monologues constructed as if they were letters written from one character to another. "My Last Duchess" is a monologue, having a speaking persona and a clearly defined dramatic audience. The dramatic situation of this poem is derived from history. The subtitle of the poem is "Ferrara," and it is likely that the persona is Browning's dramatization of Alfonso II, the fifth duke of Ferrara. Alfonso II married Lucrezia de' Medici, daughter of Cosimo I de' Medici, duke of Florence. The Medici family were newly arrived upstarts in comparison with the more ancient house of Ferrara. The duchess of Alfonso II, Lucrezia de' Medici, died at the age of seventeen in 1561, it being said that she was poisoned. Three years later Alfonso contracted to marry Barbara, niece of the count of Tyrol.

The dramatic situation of "My Last Duchess" probably involves Duke Alfonso II imagined as addressing an envoy from the count of Tyrol to negotiate the details of his wedding with Barbara. One of the main objectives of the duke's speech is to "soften up" his adversary in the negotiations so as to extract from him the maximum dowry and to exact the most dutiful compliance with his wishes by his future wife and in-laws. The reader must imagine the duke walking with his guest in the duke's art gallery while an entertainment is going on for the other guests in the lower hall of his castle. The duke pauses before a painting covered by a curtain, asks his guest to sit, and opens the curtain to display a striking portrait of his previous wife, who is dead. While the envoy contemplates the picture of the dead former wife, the duke explains that he was not completely happy with his last mate. She did not appreciate the value of his "nine hundred years old name," and so the duke "gave commands" and her annoying smiles stopped completely. She stands in the portrait as if alive, and he invites the envoy to gaze on her. Then the duke suggests that they join the party below, mentioning in passing that he is sure that the count will give him any dowry that he desires. As they descend the stairs, the duke points out a statue of the pagan god Neptune taming a sea horse, which recapitulates the struggle of the duke with the envoy. The envoy has no chance of winning a contest of will with the duke, just as the sea horse must submit to the god of the sea. The power is all in the duke's hands.

### "The Bishop Orders His Tomb at St. Praxed's Church"

"The Bishop Orders His Tomb at St. Praxed's Church" appeared in *Dramatic Romances*. Subtitled "Rome, 15—," it appears to refer to a real place, the church of St. Praxed near Rome, but unlike "My Last Duchess," it does not seem to refer to a particular person or historical event. One must construct a general idea of a worldly bishop in Italy in the sixteenth century on his deathbed speaking these lines. The dying man has his "nephews" or illegitimate sons, including his favorite, Anselm, at his bedside to communicate his last wishes to them. From the details of his speech, the reader learns that the sons' mother, the bishop's mistress, was a beautiful woman, and that the bishop had a rival for power called old Gandolf, who is buried in St. Praxed's Church. The bishop orders his sons to build him a tomb in the church that will put Gandolf's to shame by its richness. Such a tomb will be costly to build, but the dying bishop makes a shocking revelation to the boys: There was once a fire in the church from which the bishop saved an enormous semiprecious stone, a lump of lapis lazuli, which he hid. He now tells the boys where to find the buried treasure, provided they will put it on his funeral statue as a decoration.

The depiction of the bishop's character is a study in hypocrisy. One expects a churchman to be humble and honest, to deny his physical desires, and to abstain from sex and the gratification of worldly lusts. As his mind wanders and he nears death, this bishop appears to be just the opposite. Rather than living celibate, he has fathered these sons who stand around him, and he has loved their voluptuous mother. Rather than showing generosity to his enemies, even at the moment of death, he is filled with petty jealousy of old Gandolf. He has stolen the church's jewel from the conflagration. He even confuses Christianity and paganism as he describes the frieze he wants on his tomb as a mixture of erotic pagan elements and Christian scenes. Next to the depiction of the virgin martyr Saint Praxed, he wants a Bacchic orgy with "one Pan ready to twitch the Nymph's last garment off."

Works such as "The Bishop Orders His Tomb at St. Praxed's Church" were influential on the novel and the short story as well as on modern poetry, for they expanded the notion of character in fiction. Character is sometimes defined as what man habitually chooses to do. A character is said to be a liar if he usually lies. Another is a brave man if he usually refuses to run from danger. Browning writes many poems about churchmen, perhaps because their ethical character is so sharply defined. The minute one sees a character dressed as a bishop, one expects that this man will habitually act in a certain way, that his actions will be loving, self-sacrificing, humble, and Christian, and that he will not put his faith in the material world, but concern himself with heavenly goals. Browning puts such a character in a moment of unusual stress in which his expected role crumbles, and one sees through his public face to an inner set of unexpected feelings. At any other time in his life, the bishop of St. Praxed's, dressed in his robes and healthy and strong, would never have revealed that he was subject to lust, greed, pride, and all the un-Christian characteristics he reveals to his sons on his deathbed. Browning has found a moment when the bishop's public face cracks and his inner personality is revealed. The poem explores the conflict between the public role and the private personality of a man.

### "BISHOP BLOUGRAM'S APOLOGY"

In addition to "The Bishop Orders His Tomb at St. Praxed's Church," Browning wrote a number of other poems about religious hypocrites, including "Bishop Blougram's Apology," published in *Men and Women*. The dramatic situation is a nineteenth century dinner party given by Blougram for a young newspaperman who is an unbeliever. Blougram talks at length to the younger man and, perhaps a bit intoxicated by his own importance or an unusual amount of wine, confesses some things that he would not normally say in public because they do not fit the expected role of a bishop. The newspaperman Gigadibs despises Blougram because, while the bishop is intelligent enough to know that miracles and the historically untrue parts of the Bible are mere superstition, he nevertheless publicly professes to believe in them. He must therefore be a hypocrite. Apparently Gigadibs has also accused the bishop of profiting from his profession of belief and so achieving a comfortable and powerful position in life. Perhaps the poem refers to the Roman Catholic Cardinal Wiseman and Cardinal John Henry Newman, whose *Apologia pro Vita Sua* (1864) may be reflected in the title of Browning's poem.

Blougram's reply to Gigadibs's charges is important for an understanding of Browning's idea of characterization in fiction. At line 375 and following, Blougram suggests that Gigadibs thinks that a few intelligent people will always look at Blougram and "know me whether I believe in the last winking virgin, as I vow, and am a fool, or disbelieve in her and am a knave." Even so, Blougram maintains that these intelligent people will be those most fascinated with him because he maintains an impossibly contradictory balance:

You see lads walk the street . . . what's to note in that?
You see one lad o'erstride a chimney-stack; him you
must watch—he's sure to fall, yet stands! Our interest's
on the dangerous edge of things. The honest thief, the
tender murderer, the superstitious atheist . . . we watch
while these in equilibrium keep the giddy line midway:
one step aside, they're classed and done with. I, then,
keep the line.

Browning's characters are people caught in impossible
contradictions, frequently between their expected or
usual pattern of behavior and some contrary inner impulse. The situations named by Blougram as fascinating are explored in Browning's poetry: The tender murderer is Porphyria's lover, for example. As in nearly all
of Browning's dramatic poems, "Bishop Blougram's
Apology" leaves the reader struggling to find a normative judgment. Is Blougram a hypocritical exploiter of
religion for his own worldly benefit and therefore subject to scorn, or is he something else? Even though the
concluding lines of the poem are spoken as if in the
voice of Browning himself, it is still difficult to say
whether one should approve of Blougram or despise
him. In that impossible "equilibrium" the reader is fascinated.

### "ANDREA DEL SARTO"

Browning took the dramatic situation of the poem
"Andrea del Sarto" mainly from Giorgio Vasari's *Lives
of the Painters* (1550, 1568), which includes a discussion of the painter Andrea del Sarto—called the faultless painter because of the technical perfection of his
art. Andrea married a widow, Lucrezia del Fede, in
1512 and was subsequently summoned from Florence
to work at the court of Francis I of France at Fon-
tainebleau. According to Vasari's story, Francis I gave
Andrea money to purchase artworks in Florence, but he
misappropriated the funds and had to live in hiding because he allowed himself to be dominated by the artful
and wicked Lucrezia. A self-portrait of Andrea and
Lucrezia hung in the Pitti Palace at Florence while the
Brownings were residents in Italy. Elizabeth Barrett
Browning's cousin, John Kenyon, asked her husband
to send him a photograph of the painting, and so the
story goes, Browning composed and sent him this
poem instead.

The poem illustrates the idea of the "magnificent
failure," one of Browning's most important concepts.
To understand the magnificent failure, the reader must
be aware of thinking current in the 1850's concerning
the relation of art to society. For example, John Ruskin
in *The Stones of Venice* (1851-1853) makes a distinction between "slave art" and "free art." Slave art, such
as an Egyptian pyramid, sets up a simple design so that
any slave can execute it perfectly. Free art, such as a
Gothic cathedral, engages the creative impulses of every worker so that it is never completed and is marked
by the luxuriant variety of every worker's creation. A
perfect, finished, polished work of art signifies that the
artist set his or her design too low, and did not strive to
reach beyond the limits of his or her power. Perfect art
is the sign of moral degeneration. Andrea's painting is
slave's work because it is perfect.

In the poem, Andrea is speaking to his dramatic
audience, and his wife, Lucrezia, who is impatient
with him, wishes to go out in the evening to join her
"cousin," or lover, who is whistling for her in the street.
In the opening lines, the reader learns that Lucrezia is
not kind to the painter and that he must bribe her to stay
with him a few minutes. Andrea is unhappy, thinking
how his art is not of the highest order despite all its perfection. He never fails to make a perfect drawing because he never sets his design beyond his ability, "but a
man's reach should exceed his grasp, or what's a
heaven for?" He considers a painting by Raphael and
shows how the drawing of an arm in it is poor, but when
he corrects the draftsmanship, he loses all the "play, the
insight and the stretch" of the imperfect original. He laments his lost productive times when he worked in
France and regrets that he must now live in exile. He pa-
thetically asks Lucrezia to be his companion so that he
can work more and give her more money. At the conclusion of the poem, Lucrezia's "cousin" whistles for
her again while Andrea, who is a faultless painter, en-
vies the glory of less perfect artists.

Andrea paints designs that never challenge his ability and completes perfectly all his undertakings. Ironically, this perfection in art signifies his moral degeneration, for he is a slave to the beautiful but ignorant and
unfeeling Lucrezia and to the profit motive, so that he
must paint trivial works to earn gold, which Lucrezia
simply gives to her "cousin" lover. Artists such as Ra-

phael fail in their work because they set their sights so high that they can never finish or complete their designs perfectly. Although they fail, their works are magnificent. Andrea's perfect works are merely slavish.

### "CHILDE ROLAND TO THE DARK TOWER CAME"

In the middle of the nineteenth century, there was a revival of interest in knightly romances and the "matter of Britain," the ancient stories concerning King Arthur's court, evident in Tennyson's *Idylls of the King* (1859-1885) and many other poems of the period. Frequently, the failed quest of the courtly romance was a vehicle for the idea of magnificent failure. Arthur had tried to establish a court of perfect chivalry, but he had failed in the attempt. Nevertheless, his failure was more noble than a practical compromise would have been. Each of his knights must fail in some important way, suffer humiliation and death, even as Christ did, so that the nobility of their endeavor may show forth. Browning's "Childe Roland to the Dark Tower Came" is in this tradition of the courtly failed quest and the magnificent failure.

The subtitle of the poem refers to Shakespeare's *King Lear* (pr. c. 1605-1606, pb. 1608), specifically a song by the character Edgar in act 3, scene 4. Lear on the heath encounters Edgar disguised as a madman. Lear calls him a philosopher and takes him with his company. At the conclusion of the scene, Edgar pronounces some riddling or nonsense lines, including "Child Rowland to the dark tower came." These are apparently garbled snatches of traditional ballads. "Childe" means any untested knight, and Browning's poem constructs a nightmare quest for his untried knight, Childe Roland, who tells of his weird adventure. The poem is best considered a journey into the mind, a psychological rather than a physical quest. Childe Roland tells of his perilous journey across a wasted land in which a cripple advises him to turn into an "ominous tract" where the Dark Tower hides. As soon as he leaves the road, it vanishes. Everything in the enchanted land is sick, wounded, and in torment. Childe Roland thinks of his companions who have failed before him. He crosses a river and stumbles unaware on the "round squat turret." He imagines he sees all his dead companions ranged along the hillside over-

looking the arena, yet "dauntless" he sets his horn to his lips and blows the cry, "Childe Roland to the Dark Tower Came."

Like many of Browning's poems, this work seems laden with ambiguity. There are at least three possibilities: The tower is not the true object of a knight's quest, and thus Childe Roland is lost when he takes the advice of the cripple to leave the high road, and he is punished for deviating from his proper goal; or, the tower is the true quest, but Childe Roland's discovery is that it is worthless and ugly when he finds it (therefore, his life is wasted); or, the tower is the quest and is in itself meaningless, but the dedication of Roland creates success out of failure—although the tower is "squat" and ugly, he has played his proper role and even in the face of overwhelming forces, he blows defiance, dauntless to the last.

"Childe Roland to the Dark Tower Came" invites comparison with the surrealist nightmares of Franz Kafka, and Browning's use of a wasteland as a symbol for humankind's alienation and his evocation of a failed courtly quest foreshadow Eliot's *The Waste Land*. "Childe Roland to the Dark Tower Came" is one of Browning's most interesting works, and it foreshadows developments in the modernist revolution some fifty years after its publication.

### THE RING AND THE BOOK

*The Ring and the Book* is Browning's most important poem. Written in blank verse, rhymed iambic pentameter, it appeared in four volumes between November, 1868, and February, 1869. In 1860, Browning came across in Florence a collection of old documents and letters telling the story of the murder trial of Guido Franceschini, who was executed in Rome in 1698. Browning called this volume *The Old Yellow Book*; it was translated into English by Charles W. Hodell and was published in 1911.

From the lawyers' arguments and other documents emerges a particularly sordid case of "divorce Italian style." In 1693, Count Guido Franceschini, an impoverished nobleman forty years old, from the north of Italy, married a thirteen-year-old commoner, Francesca Pompilia, in Rome. She was the daughter of Pietro and Violante Comparini. Pietro had opposed the marriage, knowing that the count was not as wealthy as he seemed. His wife, however, was attracted by the possibility of a nobleman for a son-in-law and contrived to have the marriage take place. The Comparini family gave all their possessions as dowry to Count Guido, expecting to live in comfort on his estate. The count, angry to find that the Comparini family was less wealthy than he imagined, harassed them until they were forced to flee from his house. They sued for the return of Pompilia's dowry on grounds that she was not their natural daughter, but a common prostitute's child whom they had adopted. Count Guido increased his cruelty to his child bride, even though she sought help from the local bishop and governor. Pompilia fled from Count Guido's castle with the dashing young priest Caponsacchi in 1697, but Count Guido apprehended the couple near Rome on April 28, 1697. They were charged with adultery; Caponsacchi was banished, and Pompilia was confined to a nunnery from which she was released on bond to bear her child, a son, at the house of the Comparini on December 18, 1697, almost exactly nine months after her flight from Guido's castle with Caponsacchi. Her son Gaetano stood to inherit the count's name and estate. Two weeks later, Count Guido broke into the Comparini house and murdered Pietro and Violante, and left Pompilia mortally wounded. Pompilia lived four more days, long enough to accuse Count Guido of the assault. He and his companions were arrested fleeing toward his estate.

The bulk of *The Old Yellow Book* presents the legal arguments in this dark case. The murders were admitted, but Count Guido claimed that he was justified as an injured husband in defending his honor. When he was found guilty, he appealed to the pope, who refused to intervene. Count Guido was beheaded February 22, 1698, in Rome, while his accomplices were hanged. Finally, a convent brought suit to claim the estates forfeited by Pompilia's allegedly adulterous action, but a court ruled that she was innocent and gave all property to her son Gaetano.

Browning converted the material of *The Old Yellow Book* into one of the first relativistic narrative masterpieces. Some authors tell their readers what to think about their characters; others make their readers think for themselves. Browning is one of the latter, presenting his readers with questions rather than giving them

answers. In twelve books, Browning tells and retells the story of Pompilia, Count Guido, and the priest Caponsacchi, through their eyes and through the eyes of their lawyers, the eyes of the pope considering Guido's appeal, and the eyes of three factions of the vulgar population of Rome. Naturally, when Guido explains his action, he not only argues in defense of what he did but also actually believes that he is right. In his own mind, he is blameless. Likewise, when the reader sees through the limitations and prejudices of Pompilia or of Caponsacchi, the point of view dictates what is right and what is wrong. Many readers coming to Browning's text try to penetrate the tangle of conflicting judgments and opinions presented in these twelve books, and try to say that Browning's sympathy lies with Pompilia or that the pope speaks for the author. However, if there is a single, clear-cut normative judgment, why did Browning feel compelled to write the contradictory monologues that argue against it? More likely, Browning intentionally created a powerful experimental literary form, rather like the limited narration novels of Henry James. Browning's text provides a complicated stimulus, but each reader constructs in his or her mind a personal evaluation of the relative guilt or justification of Count Guido, Pompilia, Caponsacchi, the pope, and the Comparini family.

Stories are sometimes said to fall into two classes. There are stories such as mediocre mystery tales that cannot bear a second reading. Once the audience has heard the tale to its end, they know "who done it." All questions are solved, so that a second reading would be unnecessary and boring. On the other hand, there is a second kind of story that is so constructed that each reading only deepens the questions in the readers' minds. Every reader is drawn back to the text over and over, and the third or fourth reading has as much interest as the first. In *The Ring and the Book*, Browning converted a gruesome but mediocre mystery tale into a work of this second type, which poses troubling questions about right and wrong, judging and pardoning. Every character evokes some spark of sympathy when allowed to speak for himself or herself. Every character seems subject to guilt when seen through hostile eyes.

*The Ring and the Book* illustrates Browning's concern with the infinite moment, the instant when a character can act decisively to break out of his or her characteristic pattern of expected behavior and do the unforeseen. The priest Caponsacchi's flight with the count's child-bride is an example of the dizzy equilibrium between expected social behavior and contradictory impulse. The reader asks, "How could he do it and still be a priest of God, forsaking his vows of celibacy and all his ordinary rules of conduct?" The reader can imagine what it is to be a priest and what it is to be a lover, but how can there exist such a contradictory character as a lover/priest? The same question can be posed for Pompilia, the childlike innocent yet renegade wife, who is the final winner of them all eventually when her son inherits the estate. The reader has seen many times in literature the childlike, innocent woman, and equally often has encountered the sexual sharpster, but how can these contradictory roles be balanced in a single character?

OTHER MAJOR WORKS

PLAYS: *Strafford*, pr., pb. 1837; *Pippa Passes*, pb. 1841; *King Victor and King Charles*, pb. 1842; *A Blot in the 'Scutcheon*, pr., pb. 1843; *The Return of the Druses*, pb. 1843; *Colombe's Birthday*, pb. 1844; *Luria*, pb. 1846; *A Soul's Tragedy*, pb. 1846.

NONFICTION: *The Letters of Robert Browning and Elizabeth Barrett Barrett, 1845-1846*, 1926 (Robert B. Browning, editor); *Intimate Glimpses from Browning's Letter File: Selected from Letters in the Baylor University Browning Collection*, 1934; *Browning's Essay on Chatterton*, 1948 (Donald A. Smalley, editor); *New Letters of Robert Browning*, 1950 (W. C. DeVane and Kenneth L. Knickerbocker, editors); *The Letters of Robert Browning and Elizabeth Barrett Barrett, 1845-1846*, 1969 (Elvan Kintner, editor).

MISCELLANEOUS: *The Works of Robert Browning*, 1912 (10 volumes; F. C. Kenyon, editor); *The Complete Works of Robert Browning*, 1969-1999 (16 volumes).

BIBLIOGRAPHY

Bloom, Harold, ed. *Robert Browning*. New York: Bloom's Literary Criticism, 2009. A collection of literary criticism on the works of Browning.

Finlayson, Iain. *Browning: A Private Life*. New York: HarperCollins, 2004. A biography of Browning based partly on his correspondence with his wife. Looks at Browning's literary works, examines the contradictions posed by the private and public man, and spends much time examining the Brownings' marriage.

Garrett, Martin. *A Browning Chronology: Elizabeth Barrett Browning and Robert Browning*. New York: St. Martin's Press, 2000. A chronology of the works of Elizabeth Barrett Browning and Robert Browning. Bibliography and index.

_____, ed. *Elizabeth Barrett Browning and Robert Browning: Interviews and Recollections*. New York: St. Martin's Press, 2000. A collection of interviews recalling Browning and his famous wife. Bibliography and index.

Hawlin, Stefan. *The Complete Critical Guide to Robert Browning*. New York: Routledge, 2002. A reference work that provides comprehensive critical analysis of Browning's works and information on his life. Bibliography and indexes.

Kennedy, Richard S., and Donald S. Hair. *The Dramatic Imagination of Robert Browning: A Literary Life*. Columbia: University of Missouri Press, 2007. This biography draws from his letters and diaries and from memoirs of his contemporaries to create a literary biography of Browning. It tracks his reputation and development as a poet, providing a reexamination of his later works.

Loucks, James F., and Andrew M. Stauffer. *Robert Browning's Poetry: Authoritative Texts, Criticism*. 2d ed. New York: W. W. Norton, 2007. A collection of criticism of Browning's poetic works.

Neville-Sington, Pamela. *Robert Browning: A Life After Death*. London: Weidenfeld & Nicolson, 2004. Argues that Browning's marriage to Elizabeth Barrett Browning overshadowed his career and looks at his life after her death, particularly his literary works and relationships with women.

Wood, Sarah. *Robert Browning: A Literary Life*. New York: Palgrave, 2001. A biography of Browning that focuses on his literary works. Bibliography and index.

*Todd K. Bender*

# BASIL BUNTING

**Born:** Scotswood-on-Tyne, Northumberland,
England; March 1, 1900
**Died:** Hexham, England; April 17, 1985

PRINCIPAL POETRY

*Redimiculum Matellarum*, 1930
*Poems: 1950*, 1950
*First Book of Odes*, 1965
*Loquitur*, 1965
*The Spoils: A Poem*, 1965
*Briggflatts*, 1966
*Two Poems*, 1967
*What the Chairman Told Tom*, 1967
*Collected Poems*, 1968 (new edition 1978)
*Descant on Rawley's Madrigal (Conversations with
    Jonathan Williams)*, 1968
*Uncollected Poems*, 1991
*The Complete Poems*, 1994

OTHER LITERARY FORMS

Basil Bunting wrote little aside from poetry. Although he claimed that he had no use for literary criticism, he did write a small amount of critical prose. With Ezra Pound, Bunting edited the *Active Anthology* (1933), which contained a number of his poems. He contributed prose to *Agenda* and *Poetry*. In an article titled "English Poetry Today" (*Poetry*, February, 1932), Bunting descants on the poetry of the time. His remarks reveal much about his own poetic practice. The poet also elaborates upon his attitudes in an interview titled "Eighty of the Best . . ." (*Paideuma*, Spring, 1980).

ACHIEVEMENTS

Basil Bunting, in his own self-deprecating estimation, was a "minor poet, not conspicuously dishonest." His poetic career, like his life, was quixotic. He began in the tradition of the 1920's, following the lead of Pound and Louis Zukofsky, but his work did not appear in print until a limited edition of 1930 was published in Milan. His adherence to the school of Pound and the relative obscurity of his work kept him from being read by a British audience who had turned to the new men of the 1930's such as W. H. Auden, Louis MacNeice, and Stephen Spender. A collection of his poems published twenty years later in Texas (the poet himself was residing in Persia) did little to widen his audience. It was not until the 1960's, especially with the publication of *Briggflatts*, that Bunting was rediscovered.

Bunting was quick to acknowledge the influence of Pound and Zukofsky. He was a close friend of Pound, who dedicated *Guide to Kulchur* (1938) jointly to Bunting and Zukofsky. Bunting's early poems exhibit the brittle precision, vigor, and social commentary of Pound's *Cantos* (1925-1972). In these early poems, one also finds, ingeniously rendered in modern idiom, showpiece passages of Horace, Lucretius, Niccolò Machiavelli, the Persian poet Firdusi, Rūdakī of Samarkand, and others (Bunting was a master of languages). Such "translations" are actually free resurrections in English of the poetry of another language. Again after the manner of Pound, Bunting skillfully captures the character of the speaker in Browningesque dramatic monologues. T. S. Eliot's influence looms large in Bunting's use of literary allusion and his expression of the bleaker side of existence. Bunting frequently echoed Eliot's style, but with satiric intent. He believed Eliot's later poetry to be dishonest in its support of reactionary social and literary institutions. Nevertheless, he owed much to Eliot both in his use of allusion and in the creation of mood.

Bunting's place in letters is secured through his handling of rhythm, rhyme, meter, assonance, consonance, alliteration—in short, the sounds of poetry. He claimed Edmund Spenser as an influence. His emphasis was on everything that a poem gains by being spoken aloud. In his early Latin translations, he experimented with meters difficult to employ in a stressed language such as English. Later poems exhibit a free play of heavy stresses filled with spondees, trochees, and dactyls, against no identifiable iambic background. Rather, stress corresponds to the meaning of the words. Some critics have doubted the existence of recognizable rhythms in Bunting's mature poetry, but the presence of so many stressed syllables creates its own kind of meter. The poet himself has suggested that his dominant meter is the four-beat line of Old English oral poetry. In his most accomplished poem, *Briggflatts*, rough monosyllables force precise speech; the reader finds that he must articulate each consonant, exaggerating frequent stresses. The effect is not the contortions of Gerard Manley Hopkins's sprung rhythm, but rather the ictus of a pagan drum beat—without the monotony of Rudyard Kipling's meter. Against his line of strong stress the poet plays a counterpoint of assonance, consonance, internal rhyme, and alliteration. This play of sounds does much to achieve a music that, according to Bunting, is the being of poetry.

Bunting's poetic career blossomed late, with the publication of *Briggflatts*, an autobiographical poem in which he triumphantly reclaims the speech of his native Northumbria. The influence of William Wordsworth is clear in this poem, and one feels that more than any other modern poet Bunting was able to achieve the Romantic ideal of using the language of ordinary men. With flinty precision, this language of real men is forged into masculine, heavily stressed lines that resonate sounds and themes from one to another. This is Bunting's major poetic accomplishment.

## BIOGRAPHY

Basil Cheesman Bunting was born in Scotswood-on-Tyne, Northumberland, on March 1, 1900. He was reared and educated a Quaker and spoke fondly of the Briggflatts Meeting House, constructed by the Friends in 1675. When he was eighteen, Bunting refused the draft and was imprisoned in Wormwood Scrubs Prison for a year. Glimpses of the harsh prison conditions can be found in the poem "Villon" (1925). After release, he studied at the London School of Economics. At about the same time, he began to write Imagist poetry. This early work contains, in the manner of Pound, dramatic monologues and vignettes from other poets, but the influence of Eliot, whom he met in the mid-1920's, also makes itself known. Bunting left for Paris in 1923, beginning an odyssey that kept him out of England for much of the next fifty years. From Paris, he joined Pound in Rapallo, where the two became close friends. There he met and married Marian Culver, an American. The marriage lasted until 1935 and produced three children.

In the late 1920's, Bunting was for a short time music critic of *The Outlook* in London. He returned to It-

aly, where he lived until 1933. In Rapallo, Bunting and Pound edited the *Active Anthology*, which contained a number of Bunting's earliest poems. These are the most Poundian of Bunting's work. In the 1930's, he lived in the United States, and from 1937 to 1939, he earned a living as captain of a private yacht that sailed the Mediterranean and crossed to the United States. The rise of Adolf Hitler overcame his pacifism, and in 1939, he returned to England to join the Royal Air Force. Bunting spent most of the war in Iran, where his facility with languages was put to good use in Intelligence. After the war, he stayed in Iran as Persian correspondent for *The Times*. In 1948, he married an Iranian, Sima Alladadian. Many of his Middle Eastern experiences are captured in *The Spoils*, a poem written in 1951 but not published until 1965. In 1951, he returned to England. In the mid-1960's, the Pound critic Hugh Kenner was instrumental in bringing Bunting to the University of California, Santa Barbara, where he taught until he accepted a position at the University of Durham, England. He subsequently retired to Black Fells Village, Northumberland, England. Bunting died in Hexham, England, in 1985.

## ANALYSIS

Until the publication of *Briggflatts*, Basil Bunting's poetry was largely ignored, both because it had been published obscurely and because it was viewed as highly derivative—mere Poundian pastiche. In retrospect, the poems of the 1920's and 1930's show to what extent this estimation is unjustified. It is impossible to deny that—on the road to developing his own voice—Bunting wrote poems that were strongly influenced by Eliot's manner and, more particularly, Pound's. Even in his earliest work, however, Bunting can be identified by the sound of his lines, especially by the cadence of stresses that alliteration reinforces and to which assonance and internal rhyme frequently add counterpoint. This attention to sound is very characteristic of his work. In his own estimation, while music is not all there is to a poem, it is the one essential ingredient. In the *Collected Poems*, he classified his short lyrics as "Odes" and his longer poems as "Sonatas." (More than one critic has denied any but a metaphorical connection between music and poetry.) By "music," Bunting seems to be making a claim for a special interplay between the sound and meaning of words in a poem; his use of the word "ode" seems to be an appeal to poetry's source in the chants and dances of the Greek chorus. While Bunting did not appropriate the strophe and antistrophe format in the manner of Pindar, his heavily stressed meter resembles those complex rhythms best expressed in dance. In fact, Bunting claimed that, aside from its use in poetry, meter is perhaps best expressed through physical movement. Bunting's heavily stressed lines can be best appreciated in a comparison with the oral chants that accompany primitive dance.

### Overdrafts

Perhaps the best way to approach Bunting is by way of the loose verse translations he calls "overdrafts." Here Bunting follows Pound's lead, attempting to revive in the idiom of modern English the spirit of a foreign poem. As David Gordon has shown (*Paideuma*, Spring, 1980), Bunting was able, in a 1931 translation from Horace, to create an English accentual syllabic version of *ionic a minore* meter. In this and other similar performances, the poet extends the range of English metrics and prepares himself for the heavily stressed line that distinguishes his poetry. Not only is the meter of the original poem revitalized, but also the words of the poem are rendered in a modern idiom that sometimes defies the sense and historical/cultural setting of the original. Thus, the lady in the Horatian passage is deprived of "gin." She has mislaid her "workbox." Her lover is a "middle-weight pug" who wears "track-shorts." In the notes to the *Collected Poems*, the poet indicates that such "mistranslation" is intentional.

The "overdrafts" record something of the poet's interests over the years. In 1927, he translated a passage of Lucretius, and in 1931, two by Horace. In 1932, he rendered a few lines of Louis Zukofsky into Latin. He translated Catullus into English in 1933, the Persian poet Firdusi in 1935, Rūdakī of Samarkand in 1948, Manuchehri in 1949, and Saʾdī in 1949. Perhaps the most striking translation is a passage from Machiavelli titled "How Duke Valentine Contrived" (1933). This short narrative of Italian intrigue is presented in delightfully colloquial English. Duke Valentine, the reader is told admiringly, was a "first rate humbug" who fools his enemies with "rotten promises." When

the duke decides to "put an end" to his enemies, one of them is seen "blubbering" over his fate. Such unobtrusive use of colloquialism revitalizes the story for modern readers.

From the earliest odes, Bunting's style is characterized by its concentration. Although these short poems owe much to Pound, they sometimes lack the clarity of visual impression native to Imagist poetry. Nevertheless, they frequently capture an emotion with sleight of hand, as when they speak of the "pangs of old rapture," the "angriness of love," and the "savour of our sadness," and they frequently exhibit tactile and auditory images not easily achieved in poetry. For Bunting, waves of the sea consist not only in their visual impression but also in their sound, "crying a strange name." A rainstorm is seen in a "mudmirrored mackintosh," but its dampness is also "wiped and smeared" in tactile experience. Grass is "silent," a lake "slinks," children are "scabby." Visual images are never really separate from sound and touch. Thus, the mosaic of the Imagist poem is felt as "stone shouldering stone." Many of the odes might be classified as love poetry, but their view of human emotion and sexuality is as stark as their rough meter suggests.

### Sonatas

Bunting's longer poems, his "Sonatas," exhibit the same concentration as his "Odes." Some readers have objected that their "musical" qualities require too much of mind and memory for even the most avid reader. "Villon" has been accused of obscurity, lacking both a central persona and a metrical norm through which a reader might trace musical variations. In the early poetry, the use of voices rather than a persona shows the influence of Eliot rather than that of Pound. Bunting's is a poetry of mood and allusion. "Villon," a meditation on life and death, salutes a kindred spirit who lives after death only in the tracings of poetry. In the poem, the poet's own experiences in prison are incorporated in an appreciation of Villon's loneliness and suffering. Bunting's close identification with Villon the man arises from his own experiences in prison. Like Villon, Bunting saw himself as a powerless outsider commenting on the characters who people social institutions. The poem is a fit beginning for a poetic career that casts a dour eye on human life.

The wit of Bunting's social commentary is reminiscent of that of George Bernard Shaw, though it contains more of the spirit of George Orwell (in prose) and of Charles Chaplin (in motion pictures). In "Chomei at Toyama" (1932), the reader is given a delightful picture of human society, painted by a man who chooses to live poor and alone rather than be the editor of "the Imperial Anthology." Bunting enjoys making fun of the petty official (see ode 23 "The Passport Officer") and the artist who sells himself to the party line. Especially biting is the portrait of the playwright (in "Aus Dem Zweiten Reich," 1931) who is known for having written more plays than William Shakespeare. This caricature of a man is able to speak about plays, politics, and poetry without saying anything at all. For Bunting, poetry requires honesty. He gives no quarter to the humbug, cheat, cheapjack, and boaster.

Bunting saw in Eliot's lighter verse and in his conversion to institutional Christianity a wandering from the honesty that true poetry requires. More important, he disliked what he considered Eliot's lack of economy. He preferred William Butler Yeats's greater concentration but denounced what he considered to be Yeats's own posturing. Bunting criticized the word "horseman" in Yeats's epitaph as a pandering to social elitism as well as an improper violation of the meter of the line. Much of Bunting's career can be seen as an effort to escape a natural inclination to write in the manner of Eliot. "Attis: Or Something Missing" (1931) is a satirical pastiche capturing Eliot's technique in ways that Bunting could never expunge from his own poetry. For Bunting, what seems to be "missing" from Eliot's work is the inner fortitude to denounce imposture in a corrupt social establishment of which Eliot so much wanted to be a part. Here the sharp meter and concentrated images that Bunting learned from Pound do much to hide Eliot's influence. In "The Well of Lycopolis" (1935), Bunting presents a wasteland more dour than that of Eliot. It is Dante's *Inferno* (in *La divina commedia*, c. 1320; *The Divine Comedy*, 1802) transposed to the ordinary world, an *Inferno* without metaphysical extension, with neither *Purgatorio* nor *Paradiso*. Against the relief of Bunting's poetry, Eliot's Romanticism becomes glaringly obvious.

## THE SPOILS

The lengthy sonata titled *The Spoils* is frequently read as a transition to the poetry of *Briggflatts*. In its own right, *The Spoils* is a poem of great beauty, capturing the essence of Middle Eastern life and culture. In this poem, Bunting follows his former practice of including his own experiences—gathered during and after the war—with the literature and history that created the spirit of the region. The images of the poem are, in fact, "the spoils" that the poet brings back in his native tongue. Bunting's feeling for the interconnectedness of poetry and dance shows in allusions to the biblical Song of Songs, which arose, so scholars conjecture, as a play or chant probably enacted at the wedding service. It is in *The Spoils* that the distinctively Anglo-Saxon meter (characteristic of *Briggflatts*) begins to predominate. By easing the line and allowing more unstressed syllables back into his verse, the poet is able to capture the rhythms of an ancient chant. In such lines, the effect is heightened by the use of pure English monosyllables. The result is not a predictable iamb, but instead a line of three and four heavy stresses thrown in sharp relief.

## BRIGGFLATTS

Bunting conquers the heavily stressed line in *Briggflatts*, a poem that returns to claim the poet's birthright in the language of Northumberland and the beat of Anglo-Saxon poetry. This autobiographical poem no longer merely incorporates Bunting's experience. *Briggflatts* is a return to roots, not only to the language and countryside of Northumbria, but also to the Romantic project of expressing the poet in the poetry. Here Bunting's professed debt to Wordsworth, a "Northerner," becomes apparent in the sweetly recounted spots of childhood memory, in the employment of the language of the common man, and in the identification with place by which a man can measure the unfolding of his life. *Briggflatts* records the poetic life of Bunting. Pound is there, and Eliot too. Their voices are now muted, however, against Bunting's own clear Northumbrian song. The poem is composed of simple English monosyllables that are artfully placed together with precision and condensation. To use the poet's own image, the pebbles are arranged in a mosaic. Most important is the seeming artlessness of the whole; gone are the set pieces and the satiric pastiche. In their place is the compact music of Domenico Scarlatti, with "never a boast or a see-here."

OTHER MAJOR WORKS

NONFICTION: *Basil Bunting on Poetry*, 1999.

EDITED TEXTS: *Active Anthology*, 1933 (with Ezra Pound); *Selected Poems*, 1971 (by Ford Madox Ford); *Selected Poems of Joseph Skipsey*, 1976.

BIBLIOGRAPHY

*Agenda* 8 (Autumn, 1966). The entire issue is devoted to Bunting's poetry and includes essays by established critics and poets. Kenneth Cox discusses Bunting's economy of language and willingness to take risks with unexpected word choice. Robert Creeley notes Bunting's deep English roots and his ear for the English language. Sir Herbert Read comments on Bunting's insistence on music in poetry, and Charles Tomlinson explores the roots of that music in the work of Ezra Pound and William Carlos Williams and examines the musical structure of *Briggflatts*.

*Agenda* 19 (Spring, 1978). Another special issue on Bunting and his poetry. Peter Dale sets out to attack Bunting's analogy of poetry with music and tries to find meaning instead, while Roland John discusses why the critics have neglected Bunting's work. Peter Makin wonders to what degree the sound of a poem can communicate emotion, and Anthony Suter wonders also whether Bunting neglects meaning in his pursuit of sound. Also examines Bunting's creative process in an interview with Peter Quartermain.

Alldritt, Keith. *The Poet as Spy: The Life and Wild Times of Basil Bunting*. London: Aurum Press, 1998. This biography of Bunting chronicles the poet's early and lasting struggle to attain recognition for his talents, covering his imprisonment in 1918 for his role as conscientious objector to his travails in England, Iran, and Italy. Discusses the influence of Ezra Pound on his career and work, and their eventual split.

Bunting, Basil. *Basil Bunting on Poetry*. Edited by Peter Makin. Baltimore: The Johns Hopkins University Press, 1999. A collection of the lectures on poetry that Bunting gave in 1968 and 1974. The lectures trace the development of poetry but concentrates on writing and hearing poetry. Sheds light on Bunting's own poetry.

Forde, Victoria. *The Poetry of Basil Bunting*. Newcastle upon Tyne, England: Bloodaxe Books, 1991. This volume is a revision of the author's 1972 Ph.D. thesis. Includes a useful biography of the poet, accompanied by more than thirty photographs of and by Bunting. Covers the marital and financial troubles faced by the Bunting family and the effect these had on his writing. The commentary stays close to the texts, elucidating Bunting largely through his own statements.

Makin, Peter. *Bunting: The Shaping of His Verse*. Oxford, England: Clarendon Press, 1992. Makin's biography covers many of the same aspects of Bunting's life as Forde's, but more penetratingly. Makin's discussion of the poetry is more in-depth, and his scholarship is unassailable.

*Paideuma* 9 (Spring, 1980). This issue gathers essays on, and tributes to, Bunting. In the analysis of "Villon," Peter Dale considers three ways of using musical form in poetry, David Gordon charts the use of rhythm and idiom in Bunting's career, and Hugh Kenner pays tribute to Bunting's distinctive reading voice. One of the best and most enjoyable essays is Carroll Terrell's "Basil Bunting in Action," which is a mixture of criticism, memoir, biography, and documentary.

Quartermain, Peter. *Basil Bunting: Poet of the North*. Durham, N.C.: Basil Bunting Poetry Archive, 1990. This twenty-four-page pamphlet is the text of a lecture delivered on Bunting's poetry. The talk was given in the Mountjoy lecture series.

Terrell, Carroll F. *Basil Bunting: Man and Poet*. Orono, Maine: National Poetry Foundation, 1981. Contains an introduction by the editor as well as an annotated bibliography of critical works. The first three essays are biographical and are followed by essays on Bunting's "Sonatas" and the odes. A five-essay section on *Briggflatts* is followed by sections on his criticism and translations. Supplemented by a primary bibliography and an index.

Weatherhead, Andrew Kingsley. *The British Dissonance: Essays on Ten Contemporary Poets.* Columbia: University of Missouri Press, 1983. Weatherhead discusses Bunting's poetry in an essay alongside that of other British poets such as Ted Hughes, Anselm Hollo, Charles Tomlinson, and Matthew Mead. Supplemented by an index and a bibliography of works by the poets.

*Wm. Dennis Horn*

# ROBERT BURNS

**Born:** Alloway, Ayrshire, Scotland; January 25, 1759
**Died:** Dumfries, Scotland; July 21, 1796

PRINCIPAL POETRY

*Poems, Chiefly in the Scottish Dialect*, 1786 (Kilmarnock edition), 1787 (Edinburgh edition), 1793 (2 volumes)
*The Canongate Burns*, 2001 (Andrew Noble and Patrick Scott Hogg, editors)

OTHER LITERARY FORMS

As a pure poet, Robert Burns had neither the time nor the desire for other literary forms. For *The Scots Musical Museum*, edited by James Johnson between 1787 and 1803, he wrote "Notes on Scottish Song," wherein he tried to collect all the information he could about the poetic tradition of his native land. He suggested possibilities for authorship, identified the poems' native regions and the occasions of their composition, cited fragments and verses of traditional songs, and set forth critical comments and engaging anecdotes.

Following the publication and success of the 1786 edition of his *Poems*, Burns set off on a series of trips that carried him over much of Scotland. Narratives of two of those journeys, *Journal of a Tour in the Highlands Made in 1787* and *Journal of the Border Tour*, eventually found their way into print in 1834.

ACHIEVEMENTS

Robert Burns's most significant poetry was written in what may loosely be termed Scots—the northern dialect of English spoken regularly by Scottish peasants and informally by Scottish gentry. When the poet attempted to write in standard eighteenth century British English, he came forth as a different person: stiff, conventional, and genteel, seemingly trying too hard to find his place within the poetic tradition of his day. No matter what the dialect, however, literary historians have termed Burns a "pre-Romantic," a poet who anticipated William Wordsworth, gave new life to the English lyric, relied heavily upon literary forms and legends peculiar to the Scottish folk culture, and (certainly the most Wordsworthian quality of them all) wrote in the actual language of the common people. Few realize, however, that the pre-Romantic label is based primarily on Burns's songs, while the bulk of his poetry was written in the forms favored by the majority of eighteenth century poets. He also wrote satire, verse epistles to friends and fellow poets, and even a variation on the mock-epic narrative ("Tam O'Shanter"). An argument could easily be advanced that Burns ranks as a first-rate practitioner of those forms.

Nevertheless, as a writer of satire, epistle, and mock-heroic, Burns does not belong entirely to the neoclassical mainstream which followed John Dryden, Alexander Pope, and Oliver Goldsmith. With his dialect and intricate stanza forms, his poems evinced a heartiness and exuberance, and even a certain "roughness." Burns had little use for Horace, Homer, and the other models for English neoclassicism; instead, he turned to a clearer tradition that had been established during the so-called golden age of Scottish poetry by the major Scottish Chaucerians: Robert Henryson (1430-1506), William Dunbar (c. 1460-c. 1525), and Gavin Douglas (c. 1474-1522). Following the efforts of Allan Ramsay (1686-1758) and Robert Fergusson (1750-1774)—earlier Scottish poets who had collected the ancient poems and had written new ones based on the older models—Burns committed himself to the bards and songs of his native land. He refined the work of his eighteenth century predecessors, but he was also perceptive enough to learn from them and to retain characteristic subjects, forms, stanza patterns, and language.

No matter how academic, the discussion of Burns's poetry seems never to circumvent his songs. Almost to a line, those short pieces have gained wider fame and prompted more discussion than have his longer poems. Burns wrote more than three hundred songs on every subject imaginable within the context of late eighteenth century Scotland. Within the confines of those songs, Burns gave himself almost totally to the emotions of the moment; he reached out, touched the essence of rural Scotland, and brought it lyrically to life. He gave his readers the excitement and the genuineness of love, work, friendship, patriotism, and even inebriation (a point that has been greatly overemphasized). He portrayed universal character types, national heroes as well as lowly tavern revelers, and he took delight in sketching the grand parades of humanity as they passed before his vivid and lyrical imagination. Thus, Burns's poetic achievement was really very simple. He assumed the mantle of Scotland's national poet at a time when the country was struggling to preserve its cultural identity. However, if Burns spoke for Scotland, he stood also for all English-speaking people, who, as they

prepared to undergo the political and technological traumas of the nineteenth century, needed frequent reminders of their national, political, and artistic heritage.

## BIOGRAPHY

Robert Burns was born on January 25, 1759, in Alloway, some three miles south of the seaport town of Ayr. He was the first son of William Burnes (the original spelling of the family name that the poet eventually altered) and Agnes Broun. The father belonged to a lowly class of Scots agricultural society: He was a cotter, one who occupied a cottage on a farm in exchange for labor. As such, he engaged in a constant struggle to keep himself, his illiterate wife, and their seven children fed and clothed. In 1766, the elder Burnes leased seventy acres near Ayr and committed his family to farming. High rents and poor soil, however, only increased the size of the family debt.

Young Robert studied at a small village school, where, for three years, he read English literature, wrote essays, and learned mathematics. After the practicalities of elementary education had been mastered, further learning came only as time would permit. The local schoolmaster, John Murdock, managed to teach the boy some French, and in 1775, the sixteen-year-old Burns journeyed across the Doon River to Kirkoswald, where he studied the rudiments of surveying. At home, the senior Burnes assumed responsibility for the balance of his son's education: geography, history, devotional and theological literature, and more mathematics. Although chores related to the family farm assumed a high priority, young Burns managed to find time for the Bible, Presbyterian theology, and any books he could beg or borrow from friends and neighbors.

In 1777, William Burnes moved his family some twelve miles to the northwest, to Lochlie Farm, between Tarbolton and Mauchline. There, eighteen-year-old Robert emerged as a sociable, sensitive, and handsome young man. He debated in the Tarbolton Bachelors' Club, a group of serious albeit boisterous young men; he joined the Freemasons; and he discovered women. In 1781, he attempted to embark upon a business career in the flax-dressing industry at Irvine, on the coast. The venture proved to be a failure, and for the most part Burns rooted himself to the family farm in central Ayr-

*Robert Burns* (Library of Congress)

shire, where he remained until the publication of the Kilmarnock edition of his *Poems, Chiefly in the Scottish Dialect* in 1786. William Burnes died in 1784, leaving his family heavily in debt. Robert and his brother Gilbert remained on the farm, however, and the poet's early verse indicates the degree to which he involved himself in the activities, associations, and gossip of the local people.

Burns had begun to write poetry around 1773, when he was fourteen. The poems tended, primarily, to be song lyrics in the Scots vernacular, although (probably as a result of Murdock's influence) he tried his hand at some moral and sentimental pieces in standard English. The manuscripts of those poems reveal considerable roughness. Burns needed models, and not until he came upon the work of two Scots poets, Robert Fergusson and Allan Ramsay, did he learn how to write nonlyrical poetry in the Scots vernacular that would appeal to the hearts and minds of his countrymen. Three years prior to the publication of the Kilmarnock edition, he put together a commonplace book (several versions of which have been published), containing both his poems and remarks concerning his poetic development. Thus, the period 1785-1786 marked Burns's most significant literary output. It also proved to be the time when he would have to pay dearly for liaisons with various young women of the area. In May, 1785, his first daughter was born to Elizabeth Paton, a former servant; in all, he fathered nine illegitimate children, four by his future wife, Jean Armour (those were two sets of twins). He accepted responsibility for rearing and supporting all of them. Another affair with a servant girl, Mary Campbell—the "Highland Mary" of the song—ended tragically when the girl died giving birth to another Burns child.

Despite these domestic problems, the Kilmarnock edition of poems was published, bringing Burns success and some money. More important, the volume took him out of Ayrshire and into Edinburgh, where he gained the praise of the critic Henry Mackenzie (1745-1831) and the publisher William Creech (1745-1815), and where he arranged for publication and subscriptions for a new edition of his poems. From November, 1786, to mid-1788, Burns lived in Edinburgh, seeking to establish himself in its social and intellectual atmo-

sphere. Although his congenial personality and intellectual curiosity appealed to the upper levels of Edinburgh society, they were not enough to erase the stigma of low social birth. The upper classes ultimately rejected him. Thus, the young poet drifted to the late-hour social clubs frequented by printers, booksellers, clerks, and schoolmasters. Through it all, he pondered about how to earn a living, since neither poetry nor social contacts enabled him to meet his financial obligations. Four separate tours throughout Scotland and the editorship of James Johnson's *The Scots Musical Museum* yielded no relief from financial pressures.

In March, 1788, Burns rented a tract of land for farming in Ellisland, Dumfriesshire, after which he finally married Jean Armour. He then began a struggle to support his family, a contest that was not eased even upon his securing an appointment (September, 1789) as tax collector and moving to Dumfries. His literary activities were limited to collecting and writing songs, in addition to the composition of some nonlyric pieces of moderate quality. Although "Tam O'Shanter" belongs to this period, Burns misused his talents by trying to emulate the early eighteenth century poets—composing moral epistles, general verse satires, political ballads, serious elegies, and prologues for theatrical pieces.

Burns died on July 21, 1796, the result of a heart condition that had existed since his youth. The details of his life have been much overstated, particularly the gossip about his drinking and his excessive sexual appetite. For serious students of his poetry, Burns's autobiography can be found within the sound and the sense of his writing.

ANALYSIS

To an extraordinary degree, Robert Burns is the poet of Scotland, a Scotland that—despite its union with England—remained for him and his readers a totally independent cultural, intellectual, social, and political entity. Undoubtedly, Burns will always be identified exclusively with Scotland, with its peculiar life and manners communicated to the outside world through its distinctive dialect and fierce national pride. He justly deserves that identification, for he not only wrote about Scottish life and manners but also sought his inspiration from Scotland—from his own Ayrshire neighborhood, from its land and its people.

### INFLUENCE OF SCOTLAND

Scotland virtually drips from the lines of Burns's poetry. The scenes of the jocular "Jolly Beggars" have their source in Poosie Nansie's inn at Mauchline, while the poet and Tam O'Shanter meet the witches and the warlocks at midnight on the very real, local, and familiar Alloway Kirk. Indeed, reality obscures even the boldest attempts at erudite romanticism. Burns alludes to actual persons, to friends and acquaintances whom he knew and loved and to whom he dedicated his songs. When he tried his hand at satire, he focused upon local citizens, identifying specific personages or settling for allusions that his eighteenth century Scottish readers would easily recognize. In "The Cotter's Saturday Night"—which features a clear portrait of his own father—the poet reflects his deep attachment to and sincere pride in the village of Alloway and the rural environment of Ayrshire. He viewed the simple scenes in "The Cotter's Saturday Night" as the real essence of Scotland's heritage. Burns began with a sincere love and respect for his neighbors, and he sustained that attitude throughout his life and his work. Without the commitment to Scotland, he never would have conquered the hearts of its native readers or risen to become the acknowledged national poet of the land north of the Tweed.

Burns's poetry gained almost immediate success among all classes of the Scottish population. He knew of what he wrote, and he grasped almost immediately the living tradition of Scottish poetry, assimilating the qualities of that tradition into his own verse forms and distinct subject matter. For example, the stanzaic forms in such poems as "To a Mouse" (and its companions) had been in existence for more than three hundred years. Burns early had become familiar with the Scottish Chaucerians (John Major, James I of Scotland, Henryson, Dunbar, Douglas, Sir David Lyndsay) and the folk poets closer to his own day (Ramsay, James Macpherson, Fergusson); he took the best from their forms and content and made them his own. Thus, he probably could not be termed an "original" poet, although he had to work hard to set the tone and style to his readers' tastes. His countrymen embraced his poetry because they found the cadence, the music, and the dialect to be those of their own hearts and minds. The vigor and the deep love may have been peculiar to Burns, but the remaining qualities had existed longer than anyone could determine.

Still, writing in the relatively remote confines of Scotland at the end of the eighteenth century, Burns was not totally alien to the neoclassical norm of British letters. If Alexander Pope or Henry Fielding or Tobias Smollett could focus upon reality and write satires to expose the frailties of humankind, so could Burns be both realistic and satiric. In his most forceful poems—such as "Holy Willie's Prayer," "The Holy Fair," and "Address to the Unco Guid"—he set out to expose the religious hypocrites of his day, but at the same time to portray, clearly and truthfully, both the beautiful and the ugly qualities of Scottish life and character. Burns's poetry may not always be even in quality or consistent in force, but it certainly always conveys an air of truthfulness.

If Burns's poetry reverberates with the remoteness of rural Scotland, it is because he found the perfect poetic environment for the universal themes of his works. In 1803, William Wordsworth stood beside his grave and contemplated "How Verse may build a princely throne/ On humble truth." The throne was carved out of Burns's understanding of the most significant theme of his time—the democratic spirit (which helps to explain Wordsworth's tribute). Throughout, the Scottish bard salutes the worth of pure "man," the man viewed outside the context of station or wealth. Certainly, Burns was sensitive to the principles and causes that spawned the revolutions in America and in France; in fact, closer to home, the Jacobite rebellion sparked by the landing of the Young Pretender from France had occurred only nine years before the poet's birth. By nature, he was a political liberal, and his poems take advantage of every opportunity for humans or beasts to cry for freedom. Again, it was Wordsworth who identified Burns as a poet of the literary revolution—Romanticism—that later rushed through the open gates and into the nineteenth century.

### POETIC QUALITIES

Few will question that, ultimately, Burns's strength as a poet is to be found in the lyrical quality of his songs.

That quality simply stood far above his other virtues—his ability to observe and to penetrate until he discovered the essence of a particular subject, his skill in description and satire, and his striving to achieve personal and intellectual independence. In his songs, he developed the ability to record, with the utmost ease, the emotions of the common people of whom he wrote. Burns's reliance on native Scottish tradition was both a limitation and a strength. For example, although he genuinely enjoyed the poetry of James Thomson (1700-1748), the Edinburgh University graduate who ventured to London and successfully challenged the artificiality of English poetry, Burns could not possibly have written a Scottish sequel to *The Seasons* (1730, 1744). Instead, he focused upon the simple Scottish farmer, upon the man hard at work and enjoying social relationships, not upon the prevalent eighteenth century themes of solitude and retirement. In Burns, then, the reader sees strong native feeling and spontaneous expression, the source of which was inherited, not learned.

Another quality of Burns's poetry that merits attention is his versatility, the range of human emotions that exists throughout his verse. He could function as a satirist, and he could sound the most ardent notes of patriotism. His humor was neither vulgar nor harsh, but quiet, with considerable control—as in "Address to the Deil," "To a Mouse," and "To a Mountain Daisy." As a lover, as one who obviously loved to love and be loved, he wrote lyrical pieces that could capture the essence of human passion. The lyric forms allowed for the fullest expression of his versatility, most of which came about during the last ten years of his relatively short life.

## CAPTURING NATIONAL SPIRIT

From 1787 until his death in the summer of 1796, Burns committed himself to steady literary activity. He became associated with James Johnson, an uneducated engraver and enthusiastic collector and publisher of Scottish songs. From 1787 to 1804, Johnson gathered those songs into a five-volume *Scots Musical Museum*, and Burns served as his principal editor. Then the poet became associated with George Thomson, whose *Select Collection of Scottish Airs* reached six volumes between 1793 and 1811. Burns's temperament seemed suited to such a combination of scholarly activity and

poetic productivity, but he never accepted money for his contributions. The writing, rewriting, and transformation of some three hundred old songs and ballads would serve as his most singular gift to his nation. In reworking those antiquated songs and popular ballads, he returned to Scotland, albeit in somewhat modified form, a large portion of its culture that had for so long remained in obscurity. Thus, an old drinking song emerged as "Auld Lang Syne," while a disreputable ballad became "John Anderson My Jo." Finally, the Johnson and Thomson collections became outlets for certain of his more famous original songs: "For A' That and A' That" and "Scots, Wha Hae wi' Wallace Bled," as well as such love lyrics as "Highland Mary" and "Thou Lingering Star." Because of his love of and gift for the traditional Scots folk songs and ballads, Burns wrote and sang for Scotland. He became the voice and the symbol of the people and captured the national sentiment.

## MELANCHOLY STRAINS

It would be a mistake, however, to assume that all is happily rustic, nationalistic, or patriotic with Burns. On the contrary, he has a decidedly melancholy or mournful strain. A look at such poems as "A Bard's Epitaph" and the "Epistle to a Young Friend" demonstrates that the intellect and the passion of the poet were far from being comfortably adjusted. A conflict raged within the mind and heart of Burns as the sensibilities of an exceedingly gifted soul vied with the sordid lot that was his by birth and social position (or the lack of it). Despite the appearance and even the actuality of productivity during his last five years, the final stage of Burns's career reflects, in the soberest of terms, the degradation of genius. Nevertheless, his muse remained alive and alert, as his passions seethed within him until they found outlets in rhyme.

Burns controlled his passion so that, particularly in his songs, there is abundant evidence of sense and beauty. To his credit, he remained aware of the conflict within him and drew strength from the clash of experiences, of habits, and of emotions which, somehow, he managed to regulate and harmonize. Few will argue that certain of the songs ("Mary Morison," "My Nanie O," and "Of A' the Airts the Wind Can Blow") hang heavy with serious and extremely pathetic and passionate strains. Since such heaviness had its origin in the Scottish tradition, Burns could effectively hide his own melancholy behind the Lugar or the banks of Bonnie Doon.

### MORAL ELEMENT

Such conclusions invariably lead to the question of a religious or moral element in Burns's poetry. Assuredly, the more religious among Burns scholars have difficulty with such poems as "The Holy Fair," "Holy Willie," and the satiric pieces in which the poet ridiculed religious and ecclesiastical ideals and personages. No doubt Burns's own moral conduct was far from perfect, but the careful reader of his poetry realizes immediately that Burns never ridiculed religion; rather, he heaped scorn only upon those religious institutions that appeared ridiculous and lacked the insight to recognize obvious weaknesses. Indeed, the poet often seems to be looking for virtue and morality, seeking to replace the sordid scenes of his own world with the piety of another time and place. He sought a world beyond and above the grotesqueness of his own debauchery, a world dominated by order, love, truth, and joy. That is about the best he could have done for himself. Even had Burns been the epitome of sobriety, morality, and social and religious conformity, religious expression would probably not have been high on his list of poetic priorities. He inherited the poetic legacy of Scotland—a national treasure found outside the limits of the Kirk, a vault not of hymns and psalm paraphrases, but of songs and ballads. Such were the constituent parts of Burns's poetic morality.

Burns's language and poetic methods seem to distract only the impatient among his readers. To begin with, he believed that the vernacular ought never to be seen as low or harsh, or even as prostituted English. Rather, Burns came to know and to understand the Scots dialect and to manipulate it for his own poetic purpose. At the outset, he claimed to have turned his back upon formal bodies of knowledge, upon books, and to have taken full advantage of what he termed "Nature's fire" as the only learning necessary for his art. Nature may have provided the attraction toward the Scots dialect, but Burns himself knew exactly what to do with it.

Close attention to his letters and to the details of his life will yield the steps of his self-education. He read Thomas Salmon's *Geographical and Historical Grammar* (1749) and a *New System of Modern Geography, History, and Modern Grammar* (1770), by William Guthrie (1708-1770), both of which provided descriptions and examples of Scotland's traditions and language, although nothing of poetic contexts. Then he turned to Jethro Tull (1680-1740), the Hungerford farmer and inventor, who wrote several volumes on the general subject of "horse-hoeing husbandry" (1731-1739), and to the Reverend Adam Dickson of Edinburgh, who wrote *A Treatise on Agriculture* (1762, 1765, 1769) and the two-volume *The Husbandry of the Ancients* (1788). Thus, Burns was well versed in the specifics of rural Scotland by the time he discovered his most helpful source, the poetry of Robert Fergusson, who had managed successfully to capture the dialect of enlightened Edinburgh. Burns had his models, and he simply shifted the sounds and the scenes from Scotland's capital to rural Ayrshire.

### POEMS

To simplify matters even further, Burns himself had actually stood behind the plow. Little wonder, then, that the Kilmarnock edition of the *Poems* succeeded on the basis of such pieces as "The Twa Dogs," "The Holy Fair," "Address to the Deil," "Halloween," "The Cotter's Saturday Night," "To a Mouse," and "To a Mountain-Daisy." Burns had effectively described Scottish life as Scots themselves (as well as those south of the Tweed) had come to know it. More important, the poems in that initial collection displayed to the world the poet's full intellectual range of wit and sentiment, although his readers received nothing that had not already been a part of their long tradition. Essentially, the Edinburgh edition of the following year gave the world more of the same, and Burns's readers discovered that the poet's move from Ayrshire to Edinburgh had not changed his sources or his purpose. The new poems— among them "Death and Dr. Hornbook," "The Brigs of Ayr," "Address to the Unco Guid," "John Barleycorn," and "Green Grow the Rushes"—still held to the pictures of Scottish life and to the vernacular, still held to the influence of Robert Fergusson's *Scots Poems* (1773).

By the time Burns had done some substantive work

on James Johnson's *The Scots Musical Museum*, however, his art had assumed a new dimension, the writing and revision of the Scots song. The poet became a singer, providing his own accompaniment by the simple means of humming to himself as he wrote, and trying (as he explained) to catch the inspiration and the enthusiasm so strongly characterized in the traditional poetry. He set out to master the tune, then to compose for that particular strain. In other words, he demanded that for the song, musical expression must dictate the poetic theme. Nevertheless, Burns was the first to admit his weakness as a musician, making no claims even to musical taste. For him, as a poet, music was instinctive, supplied by nature to complement his art. Thus, he felt unable to deal with the technical aspects of music as a formal discipline. What he *could* do, however, was to react quickly to what he termed "many little melodies" and to give new and fresh poetic and musical expression to something like "Scots Wha Hae," one of the oldest of Scottish airs. Through the songs, Burns clearly preserved tradition, while, at the same time, he maintained his originality. This tradition was the genuine expression of the people who, from generation to generation, echoed the essence of their very existence; Burns gave it sufficient clarity and strength to carry it forward into the next century and beyond. The effect of those more than three hundred songs was, simply, to cede Burns the title of Scotland's national poet—a title that he earned because of his poetic rather than his political voice.

### "TAM O' SHANTER"

Perhaps the one poem that demonstrates Burns's ability as a serious and deliberate craftsman, a true poet, is "Tam O' Shanter" (1790, 1791). More than anything else, this piece of 224 lines transports its creator away from the "Heaven-taught plowman" image, from the label of the boy genius whose poetry is nothing more than one large manifestation of the spontaneous overflow of his native enthusiasm. Burns wrote "Tam O' Shanter" for a volume on Scottish antiquity and based it on a witch story told about Alloway Kirk, an old ruin near the poet's house in Ayr. However, he turned that tale into a mock-heroic rendering of folk material that comes close, in genre and in poetic quality, to Geoffrey Chaucer's "The Nun's Priest's Tale." Burns specifi-

cally set out to construct his most sustained and most artistic production; in his own words, he remained aware of the "spice of roguish waggery" within the poem, but he also took considerable pains to ensure that the force of his poetic genius and "finishing polish" would not go unrecognized. Burns's manipulation of his dipsomaniacal hero and his misadventures constitutes a masterful blending of the serious and the comic. The moralists of his day objected vehemently to the ribald elements of the poem. Early in the next century, William Wordsworth, whose strongest drink was probably water, attacked the attackers of "Tam O' Shanter" (as well as those who objected to all of Burns's poetry on moral grounds) by labeling them impenetrable dunces and narrow-minded puritans. Wordsworth saw the poem as a delightful picture of the rustic adventurer's convivial exaltation; if the poem lacked clear moral purpose, maintained England's laureate, it at least provided the clearest possible moral effect.

### LEGACY

The final issue raised by Burns's poetry is his place in literary history—an issue that has always prompted spirited debate. There is no doubt that Burns shares common impulses with Wordsworth and the Romantic movement, particularly in his preoccupation with folklore and the language of the people, yet neither is there any evidence of Burns's fundamental dissatisfaction with the dominant critical criteria and principal literary assumptions of eighteenth century England. The readers of his songs will be hard put to discover lush scenery or majestic mountains, or even the sea—although all were in easy reach of his eye and his mind. If he expressed no poetic interest in such aspects of nature close at hand, however, he turned even less in the direction of the distant and the exotic.

Instead, he looked long and hard at the farmer, the mouse, and the louse, and he contemplated each; the mountains, the nightingale, the skylark he also saw, but chose to leave them to the next generation of poets. In other words, Burns did not seek new directions for his poetry; instead, he took full advantage of what existed and of what had come before. He grasped literary imitation firmly and gave that form the most significance and prominence it had enjoyed since the late Restoration and the Augustan Age. Burns wrote satire and he wrote songs, but he invented neither. Rather, he served as an exploiter of tradition; he gathered inherited motifs, rhetorical conventions, and familiar language and produced art. The reader of the present century should see no less or expect no more from Burns's poetical character.

## OTHER MAJOR WORKS

NONFICTION: *Journal of a Tour in the Highlands Made in 1787*, 1834 (Allan Cunningham, editor); *Journal of the Border Tour*, 1834 (Cunningham, editor); *The Letters of Robert Burns*, 1931 (2 volumes; John De Lancey Ferguson, editor).

## BIBLIOGRAPHY

Bentman, Raymond. *Robert Burns*. Boston: Twayne, 1987. This complete introduction to the life and works of Robert Burns describes Burns's background, analyzes his poetry and songs, then places him in the context of late eighteenth century literature. Includes an annotated secondary bibliography and is suitable for high school students and college undergraduates.

Daiches, David. *Robert Burns and His World*. New York: Viking Press, 1972. A brief but very thorough account of Burns's life and times. Sections placing him in the Scottish literary and social traditions are particularly useful. The atmosphere of Burns's Scotland is well conveyed by the many well-chosen illustrations.

Jack, R. D. S., and Andrew Noble, eds. *The Art of Robert Burns*. London: Vision Press, 1982. The nine essays contained in this book place Burns in a wide social and literary context, outside his native Scotland. They seek to show Burns as a complex writer, and not merely a "cosy representative of Scottish virtues." Suitable for intermediate and advanced students.

McGuirk, Carol. *Robert Burns and the Sentimental Era*. Athens: University of Georgia Press, 1985. A study of Burns's work in the context of his literary contemporaries. McGuirk persuasively maintains that Burns's flaws were a result not of his lesser skill in standard English but of the sentimentality of thought and diction shared in varying degrees by most eighteenth century poets. Good bibliography, arranged by topics.

McIntyre, Ian. *Dirt and Deity: A Life of Robert Burns*. New York: HarperCollins, 1995. Written for the bicentenary of Burns's death, this biography organizes previous research into Burns's life, telling its story as much as possible through Burns's letters and the correspondence and memoirs of those who knew him.

Noble, Andrew. *Robert Burns and English Romanticism*. Brookfield, Vt.: Ashgate, 2001. Scholarly examination of Burns in the context of the great literary tradition of his time.

Skoblow, Jeffrey. *Dooble Tongue: Scots, Burns, Contradiction*. Cranbury, N.J.: Associated University Presses, 2001. Places Burns and his poetics in historical and Scottish cultural context. Bibliographical references, index.

*Samuel J. Rogal*

# SAMUEL BUTLER

**Born:** Strensham, England; February 8, 1612
**Died:** London, England; September 25, 1680

## PRINCIPAL POETRY

*Hudibras*, 1663, 1664, 1678 (parts 1-3)

## OTHER LITERARY FORMS

Samuel Butler wrote essays and prose in addition to verse. His best-known essay is "The Case of King Charles I Truly Stated," which argues that the execution of Charles I was unjustified. Butler's essay was published in Robert Thyer's *The Genuine Remains in Verse and Prose of Samuel Butler* (1759), and it displays his excellent understanding of English law—an understanding that plays an important role in *Hudibras*—and his ability to pick apart a point of view, a trait manifested in his carefully reasoned satire.

Of greater literary significance are his "characters," which were probably composed during 1667 to 1669, and nearly two hundred of which have been uncovered since Butler's death. The most complete edition of his characters was edited by Charles W. Daves in 1970 as *Samuel Butler, 1612-1680: Characters*. As with *Hudibras*, Butler took a popular literary form of the seventeenth century and modified it to suit his satiric purposes. His "characters" feature politicians, judges, lovers, and zealots, and in each sketch, he demonstrates his abhorrence of immoderation, his contempt for hypocrisy, his disgust with irrational thought, and his willingness to expose fraud and ostentation wherever they might be found. Although some of the characters were intended for publication, others were probably intended to serve as raw material which Butler could mine for his poetry.

## ACHIEVEMENTS

Samuel Butler's greatest achievement was to embody in a single work the failures, hypocrisy, and foolishness of an age. *Hudibras* captures the dark spirit of seventeenth century England, and the wit which made his contemporaries regard Butler as a great comic satirist also reveals the flaws in their philosophies. In Butler's stingingly accurate portrait of his time lies much of his literary strength and weakness. If one reads and understands *Hudibras*, one learns to understand the culture of Oliver Cromwell's England and of Restoration England. Butler's misanthropic point of view illuminates his society; even though he was a Loyalist, and the surface thrust of *Hudibras* is an attack on Cromwellian Puritans, Butler spares no one from his sharp insights. *Hudibras* is necessarily specific, and Butler's allusions to events and people were readily recognized in his time. Such particularity has made Butler's satire dependent on his readers' understanding of the 1600's. Thus, what made Butler's contemporaries laugh and wince may puzzle modern readers.

*Hudibras* brought Butler fame; he became known as Hudibras Butler, or simply as Hudibras. Such verse is still called Hudibrastic, and its imitations are called Hudibrastic satires. The poem stands out not only as one of the great achievements in satire but also as a work that inspired multitudes of imitations and helped to shape the forms of satire after its time. Its influence stretched from the seventeenth century to America after the revolution. Indeed, the poem's assault on cul-

*Samuel Butler* (Hulton Archive/Getty Images)

tural elitism appealed to antimonarchists and egalitarians, in spite of Butler's evident Loyalist views. Butler expanded the bounds of satire, writing in verse when contemporary literary theorists said satire was best suited to prose. Critics still argue over whether *Hudibras* is satire, burlesque, heroic satire, satirical burlesque, or something else entirely. Butler showed that satire could, like Miguel de Cervantes's *El ingenioso hidalgo don Quixote de la Mancha* (1605, 1615; *The History of the Valorous and Wittie Knight-Errant, Don Quixote of the Mancha*, 1612-1620; better known as *Don Quixote de la Mancha*) mock a literary genre, expose the foibles of a class of people, and provide insights into the intellectual controversies of an era. Butler influenced the satirists who followed him, although few produced works that could match *Hudibras* for wit, insight, and bitterness.

## BIOGRAPHY

Two distinct portraits of Samuel Butler have developed since his death—one traditional and the other historical. Most sketches of Butler's life rely on the traditional version, based primarily on the accounts of John

Aubrey, who knew him, and Anthony à Wood, a contemporary of Butler who admitted that he was uncertain of his facts. One reason why most short biographies rely on the traditional accounts is that the historical ones have been uncertain and contradictory. Evidence in the form of letters, notes, and public documents has been hard to come by, and new evidence sometimes contradicts the old. Only since the mid-twentieth century has historical evidence begun to supplant the traditional version of Butler's life.

Both versions agree on the major aspects of Butler's youth. He was born in Strensham, England, on February 8, 1612, and was baptized on February 14. His father, also named Samuel, was a farmer who rented property from the local gentry and had a home and lands in Barbourne. The elder Butler was evidently learned and maintained a large and diverse library that he left to his eight children when he died. Samuel was then only fourteen years of age.

Butler probably attended King's School in Worcester, north of Strensham. Tradition claims that he also attended college—perhaps Oxford, although records show no evidence of his having continued his formal education after leaving King's School. He probably became a secretary for various gentlemen and gentlewomen. Through these people, he became acquainted with some of the leading minds of his day, possibly including John Seldon, a legal historian who knew Ben Jonson, Thomas Hobbes, and others. Butler had ample opportunity to observe the pretentiousness of England's social and intellectual elite, and he may have learned about England's laws and theology from such people as Seldon.

In 1642, King Charles I raised his standard at Nottingham; in 1649, he was executed. Tradition has it that during these tumultuous years, Butler served as a clerk to Sir Samuel Luke, a member of Parliament from Bedfordshire, and that Luke served as the model for the character Hudibras. Other models have been suggested by historians, yet Butler probably used several Puritans as inspiration for Hudibras. He might have begun *Hudibras* before 1649, and it might have been his response to having to survive by serving parliamentarians while harboring loyalist sentiments.

Some accounts indicate that fragments of *Hudibras* were copied and circulated before the Restoration. Butler had already written essays defending the monarchy and was almost certainly working on *Hudibras* when Oliver Cromwell died in 1658. Charles II entered London in 1660, at which time works by Loyalists became popular. When *Hudibras*, part 1, was published in late 1662 (it was postdated 1663), it caught the fancy of the public and of the king; Charles II was said to quote from the poem from memory. Butler probably made enough money from the sale of *Hudibras*, part 1, and later *Hudibras*, part 2, to live well.

Butler apparently invested his money unwisely, or perhaps he spent it too rapidly. Some accounts assert that Charles II gave Butler three hundred pounds as a royal grant. Other accounts maintain that Charles II gave Butler a one-hundred-pound annuity. Others assert that both were given; still others mention neither. What seems likely is that Charles II was dilatory in fulfilling any promises he made to Butler. By 1673, Butler had become secretary to the duke of Buckingham. Not until 1677, apparently, did Charles II provide Butler with any monetary support. In 1678, *Hudibras*, part 3, was published, in part to provide Butler with income beyond that which came from his secretarial work.

Tradition holds that Butler was unjustly neglected by an ungrateful king who failed to fulfill promises made to the poet. History indicates that Charles II was freer with his promises than with his money. Butler's own sharp misanthropic wit may have cost him royal and noble help; he seems to have found fault with everyone he knew—a practice that might have alienated potential patrons. Regardless of what he was promised and what he actually received, he lived in a poor part of London and died on September 25, 1680, in genuinely miserable poverty. He was buried in the graveyard of St. Paul's, in Covent Garden. A bust of him resides in the Poets' Corner of Westminster Abbey.

ANALYSIS

Samuel Butler's stature as a poet is founded on one work: *Hudibras*. In it, he demonstrates considerable skill in prosody, yet many critics are uncertain about the work's status as poetry, describing it as doggerel. One of Butler's objectives in *Hudibras* is the debasement of heroic verse; thus, although he is undoubtedly a poet, his verse is not what is commonly thought of as poetry. This contradiction is one of many inherent in Butler's great work. He displays a broad knowledge of literature and philosophy—a knowledge which is the product of an inquisitive and thoughtful mind—yet he presents his knowledge only to portray it as foolish. Although *Hudibras* became famous as a political satire and remains best known for its portrayal of seventeenth century English politics, two of its three parts are devoted to social satire. It is above all distinguished by its verse, which spawned a school of imitations called Hudibrastic, and its wit and vigor, which make for a lively narrative. Its satire is unusually sophisticated and wide-ranging, attacking a poetic genre, a style of verse, and the politics, theology, and manners of Butler's society.

### METER AND VERSIFICATION

*Hudibras* is written in rhyming tetrameter couplets, a verse form that in Butler's day was associated with heroic poetry. Philosophically a rationalist, Butler objected to poetry which defied probability by describing magic, fairies, enchanted castles, flying horses, and other fantastic places, creatures, and events. Thus, he took a verse form that would be familiar to his audience and subverted it by using it to describe false heroes and sordid events and by employing strange rhymes and odd plays on words. *Hudibras* abounds with such irreverent rhymes as: "And Pulpit, Drum Ecclesiastik,/ Was beat with fist, instead of a stick," from part 1; and from part 2,

> Quoth *Hudibras*, You lie so ope,
> That I, without a *Telescope*,
> Can find your Tricks out, and descry
> Where you tell truth, and where you lie

Throughout his poem, Butler's verse is exuberantly barbaric; the rhymes are wildly original, and the wordplay is rapid and clever. Instead of romantic language, Butler creates witty wordplay, thus trivializing heroic verse.

### LANGUAGE

Much of Butler's brilliance as a poet is manifested in his mutilation of language. By deliberately using his couplets to present doggerel, he subverts the ideas he wishes to attack with his diction. Analytically gifted

and capable of perceiving truth in the folly of others, he insists on expressing his rationalist understanding of truth by exposing the particulars of folly. His analytical character and rationalist point of view make him seem more part of the modern era than of the English Renaissance that nurtured him. His models were works such as Edmund Spenser's *The Faerie Queene* (1590, 1596) and Cervantes' *Don Quixote de la Mancha*, but he could not empathize with *The Faerie Queene* as he could with *Don Quixote de la Mancha*. Thus, he mocks Spenser's epic work and its kin with satire more harsh than that found in Cervantes' satirical romance. Butler's verse mocks not only ideas but also the very modes in which they are expressed.

### SATIRIC CONTENT

Butler includes careful allusions to *The Faerie Queene*, the masterwork of English Renaissance heroic verse, to emphasize his implicit intent to satirize the Arcadian romances of his sixteenth century predecessors. Each canto of *Hudibras* begins with an "argument," as does each canto of *The Faerie Queene*. More important, the name *Hudibras* is taken from Spenser's poem: "He that made loue vnto the eldest Dame,/ Was hight Sir *Huddibras*, an hardy man;/ Yet not so good of deedes, as great of name." Butler takes this character who was "not so good of deedes" and places him in Puritan England. This act, coupled with his perverse versification, makes *Hudibras* satirical in its most fundamental elements: language and character.

The first part of *Hudibras* is organized by the elements of an epic quest. Like Cervantes' *Don Quixote de la Mancha, Hudibras* features a knight-errant who misperceives his world. Hudibras, the character, seems much like Don Quixote; he seeks to right wrongs, is afflicted by low characters whose natures he misapprehends, and is accompanied by a sort of squire. Even his fatness seems, in context, to be in deliberate contrast to Quixote's thinness. However, for all the seeming borrowing from *Don Quixote de la Mancha*, Hudibras is significantly different from his predecessor, just as Butler's misanthropic view of life is different from that of Cervantes. Given the misery inflicted on Cervantes, one might expect him to have a cold view of the world, but *Don Quixote de la Mancha* is a gentle satire and readers can sympathize with its unfortunate protagonist. Hudibras is an inherently unsympathetic character; he is boorish, greedy, cowardly, and self-righteous. Don Quixote seeks giants; Hudibras seeks nonconformity with Puritanical notions of virtue. One tries to combat the masters of evil; the other bullies only those who appear weak. In addition, Don Quixote's companion, Sancho Panza, is a slow but good-natured man, while Hudibras's companion, Ralph, is an angry man who despises Hudibras and rivals his master in greed, deceit, and foolishness. Butler's treatment of his characters is cold, dispassionate, and often harsh; Cervantes' compassion is a notable feature of his work.

Whatever the origins of Butler's misanthropy, his evenhanded scorn makes *Hudibras* curiously egalitarian. Butler, a royalist, leaves no character unscathed, and no idea is introduced for purposes other than to expose its emptiness. Hudibras, the Puritan, is an obvious target of Butler's antipathy, but Ralph is a religious Independent and receives the same treatment from Butler, who describes Ralph's manner of learning as one "that costs no pains/ Of Study, Industry, or Brains." Their antagonists are often cruel and usually equally self-righteous, no matter what their political leanings.

## PLOT

The plot of *Hudibras* follows a traditional pattern of romance. A knight-errant, spurned by a woman, seeks to lose his sense of loss in questing. While on his quest, he encounters dangers and assorted exotic characters. Eventually, he wins the attentions of a woman. In the case of questing Hudibras, his first adventure involves an encounter with bearbaiters and a fiddler with a wooden leg. Hudibras sees a village audience dancing merrily to the fiddler Crowdero's music and watching the bear. As a good Puritan magistrate, he is offended by the frivolity of the dancers and the immorality of the bearbaiters. Further, he recognizes the public merrymaking as a threat to public order and thus to the government. As a good logician, Hudibras deduces that such a threat represents a Roman Catholic plot to overthrow the Protestant government; the merrymakers are conspirators, and Crowdero is their leader. Hudibras seeks to arrest the fiddler and a fight ensues. In the melee, the knight-errant falls from his mount onto the bear, angering the animal. It escapes its keeper and scatters the mob. Victorious, Hudibras and Ralph place Crowdero in the village stocks. Trulla, a physically powerful woman, leads the villagers in a counterattack. After much confusion, Hudibras and Ralph are defeated and replace Crowdero in the stocks. The first part of the poem ends with the Puritan and the Independent debating both the blame for their failure and the relative importance of logic and inspiration.

## SOCIOPOLITICAL CONTEXT

No great imagination is required for one to understand how the tale of the follies of a Puritan would have appealed to King Charles II and the Royalists. Some of Butler's contemporaries read specific political figures into the roles of the villagers, yet Butler's satire is too general to support such identifications. Ideas are the targets of his satirical wit; thus, Hudibras's reasoning is more representative of Butler's satire than are the comic characters that people his narrative. Hudibras, the Puritan, sees a Popish plot where none could possibly be; he is so consumed by theory and prejudice that he does not understand reality. This notion is the heart of Butler's satire. In the crazy behavior of Hudibras in part 1, Butler expresses his contempt for the way the Puritans interpreted reality. If his satire is taken as a portrait of ideas, then Butler finds the ideas of the Puritans to be empty, hypocritical, and warped.

In parts 2 and 3, Butler's satire shifts from the political to the social. In this shift, Butler anticipates the thematic thrust of Restoration comedy, which focused on society and on the relationship between men and women. Hudibras is released from the stocks through the intercession of the Widow, who helps Hudibras on the basis of his promise to take a whipping as punishment for his misbehavior. Hudibras plans for Ralph to take his whipping for him and plots to marry the Widow, who is rich. Ralph also wants the Widow for himself. Much of the narrative focuses on the efforts of Hudibras to evade a whipping and to woo the Widow. In the process, Butler reveals the ethical depravity not only of Hudibras but of the other characters as well, and he exposes the emptiness of the love conventions of the epic romance. Even the intended victim of Hudibras and Ralph, the Widow, is no innocent. She does not mind someone marrying her for her money if he is open about it. Her objections to Hudibras and Ralph are based on their subterfuges: the lies about the whipping, the pretense of love, and the general duplicity. The decreased contemporary popularity of parts 2 and 3, in comparison to part 1, was probably a tribute to the accuracy of Butler's satire rather than a reflection of any loss of inspiration. While part 1 exposed the falseness of the preceding generation, parts 2 and 3 illustrated the hypocrisies of its intended readership; Butler's audience was asked to see its own falseness, thus anticipating Alexander Pope's *The Dunciad* (1728-1743), Jonathan Swift's satires, and the more gentle comedies of William Wycherley, William Congreve, and Richard Brinsley Sheridan.

OTHER MAJOR WORKS

MISCELLANEOUS: *The Genuine Remains in Verse and Prose of Samuel Butler*, 1759 (Robert Thyer, editor); *Characters, Observations, and Reflexions from the Notebooks*, 1908 (A. R. Waller, editor); *Samuel Butler, 1612-1680: Characters*, 1970 (Charles W. Daves, editor).

BIBLIOGRAPHY

Henderson, Philip. *Samuel Butler: The Incarnate Bachelor*. Bloomington: Indiana University Press, 1954. One of the best biographies of Butler and the first to deal with Butler's private life. Focuses on Butler's personality rather than his work. Readable and illuminating. Argues against such mistaken prevailing views that Butler hated his father. Contains a detailed chronology.

Holt, Lee. *Samuel Butler*. Rev. ed. Boston: Twayne, 1989. In his critical evaluation, Holt summarizes and quotes extensively from a wide range of Butler's work, much of it no longer available. Extends the reader's knowledge of Butler's varied accomplishments. Includes biographical information, a chronology, notes, references, a lengthy selected bibliography, and an index with brief annotations.

Parker, Blanford. *The Triumph of Augustan Poetics: English Literary Culture from Butler to Johnson.* New York: Cambridge University Press, 1998. Written for an audience familiar with seventeenth and eighteenth century history and thought, yet accessible to the nonspecialist. Parker's study includes a chapter on Samuel Butler and his part in a vigorous, tumultuous, and original period in English culture. Includes bibliographic references.

Raby, Peter. *Samuel Butler: A Biography*. Iowa City: University of Iowa Press, 1991. This biography makes much of the suffering in Butler's youth, which was occasioned by repeated whippings by his father for the slightest infractions and his grandfather's long headmastership of a school at which Butler was enrolled. Includes a bibliography.

Richards, Edward Ames. *"Hudibras" in the Burlesque Tradition*. Reprint. New York: Octagon Books, 1972. Explores the burlesque elements in Butler's *Hudibras*. Bibliography.

Snider, Alvin Martin. *Origin and Authority in Seventeenth Century England: Bacon, Milton, Butler*. Toronto, Ont.: University of Toronto Press, 1994. Explores the way in which Francis Bacon, John Milton, and Butler shared thematic interest and discourse in the genesis of ideas by focusing on their signature works: *Novum Organum*, *Paradise Lost*, and *Hudibras*, respectively.

Swartchild, William G. *The Character of a Roundhead: Theme and Rhetoric in Anti-Puritan Verse Satire, from 1639 Through "Hudibras."* New York: Russell and Russell, 1966. Provides history and criticism of English satire and the influence of Puritan mores within the genre, using Butler's work as a focal point for the discussion.

Veldkamp, Jan. *Samuel Butler: The Author of "Hudibras."* Reprint. Folcroft, Pa.: Folcroft Library Editions, 1977. Offers analysis of the religious aspects of Butler's seminal work, *Hudibras*.

Wasserman, George W. *Samuel "Hudibras" Butler*. Boston, Mass.: Twayne, 1976. Provides criticism and interpretation of Butler's most noted work.

*Kirk H. Beetz*

# LORD BYRON
## George Gordon

**Born:** London, England; January 22, 1788
**Died:** Missolonghi, Greece; April 19, 1824

PRINCIPAL POETRY

*Fugitive Pieces*, 1806
*Hours of Idleness*, 1807
*Poems on Various Occasions*, 1807
*Poems Original and Translated*, 1808
*English Bards and Scotch Reviewers*, 1809
*Hints from Horace*, 1811
*The Curse of Minerva*, 1812
*Childe Harold's Pilgrimage*, 1812-1818 (cantos 1-
    4), 1819 (the 4 cantos together)
*The Bride of Abydos*, 1813
*The Giaour*, 1813
*Waltz: An Apostrophic Hymn*, 1813
*The Corsair*, 1814
*Lara*, 1814
*Ode to Napoleon Buonaparte*, 1814
*Hebrew Melodies Ancient and Modern*, 1815
*Monody on the Death of the Right Honourable R. B.
    Sheridan*, 1816
*Parisina*, 1816
*Poems*, 1816
*The Prisoner of Chillon, and Other Poems*, 1816
*The Siege of Corinth*, 1816
*The Lament of Tasso*, 1817
*Beppo: A Venetian Story*, 1818
*Mazeppa*, 1819
*Don Juan*, 1819-1824 (cantos 1-16), 1826 (the 16
    cantos together)
*The Prophecy of Dante*, 1821
*The Vision of Judgment*, 1822
*The Age of Bronze*, 1823
*The Island*, 1823
*The Complete Poetical Works of Byron*, 1980-1986
    (5 volumes)

OTHER LITERARY FORMS

It should be noted that the titles of Lord Byron's principal poetic works include dramatic as well as lyrical and narrative works. Byron wrote eight plays in all, most of which focused on either speculative or historical subjects and were never intended for the stage. He designated them "mental theatre," or closet drama modeled after classical principles, and clearly regarded the plays as among his most important productions. Complementing Byron's extraordinarily prolific and diverse career as a poet is his versatility as a writer of epistolary prose. During his lifetime Byron composed more than twenty-nine hundred letters, which have been scrupulously edited by Leslie A. Marchand and published between 1973 and 1982 in twelve volumes under the title *Byron's Letters and Journals*. The sheer immensity of this correspondence is matched only by the unlimited range and immediacy of Byron's voice as he speaks without reserve on a variety of topics. In addition to these private documents, along with John Keats's letters the most revealing correspondence of the British Romantic poets, Byron also published the combative *Letter to [John Murray] on the Rev. W. L. Bowles' Strictures on the Life and Writings of Pope* (1821) and, in the first number of Leigh Hunt's *The Liberal* (1822), "A Letter to the Editor of 'My Grandmother's Review.'" *The Parliamentary Speeches of Lord Byron*, comprising three addresses he made while a member of the House of Lords, was issued in 1824, well after he had grown disillusioned with what he called "Parliamentary mummeries."

ACHIEVEMENTS

If poets can be judged by the intellectual and cultural myths which they inspire, then Lord Byron must be deemed the most broadly influential of the Romantic writers. Through his creation of a brooding and defiant persona known as the Byronic Hero—according to Peter L. Thorslev, Jr., a composite blend of the attributes of Cain, Ahasuerus, Satan, Prometheus, Rousseau's Child of Nature, the Man of Feeling, the Gloomy Egoist, the Gothic Villain, and the Noble Outlaw—Byron exerted a profound impact on the entire nineteenth century and its conception of the archetypal Romantic sensibility. The essential trait that came to be associated with Byronism is what Bertrand Russell, in his *History of Western Philosophy* (1945), identifies as "Titanic cosmic self-assertion." Signifying less a specific stance than a generalized attitude, the phrase denotes a proud, often despairing, rebellion against any institutional or moral system that threatens to rob the self of its autonomy, centrality, and independence. Something of the extent to which this outlook captured the imagination of the age can be gauged from a brief list of artists and thinkers whose works reflect Byron's influence: in Germany, Johann Wolfgang von Goethe, Heinrich Heine, Ludwig van Beethoven, and Friedrich Nietzsche; in France, Honoré de Balzac, Stendhal, Hector Berlioz, and Eugène Delacroix; in Russia, Alexander Pushkin and Fyodor Dostoevski; and in America, Herman Melville. Even Matthew Arnold, that most Wordsworthian of Victorian critics, admitted in his 1850 poem "Memorial Verses" that the collective English soul "Had *felt* him like the thunder's roll." Thirty-one years later, Arnold's view had not changed: "The power of Byron's personality," he wrote, approvingly quoting Algernon Charles Swinburne, "lies in . . . '*the excellence of sincerity and strength.*'"

What fascinated nineteenth century audiences about Byron was not simply the larger-than-life character of the man transmuted into art but also the flinty integrity of his mind that penetrated all deception and constantly tested the limits of skepticism. In this respect Byron seems peculiarly modern. Although often considered a Romantic paradox because of various antitheses in his nature (he led the Romantic revolution toward "expression" in poetry, for example, but was thoroughly Augustan in his literary ideals and a lifelong admirer of Alexander Pope), he rarely succumbs to the temptation of believing his own fictions and always examines his experience with obsessive honesty. In conversations with his friend and confidante Lady Blessington, Byron thus confessed to being "so changeable . . . such a strange *mèlange* of good and evil, that it would be difficult to describe me," but he goes on to say: "There are but two sentiments to which I am constant—a strong love of liberty, and a detestation of cant." These last qualities undoubtedly explain why the vein of satire was so congenial to him as a poet. In both the barbed heroic couplets of *English Bards and Scotch Reviewers*, the scathing burlesque that launched his career, and the seriocomic use of ottava rima in *Don Juan*, the epic satire that he did not live to complete, Byron sought to ex-

pose the smug complacencies and absurd pretensions of his time and, if possible, to restore to it the ability to see itself objectively. The dark *Weltschmerz* of poems such as *Childe Harold's Pilgrimage* may attest his personal despair over whether that goal could ever be accomplished, but in all his variegated moods he writes with energetic conviction born of "sincerity and strength." Byron's seminal achievement, therefore, may be his capacity for embodying the strivings of a deeply restless age, for articulating those longings and doing what all great poets do—namely, to return the imagination to the world.

## BIOGRAPHY

George Gordon, the sixth Lord Byron, was born with a clubbed right foot, a deformity that caused him considerable suffering throughout his life and did much to shape his later character. He was descended from two aristocratic and colorful families: His father, who died when Byron was three years old, was Captain John ("Mad Jack") Byron, a rake and fortune hunter who traced his ancestry back to the time of William the

*Lord Byron* (Library of Congress)

Conqueror; his mother, Catherine Gordon of Gight, was the irascible and outspoken heiress who liked to boast of her lineal connection to James I of Scotland. After her husband squandered the Gordon inheritance, Catherine moved to Aberdeen, where she reared her son under straitened financial circumstances and the Calvinistic creed of Scottish Presbyterianism. With the death of his great-uncle in 1798, the ten-year-old Byron became a titled English peer and took up residence at the patrimonial estate of Newstead Abbey in Nottingham. During this period the precocious young lord fell in love with two cousins named Mary Duff and Margaret Parker, was initiated into premature sexual dalliance by a nurse, and began his zealous regimen of swimming, boxing, fencing, and horsemanship to compensate for his physical lameness.

While at Harrow (1801-1805) and subsequently at Cambridge (1805-1807), Byron started to develop some of the strong attachments and habits that remained with him into adulthood. Though he little relished formal schooling, he periodically immersed himself in reading, became infatuated with Mary Chaworth, and cultivated lasting friendships with his half sister Augusta Leigh as well as with John Cam Hobhouse, Scrope Davies, Francis Hodgson, and others. He also incurred sizable debts for his extravagant revelries at Newstead during college vacations, and, simultaneously, he was entering the arena of literary authorship. His first few volumes of juvenilia, *Fugitive Pieces* and *Poems on Various Occasions*, were privately printed and circulated; *Hours of Idleness*, however, his ensuing venture into the public domain, prompted caustic notice by Henry Brougham, which in turn fueled the retaliatory satire of *English Bards and Scotch Reviewers*. Shortly thereafter, tiring of his life of routine dissipation, Byron prepared to leave England.

The next seven years were momentous ones in Byron's life. Before committing himself to what he thought might eventually be a Parliamentary career, he determined to broaden his education by visiting other lands and peoples. Accordingly, in 1809 he embarked with Hobhouse on an exhilarating tour through Portugal, Spain, Malta, Albania, Greece, and Asia Minor. The vivid scenes and experiences of this two-year excursion provided Byron with the materials for cantos 1-2

of his autobiographical travelogue *Childe Harold's Pilgrimage* and his several Eastern tales in verse. Eight months after his return to England in 1811, part of *Childe Harold's Pilgrimage* was published and Byron became an overnight celebrity: "I awoke one morning," wrote the nobleman-poet, "and found myself famous." Because Byron was readily identified with the melancholic, jaded, and quasi-erotic hero of his poem, he was besieged by ladies of fashion and lionized by the beau monde of Regency London. Foremost among those giddily vying for the attentions of the handsome and aristocratic young author was Lady Caroline Lamb, a flamboyant, decidedly eccentric woman who to her delight discovered Byron to be "mad—bad—and dangerous to know." Perhaps as much to escape such frenzied pursuit as for any other reason, Byron in early 1815 married Annabella Milbanke, a demure and somewhat priggish "bluestocking" whom Byron dubbed "my Princess of Parallelograms." The ill-fated marriage dissolved a year later, after the birth of a daughter, Augusta Ada, when Lady Byron learned of her husband's incestuous relations with his half sister. Socially ostracized by all but his close friends and beset by creditors, Byron left England on April 25, 1816, never to return.

The legendary final phase of Byron's career, which saw his full maturation as a poet, was crowded with events that ensured his lasting renown. Journeying through France to Switzerland, he spent his first summer in exile near Geneva, where he met two other expatriates, Percy Bysshe Shelley and Mary Shelley, with whom he enjoyed many evenings of intellectual conversation. While there, Byron also completed canto 3 of *Childe Harold's Pilgrimage*, began *Manfred* (pb. 1817), and tried unsuccessfully to stay uninvolved with Mary Shelley's persistent stepsister Claire Clairmont. In January, 1817, Clairmont and Byron had a child, a daughter they named Allegra. By the spring of that year Byron had established himself in Venice, "the greenest isle" of his imagination, where he diverted himself with numerous affairs while periodically exploring the antiquities of Florence and Rome.

The atmosphere of Italy did much to stimulate his literary creativity in new directions. By the end of 1817 he finished canto 4 of *Childe Harold's Pilgrimage*, an elegiac canto signaling Byron's decisive break with the past, and, influenced by John Hookham Frere's *Whistlecraft* (1817), a mock-heroic satirical poem in the flexible form of ottava rima, he completed the experimental *Beppo*, which looks forward to the narrative style of *Don Juan*. The period from 1818 to 1822 brought additional changes. Wearying of his promiscuous debaucheries on the Grand Canal in Venice, Byron met Countess Teresa Guiccioli of Ravenna, then nineteen years old, and soon became her devoted *cavalier servente*. This attachment, in turn, drew him into the revolutionary Carbonari struggle against Austrian rule in northern Italy, an interest reflected in his political dramas (*Marino Faliero, Doge of Venice*, pr., pb. 1821; *The Two Foscari*, pb. 1821; and *Sardanapalus*, pb. 1821). With the defeat of the Carbonari movement in 1821, Byron followed the Gambas, Teresa's family, to Pisa, where he again joined the Shelley circle, which now included Edward John Trelawny and Thomas Medwin, and composed his devastating satire *The Vision of Judgment*. News of Shelley's drowning in July, 1822, however, stunned and sobered Byron. Shortly thereafter, he left for Genoa with Countess Guiccioli, but found his thoughts increasingly preoccupied with the Greek War of Independence. The final chapter of his life, always dominated by the trait that Lady Blessington called "mobility," forms a fitting memorial to Byron's restless spirit. Elected a member of the London Greek Committee, a Philhellene organization, the poet felt obligated to translate his political convictions into action. Despite skepticism concerning various Greek leaders' loyalty to the cause and despite a sense of his own imminent death, Byron set forth to do what he could. Sailing for Missolonghi in late December, 1823, he devoted his personal fortune and energy to forming a united front against the Turks. Four months later he died of a fever; to this day he is hailed as a national hero by the Greek people.

### ANALYSIS

The history of the poetic development of Lord Byron intersects at every stage with the saga of his life; yet it is only one of many paradoxes that he valued the writing of poetry primarily for the opportunity it afforded him to escape what he termed "my own wretched identity." More than anything else, poetry for Byron was a means

both of sublimation and, ultimately, of self-realization. In his letters he thus suggests the former function when he speaks of poetry as "the lava of the imagination whose eruption prevents an earthquake," the volcanic metaphor signifying the cathartic release that the process of writing afforded him. The precise way in which it fulfilled the second function, however, is less obvious. Through the dynamics of self-projection, of investing much of his own multifaceted character in his personae, Byron strives to transcend the narrow limits of "personality" and achieve a more comprehensive perspective on himself and his experience. The essential goal of this artistic quest, which constitutes a progressive ontology, is delineated in canto 3 of *Childe Harold's Pilgrimage*: "'Tis to create, and in creating live/ A being more intense." To trace Byron's growth as a poet, therefore, is to witness him reaching beyond subjectivism and attempting to realize that intensity of being that comes about through the continuous act of self-creation.

### HOURS OF IDLENESS

Any account of Byron's achievement must begin with the poems collected in *Hours of Idleness* and the early satires. In the preface to the 1807 miscellany, the nineteen-year-old Byron calls attention to himself by posing as an unlikely author (one "accustomed, in my younger days, to rove a careless mountaineer on the Highlands of Scotland"), by minimizing the merits of his literary endeavor ("to divert the dull moments of indisposition, or the monotony of a vacant hour, urged me 'to his sin'"), and by passing preemptive judgment on his work ("little can be expected from so unpromising a muse"). Such ingenuous posturing is clearly meant to invite, under the guise of dismissing, public recognition and acclaim. Despite the transparency of the subterfuge, the poems within *Hours of Idleness* form a revealing self-portrait in which Byron, while paraphrasing past idioms in poetry and exploiting eighteenth century literary conventions, obliquely seeks to discover a mythologized pattern for his emerging sense of himself. The one theme sounded repeatedly is what Robert F. Gleckner designates "the ruins of paradise," or the fall from youthful innocence. As he explores the experience of spiritual loss and shattered illusions, Byron can be seen moving toward this latter belief that "the great object of life is Sensation—to feel that we exist—even though in pain."

Admittedly imitative in style, often to the point of mannerism, *Hours of Idleness* revolves around several episodes of separation and disenchantment that, for the speaker, spell the end of an idealized, prelapsarian past. The short poem "Remembrance," composed in 1806 but not published until 1832, epitomizes both the tone and outlook of the volume as a whole:

> My days of happiness are few:
> Chill'd by misfortune's wintry blast,
> My dawn of life is overcast,
> Love, Hope, and Joy, alike adieu!—
> Would I could add Remembrance too!

Although the lines verge on doggerel, the same mood of melancholic nostalgia informs such other generally more successful poems as "On Leaving Newstead Abbey," "The First Kiss of Love," "On a Distant View of the Village and School of Harrow on the Hill," and "Lachin y Gair." In all these works Byron cannot disown the power of memory because, though denounced as a curse, it alone provides glimpses of what in "Childish Recollections" he refers to as "the progress of my youthful dream," the foundation for his concept of self. This tension gives rise in other lyrics to a plangent wish to escape the "dark'ning shades" of maturity, regaining the uncompromised or "freeborn soul." Knowing the fatuity of the desire, however, the poet resorts at last to a kind of protective cynicism. In "To Romance," for example, abandoning what he derides as the "motley court" of "Affectation" and "sickly Sensibility," he admits that "'tis hard to quit the dreams,/ Which haunt the unsuspicious soul" but abjures the past as illusory and refuses any longer to be the dupe of his romantic fancy. Embittered by his early discovery, as Byron was later to write in canto 3 of *Childe Harold's Pilgrimage*, that "life's enchanted cup but sparkles near the brim," the poet in *Hours of Idleness* fluctuates between moments of elegiac regret and tenacious hope, the ambivalent response itself prefiguring the skeptical idealist of the major poems to follow.

### POETIC ACRIMONY

The Popean satires, which were composed shortly after the 1807 collection, disclose Byron's reaction to his disillusionment and punctured faith. In *English Bards and Scotch Reviewers*, *Hints from Horace*, and *The Curse of Minerva*—all written during the next four years—Byron lashes out at various individuals whom he regarded as typifying the literary and moral shortcomings of his age. The motto of "these degenerate days," he announces in *English Bards and Scotch Reviewers*, is "Care not for feeling," and so in arraigning nearly all his contemporaries except Samuel Rogers and Thomas Campbell he poses as the hardened realist determined to expose error on every hand: "But now, so callous grown, so changed since youth,/ I've learned to think, and sternly speak the truth." In the diatribe Byron often vents his anger indiscriminately, but the acrimony of his attack stems from a keen sense of embarrassment and outrage at the reception accorded *Hours of Idleness* by such critics as Henry Brougham in the *Edinburgh Review*. Thus, before indicating all those "afflicted," as his preface charges, "with the present prevalent and distressing *rabies* for rhyming," Byron debunks himself as well:

> I, too, can scrawl, and once upon a time
> I poured along the town a flood of rhyme,
> A school-boy freak, unworthy praise or blame;
> I printed—older children do the same.
> 'Tis pleasant, sure, to see one's name in print;
> A Book's a Book, altho' there's nothing in't.

The same irreverent or iconoclastic spirit pervades *Hints from Horace*, a mocking jab at contemporary literary practice from the vantage point of Horace's *Ars Poetica* (13-8 B.C.E., *The Art of Poetry*), and *The Curse of Minerva*, a Swiftian condemnation of Lord Elgin for his despoiling Greek sculpture. In these strident satires Byron alters his earlier poetic stance through two mechanisms: by adopting the voice of savage indignation and by spurning the accepted standards of his age. The detachment that he tries to win through both devices is another step toward his large aesthetic goal of self-realization.

### INTERTWINED MODALITIES

A crucial phase in that ongoing process involves the composition, spanning the period from 1809 to 1817, of *Childe Harold's Pilgrimage* and, to a lesser extent, of the exotic Oriental tales that include *The Giaour*, *The Bride of Abydos*, *The Corsair*, and *Lara*. These verse narratives are significant because in them two sides of Byron's complexity as an artist are counterbalanced— the usually antithetical modes that Keats, in his letters, conceptualizes as the "egotistical sublime" and "the camelion [sic] Poet." Though Keats associated the first quality with William Wordsworth, the element of the "egotistical sublime" in Byron reveals itself in the highly developed reflexivity of his semiautobiographical poems and in his tendency to concentrate on his own immediate thoughts and emotions. At the same time, however, there emerges an equal but opposite impulse that reflects Byron's essentially centrifugal rather than centripetal habit of mind. This is his characteristic propensity for employing a gamut of masks or personae through which he endeavors to escape the restrictive confines of self-consciousness, especially as molded by memory, and to achieve the intensity of being that comes with self-transcendence. Together, these intertwined modalities, the "egotistical" and the "chameleonic," make up the unique "strength" of Byron's imagination.

Readers of the time were nevertheless inclined to recognize only the former tendency in his works and so to find him guilty of facile exhibitionism. Certainly when Byronism was rampant, no one impersonated Byron better than Byron himself; yet, if one allows for this susceptibility, the earnestness with which the poet responded to his detractors is instructive. Echoing the well-known protest lodged in his 1820 "Reply to Blackwood's *Edinburgh Magazine*," he expostulated a year later to Thomas Moore that "a man's poetry is a distinct faculty, or soul, and has no more to do with the every-day individual than the Inspiration with the Pythoness when removed from her tripod." Similarly, in the privacy of his journal for 1813, while writing the very poems that incurred the charge, he remarks: "To withdraw *myself* from *myself* (oh that cursed selfishness!) has ever been my sole, my entire, my sincere motive in scribbling at all; and publishing is also the continuance of the same object, by the action it affords to the mind, which else recoils upon itself." The vehemence of these statements should not be allowed to obscure Byron's clear point regarding the psychology of composition. The vicarious world of poetry, as he views it, makes possible a release from the concentricity of the mind that otherwise, to borrow two of his fa-

vorite images in *Childe Harold's Pilgrimage*, would sting itself to death like the scorpion ringed by fire or consume its scabbard like a rusting sword.

## CHILDE HAROLD'S PILGRIMAGE

Byron first expands upon this aesthetic in cantos 3-4 of *Childe Harold's Pilgrimage*, but some attention to the earlier cantos is prerequisite to understanding the later two. When he began the travelogue in 1809 while touring Europe and the Levant, Byron conceived of a work in Spenserian stanza form which would depict, in the eighteenth century tradition of topographical or "locodescriptive" poetry, his vivid impressions of the scenes and peoples he visited, intermixed with meditative reflections. "For the sake of giving some connection to the piece," which otherwise, according to the preface, "makes no pretension to regularity," Byron introduces the "fictitious character" of Harold, who serves as the nominal hero-protagonist, although this syntactical function is about all that can be claimed for him. Out of "the fulness [*sic*] of satiety," it is true, Harold "resolve[s]" to leave England behind, having run through "Sin's long labyrinth"; yet in his wandering pilgrimage through Spain, Portugal, Albania, and Greece he remains a curiously static, one-dimensional figure and is little more than a partial projection of Byron's darker moods (for example, misanthropy, remorse, cynicism, and forced stoicism). As such, he adumbrates the explicit theme of cantos 1-2: that is, "Consciousness awaking to her woes." Neither Harold nor Byron, however, has yet learned "what he might be, or he ought," and it is somehow fitting that canto 2 should close in a Greece stripped of its ancient grandeur and heroes.

Throughout this half of the poem, Byron's protagonist bears a marked resemblance to the poet himself, but it is well not to overlook the punning assertion made in the 1812 preface that Harold is "the child of imagination." Shortly before the publication of cantos 1-2, in a letter to Robert Charles Dallas, Byron reinforces the distinction between himself and his central character: "If in parts I may be thought to have drawn from myself, believe me it is but in parts, and I shall not own even to that . . . I would not be such a fellow as I have made my hero for all the world." The disclaimer has not won wide acceptance, largely because in the holograph copy of the poem Byron initially christened his protagonist "Childe Burun"; yet the first two cantos themselves substantiate the dissociation which Byron's comment to Dallas emphasizes. On one hand, they dramatize the alienated figure of Harold, who, like the tortured hero of *Lara*, is portrayed as "a stranger in this breathing world,/ An erring spirit from another hurled;/ A thing of dark imaginings"; on the other hand, they are mediated by a separate narrator who, distanced from the foreground, objectively recognizes that "the blight of life" that overtakes men like Harold is "the demon Thought," or the canker of self-consciousness. In actuality, both entities are Byron, and through the dichotomy he seeks to plumb his own contradictory nature.

By the time that Byron came to write canto 3, however, life had paradoxically imitated art: Exiled from England by public vilification for his alleged cruelty toward his wife, the poet became that which before he had only imagined. This turn of events contributed to a new coalescence or ironic similarity between the author and his persona. Byron still does not identify himself completely with his titular hero, but he is now able to assimilate Harold as an exponent of himself without capitulating to the kind of Haroldian angst that suffuses cantos 1-2. He seems to register this altered orientation in the following lines: "Yet am I changed; though still enough the same/ In strength to bear what time can not abate,/ And feed on bitter fruits without accusing Fate." Implicit in the passage, with its allusion to John Milton's *Paradise Lost* (1667, 1674), is an undertone of confidence that even despair can be transformed into a source of stimulation and proof of his endurance. Byron now is speaking *in propria persona*. No longer rhapsodizing as in canto 1 "a youth,/ Who ne in virtue's ways did take delight," he is instead dealing with himself as a social and moral pariah—"the wandering outlaw of his own dark mind." The full assurance that he can avoid entrapment from within remains to be found, but the seeds of spiritual recovery are before him.

The groundwork is laid at the start of canto 3 when, after the framing device of an apostrophe to his daughter, Byron declares his artistic manifesto for the work: "'Tis to create, and in creating live/ A being more intense, that we endow/ With form our fancy, gaining as we give/ The life we image, even as I do now." Reflect-

ing Shelley's influence on Byron in 1816, the passage continues and reveals that the poet now views his quotidian identity as "Nothing," as a hollow fiction, while the project of art discloses to him an ideal "other" or truer self which he will appropriate through the act of creating. The poem itself, in short, becomes the vehicle for self-discovery. Thus, although Harold continues to be much the same character as he was in cantos 1-2, what has changed greatly is Byron's positioning of himself as artist vis-à-vis the poem. He no longer depends on his protagonist as a surrogate or alter ego; even though the disease of self-consciousness has not been expunged, his faith has been restored in the imagination's ability to locate new horizons of meaning in an otherwise entropic world.

Both the third and fourth cantos of *Childe Harold's Pilgrimage* contain clear evidence of his shift in outlook. The two major scenes visited in canto 3 are Waterloo and the Swiss Alps, locales which by their historical associations stand symbolically opposed. In the former, Byron finds only the tragic vanity of life and the futility of worldly ambition; in the latter, he surveys the benign sublimity and undisturbed repose of nature. Initially, it would seem that he is elevating one sphere above the other, idealizing the serenity of "throned Eternity" in contrast to the agitation of "earth-born jars." He is, to some extent, but in a unique manner. Rather than treating these landscapes as discrete alternatives, Byron exploits them as provisional constructs for raising questions and defining some of his own misgivings about the human condition. Thus, if at Waterloo he rejects the "wretched interchange of wrong for wrong" within society, in the Alps he sees nothing "to loathe in nature, save to be/ A link reluctant in a fleshly chain."

In much the same way, he responds ambivalently to the fallen figureheads of each domain—Napoleon Bonaparte and Jean-Jacques Rousseau—whom he envisions as variants of himself. Both the Napoleon who was "conqueror and captive of the earth" and the "inspired" Rousseau whose oracles "set the world in flame" were men of unbounded energy, yet each was responsible for the shambles of the French Revolution and each was subverted by "a fever at the core,/ Fatal to him who bears, to all who ever bore." Byron recognizes their failure as potentially his own as well: "And *there* hath been thy bane," he proclaims. The stanza's rhetoric reverberates with his affinity for these individuals and suggests that Byron, as Jerome J. McGann observes in *Fiery Dust* (1968), is coming to the realization that "to 'know oneself' one must submit to immediate and partial acts of perception." Within canto 3 of *Childe Harold's Pilgrimage*, therefore, the poet moves further toward the understanding that to be human means to be a pilgrim, but a pilgrim ever in the process of redefining himself and the world that he inherits.

Canto 4 continues the archetypal pattern of the journey, in this case one extending from Venice to Rome, but broadens at the end to reveal a significantly matured Byron arriving at the genuine goal or embodiment of his questing spirit. Centered around the elegiac motif or *sic transit gloria mundi*, the last canto weighs the respective claims of both art and nature to permanence as Byron tries to decipher the enigma of humanity's existence. "The moral of all human tales," he postulates, is the inevitability of ruin and unfulfilled hopes, such that "History, with all her volumes vast,/ Hath but *one* page." This stark lesson occasionally moves the poet to invective, as when he declares that "Our life is a false nature—'tis not in/ The harmony of things." Nevertheless, in the poetry of Torquato Tasso, the sculpture of Venice, and the Colosseum in Rome, he discerns a grandeur and genius which transcend the melancholy attrition of time. That discovery, in turn, rekindles conviction as to the vitality of his own essential self, a realization heightened when Byron finds that he has outgrown the fictive prop of Harold:

> But where is he, the Pilgrim of my song,
> The being who upheld it through the past?
>
> .   .   .   .   .   .   .   .   .   .   .   .   .   .   .
>
> He is no more—these breathings are his last;
> His wanderings done, his visions ebbing fast,
> And he himself as nothing. . . .

In the poem's concluding apostrophe to the sea near Albano, conceived as a "glorious mirror" and thalassic "image of Eternity," Byron achieves the true goal toward which he has been tending all along. Awesome in its untrammeled energy, the ocean becomes the symbol of the creating self that the poet has reclaimed. "My Pilgrim's shrine is won," writes Byron, for "I am not now/

That which I have been." With that declaration, Byron enters upon the last great phase of his poetic career.

### DON JUAN

The monumental epic *Don Juan* forms the inspired climax to Byron's evolution as an artist, but to understand how this is so requires brief attention to a disturbing undercurrent in *Childe Harold's Pilgrimage*. Despite the general movement toward self-apprehension in that work, there yet occur moments when the inadequacy of language to articulate "all I seek,/ Bear, know, feel" subverts the poet's faith in his enterprise. Thus, although in canto 3 he would willingly believe that "there may be/ Words which are things," he has not found them; nor is he able to disguise from himself the knowledge that language is part of the disintegrated syntax of a fallen world. Along the same lines, after pondering in canto 4 the disappointed ideals of such poets as Dante and Petrarch, he ruefully admits that "what we have of feeling most intense/ Outstrips our faint expression." The intransigence of language, its inherent circularity as an instrument of meditation, was for Byron tied to the kind of Metaphysical despair dramatized in *Manfred* and *Cain* (pb. 1821), and by way of overcoming those quandaries he adopts in *Don Juan* a more radically versatile poetics.

The chief difference between *Childe Harold's Pilgrimage* and his later "epic of negation," as Brian Wilke describes *Don Juan* in *Romantic Poets and Epic Tradition* (1965), lies in Byron's refusal any longer to be controlled by "the stubborn heart." After opening with the farce of Juan's sexual initiation, before which he pauses to berate Plato as a charlatan, Byron makes his new outlook resoundingly clear:

> No more—no more—Oh! never more, my heart,
> Canst thou be my sole world, my universe!
>
> .   .   .   .   .   .   .   .   .   .   .   .   .   .   .
>
> The illusion's gone for ever, and thou art
> Insensible, I trust, but none the worse,
> And in thy stead I've got a good deal of judgment,
> Though heaven knows how it ever found a lodgement.

Cognizant of the fictiveness of all experience, he plans to make his rambling medley of a poem mirror the manifold delusions and deceptions that man allows to impose upon his right of thought. In the face of such knowledge "Imagination droops her pinion," turning "what was once romantic to burlesque"—lines aptly capturing the shift from his stance in *Childe Harold's Pilgrimage*. In composing his "versified Aurora Borealis," however, Byron obviously sensed a creative exhilaration linked to his complete separation of himself from his hero. His letters written during the work's early stages reveal an exuberant confidence in the undertaking which, as he told Thomas Moore, was "meant to be a little quitely facetious upon every thing." Thus, addressing his old friend Douglas Kinnaird in 1819, he expressed a typically high-spirited opinion of his achievement: "As to 'Don Juan'—confess—confess— you dog—and be candid—that it is the sublime of *that there* sort of writing—it may be bawdy . . . but it is not *life*, is it not *the thing*?—Could any man have written it—who has not lived in the world?"

Byron's governing purpose in *Don Juan* is to "show things really as they are,/ Not as they ought to be." Toward that end he does not forbear lampooning all the assorted follies and philistine pretenses of "that microcosm on stilts,/ Yclept the Great World," for he sees its attachment to illusion as the root cause of men's inability to recognize or accept the truth about themselves. Byron's attack is all the more effective because he exempts neither himself as poet nor the function of language from his skeptical scrutiny. Overturning all conventional notions of structure and voice in poetry, he is intent upon making his "nondescript and ever-varying rhyme" demystify itself at every turn. Both serious and cynical, he consequently avers that compared to the epic myths of Vergil and Homer "this story's actually true," then later reminds his audience that his work "is only fiction,/ And that I sing of neither mine nor me." Nearly every stanza of *Don Juan* unmasks itself in similar fashion through the whimsical freedom of Byron's style. Fearless of incongruities in a world permeated by fraud, the poem's narrator defends his fluid cynicism in the name of verisimilitude (his aim is to "show things existent") while simultaneously debunking traditional concepts of authorial integrity: "If people contradict themselves, can I/ Help contradicting them, and everybody,/ Even my veracious self?" True "sincerity" in these terms is equated with inconsistency, paradox, and radical doubt, an outlook anticipated as early as 1813

when Byron, with uncanny self-knowledge and prescience, remarked in his journal that "if I am sincere with myself (but I fear one lies more to one's self than to any one else), every page should confute, refute, and utterly abjure its predecessor." By constantly deflating the artifices on which his own poem is built, Byron seeks to generate a self-critical model for exposing the larger abuses of his society.

*Don Juan* is, as William Hazlitt was quick to note in *The Spirit of the Age* (1825), a "poem written about itself," but foremost among the vices it satirizes are the contemporary prevalence of cant and the moral blindness or hypocrisy which it fosters. Both traits are first encountered in the character of Donna Inez, Juan's mother, in canto 1. A prodigy of memory whose brain is filled with "serious sayings darken'd to sublimity," she is walking homily—"Morality's prim personification"— who sees to it that her son is taught from only the most carefully expurgated classics. Unable to find anything to censure or amend in her own conduct, Donna Inez nevertheless carries on a clandestine affair with Don Alfonso, the husband of her close friend Julia, and later writes in fulsome praise of Catherine the Great's "maternal" attentions to Juan. Such self-deceiving and myopic piety moves Byron to wish for "a *forty-parson power* to chant/ Thy praise, Hypocrisy," the vice that he regards as endemic to his age and culture at all levels.

On a larger scale, Byron dramatizes the disastrous consequences of cant and its ability to obscure human realities in the Siege of Ismail episode beginning in canto 7. Here his target is in part the gazettes and their debased glorification of war, particularly as they promote "the lust of notoriety" within modern civilization. Spurred on by the hope of being immortalized in the newspapers or war dispatches, a polyglot collection of soldiers join with the Russians in devastating the Turkish fortress. Before recounting scene after scene of the mindless butchery, in which thirty thousand are slain on both sides, Byron reflects on whether "a man's name in a *bulletin*/ May make up for a *bullet in* his body." The final irony is that the gazettes, preoccupied with trivial gossip of the beau monde at home, generally garble the names of the dead and thoroughly distort the facts of the campaign. Determined to unriddle "Glory's dream," Byron shows that it is founded on nothing more than an abject appetite for fame and conquest. His greatest ire is reserved for someone such as the Russian leader Aleksandr Suwarrow, who, in a dispatch to Catherine after the slaughter, can glibly write, "'Glory to *God* and to the Empress!' (*Powers/ Eternal! such names mingled!*) 'Ismail's our's.'" The same purblind insensitivity, he charges, makes it possible for Wordsworth to speak of carnage as "God's daughter." In all these instances, Byron shows how language is a ready instrument for the perversion of thought and action.

His own aesthetic in *Don Juan* thus bases itself on an unswerving respect for truth, "the grand desideratum" in a society glutted with cant and equivocation. Early in the poem he comments that his is "the age of oddities let loose," such that "You'd best begin with truth, and when you've lost your/ Labour, there's sure market for imposture." The lines also echo his mocking dedication of the work to Robert Southey, who succeeded Henry James Pye as poet laureate in 1813, and his arraignment there of the other so-called Lake Poets. Having disowned the radical politics of their youth, they are depicted as comprising a "nest of tuneful persons" who now warble sycophantic praise for the Tory regime of King George III. Their apostasy in Byron's eyes is all the more reprehensible because they have, in effect, become the hirelings of the "intellectual eunuch Castlereagh," a master of oratorical "trash of phrase/ Ineffably—legitimately vile." To counteract this mounting Tower of Babel in his age, Byron persistently explodes the enchantment of words and their tendency to falsify reality. There is, accordingly, an underlying method to his chameleonic *mobilité* and digressiveness in the poem, for he demonstrates that only by doubting the language-based constructs, which people impose upon experience, can he, like the poet himself, avoid the pitfall of "universal egotism." Viewed in this light, the whole of *Don Juan* becomes an open-ended experiment in linguistic improvisation, a poem that demythologizes the very act by which it comes into being.

Because Byron's mock-epic attempts to encompass no less than "life's infinite variety," any synopsis of its innumerable subjects and themes is doomed to failure. From the opening line in which the narrator declaims "I want a hero" and then seems arbitrarily to settle on "our ancient friend Don Juan," it is evident that the ensuing comedy will follow few established conventions or patterns. This impression is reinforced later, in canto 14, when Byron points out his technique in composing *Don Juan*: "I write what's uppermost, without delay." The stated casualness in approach, however, belies the artistic integrity of the satire. Jerome J. McGann, in *Don Juan in Context* (1976), convincingly shows that the poem is "both a critique and an apotheosis of High Romanticism," primarily because it implicitly denies that any imaginative system can be an end unto itself while also endeavoring to reinsert the poetic imagination back into the context of a fallen world. If there is one crux around which the entire mosaic turns, it is that of the fundamental opposition between nature and civilization. After Juan's idyllic love affair with Haidée, "Nature's bride," is destroyed by her jealous father in canto 4, Byron suggests that the Fall is humanity's permanent condition; he conducts his hero into slavery at Constantinople in canto 5, into the bloodbath of the Siege of Ismail in cantos 7-8, into the lustful tyranny of the Russian empress in cantos 9-10, and finally into the fashionable corruptions of English society in cantos 11-17. Not all, however, is moral cannibalism. By the introduction of such unspoiled figures as Haidée at the start and Aurora Raby at the end, Byron ascribes a certain redemptive value to natural innocence that offsets, even if it does not quite counterbalance, the ruling vices of society. *Don Juan* thus immerses itself in all the unflattering details of "life's infinite variety," but always with the purpose of embodying the human realities with which the artist must deal. Byron distills the complexity of the matter in a few words: "I write the world."

## LEGACY

Byron has often been criticized as a poet for his many supposed failures—for not projecting a coherent metaphysic, for not developing a consistent attitude to life, for not resisting the Siren call of egotism, for not paying sufficient attention to style, and for not, in short, being more like Wordsworth, Samuel Taylor Coleridge, Keats, and Shelley. Because he did not adopt the vatic stance of his contemporaries or espouse their belief in organicism, he has been labeled the leading exemplar of Negative Romanticism. Common to such estimates, however, is a reluctance to recognize or concede Byron's uniqueness as a poet. Although he did not share with others of his time an exalted conception of the imagination as being equivalent, in Keats's metaphor, to "Adam's dream," he was able ultimately to do what the other four poets generally could not—namely, to accept the mixed quality of human experience. Through his ironic detachment and comic vision he permanently enlarged the domain of poetry and made it meaningful in a fresh way. This he accomplished through his skeptical idealism and his acceptance of his own paradoxes as a man and poet. "I am quicksilver," he wrote to a friend in 1810, "and say nothing positively." Therein lies perhaps the essence of his "sincerity" and "strength," traits that continue to make him an enduring cultural force.

## OTHER MAJOR WORKS

PLAYS: *Manfred*, pb. 1817 (verse play); *Cain: A Mystery*, pb. 1821 (verse play); *Marino Faliero, Doge of Venice*, pr., pb. 1821 (verse play); *Sardanapalus*, pb. 1821 (verse play); *The Two Foscari*, pb. 1821 (verse play); *Heaven and Earth*, pb. 1822 (fragment; verse play); *Werner: Or, The Inheritance*, pb. 1823 (verse play); *The Deformed Transformed*, pb. 1824 (fragment; verse play).

NONFICTION: *Letter to [John Murray] on the Rev. W. L. Bowles' Strictures on the Life and Writings of Pope*, 1821; "A Letter to the Editor of 'My Grandmother's Review,'" 1822; *The Blues: A Literary Eclogue*, 1823; *The Parliamentary Speeches of Lord Byron*, 1824; *Byron's Letters and Journals*, 1973-1982 (12 volumes; Leslie A. Marchand, editor).

## BIBLIOGRAPHY

Brewer, William D., ed. *Contemporary Studies on Lord Byron*. Lewiston, N.Y.: Edwin Mellen Press, 2001. A collection of essays on the works of Byron. Bibliography and index.

Crane, David. *The Kindness of Sisters*. New York: Alfred A. Knopf, 2003. A study of Byron's reputation after his death, exploring bitter and conflicting accounts by the woman he divorced and the half sister he seduced.

Eisler, Benita. *Byron: Child of Passion, Fool of Fame*. New York: Alfred A. Knopf, 1999. A narrative biography that does justice to the love affairs that made Byron notorious while giving ample coverage of the reasons Byron is an influential and important poet. Includes bibliographic references.

Franklin, Caroline. *Byron: A Literary Life*. New York: St. Martin's Press, 2000. A study of Byron's career, examining both his poetry and plays.

MacCarthy, Fiona. *Byron: Life and Legend*. New York: Farrar, Straus and Giroux, 2003. A biography that reexamines the life of the poet in the light of MacCarthy's assertion that Byron was bisexual, a victim of early abuse by his nurse.

Marchand, Leslie A. *Byron: A Portrait*. Chicago: University of Chicago Press, 1970. The best biography for the general reader. It is based on Marchand's definitive three-volume biography published in 1957 but includes research done in the 1960's. Marchand's portrait of Byron is balanced and free of bias. Includes fifty-six illustrations, genealogical tables, and two maps showing Byron's travels from 1809 to 1811, and Byron's Greece.

Martin, Philip. *Byron: A Poet Before His Public*. New York: Cambridge University Press, 1982. This biographical-historical analysis of Byron's works places Byron's work within the context of his contemporaries of the second generation of Romantic poets. Contains a number of illustrations and a complete bibliography.

O'Brien, Edna. *Byron in Love: A Short, Daring Life*. New York: W. W. Norton, 2009. Distinguished Irish writer O'Brien provides a biography of Byron that is perceptive and well written. O'Brien approaches the artist as a character rather than as a subject, producing a novelistic portrait of the poet.

Peters, Catherine. *Byron*. Stroud, Gloucestershire, England: Sutton, 2000. A concise biography of Byron that covers his life and works. Bibliography.

Wilson, Frances. *Byromania: Portraits of the Artist in Nineteenth- and Twentieth-Century Culture*. New York: St. Martin's Press, 1999. These eleven essays shed light on the scandalous nature of Byron's fame, including his carefully wrought self-presentation, as well as the extraordinary popularity of his work and persona. The poet is viewed through multiple, if sometimes contradictory, perspectives, the essays varying in tone from academic to humorous.

*Robert Lance Snyder*

# C

## CÆDMON

**Born:** Northumbria (now in England); early seventh century

**Died:** Whitby Abbey, Northumbria (now in England); c. 680

PRINCIPAL POETRY
"Hymn," c. 670

OTHER LITERARY FORMS

The "Hymn" is the only work that has been definitely attributed to Cædmon (KAHD-muhn).

ACHIEVEMENTS

The history of Cædmon, the first voice in English poetry, is passed down through the cleric and historian Saint Bede the Venerable who, in his *Ecclesiastical History of the English People* (731), tells the story of the humble layman to whom the gift of poetry was given one night in a dream. Bede lists many works composed by Cædmon; the only piece that can be identified with any certainty, however, is the nine-line "Hymn" fragment in praise of God the Creator.

Brief though it is, this poem defines and directs the course of English poetry, combining for the first time the meters of Nordic heroic poetry with the subject matter of the Scriptures, Christianizing the literary tradition and speaking for a culture. That the "Hymn" was held in great esteem is evidenced by the fact that versions of it exist in seventeen manuscripts ranging from the early eighth to the later fifteenth century; Cædmon's "Hymn" is the only piece of early poetry to have been preserved in this manner. Cædmon is a figure of shadow and legend, with a single biographical source and no written records; his hymn is a rich and appropriate beginning for the English poetic tradition.

BIOGRAPHY

The single source for the life of Cædmon, Bede's *Ecclesiastical History of the English People*, was completed in 731. Written in Latin and later translated into Old English, Bede's history describes the Abbey of Whitby in Northumbria, founded by Saint Hilda and ruled by her from 658 until 680. Twin communities, one for men and one for women, flourished under the direction of the abbess. To this abbey came the layman Cædmon, not to test a religious vocation but to seek employment in caring for the monastery animals. Cædmon was not young when he came to Whitby, Bede comments, but no mention is made of his earlier life. Humble and unassuming, Cædmon had his quarters with the farm animals and lived almost unnoticed by the other monastery residents.

Because of his extreme shyness, the story continues, Cædmon was never able to take his turn at the recitation and singing when, as was the custom, the harp was passed around after the communal evening meal. In order to avoid embarrassment, Cædmon would always find some excuse to leave the gathering and tend the animals, knowing that he would not be able to sing and entertain the others should the harp be passed to him. Bede's account, it should be remarked, is an invaluable description of this culture; the secular (not religious) music, the gathering to drink beer together, the shared responsibility for entertainment—all these facets of early English life are clarified in the *Ecclesiastical History of the English People*.

One evening, having left the gathering, Cædmon was sleeping when he had a dream. "Someone" came to him and commanded, "Cædmon, sing me something." When Cædmon protested, the visitant repeated the direction, asking that Cædmon sing of "the beginning of created things." Still in his dream, Cædmon obeyed the vision, breaking into song of the "first-shaping." The vision vanished.

When he awakened, unsure of what had happened, Cædmon found that he was able to recall the entire song. Still led by divine urgings, he went to the abbess, sang the "Hymn" for her, and explained the occurrence of the night before. Saint Hilda, realizing that the powers of God were involved, encouraged Cædmon, ex-

*Cædmon* (Hulton Archive/Getty Images)

Cædmon's gift, or, more likely, that later writers were moved to continue the tradition. The remarkable care taken to preserve the hymn suggests that it was widely regarded as the first piece of English alliterative poetry.

According to Bede, Cædmon died in the monastery at Whitby after receiving the Eucharist and falling into a peaceful slumber. Given his story, it would be surprising if Bede were to record any other sort of death, for he clearly intends to shape the Cædmon narrative to an argument for the religious inspiration of poetry.

ANALYSIS

Although Bede's *Ecclesiastical History of the English People* details the composition of Cædmon's "Hymn," it does not reproduce it, giving instead a prose paraphrase. Bede, himself a fine stylist, remarks quite accurately that his Latin prose cannot reproduce a vernacular hymn; poetry, he points out, does not translate well. In most of the early manuscripts of the *Ecclesiastical History of the English People*, however, the poem itself is included, often as a marginal gloss but occasionally in the body of the manuscript itself. There are seventeen of these manuscripts, both in Cædmon's own Northumbrian and in West Saxon, with the majority in the latter.

horting him to devote his life to composing music for the glory and praise of God.

Thereafter Cædmon became a monk, spending his days composing music. His gift stayed with him always, although he never learned to read or write. Others in the monastery would read the Scripture aloud; Cædmon would then make a metrical paraphrase of what he had heard. Because the gift of inspiration was to serve God's glory, Bede explains, Cædmon was able to compose only religious verse. Bede lists many of Cædmon's compositions, all of them biblical; poems of similar subject matter appeared in a 1655 Junius Manuscript by François Dujon. Dujon believed that the four scriptural poems were originals from Cædmon; modern scholarship, however, rejects any such claim. It may be that other members of the monastery imitated

In his *Anglo-Saxon Poetry* (1980), Jeff Opland terms Bede's story of Cædmon "a source of unparalleled importance in any attempt to reconstruct the history of oral poetry in Anglo-Saxon times." The claim is not extravagant. Cædmon's fragment reaches back into the heroic tradition for meter and form, blends it with Christian myths for inspiration and story, and originates English poetry as it is now known. Histories of English literature rightly devote major sections to such great figures as Geoffrey Chaucer, William Shakespeare, and John Milton. Nearly eight hundred years before Chaucer burst into joyous couplets, Cædmon, the precursor, burst into praise.

**"HYMN"**

The nine lines of the "Hymn" are given here in a modern English translation:

> Now let us herald heaven-kingdom's guardian,
> Maker of might and his mind-thoughts,
> The work of the wonder-Father when he of wonders,
>   each one
> Eternal Lord established in the beginning.
> He first shaped for the sons of men
> Heaven as a roof the holy Creator;
> And then the middle-earth for mankind, the Protector
> Eternal Lord, afterwards made
> For men, this firmament, Our Father almighty.

The "Hymn" is a kind of early English psalm; it sings the praises of God, invites the hearers to join in, details the specifics of creation, and moves to a realization that all life has been created not only for God's glory but also for the "sons of man," those who revere and love God. Although Cædmon had been instructed to sing of the "making of things," he chooses—or is inspired to choose—lyric rather than narrative, praise rather than instruction.

It is not surprising to the contemporary reader that Cædmon would sing a song in praise of God in response to a dream vision, but it is significant in the history of English poetry that formal Christianity had been introduced in England less than a century before. The Romans who had occupied the island had been Christians, but without formal practice of the religion, Christianity had nearly died out, preserved only in small pockets. Not until Pope Gregory sent Saint Augustine of Canterbury to the island in 597 did a formal mission begin; by Cædmon's time, England had reverted to Christianity, and the great monastic tradition which was to stimulate learning was beginning to flower.

### INSPIRATION

Critical debate flourishes over the nature of Cædmon's inspiration. Was he inspired to "remember" songs and rhythms he had already heard? Was he moved to sing a hymn whose words he may not have understood? Was he simply an instrument for God's power? Was he indeed a deliberate composer? It is of course tempting to align Cædmon with both the biblical tradition of the unknowing prophet who speaks the words God puts in his mouth and the "seer" who sees and describes but does not always understand. Bede clearly identifies Cædmon as the one selected by God not only for divine glory but also to begin a tradition;

because Bede was writing almost fifty years after Cædmon lived, he had an interesting perspective. Whatever one's theories of critical inspiration, the Cædmon "Hymn" holds irresistible appeal for the scholar who finds the Christian tradition and metrical artistry in such a rich blend.

### GOD AS KING

Cædmon's words describe God as king and father, powerful and provident, clearly reflecting the concept of king as the one responsible for his people's welfare and who, in return for praise and veneration, will reward his subjects with care for their needs. The creation references suggest a sort of giant mead hall, with heaven as a roof; the sons of men are all enclosed, safe from enemies, and singing their gratitude. This same anthropomorphism runs throughout most early English poetry; God is like his people in the most literal sense. At the same time, there is a strong suggestion of transcendence or otherness. Twice God is described as eternal, and the focus of the poem is clearly on the marvels and wonders of this incomprehensible but splendid "wonder-Father." The poem is charged with energy; there is something peculiarly English about the emphasis on God's actions and deeds: God establishes, shapes, makes—words suggesting concrete and deliberate actions. The deeds, however, are more than mere activities; they are "mind-thoughts," concepts put into reality by the creativity of God. The creative outburst of the poet in hymns is like the creative energy of the first Shaper. The poet, both as an inspired mystic and as a worker dependent on the lord of the monastery for sustenance, shines through these lines.

This first voice in English poetry, therefore, is essentially religious in its themes. Like the voice in the psalms, the speaker views the array of creation and claims it "for the sons of men," echoing the Genesis story as well. It is not surprising that the scriptural stories which appear in early poetry are elemental tales of creation, providence, and power; they are also, however, dramatic narratives which eventually were incorporated into the saints' legends and traditions. Although Bede explains that all of Cædmon's poetry was religious and rooted in Scripture, the nine-line fragment which begins the tradition is an especially appropriate inauguration.

## "HYMN" COMPOSITION

The Cædmon "Hymn" has far greater significance for the student of literature as the first example of the poetic form that would influence English poetry through the fifteenth century, recurring from time to time in later writers even into the twentieth. The four-stress, alliterative line, here less precise and sophisticated than in *Beowulf* (c. 1000) and in much later works of writers such as William Langland and the Pearl-Poet, gives to English poetry a grace and strength which bring the ancient Nordic heroic literature into the developing English language.

Essentially, the poetry works in this way: Each line has four stresses, two on each side of the pause or caesura. Unstressed syllables are not significant and may occur in any quantity or, occasionally, not at all. Of the four stresses, two or more will alliterate with one another, the stress directly after the pause serving as the "rhyme-giver" or alliterative key. Vowels assonate with other vowels. The first four lines of Cædmon's hymn, then, move as follows, with stresses italicized:

| | |
|---|---|
| Nu *sc*ulon *he*rigan | *he*ofonrices *we*ard |
| *Me*todes *me*ahte | and his *mo*dgepanc, |
| *We*orc *wu*ldorfaeder, | swa he *wu*ndra geh*wa*es, |
| *Ec*e *dr*ihten, | *or on*stealde. |

The pace is majestic, deliberate; the unstressed syllables, falling as they do in two's and three's, give an almost chantlike tone to the poetry. The alliteration serves the singer, who would be using a small harplike instrument for accompaniment, and unifies the poem, setting up expectations and satisfying them in more than one way. Although the poem does not formally play with rhyme, it does make use of several sound devices; some later verse in this tradition uses internal and occasionally external rhyme as well. The alliterative rhythms, however, give the poem its most definitive structure.

The poem also shows the first use of kennings, rich figures of speech that make tiny metaphors, usually hyphenated, for common terms. Here the kennings are relatively simple; later, in *Beowulf*, for example, they become more graphic. The more complex the notion, the more apt are the kennings: Heaven, for example, becomes "heaven-kingdom"; God is "wonder-Father";

earth becomes "middle-earth." God's creative word-become-act is "mind-thought," the most complex of the kennings.

BIBLIOGRAPHY

Bessinger, Jess B., Jr., and Stanley J. Kahrl, eds. *Essential Articles for the Study of Old English Poetry.* Hamden, Conn.: Archon Books, 1968. A collection of twenty-six articles on Old English poetry. Offers general studies of stylistics, themes, oral influences, and metrics as well as studies of individual poets and works. The "Hymn" is mentioned numerous times, but the book is most valuable for C. L. Wrenn's comprehensive analysis in "The Poetry of Cædmon." Articles by Morton W. Bloomfield, Francis P. Magoun, Jr., and Robert D. Stevick also treat the "Hymn" in important ways.

Fry, Donald K. "Cædmon as a Formulaic Poet." In *Oral Literature: Seven Essays*, edited by Joseph J. Duggan. New York: Barnes & Noble, 1975. Drawing on Bede's *Ecclesiastical History*, Fry presents Cædmon's "Hymn" as an oral composition and Cædmon as the founder of "Old English Christian vernacular poetry." Fry accomplishes this by examining the Latin and Old English versions of the "Hymn" to determine the genesis of diction.

_____. "The Memory of Cædmon." In *Oral Traditional Literature: A Festschrift for Albert Bates Lord*, edited by John Miles Foley. Columbus, Ohio: Slavica, 1981. Fry proposes that Cædmon's "Hymn" was written on a formulaic basis. He defines "formulaic" as the "typical traditionally expressed" and states that this type of poetry is easy to memorize and, therefore, is more easily disseminated to the nonliterate public.

Greenfield, Stanley B., and Daniel G. Calder. *A New Critical History of Old English Literature.* New York: New York University Press, 1986. Although devoting only thirteen pages of text to Cædmon, this book provides excellent insight into Cædmon's "Hymn" and problems that have confronted scholars for centuries. Useful for a broad overview of Old English literature.

Gurteen, Stephen Humphreys. *The Epic Fall of Man: A Comparative Study of Cædmon, Dante, and Milton.*

1896. Reprint. New York: Haskell House, 1964. Temecula, Calif.: Reprint Services, 1992. Gurteen is primarily concerned with a particular aspect of Christian poetic literature of England but has included in this study Dante's *Inferno* (in *La divina commedia*, c. 1320; *The Divine Comedy*, 1802) in contrast with the strong and weak points in Cædmon's and John Milton's treatments of the subject. Thirty-eight illustrations.

Hieatt, Constance B. "Cædmon in Context: Transforming the Formula." *Journal of English and Germanic Philology* 84 (October, 1985): 485-497. Supplies evidence that Cædmon's "Hymn" may draw not only from traditional pagan themes as background for its Christian base but also from inherited oral tradition, therefore echoing the established "type-scene."

Ireland, Colin. "An Irish Precursor of Cædmon." *Notes and Queries* 44, no. 1 (March, 1997): 2-4. Ireland discusses Colman mac Leneni and Cædmon and the traits they shared.

Kennedy, Charles W., trans. *The Cædmon Poems*. New York: E. P. Dutton, 1916. This older translation offers a host of supporting materials, including the translator's introduction, other major Anglo-Saxon poems, reproductions of the drawings of the Junius Manuscript, and a bibliography.

O'Keeffe, Katherine O'Brien. "Orality and the Developing Text of Cædmon's 'Hymn.'" In *Visible Song: Transitional Literacy in Old English Verse*. New York: Cambridge University Press, 1990. O'Keeffe analyzes the composition of most extant versions of the poem, with attention to such matters as spacing, spelling, punctuation, word division, and capitalization. She relates Cædmon's "Hymn" to the rich tradition of oral poetry and explores scribal awareness of the distinctions between Old English transcription and classical Latin verse.

Smith, A. H., ed. *Three Northumbrian Poems*. New York: Appleton-Century-Crofts, 1968. Smith provides texts of and extensive commentary on three Old English poems: Bede's *Death Song*, Cædmon's "Hymn," and *The Leiden Riddle*, a poem related to a Latin riddle of Aldhelm. The commentary on each discusses authorship, manuscripts, date, and location of the extant texts, and spelling and variants of the existing texts. Heavily annotated; includes a glossary, a bibliography, and an index, along with the important manuscript versions of each poem in the original language.

Stevens, Martin, and John Mandell, eds. *Old English Literature: Twenty-two Analytical Essays*. Lincoln: University of Nebraska Press, 1968. Contains several essays that treat Cædmon in passing. G. L. Brook's "Old English" analyzes texts of the two dialect versions. Robert D. Stevick in "The Oral-Formulaic Analyses of Old English Verse" explores how the "Hymn" can be classified as formulaic. In an important article, "Cædmon's 'Hymn,'" Bernard F. Huppé offers a skeptical reading of Bede's narrative account and a careful analysis of the "Hymn."

Wrenn, C. L. *A Study of Old English Literature*. New York: W. W. Norton, 1967. In a readily accessible, chronologically arranged study of Old English, Wrenn offers a highly informed overview of Anglo-Saxon literature. The chapter on Cædmon, "Cædmon and the Christian Revolution in Poetry," relates the poet to his time, assesses his contribution, and offers a thorough analysis of the poem and its background.

Zimmermann, Gunhild. *The Four Old English Poetic Manuscripts: Texts, Context, and Historical Background*. Heidelberg, Germany: C. Winter, 1995. In addition to the Cædmon manuscript, includes and comments upon the Exeter book, the Vercelli book, the Nowell codex, and Old English poetry in general.

*Katherine Hanley*

# THOMAS CAMPION

**Born:** London, England; February 12, 1567
**Died:** London, England; March 1, 1620

PRINCIPAL POETRY

*Poemata*, 1595
*A Booke of Ayres*, 1601 (with Philip Rosseter)
*Songs of Mourning*, 1613
*Two Bookes of Ayres*, 1613
*The Third and Fourth Booke of Ayres*, 1617
*The Ayres That Were Sung and Played at Brougham Castle*, 1618
*Thomae Campiani Epigrammatum Libri II*, 1619
*Selected Poems of Thomas Campion, Samuel Daniel, and Sir Walter Ralegh*, 2001 (with others)

OTHER LITERARY FORMS

Thomas Campion (KAM-pee-uhn) wrote a critical essay of poetics, *Observations in the Art of English Poesie* (1602), and a book of music theory, *A New Way of Making Fowre Parts in Counter-point* (c. 1617), the one work of his that remained in print throughout the seventeenth century.

ACHIEVEMENTS

England has always had a strong claim to one of the finest literatures in the West. Most critics agree, moreover, that the literature of the late English Renaissance—stretching from Edmund Spenser through William Shakespeare to John Milton—was the true golden age. With music, however, it is a different story; usually England imported rather than exported musical ideas. The Germans, George Frideric Handel (later naturalized as a British subject) in the eighteenth century and Felix Mendelssohn in the nineteenth, dominated English music. For two brief periods, however, England was Europe's musical innovator—the mid-fifteenth century, when John Dunstable's music taught Continental composers the new style, and the decades spanning the sixteenth and seventeenth centuries, when William Byrd, Thomas Morley, Thomas Wheelkes, and especially John Dowland ushered in England's

musical golden age. Baldassare Castiglione's *Il Cortegiano* (1528; *The Courtier*, 1561) advises the Renaissance gentleman to be adept at both poetry and music, and most educated persons had some level of expertise in both, but only one man in that twin golden age deserves to be called both a first-rate poet and a first-rate composer: Thomas Campion. Most composers would either set words by others, as John Dowland did—often producing truly moving music to inferior words, as in his famous "Come heavy sleep"—or they would write their own words with even worse literary results, as Campion's friend Philip Rosseter did in his half of *A Booke of Ayres*, which he jointly produced with Campion. Most poets would entitle a work, hopefully, "Song" and wait for a composer to do his share—as John Donne did, for example, in "Song: Goe and Catch a Falling Star." Campion, however, wrote both words and music and thus is the distillation of the English Renaissance.

BIOGRAPHY

Thomas Campion was born into a circle of lawyers. His father, John Campion, was a legal clerk in the Chancery Court, with social ambitions left unrealized at his death in 1576, when his son was nine years old. Campion's mother, Lucy, was a middle-class woman with some property inherited from her family. She had earlier married another lawyer, Roger Trigg, and had a daughter, Mary. Trigg died in 1563, and a year later, she married John Campion, bearing Thomas and his sister Rose. After John's death, she again waited a year and married yet another lawyer, Augustine Steward. When she died and Steward married a woman named Anne Sisley, Campion was left orphaned at the age of fourteen, living with foster parents, who immediately (1581) sent him with Thomas Sisley, Anne's child from a previous marriage, to Peterhouse, Cambridge.

While at Cambridge, Campion was a friend of Thomas Nashe and may have met other literary figures there also—fellow students Christopher Marlowe, Thomas Kyd, and Robert Greene, as well as Edmund Spenser's friend, the don Gabriel Harvey, who theorized about quantitative meter. Cambridge, the nurturing ground of early Puritanism, left Campion uninterested in religion—a fact that may have contributed to his decision to leave in 1584 without the usual clerical degree—but it was there that he first developed an interest in literature and music.

After a hiatus of nearly two years, Campion resumed his education by entering Gray's Inn, London, to study law—a move that his family connections made nearly inevitable. At Gray's Inn, however, Campion preferred literature and music to his legal studies, earning no degree in his eight years there and seemingly being interested mostly in the periodic revels, especially student dramatic productions. He contributed some songs to masques—good preparation for his later career as masque writer to the Jacobean nobility. It is possible that Campion met William Shakespeare at this time, for *The Comedy of Errors* was performed at Gray's Inn between 1592 and 1594, shortly before Campion left. Like his younger contemporary and fellow law student, John Donne, Campion was circulating his poetry privately and gaining a solid reputation as a poet before he appeared in print; it is also probable that Campion was singing his songs to his own lute accompaniment at this time. Five of these songs appeared pseudonymously at the end of the 1591 edition of Sir Philip Sidney's *Astrophel and Stella*.

During his years at Gray's Inn, Campion accompanied the military expedition led by the earl of Essex to Brittany to help the French fend off a Spanish invasion (1591). His poetic achievements there were more notable than his military ones: No record of his activities survives aside from two Latin poems he composed about his experiences, the epigrams "De Se" and "In Obitum Gual. Devoreux fratris clariss. Comitis Essexiae." Latin, indeed, was Campion's favored language at this time; his first published volume of poetry, *Poemata*, is a lengthy volume of Latin poems, mostly epigrams.

Soon after he abandoned law and Gray's Inn, he met the lutenist Philip Rosseter, who remained Campion's closest friend for the rest of his life. It was Rosseter who changed the direction of Campion's career. Latin was a fashionable language in the English Renaissance for those with literary ambitions; even as late as Milton, poets were expected to produce in Latin as well as English. Its accessibility to the general public, however, was limited. At this time, Campion began serious pro-

duction of poetry whose main intent was to entertain—first his lute songs and then his masques. In 1601, he published jointly with Rosseter *A Booke of Ayres*, containing forty-two songs, the first twenty-one by Campion and the last twenty-one by Rosseter.

The following year, Campion published a work in prose that gained him some fame—*Observations in the Art of English Poesie*. Possibly a reflection of the literary interests of his Cambridge days, the treatise is the last—and best—defense of quantitative meter in English verse. In the 1580's, a group of men led by Gabriel Harvey, Edmund Spenser, and Sir Philip Sidney began an attempt to rescue English poetry from the dreary fourteeners and poulter's measures that everyone seemed to be writing. Influenced by French theorists, they tried to write poetry based on duration (quantity) of syllables rather than stress (accent). Such an attempt was, perhaps, inevitable in the English Renaissance, for, like so much else, it was based on Greek and Latin models. The failure of the attempt, however, was inevitable because English inherited the strong Germanic accent from the Anglo-Saxon language and thus could not be forced to do what Greek and Latin, without the strong Germanic accent, could do naturally. Some of Spenser's and Sidney's more unreadable pieces are quantitative; then they abandoned the attempt and became great poets. Campion's *Observations in the Art of English Poesie* is actually a resurrection of this dead theory, and as a resurrected body should be, his theory was considerably stronger than the dead one. Instead of calling for an exacting measurement of long and short vowels and count of neighboring consonants, Campion appealed to variety: Use of the eight basic feet of quantitative meter would rescue English poetry from the monotony of the unending alternation of stresses and non-stresses. Campion made two mistakes in his treatise, however: First, he overlooked the fact that varying stressed instead of quantitative feet would do the job better, and second, he called the drab accentual verse that he was arguing against "rhyme." Samuel Daniel thus responded with his eloquent *The Defence of Ryme* (1603) and finally put to rest the English quantitative theory without a reply from Campion.

Campion, however, had left the field. Late in 1602 or thereabouts, he went to France and enrolled in the

University of Caen to study medicine. One might expect that Campion's stay at Caen would be similar to those at Cambridge and Gray's Inn, especially considering Caen's reputation for revels and entertainments of all sorts. This time, however, Campion persevered and received his degree, returning to London in 1605 to establish a medical practice. His reputation as a poet and musician was still strong, and this perhaps attracted sufficient patients among the nobility to keep his practice going on a secure if not lucrative level. His later verse reveals an occasional medical metaphor.

Campion wrote little during the next few years while he was establishing himself in his profession, publishing nothing between his *Observations in the Art of English Poesie* in 1602 and his five major works in his most productive year of 1613, except for *Lord Hay's Masque* in 1607. With the accession of James I to the English throne in 1603, the masque moved from the universities and inns of court to the homes of the fashionable nobility. Prospero's masque celebrating the engagement of Miranda and Ferdinand in act 4 of Shakespeare's *The Tempest* (pr. 1611) gives a good indication of the nature and function of the masque to the Jacobeans: A noble family would celebrate an important occasion, especially a wedding, with an entertainment combining music, drama, and visual spectacle, based on classical myth and employing allegory. Campion, Ben Jonson, and a number of other poets became popular as masque writers in the early seventeenth century, Campion producing five masques or masquelike entertainments, three of them in 1613.

One of the three, *The Somerset Masque* (pr. 1613), involved Campion in one of Jacobean England's worst scandals. In 1611, Robert Carr, King James's favorite and later earl of Somerset, began a liaison with Frances Howard, the countess of Essex. The relationship was partly a political one, since it was part of an attempt by the powerful Howard family to gain more power. The countess's marriage to Essex was annulled, and Somerset, against the advice of his close friend Sir Thomas Overbury, married her in late 1613. Campion's *The Somerset Masque* provided part of the nuptial entertainment. Out of spite, Somerset and his wife maneuvered Overbury into insulting the king and thus landed him in the Tower of London, where their agents slowly poisoned him to death. Part of the money paid by Somerset to the agents was conveyed by two unwitting accomplices, Sir Thomas Munson and Thomas Campion. At the subsequent trial, Campion was questioned, but no charges were brought against him, while Munson was wrongly sentenced to imprisonment in the Tower. He was imprisoned until 1617, when he was exonerated, but by that time his health had broken. Campion was the physician who attended him.

In addition to his courtly entertainments, Campion published four books of *ayres* to add to his earlier one: *Two Bookes of Ayres* published jointly in 1613 and *The Third and Fourth Booke of Ayres*, also published jointly, in 1617. The third book was dedicated to the recently released Munson and the fourth book to Munson's son, indications of Campion's loyalty to his friends. In 1618, he published *The Ayres That Were Sung and Played at Brougham Castle*—in honor of the king's visit there—a hybrid work sharing characteristics with his other books of airs and also his masques. His last work, generating a symmetry of closure, was similar to his first: *Thomae Campiani Epigrammatum Libri II*, a long collection of Latin poems, mostly epigrams, some of which appeared in his earlier volumes.

One other publishing event in Campion's life, however, needs to be mentioned. The date of *A New Way of Making Fowre Parts in Counter-point* has not yet been determined by scholars, some preferring 1617-1619 and others 1613-1614. The work is a short treatise on music theory and thus is a complement to his *Observations in the Art of English Poesie*. Before Campion, music was largely polyphonic, with each voice contributing its own melody to a rather complex whole. Campion's system minimized the melodic independence of the three lower voices. It seemed to work well enough, for it produced pleasant music, and his treatise was included in John Playford's popular *Introduction to the Skill of Music* (1660) and appeared in subsequent editions of that book until 1694, when a treatise by Henry Purcell replaced it.

Campion died on March 1, 1620. He was fifty-three years old, a lifelong bachelor. He left his very modest estate, valued at twenty-two pounds, to his friend and collaborator, Philip Rosseter.

ANALYSIS

In one sense, Thomas Campion was typically Elizabethan: Classical mythology, amorous encounters with either distant courtly ladies or willing country maids, and superficial religious emotions provided his subjects and themes. Although much of his verse lacks the substance of that of William Shakespeare, Ben Jonson, and John Donne, it is highly musical poetry, in which the careful modulation of sounds produces the illusion of music even when divorced from a musical setting. Campion's poetry depends, in short, on the ear more than most; if one is not fortunate enough to have a recording of "Never Weather-Beaten Sail" or "I Care Not for These Ladies," one should at least read these poems aloud to gain some idea of their music. This is the quality that draws Campion out of the ranks of mediocre Renaissance poets who wrote on similar conventional themes.

Campion was most successful in the writing of short poems. His airs, on which his reputation rests, include some of the best art songs written in English. Even his longer masques are appealing because they are essentially a succession of short pieces linked together; their mythological/allegorical plots contribute little to their success, for the frequent beautiful songs and the occasional interesting speech generate the ceremonious pageantry necessary to the masque. Critics have called Campion a miniaturist, and that description is apt.

Campion learned quantitative meter at first hand by studying and writing Latin poetry. His two volumes of Latin verse, which stand at opposite ends of his creative life, largely consist of epigrams and occasional poems. Epigrams poking fun at his friend, the inept poet Barnabe Barnes, praising famous people such as Francis Drake, Prince Henry, Sir Philip Sidney, William Camden, and Francis Bacon, consoling his friend Thomas Munson, extolling imaginary ladies with Roman names, and celebrating ordinary objects such as portable clocks, remind one of Ben Jonson's similar works in English. One rather long epigram, "In Obitum Gual. Devoreux fratris clariss. Comitis Essexiae," is an elegy for Walter Devereux, brother of the second earl of Essex, who died at the siege of Rouen (1591); Campion was there and wrote the poem while the battle was still in progress. One particularly short epigram, interesting for its subject, provides a good example:

About the Epigram
Similar to biting pepper, the acid epigram
Is not gracious to each taste: no one denies its use.

Among these short, useful, and sometimes acrid poems, Campion included several longer, more ambitious works, including a somewhat epic poem of 283 lines, "Ad Thamesin," celebrating the English victory over the Spanish Armada, and the 404-line Ovidian *Umbra* (1619), recounting the story of Iole, who conceived a child by the god Phoebus while she was asleep—an erotic situation that recurs in Campion's airs. These longer pieces lack the pungency of the short epigrams and are by no means first-rate poems. They do, however, contain some of the music of Campion's English airs and represent his longest productions of purely quantitative meter. The relative lack of success of these longer poems, together with the appeal of many of the shorter ones, is an indication that Campion was a miniaturist in both languages.

The famous argument between Jonson and his stage designer Inigo Jones about which element of the masque was the more important—the plot or the mechanical contrivances generating the masque's spectacle—could easily have had Campion as a third participant. Campion's masques are distinguished neither for their elaborate stage design, even though the ingenious Jones was his frequent collaborator, nor for their drama, but for their music. In contrast to Jonson's masques, Campion's appear dramatically thin: There is never a plot, only a situation, and characters are little more than mouths to deliver speeches and sing songs. It is arguable, however, that the success of a masque depends only on those qualities generating pageantry, and dramatic energy is not necessarily one of them.

LORD HAY'S MASQUE

Campion's *Lord Hay's Masque* was presented in 1607 to celebrate the marriage of King James's favorite, the Scotsman James Hay, and the English lady Honora Denney. The political situation of a recently crowned Scottish king on the English throne attempting to consolidate his two realms provides the background for this, Campion's most successful masque. There are thus three levels of meaning in the masque: the marriage of Hay and Denney, the union of Scotland and England, and the mythological reconciliation between Diana (allegorically Queen Elizabeth), who wished to keep her maids of honor virgins, and Apollo (allegorically King James), who wished to marry them to his knights. In anger, Diana has changed Apollo's knights into trees, and in the course of the masque, they regain their rightful shapes. Campion's song "Now hath Flora rob'd her bowers" is a moving poem in praise of marriage; its music is best described as majestic.

### THE LORD'S MASQUE

*The Lord's Masque*, presented as part of the ceremonies attending Princess Elizabeth's wedding to Frederick, elector of Palantine (February 14, 1613), and *The Caversham Entertainment*, presented the following April to entertain Queen Anne on her way to Bath to recover from her depression brought on by the wedding, are related pieces, this circumstantial link being strengthened by their joint publication. *The Lord's Masque* is a stately allegory in which Orpheus, representing music, frees Entheus, representing "poetic fury," from the control of Mania, or madness. The result of that liberation is a Latin poem recited by a Sybil praising the marriage of the young couple. *The Caversham Entertainment*, in contrast, is lighthearted and totally lacking in plot. A Cynic, a Traveller, and a Gardener appear severally and together before the queen, sing some rural songs, and debate issues such as the necessity of human companionship and the value of music.

### THE SOMERSET MASQUE

*The Somerset Masque* is unintentionally ironic, given the outcome of the sorry marriage it celebrates. Delegates from the four corners of the globe are attacked by the allegorical figures Error, Rumour, Curiosity, and Credulity as they sail toward England to attend the marriage. The allegorical characters cause confusion and chaos until the Fates, Eternity and Harmony, appear to restore order. The irony is that the rumors circulating about Robert Carr and his bride Frances Howard and the murder of Sir Thomas Overbury were true. A further irony is that with this masque, Campion's career as entertainer to the Jacobean nobility came to an end; it is unprovable but likely that his connection with Lord Somerset was the reason.

### A BOOKE OF AYRES, TWO BOOKES OF AYRES, AND THE THIRD AND FOURTH BOOKE OF AYRES

Campion's five books of airs—*A Booke of Ayres*, *Two Bookes of Ayres*, and *The Third and Fourth Booke of Ayres*—are somewhat misleadingly titled because the first, published jointly in 1601 with Rosseter, stands apart from the numbering, which starts with his second. All five are fairly homogeneous, containing a mixture of amorous and religious verse, between twenty-one and twenty-nine airs per book. The Rosseter collection contains, perhaps, the highest proportion of truly first-rate airs. The later books contain slightly more religious airs than the earlier (except for the first book, which is solely religious, and the second book, which is solely amorous), but this is counterbalanced by the increased earthiness of the later amorous airs, as for example in "Beauty, since you so much desire," from the fourth book, which is an almost word-for-word rendition of "Mistress, since you so much desire" from the Rosseter collection except for the important fact that the seat of "Cupid's fire" is no longer in the lady's eyes but in her genitals. Campion is even called on to apologize for some of these lyrics, telling the reader that he may turn the page if he wishes and that Chaucer was guilty of greater breaches of taste than he is.

Campion's airs are his most important contribution to literature. They are short poems, usually two or three stanzas, on conventional Renaissance subjects characterized by sensitive modulations of sound, especially vowels. They are, moreover, set to music exceptional for both melodic skill and aptness to the words. The technique of mirroring in music what is stated in words is called word painting, and Campion was a master of it. For example, in "Fire, fire, fire" from the third book, the refrain contains the repeated words "O drown both me, O drown both me," and the music descends from a higher to a lower pitch. Similarly, in "Mistress, since you so much desire" from the Rosseter collection and its revision "Beauty, since you so much desire" from the fourth book, the refrain repeats the words "But a little higher" four times, each time ascending the scale. Again, in "When to her Lute Corinna Sings" from the Rosseter collection, the line "the strings do break" is set with a quick sixteenth note musical phrase; in order to maintain the tempo, a lutenist would play this measure percussively.

This type of word painting, clever as it is, is not without dangers, as Campion himself admits in his prologue to the Rosseter collection, likening the excessive word painting of some of his contemporaries to an unskilled actor who, whenever he mentions his eyes, points to them with his finger. Much of Campion's word painting is subtle, as in "Though you are young," from the Rosseter collection, where the air's main theme, the strength of age as compared to the ephemerality of youth, is mirrored in the lute accompaniment that repeats a chord in an inverted position, that is, a lower string sounding a note higher than its next highest neighbor. Subtle in a different way is Campion's famous and much anthologized "There is a Garden in Her Face" from the fourth book. Part of the refrain, "Till cherry ripe," is repeated several times to a London street-seller's cry, with the indication that the lady celebrated in this air may be had for a price—an irony lost to the reader innocent of the music. "Never weather-beaten sail" from the first book is, perhaps, Campion's most subtle and most successful attempt at word painting. The subject of the air is the world-weariness of the singer and his desire to die and thus, like a storm-tossed ship, reach a safe harbor. A lesser composer would have set the words to music mirroring the distress and weariness of the words, but Campion writes a melody that can be described only as confident and joyous—a tension creating two perspectives, the earthly and the heavenly, and forcing the listener to see earthly troubles from a divine point of view.

OTHER MAJOR WORKS

PLAYS: *Lord Hay's Masque*, pr., pb. 1607; *The Caversham Entertainment*, pr. 1613 (masque); *The Lord's Masque*, pr., pb. 1613; *The Somerset Masque*, pr. 1613.

NONFICTION: *Observations in the Art of English Poesie*, 1602; *A New Way of Making Fowre Parts in Counter-point*, c. 1617.

BIBLIOGRAPHY

Booth, Mark W. *The Experience of Songs*. New Haven, Conn.: Yale University Press, 1981. Booth's chapter "Art Song" is an exhaustive reading of the musical and lyrical aspects of Campion's "I Care Not for These Ladies," an "anticourtly" pastoral song. Although he devotes some attention to the music of the poem, Booth focuses on the lyrics, finding them more complex than earlier critics had believed.

Coren, Pamela. "In the Person of Womankind: Female Persona Poems by Campion, Donne, Jonson." *Studies in Philology* 98, no. 2 (Spring, 2001): 225-250. Analysis of the use of the female persona in Campion's "A Secret Love or Two, I Must Confesse."

Davis, Walter R. *Thomas Campion*. Boston: Twayne, 1987. Devotes separate chapters to Campion's biography, poetry, music, theory, masques (the Renaissance "multimedia show"), and reputation. Contains a two-page chronology, extensive notes, a selected bibliography with brief annotations, and an index. Essential for Campion scholars.

Lindley, David. *Thomas Campion*. Leiden, the Netherlands: E. J. Brill, 1986. Discusses Campion's poetry, his music, the relationship between his music and poetry, and his masques. Provides literary, musical, and political contexts but focuses on the works. Contains extensive analyses of individual masques and poems and a select bibliography.

Lowbury, Edward, Timothy Salter, and Alison Young. *Thomas Campion: Poet, Composer, Physician*. New York: Barnes & Noble, 1970. Despite its title, the book stresses music. Reviews Campion's critical reputation, provides a biographical chapter, discusses the relationship between music and poetry, and examines his masques, his poem/songs, and his literary and music criticism. Six pages are devoted to "interactions." Select bibliography.

Ryding, Erik S. *In Harmony Framed: Musical Humanism, Thomas Campion, and the Two Daniels*. Kirksville, Mo.: Sixteenth Century Journal Publishers, 1993. Contrasts the poetic and musical work of the Daniel brothers, John and Samuel, with Thomas Campion. The author categorizes Campion with the Renaissance humanists. Includes a bibliography.

Wilson, Christopher. *Words and Notes Coupled Lovingly Together: Thomas Campion—A Critical Study*. New York: Garland, 1989. Contains a biographical outline, a review of Campion's scholarship, an examination of the Campion canon, brief discussions of the poetry and the music, and thorough treatments of *Observations in the Art of English Poesie* and his musical theories. Includes an extensive commentary on the masques and a comprehensive bibliography.

*Robert E. Boenig*

# THOMAS CAREW

**Born:** West Wickham, Kent, England; 1594
**Died:** London, England; March 22, 1640

PRINCIPAL POETRY

*Poems*, 1640, 1642
*Poems, with a Maske, by Thomas Carew Esquire*, 1651
*Poems, Songs and Sonnets, Together with a Masque*, 1671
*The Poems of Thomas Carew with His Masque*, 1949 (Rhodes Dunlap, editor)

OTHER LITERARY FORMS

Thomas Carew (KEHR-ee, also kuh-REW) wrote a number of songs for plays that were presented at the court of Charles I. The only other major work he produced, however, was his masque *Coelum Britannicum* (pr. 1634).

ACHIEVEMENTS

To discuss the achievements of Thomas Carew is a difficult, if not an impossible, task because the first printed edition of his work did not appear until after his death. As a result, his poems were not widely known—which is no reflection on their merit. Whatever impact he had on the literary climate of the Caroline period was limited to a small audience at court who knew his poems from the manuscript copies that were circulated. With this qualification in mind, Carew's accomplishments can be counted as significant. Although Carew was a minor poet, he was one of the best writing at a

time when minor poetry had reached a high level. Certainly Carew achieved this high level in "An Elegie upon the Death of the Deane of Pauls, Dr. John Donne," his unquestioned masterpiece. He more often produced verse that was trite or contrived. Somewhere between these two levels of achievement, however, lies a body of genuinely agreeable poetry that is valuable to the student of literature not so much because of its own innate merit but because it so effectively captures the spirit of Cavalier poetry. Indeed, one can gain a satisfactory knowledge of the themes and techniques of the Cavaliers through reading Carew alone, for he is in a sense the perfect example of the court poet during the reign of Charles I.

BIOGRAPHY

Despite the recurring popularity of his verse and his reputation as a significant Cavalier poet, little is known about the life of Thomas Carew other than that which one might infer from his poems or speculate about the life of a courtier at the court of Charles I. Carew was born in Kent in 1594. His father, Matthew, was a master in Chancery, and his mother, Alice Rymers, was descended from a noble family. Although nothing is known of Carew's boyhood, there is a record of his having begun study at Merton College, Oxford, in 1608. In 1610, he entered Cambridge, and apparently he took his degree in 1612. Again, one can only speculate about Carew's academic career, but he no doubt studied the basic curriculum in rhetoric, mathematics, and philosophy.

After graduating from Cambridge, Carew studied law, although his father's letters about his son's preparation for the bench suggest that Carew's inclinations were not toward a legal career. Rhodes Dunlap, in *The Poems of Thomas Carew* (1949), speculates that Carew may have been distracted by the notoriously frivolous life of an Inns of Court student. Matthew Carew shared this and other concerns with his friend Sir Dudley Carleton, English ambassador to Italy, who, at the request of his friend, employed the youthful Carew in 1613. Although records do exist about Carleton's Italian activities, no mention is made of Carew. No doubt the intelligent and lively Carew availed himself of the opportunities for learning and licentiousness that Italy offered until he was released from Carleton's employ in 1616, apparently the result of Carew's making a rather foolish suggestion in writing about Lady Carleton's lack of fidelity to her husband.

Carew returned to England, where he apparently fell ill with syphilis. Perhaps it was this bout with the illness that led to one of the better anecdotes concerning Carew. Apparently thinking himself to be dying, he sent for John Hale, a former school fellow from Merton College who had gone into the ministry. On his deathbed, or so he thought, Carew asked for absolution and repented his wayward life. Carew recovered and continued his ways. When he again lay ill and sent for Hale, he was refused by his former friend.

Matthew Carew tried to heal the wounds between his son and Carleton, but to no avail. No doubt the elder Carew was still completely frustrated with his son when he died in 1618.

A year later, Carew attended Sir Edward Herbert on his embassy to Paris. In 1624, Carew was recalled to England, and soon after his poetry began to circulate in manuscript form (only a few of his poems were published during his lifetime). In 1630, Carew was appointed to a court position, where he remained until his death.

Little is known about Carew's life at court. In 1634, his masque *Coelum Britannicum* was presented there; the designer was the famous architect Inigo Jones, who had worked closely with Ben Jonson. Carew was highly regarded by contemporary literary figures, counting among his friends John Donne, Ben Jonson, Sir William Davenant, James Shirley, and Richard Lovelace, with whom he apparently had a close relationship. Like so many of the Tribe of Ben, Carew was a staunch Royalist.

Another interesting anecdote told about Carew is that he saved the queen from being caught in a compromising position with Jermyn, Lord Saint Albans. He had obviously learned something from the affair with Lady Carleton. For saving her secret, the queen apparently rewarded Carew with her highest devotion.

Carew died in 1640, probably after joining the king in his Scottish campaign. He was buried next to his father at St. Anne's Chapel. No trace of either grave is discernible today.

*Thomas Carew* (Getty Images)

ANALYSIS

A man with many masters—Donne, Jonson, Giambattista Marino—Thomas Carew was slave to none, although as a Cavalier poet he has been generally regarded as one of Jonson's followers. Like Jonson, Carew commanded many lyric forms, and his lines often read as beautifully as do those of Jonson. In fact, many of Carew's verses have been effectively set to music. Proficiency with meter, however, was only part of Carew's art. He used the conceit effectively, although at times his images strain to such an extent as to warrant Samuel Johnson's attacks on the Metaphysical poets. Carew more effectively associated himself with the Metaphysical school with his use of paradox and argument, adding an intellectual quality to his poems that he so highly valued in Donne.

Jonson and Donne account for the main influences on Carew. He was equally capable of borrowing from Petrarch, Edmund Spenser, or Marino, however, for both theme and technique. In fact, because most of

Carew's poems deal with the theme of love, the forsaken lover in particular, writers such as Petrarch and Spenser were often models better suited to his purpose.

### "UPON SOME ALTERATIONS IN MY MISTRESS, AFTER MY DEPARTURE INTO FRANCE"

There has been a fair amount of speculation about whether Carew's love poems, particularly those addressed to Celia (probably a pseudonym) or to the unidentified mistress, have an autobiographical basis. Such speculation aside, the poems are interesting for both their lyric excellence and their range of themes. The peak of Carew's lyric accomplishment occurs in "Upon some Alterations in my Mistress, after my Departure into France," where the central image of the lover lost on the troubled ocean of his lady's altered affections is enhanced by the equally varying meters, thus well fusing theme and structure. Thematically, one sees in Carew a movement from Petrarchan despair to bitter vindication against his inconstant mistress. The very range of Carew's work thus demands admiration.

What this brief analysis suggests is that Carew's work reveals many of the themes and techniques that had dominated Elizabethan and Jacobean poetry and that were equally important to the Caroline poets. Carew also polished his use of the rhyming couplet in anticipation of the Augustan Age. Despite his limitations, Carew paints an accurate picture of poetic achievement and direction in the late Renaissance.

"Upon some Alterations in my Mistress, after my Departure into France" warrants comment, first, because it demonstrates an attitude in love poetry that Carew would reject for the bitter vindictiveness of later poems, such as "Disdaine returned," and second, because Carew's technique in the poem, even when not effective, is interesting. The poem is more likely autobiographical than are many of his other love poems. The poem appears to be Carew's response to his mistress's change of feeling after he had gone to France with Sir Edward Herbert. Unlike later works showing Carew bitter about his lady's rejection, this short lyric poem presents the poet as a forlorn Petrarchan lover. Appropriately, its theme is developed in the extended image of a poet lost on the troubled ocean of inconstant love and his lady's waning affections.

Carew's use of the extended image is interesting not only because it is so typical of Petrarchan poetry, but also because this technique varies from his general approach, which, like Donne's, usually fuses diverse elements. In this poem, the first stanza quickly presents the image that will be elaborated:

> Oh gentle Love, doe not forsake the guide
> Of my fraile Barke, on which the swelling tide
> Of ruthless pride
> Doth beat, and threaten wrack from every side.

It was a well-worn figure by the time Carew came to employ it, and Carew in no way used it with originality. The varied line lengths and metrical feet, however, suggesting the tempestuous seas, show Carew effectively combining idea and form.

Carew's reference to the "mystie cloud of anger" in the second stanza identifies the alterations to which the title refers. Still, Carew follows this line by calling his lady his "faire starre," seeming to say that despite her alterations, she remains for him a guiding passion. The last line of the poem, however—"In the deep flood she drown'd her beamie face"—suggests the more defiant train of thought of his later poems as he turns his back on his lady and tells her that her own treatment of him will be her destruction.

### "SONG, TO MY INCONSTANT MISTRESS"

In Carew's "Song, To my inconstant Mistress," as in "Disdaine returned," he pictures himself as the scorned Petrarchan lover, though, rather than suffering in frustration, he methodically points out why his mistress will at some point regret her attitude. This intellectual response to an emotional situation is characteristic of the school of Donne, while the lyric excellence of the poem, in five-line tetrameter stanzas rhyming *ababb*, follows the influence that governed the Tribe of Ben. Carew thus illustrates his ability to absorb diverse influences.

Underlying the entire thematic structure of "Song, To my inconstant Mistress" is the poet's paralleling of love and religion. The opening stanza portrays him as a man with a "strong faith," while his mistress is a "poor excommunicate." These early parallels suggest a point that the poet will later develop: that true faithfulness in love will, as in religion, be rewarded by salvation. The focus of this poem, however, is on the damning of the unfaithful mistress.

The second stanza develops one of Carew's typical themes, that love demands an equal commitment by both parties. The poet says that his inconstant mistress will be replaced by a "faire hand" and that this new love and the poet will be "both with equall glory crown'd." At this point, Lynn Sadler suggests, the tone of the poet has something of the "swagger of bravado." The point is well taken; moreover, the swagger is to become more bitter in the final stanza.

In the third stanza, the implications of the first are at last fulfilled. The poet has already established the bliss he will enjoy because of his constancy to the ideal of love. His main point, however, is to show the despair that awaits the one who has violated the spirit of love. Her reward, moreover, will be equal to her sin, for she will suffer to the degree that she caused suffering. Finally, again in religious terms, she will be "Damn'd for (her) false Apostasie."

"Song, To my inconstant Mistress" is one of Carew's best lyric love poems. His fusion of religious and erotic imagery enhances the latter without mocking or trivializing the former, an achievement that distinguishes the poem from the common run of Cavalier lyrics.

### "DISDAINE RETURNED"

One of Carew's best-known poems, "Disdaine returned," demonstrates two significant aspects of his art: the lyric beauty that he inherited from Jonson and his smooth integration of several typical Elizabethan and Jacobean themes. The basic structure of the poem is simple. It has three six-line stanzas in tetrameter, rhyming *ababcc*. In the last stanza, however, the closing couplet varies slightly in its meter and thus draws the poem to a decisive close, suggesting that the poet has cured himself of his lovesickness. Unlike many of the other Celia poems in which Carew expounds the poet's frustrations in love with a typical Petrarchan lament, "Disdaine returned" shows the spirit and style that were characteristic of Donne in such poems as "The Broken Heart." The poem opens with a carpe diem statement, "As old Time makes these decay/ So his flames must waste away." Rather than using these lines to make the basic live-for-the-moment argument, however, Carew sug-

gests a feeling of depressed reconciliation; his lady has lost the opportunity for a genuine love that would not fade with the passing of time or the loss of beauty. The second stanza justifies the claim as Carew defines in basically Platonic terms his ideas about love that his mistress has not been able to accept: "Hearts with equal love combined kindle never-dying fires."

In the third stanza, the frustrated poet, whose love is genuine, is forced to return his lady's rejection. As the second stanza suggests, there must be equal commitment for the relationship to prosper. The poet says, however, that he has not found his love returned: "I have searched thy soul within/ And find naught but pride and scorn." He decides to return these feelings of disdain, ending his pointless suffering.

### "AN ELEGIE UPON THE DEATH OF THE DEANE OF PAULS, DR. JOHN DONNE"

Generally accepted as Carew's best poem, "An Elegie upon the Death of the Deane of Pauls, Dr. John Donne" is one of the few poems by Carew to be published during his own lifetime. It was published in 1633, although it was probably written much nearer the time of Donne's death in 1631.

The poem opens with an indictment of an age that finds only "unkneaded dowe-bak't prose" to praise the loss of its greatest poet. Carew's frustration with this situation is intensified throughout the poem as he reviews the many changes in the use of language that Donne had wrought. He freed the poet from "senile imitation" of the ancients and then "fresh invention planted." Carew devotes a large part of the poem, in fact, to making this point, using a concept that Donne would have appreciated: Donne paid the "debts of our penurious bankrupt age," which had so long struggled in borrowed images and forms. So great was Donne's power, Carew says, that "our stubborne language bends, made only fit/ With her tough-thick-rib'd hoopes to gird about/ Thy Giant phansie."

Because Donne is gone, Carew declares, the advances that he initiated are vanishing as well, since they are "Too hard for Libertines in Poetrie." To further build on this theme, the poet uses the image of the wheel that will cease to turn after losing its "moving head." Still, Carew's final image is that of the phoenix, a popular image in Donne's poetry, to suggest that perhaps from the ashes the spirit of Donne will rise in another era.

Finally, Carew apologizes for his poor effort by saying that Donne is "Theme enough to tyre all Art." He then presents the closing epitaph:

> Here lies a King, that rul'd as hee thought fit
> The universall Monarchy of wit;
> Here lie two Flamens, and both those, the best,
> Apollo's first, at last, the true God's Priest.

This best of Carew's poems is a rather accurate projection of what would be the course of poetic achievement after the death of Donne. Not until Alexander Pope, about one hundred years later (excluding John Milton), did England see a genius to compare with Donne, yet between these two giants, such poems as this one by Carew kept alive the spirit of poetic achievement that distinguished the Renaissance.

OTHER MAJOR WORK

PLAY: *Coelum Britannicum*, pr. 1634 (masque).

BIBLIOGRAPHY

Benet, Diana. "Carew's Monarchy of Wit." In *"The Muses' Common-Weale": Poetry and Politics in the Seventeenth Century*, edited by Claude J. Summers and Ted-Larry Pebworth. Columbia: University of Missouri Press, 1988. Argues that Carew, using the absolutist rhetoric of James and Charles, consciously constructs a realm of wit in which the writer reigns supreme. Shows the problems faced by writers in the Stuarts' attempts to limit free speech.

Corns, Thomas N., ed. *The Cambridge Companion to English Poetry: Donne to Marvell*. New York: Cambridge University Press, 1993. Presents a brief but balanced biography of Carew and an analysis of his work.

Parker, Michael P. "'To my friend G. N. from Wrest': Carew's Secular Masque." In *Classic and Cavalier: Essays on Jonson and the Sons of Ben*, edited by Claude J. Summers and Ted-Larry Pebworth. Pittsburgh, Pa.: University of Pittsburgh Press, 1982. Surveys the seventeenth century genre of the country-house poem and places Carew's piece as the turning point between Jonson's "To Penshurst" and Marvell's "Upon Appleton House." Supplies information about Wrest and its owners, which was for many years obscured through historical error. Shows how the structure of the poem owes much to the masque tradition.

Ray, Robert H. "The Admiration of Sir Philip Sidney by Lovelace and Carew: New Seventeenth Century Allusions." *ANQ* 18, no. 1 (Winter, 2005): 18-22. Notes how Richard Lovelace and Carew were influenced by Sidney and examines Carew's poem "To My Worthy Friend Master George Sandys, on His Translation of the Psalmes."

Sadler, Lynn. *Thomas Carew*. Boston: Twayne, 1979. This critical biography presents a straightforward introduction to Carew's life, times, and works. Covers his entire output, emphasizing the better-known lyrics at the expense of the country-house poems and Carew's masque. Perhaps the most accessible single work on Carew for the general reader. Includes a well-selected bibliography with annotations.

Selig, Edward I. *The Flourishing Wreath*. New Haven, Conn.: Yale University Press, 1958. Reprint. Hamden, Conn.: Archon Books, 1970. The first full-length serious study of Carew's verse, this remains the most thorough attempt to justify Carew's fame in his own time. Selig's chapter on the poet's song lyrics is still valuable; he points out that a third of Carew's poems were written for singing, and sixty settings survive. The book's examination of patterns of imagery in Carew is also useful.

Semler, L. E. *The English Mannerist Poets and the Visual Arts*. Madison, N.J.: Fairleigh Dickinson University Press, 1998. Includes an introduction to mannerism as it applies to visual as well as poetic work. Each of the five poets covered, including Carew, is shown to have one or more of the characteristics of the mannerist style.

Sharpe, Kevin. "Cavalier Critic? The Ethics and Politics of Thomas Carew's Poetry." In *Politics of Discourse: The Literature and History of Seventeenth-Century England*, edited by Kevin Sharpe and Steven Zwicker. Berkeley: University of California Press, 1987. Distances Carew from the usual image of the Cavalier and argues that he was a serious writer with an orderly and hierarchical vision of a kingdom of nature and love. Emphasizes Carew's often misunderstood, positive view of marriage and connects this idea to his political vision.

Walton, Geoffrey. "The Cavalier Poets." In *From Donne to Marvell.* Vol. 3 in *New Pelican Guide to English Literature*, edited by Boris Ford. New York: Penguin Books, 1982. Stresses Carew's complexity and range, and singles out for praise the sense of social responsibility shown in Carew's two country-house poems, "To Saxham" and "To my friend G. N., from Wrest."

*Gerald W. Morton*

---

# LEWIS CARROLL
## Charles Lutwidge Dodgson

**Born:** Daresbury, Cheshire, England; January 27, 1832

**Died:** Guildford, Surrey, England; January 14, 1898

PRINCIPAL POETRY

*Phantasmagoria, and Other Poems*, 1869

*The Hunting of the Snark: An Agony in Eight Fits*, 1876

*Rhyme? and Reason?*, 1883

*Three Sunsets, and Other Poems*, 1898

*The Collected Verse of Lewis Carroll*, 1932 (also known as *The Humorous Verse of Lewis Carroll*, 1960)

*For "The Train": Five Poems and a Tale*, 1932

OTHER LITERARY FORMS

Lewis Carroll is remembered for his long fiction, the children's classics *Alice's Adventures in Wonderland* (1865) and *Through the Looking-Glass and What Alice Found There* (1871). Immediate popular and critical successes, they are now among the world's most quoted and translated books, enjoyed by children and adults alike, and their characters are part of the world's folklore. His sentimental and tendentious *Sylvie and*

*Bruno* (1889) and *Sylvie and Bruno Concluded* (1893) were far less successful.

Carroll's prose fiction is best classified as anatomy, which, unlike the novel, is about ideas rather than people and engages the mind rather than represents life realistically. The characters of *Alice's Adventures in Wonderland* and *Through the Looking-Glass and What Alice Found There* are personifications of philosophical or linguistic problems and function, much as counters in a game whose rules change according to Carroll's fancy. The books have rudimentary characteristics of the bildungsroman—Alice's changes in size or status suggesting puberty and development—but Alice herself is static. Like Gulliver or Candide, she is the "straight man" in the comedy, less important as a character than as a stabilizing perspective—that of the "normal" child in a mad world. The anatomy's distinguishing formal characteristic is, paradoxically, its refusal to take any one form—its protean, adaptive quality. In *Alice's Adventures in Wonderland* and *Through the Looking-Glass and What Alice Found There*, the dream-narrative dissolves into a structure of dialectic or symposium that is almost infinitely transformable—into poetry, parody, literary criticism, riddles, or verbal games for the sake of the play.

The tendency of Carroll's work to turn into wordplay is not confined to his fiction and poetry. He published more than three hundred separate works, consisting of formal mathematical and logical treatises, essays on cranky subjects, satires on Oxford's academic politics, numerous acrostics, puzzles, and trivia. In addition, he wrote faithfully in his diaries, now published, and composed delightful letters, also published. His work in formal mathematics is sober, systematic, and unoriginal. His contribution in logic was made indirectly and intuitively by way of his "nonsense," which dramatized in paradoxes and wordplay concepts later taken up by linguistic philosophers such as Bertrand Russell and Ludwig Wittgenstein. In general, Carroll wrote best when least serious and when working in a hybrid form somewhere between linguistic analysis and literature. In his best art, in works such as *A Tangled Tale* (1885), a cross between narrative and mathematics, or the philosophical dialogue "What the Tortoise Said to Achilles," the logician and poet combine forces.

ACHIEVEMENTS

Lewis Carroll created a new kind of children's literature that was sheer fun in the most serious sense; its combination of fantasy, humor, and wordplay stimulated the mind and the imagination. In rejecting the rational, moralistic approach of the children's literature of the eighteenth and nineteenth centuries, Carroll turned the trend toward lesson-free imaginative literature in the twentieth.

Now that Alice is known to children largely through the popular media, Carroll's books have become the territory of adults—adults from a considerable range of intellectual disciplines. Physicists, psychologists, philosophers, linguists, and computer scientists, as well as mathematicians and literary critics, have written about or in response to his work. In the twentieth century, his view of the world as a fascinating if unsolvable puzzle continued to grow on readers, presenting a difficulty in classifying his literary influence. Theoretically, "nonsense" is humor's equivalent of Symbolist poetry or abstract painting in its concern with the play of verbal surfaces and textures rather than function or content. As nonsense's purest and best practitioner, Carroll is a forerunner of Surrealism, Dadaism, and similar schools. Certainly, Carroll has made connections, directly or indirectly, with the most important of the modernists and postmodernists. T. S. Eliot, James Joyce, Franz Kafka, Wallace Stevens, Jorge Luis Borges, and Vladimir Nabokov all owe something to the nonsense perspective: alinear structure, the play of intellectual wit, the view of literature as a game of language, and the concept of autonomous art.

Carroll contributed the Mad Hatter, the Cheshire Cat, and the Jabberwock to the world's folklore; provided an abundance of popular quotations; and added several new words to the English language. While other, more ambitious works of the era have become dated, *Alice's Adventures in Wonderland*, *Through the Looking-Glass and What Alice Found There*, and *The Hunting of the Snark* survive and seem inexhaustible. This is because Carroll's gift was a language that opened minds to the infinity of worlds within words.

*Lewis Carroll* (Library of Congress)

BIOGRAPHY

Charles Lutwidge Dodgson's literary achievement under the pseudonym of Lewis Carroll is often separated from his career as a Victorian mathematician and don. As Dodgson the reserved bachelor, he lived an extremely regular life, most of it at Christ Church College, Oxford, where he matriculated in 1850, taught mathematics from 1855 until 1881, and thereafter served as curator of the Senior Common Room. Despite the academic conventionality of these externals, Dodgson had diverse interests: photography, at which he excelled in his special interest areas (children and celebrities); visits with his child-friends; theatergoing; occasional preaching; and writing. As Lewis Carroll, he wrote what he, to some extent, considered children's humor, indeed calling it "nonsense," and this side of his work is often viewed as a form of sublimation. Carroll thus becomes the rebel who escaped from the tedium of being Dodgson. Certainly, Dodgson had his part in confining Carroll to the nursery: He allowed only little girls to use his pseudonym and refused in later life to acknowledge letters addressed to Lewis Carroll at his quarters. The Dodgson/Carroll split is too simple in one respect, however; at his best and most distinctive, he merges the perspectives of the logician and the poet. His intellectual agility is behind the playfulness that inspires the word magic.

Dodgson was the third child and eldest son of the eleven children of the Reverend Charles Dodgson and Frances Jane Lutwidge. His authoritarian father may have contributed to the reserved character of his later public image. His affection for his mother was unusually strong and may have hindered his ability to develop attachments to grown women. A lifelong stammer contributed to his introversion but also may have had something to do with his fascination with portmanteau words, funny sounds, puns, and nonsense in general.

As a child educated at home until he was twelve, Dodgson was happy and precocious. To entertain his siblings, he invented games with whimsically elaborate systems of rules, wrote and staged marionette plays for home theatricals, and edited and illustrated several family magazines that contain the early expressions of the logician and poet in puzzles, nonsense, and parodies. He continued producing and contributing to these family periodicals until he was twenty-three.

Although he went on to Richmond Grammar School and Rugby, where he suffered the usual fate of the introverted egghead, the precocious child of Dodgson's idyllic years in a sense never grew up. He turned into Lewis Carroll, the persona who talked only to "child-friends," as he called the little girls whose friendship he cultivated until they reached puberty. These friendships began with Alice Liddell, daughter of the dean of Christ Church, who became Alice of Wonderland. Collectively, the girls became the inspiration, ideal readers, and mediating perspective for most of Carroll's works. This absolutely sure sense of his audience—beginning with his siblings and continuing with his child-friends—has much to do with what makes Carrollian nonsense work. It provided a creative rapport that directed him in transforming what might have been unlikely material—mathematics, logic, and linguistics, as well as wild fantasies—into poetry.

ANALYSIS

The name of Lewis Carroll is now almost synonymous with "nonsense." Carroll did not invent nonsense verse, for it is as old as children's games and nursery rhymes. With Carroll, however, it grows up and becomes something more than nonsense as that term is usually defined. The term refers to humorous verse that does not make sense, which in turn suggests a kind of nonpoetry, verse with all the surface characteristics of poetry—rhyme, meter, and figures of speech—but without meaning. As the title of Carroll's *Rhyme? and Reason?* implies, it is sound gone berserk and completely overtaking sense. Superficially, this definition fits his "Jabberwocky," which seems to have the authentic ring of a brilliant poem in a foreign language that does not exist. As such nonsense, "Jabberwocky" is a piece of ingenuity but little more. The reader's appreciation of Carroll's poetry is far more complex than the term will admit, however, as the enduring popularity of "Jabberwocky" suggests.

The fact that Carroll, a mathematician and logician, felt most alive when playing or inventing games, puzzles, stories, and rhymes with children leads to the uncommon meaning of his nonsense. As his life seems to show (and in an analogy suggested by Kathleen Blake and Carroll critic Richard Kelly), he viewed the world as a vast puzzle that could never be solved but which must be worked to the end, for the sake of the game itself. Through wordplay of all sorts, from conundrums and acrostics to parodies and paradoxes, Carroll's poetry engages the reader in that game. His nonsensical poetry is like that unsolvable puzzle of the world in inviting and resisting interpretation simultaneously. To solve it or extract a meaning would be to end the game and destroy the poem.

**ALICE'S ADVENTURES IN WONDERLAND**

As quirky as Carroll might seem, his development as a poet follows a common pattern: He began writing what is predominantly parody, in his juvenilia and *Alice's Adventures in Wonderland*, and moved on to poems that are complete in themselves, "Jabberwocky" and *The Hunting of the Snark*. Most of the poems of *Alice's Adventures in Wonderland* are parodies of popular verses and songs that Victorian children were taught and often called on to recite. In Wonderland, where the world is out of joint, these are consistently misquoted, either by the Wonderland characters, who are all mad, or Alice, whose verbal memory is understandably deranged.

Soon after falling down a rabbit hole and experiencing sudden and strange changes in size, Alice attempts to remember who she is, trying out the names of various friends. As a final effort to regain her identity, she tries to recite Isaac Watts's "Against Idleness and Mischief," which begins "How doth the little busy bee," the bee providing nature's model of virtuous industry. The resulting parody is "How doth the little crocodile," which turns Watts's pathetic fallacy into a sadistic one. The crocodile's work, in contrast to the bee's, consists of floating passively with "gently smiling jaws" open to welcome "little fishes in." In place of Watts's cozy wholesomeness, Alice seems to have constructed a Darwinian world of "Nature red in tooth and claw" or a Freudian one of oral aggression.

To extract "Eat or be eaten" as Carroll's moral would be missing the point, however, even though this theme arises in almost every parody and episode in the book. In Wonderland, as in slapstick comedy, violence is the rule, but it remains, with emotions, on a purely verbal level, as in the case of the Queen of Hearts's universal panacea, "Off with your head!" Although Carroll juxtaposes the law of the jungle against the tea-and-bread-and-butter decorum of the Victorian nursery, the point is to disrupt the normal or preconceived order. Even the trauma of Alice's loss of identity is short-lived. After misquoting the poem, she cries a pool of tears that becomes an ingenious obstacle course for the next episode.

The parodied poems are easy targets, insipid and platitudinous doggerel, and the parodies themselves are part of a larger satire on Victorian children's literature and spoon-fed education, as suggested elsewhere in the Mock Turtle's curriculum of "Reeling and Writhing" and "Ambition, Distraction, Uglification, and Derision." Carroll's parody tends to get broader, as satire on specific children's literature diffuses into satire on education and moral instruction in general, and then into wordplay that does violence on language itself and all its rules. In the parodies as a whole, the target is didacticism, but the main reason for reading is to

engage in a game of transformation that surprises and stimulates.

The dramatic situation, in which Alice is called on to recite and invariably delivers a parody, itself becomes a game, especially for Victorian readers, who immediately recognized the parodied poems and appreciated the play of the parody against the original. The episode in which Alice is told to recite "Father William" by the hookah-smoking caterpillar must have further delighted children who could share her cool upward glance at the adult world, with its arbitrary orders and rules. Her recitation, "wrong from beginning to end," as the Caterpillar comments condescendingly afterward, begins as Robert Southey's "The Old Man's Comforts," a strenuously righteous portrait of old age: "In the days of my youth I remember'd my God/ And He hath not forgotten my age." Carroll's Father William is a slapstick character; eccentrically and wonderfully athletic, he maintains his strength by standing on his head or balancing eels on his nose. He is also voracious, eating a goose with "the bones and the beak," and short tempered: The poem ends as he shouts at his son, "'Be off, or I'll kick you down stairs.'"

In this and the next parody, also on the subject of that Victorian shibboleth, the home and family, Carroll's antididacticism is at its wildest. The Duchess's lullaby is a parody of G. W. Langford's morbidly sentimental "Speak gently to the little child!/ . . . It may not long remain." Carroll inverts this advice (rule by love rather than by fear) into the loudly comic violence of "Speak roughly to your little boy,/ And beat him when he sneezes." The onomatopoeic chorus of "Wow! Wow! Wow!" is a cacophonous child-pleaser. One feels no sympathy for the Duchess's baby, to whom this advice is applied, because his feelings, like the parodied poem, are turned into a sound effect. As soon as Alice takes pity on him, he turns into a pig.

By the mad tea party episode, at which point in the narrative most of the foundations of Alice's normal, above-ground order have been destroyed, the parodies get broader and more irrelevantly playful. The Mad Hatter's song is a misquotation of Jane Taylor's "Twinkle, twinkle, little star," but it surprises and entertains as a piece of sheer incongruity. Arbitrarily, it seems, the Hatter substitutes "bat" for "star" and "tea-tray" for "diamond," producing "Twinkle, twinkle, little bat!/ How I wonder what you're at!/ Up above the world you fly,/ Like a tea-tray in the sky." The images surprise by failing to relate, either to reality or to one another. Not only do bats fail to "twinkle," but also they have nothing in common with tea-trays. Much as the Duchess's baby is turned into a thing—a sound effect and then a pig—the potential simile is neutralized, its images turning back into discrete, therefore unpoetic and senseless, objects.

Surprise and laughter are nonsense's equivalent of poetic emotion. Its "sense" is more difficult to explain. The Mad Hatter's song, however, makes Wonderland sense in several ways. As a mad inversion of a sentimental song, it corresponds with the mad tea party as the counterpart of Victorian high tea. It is also the perfect expression of the Mad Hatter, who challenges Alice's sense of time, logic, and decorum. The tea tray in the sky is the appropriate marker in the Hatter's world of eternal teatime, and the indecorous but twinkling little bat fits in with his tea-drinking companions, the March Hare and, especially, the Dormouse, who tells a story of little girls who live at the bottom of a treacle well ("well in") and draw things beginning with "M." The meaning of the Hatter's song is like that of his riddle with no answer, "Why is a raven like a writing-desk?" Through arbitrary or nonsense correspondences, the words take the reader on an exhilarating trip to nowhere and everywhere at the same time.

The Mock Turtle's two songs, which come just before the book's conclusion in the trial scene, are more playfully nonsensical, musical, and complete than the previous poems, and so prevent one's reading any moral into Wonderland. The songs also prepare for Alice's awakening, precipitated by her "Stuff and nonsense!" response to the increasingly irrational court, which, as she suddenly realizes, is "nothing but a pack of cards."

The first song upsets the previously established pattern by turning a sadistic poem into harmless play. It parodies the meter and obvious dramatic situation of Mary Howitt's "The Spider and the Fly," in which the spider invites the fly into her "prettiest little parlour." Carroll adapts Howitt's inappropriately rollicking rhythm to a fittingly gay song and dance, the "Lobster Quadrille." "Will you walk a little faster?" says a whiting to a snail, who is then exhorted to join in a "delightful" experience. Lest the snail, like the fly, fear danger—indeed, the dance involves being thrown out to sea—he is told to be adventurous and reminded that "The further off from England the nearer is to France—." The song ends jollily enough as the invitation extends to Alice and the reader: "Will you, won't you, will you, won't you, won't you join the dance?"

Similarly, "Turtle Soup" teases the reader with hints of danger and opportunities for morals, only to cancel them out. The situation reeks with dramatic irony: The Mock Turtle sings about his destiny as food and sobs all the while. However, the verbal connection between Mock Turtle and turtle soup that makes the irony possible has a fallacy embedded in it. A mock turtle cannot be made into turtle soup—or any soup, for that matter. Realizing that the implied relationship is pure wordplay, the reader is reminded that, as his name suggests, the character and indeed the whole book is a fiction. "Mock" also suggests fakery and underscores the character's sentimentality, another level of unreality. "Mock" additionally suggests ridicule, and this turtle's song is a parody of James Sayles's treacley "Star of the Evening," with lowly and also rather sloppy soup substituted for the star. Finally, riddled with too many ironies and puns of which to make sense, "Turtle Soup" turns, like the previous song, into an invitation—to eat, slurp, and sing: "Beau—ootiful Soo—oop!/ Soo—oop of the e—e—evening,/ Beautiful, beauti—FUL SOUP!"

## THROUGH THE LOOKING-GLASS AND WHAT ALICE FOUND THERE

Carroll's parody becomes a sustained and sophisticated art, and perhaps something more than parody, in *Through the Looking-Glass and What Alice Found There*, but only once, in the White Knight's ballad, which adapts the rhyme and meter of Thomas Moore's "My Heart and Lute" to the content of William Wordsworth's "Resolution and Independence." In its comment on Wordsworth's profoundly serious treatment of an experience that can strike one as less than edifying, the story shows Carroll's keen sense of the absurd. Wordsworth's narrator meets an old man on the moor, comments on the fine day, and asks him his occupation.

As the old man feebly and wanderingly answers, his words, compared to a stream, flow into one another, and his interrogator gets lost in elevated meditation. When, after further interrogation, the message finally comes through, it is merely that he wanders and gathers leeches and makes do. The leech-gatherer then becomes a symbol of independence and sanity to comfort the narrator in anxious times.

So summarized, the poem sounds like a non sequitur, an effect that Carroll intensifies through sustained nonsensical dialogue and slapstick. When Carroll's "aged, aged man," sitting precariously on a gate, mumbles so incoherently that his words trickle away "like water through a sieve," his interrogator repeatedly shouts "How is it that you live?" and thumps him on the head. Wordsworth's symbol of sanity turns into Carroll's decidedly eccentric inventor of such things as mutton pies made of butterflies and waistcoat buttons out of haddocks' eyes. Like Wordsworth's, Carroll's speaker is moved to emotional recollection of the aged man, but in moments of clumsiness rather than tranquillity—when he drops something on his toe or shoves "a right-hand foot" into a "left-hand shoe." In the *buffo* finale, Carroll maintains one rhyme for twelve lines to create an unforgettable impression of that old man he "used to know," whose "look was mild, whose speech was slow," who "muttered mumblingly and low/ As if his mouth were full of dough."

In the early and more hostile 1856 version entitled "Upon the Lonely Moor," the parody's targets were sentimentality and Wordsworth. In *Through the Looking-Glass and What Alice Found There*, the parody becomes a joke on the White Knight and then, through a hierarchy of analogies, on Carroll himself. The poem is about an eccentric inventor whom the speaker cannot forget. The White Knight is a similar eccentric inventor whom Alice cannot forget, and the quixotic White Knight is often seen as a caricature of Carroll (in life as well as in art, an eccentric inventor) who hopes Alice Liddell will not forget him. Carroll was fond of reversals and regressions such as this series, which works like a mirror reflecting the mirror reflection of an object ad infinitum. This reversal turns a hilarious but rather mean parody into a self-referential joke. Finally, it turns that joke into a poem, as the leech-gatherer, Wordsworth, the "aged, aged man," the White Knight, and Carroll become an unfolding series of mild and mumbling quixotic inventors who hope to stumble onto the key to the treasure of the universe. The poem comments on itself as poetry, for each of these figures is a poet in some questionable sense, beginning with the leech-gatherer whose feeble words transcend themselves and on through the White Knight and Carroll (both of whom, as Alice detects, got the "tune" from somebody else). By reflecting backward and forward, the parody inverts itself into a poetically suggestive surface.

As a rule, the poems of *Through the Looking-Glass and What Alice Found There* are not parodies or, like the White Knight's ballad, become something else through the reflective magic of the mirror—its main structural principle as well as the device behind the "logic" of its poetry. The book begins by reversing Wonderland's premises. Instead of a spring day's dream about falling down a rabbit hole, the sequel is a logically constructed game of "Let's pretend" that takes place indoors on a November afternoon. Though Wonderland is chaos, the universe behind the Looking Glass is determined, artificial, and abstract. The mirror principle means that everything goes backward, and reversal extends to the relationship between words and reality.

The mirror world corresponds roughly with philosophical idealism; thus, Alice becomes a figment of a dream of the Red King, who plays George Berkeley's God. Similarly, language and art shape life, and poems can make things happen. Nature imitates art in comical ways when imported nursery-rhyme characters must act out their lines. Egghead Humpty-Dumpty persists in sitting on his wall; Tweedledum and Tweedledee periodically take up arms over a rattle. Looking-Glass insects are like concrete poems, as the Bread-and-Butterfly and the Rocking-horse Fly are materialized words. Trees bark by saying "Bough-wough." Poetry is part of the logician's demonstration of how language can create self-contained worlds.

### "JABBERWOCKY"

Shortly after Alice steps through the mirror, she discovers a book that appears to be in a foreign language, but she soon realizes that it is a Looking-Glass book.

Holding it to the mirror, she reads the poem "Jabberwocky." Carroll originally planned to print the entire poem in reverse, which would have made reading it a visual joke, an infinite regression of text within text. Even when read in normal order, "Jabberwocky" works according to the rule of the world behind the mirror. The meanings one derives from it refer one back to its surface, obliterating the usual distinctions between form and content. As the title suggests, "Jabberwocky" is gibberish about the Jabberwock, which is identified with the same gibberish. As a poetry of surfaces, this nonsense works much like abstract painting or music; the play of patterns, textures, and sounds is the point.

The first quatrain, like all of Carroll's poetry, has a deceptive simplicity; it is a common ballad stanza in clear English syntax. Therefore 'Twas brillig, and the slithy toves/ Did gyre and gimble in the wabe" seems to say something but does not—quite. Later on in the book, Carroll has Humpty-Dumpty provide an elaborate interpretation—made suspect from the beginning by his assertion that he can explain all poems, even those that "haven't been invented." Defining some of the coinages as "portmanteau" words—two words combined to make a new one—he seems to clear up "mimsy" (miserable and flimsy) and "slithy" (slimy and lithe), but the principle fails with "toves" as a fusion of badger, lizard, and corkscrew, and "brillig" as the time "when you begin broiling things for dinner." If one takes Humpty-Dumpty's analysis in all seriousness, one ends up with another Mad Hatter's song composed of disparate objects such as bats and tea-trays. Its main purpose is to combine insights with false leads and so lure the reader into the game.

The puzzling first quatrain made its first appearance in 1855 in *Mischmasch*, the last of the family periodicals, in a quaint, archaic-looking script, under the heading "Stanza of Anglo-Saxon Poetry." Evidently, from the beginning Carroll wanted a mock-medieval effect. To turn it into "Jabberwocky," he added five middle stanzas—with a motif deriving, perhaps, from *Beowulf* (c. 1000) and from Saint George—and framed them with the repeated first stanza, thus turned into a refrain. To genre and structure, Carroll has applied the portmanteau principle, creating a clever mishmash of epic and ballad—a mock-epic ballad.

Thus identified, the poem does mean something— or, at least, it provides at strategic points just enough to lead the reader on. As Alice says, it gives its readers ideas, even though they "don't know exactly what they are!" The story line, starting with the second stanza, is easy to follow, having a beginning, middle, and end, as Alice perceives when she says that *somebody* killed *something*." A young man is warned by his father of the Jabberwock, goes off and kills it, and returns to the praises of his father. The elements of the epic are also present, abstracted and compressed into a balladlike miniature, a toy. Carroll uses the mock-heroic for the "pure" purpose of reducing content to patterns or game structures with which to play.

The poem includes the ominous warning of the seer; the chimerical beast and its familiars, the Jubjub and the Bandersnatch; the quest, with its dark night of the soul by the Tumtum tree; the confrontation, battle, and victory; and the glorification of the hero. In good nonsense fashion, Carroll understates motivation—for example, the hero's object in killing the creature—reducing it to the simplest of elements: He is a subject, and it is the direct object. Carroll also foreshortens significant episodes with humorous effect. The interminable quest is dismissed in a mechanically efficient line, "Long time the manxome foe he sought—" and the Jabberwock's appearance and slaying are anticlimactic. Its "eyes of flame" are stereotypical dragon paraphernalia, and it comes "whiffling" and "burbling" asthmatically rather than horrifically. The battle takes all of two lines, and it is as easy as "One, two! One, two! And through and/ through"—so easy that the only sound comes from the final, decapitating blow: "snicker-snack!"

As a "silly" epic in miniature, these five stanzas make perfect sense. The nonsense words, most of them adjectives, nouns, or onomatopoeic verbs, are coined and arranged to produce a single impression. It is difficult not to see the "beamish" hero who has "uffish" thoughts and "gallumphs" as a high-spirited boy, because the "new" words are close enough to real ones suggestive of emotional states (gruff, beaming, and gallop). He is left as merely an impression, moreover, as one means of conveying the playful spirit in which the poem is intended to be read. Similarly, the Jabberwock is reduced from a monster to a sound machine producing wonderful gibberish: whiffles, burbles, and ultimately, of course, jabberwocky. "Snicker-snack" is thus the appropriate blow for finishing it off. Not only is it a toylike sound, but also it is no more than a sound. The monster is thus reduced to a noise destroyed by a sound that "snickers" in gleeful triumph. Similarly, the story line ends in the father's joyous "chortle" (chuckle and snort).

As in the parodies, Carroll neutralizes potentially disturbing events and forces the reader's attention on the patterns and words. In doing so, he opens worlds of experience shut off from Victorian readers accustomed to a literary climate of "high seriousness" and utilitarian purpose. "Jabberwocky" thus had the effect of renewing poetry and language. It continues to do so each time it is read. Even through mock Anglo-Saxon, it brings back the feel of the incantatory power of oral alliterative verse and the liberation of a primal lyrical utterance. Indeed, the mockery, the fact that it contains words that remain "foreign," makes it more magical, for what "gibberish" there is in the poem offers the child in every reader the experience of creating his own inner language. In reading the coined words, and regardless of whether they translate as portmanteaus, one makes old sounds and meanings into new ones, recreating language in one's own image. So the reader is allowed to return momentarily to that purest creative experience, the act of uttering, naming, and making worlds out of words.

The notion that "Jabberwocky" is a meaningless poem is thus both false and true. Its "nonsense" is perhaps best thought of as pure or uncommon sense. Carroll, moreover, structured his ballad to ensure that no moral or theme could be derived from it other than an experiencing of the primacy of the word. At precisely the point in the poem at which one expects the emergence of a theme, when the Jabberwock is conquered and the father rejoices, one is back where one started—with "'Twas brillig" leading further back through the "borogroves" to the pure nowhere of "the mome raths outgrabe." For those who continue to play the game, content keeps leading back to the verbal surface, the Jabberwock to Jabberwocky, ad infinitum. As with a Möbius strip, neither side is up. Because it behaves so much like the Looking-Glass cake that must be handed around before it can be cut, whereupon it is no longer there, "Jabberwocky" might seem to make frustrating reading. By so resisting interpretation, paradoxically, the poem does teach a lesson—that a poem should not *mean* but *be*. Carroll's nonsense at its best shows how poetry should be read as a linguistic artifact—a premise taken seriously by the modernist poets and the New Critics.

In the poetry of nonsensical double-talk, Carroll was preceded by Edward Lear and followed by the Dadaists, Surrealists, Italian Futurists, Gertrude Stein, and E. E. Cummings, among others. No one, including Carroll himself, has since achieved the artless perfection of "Jabberwocky." One reason is that his followers were not playing; hyperconscious of having a serious theme to impart, they used nonsense in its various forms as a metaphor for meaninglessness in a fundamental philosophical sense. Carroll reduces, dehumanizes, and demystifies the content of his poem to make a toy or game out of it. Modernists such as T. S. Eliot used similar techniques, in the "Sweeney" poems or the game of chess in *The Waste Land* (1922) for example, to comment on the deracination of modern urban humans and the failure of communication in a world bereft of external standards of value. *The Hunting of the Snark*, Carroll's longest and most elusive poem, is more problematic, however, and has perhaps justifiably invited comparison with modern literature of the absurd.

### THE HUNTING OF THE SNARK

In the preface to *The Hunting of the Snark*, Carroll hints playfully that his new poem is "to some extent" connected with "the lay of the Jabberwock" and thus is sheer nonsense. He also directs attention to Humpty-Dumpty's portmanteau principle, suggesting that *The Hunting of the Snark* will be a sequel, a culmination of that delightful form of wordplay. Readers are likely to feel misled. The only new words are its principle terms, "Snark" (snail and shark, snarl and bark) and "Boojum" (boo, joke, and hokum?); the rest of the coined words are stale borrowings from "Jabberwocky." In other important ways, the similarities that Carroll leads his readers to expect only set off the differences.

"Jabberwocky" is quintessentially innocent wordplay; *The Hunting of the Snark*, appropriately subtitled

*An Agony in Eight Fits*, is embedded with elaborately juxtaposed systems of rules, involving syllogistic logic, numerical and alphabetical sequences, equations, diagrams, paradoxes, acrostics, and puns, none of which is consistent with common sense, one another, or their own terms. All this is the stuff of Wonderland, but Alice's mediating perspective is missing here. In Snarkland, the reader plays Alice's role, which consists of searching for the rules of a game that defies logic. Reading the poem is like being at a Mad Hatter's tea party culminating in a riddle with no answer, or worse—a joke at the reader's expense.

In *The Hunting of the Snark*, Carroll has reversed the terms of "Jabberwocky." It is a mad sea adventure and another mock-heroic quest in ballad form for an elusive monster that associates with the Bandersnatch and the Jubjub bird. However, while the Jabberwock is dispensed with promptly, the Snark is never even seen, unless by the nearest thing to a protagonist, the Baker, who vanishes before he can reveal what he has perhaps found. The search and the monomania inspiring it are the whole story until the very end, where the poem more or less self-destructs. In short, the Snark or, as it turns out to be, Boojum wins, and in a most disconcerting way.

The narrative begins in medias res as the Bellman lands his crew on an island that he swears three times is "just the place for a Snark," reasoning backward that "what I tell you three times is true." The reader learns that this sort of reasoning is typical, and not only of the Bellman: The chart he has provided for his approving crew, who scorn conventional signs, is an absolute blank, and his only "notion for crossing the ocean" is to tinkle his bell. Circular reasoning also seems to be behind the plot, which veers off into digressions and returns to confirm a course that it has arbitrarily taken. The reader finds that the Baker's uncle has warned his nephew that some Snarks are Boojums, which if met with, make one "softly and suddenly vanish away." The Baker sees a Snark, whereupon he "softly and suddenly vanishe[s] away" along with the Snark, who "*was* a Boojum, you see," as the narrator smugly informs the reader. The tale is uniquely anticlimactic. The reader is not disappointed, satisfied, or surprised; one laughs partly in bewilderment. It is not only that the

Snark—or Boojum—wins, but also one is never quite sure what it is other than the visible darkness that swallows the Baker, much less why it is. Carroll's answer seems to be a mocking "why not?"

It is no wonder that some of its early critics found this agony in eight fits less than funny. Carroll, besieged with questions as to whether it contained a hidden moral, answered inconsistently, saying alternately that it was nonsense, that he did not know, and, in two letters of 1896, that it concerned the search for happiness. As his response suggests, the poem almost demands allegorization but resists it just as strongly. The problem is shown in the wide divergence and crankiness of the various attempts to explain the poem. One explanation of the poem is that it is an antivivisectionist tract, another idea is that it is a tragedy about a business slump; other suggestions have been that the poem is a satire on Hegelian philosophy, an Oedipal quest, or an existentialist piece.

If the poem is regarding a search for happiness, as Carroll suggested, then the existentialist reading (offered by Carroll scholar Martin Gardner) seems inevitable, for the threat of annihilation is an undercurrent in all Carroll's major works. Accordingly, the search becomes life, the Snark an illusory goal, and the Boojum the absurd reward—the vanishing signifies nothingness, the void. If the poem has symbols, they certainly point in an absurd direction. The Bellman's blank map suggests the human condition of knowing nothing, neither where humanity is nor where it is going. Because the bowsprit gets mixed with the rudder, the ship goes backward, and considering the entire absence of dimension or direction, it goes nowhere other than the route that is the Bellman's arbitrary choice. The Baker, Everyman, dreams each night of a "delirious fight" with the Snark and thus exists in a state of eternal anxiety, dreading his inevitable extinction. He is so anxious, in fact, that he stammers, "It is this, it is this" three times before he can state precisely the "notion" that he "cannot endure."

## LOGIC AND LANGUAGE

Carroll would not have been able to endure such an allegory, however, for he had a slightly different notion of the absurd: the agonizing but strangely pleasing illogicality of language. Moreover, he consistently evaded or sublimated his existential concerns in the game of logic and language. Carroll was less Sartrean than Wittgensteinian, concerned less with the philosophical absurd, the fundamentals of being and nothingness, than with the epistemological absurd, the problem of how humankind knows and does not know, and knowledge's fallacy-prone medium, language. His direction is indicated in what absorbs the reader's attention, the poem's labyrinth of nonsense structures. The title refers to the reader's hunting of the Snark, and the Snark is the problem of the poem, its "hidden meaning" which "vanishes" or was a Boojum, nothing, all along.

The peculiar way the poem was composed—backward—suggests how it should be read, as a puzzle or riddle. The last line flashed into Carroll's mind when he was out strolling. He wrote a stanza to fit the nonsense line and made up the poem to fit the stanza. In other words, he derived the poem's premises (If the Snark is a Boojum, you will vanish away) from its conclusion: "For the Snark *was* a Boojum, you see." The poem works much like the absurd syllogisms found in his *Symbolic Logic: Part I, Elementary* (1896). Its premises are fallacious, its conclusion a joke, and its terms absurd; a parody of systematic reasoning, it exists to be puzzled out.

Language is frequently the culprit, for it can generate systems that relate to nothing but themselves. The prefatory poem to Gertrude Chataway is a key to showing how language works in *The Hunting of the Snark*. The preface at first appears to be a nostalgic meditation on childhood, but on second reading it turns up an acrostic spelling Gertrude's name, and on third reading a double acrostic: The first word of each quatrain spells out "Girt Rude Chat Away." The surface poem has been generated from an arbitrary system, in a sense another language, imposed on it, and it exists primarily for the sake of the game, the search for correspondences. It means little more than the playful joke that it is.

Similarly, in *The Hunting of the Snark*, one tries to follow the arbitrary systems embedded in it to learn the rules of the game. The rules are not only made arbitrarily but also applied inconsistently, continuously bringing one back to the primary fact of the poem. The rule underlying the plot follows the Bellman's example

of going nowhere; the quest veers off into tales within the tale as the various crew members pursue their monomanias. The Butcher and Beaver cross paths and become diverted from the Snark hunt at first by what they take to be the "voice of the Jubjub," then by the Butcher's threefold mock-syllogistic proof that it is the voice of the Jubjub, then by his elaborately circular equation for proving his proof is threefold, and finally in a natural history lesson on the attributes of the Jubjub. The pair's memory of the Jubjub's song, the reader learns later, has cemented their friendship, but whether they heard it or whether it ever existed is impossible to know. "The Barrister's Dream" turns the Snark hunt into another level of unreality and logical absurdity. It is about a Kafkaesque trial in which the Snark, the defending lawyer, takes over the functions of prosecution, jury, and judge, and pronounces the defendant, a pig who is already dead, guilty. In this sequence, as in the poem as a whole, the Snark symbol takes on so many potent meanings that it becomes meaningless.

As a dream and a tale within the tale, the mad trial is less bewildering than the "rule of three" motif with which the poem begins. Three is a teasing potential symbol, suggestive of the Trinity, but Carroll sets up the Bellman's absurd rule of "What I tell you three times is true" as a parody of the syllogism, reducing it to a kind of ultimate question-begging. Not only does it fail logically, but also no one applies it the same way, so that no conclusions whatsoever can be drawn. The Baker is on the verge of confessing and thus effecting his ultimate fear of extinction when he stammers three times "It is this, it is this," but never says what "It" is. The incident becomes a mock omen of sorts, but one that finally mocks the reader's utter inability to establish a causal relation. Similarly, the Butcher applies the rule to prove that he hears the "voice of the Jubjub" but alters his terms to "note" and "song," leaving the Jubjub somewhere between reality and fiction. The final absurdity is that the rule apparently works, if at all, only for the Bellman, who has said, "What *I* tell you three times is true" (italics added).

In Snarkland, classification is subordinate to the arbitrary principle of alphabetical priority. The normal impulse is to view the motley crew as a microcosm, the world satirized as a "ship of fools," especially when the crew members are designated by their occupations: the Bellman, Baker, Barrister, Billiard-marker, Banker, Bonnet-maker, Broker, Boots, Butcher—and absurdly, the Beaver, who is a lacemaker designated by species. The Beaver's inclusion signals that the whole crew "means" no more than the "rule of B." Even the "rule of B" fails, however, when one applies it to characters in general—perhaps to conclude that the Snark was a Boojum by alphabetical priority. The Jubjub bird is the one exception. One is reminded of that other sea tale of the nursery, "Rub a dub dub,/ Three men in a tub,/ The Butcher, the Baker, the Candlestick-maker," in which the characters exist for the sake of rhyme rather than reason.

The Baker, however, throws out classification altogether, for he is of the null class, Nobody. He can bake only bride-cake, for which there are no ingredients; therefore he is a nonbaker. He is distinguished for the number (forty-two) of items he has left behind upon boarding ship: his umbrella, watch, jewels, clothes—and, worst of all, his name. He is therefore called anything from "Thing-um-a-jig" to "Toasted-cheese."

The Snark is the Baker in reverse in this respect; a hodgepodge of identities and attributes, it has five "unmistakable" marks: its hollow but crisp taste, its habit of rising late, its slowness in taking a jest, its fondness for bathing machines, and its ambition. The methods of hunting a snark are equally disparate and unrelated to its marks. One may seek it with thimbles, care, forks, hope, a railway-share, smiles, and soap. The final absurdity is that all this information fails to connect with the main problem, the Boojum—with one notable exception.

For those searching for a solution to the puzzle, Carroll ended the poem with a multileveled joke that refers back to the poem itself as a joke. The third characteristic of a snark is its "slowness in taking a jest." Should "you happen to venture on one,/ It will sigh like a thing that is deeply distressed," and it is particularly antagonized by a pun, at which it "looks grave." The poem ends in a grand mock apocalypse except for the intrusion, between the sighting of the Snark and the vanishing, of a pun, the worst of all bad jokes, which appears to have been the fatal provocation. As the

Baker ecstatically wags his head, accompanied by the cheers and laughter of the crew, the Butcher puns, "He was always a desperate wag." The Baker then vanishes in the middle of the awful word, squeaking out "It's a Boo—" before "jum" is absorbed into a sound that "some fancied" a vast "weary and wandering sigh."

Carroll turns his mock-epic ballad into something like a conundrum, a riddle with an answer buried in an absurd pun. In so ending the hunt, he makes the poem dissolve like the Cheshire cat, leaving the reader with no more than the mocking terms of the last line: "For the Snark *was* a Boojum, you see." The pun refers back through the poem, reverberating mockery. "Wag" reminds the reader that the Baker is a joker, a joke, and thus nobody, really. His annihilation therefore means nothing; he never *was* to begin with, except as a figment in the dream of Carroll, the "wag" desperate to end a "bad" joke. A conundrum that puns on its being a bad joke, *The Hunting of the Snark* is the most dazzling of Carroll's infinite regressions. It regresses back into "Boojum," a metaphor for nothing, specifically the nothing that the poem means other than what it sounds like: "Boo!" enunciated jokingly and with a little hokum tossed in.

Because the poem was, as the Bellman suggests in the second fit, "so to speak, 'snarked'" from the beginning, it also teaches a lesson in the illogic of language. If one "solves" the riddle in the planted conundrum, one commits an error of the post hoc variety, moreover resting the burden of proof on the arbitrary connotations of language—puns on the "grave" look of the Snark and the purely speculative meanings of the "weary and wandering sigh" that "some fancied" they heard. The poem shows how language can seem to tell how and why the Boojum, happened but also tells nothing. This elaborate riddle is a metaphor for the impossibility of knowing final causes, and the Snark's vanishing into a Boojum is the palpable unknown.

*The Hunting of the Snark* illustrates Carroll's nonsense technique at its most complex, correlating fundamental philosophical paradoxes with semantic play. Here as elsewhere, he turns a "joke" into a poem by turning the joke on itself, thus making it embody the elusive thing that it is about. This antididactic "nonsense" has sometimes been seen as an evasion of the poem's responsibility to mean—and an evasion of the issue of meaninglessness that it raises, as well.

Paradoxically, it is precisely because it *is* that evasion that the poem speaks so well to modern readers. By sublimating his anxiety in a logician's "agony," Carroll's formal and semantic absurdities embody the urgent epistemological issues of the modern world. In another sense, then, Carroll's humor is not an evasion but rather a metaphor for what everyone must do if they do not drop out: play the game. As such, Carroll's point corresponds with that of James Joyce and the postmodern fabulators, who explore the absurd facility through which language creates reality and meaning.

OTHER MAJOR WORKS

LONG FICTION: *Alice's Adventures in Wonderland*, 1865; *Through the Looking-Glass and What Alice Found There*, 1871; *The Wasp in a Wig: The "Suppressed" Episode of "Through the Looking-Glass and What Alice Found There,"* 1977.

SHORT FICTION: "Bruno's Revenge," 1867.

NONFICTION: *A Syllabus of Plane Algebraical Geometry*, 1860; *An Elementary Treatise on Determinants*, 1867; *Euclid and His Modern Rivals*, 1879; *Twelve Months in a Curatorship*, 1884; *Three Months in a Curatorship*, 1886; *The Game of Logic*, 1887; *Curiosa Mathematica, Part I: A New Theory of Parallels*, 1888; *Curiosa Mathematica, Part II: Pillow Problems Thought During Wakeful Hours*, 1893; *Symbolic Logic, Part I: Elementary*, 1896; *Feeding the Mind*, 1907; *The Diaries of Lewis Carroll*, 1954; *The Unknown Lewis Carroll*, 1961; *The Magic of Lewis Carroll*, 1973; *The Letters of Lewis Carroll*, 1979 (Morton N. Cohen, editor); *The Oxford Pamphlets, Leaflets, and Circulars of Charles Lutwidge Dodgson, Vol. 1*, 1993; *The Mathematical Pamphlets of Charles Lutwidge Dodgson and Related Pieces*, 1994.

CHILDREN'S LITERATURE: *A Tangled Tale*, 1885; *Sylvie and Bruno*, 1889; *Sylvie and Bruno Concluded*, 1893; *"The Rectory Umbrella" and "Mischmasch,"* 1932; *The Pig-Tale*, 1975.

BIBLIOGRAPHY

Ackerman, Sherry L. *Behind the Looking Glass*. Newcastle, England: Cambridge Scholars, 2008. Ackerman analyzes the works of Carroll and discusses his life.

Bloom, Harold, ed. *Modern Critical Views on Lewis Carroll*. New York: Chelsea House, 1987. Part of a standard series of literary essays, the selections are good but contain specialized studies that may not help the beginner. Bloom's brief introduction is a good starting point in critically assessing Carroll.

Carroll, Lewis. *The Annotated "Hunting of the Snark": The Full Text of Lewis Carroll's Great Nonsense Epic "The Hunting of the Snark."* Edited with a preface and notes by Martin Gardner. New York: W. W. Norton, 2006. Contains numerous notes on the work and descriptions of Carroll's world and life.

Cohen, Morton N. *Lewis Carroll: A Biography*. New York: Random House, 1995. Cohen has devoted more than three decades to Carroll scholarship. Using Carroll's letters and diaries, he has provided what many regard as a definitive biography. Illustrated with more than one hundred of Carroll's photographs and drawings.

Fordyce, Rachel, ed. *Lewis Carroll: A Reference Guide*. Boston: G. K. Hall, 1988. An exhaustive annotated bibliography of primary and secondary material on Carroll.

Gray, Donald J., ed. *Alice in Wonderland*. New York: Norton, 1992. This Norton critical edition is an ideal starting point for the beginner, not only because of the nearly two hundred pages of background and critical essays, but also because of the helpful annotations on the two *Alice* novels. Many of the best essays from other collections are reprinted here, making it a reference work of first resort.

Jones, Jo Elwyn, and J. Francis Gladstone. *The Alice Companion: A Guide to Lewis Carroll's Alice Books*. New York: New York University Press, 1998. Full of information, a commentary on the people and places that make up Carroll's and Alice Liddell's world in mid-nineteenth century Oxford, and a sourcebook to the extensive existing literature on this period in Carroll's life.

_____. *The Red King's Dream: Or, Lewis Carroll in Wonderland*. London: Jonathan Cape, 1995. A look at Carroll in his life and times, including his literary milieu, friends, and influences. Bibliographical references, index.

Leach, Karoline. *In the Shadow of the Dreamchild: A New Understanding of Lewis Carroll*. Chester Springs, Pa.: Peter Owen, 1999. Leach uses new research to argue that the long-standing image of Lewis Carroll, his exclusively child-centered and unworldly life, his legendary obsession with Alice Liddell, and his supposedly unnatural sexuality, are nothing more than myths.

Thomas, Donald. *Lewis Carroll: A Portrait with Background*. London: John Murray, 1996. Thomas surmises the formative influences on Carroll's personality and intellect as he describes Victorian England. An invaluable guide for readers who want to understand how manners and ideas changed during Carroll's lifetime.

*Linda C. Badley*

# ANNE CARSON

**Born:** Toronto, Ontario, Canada; June 21, 1950

PRINCIPAL POETRY

*Short Talks*, 1992
*Glass, Irony, and God*, 1995
*Plainwater: Essays and Poetry*, 1995
*Autobiography of Red: A Novel in Verse*, 1998
*Men in the Off Hours*, 2000
*The Beauty of the Husband: A Fictional Essay in Twenty-nine Tangos*, 2001
*Decreation: Poetry, Essays, Opera*, 2005
*Nox*, 2010

OTHER LITERARY FORMS

Anne Carson is a crossover artist. In addition to being a prizewinning poet, she is an accomplished essayist and has a deep understanding of drama and storytelling. The subtitles of her books show her determination to think across genres and even art forms. *Autobiography of Red*, her work based on poetry fragments by ancient Greek poet Stesichoros, is presented as "a novel in

verse," while *The Beauty of the Husband*, her meditations on the relation of beauty and truth in the poetry of John Keats, becomes "a fictional essay," and the poems that make up this essay are conceived as verbal parallels to the tango in music and dance. Carson writes essays in the word's original sense of "attempts" or "trials." Her essays grow out of a deep scholarly knowledge of classical texts, especially in Greek, but show a wide eclectic knowledge of world literature and an eye for resemblances across centuries and between languages.

ACHIEVEMENTS

Anne Carson first found a wide audience with "Kinds of Water," an essay on the pilgrimage route to Compostella in northern Spain. Written as a pilgrim's diary and presenting a series of epigrammatic reflections on pilgrimage as a metaphor, the essay was chosen for inclusion by essayist Annie Dillard in *The Best American Essays of 1988* (1988), edited by Dillard and Robert Atwan. Over the next decade, Carson contributed many poems to journals. After they were collected in her first major book of poetry, *Glass, Irony, and God*, Carson won many awards, including a Lannan Literary Award for Poetry in 1996, the Pushcart Prize in 1997, the Griffin Poetry Prize in 2001 for *Men in the Off Hours*, and both the Los Angeles Times Book Prize and the T. S. Eliot Prize for Poetry in 2001 for *The Beauty of the Husband*. She also won a Guggenheim Fellowship in 1998 and a MacArthur Fellowship in 2000.

BIOGRAPHY

In interviews, Anne Carson has been extremely reticent about her private life. The few details she has let slip, mostly in her poems, suggest why: frequent moves in childhood, a father who developed Alzheimer's, a brother with a serious drug addiction, an early marriage that ended in divorce, and much loneliness. She has, however, talked about the influence of religion in her earliest years. Raised by middle-class parents in Toronto and other towns in the province of Ontario, she was a devout Roman Catholic as a child. She was fascinated by stories of saints and pilgrims and by the imagery associated with cults of the saints. She became an ardent reader and thought deeply about words.

In high school, Carson began to study ancient Greek, guided by her Latin teacher. After graduating, she entered St. Michael's College in the University of Toronto, where she found the student revolution in full swing. She dropped out periodically but always continued her education elsewhere, sometimes at an art school, sometimes in another city. She married and for a while used the surname Giacomelli. Nevertheless, she persisted in her study of Greek and completed a bachelor of arts in classics at the University of Toronto in 1974. Guided by Emmet Robbins, the "beloved teacher" to whom she later dedicated a volume of translations, she then earned both a master's degree (1975) and a doctorate (1981) in classics.

Carson wrote her doctoral thesis on love lyrics in ancient Greek. Its playful title, "Odi et Amo Ergo Sum," shows her penchant for thinking across centuries and disciplines, for it combines two Latin tags—from the Roman poet Catullus and the French philosopher René Descartes—to say, "I hate and love, therefore I am." Behind the clever line is the serious proposition that people form their sense of identity through the power of and often interrelated emotions of hatred and love. While teaching at Princeton University, Carson reduced the proposition to a single word: "bittersweet," the English equivalent of Sappho's *glukopikron* (literally, "sweet-bitter"). She reworked her study of bittersweet love in ancient poetry into a book of short essays, *Eros the Bittersweet: An Essay*, published by Princeton University Press in 1986. The book was widely praised and led to a professorship at McGill University and a series of visiting professorships at American universities from Emory University to the University of California, Los Angeles.

While living in New York in the mid-1980's, Carson met Ben Sonnenberg, the founder of the literary magazine *Grand Street*, and showed him her nonacademic writings. He gave her the encouragement she needed to persist in her penchant for blurring genres and crossing over from literary to nonliterary topics.

In the 1990's, she came to the attention of Gordon Lish, the legendary editor at Alfred A. Knopf, best known for his hand in the stories of Raymond Carver. Lish encouraged the crossing of boundaries and the mixing of genres, and drawing from a wide variety of

her writings, creative and classical, he helped her fashion *Plainwater*, a series of poems and essays. Other volumes followed from Knopf, including *Autobiography of Red*, an attempt to create the inner life of the ancient poet Stesichoros, of whose writings only fragments survive, *The Beauty of the Husband*, a series of verses inspired in part by the poetry of Keats; and *Decreation*, a collection that includes the opera libretto of that title as well as poems, short essays, and even a film script. With the books came influence, especially for the rethinking of eros in Western culture, and celebrity unusual for such a cerebral poet, including mention in an episode of the television series *The L Word* (2004-2009).

## ANALYSIS

Anne Carson was hardly the first to blur genres. Some of her "short talks" recall the stories of Virginia Woolf, the parables of Franz Kafka, or the sayings of Gertrude Stein, who are indeed among her favorite authors. There is even a tradition of classicists, from Friedrich Nietzsche onward, who have brought the insights of their scholarship to original writing, including Norman O. Brown and Peter Kingsley, and a similar tradition of poets such as Ezra Pound and H. D., who have insisted on bringing the translator or commentator into their work.

Carson's special fascination is with fragments— lines of ancient poetry that survive only in quotations and testimonials by other ancient writers. She especially likes those fragments that, like those she has translated from Stesichoros, contain the germ of whole stories and lie open to a range of interpretations.

Critics have responded differently to Carson's poetic technique. Some have found it amazingly refreshing, while others have contended that she hides behind myth and allusion or uses them to isolate herself from both her readers and the personal pain out of which many of her best poems seem to have emerged.

### PLAINWATER

*Plainwater*, subtitled "Essays and Poetry," opens with a series of poems inspired by fragments from an ancient poet, to which are added "interviews" with the poet. The volume ends with a long prose piece on "The Anthropology of Water" (the human significance of water), which is subdivided into three parts. The celebrated "Kinds of Water" is about the pilgrim road to Compostella, with a personal introduction; "Just for the Thrill: An Essay on the Difference Between Men and Women" is a parallel study of camping in North America; "Swimming" is a brief essay that acts as a kind of memoir of Carson's older brother, as if he were the author as well as the swimmer. "Short Talks" could be characterized as a series of prose poems, but also as a series of essays. Selections have been reprinted in anthologies of American poetry and short stories. The lyrics gathered in "The Life of Towns" offer three dozen different lines of perspective on the phenomenon of a collective character. Those in "Canicula di Anna" (literally, "the dog days of Anna") have fifty-three carefully imagined moments in the life of a woman in sixteenth century Italy.

### AUTOBIOGRAPHY OF RED

Carson's most sustained effort at creating new poetry out of old is *Autobiography of Red*, her "autobiography" of a sixth century B.C.E. poet. Although the name Stesichoros means "chorus master" and suggests that he wrote festival songs before the birth of Greek drama, the autobiography concentrates on the fragments that survive from his epic poem on the mythological figure of Geryon, Medusa's grandson who herded red cattle on a red island at the world's edge. In addition to learned commentaries on Stesichoros's other fragments, notably concerning Helen of Troy, Carson adds what only a fertile imagination can provide: his autobiography, written in forty-seven poems and an "interview" with the Greek poet.

### THE BEAUTY OF THE HUSBAND

Carson takes autobiography much more literally in *The Beauty of the Husband*, a sequence of twenty-nine numbered poems about her relationship with the handsome boy she married out of high school and loved for years after their divorce. The beauty in the book's title is at once the source of her husband's power over her and the transcendent quality that the English Romantic poet Keats found in his "Ode on a Grecian Urn," in which he stated that "Beauty is truth, truth beauty." In the last poem in the collection, Carson says, "To say Beauty is Truth and stop// . . . This was my pure early thought." In other words, her first intent was to enjoy

beautiful things for their own sake; however, she has learned that the beauty was within her from the beginning and, therefore, could not just be apprehended. What remains is the memory of conversations that went nowhere, usually in alternating lines. For example:

> Listen I only wanted one thing to be worthy of you.
> Are you mad.
> No yes it doesn't matter.
> You live a counterfeit life.
> Yes yes but for you.

The first speaker is the husband. For all his absences and infidelities, he is not a villain. He is presented rather as what an impersonal fate has given the poet.

### OTHER MAJOR WORKS

PLAY: *The Mirror of Simple Souls: An Opera Installation*, 2003 (opera libretto).

NONFICTION: *Eros the Bittersweet: An Essay*, 1986; *Economy of the Unlost: Reading Simonides of Keos with Paul Celan*, 1999.

TRANSLATIONS: *Electra*, 2001 (of Sophocles' play); *If Not, Winter: Fragments of Sappho*, 2002 (of Sappho's poetry); *Grief Lessons: Four Plays by Euripides*, 2006; *An Oresteia*, 2009 (of Aeschylus, Sophocles, and Euripides).

### BIBLIOGRAPHY

Baker, David, and Ann Townsend, eds. *Radiant Lyre: Essays on Lyric Poetry*. Saint Paul, Minn.: Graywolf Press, 2007. Includes essays that discuss Carson's treatment of eros, her love poems, and her influence.

Carson, Anne. "Gifts and Questions: An Interview with Anne Carson." Interview by Kevin McNeilly. *Canadian Literature/Littérature canadienner* (Spring, 2003): 12-25. Touches on Carson's ways of drawing inspiration from her childhood and her surroundings, as well as her extreme reluctance to talk about her personal life.

Davenport, Guy. Introduction to *Glass, Irony, and God*, by Anne Carson. New York: New Directions, 1995. Compares Carson to such literary modernists as T. S. Eliot, James Joyce, and Ezra Pound, who also drew on classical poets and philosophers. Written by a poet who shares Carson's background in the classical studies.

Pérez Gómez, Alberto. *Built upon Love: Architectural Longing After Ethics and Aesthetics*. Cambridge, Mass.: MIT Press, 2006. Extends Carson's thoughts about eros to architectural form and practice. Includes a discussion of urban imagery in her poems.

Roth, Michael S. "The Art of Losing Oneself." *Raritan* 27, no. 3 (Winter, 2008): 158-167. Discusses Carson's capacity to connect disparate literary and artistic figures across cultures and centuries, opening these figures up to new possibilities of understanding.

Solway, David. "What's Wrong with Annie?" In *Director's Cut*. Erin, Ont.: Porcupine's Quill, 2003. Playing devil's advocate, Solway suggests that Carson's recent fame as a poet is undeserved. Accuses her of "frivolity and affectation" and her supporters of celebrating mediocrity.

Upton, Lee. *Defensive Measures: The Poetry of Niedecker, Bishop, Glück, and Carson*. Lewisburg, Pa.: Bucknell University Press, 2005. Emphasizes Carson's use of myth and archetype to bring other times into conjunction with her own. Considers this a form of "defense" against the demands modern society places on artists.

*Thomas Willard*

---

# GEORGE CHAPMAN

**Born:** Near Hitchin, Hertfordshire, England; c. 1559
**Died:** London, England; May 12, 1634

PRINCIPAL POETRY

*The Shadow of Night*, 1594
*Ovid's Banquet of Sense*, 1595
*Hero and Leander*, 1598 (completion of Christopher Marlowe's poem)
*Euthymiae Raptus: Or, The Tears of Peace*, 1609
*An Epicede or Funerall Song on the Death of Henry Prince of Wales*, 1612

*Eugenia*, 1614
*Andromeda Liberata: Or, The Nuptials of Perseus and Andromeda*, 1614
*Pro Vere Autumni Lachrymae*, 1622

OTHER LITERARY FORMS

In his own time, George Chapman was equally well known for his poetry and plays. As a leading playwright for the children's companies that performed at the Blackfriars Theatre, he achieved distinction in both tragedy and comedy. His greatest success in tragedy was *Bussy d'Ambois* (pr. 1604, 1641), followed by a sequel, *The Revenge of Bussy d'Ambois* (pr. c. 1610). His other tragedies include the two-part *The Conspiracy and Tragedy of Charles, Duke of Byron* (pr., pb. 1608), as well as *The Tragedy of Chabot, Admiral of France* (pr. c. 1635; with James Shirley) and *The Wars of Caesar and Pompey* (pr. c. 1613). Chapman also composed the first comedy of humors, *An Humourous Day's Mirth* (pr. 1597), and romantic and satiric comedies, including *The Blind Beggar of Alexandria* (pr. 1596), *The Gentleman Usher* (pr. c. 1602), *All Fools* (pr. c. 1604), *Monsieur d'Olive* (pr. 1604), *The Widow's Tears* (pr. c. 1605), and *May Day* (pr. c. 1609).

ACHIEVEMENTS

George Chapman regarded his English translations of Homer's *Odyssey* (c. 725 B.C.E.; English translation, 1614) and *Iliad* (c. 750 B.C.E.; English translation, 1611) as "the work that I was born to do." An arduous, demanding task that occupied him for thirty years, his translation was commissioned by the youthful son of James I, Prince Henry, whose untimely death at the age of eighteen left the poet without a patron. Although he continued to work in spite of the lack of patronage, he turned to the stage and to original verse to make his living. That John Keats found looking into Chapman's Homer a thrilling discovery, which he subsequently immortalized in a sonnet, is a tribute to the quality of this work, which has not been generally admired. Chapman's translation has receded into obscurity as an archaic and quaint achievement.

Chapman's original poetry, which is characterized by a remarkable range of theme and style, is often considered difficult or even obscure for the modern reader. A largely philosophical poet, Chapman incorporates challenging intellectual concepts and images in his verse. Some of his more explicitly philosophical poems, such as *The Shadow of Night*, are rich in Neoplatonic thought, an abstruse subject. Others, such as his continuation of Christopher Marlowe's unfinished *Hero and Leander*, convey ideas through emblematic and iconographic techniques. In the poem *Ovid's Banquet of Sense*, he writes partly in the manner of the erotic epyllion and partly in the more Metaphysical vein of sharply intellectual conceits, while in *Euthymiae Raptus*, he writes more in the style of satiric allegory, with pointed, polished heroic couplets. Some of his poems are occasional, such as the *Andromeda Liberata*, which celebrates the notorious marriage of the king's favorite, Robert Carr, to Lady Frances Howard, later implicated in the murder of Thomas Overbury. Chapman's choice of the Andromeda myth to represent Frances's unconsummated marriage with the young earl of Essex was extremely tactless, and the poet had to publish a justification and explication of what was interpreted as an insulting poem. Some of his poems are mystical, as is the first section of *Euthymiae Raptus*, where he relates his encounter with the flaming vision of Homer's spirit, which inspired him to his translation, and as is the "Hymn to Our Savior," included in the collection called *Petrarch's Seven Penitential Psalms* (1612), and concerned with the theme of transcending fleshly experience. Finally, Chapman also wrote two fine elegies, *Eugenia*, written on the death of Lord Russell, and *An Epicede or Funerall Song on the Death of Henry Prince of Wales*, on the death of the much loved and genuinely lamented Prince Henry.

## BIOGRAPHY

Although George Chapman was born into a fairly wealthy and well-connected family, it was his fate to suffer poverty because he was the younger son. Not much is known about his early years. He spent some time at Oxford but did not take a degree there. After a brief period of service in the household of a nobleman, he saw military action on the Continent, participating in the Low Country campaigns of 1591-1592. His first literary accomplishment was the publication of *The Shadow of Night*, an esoteric poem reflecting his association with a group of erudite young scholars, including Sir Walter Ralegh, all of whom reputedly dabbled in the occult. His publication of a continuation of Marlowe's *Hero and Leander* clearly established his relationship with the ill-fated younger playwright.

His own early career as a playwright barely supported him, and he was imprisoned for debt in 1600. After his release, he attempted to supplement his income from the stage by seeking patronage for his nondramatic poetry. The youthful Prince Henry, a genuine patron of the arts, offered to support Chapman's proposed translation of the complete works of Homer. Unfortunately, the death of the young prince put an end to such hopes, and Chapman was never to be completely free from the specter of poverty. When he collaborated with Ben Jonson and John Marston on the city comedy *Eastward Ho!* (pr., pb. 1605), Chapman found himself in prison again, this time for the play's supposed slander against Scots. Largely through his own epistolary efforts directed toward both the king and other dignitaries, Chapman and fellow prisoner Jonson were released without having their noses slit, the usual punishment for the given offense.

After his release from prison, Chapman continued to write both plays and poetry and to continue the laborious work of translation even without the aid of patronage. He eventually became an acknowledged literary success in all these endeavors, honored in Joshua Poole's *The English Parnassus* (1657), lauded by the critic Francis Meres as one of the best in both comedy and tragedy, and believed by some modern critics to have been the "rival poet" of William Shakespeare. Although little is known about his later years, historian Anthony à Wood's description of the elderly poet as "reverend, religious, and sober" suggests his continuing dedication to the serious art of poetry and to the subtle art of life.

When Chapman died at the age of seventy-four, his monument was fashioned by Inigo Jones, the noted theatrical designer with whom Chapman had collaborated on court masques. His Latin inscription was "Georgis Chapmanus, poeta Homericus, Philosophers verus (etsi Christianus poeta)."

ANALYSIS

George Chapman's poetry is unusually diversified. It does not reveal a consistent individual style, technique, or attitude, so that an initial reading does not immediately divulge a single creative mind at work. A skilled experimenter, Chapman tried the Metaphysical style of John Donne and the satirical heroic couplet in a manner anticipating John Dryden, and in his translations reverted to the archaic medieval fourteener. His poetry is also unusually difficult. His allusions are often esoteric, his syntax strained or convoluted, and his underlying ideas verging on the occult. His is not primarily a lyrical voice, and his verses are almost never musical. For Chapman, the content of poetry is supreme, and the poet's moral calling is profound. His work, in consequence, is essentially didactic.

Chapman's poetics, as expressed in scattered epistles and dedications attached to his verses, help clarify his intentions and to reveal the purpose behind what may strike the reader as willful obscurity. Philosophically, Chapman was a Platonist, and he was well read in Neoplatonic writings. His poetic theories are a metaphorical counterpart to Platonic dualism. The fact that precious minerals are buried in the ground rather than easily available on the surface suggests to Chapman that the spirit of poetry must lie beneath the obvious surface meaning of the words. The body of poetry may delight the ear with its smooth, melodious lines, but the soul speaks only to the inward workings of the mind. Thus, Chapman rejects the Muse that will sing of love's sensual fulfillment in favor of his mistress Philosophy, who inspires the majesty and riches of the mind. The reader must not be misled by the outer bark or rind of the poems, to use another of his analogies, but should rather seek the fruit of meaning deep within. Scorning the profane multitude, Chapman consecrates his verses to those readers with minds willing to search.

### ALLEGORY AND EMBLEM

Two of the techniques that Chapman employs most often to achieve his somewhat arcane didactic purposes are allegory and emblem. His poems are frequently allegorical, both in the sense that he introduces personified abstractions as spokespeople for his ideas and in the sense that a given event or personage stands for another. He reveals his allegorical cast of mind in dealing with such objects as love, war, or learning by envisioning them as personified abstractions, clothing them in appropriate iconographical garments, and situating them in emblematic tableaux. His use of emblems thus grows out of his allegorical mode of thought. Drawing on the popular emblem books of the Renaissance, he depicts scenes or images from nature or mythology as iconographic equivalents of ideas. A torn scarf, for example, becomes a confused mind, and an uprooted tree a fallen hero. The technique is symbolic and highly visual, but static rather than dramatic.

Since Chapman regarded his Homeric translations as his major poetic mission in life, he did not consider his own poetry as a great achievement. He regarded the calling of the poet with great seriousness, however, and his poems as a result have much of importance to say. In spite of their difficulty and partly because of it, his unusual poems speak to the sensitive reader willing to dig below the often formidable surface.

### THE SHADOW OF NIGHT

Chapman's first published poem, *The Shadow of Night*, consists of two complementary poems, "Hymnus in Noctem" and "Hymnus in Cynthiam." The first is a lament, the second a hymn of praise. The first is concerned with contemplation, the second with action. Both celebrate the intellect and assert the superiority of darkness over daylight. Sophisticated in structure, esoteric in allusion, and steeped in the philosophy of Neoplatonism, the work is a challenge to the general reader.

The object of lament in "Hymnus in Noctem" is the fallen state of the world. Chapman contrasts the debased world of the present day, rife with injustice, to the primal chaos that existed when night was ruler. In that time before creation, there was harmony, for chaos had soul without body; but now bodies thrive without soul. Humans are now blind, experiencing a "shadow" night of intellect that is a reversal of genuine night. The poet then calls upon the spirit of night to send Furies into the world to punish humans for their rampant wickedness. He will aid the Furies by castigating sinful humankind in his verses and by writing tragedies aimed at moral reformation.

As night is praised for its creative darkness, the source of inner wisdom, daylight is regarded negatively, associated with whoredom, rape, and unbridled lust. Chapman warns the great virgin queen, here equated with the moon goddess, that an unwise marriage would eclipse her virtue, removing her from the wise mysteries of the night and exposing her to brash daylight. The poem ends with an emblematic scene, as Cynthia appears in an ivory chariot, accompanied by comets, meteors, and lightning.

"Hymnus in Cynthiam" proclaims praise for Cynthia as pattern of all virtue, wisdom, and beauty, at once moon goddess, divine soul of the world, and Queen Elizabeth I. Cynthia is portrayed here in her daytime role, and the active life of daylight is contrasted to night as the time for contemplation. During the day, Cynthia descends from the moon to earth, where she fashions a nymph named Euthymia, or Joy, out of meteoric stuff. Out of the same vapors, she creates a hunter and his hounds. Chapman's narrative of a shadowy hunting scene is probably based on the myth of Acteon and his hounds. The poet's allegorical version of the myth depicts the hunt as appropriate to the daylight, a time of sensual and otherwise sinful behavior. The object of the hunt is debased joy, which attracts the base affections (the hunting hounds), and the rational souls, submitting to passion (the hunters on their horses), follow after. This pageant of desire is essentially unreal, however, as daytime itself is unreal, and Cynthia promptly disposes of the hounds when night arrives. The mystical darkness offers an opportunity for true joy found only in the spiritual and intellectual fulfillment made possible by contemplative, nocturnal solitude.

The major themes of this two-part poem are thus the Platonic vision of inward contentment, the true joy afforded by contemplation, and the superiority of darkness over daylight. Writing partly in the ancient tradition of the Orphic hymns, Chapman veils his meaning in a mysterious religious atmosphere. The allegorical hunt and the emblematic scenes are, however, vividly described and poetically clear. The poem ends with a tribute to the immutability of Cynthia. Although the original harmony of primal darkness is gone, Cynthia will try to restore virtue to the degenerate world.

### OVID'S BANQUET OF SENSE

Prefacing the volume of poems featuring Chapman's next major poem, *Ovid's Banquet of Sense*, is a brief statement of the poet's convictions about his craft.

Here he admits that he hates the profane multitude, asserts that he addresses his intentionally difficult poetry to a select audience, and appeals to those few readers who have a "light-bearing intellect" to appreciate his arcane verses. At first reading, the 117 stanzas of this poem do not seem very esoteric at all. Ostensibly, *Ovid's Banquet of Sense* follows the currently popular mode of the erotic epyllion, as exemplified in William Shakespeare's *Venus and Adonis* (1593). If one follows Chapman's warning, however, one feels committed to search beneath the surface for deeper meaning.

The narrative structure of the poem follows the experience of Ovid in the garden of his mistress Corinna. In the garden, he is able to feast his senses on her while he remains hidden from her view. The first of his senses to be gratified is hearing, or *auditus*, as Corinna plays on her lute, fingering the strings and sweetly singing delightful lyrics. Then, as Ovid draws somewhat nearer to where she is seated at her bath, he is greeted by the overpowering fragrance of the spices she uses in bathing her body. His sense of smell, or *olfactus*, is now enchanted. Moving closer to the arbor to see her more clearly, Ovid is next able to feast his eyes on her inviting nakedness. The longest section of the poem is devoted to this languorous satisfaction of sight, or *visus*. The poet indulges in lavish sensual imagery to describe the experience. Ovid's intense pleasure in the sight of his unclothed mistress ends abruptly, however, when she looks into her glass and suddenly sees him staring at her. Quickly wrapping herself in a cloud, she reproaches him for his immodest spying on her private bath. Ovid defends himself very convincingly, arguing that since his senses of hearing, smell, and sight have already been satisfied, he has a right to ask for a kiss to satisfy his sense of taste, or *gustus*. She grants him the kiss, which is also described in richly provocative language, but the ingenious would-be lover then argues for gratification of the ultimate sense, touch, or *tactus*.

Corinna is responsive to Ovid's seductive plea, and when he lightly touches her side, she starts as if electrified. Like Ovid, the reader is aroused by the prolonged erotic buildup, but both are doomed to a letdown. At this climactic moment, the scene is interrupted by the sudden appearance of several other women, Corinna's friends, who have come to paint in the garden. Having led both his hero and his reader to expect more, the poet now drops the narrative with a somewhat smug remark that much more is intended but must be omitted.

In the final stanza, Chapman refers to the "curious frame" of his poem, suggesting that it resembles a painting, wherein not everything can be seen and some things having to be inferred. The meaning beneath the surface, about which Chapman warned the reader, emerges from this awareness. The reader, like Ovid, has been put in the position of voyeur. Chapman has tricked the reader into false expectations and into assuming a morally ambiguous role. Indeed, the frustration seems worse for the suspenseful reader than for the abandoned lover, for Ovid is not disappointed by the anticlimax but instead is inspired to write his _Ars amatoria_ (c. 2 B.C.E.; _Art of Love_, 1612). It is the reader who is trapped forever inside the curious frame. In spite of this trickery, _Ovid's Banquet of Sense_ is likely to be one of Chapman's most appealing poems for the general reader. The primarily pictorial imagery, the undercurrent of irony, the escalating narrative movement through the five sensory experiences, and the vivid sensuality of Ovid's responsiveness to his mistress combine to make it at once a dramatic and lyrical reading, unlike Chapman's usual heavy didacticism.

### "A CORONET FOR HIS MISTRESS PHILOSOPHY"

The didactic point of view is supplied by "A Coronet for His Mistress Philosophy," the series of interlinked sonnets that follow _Ovid's Banquet of Sense_. Offering a moral perspective on the ambiguity of _Ovid's Banquet of Sense_, this series is circular, as its title implies, with the last line of each sonnet becoming the first line of the next, coming full circle at the end by repeating the opening line. Here Chapman renounces the Muses that sing of love's "sensual emperie" and rejects the violent torments of sexual desire in favor of devotion to the benevolent mistress, Philosophy. The poet's active and industrious pen will henceforth devote itself to the unchanging beauty of this intellectual mistress, whose virtues will in turn inspire him to ever greater art.

### HERO AND LEANDER

Chapman's continuation of Christopher Marlowe's _Hero and Leander_ is also a narrative love poem. Marlowe's premature death in 1594 left unfinished his po-

etic version of this tragic love story from the classical world. What survives of Marlowe's work is two sestiads, which leave the narrative incomplete. Chapman undertook to finish the poem, publishing his own four sestiads in 1598. Chapman claims that he drank with Marlowe from the fountain of the Muses, but acknowledged that his own draft inspired verse more "grave" and "high." Whereas Marlowe had been concerned with the physical beauty of the lovers and exalted their passion, Chapman takes a moral approach to their relationship, condemning their failure to sacramentalize physical love through marriage.

In the third sestiad, the goddess Ceremony descends from heaven to reproach Leander. Her body is as transparent as glass, and she wears a rich pentacle filled with mysterious signs and symbols. In one hand, she carries a mathematical crystal, a burning-glass capable of destroying Confusion, and in the other, a laurel rod with which to bend back barbarism. Her awesome reproof of Leander likens love without marriage to meat without seasoning, desire without delight, unsigned bills, and unripened corn. Leander immediately vows to celebrate the requisite nuptial rites. Meanwhile, Hero lies on her bed, torn between guilt and passion. Her conflict gradually gives way to resolution as thoughts of her lover's beauty prevail over her sense of shame. In the end, love triumphs over fear.

In the fourth sestiad, Hero offers a sacrifice to the goddess Venus, who accuses her devotee of dissembling loyalty to her. Venus darts fire from her eyes to burn the sacrificial offering, and Hero tries to shield herself from the rage of the deity with a picture of Leander. The divinely repudiated offering is clearly a bad omen.

The fifth sestiad is introduced with Hero's expression of impatience for night to bring her lover. The marriage theme is also reinforced in the form of an allegorical digression about a wedding staged and observed by Hero to make the time seem to pass more quickly and pleasantly. The wedding scene also introduces a wild nymph, Teras, a name given to comets portending evil. Teras sings a tale to the wedding party, following it with a delicately lyrical epithalamium. As she finishes the song, however, she suddenly assumes her comet nature, and with her hair standing on end, she glides out of the company. Her back appears black, striking terror into the hearts of all, especially Hero, who anxiously awaits her lover.

Night finally arrives in the sixth sestiad, bringing with it the tragic climax of the poem. Determined to swim the Hellespont to see Hero, Leander takes his fatal plunge into the stormy sea. Vainly he calls upon first Venus, then Neptune, for help against the violent waves tormenting his body, but the swimmer is doomed. Angry Neptune hurls his marble mace against the fates to forestall the fatal moment, but to no avail. The god then brings the drowned body of Leander on shore, where Hero sees him and, grief-stricken, dies calling his name. Moved by pity, the kindly god of the sea transforms the lovers into birds called Acanthides, or Thistle-Warps, which always fly together in couples.

Although Chapman's continuation lacks the classical grace and sensuous imagery of Marlowe's first two sestiads, it is poetically successful. His poem has a variety of styles, ranging from classical simplicity to Renaissance ornateness. The inevitable tragic plot is deepened by Chapman through the theme of moral responsibility and the role of form and ritual in civilization. He uses personified abstractions effectively, as in the case of the imposing goddess Ceremony, and he demonstrates his mythmaking skills in the person of the comet-nymph Teras. His emblematic verse intensifies the visual effects of the poem, often making it painterly in the manner of *Ovid's Banquet of Sense*. In his poem, his didacticism is happily integrated with story and character rather than being imposed from without. Of all of Chapman's poems, *Hero and Leander* is the most accessible to the contemporary reader.

### EUTHYMIAE RAPTUS

*Euthymiae Raptus* is a substantial (1,232-line) allegorical poem. The immediate occasion that called it forth was the truce in the war with the Netherlands, which had been brought about through the mediation of King James, and the poem is dedicated to the young Prince Henry. It is, however, much more than an occasional poem. Partly autobiographical and partly philosophical, as well as partly topical, it is a major achievement.

The opening *inductio* has primary autobiographical value. Here Chapman relates his personal, mystical encounter with the spirit of Homer. The poet had been meditating when he suddenly perceived a figure clothed in light with a bosom full of fire and breathing flames. It is at once obvious that the apparition is blind, though gifted with inward sight. The spirit then identifies itself as Homer, come to praise Chapman for his translations and to reveal the reason why the world has not achieved a state of peace. Invisible until this moment, Homer has been inspiring Chapman's poetry for a long time. At the end of this section, Homer shows Chapman a vision of the lady Peace mourning over a coffin, despairing the death of Love. A brief *invocatio* follows, spoken by the poet, while Peace, pouring out tears of grief, prepares to speak.

The third and major section of the poem is structured as a dialogue between Peace and the poet as Interlocutor. This section is essentially a thoughtful and impassioned antiwar poem. Typical of Chapman's philosophical cast of mind, the poem probes the cause of war throughout human history. Peace's lament for Love clearly relates the fact of war to the death of Love, but why has Love died? Peace attributes the demise of Love to lack of learning among people in general. Genuine learning, according to Peace, implies a capability for original thought, without which humans can never arrive at a true knowledge of God. It is this deprived state of mind and soul that has made war possible. The failure of learning keeps humans from knowing God, thereby bringing about the end of Love, and Love is necessary to sustain Peace.

The concept of learning elucidated in this poem is not so much intellectual as ethical. Learning is viewed as the art of good life. Chapman cites three classes of men in particular who are dangerous enemies of this ideal: first, the active men, who aim only at worldly success and reject learning in favor of ruthlessly pursuing ambition; second, the passive men, who simply neglect learning while they waste time in mere pleasures; and, finally, the intellective men, who debase learning because they pursue their studies only for the sake of social and financial reward. Genuine learning, to be attained for its own sake, empowers the soul with control over the body's distracting passions and perturbations. Those who are called scholars in this world are all too often mere "walking dictionaries" or mere "articulate clocks" who cannot "turn blood to soul" and who will therefore never come to know God. These three categories of nonlearners and perverters of learning willingly enter the destructive toils of war.

### LEGACY

These four long poems, along with the elegies *Eugenia* and *An Epicede or Funerall Song on the Death of Henry Prince of Wales* and the occasional pieces, *Andromeda Liberata* and *Pro Vere Autumni Lachrymae*, represent most of Chapman's original verse. There are also a few short pieces called *Petrarch's Seven Penitential Psalms*, consisting largely of translations. The body of Chapman's original poetry is thus limited in scope but impressive in quality. Although *The Shadow of Night* is occasionally obscure in poetic diction, and although *Euthymiae Raptus* at times proves slow going in its didacticism, both of these poems are nevertheless rich in thought and are distinguished by several passages of high poetic caliber. *Ovid's Banquet of Sense* and *Hero and Leander* are actually two of the finest narrative poems of the English Renaissance.

The modern reader has much to gain from Chapman. His subtlety and irony appeal to the intellect, and his emblematic and metaphorical language pleases the aesthetic imagination. His is a distinctive Renaissance voice not circumscribed by the formulaic patterns of that highly conventional age. He is above all a serious writer, committed to the lofty calling of poetry as a vehicle of ideas through the medium of figurative language.

### OTHER MAJOR WORKS

PLAYS: *The Blind Beggar of Alexandria*, pr. 1596 (fragment); *An Humourous Day's Mirth*, pr. 1597; *Sir Giles Goosecap*, pr. c. 1601 or 1603; *The Gentleman Usher*, pr. c. 1602; *All Fools*, pr. 1604 (wr. 1599; also known as *The World Runs on Wheels*); *Bussy d'Ambois*, pr. 1604, 1641; *Monsieur d'Olive*, pr. 1604; *Eastward Ho!*, pr., pb. 1605 (with John Marston and Ben Jonson); *The Widow's Tears*, pr. c. 1605; *The Conspiracy and Tragedy of Charles, Duke of Byron*, pr., pb. 1608; *May Day*, pr. c. 1609; *The Revenge of Bussy d'Ambois*, pr. c. 1610; *The Masque of the Middle Temple and Lincoln's Inn*, pr. 1613 (masque); *The Wars of Caesar and Pompey*, pr. c. 1613; *The Ball*, pr. 1632 (with James Shirley); *The Tragedy of Chabot, Admiral of France*, pr. 1635 (with Shirley).

TRANSLATIONS: *Iliad*, 1598, 1609, 1611 (of Homer); *Petrarch's Seven Penitential Psalms*, 1612; *Odyssey*, 1614 (of Homer); *Georgics*, 1618 (of Hesiod); *The Crown of All Homer's Works*, 1624 (of Homer's lesser-known works).

### BIBLIOGRAPHY

Beach, Vincent W. *George Chapman: An Annotated Bibliography of Commentary and Criticism*. New York: G. K. Hall, 1995. A reference work providing extensive bibliographical information on Chapman. Index.

Bradbrook, Muriel C. *George Chapman*. London: Longman, 1977. This brief general overview of Chapman's life and work contains sections on the lyric poetry, including *Hero and Leander* and the translations of Homer and Hesiod. The individual chapters on the comedies and tragedies conclude that Chapman's modern reputation will have to be based on only the best of the lyrics plus two tragedies, *Bussy d'Ambois* and the two parts of the Byron play.

Donno, Elizabeth Story. "The Epyllion." In *English Poetry and Prose, 1540-1674*, edited by Christopher Ricks. New York: Peter Bedrick Books, 1986. Donno's essay provides an excellent introduction to Elizabethan narrative poetry, especially the mythological variety. Her account of Chapman's narrative verse is sound; another chapter covers his dramatic poetry. The index offers good cross-referencing. Includes a select bibliography.

Hulse, Clark. *Metamorphic Verse: The Elizabethan Minor Epic*. Princeton, N.J.: Princeton University Press, 1981. Hulse has accomplished the most complete redefinition of Elizabethan narrative poetry of modern times. His account of Chapman and his contribution is thorough and complete. The bibliographical apparatus is professional.

Huntington, John. *Ambition, Rank, and Poetry in 1590's England*. Urbana: University of Illinois Press, 2001. Huntington uncovers a form of subtle social protest encoded in the writings of aspiring Elizabethan poets, and argues that these writers invested their poetry with a new social vision that challenged a nobility of blood and proposed a nobility of learning instead. Huntington focuses on the early work of Chapman and on the writings of others who shared his social agenda and his nonprivileged status.

Kermode, Frank. "The Banquet of Sense." In *Shakespeare, Spenser, Donne*. London: Routledge & Kegan Paul, 1971. Presents a revelatory commentary on Chapman's narratives; the insights are simply unparalleled. Includes substantial notes, a bibliography, and an index.

MacLure, Millar. *George Chapman: A Critical Study*. Toronto, Ont.: University of Toronto Press, 1966. This full-scale critical analysis of all of Chapman's writings includes extensive coverage of his narrative poetry and integrates it well with the rest of his life's work. MacLure pays particular attention to his diction and his use of poetic devices. Contains an index, notes, and a bibliography.

Snare, Gerald. *The Mystification of George Chapman*. Durham, N.C.: Duke University Press, 1989. The title is slightly misleading. This first-rate critical analysis actually attempts to demystify Chapman and his work, which had suffered from a prevailing view that it was unnecessarily obscure and contorted. Snare's discussions are lucid. Includes good notes, an index, and a bibliography.

Spivack, Charlotte. *George Chapman*. New York: Twayne, 1967. An admiring study accessible to the nonspecialist, the book begins with a biographical section and then reviews Chapman's literary work. Spivack considers him an important poet, a great playwright, and a consistent philosopher—a more favorable assessment than that of other critics.

Striar, Brian. "Chapman's *Hero and Leander* V. 62." *Explicator* 66, no. 4 (Summer, 2008): 202-204. A focused analysis of the phrase, "Teras with the ebon thigh," in *Hero and Leander*, in which the author suggests that Chapman might have meant "ebur," short for "eburin" (ivory and ox-blood), instead.

Waddington, Raymond B. *The Mind's Empire: Myth and Form in George Chapman's Narrative Poems*. Baltimore: The Johns Hopkins University Press, 1974. Focuses exclusively on Chapman's poems; analyzes them exhaustively and relates them to their cultural and historical backgrounds. Emphasis is on structural analysis. Contains an extensive bibliography, index, and complete notes.

*Charlotte Spivack*

---

# THOMAS CHATTERTON

**Born:** Bristol, Gloucestershire, England; November 20, 1752
**Died:** London, England; August 24, 1770

PRINCIPAL POETRY

*Poems Supposed to Have Been Written at Bristol, by Thomas Rowley, and Others in the Fifteenth Century*, 1777 (Thomas Tyrwhitt, editor)
*Poetical Works*, 1871 (Walter Sheat, editor)

OTHER LITERARY FORMS

Thomas Chatterton, obsessed with the creation of antique literature, did not limit his artistic output to the poetry he pretended was written by the fictional fifteenth century cleric Thomas Rowley, even though any claim for his literary recognition is based on the Rowley collection. Although Chatterton's prose writings are generally imitative and unoriginal, at a time of rampant literary forgeries, he created a pastiche of spurious historical manuscripts, maps, drawings, genealogies, and pedigrees for credulous, if historically ignorant, dilettantes seeking to restore the lost treasures of Great Britain. Such exotic esoterica served two purposes: substantiation of his insistent claim of authenticity for his fraudulent poetry, and a means to ingratiate himself with the circle of those who passed as the literate antiquarians in Bristol. In 1768, at the dedication of the new Bristol Bridge across the Severn River, he fabricated and had published a minutely detailed account of the three-hundred-year-old ceremonies on the occasion of the opening of the old bridge; the manuscript, he attested, was found in St. Mary Redcliffe Church and appeared to be written in authentic Old English.

In exploring various modes for presenting the life

and character of his medieval hero William Canynges (Chatterton dropped the final "s"), a famous mayor of Bristol under Henry VI in the fifteenth century, Chatterton created illuminating letters from both him and his wholly fictional priest-confessor, the poetic monk Thomas Rowley. Such epistolary prose develops both the historical fabric of the era, the War of the Roses, and the vivid characters of the correspondents. Another nonpoetic aspect of Chatterton's work was his political essays and letters, similar to those of the infamous and anonymous eighteenth century satirist "Junius." The influence of Alexander Pope is certainly obvious in these epistles. Two other curious prose works of Chatterton deserve special notice. One is "The Ryse of Peyncteynge yn Englande wroten bie T. Rowleie, 1469, for Mastre Canynge," a work the unknown adolescent sent to the famed antiquarian Horace Walpole, hoping he would include it in his *Anecdotes of Painting in England* (1762-1771). The other is *The Last Will and Testament of Me, Thomas Chatterton, of the City of Bristol* (1770), enabling him to break his indenture to a lawyer by accompanying it with the threat of suicide.

During his final brief episode in 1770 as a Grub Street hack writer in London, Chatterton wrote whatever the journalistic market would bear; short stories and musical works attest his creative versatility. The prose selections fall roughly into two classes, the sentimental and the comic. Examples of the former were often moralistic: "Maria Friendless," a plagiarism from Samuel Johnson; "The False Step"; and "The Unfortunate Fathers," each filled with pathos and appeals to conventional emotional response. Comic works were generally picaresque tales in the manner of Tobias Smollett, reflecting Chatterton's own necessity to live by his wits. Had these short stories been refined, rather than turned out hastily in a desperate bid for recognition and remuneration, Chatterton might have developed into a skilled and entertaining writer of fiction.

At this time of frenetic literary activity in London, Chatterton completed one satiric burletta and several other fragments. This dramatic form, a popular eighteenth century version of the pantomime, was generally a drama in contemporary English rhyme, and Chatterton's contribution to this genre was *The Revenge* (pr.

1770), a low burlesque opera with mythological characters as well as miscellaneous songs. He also wrote several scenes of another set in the London social scene entitled *The Woman of Spirit* (pb. 1770).

## ACHIEVEMENTS

Riding the crest of popular Gothic taste, Thomas Chatterton freed himself of the excessive mannerisms of that eighteenth century genre—those narratives stressing only terror—and instead created tales portraying a benevolent and simple medieval world of minstrelsy where courtesy, beauty, and honor were the hallmarks. There can be little question, however, that far more significant than the value of any of his literary works is his sensational, intriguing, and complex life viewed from the standpoint of his influence as a precursor of those poets and other artists who venerated him as a heroic martyr in the cause of aesthetic creativity. Born in the age of neoclassicism, Chatterton, because of his incredible dedication to the medieval world, tapped that vein of primitive wonder, escape, and sensibility to both nature and humanity that would become Romanticism.

From Chatterton, the major Romantic writers took the inspiration to defy not only what many increasingly saw as rampant philistinism but also many of their themes, modes, and structural forms. Samuel Taylor Coleridge's "Kubla Khan," John Keats's "To Autumn," and William Wordsworth's "Resolution and Independence" are only several of the major Romantic works in which Chatterton's influence echoes. It was not from his poetry, however, that the Romantics took greatest inspiration. The notion of isolated genius, neglected and scorned by unfeeling worldly hypocrites, coalesced around the mythic circumstances of the life and death of Chatterton; sympathetic artists championed as their epitome the poet who died so young. Wordsworth's reference to him as "the marvellous Boy" represents the esteem in which he was held, and Keats especially appears inspired both personally and poetically by the youth, for his "Endymion" was "inscribed to the memory of Thomas Chatterton."

The influential Victorian Robert Browning sought to vindicate Chatterton, citing his abandonment of the fraudulent Rowleyan world and his determined attempt to begin a new, creative life in London as evidence of a different direction from that as a literary forger. To the romantic Pre-Raphaelites, at the height of England's industrialization, Chatterton persisted as a symbol of escape from an increasingly hostile society, and it is the pathos-filled painting of Chatterton's death scene by one of its members, Henry Wallis, that has forever fixed the young poet's fate in the conscience of the world. Late nineteenth century devotion to Chatterton might be viewed as a projection of unresolved contemporary dilemmas, but for whatever reason, the eighteenth century poet's myth began to fade with the rising popularity of realism. Perhaps it is only now, when people strive to assert their identity in the face of technological anonymity, and when the cult of the youthful dead apotheosizes its casualties, that the image of Chatterton will again rise, not as the desperate literary impostor, not even as a poet, but as one who sacrificed everything on the altar of creative individualism.

## BIOGRAPHY

No consideration of Thomas Chatterton can proceed without first relating the poet to Bristol, the city of all but the final four months of his brief life, particularly the environs of the St. Mary Redcliffe Church. Born in its shadow, Chatterton was the posthumous son of another Thomas, a sometime schoolmaster, choir singer, and sexton of the imposing edifice. His mother, a colorless woman of whom little is known, struggled after her husband's death to maintain the household, which also included her mother and a daughter. Poverty haunted the family, and young Thomas was forced to be educated in charity schools.

Judged dull and unteachable at the age of five at the schoolhouse in which he had been born, the child retreated into a private world of his own, haunting the church and yard of St. Mary Redcliffe, to whose legends and corners he was introduced by his uncle, a sexton. He taught himself to read from a huge black-letter Bible and soon became an omnivorous reader. The solitary child early discovered Edmund Spenser's *The Faerie Queene* (1590, 1596) and scraps of history books, and they, along with the church building and his family, were his life.

When he was eight, Chatterton was admitted to a

*Thomas Chatterton* (Time & Life Pictures/Getty Images)

charity school at Colston Hospital, a seemingly benevolent yet oppressive situation, especially to one of Chatterton's sensitivity. At the school, little more than a training prison, success in the mercantile world was the only goal of the exhausting regime, and after seven difficult years, young Chatterton's nature took logical form as a result: the dreamy, romantic escapist coexisting with the cynical, expedient realist. In the eighteenth century, Bristol physically resembled a medieval city with its walls, gates, winding narrow streets, and primitive facilities. The spirit of the city, however, was far from that of the Middle Ages, for it bustled with industry and the overpowering necessities of mercantilism. The getting and spending of money were the bases of both civic and personal status, and in such a competitive environment, young Chatterton soon realized that he must find a way to secure both fame and wealth as a means of escaping unimaginative, prosaic contemporary Bristol.

At age fourteen, he was indentured for a term of seven years to a local attorney, John Lambert, as a scrivener apprentice. Although the work was not arduous, the youth chafed in his position, his excessive pride suffering as he saw himself a slave. With little to do in the office, Chatterton had plenty of time to pore over what volumes of ancient lore he could find, as well as to write voluminously. It was from Lambert's office that he sent forth his fabricated history of the old Bristol Bridge as well as the myriad other "antique" manuscripts and other documents that filled both his time and imagination. It was also in Lambert's office that the mythical fifteenth century priest-poet Thomas Rowley first appeared; Chatterton calculated that fame was far easier to attain for a fifteenth century monk than for an obscure eighteenth century youth.

Also, while serving as Lambert's clerk, Chatterton found an eager market for his fraudulent historical documents among the tradespeople of Bristol who entertained a taste for antiquity; he palmed off bogus pedigrees as well as manufactured manuscripts that found their way into a history of Bristol then being written. It is important to recognize that eighteenth century Bristol was a provincial, middle-class citadel with few intellectual resources. Even elsewhere in England knowledge of that country's history was sketchy and legend-riddled, especially of that period before Elizabeth's reign. Only because true scholarship was practically nonexistent could the amateurish and naïve forgeries of Chatterton go undetected.

Every free moment that Chatterton could escape from the watchfulness of his master, he spent roaming around Bristol, especially in the precincts of St. Mary Redcliffe, with its hidden manuscript-filled chests. It was there, in the so-called muniment room over the North Porch, that he claimed he found the Rowley manuscripts that he wanted to share with the world.

Chatterton's life as a drudging scrivener increasingly oppressed him. He felt he must escape and be free to pursue his creative work, and one means seemed to be recognition by the literary world with its consequent rewards. In an attempt to effect this goal, the young apprentice offered "ancient poems" to James Dodsley, the London publisher of Thomas Percy's *Reliques of Ancient English Poetry* (1765), a relatively successful collection of authentic old ballads as well as some spurious additions. Receiving no reply, Chatterton then audaciously, but anonymously, wrote to Horace Walpole,

a titled and wealthy literary figure, seeking to secure him as a patron, much in the same relationship as William Canynge's to Rowley.

Initially intrigued, Walpole responded to Chatterton's letter enthusiastically, but then the youth ill-advisedly revealed his identity and position in life, enclosing several Rowleyan manuscripts. The patrician Walpole recoiled from the brash youth, sensing a hoax, especially in the light of the current literary furor swirling around the Ossianic poems claimed by James Macpherson to be translated from third century bardic writings. Walpole himself had also exploited the rage for the antique, for the first edition of his popular *The Castle of Otranto* (1765) masked the author's true identity with the claim that the medieval terror story was "translated by William Marshal, Gent, from the original Italian of Onuphrio Muralto" and supposedly first printed "at Naples in the black letter, in the year, 1529."

Because Walpole was famous, influential, and wealthy, because he had a private printing press at his "Gothick" estate, Strawberry Hill, and because he too had perpetrated literary imposture, Chatterton had sensed that he would be enthusiastic about the Rowley poems. In point of fact, the ingenious Bristol youth could not have been more mistaken. After consulting other literary figures to confirm his suspicions, Walpole self-righteously and vindictively condemned Chatterton's work as fraudulent and wrote the youth an insulting letter advising him to stick to his trade as a scrivener. Walpole, however, kept Chatterton's manuscripts for several months, despite three importuning letters requesting their return; Walpole eventually complied with no word of explanation for the delay.

His hopes for publication and patronage shattered, Chatterton became more determined to escape Bristol by any means he could, assuming that if he could work in London, he would find an appreciative audience. However, service to Lambert bound him, so he devised a plot to threaten suicide, including execution of a last will and testament. The lawyer now had suffered enough from his difficult and insolent apprentice, so the indenture was broken, and Chatterton departed immediately for London. He was seventeen years old.

Demonstrating herculean efforts to secure literary recognition and a means to survive there, the youth undertook a spartan existence, accepting any and all menial writing jobs he could locate. Still proud and unyielding, however, and writing falsely optimistic letters home, he refused help from those who recognized his increasingly desperate situation, and four months after he arrived in London, starving, alone, and ill, he drank arsenic and died at the age of seventeen.

ANALYSIS

At the outset, the troubling problem of Thomas Chatterton's identity as a literary forger must be faced. Traditionally, critics either piously indict him as an outcast and impostor in the history of belles lettres or else strain to rationalize the situation and dismiss his fabrications as only a boyish prank. Resolution of these biased positions is both impossible and unnecessary, for moral judgments are outside the task of criticism, the works themselves providing its proper basis. Thomas Rowley, like any of Chatterton's other characters, stands beside Hamlet or Huckleberry Finn as a literary creation; the fraudulent means by which he was introduced to the world are irrelevant.

Chatterton's poetry falls into three loose classes: the Rowley cycle, the non-Rowleyan miscellany, and that of the final stage in both Bristol and London. In all, there is evidence of Chatterton's remarkable but uneven efforts to vary his modes and to perfect his poetic skills to secure patronage and an audience. In the Rowley poems, he seeks to glorify his idealized patron figure, the fifteenth century William Canynge, and to represent both the reality and spirit of the imaginary Bristol as an enlightened cultural center in those times under his leadership. It is here that Chatterton's greatest artistic gifts lie: in his ability both to realize fresh and imaginative worlds of experience within realistic temporal and geographic frames, and to offer brief but beautiful glimpses into the pleasures of living in such a Camelot-like society.

Certainly much poetry that Chatterton wrote is lost, for he was not careful to preserve his work. Also, when depressed, he frequently tore his poems to bits. It is not surprising that a boy as precocious as Chatterton would be this erratic or that he would begin composing at a very early age, even though such juvenilia, whether religious hymns, didactic fables, or satiric verses, is

highly derivative. The most noteworthy of these early works is "Eleanoure and Juga." Although the controversy over the date of its composition is as yet unresolved, most critics place it in 1764, making it the first of Chatterton's poems of antiquity. Also, it was the only Rowley poem published during the lifetime of the poet, appearing in *Town and Country Magazine* in 1769. A simple pastoral ballad in form, with a vivid setting but little characterization or plot, it features two speakers, young maidens left alone by the deaths of their lovers in the Wars of the Roses, who relate their sorrows to each other, futilely seeking comfort in their mutual loss.

THE BLANK YEARS

All his early work was completed by 1764, and then for a four-year period—what has been called his blank years—no Chatterton literary production remains. The boy poet apparently was totally occupied in creating in his imagination the idealized Bristol of the fifteenth century, the incredibly detailed setting for Thomas Rowley's poems, as well as perfecting the special antique language in which he could express himself through Rowley. The minor poems that began to appear in 1768 are mostly nonlyrical and include several satires, both anti-Tory diatribes and attacks on specific individuals. Chatterton also wrote a number of insipid love lyrics for another youth to use in his courtships, but critics suggest that they too are in fact satiric, with only the poet recognizing them for what literary mockery is there. Quite moving is a 1769 elegy on the death of the poet's good friend Thomas Phillips: "Now rest, my muse, but only rest to sleep." Another side of his genius is found in his lines addressed to Horace Walpole after the connoisseur's denial of help, even though the youth was persuaded not to send them to his would-be patron. He scorns Walpole's mean heart and accuses him of perpetrating the same scheme—literary deceit—for which he now scorns Chatterton. Finally, the poet asserts that he and Rowley will stand united forever, even after Walpole has gone to hell.

NON-ROWLEYAN POEMS

Significant among the later non-Rowleyan poems of 1770 were the three "African Eclogues," the first written in Bristol and the final two in London. These poems indicate Chatterton's sensitivity to the plight of blacks and perhaps his identification with them as victims of unwarranted cruelty. Also part of the final Bristol period were the long, trenchant, satiric poem "Resignation," assailing contemporary governmental crises, and the philippic "Kew Gardens" (originally conceived as "The Whore of Babylon"), a malicious attack on the unpopular dowager princess of Wales. "The Exhibition: A Personal Satyr" was the initial Chatterton London poem, an extended prurient and vulgar treatment of the trial of a Bristol cleric on morals charges. Shortly thereafter, Chatterton returned to his concern with African suffering in the sensuous and primitive "Narva and Mored" and "The Death of Nicou."

### "AN EXCELENTE BALADE OF CHARITIE . . ."

The last Rowley poem, "An Excelente Balade of Charitie, as wroten by the gode Prieste Thomas Rowley, 1464," was in fact written in July, 1770, little more than a month before the poet's suicide. As in much of Chatterton's work, the style and dramatic imagery is more Elizabethan than medieval. The stanzaic form is rime royal, with occasional modifications of the iambic pentameter lines with a Spenserian Alexandrine. A fifteenth century version of the biblical Good Samaritan story, it is more personal than anything Chatterton had previously written. He alludes poignantly to his own helplessness and need in that of the "moaning pilgrim" with no home, friends, or money. Most critics now view it as one of his finer achievements, even though it was rejected when Chatterton offered it for publication.

### ROWLEYAN YEARS

Other than the early "Eleanoure and Juga" and the late "An Excelente Balade of Charitie," the main body of the poems Chatterton wrote and attributed to the Bristol monk Rowley are of the year beginning in the summer of 1768, and on this Middle Ages romance cycle rests any claim to genius that might be sought for the precocious youth. Chatterton even fabricated a prose biography to authenticate his ancient poet, having him born in Somersetshire at Norton Malreward, a loyal servant of the Yorkist monarch Edward IV and a dutiful parish priest. In the prose narrative "The Storie of Wyllyam Canynge," the priest describes in the first person his lifelong friendship and patronage with the Bristol mayor, making continual reference to Canynge's

enthusiastic reception of certain of his dramatic poems. In Rowley's words, here Chatterton seems to be describing Canynge as the character of the father-patron figure of his own dreams. Chatterton's main concern in the Rowleyan works was with heroism, both traditional and particular, especially that exemplified by the secular mayor Canynge. Several of the poems glorify heroes of old, pointing to obvious correspondences with the bourgeois Canynge, while villains demonstrate negatively those characteristics absent in this fifteenth century paragon.

If the juvenile effort "Eleanoure and Juga" is considered as outside the Rowley canon by nature of its probable composition by a twelve-year-old poet, then the highly dramatic "Bristowe Tragedie: Or, The Death of Syr Charles Bawdin" is the first extant Rowley poem. A vivid and dramatic character portrayal, the story is told in slow-moving ballad stanzas of the authentic political execution of the brave Sir Charles and his fellow conspirators for high treason against the obdurate King Edward IV, despite the moving intercession for clemency by William Canynge. Bawdin's defiance and courage as he stood fast by his principles under duress form the bulk of the narrative, but Canynge too demonstrates bravery and loyalty to his friends at considerable personal risk. Chatterton here employs all the stock ballad features as they were utilized by poets seeking to revive the medieval form, and to a certain degree, he succeeds in dramatizing a historical event of epic dimensions.

The next four Rowleyan works are all fragmentary: "Ynn Auntient Dayes," "The Tournament" (also known as "The Unknown Knyght," and the "Battle of Hastyngs," I and II. Metrically in all these epics except "The Tournament," Chatterton uses a pentameter line, while the stanza forms vary. Subject matter still concerns itself with heroic fifteenth century Bristol happenings and characters, and the familiar St. Mary Redcliffe Church looms dominantly in the settings, especially in "Ynn Auntient Dayes." Heraldic trappings and pageantry obviously form the background for "The Tournament," but even several rewritings failed to give life to this linear narrative of medieval competition. In dealing initially with the Battle of Hastings, Chatterton tackled a familiar and difficult topic, much inspired by

Alexander Pope's handling of the Trojan siege in his 1715 to 1718 translation of Homer's *Iliad*, but the vast material was more than he could handle, particularly the repetitious and overly realistic butchery of the combatants. Despite the scale of the battle, however, little heroic fervor was generated in his first effort, so bloodthirsty in tone. Sensing increasing powers, he again took up the subject, but the second digressive version, in truth, is little better than the first, except for a few isolated instances of well-handled poetic passages, especially the descriptions of Stonehenge and the Salisbury Plain.

At the same time that Chatterton was undertaking and then abandoning these four ambitious works, he also wrote four celebrations of traditional heroes in the lyric mode, thereby exalting the role of the hero into which he intended Canynge to take his place. These poems are significant for reasons both biographic and aesthetic: Two based on fictional saints associated with the glorification of Saint Mary Redcliffe were designed to accompany Chatterton's spurious prose "Bridge Narrative" and enhance his reputation as an antiquarian to secure local patronage; another, the Pindaric ode "Songe toe Ella," introduces the Bristol Castle lord, the Saxon hero of the tragic poem "Aella: A Tragycal Enterlude," Chatterton's most ambitious and successful Rowleyan work; the fourth was probably bait for Horace Walpole; and all reveal a new spirit of experimentation, a higher degree of complexity in Chatterton's formulation of the Rowleyan language, and the growth of confidence in the poet.

Chatterton produced five Rowleyan verse dramas: the comic "The Merrie Tricks of Laymyngetowne," the Bristol local-color-filled "The Parlyamente of Sprytes" that celebrated Canynge's heroic deeds, "Aella," "The Tournament: An Interlude," and the fragmentary "Goddwyn: A Tragedie." Other than in occasional successful passages—for example, in the ringing martial chorus with its startling personifications praising Saxon freedom and the heroic Harold in "Goddwyn"—in none of these works, with the exception of "Aella," does Chatterton handle his material maturely and produce memorable poetry. "Aella," his masterpiece, stands alone as his most ambitious and successful verse drama and demonstrates his ability to sustain complex

dramatic interest. For these reasons some attention should be given to its plot.

### "AELLA"

The brave Aella, warden of Bristol Castle, marries the lovely Saxon Birtha, who is secretly loved by his friend, the dishonorable Celmonde. After the newlyweds are serenaded by minstrels at their wedding banquet, a messenger announces a new Danish invasion threatening the West Country, and Aella, although torn by love for his bride, responds to the call to arms. At Watchet, scene of the ensuing battle, the Danish leaders argue but are soon routed by the heroic forces led by Aella, who is wounded in the fray. Meanwhile, Birtha's attendants attempt to cheer the lonely bride with more minstrelsy, but she cannot respond.

Celmonde bursts into the room to tell her in private of her husband's wounds, which he deceitfully says are mortal, and begs her to leave with him to rush to Aella's side before it is too late. She complies impetuously, telling no one the reason for her flight. Once in the dark woods, the base traitor professes his love and attempts to ravish Birtha, but her screams attract the scattered Danish forces under their defeated leader Hurra, and in the scuffle, Celmonde is killed. Birtha identifies herself to the Danish leader, who chivalrously promises her safe conduct back to Bristol.

Aella, however, was able to return to the castle, and finding Birtha missing, he succumbs to jealousy and what he conceives as wounded honor by Birtha's departure with another man, and he stabs himself. Birtha returns and, finding her husband dying, explains her actions, and they are reconciled. As the hero dies, his bride faints over his dead body, and the play ends.

The minstrel's songs interspersed in the narrative are some of Chatterton's best-known and finest lyrics, particularly the skillfully rendered lyric with the refrain "Mie love ys dedde,/ Gon to hys death-bedde,/ Al under the wyllowe tree." Perhaps Chatterton's musical inheritance here is manifest in these poetic lines.

No reader of "Aella" could miss its primarily Shakespearean derivation. Aella is Othello, foiled by the treacherous Celmonde-Iago, and Birtha is Desdemona. Other Shakespearean plays also echo in "Aella": *Henry V* (pr. c. 1598-1599), *Hamlet, Prince of Denmark* (pr. c. 1600-1601), and *The Tempest* (pr. 1611) have been traced in Chatterton's lines. Ultimately, however, it is not in its sources but in its original execution that the merit of "Aella" lies. Chatterton's shaping of the material demonstrates particularly well his lyrical imagery, especially in the minstrel songs, and has rarely been excelled in English poetry.

The few remaining works of the Rowley cycle are notable in that Chatterton continues the overriding theme of exalting Canynge's greatness. Probably the most effective of these shorter Rowley poems is another celebration in verse, "The Storie of Wyllyam Canynge," presented by means of a lovely visionary dream related by the elderly Rowley, who traces the life of his paragon and recalls valorous deeds of not only Canynge but also other heroes of Bristol. In all, these final, relatively brief but successful lyrics, which also include "The Accounte of W. Canynges Feast," "Englysh Metamorphosis," "The Worlde," and several eclogues ("Robert and Raufe," "Nygelle," and "Manne, Womanne, Syr Rogerre") support the overall image and spirit of ancient Bristol and of Canynge that Chatterton meant to portray and glorify. Taken as a whole with the rest of the Rowleyan works, the cycle forms the youthful Chatterton's finest, most astonishing accomplishment.

OTHER MAJOR WORKS

PLAYS: *The Revenge*, pr. 1770 (opera); *The Woman of Spirit*, pb. 1770 (burletta).

NONFICTION: *The Last Will and Testament of Me, Thomas Chatterton, of the City of Bristol*, 1770.

MISCELLANEOUS: *The Complete Works of Thomas Chatterton: A Bicentenary Edition*, 1971 (2 volumes; Donald S. Taylor and Benjamin Hoover, editors).

BIBLIOGRAPHY

Bronson, Bertrand H. "Thomas Chatterton." In *The Age of Johnson: Essays Presented to Chauncey Brewster Tinker*, edited by Wilmarth S. Lewis. New Haven, Conn.: Yale University Press, 1949. This relatively short study is filled with useful information about the larger context in which Chatterton's work appeared. Examines not only biographical curiosities but also critical issues brought up by the poems themselves.

Fairchild, Hoxie Neale. "Aesthetic Sentimentalists." In *Religious Trends in English Poetry: Religious Sentimentalism in the Age of Johnson, 1740-1780*. Vol. 2. New York: Columbia University Press, 1939. Takes a special approach to Chatterton by concentrating on the religious elements in his poetry. The popular religious influences of the age, combined with the interest in medieval and gothic cultures, provide color and arresting images which make Chatterton's poems richly textured, even if they are not theologically deep.

Folkenflik, Robert. "Macpherson, Chatterton, Blake, and the Great Age of Literary Forgery." *Centennial Review* 18 (1974): 378-391. This brief survey of the pre-Romantic period places Chatterton's work in context with that of another minor poet, James Macpherson, and with the great poet William Blake. All three of these poets worked with assumed identities and created personas with whom they identified in varying degrees.

Groom, Nick. *The Forger's Shadow: How Forgery Changed the Course of Literature*. London: Picador, 2002. Contains a discussion of literary forgery, including that of Chatterton.

_____, ed. *Thomas Chatterton and Romantic Culture*. New York: St. Martin's Press, 1999. A collection of diverse essays by scholars, critics, and writers such as Peter Ackroyd and Richard Holmes. They show the mercurial Chatterton in exciting new contexts and restore him as a seminal figure in English literature. Includes bibliographical references and index.

Heys, Alistair, ed. *From Gothic to Romantic: Thomas Chatterton's Bristol*. Bristol, England: Redcliffe, 2005. An examination of Chatterton's work that focuses on his portrayal of Bristol.

Kelly, Linda. *The Marvellous Boy: The Life and Myth of Thomas Chatterton*. London: Weidenfeld & Nicolson, 1971. Building on earlier studies, this comprehensive biography draws its title from a line in William Wordsworth's "Resolution and Independence." Kelly seeks to show that Chatterton was more than a literary oddity and to examine his place in the development of English Romantic poetry.

Meyerstein, E. H. W. *A Life of Thomas Chatterton*.

London: Igpen and Grant, 1930. Although this study is old, it is not out of date and is considered essential to the study of Chatterton. It is objective and comprehensive, as opposed to the sentimentalized biographies of former eras.

*Maryhelen Cleverly Harmon*

# GEOFFREY CHAUCER

**Born:** London(?), England; c. 1343
**Died:** London, England; October 25(?), 1400

PRINCIPAL POETRY

*Book of the Duchess*, c. 1370
*Romaunt of the Rose*, c. 1370 (translation, possibly not by Chaucer)
*House of Fame*, 1372-1380
*The Legend of St. Cecilia*, 1372-1380 (later used as "The Second Nun's Tale")
*Tragedies of Fortune*, 1372-1380 (later used as "The Monk's Tale")
*Anelida and Arcite*, c. 1380
*Parlement of Foules*, 1380
*The Legend of Good Women*, 1380-1386
*Palamon and Ersyte*, 1380-1386 (later used as "The Knight's Tale")
*Troilus and Criseyde*, 1382
*The Canterbury Tales*, 1387-1400

OTHER LITERARY FORMS

In addition to the early allegorical dream visions, the "tragedy" of *Troilus and Criseyde*, and the "comedy" *The Canterbury Tales*, Geoffrey Chaucer (CHAW-sur) composed various lyrical poems, wrote a scientific treatise in prose, and translated two immensely influential works from Latin and Old French into Middle English. The shorter works have received little attention from critics. "An ABC," Chaucer's earliest poem adapted from the French of Guillaume Deguilleville, and the various ballades, roundels, and envoys are in the French courtly tradition. They also reflect the influence of the Roman philosopher Boethius and often include moral advice and standard *sententiae*. Somewhat longer are the *Anelida and Arcite* and the complaints to Pity and of Venus and Mars, which develop the conventions of the languishing lover of romance.

The prose works include the interesting astrological study *A Treatise on the Astrolabe* (1387-1392), written for "little Lewis my son," and the *Boece* (c. 1380), a translation of Boethius's *De consolatione philosophiae* (523; *The Consolation of Philosophy*, late ninth century), which particularly influenced Chaucer's *Troilus and Criseyde* and "The Knight's Tale." The prologue to *The Legend of Good Women* notes that Chaucer also translated *Romaunt of the Rose* (c. 1370). Certainly the great Old French dream vision, particularly the first part by Guillaume de Lorris, influenced Chaucer's early dream allegories as well as his portrayal of certain characters and scenes in *The Canterbury Tales*—the Wife of Bath, for example, and the enclosed garden of "The Merchant's Tale." Scholars, however, are uncertain whether the extant Middle English version of *Romaunt of the Rose* included in standard editions of Chaucer is by the poet.

ACHIEVEMENTS

Seldom has a poet been as consistently popular and admired by fellow poets, critics, and the public as has Geoffrey Chaucer. From the comments of his French contemporary Eustache Deschamps (c. 1340-1410) and the praise by imitation of the fifteenth century Chaucerians to the remarks of notable critics from John Dryden and Alexander Pope to Matthew Arnold and C. S. Lewis, Chaucer has been warmly applauded if not always understood. His poetic talent, "genial nature," wit, charm, and sympathetic yet critical understanding of human diversity are particularly attractive. To D. S. Brewer, Chaucer "is our Goethe, a great artist who put his whole mind into his art."

However, sometimes this praise has been misinformed, portraying Chaucer rather grandly as the founder of English literature and the prime shaper of the English language. In fact, English literature had a long and illustrious tradition before Chaucer, and the development of Modern English from the London East Midland dialect of Chaucer has little to do with the poet. Chaucer has also been credited with a series of firsts. G. L. Kittredge identified *Troilus and Criseyde* as "the first novel, in the modern sense, that ever was written in the world." Its characters, to John Speirs, are also poetic firsts: Pandarus "the first rounded comic creation of substantial magnitude in English literature," and Criseyde "the first complete character of a woman in English literature." Others see Chaucer's poetry as "Renaissance" in outlook, a harbinger of the humanism of the modern world. Such views reveal an element of surprise on the critics' part that from the midst of Middle English such a poetic genius should emerge. In fact, typical discussions of Chaucer's career, dividing it into three stages as it develops from French influence (seen in the dream allegories) to Italian tendencies (in *Troilus and Criseyde*, for example) and finally to English realism (in *The Canterbury Tales*), imply an evolutionary view not only of Chaucer's poetry but also of English literary history. These stages supposedly reflect the gradual rejection of medieval conventionalism and the movement toward modern realism.

Whatever Chaucer's varied achievements are, the rejection of conventions, rhetoric, types, symbols, and authorities is not among them. Charles Muscatine has

*Geoffrey Chaucer* (Library of Congress)

shown, moreover, that Chaucer's "realism" is as French and conventional as are his early allegories. Chaucer's poetry should be judged within the conventions of his time. He did experiment with verse forms, establishing a decasyllabic line that, to become the iambic pentameter of the sonnet, blank verse, and heroic couplet, is English poetry's most enduring line. His talent, however, lies in manipulating the authorities, the rhetoric, and conventional "topics" and in his mastery of the "art poetical." As A. C. Spearing notes, "Once we become aware of Chaucer's 'art poetical,' we gain a deeper insight into his work by seeing how what appears natural in it is in fact achieved not carelessly but by the play of genius upon convention and contrivance."

Such an approach to Chaucer will recognize his achievement as the greatest poet of medieval England, not as a forerunner of modernism. It will note his remaking of French, Latin, and Italian sources and treatment of secular and religious allegory as being, in their own way, as original as his creation of such characters as the Wife of Bath and the Pardoner. Chaucer's achievement is in his ability to juxtapose various medieval outlooks to portray complex ideas in human terms, with wit and humor, to include both "heigh sentence" and "solaas and myrthe," and to merge the naturalistic detail with the symbolic pattern. In this attempt to synthesize the everyday with the supernatural and the homely with the philosophical, and in his insistence on inclusiveness—on presenting both the angels and the gargoyles—Chaucer is the supreme example of the Gothic artist.

BIOGRAPHY

For a medieval poet, much is known about Geoffrey Chaucer's life, his association with the English court, his diplomatic activity on the Continent, and his public appointments. He was born in the early 1340's, the son of John Chaucer, a London wine merchant. He spent time in the military, serving with the English forces in France, where he was captured in 1359; he was ransomed in 1360. Around 1366, he married Philippa Roet and probably fathered two sons. He served the crown most of his life. Originally (c. 1357), he was connected to the household of Princess Elizabeth, who was married to Prince Lionel, the son of King Edward III. He also served another son of the king, John of Gaunt, the duke of Lancaster, who later married Chaucer's sister-in-law, Katherine Swynford. Chaucer's public service survived the death of Edward III and the tumultuous reign and deposition of Richard II. It included numerous diplomatic missions to the Continent, his appointment as controller of customs and subsidy for the port of London (1374-1386), his service as a justice of the peace and member of Parliament for Kent (1386), his demanding duties as clerk of the King's Works (1389-1391), and, finally, his appointment after 1391 as deputy forester of North Petherton royal forest in Somerset. Chaucer lived in London, Greenwich, and Calais, the French port then controlled by the English. In 1399, he leased a house in the garden of Westminster Abbey. He probably died on October 25, 1400, and was buried in the nearby abbey, the first of a long line of English authors to rest in the Poets' Corner.

These biographical details provide little evidence of Chaucer's position as a poet, although in a general way they do cast light on his poetry. Chaucer's association with courtly circles must have provided both the inspiration for and the occasion of his early poetry. It is certain that he wrote the *Book of the Duchess* to commemorate the death of Blanche, the wife of John of Gaunt. He probably also composed *The Legend of Good Women* for a courtly patron (the queen, according to John Lydgate) and read *Troilus and Criseyde* to a courtly audience, as he is portrayed doing in a manuscript illustration. In more general terms, his early poetry reflects the French literary taste of the English court.

Chaucer's public career, furthermore, reveals that he was far from being the withdrawn versifier of artificial courtly tastes. His duties at the port of London and as chief supervisor of royal building projects suggest that he was a practical man of the world. Certainly these responsibilities brought him into contact with a wide variety of individuals whose manners and outlooks must have contrasted sharply with those of members of the court. In the past, such scholars as J. M. Manly searched historical records to identify specific individuals with whom Chaucer dealt in an attempt to locate models for the portraits of the pilgrims in *The Canterbury Tales*. Like any artist, Chaucer was no doubt in-

fluenced by those with whom he worked, but such research gives a false impression of Chaucer's characters. Even his most "realistic" creations are often composites of traditional portraits. Nevertheless, the studies of J. A. W. Bennett (*Chaucer at Oxford and at Cambridge*, 1974) show that careful attention to the records of fourteenth century England can enlighten modern understanding of the social, intellectual, and cultural trends of Chaucer's time and thus provide a setting for his life and work.

One aspect of Chaucer's public career must certainly have influenced his poetry. Repeatedly from 1360 to 1387, Chaucer undertook royal missions on the Continent. During these journeys, he visited Flanders, Paris, and perhaps even Spain. More important, in 1373 and again in 1378, he visited Italy. These trips to what in the fourteenth century was the center of European art brought him into contact with a sophisticated culture. They may have also introduced him to the work of the great Florentine poets, for Chaucer's poetry after these visits to Italy reflects the influence of Dante, Petrarch, and particularly Giovanni Boccaccio. Finally, the diplomatic missions suggest certain features of Chaucer's personality that lie behind his poetry, although these features seem deliberately masked by his self-portraits in the poetry. Of middle-class origin, expert in languages, and trusted at court, Chaucer as a diplomat sent on at least seven missions to the Continent must have been not only convivial and personable—the usual view of the poet—but also self-assured, intelligent, and a keen judge of character.

ANALYSIS

When reading Geoffrey Chaucer's works, one is struck by a sense of great variety. His poetry reflects numerous sources—Latin, French, and Italian—ranging from ancient authorities to contemporary poets and including folktales, sermons, rhetorical textbooks, philosophical meditations, and ribald jokes. Equally varied are Chaucer's poetic forms and genres: short conventional lyrics, long romances, exempla, fabliaux, allegorical dream visions, confessions, saints' legends, and beast fables. The characters he creates, from personified abstractions, regal birds, and ancient goddesses to the odd collection of the Canterbury pilgrims and the naïve persona who narrates the poems, are similarly varied. Finally, the poems present a wide variety of outlooks on an unusual number of topics. Like the Gothic cathedrals, Chaucer's poetry seems all-inclusive. Not surprisingly, also like the Gothic cathedrals, his poems were often left unfinished.

"Experience, though no authority," the Wife of Bath states in the prologue to her tale, "is good enough for me." Unlike her fifth husband, Jankin the clerk, the Wife is not interested in what "olde Romayn gestes" teach, what Saint Jerome, Tertullian, Solomon, and Ovid say about women and marriage. She knows "of the woe that is in marriage" by her own experience. This implied contrast between, on one hand, authority—the established positions concerning just about any topic set forth in the past by Scripture, ancient authors, and the Church fathers and passed on to the present by books—and, on the other hand, the individual's experience of everyday life is central to medieval intellectual thought. It is a major theme of Chaucer's poetry. Often Chaucer appears to establish an authority and then to contrast it with the experience of real life, testing the expected by the actual. This contrast may be tragic or comic; it may cast doubt on the authority or further support it. Often it is expressed by paired characters—Troilus and Pandarus, for example—or by paired tales, the Knight's and the Miller's. The characters' long recital of authorities may be ludicrous and pompous, Chaucer's parody of the pedant, but the pedant may be right. After Chanticleer's concern with what all the past has said about the significance of dreams, readers probably sympathize with Pertelote's comment that he should take a laxative. Nevertheless, once the rooster is in the fox's mouth, the authorities are proven correct. Similarly, the sum total of the Wife of Bath's personal experience is merely the proving, in an exaggerated form, of the antifeminist authorities. As Chaucer states in the prologue to the *Parlement of Foules*, out of old fields comes new corn, and out of old books new knowledge.

Related to the contrast between authority and experience are a series of other contrasts investigated by Chaucer: theological faith versus human reason, the ideal versus the pragmatic, the ritual of courtly love versus the business of making love, the dream world versus everyday life, the expectations of the rule versus the actions of the individual, and the Christian teaching of free will versus humankind's sense of being fated. Again, these contrasts may be treated seriously or comically, may be represented by particular characters, and may be brought into temporary balance. Seldom, however, does Chaucer provide solutions. The oppositions are implicit in human nature, in the wish for the absolute and the recognition of the relative. As novelist and critic Arthur Koestler comments on a modern political version of this dilemma (as represented by the extremes of the Yogi and the Commissar), "Apparently the two elements do not mix, and this may be one of the reasons why we have made such a mess of our History." Chaucer's poetic and highly varied treatment of these nonmixers may help to explain why his poetry continues to speak to readers today.

Chaucer's concern with these topics—a fascination not unusual in the dualistic Gothic world—imbues his poetry with a sense of irony. Since the 1930's, readers have certainly emphasized Chaucer's ironic treatment of characters and topics, a critical vogue that may be due as much to the fashions of New Criticism as to the poetry itself. However, Chaucer's characteristic means of telling his stories clearly encourages such readings. One can never be sure of his attitude because the poet stands behind a narrator whose often naïve attitudes simply cannot be identified with his creator's. Perhaps the creation of such a middleman between the poet and his audience was necessary for a middle-class poet reading to an aristocratic audience, or perhaps it is the natural practice of a diplomatic mind, which does not speak for itself but for another. Whatever the reasons, Chaucer's narrators are poetically effective. They provide a unifying strand throughout his varied work. Scholar A. C. Spearing notes that "the idiot-dreamer of *The Book of the Duchess* develops into the idiot-historian of *Troilus and Criseyde* and the idiot-pilgrim of *The Canterbury Tales*." Later, he comments that when Chaucer assigns the doggerel poem "The Tale of Sir Thopas" to Chaucer the pilgrim as a joke, he "takes the role of idiot-poet to its culmination."

One result of the use of such narrators is that, in contrast with the contemporary dream vision, *The Vision of William, Concerning Piers the Plowman* (c. 1362, A

Text; c. 1377, B Text; c. 1393, C Text; also known as *Piers Plowman*)—with its acid attacks on English society, the failures of government, and the hypocrisy of the church—Chaucer's poetry seems aware of human foibles yet accepting of human nature. He implies rather than shouts the need for change, recognizing that in this world, at least, major reform is unlikely. His essentially Christian position, hidden behind the naïve narrator and his concern with surface details, naturalistic dialogue, and sharp description, is implied by the poem's larger structures. They often provide symbolic patterning. The contrasts in the *Parlement of Foules* between the steamy atmosphere of the temple of Venus and the clear air of Nature's dominion or in *Troilus and Criseyde* between the narrator's introductory devotion to the god of love and his concluding epilogue based on Troilus's new heavenly point of view imply Chaucer's position concerning his favorite topic, human love. Similarly, the traditional Christian metaphor identifying life as a pilgrimage and the Parson's identification of Canterbury with the New Jerusalem suggest that the pilgrimage from a pub in Southwark to a shrine in Canterbury is a secular version of an important traditional religious theme. The reader of Chaucer, while paying careful attention to his realism that has been found so attractive, should also be aware of the larger implications of his poetry.

Behind the medieval interest in dreams and the genre of dream visions lies a long tradition, both religious and secular, originating in biblical and classical stories and passed on in the Middle Ages in the works of Ambrosius Theodosius Macrobius and Boethius. As a literary type, the dream vision, given impetus by the *Romaunt of the Rose*, was particularly popular in fourteenth century England. The obtuse dreamers led by authoritative guides found in such works as *Piers Plowman* and *The Pearl* (c. 1400) are typical of dream visions and may have suggested to Chaucer the creation of his characteristic naïve narrator. Certainly Chaucer's four dream visions, as different as they are from one another, already develop this narrative voice as well as other typical Chaucerian characteristics.

### BOOK OF THE DUCHESS

The earliest of Chaucer's very long poems, *Book of the Duchess* (1,334 lines), is a dream elegy in memory of the duchess of Lancaster. The poem begins with the narrator reading in bed about dreams, specifically the Ovidian story of the tragic love of Ceyx and Alcyone. After her husband's death, Alcyone is visited in a dream by Ceyx, leading to Alcyone's eventual brokenhearted death. This introductory section, which as usual refers to numerous authorities on dreams, combines Chaucer's concern with both dreams and love. These authorities provide background for the narrator's experience in a dream. After praying to Morpheus, the narrator falls asleep to dream of another couple divided by death, a man in black (John of Gaunt) and his lost lover, "faire White" (Blanche). The dreamer's foolish and tactless questions allow the grieving knight to express his love and sense of loss, sometimes by direct statement, on other occasions by such elaborate devices as describing a game of chess in which fortune takes his queen. The traditionally obtuse dreamer is here used in a remarkably original way. The poet is able to place the praise of the dead and the feelings of anguish in the mouth of the bereaved. Thus, this highly conventional poem, with its conscious borrowing from Ovid, *Romaunt of the Rose*, Jean Froissart, and Guillaume de Machaut, is an effective elegy in the restrained courtly tradition.

### HOUSE OF FAME

The *House of Fame*, Chaucer's second dream vision, breaks off suddenly after 2,158 lines. It creates a series of allegorical structures and figures in an analysis of the relationship between love, fame, rumor, fortune, and poetry. The dreamer is here provided with a guide, Jupiter's eagle, that probably derives from Dante's *Purgatorio 9*. In book 1 he relates the romance of Aeneas and Dido, two lovers of some poetic fame whose story is portrayed in panels on a temple of glass dedicated to Venus. This temple is contrasted with the house of Fame that the dreamer sees in book 3 when the eagle rather unceremoniously whisks him into the heavens. In this second allegorical structure, the dreamer views the goddess Fame surrounded by the great poets of antiquity on pedestals. They represent the authorities who, like Vergil, record the stories of such lovers as Aeneas and Dido. The dreamer realizes, however, that Fame (and thus presumably the poets of Fame) deals out good and bad at random, suggesting that there is little relationship between actuality and reputation. He next sees the house of Rumor. Full of noise and whispering people, it is perhaps an allegorical representation of the character of everyday life. In any case, this chaotic structure is no more attractive than the house of Fame. Still searching for "tydinges of Loves folk," the dreamer sees "a man of greet auctoritee," but the poem breaks off before the man can speak. The reader, like the dreamer, is left in the air; the poem is left without an ending. As Muscatine comments, "It is hard to conceive of any ending at all that could consistently follow from what we have." In fact, the poem lacks a sense of unity. Its multiple topics and elaborate descriptions are best studied as set pieces. Of particular interest is the often comic dialogue between the dreamer and the eagle in book 2.

### PARLEMENT OF FOULES

The *Parlement of Foules* (699 lines) is a more satisfactory poem, although it shares much in common with *House of Fame*, including a series of allegorical portraits and locales, a guide who tends to shove the dreamer around, and birds as characters. A poem describing the mating of birds on Saint Valentine's day, the *Parlement of Foules* begins, like the *Book of the Duchess*, with the narrator reading a book about a dream. The book is Cicero's "Dream of Scipio," the standard textbook on dreams, found in the last part of *De republica* (51 B.C.E.; *On the State*, 1817). Its guide, Scipio Africanus the elder, becomes the dreamer's guide in the *Parlement of Foules*. He dreams of the typical enclosed garden of romance, guarded by a gate. The gate's contrasting inscriptions alluding to the gates of Dante's *Inferno* suggest the dual nature of love: bliss, fertility, and "good aventure" on one hand, and sorrow, barrenness, and danger on the other. Within the garden, the dreamer again sees two versions of love, although, as naïve as ever, he seems bewildered and unsure of what he witnesses.

Like the Renaissance masterpiece painting of "Sacred and Profane Love by Titian," the poem contrasts two traditional ideals of love. One is symbolized by Venus, whose entourage includes Flattery, Desire, and Lust as well as Cupid, Courtesy, and Gentleness. Her religion of love is the subject of the poets and ancient authorities whom the narrator so often reads. Her pal-

ace is dark and mannered, painted with the tragic stories of doomed lovers. In contrast, the dreamer next sees in the bright sunlight "this noble goddesse Nature," who presides over the beauty of natural love and mating of the birds. These ceremonies include description of all levels of the hierarchy of the birds, from the pragmatic arrangements of the goose and the love devotion of the turtledove to the courtly wooing of the former by the eagles. The language of the birds, often comic, similarly ranges from the sudden "kek, kek!" and "kukkow" to elaborate Latinate diction. Although lighthearted and sometimes chaotic, the openness and social awareness of Nature's realm is clearly to be preferred to the artificiality and self-absorption of the temple of Venus. The poem ends under Nature's skillful guidance as the birds sing a song of spring, which awakens the dreamer. In the prologue, the narrator states that he wishes to learn of love. This dream has provided much to learn, yet he seems in the end unchanged by his experience and once again returns to his authorities.

### THE LEGEND OF GOOD WOMEN

Of great interest as a forerunner of *The Canterbury Tales*, *The Legend of Good Women* is Chaucer's first experiment with decasyllabic couplets and with the idea of a framed collection of stories. Like the much grander later collection, it begins with a prologue and then relates an unfinished series of stories. Although the prologue plans nineteen stories, the poem breaks off near the conclusion of the ninth, after 2,723 lines. Unlike "The General Prologue" to *The Canterbury Tales*, with its detailed portraits of the pilgrims set in the Tabard Inn, the prologue to *The Legend of Good Women* is set as yet another dream. It presents the god of love and his daisy queen in conversation with the Chaucerian narrator. Once again, the narrator is a reader of books eager to learn from life about love. More interesting, he is here also a writer of books and is harassed by the god of love for not presenting lovers in a good light in his poetry. Specific reference is made to his translation of the *Romaunt of the Rose* and to *Troilus and Criseyde*. As penance for his grievous sins against the religion of love, the narrator promises to write about the faithful lovers of ancient legend.

Comparisons with *The Canterbury Tales* are perhaps unfair, but the poem, lacking the dynamic characters and varied tales of the later collection, seems grievously repetitious. Its recital of love tragedies is borrowed from Ovid and other authorities. Nevertheless, the legends do encompass a wider range of classical stories than might at first be expected, including the stories of Cleopatra and Medea, who to the modern reader, at least, hardly qualify as "good women." The luscious yet natural scenery of the prologue is superb. Furthermore, the work is fulfillment of Chaucer's poetic development in the courtly tradition. Whatever the poem's weaknesses, it is unlikely that Chaucer would have agreed with Robert Burlin's judgment that the poem was "a colossal blunder."

### TROILUS AND CRISEYDE

In his elaborate panegyric, the French poet Émile Deschamps refers to Chaucer as a "Socrates, full of philosophy, Seneca for morality . . . a great Ovid in your poetry." The poem that most fully deserves such praise is *Troilus and Criseyde*, Chaucer's longest complete poem (8,259 lines) and, to many readers, his most moving work. Here for the first time in a long poem, Chaucer turns from the dream-vision form and the participating narrator but not from his concern with authorities and the nature of love. He now adds, however, a Boethian philosophical touch. Although it is a poem about love, Fortuna rather than Venus is the controlling goddess of Chaucer's "little tragedy." Although the career of Troilus is based on Boccaccio's *Filostrato* (c. 1335-1340), it would seem that *The Consolation of Philosophy* exerted the greatest influence on the poem.

The five books of *Troilus and Criseyde*, rather than being, as modern critics like to assert, the first novel or a drama in five acts, represent the various stages of Troilus's tragic love affair. Describing the "double sorrow" of Troilus, the son of King Priam of Troy, the poem begins with his initial love-longing, then traces his increasingly successful courtship of Criseyde culminating in their fulfilled love, the intervention of the Trojan War in the midst of their happiness, their forced separation, Criseyde's eventual acceptance of the Greek Diomede, and finally Troilus's gallant death at the hand of Achilles. While telling this story, Chaucer paints a series of scenes, both comic and serious, sometimes absurd, often movingly romantic, examining various outlooks on human love. Troilus's excessive idealism seems to parody the courtly lovers of French romances, whereas the pragmatic, often cynical attitudes of Pandarus, the uncle of Criseyde and confidant of Troilus, remind one of the waterfowl in the *Parlement of Foules* and the later fabliaux of *The Canterbury Tales*. Criseyde's views of love shift between these two extremes, varying according to her feelings and the exigencies of circumstance.

Calling *Troilus and Criseyde* Chaucer's "great failure," Ian Robinson (*Chaucer and the English Tradition*, 1972) believes that the poem includes "many great parts but they don't cohere into a great whole." However, the poem does have a unifying structure, based on the rising and falling stages of the Wheel of Fortune. The notion of Fortune turning a wheel that sometimes takes humans to the height of success and sometimes drags them down to failure is standard in medieval thought and very popular in both literature and art. The stages of the wheel, along with the poem's narrative units, are set forth in the invocations that introduce the books of *Troilus and Criseyde*. In the first, when Troilus is at the bottom of the wheel, the narrator invokes Tesiphone, "thou cruel fury." As Morton Bloomfield comments ("Distance and Predestination in *Troilus and Criseyde*"), Tesiphone was characterized as the "sorrowful fury" who laments her torments and pities those whom she torments. The choice is thus appropriate for the description in book 1 of the hero's initial love torments and for the events of the entire poem. The Chaucerian narrator presents himself as "the sorrowful instrument" of love, required to tell the "sorrowful tale."

The invocation in book 2, to Clio the Muse of history, suggests that the second stage represents a rather neutral and objectively historical description of the rise of Troilus on the wheel, whereas the invocation to Venus in book 3 is appropriate for the stage when the lovers are at the top of the wheel and consummate their love. As all readers of Boethius know, however, if one chooses to ride to the top of the wheel, one in all fairness cannot be surprised when the wheel continues to turn downward. Thus, book 4 begins with an invocation to Fortune and her wheel, which throws down the hero and sets Diomede in his place. There is also an appropriate reference to Mars, suggesting the growing influence of the war on the romance. Book 5 follows without an invocation, probably because it is a continuation of the fourth book and implying that the down ward movement of the wheel is one continuous stage. Certainly the poem's last book does not introduce any new elements. Its major concerns are Troilus's fatalism and the details of the Trojan War.

This pattern clearly interweaves two problems that dominate the poem: the perplexities of human love and humanity's sense of being fated. Troilus is the character overwhelmed by both problems. Although many critics are fascinated by the inscrutable Criseyde and attracted by the worldly-wise Pandarus, Troilus is the poem's central figure. Readers may become frustrated by his passive love-longing and swooning and his long-winded and confused discussion of predestination and free will; however, he is treated sympathetically and his situation must be taken seriously. One can argue, using Boethius as support, that the solution to the human predicament is simply never to accept the favors of Fortune—to stay away from her wheel—but what man would not do as Troilus did for the love of Criseyde? Similarly, one can agree with the moralizing narrator at the poem's conclusion that the solution is to avoid worldly vanity and the love associated with Venus and to look instead to heavenly love.

Certainly Troilus recognizes this view as his soul ascends to the seventh sphere. However, the poem as a whole hardly condemns the love of the two Trojans. On the contrary, it describes their long-awaited rendezvous in bed with great sensitivity and poetic beauty, with warmth and sensuous natural imagery. As Spearing states, "There is probably no finer poetry of fulfilled love in English than this scene." In this great tragic romance, Chaucer seems to juxtapose human and divine love and to intermingle the sense of predestination and the Christian teaching of free will; not until the end does he speak as the moralist and condemn worldly vanity. Perhaps the tragedy of Troilus and of the human situation in general is that the distinctions are not sufficiently clear until it is too late to choose.

## THE CANTERBURY TALES

Near the end of *Troilus and Criseyde*, Chaucer associates his "little tragedy" with a long line of classical poets and then asks for help to write "some comedie." Donald Howard and others have seen this as a reference to the poet's plans for *The Canterbury Tales*. Whether Chaucer had this collection planned by the time he had completed *Troilus and Criseyde*, *The Canterbury Tales* can certainly be understood as his comedy. If, as the Monk notes at the beginning of his long summary of tragic tales, a tragedy deals with those who once "stood in high degree, and fell so that there was no remedy," in the medieval view comedy deals with less significant characters and with events that move toward happy endings. *The Canterbury Tales* is thus a comedy, not because of its comic characters and humorous stories—several tales are actually tragic in tone and structure—but because its overall structure is comic.

Like Dante's *La divina commedia* (c. 1320, 3 volumes; *The Divine Comedy*, 1802), which traces the poet's eschatological journey from Hell through Purgatory to Heaven, shifting from a pagan guide to the representatives of divine love and inspiration, and concluding with the beatific vision, Chaucer's comedy symbolically moves from the infernal to the heavenly. From the worldly concerns of the Tabard Inn in Southwark and the guidance of the worldly-wise Host, through a variety of points of view set forth by differing characters on the pilgrimage road, the poem moves to the religious goal of the saint's shrine in Canterbury Cathedral and the Parson's direction of the pilgrims to "Jerusalem celestial."

Although with differing effects, since the Christian perspective of *Troilus and Criseyde* lies beyond the narrative itself, Chaucer's tragedy and comedy thus share a similar moral structure. Like the tragedy, *The Canterbury Tales* moves from an ancient story of pagan heroes to a Christian perspective. In *Troilus and Criseyde*, the narrator develops from being the servant of the god of love to being a moralist who condemns pagan "cursed old rites" and advises the young to love him who "for love upon a cross our souls did buy." The collection of tales similarly moves from the Knight's "old stories" set in ancient Thebes and Athens and relating the fates of pagan lovers to the Parson's sermon beginning "Our swete lord god of hevene." In contrast with the earlier poem, *The Canterbury Tales* is a comedy because its divine perspective is achieved within the overall narrative. As in the earlier poem, however, this divine perspective at the end does not necessarily cancel out the earlier outlooks proposed. The entire poem with its multiplicity of characters and viewpoints remains.

Such an approach to *The Canterbury Tales* assumes that, although unfinished, the poem is complete as it stands and should be judged as a whole. Like the Corpus Christi cycles of the later Middle Ages, which include numerous individual plays yet can (and should) be read as one large play tracing salvation history from creation to doomsday, *The Canterbury Tales* is more than the sum of its parts. "The General Prologue," that masterpiece of human description with its fascinating portraits of the pilgrims, establishes not only the supposed circumstances for the pilgrimage and the competition to tell the best story but also the strands that link the tales to the characters and to one another. Although only twenty-four tales were finished, their relationship to one another within fragments and their sense of unity within variety suggest that Chaucer had an overall plan for *The Canterbury Tales*.

The famous opening lines of "The General Prologue," with the beautiful evocation of spring fever, set forth both the religious and the secular motivations of the pilgrims. These motivations are further developed in their description by the pilgrim Chaucer. He again is the naïve narrator whose wide-eyed simplicity seems to accept all, leaving the discriminating reader to see beyond the surface details. Finally, in his faithful retelling of the stories he hears on the way to Canterbury—for once his experience has become an authority to which, he explains, he must not be false—the narrator again unwittingly implies much about these various human types. Several of the prologues and tales that follow then continue to explore the motivations of the individual pilgrims. The confessional prologue of "The Pardoner's Tale" and its sermon filled with moral exempla, for instance, ironically reflects the earlier description of the confidence man, Pardoner, as one "with feigned flattery and tricks, made the parson and the people his apes."

It would be a mistake, however, to interpret the various tales simply as dramatic embodiments of the pilgrims. Certainly Chaucer often fits story to storyteller. The sentimental, self-absorbed, and prissy Prioress tells, for example, a simplistic, anti-Semitic tale of a devout little Christian boy murdered by Jews. The implications of her tale make one question the nature of her spirituality. The tales given the Knight, Miller, and Reeve also reflect their characters. The Knight tells at great length a chivalric romance, a celebration of his worldview, whereas the Miller and Reeve tell bawdy stories concerning tradesmen, clerks, and wayward wives.

However, these tales also develop the larger concerns of *The Canterbury Tales* implied by Chaucer's arrangement of the tales into thematic groups. "The Knight's Tale," with its ritualized action and idealized characters, draws from Boethian philosophy in its symmetrically patterned examination of courtly love, fate, and cosmic justice. The Miller then interrupts to "quite" or answer the Knight with a bawdy fabliau. Developing naturalistic dialogue and earthy characters, it rejects the artificial and the philosophical for the mundane and the practical. In place of the Knight's code of honor and courtly love, elaborate description of the tournament, and Stoic speech on the Great Chain of Being, the drunken Miller sets the stage for sexual conquest, a complex practical joke, and a "cherles tales" involving bodily functions and fleshly punishment. In "The Miller's Tale," justice is created not by planetary gods but by human action, each character getting what he deserves. The Reeve, offended by both the Miller and his tale, then follows with another fabliau. His motivations are much more personal than those of the Miller: The Reeve feels that the Miller has deliberately insulted him, and he insists on returning the favor. However, even in this tale Chaucer provides another dimension to the issues originally set forth by the Knight.

The clearest example of Chaucer's thematic grouping of tales is the so-called Marriage Cycle. First noted by G. L. Kittredge and discussed since by various critics, the idea of the cycle is that Chaucer carefully arranged particular tales, told by suitable pilgrims, so that they referred to one another and developed a common theme, as in a scholarly debate. The Marriage Cycle examines various viewpoints on love and marriage, particularly tackling the issue of who should have sovereignty in marriage, the husband or the wife. The cycle is introduced by the Wife of Bath's rambling commentary on the woes of marriage and her wishful tale of a young bachelor who rightly puts himself in his wife's "wyse governance." After the Friar and Summoner "quite" each other in their own personal feud, the cycle continues with an extreme example of wifely obedience, "The Clerk's Tale" of patient Griselda. Such an otherworldly portrait of womanly perfection spurs the Merchant, a man who is obviously unhappy in marriage, to propound his cynical view of the unfaithful wife. The saint's legend of the scholarly Clerk is thus followed by the fabliau of the satirical Merchant, and the debate is no nearer conclusion. Finally, the Franklin appears to "knit up the whole matter" by suggesting that in marriage the man should be both dominant as husband and subservient as lover. However, the Franklin's view is hardly followed by the characters of his tale. Interestingly, the two solutions to the issue of sovereignty proposed—those of the Wife of Bath and of the Franklin—are developed in Breton lays, short and highly unrealistic romances relying heavily on magical elements. Is it the case that only magic can solve this typically human problem? Chaucer, at least, does not press for a definitive answer.

The great sense of variety, the comic treatment of serious issues, the concern with oppositions and unsuccessful solutions, and the lively and imaginative verse that so typifies *The Canterbury Tales* are best exemplified by "The Nun's Priest's Tale." A beast fable mocking courtly language and rhetorical overabundance, the tale at once includes Chaucer's fascination with authorities, dreams, fate, and love and marriage, and suggests his ambivalent attitudes toward the major philosophical and social concerns of his day. The elevated speeches of Chanticleer are punctuated by barnyard cries, and the pompous world of the rooster and hen are set within the humble yard of a poor widow.

Here the reader is provided with a comic version of the detached perspective that concludes *Troilus and Criseyde*. After deciding that dreams are to be taken seriously and refusing to take a laxative, Chanticleer disregards his dream and its warning and makes love to his favorite wife in a scene that absurdly portrays chickens as courtly lovers. Interestingly, Chanticleer now cites a standard sentiment of medieval antifeminism: *In principio/ Mulier est hominis confusio* ("In the beginning woman is man's ruin"), which alludes to the apostle John's famous description of the creation (John 1:1). The learned rooster, moreover, immediately mistranslates the Latin as "Womman is mannes ioye and al his blys," perhaps the Priest's subtle comment on the Nun he serves or the rooster's joke on Pertelote. The joke ultimately is on Chanticleer when "a colfox ful of sley iniquitee" sneaks into this romance "garden." Noting that the counsel of woman brought woe to the world "And made Adam from paradys to go," the Nun's Priest then relates the temptation and fall of Chanticleer and the subsequent chasing of the fox and rooster out of the barnyard. The adventure is full of great fun, a hilarious scene, yet strangely reminiscent of the biblical story of the Fall of Man. It is not clear what one is to make of such a story.

Although Chaucer was not the first author to create a framed collection of stories, *The Canterbury Tales* is assuredly the most imaginative collection. Earlier the poet had experimented with a framed collection in *The Legend of Good Women*. His Italian contemporary, Boccaccio, also created a collection of stories in *The Decameron* (c. 1348-1353), although scholars cannot agree whether Chaucer knew this work. Earlier collections of exempla and legends were probably known by the poet, and he certainly knew the great collection of Ovid, *Metamorphoses* (c. 8 C.E.; English translation, 1567). Like Ovid's collection, *The Canterbury Tales* is organized by thematic and structural elements that provide a sense of unity within diversity. Chaucer's choice of the pilgrimage as the setting for the tales is particularly effective, since it allows the juxtaposition of characters, literary types, and themes gathered from a wide range of sources and reflecting a wide range of human attitudes.

Here, perhaps, is the key to Chaucer's greatness. Like the medieval view of the macrocosm, in which constant change and movement take place within a relatively unchanging framework, Chaucer's view of the microcosm balances the dynamic and the static, the wide range of individual feeling and belief within unchanging human nature. *The Canterbury Tales* is his greatest achievement in this area, although earlier poems, such as the *Parlement of Foules*, with its portrayal of the hierarchy of birds within nature's order, already show Chaucer's basic view. Ranging over human nature, selecting from ancient story and supposed personal experience, with a place for both the comic and the tragic, Chaucer's poetry mixes mirth and morality, accomplishing very successfully the two great purposes of literature, what the Host calls "sentence and solas," teaching and entertainment.

## OTHER MAJOR WORKS

NONFICTION: *Boece*, c. 1380 (translation of Boethius's *The Consolation of Philosophy*); *A Treatise on the Astrolabe*, 1387-1392.

MISCELLANEOUS: *Works*, 1957 (second edition; F. N. Robinson, editor).

## BIBLIOGRAPHY

Ackroyd, Peter. *Chaucer*. New York: Nan A. Talese/ Doubleday, 2005. A biography of Chaucer that brings the medieval world to life and relates Chaucer's life to his poetry.

Blamires, Alcuin. *Chaucer, Ethics, and Gender*. New York: Oxford University Press, 2006. This volume examines not only Chaucer's treatment of women, but also how gender affects the moral tone of his works. Blamires offers a new perspective on Chaucer's writing as he uses philosophical questions of ethics and morality to view the traditionally fixed notions of gender in Chaucer's works. With his lucid writing style, Blamires makes the difficult subject matter easy to fathom and puts a new spin on issues of gender in Chaucerian studies.

Borroff, Marie. *Traditions and Renewals: Chaucer, the Gawain-Poet, and Beyond*. New Haven, Conn.: Yale University Press, 2003. A collection of essays that provide a fresh and different analysis of Chaucer's work.

Brewer, Derek. *The World of Chaucer*. Rochester, N.Y.: D. S. Brewer, 2000. An illustrated look at Chaucer's work and the intellectual life of his time. Includes bibliography and index.

Brown, Peter, ed. *A Companion to Chaucer*. Malden, Mass.: Blackwell, 2000. Part of the Blackwell Companions to Literature and Culture series. Offers broad and detailed essays by scholars of Chaucer and his era.

Condren, Edward I. *Chaucer and the Energy of Creation: The Design and the Organization of "The Canterbury Tales."* Gainesville: University Press of Florida, 1999. Examines the motives behind Chaucer's layout of the stories.

Hirsh, John C. *Chaucer and the "Canterbury Tales": A Short Introduction*. Malden, Mass.: Blackwell, 2003. An introduction to *The Canterbury Tales* for the general reader.

Lynch, Jack, ed. *The Canterbury Tales*. Pasadena, Calif.: Salem Press, 2010. Original essays and classical criticism provide a unique insight into Chaucer's tales.

Rossignol, Rosalyn. *Chaucer A to Z: The Essential Reference to His Life and Works*. New York: Facts On File, 1999. An indispensable guide for the student of Chaucer.

West, Richard. *Chaucer, 1340-1400: The Life and Times of the First English Poet*. New York: Carroll & Graf, 2000. A discussion of the history surrounding Chaucer's achievements and the events of his life. Chapters take up such matters as the Black Death's impact on the anti-Semitism evident in "The Prioress's Tale" and the impact of the great English Peasants' Revolt of 1381 on Chaucer's worldview.

*Richard Kenneth Emmerson*

# JOHN CLARE

**Born:** Helpston, Northamptonshire, England; July
   13, 1793
**Died:** Northampton, Northamptonshire, England;
   May 20, 1864

PRINCIPAL POETRY

*Poems Descriptive of Rural Life and Scenery*, 1820
*The Village Minstrel, and Other Poems*, 1821
*The Shepherd's Calendar*, 1827
*The Rural Muse*, 1835
*The Later Poems of John Clare*, 1964 (Eric
   Robinson and Geoffrey Summerfield, editors)
*The Shepherd's Calendar*, 1964 (Robinson and
   Summerfield, editors)
*Selected Poems and Prose of John Clare*, 1967
   (Robinson and Summerfield, editors)
*The Midsummer Cushion*, 1979
*The Later Poems of John Clare, 1837-1864*, 1984
*The Early Poems of John Clare, 1804-1822*, 1988-
   1989

OTHER LITERARY FORMS

John Clare attempted little systematically except poetry. He left manuscript drafts of several unfinished essays, and part of what was intended as a natural history
of Helpston. He wrote two lengthy autobiographical
essays, one of which was published in 1931: *Sketches
in the Life of John Clare, Written by Himself.* The other
appeared in a collection of his prose in 1951. He also
left one year of a journal in which he recorded his reading and his speculations on religion, politics, and literature. His best-known essay is probably his "Journey
Out of Essex," an account of his escape from an asylum
and his harrowing journey home on foot with no food
or shelter; it has been published several times.

ACHIEVEMENTS

John Clare overcame obstacles that would have defeated most other people and became an important poet
of the Romantic period in England. His family was illiterate and desperately poor though ambitious for their
son to rise in the world. His formal schooling was mini-

mal, and he lived all his life isolated from the literary
currents of his day. His editors censored his work
heavily, misled him about royalties, and were generally
insensitive to what he was trying to do in his verse. He
suffered for years from malnutrition and then from in-
curable mental illness. Despite everything, he not only
was enormously prolific as a poet—more than three
thousand poems in a fifty-five-year career that began at
the age of sixteen—but also wrote a number of poems
that may deservedly be called masterpieces. In particular, his descriptive poems have come to be recognized
for their originality and anticipation of certain trends in
twentieth century nature poetry. His dedication to poetry was intense, surviving, in addition to all other trials, the almost complete financial failure of three of the
four books he published during his lifetime. His *The
Shepherd's Calendar* is one of the truest and most delightful evocations of English rural life ever written.
The "animal" poems of his middle years (the most famous of which is probably "Badger") are stark and
powerful expressions of his increasing alienation and
despair. He carried his dedication to poetry undiminished into confinement in an asylum, where he wrote
poems which show his "sane" grasp of his own insanity. These later poems rise to a universality that has
made them widely admired ever since some of them
were published in 1873.

Clare was almost completely ignored by the critics
until the commentary of Arthur Symons in 1908, and
the first textually reliable selection of his poems did not
appear until 1920. Even at that, the student of Clare
must still exercise extreme caution when using certain
editions. In particular, the largest existing selection of
his poems, the most complete editions of his prose, and
the only one of his letters (all edited by J. W. and Anne
Tibble), as well as one of the two existing selections of
his asylum poems (edited by Geoffrey Grigson), contain serious misprintings of the manuscripts on almost
every page. Much better selections have appeared, published by the Oxford University Press. His reputation
began to rise after the work of Symons and especially
after the edition by Edmund Blunden in 1920. Much
criticism and analysis has appeared since the centennial
of Clare's death in 1864, and his reputation has risen
rapidly since then.

BIOGRAPHY

John Clare's childhood was spent laboring in the fields near his native village and in the "dame schools" that provided a rudimentary education for those of the rural poor who understood their value. Clare's father was a ballad singer of some local note, and this early exposure to village folk culture, together with his bent for reading, provided a solid base for his later accomplishments. His interest in writing seems to have awakened at the age of sixteen when he acquired a copy of James Thomson's narrative-descriptive poem *The Seasons* (1730, 1744). Finding time and opportunity to write at all, however, proved difficult. Unable to afford much paper, he recorded his earliest efforts on scraps kept in his hat; thus they were easily lost or damaged. The extremely long hours of an agricultural laborer and the distrust of learning among his fellow villagers restricted him further. Nevertheless, by his early twenties, he had assembled a fairly substantial body of work that he showed to a nearby storekeeper with literary connections in London. His first book, *Poems Descriptive of Rural Life and Scenery*, was brought out in 1820 by John Taylor, publisher of Charles Lamb and John Keats. It was an immediate success, going through four editions within a year. Taylor then published a second volume, *The Village Minstrel, and Other Poems*, in 1821, but its sales were disappointing. Clare's first book had caught the very end of a craze for "peasant poets," Over the next several years, he made a few trips to London, meeting and socializing with Lamb, William Hazlitt, Thomas De Quincey, and others. Nevertheless, problems quickly developed. He began to have disagreements with his publishers over the editing of his poems, the size of his family increased rapidly (he had married a local woman in 1820), and so did his debts. He could not seem to get an accurate or satisfactory explanation of how much of his royalties were needed to pay publishing expenses.

From then until 1837, Clare lived in Helpston almost without interruption, writing increasingly good poetry with almost no public recognition at all. A third volume, *The Shep-*

*herd's Calendar*, was finished in 1823 but not published until four years later when it, too, sold poorly. He suffered from malnutrition and his mental health began to deteriorate. Regular employment was scarce in his region, and a move to a neighboring village in 1832 (to a cottage given him by a patron) did not substantially alter his prospects. His sense of place was so strong that he found it difficult to adjust to the move, and he grew increasingly deluded. In 1835, he managed to have a fourth volume published, *The Rural Muse*. The book was well received by the critics but did not sell well.

Finally, in late 1837, he was taken to Matthew Allen's experimental asylum at High Beech, in the Epping Forest near London. There he was well-treated and recovered some of his physical health, but he wrote little for several years. In the spring of 1841, he began writing poetry again, and he escaped in July. He made his way home by walking for several days, surviving by eating grass along the roadside. Although he was not violent, he was clearly not sane, and in late 1841, he

*John Clare* (Hulton Archive/Getty Images)

was again committed, this time nearer home at the asylum in Northampton. There he remained until his death in 1864 at the age of seventy. His asylum poetry was written almost entirely in the last few months at High Beech and during the brief stay at home and the first several years at Northampton. When a sympathetic asylum supervisor who had preserved his work departed in 1850, his deteriorating condition and lack of encouragement from the staff seemingly closed off his inspiration.

ANALYSIS

The poetry of John Clare shows throughout its development the influence of three forces: the culture of his village and social class, nature, and the topographical and pastoral poetry of the eighteenth century. Clare's view of human life as lived in close relationship with nature is presented in his poetry as a series of contrasts between the freer, socially more equal, open-field village of his childhood and the enclosed, agriculturally "improved," and socially stratified village of his manhood; between the Eden of a wild nature untouched by human beings and the fallen nature of fences, uprooted landmarks, and vanished grazing rights; between the aesthetic response to nature that loves it for what it is and the scientific response that loves it for profit and social status. Further, as a self-educated poet in a land of illiterate laborers, Clare had difficulty resolving the tension between his temptation to idealize village life and his equally strong temptation to expose its squalid ignorance. One evidence of this is the fact that he wrote *The Shepherd's Calendar*, a celebration of the beauty and activity of a village, in the same year that he wrote "The Parish," a brutally frank attack on its ignorance and cultural isolation. In his best poetry, Clare is able to see each reality as only a part of the truth.

**"GYPSIES"**

A typical Clare poem of his pre-asylum years will seek, above all, concreteness in its imagery and a structure designed to make the images reveal the maximum amount of meaning. Clare is a master at creating multiple levels of significance through what at first seems like an almost random collection of sights and sounds. A poem that well illustrates this technique is his un-

rhymed sonnet "Gypsies." It is a poem that deftly combines Clare's love of rural life with his awareness of its darker side. He begins the poem, as he does so many others, with a sense of the mystery of nature: "The snow falls deep; the forest lies alone." He immediately introduces the theme of human suffering amid the beauty: "the boy goes hasty for his load of brakes/ Then thinks upon the fire and hurries back." The cold is beautiful but potentially deadly. Then he transports the reader to the gypsy camp where there are only bushes to break the wind, where "tainted mutton wastes upon the coals," and the scrawny dog squats nearby "and vainly waits the morsel thrown away." Clare's use of internal rhyme is very successful, as "tainted" and "vainly" resonate against each other in interesting ways. In a sense, the gypsies are "tainted" in the settled village society and thus hope in vain for acceptance. Clare has provided hints of an attitude, then, while allowing the details to carry the implications. He seems to reject both the villagers' ethnic bigotry and the hopelessness of gypsy life: "'Tis thus they live—a picture to the place/ A quiet, pilfering, unprotected race." The seeming offhandedness of "'Tis thus they live" is acceptance and rejection, simultaneously, as the remaining line and one half so neatly demonstrate by balancing "quiet" against "pilfering" against "unprotected." The sudden rise from specific images to broad generalization at the end does not surprise the reader because the details have been so carefully chosen throughout. Clare refuses to idealize gypsy life just as he refuses to excuse the villagers for their prejudice The sonnet as he uses it here retains most of the traditional Shakespearean form except for the lack of rhyme. It is all the more impressive because Clare encloses his argument in a description that values the gypsies for the beauty they add to life. This determination to see life for what it is and an equal determination not to allow its bitterness to defeat him or prevent him from seeing its beauty is one of Clare's most admirable qualities as a poet and as a man.

The themes of Clare's poetry grow directly out of the ways of seeing human life and nature illustrated in "Gypsies." Perhaps the most important of his themes is the contrast between the village and landscape of the past and of the present. In making this contrast in his poetry, Clare is not simply engaging in private history making that would leave modern readers uninterested because they occupy a space and a time far removed from Clare's. Rather, he is comparing two fundamentally different approaches to the relationship between human beings and the natural world. The choice between these two approaches is as crucially important today as it was then, and for this reason alone Clare's poetry has lost none of its cogency for the modern world.

### "THE MORES"

In Clare's time, enclosure of the land for purposes of agricultural improvement was the issue that divided people in rural areas. No Clare poem speaks more eloquently to what enclosure did, psychologically as well as physically, to village life and to him as a poet than "The Mores" (that is, moors). It is written in a familiar eighteenth century form and style: the locodescriptive poem in heroic couplets. Nevertheless, Clare handles it in original ways. The heroic couplet in the eighteenth century embodies the polished wit and rational completeness that characterized the view of life held by the Age of Reason. Clare's couplet has a slow, solemn movement that is equally as impressive, though far different in effect. At the beginning of the poem, for example, the same sense of mystery in primeval nature seen in "Gypsies" is present, although that mystery is more obviously a part of the argument to be made: "Far spread the moorey ground a level scene/ Bespread with rush and one eternal green/ That never felt the rage of blundering plough." Here again is balance: the quietness of the pre-enclosure view versus a barely suppressed anger; nature's innocence and eternity against the "blundering" greed of human beings.

Clare's description is always visually precise and yet capable of entertaining several levels of meaning: "uncheckt shadows of green green brown and grey," where "uncheckt" means both "without limits" and "not in checkered patterns as enclosed fields are." A few lines later, "one mighty flat undwarfed by bush or tree/ Spread its faint shadow of immensity." Here, "flat" functions both as a noun and as a kind of suspended adjective: The reader pauses in suspense at this unusual caesura, so that the line reinforces the idea that the reader cannot see the limits of this "faint shadow of immensity/ In the blue mist the (h)orisons edge sur-

rounds." Human pride erupts into the poem, for "inclosure came and trampled on the grave/ Of labours rights." From here to the end of the poem, there is continual tension between longing for the old freedom and the reality of the new concern for boundaries, profits, and class distinctions. When these two value systems begin to clash more directly in the poem, the descriptive style becomes harsher, befitting the new dispensation: "And sky bound mores in mangled garbs are left/ Like mighty giants of their limbs bereft." Everywhere there is a pettiness, a separation rather than a communion: "Fence now meets fence in owners little bounds . . ./ In little parcels little minds to please/ With men and flocks imprisoned ill at ease."

As the poem proceeds it becomes clearer that Clare is really talking about a failure of vision: "Each little tyrant with his little sign/ Shows where man claims earth glows no more divine." The problem with the human desire to dominate nature is finally that it destroys that which makes people most human. In Clare's view, then, beauty, freedom, open fields, and social harmony have been succeeded by ugliness, fences, and social antagonism. Under these circumstances, poetic creativity becomes as difficult as any other activity requiring vision. The moors "are vanished now with commons wild and gay/ As poets visions of lifes early day." The cumulative force of the couplets, the measured movement of the lines, the masterful control over the reader's "eye" as it moves over the landscape, all create an emotional impact that makes "The Mores" typical of Clare at his best in the descriptive-narrative poem.

Clare's poetry grew increasingly lyric and less narrative-descriptive as the years passed. As was John Keats, Clare was particularly interested in taking the sonnet in new directions. They both believed that the sonnet might function as a stanza form for longer poems. In Keats's case, the result was the great odes of 1819; in Clare's, the very different but impressive poems on animals of the mid-1830's. Clare's poems had always been filled with a variety of animal life, but these poems move to a new attitude toward nature, emphasizing its otherness from human beings. By a seeming paradox, they move also toward an increased empathy with nature. The paradox is resolved by seeing that it is precisely the alienation of wild nature from human society (especially of certain hunted animals) with which Clare could identify because he, too, felt thus cut off from human understanding. The actions of animals in and around nests, caves, and hollow trees fascinated him. These were places where relatively helpless creatures might hope to escape.

### "SAND MARTIN"

In the poem "Sand Martin," for example, the bird inhabits the "desolate face" of a wasted landscape far away from people where it flits about "an unfrequented sky." Clare seems to admire most the sand martin's ability to "accept" the desolation of its habitat because of the protection it affords. The speaker of the poem feels "a hermit joy/ To see thee circle round nor go beyond/ That lone heath and its melancholy pond." Clare knew that a person's roots and his resulting sense of place might make him part of a scene that could enervate his spirit; yet, he might be unable to function in any other place. Clare is a pioneer in using the sonnet to center on a single, unified experience by ignoring the traditional octave-sestet break and using instead accumulation of detail to create meaning. Thus, his early reading in the topographical poetry of the eighteenth century, with its emphasis on a collection of images moving toward a visual as well as an emotional climax, served him well when he wished to make his poetry express through details his anguish and sense of isolation. Meaning emerges in a Clare description almost in slow motion, and it is sometimes late in the poem before the reader realizes what power the accumulated detail has acquired.

### LYRIC POEMS

Clare is one of the great lyric poets of the English language. His roots were in a culture that valued the ballad and the oral tale as art forms as well as sources of tradition. Clare himself was a lifelong collector of ballads and folk songs (noting down music as well as words), and he played the violin well. Many of his finest lyrics come from the 1830's and the asylum years, when the bulk of his output became lyric rather than narrative or descriptive. The good lyric can sometimes succeed in reaching the widest audience when it is most personal and "private." From the mid-1830's come four of Clare's best: "Remembrances," "Song's Eternity," "With Garments Flowing," and "Decay." A brief comparison of these four will serve to illustrate the command that Clare exercised over a variety of forms, moods, and themes in the lyric.

In "Remembrances," Clare uses a device so simple and well known—the stages of human life compared to the seasons of the year—that in the hands of a lesser poet it would become trite and shopworn. This ballad-like poem has octameter lines and a typical rhyme scheme of *aaabcccddd*; it is marvelously adapted to the leisurely Smemories of childhood which the poem treats. From the first line, "Summers pleasures they are gone like to visions every one," Clare manages to imbue the commonest scenes from the past with a haunting quality that the incantatory rhythm of the verse reinforces perfectly.

"Song's Eternity" is a very different kind of lyric. Instead of unusually long lines, it has unusually short ones: alternating lines of four beats and two. Rather than the expansiveness of the quasi-narrative ballad, Clare offers the crisp conciseness of

> What is song's eternity?
> Come and see.
> Melodies of earth and sky.
> Here they be.
> Songs once sung to Adam's ears.
> Can it be? . . .
> Songs awakened with the spheres
> Alive.

It is Clare's frequently heard theme of the eternity of nature that will provide the necessary stay against the confusion of modern life.

The third lyric, "With Garments Flowing," represents still another form and another purpose. It is a love lyric written in a meter often found in Clare's poetry: stanzas with alternating nine and eight syllables, all tetrameter, rhyming *ababcdcd*. It is more regular than the forms used in "Remembrances" and "Song's Eternity" and was probably chosen because he wanted the ballad-like stanza without its looseness and conversational tone together with the conciseness and rhythm of "Song's Eternity" without the absolute regularity of that poem. The success of "With Garments Flowing" lies also in the metonymy of the garments of the lover's dress standing for the lover herself. To the speaker in the poem, she is the type of all that is beautiful. However, in describing her, Clare retains homely details of village life while avoiding the sentimentality that can threaten such an attempt.

Finally, "Decay" is another quite different kind of lyric and equally successful. Clare wrote it apparently as a means of understanding what was happening to his poetic voice as a result of the move in 1832 to another village, as a way of regaining his poetic voice or at least of explaining its loss. He skillfully controls the reader's response through subtle variations in the rhyme scheme in the ten-line stanzas, as well as through modulations in the simple theme: "O poesy is on the wane/ I hardly know her face again," which acts as a kind of refrain throughout. Personification is also important in this poem: The sun is a "homeless ranger" that "pursues a naked weary way/ Unnoticed like a very stranger." The blend of the local and the universal, as is so often true in Clare's poetry, is here perfectly calculated to communicate disorientation in a coherent manner: "I often think that west is gone/ Oh cruel time to undeceive us." Time has taken away the visionary gleam: "The stream it is a naked stream/ . . . The sky hangs o'er a broken dream/ The bramble's dwindled to a bramble." The tone becomes more bitter, and the speaker more puzzled even while attaining a new understanding: "And why should passing shadows grieve us/ . . . And hope is but a fancy play/ And joy the art of true believing." Here the sarcasm and the grief somehow perfectly complement each other.

### ASYLUM POEMS

Clare's creativity followed a different pattern in the asylum years. Long periods of virtual poetic silence were followed by relatively brief times of sustained production. The dominant theme of his asylum poems is the assertion of his identity as a free man and as a poet. Indeed, Clare had always believed that freedom of the eye and of the mind were necessary preconditions of artistic creativity. His determination to be remembered as a poet, decades after his work had been largely forgotten, is probably responsible both for the quality of his asylum work and for the fact that madness did not completely engulf his mind any sooner than it did. Clare's first sustained asylum production was a continuation of Lord Byron's *Childe Harold's Pil-*

*grimage* (1812-1818, 1819), written in 1841 under the delusion that he was Byron. While it was left unfinished, the work demonstrates that his descriptive and lyric talents were not only unimpaired but also still developing. It was, however, in the first few years of his confinement at Northampton Asylum (from 1842 to about 1848) that some of Clare's finest poems were written. Three of these may be examined briefly for the light they cast on the theme of self-identity and on his level of achievement in these years.

In "Peasant Poet," Clare seems to sum up what his poetic life had been about, emphasizing, of course, simplicity and love of nature. His gift for juxtaposing images of ordinary things to achieve fresh meaning is undiminished: "the daisy-covered ground" immediately next to "the cloud-bedappled sky"; the sound of the brook leading the eye to the swallow "swimming by." This peasant poet of whom he speaks (clearly himself) was not a great achiever "in life's affairs." He was just two things: "A peasant in his daily cares/ The poet in his joy." It is a descriptive lyric containing the essence of his poetic credo: poetry as joy, transforming the face of daily life.

The second poem, "An Invite to Eternity," is Clare's most sustained attempt to define the perception of the insane mind; not to define it as a dictionary would but to re-create for the reader its vision of the world—making the reader participate in it and so identify with it. Like so many of Clare's poems, whenever written, this one begins with an invitation—in this case to a "sweet maid" who is to travel with him through the landscape of madness. In the same sort of personification seen in "Decay," both the sun and the path have forgotten where they are to go. In this "strange death of life to be," what the reader sees is inverted, made into its opposite: "Where stones will turn to flooding streams/ Where plains will rise like ocean waves." The swaying rhythm of the tetrameter lines creates an almost hypnotic effect. It is an existence without identity: being and nonbeing at the same time. In this twilight existence, they will not know each other's face, and time itself will cease to exist: "The present mixed with reasons gone/ And past and present all as one." Knowing all this, he asks the maid, can her life be led "to join the living with the dead?" If so (and he seems to await her answer with the serenity of absolute knowledge), "Then trace thy footsteps on with me/ We're wed to one eternity." Logic, time, identity, and ordinary perception of the "real" have all been suspended, to be replaced by their opposites. The perfectly ordered form of the poem, its calm account of the horrors of irrationality, provide remarkable evidence of Clare's ability at times in the asylum to view his own insanity from outside, as it were. Perhaps more important, the poem demonstrates how much he was still a poet in control of his art.

The third poem is entitled simply "I Am." If "Peasant Poet" sums up Clare's view of himself as poet, and "An Invite to Eternity" his view of himself as insane, "I Am" may be said to provide the essence of Clare as child of God. In the poem, he creates a persona supremely tragic: the good man bereft of that which gave his life purpose and left to experience the moment of self-understanding completely alone. The poem turns on the idea of existence without essence, and the first stanza reiterates the "I Am" four times in its six lines: Since no one knows anything of him except that he exists, he becomes "the self-consumer of [his] woes." They have no outlet, they meet with no understanding. The tremendous psychological pressure that this would ordinarily create is somehow controlled and made to yield calm resignation rather than anger, as the speaker surveys "the vast shipwreck of my lifes esteems." Instead, in the third and final stanza, he returns to a familiar Clare theme: the Eden of nature. There, where there is neither man nor woman, only God, peace is at last possible: "Untroubling and untroubled where I lie/ The grass below, above, the vaulted sky." In Clare's country, the two essential facts had always been the moors and the sky—both flat, immense, bare, unchanging, losing themselves at the edge in mist and shadow.

## OTHER MAJOR WORKS

NONFICTION: *Sketches in the Life of John Clare, Written by Himself*, 1931; *John Clare's Birds*, 1982; *John Clare's Autobiographical Writings*, 1983; *The Natural History Prose Writings of John Clare*, 1983; *The Letters of John Clare*, 1985; *Selected Letters*, 1988 (Mark Storey, editor).

## BIBLIOGRAPHY

Bate, Jonathan. *John Clare: A Biography*. New York: Farrar, Straus and Giroux, 2003. Scholarly biography of the writer.

Blythe, Ronald. *Talking About John Clare*. Nottingham, England: Trent, 1999. A commentary on the relationship between the English rural writer and the places that inform his work. Includes passages on many writers who are thematically associated with Clare.

Chilcott, Tim. *"A Real World and Doubting Mind": A Critical Study of the Poetry of John Clare*. Hull, England: Hull University Press, 1985. The title of this volume is taken from Clare's *The Shepherd's Calendar*. Chilcott argues that the "real world" and the "doubting mind" are two distinct aspects of Clare's poetry. Discusses the periods before and during his asylum stay. A challenging critical study recommended for readers familiar with Clare.

Chirico, Paul. *John Clare and the Imagination of the Reader*. New York: Palgrave Macmillan, 2007. This work examines Clare's poetry, his early periodical publications, and scholarly studies by others about his writing. Also examined are his role in the literary world and his relationship with his publishers.

Clay, Arnold. *Itching After Rhyme: A Life of John Clare*. Tunbridge Wells, England: Parapress, 2000. A detailed biography with bibliographical references and index.

Houghton-Walker, Sarah. *John Clare's Religion*. Burlington, Vt.: Ashgate, 2009. Discusses the religious aspect presented in Clare's poetry in the context of pastoral poetry.

Storey, Edward. *A Right to Song: The Life of John Clare*. London: Methuen, 1982. A full-length biography sympathetic to Clare that looks at the complexity of his poetic landscapes. The thoroughly researched biography stays close to his works and is recommended for Clare scholars.

Storey, Mark. *The Poetry of John Clare: A Critical Introduction*. London: Macmillan, 1974. Explicitly an introduction, this volume traces the development of Clare's poetry from his humble beginnings to his maturation. Chooses *The Shepherd's Calendar* as the focal point for an examination of Clare's mature descriptive technique. An appreciative study of Clare that highlights both the appeal and the variety of his work.

Vardy, Alan D. *John Clare: Politics and Poetry*. New York: Palgrave Macmillan, 2003. This profile examines the political and philosophical views of the poet and further investigates the role of his editor, John Taylor.

*Mark Minor*

---

# AUSTIN CLARKE

**Born:** Dublin, Ireland; May 9, 1896
**Died:** Dublin, Ireland; March 19, 1974

PRINCIPAL POETRY

*The Vengeance of Fionn*, 1917 (based on the Irish Saga "Pursuit of Diarmid and Grainne")
*The Fires of Baal*, 1921
*The Sword of the West*, 1921
*The Cattledrive in Connaught, and Other Poems*, 1925 (based on the prologue to *Tain bo Cuailnge*)
*Pilgrimage, and Other Poems*, 1929
*The Collected Poems of Austin Clarke*, 1936
*Night and Morning*, 1938
*Ancient Lights*, 1955
*Too Great a Vine: Poems and Satires*, 1957
*The Horse-Eaters: Poems and Satires*, 1960
*Collected Later Poems*, 1961
*Forget-Me-Not*, 1962
*Flight to Africa, and Other Poems*, 1963
*Mnemosyne Lay in Dust*, 1966
*Old-Fashioned Pilgrimage, and Other Poems*, 1967
*The Echo at Coole, and Other Poems*, 1968
*Orphide, and Other Poems*, 1970
*Tiresias: A Poem*, 1971
*The Wooing of Becfolay*, 1973
*Collected Poems*, 1974
*The Selected Poems*, 1976

OTHER LITERARY FORMS

Besides his epic, narrative, and lyric poetry, Austin Clarke published three novels, two volumes of autobiography, some twenty verse plays, and a large volume of journalistic essays and literary reviews for newspaper and radio. He also delivered a number of radio lectures on literary topics and gave interviews on his own life and work on Irish radio and television.

ACHIEVEMENTS

In a poetic career that spanned more than fifty years, Austin Clarke was a leading figure in the "second generation" of the Irish Literary Revival (also known as the Celtic Revival). Most of his career can be understood as a response to the aims of that movement: to celebrate the heroic legends of ancient Ireland, to bring the compositional technique of the bardic poets into modern English verse, and to bring poetry and humor together in a socially liberating way on the modern stage.

Clarke's earliest efforts to write epic poems on pre-Christian Ireland were not generally successful, although his first poems do have passages of startling color and lyric beauty that presage his later work. When, in the 1930's, he turned to early medieval ("Celtic Romanesque") Ireland, he found his métier, both in poetry and in fiction. To the celebration of the myth of a vigorous indigenous culture in which Christian ascetic and pagan hedonist coexisted, he bent his own disciplined efforts. Unlike William Butler Yeats and most of the leading writers of the Revival, Clarke had direct access to the language of the ancient literature and worked to reproduce its rich sound in modern English. In this effort he was uniquely successful among modern Irish poets.

In his later years, Clarke turned to satirizing the domestic scene, living to see cultural changes remedy many of his complaints about Irish life. Although he wrote in obscurity through most of his career, in his later life, Clarke was belatedly recognized by several institutions: He was awarded an honorary D.Litt. in 1966 from Trinity College, received the Gregory Medal in 1968 from the Irish Academy of Letters, and was the "Writer in Profile" on Radio Telifís Éireann in 1968.

BIOGRAPHY

Austin Clarke was born into a large, middle-class, Catholic, Dublin family on May 9, 1896. He was educated by the Jesuits at Belvedere College and earned a B.A. and an M.A. in English literature from University College, Dublin, in 1916 and 1917, and he was appointed assistant lecturer there in 1917. In his formative years, he was heavily impressed by the Irish Literary Revival, especially Douglas Hyde's Gaelic League and Yeats's Abbey Theatre, and his political imagination was fired by the Easter Rising of 1916. In 1920, following a brief civil marriage to Geraldine Cummins, he was dismissed from his university post; shortly thereafter, he emigrated to London and began to write his epic poems on heroic subjects drawn from the ancient literature of Ireland.

In 1930, Clarke married Nora Walker, with whom he had three sons, and between 1929 and 1938, he wrote a number of verse plays and two novels—both banned in Ireland—before returning permanently to Ireland in 1937. Since in his creative career and national literary allegiance he was from the beginning a disciple of Yeats, he was sorely disappointed to be omitted from *The Oxford Book of Modern Verse* that Yeats edited in 1936. Nevertheless, with the publication of *Night and Morning*, Clarke began a new and public phase in his creative career: The following year, he began his regular broadcasts on poetry on Radio Éireann and started to write book reviews for *The Irish Times*. Between 1939 and 1942, he was president of Irish PEN and cofounder (with Robert Farren) of the Dublin Verse-Speaking Society and the Lyric Theatre Company. Subsequently, his verse plays were produced at the Abbey and on Radio Éireann.

Clarke's prolonged creative silence in the early 1950's seems, in retrospect, oddly appropriate to the depressed state of Ireland, where heavy emigration and strict censorship seemed to conspire in lowering public morale. However, as if he were anticipating the economic revival, he published *Ancient Lights* in 1955. Here began a new phase in his poetic career, that of a waspish commentator on contemporary events, composing dozens of occasional poems, some of which can lay claim to a reader's attention beyond their particular origins. Between 1955 and his death, a collection of

these pieces appeared every two or three years, as well as two volumes of autobiography. His public profile was maintained through his radio broadcasts, his regular reviews in *The Irish Times*, his attendance at many PEN conferences, and his visits to the United States and the Soviet Union. In 1972, he was nominated for the Nobel Prize in Literature. He died on March 19, 1974, shortly after the publication of his *Collected Poems*.

ANALYSIS

The first phase of Austin Clarke's poetic career, 1917 to 1925, produced four epic poems that are little more than apprentice work. Drawing on Celtic and biblical texts, they betray too easily the influences of Yeats, Sir Samuel Ferguson, and other pioneers of the Revival. Considerably overwritten and psychologically unsure, only in patches do they reveal Clarke's real talent: his close understanding of the original text and a penchant for erotic humor and evocative lyrical descriptions of nature. The major preoccupations of his permanent work did not appear until he assimilated these earliest influences.

Clarke's difficulties with religious faith, rejection of Catholic doctrine, and an unfulfilled need for spiritual consolation provide the theme and tension in the poems from *Pilgrimage, and Other Poems* and *Night and Morning*. These poems arise from the conflicts between the mores of modern Irish Catholicism and Clarke's desire for emotional and sexual fulfillment. These poems, therefore, mark a departure from his earlier work in that they are personal and contemporary in theme, yet they are also designedly Irish, in setting and technique.

In searching for a vehicle to express his personal religious conflicts while keeping faith in his commitment to the Irish Literary Revival, Clarke found an alternative to Yeats's heroic, pre-Christian age: the "Celtic Romanesque," the medieval period in Irish history when the Christian Church founded by Saint Patrick was renowned for its asceticism, its indigenous monastic tradition, its scholastic discipline, its missionary zeal, and the brilliance of its art (metalwork, illuminated manuscripts, sculpture, and devotional and nature poetry). Although this civilization contained within it many of the same tensions that bedeviled

Clarke's world—those between the Christian ideal and the claims of the flesh, between Christian faith and pagan hedonism—it appealed to his imagination because of his perception of its independence from Roman authority, the separation of ecclesiastical and secular spheres, and its respect for artistic excellence. This view of the period is selective and romanticized but is sufficient in that it serves his artistic purposes.

Clarke's poetry is Irish also in a particular, technical sense: in its emulation of the complex sound patterns of Gaelic verse, called *rime riche*. In this endeavor, he was following the example set by Douglas Hyde in his translations of folk songs and by the poems of Thomas MacDonagh. This technique employs a variety of rhyming and assonantal devices so that a pattern of rhymes echoes through the middles and ends of lines, playing off unaccented as well as accented syllables. Relatively easy to manage in Gaelic poetry because of the sound structure of the language, *rime riche* requires considerable dexterity in English. However, Clarke diligently embraced this challenge, sometimes producing results that were little more than technical exercises or impenetrably obscure, but often producing works of unusual virtuosity and limpid beauty. Clarke summed up his approach in his answer to Robert Frost's inquiry about the kind of verse he wrote: "I load myself with chains and I try to get out of them." To which came the shocked reply: "Good Lord! You can't have many readers."

Indeed, Clarke is neither a popular nor an easy poet. Despite his considerable output (his *Collected Poems* runs to some 550 pages), his reputation stands firmly on a select number of these. Of his early narrative poems, adaptations of Celtic epic tales, only a few passages transcend the prevailing verbal clutter.

## PILGRIMAGE, AND OTHER POEMS

With the publication of *Pilgrimage, and Other Poems*, however, the focus narrowed, and the subjects are realized with startling clarity. Perhaps the most representative and accomplished poem in this volume is the lyric "Celibacy." This treatment of a hermit's struggle with lust combines Clarke's personal conflicts with the Catholic Church's sexual teachings and his sympathy with the hermit's spiritual calling in a finely controlled, ironic commentary on the contemporary Irish suspi-

cion of sex. Clarke achieves this irony through a series of images that juxtapose the monk's self-conscious heroism to his unconscious self-indulgence. The rhyming and assonantal patterns in this poem are an early example of the successful use of the sound patterns borrowed from Gaelic models that became one of the distinctive characteristics of his work.

## NIGHT AND MORNING

With the publication of *Night and Morning*, there is a considerable consolidation of power. In this collection of sterling consistency, Clarke succeeds in harnessing the historical elements to his personal voice and vision. In the exposition of the central theme of the drama of racial conscience, he shows himself to be basically a religious poet. The central problems faced here are the burden to the contemporary generation of a body of truth received from the centuries of suffering and refinement, the limitations of religious faith in an age of sexual and spiritual freedom, and the conflicts arising from a sympathy with and a criticism of the ordinary citizen. Clarke's own position is always ambivalent. While he seems to throw down the gauntlet to the dogmatic Church, his challenge is never wholehearted: He is too unsure of his position outside the institution he ostensibly abjures. This ambivalence is borne out in the fine title poem in this volume, in the implications of the Christian imagery of the Passion, the candle, the celebration of the Mass, the Incarnation, and the double lightning of faith and reason. A confessional poem, "Night and Morning" protests the difficulties in maintaining an adult faith in the Christian message in a skeptical age. Although it criticizes the lack of an intellectual stiffening in modern Irish Catholicism and ostensibly yearns for the medieval age when faith and reason were reconciled, the poem's passion implies an allegiance to the Church that is more emotional than intellectual. These ambiguities are deftly conveyed by the title, design, tone, and imagery of the poem.

Almost every poem in this volume shows Clarke at his best, especially "Martha Blake," "The Straying Student," and "The Jewels." In "Martha Blake," a portrait of a devout daily communicant, Clarke manages multiple points of view with lucidity and ease. From one perspective, Martha's blind faith is depicted as heroic and personally valid; from another, Martha is not very aware of the beauty of the natural world around her, although she experiences it vicariously through the ardor of her religious feelings; from a third, as in the superb final stanza, the poet shares with his readers a simultaneous double perspective that balances outer and inner visions, natural and supernatural grace. The ambiguity and irony that permeate this last stanza are handled with a sensitivity that, considering the anguish and anger of so much of his religious verse, reveals a startling degree of sympathy for ordinary, sincere Christians. He sees that a passionate nature may be concealed, and may be fulfilling itself, beneath the appearances of a simple devotion.

### ANCIENT LIGHTS

When, after a long silence, *Ancient Lights* appeared in 1955, Clarke had turned from his earlier historical and personal mode to a public and satirical posture. These poems comment wittily on current issues controversial in the Ireland of the early 1950's: the mediocrity and piety of public life, "scandalous" women's fashions, the domination of Irish public opinion by the Catholic Church, the "rhythm" method of birth control, and the incipient public health program. Many of these poems may appear quaint and require annotations even for a post-Vatican II Irish audience. The lead poem, "Celebrations," for example, in criticizing the smug piety of postrevolutionary Ireland, focuses on the Eucharistic Congress held in Dublin in 1932. The poem is studded with references to the Easter Rising of 1916, its heroic antecedents and its promise for the new nation. These are set in ironic contrast with the jobbing latter-day politicians who have made too easy an accommodation with the Church and have thus replaced the British with a native oppression. Clarke vehemently excoriates the manner in which the public purse is made to subscribe to Church-mandated institutions. Despite its highly compressed content, this poem succeeds in making a direct statement on an important public issue. Unfortunately, the same is not true of many of Clarke's subsequent satires, which degenerate into bickering over inconsequential subjects, turn on cheap puns, or lapse into doubtful taste.

This cannot be said, however, of the title poem of this volume, one of Clarke's best achievements. Autobiographical and literally confessional, it can be profit-ably read in conjunction with his memoir, *Twice 'Round the Black Church: Early Memories of Ireland and England* (1962), especially pages 138-139. It begins with the familiar Clarke landscape of Catholic Dublin and the conflict between adolescent sex and conscience. Having made a less than full confession, the persona guiltily skulks outside, pursued by a superstitious fear of retribution.

Emerging into the light like an uncaged bird, in a moment reminiscent of that experienced by James Joyce's Stephen Daedalus on the beach, the protagonist experiences an epiphany of natural grace that sweeps his sexual guilt away. The Church-induced phobias accumulated over the centuries drop away in a moment of creative self-assertion. This experience is confirmed in nature's own manner: driven by a heavy shower into the doorway of the Protestant black church (for the full significance of the breaking of this sectarian taboo, see again his memoir), he experiences a spiritual catharsis as he observes the furious downpour channeled, contained, and disposed by roof, pipe, and sewer. With the sun's reappearance, he is born again in a moment of triumphant, articulate joy.

The narrative direction, tonal variety, and especially the virtuosity of the final stanza establish this poem as one of Clarke's finest creations. It weaves nostalgia, humor, horror, vision, and euphoria into a series of epiphanies that prepare the reader for the powerful conclusion. This last stanza combines the images of penance with baptism in a flood of images that are precisely observed and fraught with the spiritual significance for which the reader has been prepared. It should be noted, however, that even here Clarke's resolution is consciously qualified: The cowlings and downpipes are ecclesiastical, and the flood's roar announces the removal of but "half our heavens." Nevertheless, in the control and energy of its images and sound patterns, the poem realizes many of Clarke's objectives in undertaking to write poetry that dramatizes the proverbial tensions between art, religion, and nature in the national conscience.

### SATIRE AND IRONY

In the nineteen years following the publication of *Ancient Lights*, Clarke produced a continuous stream of satires on occasional issues, few of which rise above their origins. They are often hasty in judgment, turgid almost beyond retrieval, or purely formal exercises. These later volumes express a feeling of alienation from modern Ireland, in its particular mix of piety and materialism. Always mindful of the myths lying behind Irish life, his critique begins to lose its currency and sounds quixotically conservative. Then in the early 1960's, with the arrival of industrialization in Ireland, relative prosperity, and the Church reforms following Vatican II, many of Clarke's criticisms of Irish life become inapplicable and his latter-day eroticism sounds excessively self-conscious and often in poor taste. Nevertheless, some of his later lyrics, such as "Japanese Print," and translations from the Irish are quite successful: lightly ironic, relaxed, matching the spirit of their originals.

### MNEMOSYNE LAY IN DUST

The most impressive personal poem of this last phase in his career is the confessional *Mnemosyne Lay in Dust*. Based on his experiences during a lengthy stay at a mental institution some forty years before, it recrosses the battleground between his inherited Jansenism and his personal brand of secular humanism. In harrowing, cacophonic verse, the poem describes the tortured hallucinations, the electric shock treatment, the amnesia, the pain of rejection by "Margaret" (his first wife), the contemplated suicide, and the eventual rejection of religious taboos for a life directed to the development of reason and human feeling. For all its extraordinary energy, however, this poem lacks the consistency and finish of his shorter treatments of the same dilemma.

### FINAL PHASE

The last phase of Clarke's poetic career produced a group of poems on erotic subjects that affirm, once again, his belief in the full right to indulge in life's pleasures. The best of these—such as "Anacreontic" and "The Healing of Mis"—are remarkably forthright and witty and are not marred by the residual guilt of his earlier forays into this subject.

Clarke's oeuvre is by turns brilliant and gauche. Learned and cranky, tortured and tender, his work moves with extraordinary commitment within a narrow range of concerns. His quarrels with Irish Catholicism and the new Irish state, his preoccupation with problems of sexuality and with Irish myth and history, and his technical emulation of Irish-language models set him firmly at the center of Irish poetry after Yeats. These considerations place him outside the modernist movement. In Ireland, he has been more highly rated by literary historians than by the younger generation of poets. Recognition abroad is coming late: In about twenty poems, he has escaped from his largely self-imposed chains to gain the attention of the world at large.

### OTHER MAJOR WORKS

LONG FICTION: *The Bright Temptation*, 1932, 1973; *The Singing Men at Cashel*, 1936; *The Sun Dances at Easter*, 1952.

PLAYS: *The Son of Learning*, pr., pb. 1927 (pr. 1930 as *The Hunger Demon*); *The Flame*, pb. 1930; *Sister Eucharia*, pr., pb. 1939; *Black Fast*, pb. 1941; *As the Crow Flies*, pr. 1942 (radio play), pr. 1948 (staged); *The Kiss*, pr. 1942; *The Plot Is Ready*, pr. 1943; *The Viscount of Blarney*, pr., pb. 1944; *The Second Kiss*, pr., pb. 1946; *The Plot Succeeds*, pr., pb. 1950; *The Moment Next to Nothing*, pr., pb. 1953; *Collected Plays*, pb. 1963; *The Student from Salamanca*, pr. 1966; *Two Interludes Adapted from Cervantes: "The Student from Salamanca" and "The Silent Lover,"* pb. 1968; *The Impuritans: A Play in One Act Freely Adapted from the Short Story "Young Goodman Brown" by Nathaniel Hawthorne*, pb. 1972; *The Visitation*, pb. 1974; *The Third Kiss*, pb. 1976; *Liberty Lane*, pb. 1978.

NONFICTION: *Poetry in Modern Ireland*, 1951; *Twice 'Round the Black Church: Early Memories of Ireland and England*, 1962; *A Penny in the Clouds: More Memories of Ireland and England*, 1968; *The Celtic Twilight and the Nineties*, 1969; *Growing Up Stupid Under the Union Jack: A Memoir*, 1980.

### BIBLIOGRAPHY

Algoo-Baksh, Stella. *Austin C. Clarke: A Biography.* Toronto, Ont.: ECW Press, 1994. Combines a narrative of Clarke's life with thoughtful interpretations of some of his major works. Gives a portrait of his public persona but few details of his personal life. Includes bibliographical references and index.

Corcoran, Neil. *Poets of Modern Ireland.* Carbondale:

Southern Illinois University Press, 1999. Contains an essay on Clarke, which focuses on his poetic achievements.

Garratt, Robert F. *Modern Irish Poetry: Tradition Continuity from Yeats to Heaney.* Berkeley: University of California Press, 1986. This important book devotes a chapter to Clarke, the main figure of transition for twentieth century Irish poetry. Clarke's early poetry followed William Butler Yeats in retelling Irish myths, his middle work focused on medievalism, and his later poems echoed James Joyce in their critical analysis of religion. Contains an index and select bibliography that includes material on Clarke.

Halpern, Susan. *Austin Clarke: His Life and Work.* Dublin: Dolmen Press, 1974. This survey of Clarke's prolific output in prose and verse concentrates on the verse. Substantial bibliography.

Harmon, Maurice. *Austin Clarke, 1896-1974: A Critical Introduction.* Dublin: Wolfhound Press, 1989. The introduction covers the life of Clarke, the contexts for his writing, his Catholicism, and his participation in nationalist movements. Two phases are then examined: first, his prose, drama, and poetry from 1916 to 1938; second, his sustained work in poetry, short and long, from 1955 to 1974. Supplemented by a portrait, notes, a bibliography, and an index.

*Irish University Review* 4 (Spring, 1974). This special issue on Clarke contains a detailed account of his involvement with, and artistic contributions to, the Dublin Verse-Speaking Society and the Lyric Theatre Company, and it provides a complete list of the two organizations' productions.

Murphy, Daniel. "Disarmed, a Malcontent." In *Imagination and Religion in Anglo-Irish Literature, 1930-1980.* Blackrock, Ireland: Irish Academic Press, 1987. Analyzes Clarke's lyrics and satires. Also examines religious tensions in *Mnemosyne Lay in Dust*, reviews Clarke's use of history, examines Clarke's satirical style, and finally sketches Clarke's use of nature. The chapter is supplemented by notes and a bibliography. The book contains an index.

Ricigliano, Lorraine. *Austin Clarke: A Reference Guide.* New York: Maxwell Macmillan International, 1993.

A chronology of the major works by Clarke; an alphabetical list of all the individual poems and plays in the volumes cited; and a secondary bibliography, also arranged chronologically from 1918 to 1992, with descriptive annotations.

Schirmer, Gregory A. *The Poetry of Austin Clarke.* Notre Dame, Ind.: University of Notre Dame Press, 1983. A critique of Clarke's poetry. Bibliography and index.

Tapping, G. Craig. *Austin Clarke: A Study of His Writings.* Dublin: Academy Press, 1981. After calling Clarke's tradition "modern classicism," Tapping sketches a background of Romanticism to "Celto-Romanesque." Five chapters study the poetic drama, the novels, the poetry from 1938 to 1961, the poetry of the 1960's, and the new poems as treatments of old myths. Augmented by bibliographies, notes, an appendix, and an index.

*Cóilín Owens*

---

# ARTHUR HUGH CLOUGH

**Born:** Liverpool, England; January 1, 1819
**Died:** Florence, Italy; November 13, 1861

PRINCIPAL POETRY
*The Bothie of Tober-na-Vuolich*, 1848 (first published as *Toper-na-Fuosich*)
*Ambarvalia*, 1849 (with Thomas Burbridge)
*Amours de Voyage*, 1858 (serial)
*Mari Magno*, pb. 1862 (wr. 1861)
*Poems*, 1862
*Dipsychus*, pb. 1865 (wr. 1850)
*The Poems of A. H. Clough*, 1951 (H. F. Lowry, editor)

OTHER LITERARY FORMS
Arthur Hugh Clough (kluhf), although primarily a poet, was also a distinguished essayist. Clough's essays tend to cluster around two topics—literary criticism, and social, especially religious, issues. His prose works appeared primarily in newspapers and periodicals.

They have been collected in *The Poems and Prose Remains of Arthur Hugh Clough* (1869) and *Selected Prose Works* (1964).

ACHIEVEMENTS

Most assessments of Arthur Hugh Clough's achievements raise the question, "Why did he not achieve more?" This question originated with his contemporaries and reflects the social attitudes and professional expectations of Victorian times. A young man who was well begun, that is, one who graduated from Oxford or Cambridge and who enjoyed the respect of his colleagues, was expected to rise to eminence in his profession. Clough began with these high expectations. Subsequently, however, he surrendered a fellowship at Oxford, took an administrative post at the University of London, became an examiner in the Education Office, and, finally, an aide to the famous nurse Florence Nightingale. Contemporaries saw this path as a continual falling off. Furthermore, his real accomplishments in poetry occur in just a single decade of his life. Perhaps a more generous way of assessing Clough's achievement is to concentrate on his creative work itself.

His writing reveals a ferocious intellectual honesty that, by its clarity of vision, allows subsequent generations to see more clearly what were the inner tensions of the reflective person in an age of religious, scientific, and political ferment. Clough is an articulate observer of the age that witnessed the rapid spread of evangelicalism, the sharp reaction against it by the Oxford Movement, the open attacks on historic Christianity, and the fervent reply of a beleaguered orthodoxy. Moreover, he is not only an observer; he is also a sympathetic participant drawn in painfully divergent directions by the conflicts of his times.

BIOGRAPHY

When Arthur Hugh Clough was three years old, his family moved from Liverpool to Charleston, South Carolina. During the six years he spent in the United States, he lived under the constant influence of his mother's evangelical piety. In spite of a subsequent religious disillusionment, the concerns and temperament of the evangelical disposition marked Clough's poetry for the rest of his life.

*Arthur Hugh Clough* (Hulton Archive/Getty Images)

In 1828, Clough was sent back to England for his education. The following year, he entered Rugby and so fell under another of the dominant influences on his life and work—namely, the family of the headmaster, Thomas Arnold. Arnold and his two sons Tom and Matthew Arnold (who became a poet) fostered in Clough the ideals of a commitment to reason, rigorous self-discipline in pursuit of high goals, and a deep moral sobriety in contemplating public affairs. At Rugby, Clough was editor of the *Rugby Magazine* and head of the School House.

Clough won a prestigious scholarship to Balliol College, Oxford, which he entered in 1827. In 1841, he earned a second-class degree, to the considerable surprise of friends who had expected more, and he was denied a fellowship in his own college after his graduation. Nevertheless, he was elected to a fellowship in Oriel College and so remained at Oxford, where he became one of the most popular tutors.

Throughout Clough's years at Oxford, he had watched the progress of the Oxford Movement. The polemical context of religious discussions on the Oxford campus at the time may have contributed to a growing skepticism, which culminated in Clough's resigning the Oriel Fellowship in 1848 as an act of conscience. He could not endorse the Thirty-nine Articles (the Creed of the Anglican Church), as Oxford dons were expected to do. The soul-searching struggle of his departure from Oxford may be intimated in his poem *The Bothie of Tober-na-Vuolich*, written shortly thereafter.

Clough was not "ruined" in English education, however, and in 1849, after a trip to Italy during which he witnessed the French suppression of Giuseppe Mazzini's Roman Republic, he became the principal of University Hall, University College, London. From the Italian trip came his *Amours de Voyage*. He returned to Italy the following year and, while there, began his long and perhaps best-known poem, *Dipsychus* (first published in *Letters and Remains*, 1865).

In 1852, Clough resigned his duties at University Hall in a dispute over the manner in which religious instruction should be administered and over his refusal to actively recruit students in this prototype of a modern university. He set sail for the United States, where he enjoyed some reputation for his *The Bothie of Tober-na-Vuolich*, and the favor of such American literary figures as Ralph Waldo Emerson, James Russell Lowell, Henry Wadsworth Longfellow, and Charles Eliot Norton. Nevertheless, he could not find a position that would allow him an income sufficient to marry the girl he had left in England—Blanche Smith. Thus, he returned to England when Thomas Carlyle secured for him a position with the Education Office.

Clough and Blanche Smith were married in June, 1854, and for the remaining seven years of his life, he continued his rather routine work as a bureaucrat. This employment, compounded by the increasing duties he performed for Florence Nightingale, Blanche's cousin, crowded out his efforts at poetry. This busy employment helps to account for the fact that Clough's most prolific period of creativity was confined to a single decade of his life.

During 1859, Clough was stricken ill with scarlatina. Traveling about the Continent in an effort to recover his health gave him opportunity to think of poetry once again. He had written a good deal of the unfinished *Mari Magno* (first published in *Poems*, 1862) when he died in Florence in 1861. He was buried in the Protestant cemetery there, just four months after Elizabeth Barrett Browning had been interred in the same place.

## ANALYSIS

Arthur Hugh Clough's poetry is the effort of a man reared in deep religious faith to discover whether, following his apostasy, an honest skepticism could produce high-minded contentments equal to those of the idealism he had repudiated.

### THE BOTHIE OF TOBER-NA-VUOLICH

Although he wrote occasional poems throughout his life and published a number in the school magazine at Rugby, Clough's career as a serious poet extends only from 1848 to 1858, with a resurgence of activity in the last year of his life, 1861. *The Bothie of Tober-na-Vuolich*, his first major work, appeared at the end of a long year of soul searching. Early in 1848, he had resigned as tutor, and in October, he resigned his fellowship at Oriel. In November, the poem appeared. It is a long account of a group of Oxford scholars who retire to the Scottish highlands to read for examinations. The most distinctive member of the party, Philip Hewson, is a freethinking radical who falls in love three different times during the extended stay—the last time with the girl who lives in the bothie (cottage) at Tober-na-Vuolich. Philip's various personal experiences have a softening effect on his political views. Early in the poem, he makes a high-strung and doctrinaire attack on the privileged classes, but the women he meets have to be dealt with as actual and complex beings. When he finally falls in love with the peasant girl Elspie, he comes to realize that his economic account of the peasantry is far too simple to explain the living person. In the belief that Oxford scholasticism is too far removed from the life of experience, Philip declines to return—for reasons similar to those of the poet himself. Even Philip's skepticism now seems to him too doctrinaire to account for the stress of his inner life, and the poem ends with Philip and Elspie emigrating to New Zealand where he "hewed and dug; subdued the earth and his spirit." Clough suggests that his late skepticism might be as doctrinaire as his early faith, and he looks to the leavening of actual experience to moderate his own abstract scholasticism.

*The Bothie of Tober-na-Vuolich* is written in hexameters. This fact has produced a long-running controversy over the metrical effects of the poem. Wendell Harris has given a comprehensive account of the arguments (*Arthur Hugh Clough*, 1970). Clough's defenders—such as Matthew Arnold—believe that his use of hexameters gives his poem the primitive, homespun forcefulness that is also to be found in the poetry of classical antiquity—in Homer's *Iliad* (c. 750 B.C.E.; English translation, 1611) for example: "So in the golden morning they parted and went to the westward." Critics of the poem believe that for a sustained work the meter, tending to "break down into anapests" (Harris), flows against the natural iambs of English narrative discourse. It falls somewhere between prose and poetry: "So in the cottage with Adam the pupils live together/ Duly remained, and read, and looked no more for Philip." If there is to be found a justification for the meter, it is in Clough's expectation that the rough-hewn meter would reinforce his theme: the rejection of doctrinaire scholasticism (and the modern poetic conventions) in favor of an experientially authenticated sense of love and social justice.

### AMBARVALIA

*Ambarvalia* appeared in January, 1849—only three months after *The Bothie of Tober-na-Vuolich*. *Ambarvalia* is a collection of poems on several topics. The title refers to an ancient Roman festival in which animals were sacrificed to ensure the fertility of the fields. By this title, Clough may have intended to remove himself from a sectarian Christian ideal of the world and to evoke the image of a mythology at once more primitive and closer to nature. The leading poem of the collection implies this sort of skepticism; it is called "The Questioning Spirit." In it, one human spirit confronts all the others with troubling questions, and they reply that they neither know nor need to know the solution to such rarefied philosophical problems. The poem is an attack on a mindless sort of orthodoxy: "Only with questionings pass I to and fro,/ Perplexing these that sleep, and in their folly/ inbreeding doubt and sceptic melancholy." That melancholy questioning, coupled with a

persistent but vague hope that always attends his agnosticism, could be the theme of Clough's entire poetry. The poem "Why Should I Say I See the Things I See Not" is a well-nigh militant refusal to say that reality rests on things not manifest, "Unfit, unseen, unimagined, all unknown." The last of the twenty-nine poems in *Ambarvalia* asks the ancient question whether there actually are gods who treat human beings in the apparently shabby ways that fate seems to dictate. He answers his own question in this problematical way:

> If it is so let it be so
> And we will all agree so;
> But the plot has counterplot,
> It may be, and yet be not.

### DIPSYCHUS

In 1850, Clough began his long poem *Dipsychus*. Although it did not appear until 1865 (indeed it was never truly finished), this poem has since become Clough's best-known work. It consists of fourteen scenes, an epilogue, and four more scenes of a continuation. The poem is set in Venice. Its protagonist is Dipsychus, the divided soul, who is engaged in a lengthy dialogue with Spirit (who, as the reader later learns, is Mephistopheles). Some readers have believed that the Spirit is the projected voice of the skeptical "half" of Dipsychus's mind. A better reading seems to be that Dipsychus represents the mind torn between faith and doubt, and Spirit represents the distractions that would alleviate his inward tensions through the pleasures of everyday life: sex, wealth, the struggle for power, and the like. Dipsychus, however, does not want to be merely mollified; he wants to know the honest truth of the world.

*Dipsychus* not only is reminiscent of Johann Wolfgang von Goethe's *Faust: Eine Tragödie* (pb. 1808, 1833; *The Tragedy of Faust*, 1823, 1838) but also challenges comparison. Goethe's poem has more action and pageantry, a grander scale and more subtle inquiry, but Clough's poem presents the issues with a bold forthrightness that marks the possibility of a clearly skeptical voice in Victorian society even before the publication of Charles Darwin's *On the Origin of Species* (1859). The clause "Christ is not risen" becomes a recurring refrain in the opening scenes. Spirit (Mephistopheles) replies that if such is the case, all Dipsychus's metaphysics would be futile and he might as well console himself with the pleasures of the flesh:

> This lovely creature's glowing charms
> Are gross illusion, I don't doubt that;
> But when I pressed her in my arms
> I somehow didn't think about that.

Finally, Dipsychus, having succumbed to Spirit's temptation to "Enjoy the minute," despairs of a metaphysic that will give authenticity to his actions and resigns himself to living the common life. In the continuation, however, when he has lived long and become a successful Lord Chief Justice, he must face the woman he debauched thirty years earlier. He must face the fact that even if his actions seem not to be subject to the guidance of metaphysics, they nevertheless have consequences: "Once Pleasure and now Guilt." The poem ends with the inference that because actions have results, experience may after all generate meanings and values even when doctrinaire ideologies fail.

### AMOURS DE VOYAGE

*Amours de Voyage* was written in 1849, although it did not appear publicly until 1858. In this poem, Clough is still trying to make hexameters carry a rather plain narrative. Structurally, the poem is a series of letters, one group from Claude to Eustace describing his travels in Italy and his infatuation for an English girl he has encountered. The interspersed letters are from Georgiana Trevellyn to Louisa. Georgiana's letters are filled with girlish gossip and observations on political affairs, but such comments give way to an increasing preoccupation with the Trevellyns' new acquaintance—Claude. In postscripts to Georgiana's letters and then in a correspondence of her own, Mary Trevellyn describes first her contempt, then her aloofness, then her interest, then her obsession with Claude. Their first acquaintance, which left them at cross-purposes, gives way to real love for each other. Claude and Mary miss connections at various Continental watering places until Mary reports that she is returning to England, and the reader concludes that the protagonists have missed their chance for love, because Claude is going to Egypt.

The letters, however, are about not only an ironic love affair that never occurred, but also the events that undermine other features of Claude's high-minded idealism. In this regard, *Amours de Voyage* is much like Friedrich Schiller's philosophical letters. Claude decides to leave Europe not merely because he cannot locate Mary but also because "Rome will not suit me; the priests and soldiers possess it." The authoritarian spirit of European orthodoxy and the militant spirit of European politics offer no consolation to a young freethinker who sees that Europe is going to miss its chance for peace as he has missed his chance for love.

### MARI MAGNO

Clough worked little at poetry after 1858 until it became evident that his failing health was not yielding to treatment. At the time of his death, he was hard at work on *Mari Magno*. The poem is a Chaucerian collection of tales told by travelers aboard a transatlantic ship bound for the United States, across the "great sea." The tales are told on six different nights of the voyage. The clergyman tells two, the lawyer two, an American one, the narrator one in his own voice, and the mate one.

At this late hour of his life, Clough's stories tell of love missed or nearly missed. The failure of idealized love and the necessity of going on with practical life are forced on the protagonists by impersonal chance, by odd coincidences, a too-late arrival at a rendezvous, a ship that leaves too soon. There is little searching here for the great idea, no return to the struggle for a secular metaphysic that will justify actions and values. Rather, there is merely a plaintive lament for a lost idealism that has no home in this pragmatic world, and a sad sense that even true hearts and high-minded spirits must come to grips with a world of unkept promises and missed appointments. A poignant longing for this hopeless idealism is balanced against the tranquillity that comes from a resignation to life as it is.

### LEGACY

Clough's poetry, taken altogether, considers the common themes of love, faith, and learning; makes them vulnerable to the disillusionments of modern skepticism; and then asks certain questions. First, does intellectual honesty necessarily erode the authority of these traditional ideals? Second, is there some new, coherent perception of the world (in *Dipsychus* he calls it a "Second Reverence") that will satisfy the demands of both a rigorous honesty and the spiritual needs that ideals have traditionally satisfied? These questions make Clough a representative figure among the young intellectuals of mid-nineteenth century Europe. His friend Matthew Arnold described his dilemma as a struggle "between two worlds, one dead the other powerless to be born." Clough does seem to have acquired some tranquillity in the years following his marriage, and critics disagree whether he found it because he quit struggling or because he discovered what he was looking for—a high-minded skepticism that was humane and satisfying. Perhaps the safest way to interpret his life and work is to affirm that their outward expressions suggest an inward acceptance complex enough to tantalize biographers, effectual enough to redeem Clough's sense of well-being.

OTHER MAJOR WORKS

NONFICTION: *Letters and Remains*, 1865 (Mrs. Clough, editor); *Prose Remains*, 1888; *Selected Prose Works*, 1964 (B. B. Trawick, editor).

MISCELLANEOUS: *The Poems and Prose Remains of Arthur Hugh Clough*, 1869 (2 volumes).

BIBLIOGRAPHY

Biswas, Robindra Kumar. *Arthur Hugh Clough: Towards a Reconsideration*. Oxford, England: Clarendon Press, 1972. This somewhat laborious biographical-critical study of Clough makes a case for his success around the period 1847-1852, particularly in *Amours de Voyage*, in which Clough "confidently fulfills his potential as a poet." His is a "minor key," or "a footnote" illuminating a "major argument" in the text of Victorian poetry. Good bibliography.

Chorley, Katharine. *Arthur Hugh Clough: The Uncommitted Mind*. Oxford, England: Clarendon Press, 1962. This biography assumes that "Clough wrings his criticism of life out of his own experience." His poetry is a fight to "save himself" from his own intellectual honesty by fixing on some faith, but he "dared not commit himself to any answer," because of an Oedipal conflict with the authority of his mother.

Christiansen, Rupert. *The Voice of Victorian Sex: Arthur H. Clough, 1819-1861*. London: Short Books, 2001. A brief biography focused on the interior, psychological aspects of Clough and his work. He is placed in context in Victorian England, and Christiansen details Clough's struggle with natural physical urges and the shame they caused him all his life.

Greenberger, Evelyn Barish. *Arthur Hugh Clough: The Growth of a Poet's Mind*. Cambridge, Mass.: Harvard University Press, 1970. Studies Clough's prose writings on political and religious matters and shows him in a new light, as an energetic reformer and committed thinker. Traces his growth from naïve abstractions through active polemics and some disappointment to a greater wisdom concerning individual virtue within the social structure.

Harris, Wendell V. *Arthur Hugh Clough*. New York: Twayne, 1970. A brief, sound, introductory study of the poet's career. Most revaluations of Clough see him as a poet of Victorian doubt who quit poetry when he found no resolution. Harris argues that when Clough had "beaten out a form of belief he could accept, the anvil ceased to ring." Contains a chronology and a bibliography with helpful annotations.

Houghton, Walter E. *The Poetry of Clough: An Essay in Revaluation*. New Haven, Conn.: Yale University Press, 1963. Houghton's book is still the best discussion of Clough's poetry and poetics, with a focus on technique. A master of the "intellectual lyric," Clough streamlined his language and rhetoric in his search for certainty, his idiomatic and straightforward style qualifying him as "one of the best of Victorian poets" and "perhaps the most modern."

Kenny, Anthony. *Arthur Hugh Clough: A Poet's Life*. New York: Continuum, 2005. This biography delves into the links between Clough's personal life and his poetry, and examines his various relationships with women.

Moore, Richard. "Arthur Hugh Clough." *Notes and Queries* 46, no. 1 (March, 1999): 53-55. A discussion of two previously unpublished letters by Clough sent to Lady Harriet Ashburton that clarify some details in his biography.

Thorpe, Michael, ed. *Clough: The Critical Heritage*. New York: Barnes & Noble, 1972. This volume in the Critical Heritage series contains contemporary letters, views, and reviews of Clough from 1847 to 1869, as well as posthumous reactions up to 1920. Contributors include Matthew Arnold, Ralph Waldo Emerson, Algernon Charles Swinburne, and E. M. Forster.

Timko, Michael. *Innocent Victorian: The Satiric Poetry of Arthur Hugh Clough*. Athens: Ohio University Press, 1966. Concentrates on Clough's satire and emphasizes the importance of placing the poet within the context of the "vital influence" of the society that is his satire's target. The poetry is driven by a "moral aesthetic" of "positive naturalism," which not only recognizes but also embraces human contradictions and limitations.

*L. Robert Stevens*

# LEONARD COHEN

**Born:** Montreal, Quebec, Canada; September 21, 1934

PRINCIPAL POETRY

*Let Us Compare Mythologies*, 1956
*The Spice-Box of Earth*, 1961
*Flowers for Hitler*, 1964
*Parasites of Heaven*, 1966
*Selected Poems, 1956-1968*, 1968
*The Energy of Slaves*, 1972
*Credo*, 1977
*Death of a Lady's Man*, 1978
*Book of Mercy*, 1984
*Stranger Music: Selected Poems and Songs*, 1993
*Dance Me to the End of Love*, 1995
*God Is Alive, Magic Is Afoot*, 2000
*Book of Longing*, 2006

OTHER LITERARY FORMS

In addition to poetry, Leonard Cohen wrote two works of fiction, *The Favorite Game* (1963) and *Beautiful Losers* (1966). However, he is best known as a songwriter and singer.

ACHIEVEMENTS

Leonard Cohen has been primarily recognized for his music rather than his poetry, although that distinction is misleading. The lyrics to most of his songs can be read as poems, and his poems often have a musical quality. In 1968, Cohen won the Canadian Governor General's Award for English-language poetry for *Selected Poems, 1956-1968*, but he refused the honor, saying that the very nature of his work would have been sullied had he accepted the honor.

Canada has found other ways to honor Cohen. He was inducted into the Canadian Music Hall of Fame in 1991 and won JUNO Awards in 1993 for Male Vocalist of the Year and Best Video and in 1994 for Songwriter of the Year. In 1993, he also received the Governor General's Performing Arts Award. In 2003, he was made a Companion of the Order of Canada, the country's highest civilian honor, and in 2006 was inducted into the Canadian Songwriters Hall of Fame. He was made a Grand Officer of the National Order of Quebec in 2009.

In the United States, Cohen was a featured artist on Herbie Hancock's *River: The Joni Letters*, which won a Grammy Award for album of the year in 2007. In 2008, Cohen was inducted into the U.S. Rock and Roll Hall of Fame. In 2010, the Recording Academy awarded Cohen with the Lifetime Achievement Award.

BIOGRAPHY

Leonard Norman Cohen was born in 1934 in Montreal, Canada, to a middle-class Jewish clothing store owner, Nathan Cohen, and his wife, Marsha Kinitsky Cohen. His childhood was privileged, although he lost his father when he was just nine. Even at that age, the boy accepted death matter-of-factly, as an unfortunate part of life. He attended a Jewish high school and graduated from McGill University in 1955. He enrolled in Columbia University, but after a short while returned to Montreal to write a book (unpublished) and to read his poetry in coffeehouses.

He published his first poetry collection, *Let Us Compare Mythologies*, when he was just twenty-one. It was republished as a facsimile edition in 2007 by Ecco Press. His second poetry collection, *The Spice-Box of Earth*, was well received and earned him notice among

*Leonard Cohen* (Redferns/Getty Images)

Canadian poets. He visited Cuba in 1961 and later traveled in Europe. He eventually settled on the isle of Hydra in Greece, in what he called "creative seclusion," a stay broken up by returns to Montreal to renew his "neurotic affiliations." In 1969, he met Suzanne Elrod (not the "Suzanne" of his poetry), with whom he had two children.

In the 1960's, Cohen began to blend his poetry with music, releasing the album *Songs of Leonard Cohen* in 1967. The 1970's were a productive time for Cohen, who became a popular singer-songwriter and continued to publish works of poetry, including *The Energy of Slaves* and *Death of a Lady's Man*, a mixture of prose and poetry whose title was adapted from that of *Death of a Ladies' Man*, an album released in 1977. In the 1980's, he published *Book of Mercy*, which contained prayers, meditations, and psalms, and released the album *I'm Your Man* (1988).

In 1993, Cohen moved to California and began to explore Buddhism under the tutelage of Kyozan Joshu Sasaki (Roshi). He spent the next five years in seclusion in a Rinzai Zen monastery atop Mount Baldy in the San Gabriel Mountains near Los Angeles. By 1996, he had become an ordained Rinzai Buddhist monk and was given the name Jikan, meaning "silent one." In 1998, he emerged from the monastery, less outwardly frantic, but still awash in sadness. In "Titles," from the *Book of Longing*, Cohen describes his experience:

> For many years
> I was known as a Monk
> I shaved my head and wore robes
> and got up very early
> I hated everyone
> but I acted generously
> and no one found me out.

Although the monastery apparently did not completely fulfill Cohen's religious needs, his experience brings to mind the Buddhist sutra that says "attainment is emptiness but the search for it is still worthwhile."

After Cohen left the monastery, he returned to music, releasing the album *Ten New Songs* in 2001. However, he came back to a world of emotionally wrenching situations in which he was betrayed by people he trusted. His business manager of seventeen years, Kelley Lynch, had used his absence to abscond with $5 million from his retirement savings, investments, and personal accounts. Cohen was hurt by this betrayal, all the more so because he and Lynch had been lovers fifteen years earlier. He was awarded a $9.5 million judgment against her in 2006.

Cohen—sometimes known as the Godfather of Gloom, the Grocer of Despair, and the Merchant of Misery—has been afflicted with a lifelong depression, never quite understanding where his dark episodes originated but usually finding temporary solace in bars, drugs, and women. He has been called a womanizer, but Cohen claims to have appreciated all his partners, and he memorialized many in his poetry and lyrics. His depression has eased with age, something he attributes to a natural process whereby anxiety-producing brain cells die off. His biggest regret is that he had to grow old with his "friends . . . gone, and [his] hair . . . grey," and he "ache[s] in the places where [he] used to play," ("The Tower of Song," from the album *I'm Your Man*). Although he feels better mentally, he has more reasons to write about physical decay, loss of sexual appeal, and fear of death. He says he still has the same desires and still wants to surround himself with beauty, but he notes that women are gentler now, asking him to enjoy the sight of their naked bodies and then bending over his bed and covering him with a blanket, as they would a child.

ANALYSIS

Leonard Cohen celebrates the personal, historical, and sexual. He sees an interconnectedness in religion, sexual union, and the freeing of the spirit. He writes not only of all those who experience angst as they lose love, grow old, and watch all around them decay, but also of those who seek solace in religion and can emerge for a moment or two from their deep despair and test the waters of joy. His lyrics and poetry are a record of his life; they demonstrate self-mockery, humor, and his sense that nothing has value, and can be deliberately offensive or self-annihilating.

His poems and lyrics both embody a kind of zen poetry of being and contain tension and energy. His poems on aging reflect a personal and deep sense of loneliness and misery. His early works deal with opposites: guilt and sexual freedom, violence and beauty, and love and loss. They follow a conventional meter and form but contain intense messages that create a startling contrast. His later works delve into social and historical issues.

The anachronistic title of Cohen's third book of poetry, *Flowers for Hitler*, perhaps gives the reader a sense of Cohen as a poet: Who would pay tribute to a monster like Hitler with a gift of flowers? Is Cohen an unreconstructed Nazi or a neo-Nazi? Certainly not. Why then does the poet even suggest that a mass murderer is worthy of colorful blooms? Similarly alarming visual images appear in the poem "Lovers" (from *Let Us Compare Mythologies*), which describes death in a concentration camp: "And at the hot ovens they/ Cunningly managed a brief/ Kiss before the soldier came/ To knock out her golden teeth." Cohen excels at capturing the moment, the horror of the times. He goes on to write: "And in the furnace itself/ As the flames flamed higher,/ he tried to kiss her burning breasts/ As she burned in the fire." Few images could be more powerful than this. His poetry and lyrics have always dealt with love and loss, with longing for an elusive something.

STRANGER MUSIC

In *Stranger Music*, Cohen included poetry from all his previously published books and added the lyrics from selected songs from many of his albums. Three particularly noteworthy songs admired partly for their lyrics are "Suzanne" (from *Songs of Leonard Cohen*), "Anthem" (from *The Future*, 1992), and "Hallelujah" (from *Various Positions*, 1985).

"SUZANNE" AND "ANTHEM"

*Parasites of Heaven* included the poem "Suzanne Takes You Down," which became the song "Suzanne," one of the best known of Cohen's compositions. Vocalist Judy Collins recorded this song in 1966, becoming the first of many to cover it, and provided a boost to Cohen's musical career. The Suzanne portrayed in the poem was a friend's wife, and thus Cohen could not become involved with her. Also, neither he nor the woman wanted to ruin the deep feelings and appreciation they had for each other. Hence the line "For he's touched her perfect body with his mind."

If Cohen has a philosophy, it could be the words from "Anthem": "There is a crack, a crack in everything/ That's how the light gets in." In an interview, he said, "That's the closest thinking I could describe to a credo. That idea is one of the fundamental positions behind a lot of the songs."

### "HALLELUJAH"

The song "Hallelujah" has had more written about it than any of Cohen's other works. It has been sung by many leading artists, with all the emotion and passion it deserves. There are pages of responses to it on the Internet. The fact that some of the lyrics are difficult to decipher and can be interpreted in many ways adds to the challenge and also poses the question of whether meaning has to be spelled out clearly to convey feeling.

All five stanzas of the song end with repetition of the word "hallelujah," each in response to a different situation. "Hallelujah," a word denoting celebration or gratitude, is Cohen's natural response to any situation alive with emotion; he seems to suggest that life itself, both the good and the bad, is worthy of praise. The poem starts with a biblical reference to King David playing a "chord" that "pleased the Lord." In the second stanza, Cohen again mentions a biblical figure: Delilah, angered by Samson's weakness for women, cuts his hair, the source of his physical power, and "from [his] lips she drew the Hallelujah." Perhaps he becomes more human without his force. In the third stanza, the poet has taken up with a lover but wants to make it clear to her that he is loathe to commit, that such a relationship would stymie his creativity. Loss and despair free him to explore his imaginative mind. He has seen her raise her victory flag upon moving in with him, but notes: "Love is not a victory march/ It's a cold and it's a broken Hallelujah." Although he is not committed to the relationship any longer, any experience, even a cold and broken one, is worthy of praise because out of despair comes creativity. The next stanza is both sexual and religious, a combination with which Cohen is quite comfortable. He believes that sexual union is a religious experience, and that

while the relationship lasted, "every breath we drew was Hallelujah."

### THE BOOK OF LONGING

*The Book of Longing* contains poems from the 1970's and from 1993 to 1998 (his five years in the monastery) and spans a wide range of subjects, attitudes, and poetic forms. The poems fall into the general categories of autobiographical, love, short and comic, and religious verse. Many of the poems are melancholy, but Cohen can still be humorous, even when writing about his loss of physical powers and betrayals in love. His illustrations further evoke a serious/playful mood. Each poem could be set to music, and American composer Philip Glass created a song cycle based on the book in 2007.

The title poem, "The Book of Longing," starts with Cohen lamenting his weakness in old age but expressing gratitude for medication that helps. He writes in four rhymed stanzas in traditional form: "I can't make the hills/ the system is shot/ I'm living on pills/ for which I thank G-d." He then describes his life: "I followed the course/ From chaos to art/ Desire the horse/ Depression the cart." Desire moved him forward, but depression followed. In "Roshi at Eighty-nine," Cohen says of Joshu Sasaki, his spiritual leader: "His stomach's very happy/ The prunes are working well. " Clearly, to Cohen, it all comes down to bodily functions.

In "A Life of Errands," he conveys the idea that the pleasures in old age are not as intense as they were when he was young, but, in their simplicity, are perhaps more satisfying. For example, a smile from a young cashier can give him the incentive to go on for another day. "The Old Automat on 23rd St." is a silly, but strangely effective poem expressing satisfaction with the way things are: "The meatballs were round/And the pancakes were flat/ I asked G-d in heaven/ to keep it like that." Despite some pleasures, life still contains melancholy for Cohen. In "The Tradition," he notes that "He will never untangle/ Or upgrade/ The circumstances/ That fasten him to this loneliness."

OTHER MAJOR WORKS

LONG FICTION: *The Favorite Game*, 1963; *Beautiful Losers*, 1966.

BIBLIOGRAPHY

Boucher, David. *Dylan and Cohen: Poets of Rock and Roll*. New York: Continuum, 2004. Examines the careers of Bob Dylan and Cohen, two musicians who were admired for their lyrics and poetry.

Cohen, Leonard. *A Book of Longing*. New York: Harper Collins, 2006. This collection is so autobiographical—giving a step-by-step accounting of the man's life during a seminal period—that it can reveal more about him than any biographer's account.

_____. "Leonard Cohen." http://www.leonardcohen .com. The official Web site of Cohen contains a biography and considerable information about his music, including appearances.

Footman, Tim. *Leonard Cohen: Hallelujah—A New Biography*. New Malden, England: Chrome Dreams, 2009. Footman interviewed colleagues of Cohen to provide a fresh perspective on Cohen's life. Covers topics such as depression, sex and relationships, politics, and his poetic and musical development.

The Leonard Cohen Files. http://www.leonardcohen files.com. This Web site is a combined effort between fans and Cohen's office. It is thoroughly comprehensive, containing a chat room, message board, videos, unpublished poems, a short film starring Quentin Tarantino, an excellent British Broadcasting Corporation (BBC) documentary, interviews, indexes to songs and lyrics, master poems, many pictures of Cohen, drawings and paintings, and a filmography.

Locke, Jack, and the Foundation for Public Poetry. *Leonard Cohen, You're Our Man: Seventy-five Poets Reflect on the Poetry of Leonard Cohen*. Montreal: Foundation for Public Poetry, 2009. Features poems inspired by Cohen and gathered together to honor his seventy-fifth birthday.

Nadel, Ira B. *Various Positions: A Life of Leonard Cohen*. 1996. Reprint. Austin: University of Texas, 2007. A scholarly account based on thorough research. Nadel explains Cohen's work habits and his feeling that he is documenting his life through his poetry and lyrics. He observes that Cohen seeks beauty but cannot hold on to it without feeling entrapped. He prefers "a clean slate."

Sheppard, David. *Leonard Cohen*. New York: Thunder's Mouth Press, 2000. This biography looks at Cohen's life and the influences on it—his Jewish beginnings, drugs, sex, alcohol, and Buddhism—and finds in Cohen an ability to express heartfelt truth.

*Gay Pitman Zieger*

# SAMUEL TAYLOR COLERIDGE

**Born:** Ottery St. Mary, Devonshire, England;
October 21, 1772
**Died:** Highgate, London, England; July 25, 1834

PRINCIPAL POETRY

*Poems on Various Subjects*, 1796, 1797 (with Charles Lamb and Charles Lloyd)
*A Sheet of Sonnets*, 1796 (with W. L. Bowles, Robert Southey, and others)
*Lyrical Ballads*, 1798 (with William Wordsworth)
*The Rime of the Ancient Mariner*, 1798
*Christabel*, 1816
*Sibylline Leaves*, 1817
*The Complete Poetical Works of Samuel Taylor Coleridge*, 1912 (2 volumes; Ernest Hartley Coleridge, editor)

OTHER LITERARY FORMS

The original verse dramas of Samuel Taylor Coleridge (KOHL-rihj, also KOH-luh-rihj)—*The Fall of Robespierre* (pb. 1794, with Robert Southey), *Remorse* (pr., pb. 1813, originally *Osorio*), and *Zapolya* (pb. 1817)—are of particular interest to readers of his poetry, as is *Wallenstein* (1800), his translation of two dramas by Friedrich Schiller. His major prose includes the contents of two periodicals, *The Watchman* (1796) and *The Friend* (1809-1810, 1818), two lay Sermons, "The Statesman's Manual" (1816) and "A Lay Sermon" (1817), the *Biographia Literaria* (1817), "Treatise on Method," originally published in *The Encyclopaedia Metropolitana* (1818), and a series of metaphysical aphorisms, *Aids to Reflection* (1825). His lectures on politics, religion, literature, and philosophy have been collected in various editions, as have other short essays, unpublished manuscripts, letters, records of conversations, notebooks, and marginalia. These prose works share common interests with his poetry and suggest the philosophical context in which it should be read. Coleridge's literary criticism is particularly relevant to his poetry.

## ACHIEVEMENTS

It is ironic that Samuel Taylor Coleridge has come to be known to the general reader primarily as a poet, for poetry was not his own primary interest and the poems with which his name is most strongly linked—*The Rime of the Ancient Mariner*, "Kubla Khan," and *Christabel*—were products of a few months in a long literary career. He did not suffer a decline in poetic creativity; he simply turned his attention to political, metaphysical, and theological issues that were best treated in prose. That Coleridge is counted among the major poets of British Romanticism is, for this reason, all the more remarkable. For most poets, the handful of commonly anthologized poems is a scant representation of their output; for Coleridge, it is, in many instances, the sum of his accomplishment. His minor verse is often conventional and uninspired. His major poems, in contrast, speak with singular emotional and intellectual intensity in a surprising range of forms—from the symbolic fantasy of *The Rime of the Ancient Mariner* (which first appeared in *Lyrical Ballads*) to the autobiographical sincerity of the conversation poems— exerting an influence on subsequent poets far beyond what Coleridge himself anticipated.

## BIOGRAPHY

Samuel Taylor Coleridge was born October 21, 1772, in the Devonshire town of Ottery St. Mary, the youngest of ten children. His father, a clergyman and teacher, died in October, 1781, and the next year Coleridge was sent to school at Christ's Hospital, London. His friends at school included Charles Lamb, two years his junior, whose essay "Christ's Hospital Five-and-Thirty Years Ago" (1820) describes the two sides of Coleridge—the "poor friendless boy," far from his home, "alone among six hundred playmates"; the preco-

cious scholar, "Logician, Metaphysician, Bard!," holding his auditors "entranced with imagination." Both characteristics—a deep sense of isolation and the effort to use learning and eloquence to overcome it— remained with Coleridge throughout his life.

He entered Cambridge in 1791 but never completed work for his university degree. Depressed by debts, he fled the university in December, 1793, and enlisted in the Light Dragoons under the name Silas Tompkyn Comberbache. Rescued by his brothers, he returned to Cambridge in April and resumed his studies. Two months later, he met Robert Southey, with whom he soon made plans to establish a utopian community ("Pantisocracy") in the United States. Southey was engaged to marry Edith Fricker, and so it seemed appropriate for Coleridge to engage himself to her sister Sara. The project failed, but Coleridge, through his own sense of duty and Southey's insistence, married a woman he had never loved and with whom his relationship was soon to become strained.

As a married man, Coleridge had to leave the university and make a living for his wife and, in time, children—Hartley (1796-1849), Berkeley (1798-1799), Derwent (b. 1800), and Sara (1802-1852). Economic survival was, it turned out, possible only with the support of friends such as Thomas Poole and the publisher Joseph Cottle and, in 1798, a life annuity from Josiah and Tom Wedgwood. The early years of Coleridge's married life, in which he lived with his family at Nether Stowey, were the period of his closest relationship with the poet William Wordsworth. Inspired by Wordsworth, whom he in turn inspired, Coleridge wrote most of his major poetry. Together, the two men published *Lyrical Ballads* in 1798, the proceeds of which enabled them, along with Wordsworth's sister Dorothy, to spend the winter in Germany, where Coleridge studied metaphysics at the University of Göttingen.

Returning to England the following year, Coleridge met and fell deeply in love with Sara Hutchinson, a friend of Dorothy who later became Wordsworth's sister-in-law. This passion, which remained strong for many years, furthered Coleridge's estrangement from his wife, with whom he moved to Keswick in the Lake District of England, in July, 1800, to be near the Wordsworths at Grasmere. Coleridge's health had always been poor, and he had become addicted to opium, which, according to standard medical practice at the time, he had originally taken to relieve pain. Seeking a change of climate, he traveled to Malta and then Italy in 1804 to 1806. On his return, he and his wife "*determined* to part absolutely and finally," leaving Coleridge in custody of his sons Hartley and Derwent (Berkeley had died in 1799).

In 1808, Coleridge gave his first public lectures and in the next two years published the twenty-seven issues of *The Friend*. By now, he was a figure of national standing, but his private life remained in disarray. Sara Hutchinson, who had assisted him in preparing copy for *The Friend*, separated herself from him, and in 1810, he quarreled decisively with Wordsworth. (They were later reconciled, but the period of close friendship was over.) Six years later, after various unsuccessful attempts to cure himself of opium addiction and set his affairs in order, he put himself in the care of James Gillman, a physician living at Highgate, a northern suburb of London. Under Gillman's roof, Coleridge was once again able to work. He wrote the two lay Sermons, "The

*Samuel Taylor Coleridge* (Library of Congress)

Statesman's Manual" and "A Lay Sermon"; completed the *Biographia Literaria*, originally planned as an autobiographical introduction to *Sibylline Leaves* but ultimately two volumes in its own right; and revised the essays he had written for *The Friend*, including among them a version of the "Treatise on Method," which he had composed for the first volume of *The Encyclopaedia Metropolitana*. He also resumed his public lectures on philosophy and literature and in time became a London celebrity, enthralling visitors with his conversation and gradually attracting a circle of disciples. Meanwhile, he worked at the magnum opus that was to synthesize his metaphysical and theological thought in a single intellectual system. This project, however, remained incomplete when Coleridge died at Highgate, July 25, 1834.

ANALYSIS

Samuel Taylor Coleridge's major poems turn on problems of self-esteem and identity. Exploring states of isolation and ineffectuality, they test strategies to overcome weakness without asserting its antithesis—a powerful self, secure in its own thoughts and utterances, the potency and independence of which Coleridge feared would only exacerbate his loneliness. His reluctance to assert his own abilities is evident in his habitual deprecation of his own poetry and hyperbolic praise of William Wordsworth's. It is evident as well in his best verse, which either is written in an unpretentious "conversational" tone or, when it is not, is carefully dissociated from his own voice and identity. By means of these strategies, however, he is often able to assert indirectly or vicariously the strong self he otherwise repressed.

**"THE EOLIAN HARP"**

Writing to John Thelwall in 1796, Coleridge called the first of the conversation poems, "The Eolian Harp" (written in 1795), the "favorite of *my* poems." He originally published it, in 1796, with the indication "Composed August 20th, 1795, At Clevedon, Somersetshire," which dates at least some version of the text six weeks before his marriage to Sara Fricker. Since Sara plays a role in the poem, the exact date is crucial. "The Eolian Harp" is not, as it has been called, a "honeymoon" poem; rather, it anticipates a future in which

Coleridge and Sara will sit together by their "Cot o'ergrown/ With white-flower'd Jasmin." Significantly, Sara remains silent throughout the poem; her only contribution is the "mild reproof" that "darts" from her "more serious eye," quelling the poet's intellectual daring. However, this reproof is as imaginary as Sara's presence itself. At the climax of the poem, meditative thought gives way to the need for human response; tellingly, the response he imagines and therefore, one must assume, desires, is reproof.

"The Eolian Harp" establishes a structural pattern for the conversation poems as a group. Coleridge is, in effect, alone, "and the world *so* hush'd!/ The stilly murmur of the distant Sea/ Tells us of silence." The eolian harp in the window sounds in the breeze and reminds him of "the one Life within us and abroad,/ Which meets all motion and becomes its soul." This observation leads to the central question of the poem:

> And what if all of animated nature
> Be but organic Harps diversely fram'd,
> That tremble into thought, as o'er them sweeps
> Plastic and vast, one intellectual breeze,
> At once the Soul of each, and God of all?

Sara's glance dispells "These shapings of the unregenerate mind," but, of course, it is too late, since they have already been expressed in the poem. (Indeed, the letter to Thelwall makes it clear that it was this expression of pantheism, not its retraction, that made the poem dear to Coleridge.) For this reason, the conflict between two sides of Coleridge's thought—metaphysical speculation and orthodox Christianity—remains unresolved. If the poem is in any way disquieting, it is not because it exemplifies a failure of nerve, but because of the identifications it suggests between metaphysical speculation and the isolated self, religious orthodoxy and the conventions—down to the vines covering the cottage—of married life. Coleridge, in other words, does not imagine a wife who will love him all the more for his intellectual daring. Instead, he imagines one who will chastise him for the very qualities that make him an original thinker. To "possess/ Peace, and this Cot, and thee, heart-honour'd Maid!," Coleridge must acknowledge himself "A sinful and most miserable man,/ Wilder'd and dark." Happiness, as well as poetic closure, de-

pends on this acceptance of diminished self-esteem. Even so, by embedding an expression of intellectual strength within the context of domestic conventionality, Coleridge is able to achieve a degree of poetic authority otherwise absent in the final lines of the poem. The ability to renounce a powerful self is itself a gesture of power: The acceptance of loss becomes—as in other Romantic poems—a form of strength.

The structure of "The Eolian Harp" can be summarized as follows: A state of isolation (the more isolated for the presence of an unresponsive companion) gives way to meditation, which leads to the possibility of a self powerful through its association with an all-powerful force. This state of mind gives place to the acknowledgment of a human relationship dependent on the poet's recognition of his own inadequacy, the reward for which is a poetic voice with the authority to close the poem.

### "THIS LIME-TREE BOWER MY PRISON"

This pattern recurs in "This Lime-Tree Bower My Prison" (1797). The poem is addressed to Charles Lamb, but the "gentle-hearted Charles" of the text is really a surrogate for the figure of Wordsworth, whose loss Coleridge is unwilling to face head-on. Incapacitated by a burn—appropriately, his wife's fault—Coleridge is left alone seated in a clump of lime trees while his friends—Lamb and William and Dorothy Wordsworth—set off on a long walk through the countryside. They are, like Sara in "The Eolian Harp," there and yet not there: Their presence in the poem intensifies Coleridge's sense of isolation. He follows them in his imagination, and the gesture itself becomes a means of connecting himself with them. Natural images of weakness, enclosure, and solitude give way to those of strength, expansion, and connection, and the tone of the poem shifts from speculation to assertion. In a climactic moment, he imagines his friends "gazing round/ On the wide landscape" until it achieves the transcendence of "such hues/ As veil the Almighty Spirit, when yet he makes/ Spirits perceive his presence."

As in "The Eolian Harp," the perception of an omnipotent force pervading the universe returns Coleridge to his present state, but with a new sense of his own being and his relationship with the friends to whom he addresses the poem. His own isolation is now seen as an end in itself. "Sometimes/ 'Tis well to be bereft of promised good," Coleridge argues, "That we may lift the soul, and contemplate/ With lively joy the joys we cannot share."

### "FROST AT MIDNIGHT"

"Frost at Midnight," the finest of the conversation poems, replaces silent wife or absent friends with a sleeping child (Hartley—although he is not named in the text). Summer is replaced by winter; isolation is now a function of seasonal change itself. In this zero-world, "The Frost performs its secret ministry,/ Unhelped by any wind." The force that moved the eolian harp into sound is gone. The natural surroundings of the poem drift into nonexistence: "Sea, and hill, and wood,/ With all the numberless goings-on of life,/ Inaudible as dreams!" This is the nadir of self from which the poet reconstructs his being—first by perception of "dim sympathies" with the "low-burnt fire" before him; then by a process of recollection and predication. The "film" on the grate reminds Coleridge of his childhood at Christ's Hospital, where a similar image conveyed hopes of seeing someone from home and therefore a renewal of the conditions of his earlier life in Ottery St. Mary. Even in recollection, however, the bells of his "sweet birth-place" are most expressive not as a voice of the present moment, but as "articulate sounds of things to come!" The spell of the past was, in fact, a spell of the imagined future. The visitor he longed for turns out to be a version of the self of the poet, his "sister more beloved/ My playmate when we both were clothed alike." The condition of loss that opens the poem cannot be filled by the presence of another human being; it is a fundamental emptiness in the self, which, Coleridge suggests, can never be filled, but only recognized as a necessary condition of adulthood. However, this recognition of incompleteness is the poet's means of experiencing a sense of identity missing in the opening lines of the poem.

"Frost at Midnight" locates this sense of identity in Coleridge's own life. It is not a matter of metaphysical or religious belief, as it is in "The Eolian Harp" or "This Lime-Tree Bower My Prison," but a function of the self that recognizes its own coherence in time. This recognition enables him to speak to the "Dear Babe" who had been there all along, but had remained a piece of the setting and not a living human being. Like the friends of "This Lime-Tree Bower My Prison," who are projected exploring a landscape, the boy Hartley is imagined wandering "like a breeze/ By lakes and sandy shores." The static existence of the poet in the present moment is contrasted with the movement of a surrogate. This movement, however, is itself subordinated to the voice of the poet who can promise his son a happiness he himself has not known.

In all three poems, Coleridge achieves a voice that entails the recognition of his own loss—in acknowledging Sara's reproof or losing himself in the empathic construction of the experience of friend or son. The act entails a defeat of the self, but also a vicarious participation in powerful forces that reveal themselves in the working of the universe, and through this participation a partial triumph of the self over its own sense of inadequacy. In "Frost at Midnight," the surrogate figure of his son not only embodies a locomotor power denied the static speaker, but also, in his capacity to read the "language" uttered by God in the form of landscape, is associated with absolute power itself.

### THE RIME OF THE ANCIENT MARINER

Although written in a very different mode, *The Rime of the Ancient Mariner* centers on a similar experience of participation in supernatural power. At the core of the poem is, of course, the story of the Mariner who shoots the albatross and endures complete and devastating isolation from his fellow man. The poem, however, is not a direct narrative of these events; rather, it is a narrative of the Mariner's narrating them. The result of the extraordinary experience he has undergone is to make him an itinerant storyteller. It has given him a voice, but a voice grounded on his own incompleteness of self. He has returned to land but remains homeless and without permanent human relationships. In this respect, *The Rime of the Ancient Mariner* is Coleridge's nightmare alternative to the conversation poem. As "conversations," they suggest the possibility of a relationship with his audience that can in part compensate for the inadequate human relationships described in the poem. The Mariner's story is a kind of conversation. He tells it to the Wedding-Guest he has singled out for that purpose, but the relationship between speaker and audience can scarcely be said to compensate for the Mariner's lack of human relationships. The Wedding-Guest is compelled to listen by the hypnotic power of the Mariner's "glittering eye." He "beats his breast" at the thought of the wedding from which he is being detained and repeatedly expresses his fear of the Mariner. In the end, he registers no compassion for the man whose story he has just heard. He is too "stunned" for that—and the Mariner has left the stage without asking for applause. His audience is changed by the story—"A sadder and a wiser man,/ He rose the morrow morn"—but of this the Mariner can know nothing. Thus, the power of the Mariner's story to captivate and transform its audience simply furthers his alienation from his fellow human beings.

Structurally, the poem follows the three-stage pattern of the conversation poems. A state of isolation and immobility is succeeded by one in which the Mariner becomes the object of (and is thus associated with) powerful supernatural agencies, and this leads to the moralizing voice of the conclusion. Unlike the conversation poems, *The Rime of the Ancient Mariner* prefaces individual isolation with social isolation. The Mariner and his shipmates, in what has become one of the most familiar narratives in English literature, sail from Europe toward Cape Horn, where they are surrounded by a polar ice jam. An albatross appears and accepts food from the sailors; a fair wind springs up, and they are able to resume their journey northward into the Pacific Ocean; the albatross follows them, "And every day, for food or play,/ Came to the mariner's hollo!"—until the Mariner, seemingly without reason, shoots the bird with his crossbow. Coleridge warned readers against allegorizing the poem, and it is fruitless to search for a specific identification for the albatross. What is important is the bird's gratuitous arrival and the Mariner's equally gratuitous crossbow shot. The polar ice that threatens the ship is nature at its most alien. Seen against that backdrop, the albatross seems relatively human; the mariners, accordingly, "hailed it in God's name"; "As if it had been a Christian soul." Like the "film" in "Frost at Midnight"—a poem in which crucial events are also set against a wintry backdrop—the bird offers them a means of bridging the gap between humans and nature, self and nonself,

through projecting human characteristics on a creature of the natural world. By shooting the albatross, the Mariner blocks this projection and thus traps both himself and his shipmates in a state of isolation.

The Mariner's act has no explicit motive because it is a function of human nature itself, but it is not merely a sign of original sin or congenital perversity. His narrative has until now been characterized by a remarkable passivity. Events simply happen. Even the ship's progress is characterized not by its own movement but by the changing position of the sun in the sky. The ice that surrounds the ship is only one element of a natural world that dominates the fate of the ship and its crew, and it is against this overwhelming dominance that the Mariner takes his crossbow shot. The gesture is an assertion of the human spirit against an essentially inhuman universe, aimed at the harmless albatross.

He is punished for this self-assertion—first, by the crewmen who blame him for the calm that follows and tie the albatross around his neck as a sign of guilt. It is only after this occurs that the Mariner, thirsty and guilt-ridden, perceives events that are explicitly supernatural, and the second stage of his punishment begins. However, the Mariner's isolation, even after his shipmates have died and left him alone on the becalmed ship, remains a consequence of his assertion of self against the natural world, and the turning point of the poem is equally his own doing. In the midst of the calm, the water had seemed abhorrently ugly: "slimy things did crawl with legs/ Upon the slimy sea," while "the water, like a witch's oils,/ Burnt green, and blue and white." Now, "bemocked" by moonlight, the same creatures are beautiful: "Blue, glossy green, and velvet black,/ They coiled and swam; and every track/ Was a flash of golden fire." In this perception of beauty, the Mariner explains, "A spring of love gushed from my heart,/ And I blessed them unaware." At the same moment, he is once again able to pray, and the albatross falls from his neck into the sea. Prayer—the ability to voice his mind and feelings and, in so doing, relate them to a higher order of being—is a function of love, and love is a function of the apprehension of beauty. In blessing the water snakes, it should be noted, the Mariner has not returned to the viewpoint of his shipmates when they attributed human characteristics to the albatross. When he conceives of the snakes as "happy living things," he acknowledges a bond between all forms of organic life, but their beauty does not depend on human projection.

However, achieving this chastened vision does not end the Mariner's suffering. Not only must he endure an extension of his shipboard isolation, but also when, eventually, he returns to his native land, he is not granted reintegration into its society. The Hermit from whom he asks absolution demands quick answer to his own question, "What manner of man art thou?" In response, the Mariner experiences a spasm of physical agony that forces him to tell the story of his adventures. The tale told, he is left free of pain—until such time as "That agony returns" and he is compelled to repeat the narrative: "That moment that his face I see,/ I know the man that must hear me:/ To him my tale I teach." The Mariner has become a poet—like Coleridge, a poet gifted with "strange power of speech" and plagued with somatic pain, with power to fix his auditors' attention and transform them into "sadder and wiser" men. However, the price of this power is enormous. It entails not only the shipboard suffering of the Mariner but also perpetual alienation from his fellow human beings. Telling his story is the only relationship allowed him, and he does not even fully understand the meaning of his narration. In the concluding lines of the poem, he attempts to draw a moral—

> He prayeth best, who loveth best
> All things both great and small;
> For the dear God who loveth us,
> He made and loveth all.

These words are not without bearing on the poem, but they overlook the extraordinary disproportion between the Mariner's crime and its punishment. Readers of the poem—as well as, one supposes, the Wedding-Guest—are more likely to question the benevolence of the "dear God who loveth us" than to perceive the Mariner's story as an illustration of God's love. Thus, the voice of moral authority that gave the conversation poems a means of closure is itself called into question. The soul that acknowledges its essential isolation in the universe can never hope for reintegration into society. The poet whose song is the tale of his own suffering can

"stun" his reader but can never achieve a lasting human relationship. His experience can be given the aesthetic coherence of narrative, but he can never connect the expressive significance of that narrative with his life as a whole.

It is in part the medium of the poem that allows Coleridge to face these bleak possibilities. Its ballad stanza and archaic diction, along with the marginal glosses added from 1815 to 1816, dissociate the text from its modern poet. Freed from an explicit identification with the Mariner, Coleridge is able both to explore implications of the poet's role that would have been difficult to face directly and to write about experiences for which there was no precedent in conventional meditative verse.

### "KUBLA KHAN"

A similar strategy is associated with "Kubla Khan," which can be read as an alternative to *The Rime of the Ancient Mariner*. The poem, which was not published until 1816, nearly two decades after it was written, is Coleridge's most daring account of poetic inspiration and the special nature of the poet. In the poem, the poet's isolation is perceived not as weakness but strength. Even in 1816, the gesture of self-assertion was difficult for Coleridge, and he prefaced the poem with an account designed to diminish its significance. "Kubla Khan" was, he explained, "a psychological curiosity," the fragment of a longer poem he had composed in an opium-induced sleep, "if that indeed can be called composition in which all the images rose up before him as *things*, with a parallel production of the correspondent expressions, without any sensation or consciousness of effort." Waking, he began to write out the verses he had in this manner "composed" but was interrupted by a visitor, after whose departure he found he could no longer remember more than "the general purport of the vision" and a few "scattered lines and images."

The problem with this explanation is that "Kubla Khan" does not strike readers as a fragment. It is, as it stands, an entirely satisfactory whole. Moreover, the facts of Coleridge's preface have themselves been called into question.

Just what was Coleridge trying to hide? The poem turns on an analogy between the act of an emperor and the act of a poet. Kubla Khan's "pleasure-dome" in Xanadu is more than a monarch's self-indulgence; symbolically, it attempts to arrest the process of life itself. His walls encircle "twice five miles of fertile ground," in the midst of which flows "Alph," the sacred river of life, but they control neither the source of the river nor its conclusion in the "lifeless ocean" to which it runs. The source is a "deep romantic chasm" that Coleridge associates with the violence of natural process, with human sexuality, and with the libidinal origins of poetry in the song of a "woman wailing for her demon lover." Kubla's pleasure-dome is "a miracle of rare device," but it can exert no lasting influence. The achievement of the most powerful Oriental despot is limited by the conditions of life, and even his attempt to order a limited space evokes "Ancestral voices prophesying war!"

In contrast, the achievement of the poet is not bounded by space and time and partakes of the dangerous potency of natural creativity itself. The nature of inspiration is tricky, however. The speaker of the poem recollects a visionary "Abyssinian maid" playing a dulcimer, and it is the possibility of reviving "within me/ Her symphony and song" that holds out the hope of a corresponding creativity: "To such a deep delight 'twould win me,/ . . . I would build that dome in air, . . ." The poet's act is always secondary, never primary creativity. Even so, to re-create in poetry Kubla's achievement—without its liabilities—is to become a dangerous being. Like the Mariner, the inspired poet has "flashing eyes" that can cast a spell over his audience. His special nature may be the sign of an incomplete self—for inspiration depends on the possibility of recovering a lost recollection; nevertheless, it is a special nature that threatens to re-create the world in its own image.

## CHRISTABEL

Nowhere else is Coleridge so confident about his powers as a poet or writer. *Christabel*, written in the same period as *The Rime of the Ancient Mariner* and "Kubla Khan," remains a fascinating fragment. Like "Kubla Khan," it was not published until 1816. By then, the verse romances of Sir Walter Scott and Lord Byron had caught the public's attention, and among Coleridge's motives in publishing his poem was to lay

claim to a poetic form he believed he had originated. More important, though, his decision to publish two parts of an incomplete narrative almost two decades after he had begun the poem was also a means of acknowledging that *Christabel* was and would remain unfinished.

To attribute its incompletion to Coleridge's procrastination evades the real question: Why did the poem itself preclude development? Various answers have been offered; the most convincing argue a conflict between the metaphysical or religious significance of Christabel—whose name conflates Christ and Abel—with the exigencies of the narrative structure in which she is placed. As Walter Jackson Bate explains it, the "problem of finding motives and actions for Christabel . . . had imposed an insupportable psychological burden on Coleridge." The problem that Coleridge fails to solve is the problem of depicting credible innocence. Christabel, the virgin who finds the mysterious Lady Geraldine in the forest and brings her home to the castle of her father, Sir Leoline, only to fall victim to Geraldine's sinister spell, is either hopelessly passive and merely a victim, or, if active, something less than entirely innocent. At the same time, Geraldine, who approaches her prey with "a stricken look," is potentially the more interesting character. Christabel is too much like the albatross in *The Rime of the Ancient Mariner*; Geraldine, too much like the Mariner himself, whose guilt changes him from a simple seaman to an archetype of human isolation and suffering. Christabel's name suggests that Coleridge had intended for her to play a sacrificial role, but by promising to reunite Sir Leoline with his childhood friend, Roland de Vaux of Tryermaine, whom she claims as her father, Geraldine, too, has a potentially positive function in the narrative. Whether or not her claim is true, it nevertheless initiates action that may lead to a reconciliation, not only between two long-separated friends but also between Sir Leoline's death-obsessed maturity and the time in his youth when he was able to experience friendship. There is, therefore, a suggestion that Geraldine is able to effect the link between childhood and maturity, innocence and experience, of particular concern to Coleridge—and to other Romantic poets as well. If Christabel and Geraldine represent the passive and active sides of Coleridge, then his failure to complete the narrative is yet another example of his inability to synthesize his personality—or to allow one side to win out at the expense of the other.

A few other poems from 1797 to 1798 deserve mention. "The Nightingale" (1798), although less interesting than the other titles in the group, conforms to the general structure of the conversation poems and so confirms its importance. "Fears in Solitude" (1798) is at once a conversation poem and something more. Like the others, it begins in a state of isolation and ends with social reintegration; its median state of self-assertion, however, takes the form of a public political statement. The voice of the statement is often strident, but this quality is understandable in a poem written at a time when invasion by France was daily rumored. "Fears in Solitude" attacks British militarism, materialism, and patriotism; however, it is itself deeply patriotic. "There lives nor form nor feeling in my soul," Coleridge acknowledges, "Unborrowed from my country," and for this reason the poem is not a series of topical criticism but an expression of the dilemma of a poet divided between moral judgment of and personal identification with his native land.

### "DEJECTION"

When Coleridge returned from Germany in the summer of 1799, his period of intense poetic creativity was over. The poems that he wrote in the remaining years of his life were written by a man who no longer thought of himself as a poet and who therefore treated poetry as a mode of expression rather than a calling. "Dejection: An Ode," which Coleridge dated April 4, 1802, offers a rationale for this change and seems to have been written as a formal farewell to the possibility of a career as a poet. The poem's epigraph from the *Ballad of Sir Patrick Spence* and its concern with perception link it with *The Rime of the Ancient Mariner*; its use of the image of the eolian harp links it with the poem by that name and, by extension, with the free-associational style of the conversation poems as a group. Its tone and manner are also close to those of the conversation poems, but its designation as an ode suggests an effort to elevate it to the level of formal statement. At the same time, its recurrent addresses to an unnamed "Lady" (Sara Hutchinson) suggest that the poem was primarily

intended for a specific rather than a general audience, for a reader with a special interest in the poet who will not expect the poem to describe a universal human experience. Thus, the poem is at once closely related to Coleridge's earlier verse and significantly different from it.

In keeping with the conversation-poem structure, "Dejection" begins in a mood of solitary contemplation. The poet ponders the moon and "the dull sobbing draft that moans and rakes/ Upon the strings of this Aeolian lute." Together, they portend a storm in the offing, and Coleridge hopes that the violence of the "slant night shower" may startle him from his depression. His state, he explains, is not merely grief; it is "A stifled, drowsy, unimpassioned grief,/ Which finds no natural outlet, no relief,/ In word, or sign, or tear." All modes of emotional expression are blocked: He is able to "see" the beauty of the natural world, but he cannot "feel" it, and thereby use it as a symbol for his own inner state. He has lost the ability to invest the "outward forms" of nature with passion and life because, by his account, his inner source of passion and life has dried up. This ability he calls "Joy"—"the spirit and the power,/ Which wedding Nature to us gives in dower/ A new Earth and new Heaven." The language of apocalypse identifies "Joy" with religious faith; the notion of language suggests a more general identification with the expressive mode of his earlier poetry and its ability to transform an ordinary situation into an especially meaningful event. To have no "outlet . . ./ In word" is to have lost the voice of that poetry; to make the observation within a poetic text is to suggest one more difference between "Dejection" and Coleridge's earlier poetry.

"Dejection" may seem like a restatement of the notion of a possible harmony—now lost—between nature and the human that was expressed in the earlier poetry. In fact, "Dejection" denies the grounds of the harmony advanced in the earlier poems. In "Frost at Midnight," for example, the "shapes and sounds" of the natural world are perceived as an "eternal language, which thy/ God utters." In "The Eolian Harp," man is conceptualized (tentatively) as only one of the media through which the eternal force expresses itself. "Dejection," in contrast, identifies the source of "Joy" in man himself. In feeling the beauty of nature, "we in ourselves rejoice." Although the earlier poems toyed with pantheism, this focus on the state of mind of the individual soul is squarely orthodox, but the religious conservatism of "Dejection" does not in itself explain the termination of Coleridge's poetic career.

Coleridge himself attributes this termination to his own self-consciousness. As he explains in "Dejection," he had sought "by abstruse research to seal/ From my own nature all the natural man." This scientific analysis of the self got the better of him, however, and now his conscious mind is compelled to subject the whole of experience to its analytic scrutiny. Nothing now escapes the dominance of reason, and insofar as the power of Coleridge's greatest poetry lay in its capacity to dramatize or at least imagine a universe imbued with supernatural meaning, the power is lost. Theologically, this capacity can be associated with pantheism or the vaguely heterodox natural theology of the conversation poems; psychologically, its potency, derived from primal narcissism, is related to the animism given explicit form in the spirits who supervise the action in *The Rime of the Ancient Mariner*. The power of this poetry, it can be argued, lies in its ability to recapture a primitive human experience of the world.

The psychological awareness that Coleridge gained by his own self-analysis made this primitive naïveté impossible. "Dejection" is thus potentially a poem celebrating the maturity of the intellect—its recognition that its earlier powerful experience of nature, even when attributed to a Christian deity, was a matter of projection and therefore a function of his need to associate himself with an objective expression of his own potency. If the poem is not celebratory, it is because the consequences of this recognition amount to an admission of the importance of his individual self at odds with Coleridge's need for social acceptance. At the same time, it deprives him of that powerful confirmation of self derived from the illusionary sense of harmony with the animistic forces of the natural world. "Dejection" should have been a poem about Coleridge's internalization of these forces and triumphant recognition of his own strength of mind. Instead, he acknowledges the illusion of animism without being able to internalize the psychic energy invested in the animistic vision.

In disavowing belief in a transcendental power inherent in nature, Coleridge disavows the power of his own earlier poetry. "Dejection" lacks the ease and confidence of the conversation poems, and its structure is noticeably mechanical. The storm that ends "Dejection" replaces the voice of authority that defined their closure, but, despite being anticipated by the opening stanzas, it is a deus ex machina without organic connection with the poet. For reasons that the poem itself makes clear, it can effect no fundamental transformation of his being. Hence, it is simply unimportant, and to expect it to have greater effect is, in the words of "The Picture" (1802), to be a "Gentle Lunatic."

## LATER POETRY

Having forgone "Gentle Lunacy," the best of Coleridge's later poetry speaks with an intense but entirely naturalistic sincerity. In poems such as "The Blossoming of the Solitary Date-Tree" (1805), "The Pains of Sleep" (1815), and "Work Without Hope" (1826), Coleridge makes no attempt to transform his poetic self into the vehicle for universal truth. He simply presents his feelings and thoughts to the reader. He complains about his condition, but there is no sense that the act of complaint, beyond getting something off his chest for the time being, can effect any significant alteration of the self. Other poems lack even this concern for the limited audience whom he might have expected to be concerned with his personal problems. Poems such as "Limbo" (1817) and "Ne Plus Ultra" (1826?) are notebook exercises in conceiving the inconceivable— in this case, the states of minimal being, in which even the Kantian categories of space and time are reduced to uncertain conceptions, and absolute negation, "The one permitted opposite of God!" With other poems written for a similar private purpose, they are remarkable for the expressive power of their condensed imagery and their capacity to actualize philosophical thought. Coleridge's mastery of language never deserted him.

The greatness of the half dozen or so poems on which his reputation is based derives, however, from more than mastery of language. It derives from a confidence in the power of language that Coleridge, for legitimate reasons, came to doubt. Those half dozen or so poems assume that Coleridge is not a great poet, but that the grounding medium of poetry, like the "eternal language" of nature, is itself great. The very fact of his achievement from 1797 to 1798 presented to him the possibility that it was Coleridge and not poetry in which greatness lay; and, given that possibility, Coleridge could no longer conceive of himself as a poet. He would continue to write, but in media in which it was the thought behind the prose, and not the thinker, that gave meaning to language.

OTHER MAJOR WORKS

PLAYS: *The Fall of Robespierre*, pb. 1794 (with Robert Southey); *Remorse*, pr., pb. 1813 (originally *Osorio*); *Zapolya*, pb. 1817.

NONFICTION: *The Watchman*, 1796; *The Friend*, 1809-1810, 1818; "The Statesman's Manual," 1816; *Biographia Literaria*, 1817; "A Lay Sermon," 1817; "Treatise on Method," 1818; *Aids to Reflection*, 1825; *On the Constitution of the Church and State, According to the Idea of Each: With Aids Toward a Right Judgment on the Late Catholic Bill*, 1830; *Specimens of the Table Talk of the Late Samuel Taylor Coleridge*, 1835; *Letters, Conversations, and Recollections of S. T. Coleridge*, 1836; *Letters of Samuel Taylor Coleridge*, 1855 (2 volumes; Ernest Hartley Coleridge, editor); *Coleridge's Shakespearean Criticism*, 1930; *Coleridge's Miscellaneous Criticism*, 1936; *Notebooks*, 1957-1986 (4 volumes).

TRANSLATION: *Wallenstein*, 1800 (of Friedrich Schiller's plays *Die Piccolomini* and *Wallensteins Tod*).

MISCELLANEOUS: *The Collected Works of Samuel Taylor Coleridge*, 1969-2001 (13 volumes; Kathleen Coburn et al., editors).

BIBLIOGRAPHY

Alexander, Caroline. *The Way to Xanadu*. New York: Knopf, 1994. The author relates her travels to the places that inspired Coleridge's "Kubla Khan" and describes the texts that inspired Coleridge.

Ashton, Rosemary. *The Life of Samuel Taylor Coleridge: A Critical Biography*. Cambridge, Mass.: Blackwell, 1996. Examines Coleridge's complex personality, from poet, critic, and thinker to feckless husband and guilt-ridden opium addict. Coleridge's life is placed within the context of both British and German Romanticism.

Blades, John. *Wordsworth and Coleridge: "Lyrical Ballads."* New York: Palgrave Macmillan, 2004. Detailed analysis of the poems in the literary and historical contexts in which *Lyrical Ballads* was first conceived and created. Documents the revisions made for the second edition and traces the literary criticism of the work in the following decades.

Bloom, Harold, ed. *Samuel Taylor Coleridge*. New York: Chelsea House, 2009. A collection of essays that provide literary criticism of the works of Coleridge.

Christie, William. *Samuel Taylor Coleridge: A Literary Life*. New York: Palgrave Macmillan, 2006. Part biography, part literary criticism, this text provides readers with an in-depth account of Coleridge's personal life and his progression as a writer. Christie helps readers understand Coleridge's works by placing them into the context of his life and providing their publication history. Drawing on the author's notebooks and letters, Christie presents his own interpretation of Coleridge's writing, and discusses other critics' texts, as well.

Holmes, Richard. *Coleridge: Early Visions, 1772-1804*. New York: Viking Press, 1990. The first volume of a two-volume biography. Covers Coleridge's life up to his departure for Malta in 1804. This splendid book is virtually everything a biography should be: well researched, lively, full of insight, and sympathetic to its subject without ignoring other points of view. Fully captures Coleridge's brilliant, flawed, fascinating personality.

_____. *Coleridge: Darker Reflections, 1804-1834*. London: HarperCollins, 1998. In this second, concluding volume of his biography of Coleridge, Holmes traces the tragedies and triumphs of the poet's later career.

Perry, Seamus. *Samuel Taylor Coleridge*. New York: Oxford University Press, 2003. This biography of Coleridge traces his life from its early beginnings through the end of his life. Examines his friendships with Southey and Wordsworth and his numerous careers.

Sisman, Adam. *The Friendship: Wordsworth and*

*Coleridge*. New York: Viking, 2007. An intimate examination of their friendship and its deterioration.

Vigus, James, and Jane Wright, eds. *Coleridge's Afterlives*. New York: Palgrave Macmillan, 2008. Thirteen essays that examine the influence of Coleridge's writings on imagination, narrative structure, and other topics.

*Frederick Kirchhoff*

# WILLIAM COLLINS

**Born:** Chichester, Sussex (now in West Sussex), England; December 25, 1721
**Died:** Chichester, Sussex (now in West Sussex), England; June 12, 1759

PRINCIPAL POETRY

*Persian Eclogues*, 1742
*An Epistle: Verses Humbly Address'd to Sir Thomas Hanmer on His Edition of Shakespeare's Works*, 1744
*Odes on Several Descriptive and Allegoric Subjects*, 1746 (dated 1747)
*An Ode on the Popular Superstitions of the Highlands of Scotland, Considered as the Subject of Poetry*, 1788 (wr. 1749)

OTHER LITERARY FORMS

The form of William Collins's literary accomplishments was limited to poetry.

ACHIEVEMENTS

William Collins's achievements in poetry do not embody the results of careful observation of life, his best poems being descriptive and allegorical. His feelings were intense when he contemplated abstractions such as simplicity, an aesthetic ideal to which his ode gives subtle definition by means of description. His ability to think about abstractions and intellectual concepts in pictorial terms was his most remarkable gift. A second gift was his ability to link every part of his poem

to the next, so that the poem flows along in an unbroken stream.

His best work was done in the ode. Of the twelve such pieces published under the title *Odes on Several Descriptive and Allegoric Subjects* in 1746, three stand out for special effects. The "Ode on the Poetical Character" roughly approximates the true Pindaric ode and, unlike Augustan forms, shows the poet to be an inspired creator and projects imagination as the prime essential of a true poet. "The Passions, an Ode for Music" is a pseudo-Pindaric ode in the tradition of John Dryden's "Alexander's Feast." Its richness of image and appropriate variety of movement have made it the poet's most popular piece. *An Ode on the Popular Superstitions of the Highlands of Scotland, Considered as the Subject of Poetry* is Collins's longest poem, containing his invention of the seventeen-line stanza of iambic pentameter ending with an Alexandrine. It was also the first significant attempt in English literature to concentrate on the Romantic elements of Scottish legend and landscape.

Collins's themes are significant because they anticipate the interests of the early nineteenth century Romantic poets and thus the broad concerns found in modern poetry. Five themes are noteworthy. First, Collins is concerned with the role of imagination in poetry. He believes that imagination rather than reason, an Augustan concern, is the essential trait of the poet. Second, he is a critic of literature, one whose commentary is conditioned by his concern for the imagination. Third, Collins shows a strong interest in folklore and its relation to literature, anticipating Samuel Taylor Coleridge and William Wordsworth. Fourth, he often emphasizes patriotic and political themes, themes that promote ideas of freedom, liberty, and justice, all special concerns of the early Romantic writers. Finally, Collins continually expresses concern for psychological issues in his poetry. All these themes are tied directly to the problem of imagination.

BIOGRAPHY

William Collins was born at Chichester in Sussex in December, 1721. His early years seem to have been those of a favored child. Whether Collins attended a school or learned his first letters at home or under the tutelage of a local curate, he was well enough prepared by the time he was eleven to be admitted as a scholar to Winchester College. His years at Winchester were important. It was there that he made friendships with Joseph Warton, William Whitehead, and James Hampton, and studied mythology and legend in Homer and Vergil. He wrote and published his first poems while at Winchester.

Some scholars believe that it was Warton's friendship and influence that led Collins to become interested in literature. The Warton family was thoroughly literary, and it is possible that Joseph's example first persuaded the youth from his Chichester home and encouraged him to begin cultivating his literary interests. In any case, Collins's literary powers developed while he was at Winchester. One of the poems he wrote during these years, "Sonnet," was published in the *Gentlemen's Magazine* in October, 1739.

After completing his studies at Winchester, Collins was admitted to Queen's College, Oxford, on March 21, 1740. On July 29, 1741, he was appointed demy of Magdalen College, allowing him some stipend, and in 1743, he took the bachelor's degree and left Oxford. Before leaving college, he had published his *Persian Eclogues*, and although the work was published anonymously, the publication was Collins's first serious claim to public notice and ironically remained his chief popular accomplishment during his lifetime. While at Oxford, Collins also published *An Epistle*, which, like *Persian Eclogues*, was well received. The book went into a second edition in 1744, which in itself might have been the inspiration that caused Collins to leave for London to try his hand at the literary life. He moved to the city for a brief period, but eventually settled in Richmond, where he worked for a time and established new friendships, in particular one with James Thomson.

When Bonnie Prince Charles landed in Scotland in 1745 and sounds of war spread, Collins turned to writing patriotic verse. During the early part of 1746, Collins was working on his odes. Perhaps they had been in progress for some time; in any event, scholars are quite sure that by the summer of 1746 they were nearing the form in which they now exist. It may have been at this time that Collins traveled to the Guildford races, where

he met Joseph Warton. In time they mutually decided to publish their poems. The publication of his *Odes on Several Descriptive and Allegoric Subjects* in 1746 was the high-water mark of Collins's life, even though he probably did not realize it at the time, primarily because the public took very little note of them. Scholars do not know what his reaction to this relative failure may have been, but they do know that he was engaged in various literary projects in 1747 and that he remained active in literary circles. The depressing malady to which Thomas Warton refers in one of his letters did not begin to afflict Collins until 1750 at the earliest.

Collins began disposing of his share of the family property in Chichester in 1749, and when he made his last trip there in October for final legalities, he met John Home, beginning another fertile creative period in his life. By 1750, there were announcements that a new translation by Mr. William Collins of Torquato Tasso's *Jerusalem Delivered* (1575) would appear. Although no copy seems to exist, there is every reason to believe that Collins did translate the poem. After meeting Home, Collins also went on to write the famous ode on the superstitions of Scotland.

It must have been about the end of 1750 or in 1751 that Collins's illness began. Eventually he was committed to an insane asylum. Warton mentions that at Easter, 1751, Collins was "given over and supposed to be dying." Samuel Johnson's account is probably substantially accurate—except that he has him dying in 1756 rather than in 1759. No one since the eighteenth century has added to the knowledge of the last period of Collins's life.

ANALYSIS

Although the heroic couplet had achieved its dominance by the time of William Collins, lyric poetry was still alive, albeit somewhat in reserve as a popular mode of expression. The lyric poet of the second quarter of the eighteenth century had available a number of traditional forms: the Pindaric ode for exalted subjects, the Horatian ode for a variety of urban and meditative themes, the elegy, and the song. A new type appeared, another type of "ode" that centered on a personified abstraction treated in a descriptive way. Borrowing from John Milton's style in "L'Allegro" and "Il Penseroso," the Wartons and Collins played a major role in developing this form.

Collins did not achieve fame with his odes during his lifetime, and perhaps this lack of recognition contributed to his early mental instability and eventual death at thirty-seven. His odes never attain warmth and personal intimacy, but they do achieve particular effects that are unsurpassed in eighteenth century poetry: pensive melody, emotionally charged landscape, vigorous allegory, and rich romanticism.

Collins, like his friends the Wartons, advocated concepts of poetry that would eventually dominate poetic thought by the turn of the nineteenth century. His belief that poetry should be freely imagined and passionately felt, that it should be blessed with *furor poesis*, puts him basically into the Wordsworthian camp. His formalism and abstraction, ties to his Augustan background, obviously hamper his style. Collins is much like Edwin Arlington Robinson's Miniver Cheevy, born out of time. He has one poetic foot in the past, but the other, much larger one, extends far into the future, since it would be some forty years after his death before the publication of William Wordsworth and Samuel Taylor Coleridge's *Lyrical Ballads* (1798), the recognized *locus classicus* of Romanticism. Collins has been compared with the early nineteenth century poet Percy Bysshe Shelley in his use of abstraction; in the work of both poets, personifications become real figures that help express a delicate mood without recourse to great detail: "Spring with dewey fingers cold" and "Freedom a weeping hermit" illustrate the method well. This personification of natural phenomena in eighteenth century verse for the most part symbolizes affective states, where the allegorical figure sums up the meaning that the phenomenon has for the poet.

Collins does seem at times to strive for scholarly classicism. His mixture of classical and medieval sources illustrates his "two voices" long before Alfred, Lord Tennyson's metaphor and poems come into overt expression. He was the most free of all the early precursors of Romanticism, and his predominant concern was the spirit of beauty. Most critics compare Collins favorably with his contemporaries, especially with Thomas Gray, generally agreeing with William Hazlitt's assessment. Hazlitt argued that Collins possessed genu-

ine inspiration, and that even though his work is marred by affectation and certain obscurities, "he also catches rich glimpses of the bowers of paradise."

## "ODE ON THE POETICAL CHARACTER"

Perhaps the best guide to Collins's attitude toward inspiration and imagination is his "Ode on the Poetical Character." Early in the ode, Collins asserts that the true poetical character is godlike, for the bard is one "prepared and bathed in heaven." Following this apotheosis, Collins pursues the idea by describing God's creation of the world as analogous to the poet's act of creation. A bit of sixteenth century pagan/Christian syncretism is reflected in his analogy: God was the original type of all poets and the contemporary poet imitates his divine power. Collins, however, adds allegorical layers to this analogy. He suggests that Fancy is a separate female entity and not merely an attribute of God, and he adds the rather confusing metaphor of a girdle of poetic imagination.

Collins turns to the examples of John Milton and Edmund Spenser, suggesting that the true poet will find his voice in a kind of wedding of their diverse styles. One finds such a poet, according to stanza 3, "high on some cliff . . . of prospect wild," accompanied by holy genie and surrounded by an Eden-like environment. In this ode there is a sense of a new aesthetic attitude that later comes to be described as "Romantic"; John Langhorne says that the ode is so wild it seems to have been written under the Romantic tyranny of the imagination.

## PERSIAN ECLOGUES

The wedding of the styles of Spenser and Milton that results in this strong emotional verse can be related to Collins's earlier work entitled *Persian Eclogues*. He prefaces his eclogues with the statement that "The style of my countrymen is as naturally strong and nervous as that of an Arabian or Persian is rich and figurative." Spenser is a writer whom Collins associates with Persian genius because of his luxuriously expansive style. Following the contemporary attitude toward Hebraic poetry as being energetic but brief rather than copious, Collins thinks of Milton as an example. The fusion of these two styles results in rich, emotional verse.

*Persian Eclogues* was published in 1742 while Collins was at Oxford, but the individual eclogues had been written sometime between his birthday in 1738 and the winter of 1740. According to Joseph Warton, Collins wrote them at a time when he was studying Persian history. In Collins's time, exotic Eastern interests were becoming popular, and features of Oriental poetry had become fascinating to the post-Augustan generation. Thomas Rymer comments that fancy dominated Oriental verse, "wild, vast and unbridled." Obviously, such a style met with Collins's approval; the pretense that he was actually translating Persian poetry allowed him to attempt a rich elegance and wildness of thought, traits that became characteristic of his mature Romanticism.

Most critics agree that the eclogues contain little genuine Orientalism. In diction and structure they closely follow conventions of the eighteenth century pastoral, especially those of Alexander Pope. There are several significant differences, however, between Pope and Collins, the first of which is simply that Collins's setting is exotic, not English. Also, there is a difference in theme; although both writers follow the conventional emphasis on the power of time, Collins's tone is secular rather than Christian, as in Shelley's pastoral elegy "Adonais." Collins does not see the essence of pastoral as the recognition of humanity's fall and of modern humans' desire to repudiate Adam and inherited sin. By using the seasons, Pope, for example, is able to trace humanity's decline from a golden age to an age of error, with a final eclogue showing the transforming power of Christ, who can bring the golden age back for all humankind. Collins does not use the seasons for his structure and he does not use the sacred closing eclogue. Rather, he suggests that the usable values of the past should be put into practice in contemporary society.

There is little borrowing from other sources in *Persian Eclogues*. The third eclogue may be a variation of a story of a king of Persia who, after witnessing the simple life of his peasant subjects, gives up his kingship for a time to live with shepherds. The king eventually returns to court with a favorite shepherd, who in turn longs continually for his rural home. This story appeared in Ambrose Phillips's periodical *The Free-Thinker* in 1719 and 1739, thus making it possible for Collins to have seen it.

## "ODE TO LIBERTY"

Another poem reflecting Collins's orientation toward Romanticism is the 1746 "Ode to Liberty." The background for the ode is the War of the Austrian Succession. The war with France saw the city of Genoa fall prey to allied invasion because of Austrian occupation: Genoa is another example of the democratic fight for liberty, paralleling Austria's own William Tell who refused to bow to the dictatorial governor's demands. The "Ode to Liberty" suggests a desire for peace, implying throughout a great sympathy for those who suffer innocently. Collins's question in strophe 1, perhaps alluding to the exhortations of Tyrtaus to the Spartans in the Second Messenian War to fight with courage, stresses the disgrace of cowardice and the glory of patriotism. He also alludes to William Tell in epode 1, and his closing remarks suggest that England will welcome to its shores for peaceful play the dedicated youth who fought so bravely.

## AN ODE ON THE POPULAR SUPERSTITIONS OF THE HIGHLANDS OF SCOTLAND

It is generally observed that the ode that expresses Collins's Romantic temperament at its best is one of his last works, originally entitled *Ode to a Friend on His Return* but published posthumously in 1788 as *An Ode on the Popular Superstitions of the Highlands of Scotland, Considered as the Subject of Poetry*. The ode was addressed to a friend and fellow writer, John Home, who was leaving London after his failure to place one of his plays on the London stage.

The Romantic nature of the piece is seen in the opening lines as Collins asks his friend to rediscover a region inhabited by "Fairy People" and ruled by "Fancy." The ancient bards seem to rise in masque-like manner around Home, whose mind is "possest" by strange powers. The "matted hair with bough fantastic crown'd" enhances the supernatural mood that Collins establishes. Collins admonishes Home to make use of such forces in writing his plays. By employing supernatural tales such as are found in the folklore of Scotland, Collins says, the modern poet can partake of the visionary power found therein and share in its creative force. Probably the most alluring section of the ode is the story of the hapless swain caught up in the force of the kelpie's wrath. The swain is led astray by glimmering mazes that cheer his sight. These lights are actually the will-o'-the-wisps, a vision deluding and drawing him to the water monster, whose malignant design becomes obvious to the reader at this point. The poor swain becomes a passive, helpless wretch in the clutches of the evil kelpie. His death leads to his transformation into a supernatural being, unable to bridge the gap between his former and his present life.

In the closing lines, Collins invokes a natural environment that is sustained by supernatural traditions. The ode is undoubtedly a celebration of the new visionary source which would further liberate poetry in the Romantic period.

BIBLIOGRAPHY

Doughty, Oswald. *William Collins*. London: Longmans, Green, 1964. A brief, handy book recommended for its accessibility. A view of Collins's life is followed by succinct readings of his major poems. Includes a useful bibliography.

Jung, Sandro. "Collins's 'Ode to Evening.'" *Explicator* 64, no. 1 (Fall, 2005): 19-25. Analyzes Collins's use of "to rove" in his poem "Ode to Evening." Notes the poet's originality in his use of the verb.

Sherwin, Paul S. *Precious Bane: Collins and the Miltonic Legacy*. Austin: University of Texas Press, 1977. Sherwin's "anxiety of influence" approach, though perhaps inapplicable to all poets, is certainly applicable to Collins and the poets of the age of sensibility, who consciously looked back to the towering figures of Edmund Spenser, William Shakespeare, and John Milton. The reading of Collins's "Ode on the Poetical Character" is particularly recommended.

Sigworth, Oliver F. *William Collins*. New York: Twayne, 1965. This is a very good introduction to the life and work of Collins. Lodged between a biographical account of Collins and a long treatment of the poetry is a particularly useful consideration of "the poetry and the age." Supplementing the text are a chronology, notes, and a bibliography.

Sitter, John. *Literary Loneliness in Mid-Eighteenth-Century England*. Ithaca, N.Y.: Cornell University Press, 1982. Sitter is a major authority on the so-called Age of Sensibility in England during the 1740's and 1750's—the period that Collins has come to exemplify. Contains excellent discussions of other writers important to the period, as well as an extended treatment of Collins and his poetry.

Weiskel, Thomas. *The Romantic Sublime: Studies in the Structure and Psychology of Transcendence*. Baltimore: The Johns Hopkins University Press, 1976. An impressive book, demanding and difficult but containing an important reading of Collins and his poetry, especially the crucial "Ode on the Poetical Character."

Wendorf, Richard. *William Collins and Eighteenth-Century English Poetry*. Minneapolis: University of Minnesota Press, 1981. Also an editor of Collins, Wendorf begins with an informed, sensible treatment of Collins's "madness"—for years a critical and biographical stumbling block—then moves on to consider Collins's career and poetry. The treatment of Collins's "musical odes" is highly interesting. A useful "note" on modern criticism of Collins is included.

White, Deborah Elise. *Romantic Returns: Superstition, Imagination, History*. Stanford, Calif.: Stanford University Press, 2000. Intended for readers with a background in literary theory, the book covers the theorization and operation of "imagination" in pre-Romantic and Romantic writing. The ways in which the aesthetics of Romanticism inform its political and economic speculations are explored in an analysis of the poetry and prose of William Collins, William Hazlitt, and Percy Bysshe Shelley.

Woodhouse, A. S. P. "Collins and the Creative Imagination: A Study in the Critical Background of His Odes (1746)." In *Studies in English by Members of University College, Toronto*, edited by M. W. Wallace. Toronto, Ont.: University of Toronto Press, 1931. A classic early study of Collins, still vital for Woodhouse's discussion of the ode in the mid-eighteenth century and his treatment of Collins's most important poem, the "Ode on the Poetical Character."

*John W. Crawford*

# PADRAIC COLUM

**Born:** County Longford, Ireland; December 8, 1881

**Died:** Enfield, Connecticut; January 11, 1972

PRINCIPAL POETRY

*Wild Earth: A Book of Verse*, 1907
*Dramatic Legends, and Other Poems*, 1922
*Creatures*, 1927
*Way of the Cross*, 1927
*Old Pastures*, 1930
*Poems*, 1932
*The Story of Lowry Main*, 1937
*Flower Pieces: New Poems*, 1938
*The Collected Poems of Padraic Colum*, 1953
*The Vegetable Kingdom*, 1954
*Ten Poems*, 1957
*Irish Elegies*, 1958
*The Poet's Circuits: Collected Poems of Ireland*, 1960
*Images of Departure*, 1969
*Selected Poems of Padraic Colum*, 1989 (Sanford Sternlicht, editor)

OTHER LITERARY FORMS

Padraic Colum (KAWL-uhm) was a prolific writer who expressed himself in many different genres during the first seven decades of the twentieth century. He helped found the Abbey Theatre in Dublin with William Butler Yeats, and he wrote three major plays: *The Land* (pr., pb. 1905), *The Fiddler's House* (pr., pb. 1907), and *Thomas Muskerry* (pr., pb. 1910). All three plays deal with the dignity of Irish farmers. He wrote numerous short stories; two major novels, *Castle Conquer* (1923) and *The Flying Swans* (1957); and numerous essays on Irish history and politics. After his immigration to the United States in 1914 with his wife, Mary Colum, he became especially famous for his elegant retelling of folk tales for children. Some of his most admired books for children are *The King of Ireland's Son* (1916), *The Golden Fleece and the Heroes Who Lived Before Achilles* (1921), and *Legends of Hawaii* (1937).

ACHIEVEMENTS

Unlike other great writers of the literary movement called the Irish Renaissance (also the Celtic Revival), such as William Butler Yeats, Lady Augusta Gregory, and James Joyce, who were his friends, Padraic Colum was from a peasant background. He understood profoundly the beliefs and moral values of Irish farmers. Although he moved to the United States in 1914, his thoughts never really left the Irish countryside of his youth. In his poetry and prose, he wrote in a deceptively simple style. His poetry captured the simple dignity of Irish peasants, whose emotions and struggles he presented as representations of the rich diversity of human experience. Some of his poems, including "An Old Woman of the Roads" and "A Cradle Song," have been learned by heart by generations of Irish and Irish American students. His poetry is immediately accessible to young readers, but more mature readers also appreciate the simple eloquence and evocative power of his poems. He captured the essence of Irish folklore and popular culture and transmitted to readers its profound universality. He became a member of the American Academy of Arts and Letters in 1948 and served as chancellor for the Academy of American Poets from 1950 to 1951. In 1952, Colum won an Academy of American Poets Fellowship. He received the Gregory Medal of the Irish Academy of Letters in 1953 and the Regina Medal in 1961.

BIOGRAPHY

Padraic Colum was born in a workhouse in Ireland's County Longford on December 8, 1881. His original name was Patrick Columb, but in his early twenties, he changed his name to Padraic Colum to make it sound more Irish and less English. He was the first of eight children born to Susan and Patrick Columb. During his youth, he learned about Irish folklore and traditions by listening to the oral tales told by those who lived in County Longford. He never wavered in his commitment both to the Catholic faith of his ancestors and to the values of Irish peasant culture. His formal education ended when he was sixteen, and he was in many ways a self-educated man.

His family moved to Dublin in 1891, and after his studies ended, Colum became a clerk for the Irish railroads. He soon developed a deep interest in Gaelic culture and discovered his abilities as a writer. With the encouragement of Yeats and Lady Augusta Gregory, he wrote plays for the newly founded Abbey Theatre in Dublin as well as lyric poetry. A monetary grant in 1908 from American businessman Thomas Kelly enabled Colum to resign from his job with the railroads and to concentrate solely on his writing. From then on, Colum earned his living as a writer. He married Mary Maguire in 1912, and they moved to the United States two years later.

While in the United States, the Colums often wrote together. They were popular lecturers and visiting professors at various American universities, especially at Columbia University, where they taught literature for many years. They spent most of their time in New York City, but they traveled frequently. Although they had no children, Colum earned his living largely by retelling folktales for children. These books were enormously popular. In 1924, the provincial legislature in Hawaii decided to preserve traditional Hawaiian folktales, and it decided that Colum was the most qualified person to undertake this project. The Colums spent two years in Hawaii, where Padraic learned Hawaiian and became so erudite in Hawaiian culture that he gave numerous lectures on Hawaiian history and culture in Honolulu's Bishop Museum.

During his nearly six decades in the United States, Colum remained a prolific writer. He was a humble man who preferred speaking about his wife and their numerous fellow writers, especially their close friend James Joyce, to talking about himself. One year after Mary's death in 1957, Colum completed a biography the two of them had been writing of Joyce, which he titled *Our Friend James Joyce*. At that time Colum began receiving care from his nephew Emmet Greene, who assisted him in his many trips around the New York area. Although Colum never wrote an autobiography, American scholar Zack Bowen recorded a series of interviews with him in the 1960's. In the interviews, Colum spoke extensively of his literary career. Bowen relied on these interviews for his 1970 biography of Colum, and he donated these tapes to the library of the State University of New York, Binghamton, which houses Colum's papers. Colum died in a nursing home

*Padraic Colum* (Library of Congress)

in Connecticut on January 11, 1972. His body was flown to Ireland, where he was buried next to his beloved Mary.

ANALYSIS

In nineteenth century British and American plays, a common character type was the "stage Irishman." This artificial Irish character was not very bright or sensitive. He tended to be a buffoon whose major interest in life was drinking. These plays revealed no understanding of the harsh reality of colonial rule and economic exploitation in rural Ireland. Until the very end of the nineteenth century, Catholics could not own land in Ireland, and farmers were forced to pay rent to absentee landlords. A desire for stability and a profound love of the land were deeply felt by Irish peasants. Padraic Colum expressed their feelings in a poetic voice that was authentic.

### "AN OLD WOMAN OF THE ROADS"

Colum's 1907 book *Wild Earth* includes some of his most admired poems. The very title suggests that generations of Irish peasants had resisted British efforts to suppress their culture and their Catholic faith. One of Colum's most famous early poems is "An Old Woman of the Roads." Its title refers to so-called tinkers, itinerant peddlers who traveled the roads of Ireland in their wagons and sold their goods. Because of their trade, tinkers did not develop roots in a specific village. In this twenty-four-line poem, which is composed of six four-line stanzas, the old woman speaks in the first person. She is a humble but proud woman with simple desires. She dreams of having a house with a hearth, heated by sod, in which she could have a bed and a dresser. She imagines that this house would also be her store, in which she could display her goods to eager customers. She is tired of endless traveling in her wagon, and she dreams of stability, which she associates with peace. Like almost all Irish peasants, she is deeply committed to the Catholic faith that gives her the strength to endure suffering with quiet dignity. In the final stanza, the old woman realizes that she may never have a house in this life, but she still dreams of paradise, where she will be "out of the wind's and the rain's way." As she travels the roads of Ireland, she prays to God "night and day."

As for other Irish peasants, God's presence in their daily lives and the resurrection are realities that she does not question. She is tired of the constant struggle to survive in abject poverty, but she never forgets that God loves her, and she believes that she will eventually return to her true "house" in heaven. With many different uses of the word *house*, Colum enables his readers to appreciate the quiet dignity and profound spirituality of ordinary Irish people. It is not at all surprising that "An Old Woman of the Roads" remains a poem beloved by generations of Irish readers and readers of Irish descent.

### "A CRADLE SONG"

Another 1907 poem that has remained popular is the sixteen-line poem "A Cradle Song." As in "An Old Woman of the Roads," each stanza contains four lines of free verse. The scene evoked in this poem is universal. Parents around the world sing to their babies to calm them and to help them sleep. Just as in "An Old Woman of the Roads," Colum includes a clear religious reference because the mother of whom he speaks in "A Cradle Song" is the Virgin Mary.

Colum transfers the infancy of Christ to an Irish country setting, and he refers to Mary by the Irish term of endearment "Mavourneen," which means "darling." The Gospel according to Saint Matthew tells how three wise men, or magi, came to adore the infant Jesus just after Mary had given birth. In "A Cradle Song," Colum transforms these wise men into "men from the fields" whom a new mother has invited to come see her infant son, whom she has protected with "her mantle of blue." The great respect due Christ and all babies and mothers requires that the "men from the fields" enter the house "gently" and "softly," lest they disturb the mother or child. Colum evokes the poverty of these surroundings by pointing out that the floor in this house is cold, and farm animals are "peering" at the mother and baby "across the half door." Despite the lack of material comfort, the mother is incredibly happy because she is experiencing the miracle of a new life. In this poem, Colum expresses very eloquently to his readers the incredible joy that new life brings.

### "ROGER CASEMENT"

Colum wrote several elegies in praise of distinguished Irish people who had died. His most famous elegy was for the Irish patriot Roger David Casement (1864-1916), whom the British hanged on a charge of treason. Colum and others who favored Irish independence from Great Britain never believed the accusations against Casement, whom they considered to be a martyr. This elegy contains two eight-line stanzas. Four of the sixteen lines contain the Gaelic words for mourning, "ochone, och, ochone, ochone!" One could translate the word *ochone* as "alas," but these are words people say at an Irish country burial. Casement was hanged in a British jail, but Colum imagines that Irish peasants have reserved for him the honors owed to a worthy person who has left this earth to spend eternity in heaven. Colum states that those who respect Roger Casement's memory are not respectable English people named Smith, Murray, or Cecil, who approved of the execution of an Irish hero, but rather "outcast peoples . . . who laboured fearfully." These social outcasts, whom the British disdain and with whom Colum identifies, will "lift" Casement "for the eyes of God to see."

Although Casement was executed for treason, Colum reminds his readers that although a colonial power can reduce individuals to silence by killing them, it can never destroy in the minds of ordinary people the martyr's dignity. Casement's heroism in the face of death serves only to remind Irish people of his "noble stature . . . courtesy and kindliness" that Colum evokes in this very powerful elegy.

### "AFTER SPEAKING OF ONE WHO DIED A LONG TIME BEFORE"

Although Colum wrote poems of very high quality for seventy years, just three years before his death, he completed an extraordinary collection of twenty poems, titled *Images of Departure*. These exquisite poems express the joy of life felt by an eighty-eight-year-old poet who had survived his wife and almost all his friends. Perhaps the finest poem in this collection is the twenty-four-line poem "After Speaking of One Who Died a Long Time Before." This short poem is composed of an eleven-line stanza and a thirteen-line stanza. He links his personal loss of his beloved wife and best friend, Mary, with the "tenderness and grief" simultaneously felt by people when they think of dead loved ones who profoundly touched their lives. Near the very end of his long life, Colum still demonstrated his masterful ability to use ordinary words and images to help his readers appreciate the rich complexity of human emotions.

### OTHER MAJOR WORKS

LONG FICTION: *Castle Conquer*, 1923; *The Flying Swans*, 1957.

SHORT FICTION: *Selected Short Stories of Padraic Colum*, 1985 (Sanford Sternlicht, editor).

PLAYS: *The Children of Lir*, pb. 1901 (one act); *Broken Soil*, pr. 1903 (revised as *The Fiddler's House*, pr., pb. 1907); *The Land*, pr., pb. 1905; *The Miracle of the Corn*, pr. 1908; *The Destruction of the Hostel*, pr. 1910; *Thomas Muskerry*, pr., pb. 1910; *The Desert*, pb. 1912 (revised as *Mogu the Wanderer: Or, The Desert*, pb. 1917); *The Betrayal*, pr. 1914; *Three Plays*, 1916, 1925, 1963 (includes *The Land*, *The Fiddler's House*, and *Thomas Muskerry*); *The Grasshopper*, pr. 1917 (adaptation of Eduard Keyserling's play *Ein Frühlingsofer*); *Balloon*, pb. 1929; *Moytura: A Play for Dancers*, pr., pb. 1963; *The Challengers*, pr. 1966

(3 one-act plays: *Monasterboice*, *Glendalough*, and *Cloughoughter*); *Carricknabauna*, pr. 1967 (also as *The Road Round Ireland*); *Selected Plays of Padraic Colum*, 1986 (includes *The Land*, *The Betrayal*, *Glendalough*, and *Monasterboice*; Sternlicht, editor).

SCREENPLAY: *Hansel and Gretel*, 1954 (adaptation of Engelbert Humperdinck's opera).

NONFICTION: *My Irish Year*, 1912; *The Road Round Ireland*, 1926; *Cross Roads in Ireland*, 1930; *A Half-Day's Ride: Or, Estates in Corsica*, 1932; *Our Friend James Joyce*, 1958 (with Mary Colum); *Ourselves Alone: The Story of Arthur Griffith and the Origin of the Irish Free State*, 1959.

CHILDREN'S LITERATURE: *A Boy in Eirinn*, 1913; *The King of Ireland's Son*, 1916; *The Adventures of Odysseus*, 1918; *The Boy Who Knew What the Birds Said*, 1918; *The Girl Who Sat by the Ashes*, 1919; *The Boy Apprenticed to an Enchanter*, 1920; *The Children of Odin*, 1920; *The Golden Fleece and the Heroes Who Lived Before Achilles*, 1921; *The Children Who Followed the Piper*, 1922; *At the Gateways of the Day*, 1924; *The Island of the Mighty: Being the Hero Stories of Celtic Britain Retold from the Mabinogion*, 1924; *Six Who Were Left in a Shoe*, 1924; *The Bright Islands*, 1925; *The Forge in the Forest*, 1925; *The Voyagers: Being Legends and Romances of Atlantic Discovery*, 1925; *The Fountain of Youth: Stories to Be Told*, 1927; *Orpheus: Myths of the World*, 1930; *The Big Tree of Bunlahy: Stories of My Own Countryside*, 1933; *The White Sparrow*, 1933; *The Legend of Saint Columba*, 1935; *Legends of Hawaii*, 1937; *Where the Winds Never Blew and the Cocks Never Crew*, 1940; *The Frenzied Prince: Being Heroic Stories of Ancient Ireland*, 1943; *A Treasury of Irish Folklore*, 1954; *Story Telling, New and Old*, 1961; *The Stone of Victory, and Other Tales of Padraic Colum*, 1966.

### BIBLIOGRAPHY

Bowen, Zack. *Padraic Colum: A Biographical-Critical Introduction*. Carbondale: Southern Illinois University Press, 1970. This excellent introduction to Colum's works was based on a careful study of his writings but also on extensive interviews between Colum and Zack Bowen in the 1960's.

Colum, Mary. *Life and the Dream*. Garden City, N.Y.:

Doubleday, 1947. A firsthand account by Colum's wife of the impact of the Irish Literary Revival. The events and personalities of that creative period are regarded nostalgically and rather uncritically.

Hogan, Robert, Richard Burnham, and Daniel P. Poteet. *The Rise of the Realists*. Atlantic Highlands, N.J.: Humanities Press, 1979. This volume concentrates on the years of Colum's involvement with the Abbey Theatre and the national theater movement. Although it focuses on the plays, it sheds light on Colum's poetry.

*Journal of Irish Literature* 2, no. 1 (January, 1973). This special issue on Colum contains a miscellany of Colum material, including tributes from a number of Irish scholars, a substantial interview, and articles surveying Colum's achievements. Also included is a portfolio of work by Colum, including two plays, poems for children and other verse, and various prose pieces, one of which is a self-portrait.

Murphy, Ann. "Appreciation: Padraic Colum (1881-1972), National Poet." *Eire-Ireland: A Journal of Irish Studies* 17, no. 4 (Winter, 1982): 128-147. A thoughtful essay that describes well the important place of Colum in twentieth century Irish poetry.

Murray, Christopher. "Padraic Colum's *The Land* and Cultural Nationalism." *Hungarian Journal of English and American Studies* 2, no. 2 (1996): 5-15. A short but accurate description of Colum's support for Irish independence from Great Britain.

"Poet to the Eye, Giant in the Canon." *Irish Times*, December 11, 2006, p. 14. This article, written after the 135th birthday of the poet, argues that Colum's skills as a poet should be more highly recognized.

Sternlicht, Sanford. *Padraic Colum*. Boston: Twayne, 1985. An introductory study of Colum's long life and various literary achievements. Much attention is given to the poems. Also contains a detailed chapter on the prose and another on Colum's works of mythology, which are associated with his children's writing. Includes a chronology and a bibliography.

_____. "Padraic Colum: Poet of the 1960's." *Colby Literary Quarterly* 25, no. 4 (1989): 253-257. A short but insightful analysis of *Images of Departure* elegies written by Colum in the 1960's.

*Edmund J. Campion*

# WILLIAM CONGREVE

**Born:** Bardsey, Yorkshire, England; January 24, 1670

**Died:** London, England; January 19, 1729

PRINCIPAL POETRY

"To Mr. Dryden on His Translation of Persius," 1693

*Poems upon Several Occasions*, 1710

OTHER LITERARY FORMS

The major works of William Congreve (KAWN-greev) are his plays: four comedies, *The Old Bachelor* (pr., pb. 1693), *The Double-Dealer* (pr. 1693), *Love for Love* (pr., pb. 1695), and *The Way of the World* (pr., pb. 1700), and one tragedy, *The Mourning Bride* (pr., pb. 1697). Congreve also wrote criticism, *Amendments of Mr. Collier's False and Imperfect Citations* (1698); a novella, *Incognita: Or, Love and Duty Reconcil'd* (1692); a masque, *The Judgement of Paris* (pr., pb. 1701); and an opera, *Semele* (pb. 1710). Some of his letters were published in a collection edited by John Dennis (1696). His other miscellaneous writings include contributions to *The Gentleman's Journal* (1692-1694), an essay for *The Tatler* (February 13, 1711), and the "Dedication to John Dryden's *Dramatick Works*" (1717).

ACHIEVEMENTS

In his own day, William Congreve had a considerable reputation as a poet. John Dryden, in his poem "To My Dear Friend Mr Congreve," crowned him as his successor, and as a political poet supporting William III, Congreve performed much the same function as Dryden did for Charles II and James II. Contemporary writers such as Jonathan Swift and the lesser known Charles Hopkins and William Dove praised Congreve's verse extravagantly. Almost all this praise, however, stemmed from Congreve's reputation as a dramatist and from his pleasing personality. By the middle of the eighteenth century, critics began looking at Congreve's poetry in isolation and harshly condemned it. In the nineteenth century, Thomas Macaulay pronounced Congreve's poetry to be of little value and long forgotten, and Edmund Gosse concentrated on Congreve the man, giving no very favorable judgment. After such a great fall in Congreve's reputation, critical judgment of his poetry has settled: He is considered an elegant minor poet, whose real fame rests on his plays. His best poems are his light love songs and his witty prologues; his greatest contribution to poetry was his condemnation of the irregular Cowleyan Pindaric, a form that had led to much laxness and mediocrity in poetry.

## BIOGRAPHY

William Congreve was born in Yorkshire but grew up in Ireland, where his father served as an army lieutenant. Unlike many poets of his day, he belonged to the gentry: His grandfather was squire of Stretton Hall in Staffordshire. Congreve attended Kilkenny College, where he is reported to have written his first poem on the death of his headmaster's magpie. Swift was an older classmate of Congreve at Kilkenny and later at Trinity College, Dublin. After college, Congreve moved to London to study law but soon became entranced by the literary life. He frequented Will's coffeehouse, published a novel, and began writing odes and songs. His translations of Homer won Dryden's praise and friendship, and Dryden edited and then sponsored Congreve's first play, *The Old Bachelor*. During the play's run, Congreve fell in love with the young actress Anne Bracegirdle, for whom he wrote many poems and the part of Millamant in *The Way of the World*. For his promise as a propagandist for William III, Congreve was given his first of a long series of political posts, commissioner for hackney coaches; in gratitude, he produced the standard celebratory odes. *The Mourning Bride*, Congreve's only tragedy, was his greatest popular success, although he is most acclaimed now for *The Way of the World*, a relative failure in its own day.

After the less-than-rapturous reception of *The Way of the World*, suffering from increasing blindness and painful gout, Congreve declined to expend the enormous amount of energy and concentration needed to write plays. He continued to write verses on occasion and became a gentleman about town, friend of prominent writers, and gallant of Henrietta, duchess of

Marlborough. Although he stopped writing for the theater, his love for it never waned; in 1705, he became the director of the new Haymarket Theater. His government posts continued; in 1714, he was made searcher of customs and then secretary to the island of Jamaica, an office that gave him an adequate income for the rest of his life. He died in 1729 and was buried in Westminster Abbey, where the duchess was buried beside him a few years later.

## ANALYSIS

William Congreve's best poetry, like his plays, brings Restoration society to life: the intricacies of the courtship dance and the war in the theaters between playwrights and critics. When Congreve strays from his own milieu into political propaganda, however, or makes attempts at the sublime, his poetry rarely rises above the mediocre.

### COURTSHIP

Congreve's poems, particularly his songs, reveal the feelings of both partners in the courtship dance. His men are not confident and promiscuous Horners who accumulate conquest after conquest but insecure young men who often have been hurt or discarded by women. One song, in anapests, mimics the headstrong impetuosity and lumbering clumsiness of a young man in love: "I Look'd, and I sigh'd, and I wish'd I cou'd speak." Another song, "The Reconciliation," reminds one of John Donne's "Go and Catch a Falling Star": A cynical young man insists that women prove ungrateful whenever men are true and claims that the joys women give are "few, short, and insincere." "Song," one of Congreve's best-known and most-liked poems, purportedly composed for Anne Bracegirdle, is written in the calm yet bittersweet manner of Sir Thomas Wyatt. A lover, remembering the past joys of his inconstant mistress, determines not to seek revenge but to be grateful for what has been. Many of Congreve's songs sound this same theme of a young man bemoaning his lost love.

Congreve's women fall into two categories: honorable women torn between their desire to love and be loved and their need to maintain their virtue and inconstant women who leave heartbroken, hapless men in their wake. Congreve shows great sensitivity to the

*William Congreve* (Library of Congress)

plight of women in the love-honor struggle of Restoration society. In "Song in Dialogue, for Two Women," the two women speakers decide whether to yield to their lovers' enticements. The first speaker claims she will but changes her mind after listening to the second. Both sing a chorus that acknowledges how quickly men can lose interest: "And granting Desire,/ We feed not the Fire,/ But make it more quickly expire." In another song, Selinda is caught between her religious desire for purity and her secular desire to keep her lover: She runs to the church if he asks her favor yet cries when she thinks he will leave her. Selinda's lover wittily reveals the pressure put on a Restoration woman: "Wou'd she cou'd make of me a Saint,/ Or I of her a Sinner."

Like Alexander Pope, Congreve has his essay on women: three short poems on Amoret, Lesbia, and Doris. "Doris," which was much praised by Sir Richard Steele, presents a fully rounded picture of a promiscuous "Nymph of riper Age" who shines on various lovers in the night and quickly forgets them the next day.

"Lesbia" describes a young man's discovery of the empty head of the idol he worships: the "trickling Nonsense" from her coral lips like balm heals his heart wounded by love. "Amoret" presents a contradictory young woman, who affects "to seem unaffected" and laughs at others for what she prizes in herself. A blind hypocrite, she does not see that "She is the Thing that she despises."

Congreve claimed to be a moralist, exposing the vice and folly of his society. He is indeed harsh in his condemnation of unfaithful, hypocritical wives. In his epilogue to Thomas Southerne's *Oroonoko* (1695), he satirizes town ladies who profess to be Christian and virtuous yet despise their spouses and take their marriage vows lightly. Promiscuous single women may leave angry, unhappy men, but they do not undermine the foundations of society—marriage and family.

### PROLOGUES AND EPILOGUES

Congreve's prologues and epilogues, though less vigorous and daring than Dryden's, comment on the state of the theater and society through the use of witty imagery. His prologues are fitting appetizers for the feasts that follow: forgetting lines, pleading with the audience to like the play, and running offstage in confusion.

Critics habitually drew the ire of Restoration playwrights, and Congreve regularly traded insults with them. The epilogue to *The Old Bachelor* sandwiches a witty comparison of young women and playwrights between the standard pleading to be approved and the standard insulting of the critics ("If he's an ass, he will be tried by's peers"). Once the end is gained, both women and playwrights are damned (discarded).

The prologue to *The Double-Dealer* is more sophisticated, with fewer drops in tone. It compares the play to a Moorish infant, thrown by its father (the playwright) into the sea (the pit) to prove its legitimacy. The image serves Congreve well; he can describe the pit as tempestuous and call the critics sharks. The epilogue to *The Double-Dealer* classifies the audience of the Restoration theater, critics all: the men of learning, the pit, the ladies, the beaux, and the witlings, each of whom has different exacting requirements for a successful play. The same theme recurs in Congreve's epilogue to *Oroonoko*. The poet divides his time among the different tastes; his one foot wears the sock, the other the buskin, and in striving to please, he is forced to hop in a single boot.

In addition to condemning the critics and the problems they create for authors, Congreve condemns the amateur playwrights who at the time were drowning the stage. He laments that the theater has become a church whose main activity is funerals, not christenings. In another witty metaphor, he tells the wits that Pegasus—that is, the art of writing—has tricks that take more to master than merely getting up and riding. He ridicules the lady playwrights in lines as good as Pope's in *The Dunciad* (1728-1743): "With the same Ease, and Negligence of Thought,/ The charming Play is writ, and Fringe is wrought." One important theme of Congreve is the hard task serious writers have, not in writing itself but in presenting their works, when they are assailed by ignorant critics and torpedoed by amateurish mishmash.

Jeremy Collier attacked Congreve's licentiousness in his "Short View of the Immorality and Profaneness of the English Stage," but Congreve blamed the audience for the type of plays that were popular. Reciting his "Epilogue at the Opening of the Queen's Theatre," Bracegirdle told the audience that the beaux may find it hard to spend one night without smutty jests, but she promises them soon "to your selves shew your dear selves again" and display "in bold Strokes the vicious Town." Congreve whirls in defensive fury against the pseudoreformers. In "Prologue, to the Court, on the Queen's Birthday," he claims that playwrights seek to war against vice and folly but reformers force the Muse to assume the very forms she has been fighting. Reformers break the mirror (the plays), which reflects their own ignorance and malice. Congreve renounces the stage, saying his Muse will now pursue the nobler tasks of painting the "Beauties of the Mind" and, by showing the court the virtues of one such as the queen, "shame to Manners an incorrigible Town." He says he will remain a moralist although his means have changed. Unfortunately, when he praises the virtuous queen, his lines lack the strength of the earlier diatribe: The only line in this prologue that matches the eloquence of his fury is one in which the Muse "secretly Applauds, and silently Admires" the queen.

## IMAGERY

When Congreve leaves writing for the stage or writing about the stage, his poetic powers by and large desert him and his claim of remaining a moralist is specious; it is hard to find any morality in "poet laureate" praises. The only thing that redeems Congreve's laudatory verses to William and to Mary is his imagery, which leaps out from the sycophantic meanderings. In "To the King, on the Taking of Namure," Congreve admits that his proper sphere is singing simple love songs, but he underestimates his own abilities. His description of the Battle of Namure rises above the commonplace, with its discordant consonants imitating the clash and clang of battle (before Pope's strictures on sound and sense) and his images of the earth in labor giving birth to the "dead Irruptions" and the air tormented by the cannon fire and smoke. Warlord man is shown to victimize nature.

On the other hand, nature befriends human beings when they are gentle. In "The Mourning Muse of Alexis, Lamenting the Death of Queen Mary," Congreve describes the beauty and peace of nature mourning Queen Mary: Sable clouds adorn the chalk cliffs, bees deposit their honey on Mary's tomb, and glowworms light the dirges of fairies. The imagery is beautiful, but if one comes to the poem with the expectation that it will give solace, it is disappointingly silly.

Although the classical set pieces in Congreve's poems to King William are disastrous, the set piece in the irregular ode "On Mrs. Arabella Hunt, Singing" works well. Much like Pope's portrayal of dullness in *The Dunciad*, Congreve's mighty god Silence is wrapped in a melancholy thought, wreathed by mists and darkness, lulled by poppy vapors, and sitting on an "ancient" sigh. Silence is vanquished by the beauty of Hunt's singing, and her listeners are left in a state reminiscent of the lovers on John Keats's Grecian urn, "For ever to be dying so, yet never die."

Congreve's "A Hymn to Harmony, in Honour of St. Cecilia's Day, 1701" and Pope's "Ode for Musick, on St. Cecilia's Day," when compared, illustrate the difference between a great poet and a minor one. In both poems, the authors describe the ability of music to soothe troubled minds. Congreve says that the Muses with balmy sound assuage a wrathful and revengeful mind, while Pope turns the idea into a concrete image, personifying melancholy, sloth, and envy and showing rather than explaining the effect of music on them. Pope may have mined Congreve's ore for ideas, but he cut, polished, and presented the more beautiful gems.

Congreve's technical abilities never equal the power of his imagery. He squirms and struggles under the burden of rhyming. To achieve his rhymes, he often destroys his syntax or creates a jingle of sound rather than a flow. Even when he does find a rhyme, it frequently is only an eye-rhyme or a jarring approximation of a rhyme. Perhaps one reason that Congreve was able to create exquisite poetry in *The Mourning Bride*, lines that Samuel Johnson called "the most poetical paragraph" in the "whole mass of English poetry," is that he was not forced into rhyme and could write blank verse.

Like other writers who experiment in genres other than their major ones, Congreve does not repeat the brilliance of his plays in his poetry. Lacking technical virtuosity, flawed by absurd and frozen set pieces, and distinguished by no more than ordinary political praise, his poems nevertheless can sparkle with striking imagery and wit. Above all, Congreve's poems, with their views of the theater and of love and honor in Restoration society, add to the reader's understanding of his plays.

## OTHER MAJOR WORKS

LONG FICTION: *Incognita: Or, Love and Duty Reconcil'd*, 1692 (novella).

PLAYS: *The Double-Dealer*, pr. 1693; *The Old Bachelor*, pr., pb. 1693; *Love for Love*, pr., pb. 1695; *The Mourning Bride*, pr., pb. 1697; *The Way of the World*, pr., pb. 1700; *The Judgement of Paris*, pr., pb. 1701 (masque); *Squire Trelooby*, pr., pb. 1704 (with Sir John Vanbrugh and William Walsh; adaptation of Molière's *Monsieur de Pourceaugnac*); *Semele*, pb. 1710 (libretto), pr. 1744 (modified version); *The Complete Plays of William Congreve*, 1967 (Herbert Davis, editor).

NONFICTION: *Amendments of Mr. Collier's False and Imperfect Citations*, 1698; *William Congreve: Letters and Documents*, 1964 (John C. Hodges, editor).

TRANSLATIONS: *Ovid's Art of Love, Book III*, 1709; *Ovid's Metamorphoses*, 1717 (with John Dryden and Joseph Addison).

MISCELLANEOUS: *Examen Poeticum*, 1693; *The Works of Mr. William Congreve*, 1710; *The Complete Works of William Congreve*, 1923 (reprint, 1964; Montague Summers, editor; 4 volumes).

## BIBLIOGRAPHY

Bartlett, Laurence. *William Congreve: An Annotated Bibliography, 1978-1994*. Lanham, Md.: Scarecrow Press, 1996. A bibliography of works concerning Congreve. Index.

Hodges, John C. *William Congreve: The Man*. New York: Modern Language Association of America, 1941. Though somewhat dated, this is still a good standard biography of Congreve. Hodges traces Congreve's youth in Ireland, his college years at Trinity College, Dublin, his life among the coffeehouses and theaters of London, and his relationships with the actress Annie Bracegirdle and the duchess of Marlborough. A readable introduction to Congreve's life, this volume also briefly discusses his major works.

Lindsay, Alexander, and Howard Erskine-Hill, eds. *Congreve: The Critical Heritage*. New York: Routledge, 1989. An anthology of critical material on Congreve, divided into three sections: "The Early Reception, 1691-1700," "The Eighteenth-Century Response, 1701-1793," and "The Nineteenth Century and After, 1802-1913." Included are many interesting pieces by contemporaries such as John Dryden and Joseph Addison, and a poem praising Congreve by his friend Jonathan Swift. Though no modern criticism is included, this volume is invaluable as a record of responses to Congreve's work in literary history.

Novak, Maximillian E. *William Congreve*. New York: Twayne, 1971. After a detailed introduction to Congreve's life, Novak discusses each of Congreve's five plays and devotes a concluding chapter to Congreve's poetry and other writings. Supplemented by an excellent select bibliography (including secondary sources), notes, an index, and a chronology.

Thomas, David. *William Congreve*. New York: St. Martin's Press, 1992. A good introduction to the life and works of Congreve. Includes bibliographical references and an index.

Williams, Aubrey L. *An Approach to Congreve*. New Haven, Conn.: Yale University Press, 1979. This insightful study provides a discussion of the historical context from which Congreve's work emerged, as well as discussions of Congreve's five plays and one novella. Supplemented by notes and an index.

*Ann Willardson Engar*

# HENRY CONSTABLE

**Born:** Flamborough(?), England; 1562
**Died:** Liège, France; 1613

PRINCIPAL POETRY
*Diana*, 1592, 1594
*Spiritual Sonnets*, 1815
*The Poems of Henry Constable*, 1960 (Joan Grundy, editor)

OTHER LITERARY FORMS

Henry Constable's other writings were political and religious prose works. While still a Protestant, he wrote a pamphlet called *A Short View of a Large Examination of Cardinall Allen His Trayterous Justification of Sir W. Stanley and Yorck* (c. 1588). This was an answer to a work of 1587 in which the Roman Catholic cardinal had justified the surrender of Daventer to the Spaniards by Stanley, one of Leicester's chief officers. Constable answered specific arguments of Allen's work with arguments based on justice and Protestant theology. He mocked the cardinal, implying that he was a "purple whore." He also wrote the *Examen pacifique de la doctrine des Huguenots* (1589, *The Catholike Moderator: Or, A Moderate Examination of the Doctrine of the Protestants*, 1623), published anonymously in Paris. The work was pro-Huguenot, but in it, the author pretended to be a Catholic. The work was an enlargement of a response that he wrote to another tract. Again, Constable was concerned with politics, theology, and justice, but he also indicated that he desired the union of the Protestant and Roman Catholic churches. Constable was soon to become a Catholic. He wrote an unpub-

lished theological work (c. 1596) that has been lost, and another work on English affairs (c. 1597). He is presumed to be the author or coauthor of an anonymous book in defense of King James's title in 1600, which was an answer to another work supporting Spain that was erroneously attributed to him. He also collaborated with Dr. W. Percy on a work against the Spanish and Jesuits in 1601. It is clear that Constable was deeply involved in the political and religious matters of his day. His religious interests were to affect greatly his life and his poetry, and he wrote an important group of religious sonnets after his conversion to Catholicism. As the prose works mentioned above showed his commitment to the Protestant cause, his religious sonnets showed his strong feelings for the Catholic faith.

ACHIEVEMENTS

In his best-known work, *Diana*, Henry Constable wrote highly polished courtly sonnets. Some modern critics consider his undated *Spiritual Sonnets*, which appeared only in manuscript, to be superior to *Diana* in their originality and strong sense of feeling. Both his secular and his religious poems, however, were sonnets of praise. His love of argument is evident in the logical patterns of his sonnets, particularly in his use of symmetrical antitheses, often with accompanying alliteration. The openings of many of his sonnets are striking, and he made use of clever conceits, including some of the extended Metaphysical variety that are memorable. His diction was simple and unaffected, though his style was marked by considerable repetition.

Although he has come to be regarded as a minor poet, he was viewed as a major talent by his contemporaries. He was one of the earliest of Elizabethan sonnet writers and helped to create the fashion. Many of his sonnets had been written before 1591, when Sir Philip Sidney's *Astrophel and Stella* was published. The *Diana* of 1592 was one of the earliest collections of sonnets. Samuel Daniel, the author of *Delia* (1592), may have been influenced by Constable rather than the other way around. William Shakespeare seems to have borrowed specific details from Constable, and Michael Drayton also showed Constable's influence. Francis Meres in *Palladis Tamia* (1598) praised him highly. Ben Jonson's "An Ode" (c. 1600) listed Constable with

Homer, Ovid, Petrarch, Pierre de Ronsard, and Sidney, and his name is mentioned in the company of excellent poets by Drayton and Gabriel Harvey. In the anonymous play *Returne from Parnassus* (c. 1600), he is spoken of as "Sweate Constable." Edmund Bolton in the *Hypercritica* (1618) termed Constable "a great master in the English Tongue, nor had any Gentleman of our Nation a more pure, quick, or higher Delivery of Conceit. . . ." The contemporary poet Alexander Montgomerie wrote a Scottish version of one of his poems, and a Latin translation of another is included in the *Poemata* (1607) of Dousa (Filius). After his own time, he was largely unknown until the nineteenth century, when his poetry was edited by W. C. Hazlitt and was included in anthologies of Elizabethan sonnets.

BIOGRAPHY

Henry Constable came from a line of distinguished ancestors on both his father's and his mother's side. The surname originated from the office of Constable in Chester, which had been held by members of his father's family since the time of William the Conqueror, although his father's branch of the family had settled in Yorkshire. The poet must have been born in 1562, since he was thirteen years old in 1575, and was presumably born at Flamborough. There is no information about his childhood. He attended St. John's College, Cambridge, his rank being recognized there by special distinctions. After receiving his bachelor's degree in 1579 or 1580 by a special grace, the reason not made clear, he was admitted to Lincoln's Inn on February 21, 1583. Later in the same year, a letter he wrote to his father indicates that he was with the English ambassador, Sir Francis Walsingham, in Scotland. Walsingham recommended the young Constable to the English ambassador in Paris, who was distantly related to Constable, and he became an emissary. He seems to have been a proponent of the Protestant cause at Paris, remaining there until 1585. He wrote indignantly about the actions of English Catholics in Paris, and he was recommended to Walsingham by Stafford as a good choice to help the Protestant Henry of Navarre stand firm in the face of Catholic arguments. After Constable left Paris, he traveled to Heidelberg, to Poland, to Italy, perhaps to Hamburg, and probably to the Low Countries. His pamphlet

in answer to a work by Cardinal Allen was probably written in 1588.

It seems likely that Constable spent the years 1588 and 1589 at court, and he was said to have been a favorite of the queen. He wrote sonnets, including ones to Penelope Rich, and was much in the company of Arabella Stuart. He was friendly with many Protestants of the Continent, including followers of Henry of Navarre. One of these, Claude d'Isle, Seigneur de Marivaux, sent several letters by James VI of Scotland to their destination by way of Constable. Another follower of Henry of Navarre and friend of Constable was Jean Hotman, who wished to see the Protestant and Roman Catholic Churches united. Constable was involved with him and others, including Penelope Rich, in an intrigue to obtain the favor of James VI for the earl of Essex. Constable met with the king and assured him of his loyalty despite the fact that Arabella Stuart was the chief rival of James in his claims to the throne of England. The scheme was, however, not successful. Constable was at the Scottish court some weeks before October 21, 1589, when he returned to London. While at the Scottish court, he of course met the members of James's literary circle. In 1589, he also wrote the work defending the Huguenots in which he pretended to be a Catholic.

By 1590, Constable had decided to become a Roman Catholic. By the end of that year, all his secular sonnets had probably been written and collected. In 1591, he went to France with Essex on an expedition to assist Henry IV militarily. Not long afterward, however, he apparently joined the other side and publicly became a Catholic. His father was said to have died as a result. Constable wrote a letter to the Countess of Shrewsbury, protesting that if his safety in England were not assured, he would stay in France. After a trip to Rome, he remained in France, living in Paris, occasionally traveling to Rouen, Scotland, Rome, Antwerp, and Brussels. He was often in need of money, although he had an irregular pension from Henry IV. Although he was a Catholic exile, he did not support the claim of Spain to the throne of England. He supported instead the claim of James VI of Scotland, from whom Catholics at least hoped for tolerance. For several years, Constable schemed to ensure the safety of English Catholics, the return of England to the Roman Catholic Church, and the union of Catholics and Protestants. He tried to use the influence of Henry IV to secure some toleration for Catholics in England. He was part of a plot to convert the Queen of Scots to Catholicism, and he tried to convert James IV as well. He wrote some theological and political pieces, and in 1600, he went to Rome to persuade the pope to support him in another excursion to Scotland. The attempt failed.

Constable returned to England after James I became king in 1603 and was permitted to possess his family's lands. He hoped, with the help of others, to convert James I, but in 1604, he was committed to the Tower of London after some letters revealing the scheme had been seized in France and sent back to England, probably by the king of France. Released in a few months, Constable was confined to his house. Once more deprived of his inheritance, he became dependent on kinsmen. For the next few years, he was in and out of prison, until in 1610, he was either banished or simply permitted to leave the country.

After Henry IV's death, Constable returned to France. He died at Liège in 1613 after going there to help convert a Protestant minister. He lay meditating on the crucifix for several days before he died, demonstrating the truth of the words he had written while imprisoned in the Tower of London: "whether I remayn in prison, or go out, I have learned to live alone with God."

ANALYSIS

In his courtly sonnets, collected in *Diana*, Henry Constable used the traditional conventions of the Petrarchan sonnet. He was also influenced by the French and Italian sonnets of his contemporaries, particularly Philippe Desportes. The title *Diana* is borrowed from Desportes's chief sonnet sequence, and the Italian headlines in the work (sonnetto primo and so on) reveal the Italian influence.

Joan Grundy, one of Constable's editors, considers the Todd manuscript of this work to be the closest thing to an authoritative text, having been assembled before Constable's departure from England from poems that had been written over a period of time. There is an elaborate framework divided into three parts; these parts are then further divided into groups of seven sonnets. Constable provided explanatory titles, some notes on numerical symbolism, and the disclaimer that the sonnets are "vayne poems." In all his sonnets, Constable used the Petrarchan sonnet form *abba abba cde cde*, with variations.

DIANA

Many of the sonnets in *Diana* are love poems. In the sonnet "To his Mistrisse," which begins, "Grace full of grace," he declares that although these verses include love complaints to others, he now loves only her. The last three lines play on the word "grace" again, vowing that he flies to God for grace that he may live in delight or never love again. Grace was a theological concept with varying interpretations, as well as being part of a noble address and a woman's name. Louise Imogen Guiney in *Recusant Poets* (1939) speculated that the "Grace" might be Grace Talbot, youngest daughter of George Talbot, sixth earl of Shrewsbury. The last sonnet in the manuscript is "To the diuine protection of the Ladie Arbella the author commendeth both his Graces honoure and his Muses aeternitye." Arabella Stuart was the granddaughter of the countess of Shrewsbury. Constable's sonnet "To the Countesse of Shrewsburye vpon occasion of his dear Mistrisse whoe liu'd vnder her gouer[n]ment" (part 3, group 3, sonnet 2), indicates that he loved someone in her company. It is not even certain, however, whether the sonnet was written to the countess or to the dowager countess. The countess has also been suggested as a candidate for Constable's Diana, and even Mary, Queen of Scots, has been mentioned because she was in the custody of the dowager countess at one time. Another possibility is Penelope Rich. The Harrington manuscript consists of twenty-one sonnets appearing under the title "Mr. Henry Constable's sonetes to the Lady Ritche, 1589." Penelope Rich had requested Constable in a letter to Hotman "qu'il ne soit plus amoureux." This lady was Philip Sidney's Stella, and she was involved in political intrigue with Constable.

In part 1, group 1, sonnet 3, which deals with the "variable affections" of love, Constable uses repetition to great effect, combining it with antithesis. The first, fifth, and ninth lines begin, "Thyne eye," and the second, sixth, and tenth lines begin, "Myne eye." Her eye, he declares, is the mirror in which he sees his heart, and his eye is a window through which her eye may see his heart; there, he says, she may see herself painted in bloody colors. Her eye is the "pyle" or pointed tip of a dart, and his eye is the aiming-point she uses to hit his heart. "Myne eye thus helpes thyne eye to work my smarte." Her eye is a fire and his eye a river of tears, but the water cannot extinguish the flames, nor can the fire dry up the streams from his eye. Constable's technique in this poem is to proceed by a series of parallel and antithetical metaphors. Some of them are traditional, but "thine eye the pyle" is presumably original, at least in English, since the *Oxford English Dictionary* cites this poem as the earliest example of the word's usage. Shakespeare is thought to have imitated lines 1-4 of this poem in his sonnet 24. Constable's contemporary, Alexander Montgomerie, wrote a Scots version of the sonnet.

In the first sonnet of the second group, "An Exhortation to the reader to come and see his Mistrisse beautie," Constable combines repetition with hyperbole. He repeats the word "come" twice in both line 1 and line 6, while in the sestet, "millions" becomes the dominant note, being repeated in lines 9, 10, and 12. Here he uses hyperbole ingeniously to praise the subject of the poem, who is a wonder of nature. He exhorts the reader to come and see her in order to write about her so that the next generation will lament being born too late to see her. Everyone should come and write about her, he protests, for the time may be too short and men too few to write the history of her least part, even though they should write constantly and about nothing else. In the sestet, he declares that the millions who write about her are too few to praise one of her features and can only write about one aspect of her eye, her lip, or her hand, such as "the light or blacke the tast or red the soft or white." This poem was inspired by Petrarch's sonnet 248.

While the first part of *Diana* is about the "variable affections of loue," Constable points out in his "The order of the booke" that the first seven poems are about the beginning of love, the second seven are in praise of his mistress, and the third seven concern specific events in his love experience. In the second sonnet of this third set, "Of his Mistrisse vpon occasion of her walking in a

garden," he personifies some of the flowers, making the roses red because they blush for shame when they see her lips and the lilies white because they become pale with envy of her. He indicates his own love by stating that the violets take their color from the blood his heart has shed for her. In the sestet, she becomes a kind of nature goddess. All flowers take their "vertue" from her and their smells from her breath; the heat from her eyes warms the earth, and she manages to water it as well by making him cry. Shakespeare imitated the opening of this sonnet in *The Rape of Lucrece* (1594), lines 477-479.

In the second sonnet of that same set, "To his Ladies hand vpon occasion of her gloue which in her absence he kissed," Constable uses a traditional theme, for there were many French and Italian poems addressed to the lady's hand, with the theme going back to Petrarch's sonnet 199. The idea of the hand shooting out arrows was also traditional, but Constable goes on to compare his five wounds caused by her five ivory arrows (her fingers) with the stigmata of Saint Francis. This poem, then, uses remarkably specific religious imagery. The stigmata were the impressions of the five wounds of Christ that Saint Francis received on his flesh. Constable uses contrasts cleverly here, declaring that Saint Francis did not feel the wounds, while he (Constable) lives in torment, and that the wounds of Saint Francis were in his hands and feet, while his own wounds are in his heart. The metaphor becomes an elaborate conceit, for if he is therefore a saint like Saint Francis, the bow that shot the shafts is a relic, and thus her hand should be kissed. Her glove is a divine thing because it is the quiver of her arrows (the covering of her hand) and the shrine of a relic (her hand).

## SPIRITUAL SONNETS

Constable's *Spiritual Sonnets* praise God and his saints rather than an earthly love. The sequence begins with three sonnets to God the Father, the Son, and the Holy Ghost. The one praising God the Father begins by declaring that his essence and his existence are the same, the terminology being derived from scholastic philosophy. The essence of a being was the nature of the being, and existence was the actuality of the being. God's nature was to exist, for he was contingent on no other cause. The next lines reflect the idea that the mind of God reflects God, and thus that the Son of God is the image of God the Father. The doctrine is based on Saint Paul's description in Hebrews of the Son as "being the brightness of his glory, and the express image of his person." Constable makes use of this material in the poem, saying that there is mutual love between Father and Son, as the sighs of lovers become one breath, while both breathe one spirit of equal deity, the Holy Ghost. That the Holy Ghost proceeds from both the Father and the Son was orthodox Catholic doctrine. Constable ends the poem by asking God the Father, who wishes to have the title of Father, to engrave his mind with heavenly knowledge so that it may become his Son's image (continuing the image figure but applying it to himself), and by praying that his heart may become the temple of the spirit, thus neatly linking the abstract theological discussion of the early part of the sonnet with the individual experience of God.

"To God the Sonne," the middle sonnet, is less abstract. The poet addresses Christ as "Great Prynce of heaven," begotten of the King and of the Virgin Queen, descendant of King David. After this royal beginning, he contrasts the angels singing at his birth with the shepherds playing their pipes; likewise, kings become like humble shepherds for Christ's sake. Heaven and earth, high and low estate, all have a claim to Christ's birth, for he was begotten in heaven, was of kingly race on his mother's side, and was poor. In "To God the Holy Ghost," Constable becomes more abstract and theological again by way of allegorical personification, likening the Holy Ghost in heaven to the love with which the Son and the Father kiss. He describes how the Holy Ghost took the shape of a dove and of fiery tongues and asks the Holy Ghost to bestow on his love of God his wings and His fire, so that he may appear a seraphim in his sight. The burning quality of the seraphim in theological writings, such as Pseudo-Dionysius the Areopagite's *De caelesti hierarchia* (c. 500; *The Celestial Hierarchy*, 1894), is here in keeping with the fiery nature of the Holy Ghost, for Constable asks the Holy Ghost for his wings and fire, two qualities of the seraphim that he wants to possess. This trinity of poems has sources in such writers as Saint Augustine and Thomas Aquinas, but each poem is a personal prayer addressed to an aspect of God.

In "To the Blessed Sacrament," Constable relates the red wine and white Eucharist of the communion service to the red blood and white body of Christ, the body pale because of the shedding of blood. Christ's body is now veiled in white to be received by Constable in the Eucharist, as though in his burial sheet, making Constable into a burial vault or monument for the corpse. He prays that the Christ whom he has received into his body in the Eucharist will appear to his soul, which is imprisoned in earth the way his forefathers were suspended in Limbo when Christ gave them light. He asks Christ to clear his thoughts and free him in a similar way from the flames of evil desire. The poem is a unified sequence of Metaphysical conceits.

In "To the Blessed Lady" (the first of his poems with that title), Constable speaks of the Virgin Mary as a Queen of Queens, born without Original Sin. God the Father provided his Spirit for her spouse, and she conceived his only Son, and so she was linked with the whole Trinity. Queens of this earth should no longer glory in their role, for much greater honor is due the queen "who had your God, for father, spowse, & sonne." Constable here delights in the realization of Mary's multiple relationships with God, an intellectual concept that holds the element of surprise.

At the beginning of the first of Constable's four poems on Mary Magdalen, he alludes to the saint's legendary retiring to a penitential life in Provence, saying that "for few nyghtes solace in delitious bedd," she did penance "nak'd on nak'd rocke in desert cell" for thirty years. He speaks directly to her in the poem, saying that for each tear she shed, she has a sea of pleasure now. The poem develops through a series of contrasts. In one of his other poems to the same saint, he begins by saying that she can better declare to him the pleasures of heavenly love than someone who has never experienced any other loves or than someone who is not a woman, for his soul will be like a woman once moved by lust but then betrothed to God's Son. His body is "the garment of my spryght" in the daytime of his life, and death will bring "the nyght of my delyght." His soul will be "vncloth'd," and resting from labor, "clasped in the armes of God," will "inioye/ by sweete coniunction, everlastying ioye." The poem proceeds by a complicated sequence of analogies and contrasts:

Mary Magdalen knew earthly love, knew heavenly love; his soul is like her, having experienced lust and spiritual love; in the day, his soul is covered with the garment of his body, but in the night of mystical union with God it will be naked.

In his sonnets, Constable praises his subjects, both secular and religious, by comparisons (some traditional and some highly original and Metaphysical), and often by ironic contrasts expressed with grammatical parallelism. His wording is simple, and there is much deliberate repetition. Through his carefully reasoned and highly polished sonnets he communicates very well both his love of Diana and his love of God.

## OTHER MAJOR WORKS

NONFICTION: *A Short View of a Large Examination of Cardinall Allen His Trayterous Justification of Sir W. Stanley and Yorck*, c. 1588; *Examen pacifique de la doctrine des Huguenots*, 1589 (*The Catholike Moderator: Or, A Moderate Examination of the Doctrine of the Protestants*, 1623).

## BIBLIOGRAPHY

Cousins, A. D. *The Catholic Religious Poets from Southwell to Crashaw: A Critical History*. London: Sheed and Ward, 1991. Contains a chapter on Constable and William Alabaster, which looks at *Spiritual Sonnets* in depth.

Fleissner, Robert F. *Resolved to Love: The 1592 Edition of Henry Constable's "Diana."* Salzburg: Institute of English and American Studies, University of Salzburg, 1980. Part of the Salzburg Studies in English Literature series, this monograph is one the few book-length studies of Constable.

Grundy, Joan. *Henry Constable*. Liverpool, England: Liverpool University Press, 1960. A comprehensive work that includes a biographical essay, complete facsimiles of his poems, discussions about his life, poems, and texts, and evaluations of his influence and reputation. Further increasing the value of this book are its exhaustive footnotes and bibliographic entries.

Miola, Robert S. *Early Modern Catholicism: An Anthology of Primary Sources*. New York: Oxford University Press, 2007. Contains a chapter on Ca-

tholicism in poetry that looks at the poetry of Constable, among others. Contains several poems by Constable.

Parker, Tom W. N. *Proportional Form in the Sonnets of the Sidney Circle: Loving in Truth*. New York: Oxford University Press, 1998. Chapter examines the life of Constable and his poetry in *Diana* and *Spiritual Sonnets*.

Richardson, David A., ed. *Sixteenth-Century British Nondramatic Writers: Second Series*. Vol. 136 in *Dictionary of Literary Biography*. Detroit: Gale Research, 1994. Contains a short biographical entry on Constable, along with some literary analysis.

Shell, Allison. *Catholicism, Controversy, and the English Literary Imagination, 1558-1660*. New York: Cambridge University Press, 1999. The chapter on Elizabethan writers who were Catholic loyalists contains considerable discussion of Constable and his work.

# CHARLES COTTON

**Born:** Beresford Hall, Staffordshire, England; April 28, 1630
**Died:** London, England; February 16, 1687

## PRINCIPAL POETRY

"An Elegie upon the Lord Hastings," 1649
*A Panegyrick to the King's Most Excellent Majesty*, 1660
"The Answer," 1661
*Scarronides: Or, Virgile Travestie*, 1664
*A Voyage to Ireland in Burlesque*, 1670
*Horace*, 1671 (translation of Pierre Corneille's play; with original lyric poetry)
*Burlesque upon Burlesque*, 1675
"To my dear and most worthy Friend, Mr. Izaak Walton," 1675
"The Retirement," 1676
*The Wonders of the Peake*, 1681
*Poems on Several Occasions*, 1689
*Genuine Works*, 1715

## OTHER LITERARY FORMS

Apart from his original poetry, Charles Cotton also published translations and burlesques (now of minor interest), books on planting and gaming, and a treatise on fly-fishing that became *The Compleat Angler, Part II* (1676), the second part of Izaak Walton's *The Compleat Angler: Or, The Contemplative Man's Recreation* (1653) in its fifth edition. He is not known to have written fiction, essays, or pamphlets. As with most seventeenth century figures, he left no diary and not much correspondence. Consequently, information on Cotton's day-to-day life is sparse, and many of his poems (which circulated in manuscript) cannot be precisely dated.

## ACHIEVEMENTS

During his lifetime and throughout the eighteenth century, Charles Cotton was known almost exclusively as a writer of burlesques and translations. His rendering of Michel Eyquem de Montaigne into idiomatic English prose was particularly admired. Cotton has come to be esteemed as a congenial minor poet of the Restoration period who anticipated aspects of Romanticism in his verse and who collaborated belatedly with Walton to produce one of the most popular books in English literature. However, Cotton is a significant landscape poet, a perceptive observer of rural life, an often graceful lyricist, and a distinguished regionalist.

Not until the Romantic period was Cotton taken seriously as an original versifier. Charles Lamb, a lover of old books, rediscovered Cotton's *Poems on Several Occasions* more than a century after their publication and quoted several of them delightedly in a letter of March 5, 1803. He selected four examples of Cotton's work to be included in Robert Southey's *Specimens of the Later English Poets* (1807): "Song. Montross," "The Litany," "The Retirement," and the "Morning" quatrain. William Wordsworth discussed, praised, and quoted Cotton's "Winter" quatrains in his famous preface to his *Poems* (1815). Samuel Taylor Coleridge extolled Cotton's *Poems on Several Occasions* in *Biographia Literaria* (1817), chapter 19. Lamb called special attention to Cotton's poem "The New Year" in his essay "New Year's Eve" (*Essays of Elia*, 1823), and with this, Cotton's poetic reputation reached its peak. Cot-

*Charles Cotton* (©Michael Nicholson/CORBIS)

ton lost favor during the Victorian years and proved less interesting to the earlier twentieth century than more complicated Metaphysical poets such as John Donne. Though he holds a place in the literary history of seventeenth century England, Cotton has never been regarded as a major writer.

## BIOGRAPHY

Charles Cotton was born at Beresford Hall, Staffordshire, on April 28, 1630. The only child of Charles and Olive Stanhope Cotton, he was, like his father, a country squire with literary interests—and a Royalist. The English Civil War, which began when he was twelve, inspired Cotton with a vision of worldwide chaos that he soon expressed in verse through descriptions of the adjacent Peak District scenery in Derbyshire. From about 1648 to 1655, young Charles was tutored by Ralph Rawson, who is mentioned in several of Cotton's early poems and who in turn addressed a poem to him. Cotton's first published poem was "An Elegie upon the Lord Hastings," which appeared in 1649; Hastings had died earlier that year at the age of nineteen. Other poems lamenting Hasting's death were written by John Dryden, Robert Herrick, Andrew Marvell, John Denham, Sir Aston Cokayne, Alexander Brome, and John Bancroft. It cannot be said that Cotton's was the best. In 1651, he wrote another elegy, on Lord Derby, a Royalist who was captured after the Battle of Worcester and beheaded on October 15, 1651. His strong political feelings were made further apparent in "The Litany" and in "To Poet E—— W——," the latter castigating Edmund Waller for his servile obsequiousness in the face of the Cromwellian regime. Cotton wrote all these potentially seditious poems as a young bachelor in his twenties. Like almost all his shorter verse, they remained unpublished during his lifetime.

Throughout the winter of 1655-1656, Cotton was in France. From there, he addressed several poems of amorous longing to Isabella "Chloris" Hutchinson, whom he married on June 30, 1656, and who bore him nine children before her death in 1669. She may also have been the inspiration for "On Christmas-Day, 1659," which is the only one of Cotton's major poems to be concerned with orthodox religion. Its happy mood anticipated the impending restoration of the monarchy, which took place on May 29, 1660; Cotton then wrote *A Panegyrick to the King's Most Excellent Majesty*, celebrating a day that must have been as exhilarating to him as that of his own wedding.

For the next twenty-five years, Cotton published the literary works (not all of them precisely datable) upon which his immediate reputation would rest. Thus, in 1661, "The Answer" (to Alexander Brome) celebrated that "dusty corner of the World" which Cotton called his own and the return of his humble Muse, which for the next few years manifested itself primarily in translations. A prose translation of *The Morall Philosophy of the Stoicks* (1664), from the French of Guillaume Du Vair, preceded Cotton's famous *Scarronides*, a daringly bawdy verse burlesque of Vergil. Named for a previous French work (Paul Scarron's *Virgile travesti*, 1648), it became Cotton's most popular poem, which Samuel Pepys, among others, thought "extraordinary good" (*Diary*, March 2, 1664). To a modern critic such as James Sutherland, on the other hand, it seems nothing more than a "crude, sniggering, schoolboy denigration" of an immortal poet whom force-fed students of the classics were all too willing to disparage. Whatever its worth as literature, *Scarronides* remained central to Cotton's reputation until the nineteenth century. In 1666, however, he wrote the "Winter" quatrains, which were later to be praised by Wordsworth.

When his wife died in 1669, Cotton (who married again five years later) left Beresford Hall long enough to head a military expedition to Ireland, with his agreeable poetic narrative *A Voyage to Ireland in Burlesque* the only significant result. Consisting of three cantos of rhymed hexameters, *A Voyage to Ireland in Burlesque* is a good-hearted diary of travel vexations, candid and earthy. Cotton's translation of Pierre Corneille's drama *Horace* (pb. 1671), appearing the next year, included ten songs and choruses of his own, the largest body of Cotton's lyric poetry to be published in his lifetime. He was now at the height of his literary productivity. In 1674, Cotton published more translations from the French, including one of Blaize de Montluc, and an original work in prose, *The Compleat Gamester*, which was reprinted at frequent intervals for the next fifty years. *The Planters Manual* (1675), also an original prose work, was less successful, being only a guide to successful horticulture. His next major success was a burlesque in verse of the Roman poet Lucian. Called *Burlesque upon Burlesque*, it was written in Hudibrastic tetrameter (imitating Samuel Butler). Having created a taste for such literary travesties with his earlier demolitions of Vergil, Cotton now replied to his own imitators by providing them with a further model from which to steal.

These were also the years of his close friendship with Izaak Walton, whose *The Compleat Angler* had already influenced Cotton's *The Compleat Gamester* of 1674. That same year, Cotton built the famous fishing house in which his initials and Walton's were intertwined over the front door. He published one of his best poems, "To My Dear and Most Worthy Friend, Mr. Izaak Walton," in the 1675 edition of Walton's *Lives* (of Donne, Richard Hooker, and George Herbert) after having written it three years earlier. When Walton's *The Compleat Angler* was next published (1676, fifth edition), it included a second part by Cotton, the treatise on fly-fishing that is surely his best-known and most-read work today. Cotton's idyllic poem "The Retirement," published in the same volume, ends with Cotton's hope of living "sixty full years." He actually died just short of fifty-seven.

In 1678, the philosopher Thomas Hobbes published *De Mirabilibus Pecci*, a Latin poem extolling the already well-known wonders of the Peak District in Derbyshire, including caverns, springs, and a great house. Alongside the Latin in this edition there was an English translation "by a person of Quality" who may have been Cotton but probably was not. In any case, Hobbes's versified horseback journey through this anomalous landscape led Cotton to compose his longest poem, *The Wonders of the Peake*, published in 1681. The year of its appearance was also one of almost unbearable financial stress for Cotton, who had inherited a deeply entailed estate from his father (died 1658) and could no longer cope with the accumulated debts. He was therefore obliged to sell Beresford Hall at auction. Fortunately, it was immediately purchased by his cousin John Beresford, who allowed Cotton to remain until his death six years later. It was thus an ebullient Cotton who cheerfully defied the severe winter of 1682-1683 in a "Burlesque upon the Great Frost," addressed of John Bradshaw. Much of his confinement was probably devoted to his translation of Montaigne (1685), which eighteenth century readers generally considered to be the most notable of all his works. Two memorable late poems were "To Astraea" (1686), addressed to Aphra Behn, the first professional woman author in England, and the "Angler's Ballad," which, with its reference to King James II (reigned 1685-1688), is usually regarded as Cotton's last. These and others were collected as *Poems on Several Occasions* in 1689, two years after Cotton's death, and the *Genuine Works* followed in 1715. Alexander Chalmers published "The Poems of Charles Cotton"—including almost all his poetry—in *The Works of the English Poets* (1810), and Thomas Campbell included selections in *Specimens of the British Poets* (1819). There were no further substantial editions of Cotton's poetry until the twentieth century.

ANALYSIS

When Charles Cotton was twelve years old, Puritan insurgents overthrew the monarchy of Charles I and es-

tablished a Presbyterian commonwealth in its place. During the last years of his life, James II sought to restore Roman Catholicism, and Cotton just missed seeing the Bloodless Revolution of 1688, which banished James to the Continent and returned the monarchy to Protestantism. Of these momentous events, Cotton had surprisingly little to say. While "The Litany," for example, is outspokenly anti-Cromwellian, it regards the Protector only as a vile nuisance, on a level with "ill wine" and "a domineering Spouse." Similarly, Cotton was even more predisposed to ignore the religious controversies of his time. Only "On Christmas-Day, 1659" is significantly Christian; even in his several elegies, there is no specifically Christian consolation. Of the great subjects available to him, Cotton did little with politics (after 1651), very little with religion, and nothing with discovery or science.

Cotton's subjects are the traditionally Horatian ones of leisure, relaxation, friendship, love, and drinking, with some special attention in his case to the river Dove, fishing, his fellow poets, and the scenery of the Peak District. He is also especially observant of rural life, so that many of his poems are designedly pastoral, including eclogues in which Cotton himself appears as a lovesick shepherd. When sadness intrudes upon these idyllic scenes, it is generally economic in origin: Poverty is another of Cotton's themes, especially as it affects the literary life.

For all his love of retirement and solitude, Cotton was not a literary elitist. There are few barriers to the enjoyment of his poems, which are straightforwardly written in plain, colloquial English, as was thought appropriate to pastoral and the burlesque. Though influenced by his Metaphysical predecessors, John Donne especially, Cotton is more akin to Robert Herrick. Both Cotton and Herrick, for example, are observant regionalists particularly ready to celebrate the rewarding, if seemingly inconsequential, joys of rural life and of the milder emotions. Thus, Cotton generally prefers well-observed pastoral details and witty asides to complex imagery or erudite mythology. His contempt for classical learning was probably quite real. There is throughout Cotton's work a serene complacency regarding the adequacy of his own lighthearted perceptions and the healthiness of his instincts. While Romantic critics such as Charles Lamb appreciated the accuracy and vigor of Cotton's outlook, Victorians (such as the American James Russell Lowell) were frequently dismayed by his unapologetic "vulgarity" regarding bodily parts and functions.

A more serious objection to Cotton's verse is its apparent lack of substance. Without quite achieving the epigrammatic quotability of, for example, Richard Lovelace or Andrew Marvell, Cotton resembles both in his largely traditional thematic concerns. He writes most obviously to amuse himself and sometimes to amuse, compliment, or insult others, but rarely to inspire deep feeling or thought. In several instances, his poems are overlong and drift into lower reaches of the imagination. In others, potentially fine lyrics are marred by inadequacies that a more serious poet would have been at pains to remove. Because poetry for Cotton was private and usually recreational, his work often lacks finality and polish. From a generic point of view, Cotton was most original in bringing to public notice the burlesque and the travel narrative as poetic forms. The other forms that he uses are generally conventional and had been used by his immediate predecessors. His lyrics, for example, are in form, technique, and substance, largely unoriginal, except insofar as they are infused by a unique and engaging personality.

Ultimately, this personableness is his greatest strength. Within his best poems (and his prose addition to Walton), Cotton is superbly himself, and nowhere more so than in "The Answer," a verse epistle to Alexander Brome, whose minor verse helped to reawaken Cotton's neglected Muse, which thrived on solitude. "No friends, no visitors, no company" were desired, "So that my solace [wrote Cotton] lies amongst my grounds,/ and my best companie's my horse and hounds." In a second epistle to Brome, also in heroic couplets, Cotton laments the neglected poet who "knows his lot is to be Poor." A related panegyric, "On the Excellent Poems of My Most Worthy Friend, Mr. Thomas Flatman" (another minor poet of the time), is Cotton's fullest statement of his own concept of poetry, which involves the balancing of old and new, judgment and wit, knowledge and feeling, naturalness and style, propriety and vigor. In many of his literary poems, however, Cotton denigrates his own poetic abilities and

himself. If his burlesques are often mock-heroic, he is sometimes even antiheroic in his lyrics. Thus, in his "Epistle to John Bradshaw Esq.," Cotton describes his return to Beresford Hall after a four-month business trip to London. He remains

> The same dull Northern clod I was before,
> Gravely enquiring how Ewes are a Score,
> How the Hay-Harvest, and the Corn was got,
> And if or no there's like to be a Rot;
> Just the same Sot I was e'er I remov'd,
> Nor by my travel, nor the Court improv'd.

Cotton is at his best when most incorrigible.

### The Wonders of the Peake

*The Wonders of the Peake*, probably written two years before its publication, is Cotton's longest original poem, being almost fifteen hundred lines of his favorite heroic couplets. In organization and substance, it is straightforward, as the reader is led to visit each of the seven "wonders" (traditional before Cotton) in turn: Poole's Hole, a cave; St. Anne's Well, a spring; Tydes-well, another spring; Elden-Hole, a second cave; Mam-Tor, a disintegrating mountain; Peak Cavern ("Peake's-Arse"), the third and most important cave; and Chatsworth, seat of the duke of Devonshire, a splendid mansion inexplicably situated in this wilderness of geological oddities. Although undistinguished as verse, the poem is of major historical significance as a journey poem, when examples in that genre were unusual, and as a then rare attempt to describe an uncultivated landscape in English verse.

Prior to the seventeenth century, landscape was generally neglected in British literature and art (consider William Shakespeare's plays). Only following the Restoration in 1660 did scenery in literature become increasingly common. Among the reasons for its popularity were the influence of Dutch landscape painting (with an Italian influence following somewhat later), the popularity of Vergil, the rise of Baconian science, and a new naturalism (as in the thought of Thomas Hobbes, whose Latin poem on the Peak preceded Cotton's English one). As Marjorie Hope Nicolson has shown (in her book *Mountain Gloom and Mountain Glory*, 1959), with some understandable oversimplification, Cotton is of special interest in the history of

British landscape aesthetics because *The Wonders of the Peake* articulates so powerfully the genuine disgust, and yet interest, which irregular terrain such as that of Derbyshire evoked. For Cotton, the limestone caverns of the Peak are both sexual and theological. They are also theaters of the imagination, wherein the mind is invited to transform ambiguously shaped dripstone formations into what it will. Cotton, in other words, substantially discovered the cavern imagery that many later poets, William Blake especially, would use in discussing the subconscious mind. Thus, Cotton was a precursor of eighteenth century landscape aesthetics and of Romantic landscape imagery.

### SHORTER POEMS

Cotton's shorter poems, almost all of them published posthumously in 1689 from an uncertain text, are easily categorized (since they cannot be dated) into form and subject areas: poems of nature and the rural life, love poems, odes, elegies and epitaphs, epistles, epigrams, narratives, and burlesques and satires. The nature poems include "The Retirement"; sets of quatrains to morning, noon, evening, and night; various eclogues; and "Winter," which consists of fifty-three quatrains of tetrameter couplets full of the rural imagery and controlled understatement that Wordsworth admired; it is probably Cotton's best poem.

The love poems include songs, odes, madrigals, sonnets, and a rondeau. Those addressed to "Chloris," his future wife, and others inspired by her (such as "The Separation") are among Cotton's finest works, reaching a depth of feeling that he seldom again achieved. However, other poems by him addressed to or concerning women are crudely sensual and even misogynistic, if maliciously funny. Thus, "Resolution in Four Sonnets, of a Poetical Question put to me by a Friend, concerning four Rural Sisters" estimates the relative ability of each to be seduced, while "To Aelia" (which begins "Poor antiquated slut, forbear") admonishes an over-aged debauchee.

Though Cotton wrote odes on many subjects, particularly love, he also composed a series of Pindaric ones on hope, melancholy, women, beauty, contentment, poverty, and death. Those to hope, melancholy, and death are serious poetry reminiscent of Donne and Herbert. Some of his earliest poems were elegies; those

still capable of moving modern readers were written in honor of his first wife ("Gods! are you just?") and of his fellow poet Richard Lovelace.

Several of the epitaphs, like that on Robert Port, are long enough to compete with the elegies; that on M. H., a whore, is a macabre evocation of necrophilia and grief. The shorter epitaphs and Cotton's epigrams are generally ineffective. His narrative poems, such as those on Ireland and the Peak, grade into his epistles, as in "A Journey into the Peak. To Sir Aston Cockain." Finally, several of the odes and epistles are really drinking songs, as Cotton in his later years cheerfully faced the prospects of poverty and old age.

### POEMS ON SEVERAL OCCASIONS

Despite its variety and excellence, Cotton's *Poems on Several Occasions* was little noticed in its own time, even though, as James Sutherland has suggested, it contained "more and better poetry . . . than is to be found in any other minor poet of the Restoration." By the time it appeared, naturalness and honesty were out of fashion, and Cavalier morality had been circumscribed. Though Cotton's burlesques continued to be read, his accomplishments in more important genres were almost totally forgotten until appreciative Romantic readers established a new assessment of Cotton that has since become the basis for his modern reputation.

OTHER MAJOR WORKS

PLAY: *Horace*, pb. 1671 (translation of Pierre Corneille's play; with original lyric poetry).

NONFICTION: *The Compleat Gamester*, 1674; *The Planters Manual*, 1675; *The Compleat Angler, Part II*, 1676.

TRANSLATIONS: *The Morall Philosophy of the Stoicks*, 1664 (of Guillaume Du Vair); *The History of the Life of the Duke of Espernon*, 1670; *The Commentaries of Messire Blaize de Montluc, Mareschal of France*, 1674; *The Fair One of Tunis*, 1674; *Essays of Michael Seigneur de Montaigne*, 1685; *Memoirs of the Sieur De Pontis*, 1694.

BIBLIOGRAPHY

Beresford, John, ed. *The Poems of Charles Cotton, 1630-1687*. New York: Boni and Liveright, 1923.

The introduction to this selection contains a lengthy biography, with primary source material, and draws on the poems themselves as biographical sources. Includes an overview of the poet's general qualities and the range of his subjects. Examines the publication history and the credibility of the original 1689 edition of the poems.

Buxton, John, ed. *The Poems of Charles Cotton*. Cambridge, Mass.: Harvard University Press, 1958. The introduction updates and expands on John Beresford's earlier biographical notes. Explains the editor's selections, which include important material from a previously lost manuscript. A section of critical commentary on Cotton contains notes, verse tributes, and references by other writers. The introductory material accompanies a good selection of the poet's work.

Cotton, Charles. *Charles Cotton's Works, 1663-1665: Critical Editions of "The Valiant Knight" and "Scarronides."* Edited by A. I. Dust. New York: Garland, 1992. Editor Dust provides a close look at two burlesques by Cotton.

Hartle, P. N. "Mr. Cotton, of Merry Memory." *Neophilologus* 74 (October, 1989): 605-619. This excellent essay examines the range of styles and the high quality found in Cotton's poetry. Points out Cotton's particular skill as a writer of burlesques and his sometimes obscene sense of humor. Contains quotations from *Scarronides* and *Burlesque upon Burlesque*. This lively piece captures the spirit of the writer in a most engaging way.

Nicolson, Marjorie Hope. *Mountain Gloom and Mountain Glory*. Ithaca, N.Y.: Cornell University Press, 1959. The author explores the reasons behind the differing perceptions of mountains in seventeenth, eighteenth, and nineteenth century thought. The short reference to Cotton concerns only one poem, *The Wonders of the Peake*, and examines his attitude toward nature.

Robinson, Ken, ed. *Charles Cotton: Selected Poems*. Manchester, England: Fyfield Books, 1983. This representative selection of poems includes a handy chronological table and an introduction with explanatory textual notes. Places Cotton in a historical, social, and intellectual context, characterizing

him as a classical skeptic. The author also looks at the simplicity in both his style and his worldview.

Sembower, Charles Jacob. *The Life and the Poetry of Charles Cotton*. 1911. Reprint. New York: New Library Press, 2007. This work examines Cotton's life and how it shaped his poetry.

*Dennis R. Dean*

---

# ABRAHAM COWLEY

**Born:** London, England; 1618
**Died:** Chertsey, England; July 28, 1667

## PRINCIPAL POETRY

*Poeticall Blossomes*, 1633
*The Mistress: Or, Several Copies of Love Verses*, 1647
*Poems*, 1656 (also known as *Miscellanies*)
*Verses Lately Written upon Several Occasions*, 1663
*Poemata Latina*, 1668

## OTHER LITERARY FORMS

From time to time, Abraham Cowley (KOW-lee) interrupted his poetic activity with bits of drama and prose. The former were light, immature attempts: a pastoral drama, *Loves Riddle* (pb. 1638); a Latin comedy entitled *Naufragium Joculare* (pr., pb. 1638); another comedy, *The Guardian* (pr. 1641), hastily put together when Prince Charles passed through Cambridge, but rewritten as *Cutter of Coleman-Street* (pb. 1663). His serious prose is direct and concise, although the pieces tend to repeat the traditional Renaissance theme of solitude. His most notable prose work was a pamphlet, *A Proposition for the Advancement of Experimental Philosophy* (1661), which may have hastened the founding of the Royal Society.

## ACHIEVEMENTS

In the 1930's, the respected critic and literary historian Douglas Bush suggested that Abraham Cowley needed to be seen and understood as a man of his own age, rather than as an artist whose appeal is timeless. That statement may well be the key to assessing Cowley's achievement. During his own day, he secured a considerable reputation as a poet that endured well into the eighteenth century. Then, in 1779, Samuel Johnson issued, as the initial piece to what became *Lives of the Poets* (1779-1781), his *Life of Cowley*. With his usual rhetorical balance, Johnson described Cowley as a poet who had been "at one time too much praised and too much neglected at another." The London sage, through laborious comparison, classified his subject among the Metaphysical poets of the first half of the seventeenth century—a group that he could not always discuss in positive terms. Johnson, however, did single out Cowley as the best among the Metaphysicals and also the last of them. In general, Johnson praised the "Ode of Wit" (1668), turned a neutral ear toward the *Pindarique Odes* (1656), and evaluated the prose as possessing smooth and placid "equability." Cowley was all but forgotten during the nineteenth century, and not until after World War I, when critics such as Sir Herbert J. C. Grierson and T. S. Eliot began to rediscover Metaphysical verse, did his achievement begin to be understood.

Perhaps Cowley's greatest achievement as a poet was that, even in retirement, he stood willing to consider the intellectual challenges of a new world, a world at the edge of scientific and political revolution. He seemed extremely sensitive to the need for the poem as a means for expressing the intellectual essence of that new world, yet he never forsook the Renaissance tradition in which he had been taught. Cowley gave to English poetry a sensible mixture of seriousness, learning, imagination, intelligence, and perception. Although he often wrestled with himself, caught between authority and reason, between the rational and the imaginative, between the rejected past and the uncertain future, he managed to control his art, to triumph over the uncertainty and confusion of his time. Through poetry, Cowley searched for order; through poetry he achieved order—classical, scientific, and religious order—in a world that had itself become worn from passion. The achievement of Cowley is that he showed his successors—especially the Augustans of the early eighteenth century—that a poet should seek and find new material

and new methods without having to sever the strong cord of the past.

BIOGRAPHY

Abraham Cowley was born in the parish of St. Michael le Quern, Cheapside, in London, sometime after July, 1618, the seventh child and fifth son (born posthumously) of Thomas Cowley, a stationer and grocer, who left £1000 to be divided among his seven children. His mother was Thomasine Berrye, to whom Thomas Cowley had pledged his faith sometime in 1581. The widow did the best she could to educate her children through her own devices and then managed to send the boys off to more formal institutions. Thus, she obtained young Abraham's admission as a king's scholar at Westminster School, to which he proceeded armed with some acquaintance with Edmund Spenser. By the age of fifteen, he was already a published poet; his first collection of five pieces, entitled *Poeticall Blossomes*, was followed by a second edition three years later. One of the poems, "Pyramus and Thisbe," some 226 lines long, had been written when he was ten; another, "Constantia and Philetus," was written during the poet's twelfth year.

Cowley's scholarly skills unfortunately did not keep pace with the development of his poetic muse. Apparently the boy balked at the drudgeries of learning grammar and languages; furthermore, his masters contended that his natural quickness made such study unnecessary. In the end, he failed to gain election to Cambridge University in 1636 and had to wait until mid-June of the following year, at which time he became a scholar of Trinity College. Cambridge proved no deterrent to young Cowley's poetic bent; in 1638, he published a pastoral drama, *Loves Riddle*, written at least four years previously. Then, on February 2, 1638, members of Trinity College performed his Latin comedy, *Naufragium Joculare*, which he published shortly thereafter. After taking his B.A. in 1639, Cowley remained at Cambridge through 1642, by which time he had earned the M.A. The year before, when Prince Charles had passed through Cambridge, the young poet had hastily prepared for the occasion a comedy entitled *The Guardian*; the piece was acted a number of times before its publication in 1650 and it continued to be performed, privately, of course, during the Commonwealth and the suppression of the theaters.

Leaving Cambridge in 1643, Cowley continued to write poetry, principally at St. John's College, Oxford, where he had "retired" and become intimate with Royalist leaders. Joining the family of Jermyn (later St. Albans), he followed the queen to France in 1646, where he found a fellow poet, Richard Crashaw. The exiled court employed Cowley for a number of diplomatic services, particularly on missions to Jersey and Holland; other activities included transmitting a correspondence in cipher between Charles I and his queen. During this period, several of Cowley's works appeared in London, including a collection of poems entitled *The Mistress*. His poetic output was restricted, however, because his diplomatic work occupied all his days and most of his evenings. In 1656, his employers sent him to England on what can only be termed an espionage mission under the guise of seeking retirement. He was arrested, but only because the authorities mistook him for someone else; released on bail, he remained under strict probation until Charles II reclaimed the throne of England in 1660.

For Cowley, however, the big event of 1656 was the publication of his most important collection, *Poems*— including the juvenile pieces, the elegies to William Hervey and Crashaw, *The Mistress*, the *Pindarique Odes*, and *Davideis*. The last item, an epic of four books (out of twelve that he had originally planned), actually belonged to the poet's Cambridge period, and Cowley finally admitted that he had abandoned plans to complete it. After the publication of the *Poems*, Cowley, still in the employ of the exiled Royalists in France, suddenly took up the study of medicine—as a means of obscuring his espionage activities. Seemingly without difficulty, he earned his medical doctor's degree at Oxford in December, 1657, and then retired to Kent, where he studied and produced a Latin poem, "Plantarum Libri duo" (published in 1662). After the Restoration, Cowley's best poetry and prose appeared: "Ode upon the Blessed Restoration" (1660), *A Vision, Concerning His Late Pretended Highnesse, Cromwell the Wicked* (1661), *A Proposition for the Advancement of Experimental Philosophy*, "Ode to the Royal Society" (1661), and *Verses Lately Written upon Several Occasions*.

Cowley's early employer, Jermyn, by then the earl of St. Albans, helped to obtain for him some royal land at Chertsey, where he could spend the remainder of his days in easy retirement. There he settled in April, 1665. His health began to decline, however, and the fact that his tenants balked at paying their rents did little to improve his physical and emotional condition. In late July, 1667, after being outdoors longer than necessary, he caught a severe cold; he died on the twenty-eighth of that month. Cowley was buried with considerable ceremony in Westminster Abbey, near Geoffrey Chaucer and Edmund Spenser, and for the rest of the seventeenth century, poets and critics continued to view him as the model of cultivated poetry.

ANALYSIS

Abraham Cowley is a transitional figure, a poet who tended to relinquish the emotional values of John Donne and George Herbert and grasp the edges of reason and wit. He was more versatile than the early Metaphysicals: He embraced the influence of Donne and Ben Jonson, relied on the Pindaric form that would take hold in the eighteenth century, conceived of an experimental biblical epic in English (*Davideis*) well in advance of John Milton's major project, and demonstrated an open-mindedness that allowed him to write in support of Francis Bacon, Thomas Hobbes, and the Royal Society. Cowley's elegies on the deaths of William Hervey and Richard Crashaw are extremely frank poems of natural pain and loss, while at the same time the poet recognized the need for the human intellect to be aware of "Things Divine"—the dullness of the earthly as opposed to the reality of the heavenly.

Indeed, Cowley's versatile imagination ranged far and wide, and he easily adapted diverse subjects to fit his own purposes. Unlike the poets of the Restoration and the early eighteenth century who followed him, he ignored various current fashions and concentrated on economy, unity, form, and imagination; he did not have to force the grotesque on his readers, nor did he have to inundate them with a pretense of art. Cowley was a master at what Bishop Thomas Sprat termed, in 1668, "harmonious artistry." He turned his back on wild and affected extravagance and embraced propriety and measure; he applied wit to matter, combined philosophy with charity and religion. Even when writing amorous verse, he took inspiration both from the courtier and from the scholar—the passion of the one and the wisdom of the other.

### POETICALL BLOSSOMES

Cowley launched his career as a serious poet at the age of fifteen, while still a student at Westminster School, with the publication of *Poeticall Blossomes*. In fact, there is evidence that the volume had been prepared in some form at least two years earlier. At any rate, what appeared was a rather high level of poetic juvenilia, five pieces in which both sound and sense reflected an ability far beyond the poet's youth. The first, "Pyramus and Thisbe," 226 lines, does not differ too markedly from Ovid's tale, although Cowley's Venus seems overly malevolent and the (then) ten-year-old poet carried to extremes the desired but untasted joys of love. Otherwise, the piece evidences a sense of discipline and knowledge often reserved for the mature imagination, as young Cowley attempted to control his phrasing and his verse form. The second poem in the collection, "Constantia and Philetus," may serve as a companion to "Pyramus and Thisbe," although it is certainly no mere imitation. Cowley, now about twelve, again chose as his subject a tragic love story, keeping hold on Venus, Cupid, and other deities. However, he shifted his setting from ancient Rome to the suburban surroundings of an Italian villa, there to unfold a rather conventional poetic narrative: two lovers, a rival favored by the parents, a sympathetic brother, and a dead heroine. He adorned the entire scene with amorous conceits and characters yearning for the beauties of the country and the consolations of nature.

In addition to the larger pieces, *Poeticall Blossomes* contained an interesting trio of shorter efforts. In "A Dream of Elysium," Cowley, seemingly engaged in an exercise in poetic self-education, parades before a sleeping poet a host of classical favorites: Hyacinth, Narcissus, Apollo, Ovid, Homer, Cato, Leander, Hero, Portia, Brutus, Pyramus, and Thisbe. The final two poems of the volume constitute the young writer's first attempts at what would become, for him, an important form— the occasional poem. Both pieces are elegies: One mourns the death of a public official, Dudley, Lord

Carleton and Viscount Dorchester, who attended Westminster School, served as secretary of state, and died in February, 1632; the other was occasioned by the death of Cowley's cousin, Richard Clerke, a student at Lincoln's Inn. Naturally, the two poems contain extravagant praises and lofty figures, no doubt reflecting what the boy had read in his favorite, Spenser, and had been taught by his masters. There are those who speculate that had Cowley died in adolescence, as Thomas Chatterton did in the next century, the verses of *Poeticall Blossomes* would have sustained at least a very small poetic reputation in a very obscure niche of literary history. Cowley, however, despite a number of purely political distractions during his adult life, managed to extend his poetic talents beyond childhood exercises, and it is to the products of his maturity that one must turn for the comprehension and appreciation of his art.

### POEMS

Perhaps Cowley's most important contribution to poetry came in 1656 with the publication of his extensive collection, *Poems*, several additions to which he made during his lifetime. Of more than passing interest is the preface to this volume, wherein Cowley attempts, by reference to his own personal situation, to explain the relationship between the poet and his environment. In 1656, he had little desire to write poetry, mainly because of the political instability of the moment, his own health, and his mental state. He admitted that a warlike, unstable, and even tragic age may be the best for the poet to write about, but it may also be the worst time in which to write. Living as he did, a stranger under surveillance in his own homeland, he felt restricted in his artistic endeavors. "The soul," he complained in the preface, "must be filled with bright and delightful ideas when it undertakes to communicate delight to others, which is the main end of poesy." Thus, he had given serious thought to abandoning Puritan England for the obscurity of some plantation in the Americas, and the 1656 *Poems* was to be his legacy to a world for whose conflicts and confrontations he no longer had any concern.

The *Poems* contain four divisions: the *Miscellanies*, including the *Anacreontiques*; *The Mistress*, a collection of love poems; *Pindarique Odes*; and the *Davideis*, a heroic epic focusing on the problems of the Old Testament king. In subsequent editions, Cowley and his editors added "Verses on Various Occasions" and "Several Discourses by Way of Essays in Prose and Verse." Cowley himself informed his readers that the *Miscellanies* constituted poems preserved from earlier folios (some even from his school days); unfortunately, he made no distinction between the poor efforts and those of quality. Thus, an immature ode, "Here's to thee, Dick," stands near the serious and moving elegy "On the Death of Mr. William Hervey," in which he conveys both universal meaning and personal tragedy and loss. Cowley, however, rarely allowed himself to travel the route of the strictly personal; for him, poetry required support from learning, from scholastic comparisons that did not always rise to poetical levels. The fine valedictory "To the Lord Falkland," which celebrates the friendship between two interesting but divergent personalities, is sprinkled with lofty scientific comparisons to display the order that reigns in the crowded mind of his hero. Indeed, there are moments in Cowley's elegies when the reader wonders if the poet was more interested in praising the virtues of science and learning than in mourning the loss of friends. Such high distractions, however, do not weaken the intensity of Cowley's sincerity.

### The Mistress

*The Mistress*, originally published as a separate volume in 1647, comprises one hundred love poems, or, in Cowley's own terms, feigned addresses to some fair creature of the fancy. Almost apologetically, the poet explains in the prefatory remarks that all writers of verse must at one time or another pay some service to Love, to prove themselves true to Love. Unfortunately, Cowley evidences difficulty in warming to the occasion, perhaps held back by the prevalent mood of Puritan strictness that then dominated the art. Thus, many of his physical and psychological images of Love come from traditions rather than from the heart: Love is an interchange of hearts, a flame, a worship, a river frozen by disdain. On the other hand, Cowley's original, nontraditional images and similes are often wildly incongruous, even unintentionally comical, and lacking in true feeling.

Tears are made by smoke but not by flame; the lover's heart bursts on its object "Like a grenado shot into a magazine"; a love story cut into bark burns and withers the tree; a young lady's beauty changes from civil government to tyranny. Certainly, *The Mistress* reveals that Cowley could employ an obvious degree of playfulness in verse; he could counterfeit, with ease and ingenuity, a series of love adventures; he could sustain some semblance of unity in a seeming hodgepodge of romantic episodes; he could amuse his readers. For those of his age who took their love poetry seriously, however—for those who expected grace, warmth, tenderness, even truth—*The Mistress* must have been rather disappointing.

### Pindarique Odes

There is some confusion concerning the form of the *Pindarique Odes*. Cowley may have wanted readers to believe that he was writing the true Pindaric ode: strophe, antistrophe (alike in form), and epode (different in form from the first two divisions), with varying meter and verse lengths within a strophe, but nevertheless regular metrical schemes established for corresponding divisions. Actually, he created a new form, an irregular ode: He discarded the usual stanza patterns, varied the length of lines and the number of lines within the strophes, and varied the meter with shifts in emotional intensity. He obviously knew what he was doing and probably chose the title for the section to disguise a questionable innovation. In fact, he doubted (in the preface) whether the form would be understood by most of his readers, even those acquainted with the principles of poetry. Nevertheless, he employed sudden and lengthy digressions, "unusual and bold" figures, and various and irregular numbers. Cowley's purpose throughout was to achieve a sense of harmony between what he viewed as the liberty of the ode and the moral liberty of life, the latter combining responsibility and freedom. Through moral liberty, he hoped to find simplicity, retirement, and charm; the liberty of the ode, he thought, might allow for a greater participation in intellectual exercise.

In practice, the ode allowed Cowley the opportunity to subject his readers to a host of what he had termed "bold figures," images that would have occurred to no one other than he. Thus, on one occasion he asks his Muse to "rein her Pindaric Pegasus closely in," since the beast is "an unruly and a hardmouthed horse." At another time, the Muse appears in her chariot, with Eloquence, Wit, Memory, and Invention running by her side. Suddenly, Cowley stops the action to compare the Muse with the Creator and with the two worlds that they have created. Such comparisons, with their accompanying "bold" images, allowed the poet to display his learning, to set down explanatory notes of definition, explication, and interpretation—whether his readers needed them or not. As long as he could serve as his own explicator, there seemed no limit to his invention. Generally, though, Cowley's odes fall short of their intentions as complete pieces of poetry. The digressions—the instruments of the poet's new-found intellectual freedom—may strike and impress the reader momentarily, but they also distract and divert the attention from the main idea of the poem.

Not all of Cowley's odes fall short of the mark. He succeeded when his subject interested him enough to say something substantive about it. In both "To Mr. Hobbes" and "Brutus" he followed the serious thinkers of his time. The first poem finds him looking beyond the transitory troubles of the moment to a new day. The second allows him to observe Oliver Cromwell, the Caesar of his time and, like the conscientious Royalist of the period, seek contemplation rather than action. He looks to history and philosophy to explain the evils of tyranny and to find parallels with other evils that eventually gave way to good. In the ode to Hobbes, Cowley finds solace in the fact that all ideas and concepts of permanent value must remain young and fresh forever. In the ode to Brutus, the poet discovers that odd events, evil men, and wretched actions are not themselves sufficient to destroy or even obscure virtue. Again, the particular circumstances of the moment and his deep personal disappointment gave Cowley the conviction to express what he actually felt.

### DAVIDEIS

It is tempting to dismiss *Davideis* as another example of Cowley's juvenilia. Of the twelve books planned, only four were finished, and those were written while Cowley was still at Cambridge. By 1656, and perhaps even before, Cowley had lost his taste for the epic and determined not to finish it. If anything can be salvaged from *Davideis* it may be found in the preface, where the poet makes an eloquent plea for sacred poetry. Cowley complains that for too long wit and eloquence have been wasted on the beggarly flattery of important persons, idolizing of foolish women, and senseless fables. The time has come, he announces, to recover poetry from the devil and restore it to the kingdom of God, to rescue it from the impure waters of Damascus and baptize it in the Jordan.

Unfortunately, the epic that follows never rises to the elegance or merit of the prefatory prose. The poem simply sinks from its own weight. Cowley's Hell, for example, is a labyrinth of cosmic elements: caverns that breed rare metals; nests of infant, weeping winds; a complex court of mother waters. The journey there is indeed long and laborious, and the relationship between all those cosmic details (gold, winds, voices, tides, and tidelessness) and Hell is never made clear. Cowley himself acknowledged the immaturity and weakness of the epic, but he also saw it as an adumbration of the poetic potential of biblical history. Eleven years after the publication of *Davideis* in the collected *Poems*, John Milton published *Paradise Lost* (1667, 1674).

### "HYMN TO LIGHT"

Cowley added to the collected editions of his poems as they were issued between 1656 and his death in 1667. As with the contents of the first edition, the pieces vary in quality. In "Hymn to Light," the poet manages to achieve a proper balance between his learning and his imagination. The reader senses that Cowley has actually observed the "winged arrows" shooting from the "golden quiver of the sky," the result of a long succession of fresh and bright dawns rising in the English countryside. Those very dawns seem to have frightened "sleep, the lazy owl of night," turning the face of "cloudy care" into a "gentle, beamy smile." During those blessed years of retirement, away from the unnatural complications and intrigues of the political world, Cowley turned more and more toward the beauty of nature as a source of pleasure. Although in "Hymn to Light" he labels light an offspring of chaos, its very beams embrace and enhance the charms and beauty of the world, while at the same time tempting the selfish and inconsiderate by shining on valuable elements. Toward the end of the poem, he conceives of light as a "clear river" that pours forth its radiance from the vast ocean of the sky; it collects in pools and lakes when its course is opposed by some firm body—the earth, for example. Such a conceit may appear overly abstract and abstruse, but it is perhaps the most extreme figure of the poem, demonstrating the degree to which the mature Cowley had advanced beyond his juvenile epic endeavors.

### "Ode to the Royal Society"

There are critics who assert that with the "Ode to the Royal Society" (1667), Cowley rose to his highest level. That is debatable, but it is certainly his last important poem. The poem was written at the request of Cowley's friend, the diarist John Evelyn, who asked for a tribute to the Royal Society to complement the official history being undertaken by Thomas Sprat, bishop of Rochester. The poem, published the same year as Sprat's *History of the Royal Society*, focused not so much on the institution in question or even on science in general but on the evolution of philosophy, which Cowley placed into two chronological periods: before and after Francis Bacon. The poet dwells briefly on the constrictions of the early philosophies, which merely wandered among the labyrinths of endless discourse, with little or no positive effect on humankind. Then follows an impassioned attack on pure authority, which arrived at erroneous scientific and intellectual conclusions and stubbornly clung to them.

Cowley compares Francis Bacon—who, with his *Advancement of Learning* (1605), *Novum Organum* (1620), and *De Augmentis Scientiarum* (1623), had initiated a new age of philosophy—to Moses; men of intellect were led out of the barren wasteland of the past to the very borders of exalted wit. Only Bacon, maintains Cowley, was willing to act and capable of routing the ghostlike body of authority that had for so long misled people with its dead thoughts. The philosophers of the past were but mechanics, copiers of others' work; Bacon summoned the mind away from words, the mere pictures of thoughts, and redirected it toward objects, the proper focus of the mind. Thus, the poet paid tribute to the philosopher as the proper predecessor of the Royal Society; his investigations paved the way for the significant accomplishments of that institution. The immediate success of the poem may have been due in part to Cowley's personal ties with the Royal Society—

particularly as a friend of both Sprat and Evelyn and as the author of *A Proposition for the Advancement of Experimental Philosophy*. Those critics who have praised the piece for its pure poetic merit, however, have rightly identified it as the culmination of Cowley's contributions to the English ode.

### Legacy

Beginning with Joseph Addison's negative criticism (*The Spectator* 62, May, 1711) and extending through the critique in Samuel Johnson's *Lives of the Poets*, Cowley's reputation has endured the accusations of mixed wit and strained metaphysical conceits. Obviously, Addison and Johnson, even though they represent opposite chronological poles of the eighteenth century, were still too close to their subject to assess him objectively and to recognize him as a transitional figure. Cowley lived during the end of one intellectual age and the beginning of another. He belonged alongside John Donne, Richard Crashaw, George Herbert, Henry Vaughan, Thomas Traherne, and Andrew Marvell; he owed equal allegiance to the writers of the early Restoration, to such classicists as John Denham and Edmund Waller. Thus, his poetry reflects the traditions of one period and the freshness of another, the extravagances of youth and the freedom to combine ingenuity with reason and learning. Cowley also had the distinct advantage of a point of view resulting from the mastery of several positive sciences and of practically all the literature of Europe. Knowledge, reflection, control, clear judgment: These he carried with him from the Puritan Revolution into the Restoration and then to his own retirement. He belonged to an age principally of learning and of prose; he wrote poetry with the sustained rhetorical and emotional force that often results in greatness. Unfortunately, his meteor merely approached greatness, flaring only for a brief moment on the literary horizon.

### Other major works

PLAYS: *Loves Riddle*, pb. 1638; *Naufragium Joculare*, pr., pb. 1638; *The Guardian*, pr. 1641 (revised as *Cutter of Coleman-Street*, pb. 1663).

NONFICTION: *A Proposition for the Advancement of Experimental Philosophy*, 1661; *A Vision, Concerning His Late Pretended Highnesse, Cromwell the Wicked*,

1661; *Several Discourses by Way of Essays in Prose and Verse*, 1668.

MISCELLANEOUS: *The Works of Mr. Abraham Cowley*, 1668, 1681, 1689.

BIBLIOGRAPHY

Dykstal, Timothy. "The Epic Reticence of Abraham Cowley." *Studies in English Literature* 31, no. 1 (Winter, 1991): 95. An analysis of Cowley's *Davideis* and John Milton's *Paradise Lost*.

Hinman, Robert B. *Abraham Cowley's World of Order*. Cambridge, Mass.: Harvard University Press, 1960. Summarizes Cowley's scholarship, outlines his notions about art, examines the influence of Francis Bacon and Thomas Hobbes, reads the poems in terms of "order," and evaluates Cowley's position as a poet. Contains an extensive bibliography.

Nethercot, Arthur H. *Abraham Cowley: The Muse's Hannibal*. 1931. Reprint. New York: Russell & Russell, 1967. The definitive biography, this book discusses Cowley's literary work, citing his composition of the first religious epic in English, his development of the Pindaric ode, and his literary criticism. Includes an extensive bibliography, several illustrations, and some documents, one of which is Cowley's will.

Pebworth, Ted-Larry. "Cowley's *Davideis* and the Exaltation of Friendship." In *The David Myth in Western Literature*, edited by Raymond-Jean Frontain and Jan Wojcik. West Lafayette, Ind.: Purdue University Press, 1980. Essay concerns the friendship of David and Jonathan, which is compared to the classical friendships of Damon and Pythias, Cicero and Atticus, and Orestes and Pylades and the topical friendship of Cowley and William Hervey. Examines the friendship in *Davideis* in terms of the three-step Neoplatonic progression of love.

Revard, Stella P. "Cowley's *Pindarique Odes* and the Politics of the Inter-Regnum." *Criticism* 35, no. 3 (Summer, 1993): 391. An examination of Royalist celebration and resistance in Cowley's *Pindarique Odes*. It is assumed that these texts and the political agenda they encode were produced under censorship.

Taaffe, James G. *Abraham Cowley*. New York: Twayne, 1972. An excellent overview of Cowley's literary work. Contains readings of many of Cowley's works, with extensive commentary on *Davideis*. Of the shorter works, "The Muse," the poems on the deaths of Richard Crashaw and William Hervey, and the Cromwell poem are treated in some detail. Includes a chronology and an annotated select bibliography.

Trotter, David. *The Poetry of Abraham Cowley*. Totowa, N.J.: Rowman & Littlefield, 1979. Tends to downplay political and social contexts and to stress the role of form in Cowley's work. The lyric poems (especially *The Mistress*), the sacred poems, the Pindaric odes, and Cowley's relationship to Richard Crashaw are treated in separate chapters. Contains a helpful bibliography.

Walton, Geoffrey. "Abraham Cowley." In *From Donne to Marvell*. Vol. 3 in *A Guide to English Literature*, edited by Boris Ford. London: Cassell, 1956. Walton regards Cowley as the bridge between Metaphysical wit and neoclassical poetry and relates Cowley's poetry back to Jonson and Donne and ahead to Dryden and Pope. Walton's focus, though, is on Cowley's neoclassical verse, especially in the shaping of the Pindaric ode and the creation of the first neoclassical epic in English, *Davideis*.

Welch, Anthony. "Epic Romance, Royalist Retreat, and the English Civil War." *Modern Philology* 105, no. 3 (February, 2008): 570. Welch discusses the effect that the stalemate of Charles I's army at the First Battle of Newbury had on the Royalist epic poem that Cowley was writing about the Civil War.

Williamson, George. *Six Metaphysical Poets: A Reader's Guide*. New York: Farrar, Straus and Giroux, 1967. Williamson's chapter on Cowley provides a good overview of the metaphysical elements in Cowley's poetry. Contains several one-page discussions of individual poems and concludes with an informative comparison between Cowley and Donne. For Williamson, Cowley's love poetry is located between Donne's Metaphysical poetry and Waller's verse.

*Samuel J. Rogal*

# WILLIAM COWPER

**Born:** Great Berkhampstead, Hertfordshire, England;
    November 26, 1731
**Died:** East Dereham, England; April 25, 1800

## PRINCIPAL POETRY

*Olney Hymns*, 1779 (with John Newton)
*Poems*, 1782
*The Task*, 1785
*Completed Poetical Works*, 1907 (standard edition)

## OTHER LITERARY FORMS

The *Olney Hymns* are now commonly studied as poems. Of the sixty-four hymns contributed to the volume by William Cowper (KEW-pur), only a very few still appear in church hymnals. The hymn, however, while certainly kin to the poem, presents unique demands on the author and cannot be judged fairly by the same critical standards. The hymn must try to reflect universal Christian feelings on a level immediately recognizable to all the human souls and intellects that make up a congregation. It must be orthodox and express only the expected. It must be simple, and above all it must not reveal what is individual about the author. To the extent that Cowper's unique genius could not always be restrained by convention, he is not consistently as good a hymnist as Isaac Watts or Charles Wesley.

In the eighteenth century, the familiar letter became so artistically refined that modern literary scholars now regard it as a minor literary form. Cowper's collected correspondence fills four volumes (Wright edition, 1904) and treats an incredible range of subjects and themes with great insight, humor, and style. Literary historians regard him as one of the finest letter writers in English.

## ACHIEVEMENTS

Modern literary historians commonly assign William Cowper to the ranks of the so-called pre-Romantics, and to be sure, his subjective voice, preference for the rural to the urban, and social concern are qualities more easily discernible in the poetry of the early nineteenth century than of the late eighteenth century. Cow-per, however, was not attempting to create a literary movement. The poetry characteristic of his later years is clearly a perfection of themes and forms that occupied his attention from the first, and those early efforts are not radical departures from what is considered mainstream neoclassicism. Satire, mock-heroic, general nature description, all are present, but Cowper grew in his art and was not concerned that his growth made him into something a bit different.

Cowper's satires, for example, are notable for a measure of charity toward their subjects, charity that he saw was lacking in the satires of Alexander Pope and his contemporaries. Moreover, Cowper was greatly interested in poetic structure but also felt that the poetry of his age put too much emphasis on structure at the expense of real human personality. The canon of Cowper's work is of a very uneven quality, but his finest efforts, such as *The Task*, display an unobtrusive structure and identifiable human presence uncommon in the neoclassical age, and they are fine by the standards of any age. Perhaps his outstanding structural achievement is the conversational blank verse used in *The Task*. There is no more interesting development in that form between John Milton and William Wordsworth. However, while Cowper's critical reputation is quite good, he is not regarded as one of the major figures in English letters. The conventions of neoclassical poetry had been manipulated with greater skill by Pope, and the new directions suggested by Cowper would be shortly perfected by Wordsworth. Thus, the achievement of Cowper, by no means insignificant, is somewhat obscured by the giants who surround him.

## BIOGRAPHY

William Cowper was born on November 26, 1731, in Great Berkhampstead, Hertfordshire, England. He was the fourth child of the Reverend Dr. John Cowper, rector of Great Berkhampstead, and Ann Donne. Both parents represented distinguished families. The Cowpers had distinguished themselves by loyalty to the Crown, and John Cowper's uncle, Sir William, had been created baron in 1706 and earl in 1718. The Donnes were of even nobler lineage and traced descent from Henry III. The famous seventeenth century poet, John Donne, was of the same illustrious family. John and Ann had seven children, but only William and their last child, also named John, survived infancy. Very shortly after the birth of John, Ann died; William was only six at the time.

Cowper's father appears to have been neither a cruel nor especially loving parent. Shortly after Ann's death, young William was sent away to school. This early separation from his parent—not unusual in upper-class households—seems to have affected the poet greatly, because several years later, Cowper attacked the practice and the school system in general in a poem, *Tirocinium* (1785). While a student at Westminster, Cowper met his first love, his cousin Theodora. The affair was terminated in 1756, but it is commemorated in nineteen sentimental love poems addressed to Delia. Cowper suffered his first severe attack of depression in 1752. He was studying law at the time and was called to the bar in 1754. Although he had no great fondness for the profession, his family had thought it best that he have some livelihood.

In 1759, Cowper was appointed commissioner of bankrupts, a minor governmental post that paid very little. Out of the need for financial security, he applied for an appointment to the post of clerk of the journals of the House of Lords. When the incumbent clerk died, Cowper's appointment was put forward only to be challenged by supporters of another candidate. In 1763, Cowper learned that he would have to face an examination to determine the best applicant. This prospect greatly aggravated his already depressed state, and he experienced a severe mental breakdown during which he unsuccessfully attempted suicide. Clearly, he could not occupy a government post. The sense of rejection as a consequence of this realization joined with the recollection of his mother's death, and the broken affair with Theodora led Cowper to imagine that his exile from normal human relationships was God's sign to him that he was also excluded from the company of the blessed for all eternity.

Following an eighteen-month residence in an asylum, Cowper moved to the country, where he soon made the acquaintance of the Unwin family. He resided with that cheerful and cordial family in Huntingdon and then accompanied Mrs. Unwin in her move to the town of Olney following the sudden death of her hus-

band. Here, Cowper met the revivalist minister John Newton, and for a time, he enjoyed a useful and productive existence. He became interested in the problems of the poor and various charitable activities and joined with Newton in writing a collection of hymns that was later published as the *Olney Hymns*. In January, 1773, however, shortly before his planned marriage to the widowed Mrs. Unwin, Cowper again suffered a period of instability. Convinced by a terrifying dream that it was God's will, he once again attempted suicide. His failure only added to his distress, for now, sure that he had failed to obey God's command, he became utterly convinced of his damnation. Although he recovered from the 1773 breakdown, despair never left him.

Largely as a distraction, Cowper turned his attention to writing poetry, and in February, 1782, he published his first significant collection. The early 1780's were made happier for Cowper by his friendship with Lady Austin, who had taken up residence near Olney. It was at the suggestion of this good-humored lady that in July, 1783, he began his masterpiece, *The Task*. That

*William Cowper* (©Michael Nicholson/CORBIS)

poem provided the title for his next collection that appeared in 1785. However, whatever joy Cowper may have derived from the favorable public response to his new volume was soon erased by the death of Mrs. Unwin's son, William. This shock, plus the anxiety caused by moving from his beloved Olney to Weston, was more than Cowper could endure, and in 1787, he again lost his grip on reality.

Following his recovery, Cowper again turned to writing. He began a translation of Homer and addressed himself to social issues, especially the fight against slavery. For a few years at least, he was able to reproduce the routine and uneventful living he had enjoyed at Olney. In December, 1791, however, Mrs. Unwin suffered a stroke; in May, 1792, she suffered another that rendered her immobile and speechless. She recovered somewhat, but the guilt Cowper felt at recalling how her life had been spent in his care, plunged him again into deep melancholy. His feelings are well expressed in "To Mary," written in the fall of 1793. Not even the satisfaction of his great poetic fame and an annual pension of three hundred pounds from George III could lift him from despair or silence the voices of eternal doom that came to him at night. On December 17, 1796, Mrs. Unwin died. "The Castaway," composed in 1799, is one of the bleakest poems in English and itself sufficient comment on the last three years of Cowper's life. On April 25, 1800, after a one-month struggle with edema, he died. A witness described his last facial expression as one of "holy surprise."

ANALYSIS

William Cowper's poetic achievement is marked by a tension between subjectivity and objectivity, a tension that, at its best, produces a unique poetry defying easy classification as either neoclassical or Romantic. Cowper wrote poetry to preserve his sanity. It was a way to distract himself from the terrible brooding on the inevitability of his damnation, and even when his gloom made it impossible to focus on subjects other than his own condition, at least the very act of writing, the mechanical business of finding rhymes or maintaining meter, defused the self-destructive potential of the messages of despair that crowded his dreams and came to him in the whisperings of mysterious voices. Be-

cause the poetry was not only by Cowper but also for Cowper, it displays a subjectivity uncommon in the neoclassical tradition. Although Cowper had his own opinions about poetry and disliked the formal, elegant couplet structure that dominated the verse of his day, he was not completely a rebel. Objectivity, Horatian humor, sentimentality, respect for the classics, the very qualities that define neoclassicism are all present in Cowper's verse. Unlike William Wordsworth, he never issued a manifesto to revolutionize poetry. Indeed, the levelheaded detachment of the Horatian persona, so popular with Cowper's contemporaries, was a stance that he often tried to capture for the sake of his own mental stability. When Cowper manages a balance between the subjectivity that injects his own gentle humanity into a poem and the objectivity that allows universal significance, he is at his best.

## "ON THE RECEIPT OF MY MOTHER'S PICTURE OUT OF NORFOLK"

One of Cowper's most famous poems illustrates the poet at less than his best when he manages almost fully to withhold his own personality and allows convention to structure his message. "On the Receipt of My Mother's Picture Out of Norfolk" was written in 1790, fifty-three years after his mother's death and only ten years before his own. The poem avoids the theme of death and rather focuses on the mother with the only tool available to it: convention. The poem begins with a reference to the power of art to immortalize, a theme that might have supported some interesting content. The poet then introduces yet another worthy theme: "And while that face renews my filial grief,/ Fancy shall weave a charm for my relief"; while the art of the picture kindles an old grief, the art of the poem will provide the balm. Neither theme, however, survives beyond the first few lines of the poem. Instead, Cowper turns to the popular conventions of eighteenth century verse to produce a proper comment on a dead mother.

The verse form is the heroic couplet, the dominant form of the age. The diction is formal because the neoclassical notion of decorum—words appropriately matched to the subject matter—demanded formality in the respectful approach of a child to a parent. Ann Cowper, the poet's mother, is unrecognizable in the poem; she has no individuality, no visual reality for the reader.

Consistent with the neoclassical emphasis on the general and ideal rather than the particular and commonplace, Cowper creates a cloud of expected motherly virtues through which the face of Ann can be seen but dimly. Here it should be remembered, however, that the poet is reacting to a picture, an eighteenth century portrait, not to a tangible human being, and that portrait itself would have been an idealized representation reflective of the aesthetic principle voiced by Sir Joshua Reynolds: "The general idea constitutes real excellence.... Even in portraits, the grace, and, we may add, the likeness, consists more in taking the general air than in observing the exact similitude of feature."

The poem, then, does accurately treat its subject if that subject is indeed the portrait. Still, the treatment is for the most part a catalog of hackneyed images— "sweet smiles" and "dear eyes"—mixed with a few images that need more than originality to save them, such as the extended simile that likens the mother to "a gallant bark from Albion's coast" that "shoots into port at some well-havered isle," a rather unflattering analogy if the reader attempts to use it to help visualize the mother. The overall sentimentality of the poem is also no departure from neoclassical convention. Sentimentalism in all literary genres had emerged as a popular reaction to the great emphasis placed on reason by so many eighteenth century thinkers. The universe, it was held, is logical and ordered, and all nature, including human nature, is ultimately understandable by the human ability to reason. Sentimentalism answered this by calling attention to emotions and feelings. Humanity is not merely rational; there are finer qualities beyond the power of logic to comprehend. At its best, sentiment could add an element of emotion to reason and make a work more reflective of the real human psyche. At its worst, sentiment drowned reality in maudlin fictions and saccharine absurdities. Cowper's poem does not completely sink in the quagmire of sentimental syrup. It hangs on by the thread of an idea about the immortalizing power of art, a thread that is visible at the beginning and then again at the end but which for the greater part of the poem is lost in the swamp.

All this is not to say that "On the Receipt of My Mother's Picture Out of Norfolk" is a bad poem. Indeed, it remains one of Cowper's most frequently anthologized works. If it is conventional, it is still worth studying as a good example of several aspects of the neoclassical tradition unknown to readers who name the age after Alexander Pope or Samuel Johnson. Cowper, however, was capable of doing better. The problem with the mother poem was that rather than writing about his mother, he pretended to write about his own feelings and memories. The memories after so many years were probably dim, and he seems to have chosen to avoid an expression of his dark fears and utter isolation in favor of a conventional grieving son persona.

## "THE CASTAWAY"

Cowper succeeds more fully when his reaction to a situation or event includes, but also goes beyond, the feelings most readers would experience when he injects enough of his purely subjective response to allow the reader to see a somewhat different but still believable dimension to what it is to be human. The loss of a mother is certainly an appropriate correlative to the emotions expressed in the poem. Moreover, the emotional response is certainly believable; it is not, however, unique. The loss of a seaman overboard during a storm is also an appropriate correlative to the emotions of the speaker in "The Castaway," but here Cowper does more than simply respond to a situation.

The episode of the seaman swept overboard in a storm, an account of which Cowper had read in George Anson's *Voyage* (1748) some years before writing the poem, is actually an extended metaphor for the poet's own condition. Interestingly, the analogy between poet and sailor is only briefly pointed out at the very beginning and again at the end of the poem. The metaphor, the story of the sailor, is for the most part presented with curious objectivity. The facts of the tragedy are all there: the storm, the struggles of the seaman, the futile attempts at rescue. There is also a respectable measure of grief in the subdued tone of the speaker; the reader, however, could not be misled by this seeming objectivity. It is at once apparent that the poem is really about the tragic fate of the poet, but it is precisely in this tension between the objective and subjective that the poem says so much. The effect of the long metaphor in keeping the poet's ego in the background is to illustrate that indeed the poet is an insignificant thing—a tiny, isolated being beyond the help of his fellows and the concern of his God. That curious objectivity is in fact the attitude of the universe toward Cowper. It does not seem to care, and it is not hostile. It has simply excluded Cowper from the scheme of things, a scheme that allows for the possibility of salvation for all humans.

The God in "The Castaway" seems strangely Deistic. He is unwilling to interfere with the predetermined operation of his universe, but unlike many of his contemporaries who viewed the universe with optimism, believing that if God was remote, at least the system that he set in motion was good, Cowper sees no goodness in his own portion. In "The Castaway," Cowper can neither bless nor curse his fate, for any action would detract from the utter futility he wishes to convey. "The Castaway," then, is highly subjective. The poet is in no way suggesting that the fate of the metaphorical sailor describes the universal human condition. Indeed, humanity is on board the ship, which survives the storm. Cowper is talking about himself, but the air of objectivity in the presentation stresses the futility and isolation he wishes to convey. In other words, the structure of the poem contributes greatly to its message. What is Cowper in the eyes of God? He is no more than the minimal first-person intrusion in the sixty-six lines that constitute "The Castaway."

### "The Poplar Field"

Cowper was a fine craftsperson in the structuring of poems. His collected works clearly show a fondness for experimentation, and as is to be expected, some of those experiments were more successful than others. An interesting example is "The Poplar Field," a frequently anthologized lyric that deals with the fleeting glories of this world. Here, Cowper deliberately violates decorum and adopts a sprightly, heavily accented meter. The mere four feet to a line gallops the reader through musings on various reminders of mortality. The meter seems to mock the expected seriousness of the theme to produce a parody of melancholy landscape verse. The content of the poem consists, for the most part, of uninspired platitudes and clichés, but this is the necessary fodder for parody. A less generous reading might assert that parody is not an issue. The poem is rather a straightforward presentation of the joys of melancholy, the pleasures of the contemplative life. The meter is the vehicle for communicating the pleasure idea to

the audience, and Cowper's "The Poplar Field" is really a direct descendant of John Milton's "L'Allegro." If this is the case, the trite content cannot be justified as fuel for a satiric fire and must be held to be just that: trite content. Perhaps, then, "The Poplar Field" is of the same family as "On the Receipt of My Mother's Picture Out of Norfolk": Both poems suffer from the substitution of conventions for the presence of the real Cowper.

### "The Diverting History of John Gilpin"

An experiment of unchallenged success is "The Diverting History of John Gilpin." Structure is everything in this delightful ballad about the misadventures of a linen draper on his twenty-year delayed honeymoon. The lively meter and rhyming quatrains are ideally suited to the rollicking humor of the piece. Gilpin, a rather bombastic but totally good-natured hero, has his adventure told by a narrator who is himself satirized by the deceptively careless method of his composition. It soon becomes clear that the poem is everything and that the narrator will not be stopped or the rhythm broken by such concerns as taking time to find an appropriate figure rather than a silly one or even by running out of content to fill the quatrain: "So like an arrow swift he flew,/ Shot by an archer strong;/ So did he fly—which brings me to/ The middle of my song." For Cowper, the poem lived up to its title; it seems to have diverted him indeed, for the reader familiar with Cowper's voice will look in vain for a trace of the brooding author of "The Castaway." However, beneath the funny story, the brilliant metrics, and the silly narrator, there is still the gentle poet who prefers to laugh with his characters rather than reduce them to the grotesque fools that populate so much of eighteenth century satire.

Despite the success of "The Diverting History of John Gilpin," Cowper has never been considered a leading satirist of the age. Satire, especially in the popular Horatian mode, must have had its attractions for him. The detached, witty observer who by choice leaves the herd to remark on the foibles of humanity presented an ideal persona, but it was a stance that Cowper could seldom sustain. The satirist must appear objective; the folly must appear to be a genuine part of the target and not merely in the satirist's perception of the target. Cowper could maintain that kind of objectivity only when there was really nothing at stake. Poking fun at the world of John Gilpin is harmless, for there is no suggestion that the world is real beyond the confines of the poem. When the subject is real, however, Cowper cannot stand aside. He lacks wit, in the neoclassical sense of the word. Wit consisted of the genius needed to conceive the raw material of art and the acquired good taste to know how to arrange bits of that material into a unified whole. Wit did not allow for the subjective intrusion of the author's personal problems. Cowper's genius was so intertwined with his special mental condition that he could not remain detached, and when he tried, his acquired skill could only arrange conventions, substitutes for his unique raw material. Moreover, Cowper lacked the satirist's willingness to ridicule. He had nothing against humanity. The shipmates are guiltless in the tragedy of the castaway. Humanity, to be sure, has its delusions and vanities, but Cowper preferred the deflected blow to the sharp thrust.

### THE TASK

*The Task* is Cowper's major achievement, and it is the satiric Cowper who introduces the work. His friend, Lady Austin, had suggested a sofa as an appropriate topic for a poem in blank verse. Of course, such a subject could only be addressed satirically, and Cowper elected the conventional form of mock-heroic. Specifically, he alluded to *The Aeneid* with "I sing the sofa" and thereby suggested that a modern Vergil would be hard pressed to find in eighteenth century society a topic deserving heroic treatment. However, the sofa is more than simply a mean subject, it is a quite appropriate symbol for sloth and luxury, the very qualities responsible for society's falling away from the truly heroic. Having called attention to the problem, there is little more for the sofa to do, except that it led Cowper to something worth saying, and he needed a structure less restrictive of his own involvement than the mock-heroic. So with a comment on how he prefers walks in the country to life on the sofa, Cowper shifts to an appreciation of nature theme and the *I* who had been the Vergilian persona of the satire suddenly becomes Cowper himself.

*The Task* is far too long a work for detailed analysis here. Its five thousand lines are divided into six parts: "The Sofa," "The Time-Piece," "The Garden," "The Winter Evening," "The Winter Morning Walk," and "The Winter Walk at Noon." The question of the overall unity of the work has probably attracted the greatest amount of critical attention. Cowper's own comments about the poem indicate that he was not aiming at tight thematic development; rather, the ideas were naturally suggested by immediately preceding ideas with the whole moving along with the ease of an intelligent but unplanned conversation.

Cowper's style, once the mock-heroic has been dropped, certainly suggests conversation. The diction is elegant but natural, quite different from the language of the other popular eighteenth century nature poet James Thomson, whose baroque language in *The Seasons* (1730, 1744) imitated the grand style of John Milton. Moreover, Cowper's blank verse avoids the end-stopped lines used by Thomson, which detracted from the conversational effect by their epigrammatic regularity. The deceptively artless ease of the poem with its several scenes, frequent digressions, and inclusion of highly personal material might easily lead the reader to conclude that the poet is recording a stream of consciousness with no central purpose or theme in mind. In fact, *The Task* is concerned with the need and search for balance in nature and human life. The sofa itself suggests the theme, for if it represents the scale tipping toward excessive luxury, there must somewhere in the range of experience be an ideal condition against which such excesses can be recognized and measured.

The ultimate excess to which the sofa points is the city, London, which on a physical plane reveals squalor, corruption, and insanity; its spiritual reality is sin. The opposite side of the scale also has a spiritual and physical existence. Spiritually, this extreme is the untempered wrath of God, pure divine power; on the physical level, such power is reflected in disturbances in nature and the brutalism that is the alternative to civilization. The early books explore the extremes and present the rural countryside as perhaps the best balance. This balance is insecure, however, for intrusions of both natural and human turmoil bring constant disturbance. The latter parts of the poem demonstrate the futility of finding a secure position in the physical environment. For those who enjoy God's grace, conversion can clarify the balance and bring freedom and order. The final book reveals God as the ultimate source of harmony. In his infinite kindness and infinite sternness, the Father judges all, and that judgment is perfection.

Among the landscape descriptions, character sketches, social criticism, and personal confessions, a unifying theme is perceptible if not obvious in *The Task*, and interestingly, it is the theme that best describes Cowper's life and art, the quest for a place of stability, a point of balance. In his art, he experimented to find his own voice, and he found it between the extremes of objectivity, toward which most art of his age tended, and the subjectivity that would characterize the art of the next generation. In the task of his life, he sought the balance of sanity, a quiet place of his own between the stress of urban society and the horror of being utterly alone, a castaway in a sea of despair. Tragically, he could not occupy that stable middle ground for very long; but in his best poetry, he created a remarkable sanity and said still-important things in a way that cannot easily be pigeonholed as neoclassical or Romantic but is uniquely Cowper.

## OTHER MAJOR WORKS

NONFICTION: *Correspondence, Arranged in Chronological Order*, 1904 (4 volumes); *The Centenary Letters*, 2000 (Simon Malpas, editor).

## BIBLIOGRAPHY

Brunström, Conrad. *William Cowper: Religion, Satire, Society*. Lewisburg, Pa.: Bucknell University Press, 2004. A critical study of the poet's significance. Aimed at serious scholars.

Cowper, William. *The Centenary Letters*. Edited by Simon Malpas. Manchester, England: Fyfield Books, 2000. A collection of Cowper's correspondence with a biographical introduction by Malpas.

Ella, George Melvyn. *William Cowper: Poet of Paradise*. Durham, England: Evangelical Press, 1993. Criticism and interpretation of Cowper's work with an extensive bibliography.

Free, William Norris. *William Cowper*. New York: Twayne, 1970. This 215-page work takes a biographical approach to interpretations of *The Task, Olney Hymns*, and Cowper's short poems. Norris suggests that Cowper's experiences had influence on poetic elements such as theme, structure, tone, and metaphor. Includes a lengthy bibliography, notes, and an index.

Hopps, Gavin, and Jane Stabler, eds. *Romanticism and Religion from William Cowper to Wallace Stevens*. Burlington, Vt.: Ashgate, 2006. Contains an essay on Cowper's poetry that presents his religious views and places him among the Romanticists.

King, James. *William Cowper: A Biography*. Durham, N.C.: Duke University Press, 1986. The standard biography that corrected many of the oversights and inaccuracies of early biographies. The poetical works are discussed as markers in the chronology of Cowper's life. The 340-page work includes an extensive index and notes.

Newey, Vincent. *Cowper's Poetry: A Critical Study and Reassessment*. Totowa, N.J.: Barnes & Noble, 1982. Newey's intelligent approach closely examines Cowper's work psychodramatically and sees the poet as a genius craftsperson of complex, contemporary, relevant poetry. The 358-page volume looks at *The Task*, moral satires, hymns, and comic verse. Includes a chronology and index of persons and works.

Nicholson, Norman. *William Cowper*. 1951. Reprint. London: Longman, 1970. A comprehensive critical work that primarily discusses the influence of the evangelical revival on Cowper. Nicholson sees Evangelicalism as a vigorous and emotional movement that paralleled Romanticism. Although Cowper's poetic sensibility first developed under Evangelicalism, his early poetry reflects contemporary religious and social thought and later becomes partially independent of the movement to share aspects with Romanticism.

Ryskamp, Charles. *William Cowper of the Inner Temple, Esq*. New York: Cambridge University Press, 1959. This 270-page book studies Cowper's life and works before 1786, focusing on his life and literary activities as a Templar and gentleman. Appendixes include previously uncollected letters, essays, poems, and contributions to magazines. Supplemented by illustrations, notes on Cowper's friends and relatives, and an index.

*William J. Heim*

# GEORGE CRABBE

**Born:** Aldeburgh, Suffolk, England; December 24, 1754

**Died:** Trowbridge, Wiltshire, England; February 3, 1832

PRINCIPAL POETRY
*Inebriety*, 1775
*The Candidate*, 1780
*The Library*, 1781
*The Village*, 1783
*The News-Paper*, 1785
*Poems*, 1807
*The Borough: A Poem, in Twenty-four Letters*, 1810
*Tales in Verse*, 1812
*Tales of the Hall*, 1819
*Poetical Works*, 1834 (8 volumes)

OTHER LITERARY FORMS

Little has survived of the nonverse writings of George Crabbe (krab). Extant are critical prose prefaces to various of his published verse collections, a treatise on "The Natural History of the Vale of Belvoir" that appeared in 1795, an autobiographical sketch published anonymously in *The New Monthly Magazine* in 1816, a selection of his sermons published posthumously in 1850, and certain of his letters, journals, and notebook entries that have been published in varying formats throughout the years since his death. With the exception of several of the critical prefaces, particularly that which accompanies *Tales in Verse*, and portions of the letters and journal entries, these do not shed significant light on Crabbe's poetic accomplishments. In 1801-1802, Crabbe is known to have written and subsequently burned three novels and an extensive prose treatise on botany.

ACHIEVEMENTS

The problem of assessing George Crabbe's achievements as a poet has proved a difficult one from the start. It vexed Crabbe's contemporaries and continues in some measure to vex scholars today. To a large extent this may be caused by the difficulties in classification.

His works bridge the gap between neoclassicism and Romanticism and on separate occasions—or even simultaneously—display characteristics of both movements. As the bewildering variety of labels that have been applied to Crabbe indicate, the multifaceted nature of his canon defies easy categorization. He has been termed a realist, a naturalist, an Augustan, a Romantic, a sociological novelist in verse, a psychological dramatist, a social critic, a poetic practitioner of the scientific method, a didactic moralist, a social historian, a "Dutch painter," and a human camera. Such labels, often supportable when applied to selected portions of Crabbe's work, do not appear useful in describing his total achievement. Nevertheless, it is on such restricted interpretations that estimations of Crabbe have frequently been built. While attesting to his artistic versatility and providing a focal point for isolated instances of detailed analysis and appreciation, the result has been in large part detrimental to the establishment of a sound critical tradition with respect to Crabbe, for readers of all types—and especially the critics—are most often reluctant to give serious consideration to an artist who cannot be conveniently classified.

Crabbe's earliest literary productions were clearly derivative, most often fashionable satires and other forms in the Augustan mode, but after the appearance of *The Village* one begins to find such terms as "original," "unique," and "inventive" being consistently applied to him. Samuel Johnson, who read *The Village* in manuscript, praised it as "original, vigorous, and elegant." The sensation surrounding the publication of *The Village* proved to be a mixed blessing, for while it won Crabbe many admirers, it also served to fix him in the popular imagination as an antipastoralist and as the "poet of the poor," tags that are misleading and inaccurate when applied to a large part of his work. Crabbe's art showed consistent development throughout his long writing career, particularly in the progressively sophisticated manner in which he articulated his main form, narrative verse. He experimented frequently with narrative techniques and with innovative framing concepts for his collections of verse tales and is often credited with having influenced such writers of prose fiction as Jane Austen and Thomas Hardy. On the other hand, he remained doggedly faithful to that stalwart of eighteenth century prosody, the heroic couplet, departing from it only rarely in his more than sixty-five thousand lines of published verse. Following the appearance of *The Village*, Crabbe's reputation continued to grow, despite a twenty-two-year hiatus in his publishing career, finally declining in his later years largely as a result of the predominant influence of Romantic literary tastes. In his time, he was praised highly by Johnson; Sir Walter Scott; Lord Byron, and even William Wordsworth, with whom he had little in common in either taste or technique; his most consistent and eloquent champion, however, was Francis Jeffrey, the formidable critic of *Edinburgh Review*. His harshest critics, on the other hand, were Samuel Taylor Coleridge and William Hazlitt, both of whom found him significantly deficient in "imagination" (as the Romantics were prone to define that term) owing to his meticulous attention to realistic detail. The high estimation of Crabbe's achievements drifted slowly downward throughout the course of the nineteenth century but began to revive in the twentieth century with largely favorable critical reassessments by such figures as E. M. Forster, F. L. Lucas, and F. R. Leavis. His work has been the subject of several extended critical studies, and although it is doubtful that he will ever be awarded a place among the highest ranking English poets, it appears certain that he is again being accorded some of the critical and popular esteem in which he once was held.

## BIOGRAPHY

George Crabbe was born on Christmas Eve in 1754 in Aldeburgh (or, as it was then known, Aldborough), Suffolk, the eldest son of the local collector of salt duties, who early recognized the intellectual potential of his son and endeavored to provide educational opportunities for him beyond those normally accessible to one in his station. Once a busy and prosperous seaport, Aldeburgh had dwindled in size and importance by the middle of the eighteenth century and contained a populace whose general poverty, ignorance, and ill-nature was matched by the isolated, inhospitable conditions of a seacoast plagued by tempestuous weather and surrounded by a dreary countryside consisting largely of salt marshes, heaths, and tidal flats. Crabbe's early experiences in this setting left a lasting impression:

Throughout his life, Aldeburgh retained a strong hold on his imagination. This strange mixture of fascination and repugnance formed the basis for a large number of the characters and settings that are possibly the most striking features of his poetry.

Between the ages of eight and thirteen, Crabbe's father arranged for him to attend grammar schools in Bungay and Stowmarket, both in Norfolk, where he received the foundations of a classical education and is known to have made his first attempts at composing doggerel verse. Unable to continue financing his son's education and having determined that the field of medicine would be the most suitable to his son's talents and inclinations, the elder Crabbe in 1768 engaged for George to be bound as an apprentice to an apothecary and surgeon at Wickhambrook, near Bury St. Edmund's, in Suffolk. Used more as a farmhand than as a surgical apprentice, young Crabbe was exceedingly unhappy there and, in 1771, was removed by his father to a more favorable situation in Woodbridge, Suffolk. These were to prove relatively happy years, for though he seems to have shown no great interest in his medical studies, life in Woodbridge was an agreeable contrast to what he had known in Aldeburgh and Wickhambrook. It was also during this period that he met and courted his future wife, Sarah Elmy, and saw his first poem of any consequence, *Inebriety*, appear in print in 1775.

In the summer of that year, his apprenticeship over, Crabbe returned to Aldeburgh, and after a period of uncertainty during which he worked as a common laborer on the docks (much to the dismay of his father), he finally began to practice his profession late in the year. The next four years were particularly frustrating and unhappy ones for the young doctor: It is clear that he never had any real confidence in his abilities as a physician and that he felt himself to be surrounded by people who did not appreciate him and to whom he felt in every way superior. His practice was unsuccessful, and his continuing poverty made it appear doubtful whether he would ever find himself in a position financially stable enough to marry his beloved Sarah. Thus, in early 1780, he abandoned his practice, borrowed five pounds from a local philanthropist, and journeyed to London to take his chances as a poet. Although he would never again return to the profession of medicine, the years spent in training and practice were not entirely wasted ones, for they are undoubtedly responsible for such often-noted features of his poetry as his minute attention to detail and his fascination with aberrant psychological states.

London did not treat Crabbe kindly. Although he did manage to publish *The Candidate*, a dull, unreadable poem, his attempts to secure patronage were singularly unsuccessful, and his increasingly desperate financial state brought him to the point where, by early 1781, he was threatened with debtors' prison. At this propitious moment, he found the patron he had been seeking, the influential statesman Edmund Burke, who eased his financial straits, helped him find publishers for his poetry, and introduced him to such eminent figures of the day as Sir Joshua Reynolds, Charles James Fox, and Johnson. It was Burke also who convinced Crabbe to take holy orders in the Anglican Church and who used his influence to get the young poet ordained, which occurred in 1782. Burke then secured for him a position that allowed him to pursue his duties as a clergyman while at the same time leaving sufficient leisure to write poetry.

His financial worries finally over, his career set, Crabbe entered a largely productive and happy phase in his life. He and Sarah were married in 1783, and over the years, Crabbe was assigned to various livings in Suffolk and Leicestershire. In the early 1790's, the deaths of several of their children affected Sarah's mental state in a way that would become progressively more desperate until her death in 1813. At about the same time, Crabbe began to suffer from vertigo and digestive ailments. Opium was prescribed, and he continued to use the drug for the remainder of his life. For these and perhaps other reasons, he published no poetry for a period of twenty-two years, though he is known to have continued writing poems and other literary works, the majority of which he ultimately destroyed. Crabbe's literary reemergence in 1807 marked the beginning of his most significant period of poetic production, culminating in the 1819 publication of *Tales of the Hall*. Following Sarah's death, he assumed the livings at Trowbridge, in Wiltshire, where he passed the remaining years of his life as a celebrated member of his

*George Crabbe* (Hulton Archive/Getty Images)

community, taking occasional trips to London and Suffolk to visit old friends. Though he never remarried, he maintained a lively correspondence with admiring female readers in several parts of the British Isles. Crabbe died in the rectory at Trowbridge on February 3, 1832.

ANALYSIS

No critical assessment of George Crabbe's work has ever isolated his essence more precisely than do the words he himself provided in the concluding lines of letter 1 of *The Borough*:

> Of sea or river, of a quay or street,
> The best description must be incomplete;
> But when a happier theme succeeds, and when
> Men are our subjects and the deeds of men;
> Then may we find the Muse in happier style,
> And we may sometimes sigh and sometimes smile.

Any reader who has generously sampled Crabbe's work would likely agree with the point suggested here: It is indeed people and their actions that form the central focus in the majority of his poems. Crabbe was, above all else, a narrative poet, and in the estimation of some critics second only to Geoffrey Chaucer. Paradoxically, however, his reputation in his own day (and to some extent even in the present) was not primarily based on that fact. Rather, he was seen as a painter in words—a master of highly particularized visual imagery who conjured up vivid landscapes and interior settings, most often for the purpose of emphasizing the sordid and brutal elements of existence. Though people might be present in these scenes, they were generally seen as little more than corollary features to the inanimate components dominating the whole (such as the famous description of the aged shepherd in the poorhouse found in book 1 of *The Village*). Hence, Sir Walter Scott's well-known epithet, "nature's sternest poet" ("nature" in the nineteenth century sense of the term), has come to epitomize the predominant attitude toward Crabbe as a poet. That view is indeed unfortunate, for the narrowness of its emphasis ignores the very features of Crabbe's work on which his surest claim to significance might be built. Missing in this approach, for example, is any notion of the richness and diversity of Crabbe's humor, surely one of his most delightful features. Furthermore, such a limited view fails to note the increasingly optimistic tone of Crabbe's work, in its progress from *The Village* to *Tales of the Hall*. Most important, however, the opinion reverses what surely must be the proper emphasis when considering Crabbe's poetry as a whole: People, rather than merely serving to enhance Crabbe's realistic descriptions, are in fact the subject and center of his concern. Nature and external detail, while present to a significant degree in his poetry, exist primarily to illuminate his fascination with character.

If any one reason might be cited for the disproportionate emphasis given to Crabbe's descriptive and pessimistic qualities, it would most likely be the influence of *The Village*. This poem, a sensation in its own day and still the most consistently anthologized of Crabbe's works, paints an unrelentingly bleak picture of human existence in a manner that is essentially descriptive and makes extensive use of external detail. These same concerns and techniques may also be seen to operate in large portions of Crabbe's next two major works, *The Parish Register* (which appeared in *Poems*) and *The Borough*. In all these, the influence of

Crabbe's early life, and especially his perceptions of his native town of Aldeburgh, form the controlling focus. At the same time, however, as early as *The Village* itself and certainly in the works that follow it, the perceptive reader can note Crabbe's increasing interest in character and narration. By the time *Tales in Verse* was published, the mode had become completely narrative and continued to be so throughout the poet's writing career.

Moreover, a concomitant softening of the hard lines presented in Crabbe's early poetry becomes increasingly evident as he moved more and more in the direction of a psychological and sociological examination of the factors necessary for successful human interaction. True, social criticism, human suffering, and the stultifying effects of an inhospitable environment are factors that never disappear entirely from Crabbe's writings. As time goes on, however, they retreat significantly from their earlier position of predominance and assume no more than their proportionate role in what Jeffrey referred to as "the pattern of Crabbe's arabesque."

With a canon as large as Crabbe's, it is perhaps to be expected that a remarkably large and diverse array of themes and motifs may be cataloged when examining his work as a whole. Nevertheless, certain patterns recur frequently enough in dynamic variation so as to be considered dominant. Proceeding, as they invariably do, from an intense interest in character and in human interaction, they are all rich in psychological and sociological insights. Chief among them are the problems of moral isolation, of the influence of relatives on young minds, of success and failure in matters of love, courtship and marriage, and of the search for reconciliation as an antidote to bitterness and estrangement. To watch these thematic concerns grow in texture and complexity as Crabbe explores them in a succession of tales is one of the pleasures of reading a generous and representative selection of his works. Of no less interest is the process of experimentation and refinement by which Crabbe first discovers and then seeks to perfect the stylistic and structural mechanisms best suited to his characteristic narrative voice.

### THE VILLAGE

From the moment of its first appearance in 1783 to the present, the most immediate response of critics and general readers alike has been to see *The Village* as a poem written in response to Oliver Goldsmith's *The Deserted Village* (1770), published thirteen years earlier. This is certainly understandable. The respective titles invite such comparison, and Crabbe himself explicitly alludes to Goldsmith's poem on several occasions. Furthermore, it is apparent to even the most casual reader that Crabbe's Aldeburgh (for most assuredly it is Aldeburgh that forms the model for *The Village*) is in every conceivable way the very antithesis of Goldsmith's Auburn. Although all this is true, the notion of Crabbe's poem as a simple rebuttal of Goldsmith is far too limiting; rather, it should be seen as a poem that constitutes in large part a reaction against the entire eighteenth century literary convention that governs Goldsmith's poem. The term antipastoral is a convenient label to use here, but only if one keeps in mind the fact that Crabbe's bias against the pastoral mode is somewhat specialized. It is not classical pastoralism or even its manifestations in earlier English poetry to which Crabbe objects, but rather the manner in which, in the eighteenth century, poets and public alike had irrationally come to accept the conventions of pastoral description as constituting accurate and useful representations of rural life. If it is somewhat difficult to understand the tone of outrage that underlies the cutting edge of Crabbe's realism in this poem, it is perhaps because most modern readers, unlike Crabbe, have been spared the effusions of countless minor poets, most of them deservedly now forgotten, whose celebrations of the joys of pastoral rusticity filled the "poet's corner" of many a fashionable eighteenth century magazine. He speaks to them when he says: "Yes, thus the Muses sing of happy swains,/ Because the Muses never knew their pains." Crabbe knew their pains; he had felt many of them himself, perhaps too many to assure his own objectivity. For, whatever the merits of seeing *The Village* as a realistic rejoinder to an artificial and decadent literary tradition, one must always remember that Crabbe's brand of realism may at times in itself be somewhat suspect by virtue of the conscious and unconscious prejudices he bears toward his subject matter.

*The Village* consists of two parts—books 1 and 2— but it is book 1 that has always commanded the greatest interest. This portion of the poem is dominated by a number of descriptive set pieces, perhaps the most frequently quoted passages in all of Crabbe's works. The first of these, and the one that perhaps best epitomizes the poem's uncompromisingly harsh view of rural life, concerns the countryside that surrounds the village— the coastline and adjoining heaths. It is a bleak, barren, forbidding prospect that Crabbe presents, a landscape inhospitable to people and barely capable of sustaining life of any sort. Images of decay and sickness, of despair, of almost anthropomorphic hostility pervade the descriptions, chiefly of vegetation, of this isolated sector of the East Anglian seacoast. Almost imperceptibly, Crabbe moves from this dominant sense of place to his initial, tentative descriptions of the inhabitants, the first of many instances in his poetry in which people and physical setting are juxtaposed in meaningful counterpoint.

The next of the famous set pieces in the poem is a description of the village poorhouse, the vividness and intensity of which so struck Crabbe's contemporaries that the language they frequently used to discuss it is of a sort most generally reserved for discussions of painting. Several modern commentators have argued that, in this section of the poem, Crabbe is functioning primarily as a social critic, calling into question, among other things, the prevailing Poor Laws and their administration in local parishes. This may be so; nevertheless, it is again the pure descriptive vividness of this scene that remains its most memorable feature. The details relating to the exterior and interior of the building form a backdrop to the cataloging of its miserable inhabitants. Again, the predominant images are of decay, oppressiveness, and despair. Amid these scenes of not-so-quiet desperation, Crabbe gives particular attention to one inhabitant of the poorhouse, an old shepherd, worn out, useless, lodged there to pine away his days in loneliness and frustration. Perhaps nowhere else in the poem does Crabbe so brutally and cynically mock the pastoral ideal. Book 1 ends with vicious satirical portraits of the doctor and priest who, paid by the parish to attend to the needs of the inhabitants of the poorhouse, openly and contemptuously neglect their duties.

Book 2 is considerably less successful in its execution, primarily owing to a lack of consistency in tone and format. Crabbe begins by intimating that he wishes to soften his harsh picture of village life by showing some of its gentler moments; soon, however, this degenerates into a description and condemnation of the drunkenness of the villagers, a subject that he had previously explored in the youthful *Inebriety*. Even more disturbing, however, is the poem's conclusion, which takes the form of an unrelated and lengthy eulogy on Lord Robert Manners, late younger brother of the duke of Rutland, the man whom Crabbe was currently serving as private chaplain.

Although it is probably his best-known work and contains some of his finest descriptive writing, *The Village* is hardly Crabbe's most representative poem. In his treatment of the aged shepherd, in the satiric portraits of the doctor and priest, one may sense the embryonic forms of the distinctive narrative voice that would ultimately come to dominate his poetry; before this manifested itself, however, a number of years had intervened.

### POEMS

With the exception of *The News-Paper*, a lukewarm satire on the periodical press very much in the Augustan mode, Crabbe published no poetry in the period between the appearance of *The Village* in 1783 and the release of the collection, *Poems*, in 1807. That he was not artistically inactive during this period, however, is evidenced by the vigor and diversity of the poems found in the 1807 volume, and there is ample reason to lament the many efforts in manuscript he is known to have destroyed at this time. In addition to his previously published works, the 1807 *Poems* contained a number of commendable new efforts, including "The Birth of Flattery," "The Hall of Justice," and the provocative "Sir Eustace Grey." All these works show Crabbe experimenting with various narrative techniques. The star attraction of the new collection, however, was a much longer poem entitled *The Parish Register*.

### THE PARISH REGISTER

Readers who enjoyed the angry, debunking tone of Crabbe's antipastoralism in *The Village* were probably delighted by the first several hundred lines of *The Parish Register*, which seem to signal a continuation of the same interests. "Since vice the world subdued and waters drown'd,/ Auburn and Eden can no more be found," Crabbe notes wryly and then proceeds to un-

veil a number of highly particularized descriptions, the most memorable of which outlines in vivid and often disgusting detail the vice and squalor of a poor village street. If anything, Crabbe appears to be well on his way to outdoing his previous efforts in this vein. At this point, however, the poem suddenly takes a new tack and begins to present a series of narratives that in the aggregate constitute its dominant feature.

The plan of *The Parish Register* is, in essence, simple and ingenious. A narrative voice is created by Crabbe; it is that of the parish priest of a small village who, at year's end, reviews the records in his church register and comments in varying fashion on the real-life stories that lie behind the cold names and dates. The poem has three divisions—"Baptisms," "Marriages," and "Burials"—and in each the loquacious speaker presents a number of narratives ranging in length and complexity from simple vignettes of a few lines to more ambitious efforts resembling full-blown tales. Generally, the best narratives are found in "Baptisms" and "Burials," particularly in the latter. Two stories of chief interest in the "Baptisms" section are that of Lucy, the daughter of a proud and wealthy miller, who conceives a child out of wedlock, is ostracized by her father and the community, and slowly goes mad, and that of Richard Monday, a foundling brought up and abused in the village poorhouse, who leaves the village to become an enormous success in the world and on his deathbed leaves only a pittance to his native town. "Burials" contains a number of memorable portraits, including those of the prudent, matriarchal Widow Goe and of old Sexton Dibble, who managed to outlive the five parsons he successively served. The most interesting, however, are the stories of Robin Dingley and Roger Cuff. In the first of these, Robin, a poor but contented man, becomes the victim of a clever attorney who leads him to place all his hopes on the possibility of a rich inheritance; when these are dashed, the loss drives him crazy and makes him a wanderer for life. The acuteness of Crabbe's psychological perceptions are noteworthy in this story, one of the first of a number of tales in which he explores the bases of aberrant behavior. Borrowing certain motifs from older folk tales, the story of Roger Cuff tells of a young man who has a falling out with his kin, goes off to sea, and years later, having made his fortune, returns disguised as a beggar to test the moral fiber of the surviving members of his family. Refused by the closest of them, he shares his wealth with an unpretentious distant relative who lives as a reclusive hermit in the forest. Years later, in "The Family of Love," one of the stories from his posthumous collection of tales, Crabbe returned to this theme but with significant alterations.

In *The Parish Register*, one can observe Crabbe in the process of discovering his considerable talents as a writer of narrative verse. His experimentations with frame, point of view, dialogue and character interaction, and a host of other practical and thematic considerations, point the way toward more sophisticated efforts yet to come. Even as he was finishing this poem, he was hard at work on a far more ambitious undertaking, *The Borough*.

## THE BOROUGH

One of Crabbe's longest poems—approximately eight thousand lines—*The Borough* is also one of his most perplexing and in many ways his least successful effort when considered as a whole. Within its vast scope, however, there are isolated instances of writing that rank among the poet's best. As in *The Village* and *The Parish Register*, the subject of Crabbe's third major poem is once again a thinly disguised Aldeburgh. This time, however, the scale is much more ambitious, for, as he makes clear in his lengthy prose preface and in the opening section of the poem, the aim of *The Borough* is nothing less than complete description: All aspects of the town, its buildings, trades and professions, public institutions, social activities, and inhabitants are to be revealed. Naturally, the scheme is so grandiose as to preclude its complete achievement, but the efforts that Crabbe makes in pursuing it are in themselves somewhat remarkable. The result, unfortunately, sometimes seems more akin to social history than to poetry. In structure, the poem is epistolary, consisting of a series of twenty-four verse letters written by a resident of the borough to a friend in a far distant part of the country who has requested a description of the place. Among them are some of the dullest pieces of writing in Crabbe's entire canon, including the letters on "Elections," "The Hospital and Governors," and "Schools." Paradoxically, however, this same ponderous frame-

work yields some of Crabbe's finest narrative pieces.

Letters 19 to 22, collectively entitled "The Poor of the Borough," provide the most fully developed narratives found in Crabbe's work to this point. They are, in essence, short stories in verse, each one focusing on a different character type and probing the psychological dimensions of motivation and consequence. "Ellen Orford" (letter 20), a story in which Crabbe broadens his narrative technique by having Ellen tell a large part of her own history, is an account of cumulative personal tragedy, borne stoically by a woman whose essential goodness and faith in God enable her to rise above what Hamlet termed "the slings and arrows of outrageous fortune." No such inspirational note is provided in "Abel Keene" (letter 21), in which a pious man is seduced into abandoning his faith, the process ending in despair and suicide. A fascinating study of self-deception and its disastrous results is presented in "The Parish Clerk" (letter 19), which tells the story of Jachin, the spiritually proud clerk of the parish who feels he is above sin and alienates everyone with his smug sanctimony. Tempted by his poverty and secure in the rationalizations he has constructed for his conduct as well as in the foolproof method he has devised for its implementation, Jachin begins to steal from the collection plate during services. Eventually caught and publicly disgraced, he goes the way of many of Crabbe's moral outcasts, retreating from the society of men to blend into the bleakness of the surrounding countryside, where his mental and physical energies are gradually dissipated and death comes as a welcome relief.

By most accounts, the finest story in *The Borough*, perhaps the best in all Crabbe's canon, is "Peter Grimes" (letter 22), on which Benjamin Britten based his well-known opera. The tale has so many remarkable features—its implicit attack on the abuses of the apprentice system, its subtle articulation of the notion that the ultimate responsibility for deviant behavior may rest within the society that fosters it, its powerful juxtapositions of external description and interior states of mind, and its surprisingly modern probing of the psychological bases of child abuse—that it is difficult to isolate any one of them as the key factor in assessing the impact it has had on most readers. A misanthropic fisherman who lives on the fringes of his community, Peter

Grimes emerged from a childhood in which he irrationally hated the father who loved him. As an adult, he acquires and successively destroys three young orphans from London who are bound to him as apprentices. The townspeople, aware of what is occurring, turn their backs on what they view as none of their business ("Grimes is at his exercise," they say when the cries of his victims are heard in the town's streets), until the death of the third boy proves to be more than they can ignore. Although they cannot legally punish him—nothing can be proved conclusively—Grimes is forbidden to take any more apprentices and is ostracized by the community. He withdraws into the desolation of the tidal flats and salt marshes surrounding his village, and there, brooding alone under the hot sun, he becomes possessed by wild and persistent visions of his father and the murdered apprentices, who dance on the waters and beckon him to join them in their element. His mind shattered, he sinks to death in an agony of terror and desperation. "Peter Grimes" is a story of considerable power, owing in large part to Crabbe's masterful conception of the title character, who, like William Shakespeare's Iago and Herman Melville's Claggart, taxes the limits of critical understanding.

Despite the ponderous framing device employed by Crabbe in *The Borough*, it is possible in the narrative portions of that poem to see him working toward the use of a narrator who is to a certain degree effaced, as well as toward an occasional reliance on multiple points of view. In *Tales in Verse*, which appeared in 1812, he continued those trends and abandoned, temporarily, the use of any sort of framing device. Here, in his first collection of poetry devoted entirely to narrative themes, Crabbe presents a series of twenty-one discrete verse tales in which, as he notes in his preface

> the attempt at union therefore has been relinquished, and these relations are submitted to the public, connected by no other circumstance than their being the productions of the same author, and devoted to the same purpose, the entertainment of his readers.

Ironically, what Crabbe himself half-apologetically presented as a loose compendium of disparate elements may, in fact, be his most thoroughly integrated work, for there is one factor that the vast majority of the individual tales share in common: They are, in large part, variations from every conceivable point of view on the themes of love, courtship, and marriage.

## TALES IN VERSE

In the collection *Tales in Verse*, Crabbe presents a number of his most memorable stories. One useful method of approaching the collection is to distinguish between those tales in which two persons have successfully found the basis for compatibility, avoiding the numerous pitfalls that at any point in the love-courtship-marriage continuum can destroy the entire process, and those in which the reverse has occurred. Thus, in the latter category may be grouped such tales as "Procrastination" (4), "The Patron" (5), "The Mother" (8), "Squire Thomas: Or, The Precipitate Choice" (12), and "Resentment" (17), while the former is represented by "The Parting Hour" (2), "The Frank Courtship" (6), "The Widow's Tale" (7), "Arabella" (9), "The Lover's Journey" (10), "Jesse and Colin" (13), "The Confidant" (16), and "The Wager" (18). Myriad influences may affect the delicate balance of the relationships explored in these tales, ensuring their ultimate success or failure, but two situations recur in a variety of forms. In the first of them, Crabbe explores the power, for better or for worse, that a third person may exert on a couple's life. The influence may range from a healthy one, as in the case of the emancipated aunt in "The Frank Courtship," to that which is destructive, as in "The Mother." In other situations, the influence may present an obstacle that must be overcome and resolved so that the relationship may achieve its true potential, as is demonstrated in "The Confidant." The other recurring situation, one that came to be a dominant motif in Crabbe's remaining work, is the need to seek out and establish the compassionate basis of understanding that must ultimately be the cornerstone of any successful, lasting human relationship. Frequently, this is seen in the context of a major disrupting incident in a couple's life that tests the ability of one of them to display the qualities of forgiveness and understanding necessary to keep the relationship alive. The opposite effects of this type of situation are presented, respectively, in "Resentment" and "The Confidant," as well as in certain other of the tales.

Beyond its thematic articulations, which are at once perceptive and sophisticated, "The Frank Courtship" is a tale that commands attention by virtue of its tone and stylistic qualities. Perhaps nowhere else in Crabbe's poetry is dialogue used to such delightful effect as in the courting scene between Sybil and her young suitor, Josiah; it is a piece of dramatic interchange that in the sharpness and vivacity of language reminds one of the best of Shakespeare's romantic comedies. Further, the optimistic, at times almost playful, tone of this composition may be cited as one of several memorable instances in Crabbe's poetry that serve to balance the elements of somberness and pessimism most frequently ascribed to him.

### TALES OF THE HALL

In *Tales in Verse*, while not abandoning his interests in individual psychological observation, Crabbe moved strongly in the direction of exploring the dynamics of social interaction between people. This interest carried over into his next major production, *Tales of the Hall*. One of the features most immediately apparent in *Tales of the Hall* is the author's return to the use of a comprehensive framing device for the presentation of a number of separate tales. Crabbe has integrated within the controlling frame of his new collection the same sort of thematic cohesiveness that serves to connect the individual narratives of *Tales in Verse*. Again, the great majority of the various tales (here called "books") represent diverse angles of vision from which to observe the many features inherent in the love-courtship-marriage syndrome. As if to emphasize his desire to pursue these studies from as many angles as possible, Crabbe further complicates his design by experimenting freely with multiple points of view and with other structural complexities in certain of the tales.

The frame itself is of considerable interest and, in its complex pattern of development, has led more than one critic to the conclusion that *Tales of the Hall* may justifiably be termed a novel in verse. As outlined in "The Hall" (1) and the several books that immediately succeed it, the collection is bound by the story of two half brothers, George and Richard, who after a long separation have come together on a somewhat experimental basis to see what, if anything, they might have in common. Here, on the elder brother George's recently purchased estate (the Hall), they spend some weeks together, gradually wearing away the reserve and potential

misunderstandings that at various points threaten to disturb the growing bond between their vastly differing personalities. In the course of this process, they tell tales of various sorts, some concerning themselves, others about people they have known in the past or have recently met in the surrounding area, and are frequently joined by a third companion and narrator, the local vicar. As the various tales unfold, the story of George and Richard itself develops in texture and complexity, resolving itself amicably, if somewhat flatly, in the final book. If the overall form of *Tales of the Hall* may be compared to that of the novel, however, it also bears certain affinities in substance to the type of long autobiographical poem that was proving increasingly popular among poets during this period (as, for example, those of Wordsworth and Byron). A convincing case might be made for seeing George and Richard—and to a certain extent even Jacques, the vicar—as varying projections of Crabbe's own conceptualized self-image.

The quality of the individual stories of *Tales of the Hall* is perhaps more uneven than that of *Tales in Verse*. The best of the stories, however, are definitely of a very high order. One is "Smugglers and Poachers" (21), an intricately plotted tale that, in addition to evidencing Crabbe's ongoing concern with social injustices, provides, in its depiction of the enmity between the brothers James and Robert, a bitter and dramatic counterpoint to the happier circumstances of the brothers found in the frame tale. Estrangement and failure in matters of love continue to find expression, as in the powerfully tragic "Ruth" (5) or the more philosophical "Lady Barbara: Or, The Ghost" (16); but on the whole, the tone of this collection is more consistently optimistic than in any of Crabbe's previous efforts and the note of forgiveness and reconciliation that dominates a number of the tales continues a trend first noticed in *Tales in Verse*. Two tales that illustrate this rather well are "William Bailey" (19) and the structurally complex "Sir Owen Dale" (12), both of which feature central characters who ultimately come to realize that the errors of the past cannot be allowed to poison the present forever. If there is a moral lesson to be drawn from the essentially nondidactic poetry of the later Crabbe, it is surely this point.

Two years after Crabbe's death, there appeared the most complete edition of his poetry available up to that time. Edited by his son and including as its final volume the highly readable biographical account of his father's life, the *Poetical Works* of 1834 featured a number of poems never published by Crabbe during his lifetime, many of which were obviously still in a state of manuscript revision at the time of his death. Of chief interest among them is the group known collectively as *Posthumous Tales*.

### POSTHUMOUS TALES

Actually, the twenty-two tales that constitute this final collection of narrative verse fall into two groups. Tales 6 through 22 represent what may be described as draft versions of a new collection of poems that Crabbe had tentatively entitled *The Farewell and Return*. Crabbe's organizing principle in the collection posits a situation in which a young man leaves his native town and returns many years later to find it immensely changed. Each tale is divided into two basic parts, the first of which provides a description of a person or thing at the time of the narrator's departure, while the second involves an updating on the part of a friend whom the narrator encounters on his return. The concept, while ingenious in nature and serving to demonstrate Crabbe's continuing preoccupation with the problem of narrative frames, is far from successful; the individual tales often resolve themselves into a depressingly predictable series of variations on the theme of destructive mutability. These evident shortcomings should not be judged too harshly, however, since it is reasonable to assume that, given the chance for suitable revision, Crabbe would ultimately have rendered the collection consistent with the quality of his previous work. One tale from *The Farewell and Return* group, "The Boat Race" (18), is deserving of special mention, if only by virtue of its splendidly effective description of a sudden storm on the river and its disastrous effects.

In some respects, the best narratives in the *Posthumous Tales* are found in the five unrelated tales that begin the collection, including the delightful "Silford Hall: Or, The Happy Day" (1), a highly autobiographical account of an impressionable young lad's sense of wonder and delight on receiving a guided tour of an aristocrat's palatial estate. Also of significant interest is "The Family of Love" (2), a tale in many ways reminiscent of the account of Roger Cuff found in *The Parish Register*, but with the significant difference that the central character of this later narrative finds it within himself to forgive his erring kin, reestablishing the bond of human understanding he could so easily and irrevocably destroy. In this contrasting treatment of an earlier theme, one can again gauge the distance that Crabbe has traveled in his attitude toward the potential for social fulfillment.

In the last analysis, one cannot escape the conclusion that there is a certain amount of unevenness in Crabbe's work, perhaps enough to justify his exclusion from the first rank of English poets. His occasional difficulty in blending new characters into a narrative, his sometimes annoying penchant for wordy digressiveness, his periodic lapses in tone and in the handling of dialogue, even those infrequent examples of "bad lines" that his nineteenth century detractors so loved to quote—all these and perhaps others as well might be charged to him as observable defects in technique. To dwell too long and too hard on these factors, however, is to miss the true essence of Crabbe and to a large degree his power. In his relentless scrutiny of psychological and sociological themes, from the dark, brooding malevolence of "Peter Grimes" to the delicate social harmonies of "The Frank Courtship" and the frame of *Tales of the Hall*, one can clearly see the elements that link him securely to such widely divergent masters of English storytelling as Emily Brontë and Jane Austen. A later commentator on Crabbe, Oliver Sigworth, strikes the proper balance when he notes that "we may wish for various perfections which Crabbe did not attain, but, unique as he is, some may be happy in those which he possessed."

### OTHER MAJOR WORKS

NONFICTION: "The Natural History of the Vale of Belvoir," 1795; *Selected Letters and Journals of George Crabbe*, 1985 (Thomas C. Faulkner, editor).

### BIBLIOGRAPHY

Bareham, Tony. *George Crabbe*. New York: Barnes & Noble, 1977. Examines how Crabbe's poetry reflects contemporary ideas on religion, politics, psychology, and aesthetics. Emphasizes that Crabbe was a "proper spokesman" for mainstream English thought. The 245-page text includes an index and a chronology of major events in Crabbe's career.

Crabbe, George. *The Life of George Crabbe by His Son*. 1834. Reprint. London: Cresset, 1947. This standard biography, written from the unique perspective of the poet's son, offers a benign yet candid glimpse into the poet's personality. An introduction by Edmund Blunden provides further criticism of Crabbe's poetry, including an interesting discussion on the influence that Crabbe's training as a physician and clergyman had on his writing.

Edwards, Gavin. *George Crabbe's Poetry on Border Land*. Lewiston, N.Y.: E. Mellen Press, 1990. This critical work, organized by subject, takes a social historical approach to Crabbe's poems, dealing with Crabbe's ability to reflect his time accurately. It thoroughly discusses the concept of Crabbe as a realist, suggesting his poetry has a more complex relationship to history than just simple realism.

Hatch, Ronald B. *Crabbe's Arabesque: Social Drama in the Poetry of George Crabbe*. Montreal: McGill-Queen's University Press, 1976. Attempts to show how Crabbe grew beyond being simply a social critic by focusing on his handling of social issues in his poetry. Suggests that Crabbe's development can be seen in the way his poems' dramatic structures handle conflicting questions that either clash or are reconciled. Includes a chronology of Crabbe's life, a selected bibliography, and index.

Mahood, M. M. *The Poet as Botanist*. New York: Cambridge University Press, 2008. Contains a chapter looking at the descriptions of plants in Crabbe's poetry.

Pollard, Arthur, ed. *Crabbe: The Critical Heritage*. London: Routledge & Kegan Paul, 1972. An interesting compilation of criticism of Crabbe's writings by his contemporaries, including William Hazlitt, William Wordsworth, and Samuel Taylor Coleridge, along with later commentary. Arranged by individual works, the book also contains an informative introduction on Crabbe and his writing and indexes to names, works, characteristics, and periodicals.

Powell, Neil. *George Crabbe: An English Life, 1754-1832*. London: Pimlico, 2004. A readable biography of the poet that draws largely on the biography of his son and namesake.

Whitehead, Frank S. *George Crabbe: A Reappraisal*. Cranbury, N.J.: Associated University Presses, 1995. A critical assessment of Crabbe's work with bibliographical references and an index.

*Richard E. Meyer*

# RICHARD CRASHAW

**Born:** London, England; c. 1612
**Died:** Loreto (now in Italy); August 21, 1649

PRINCIPAL POETRY
*Epigrammatum Sacrorum Liber*, 1634
*Steps to the Temple*, 1646, 1648
*Carmen Deo Nostro*, 1652
*Poems: English, Latin, and Greek*, 1927, 1957
*Complete Poetry of Richard Crashaw*, 1970

OTHER LITERARY FORMS

Richard Crashaw (KRASH-aw) wrote primarily religious poetry reflecting the life of Christ and the symbols of Christianity.

ACHIEVEMENTS

Richard Crashaw occupies his niche in literary history as a sort of maverick Metaphysical whose poetry, although displaying many of the techniques and characteristics of John Donne and George Herbert, is unique in its baroque flamboyance and its strong Roman Catholic sensibilities.

A poet of fluctuating popularity, Crashaw has had his work treated as decadent Metaphysical poetry, as an outstanding example of ornate wit, as conventional Catholic devotion, and as intensely personal expression. His poems are longer and more elaborate than those of his model George Herbert, although his themes are narrower in focus. Crashaw is sometimes ranked with Donne and Herbert as a major Metaphysical poet; alternately, he is linked with such significant but minor writers as Abraham Cowley and Henry Vaughan.

In his intense rendering of Counter-Reformation Roman Catholic spirituality, as well as in his use of powerful visual experiences, Crashaw is distinctive. His poetry, widely popular in his own day, continued to attract readers and critical appreciation through the end of the seventeenth century and early in the eighteenth; it waned with the pre-Romantics and their successors and received relatively little notice until early in the twentieth century, when a host of major critics rediscovered religious poetry.

## BIOGRAPHY

The only child of William Crashaw, Richard Crashaw was born in London in either 1612 or 1613. His mother died when he was an infant; William Crashaw's second wife, Elizabeth, died when Richard was seven.

William Crashaw, Anglican divine, seems an unlikely parent for one of England's most famous converts to Roman Catholicism. Staunchly Low Church (some say Puritan) in his theology and in his lifestyle, the elder Crashaw devoted his life to preaching and writing, partly against the Laudian or High Church excesses in the Church of England but principally against what he perceived as the far greater dangers of the Church of Rome itself. In his efforts to know the full strength of the enemy, William Crashaw amassed an impressive collection of "Romish" writings; the critic can only speculate what effect these works, as well as his father's convictions, may have had on the spiritual development of Richard Crashaw.

After two years at London's famed Charterhouse School with its austere regime and classical curriculum, Crashaw was admitted, in 1631, to Pembroke College at Cambridge University. He would receive his A.B. in 1634 and his A.M. in 1638. He came to Pembroke with something of a reputation as a poet, a reputation that grew steadily as he produced Latin and Greek epigrams as well as English models, translations of the Psalms, and various occasional verses. These works form the basis of his 1634 publication, *Epigrammatum Sacrorum Liber*, the only work Crashaw himself would see through the printing process.

In 1635, Crashaw was appointed to a fellowship at Peterhouse College and sometime shortly thereafter was ordained to the Anglican priesthood. At Peterhouse, he was in direct contact with a circle of Laudian churchmen whose devotion, emphasis on liturgical ceremony and propriety, and reverence marked another step in Crashaw's eventual spiritual journey to Rome. Between 1635 and 1643, Crashaw also learned Spanish and Italian, moving with ease into the reading of the Spanish mystics, among them Teresa of Ávila and John of the Cross, as well as the rich tradition of Italian devotional literature. This material would strongly influence his later poetry, to the extent that his work is sometimes described as Continental rather than English.

Another significant event of the Peterhouse years was Crashaw's acquaintance with the community at Little Gidding, the religious retreat founded by George Herbert's friend Nicholas Ferrar. At Little Gidding, daily communal prayers and other religious observances were prescribed and orderly; the ancient church building was restored by the community to a Laudian elegance; the sanctuary fittings were rich and reverent. Although Ferrar and his followers steadfastly maintained their allegiance to Canterbury, the community was sometimes criticized as Papist.

These same criticisms were being levied at Peterhouse, where John Cosin, master of Peterhouse and a friend of Crashaw, was restoring and adorning the college chapel with equal devotion. Reports of the candles, incense, and crucifixes at Peterhouse continued to arouse Puritan suspicions; in the early 1640's, Cosin, along with Crashaw, was censured for "popish doctrine." In 1643, Parliament, goaded by the growing Puritan forces, forbade all altar ornaments as well as all pictures of saints. In these early years of the Civil Wars, Cosin, Crashaw, and four others were formally expelled from their fellowships and forced to depart.

The last six years of Crashaw's life, the key years of his conversion and the flowering of his poetry, are difficult to trace with any certainty. In 1644, he wrote from Leyden, speaking of his poverty and his loneliness. He may have revisited England, probably only for a short period. At some point, he made the acquaintance of Queen Henrietta Maria, who, as a devout Catholic, took up his cause in a letter to Pope Innocent. Somewhere in his physical and spiritual travels, Crashaw decided—or discerned a call—to commit himself to Roman Catholicism; this central experience cannot be dated. He continued to write, completing the poems his editor would entitle *Steps to the Temple* (a humble compliment to George Herbert's *The Temple*, 1633), revising many of his earlier poems, and working on the pieces that would form his last volume, *Carmen Deo Nostro*.

Crashaw spent time in Rome and in Paris, absorbing the rich art of these cities as well as their expressions of Catholicism. In Paris, he was befriended by the poet Abraham Cowley who, appalled at his friend's physical condition, obtained care and financial assistance for him. Back in Rome, Crashaw was appointed to the service of a cardinal and subsequently was sent to Loreto, the house where, according to Catholic tradition, the Virgin Mary received word of the Annunciation. Crashaw had barely reached this Marian shrine when he fell ill; he died August 21, 1649.

## ANALYSIS

Richard Crashaw's poetry may be divided into three groups of unequal significance for the scholar: the early epigrams, the secular poetry, and the religious poetry. The early epigrams and translations are studied, meticulous, and often occasional. The 178 Latin epigrams in *Epigrammatum Sacrorum Liber* show the influence of Martial and other classical writers. Crashaw also uses biblical motifs, particularly for his several English epigrams, displaying in his treatment of these themes an example of the close reading that will underlie his later work.

As a book of poetry, these early pieces are significant for the discipline they reveal and for their fascination with wordplay—puns, quips, repetitions, conceits—which Crashaw will later elevate to such exuberance. They are finger exercises, and if they lack the genius of John Milton's college ventures, they nevertheless suggest later greatness.

## DELIGHTS OF THE MUSES

Crashaw's second body of verse, the secular or nonsacred poetry, comprises much of the work found in *Delights of the Muses*, the volume appended to and published with *Steps to the Temple*. In that volume, Crashaw displays the Donnean Metaphysical, writing poems with titles such as "Wishes. To His (Supposed) Mistress," "A Picture Sent to a Friend," "Venus Putting on Mars His Armor," and "Loves Horoscope." Witty, polished, urbane, these poems show an accomplished and sophisticated writer delighting in the possibilities of English poetry. Intensely visual, these poems often select a single image and elaborate it in a manner reminiscent of the earlier emblem tradition. The classical tradition is still strong but the metrics are clearly English.

Although the poems in *Delights of the Muses* are often Donne-like in their wit, there is a certain reticence to them. The robust speaker of Donne's songs and sonnets is absent in Crashaw; there is relatively little use of the personal pronoun and none of the speechlike abruptness that makes so many of Donne's poems memorable. The meter is usually highly regular, most often iambic tetrameter or pentameter, and the cadences are smooth. There is an unsubstantiated tradition that Crashaw was a trained musician; these poems would support that claim.

From time to time, there is a baffling half-revelation, for example in the two-line "On Marriage," when the speaker declares that he would "be married, but I'd have no wife,/ I would be married to the single life." Whether this is witty posturing, cynical disclaimer, or an honest account of his own state (Crashaw never married), the reader cannot tell. Crashaw's work would appear in anthologies even if he had written only the secular poetry, but his name would definitely be in smaller type. The poet himself spent far less effort in revising these secular poems, suggesting that he too considered them of secondary importance.

## STEPS TO THE TEMPLE AND CARMEN DEO NOSTRO

Turning to Crashaw's major works, those rich poems that he wrote and revised for the collections that would become *Steps to the Temple* and *Carmen Deo Nostro*, one is confronted with a lavish, even bewildering, highly sensuous, celebration of the Christianity that so fired the poet. If Donne argues with God in his Holy Sonnets and Herbert prays through *The Temple*, then Crashaw contemplates and exclaims. Apparently gifted with mystical experiences even in the midst of his English tradition, Crashaw's mode of prayer is much more akin to that of Teresa of Ávila than to the Book of Common Prayer. Like Teresa, who said that she could meditate for hours on the opening two words of the Lord's Prayer, Crashaw, confronted by the mysteries of Christ's life, death, and resurrection, meditates, celebrates, sorrows, refines, ponders, sees. Faced with mystery, he expresses it in paradox and strains to reconcile the opposites. Christianity does, after all, continually join flesh and spirit, God and humanity, justice and mercy, life and death. Crashaw's poetry does the same: It reveals rather than persuades. Unlike Henry Vaughan and especially Thomas Traherne, whose religious poetry is almost unflaggingly optimistic, Crashaw focuses on both the joys and sufferings of Christianity and more on the sufferings of Christ and the Virgin Mary, although he involves himself in the joyous mysteries of Christianity as well.

### "IN THE HOLY NATIVITY OF OUR LORD"

"In the Holy Nativity of Our Lord," one of Crashaw's best-known, most tightly written poems, makes a most appropriate introduction to the poet. Starting with the paradox of the revelation of Christ's birth to humble shepherds, Crashaw structures his hymn in a series of dualities and paradoxes: "Loves noone" meets "Natures night," frost is replaced by flowers, a tiny manger provides a bed for "this huge birth" of God who becomes man. The dualities in the poem are underscored by the shepherds themselves, classically named Tityrus and Thursis, who alternate verses and sing the chorus together.

The contrasts lead to the central question of the hymn, where to find a "fit" bed for the infant Jesus. When the "whitest sheets of snow" prove pure but too cold and the "rosie fleece" of angels' wings is warm but cannot "passe for pure," the shepherds return to the nativity scene to discover that the Christ child has vividly and dramatically reached his own solution:

> See see, how soone his new-bloom'd cheeke
> Twixt's mother's brests is gone to bed.
> Sweet choice (said I!) no way but so
> Not to lye cold, yet sleep in snow.

The paradox is resolved in the person of the Virgin Mother, Mary; the "I" of the shepherds becomes the "we" of all the faithful; the celebration of "Eternitie

shut in a span/ Summer in winter, day in night,/ Heaven in Earth and god in man" ends in a full chorus, followed by an anthem of liturgical joy.

Several traits elevate this poem well above the countless conventional, albeit sincere, Nativity poems of this period. The central image is vivid and personal; the Christ child is presented not as king but as nursing infant. Crashaw brilliantly takes the biblical motif of the Son of man, who has no place to lay his head, and transforms it into image. The poem moves gracefully from opening question to resolution, celebrating that resolution and concluding with the offering: "at last . . . our selves become our owne best sacrifice." It is a poem of liturgical color: The images of white and gold that weave through the stanzas are reminiscent of the vestments worn for the Christmas liturgy as well as the sunrise of Christmas Day.

One of Crashaw's simpler poems because of its traditional subject matter, "In the Holy Nativity of Our Lord" exemplifies the gifts of the poet. Crashaw is a worker with color: gold and silver, red and crimson and scarlet, and blinding white fill the poems along with modifiers such as "bright," "rosy," "radiant," and a score of others. The poet is highly conscious of textures and surfaces, forever describing his images as "soft," "rough," "slippery." Predominantly Anglo-Saxon in his diction (his most repeated nouns are monosyllables—"die," "birth," "sun," "flame," "heart," "eyes"), Crashaw betrays his early fondness for Latin in some of his favorite adjectives: "immortal," "triumphant," "illustrious," and "supernatural." He alliterates constantly, playing with vowel and consonant sounds to achieve unity of tone as well as musical qualities.

### "SAINTE MARY MAGDALEN"

Ironically, Crashaw's most characteristic gifts as a poet, particularly his enthusiasm for the refined and elaborate image, are responsible for some of his most-criticized efforts. Of these, the most famous is "Sainte Mary Magdalen: Or, The Weeper," a long poem commemorating the legend of Mary Magdalene, the sinner forgiven by Jesus, who, according to tradition, wept tears of repentance for many years. The motif is a beloved one in the seventeenth century; poems celebrating (and recommending) tears abound, often with Mary Magdalene, Saint Peter, or another grieving Christian as the focal point. Crashaw's poem is really not about Mary Magdalene at all; rather it is about the tears themselves, which, after falling from Mary Magdalene's eyes, follow a circuitous, thirty-seven stanza route, develop a speech of their own, and finally go up to Heaven to meet "a worthy object, Our Lords Feet." In between his opening salutation of Magdalene's eyes ("Ever bubling things! Thawing crystall! Snowy hills!") and the final image of Jesus, Crashaw scatters images and conceits with such abandon as to bewilder the unwary. Some of these conceits are richly apt: Magdalene is "pretious prodigall! Faire spendthrift of thy self!" Others (and there are many more of these) are extravagant, incredible, even ludicrous:

> And now where e're he strayes
>
> . . . . . . . . . . .
>
> He's follow'd by two faithfull fountaines,
> Two walking Bathes; two weeping motions;
> Portable and compendious Oceans.

"Sainte Mary Magdalen" has been cited as the prime example of all that is bad, even bathetic, in Crashaw, and surely today's reader, accustomed to a leaner poetic style and certainly to a less visible religious expression, confronts major problems. These can be partially alleviated, however, with at least some consideration of the traditions out of which Crashaw is writing. He is, in a sense, doing in "Sainte Mary Magdalen" what Teresa of Ávila is doing with the Lord's Prayer: He is taking a single image and pondering it at length, refining and embroidering and elaborating the object of his meditation until it reaches a conclusion.

Crashaw is also influenced by the Christian tradition of litanies. A litany is a long series of short prayers, each one a single phrase or epithet, often recited by a priest with responses ("pray for us" or "have mercy on us") from the congregation. A litany does what the poem does: It presents aspect after aspect of the holy person or mystery so that the faithful may, in some sense, see. The petitions of a litany are not related to one another but to the person or mystery they are celebrating: The Virgin Mary, for example, is called Ark of the Covenant, Morning Star, Mystical Rose, Tower of Ivory, not because these phrases have any relationship to one another, but because they are figures or conceits

of her. Depending on one's scriptural background or perhaps spiritual disposition, some phrases suggest more devotion than others.

Much has been said of Crashaw's affinities with the movement in art called Baroque—that richly decorative aesthetic that suggests tension, opposites pulling at each other, extravagant gestures and ornate detail, and that somehow connotes a sense of unworldliness or otherness. "The Weeper," in its maze of images and conceits, suggests that it contains a significant truth that readers cannot follow but at which they can only guess. The poem is perhaps less baroque than some of Crashaw's other works, but it has that same energy, tension, and movement.

Finally, one might consider the fact that the poem celebrates Mary Magdalene, who wept repeatedly, even for years. The poem, too, celebrates repeatedly, with a focus on image after image, indeed perhaps doing the very thing it celebrates. Like Mary Magdalene, the poem reverences the Lord again and again. Read in this sense, "Sainte Mary Magdalen" may well be a hieroglyph, the term used by Joseph Summers to describe George Herbert's poetry (*George Herbert: His Religion and Art*, 1954).

All the above is not intended as a defense of "Sainte Mary Magdalen" so much as an attempt to view Crashaw in his contexts. Like many of the mystics, he has little need for discursive structure, preferring instead the intuitive, associative mode for communicating his experiences. If some images are banal, they are still a part of his contemplation and they stay in the poem. It is an unfamiliar aesthetic but not one without some validity. It is worth noting that nearly all Crashaw's numerous revisions of his poetry are toward length; he rarely discarded and never shortened.

### SAINT TERESA POEMS

As a Roman Catholic, Crashaw was more free than his Church of England contemporaries to consider the lives of the saints. Although the biblical Mary Magdalene and the Virgin Mary were appropriate for the devotions of at least High Church Anglicans, saints such as Teresa of Ávila were less so, even though Teresa's works had appeared in English as early as 1611 and would surely have been familiar to devout readers. It is not known whether Crashaw possessed a copy of

Teresa's classic *El castillo interior: O, Tratado de las moradas* (wr. 1577, pb. 1588; *The Interior Castle,* 1852); if he did, and if he preached against it, there is an intriguing poetic justice in his son's selection of Teresa for his richest poems. The two Saint Teresa poems rank among Crashaw's finest.

The poems contrast as well as match; "A Hymn to the Name and Honor of the Admirable Saint Teresa" is a legend or story made into a lesson, whereas "The Flaming Heart" is a meditation on an image, possibly the painting by the Antwerp artist Gerhard Seghers, or perhaps the more famous Gian Lorenzo Bernini statue in the Coronaro Chapel, Saint Maria della Vittoria, Rome. Crashaw could have seen either representation, and he may well have seen both.

"A Hymn to the Name and Honor of the Admirable Saint Teresa" begins with the story of the child Teresa, who, wanting martyrdom and heaven for her faith, persuades her little brother to go off with her in search of the Moors, who will, she hopes, put them to death. The poet, meditating on the greatness of heart in the six-year-old Teresa, is both witty and moving when he breaks in, "Sweet, not so fast!" A richer, more demanding martyrdom awaits the adult Teresa; she will be called to the contemplative life, reform the Carmelite order, write magnificent works, and give herself totally to the love of God. Dying to the self in the most ancient tradition, she will indeed be a spiritual martyr. The poem combines, in the richest Metaphysical tradition, intellect and emotion, tough demands and profoundly intuitive responses. Teresa is not free to choose her martyrdom any more than were the first Christians; she can only respond to the choice that God makes for her.

In the poem, Crashaw is working in the best tradition of Anglican preaching as well as with Roman Catholic sensitivity. He begins with a story, an exemplum, good clear narrative, aphorisms ("Tis Love, not years nor limbs, that can/ Make the Martyr, or the man"), vivid drama, and a totally believable picture of the child Teresa and her ardent love of God. The regular tetrameter lines with their *aabb* rhymes move the story gracefully, even inevitably, along. Then, with "not so fast," the poet moves into a new vein altogether, summoning back Teresa—and the reader—to contemplate what giving oneself to God really means. The poetry moves

from narrative to lyrical, intuitive expression and is filled with images, exclamations, and apostrophes. Instead of martyrdom as a child, Teresa will face numerous mystical deaths, which will prepare her for the final death that brings total union with the Lord; these mystical deaths "Shall all at last dye into one,/ And melt thy soules sweet mansion." The diction becomes more and more simple as the concepts underneath the poetry become increasingly mystical. The poem concludes in a dazzling combination of Anglican neatness ("decorum") and Roman Catholic transcendence: The one who wishes to see Jesus "must learne in life to dye like Thee." The poem is simultaneously a meditation on a holy life and a lyrical celebration of one who was chosen by God to live totally for him. The women in Crashaw's poetry, whether the Virgin Mary, Magdalene, Teresa, or even that "not impossible she" of the poem "Wishes. To His (Supposed) Mistress," are all great souled, larger than life, intensely vivid, and visual. Later, Crashaw would write "An Apologie" for the hymn as "having been writt when the author was yet among the protestantes"; one wonders whether its discursive, even preachy, tone is a manifestation of this state of mind. Surely, the poem needs no "apologie."

In the second Teresa poem, "The Flaming Heart," Crashaw keeps his tetrameter rhymed couplets but adopts a totally different stance, moving from story-with-lesson to contemplation. The thirteenth century theologian Thomas Aquinas defines contemplation as simultaneously knowing and loving one of the divine mysteries, and the poem illustrates that definition. The speaker is gazing at a picture or statue of Teresa in which she is visited by a seraphim, a celestial being, who, holding a burning dart, prepares to transfix the saint. The scene is taken from Teresa's own journal account of her divine revelations and translates the momentary interior apprehension into external narration. Teresa's language is explicitly sexual; the cherub with the dart, the piercing, the pain followed by ecstatic joy, all these are a part of that long tradition that uses the language of physical love for God's encounters with his people. It is the language of Donne's Holy Sonnets. Catholic artists, directed by the Council of Trent to make the mysteries of faith more vivid for believers, are drawn to this incident; it is not surprising that the newly converted Crashaw, already enamored of image and mystery, would be drawn to the story of Teresa, another "not impossible she."

"The Flaming Heart" welcomes "you that come as friends" almost as though the readers are pilgrims to the church where the image is displayed. The faithful viewers are, however, immediately corrected by the wit of the speaker; although "they say" that one figure is the seraphim and the other is Teresa, the speaker assumes the role of correcting guide, asking, "be ruled by me." The figures must be reversed; the saint is the seraphim.

With that flashing insight, "Read HIM for her and her for him," the poet moves into the entire burden of the long poem, constantly juxtaposing Teresa and the seraph, celebrating her angelic virtues and total love of God, casting the seraph in the role of a "rivalled lover" who needs to veil his face, singing praise of the "flaming heart" of Teresa that is so afire with love. The couplets race in their eagerness to show this instant, moving from abstract to concrete, from Teresa to the seraph. The colors are rich here, crimson, golden, and fiery; the sense of pain becoming joy is almost tangible; the transcendence of the moment breaks out of the visual representation as the speaker also moves out of time and space and into the world of mystical prayer. The closing lines, perhaps Crashaw's most intense and most often cited, are litany, prayer, celebration, vision.

## BIBLIOGRAPHY

Bertonasco, Marc F. *Crashaw and the Baroque.* Tuscaloosa: University of Alabama Press, 1971. Traces Crashaw's key images to seventeenth century emblem books and finds Saint Francis de Sales's meditative method the major influence on Crashaw's spiritual development. Provides a detailed analysis of "Sainte Mary Magdalen" that demonstrates these influences. The appendix contains a review of Crashaw's scholarship, and a bibliography.

Cefalu, Paul. *English Renaissance Literature and Contemporary Theory: Sublime Objects of Theology.* New York: Palgrave Macmillan, 2007. Cefalu uses modern philosophy and cultural theory to analyze the religious poems of Crashaw, John Milton, and John Donne.

Cousins, Anthony D. *The Catholic Religious Poets from Southwell to Crashaw: A Critical History.* London: Sheed & Ward, 1991. History of the criticism and interpretation of these English poets from a Christian perspective. Bibliographical references, index.

Healy, Thomas F. *Richard Crashaw.* Leiden, the Netherlands: E. J. Brill, 1986. Explains that Crashaw's poetry owes much to his Cambridge years at Pembroke and Peterhouse, when the religious, intellectual, and poetic environment shaped his ideas and his work. Includes extended criticism of "Musick's Duell" and, particularly, "To the Name of Jesus."

LeVay, John. "Crashaw's 'Wishes to His (Supposed) Mistresse.'" *Explicator* 50, no. 4 (Summer, 1992): 205. A critique of Crashaw's "Delight of the Muses," which includes a wishful reverie of the poet's ideal woman.

Mintz, Susannah B. "The Crashavian Mother." *Studies in English Literature* 39, no. 1 (Winter, 1999): 111-129. A study of the history of critical thought regarding Crashaw's relationship to women.

Parrish, Paul A. *Richard Crashaw.* Boston: Twayne, 1980. Surveys Crashaw's life and work and contains several relatively long explications of individual Crashaw poems. Provides a biography, followed by chapters on Crashaw's early work, the secular poems, *Steps to the Temple*, the major hymns, and the Teresa poems. Includes a selected, annotated bibliography.

Sabine, Maureen. *Feminine Engendered Faith: The Poetry of John Donne and Richard Crashaw.* London: Macmillan, 1992. Examines these two poets' religious imagery and content with particular emphasis on the impact of the Virgin Mary. Contains bibliographical references, index.

Young, R. V. *Doctrine and Devotion in Seventeenth-Century Poetry.* Rochester, N.Y.: D. S. Brewer, 2000. History and criticism of Christian poetry in seventeenth century England. The works of Crashaw, George Herbert, Henry Vaughan, and John Donne are analyzed. Includes bibliographic references.

_____. *Richard Crashaw and the Spanish Golden Age.* New Haven, Conn.: Yale University Press,

1982. Places Crashaw within a metaphysical context and argues that Crashaw's poetry is impersonal and public, that he was familiar with contemporary Spanish literature, and that his poems about saints and feast days ("The Flaming Heart," "Hymn to the Name of Jesus," and "A Hymn to the Name and Honor of the Admirable Saint Teresa") deserve the extended criticism he devotes to them.

*Katherine Hanley*

# CYNEWULF

**Born:** Northumbria (now in England); 757
**Died:** Northumbria (now in England); 786
**Also known as:** Kynewulf

PRINCIPAL POETRY

*Christ II (Ascension)*, c. 800
*Elene*, c. 800
*The Fates of the Apostles*, c. 800
*Juliana*, c. 800

OTHER LITERARY FORMS

The known literary works of Cynewulf (KIHN-uh-woolf) remain the four poems attributed to him in the Exeter Book and the Vercelli Book.

ACHIEVEMENTS

Since the discovery of his name in the nineteenth century, Cynewulf's reputation, like the size of his canon, has fluctuated widely. Certainly, a prolific poet who could count *The Dream of the Rood* among his works would deserve much respect, but the Cynewulf of the four signed poems has not fared so well. Scholars have always shown great interest in Cynewulf, primarily because of his runic signatures. Daniel Calder is probably right in suggesting that critical assessment of the poet has suffered "from the need to make him more important than he is." General histories and surveys of Old English poetry, for example, devote much space to this poet with a name, but have been essentially unimpressed by the poetry itself. Some have seen it as a di-

luted version of the earlier heroic style, a breakdown of technique, and the end of a great tradition. Commenting on *The Fates of the Apostles* in his history of medieval poetry, Derek Pearsall states that the poem "has the characteristic nerveless orthodoxy of treatment which prompts one to think of Cynewulf's poems in turn as the final product of a declining old age." Even the editors of Cynewulf have not been admiring. Rosemary Woolf, editor of *Juliana*, sees the poem as bringing "Old English poetry into a blind alley." What is not certain in these and numerous other such assessments of Cynewulf is the extent to which they reflect the quality of his poetry or the critic's preference for the heroic style of earlier English poetry. The modern distaste for the hagiographic subject matter and overt didacticism of these Christian poems may also account for Cynewulf's bad notices.

Later studies approaching Cynewulf's poems within the contexts of Christian exegesis, hagiography, and iconography, however, have signaled a general reevaluation of the poems. *Elene* and *Christ II* have been especially praised. Scholars have been impressed by the "sophisticated handling" of patristic motifs in *Christ II* and the "beauty of intellectual form" of *Elene*. Comparisons of Cynewulf's poems with religious pictorial art have been especially popular. *Juliana* has been compared to an icon, *Christ* to a triptych, and *Elene* to panels on a church wall. To judge these poems against Aristotelian and nineteenth century expectations of realism is as foolish as judging a Byzantine icon or a complex design in the *Book of Kells* against Renaissance expectations of linear perspective and verisimilitude in art.

As helpful as these new approaches to the structure and characters of Cynewulf's narratives are, the poems remain to be appreciated and analyzed as poetry. Clearly, poetry was very important to Cynewulf. His runic signatures may reflect his desire to elicit prayers, but they also imply that he believed the poems deserved reward. Whereas the earlier oral poets (the scops) probably saw their poetry as common property, Cynewulf's signatures and requests for prayers suggest "that he believed that he had a permanent claim on his work" (Barbara Raw, *The Art and Background of Old English Poetry*, 1978).

In *Christ II*, Cynewulf includes poetry and song among the gifts that Christ bestows on humankind. Thus, the composition of poetry itself is considered a pious act, the development of God-given talent, the manipulation of secular technique for religious purposes. Certainly, Cynewulf so manipulated Anglo-Saxon poetic technique. In his poetry, he borrows and adapts formulaic phrases, standard motifs, and established kennings (elaborate and traditional metaphors such as "swan-road" for "sea"). He continues the tradition of alliterative and accentual verse, dividing the poetic line into two half lines containing two stresses each. These half lines are joined by alliteration, the pattern of which varies from line to line but is generally controlled by the sound of the first stressed syllable in the second half line. The pattern of stressed and unstressed syllables also varies, allowing the poet a variety of rhythmic effects.

Cynewulf's poetry does differ in many respects from the earlier heroic poetry and even from the religious verse formerly attributed to Caedmon. On occasion, Cynewulf experiments with rhyme—something very unusual in Old English, as is also his use of runes. Some of the differences may be caused by Cynewulf's dependence on Latin texts, although detailed studies of his use of sources suggest that Cynewulf actually improved and clarified the syntax of his originals. His style has been described as "classic." Cynewulf's verse is also "looser," "lighter," and more varied rhythmically, developing a great number of secondary stresses. In contrast to the elevated tone of *Beowulf* (c. 1000), it is more conversational. Some consider this effect prosaic, the end of a poetic tradition, but more recently, Raw has explained the style as a deliberate attempt at informality, an effort to follow Augustine's advice to express Christian themes in a simple style. Cynewulf does vary his style according to his subject, from meditation to set descriptive passages and formal debates.

BIOGRAPHY

The discovery of Cynewulf's name has not meant the discovery of a biography for the poet. Working from a name deciphered from runes, scholars have made tortuous attempts to discover a Cynewulf in historical records who could be identified as the poet. Candidates

have included Cenwulf, an abbot of Peterborough (died 1006); Cynewulf, a bishop of Lindisfarne (c. 780); and Cynewulf, a priest of Dunwich (c. 803). None of these identifications has been accepted, and scholars are left with what meager data can be deduced from the four poems. Based on the poetry's subject matter, dependence on Latin sources, and relationship to the liturgical calendar, scholars assume he was a literate poet, a cleric, and probably a monk. Based on dialect and linguistic analysis, Cynewulf is usually dated around the turn of the eighth and ninth centuries and placed within the broad area of the Anglian dialect, in northern and eastern England. Because the runes twice give the poet's name as "Cynewulf" and twice as "Cynwulf," suggesting a variation of spelling not known in texts from the north, scholars have further limited the dialect to Mercian. This conclusion is supported by the rhyming passages in *Elene* and *Christ II*, which are most effective when the Mercian, rather than the manuscript's West Saxon, dialect is followed.

The evidence nevertheless remains scanty. Elaborate arguments based on what the "I" persona says in the poems have suggested that Cynewulf was a wandering minstrel or that he led a riotous and sinful life until, through conversion, he became a religious poet. Such arguments misunderstand the traditions of the elegiac wanderer in Old English poetry and conventional Christian humility motifs. Like other attempts to deal with the unknown poet rather than with his known poetry, they are fruitless. As Daniel Calder concludes, after surveying what little is known,

> Barring the discovery of wholly new evidence, the pursuit of Cynewulf's identity and the spinning out of a biography remain idle tasks. He emerges from the anonymity of Anglo-Saxon poetry long enough to sign his name and then disappear again into that great obscurity he shares with all the other scops who left no trace.

ANALYSIS

Cynewulf's name is known to students of Old English poetry because, in the conclusions of the four poems that can be attributed to him with certainty, he "signed" his name in runic letters. The name, however, was not deciphered until 1840. Cynewulf did not write his name directly, but wove the runes into the concluding meditations of his poems, so that they can be read not only as letters spelling his name, but also as symbols representing words that form part of the poetry. This riddling device—with both personal and poetic purposes—is typical of Cynewulf's poetry, which often applies devices used in earlier heroic and secular poetry to his meditative religious verse.

### CYNEWULF'S CANON

Cynewulf's four poems are extant in two of the four major manuscript collections of Old English poetry, both copied around the year 1000 in the West Saxon dialect. The Exeter Book, now in the Exeter Cathedral Library, contains *Christ II* and *Juliana*; the Vercelli Book, located in the northern Italian cathedral library of Vercelli, includes *The Fates of the Apostles* and *Elene*. Nineteenth century scholars, driven by the rare discovery of a poet's name from a period of general anonymity, attributed all the religious verse in these two manuscripts to Cynewulf. Just as Caedmon was considered to be the author of the poems dealing with Old Testament subjects extant in the Junius manuscript, so Cynewulf became the author of the saints' lives and allegorical poetry of the Exeter and Vercelli manuscripts. Only *Beowulf* (c. 1000), found in the fourth major manuscript, escaped being attributed with confidence to Cynewulf.

This poetry does in some respects share stylistic and thematic features with the four poems of Cynewulf. The two *Guthlac* poems ("A" and "B") treat the life and death of the eighth century hermit Saint Guthlac. Like *Juliana*, Cynewulf's account of the martyrdom of Saint Juliana, these poems deal with a saint who was challenged and harassed by demons. Guthlac is a Mercian saint associated with Croyland Abbey in Lincolnshire, an area perhaps connected with Cynewulf. Furthermore, *Guthlac B*, based on the Latin *Vita Guthlaci* by Felix of Croyland, shares several stylistic devices with the "signed" poems. Because in the Exeter Book its conclusion is missing, it is possible that it may have closed with a passage containing Cynewulf's name.

Also stylistically related to Cynewulf's poetry is *The Dream of the Rood*. Found not only in the Vercelli Book but also in fragments inscribed in runes on the Ruthwell Cross (located in southwest Scotland), this dream vision shares certain descriptive passages with *Elene*. Whereas *Elene* describes Constantine's conversion and Saint Helena's discovery of the cross, *The Dream of the Rood* concentrates on Christ's crucifixion; nevertheless, both share a devotion to the glorious cross of victory. Now usually dated earlier than Cynewulf's poetry, *The Dream of the Rood* has been called one of the greatest religious lyrics in the English language. It certainly is the best of the "Cynewulfian group," those poems associated with, but not now attributed to, Cynewulf.

The other poems attributed by nineteenth century scholars to Cynewulf share fewer stylistic and thematic elements with the four signed poems. *Andreas*, a saint's legend based on the apocryphal Latin *Acts of Saints Andrew and Matthew*, was long tied to *The Fates of the Apostles*, a summary description of the deaths of Christ's disciples. Because *The Fates of the Apostles*—considered to be an epilogue to *Andreas*, which precedes it in the Vercelli Book—contained the runic signature, scholars reasoned that *Andreas* must also be by Cynewulf. Similarly, *Christ I (Advent)* and *Christ III (Last Judgment)* were attributed to Cynewulf before critical analysis subdivided *Christ* into three distinct poems. Although the three may be thematically related and perhaps were even brought together by Cynewulf, only *Christ II* (lines 441-866) concludes with the runic signature. It is a meditation on, and explication of, the significance of Christ's Ascension. *Christ I*, a series of antiphons for use in Vespers during the week preceding Christmas, is, according to Claes Schaar, "fairly close to Cynewulf's poetry," whereas *Christ III*, a rather uneven picture of the Last Judgment and the terrors awaiting the sinful, is definitely not by Cynewulf. *The Phoenix*, an allegorical treatment of Christ's Resurrection; *Physiologus*, a series of allegorized interpretations of natural history; and *Wulf and Eadwacer*, once understood as a riddle containing Cynewulf's name, are today not associated with Cynewulf.

Nineteenth century understanding of the Cynewulf canon had a certain balance and symmetry, which is attractive. If Caedmon dealt with the epic themes of the Old Testament, Cynewulf emphasized themes more exclusively Christian: allegories of salvation, events in the life of Christ, and the stories of the early martyrs. This poetry spanned Christian history from Palestine in the first century to England in the eighth; from Christ's birth (*Christ I*) to his death (*The Dream of the Rood*), Resurrection (*The Phoenix*), and Ascension (*Christ II*); from the foundation of the church by the first missionaries (*The Fates of the Apostles* and *Andreas*) to the suffering of the martyrs (*Juliana*), the official recognition of Christianity by the Roman Empire (*Elene*), and the continuity of the tradition of the hermit saint in England (*Guthlac*). This broad survey of Christian history not unexpectedly concluded with a description of the Last Judgment (*Christ III*).

The analyses of S. K. Das and Schaar in the 1940's, however, have limited Cynewulf's canon to the four poems containing his name, leaving one to wonder whether even these rather varied and differing works would have survived the complex and thorough stylistic and linguistic analyses if they had not concluded with a runic signature. Resembling the effect of higher criticism of the Bible, Old English scholarship has reduced Cynewulf from being the author of a large and diverse body of verse to being the composer of 2,600 lines: *The Fates of the Apostles* (122 lines), *Juliana* (731 lines), *Elene* (1,321 lines), and *Christ II* (426 lines).

### THE FOUR POEMS

Cynewulf's four poems vary in length, subject, complexity, and style, yet they may be characterized as sharing similar source materials, purposes, and themes. All four are essentially didactic Christian poems, based on Latin prose originals, probably composed with the liturgical calendar in mind, and perhaps to be read as poetic meditations accompanying other monastic readings. The poems are didactic and specifically Christian in that their major purpose is to teach or celebrate significant events of salvation history. The four reflect a variety of Latin originals and specific types of monastic readings, meditative practice, and exegetical thought. In *The Fates of the Apostles*, Cynewulf notes that he borrowed from many holy books, and he clearly takes pride in his knowledge and use of the "authorities" throughout his work.

Thematically, Cynewulf's poems reflect an interest also typical of his time and of monastic literature, the cosmic conflict between the forces of good and evil. This conflict is portrayed in both human and supernatu-

ral terms, sometimes in brief summaries of Christian suffering, sometimes in long debates and complaints. To highlight this conflict, Cynewulf establishes polarities of good and evil. The devil and his cohorts are clearly opposed to Christ and his faithful. Emperors and the wealthy persecute martyrs and the poor, and the headstrong Jews oppose the reasonable Christians. Idols contrast with Christian worship; lust attacks virginity; the law cannot conquer grace.

Characters are either black or white, symbols of good or evil rather than individual. While imprisoned, Juliana is suddenly visited by a demon pretending to be an angel. Her suitor, who in the Latin sources is merely a pragmatic Roman official, is portrayed by Cynewulf as a champion of paganism. There must be no hesitation, no sense that characters may have a divided mind. When the actors in this cosmic drama do change, they do not develop characters but flip from one extreme to another, as if shifting masks. In *Elene*, Judas shifts from being a miracle-working Christian bishop. Paralleling the career of Saul in the New Testament, whose conversion from persecutor to persecuted is signaled by a change of his name to Paul, Judas's name is changed to Cyriacus. As in the New Testament, which lies behind Cynewulf's Latin sources, there definitely is no place for the lukewarm.

Cynewulf's poems draw on the recorded victories of the faithful in the past to teach Christians in the present to uphold their inheritance of truth. This didactic purpose is accomplished by two means: Cynewulf portrays past events as types or symbols that can be applied to contemporary Christians, and he inserts personal comments in the conclusion of his poems, confessing his own need to follow the examples of the past and to repent in the present. As in the past, Christ gave power to the saints to withstand the forces of Satan, so in the continuing battle between good and evil, he gives power to overcome temptation. The monastic communities, which understood themselves to be the inheritors of the tradition begun by the martyrs, will likewise conquer evil. The cosmic battle, given personal application, is made urgent by the concluding meditations on the transitory nature of the world, on the Last Judgment, and on the joys of heaven. In the future, contemporary events will be judged according to their place in the battle lines, and those joining the forces of Christianity will be appropriately rewarded.

## THE FATES OF THE APOSTLES

Basically a catalog listing the missionary activities and deaths of Christ's twelve apostles, *The Fates of the Apostles* is based on various Latin historical martyrologies. Its brief accounts of the early Christian missionaries may have been intended for reading during November to celebrate the martyred saints. Of Cynewulf's four poems, *The Fates of the Apostles* is considered as "the least effective" and "inferior" by several critics. Such evaluations probably reflect modern contempt not only for the poem's subject but also for its form. To the Anglo-Saxon Christian community, however, sharing strong missionary impulses, interested in converting pagans, and claiming to be both historically and universally established, the poem's subject is a proclamation of legitimacy. Its form, furthermore, would not seem odd in an age when Christian chronicles were often composed in poetry and the poet was caretaker of the community's memory. Such catalogs have an honorable parentage both in the Old and New Testaments and in classical literature—in the catalogs of Homer, for example.

More appreciative critics have sought through elaborate numerical and grammatical analysis to complicate the poem, to see it as more than a simple catalog, as mannered, mystical, and even ironic. However, what seems most obvious about *The Fates of the Apostles* is its simplicity of purpose and structure. It establishes, in the clearest possible outline, the conflict between good and evil: Christian heroes, courageously obeying Christ's command to go into all nations, preach to the heathen, and suffer martyrdom. These deeds are related to the poet, his world, and his heavenly goals through the poem's prologue and epilogue.

Mentioning each of the twelve apostles in turn, Cynewulf follows a simple pattern with appropriate variations: "We have heard how X taught the people in, or journeyed to, Y and died at the hands of Z." The specific acts are introduced by a personal comment on the poet's own weariness and similarly conclude with a personal request that those who hear the poem will pray to the apostles for him. Then follows the runic signature, which inverts the spelling of his name to read "FWULCYN." The runes are woven as a riddle into a meditation on the mutability of earthly joy and wealth. The poet then refers to himself as a wanderer—a motif of long standing in Christian thought, which rejects this world as a home—and concludes with a reminder of the true home of all Christians, Heaven.

## JULIANA

Juliana is a classic saint's life. Based on a Latin prose life or one of Saint Bede's sources, the poem narrates the various human and devilish tortures and temptations withstood by Saint Juliana, who died about 305-311 and whose martyrdom is celebrated in the Christian calendar on February 16. Like *The Fates of the Apostles*, *Juliana* has not fared well with critics. To Stanley Greenfield, for example, it is "the least impressive as poetry of the Cynewulf group" (*Critical History of Old English Literature*, 1965). In contrast to *The Fates of the Apostles*, it is a lengthy and somewhat repetitious account (even though lacking approximately 130 lines) of the suffering not of numerous saints but of a single martyr.

The conflict between the opposing forces of good and evil is again drawn through stark contrasts. Juliana's suitor, Eleusius, is portrayed as possessing stores of treasure, representing earthly nobility and power. Repeatedly characterized by his wealth, he is the choice of Juliana's father, who tells the virgin that Eleusius is better, nobler, and wealthier than she, thus deserving her love. In contrast, Juliana's heart is set on a different bridegroom, the noble ruler of Heaven, possessing eternal wealth and divine power. As in the traditional love triangle of romance—what Northrop Frye calls "the secular scripture"—the father is enraged by his daughter's intransigence and gives her over to her enemies. Here, however, the love triangle leads to supernatural conflict, as Juliana contrasts her Lord with Eleusius's devils. After forcing a long confession from a demon, "the enemy of the soul," and suffering numerous torments, Juliana is killed. Eleusius, driven mad by the ordeal of dealing with a martyr, is drowned, along with his companions.

The narrative concludes by describing the hellish destiny of Eleusius and his supporters, using the language of heroic poetry to deny the rewards traditionally given to the Germanic *comitatus* (the heroic band of warriors) by its chieftain. It is as if Cynewulf uses the heroic style to condemn an old heroism and to substitute a new Christian heroism, not based on violent deeds but on faithful suffering, for the destiny of Eleusius and the pagans is contrasted to the destiny of Juliana, whose martyred body is the occasion of joy in her native Nicomedia, and continuing glory for Christians. This continuity is then extended by Cynewulf to the present when he asks for aid from Saint Juliana in his own preparation for death. Weaving his name into a meditation on death—here using three groups of runes, "CYN," "EWU," "LF"—the poet again requests prayers from those who read his poem and asks that the ruler of Heaven stand by him at the final judgment.

### ELENE

Also in the tradition of the saint's legend, *Elene* spins a more complicated narrative than does *Juliana*. Based on a version of the *Inventio Sanctae Crucis* similar to the *Acta Cyriaci*, it relates the discovery of the true cross by Saint Helena, the mother of Constantine. This event is celebrated in the liturgical calendar on May 3. *Elene* is generally considered to be Cynewulf's finest poem; its description of the glorious cross gleaming in the sky is often compared with the imagery of *The Dream of the Rood*. *Elene*'s popularity may also be the result of its development of several passages in the heroic style, including Elene's sea journey and Constantine's war against the Huns. Using the vigorous language of battle poetry, Cynewulf here develops the motif of the beasts of battle: the raven, eagle, and wolf that traditionally frequent Old English poetic battles.

Nevertheless, *Elene*'s basic theme is Christian, and although it borrows epic devices, the poem's main subject is conversion. It describes three miraculous conversions related to the discovery of the cross: Constantine's conversion following his vision of the cross; Judas's conversion leading to the discovery of the cross; and the conversion of the Jews after the discovery of the nails used to crucify Christ. In relating these conversions, the poem may strike modern readers as inexplicable and even offensive. The suffering of the Christian martyr memorialized in *Juliana* becomes here the militancy of the Christian emperor. The cross becomes the banner of war, and the nails of the cross, hammered by Roman soldiers into the flesh of Christ,

become amulets for the bridle of the Roman emperor, assuring that he will vanquish all. Similarly, in contrast to the protagonist of *Juliana*, Elene represents imperial power and can force her beliefs on others. Thus she has Judas cast into a cistern for seven days until he acknowledges the truth of Christianity. In Cynewulf's black-and-white view of salvation history, Elene is on the side of right, whereas the Jews, cursed for rejecting Christ, deserve humiliation and punishment.

An unsympathetic approach to *Elene*, however, misunderstands both the Christian background of the poem and its development of characters as types. The figure of Judas, particularly, needs careful attention. The poem introduces him after Elene asks to see the wisest among the Jews. Groups of three thousand, then one thousand, and finally five hundred wise men are rejected by Elene before Judas, "the one skilled in speeches," reducing the number of the righteous to Lot and his family. Judas shares features with Lot, for like him, he has ancient parentage and familial ties to the righteous, yet represents a doomed people. He knows the truth of Christianity from his father; furthermore, his brother was Stephen, the first Christian martyr. He refuses, however, to accept what he knows. Like his namesake, Judas Iscariot, the most despised Jew in Christian history, he rejects Christ until driven to admit the truth by Elene. Then his role is reversed, a point emphasized by the demon who appears in the poem to complain of Christian interference in the designs of evil. This new Judas—like Christ, the new Adam—provides the way to salvation through the cross. By converting to Christianity and using his wisdom to discover the cross, Judas Cyriacus saves not only himself, but also the Jewish people, whom medieval Christians believed would ultimately be converted to Christianity.

Other characters in *Elene* are similarly given typological significance. Constantine is associated with Christ and Elene with *ecclesia*, the victorious Christian Church. The confrontation between Judas and Elene thus symbolizes a standard doctrinal topic of Christian apologetic and polemical literature: the confrontation between *synagoga* and *ecclesia*, the law of Judaism and the grace of Christ. The confrontation is settled by the elevation of the cross, the visible token of Christ's redemptive act and a disastrous defeat for the devil.

Like the missionary activities of the apostles and the martyrdom of the saints, however, this confrontation is only one of a series of battles in the larger war between good and evil. It remains for the individual to take sides in the war, to join forces with *ecclasia*, as Cynewulf emphasizes in his conclusion. In a passage developing internal rhymes, he relates his own conversion from sin to the cross. The poet takes the past event and gives it personal application, for his own conversion associates him with the three conversions of the narrative. Then, after weaving his name in runes into a meditation on the mutability of this world, Cynewulf describes doomsday and the respective rewards of the righteous and evil. This concluding radical perspective explains the militancy of the Christian emperor, the conversion of the Jews, and the poet's own dedication to the cross.

## CHRIST II

Unlike Cynewulf's other poems, *Christ II* deals not with Christian saints but with a key event in the life of Christ, the Ascension. Rather than drawing from legendary sources, it closely parallels the last part of Pope Gregory's homily on the Ascension (homily 29), with some additions based on Saint Bede's *On the Lord's Ascension* (c. 700) and monastic readings for Ascensiontide. Although Claes Schaar believed that in *Christ II* "the poet is some-what overwhelmed by the rhetoric of Gregory," others have praised Cynewulf's "masterful reworking" of the homily. Daniel Calder, comparing Cynewulf's treatment of Gregory to Gregory's treatment of the Bible, notes that the poet "takes liberties with Gregory's text" to arrive at the truth concerning the Ascension, sometimes expanding, other times rearranging, his Latin source.

The result is an imaginative exposition of the significance of the Ascension combining Christian allegory and exegesis with Germanic poetic techniques. The description of Christ's six leaps in his role as humankind's savior, from incarnation to Ascension, allegorically develops the exegesis of the Song of Solomon and establishes the Ascension as the final necessary step in the long process of humankind's salvation. Christ, "the famous Prince," leaves his band of retainers on earth (the disciples) and goes to join the band of angels in Heaven. The disciples, like the wanderers of Old English elegiac poetry, are overwhelmed by the loss of

their leader, whereas the angels raise a song of joy and triumph. However, the apostles are not left helpless, for Christ bestows gifts on humankind, including not only the spiritual gifts of wisdom, poetry, and teaching, but also the physical gifts of victory in battle and seafaring.

Even the description of Christ's glorious Ascension, however, is understood in the context of the cosmic battle between good and evil. Christ is welcomed to Heaven by a song praising his harrowing of Hell, his victory against the "ancient foes." In another passage experimenting with internal rhyme, Cynewulf establishes the significance of Christ's act, which makes possible humankind's choice between salvation and damnation. The passage, reflecting the poet's pronounced dualism, contrasts Heaven and Hell, light and dark, majesty and doom, glory and torment.

Later, Cynewulf relates Christ's six redemptive leaps to humankind's need to leap by holy deeds to the rewards of Heaven. The Father of Heaven will help humankind overcome sin and will protect the faithful against the attacks of fiends in the cosmic battle. The importance of such reliance on Christ is underscored in the poem's conclusion, Cynewulf's elaborate treatment of doomsday. Introduced by his own confession of sin and fear of judgment, it includes the runic signature woven into the description of terror facing the worldly humans before the almighty judge.

Thus, as in *The Fates of the Apostles*, *Juliana*, and *Elene*, Cynewulf in *Christ II* ties the events of Christian history, developed from his Latin sources, to his contemporary world through personal confession. The poems all teach a basic concept underlying the Christian liturgy and its understanding of sacred time: the close relationship between the past, present, and future. The victories of the past in the struggle between good and evil symbolized by the ministry of Christ and the lives of the saints must be repeated in the present by the individual Christian, for in the future all people will face the judgment of God.

BIBLIOGRAPHY

Bjork, Robert E., ed. *The Cynewulf Reader*. New York: Routledge, 2001. A collection of essays that provide a comprehensive view of the Anglo-Saxon poet and his work.

Bredehoft, Thomas A. *Textual Histories: Readings in the Anglo-Saxon Chronicle*. Buffalo, N.Y.: University of Toronto Press, 2001. This discussion of Anglo-Saxon chronicles contains a discussion of Cynewulf's poetry.

Calder, Daniel G. *Cynewulf*. Boston: Twayne, 1981. This book-length critical analysis approaches its study by relating together all Cynewulf's poems. Augmented by a selected bibliography, these poems are studied for structural and thematic similarities to establish a base for in-depth examination.

Cook, Albert S., ed. *The Christ of Cynewulf*. Hamden, Conn.: Archon Books, 1964. While concentrating on the poem *Christ II*, Cook provides extensive information on the life of Cynewulf, including his theology. Supplemented by grammatical notes and a glossary, this book offers indispensable insight into this Old English poet.

Frese, Delores Warwick. "The Art of Cynewulf's Runic Signatures." In *Anglo-Saxon Poetry: Essays in Appreciation*. Notre Dame, Ind.: University of Notre Dame Press, 1975. Frese discusses how the runic signature of Cynewulf was intricately interwoven into the texts of his poetry, greatly affecting and shaping the vocabulary, imagery, and ideology.

Greenfield, Stanley B., and Daniel Calder. *A New Critical History of Old English Literature*. New York: New York University Press, 1986. Shows the importance of the writings of Cynewulf in the Old English tradition. Presents interesting background and information on Cynewulf's possible identity and analyzes his poetry as subtle Christian abstractions, reflective in their constructs.

Mann, Jill, and Maura Nolan, eds. *The Text in the Community: Essays on Medieval Works, Manuscripts, Authors, and Readers*. Notre Dame, Ind.: University of Notre Dame Press, 2006. This discussion of medieval works contains a section on Cynewulf.

Olsen, Alexandra Hennessey. *Speech, Song, and Poetic Craft: The Artistry of the Cynewulf Canon*. New York: Lang, 1984. Olsen stresses the fact that Cynewulf used poetic language to reinforce legends and used a conscious literary style to compose poems of high moral purpose. Augmented with an exhaustive bibliography.

Schaar, Claes. *Critical Studies in the Cynewulf Group*. New York: Haskell, 1967. Complemented with an excellent bibliography, this volume critically examines not only Cynewulf's poetry but also other works from the same period. Includes analysis of subject, text, style, and manner, for an in-depth look at traditional writings and poetic personalities.

Wine, Joseph D. *Figurative Language in Cynewulf: Defining Aspects of a Poetic Style*. New York: Peter Lang, 1993. A study of the use of Old English figures of speech in Cynewulf's poetry. Includes bibliography and index.

*Richard Kenneth Emmerson*

# D

## SAMUEL DANIEL

**Born:** Taunton, Somerset, England; 1562(?)
**Died:** Beckington, England; October, 1619

PRINCIPAL POETRY

*The Complaynt of Rosamonde*, 1592
*Delia*, 1592
*The First Fowre Bookes of the Civile Warres*
 *Between the Two Houses of Lancaster and*
 *Yorke*, 1595 (enlarged 1599 and 1601)
*Musophilus: Or, A Defence of Poesie*, 1599, 1601,
 1602, 1607, 1611, 1623
*Poeticall Essayes*, 1599
*Certaine Small Poems*, 1605
*Songs for the Lute, Viol and Voice*, 1606

OTHER LITERARY FORMS

In 1594, for the third edition of *Delia*—which bore the title *Delia and Rosamond augmented*—Samuel Daniel included a play, *Cleopatra*, which was written in the "Senecan mode." Actually, the author entered the piece in the Stationers' Register as early as October 19, 1593, and dedicated it to his patron, Mary Herbert, countess of Pembroke, the sister of Sir Philip Sidney. He stated that he wrote it at her request and as a companion to her own translation of the French playwright Robert Gainier's *Tragedy of Antonie* (1592). Six years later, Daniel began another play, three acts of a tragedy based on the story of Philotas, taken from Quintus Curtius, Justin, and Plutarch's *Life of Alexander*. Originally, he had intended the play to be acted at Bath during the Christmas season by certain gentlemen's sons; however, his printers urged him to complete other projects, and *The Tragedy of Philotas* was not completed and published until 1605. Daniel dedicated the work to Prince Henry, complaining that the public favor extended to him during the reign of Elizabeth had not been carried over to that of James I.

*The Tragedy of Philotas* caused Daniel some problems at Court, principally because suspicion arose that Philotas was actually a representation of the late earl of Essex. Such a conclusion meant that the author was trying to apologize for or to defend Essex's rebellion of 1601. Thus, the nobles summoned Daniel before them requesting him to explain his meaning; upon doing so, he was nevertheless reprimanded. In 1607, Daniel published a "corrected" edition of *The Tragedy of Philotas*, with an "apology" denying that his play warranted the aspersions that had been cast upon it. Finally, the poet published, in 1618, *The Collection of the Historie of England*, from the beginnings of English history to the end of Edward III's reign (1377).

ACHIEVEMENTS

Samuel Daniel's reputation has suffered the misfortune of history, the poet having lived and written during an age of literary giants. In a sense, he lies buried beneath the weight of Edmund Spenser, William Shakespeare, John Lyly, Sir Philip Sidney, Michael Drayton, Thomas Campion, and Ben Jonson. The existence of those personages was not itself sufficient to relegate Daniel to the second rank of poets; rather, the writer's own attitudes toward poetry and the state of the world contributed to his eventual position in the literary history of the later Elizabethan period. On the surface, Daniel appears to be an intelligent and thoughtful poet, gifted with imagination and literary eloquence. No one has ever questioned his dedication to the craft of poetry, as he labored to write and then to polish his verse. He embraced all the virtues associated with the best practitioners of his art: the patience to correct and revise and a sensitivity to criticism. Those very virtues, however, restricted both his artistic and personal advancements. He was by nature reluctant to burst forth upon the world. Incessant labor and untiring revision became a refuge for his hesitancy and uncertainty, and he spent much time, both in and outside his poetry, reflecting upon and developing a variety of viewpoints.

Nevertheless, that hesitancy and uncertainty, as observed from a distance of almost three centuries, may well constitute the essence of Daniel's achievement as a poet. He never saw himself other than as a poet called upon to write poetry. With that purpose in mind, he sought perfection, although he fully recognized the impossibility of ever rising to that state. For example, he revised *The Complaynt of Rosamonde* five times and *Delia* on four occasions, while *Musophilus* was altered substantially from its first appearance in 1599 through editions of 1601, 1602, 1607, 1611, and 1623—so often, in fact, that he almost ruined the piece. Still, the revisions reveal Daniel at work, striving to improve the verbal melodies of his lines, repairing what he thought were technical blemishes, purging the Elizabethan idiom from his language, and seeking conciseness at almost any cost. Indeed, in discussing these revisions and alterations, a modern editor of Daniel's poetry has referred to the writer as "something of a neoclassicist born before his time," particularly in reference to his passion for accuracy.

Daniel may have been somewhat intimidated by his contemporaries, but he certainly could stand foremost among them in terms of his patriotism—the eagerness and sincerity with which he expressed his love for his country. Patriotism was a mark of the times; still, the careful reader of his poems will readily observe that he availed himself of every opportunity to support England. In his *The First Fowre Bookes of the Civile Warres Between the Two Houses of Lancaster and Yorke*, for example, he extols the virtues of the Talbots, dukes of Shrewsbury, and of Prince Henry at Agincourt with a passion equal to Shakespeare's history plays; he blames a French woman by the name of Margaret for the murder of Henry IV's youngest son, the duke of Humphrey; and he cries out to Neptune as god of the sea and protector of his nation to shut out ungodly wiles, vile impieties, and all variety of corruption in order to keep England "meere English." Such expression, however, is not limited to patriotism for the sake of mere nationalism; indeed, Daniel recognized all aspects and varieties of patriotic virtue: the courage of the Welsh bowmen and the fortitude and religious conviction of Sir William Wallace, the principal champion of Scotland's independence. Kings are also given their due, as Daniel describes Edward I, a generous prince and Christian warrior who shed his blood for England's greatness. Richard Coeur de Lion (Richard I), on the other hand, and from a more objective point of view, is depicted as having found himself caught up in his cam-

paigns against Philip II of France in an unjust and unprofitable war, deceiving both the world and himself.

Daniel's dedication to England can be related directly to his love of the past. In that respect, he stood equal to a select band among his contemporaries, principally Sidney and Spenser. He rose in anger at allusions by others to the vaunted infallibility of the Greeks and Romans. Such proclamations, he maintained, were but passions that clouded sound men's judgments and caused them to lose respect for the traditions of their own nations. Thus, as in *Musophilus*, Daniel sought out those times that, free from classical ornamentation and deformity, fashioned the wonderful architecture of England. Standing, regretfully, before Stonehenge, he sees it as a vague symbol of the nation's birth: "The misery of darke forgetfulnesse." Similarly, he looks back upon an early day to a peaceful and devout world, in which men of learning lived in a cloistered security. What happened to that cloister? It was a bubble of illusion, burst from without by printing presses, which spread controversy, and by gunpowder, which destroyed the ancient form and discipline of medieval warfare.

In the final analysis, however, Daniel must be seen as a poet of the Renaissance whose imagination grew out of Renaissance ideals of action—to pursue learning and to reconcile the ideal of action with that of culture. Such poetry, particularly in *Musophilus*, became prophecy in which Daniel looked to a new world that would continue to emphasize the civilization of times past. In that new world, the poet (perhaps Daniel himself) rises to considerable heights when he explicates the fine qualities of that former age. Like his contemporaries, Shakespeare and Spenser, Daniel represented the true Elizabethan poet because, as did all true Elizabethans, he tried very hard to transcend the boundaries of his age. "The Starres, that have most glorie," he wrote, "have no rest."

BIOGRAPHY

Although the exact date and place of Samuel Daniel's birth remain unknown, he was probably born near Taunton, in north Somerset, in late 1562 or early 1563, the son of John Daniel, a music master. A younger brother, John, became a musician of some reputation, having earned a bachelor's degree in music in 1604 from Christ Church College, Oxford, after which he published twenty songs titled *Songs for the Lute, Viol and Voice*—with words by his poet-brother. A third brother, also named John, engaged himself in the service of the earl of Essex. He was later fined and imprisoned for having embezzled certain of Essex's letters to his wife and, in 1601, for conspiring with one Peter Bales to blackmail the countess.

Samuel Daniel entered Magdalen Hall, Oxford, in 1581, at the age of nineteen as a commoner. However, he did not remain quite long enough to earn a degree; after about three years, he found English poetry, history, and translation more to his liking than the stricter disciplines of logic and philosophy. Thus, in 1585, he published his first book, a translation of a tract on devices, or crests, titled *Imprese*, by Paolo Giovo, Bishop of Nocera. By 1586, he had obtained a position with Lord Stafford, Elizabeth's ambassador to France; in September of that year, he was found at Rye in the company of an Italian doctor, Julio Marino. If one is to trust the 1594 sonnet collection, *Delia* (numbers 47 and 48), Daniel had spent almost two years in Italy—either from 1584 to 1586, or at some period prior to 1589. Shortly after 1590, the poet became tutor to William Herbert, third earl of Pembroke, son of Sidney's sister, Mary, and the patron of Shakespeare. Thus, Daniel took up residence at Wilton, near Salisbury, the seat of the Pembrokes.

The real attraction for Daniel at Wilton was not his pupil, but the boy's mother, Mary Herbert, countess of Pembroke. A woman of excellent literary taste and of distinctive literary talent, she had married Henry Herbert in 1577 and became the most famous patroness of literature in her time, bestowing her favors and encouragement upon Spenser, Jonson, Shakespeare, her brother Sir Philip Sidney, and, of course, Daniel. Despite such support for his work, however, Daniel first appeared before the world without his consent or even foreknowledge. At the end of the 1591 edition of Sidney's *Astrophel and Stella*, the printer (or editor) attached twenty-seven of Daniel's sonnets; what really bothered Daniel, however, was the fact that the pieces contained typographical errors that offended his sense of correctness. He countered by issuing, in February,

1592, his volume of *Delia*, with fifty sonnets dedicated to the countess of Pembroke. The volume was well received, with the result that Daniel published a new edition later the same year (with four new sonnets and *The Complaynt of Rosamonde*, a long narrative poem) and a third edition in 1594. In the latter collection, he replaced the prose dedication to the countess of Pembroke with a sonnet, added a number of sonnets and deleted others, enlarged *The Complaynt of Rosamonde* by twenty-three stanzas, and included his Senecan tragedy, *Cleopatra*.

Daniel's reputation grew and attracted Spenser's attention, the epic poet thinking highly of him and encouraging him to write tragedy. Daniel was not interested in such projects, however; instead, he produced a long historical poem, *The First Fowre Bookes of the Civile Warres Between the Two Houses of Lancaster and Yorke*; on the model of Lucan's *Bellum civile* (60-65 C.E.; *Pharsalia*, 1614). For the next five years (1595-1599), Daniel published nothing new, principally because he was busily engaged at Skipton, Yorkshire, in tutoring Anne Clifford, daughter of the countess of Cumberland, then eleven years of age. He enjoyed the relationship with the family but felt restricted by the work that kept him from writing poetry—especially the completion of his *Civile Warres*. Nevertheless, he managed to wrench himself free long enough to compose, in 1599, his poem *Musophilus* and a verse *Letter from Octavia to Marcus Antonius*. Two years later, he published the first collected edition of his works, *Poeticall Essayes*. That was followed by a complete edition later in 1601, *The Works of Samuel Daniel*.

There are those who would maintain that, upon Spenser's death in 1599, Daniel succeeded him as poet laureate of England. However, before Jonson received his patent and pension in February, 1616, the official position of poet laureate did not really exist. True, Spenser had received £50 a year from Queen Elizabeth, but that sum signified informal royal recognition rather than payment for a distinct position or office. Although Daniel occupied no formal position as a poet, he visited often at Court early in the reign of James I, where friends received him well. Further, Daniel had determined to be one of the first to congratulate James on the king's arrival in England; thus, he sent him *A Panegyricke Congratulatorie* while he traveled toward London. In 1602, the poet had dedicated a sonnet to "Her Sacred Majestie," Queen Anne. With his political fences fairly secure, he turned his attention to *The Tragedy of Philotas*.

Daniel spent the better part of his later years reviewing his early poetry, preparing editions of his works, and writing second-rate entertainments for Court festivities: *The Vision of the Twelve Goddesses* (pr., pb. 1604), *The Queenes Arcadia* (pr., pb. 1606), *Tethys Festival: Or, The Queenes Wake* (pr., pb. 1610), and *Hymens Triumph* (pr. 1614, pb. 1615), the last piece to be published by Daniel during his lifetime. Such efforts yielded some reward, for he received the appointment of inspector of the children of the queen's revels, a post that he gave over to his brother John in 1619. In 1607, the poet served as a groom of the queen's privy chamber, which meant a stipend of £60 a year. He had moved out of London in 1603 and rented a farm in Wiltshire, near Devizes. There, in June, 1618, he wrote his last poem "To the Right Reverend Father in God, James Montague, Lord Bishop of Winchester," Dean of the Chapel and a member of the Privy Council, the purpose of which was to console the cleric during his sickness. Daniel himself died in October, 1619.

ANALYSIS

Perhaps the most sensible point at which to begin an analysis of Samuel Daniel's poetry is the commentary of his contemporaries. The poets of his day saw considerable quality in his work. Francis Meres, a rector, schoolmaster, and literary reviewer, believed that in the *Delia* sonnets, Daniel captured the matchless beauty of his titled subject, while the individual's passion rose at the reading of the distressed Rosamond's death. Meres also found the *Civile Warres* to be equal to Lucan's *Pharsalia*. The lyric poet and writer of romances Thomas Lodge gave him the highest praise for invention and choice of language, while Thomas Carew, one of Jonson's principal disciples, labeled him the English Lucan. Daniel's rhyme caught the attention of the Scots pamphleteer and versifier William Drummond of Hawthornden, who believed it second to none, and a number of lesser poetic lights during the reigns of Eliz-

abeth and James I heaped praise upon Daniel's sharp conceits, pure English, and choice of words. There were, of course, a like number of detractors, foremost among them being Jonson, the dramatist John Marston, and Drayton, who claimed that Daniel was only a historian in verse who should have written prose rather than poetry. Interestingly, the judgments of Daniel's contemporaries, both positive and unfavorable, were not too far off the mark.

Daniel's career as a poet must be viewed in two stages. In his early period, the poet committed himself to pageantry and the patriotism of Elizabethan England. He sought to glorify his nation, applying his imagination to its ideals and achievements. As he matured, however—as his experiences widened and his intellect developed and deepened—he learned how to control the complex combination of poetry and history. Further, he learned about the language of poetry. Once in command of the poet's art of language, he began to understand the conflicts in which all Elizabethan poets engaged: confidence in and concern for the ability to write poetry; dedication to the notion of England, but doubt of the events of history; and trust in beauty, but skepticism about surface materialism. Still, with all these conflicts, Daniel managed to succeed as a poet because, in the end, he appealed to custom and nature, both of which provided him "wings" to carry him "not out of his course, but as it were beyond his power to a faire happier flights."

DELIA

Daniel reached the height of his stature as a poet with the publication of his sonnet sequence, *Delia*, and its apparent companion piece, the long narrative poem *The Complaynt of Rosamonde*. Although the poet, by 1592, might have been expected to demonstrate some evidence of having been influenced by Sidney and his sister, the countess of Pembroke, *Delia*, in particular, differs significantly from *Astrophel and Stella*. The former contains little of the drama and personal tension found in Sidney's sequence, but it has considerably more melody and clear imagery. The majority of the sonnets follow the English (or Shakespearean) pattern, with three quatrains and a final couplet. Unlike those of Shakespeare, however, the poems lack any bursts of emotional surge or lift. Instead, Daniel clung to this pure diction, serene rhythms, and sparkling clarity that allowed his reader to see, without difficulty, such objects as a clear-eyed rector of a holy hill, a modest maid decked with the blush of honor, and the green paths of youth and love. True, the sonnets are supposed to reflect the passionate love adventures of the poet's youth; obviously, however, time, a series of careful revisions for later editions, and the quiet and placid nature of maturity created a unified series of sober, restrained, and mediated utterances. There are a number of interesting biographical and source problems surrounding *Delia*, particularly the identity of the lady of the title and accusations of plagiarism from several French sonneteers; these remain debates of a speculative nature and ought not to detract from the true poetic force of the complete sequence.

### THE COMPLAYNT OF ROSAMONDE

*The Complaynt of Rosamonde* first appeared in 1592, bound with the authorized edition of *Delia*. Thus, scholars have quickly labeled it a companion to the sonnets, although it might be more accurately termed a transition. On one hand, its style and content relate it to *Delia*, but it also moves in the opposite direction, toward the serious, contemplative tone of later poems. In 106 seven-line stanzas, Daniel relates the story of Rosamond Clifford, mistress of Henry II, but the poet does not forget entirely the Delia of his sonnets. The ghost of Rosamond, while pleading with the poet to attempt to relate her narrative, apologizes for intruding upon his own private griefs. However, the spirit strongly suggests that Delia's heart may be moved by evidence of poetic sympathy for one of her sex—namely, Rosamond. Before vanishing, the ghost appeals to Delia for a sigh to help her pass to a sweet Elysian rest. Thus, Daniel finds himself alone with his own sorrows concerning the errors of his youth. In another context, the despondent Rosamond reflects upon the cruelty of isolating beauty from the admiration of the world. She points to the beautiful women who come to town to display their loveliness—all except Delia, who has been left in a remote part of the country. *The Complaynt of Rosamonde* demonstrates the skill with which Daniel could construct a long narrative poem containing both story and moral, uncluttered with social, religious, or political complications. In *The*

*Complaynt of Rosamonde*, he concentrated almost exclusively on the theme of personal tragedy and the contrast between exaltation and misery. Such concentration permitted him to develop a character, write a story reflecting universal melancholy, and place both in a context appropriate to and worthy of the term "complaint."

### CLEOPATRA

Daniel's *Cleopatra* is a carefully formed Senecan tragedy in alternate rhyme, justifiably dismissed as drama but not sufficiently appreciated for its poetry. The play, which focuses mainly on events subsequent to Anthony's death, was dwarfed by Shakespeare's *Antony and Cleopatra* (pr. c. 1606-1607), which swept all rivals from the field. Nevertheless, Daniel's *Cleopatra* can be appreciated as literature. It contains an abundance of human feeling from which the reader may derive dramatic and poetic pleasure; further, its form and diction have been compared with that of Shakespeare's *Antony and Cleopatra* and John Dryden's *All for Love: Or, The World Well Lost* (pr. 1677). Daniel concentrates his attention on Cleopatra to examine her at a moment of significant crisis, to view her from various perspectives. For example, he weaves into his verse drama a number of seemingly peripheral scenes that function as comments on Cleopatra's resolve to die. Such scenes—Arius saving Philostratus from death and Philostratus being ashamed of clinging to life so eagerly in time of national disaster—place the story of individual persons into the larger, more important context of politics and society. Certainly there is much to observe in the conflict between Cleopatra as queen and as mother. Daniel, however, does not lose sight of the "higher" moral issues: pride and riot out of control, government and citizens overcome by impiety and false security, and the entire society wallowing in what he terms "fat-fed pleasure."

### CIVILE WARRES

Certainly, the historical and political issues in *Cleopatra* helped establish Daniel's interest in those areas, and he never lost sight of his mission to give the world a memorable historical epic. Thus, almost exactly a year after entering *Cleopatra* in the Stationers' Register, the poet issued the initial version of his *Civile Warres*. After almost fifteen years of labor, beginning in 1594,

Daniel managed to produce eight books amounting to about seven thousand ottava rima lines. The work began with Richard II in 1377 and was supposed to end with the marriage of Henry VII to Elizabeth of York in January, 1486, but the poet fell slightly short of the mark and arrived only at 1464 and the marriage of Edward IV and Lady Elizabeth Grey. Although it would be a disservice to Daniel's motives to term the project a mistake, it may well have been too ambitious an undertaking for one who was not a fully committed historian. Daniel set out to versify the truth, not to write a poem; he hoped that the result would serve all his countrymen, a national epic that seemed right for the time. Unfortunately, his contemporaries viewed the *Civile Warres* as a verse chronicle, not as an epic poem. In fact, Jonson complained that Daniel had written a poetic commentary on the civil wars, but had failed to include a single battle—a comment that was more figurative than factual.

Actually, the problems arising from the project were not entirely of Daniel's own making. He originally intended to establish himself as a legitimate epic poet and a loyal subject of Elizabeth by anchoring the *Civile Warres* to Tudor myth and history. Although the blood factions of the nation produced a bloody war, good eventually came from the evil. Elizabeth would serve as a symbol of peace following the civil strife, thus inspiring poets to record and comment upon the events. By 1609, however, prior to completing the final book of the *Civile Warres*, Daniel found himself without a subject: Elizabeth was dead. He had by that time, however, directed his attention to other forms of historical writing, especially prose, and he simply lost interest in the epic, as well as in the historical period he was attempting to versify.

### MUSOPHILUS

History was not the only study to capture Daniel's interest and muse. His *Poeticall Essayes* of 1599 contain one of his most characteristic poems, *Musophilus*. It is certainly a very personal piece, yet it stands as a fine example of the verse dialogue. On the personal level, the poet contends that he must develop and defend his own art, not only for the benefit of those who are contemptuous of it but also to reestablish his faith in himself and in the career of letters to which he has dedicated himself. That personal level, then, dictates the

structure of the poem. Philocosmus, the unlettered man of action, confronts Musophilus, the defender of culture and of all learning. Daniel maintained that the idea for the poem was his—from his own heart—but there are clear connections to Count Baldassare Castiglione's *Il Cortegiano* (1528; *The Courtier*, 1561). At any rate, Philocosmus (like the French) reflects the great heresy of knowing only the nobility of arms; he ignores and also abhors letters, and considers learned men rascals. Such thinking is of course countered with the idea of letters being profitable and necessary for life and culture. The mind, therefore, enters the contest against materialism and narrow utilitarianism in order to preserve reverence. Daniel seriously believed that religious innovation and reform would eventually alter all priorities—the good as well as the bad—thus eradicating the sacred traditions of religion. In other words, in defending poetry and learning, the lines of *Musophilus* clearly echo the poet's fear of the scientific spirit, of an arrogance wherein people strive to talk rather than to worship. The ideal for Daniel was for humility and modesty to accompany knowledge and learning.

### OTHER MAJOR WORKS

PLAYS: *Cleopatra*, pb. 1594; *The Tragedy of Philotas*, pb. 1605.

NONFICTION: *The Defence of Ryme*, 1603; *The Collection of the Historie of England*, 1618.

MISCELLANEOUS: *The Works of Samuel Daniel*, 1601; *The Complete Works in Verse and Prose of Samuel Daniel*, 1885-1896, 1963 (5 volumes; Alexander B. Grosart, editor).

### BIBLIOGRAPHY

Attreed, Lorraine. "England's Official Rose: Tudor Concepts of the Middle Ages." In *Hermeneutics and Medieval Culture*, edited by Patrick J. Gallacher and Helen Damico. Albany: State University of New York Press, 1989. Attreed places Daniel at the end of a tradition of Tudor apologists concerned with the legend of Tudor achievement and with the mythical connection to King Arthur, and she traces Daniel's growing discomfort with the simplistic tendencies of such historiography. Although not concerned exclusively with Daniel, this article provides important context for much of his historical writing in both verse and prose.

Bergeron, David M. "Women as Patrons of English Renaissance Drama." In *Patronage in the Renaissance*, edited by Guy Fitch Lytle and Stephen Orgel. Princeton, N.J.: Princeton University Press, 1981. Chronicling the importance of women as patrons of dramatic works, Bergeron shows the particular importance to Daniel of both Lucy Russell, the countess of Bedford, and Mary Herbert, the countess of Pembroke. The former arranged for Daniel to be commissioned to write *The Vision of the Twelve Goddesses*, and the latter made him part of her circle at Wilton. Both patrons were major influences on Daniel's career.

Galbraith, David. *Architectonics of Imitation in Spenser, Daniel, and Drayton*. Toronto, Ont.: University of Toronto Press, 2000. Galbraith examines Daniel's *Civile Warres*, Edmund Spenser's *The Faerie Queene* (1590, 1596), and Michael Drayton's *Poly-Olbion* (1612-1622) to explore the boundaries between history and poetry.

Harner, James L. *Samuel Daniel and Michael Drayton: A Reference Guide*. Boston: G. K. Hall, 1980. Harner collects all the major scholarly treatments of Daniel and Michael Drayton from 1684 through early 1979 and annotates each one briefly. The two poets are treated separately.

Helgerson, Richard. "Barbarous Tongues: The Ideology of Poetic Form in Renaissance England." In *The Historical Renaissance: New Essays on Tudor and Stuart Literature and Culture*, edited by Richard Strier and Heather Dubrow. Chicago: University of Chicago Press, 1988. Tracing the sixteenth century argument for quantitative verse to a choice for the civilized tradition of Greece and Rome over the barbarous one of the Goths, Helgerson shows how Daniel answers that argument by repudiating the classical model and by celebrating the gothic origins of the English language and its poetry. Daniel's choice of rhyme is therefore patriotic as well as theoretical. Helgerson sees this choice in a consciously political context, coming as it does in 1603, the year of Queen Elizabeth's death.

Hiller, Geoffrey A., and Peter L. Groves, eds. *Daniel Samuel: Selected Poetry and "A Defense of Rhyme."* Asheville, N.C.: Pegasus Press, 1998. Annotated edition of Daniel's major poetry and selected prose which expands in scope and detail the Sprague 1930 edition. Spelling and punctuation have been modernized. Some selections are prefaced by a discussion of their literary characteristics, publication history, and thematic content.

Himelick, Raymond. Introduction to *"Musophilus": Containing a General Defense of All Learning*. West Lafayette, Ind.: Purdue University Press, 1965. After a brief biographical introduction, Himelick explains the main argument of Daniel's philosophical poem and examines its sources and analogues, the poet's revisions, and the style. This volume is a helpful commentary on a rather difficult and abstract work.

Quinn, Kelly A. "Fulke Greville's Friendly Patronage." *Studies in Philology* 103, no. 4 (Fall, 2006): 417-426. Examines the patronage relationship between Greville and Daniel, saying it was broad enough to be more of a friendship and to include some disagreement.

Rees, Joan. *Samuel Daniel: A Critical and Biographical Study*. Liverpool, England: Liverpool University Press, 1964. Placing Daniel and his works in detailed biographical and historical context, Rees explains important influences on the poet and elucidates his main ideas. She is particularly informative on patronage and its effects on Daniel. Unlike many critics, Rees defends Daniel's play *Cleopatra*, but on the other hand, she thinks his masques show unease with the form and its symbolism. Contains four illustrations and a good, though not annotated, select bibliography.

Seronsy, Cecil. *Samuel Daniel*. New York: Twayne, 1967. This basic critical biography of Daniel is clearly and simply presented. Shows the development of Daniel as a poet over the course of many years. The final chapter, "Poet and Thinker," offers an excellent introduction to Daniel's versification, characteristic imagery, and ideas. Includes an annotated short bibliography.

*Samuel J. Rogal*

# GEORGE DARLEY

**Born:** Dublin, Ireland; 1795
**Died:** London, England; November 23, 1846

PRINCIPAL POETRY

*The Errors of Ecstasie: A Dramatic Poem with*
*Other Pieces*, 1822
*Nepenthe*, 1835
*Poems of the Late George Darley*, 1890
*The Complete Poetical Works of George Darley*,
1908 (Ramsey Colles, editor)

OTHER LITERARY FORMS

George Darley might be called a literary hack. The profession of writer in the early nineteenth century was a precarious one, and Darley tried his hand at most of the popular literary forms of his time. Although his work was usually unsigned, in keeping with the tradition of anonymous reviewing and publishing at the time, Darley can be credited with lyrical dramas, or masques, in the Elizabethan style, and a large number of reviews of art exhibits and current plays.

Among Darley's major literary works were a series of "dramatic" poems, *Sylvia: Or, The May Queen, a Lyrical Drama* (pb. 1827); and two tragedies: *Thomas à Becket: A Dramatic Chronicle in Five Acts* (pb. 1840) and *Ethelstan: Or, The Battle of Brunaburh, a Dramatic Chronicle in Five Acts* (pb. 1841). The titles of Darley's dramatic pieces suggest that they were written to be publicly staged, but none ever made it to the theater. Finally, Darley's letters should be noted as a highly valuable commentary on the life of a professional writer at a critical phase in English literature. His letters, even more than his various essays on literature and art, provide a useful series of insights into the events and problems of the era. In spite of Darley's shy disposition, he met many of the most famous poets and critics of his time, read widely in the literature of his day, and was a fair commentator on many pressing social issues.

It should be noted that Darley spent his last five years writing scientific textbooks for the use of students of secondary age. He may also have written a *Life of Virgil*, which is ascribed to him in the British Museum catalog.

ACHIEVEMENTS

George Darley never attained the recognition for his poetry and dramatic works that he earnestly sought throughout most of his adult life, although he pretended to be indifferent to the poetic fame that invariably eluded him and demanded that his friends be unsparing of his feelings in making their comments on his work. In truth, his poetry was seldom reviewed or even noticed by anyone outside the immediate circle of his friends. It is difficult to find references to his ideas or to his poetry in anything but the most exhaustive surveys of English Romanticism. Still, within the circle of Darley's friends, he was regarded as something of a poetic genius—the poet who would bring forth a new era of poetry. Charles Lamb, Thomas Lovell Beddoes, and John Clare were enthusiastic readers of his work and did their best to secure attention from the critical reviews. Even the proverbially churlish Thomas Carlyle remarked that Darley was one of the few poets of his day who really understood the spirit of Elizabethan tragedy, to the extent of being able to imitate it with any kind of success. Despite these favorable opinions, Darley never achieved more than a marginal place among the English poets of the early nineteenth century.

It was only some forty years after his death that readers took up Darley's poetry with interest. Part of this interest derived from the Celtic renaissance, but part also derived from Darley's ultimate claims to be read as a good minor poet.

BIOGRAPHY

George Darley was born in Dublin, Ireland, in 1795. He was the oldest of seven children of Arthur and Mary Darley. His parents were of the upper class, and for unknown reasons went to America for an extended visit when Darley was about three. The boy was reared by his grandfather, and he always referred to this period of his life as the "sunshine of the breast." At this time in his life, Darley acquired an extreme stammer, so severe that even in his later years, his closest friends could scarcely make out what he was saying. The stammer may have been important in determining his later career as a poet, and it partly accounts for one of the most common themes in the poetry: the isolation of the poet.

In 1815, Darley entered Trinity College, Dublin. He apparently made few friends there and, curiously, never mentioned the school in his later correspondence. The stammer interfered with his examinations, but he received his degree in 1820 and immediately left for London. Despite his speech defect and chronic shyness, Darley made friends with a number of writers who were emerging in the 1820's. His friends encouraged his work, and the letters he exchanged with such poets as Clare and Beddoes reveal their high regard for his work.

Darley spent almost ten years in London working at various literary and scientific projects, but late in 1830, he determined to go to France. He wrote occasional essays on art for the *Athenaeum* and (perhaps) another journal, titled *The Original*, but there are few records of his life in Paris or his tours to Italy. It is significant, however, that several members of the Darley family were, for a while, reunited. The older brothers toured Italy together, and later Germany. Darley had always been sickly and generally poor, but he was a good tourist, and the letters from this period are among his best.

Darley continued to review books on various subjects for the *Athenaeum*, earning a reputation for extreme severity. He adopted the role in his private life of a vivacious and often bitter critic; he died in November, 1846, having never revisited Ireland, which constituted the one subject that was above criticism.

## ANALYSIS

George Darley's best poetry is the work of a man seeking escape from the world. The sorrows of his life—his poverty and his lack of recognition—are for the most part not present in his poetry. Many of his poems are about love, beautiful women, and the death of innocent women. This preoccupation suggests one of the more common Romantic motifs: the separation between a desirable realm of creativity and fertility and the sterile existence of the poet's life. In Darley's love poems, there is a continuing search for perfection—the perfect woman, the perfect love. These poems show the influence of the Cavalier poet Thomas Carew, and it might be noted that one of Darley's most successful poems ("It Is Not Beauty I Demand") was published in the *London Mag-*

*azine* with the name Carew appended to it. The fraud was not discovered until much later, after Francis Palgrave had included the poem in *The Golden Treasury*.

The women in Darley's poems are not the sentimental idols of so much nineteenth century love poetry, yet these lyrics are marred by Darley's frequent use of Elizabethan clichés: lips as red as roses, breasts as white as snow, hair as golden as the sun. In setting and theme as well, Darley's love poems are excessively conventional.

### NATURE POEMS

In his nature poetry, Darley was able to achieve a more authentic style and tone. His early years in the Irish countryside had given him an almost pantheistic appreciation of nature as the ultimate source of comfort; many of his nature poems border on a kind of religious veneration. It is nature that comforts humanity, not the Church; it is nature that speaks with an "unerring voice" and will, if attended to, provide humans with the lessons in morality that they require.

"A Country Sunday," one of Darley's finest nature poems, illustrates this idea of God-in-nature. The poem, given its reference to Sunday, is curiously barren of any directly religious references. It is the sun that gives joy and the wind that serves as the vehicle of prayer. Nature serves as the great link between humanity's sordid existence and heaven.

### "IT IS NOT BEAUTY I DEMAND"

In several of the lyric poems the themes of nature and love are fused. "It Is Not Beauty I Demand"—Darley's one assuredly great poem—illustrates the blending of nature and love, though the intent of the poet is to raise human love to a level beyond anything that might be found in nature. Darley's method is to use many of the standard phrases about women's beauty ("a crystal brow"; "starry eyes"; "lips that seem on roses fed") in a series of ten rapidly moving quatrains, with eight beats to each line, and a simple rhyme scheme of *abab cdcd* through the whole of the poem. The quatrains move rapidly, in part because Darley uses the syntax and diction of one who is speaking directly to his reader.

In "It Is Not Beauty I Demand," the natural beauties of the perfect woman are rejected as mere ornaments, or "gauds." In the fourth stanza, Darley breaks from the

Cavalier tradition of "all for love" and inserts a fairly traditional moral into the poem. Thus, the red lips are rejected because they lead to destruction, like the red coral "beneath the ocean stream" upon which the "adventurer" perishes. The same moral argument is continued in the following stanzas, in which the white cheeks of the woman are rejected because they incite "hot youths to fields of blood." Even the greatest symbol of female beauty—"Helen's breast"—is rejected because Helen's beauty provoked war and suffering.

Darley's ideal woman would be a companion, a comforter, one with "a tender heart" and "loyal mind." Despite Darley's obvious affinities in this poem with Carew and other Cavalier poets, the poem represents a rejection of the Cavalier ideals of going off to battle to prove one's love and honor; it also represents a challenge to the rich sensuality of much Romantic poetry. With its emphasis on the intellectual virtues of women and the pleasures of companionship (versus sex), "It Is Not Beauty I Demand" is an affirmation of the ideals of love and marriage associated with the Victorians.

### VERSE DRAMAS VERSUS LYRICS

Mention must be made of Darley's two tragedies, which in spite of their obvious failure as stage plays represent his most sustained creative effort. Darley had always been an enthusiastic reader of William Shakespeare and other Elizabethan dramatists; one of the most striking themes in his dramatic reviews was the death of tragedy in his own time. He was especially sickened by the rise and popularity of domestic tragedy; he reviewed one of the most popular tragedies of his time (*Ion*) in an almost savage manner for its sentimentality. Darley was not able to reverse the tendencies of Victorian playwriting, but his two tragedies, *Thomas à Becket* and *Ethelstan*, whatever their shortcomings as plays (they can be characterized as dramatic verse), illustrate what he thought a tragedy ought to be. He invoked the Elizabethan ideal of a man in high place who is brought to his death through his own error and the malice of others. Darley, however, was not able to write dialogue, and his characters are much given to lengthy, histrionic speeches. In many instances, the speeches cover entire scenes. As far as the plays have merit, they serve to illustrate the Victorian preoccupation with the "great man." Darley's heroes and villains are indeed on

the heroic scale, but they lack credibility and the blank verse is frequently bathetic.

By contrast, Darley's lyrics, his only lasting achievement, have a genuine but limited appeal. His speech impediment, aloofness, and chronic shyness seemed to have forced him into a career that would serve as a natural release to his emotions. In his poetry, Darley created a world of fantasy, of benevolent nature and beautiful maidens, an ordered universe that the poet never found in real life.

### OTHER MAJOR WORKS

PLAYS: *Sylvia: Or, The May Queen, a Lyrical Drama*, pb. 1827; *Thomas à Becket: A Dramatic Chronicle in Five Acts*, pb. 1840; *Ethelstan: Or, The Battle of Brunaburh, a Dramatic Chronicle in Five Acts*, pb. 1841.

NONFICTION: *The Life and Letters of George Darley*, 1928 (Claude Abbott, editor of letters).

### BIBLIOGRAPHY

Abbott, Claude Colleer, ed. *The Life and Letters of George Darley, Poet and Critic*. 1928. Reprint. Oxford, England: Clarendon Press, 1967. A rare biography of Darley, which presents him as a poet and critic of distinction. Includes a full analysis of Darley's lyric poetry and of his major work *Nepenthe*. Notes the weakness in the structure of his work and suggests that it should be read as a series of lyric episodes expressing the theme of spiritual adventure. Includes a complete bibliography of works by Darley.

Bloom, Harold. *The Visionary Company: A Reading of English Romantic Poetry*. 1961. Rev. ed. Ithaca, N.Y.: Cornell University Press, 1971. This brief analysis is important because Bloom is one of the most influential of modern literary critics. He pays Darley a high compliment by including him in the "visionary company" of Romantic poets. Includes a reading of *Nepenthe*, which Bloom sees as a quest-romance in the tradition of Percy Bysshe Shelley's *Alastor* (1816) and John Keats's *Endymion: A Poetic Romance* (1818).

Brisman, Leslie. *Romantic Origins*. Ithaca, N.Y.: Cornell University Press, 1978. The most extensive treatment of Darley by a modern critic, although it makes difficult reading. Brisman argues that Darley's awareness of his rank as a minor poet provides him with a recurring theme: He deliberately cultivates a "myth of weakness." This is particularly noticeable in *Nepenthe*, a poem in which Darley transforms the romantic quest "into a search for images of poetic diminutiveness."

Heath-Stubbs, John F. *The Darkling Plain: A Study of the Later Fortunes of Romanticism in English Poetry from George Darley to W. B. Yeats*. 1950. Reprint. Philadelphia: R. West, 1977. Perhaps the best brief overview of Darley's work, particularly *Nepenthe*. Heath-Stubbs links *Nepenthe* to works by Keats and Shelley, and also those by William Blake. Argues that in its "continuous intensity of lyrical music and vivid imagery" *Nepenthe* is unlike any other poem of similar length in English.

Jack, Ian. *English Literature, 1815-1832*. Oxford, England: Clarendon Press, 1963. Brief assessment in which Jack argues that Darley was a better critic than he was poet. Of his poetry, Darley's lyrics are superior to his long poems, although his diction was often flawed. He may, however, have had an influence on Alfred, Lord Tennyson. One of Darley's weaknesses was that he did not have anything original to say.

*John R. Griffin*

---

# SIR WILLIAM DAVENANT

**Born:** Oxford, England; February, 1606
**Died:** London, England; April 7, 1668
**Also known as:** William D'Avenant

PRINCIPAL POETRY

*Madagascar: With Other Poems*, 1638
*Gondibert*, 1651 (unfinished)
*The Seventh and Last Canto of the Third Book of Gondibert*, 1685
*The Shorter Poems and Songs from the Plays and Masques*, 1972 (A. M. Gibbs, editor)

OTHER LITERARY FORMS

Although he produced a considerable body of lyric and epic poetry, the bulk of the literary work of Sir William Davenant (DAV-uh-nuhnt) was designed for the stage. His early dramas, heavily indebted to William Shakespeare and Ben Jonson, included the tragedy *The Cruell Brother* (pr. 1627), the comedies *The Witts* (pr. 1634) and *News from Plimouth* (pr. 1635), and the pastoral romance *The Platonick Lovers* (pr. 1635). In the mid-1630's, he began writing masques; the best and most elaborate of these, *Britannia Triumphans* (pr., pb. 1638), was done in collaboration with Inigo Jones. *Salmacida Spolia* (pr., pb. 1640), also with Jones, was the last masque in which Charles I performed. After the Civil War, Davenant produced a series of dramatic entertainments, comprising a mixture of set speeches, scenes, and musical interludes, designed to circumvent the Puritan prohibition of conventional drama. The first was *The First Days Entertainment at Rutland House* (pr. 1656). In more sophisticated pieces on heroic themes, *The Siege of Rhodes* (pr., pb. 1656) and *The Cruelty of the Spaniards in Peru* (pr., pb. 1658), Davenant collaborated with such composers as Henry Lawes and Matthew Locke to create the English opera. After the Restoration, he devoted much of his time to rewriting Shakespeare, and in 1667, in collaboration with John Dryden, he produced an immensely popular comic travesty of *The Tempest*.

ACHIEVEMENTS

Sir William Davenant's lyric poetry, although essentially derivative from John Donne, Jonson, and the Cavalier mode, is both skillful and varied. Davenant's longest poem, the unfinished *Gondibert*, is competent but undistinguished in its artistry. Nevertheless, it is of major importance when considered in conjunction with *The Preface to Gondibert with An Answer by Mr. Hobbes* (1650). *Gondibert* was one of the first neoclassical poems. Here Davenant advocates such neoclassical precepts as the importance of restraint in metaphor, image, and sentiment; the use of the balanced, closed line; and the importance of probability. His popularization of neoclassical decorum and his development of the opera and the heroic drama are Davenant's major achievements.

BIOGRAPHY

Sir William Davenant, or D'Avenant, as he styled himself in later years, lived a life that seems to cry out to be the subject of a historical novel. Born into the middle class, destined to be a tradesman, he rose to become one of the most honored poets and playwrights of his day, a general in the army of Charles I, a successful diplomat, and the friend and companion of some of the most glamorous men and women of his age.

John Davenant, a vintner, was mayor of Oxford in 1606, the year of his son William's birth. Shakespeare was supposedly a regular visitor at the Davenant tavern and was reputed to be the boy's actual father, a rumor that the young poet actively fostered. Intended for apprenticeship to a London merchant, Davenant, at his father's death in 1622, was instead preferred to the powerful duchess of Richmond as a page. At the duke of Richmond's death in 1624, Davenant took service with Fulke Greville, Lord Brooke, opening even further the doors of patronage and preferment. The elder poet was an early supporter of his talent, and by 1627, Davenant was a working playwright with his first tragedy, *The Cruell Brother*, licensed for performance. New plays followed quickly, but in 1630, Davenant fell silent for several years, the victim, it is believed, of a nearly fatal case of syphilis, an illness that cost him his nose. By 1633, however, Davenant had returned to the stage, writing a number of successful plays, gaining a reputation as a poet, and in the later years of the decade, achieving great success as a writer of court masques. In 1638, he was named poet laureate.

Davenant served with distinction in the Bishop's Wars of 1640 and was later implicated in the First Army Plot against Parliament. When the Civil War broke out, he served under the duke of Newcastle as lieutenant-general of ordinance and later fought with the king's army, being knighted in 1642 at the Siege of Gloucester. In the later years of the war, he specialized in procuring arms and ammunition, making several dangerous trips to the Continent. Eventually, on the collapse of the Royalist cause, he fled to France and became one of Queen Henrietta-Maria's most trusted servants.

In France, Davenant began the collaboration with Thomas Hobbes that was to be instrumental in the de-

*Sir William Davenant* (New York Public Library)

velopment of neoclassical theory. In 1650, they published *The Preface to Gondibert with An Answer by Mr. Hobbes*. Meanwhile, Davenant was appointed governor of Maryland by the exiled Charles II, but his ship to the New World was captured by privateers commissioned by Parliament. He spent the next two years in prison. Although released in 1652, at John Milton's intervention according to one tradition, Davenant spent the next few years in poverty and was again arrested, for debt, in 1654.

In 1656, Davenant returned to writing for the stage and, in his attempt to circumvent Puritan restrictions, developed the rambling art form that was the direct ancestor of both modern opera and Dryden's heroic drama. His career for the next few years was a series of successes, although he has been accused of selling out to the Puritan government. After the Restoration, his popularity continued, but he was never reinstated in his laureateship. Charles II frequently attended his plays, and at the time of his death on April 7, 1668, Davenant was one of the two most successful theater managers in London.

ANALYSIS

Sir William Davenant began his career as a versatile, technically competent poet, adept at producing *à la mode* verse guaranteed to please his patrons. His shorter works, many of them clearly bearing the stamp of Donne's or Jonson's influence, cover the entire range of forms fashionable in Caroline England: odes, satires, panegyrics, songs, and occasional poems. His themes were essentially what one would expect from a man destined to become poet laureate: the heroism of Prince Rupert and the king, the importance of friendship and the good life, the nobility of any number of aristocrats, and the beauty of a variety of noble ladies, especially the queen. As a lyric poet, Davenant was a competent craftsman, one of the best of that "mob of gentlemen who wrote with ease" and who surrounded Charles I. In later years, however, he became a trailblazer, and his heroic poem, *Gondibert*, taken in conjunction with its *The Preface to Gondibert with An Answer by Mr. Hobbes*, is one of the most important poems of the middle years of the seventeenth century.

## MADAGASCAR

Although many of his early verses had appeared in poetic miscellanies or editions of his or others' plays, the first collection of Davenant's poems to be printed was *Madagascar* in 1638. It consisted of the long (446-line) title poem and forty-two shorter pieces, including poems addressed to the king and queen, to aristocrats such as the duchess of Buckingham and the earls of Portland and Rutland, and to friends such as Endymion Porter, Henry Jermyn, and Thomas Carew. Also present are satiric works, several poems commemorating deaths, including those of Shakespeare, Jonson, and Davenant (a false rumor), and a number of prologues, epilogues, and songs from plays. The volume opens with commendatory verses from Porter, Sir John Suckling, Carew, and William Habington.

Like Michael Drayton's "To the Virginian Voyage" of 1606, Davenant's "Madagascar" is a patriotic poem designed to stir Englishmen to great deeds of exploration and conquest. Whereas Drayton's poem is occasional—although three voyages were undertaken to Virginia in the year the work appeared—Davenant's piece honors a nonevent, Prince Rupert's proposed but never attempted expedition to South Africa, a voyage

that his uncle Charles I eventually forbade and that Rupert's mother compared to an adventure of Don Quixote.

As the poem opens, Davenant recounts his soul's dream journey south to the tropics, where he beholds Rupert, his "mighty Uncles Trident" in hand, disembarking on the island of Madagascar with an army. The natives immediately surrender, awed as much by Rupert's beauty as by his military prowess. Other Europeans, perhaps Spaniards, also invade, and each side chooses two champions to determine ownership of the island by single combat. The English champions, for whom "The God-like *Sidney* was a Type," are Davenant's friends Porter and Jermyn. Their conflict is recounted in typically "high, immortall verse," charged with elaborate conceits. The English champions are victorious, but the treacherous Spaniards renege on their vow to surrender, thus proving the justice of the English claim and providing Davenant with material for further elaborately depicted battle scenes. Eventually, Rupert is proclaimed "The first true Monarch of the *Golden Isle*" and Madagascar's great riches are described at length, its value to the English crown confirmed. Exhausted, the poet's soul returns to his body.

At bottom, the Madagascar proposal was not very well thought out, and when it was submitted to the East India Company, that body responded with what Davenant's biographer, A. H. Nethercot, calls "diplomatic caution," essentially refusing to have anything to do with it. Virtually all of Charles I's advisers pointed out the impossibility of the project, and Archbishop Laud even went so far as to offer Rupert a bishopric to replace his supposed governorship. Thus, the historical background lends to the poem a faint air of the ridiculous. Perhaps realizing this, Davenant concluded it with a whimsical description of himself, twirling a chain of office, growing goutish, sitting on the island's judicial bench. The poem's intent, however, is clear. With an eye toward the main chance of preferment, the soon-to-be poet laureate was quite obviously cultivating Rupert, the rising young star of the Caroline court.

Many of the poems that Davenant addressed to individual courtiers and noblemen, such as the typically if somewhat simplemindedly Jonsonian "To the King on New-years day 1630," are occasional verse. This poem begins by praising Charles I as a ruler who teaches by example, and by offering him all the joy inherent in such standard Cavalier touchstones as "Youth . . . Wine, and Wealth." It continues by wishing the king and the nation, first, peace, but peace "not compass'd by/ Expensive Treaties but a Victorie," and, second, a successful Parliament, one consisting of "such who can obey./ . . . not rebell." These veiled references to recent and only partially successful treaties with France and Spain and to Charles's dissolving of Parliament in March of 1629 typify Davenant's method and belief with regard to politics. He was essentially a "yes-man," defending Charles I's actions without reservation, or, if differing at all with the king's policy, arguing on the side of action, the side of victory without compromise.

Other poems in the volume include "Elizium, To the Duchess of Buckingham," which begins by describing one of those Arcadian utopias of friendship, love, and beauty so popular with Cavalier poets, and finishes by eulogizing the dead duke of Buckingham; "A Journey into Worcestershire," a mock travelogue of the sort popularly used to satirize the foibles and follies of country bumpkins, Puritans, and the author and his friends; "Jeffereidos," a satire recounting the kidnapping of Jeffery Hudson, the queen's dwarf; and a pastoral lament, "Written When Colonel Goring Was Believ'd to be Slaine," in which two swains, Porter and Jermyn, again bemoan Goring's supposed death, juxtaposing fairly standard pastoral and heroic references to Achilles, Hector, and Elizium with references to Christopher Columbus and Ferdinand Magellan, and a complex, Donne-like nautical conceit. References to ships, compasses, charts, and exploration appear over and over again in Davenant's work. Indeed the nautical world is his favorite source of metaphors.

### WORKS

Between 1660 and 1663 Davenant published three short panegyric poems, *To His Excellency the Lord General Monck* (1660), *Upon His Sacred Majestie's Return to His Dominions* (1660), and *To the King's Most Sacred Majesty* (1663). These are minor pieces, very much the sort of thing every other poet of the day was writing. They were republished in the 1673 *Works* along with *Poems on Several Occasions*, a volume of Davenant's short pieces that had been intended for sep-

arate publication in 1657 but that had never seen print. *Poems on Several Occasions* includes the long (624-line) *To the Earl of Orrey*, an elaborate panegyric written in the 1650's. Davenant praises Orrey, a noted statesman and soldier who was later to be instrumental in restoring Charles II to the throne, in an elaborate conceit in which the poet is an explorer sailing the marvelous coastline of the earl's genius.

There are fifty shorter pieces in *Poems on Several Occasions*, some of them dating from the 1630's; most of them, like the *Madagascar* poems, are easily classifiable as occasional pieces, lyrics, and satires. Perhaps the finest verses in *Poems on Several Occasions* are the short lyrics. Davenant's "The Lark now leaves his watry Nest" is a lovely compliment, more Elizabethan than anything else, in which the standard metaphor of the lady's awakening being like the sun's rising is handled with uncommon grace. Another lyric, "Endimion Porter and Olivia," contemplates the fate of lovers after death and the danger of their being separated.

### GONDIBERT

Davenant is remembered today primarily as the author of *Gondibert*. This heroic poem relates the maneuverings and martial engagements involved in establishing the successor to the aging Aribert, eighth century king of the Lombards. The king's heir is the beautiful Rhodalind, and the king wishes her to wed Duke Gondibert, a knight who equals her in excellence. Unfortunately, the immoral but otherwise extremely capable Prince Oswald also aspires to the princess's hand and will fight to gain it. Oswald's followers are all hardened veterans of many campaigns. Gondibert's, by contrast, are mere youths, brave, but inexperienced, and devout worshipers at the shrine of Love.

One day Oswald and his troops ambush Gondibert while he is returning from the hunt. Disdaining to take advantage of his superior numbers, the prince offers to meet the duke in single combat. Soon the several leaders of the two factions are similarly engaged, and Davenant describes the battle in great detail and with considerable relish. Oswald and his men are noble foes, but because virtue and Gondibert must triumph, Oswald is killed. As was the case in the duel in "Madagascar," which clearly served as a thematic, though not a stylistic, rough sketch for the heroics of *Gondibert*, the defeated faction refuses to abide by its leader's promise and attacks the duke's small party. Gondibert, wounded, nonetheless defeats them, and although they have already proved doubly treacherous, he gallantly lets them depart.

The poem goes on to relate the hero's recovery from his wounds at the palace of Astragon, a scientist-philosopher modeled on Sir Francis Bacon or Sir William Gilbert. While civil war is brewing, Gondibert dallies with Astragon's daughter, Birtha, and falls in love with her shortly before discovering that he has been proclaimed fiancé to Rhodalind. Soon after, the work breaks off. Although he lived another seventeen years, Davenant never returned to it.

*Gondibert*'s importance lies not so much in its innate excellence as in the theory behind it. In its own day, it provoked both controversy and ridicule. The poem was praised by Hobbes, who had something of a stake in it, and by both Edmund Waller and Abraham Cowley; but the more common reaction was highly negative. Some, like John Denham, were reduced to obscenities.

### THE PREFACE TO GONDIBERT WITH AN ANSWER BY MR. HOBBES

In the all-important *The Preface to Gondibert with An Answer by Mr. Hobbes*, Davenant argues that Homer, despite his greatness, erred when he introduced the supernatural into poetry. It is acceptable, for example, for the poet to petition his Muse metaphorically, when it is clear that he is really speaking to what Davenant calls his "rationall Spirit," but it is not acceptable for the poet to treat the Muse as a person in her own right. Vergil is similarly at fault and, even more so, Torquato Tasso and Edmund Spenser, the great modern heroic poets, because they as Christians should know better. Davenant generally follows his own advice in *Gondibert*, grounding his characters' actions not in motivation provided by meddling deities, but in the desire for power, martial exercise, and love. He does, however, include an enchantress in the poem, and has the Duke give Birtha a magic emerald that will change color if he is unfaithful.

Davenant saw the heroic poem as, at least in part, a didactic tool and resolved to display characters who exemplified active Christian virtues, although his con-

flicting desire to promote the Cavalier virtue of martial prowess occasionally led him to extremes. To convey the moral message and to please the reader were for Davenant the first requirements of the heroic poem, and anything standing in the way was to be condemned. Thus, Spenser could be faulted for his archaic language, complex stanzas, and obscure allegories. Davenant's own language is lofty but contemporary, his stanza a simple four-line iambic pentameter, rhyming *abab*.

Davenant was attempting to define and put to use what is now thought of as the neoclassical poetic. Breaking with his own early use of the metaphysical manner, he emphasized decorum, arguing against extremes, whether of language, sentiment, metaphor, or wit, and insisting on the superiority of the familiar and the real. With Hobbes's aid, Davenant set out to develop an active poetic that repudiated all use of the supernatural even in epic or heroic forms, and which insisted on a rationalist approach to human nature. The word "wit" had meant something very different to Donne from what it was to mean to Alexander Pope, and it was in Davenant's *The Preface to Gondibert with An Answer by Mr. Hobbes* that many of the arguments were first expounded that were eventually to lead to that change.

OTHER MAJOR WORKS

PLAYS: *The Cruell Brother*, pr. 1627; *The Just Italian*, pr. 1629; *The Siege: Or, The Collonell*, pr. 1629; *The Tragedy of Albovine, King of the Lombards*, pb. 1629; *Love and Honour*, pr. 1634; *The Witts*, pr. 1634; *News from Plimouth*, pr. 1635; *The Platonick Lovers*, pr. 1635; *The Temple of Love*, pr., pb. 1635 (masque); *The Triumphs of the Prince d'Amour*, pr., pb. 1636 (masque); *Britannia Triumphans*, pr., pb. 1638 (masque); *The Fair Favorite*, pr. 1638; *Luminalia: Or, The Festival of Light*, pr., pb. 1638; *The Unfortunate Lovers*, pr. 1638; *The Distresses*, pr. 1639 (also known as *The Spanish Lovers*); *Salmacida Spolia*, pr., pb. 1640 (masque); *The First Days Entertainment at Rutland House*, pr. 1656 (music by Henry Lawes); *The Siege of Rhodes, Part I*, pr., pb. 1656 (*Part II*, pr. 1659); *The Cruelty of the Spaniards in Peru*, pr., pb. 1658; *The History of Sir Francis Drake*, pr., pb. 1659; *Hamlet,* pr. 1661 (adaptation of William Shakespeare's play); *Twelfth Night*, pr. 1661 (adaptation of Shakespeare's play); *The Law Against Lovers*, pr. 1662; *Romeo and Juliet*, pr. 1662 (adaptation of Shakespeare's play); *Henry VIII*, pr. 1663 (adaptation of Shakespeare's play); *Macbeth*, pr. 1663, (adaptation of Shakespeare's play); *The Playhouse to Be Lett*, pr. 1663; *The Rivals*, pr. 1664; *The Tempest: Or, The Enchanted Island*, pr. 1667 (with John Dryden; adaptation of Shakespeare's play); *The Man's the Master*, pr. 1668; *Dramatic Works*, 1872-1874 (5 volumes; James Madiment and W. H. Logan, editors).

NONFICTION: *The Preface to Gondibert with an Answer by Mr. Hobbes*, 1650 (with Thomas Hobbes).

MISCELLANEOUS: *Works*, 1673 (3 volumes), 1968 (reprint).

BIBLIOGRAPHY

Blaydes, Sophia B., and Philip Bordinat. *Sir William Davenant*. Boston: G. K. Hall, 1981. Begins with a chapter on Davenant's life and times and then surveys the early plays, the masques, and the Restoration plays. The bibliography is excellent, including even dissertations and theses as well as the usual primary and secondary sources. A good place to begin studying Davenant.

_____. *Sir William Davenant: An Annotated Bibliography, 1629-1985*. New York: Garland, 1986. This bibliography casts a wide net in 365 pages. The primary bibliography is divided into "Collected Works," "Separate Works," and "Miscellaneous Works." The secondary bibliography is broken down into four sections, treating Davenant century by century, and the last section is subdivided into decades. An exceptionally useful tool for Davenant scholars.

Bold, Alan. *Longman Dictionary of Poets*. Harlow, England: Longman, 1985. The entry on Davenant postulates that he may have been William Shakespeare's godson. Cites "The Souldier Going to the Field" as his best-known poem and asserts that it is a "tender expression of regret on leaving love for war."

Edmond, Mary. *Rare Sir William Davenant*. New York: St. Martin's Press, 1987. A scholarly study, with rich notes, that treats the subject's whole career. Davenant as man of the theater is considered in chapters treating the early plays and masques, *Gondibert*, the opera, the formation of the "Davenant/Killigrew stage monopoly," and Davenant as theater manager and stage director. Includes helpful bibliography.

Harbage, Alfred. *Sir William Davenant: Poet Venturer, 1606-1668*. New York: Octagon Books, 1971. A full-length, sympathetic study of Davenant, whom Harbage calls the "most conspicuous of the Cavalier poets" and whose poetry was "sometimes inspired." Contains extensive coverage of his early life, his plays, and his poems, with a chapter devoted to *Gondibert*.

Lewcock, Dawn. *Sir William Davenant, the Court Masque, and the English Seventeenth-Century Scenic Stage, c1605-c1700*. Amherst, N.Y.: Cambria Press, 2008. While this work is about Davenant's dramatic work, it also deals with his poetry.

Nethercot, Arthur H. *Sir William Davenant: Poet Laureate and Playwright-Manager*. Chicago: University of Chicago Press, 1938. Reprint. New York: Russell and Russell, 1967. The longest and most detailed study of Davenant. Besides focusing on Davenant as a man of the theater world, Nethercot includes scholarly appendixes on the questions of Davenant's wife as Shakespeare's "Dark Lady," the Chancery Suit against Urswick, Mary Davenant's will, and Thomas Warren's death.

*Michael M. Levy*

---

# DONALD DAVIE

**Born:** Barnsley, South Yorkshire, England; July 17, 1922
**Died:** Exeter, Devon, England; September 18, 1995

PRINCIPAL POETRY
*Brides of Reason*, 1955
*A Winter Talent, and Other Poems*, 1957
*The Forests of Lithuania*, 1959

*New and Selected Poems*, 1961

*A Sequence for Francis Parkman*, 1961

*Events and Wisdoms: Poems, 1957-1963*, 1964

*Essex Poems, 1963-1967*, 1969

*Six Epistles to Eva Hesse*, 1970

*Collected Poems, 1950-1970*, 1972

*The Shires*, 1974

*In the Stopping Train, and Other Poems*, 1977

*"Three for Water-Music" and "The Shires,"* 1981

*The Battered Wife, and Other Poems*, 1982

*Collected Poems, 1970-1983*, 1983

*To Scorch or Freeze: Poems About the Sacred*, 1988

*Poems and Melodramas*, 1996

*Selected Poems*, 1997

*Collected Poems*, 2002 (Neil Powell, editor)

## OTHER LITERARY FORMS

Donald Davie (DAY-vee) was a highly respected man of many letters. In addition to his poetry, he published numerous works of literary theory and criticism, including important books on Ezra Pound and Thomas Hardy, and an abundance of material on various British, American, and European authors. He also wrote several cultural histories that discuss the impact of religious dissent on culture and literature and edited a number of anthologies of Augustan and Russian poetry; in addition, he published biographical essays and translated Russian poetry.

## ACHIEVEMENTS

Donald Davie's high reputation in the United States is apparent in the many awards and other academic appointments he received. He was the recipient of three awards in 1973—a Guggenheim Fellowship, an honorary fellowship at St. Catharine's College in Cambridge, and a fellowship in the American Academy of Arts and Sciences. In 1978, he earned a doctorate in literature from the University of Southern California and was made an honorary fellow at Trinity College in Dublin, Ireland.

## BIOGRAPHY

Donald Alfred Davie was born July 17, 1922, into a lower-middle-class Baptist family, the son of a shop-keeper and the grandson of domestic servants. He grew up amid the slag heaps of industrial West Riding. His mother frequently recited poetry, and, according to Davie, "Robin Hood . . . surely did more than any other single text to make me a compulsive reader for ever after." His father, a lively and emotionally expressive man, encouraged the young boy to take piano lessons. Even as a child, however, Davie rankled at the pretensions and philistinism of his more well-to-do neighbors.

In 1940, Davie began his studies of seventeenth century religious oratory and architecture at St. Catharine's College, Cambridge. He joined the Royal Navy in 1941 and between 1942 and 1943 was stationed in northern Russia, where he studied the poetry of Boris Pasternak, who was to become an important and lasting influence. He married Doreen John, from Plymouth, in 1945; they had three children. Davie returned to Cambridge in 1946 and studied under F. R. Leavis; he earned his B.A. in 1946, his M.A. in 1949, and his Ph.D. in 1951. Between 1950 and 1957, he taught at Trinity College, Dublin, where he met the writers and poets Joseph Hone, Austin Clarke, and Padraic Fallon. He spent 1957-1958 as visiting professor at the University of California, Santa Barbara, where he was introduced to Yvor Winters, Thom Gunn, and Hugh Kenner (whose teaching post he actually filled for the year); it was during this period that he joined the Reactionary Generation of poets.

In 1958, he returned to Cambridge as a lecturer in English at Gonville and Caius Colleges, worried about how the "sentimental Left occupied all the same positions." Commenting further on his isolation during this time, he said: "The politics of envy . . . [and] self-pity had sapped independence, self-help, and self-respect." In 1964, he cofounded and became professor at the University of Essex (he later became pro-vice-chancellor there). Then, only four years later, feeling utter disillusionment with a declining British society and the philistinism of even his fellow poets, and also feeling totally alienated from his university colleagues, he moved to the United States and joined the faculty of Stanford University, where he remained until 1978. In 1978, he became Andrew W. Mellon Professor of Humanities at Vanderbilt University. He retired from

Vanderbilt in 1988 and returned full-time to the Devonshire village where for many years he had spent his summers. "I take retirement seriously, in a way that puzzles others, including my wife. I mean that I seldom find reasons for leaving this village." His writing slowed during this period and he died in Exeter, Devon, on September 18, 1995.

ANALYSIS

In both his poetry and his critical commentary, Donald Davie advocated a poetry of formal structure and prose syntax, along with restrained metaphor and feeling. He urged repeatedly that art communicate rational statement and moral purpose in technically disciplined forms. His work, usually highly compressed, erudite, and formally elegant, is sometimes criticized for its lack of feeling and for tending toward the overly academic—in short, for the notable absence of the personal element. Davie, nevertheless, stood firm in his position that the poet is responsible primarily to the community in which he writes for purifying and thus correcting the spoken language: "The central act of poetry as of music, is the creation of syntax, of meaningful arrangement." The poet thus helps one understand one's feelings; he improves the very process of one's thinking, and hence one's subsequent actions. Ultimately, the poet helps correct the moral behavior of the community at large.

Davie's poetry, frequently labeled neo-Augustan, is characterized by formal elegance, urbane wit, technical purity, and plain diction. A widely respected poet, Davie pursued a refined and austere art to counter the disorder of the modern world. Shortly after publishing his *Collected Poems, 1950-1970*, he described the spirit of mid-century as "on the side of all that was insane and suicidal, without order and without proportion, *against* civilization." To Davie, the artist's purification of the word might restore moderation, propriety, and control—the very values that inspire integrity and courage. The poet, by improving the spoken language of his society, might actually inspire the creative, moral, and social betterment of civilization. Again and again, Davie explained that "the abandonment of syntax testifies to . . . a loss of confidence in the intelligible structure of the conscious mind, and the va-

lidity of its activity." The main activity of the mind is moral and social.

Davie gained recognition with the *New Lines* anthology published in 1956 and the Movement of the 1950's. His name was linked with John Wain, Kingsley Amis, Philip Larkin, Gunn, Robert Conquest, D. J. Enright, Elizabeth Jennings, and John Holloway, along with the other reactionary poets who stood against the romantic excesses, "tawdry amoralism," and Imagism and Symbolism of the British poets of the 1940's, such as Dylan Thomas, T. S. Eliot, and Ezra Pound. The Movement argued for a return to conventional prose syntax and a more formal poetry that utilized the conservative metaphors of the eighteenth century Augustans. These poets, who shared a similar class background, as well as similar educational and professional goals, were, in addition, linked to various Reactionary Generation Americans such as Winters, Louise Bogan, the Fugitives, and even Hart Crane, and to those poets who were pursuing concrete poetry, such as H. D. and Pound. For Davie and the Movement, a decorous diction was to be selected according to subject or genre; so, too, structure was to be logical rather than musical.

**BRIDES OF REASON**

The first poem of Davie's first volume, *Brides of Reason*, introduces a theme that persisted throughout his career—English identity abroad: the would-be-exile-becomes-hero, the poet inhabiting and striving to unite two different national psyches. Now in Ireland, he describes his "Hands [as] acknowledging no allegiance./ Gloved for good against brutal chance" ("Demi-Exile. Howth"). He also wrote, again in neo-classical form, that his work is intended to appeal to the "logic" in his reader, so that "poets may astonish you/ With what is not, but should be, true,/ And shackle on a moral shape" ("Hypochondriac Logic"). The frequent obscurities and ambiguities of this volume reflect the influence of William Empson and F. R. Leavis, although more noteworthy is Davie's debt to the Augustans William Cowper, Oliver Goldsmith, Samuel Johnson, and Christopher Smart. "Homage to William Cowper," which proposes that "Most poets let the morbid fancy roam," goes on to insist that "Horror starts, like Charity, at home." Davie, admitting that he is "a pasticheur of late-Augustan styles," would work with rhetoric of the eighteenth century and attempt a rational structure through absolute clarity of premeditated logic. In "Zip!" he wrote:

> I'd have the spark that leaps upon the gun
> By one short fuse, electrically clear;
> And all be done before you've well begun.
> (It is reverberations that you hear.)

"On Bertrand Russell's 'Portraits from Memory'" begins with a familiar Davie verse:

> Those Cambridge generations, Russell's, Keynes' . . .
> And mine? Oh mine was Wittgenstein's, no doubt:
> Sweet pastoral, too, when some-one else explains,
> Although my memories leave the eclogues out.

Davie's early poetry was frequently compared to Charles Tomlinson's because of their mutual equation of form and morality. Poise, control, and clarity of statement, both poets maintained, reflect moral imperatives and contribute toward the establishment of a society of common sense, human decency, and high moral principle. Nevertheless, with his admittedly high moral stance, Davie began a long isolation from his more fashionable contemporaries—from the early Thomas to the confessional poetry of Theodore Roethke, Sylvia Plath, and Robert Lowell. Throughout his career, Davie remained aloof from even the great William Butler Yeats and Eliot, in whose vast mythmaking he sensed a distancing from the human condition. For Davie, the poet must speak directly to his reader and take on the role of "spokesman of a social [not mythic] tradition"; the poet is responsible for the rescue of culture from decline by "making poetry out of moral commonplace." Interestingly, although Davie's aims were not entirely unlike those of Yeats and Eliot—to inspire action and change in a philistine and unimaginative contemporary world—he would accomplish his ends not through imaginative participation in myth, but rather through conscious control of language, and thus thought and, finally, action. Responding to Davie's example of proper diction and traditional meter and syntax, for example, one might feel inclined to affirm the proper values of a more stable and civilized past. In "Vying," Davie wrote:

> There I, the sexton, battle
> Earth that will overturn
> Headstones, and rifle tombs,
> And spill the tilted urn.

Over the years, Davie gradually moved toward shorter and brisker lines, as well as a less obscure poetry. There was also an increasing display of emotion and a greater revelation of self—a closer relationship between the speaker and his landscape, history, and metaphor. The specific and general became more closely integrated. His rejection of a poetry consumed with the "messy ego," nevertheless, remained absolute, like his insistence that language remain the starting point of moral betterment. He therefore continued to reject accepted modern usage: "the stumbling, the moving voices," "the Beat and post-Beat poets,/ The illiterate apostles" ("Pentecost"). What is wanting and necessary, instead, is a "neutral tone" ("Remembering the 'Thirties"), reasonableness, and common values.

### A SEQUENCE FOR FRANCIS PARKMAN

*A Sequence for Francis Parkman*, Davie's response following his first visit to North America during 1957-1958, contains brief profiles of Sieur de La Salle, the Comte de Frontenac, Louis Joseph de Montcalm, Pontiac, and Louis Antoine de Bouganville, as Davie adapted them from the historiographer Francis Parkman.

*A Sequence for Francis Parkman* reveals Davie's fascination with the openness of North America with its empty and uncluttered spaces that lack the detritus of a long history of human failure. The continent functions not unlike a grand tabula rasa on which the poet can project his meditations. He wrote in "A Letter to Curtis Bradford":

> But I only guess,
> I guess at it out of my Englishness
> And envy you out of England. Man with man
> Is all our history; American,
> You met with spirits. Neither white nor red
> The melancholy, disinherited
> Spirit of mid-America, but this,
> The manifest copiousness, the bounties.

### EVENTS AND WISDOMS AND ESSEX POEMS, 1963-1967

The volume *Events and Wisdoms*, while retaining Davie's witty, epigrammatic style, also introduces a more sensual imagery in its precise descriptions of nature. In "Low Lands," for example, Davie describes a river delta

> Like a snake it is, its serpentine iridescence
> Of slow light spilt and wheeling over calm
> Inundations, and a snake's still menace
> Hooding with bruised sky belfry and lonely farm.
> The grasses wave on meadows fat with foison.

Both *Events and Wisdoms* and *Essex Poems, 1963-1967* illustrate Davie's pastoral-elegiac mode ("I smell a smell of death," "July, 1964"). He focused on death and emptiness, moving away from the more self-conscious literary subject matter of the Movement poetry. In the well-known "Winter Landscapes," he wrote:

> Danger, danger of dying
> Gives life in its shadows such riches.
> Once I saw or I dreamed
> A sunless and urbanized fenland
> One Sunday, and swans flying
> Among electric cables.

The sense of exile both within and outside his native country was also pronounced in poems such as "Rodez" and "The North Sea." Davie once again projected a concrete geography upon which to elaborate his meditations on human history and personal conduct. There is even an immersion in the external world of human event and interaction. Like Pound, who exerted a complex influence upon him, Davie wandered through the traditions of history, reexamining and restating human values worthy of restoration. "Rodez" admits "Goodbye to the Middle Ages! Although some/ Think that I enter them, those centuries/ Of monkish superstition, here I leave them/ With their true garlands, and their honest masks." Davie also accepted Pound's regard for nonhuman nature in its purposive indifference and essential *quidditas*. The poems in this volume, many composed in his most direct and sparsest language, retain Davie's essential urbanity, what Eliot called "the perfection of a common language"—imper-

sonal, distinguished, and well mannered—a language sometimes called by Davie's detractors uninspiredly chaste, versified prose, an academic and excessively moralistic statement removed from sense experience. Nevertheless, "The practise of an art," he insisted, "is to convert all terms/ into the terms of art" ("July, 1964").

### SIX EPISTLES TO EVA HESSE

*Six Epistles to Eva Hesse* again reflects Pound's rich influence on Davie. Like Pound, Davie incorporated the influences of numerous older and foreign literary traditions; he remained, like Pound, the traveler through history—the connoisseur of historical value, time, place, and event. Davie, however, retained his rage against disorder and freewheeling individuality, along with a rejection of Pound's experimental dislocations of traditional syntax. *Six Epistles to Eva Hesse*, addressed to Pound's German translator, is, in fact, Davie's "Essay on Criticism." He asked rhetorically

> Is it time
> For self-congratulating rhyme
> To honour as established fact
> the value of the artefact?
> Stoutly to trumpet Art is all
> We have, or need, to disenthrall
> Any of us from the chains
> History loads us with?

Again utilizing the verse epistle form and experimenting with a mixture of didactic narrative, satire, and a fluid octosyllabic couplet structure, Davie contemplated the new and old:

> Confound it, history . . . we transcend it
> Not when we agree to bend it
> To this cat's cradle or that theme
> But when, I take it, we redeem
> This man or that one.

Thus Davie established a connection between the virtues of common sense, proportion, and compassion; linear and empirical history; and specific, fixed verse forms.

### COLLECTED POEMS, 1950-1970

The highly praised *Collected Poems, 1950-1970* draws on Davie's experiences in both England and the United States. He applauded the "Atlantic" as a "pond" in "a garden." At the same time, he reiterated his "faith that there are still distinctively English—rather than Anglo-American or 'international'—ways of responding imaginatively to the terms of life found in the twentieth century." One is reminded of Davie's Baptist roots and the stern demand of his faith. "Dissentient Voice," with its clear reference to Dylan Thomas's "Fern Hill," reminds one of the severities of Davie's childhood. "When some were happy as the grass was green/ I was as happy as a glass was dark." "England" recalls the bitterness of expatriation: On his way back from the United States to Great Britain, Davie confessed:

> I dwell, intensely dwell
> on my flying shadow
> over the Canadian barrens,
> and come to nothing else
>
> . . . . . . . .
>
> Napoleon was right:
> A nation of purveyors.
> Now we purvey ourselves
> . . . [with] brutal manners, brutal
> simplifications as
> we drag it all down.

To be sure, many of Davie's poems focus on England, and many compare the Mediterranean and Northern worlds. *The Forests of Lithuania*, written earlier (1959), however, and based on Adam Mickiewicz's romantic epic *Pan Tadeusz* (1834; English translation, 1917), focuses on Lithuania during its 1811-1812 Russian occupation. In this experimental poem, Davie utilized novelistic techniques, explaining that his goal was to deal with "common human experiences in the way they are commonly perceived, as slowly and gradually evolving amid a wealth of familiar and particular images" in the effort to "win back some of this territory from the novelist." "The Forest," for example, builds upon a series of lush and classical descriptions, as the poet conveys the sensual, as well as visual and tactile, richness of the landscape:

> Currants wave their hop-crowned tresses,
> Quickbeams blush like shepherdesses,
> The hazel in a maenad's shape
> Crowned with her nuts as with the grape
> Twirls a green thyrsus, and below
> The striplings of the forest grow—

## THE SHIRES

Davie's tour de force, told entirely about England, is the complex autobiographical *The Shires*. Consisting of forty poems, one for each county in England, it is arranged in alphabetical order from Bedfordshire to Yorkshire. *The Shires* consists primarily of reveries about English geography and history, and as Davie lamented the unfulfilled potential of entire communities, as well as of individuals, he revealed the influence of Thomas Hardy. Also, in a voice that ranges from the formal to the informal, Davie filled the landscapes with personal (sometimes obscure) allusions. He speaks of Monmouthshire, for example, as the location of England's "wedding" to Wales and his marriage to a Welsh woman. The volume treats major and minor events, the tragic and the trivial. At times, Davie is serious and bitter about the modern world; at other times, he is resigned, wry, and even witty. These are poems of dissent and praise, as they treat his own experience and contemporary and historical England. Their predominant subject, however, is human and social neglect, and the waste ultimately brought on by the indifference to precise language and thought.

In "Suffolk," Davie admitted, "My education gave me this bad habit/ Of reading history for a hidden plot/ And finding it; invariably the same one,/ Its fraudulent title always, 'Something Gone.'" The poems resound with historical and literary echoes and august figures such as Lord Nelson, Tom Paine, Robert Walpole, Sir Francis Drake, Jane Austen, William Wordsworth, A. E. Housman, W. H. Auden, and John Fowles. Compared with the past, the contemporary world is vulgar and uninspired: "We run through a maze of tunnels for our meat/ As rats might . . ./ Drake,/ This is the freedom that you sailed from shore/ To save us for?" ("Devonshire"). Once again, Davie blended the particular and the abstract. Each shire reveals its own lesson. "Essex," where Davie taught, speaks of how language—the means of experiencing order of the self and society—is corrupted: "Names and things named don't match/ Ever." "Cornwall" describes the decline of imagination and intelligence: People live, said the poet, with "black patches on both eyes." "Devonshire" treats the corruption of community, and in "Staffordshire," the unrealized potential of the past has blighted the future.

The "Dorset" sequence, of particular interest, is organized in the manner of Pound's *The Pisan Cantos* (1948), with reveries and shifts of perspective and multileveled allusions to scholarship, history, culture, and autobiography. In "Sussex," however, one truly hears the poet's elegiac sadness for the general vacancy and lovelessness that has blanketed all the shires and that extends into the future. He writes:

> The most poeticized
> Of English counties . . .
>
> "Brain-drain" one hears no more of,
> And that's no loss. There is
> Another emigration:
> Draining away of love.

Throughout, the modern world is characterized by empty ceremony, diminished political acumen, and imprecise language. Davie also portrayed a physically vast, industrialized, polluted, and drab landscape.

The extraordinary "Trevenen" is a verse biography and tragedy, composed in octosyllabic couplets. It tells the story of the late-eighteenth century Cornish naval officer who, after a heroic career, was driven mad by those he served. Trevenen lived in "an age much like our own;/ As lax, as vulgar, as confused;/ . . ./ Where that which was and that which seemed/ Were priced the same, where men were duped/ And knew they were." Davie's portrayal of Trevenen's naïveté, heroism, and death are among his most moving lines. The octosyllabic line is truncated to three stresses in four or six syllables:

> Aware man's born to err,
> Inclined to bear and forebear.
> Pretense to more is vain.
> Chastened have they been.
> Hope was the tempter, hope.
> Ambition has its scope
> (Vast: the world's esteem);
> Hope is a sickly dream.

## IN THE STOPPING TRAIN, AND OTHER POEMS

In his poems after the mid-1970's, Davie moved toward a more open and personal statement, although his commitment to perfect language and syntax remained, he said, less for the purpose of strengthening social and moral law than as a means of coming to terms with his personal life, which, he also confessed, was "the man going mad inside me." The title piece of *In the Stopping Train, and Other Poems*, for example, is clearly less obscure and more emotionally expansive than has been his custom; it portrays a divided sensibility, an "I" and a "him." Davie admitted that the poem "is an expression of a mood of profound depression and uncertainty about what it has meant for me personally, and for people close to me, that for so many years I have devoted myself to this curious activity we call poetry." The poet boards a slow train in a journey of personal and historical reverie that moves through time and engages him in the difficult struggle to understand himself and define poetry. He is bitter about his ignorance of the world around him—the smell of a flower—and corrupted by his obsession with language:

> Jonquil is a sweet word.
> Is it a flowering bush?
> . . . . . . . .
> he never needed to see,
> . . . . . . . .
> he never needs to use his
> Nose, except for language.

Not unlike the confessional poets, from whom he has always separated himself, he indicts himself "With his false loves." Finally, he confesses, "The man going mad inside me" is rendered mad by history and must mount "a slow/ and stopping train through places/ whose names used to have virtue." Like *The Shires*, "In the Stopping Train" integrates the abstract and personal and accomplishes a tighter relationship between the human, social, and abstract. Its complex narrator is closely integrated into the vast experience of common humanity.

In "To Thom Gunn in Los Altos, California," Davie admits of the pleasures and fears of the poet-exile in search of meaning: "What am I doing, I who am scared of edges?" All the same, poetry remains an exulting experience—the means of social, and, ultimately, of spiritual transcendence, even though he knows that "Most poems, or the best/ Describe their own birth, and this/ Is what they are—a space/ Cleared to walk around in" ("Ars Poetica"). *Three for Water-Music*, which contains noticeably sensuous and colorful images, also reminds one of Eliot's *Four Quartets* (1943), with its complex philosophical subjects and difficult personal allusions set within carefully defined formal divisions. The poet contemplates specific geographies once again and specific historical dates, and from these, deals with the personal and abstract. There are "epiphanies all around us/ Always perhaps," he remarks, and his personal recollections and even mythic evocations merge within a broad variety of styles.

### THE BATTERED WIFE, AND OTHER POEMS

*The Battered Wife, and Other Poems* focuses on Davie's early life in Ireland when he was "martyred" to words. The title poem is a straightforward but unusually moving narrative about unfulfilled love. "Screech-Owl" admits that "Nightingales sang to me/ Once, and I never knew." In "Artifex in Extremis," Davie writes, "Let him rehearse the gifts reserved for age/ Much as the poet Eliot did," and then proceeds to explore the consciousness of the dying poet. He measures his success "to confess" that "The work that would . . . speak for itself/ Has not, [and this awareness] comes hard." The poems have an unusual intimacy about them, and the reader can sense a lament for the time and passion that have passed and forever been lost.

As a critic, Davie's remarks shed an interesting perspective on his poetry and reinforced his continuing concerns. For example, in *Purity of Diction in English Verse* (1952), he reaffirmed that the

> strength of statement is found most often in a chaste or pure diction, because it goes together with economy in metaphor; and such economy is a feature of such a diction. It is achieved by judgment and taste, and it preserves the tone of the centre, a sort of urbanity. It purifies the spoken tongue.

This sentiment continues through *The Poet in the Imaginary Museum: Essays of Two Decades* (1977), a collection of essays whose title refers to the artist's obligation to wander through history to absorb and utilize art in all its forms. Speaking of Pound, for example, Davie again reiterated the poet's responsibility to link poetics and politics: "One would almost say . . . that to dislocate syntax is to threaten the rule of law in the community."

### OTHER MAJOR WORKS

NONFICTION: *Purity of Diction in English Verse*, 1952; *Articulate Energy: An Enquiry into the Syntax of English Poetry*, 1955; *The Language of Science and the Language of Literature, 1700-1740*, 1963; *Ezra Pound: Poet as Sculptor*, 1964; *Thomas Hardy and British Poetry*, 1972; *Pound*, 1975; *The Poet in the Imaginary Museum: Essays of Two Decades*, 1977 (Barry Alpert, editor); *A Gathered Church: The Literature of the English Dissenting Interest, 1700-1930*, 1978; *Trying to Explain*, 1979; *English Hymnology in the Eighteenth Century: Papers Read at a Clark Library Seminar, 5 March 1977*, 1980; *Kenneth Allott and the Thirties*, 1980; *Dissentient Voice: The Ward and Phillips Lectures for 1980 with Some Related Pieces*, 1982; *These the Companions: Reflections*, 1982; *Czesław Miłosz and the Insufficiency of Lyric*, 1986; *Under Briggflatts: A History of Poetry in Great Britain, 1960-1988*, 1989; *Slavic Excursions: Essays on Russian and Polish Literature*, 1990; *Old Masters: Essays and Reflections on English and American Literature*, 1992; *The Eighteenth-Century Hymn in English*, 1993; *Essays in Dissent: Church, Chapel, and the Unitarian Conspiracy*, 1995; *With the Grain: Essays on Thomas Hardy and Modern British Poetry*, 1998 (Clive Wilmer, editor); *Two Ways Out of Whitman*, 2000 (Doreen Davie, editor); *A Travelling Man: Eighteenth-Century Bearings*, 2003; *Modernist Essays: Yeats, Pound, Eliot*, 2004 (Wilmer, editor).

TRANSLATION: *The Poems of Doctor Zhivago*, 1965 (of Boris Pasternak).

EDITED TEXTS: *The Late Augustans: Longer Poems of the Eighteenth Century*, 1958; *Pasternak: Modern Judgments*, 1969 (with Angela Livingstone); *Augustan Lyric*, 1974; *The New Oxford Book of Christian Verse*, 1981; *The Psalms in English*, 1996.

### BIBLIOGRAPHY

Dekker, George, ed. *Donald Davie and the Responsibilities of Literature*. Orono, Maine: National Poetry Foundation, 1983. Provides a good sampling of criticism on Davie.

Everett, Barbara. "Poetry and Christianity." *London Review of Books*, February 4-18, 1982, 5-7. Everett stresses the reticence of Davie's poetry. Davie avoids strong displays of emotion, enabling him to concentrate on stylistic effects. At his best, as in *Three for Water-Music*, his poetry is superlative. He strongly emphasizes the values of the English countryside and defends an ideal of Christian civilization that he regards as in decline. Many of his best effects are understated and tacit, although he often begins a poem with a sharp phrase.

Fowler, Alastair. *A History of English Literature*. Cambridge, Mass.: Harvard University Press, 1987. Fowler relates Davie to the other Movement poets such as Robert Conquest and Philip Larkin. Davie's poetry stresses local themes and avoids difficulty. The value of plain, strong syntax is rated very high by Davie, but less so, one gathers, by Fowler. Davie avoids foreign influences and adopts a no-nonsense attitude toward the problem of how poetry relates to the world. Fowler rates him below Larkin and appears to dislike the Movement poets.

Jacobs, Alan. "Donald Davie: 1922-1995." *American Scholar* 66, no. 4 (Autumn, 1997): 579-585. In this piece written to mark Davie's passing, Jacobs, a professor of English at Wheaton College, recalls a 1994 meeting with the poet. He describes him as having a contrarian temperament and discusses his poetry.

Kermode, Frank. *An Appetite for Poetry*. Cambridge, Mass.: Harvard University Press, 1989. Kermode notes a paradoxical side to Davie's poetry. Davie adopts the view that the genuine tradition of English poetry is one stressing local values. Thomas Hardy exemplifies the correct manner of writing poetry, and T. S. Eliot is regarded as aberrant. Davie considers his own work part of a counterrevolution against the modernism of Ezra Pound and Eliot. Nevertheless, his poetry displays the influence of both of those poets. Kermode contends that Davie is more cosmopolitan than Philip Larkin.

Leader, Zachary, ed. *The Movement Reconsidered: Essays on Larkin, Amis, Gunn, Davie, and Their Contemporaries*. New York: Oxford University Press, 2009. Contains essays on the members of the Movement, including Davie, Thom Gunn, Philip Larkin, and Kingsley Amis.

Powell, Neil. "Donald Davie, Dissentient Voice." In *British Poetry Since 1970: A Critical Survey*, edited by Peter Jones, et al. London: Persea Books, 1980. Powell notes that much of Davie's poetry is concerned with his English audience. His move to California indicates a disillusion with England, and *Essex Poems, 1963-1967* suffers from an undue display of anger toward his former country. In some instances, for example, in the sequence *In the Stopping Train, and Other Poems*, Davie talks to himself. Often, the shifts between "I" and "he" are bewildering. At his best, Davie is forceful and clear.

Ricks, Christopher. "Davie's Pound." *New Statesman* 69, no. 1779 (April 16, 1965): 610. Provides insights into Davie's admiration for Ezra Pound.

Rosenthal, M. L., and Sally McGall. *The Modern Poetic Sequence*. New York: Oxford University Press, 1983. The authors discuss in an illuminating way Davie's display of emotion in his poetry. His mood is usually bleak and somber. Instead of adding lyrical meditations after his narrative, in the nineteenth century tradition, Davie emphasizes the subjective throughout his poems. A detailed discussion of "After the Accident," an account of an automobile crash that nearly killed Davie and his wife, elucidates these points.

Wright, Stuart T., comp. *Donald Davie: A Checklist of His Writings, 1946-1988*. New York: Greenwood Press, 1991. A comprehensive bibliography of Davie's works.

*Lois Gordon*

# SIR JOHN DAVIES

**Born:** Chisgrove, Tisbury, Wiltshire, England; April, 1569

**Died:** London, England; December 8, 1626

PRINCIPAL POETRY
*Epigrammes and Elegies*, 1590? (with Christopher Marlowe)
"The Epithalamion of the Muses," c. 1594
*Orchestra: Or, A Poeme of Dauncing*, 1596, 1622

*Hymnes of Astraea*, 1599

*Nosce Teipsum: This Oracle Expounded in Two Elegies*, 1599

*A Contention Betwixt a Wife, a Widdowe, and a Maide*, pr. 1602

*Yet Other Twelve Wonders of the World*, pb. 1608 (wr. 1602 or 1603; also known as *The Twelve Wonders of the World*)

*The Poems of Sir John Davies*, 1941 (Clare Howard, editor)

*The Poems of Sir John Davies*, 1975 (Robert Krueger, editor)

## OTHER LITERARY FORMS

Throughout his literary career, Sir John Davies (DAY-veez) published various nonfiction prose works, including a history of Ireland and a political commentary.

## ACHIEVEMENTS

Sir John Davies' reputation as a poet has shifted radically, depending on the taste of the reading public. His epigrams and occasional poems were very popular with his contemporaries; they survive in numerous manuscript copies. *Nosce Teipsum*, his long philosophical poem, went through five editions during his lifetime. Reprinted first by Nahum Tate in 1697, it went through several more editions and remained very popular in the eighteenth century. Alexander Pope paid Davies the compliment of imitating him, and Samuel Johnson praised his skill at arguing in verse. Samuel Taylor Coleridge, in *Biographia Literaria* (1817), adapts three stanzas from *Nosce Teipsum* to explain how the poetic imagination functions. In the modern era, Davies attracted the favorable attention of poets such as T. S. Eliot and Theodore Roethke but has fared less well in academic scholarship.

In his very influential work *The Elizabethan World Picture* (1943), E. M. W. Tillyard identified Davies as a principal intellectual spokesperson for the Elizabethan "world picture" and described his verse as "typically Elizabethan." This approach to his poetry established Davies as a poet who should be read for his ideas, for the insights he offered regarding the Elizabethan mind. Davies' modern editor, Robert Krueger, takes pre-

cisely this position when he concludes his critical introduction to *The Poems of Sir John Davies* with the following statement: "Davies will never again be read for profit or pleasure; his readers will always be students of the Elizabethan world."

While it would be foolhardy to conclude that Davies is an underestimated "poet's poet," the major works of a poet who continued to receive favorable commentary from other practicing poets should not be dismissed as mediocre. His place in political history is assured: He served as attorney general of Ireland under James I and assisted in planning the "Plantation of Ulster." His literary achievements are more difficult to assess: Popular in his own day as the author of *Nosce Teipsum*, his long philosophical poem, and of salacious, satirical epigrams, Davies is now mostly remembered for his *Orchestra*.

## BIOGRAPHY

John Davies was born in 1569, just five years after William Shakespeare and two years before John Donne. His life belongs as much to the Jacobean as to the Elizabethan period. He probably became interested in writing epigrams while he was attending Winchester School. This preparatory school produced a large number of important writers of epigrams, including John Owen, Thomas Bastard, and John Hoskins, as well as Davies. After spending some time at Oxford, Davies attended New Inn, an Inn of Chancery associated with the Inns of Court, before entering the Middle Temple and formally beginning his study of the law. Located near the theaters, the Inns of Court, the four important law schools in London, attracted many young men with literary as well as legal interests. Sir Francis Bacon studied at Gray's Inn, Donne at Lincoln's Inn, and Sir Walter Ralegh and John Marston at the Middle Temple.

In the fall of 1592, Davies visited the University of Leiden, arriving a week after William Fleetwood and Richard Martin, his fellow students at the Middle Temple. William Camden, one of the leading English antiquarians, wrote a letter introducing Davies to Paul Merula, a distinguished Dutch jurist. The trip may have been partially motivated by the need to improve Fleetwood's image with the Middle Temple Benchers. He and Martin had been expelled on February 11, 1592, for their "misdemeanours and abuses to the Masters and Benchers." Davies was probably involved in the Candlemas disturbances, but he and Robert Jacob, a lifelong friend, were given the milder penalty of merely being excluded from commons.

By 1594, Davies had apparently been presented at court by Charles Blount, Lord Mountjoy, who, along with Sir Thomas Egerton, is described as Davies' patron in all the manuscript sources for his biography. Queen Elizabeth had Davies sworn her servant-inordinary and encouraged him in his studies at the Middle Temple. He then served as part of the embassy to Scotland for the christening of Prince Henry at Stirling Castle on October 30, 1594.

On July 4, 1595, Davies was "called to the degree of the Utter Bar with the assent of all the Masters of the Bench." Since his admission to the Bar came after the minimum seven years of residence and since he was called with the permission of all the Masters of the Bench, not merely by a particular reader, he must have distinguished himself as a particularly brilliant student. Much of his best poetry was written during this period. By 1595, he had probably written *Nosce Teipsum*, which he did not publish until 1599, and most of his epigrams. In 1596, he published the first printed version of *Orchestra*, an encomium of dancing, to which he attached a dedicatory sonnet to Martin, addressing him as his dearest friend.

On February 9, 1598, Davies entered the Middle Temple Dining Hall while the Benchers were seated decorously at the table, preparing for the practice court and other exercises which followed dinner. Davies walked immediately to the table where Martin was seated and broke a bastinado over his head. Before leaving, he drew his rapier and brandished it above his head. For this flagrant violation of legal decorum, he was expelled on February 10 "never to return." No entirely satisfactory explanation for this attack has been proposed.

In *John Marston of the Middle Temple* (1969), Philip Finkelpearl speculated that the attack was related to a satiric reference to Davies' descent from a tanner which was made during the Christmas revels at the Middle Temple. Martin played the Prince d'Amour,

the central figure in the festivities, but it was Matagonius, the prince's poet, who was responsible for the satire against Davies. The incident occurred on December 27, 1597, so long before Davies' attack on Martin that it is difficult to believe that the two events were closely related. Whatever the provocation, it must have seemed significant to Davies, so much so, that he was willing to risk his promising legal future for public revenge.

After his expulsion, Davies may have spent some time at Oxford. By 1601, he was serving in the House of Commons as a representative from Corfe Castle, Dorset. During the debate over monopolies, a raging controversy in this parliament, he advocated that the House of Commons proceed to pass a bill canceling the monopolies or patents. The queen's loyal supporters vigorously recommended that the House humbly petition her to redress their grievances, since granting monopolies was part of her royal prerogative. Sir Robert Cecil singled Davies out for a special reprimand. Martin also served in the parliament of 1601 and also opposed monopolies; his active support of Davies' position suggests that the reconciliation between the two men may have been genuine. Davies' own outspoken demeanor is the more surprising because he had been readmitted to the Middle Temple only about a month before the debate.

After James came to the throne of England, Davies was appointed first solicitor general and then attorney general of Ireland. After receiving a knighthood in 1603, the first concrete evidence of his progress up the social ladder occurred in 1609 when he married Lady Eleanor Audeley, the daughter of George Touchet, Lord Audeley, later the earl of Castlehaven. By 1612, Davies had been created a sergeant-at-law, and by 1613, he was well enough off financially to be listed as one of the chief adventurers in a list of investors in the Virginia Company. In 1612, he published his major prose work, a history of Ireland titled *A Discoverie of the True Causes Why Ireland Was Never Entirely Subdued, nor Brought Under Obedience of the Crowne of England, Until the Beginning of His Majesties Happie Raigne*.

However socially advantageous Davies' marriage was, it cannot have been very pleasant. Lady Eleanor's brother, Mervyn Touchet, the second earl of Castle-haven, was criminally insane. He was sentenced to death for unnatural offenses after a notorious trial in the House of Lords; Charles I temporarily improved the moral image of the aristocracy by allowing the execution to take place. Lady Eleanor herself was a religious fanatic who believed that she was the prophet Daniel reincarnated. The truth was supposedly revealed to her in anagrams which she explicated in incoherent prophecies. By her own report, three years before the end, she foresaw Davies' death and donned her mourning garments from that moment: "when about three days before his sudden death, before all his servants and his friends at the table, gave him pass to take his long sleep, by him thus put off, 'I pray weep not while I am alive, and I will give you leave to laugh when I am dead'" (*The Lady Eleanor Her Appeal*, 1646). Lady Eleanor did not mourn, but she had little reason to laugh after Davies' death. She remarried Sir Archibald Douglas in three months, but he neglected and finally deserted her. He also burned her manuscripts, and she prophesied that he, like Davies, would suffer for it. According to her reports, while taking communion, he was struck dumb so that he could only make sounds like a beast. He apparently left England.

These facts are significant for a critical analysis of the surviving biographical materials and manuscript verse of Davies. His daughter Lucy married Ferdinando Hastings and became the countess of Huntingdon. Since her uncle was criminally insane and her mother's self-righteous fanaticism verged on madness, she would naturally want to present her father as morally upright and be sure that he was remembered for his solemn philosophical poetry and weighty prose. If the "licentious" sonnets first printed in the Clare Howard edition of Davies' *Poems* (1941) had been left among Davies' papers instead of in the library at Trinity College, Dublin, it is unlikely that either Lucy or her son Theophilus would have printed them. In his biographical notes on Davies, which survive in manuscript in the Hastings Collection at the Henry E. Huntington Library, Theophilus describes each of Davies' political appointments in detail, alludes to royal favors, and devotes several paragraphs to a description of Lucy Davies' dowry: Sir John's poetry is never mentioned.

## ANALYSIS

Sir John Davies' minor poetry falls into three general classes: dramatic entertainments written for court ceremonies or celebrations, occasional poems which he sent to prominent people, and satires commenting on a literary fashion or topical scandal. Of the entertainments which can be clearly attributed to Davies, the most important are "The Epithalamion of the Muses," presented at the wedding of Elizabeth Vere, daughter of Edward Vere, earl of Oxford, to William Stanley, earl of Derby, and preserved in the commonplace book of Leweston Fitzjames of the Middle Temple; *A Contention Betwixt a Widdowe, and a Maide* presented at the home of Sir Robert Cecil on December 6, 1602, in honor of Queen Elizabeth; and *Yet Other Twelve Wonders of the World*, twelve poems in rhymed couplets which were apparently inscribed on a dozen trenchers which Davies presented to the Lord Treasurer on New Year's Day in 1602 or 1603. John Maynard set *Yet Other Twelve Wonders of the World* to music in 1611.

Davies' occasional poems were addressed to influential people such as Henry Percy, earl of Northumberland; Sir Thomas Egerton, Lord Chancellor of England; and Sir Edward Coke, attorney general; as well as King James and Queen Anne. His "Gulling Sonnets" belong to the third class of topical poetry. In these sonnets, Davies mocks the conventions of the Petrarchan sonnet sequences which were popular in the 1590's. These particular poems survived only in manuscript accompanied by a dedication to Sir Anthony Cooke. They must have been written between 1596, when Cooke was knighted, and 1604, when he died. An internal reference to *Zepheria* (1597), an anonymous sonnet sequence, suggests that they were completed by 1598. *Zepheria* was probably written by a young law student since it contains an awkward combination of learned legal terms and Petrarchan images.

In his nineteenth century Victorian edition of Davies' works, Alexander Grosart supplied a commentary on Davies which unfortunately has dominated twentieth century critical opinion of the poet's major works. *Orchestra*, a dialogue between Penelope and one of her wooers, is, according to Grosart, a *jeu d'esprit* which Davies tossed off in his youth. Grosart insisted that Davies' most valuable work was *Nosce Teipsum* and that the chief merit of this exhaustive compendium of knowledge about the soul and immortality was its originality. Responding to Grosart's claim, modern academic scholarship on Davies has largely consisted of arguments that Davies' ideas derive from Plato, Aristotle, Pierre de la Primaudaye, Philippe du Plessis-Mornay, and Michel Eyquem de Montaigne.

Underlying the approach to Davies which Grosart initiated is the assumption that a sixteenth century writer would have aimed at or even particularly valued originality. Davies, however, belonged to an age which suspected novelty, valued intellectual tradition, and sought to imitate poetic models rather than to express personal feelings. Poets consciously modeled themselves on previous poets. Edmund Spenser, who hoped to win the title of the English Vergil, began by writing pastorals just as his Latin master had done.

In *On Poetry and Poets* (1957), T. S. Eliot, in what remains the best critical appreciation of Davies' works, calls attention to his metrical virtuosity, his clarity and purity of diction, and his independence of thought. In shifting the critical issue from originality to independence of thought, Eliot demonstrates historical as well as literary insight. While Davies' ideas on the soul and immortality are not original, one should not expect them to be. His synthesis of many diverse sources shows intellectual independence.

Each of Davies' major poems has to be assessed in relation to other works in that particular genre. He consciously works with certain established poetic conventions. His *Nosce Teipsum* should be examined in relation to other long philosophical poems, such as Lucretius's *De rerum natura* (c. 60 B.C.E.; *On the Nature of Things*, 1682), Aonio Paleario's *De immortalitate animae* (1536), Samuel Daniel's *Musophilus: Or, A Defence of Poesie* (1599, 1601, 1602, 1607, 1611, 1623), and Fulke Greville's poetic treatises. *Orchestra* belongs to the genre of mythological wooing poems, which were later given the name *epyllia*, or minor epics. In writing *Orchestra*, Davies did not set out to write a poem about the Elizabethan worldview; he suggests that *Orchestra* relates a wooing episode that Homer forgot to include in the *Odyssey* (c. 725 B.C.E.;

English translation, 1614) because he wants his readers to associate the poem with other amatory poems popular in England in the 1590's. Of these, two of the most popular were Christopher Marlowe's *Hero and Leander* (1598) and Shakespeare's *Venus and Adonis* (1593). *Orchestra*, however, lacks the sensuality of these two poems and seems to resemble the more philosophical efforts in the genre, such as Michael Drayton's *Endimion and Phoebe* (1595) and George Chapman's *Ovid's Banquet of Sense* (1595). The *Hymnes of Astraea* belong to a genre treated with disdain by most modern scholars. They are acrostic lyrics intended as an Accession Day tribute to Queen Elizabeth. Like the many entertainments written to praise Elizabeth's beauty or her purity, they are intended as courtly compliments and should be approached as artful "trifles," excellent in their kind.

Finally, it is important to emphasize that Davies was a man of ideas. His poems are intended not only to delight but also to teach and to inform. Critics who associate poetry with the expression of feelings or the description of scenery may find his verse less immediately accessible. He thrived on formal restraints; to appreciate his poetry requires a sensitivity to the technical difficulties of writing verse. It also requires that the reader accept verse in which, in Eliot's words, "thought is not exploited for the sake of feeling; it is pursued for its own sake."

### EPIGRAMMES AND ELEGIES

Davies' *Epigrammes and Elegies* appeared without a date and with a title page reading "At Middleburgh." No satisfactory explanation has been offered for the posthumous combination of Christopher Marlowe's translation of Ovid's *Elegies* with Davies' *Epigrammes and Elegies*. It is unlikely that the first edition was a piracy because Epigrams 47 and 48, which balance 1 and 2 in the printed text, seem to have been written specifically for the printed edition; they are absent from all four of the most important manuscripts. Although some of the epigrams may have dated from his school days, the majority were probably written between 1594 and 1595.

The poems are obviously modeled on Martial's epigrams, but Davies supplies details of sixteenth century English life. In "Meditations of a Gull," he describes a young gentleman consumed by "melancholy," a young man uninterested in politics who wears a cloak and a "great black feather." He is clearly describing the type of young man who pretends to be an intellectual, rather than a specific caricature. Davies, in fact, claims that his epigrams tax under "a peculiar name,/ A generall vice, which merits publick blame." In June, 1599, the bishop of London and the archbishop of Canterbury ordered that "Davyes Epigrams and Marlowe's Elegyes" be burned. Since they seem less obscene than other works so condemned, it may be that one of the epigrams contained a libelous allusion unrecognizable today. Practice in this genre, which requires condensation and lucidity, assisted Davies in developing talents which he demonstrated more forcefully in *Nosce Teipsum* and *Orchestra*, but the *Epigrammes and Elegies* still have some interest because of the clever way in which they mirror life in sixteenth century London.

### NOSCE TEIPSUM

*Nosce Teipsum* was first printed in 1599, approximately one year after Davies was expelled from the Middle Temple. The poem has frequently been described as an attempt on Davies' part to "repair his fortunes with his pen," thus assuming that Davies wrote it to show that he repented his assault on Martin and that he had completed his reformation. The poem contains what could be interpreted as an autobiographical reference: Affliction is described as having taken the narrator by the ear to teach him a lesson. There is substantial evidence, however, that the poem was begun long before Davies attacked Martin and that it was revised over a period of several years.

The question of literary form has received little attention in discussions of *Nosce Teipsum*, but an understanding of the nature of the poem's form and structure is crucial. First, the argument, or organization of ideas, does not define the form. It is impossible to outline *Nosce Teipsum* thematically without reaching the conclusion that the poem is a loosely organized compendium of Elizabethan knowledge. The second elegy, for example, defines the soul in relation to the body, but then discusses the origin of the soul, the Fall of Man, and free will, before considering the way in which the powers of the soul are actually exercised in the body.

The Fall of Man is discussed at the beginning of the first elegy and then examined again in stanzas 138-186 of the second elegy. Second, the poem is divided into two elegies of very different lengths, 45 stanzas in the first and 436 in the second. In the second elegy, a description of the soul requires 273 stanzas with arguments for immortality requiring another 163 stanzas. Davies could have divided the second elegy into two separate sections; that he did not do so requires some consideration.

The relationship between the two elegies is suggested by the general title of the work, not by the separate titles of the two elegies: *Nosce Teipsum: This Oracle Expounded in Two Elegies*. The emphasis should be upon "oracle," not upon the broad tradition of self-knowledge. The first elegy, "Of Humane Knowledge," is a riddle that presents the dilemmas that individuals experience in attempting to acquire self-knowledge. Both biblical and classical illustrations are used because the riddle of self-knowledge puzzles Christians as well as pagans. The second elegy represents a solution to the riddle, and it is structured as a classical oration. Davies' structure reverses the procedure of the classical oracle in which a relatively clear question led to an enigmatic answer. Influenced by the Renaissance concept of the "oracle" as an obscure riddle, Davies intends the first elegy to represent the question put to the deity in the ancient oracles; it concludes with an enigmatic statement of human nature. The second elegy presents a clear and straightforward answer to that enigmatic statement. The relationship between the two elegies explains why the form of *Nosce Teipsum* required a break between the two poems.

The second elegy uses the seven-part format of a classical oration, following the divisions of Thomas Wilson, the sixteenth century rhetorician, rather than the six sections recommended by Cicero. The "entrance" (stanzas 1-21) invokes divine light, showing the poet's need for divine assistance by summarizing the diversity of opinions about the soul (7-15). The "narration" (22-174) consists of two parts: a definition (22-100) and a history (101-174). The soul is defined as a spirit separate from the body; then, the history of how the soul and body were created is summarized. The "proposition" (175-189) answers the questions: why the soul is related to the body, in what manner it is related to the body, and how the soul exercises its powers in the body. The answers summarize the major themes of the "history," "definition," and "division." Davies uses the "division" (190-269) literally to divide the faculties of the soul and their functions; traditionally, the division explained the disposition of the material. The arguments for the immortality of the soul are presented as the "confirmation" (274-357); the refutation of arguments against the immortality of the soul follows in the "confutation" (358-420). In the "conclusion" (421-436), Davies links the two main subjects, the soul and immortality, and then admonishes his own soul to be humble. This admonition parallels the invocation to divine light presented in the entrance.

Brilliantly using the resources of rhetoric, Davies takes the reader from darkness and ambiguity in the first elegy to light and clarity as the answer to the riddle is discovered. The vision of man as a "*proud* and yet a *wretched* thing" at the end of the first elegy is corrected in the Acclamation which precedes the arguments for immortality in the second elegy:

> O! What a lively life, what heavenly poer,
> What spreading vertue, what a sparkling fire!
> How great, how plentifull, how rich a dower
> Dost Thou within this dying flesh inspire!

## ORCHESTRA

Davies' most engaging poem, and probably his most interesting for the modern reader, is *Orchestra*, an encomium of dancing set within a Homeric frame. The poem is supposed to relate a dialogue between Penelope, Queen of Ithaca, and Antinous, one of the disorderly suitors who wants to marry Penelope. Antinous invites Penelope to dance, but she refuses, calling dancing "this new rage." He responds with a lengthy defense of dancing, its antiquity and order.

Davies successfully achieves an exuberant combination of fancy and learning by using the structure, imagery, and setting to suggest multiple levels of meaning. These levels overlap and reinforce one another, but they can be generally distinguished as philosophical, political, and aesthetic. On a philosophical level, the poem is an extended hyperbole which views the macrocosm and microcosm united in the universal dance of

life. Davies, however, treats this traditional idea playfully as well as seriously. When he extends the central image of a dancing cosmos to include the description of the veins of the earth as dancing "saphire streames," and to include the personification of Echo, the "prattling" daughter of the air, as an imperfect dancer, the reader becomes keenly aware of the poet's artifice. One is amused by these unconventional extensions of the traditional metaphor, but one does not question its basic validity. The aesthetic effect that Davies achieves is to render the tone playful without undercutting the seriousness of the message.

Similarly, Davies interweaves the themes of love and beauty in ways that enrich the philosophical and aesthetic overtones of the poem. Love is described as the father of dancing and also functions as a major figure in the poem. Stanzas 28-76 are devoted to Antinous's description of Love's speeches and actions, and Love, disguised as a page, presents Antinous with the magic mirror which reflects an idealized view of Elizabeth and her court (stanzas 109-126). In stanzas 98-108, love also becomes the central issue in the dialogue between Penelope and Antinous. She attacks Love as "of every ill the hatefull Father vile" (stanza 98), supporting this charge with mythological examples (stanzas 99-100). She concludes with a rejection of both dancing and love in stanza 101: "Unhappy may they prove,/ That sitting free, will either daunce or love." Antinous replies by distinguishing mischievous Lust from that "true Love" who invented dancing, tuned the world's harmony, and linked men in "sweet societie." In stanzas 105-108, Antinous argues that Love dances in Penelope: Her beauty is "but a daunce where Love hath us'd/ His finer cunning, and more curious art." As E. M. W. Tillyard has suggested, these stanzas allude to the Platonic ladder in which the lover is first attracted to the physical beauty of his mistress and then to her spiritual beauty and virtue; he is led up the ladder to the point at which he values virtue for its own sake. In stanza 108, the imagined vision of Penelope's virtues dancing a round dance in her soul almost puts Antinous into a trance.

The philosophical and aesthetic levels are closely related. Not only is Penelope's beauty described as a dance in which Love has used his "more curious art" but also Love's dance in Penelope is developed by artistic illustrations: Love dances in her fingers when she weaves her web (stanza 106) or when she plays "any silver-sounding instrument" (stanza 107). This type of aesthetic statement is set forth quite overtly in the poem, but there are also two digressions from the central action which function aesthetically to symbolize the entire poem: First, Antinous reports a long speech which the god Love delivered to disorderly men and women to persuade them to dance. This persuasion to dance, stanzas 29-60, is a rhetorical set piece; it is unrelated to the main action, Antinous's persuasion of Penelope to dance, and yet it mirrors it. Love's speech is a macrocosmic parallel to the microcosm in which Antinous is wooing Penelope. Second, near the conclusion of the poem (stanzas 109-126), in the second digression, Antinous summons Love disguised as a page boy to bring a magic mirror which reflects a vision of Elizabeth's court in which the sovereign moon is surrounded by dancing stars. The heavenly bodies and the court, or body politic, are united in harmonious order. Each of the above digressions comments upon the poem and underlines Davies' political intentions.

Queen Elizabeth was in her sixties when *Orchestra* was written, but she was surrounded by suitors who wished to be named as her successor. The contemporary political situation offered a close parallel to the Homeric setting, but Davies could not afford to make the comparisons too explicit. He merely hints that his own Queen Elizabeth, like Queen Penelope, is reluctant to participate in the orderly movement of the universe by assuring for a transfer of power (stanzas 60, 57-58). In the first digression, Antinous parallels Love, the god, who is attempting to persuade the disorderly men and women to learn to dance; by implication, Penelope parallels them.

The mirror, like the rhetorical set piece, symbolizes in miniature the poem. Davies' *Orchestra*, like the mirror, has displayed the timeless and ideal forms of order in the macrocosm and the microcosm. It has shown the past by describing Antinous's wooing of Penelope and hinted at the rejection of order in Penelope's refusal. The poem, like the mirror, also shows the present by describing the Queen surrounded by her courtiers as the moon surrounded by the stars, but there is no provision for the future. At the end of the poem, the reader does not know whether Queen Penelope will finally accept the invitation to dance and in so doing assure order throughout the macrocosm and microcosm. The invocation to Urania in stanza 127 is addressed to a "Prophetesse divine," not to the muse of heavenly love. This invocation, which follows the invocation in stanza 123 so closely, emphasizes that the poet cannot prophesy the future. He has shown the past, present, and the timeless ideal, but it is up to the Queen to provide for the future.

The epic trappings, in which the disorderly Antinous of the *Odyssey* becomes a spokesperson for order, invite the reader to make parallels, but they are handled so playfully that *Orchestra* could, if need arose, masquerade as a simple wooing poem. The poem invites but does not require a political interpretation. *Orchestra* is constructed so that it could pass as a *jeu d'esprit* or as a celebration of honor climaxing in a compliment to the Queen, but it was intended as Davies' "pithie exhortation" to Elizabeth to settle the succession so that an orderly transfer of power would be assured after her death.

Three versions of *Orchestra* have survived, and in each, Davies' handling of the conclusion reflects his views about the contemporary political situation. The only surviving manuscript of the poem (LF) is preserved in Leweston Fitzjames's commonplace book (Bodleian Library Add. MS. B. 97. fols. 258-38). LF contains only some stanzas of the first printed version: 1-108 plus 131. An entry in the Stationers' Register in 1594 suggests that LF preserves an early version composed in 1593-1594, a time when the publication of Father Robert Parsons's *Conference About the Next Succession to the Crown of England* had made the subject of the succession dangerous to discuss. The LF version omits the magic mirror sequence so that no celebration of order in the body politic is included in the poem.

The first printed version is titled *Orchestra: Or, A Poeme of Dauncing. Iudicially Prooving the True Observation of Time and Measure, in the Authenticall and Laudable Use of Dauncing.* This version consists of stanzas 1-131. Probably to render the political implications less explicit, Davies added stanzas 109-126, the mirror sequence, to the already complete manuscript version before he published the poem in 1596.

The final version of the poem appeared in 1622, nearly twenty years after the succession had been peacefully settled. The 1622 version substitutes a dedication to Prince Charles for the earlier one to Richard Martin, who had died a few years earlier. Stanzas 127-131, which contain veiled allusions to poets popular in the 1590's, are omitted. Following stanza 126 there is the curious note: "Here are wanting some stanzas describing Queen Elizabeth. Then follow these." Ironically, the five new stanzas (132-136) contain a description of Queen Elizabeth. The printer seems to have confused these stanzas in manuscript and not known where to insert them; to conceal his confusion he added a note suggesting that something had been left out and merely printed the stanzas at the end of the text. When the stanzas are reordered and inserted in the appropriate places, it is clear that in this version Davies did intend to suggest that Queen Penelope accepted the invitation to dance. The invocation to Urania is omitted, and the poem concludes with stanza 126. Davies, looking back nostalgically on the Elizabethan court of his youth, suggests that Elizabeth's reign was indeed England's Golden Age.

### HYMNES OF ASTRAEA

*Hymnes of Astraea*, twenty-six acrostic lyrics, celebrates Queen Elizabeth as Astraea, the just virgin, who left the earth after the end of the Golden Age; these hymns suggest that the English Virgin Queen is an embodiment of Astraea, who has returned to usher in the golden age of England. The number twenty-six was associated with the astrological sign of the constellation Virgo, and Virgo, in turn, was associated with Astraea, the just virgin. In *Orchestra*, Davies indicated that "the fairest sight that ever shall be seene" would occur when "sixe and twenty hundreth yeeres are past" (stanza 121). This reference demonstrates his awareness of the Virgo-Astraea tradition and his desire to associate it with Elizabeth, who, by deciding the succession question, could bring a new golden age to England.

*Hymnes of Astraea* is an artful and brilliantly sustained tour de force. Each of the twenty-six acrostic lyrics contains sixteen lines divided into stanzas of five, five, and six. In all twenty-six lyrics, Davies follows a regular rhyme pattern of *aabab ccdcd* in the first two stanzas, with occasional variations from the dominant pattern of *eefggf* in the third stanzas. The meter is predominantly iambic tetrameter. *Hymns of Astraea* was entered in the Stationers' Register on November 17, 1599, the Queen's Accession Day. Intended as an Accession Day tribute, the initial letters of the lines read downward spell the royal name: ELISABETHA REGINA.

### OTHER MAJOR WORKS

NONFICTION: *A Discoverie of the True Causes Why Ireland Was Never Entirely Subdued, nor Brought Under Obedience of the Crowne of England, Until the Beginning of His Majesties Happie Raigne*, 1612; *Le Premer Report des Cases et Matters en Ley*, 1615; *A Perfect Abridgement of the Eleven Bookes of Reports of the Reverend and Learned Sir Edw. Cook*, 1651; *The Question Concerning Impositions, Tonnage, Poundage, Prizage, Customs*, 1656.

### BIBLIOGRAPHY

Brink, Jean R. "Sir John Davies' *Orchestra*: Political Symbolism and Textual Revision." *Durham University Journal* 72 (1980): 195-201. Analyzes the way in which *Orchestra*, Davies' most important poem, comments both philosophically and politically upon the Elizabethan worldview. The notes offer a useful summary of previous biographical and critical discussions of Davies.

Brooks-Davies, Douglas, ed. *Silver Poets of the Sixteenth Century: Wyatt, Surrey, Ralegh, Philip Sidney, Mary Sidney, Michael Drayton, and Sir John Davies*. Rutland, Vt.: Charles E. Tuttle, 1992. Examines work by Thomas Wyatt; Henry Howard, earl of Surrey; Sir Walter Ralegh, and Davies, including the long philosophical poems *Orchestra* and *Nosce Teipsum*.

Davies, John. *The Poems of Sir John Davies*. Edited by Robert Krueger. Oxford, England: Clarendon Press, 1975. The standard edition of Davies' poetry, but as Krueger notes in the introduction, much of Davies' verse, especially his epigrams and occasional poetry, was still being recovered from manuscript at the time that this edition appeared.

Eliot, T. S. *On Poetry and Poets*. 1957. Reprint. New York: Farrar, Straus and Giroux, 2009. Eliot's essay provides a good critique of Davies' work, placing it in its time.

Helgerson, Richard. *Self-Crowned Laureates: Spenser, Jonson, Milton, and the Literary System*. Berkeley: University of California Press, 1983. Although Helgerson offers only a brief discussion of Davies, his study of the social milieu in which English Renaissance poetry was composed is important. Helgerson distinguishes Davies, a gifted amateur, from both the professionals and the would-be laureate poets.

Klemp, P. J. *Fulke Greville and Sir John Davies: A Reference Guide*. Boston: G. K. Hall, 1985. Klemp presents a chronological bibliography of works by and about Davies from 1590 to 1985. Each entry in the bibliography has been annotated.

Pawlisch, Hans S. *Sir John Davies and the Conquest of Ireland: A Study in Legal Imperialism*. New York: Cambridge University Press, 1985. Concentrates on Davies' legal and political career rather than his verse. Pawlisch argues that judge-made law offered the English monarchy a means of consolidating the Tudor conquest of Ireland.

Sanderson, James L. *Sir John Davies*. Boston: Twayne, 1975. Although the biography is out of date, this study of Davies is the only full-length discussion of his life and major poems. Sanderson comments on Davies' epigrams, *Orchestra, Nosce Teipsum*, and his religious and occasional verse.

Schmidt, A. V. C. "Whirling World, Dancing Words: Further Echoes of Sir John Davies in T. S. Eliot." *Notes and Queries* 54, no. 2 (June, 2007): 164-168. Schmidt finds evidence of Davies' dance imagery in the opening paragraph of Eliot's "Ash Wednesday" and notes other ways in which Davies influenced the poetry of Eliot.

Sneath, E. Hershey. *Philosophy in Poetry: A Study of Sir John Davies' Poem "Nosce Teipsum."* 1969. Reprint. Charleston, S.C.: Bibliolife, 2009. A rare book-length focus on Davies's poem, addressed in terms of soul and body, materialism and sensationalism.

*Jeanie R. Brink*

# CECIL DAY LEWIS

**Born:** Ballintubbert, Ireland; April 27, 1904
**Died:** Hadley Wood, Hertfordshire, England; May 22, 1972
**Also known as:** Nicholas Blake; C. Day Lewis

PRINCIPAL POETRY
*Beechen Vigil, and Other Poems*, 1925
*Country Comets*, 1928
*Transitional Poem*, 1929
*From Feathers to Iron*, 1931
*The Magnetic Mountain*, 1933
*Collected Poems, 1929-1933*, 1935
*A Time to Dance, and Other Poems*, 1935
*Overtures to Death, and Other Poems*, 1938
*Poems in Wartime*, 1940
*Selected Poems*, 1940
*Word over All*, 1943
*Short Is the Time: Poems, 1936-1943*, 1945
*Collected Poems, 1929-1936*, 1948
*Poems, 1943-1947*, 1948
*Selected Poems*, 1951, 1957, 1969, 1974
*An Italian Visit*, 1953
*Collected Poems*, 1954
*The Newborn: D.M.B., 29th April 1957*, 1957
*Pegasus, and Other Poems*, 1957
*The Gate, and Other Poems*, 1962
*Requiem for the Living*, 1964
*A Marriage Song for Albert and Barbara*, 1965
*The Room, and Other Poems*, 1965
*The Abbey That Refused to Die: A Poem*, 1967
*Selected Poems*, 1967
*The Whispering Roots*, 1970
*The Poems, 1925-1972*, 1977 (Ian Parsons, editor)
*The Complete Poems of C. Day Lewis*, 1992
*Selected Poems*, 2004

OTHER LITERARY FORMS

Cecil Day Lewis's fiction can easily be placed into three categories, the first being the novels published prior to World War II: *The Friendly Tree* (1936), *Starting Point* (1937), and *Child of Misfortune* (1939). Then, under the pseudonym of Nicholas Blake, he became a significant contributor to the popular genre of detective fiction. Finally, there are two pieces of juvenile fiction. Day Lewis's output was, however, not confined to fiction and poetry. He also produced a large body of literary criticism, editorial projects, and translations.

### ACHIEVEMENTS

Cecil Day Lewis was the most conscientious poet laureate in England's history—even surpassing Alfred, Lord Tennyson in his conception of the laureate's responsibilities. During his tenure, from 1968 until his death in 1972, a period in which he suffered from illness, Day Lewis produced a lengthy list of poems on national and topical themes, a majority of which stand on their own poetic merits, as opposed to personal and shallow tributes to specific royal personages. Indeed, during his period as the nation's laureate, Day Lewis underscored his own importance as a contributor to English poetry, as one who understood and accepted the tradition of English poetry and significantly enlarged upon it.

Day Lewis's poetic achievement was marked by a flexible attitude toward the political and social temper of his times. He never withdrew to some private shelter to ponder future poetical-political courses of action or to brood over loss or misfortune. On the contrary, he viewed poetry as being exceedingly public and the poet as being the property of that public. Thus, he tried to share himself and his work with as many people as possible through books of and about poetry for children, through lectures and radio broadcasts about poetry, and through societies and festivals for advancing the general state of the poetic art. Particularly in the later stages of his career when he served as laureate, Day Lewis spent almost as much time writing and talking about poetry as he did creating poems. His appointment, in 1951, as Professor of Poetry at Oxford allowed him, still further, to perform a distinct service to his art.

Finally, Day Lewis's achievement may be observed in the nature of his own work as a representation of what may conveniently be termed the poetry of the mid-twentieth century. His poetry indeed represents the conflict within the modern poet of that period, a conflict between the old and the new. In *A Hope for Poetry* (1934), he elaborated upon that conflict as a confrontation between the idea of the poet forging ahead to shape a new society and a new society shaping artists in its own image.

Such poems as "The Conflict," "The Double Vision," "Marriage of Two," "The Misfit," and "The Neurotic" capture effectively the degrees of uncertainty that Day Lewis sensed about people of his place and time. He understood well the old injustices that prompted, in turn, men and women to perform new injustices against one another. For him, poetry served society by asking questions about those conflicts, by probing moral problems for answers to some very difficult questions. In the act of poetic questioning, he sought not only a personal answer but also one that would best serve the social good.

*Cecil Day Lewis* (Hulton Archive/Getty Images)

## BIOGRAPHY

Cecil Day Lewis (Cecil Day-Lewis) was born in 1904 at Ballintubbert, Queen's County, in Ireland, where his father, the Reverend F. C. Day-Lewis, served as a curate. His mother, Kathleen Blake Squires, claimed distant relationship to Oliver Goldsmith, while the poet himself once reported a connection between his grandmother and the family of William Butler Yeats. The original name of the paternal family had been, simply, Day; the family later acquired the Lewis and then carried both names in hyphenated form. However, the poet discarded the hyphen for the purpose of practicing what he termed, in his autobiographical *The Buried Day* (1960), "inverted snobbery."

In 1907, when Day Lewis was only three years of age, the family severed its Irish connection and moved to England; by age six, the youngster had achieved some competence as a writer of verse. His pursuit of formal learning took him first to Sherborne School (Dorsetshire), then to Wadham College, Oxford, where he developed a particular interest in Latin poetry. He published *Beechen Vigil, and Other Poems* while still an undergraduate, and spent the years between his departure from Oxford and the onset of World War II writing poetry and teaching English in a number of public schools in England and Scotland: Summer Fields, Oxford (1927-1928); Larchfield, Helensburgh, on the Firth of Clyde (1928-1930)—where he was succeeded by W. H. Auden; and Cheltenham College, Gloucestershire (1930-1935). With the publication of *Collected Poems, 1929-1933* and *A Question of Proof* (1935, the first detective story by Nicholas Blake), Day Lewis abandoned pedagogy for full-time authorship, although he would return to teaching and lecturing on a far more sophisticated level after World War II.

During the war, the poet worked for the Ministry of Information, after which he received a number of prestigious academic appointments: Clark Lecturer, Cambridge (1946); Warton Lecturer, British Academy, London (1951); Professor of Poetry, Oxford (1951-1956); Byron Lecturer, University of Nottingham (1952); Chancellor Dunning Lecturer, Queen's University, Kingston, Ontario (1954); Sidgwick Lecturer, University of Cambridge (1956); Norton Professor of Poetry, Harvard (1964-1965); and Compton Lecturer, University of Hull (1968). Day Lewis also served as director of the publishing house of Chatto and Windus, London, from 1954 until his death, as well as a member of the Arts Council of Great Britain from 1962 to 1967. His most significant appointment and honor came in 1968, when he succeeded John Masefield (who died on May 12, 1967) as poet laureate of England. Although the list of candidates was never published, speculation as to his competition focused on such names as Richard Church, Robert Graves, Edmund Blunden, and W. H. Auden. The last named had, by then, however, become an American citizen, while the first three poets were all more than seventy years of age. As matters turned out, Day Lewis's tenure as laureate lasted only four years.

The poet's first marriage was to Constance Mary King in 1928; upon their divorce in 1951, he married Jill Balcon. His last residence was at Crooms Hill, outside London and west of Greenwich Park. After his death on May 22, 1972, Day Lewis's body was transferred for burial at Stinsford, Dorsetshire (one mile east of Dorchester), close to the remains of Thomas Hardy, whom he greatly admired.

## ANALYSIS

During his Oxford years and the period of his preparatory school teaching, Cecil Day Lewis published his first volumes of poetry: *Beechen Vigil, and Other Poems*, followed by *Country Comets*. Both constitute a high level of juvenile verse, the products of a student who had studied much about poets and poetry but who had learned little about life and had experienced even less. The two books demonstrate, however, that, prior to the age of twenty-five, Day Lewis had essentially mastered the craft of poetry. Further, the two volumes established that for him, a book of verse would emerge as a unified, thematic whole rather than merely as a collection of miscellaneous pieces.

The poet's earliest conflicts arose out of his inability to distinguish clearly the old values of his present and past worlds from the newly emerging ones of the present and the future. In two poems, for example, "Juvenilia" and "Sketches for a Portrait," the young man of privileged and comfortably secure economic class confronts a fundamental social problem: whether to continue to accept without question the comfortable conventions of his class, or to look beyond both the class and the comforts in an attempt to understand and then to identify with the problems of people who exist totally outside his sphere of experience and values. Day Lewis inserts into the poetic environment high garden walls that protect the young man's neatly manicured lawn from the grime of the outside, but, certainly, the day must come when the dirt will filter through the wall and smudge the laurel. Then what?

### TRANSITIONAL POEM

The answers to that question did not come quickly or easily. Instead, in three separate volumes, Day Lewis portrayed the complexity of human experience as it unfolded in several stages. The first, titled *Transitional Poem*, represents a form of self-analysis wherein the poet initially rejected the romantic nature worship of the preceding century as no solution to what he perceived as the mind's "own forked speculation." At the age of twenty-five, Day Lewis had little or no sympathy for those among his contemporaries who appeared as "intellectual Quixotes," propagandizing abstract values and superficial critical criteria. As a poet he sought, instead, to harness the chaos of a disordered world and beget a new age built upon the "crest of things," upon the commonplace "household stuff, stone walls, mountains and trees/ [that] Placard the day with certainties." Further, the word of the artist, of the twentieth century poet, cannot be allowed, like the Word of God, to stand remote and free from actuality. Instead, poetry must return to life: "Wrenching a stony song from a scant acre/ The Word still justifies its Maker."

### FROM FEATHERS TO IRON

Two years later, in 1931, Day Lewis continued his spiritual self-analysis in *From Feathers to Iron*. The title of the piece came from an observation by John Keats: "We take but three steps from feathers to iron," in reference to the maturation process from a theoretical perception of life to an actual understanding of human existence. In this series of lyric poems, Day Lewis considered the theme of experience within the context of marriage and parenthood. Love, he maintained, cannot endure without the presence of children; two years seems the limit for the love of husband and wife to be "marooned on self-sufficiency," and thus new dimensions must be added to the union. The poems in the volume concern fertility, the passion and the pain involved with the anguish of birth, and the hope that fatherhood may end what the poet terms the "indeterminate quarrel between a fevered head and a cold heart." The narrator of the volume occupies the long period of expectation with poems to both mother and child, while the final days seem to him "numb with crisis, cramped with waiting"; after man and wife have, together, explored the extremes of pain and fear, deliverance finally arrives and the multifaceted experience draws to a close. Day Lewis may well have been the first to attempt, in verse, a serious analysis of marriage as it relates to birth and parenthood, placing it squarely within the context of the modern world, in the midst of its complexities and technological by-products.

### THE MAGNETIC MOUNTAIN

Careful readers may sense, in the last of the three works—*The Magnetic Mountain*—the influences of Gerard Manley Hopkins and W. H. Auden. Day Lewis divided the piece into four major sections, the beginning being especially reminiscent of Hopkins's "The Windhover." The poet invokes a "kestrel joy, O hoverer in wind," as he searches "beyond the railheads of reason" for a "magnetic mountain," for truth. He proposes to follow his friends—Auden and Rex Warner—along the political path toward truth, where, in the second section, he surveys some politically reactionary types: a clinging mother, a conventional schoolmaster, a priest, and a "domestic" man. Then, in the third section, Day Lewis exposes what he believes to be the real enemies of progress: the flattering spell of love, popular education and information, the "religion" of science, and false romantic ideals. The poem ends with a series of lyrics extolling a social effort governed by the duality of twentieth century man—as soarer ("windhover") and as an earthbound creature. Criticism of *The Magnetic Mountain* focuses upon the issue of influence; some critics maintain that it contains too much of Auden's political and social thought, not enough of Hopkins's language and rhythm, and even less of Day Lewis's own voice.

### POLITICAL PHILOSOPHY

Although the emphasis in *Transitional Poem, From Feathers to Iron*, and *The Magnetic Mountain* may appear social and spiritual, the political implications of the three volumes should not be ignored. Scholars generally have been attentive to the political philosophy of the early, prewar poetry of Day Lewis, particularly in the light of the poet's interest, in company with a number of his intellectual and artistic contemporaries, in communism as the principal healing agent for an economically and politically sick world. Day Lewis's excursions along the highways of Marxist philosophy, however, do not provide an adequate background needed to evaluate his work of the 1930's. Certainly a knowledge of his communist sympathies helps to clarify certain attitudes and methods, particularly his bullying tone or even outright contempt toward middle-class men and women in pursuit of little else beyond their contented, individualistic careers. Nevertheless, standing steadily behind the signposts of political ideology can be seen the beauty and the momentum created by the language of poetry—not by the language of politics. Poetically, the pieces depend very little on their topical content, especially after the specific events mentioned have faded into the clouds of history. To his credit, Day Lewis remained a poet and held fast to the principles of his art—as did Auden and Stephen Spender, and as did George Orwell in his fiction. Although Day Lewis tried his hand at political pamphleteering, he could not function for very long in that capacity, especially when his passions gained the upper hand.

### THE 1930'S

Once Day Lewis had turned away from politics, his poetry reaped considerable artistic profit from force and economy. During the 1930's, the young poet struggled to find some use for the dominant images of the modern world, especially for modern industry and transportation. Similarly, he appeared uncomfortable, sometimes overly aggressive, in his attempts to find a place for the serenities of nature amidst the noise and the movement generated by his political themes. After 1939, however, even with the coming of world conflict, Day Lewis seemed eager to turn toward nature, to write as a true child of the provinces, as one who delighted in plowed fields, elevated tracts of land, and cloud formations, in air and in landscape; as one who sought to inject a positive spirit into his poetry after so many years of despair, disillusionment, and political frustration.

"For me there is no dismay," he announced in *Word over All*, seemingly struck "Dumb as a rooted rock" by the tragedy of world events. Nevertheless, despite his unveiled Georgian mood, he could still communicate with a nation at war, declaring, in "The Assertion," that "Now is the time we assert/ To their face that men are love. . . ." Again, in "Lidice," he recognized the complexity and the composition of humanity, the good and the evil that existed everywhere and at all times, and he understood that "The pangs we felt from . . . atrocious hurt/ Promise a time when the killer shall see/ His sword is aimed at his own naked heart."

In *From Feathers to Iron* and *The Magnetic Mountain*, despite certain inclinations toward themes of social unrest, political upheaval, and general radicalism, Day Lewis rarely lost sight of the form and function of lyric poetry, of the beauty and the rhythm of poetic language. Both during and after the war, he intensified his mastery of and reliance upon the love song, especially those tender poems in which he attempted to trace the effect of love on the personality, as in "The Lighted House" and "The Album." With his change in thematic emphasis came, of course, certain regrets, particularly over having lost the wildness, the excitement, the rapture of youth. Thus, in "The Rebuke," the love song serves well as a means of asking some penetrating questions about "the sparks at random," the "spendthrift fire, the holy fire"; all that has passed without having left its proper, natural effect, and it is now too late to do anything about it. Day Lewis's lyric poetry is firmly in the tradition of Richard Lovelace, Andrew Marvell, and Alfred, Lord Tennyson; during his later years, he never really strayed far from those models.

### AN ITALIAN VISIT

The most ambitious and impressive volume of Day Lewis's poetry appeared in 1953 under the title *An Italian Visit*. The book consists of a long work divided into seven parts: "Dialogue at the Airport," "Flight to Italy," "A Letter from Rome," "Bus to Florence," "Florence: Works of Art," "Elegy Before Death: At Settignano," and "The Homeward Prospect." In this work, Day Lewis changed his poetic mood from an austere evangelizing spirit to an acceptance of a lighter, more genial mode of existence. He describes those who flowered in the 1930's as "an odd lot," "sceptical yet susceptible,/

Dour though enthusiastic." The poem is an intellectual travel book, a voyage of discovery not only of scenes and cities but also of the latent faculties of the traveler's mind and heart. Day Lewis's traveler, however, is a composite of three people who, in turn, reflect three aspects of the poet's own personality: Tom's concern is for the present, and Dick looks to the past; Harry, on the other hand, focuses upon neither, but searches the future for the truth. Tom takes his pleasure in the immediate moment as he seeks to gratify the senses through "The real, royal, vulgar pageant—/ Time flying like confetti or twirled in rosettes." Dick, the scholar, thinker, artist, and lover of the perfect, evaluates the present through the supreme achievements of the past ("Reaching across generations to find the parent stock"), while Harry—a sociologist, rationalist, brooder upon the human condition, and seeker of reality under appearances—sees the world as a "provocative, charming/ Striptease universe."

At the conclusion of the holiday, each traveler returns to England after having experienced a different Italy: Tom returns "enriched," Dick "sobered," and Harry "lightened." Two sections of the poem, "Florence: Works of Art" and "Elegy Before Death: At Settignano," stand apart from the five. In the former, Day Lewis seems to have had a grand time practicing parodies of the styles of Hardy, Yeats, Robert Frost, Auden, and Dylan Thomas—all poets whom he enthusiastically endorsed and admired. The "Settignano" section is a stark contrast, a profoundly moving meditation on the subjects of love, time, and mortality. The ark of love embarks through a "pinprick of doubt into the dark," wherein "a whole life is drained off," while in "Rhadamanthine" moments, lovers find "a chance to make our flux/ Stand and deliver its holy spark." Merely a quick glance at the first and second generation Romantic poets of the nineteenth century reveals how well Day Lewis has extended the conventions of meditative verse and has done so without any perverse effort at originality for its own sake. For him, the traditions still hold.

Perhaps the most appealing human quality of Day Lewis's poetry is his natural hesitancy and inconsistency. Throughout his literary career, marked by political, social, and philosophical sampling and exper-

imentation, he never once embraced the banner of unwavering certainty—the standard of false intellectual pride. He was, indeed, a poet of several points of view who spoke—as in *An Italian Visit*—in and through several voices, a modest thinker and artist who needed to work within a poetic tradition.

**LATER POETRY**

In the postwar poems and beyond, Day Lewis seemed to find his tradition. He came to understand what may be termed his "Englishness," his need for skeptical inquiry into himself and his world. That tradition bred and nurtured such authors as Robert Burns, William Barnes, and Hardy. Day Lewis had learned, from Hopkins and especially from Hardy, that the poet did not have to obligate himself to the smart and the fashionable; he had learned that the poet's responsibility rested upon the freedom to create his own personal atmosphere of seriousness and charm. After he cast off the restrictive mantle of fashionable radicalism and after he endured the tragedy of world war, Day Lewis found his freedom, his tradition, and his own poetic voice.

OTHER MAJOR WORKS

LONG FICTION: *A Question of Proof*, 1935 (as Nicholas Blake); *The Friendly Tree*, 1936; *Thou Shell of Death*, 1936 (also known as *Shell of Death*; as Blake); *Starting Point*, 1937; *There's Trouble Brewing*, 1937 (as Blake); *The Beast Must Die*, 1938 (as Blake); *Child of Misfortune*, 1939; *The Smiler with the Knife*, 1939 (as Blake); *Malice in Wonderland*, 1940 (also known as *The Summer Camp Mystery* and *Malice with Murder*; as Blake); *The Corpse in the Snowman*, 1941 (also known as *The Case of the Abominable Snowman*; as Blake); *Minute for Murder*, 1947 (as Blake); *Head of a Traveler*, 1949 (as Blake); *The Dreadful Hollow*, 1953 (as Blake); *The Whisper in the Gloom*, 1954 (also known as *Catch and Kill*; as Blake); *A Tangled Web*, 1956 (also known as *Death and Daisy Bland*; as Blake); *End of Chapter*, 1957 (as Blake); *A Penknife in My Heart*, 1958 (as Blake); *The Widow's Cruise*, 1959 (as Blake); *The Worm of Death*, 1961 (as Blake); *The Deadly Joker*, 1963 (as Blake); *The Sad Variety*, 1964 (as Blake); *The Morning After Death*, 1966 (as Blake); *The Private Wound*, 1968 (as Blake).

PLAY: *Noah and the Waters*, pb. 1936.

NONFICTION: *A Hope for Poetry*, 1934; *Revolution in Writing*, 1935; *The Colloquial Element in English Poetry*, 1947; *The Poetic Image*, 1947; *The Poet's Task*, 1951; *The Poet's Way of Knowledge*, 1957; *The Buried Day*, 1960; *The Lyric Impulse*, 1965; *A Need for Poetry?*, 1968.

TRANSLATIONS: *The Georgics of Virgil*, 1940; *The Graveyard by the Sea*, 1946 (of Paul Valéry); *The Aeneid of Virgil*, 1952; *The Eclogues of Virgil*, 1963.

CHILDREN'S LITERATURE: *The Otterbury Incident*, 1948.

EDITED TEXT: *The Collected Poems of Wilfred Owen*, 1963.

BIBLIOGRAPHY

Balcon, Jill. "The Interview: Jill Balcon." Interview by Rachel Cooke. *The Observer*, May 20, 2007, p. 12. The eighty-two-year-old widow of Day Lewis discusses her marriage to the poet and the affair he had after they were married. She served as a source of information for Peter Stanford and his 2007 biography of Day Lewis.

Bayley, John. *The Power of Delight: A Lifetime in Literature—Essays, 1962-2002*. New York: W. W. Norton, 2005. The collected essays of this major critic feature one on Blake (Day Lewis) and his use of pastiche, both in poetry and in fiction. Index.

Day-Lewis, Sean. *Day-Lewis: An English Literary Life*. London: Weidenfeld & Nicolson, 1980. The first son of Blake wrote this year-by-year biography of his father within a decade of his father's death. Family members and friends contributed material to an objective but intimate portrait of the poet. Both the poetry publications and the crime novels under the name Blake are discussed.

Gelpi, Albert. *Living in Time: The Poetry of C. Day Lewis*. New York: Oxford University Press, 1998. A full-length critical study of the works of Day Lewis and a record of his poetry within the literary ferment of the twentieth century. Explores the three major periods of the poet's development, beginning with the emergence of Day Lewis in the 1930's as the most radical of the Oxford poets.

Riddel, Joseph N. *C. Day Lewis*. New York: Twayne, 1971. Riddel argues that Day Lewis should be known as more than a member of the "Auden group" of British poets of the 1930's. His poetry is considered chronologically with emphasis on the creative and radical period from 1929 to 1938. The problems of language, individual psychology, the "divided self," and the lyric impulse are enduring themes. An essential study supplemented by notes and a bibliography.

Smith, Elton Edward. *The Angry Young Men of the Thirties*. Carbondale: Southern Illinois University Press, 1975. In his first chapter, "C. Day-Lewis: The Iron Lyricist," Smith outlines the dilemma of British poets in the 1930's, a decade of worldwide economic collapse.

Stanford, Peter. *C. Day-Lewis: A Life*. New York: Continuum, 2007. In this literary biography, Stanford argues that Day Lewis's poetry is undervalued. The poet's personal life, with his lovers and wives, is discussed.

Whitehead, John. *A Commentary on the Poetry of W. H. Auden, C. Day Lewis, Louis MacNeice, and Stephen Spender*. Lewiston, N.Y.: Edwin Mellen Press, 1992. Contains critical analysis of the poetry of Day Lewis, as well as that of three other English poets.

*Samuel J. Rogal*

---

# THOMAS DEKKER

**Born:** London, England; c. 1572
**Died:** London, England; August, 1632

PRINCIPAL POETRY

*The Whole History of Fortunatus*, 1599 (commonly known as *Old Fortunatus*, play and poetry)

*The Shoemaker's Holiday: Or, The Gentle Craft*, 1600 (based on Thomas Deloney's narrative *The Gentle Craft*, play and poetry)

*The Wonderful Year*, 1603 (prose and poetry)

*The Honest Whore, Part I*, 1604 (with Thomas Middleton, play and poetry)

*The Honest Whore, Part II*, c. 1605 (play and
poetry)

*The Double PP*, 1606 (prose and poetry)

*Lanthorn and Candlelight*, 1608, 1609 (prose and
poetry; revised as *O per se O*, 1612; *Villanies
Discovered*, 1616, 1620; *English Villanies*,
1632, 1638, 1648)

*Dekker, His Dream*, 1620 (prose and poetry)

*The Virgin Martyr*, c. 1620 (with Philip Massinger,
play and poetry)

*The Witch of Edmonton*, 1621 (with William
Rowley and John Ford, play and poetry)

*The Sun's Darling*, 1624 (with Ford, play and
poetry)

OTHER LITERARY FORMS

Thomas Dekker (DEHK-ur) was a prolific author.
Although his canon is not easily fixed because of works
presumed to be lost, disputed authorship, and revised
editions, the sheer number of his publications is impressive. Dekker was primarily a dramatist. By himself, he composed more than twenty plays, and he collaborated on as many as forty; more than half of these
are not extant today. His plays come in all the genres
that theater-hungry Elizabethans loved to devour: city
comedies, history plays, classical romances, and domestic tragedies. Additionally, Dekker published about
twenty-five prose tracts and pamphlets that catered to a
variety of popular tastes: descriptions of London's low-
life, collections of humorous and scandalous stories,
and jeremiads on the nation's sins and its impending
punishment at the hands of an angry God. Dekker
found time between writing for the theater and the
printing press to compose complimentary verses on
other poets' works and to twice prepare interludes,
sketches, and songs for the pageants honoring the Lord
Mayor of London.

The best edition of the plays, *The Dramatic Works of
Thomas Dekker* (1953-1961), is edited by Fredson Bowers in four volumes. Those tracts dealing with the ca-
lamities befalling Stuart London are represented in *The
Plague Pamphlets of Thomas Dekker* (1925; F. P. Wilson, editor). The bulk of Dekker's prose and verse is collected in the occasionally unreliable *The Non-Dramatic
Works of Thomas Dekker* (1884-1886, 4 volumes; Al-

exander B. Grosart, editor). A more readable and more
judicious sampling of the tales and sketches is found in
*Selected Prose Writings* (1968; E. D. Pendry, editor).

ACHIEVEMENTS

A writer such as Thomas Dekker, so prolific in output, necessarily produces a lot of chaff with his wheat.
His plays often lack tightly knit plots and carefully pro-
portioned form; his prose works, especially those satirizing the moral lapses of contemporaries, sometimes
belabor the point. Two literary virtues, however, continue to endear Dekker to readers, virtues common to
both plays and pamphlets, to both verse and prose.

First, Dekker is always a wordsmith of the highest
rank. Although Ben Jonson complained of Dekker and
his collaborators that "It's the bane and torment of our
ears/ To hear the discords of those jangled rhymers,"
hardly any reader or critic since has shared the opinion.
Since the seventeenth century, Dekker has been universally acknowledged as a gifted poet whose lyrical ability stands out in an age well-stocked with good lyric
poets. Charles Lamb's famous pronouncement that
Dekker had "poetry for everything" sums up the commonplace modern attitude. Not only Dekker's verse in
the plays, however, but also his prose deserves to be
called poetic. Dekker's language, whatever its form, is
characterized by frequent sound effects, varied diction,
and attention to rhythm. Thoroughly at home with Renaissance habits of decorative rhetoric, Dekker seemingly thought in poetry and thus wrote it naturally,
effortlessly, and continually.

Second, Dekker's heart is always in the right place.
His sympathetically drawn characters seem to come
alive as he portrays the people, sights, and events of
Elizabethan London. Dekker is often compared with
Geoffrey Chaucer and William Shakespeare for his
sense of the *comédie humaine*, for knowing the heights
and depths of human experience and for still finding
something to care about afterward. Dekker's keen observations of life underlie his sharp sense of society's
incongruities.

BIOGRAPHY

Few specifics of Thomas Dekker's life are known.
He was probably born in 1572, although this date is

*Thomas Dekker* (Hulton Archive/Getty Images)

conjectural. He may have served as a tradesman's apprentice or a sailor before beginning (in 1595?) to write plays for companies of actors. By playwriting and pamphleteering, he kept himself alive for the next thirty-seven years. The date of his marriage is uncertain, but it is known that his wife, Mary, died in 1616. Dekker lived his life almost completely in London, first in Cripplegate and later in Clerkenwell. He was imprisoned for debt on three occasions and once for recusancy. Presumably the Thomas Dekker who was buried in August, 1632, in Clerkenwell parish was the playwright and pamphleteer.

Although Dekker's personal life is mostly subject to conjecture, his professional career can be more closely followed. It revolves around three intertwining themes: the dramatic collaborations, the pamphlets, and a lifelong struggle against poverty. No one knows how Dekker's career started, but by 1598, he was writing plays alone or jointly for Philip Henslowe. Henslowe owned and managed the Rose Theatre, where he commissioned writers to compose plays for his prime tenants, an acting company called the Lord Admiral's

Men. In 1598 alone, Dekker had a hand in fifteen plays (all now lost) that Henslowe commissioned. The sheer quantity indicates how audiences must have clamored for new productions, and some of the titles indicate the taste of the age for popularizations of history (*The First Civil Wars in France*), reworkings of classical tales (*Hannibal and Hermes*), and current stories of eccentric persons or scandalous events (*Black Batman of the North*). All the plays on which Dekker worked had catchy titles: *The Roaring Girl: Or, Moll Cutpurse* (pr. c. 1610), *The Honest Whore*, *The Witch of Edmonton*, and *Match Me in London* (pr. c. 1611-1612), to name a few.

As early as 1600, Dekker was writing for companies other than the Lord Admiral's Men. In the course of his career, he would write for the leading acting companies of the time: the Children of St. Paul's, the Prince's Men, the Palsgrave's Men, and the Players of the Revels. More varied than his employers were his collaborators: As a young man Dekker worked with Michael Drayton, Jonson, George Chapman, Henry Chettle, and even Shakespeare. When he returned to the theater as an older man, the new young scriptwriters—a veritable "Who's Who" of Jacobean dramatists, including John Ford, Samuel Rowley, John Marston, Philip Massinger, and John Webster—worked with him.

Since his employers and collaborators changed so often, it is not surprising that at least once the intense dramatic rivalry characteristic of the age embroiled Dekker in controversy. In 1600, he was drafted into the brief but vitriolic "War of the Theatres," which had begun in the previous year when Marston satirized Jonson as a boorish and presumptuous poet. Jonson returned the compliment by poking fun at Marston in two plays and tried to anticipate a Marston-Dekker rejoinder with a third play, *Poetaster: Or, His Arraignment* (pr. 1601), which compares them to "screaming grasshoppers held by the wings." Marston and Dekker retaliated with *Satiromastix: Or, The Untrussing of the Humourous Poet* (pr. 1601), an amalgam of tragic, comic, and tragicomic plots, portraying Jonson as a slow-witted and slow-working poet for hire.

In 1603, Dekker was forced to find another line of work when an outbreak of the plague closed the theaters. He produced a pamphlet, *The Wonderful Year*, which recounted the death of the queen, Elizabeth I, the accession of James I, and the coming of the disease that scourged humankind's folly. In the next six years, Dekker published more than a dozen pamphlets designed to capitalize on readers' interest in current events and the city's criminal subculture. In his pamphlets, as in his plays, Dekker provides a panorama of cutpurses, pimps, courtesans, apprentices, and similar types; he paints scenes of busy streets and records the sounds of loud voices, creaking carriages, and thumped pots. Dekker's purpose is not that of the local colorist who preserves such scenes simply because they typify a time and place. Rather, his interest is that of the moralist who sees the side of city life that the upper classes would like to ignore and that the academics shrug off as part of the necessary order of things.

Dekker himself knew this low world intimately—at least he never seems to have gotten into the higher. Unlike his fellow writers Jonson and Shakespeare or the actor Edward Alleyn, Dekker could not or did not take advantage of the aristocracy's interest in the theater to secure for himself consistent patronage and financial stability. Playwriting seems to have brought Dekker only a few pounds per play: Despite his prodigious outburst of fifteen collaborations in 1598, he was arrested for debt that year and the next. Fourteen years later, while both publishing pamphlets and writing plays, Dekker was again imprisoned for debt at the King's Bench, a prison notorious for its mismanagement. He remained in debtors' prison for six or seven years (1613-1619).

No wonder, then, that money is one of Dekker's favorite themes and gold one image to which he devotes loving attention. He neither worships the almighty guinea nor scorns sinful lucre. On one hand, Dekker likes money: His best characters make shrewd but kindly use of the stuff; they work, and their labor supports them. He sometimes sees even confidence games as offshoots of a healthy capitalistic impulse. Old Fortunatus's claim, "Gold is the strength, the sinnewes of the world,/ The Health, the soule, the beautie most divine," may be misguided, but Dekker understands the impulse. He forgives prodigals easily. On the other hand, Dekker expects generosity from moneymakers. Even virtuous persons who do not use their wealth well

come to bad ends; those who refuse to help the needy he assigns to the coldest regions of hell. According to Pendry in *Selected Prose Writings*, the use of money is for Dekker an index of morality: Virtue flows from its proper use and vice from its improper.

The last decade of Dekker's life was a repetition of the previous three. He wrote for the theater, published pamphlets, and teetered on the edge of debt. Though his life was hard and his social rank was low, Dekker generally wrote as if his literary trade was, like the shoemaker's, a truly gentle craft.

ANALYSIS

Most of Thomas Dekker's best poetry is found in his plays; unfortunately, since most of his plays were collaborations, it is often difficult to assign particular poetic passages to Dekker, and perhaps even harder to assign the larger poetic designs to him. He is, however, generally credited with most of the poetry in *Old Fortunatus* and *The Honest Whore, Parts I* and *II*. He wrote the delightfully poetic *The Shoemaker's Holiday* almost unaided. Mother Sawyer's eloquent poetry in *The Witch of Edmonton* so closely resembles portions of his long pamphlet-poem, *Dekker, His Dream*, as to make it all but certainly his. Songs and verses occupy varying proportions of his journalistic works, from a few lines in *The Wonderful Year*, to several songs in *Lanthorn and Candlelight*, to most of *The Double PP*. In all his plays, verse comprises a significant part of the dialogue.

While the quality of thought and care in organization vary from work to work and almost from line to line in a given work, the quality of the sound rarely falters. According to George Price in *Thomas Dekker* (1969), one poem long attributed to Dekker, *Canaan's Calamitie* (1598), has been excluded from the canon largely because of the inferior music of its verse. Critics often attach words such as "sweet," "lovely," "gentle," and "compassionate" to Dekker's most popular passages, and the adjectives seem to cover both sound and theme in works such as *Old Fortunatus* and *The Shoemaker's Holiday*.

OLD FORTUNATUS

An old-fashioned production in its own day, *Old Fortunatus* weaves a morality pageant in which the goddess Fortune and her attendants witness a power struggle between Virtue and Vice with a loose chronicle play about a man to whom Fortune grants a choice. Instead of health, strength, knowledge, and wisdom, old Fortunatus chooses riches. His wealth and native cunning enable him to steal knowledge (in the form of a magic hat). After Fortune claims the old man's life, his sons Ampedo and Andelocia, inheriting his magic purse and hat, make no better use of them than their father had done. Greedy Andelocia abducts a princess, plays assorted pranks at various courts, and ends up strangled by equally greedy courtiers; virtuous Ampedo wrings his hands, eventually burns the magic hat, and dies in the stocks, unmourned even by Virtue. Structurally, *Old Fortunatus* has the odd elegance of medieval drama. Fortune, Virtue, and Vice enter the human world five times, usually with song and emblematic show designed to judge men or to point out the choices open to them.

The play's allegorical pageantry demanded elaborate costuming and equally elaborate verse, ranging from songs in varied meters and tones to dialogues that are often more incantation than blank verse speech:

*Kings:* Accursed Queen of chaunces, damned sorceresse.
*The Rest:* Most pow'rfull Queen of chaunce, dread
  soveraignesse.
*Fortune:* . . . [*To the Kings*] curse on: your cries to me are
  Musicke
And fill the sacred rondure of mine eares
With tunes more sweet than moving of the Spheres:
Curse on.

Most of the chronicle play that is interwoven with the morality pageant employs blank verse liberally sprinkled with prose passages and rhymed couplets. Renaissance notions of decorum set forth rather clear-cut rules governing the use of prose and poetry. An iambic pentameter line was considered the best medium for tragedy and for kings' and nobles' speeches in comedy. Madmen, clowns, and letter-readers in tragedy and lower-class characters in comedy can speak prose. Dekker refines these guidelines. He uses prose for musing aloud, for French and Irish dialects, for talking to servants, and for expressing disappointment or depression: The sons mourn their dead father and have their most violent quarrel in prose. Dekker keys form to mood much as a modern songwriter does when he inserts a spoken passage into the lyrics. Even Dekker's prose, however, is textured like poetry; except for the lack of iambic pentameter rhythm, prose passages are virtually indistinguishable from verse. Typical are the lilting rhythms of the following passage (one of the cruelest in the play): "I was about to cast my little little self into a great love trance for him, fearing his hart was flint, but since I see 'tis pure virgin wax, he shall melt his belly full."

Sound itself is the subject of much comment in the play. Dekker's natural gift for pleasing rhythms, his knack for combining the gentler consonant sounds with higher frequency vowels, and his ear for slightly varied repetitions all combine to make *Old Fortunatus* strikingly beautiful poetry.

The fame of *Old Fortunatus*, however, rests on more than its sound. Dekker's imagery deserves the praise it consistently gets. The Princess's heartless line is one of many that connect melting with the play's values—love, fire, gold, and the sun—in ways that suggest both the purification of dross through the melting process and the fate of rich Crassus. Other images connect the silver moon and stars with music, and both precious metals with an earth producing fruit-laden trees that men use wisely or unwisely. The allegorical figures with their emblematic actions and costumes would heighten the effectiveness of such imagery for a viewing audience, just as hearing the poetry greatly magnifies its impact over silent reading.

### THE SHOEMAKER'S HOLIDAY

In *The Shoemaker's Holiday*, Dekker shows a more sophisticated use of poetry. As in *Old Fortunatus*, he shifts between poetry and prose, depending somewhat on the characters' social class but more on mood, so that in a given scene a character can slip from prose to poetry and back while those around him remain in their normal métier. In the earlier play, however, he made little attempt to connect certain characters with certain sounds or images. In *The Shoemaker's Holiday*, characters have their own peculiar music.

The play combines three plots. In the first, Rowland Lacy disguises himself as Hans, a Dutch shoemaker, to avoid being shipped off to war in France, far from his beloved Rose Otley. His uncle, the earl of Lincoln, and her father, Sir Roger Otley, oppose the love match. In the second, the shoemaker Rafe leaves his young wife, Jane, to do his country's bidding; later, lamed and supposed dead, he returns to find Jane missing. He rediscovers her just in time to stop her marriage to the rich but shallow Hammon. In the third, master shoemaker Simon Eyre, the employer of Lacy, Rafe, and a crew of journeymen and apprentices, rises by common sense and enthusiastic shop management to become London's merriest Lord Mayor.

Two relatively minor characters illustrate Dekker's poetic sense. The earl of Lincoln, despite his blank verse, speaks less poetically than most of the other characters, and Eyre's journeyman, Firke, despite his freer prose rhythms, speaks much of the best poetry. Lincoln's decasyllables in the opening scene, for example, summarize Lacy's situation with few rhetorical figures:

> 'Twas now almost a year since he requested
> To travel countries for experiences.
> I furnished him with coin, bills of exchange,
> Letters of credit, men to wait on him.

Lincoln's speech is not absolutely unpoetic. Its rhythm is varied, quickened by added syllables and made natural by inverted feet—but that is all. Lincoln has a prosaic mind; to him Lacy's love is mere nuisance, a mild threat to the family name. Dishonest about his own motives, he presumes that others are likewise motivated by self-interest. Thus, when he speaks, his words slip easily off the tongue, but rarely figure forth the imaginative connections between things that Dekker's other characters display.

By contrast, Firke's lines have more of poetry's verbal texture than does most modern free verse. Asked the whereabouts of the eloped Rose and Lacy, he answers in a pastiche of poetic allusions and a pun on the gold coin that Elizabethans called angels: "No point: shall I betray my brother? no, shall I prove *Judas* to Hans? no, shall I crie treason to my corporation? no, I shall be firkt and yerkt then, but give me your angell, your angell shall tel you." The passage shouts an emphatic dance rhythm, forcefully repeats the focal "no, shall I," employs assonance ("*Judas* to *Hans*"), allitera-

tion ("betray my brother"), and rhyme ("treason to my corporation" and "firkt and yerkt"). It speeds along, then slows to a perfectly cadenced close. The speaker, a boisterous, rowdy, practical joker, is always ready to burst into song, or something so close as to be indistinguishable from song.

Dekker gives these minor characters distinctive poetic voices. To the major characters, he gives individualizing linguistic habits. Bluff Simon Eyre's trick of repeating himself would be maddening in a less kindly fellow. He is the only character capable of speaking prose to the king. Hammon, suitor both to Rose and Jane, speaks courtly compliment in light, rhymed couplets in which vows about "life" and "wife" play too heavy a part. Though he enjoys the banter of stichomythic verse, his images are stuffily conventional. As wellborn characters, Lacy and Rose naturally speak blank verse. Lacy's voice, however, turns to a quick prose dialect when he is disguised as Hans; Rose occasionally startles by slipping out of her romantic preoccupations into a few lines of practical yet polished prose.

Perhaps the play's best poetry is that which Dekker gives to shoemaker Rafe and seamstress Jane. Surrounded by shopkeepers and unaccustomed to courtly compliment, these two must invent their own poetic images and rhythms. "I will not greeve you,/ With hopes to taste fruite, which will never fall," says Jane to Hammon. Hearing of Rafe's death, she dismisses her persistent suitor with lines remarkable for homespun grace. Rafe, in turn, gives the entire play its thematic unity in two passages that raise shoemaking from a craft to a communal act of love. As he leaves for France, Rafe gives Jane a parting gift: not the jewels and rings that rich men present their wives, but a pair of shoes "cut out by *Hodge*, Sticht by my fellow *Firke*, seam'd by my selfe,/ Made up and pinckt, with letters for thy name." The shoes are the epitome of the shoemaker's art, and they are individually Jane's. Dekker returns to the image at a pivotal point after Rafe comes home from the war. The shoes, now old and needing replacement, lead Rafe to reunion with the missing Jane. His homely poetry, the most original in a play full of original language, is more touching than preposterous:

> . . . this shoe I durst be sworne
> Once covered the instep of my *Jane:*
> This is her size, her breadth, thus trod my love,
> These true love knots I prickt, I hold my life,
> By this old shoe I shall find out my wife.

The simple language fits Rafe as well as the shoe fits Jane. In *The Shoemaker's Holiday*, craftsmen know their work as confidently as the master wordsmith Dekker knows his characters' individual voices.

Critics generally agree that the play is Dekker's poetic masterpiece. His other plays contain excellent poetry, nicely tuned to suit persona in sound, mood, and imagery, but none has the range and grace of *The Shoemaker's Holiday*. Of special interest to the student of Dekker's verse are two of the speeches in *The Honest Whore* plays. In *Part I*, Hippolito's furious diatribe against whoredom is a virtual monologue, rising in a hundred lines to a fine crescendo, which deserves careful metrical and figural analysis. Its counterpart in *Part II*, Bellafront's long argument against her former profession, deserves similar attention.

### PAMPHLETS

Dekker's pamphlets continue the habit of mixing prose and verse; most of them contain some poetry, if only in the rhymed couplets signifying closure. As early as 1603, in *The Wonderful Year*, he was writing essentially dramatic poetry. In that pamphlet, he includes two poems supposed to be the prologue and a summary of the action of a play—the "play" of England's reaction to Elizabeth I's death. The poetic section ends with three short epigrams of a deliberately homespun sort. *Lanthorn and Candlelight* further reflects the dramatic in Dekker's poetry. In the opening chapter, poems are couched in cant, a special thieves' jargon. "To cant" means "to sing," but since "canters" are strange, they sing strangely: "Enough! With boozy cove maund nase,/ Tower the patring cove in the darkman case." Dekker includes both a "Canter's Dictionary" (largely plagiarized) and "Englished" translations. His habit of using dramatic voices in poetry finds a logical conclusion in such songs.

Poetry is sporadic in most of Dekker's pamphlets; in *The Double PP* and *Dekker, His Dream*, however, it dominates. The former alternates sections of prose and

poetry in an exhibition of English nationalism as complete as Simon Eyre's. In an elaborate rhetorical figure, Dekker presents ten kinds of papists as ten chivalric shields attacked by ten well-armed classes of English Protestants. The generally shallow but occasionally penetrating stereotypes show the influence of the current fad for Overburian Characters.

### DEKKER, HIS DREAM

*Dekker, His Dream* is a much better poem. Published shortly after his release from seven years in debtor's prison, the work is ostensibly autobiographical. Dekker claims to relate a dream he had after almost seven years of imprisonment in an enchanted cave. Using lines of rhymed iambic pentameter that vary with his subject in tone and tempo, Dekker describes the last day of the world, the final judgment, heaven, and hell. Periodically he interrupts the narrative to justify his vision by quoting in prose from scripture or church authorities.

Structurally, *Dekker, His Dream* is among his best works, building slowly to a climactic conclusion in which Dekker turns out to be, as William Blake said of John Milton, "of the devil's party." The poem begins with covert reminders of what Dekker himself has recently suffered, then moves vividly through the tale of Earth's destruction. Calmly, it relates the majestic coming of Christ and the harmonious rewards given the good, then turns rather quickly to hell. (In fact, Christ and Heaven occupy eight of Dekker's fifty-two pages.) Like Dante, Dekker secures permission to walk among the damned; he finds a two-part hell. In the first, the cold region, he sees the "rich dogs" who refused to help the poor and sick. Tormented by whips, diseases, snakes, and salamanders, they react with "Yels, teeth-gnashing, chattering, shivering." Then he moves into the traditional fires to find the drunkards, gamblers, adulterers, and gluttons—"millions" of them, whipped and stung with their own longings and with the "worme of conscience." Among them is a young man cursing God and proclaiming loudly as the whips descend that he does not deserve eternal punishment. Dekker gives him a perfectly logical defense: He had only thirty years of life, fifteen of which were spent asleep, five more in childishness, and some at least in good deeds. Nature had given him little—drops of gall from her left breast instead of milk—and his sins were small. His lengthy defense contains some of Dekker's best images and rhythms; it is interrupted by a booming angelic voice that shouts about justice until the rest of the damned, angered, outshout it, waking the poet. Dekker, hands shaking from the experience, concludes that, reading the world, "I found Here worse Devils than are in Hell."

The dream vision has been largely misinterpreted, but close study of the quality of the imagery and the proportions of the whole indicate that Dekker was indeed leading his readers to question the justice shouted by the avenging angel. It is a subtly and effectively composed poem, deserving more attention than it has had.

## OTHER MAJOR WORKS

PLAYS: *Patient Grissell*, pr. 1600 (with Henry Chettle and William Haughton); *Satiromastix: Or, The Untrussing of the Humourous Poet*, pr. 1601; *Sir Thomas Wyatt*, pr. 1602 (as *Lady Jane*, pb. 1607); *Westward Ho!*, pr. 1604 (with John Webster); *Northward Ho!*, pr. 1605 (with Webster); *The Whore of Babylon*, pr. c. 1606-1607; *The Roaring Girl: Or, Moll Cutpurse*, pr. c. 1610 (with Thomas Middleton); *If This Be Not a Good Play, the Devil Is in It*, pr. c. 1610-1612 (as *If It Be Not Good, the Devil Is in It*); *Match Me in London*, pr. c. 1611-1612; *The Noble Soldier: Or, A Contract Broken, Justly Revenged*, pr. c. 1622-1631 (with John Day; thought to be the same as *The Spanish Fig*, 1602); *The Wonder of a Kingdom*, pr. c. 1623; *The Welsh Embassador: Or, A Comedy in Disguises*, pr. c. 1624 (revision of *The Noble Soldier*); *The Dramatic Works of Thomas Dekker*, 1953-1961 (4 volumes; Fredson Bowers, editor).

NONFICTION: *News from Hell*, 1606; *The Seven Deadly Sins*, 1606; *The Bellman of London*, 1608; *A Work for Armourers*, 1609; *Four Birds of Noah's Ark*, 1609; *The Gull's Hornbook*, 1609; *Penny-Wise, Pound-Foolish*, 1631; *The Plague Pamphlets of Thomas Dekker*, 1925 (F. P. Wilson, editor).

MISCELLANEOUS: *The Magnificent Entertainment Given to King James*, 1603 (with Ben Jonson and Middleton); *The Non-Dramatic Works of Thomas Dekker*, 1884-1886 (4 volumes; Alexander B. Grosart, editor); *Selected Prose Writings*, 1967 (E. D. Pendry, editor).

## BIBLIOGRAPHY

Adler, Doris Ray. *Thomas Dekker: A Reference Guide*. Boston: G. K. Hall, 1983. An annotated bibliography of works on Dekker. Index.

Champion, Larry S. *Thomas Dekker and the Tradition of English Drama*. 2d ed. New York: Peter Lang, 1987. This straightforward commentary deals primarily with the dramatic structure and tone of the plays, but also shows how Dekker often experiments with new approaches. Also discusses Dekker's links with his contemporaries.

Conover, James H. *Thomas Dekker: An Analysis of Dramatic Structure*. The Hague, the Netherlands: Mouton, 1966. Traces the development of the plots of Dekker's major plays (including *The Shoemaker's Holiday, The Honest Whore, Old Fortunatus*, and *Satiromastix*) and concludes with a chapter on the structural traits he believes are peculiar to Dekker's works.

Dekker, Thomas. *The Shoemaker's Holiday*. Edited by Stanley Wells and Robert Smallwood. 3d ed. London: Metheun Drama, 2008. More than a reprint of the play, this edition provides a study of the text and the editors' historical introduction, including an examination of the play's relationship with contemporary life and drama and its place in Dekker's work, a stage history, analysis, and a reprint of source materials.

Gasper, Julia. *The Dragon and the Dove: The Plays of Thomas Dekker*. New York: Oxford University Press, 1990. A critical analysis of Dekker's plays that focuses on his treatment of kings and rulers as well as of Protestantism. Bibliography and index.

Hoy, Cyrus Henry. *Introductions, Notes, and Commentaries to Texts in "The Dramatic Works of Thomas Dekker."* 4 vols. Edited by Fredson Bowers. 1980. Reprint. New York: Cambridge University Press, 2009. The work edited by Bowers focused on the text of the plays, but this work places the plays in their critical context and provides details of the their writing, including collaborations and sources.

Hunt, Mary Leland. *Thomas Dekker: A Study*. 1911. Reprint. Philadelphia: R. West, 1977. The first book-length study of Dekker's life and work—prose as well as plays. It remains useful not only for the critical summaries of the works but also for its chronological treatment of the poet's life. Of special interest are the comments about Dekker's friendships in the theater and his collaborators.

Price, George R. *Thomas Dekker*. New York: Twayne, 1969. Price provides all the standard virtues of the Twayne volumes: a succinct chronology, a chapter on the life, and three chapters of analysis followed by a summarizing conclusion. The detailed notes and annotated bibliography make this study an excellent starting place for students of Dekker.

Waage, Frederick O. *Thomas Dekker's Pamphlets, 1603-1609, and Jacobean Popular Literature*. 2 vols. Salzburg: University for English Language and Literature, 1977. These two scholarly volumes are full of commentary on Dekker's ideas and his life. The first chapter on Dekker's career, 1603-1609, is informative, and the seventeen-page bibliography offers researchers a good beginning point.

Wells, Stanley. *Shakespeare and Co.: Christopher Marlowe, Thomas Dekker, Ben Jonson, Thomas Middleton, John Fletcher, and the Other Players in His Story*. London: Penguin, 2007. While the main focus is William Shakespeare, this work also treats Dekker, especially in his association with Shakespeare.

*Robert M. Otten and Elizabeth Spalding Otten*

---

# WALTER DE LA MARE

**Born:** Charlton, Kent, England; April 25, 1873
**Died:** Twickenham, Middlesex, England; June 22, 1956
**Also known as:** Walter Ramal

PRINCIPAL POETRY
*Songs of Childhood*, 1902
*Poems*, 1906
*A Child's Day: A Book of Rhymes*, 1912
*The Listeners, and Other Poems*, 1912
*Peacock Pie: A Book of Rhymes*, 1913

*The Sunken Garden, and Other Poems*, 1917
*Motley, and Other Poems*, 1918
*Flora: A Book of Drawings*, 1919
*Poems 1901 to 1918*, 1920
*Story and Rhyme*, 1921
*The Veil, and Other Poems*, 1921
*Down-Adown-Derry: A Book of Fairy Poems*, 1922
*Thus Her Tale*, 1923
*A Ballad of Christmas*, 1924
*Stuff and Nonsense and So On*, 1927
*Self to Self*, 1928
*The Snowdrop*, 1929
*News*, 1930
*Poems for Children*, 1930
*Lucy*, 1931
*Old Rhymes and New*, 1932
*The Fleeting, and Other Poems*, 1933
*Poems, 1919 to 1934*, 1935
*This Year, Next Year*, 1937
*Memory, and Other Poems*, 1938
*Haunted*, 1939
*Bells and Grass*, 1941
*Collected Poems*, 1941
*Collected Rhymes and Verses*, 1944
*The Burning-Glass, and Other Poems*, 1945
*The Traveller*, 1946
*Rhymes and Verses: Collected Poems for Young People*, 1947
*Inward Companion*, 1950
*Winged Chariot*, 1951
*O Lovely England, and Other Poems*, 1953
*The Complete Poems*, 1969

OTHER LITERARY FORMS

Walter de la Mare (deh-luh-MEHR) was a prolific author of fiction and nonfiction as well as poetry. His novels include modern adult fiction, such as *Memoirs of a Midget* (1921), and fiction for children, such as *The Three Mulla-Mulgars* (1910). His short stories fit into a variety of traditional genres; many are tales of the supernatural. The interests that manifest themselves in the poetry and fiction are more explicitly revealed in de la Mare's essays and his work as an editor. Not much given to analysis, as a critic he was primarily an appreciator and interpreter, much as he was as a poet. Of the anthologies he edited, *Behold, This Dreamer!* (1939) is perhaps the most revealing of the influences that de la Mare particularly valued in his work as a poet.

## ACHIEVEMENTS

Walter de la Mare was one of the most popular poets of his time. Since his death his reputation has faded. His verse sometimes sounds too romantic for the sensibilities of a modern audience. However, his children's verse remains in print, and the best of his adult poetry remains standard for inclusion in anthologies of twentieth century English poets. The present moderate eclipse of the popularity of his poetry is probably temporary, because his best verse has those iconoclastic qualities that make such poets as William Blake stand out from ordinary poets.

De la Mare's sensibility is deeply rooted in the Romanticism of the nineteenth century, and like the works of Rudyard Kipling and George Bernard Shaw, his writings often seem reminiscent of the Victorian era. Nevertheless, his subjects were from the twentieth century, and the resultant mixture of contemporary realism and Romantic style make him special among major poets. Of the various poetic modes represented in his works, the lyric was the one with which de la Mare had his greatest artistic success; he ranks among the best lyric poets in the English language, and he may be the best English lyric poet of his era. In his mastery of poetic form and metaphor, de la Mare compares favorably with the best the English language has to offer.

His blend of romance and realism, of the supernatural with the commonplace, inspired poets of his day. The term *delamarian* was coined sometime during de la Mare's middle years, and it is still used to identify works that employ techniques that are best represented by his work. The coinage of such a term is evidence of the esteem in which de la Mare was held by many of his contemporaries, and of the unique blend of form and ideas that makes him one of the twentieth century's best poets.

## BIOGRAPHY

The first in-depth, full-length biography of Walter John de la Mare was not published until 1993. He was,

*Walter de la Mare* (Library of Congress)

by the few published accounts of those who knew him, a quiet and unremarkable man. One can reasonably infer from the absence of autobiographical material from an otherwise prolific writer that he was a private man. He seems to have lived his adventures through his writing, and his primary interests seem to have been of the intellect and the spirit.

He was born in 1873 to James Edward de la Mare and Lucy Sophia Browning de la Mare, a Scot. He attended St. Paul's Cathedral Choir School. While in school he founded and edited *The Choiristers' Journal*, a school magazine. In 1890, Walter de la Mare entered the employ of the Anglo-American Oil Company, where he served as bookkeeper until 1908. During these years, he wrote essays, stories, and poetry, which appeared in various magazines, including *Black and White* and *The Sketch*. In 1902, *Songs of Childhood*, his first book—and one of his most lastingly popular—was published. There he used the pseudonym Walter Ramal. Then, after using it also for his novel *Henry Brocken* in 1904, he dropped it. He married Constance Elfrida Igpen in 1899, with whom he had two sons and two daughters. She died in 1943.

De la Mare's employment at the Anglo-American Oil Company ended in 1908, when he was granted a Civil List pension of one hundred pounds a year. Thus encouraged, he embarked on a life of letters during which he produced poetry, short stories, essays, and one play, and edited volumes of poetry and essays. These many works reveal something of de la Mare's intellect, if not of his character. They reveal a preoccupation with inspiration and dreams, an irritation with Freudians and psychologists in general (they were too simplistic in their analyses, he believed), a love of romance, and a love for the child in people. The works reveal a complex mind that, curiously, preferred appreciation to analysis and observation to explanation.

ANALYSIS

The poetry of Walter de la Mare falls superficially into two groups: poetry for children and poetry for adults. This obvious and misleading division is unfortunate, however, because many readers have come to think of de la Mare as principally an author for children. Much of his poetry is intended for an adult readership; that which is meant for children is complex enough in theme to satisfy demanding adult readers. Much misunderstanding of the nature of de la Mare's poetry comes from its childlike response to the world. De la Mare distinguishes between the typically childlike and adult imaginations. Children, he contends, view the world subjectively, making and remaking reality according to their egocentric desires. Adults are more analytical and tend to dissociate themselves from reality; they try to observe reality objectively. De la Mare prefers the childlike view, an inductive rather than deductive understanding of the world. Reality, he believes, is revealed through inspiration, an essentially subjective aspect of human imagination. The modern vogue of discussions of "higher planes of reality" would have had little meaning for de la Mare, but he would approve the notion that there is a reality beyond that which can be objectively observed. Time and nature are tyrants

who rule humankind. Their effects can be observed, but they in themselves cannot. To understand the reality of time and nature, the poet uses his imaginative insight. In pursuit of such insight, de la Mare studied dreams; as a poet he strove to describe the world as if observing it while in a walking dream. He attempted to observe as he imagined a child might observe, and because childhood involves a continual discovery of both the physical reality and the spiritual reality of nature, de la Mare's poetry is alive with discovery, wonder, and—as discovery often brings—disappointment with the imperfections of the world.

De la Mare wrote more than a thousand poems over more than half a century. In any such body of work, written during a long lifetime, one can rightly expect to find much diversity in subject and tone. De la Mare's work is no exception. Although he was a lyric poet all his life, his work shifted from short poems to long ones, and his prosody increased in complexity. To read the body of de la Mare's poetry is to experience a mind of diverse and passionate interests, with some of those interests unifying the whole of the poet's verse. De la Mare was a careful craftsman whose verse rhythms can disturb and delight wherever the content of a poem dictates. He loved children and strove to experience the world like a child, inductively. He saw the world of everyday experience as only part of a greater universe; he believed in spirits and a supernatural world. He saw great value in nature, even if it could be indifferent to human suffering.

These beliefs and passions enliven de la Mare's work, forming a background that colors all his poems. If his poetry may be said to deliver a particular message, it is one that is at once simple and complex in its implications, like his verse: People are partly spiritual and thus should never be indifferent to evil, should love innocence, and should understand that each person is greater than he or she appears.

CHILDREN'S POETRY

De la Mare's interest in childlike inspiration led him to write poetry for children. His respect for childlike imagination is reflected in the absence of condescension in his children's verse. In fact, most of it resembles that which he wrote for adults, although his diction is at a level that children can understand. All the major concerns of de la Mare's intellectual life are expressed in his children's verse; in "The Old King" (1922), for example, he discusses death. The "old King of Cumberland" awakens in surprise and looks about his room for what had disturbed him, but all seems normal until he touches his chest "where now no surging restless beat/ Its long tale told." The King's heart has stopped and he is terrified. The whole of the poem is expressed in a manner that children can comprehend, and de la Mare makes three important points: that death is a fact, that there is a reality beyond death, and that death is dreamlike. He never means to frighten his young readers; rather, he means for them to understand. For example, in "Now, Dear Me!" (1912), he describes a fearsome ghost: "A-glowering with/ A chalk-white face/ Out of some dim/ And dismal place." The ghost turns out to be Elizabeth Ann, a child very much alive, done up to frighten her nurse. Children are invited to laugh at the very real fears that their imaginations can create.

A child is unlikely to miss the implied respect for his mind when he reads poetry that clearly states de la Mare's point of view on a subject of moral substance. "Hi!" (1930) is a lyric that presents a hunter's killing of an animal: "Nevermore to peep again, creep again, leap again,/ Eat or sleep or drink again, Oh, what fun!" De la Mare's dismay at the killing of wildlife is clear, as is his effort to speak of an important matter to his young readership. Wildlife plays an important role in his poetry. Bears and elephants and other animals are shown as friendly to children. When Elizabeth Ann takes a bath in "Little Birds Bathe" (1912), her tub is invaded by a "Seal and Walrus/ And Polar Bear." A host of other animals join them, from alligators to swans to pumas. Her bath sounds fun, and the poem is as cheerful a depiction of bathing and imagination as one could hope to read. In "Who Really?" (1930), bears and bees share a natural antagonism and similarity—they are both thieves. In "The Holly" (1930), the poet describes the natural beauty of the holly tree. Repeatedly, he depicts nature as other than frightening; it can be awesome, but a child's imagination can render it knowable.

### DREAMS AND THE SUPERNATURAL

The supernatural and dreams are significant aspects of de la Mare's poetry for youngsters. His verse spans topics from Christianity to pagan mysticism. In "Eden"

(1930), he discusses the Fall of Man from God's grace and its effect on all nature. When the sin of humanity leads to the Great Flood, trees and animals suffer the consequences. Thus, the banishment of Adam and Eve is bewailed by the nightingale.

The notion that the fates of Humanity and Nature are linked is unmistakable. Pagan mysticism in the forms of fairies and elves is common children's fare. Typical of de la Mare's respect for his young audience, he offers uncommon fairies. In "The Double" (1922), a fairy child joins a young dancer in a garden. The fairy is at once a reflection of the dancer and a part of the plants in the garden; it is at once substantial and incapable of leaving the faintest marks of its footsteps. The poem is a sad evocation of childlike imagination; the fairy child disappears beyond recalling. Fairies and their kin are evocations of the natural world; they respond to people when people respond to nature. They are ephemeral, as much the products of imagination and dreams as of tradition and myth.

"The World of Dream" (1912) takes poetic tradition and uses it to portray a child's view of sleep. When dreaming, one often seems to be floating on air or water; death is often described similarly. De la Mare takes his sleeping child on a ride in a boat equipped with "elphin lanterns," a boat with "hundreds of passengers." The misty world of sleep sounds peaceful and much like death.

### DEATH AND EVIL

The connecting of sleep and death is common in literature, yet death is not a customary topic intended for children. Although de la Mare writes for children, he spares them none of the topics that he deems important. Death is a part of nature; it is something that, as "Eden" shows, was brought into nature by humankind. Death is not inherently evil, although killing can be. In de la Mare's poetry, dreams and death are often linked, and he commonly uses dreams to reveal a truer reality than is found in the nondreaming world. Thus, death itself is not meant to be evil or even exceptionally awful.

Even so, de la Mare did perceive evil in the world, and children are not spared its presence in his poetry. Evil is not trivialized for the sake of youthful readers. The poet shows children being punished for naughty behavior, as in "This Little Morsel of Morsels Here"

(1912), but he does not lay the heavy burden of evil on the filching of gingery sweets: Bears can misbehave and so can children. Naughtiness is natural, although undesirable. True evil is profound. It can be personified as a "handsome hunting man" in "Hi!" or as the actions of a child slashing his toy sword through the grasses of a meadow in "The Massacre" (1906). The actions seem innocent, but the child imagines heads lopped off and "dead about my feet." Nature in the form of sunlight and air recoils in horror from the imaginary deeds that in a child foreshadow the potential evil of adulthood.

### POETRY FOR ADULTS

Most of de la Mare's verse was directed at an adult audience. Although his poetry for children reveals the bare forms of his poetic interests, it is primarily cheerful, concentrating on sympathetically helping children to use their imaginations; his adult poetry is more somber and even more mystical. The most famous of de la Mare's poems perhaps best exemplifies his characteristic blending of dreams, the supernatural, and the childlike imagination. "The Listeners" (1912) was once memorized by thousands of schoolchildren; it puzzled and enthralled de la Mare's contemporaries, and it is likely to survive the test of time, retaining its mystical and symbolic power.

### "THE LISTENERS"

In "The Listeners," a Traveller knocks at the door of a house that is at once empty and filled with "a host of phantom listeners." The Traveller smites the door and is answered only by echoes in empty hallways. He repeatedly calls, "Is anybody there?" and listens for replies. Even though no one answers, the Traveller senses the presence of the listeners: "And he felt in his heart their strangeness,/ Their stillness answering his cry." The Traveller strikes the door again and cries out, "Tell them I came, and no one answered,/ That I kept my word." The listeners who lurk in "the shadowiness of the still house" listen to him mount his horse and ride away. Throughout the poem, silence is as palpable as sound, and at its conclusion silence remains a part of the listeners' house. The poem exhibits the salient traits of most of de la Mare's poetry. Its tone, subject, and events all seem part of a dream, yet it is populated by mundane physical details: a horse dining on grass, the

Traveller's "grey eyes," and a "dark stair." The poem's effect is mystification and strangeness; its appeal is emotional, rather than intellectual. The theme of others who are near-human beings but cannot be seen nor heard is important to an understanding of de la Mare's work. Humanity is surrounded by spirits and fairies in his poetry. The listeners might be spirits of the dead or of the supernatural world; they might be otherworldly memories of the presences of those who dwelt in the house. Their nature is ambiguous because human experience of the spiritual is usually ambiguous.

The Traveller himself offers another context besides the supernatural. He senses the listeners and speaks to them. His purpose is at once specific and general; he comes to fulfill a promise, but the circumstances under which the promise was made and the people to whom it was made are never presented, leaving ambiguity instead of specifics. The Traveller's purpose is general enough to represent general human purpose; the Traveller is symbolic of all people. The theme of life as a journey marks much of de la Mare's most evocative work, and the idea of humanity as an aggregate of individual travelers is an important part of de la Mare's poetic vision. The Traveller represents people, and the listeners, too, can be people. In a sense, all people are both travelers and listeners, and often communication between people can be vague and uncertain. Often people's purposes are as mysterious to others as is that of the Traveller. Often people's lives are as distant from the lives of others as the listeners are from the Traveller. Typical of much of de la Mare's poetry, "The Listeners" allows multiple readings.

### "HAUNTED"

The eerie dream quality of "The Listeners" reflects de la Mare's understanding of the world. A theme that is found from his earliest to his latest poetry is that of reality as dream. The supernatural world can be more substantial than the world of common experience; dreams are at once reflective of how everyday reality compares with the more valid reality of the spirit and are connections between the natural and supernatural. Human beings are parts of both worlds because of their spiritual natures. In "Haunted" (1939), a persona—the poem's speaker—fears "Life, which ever in at window stares." His fear originates in the uncertainty of life: "You say, *This is.* The soul cries, *Only seems.*" What the conscious mind perceives as real, the spirit understands as insubstantial. The persona notes "And who, when sleeping, finds unreal his dreams?" Dreams can seem to be real, and thus earthly life can seem to be all there is to existence. However, in each person is a soul, a part of the supernatural world, and the soul perceives the danger and the reality beyond ordinary physical sensation. In "Haunted," the dangers lie in "the Fiend with his goods," who can turn a seemingly mundane activity into a spiritual threat. Those who inhabit the supernatural world have their own purposes, and human beings can miss seeing those purposes.

### "The Slum Child"

Even de la Mare's poetic depictions of contemporary life are imbued with his conception of humanity's mixed relationships with the commonplace and the otherworldly. "The Slum Child" (1933), for example, evokes with carefully selected detail the dreary, unnatural life of an urban child growing up in poverty. The poem features one of de la Mare's favorite topics, children, and one of the fundamental themes of his poetry, that nature is an important part of human experience. The youngster in "The Slum Child" suffers from lack of exposure to nature. The child lives in a world of stone, "lean-faced girls and boys," and beggary. De la Mare employs irony to convey the unnaturalness of the slum childhood, as when his speaker uses the word "harboured": "What evil, and filth, and poverty,/ In childhood harboured me." The best that can be said about childhood in a slum is that it is miserable.

A reader could interpret "The Slum Child" as simply a poem of social protest. De la Mare's love of children is well known, and his dismay at the abuse of children in the slum environment is clearly portrayed in the poem. Such a reading, however, would have to ignore the poem's last four stanzas. The poem is spiritual and consistent with de la Mare's emphasis on emotional rather than intellectual impact on his readers. He notes that within the child, "Some hidden one made mock of groans,/ Found living bread in stones." The depiction of slum life elicits anger, sadness, and feelings of hopelessness; yet the child's life is not hopeless. The poem's speaker, as an adult, looks back at his own youthful face and "I search its restless eyes,/ And, from those woeflecked depths, at me/ Looks back through all its misery/ A self beyond surmise." The soul exists beyond the body. Even in the horrible slum one can find hope in one's spirit, which exists in the cosmos as well as in the tiny microcosm of everyday life. Like most of de la Mare's best poetry, "The Slum Child" is complex; it expresses de la Mare's horror of the child's life, and it reveals the inherent hopefulness of his belief in the supernatural.

### "The Traveller"

The notion of the relative unimportance of the physical in relation to the spiritual is another theme that unifies de la Mare's poetry, from his first publications to his last. In one of his best poems, "The Traveller," this theme is symbolically presented. The Traveller himself is Everyman, and his journey is the journey that all people must take through life. The Traveller begins his journey at Titicaca, in the land of the Incas, and travels into strange places with alien landscapes. Throughout, de la Mare creates marvelously beautiful images. In the beginning, the Traveller gazes at "a vast plateau, smooth as porphyry,/ Its huge curve gradual as a woman's breast." He rides his Arabian horse onto the plateau, the surface of which is "Branched veins of sanguine in a milk-pale stone," becoming "Like night-blue porcelain." His journey takes him over "A vitreous region, like a sea asleep,/ Crystalline, convex, tideless and congealed." Eventually, the Traveller reaches "an immeasurable well/ Of lustrous crystal motionless black/ Deeped on. As he gazed . . ./ It seemed to him a presence there gazed back."

In a poem that purports to represent symbolically the life not only of each human being but of each earthly creature as well, such particular descriptions as the foregoing can be mystifying. "The Traveller" is a mixture of the implicit and the explicit. The poem's protagonist explicitly sees animals following him on his journey; he explicitly ages; he explicitly contemplates the meaning of his life: "Could Earth itself a living creature be,/ And he its transitory parasite?" As Henry Charles Duffin points out in his *Walter de la Mare: A Study of His Poetry* (1949), the poem's Earth is alive; it is an eye, and the Traveller traverses its ball and iris to its pupil, the "well." Throughout his life, from youthful determination to middle-aged contemplation to aged despair, the Traveller is watched. "Even the little ant . . . conscious may be of occult puissance near"; even, the poem states, the smallest of creatures can feel the living presence of Earth.

Some critics have emphasized the despair in the poem; the divine may be too remote from humanity and humanity too small to be noticed. They focus on de la Mare's despair and uncertainty about the existence and possible nature of God. Others find an affirmation of faith in the poem. Typical of much of de la Mare's introspective poetry, "The Traveller" depicts pain and frustration as parts of living; and typical of the poetry, Earth, nature, and each human being have spiritual aspects that can defy evil.

OTHER MAJOR WORKS

LONG FICTION: *Henry Brocken*, 1904; *The Return*, 1910; *The Three Mulla-Mulgars*, 1910 (reprinted as *The Three Royal Monkeys: Or, The Three Mulla-Mulgars*, 1935); *Memoirs of a Midget*, 1921; *At First Sight: A Novel*, 1928.

SHORT FICTION: *Story and Rhyme: A Selection*, 1921; *The Riddle, and Other Stories*, 1923; *Ding Dong Bell*, 1924; *Broomsticks, and Other Tales*, 1925; *Miss Jemima*, 1925; *Readings*, 1925-1926 (2 volumes); *The Connoisseur, and Other Tales*, 1926; *Old Joe*, 1927; *Told Again: Traditional Tales*, 1927; *On the Edge*, 1930; *Seven Short Stories*, 1931; *The Lord Fish*, 1933; *The Nap, and Other Stories*, 1936; *The Wind Blows Over*, 1936; *Animal Stories*, 1939; *The Picnic*, 1941; *The Best Stories of Walter de la Mare*, 1942; *The Old Lion, and Other Stories*, 1942; *The Magic Jacket, and Other Stories*, 1943; *The Scarecrow, and Other Stories*, 1945; *The Dutch Cheese, and Other Stories*, 1946; *Collected Stories for Children*, 1947; *A Beginning, and Other Stories*, 1955; *Ghost Stories*, 1956; *Short Stories, 1895-1926*, 1996 (Giles de la Mare, editor); *Short Stories, 1927-1956*, 2001 (Giles de la Mare, editor).

PLAY: *Crossings: A Fairy Play*, pr. 1919.

NONFICTION: *Rupert Brooke and the Intellectual Imagination*, 1919; *The Printing of Poetry*, 1931; *Lewis Carroll*, 1932; *Poetry in Prose*, 1936; *Pleasures and Speculations*, 1940; *Chardin, J.B.S. 1699-1779*, 1948; *Private View*, 1953.

EDITED TEXTS: *Come Hither*, 1923; *The Shake-*speare Songs, 1929; *Christina Rossetti's Poems*, 1930; *Desert Islands and Robinson Crusoe*, 1930; *Stories from the Bible*, 1930; *Early One Morning in the Spring*, 1935; *Animal Stories*, 1939; *Behold, This Dreamer!*, 1939; *Love*, 1943.

BIBLIOGRAPHY

Benntinck, Anne. *Romantic Imagery in the Works of Walter de la Mare*. Lewiston, N.Y.: Edwin Mellen Press, 2001. Devotes one chapter apiece to each of seven major Romantic themes or leitmotifs in de la Mare's poetry. Includes bibliography, index of works, general index.

Duffin, Henry Charles. *Walter de la Mare: A Study of His Poetry*. London: Sidgwick and Jackson, 1949. The author focuses on de la Mare's verse. He considers him a sublime visionary poet of exceptional lucidity whose excessive creative energies are diminished in the prose stories, which he also considers delightful. His main thesis is that de la Mare's poetry neither criticizes nor escapes life, but rather heightens it.

Fowler, Alastair. *A History of English Literature*. Rev. ed. Oxford, England: Basil Blackwell, 1989. Fowler considers de la Mare the strangest, most elusive poet of the early twentieth century. His interest in supernaturalism was no eccentricity, but it was the expression of a metaphysical puzzlement about the nature of reality. He was a genuine philosopher, comparable to John Donne and other Metaphysical poets. Primarily a connoisseur of darkness, he is absurdly undervalued by most critics.

Hopkins, Kenneth. *Walter de la Mare*. 1953. Rev. ed. London: Longmans, Green, 1957. This slim volume touches on de la Mare's life and his prose and verse writings. The author, who is an ardent admirer of de la Mare, briefly examines all his major writings. A useful but limited introduction to de la Mare. Supplemented by a select bibliography.

McCrosson, Doris Ross. *Walter de la Mare*. New York: Twayne, 1966. A good critical introduction to de la Mare. McCrosson examines at length the author's total literary output, concentrating particularly on the novels. The writer points out that de la Mare's fascinating quest into the mysteries of life never coalesced into a coherent vision. Complemented by a chronology and a select bibliography.

Manwaring, Randle. "Memories of Walter de la Mare." *Contemporary Review* 264 (March, 1994): 148-152. A reminiscence of a longtime acquaintance of de la Mare that comments on his style and his influence. Reflects de la Mare's childish delight in simple things that is so often reflected in his works.

Megroz, R. L. *Walter de la Mare: A Biographical and Critical Study*. London: Hodder and Stoughton, 1924. Megroz conducted the first study of de la Mare's work, "treading what is almost virgin soil," as he phrased it. The author professes his deep admiration for de la Mare, sketches a brief biography, comments on personal impressions, and then devotes his study to the poetry. His book is less a critical examination of de la Mare and more an appreciation.

Perkins, David. "Craftsmen of the Beautiful and the Agreeable." In *A History of Modern Poetry*. Vol. 1. Cambridge, Mass.: Harvard University Press, 1976. Perkins emphasizes de la Mare's complicated relationship to the Romantics. Like them, he often wrote about the world as a dream. He was aware of the conventional nature of Romantic poetry and often the poems are about conventions. Unlike certain Romantics, he does not portray evil as sublime. He is a master at interrogative conversation and anticipates the modernist stress on the accents of daily speech.

Sisson, C. H. *English Poetry, 1900-1950*. Manchester, England: Carcanet Press, 1981. Sisson mentions that de la Mare was the last of the Romantics. His poetry combines Romantic themes with the more personal themes of twentieth century verse. It is characterized by purity of language and hushed, intimate accents, and it succeeds in capturing the intimate rhythms of speech. De la Mare was at his best in a limited range of subjects. His finest work pictures life on the edge of a dream.

Whistler, Theresa. *Imagination of the Heart: The Life of Walter de la Mare*. London: Duckworth, 1993. A good biography of de la Mare. Includes bibliographical references and an index.

*Kirk H. Beetz*

# JOHN DONNE

**Born:** London, England; between January 24 and June 19, 1572
**Died:** London, England; March 31, 1631

PRINCIPAL POETRY

*An Anatomy of the World: The First Anniversary*, 1611
*Of the Progress of the Soule: The Second Anniversary*, 1612
*Poems, by J. D.: With Elegies on the Authors Death*, 1633, 1635, 1639, 1649, 1650, 1654, 1669

OTHER LITERARY FORMS

Although John Donne (duhn) is known chiefly as a lyric poet, the posthumous volume *Poems, by J.D.*, which includes the lyrics, represents only a small part of his literary output. Donne was famous in his own age mainly as a preacher; in fact, he was probably the most popular preacher of an age when preaching held the same fascination for the general public that the cinema has today. Various sermons of Donne's were published during his lifetime, and several collections were published in the following decades. Without a commitment to Donne's religious values, however, few today would want to read through many of his sermons. Donne must, however, be credited with the careful articulation of the parts of his sermons, which create a resounding unity of theme; and his control of prose rhythm and his ingenious imagery retain their power, even if modern readers are no longer disposed to see the majesty of God mirrored in such writing.

Excerpts from Donne's sermons thus have a continuing vitality for general readers in a way that excerpts from the sermons of, for example, Lancelot Andrewes cannot. In the early seventeenth century, Andrewes had been the most popular preacher before Donne, and, as bishop of Winchester, he held a more important position. He also had a greater reputation as a stylist, but for modern readers, Andrewes carries to an extreme the baroque fashion of "crumbling a text" (analyzing in minute detail). The sermons of Andrewes are now unreadable without special training in theology and classical languages. On the other hand, though also writing for an educated audience with a serious interest in divinity, Donne wears his scholarship more easily and can still be read by the general student without special preparation. His sermon to the Virginia Company is the first sermon in English to make a missionary appeal.

The single most famous of Donne's sermons was his last. *Death's Duell* (1632), preached before King Charles on February 25, 1631, is a profound meditation on mortality. Human mortality is always a major theme with Donne, but here he reaches a new eloquence. Full of startling imagery, the sermon takes as its theme the paradox that life is death and death is life—although Christ's death delivers humankind from death. When this last sermon of Donne's was published, Henry King, bishop of Chichester, remarked that "as he exceeded others at first so at last he exceeded himself."

A work of similar theme but published by Donne in his own lifetime is the *Devotions upon Emergent Occasions* (1624). Composed, as R. C. Bald has shown, with extreme rapidity during a serious illness and convalescence in 1623, this work is based on the structured meditational technique of Saint Francis de Sales, involving the sensuous evocation of scenes, although, as Thomas F. Van Laan has suggested, the work is perhaps also influenced by the *Ejercicios espirituales* (1548; *The Spiritual Exercises*, 1736) of Saint Ignatius of Loyola. It is divided into twenty-three sections, each consisting of a meditation, an expostulation, and a prayer. The work is an artfully constructed whole of sustained emotional power, but the meditations have achieved a special fame with their vivid evocations of the theme that sickness brings people closer to God by putting them in touch with their frailty and mortality. Various meditations from the *Devotions upon Emergent Occasions* present famous pictures of the tolling of the death knell, of the body as a microcosm, and of the curious medical practices of the day, for example, the application of live pigeons to Donne's feet to try to draw the vapors of fever from his head. By this last practice, Donne discovers that he is his own executioner because the vapors are believed to be the consequence of his melancholy, and this is no more than the studiousness required of him by his calling as

a preacher. Although in past centuries most readers found the work's self-consciousness and introspection alienating, the contemporary sensibility finds these characteristics especially congenial. The three meditations on the tolling of the bells have, in particular, provided titles and catchphrases for popular writers.

A posthumously published early study of mortality by Donne is *Essayes in Divinity* (1651). Written in a knotty, baroque style, the work is a collection of curiously impersonal considerations of the Creation and of the deliverance of the Israelites from bondage in Egypt. The essays show none of the fire of the sermons and of the *Devotions upon Emergent Occasions*. A very different sort of contemplation of mortality is provided in *Biathanatos* (1646). The casuistical reasoning perhaps shows evidence of Donne's Jesuit background. The same approach to logic and a similar iconoclasm are apparent in *Juvenilia: Or, Certaine Paradoxes and Problems* (1633; the first complete version was, however, not published until 1923).

The earliest of Donne's publications were two works of religious controversy of a more serious nature. These works also show Donne's Jesuit background, but in them, he is reacting against his upbringing and presenting a case for Anglican moderation in the face of Roman Catholic—and especially Jesuit—pretensions. *Pseudo-Martyr* (1610) was written at the explicit request of King James, according to Donne's first biographer, Izaak Walton. Here and throughout his subsequent career, Donne is a strongly committed Erastian, seeing the Church as properly subordinate in this world to secular authority.

The other of these early works of controversy, *Ignatius His Conclave* (1611), which appeared in Latin as well as English, is still amusing to modern readers who are unlikely to come to it with quite the strong partisan feeling of its original audience.

ACHIEVEMENTS

John Donne was a remarkably influential poet in his day. Despite the fact that it was only after his death that a substantial body of his poetry was published, the elegies and satires (and to a lesser extent the divine poems and the songs and sonnets) had already created a new poetic mode during Donne's lifetime as a result of circulating in manuscript. Thomas Carew, in a memorial elegy published in the first edition of Donne's poems, described him as ruling the "universal monarchy of wit." The poetry of the School of Donne was usually characterized in its own day by its "strong lines." This characterization seems to have meant that Donne and his followers were to be distinguished from the Sons of Ben, the poets influenced by Ben Jonson, chiefly by their experiments with rough meter and conversational syntax; Jonson, however, was also—somewhat confusingly—praised for strong lines. Donne's own characteristic metrics involve lines densely packed with syllables. He makes great use not only of syncope (dropping of an unstressed vowel within a word) and elision (dropping of an unstressed vowel at the juncture between words) but also of a device almost unique to Donne among English poets—synaloepha (speeding up of adjacent vowels at the juncture between words with no actual dropping). By hindsight, Donne, Edward Lord Herbert of Cherbury, Henry King, George Herbert, John Cleveland, Richard Crashaw, Abraham Cowley, Henry Vaughan, Andrew Marvell, and others of the School of Donne share not only strong lines but also a common fund of imagery. Eschewing for the most part classical allusions, these poets turned to the imagery of everyday life and of the new learning in science and philosophy.

In the middle of the seventeenth century, there occurred what T. S. Eliot has memorably described as a "dissociation of sensibility," after which it became increasingly difficult to see Donne's secular and religious values as part of a consistent whole. The beginnings of this attitude were already apparent in Donne's own day; in a letter, for example, he describes *Biathanatos* as the work not of Dr. Donne but of the youthful Jack Donne. Toward the end of the century, the change of perspective is complete when John Dryden describes Donne unsympathetically as one who "perplexes the Minds of the Fair Sex with nice Speculations of philosophy." The Restoration and the eighteenth century had lost Donne's sense of religious commitment and thus scrutinized a style in isolation from the content it intended to express. Donne's poetry was condemned as artificial, and his reputation disappeared almost overnight.

This was the situation when Samuel Johnson wrote the famous strictures on Donne in his *Life of Cowley*. That these remarks occur in the *Life of Cowley* is perhaps a commentary on the fallen stature of the earlier poets: Donne did not himself merit individual treatment in *Lives of the Poets* (1779-1781). Conceding that to write like Donne "it was at least necessary to read and think," Johnson describes the wit of the School of Donne—accurately enough—as the "discovery of occult resemblances in things apparently unlike." Although many readers of the earlier seventeenth century and of the twentieth century would consider the description high praise, for Johnson it was a condemnation. For him, the "most heterogeneous ideas are yoked by violence together." He popularized the term "Metaphysical poetry" for this yoking; the term had, however, been used earlier, even in Donne's own day.

Donne's stature and influence in the twentieth century and beyond are equal to his great stature and wide influence in the seventeenth century, but the attitude represented by Johnson remained the norm for the centuries between. Donne's modern-day prestige is based on values different from those that accounted for his prestige in his own day. The seventeenth century took its religion seriously but understood religion as part of the whole fabric of life. Donne's stature as a preacher was for this reason part of his prestige as a poet. In addition, the fact that he wrote love poetry and sometimes used graphic erotic imagery did not in his own day seem incongruous with his calling as a preacher.

The twentieth century did not, of course, recover the intense religiosity of the early seventeenth century, but what T. S. Eliot, Ezra Pound, and other poets of their circle had discovered in the 1920's was an aestheticism as intense as this religiosity. Their values naturally led them to praise lyric poetry in preference to epic and to prize intensity of emotion in literary work of all kinds. They disparaged the poetry of John Milton because it was an expression of ideas rather than of feeling and offered Donne as a model and a more appropriate great author for the period. The restoration of Donne's prestige was remarkably complete; but, paradoxically, precisely because the triumph of Donne was so complete, the denigration of Milton never quite occurred. The values that Eliot and others praised in Donne were looked for—and discovered—in Milton as well.

Although Donne was perhaps a more exciting figure during his mid-twentieth century "rediscovery" than he is in the twenty-first century, because to appreciate him meant to throw over the eighteenth and nineteenth century allegiance to Milton as the great poet of the language, Donne's stature as a major figure has become assured. Modern-day scholarly opinion has, however, been moving inevitably toward seeing the divine poems as the capstone of his career. Scholarly opinion has, in fact, moved beyond Eliot's position and come to value literary works simply because they have religious content, since intensity of feeling will surely be found in a poetry of religious commitment. This is not a way of appreciating Donne and the Metaphysicals that would have been understood in the seventeenth century.

BIOGRAPHY

Born in St. Nicholas Olave Parish, London, sometime between January 24 and June 19, 1572, John Donne came from a Welsh paternal line (originally Dwn) with some claim to gentility. His father, however, was an ironmonger, although important enough to serve as warden of his professional guild. On his mother's side, Donne's connections were distinguished for both their intellectual attainments and their recusancy—that is, allegiance to the Church of Rome in the face of the Elizabethan Church Settlement. Donne's maternal grandfather was the epigrammatist and playwright John Heywood. A great-grandfather, John Rastell, was a minor playwright. Two of Donne's uncles were Jesuits who died in exile for their faith, as did his great-uncle Judge William Rastell; and another great-uncle, the monk Thomas Heywood, was executed, having been caught saying Mass. Finally, a great-grandmother was the sister of Thomas More, whose skull Donne inherited and very characteristically kept as a memento mori. Donne's brother, Henry, died in prison, where he had been sent for harboring a seminary priest; and Donne justifiably said in *Pseudo-Martyr* that no family had suffered more for the Roman Church.

His father died while Donne was still in infancy. His mother married twice more. The stepfather of Donne's youth was a prominent physician. At first educated at home by Roman Catholic tutors, in 1584, Donne and his younger brother, Henry, were admitted to Hart Hall, Oxford. Although they were a precocious twelve and eleven at the time, they were entered in the register as even younger to circumvent the requirement that students of sixteen and over subscribe to the Oath of Supremacy. Donne spent probably three years at Oxford altogether.

Although records are lacking for the next period of Donne's life, one theory is that he spent some of this time in travel abroad. With his brother, Donne eventually took up residence at the Inns of Court to prepare for a legal career. Unsettled in these career plans by the arrest and death of Henry, Donne began serious study of the relative claims of the Anglican and Roman Churches and finally abandoned the study of law entirely.

In 1596, he participated in the earl of Essex's military expedition to Cadiz. Donne's affability and his growing reputation as a poet—sustained by the private circulation of some of his elegies and lyrics—recommended him to a son of Sir Thomas Egerton who had also participated in the sack of Cadiz, and Egerton, who was Lord Keeper, was persuaded to appoint Donne as his secretary. In this position and also in Parliament, where he served briefly in 1601, he had many opportunities to meet people of note, and he improved his reputation as a poet by composing satires and occasional poems as well as additional lyrics.

In 1601, Donne was already in his late twenties, and, during Christmastide, he contracted a secret marriage with Anne More, the sixteen-year-old niece of Lady Egerton. Because the marriage was contrary to her father's wishes, Donne was imprisoned for his offense; he also permanently lost his position as Egerton's secretary, and the couple were forced to live for several years on the charity of friends and relations. A comment made at the time, sometimes attributed to Donne himself, was, "John Donne, Anne Donne, Undone."

Although his career hopes had been dashed by the impetuous marriage, his winning personality and poetic skill won for him new friends in high places. He traveled abroad with Sir Walter Chute in 1605; he became a member of the salon of Lucy, countess of Bedford; and he even attracted the attention of King James, who saw what a useful ornament Donne would be to the Church and urged him to take orders. Not completely resolved in his conscience to do so, Donne, for a considerable time, temporized. However, his activity during this period led him inevitably toward this step. A substantial body of Donne's religious verse was written during this period and sent to Magdalen Herbert, mother of George Herbert and Lord Herbert of Cherbury. Finally, he committed himself to seeking advancement within the Anglican Church with the publication of *Pseudo-Martyr*, a work of religious controversy on a problem strongly vexing the King—the refusal of Roman Catholics to subscribe to the Oath of Allegiance. Thereafter, the king refused to consider Donne for any post outside the Church. In 1610, Oxford University awarded an honorary master's degree to Donne, who had been prevented by his former religion from taking an undergraduate degree.

Having composed the *Anniversaries* under the patronage of Sir Robert Drury of Hawsted, he accompanied Sir Robert to Paris and then to Frankfort. After the return of the party to England in 1612, Donne and his family resided with Sir Robert. Although he continued to write occasional verse, Donne had definitely decided to take orders. Having prepared himself through further study, he was ordained early in 1615, and numerous avenues for advancement immediately became available to him. The king made him a royal chaplain. Cambridge awarded him the degree of doctor of divinity by royal command. Lincoln's Inn appointed him reader in divinity to the Society. In addition, he was able to turn down offers of fourteen country livings in his first year as a priest, while accepting two. The one blight on his early years as a priest was the death of his wife in 1617. In 1619, Donne took time out from his regular duties to serve as chaplain accompanying Lord Doncaster on an embassy to Germany.

Donne's fame as a preacher had been immediate, and it continued to grow each year. As Walton reports, even his friends were surprised by the continuous growth of his pulpit eloquence after such a striking beginning. Such genius received its proper setting in 1621, when Donne was appointed dean of St. Paul's Cathedral. The position was also a lucrative one, and the dean's residence was as large as an episcopal palace.

The winter of 1623-1624 was a particularly eventful time in Donne's life. Having contracted relapsing fever, he was on the verge of death, but with characteristic dedication—and also characteristic self-consciousness—he kept a meticulous record of his illness as an aid to devotion. The resulting work, *Devotions upon Emergent Occasions*, was published almost immediately. During the same period, Donne's daughter, Constance, married the aging Elizabethan actor Edward Alleyn, founder of Dulwich College. From circumstances surrounding the wedding, the publishing history of *Devotions upon Emergent Occasions* has been reconstructed. It now seems clear that Donne composed this highly structured work in just a few weeks while still physically incapacitated.

In 1624, he took on additional duties as vicar of St. Dunstan's-in-the-West. After the death of King James in the following year, Donne was chosen to preach the first sermon before the new king. This and other ser-

*John Donne* (Library of Congress)

mons were printed at the request of King Charles. Also printed was his memorial sermon for Lady Danvers, as Magdalen Herbert had become.

Even when Donne again became gravely ill in 1629, he would not stop preaching. Ever conscious of his mortality during these last months, he sat for a portrait wearing his shroud. When he delivered his last sermon on Ash Wednesday in 1631, it was the famous *Death's Duell*. Walton gives a vivid account of the writing and preaching of this sermon during Donne's last illness, and some of the sermon's special urgency is perhaps explained by the fact that the king's household called it Donne's own funeral sermon. Indeed, a few weeks later, on March 31, 1631, he died, having been preceded only a few months before by his aged mother.

## Analysis

The traditional dichotomy between Jack Donne and Dr. Donne, despite John Donne's own authority for it, is essentially false. In the seventeenth century context, the work of Donne constitutes a fundamental unity. Conventional wisdom may expect devotional poetry from a divine and feel a certain uneasiness when faced with love poetry, but such a view misses the point in two different ways. On one hand, Donne's love poetry is philosophical in its nature and characterized by a texture of religious imagery; and on the other hand, his devotional poetry makes unexpected, bold use of erotic imagery. What Donne presents is two sides of a consistent vision of the world and of the mortality of man.

In the nineteenth century, when Donne's poetry did occasionally attract some attention from the discerning, it was not for the lyrics but for the satires. The satirical mode seemed the most congenial use that Donne had found for his paradoxical style. This had also been the attitude of the eighteenth century, which, however, valued metrical euphony too highly to accept even the satires. In fact, Alexander Pope tried to rescue Donne for the eighteenth century by the curious expedient of "translating" his satires into verse, that is, by regularizing them. In addition to replacing Donne's strong lines and surprising caesurae with regular meter, Pope, as Addison C. Bross has shown, puts ideas into climactic sequence, makes particulars follow generalizations,

groups similar images together, and untangles syntax. In other words, he homogenizes the works.

Although Donne's lyrics have become preferred to his satires, the satires are regarded as artistically effective in their original form, although this artistry is of a different order from that of the lyrics. Sherry Zivley has shown that the imagery of the satires works in a somewhat different way from that of the imagery of the lyrics, where diverse images simply succeed one another. With images accumulated from a similarly wide range of sources, the satires build a thematic center. N. J. C. Andreasen has gone even further, discerning in the body of the satires a thematic unity. Andreasen sees Donne as having created a single persona for the satires, one who consistently deplores the encroaching materialism of the seventeenth century.

### "Kind pity chokes my spleen"

Satire 3 on religion ("Kind pity chokes my spleen") is undoubtedly the most famous of the satires. Using related images to picture men as engaging in a kind of courtship of the truth, the poem provides a defense of moderation and of a common ground between the competing churches of the post-Reformation world. Although written in the period of Donne's transition from the Roman Catholic Church to the Anglican, the poem rejects both of these, along with the Lutheran and the Calvinist Churches, and calls on men to put their trust in God and not in those who unjustly claim authority from God for churches of their own devising.

In addition to the fully developed satires, Donne wrote a small number of very brief epigrams. These mere witticisms are often on classical subjects and therefore without the occasional focus that turns Ben Jonson's epigrams into genuine poetry. This is the only place where Donne makes any substantial use of classical allusion.

In his own day, Donne's most popular poems were probably his elegies. Although the term "elegy" is applied only to a memorial poem in modern usage, Donne's elegies derive their form from a classical tradition that uses the term, as well, for poetry of love complaint written in couplets. Generally longer than the more famous songs and sonnets, the elegies are written on the model of Ovid's *Amores* (c. 20 B.C.E.; English translation, c. 1597). Twenty or more such poems have been attributed to Donne, but several of these are demonstrably not his. On the basis of manuscript evidence, Dame Helen Gardner has suggested that Donne intended fourteen poems to stand as a thematically unified Book of Elegies and that "The Autumnal" (elegy 9), which has a different manuscript history, and "The Dream" (elegy 10), which is not in couplets, although authentic poems by Donne, do not form a part of it.

### "THE AUTUMNAL"

Elegy 9, "The Autumnal," praises older women as more seasonable to the appetite because the uncontrollable fires of their youth have passed. There is a long tradition that this poem was specially written for Magdalen Herbert. If so, it is particularly daring since, although not a seduction poem, it is frankly erotic in its praise; inasmuch as Magdalen Herbert did take as her second husband a much younger man, however, it may be supposed that she would have appreciated the general recognition that sexual attractiveness and interest can endure and even ripen. On the other hand, the poem's praises are not without qualification. The persona admires autumnal beauty, but he can see nothing attractive in the truly aged, whom he rejects as death's heads from which the teeth have been scattered to various places—to the vexation of their souls since the teeth will have to be gathered together again for the resurrection of the body at the Last Judgment. Thus the poem shows Donne's typical combination of eroticism and contemplation of mortality in a mode of grotesque humor.

### "TO HIS MISTRESS GOING TO BED"

In elegy 19, "To His Mistress Going to Bed," the persona enthusiastically directs his mistress in her undressing. Aroused, he uses his hands to full advantage to explore her body. In a famous passage, he compares his amazement to that of someone discovering a new land. He next directs her to bare her body to him as fully as she would to the midwife. This graphic request is followed by the poem's closing couplet, in which the persona points out that he is naked already to show his mistress the way and thus poignantly reveals that he is only hoping for such lasciviousness from her and not already having his wanton way. Even this poem uses religious imagery—most clearly and most daringly when it advocates a woman's baring of her body to her lover by analogy with the baring of the soul before God. In an influential explication, Clay Hunt suggests that Donne is, in fact, ridiculing the Neoplatonic school of love that could seriously advance such an analogy. If so, Donne is clearly having it both ways and making the analogy available for its own sake as well.

### "THE CANONIZATION"

The songs and sonnets, as the other love poems are usually called, although no sonnets in the conventional sense are included, show an imaginative variety of verse forms. They are particularly famous for their dramatic, conversational opening lines. In addition, these poems are a great storehouse of the kind of verbal ambiguity that William Empson has shown the modern world how to admire.

In "The Canonization," the persona justifies his love affair in explicitly sacred terms by explaining that his relationship with his beloved makes the two of them saints of love. John A. Clair has shown how the structure of "The Canonization" follows the five stages of the process of canonization in the Roman Catholic Church during the Renaissance: proof of sanctity, recognition of heroic virtue, demonstration of miracles, examination of relics and writings, and declaration of worthiness of veneration. The poem is thus addressed to a devil's advocate who refuses to see the holiness of erotic love. It is this devil's advocate in love who is asked to hold his tongue, in the famous first line. "The Canonization" illustrates Donne's typical use of ambiguity as well as paradox, not as merely decorative wit, but to reveal deepest meanings. William H. Machett suggests that, for example, when the lovers in this poem become a "piece of chronicle," the word "piece" is a triple pun meaning masterpiece, fragment, and fortress. There is also a much more obvious meaning—piece of artillery—a meaning that interacts with the title to give a richer texture to the whole poem: The poem is about not only the making of saints of love, but also the warfare between this idea and conventional notions of sex and religion. Consequently, yet another meaning of "piece" comes into play, the sexual.

### "THE FLEA"

"The Flea" is a seduction poem. Like many of the songs and sonnets, it takes the form of a logical argument making full use of the casuistries and indeed sophistries of the dialectic of Peter Ramus. In the first of the poem's three stanzas, the persona asks the lady to contemplate a flea he has discerned on her person. Because his blood and hers are mingled in the flea that has in succession bitten each of them, the mingling of the bloods that takes place during intercourse (as was then believed) has already occurred.

In the second stanza, the persona cautions the lady not to kill the flea. By joining their bloods, the flea has become the place of their joining in marriage, so for her to kill the flea would be to murder him and also to commit both suicide and sacrilege.

In the last stanza, the persona discovers that the lady has ignored his argument and killed the flea, but he is ready with another argument. When the lady triumphantly points out that they have survived this death of the flea, surely she is also showing how false her fears of sex are, because sex involves no greater loss of blood and no greater death. Implicit in these last lines is the traditional pun on "death," which was the popular term for sexual climax.

The pun and the poem as a whole illustrate Donne's characteristic mingling of the sacred and the profane. It should be noted that a love poem on the subject of the lady's fleas was not an original idea with Donne, but the usual treatment of the subject was as an erotic fantasy. Donne's originality is precisely in his use of the subject for dialectic and in the restraint he shows in ending the poem before the lady capitulates, in fact without indicating whether she does.

### "THE ECSTASY"

"The Ecstasy," the longest of the songs and sonnets, has, for a lyric, attracted a remarkable range of divergent interpretations. The poem is about spiritual love and intermingling as the culmination of physical love, but some critics have seen the Neoplatonism, or spiritualizing of love, as quite serious, while others have insisted that it is merely a patently sophistical ploy of the persona to convince his mistress that, since they are one soul, the physical consummation of their love is harmless, appropriate, inevitable. If the critics who see "The Ecstasy" as a seduction poem are right, the conclusion is even more salacious than they have supposed, since it calls on the addressee to examine the lovers closely for

the evidence of true love when they have given themselves over to their bodies—in other words, to watch them make love. In fact, the poem, like so many of Donne's, is quite content to be theological and erotic by turns—beginning with its very title, a term used of both religious experience and sexual experience. That the perfect soul brought into being by the union of the lovers should combine the flesh and spirit eternally is an understandable religious hope and also a good sexual fantasy. In this way, the poem illustrates Donne's philosophy of love. Although not all his poems use this theme, Donne has, in fact, a unique ability for his day to perceive love as experienced by equals.

### "A VALEDICTION: FORBIDDING MOURNING"

Another famous poem of love between equals is "A Valediction: Forbidding Mourning." The poem rushes through a dazzling spectrum of imagery in just the way deplored by Samuel Johnson. In addition, in the *Life of Cowley*, Johnson singles out the poem for his ultimate condemnation, saying that in the extended metaphor of the last three stanzas "it may be doubted whether absurdity or ingenuity has the better claim." During the present century, ingenuity has once again become respectable in poetry, and modern readers come with more sympathy than Johnson did to this famous extended metaphor, or conceit, comparing lovers who have to suffer a temporary separation to a pair of pencil compasses. Even the improbability of the image—which Johnson castigated as absurdity—has been given a context by modern scholarship. W. A. Murray, for example, has shown that the circle with a dot in the center, which is inscribed by the compasses reflecting the lovers who are separated yet joined, is, in fact, the alchemical symbol for gold, mentioned elsewhere in the poem and a traditional symbol of perfection. More ingeniously, John Freccero has seen Donne's compasses as inscribing not simply a circle but, as they close, a spiral. The spiral has some history of use in describing the motion of the planets. Because the spiral is also a conventional symbol of humanity, this spiral reading helps readers see in "A Valediction: Forbidding Mourning" Donne's characteristic balance of the celestial and the personal.

In fact, Donne's inclusiveness is even wider than it is usually assumed to be. He collapses not only physical and spiritual but also male and female. Donne has the unusual perspicacity to make the persona of "Break of Day" explicitly female, and although no critic has made the point before, there is nothing to prevent seeing a similar female persona in "A Valediction: Forbidding Mourning." Such a reading has the advantage of introducing some erotic puns in the compass conceit as the man (the fixed center in this reading) harkens after his beloved as she roams and then grows erect when she returns to him. More important, such a reading makes further sense out of the image of a circle inscribed by compasses. The circle is a traditional symbol of woman, and woman's life is traditionally completed— or, as the poem puts it, made just—with a man at the center. Because the circle is a natural sexual image for woman, in this reading, the poem illustrates the practical sex as well as the theoretical sociology behind its imagery as the lover's firmness makes the woman's circle taut. An objection that might be made to this reading is that the poem's various references to parting show that it is the speaker who is going away. Although a woman of the seventeenth century would be unlikely to do extensive traveling apart from her lover (or even in his company), a woman may have to part as well as a man, and lovers might well think of themselves as roaming the world when kept apart only by the daily round of pedestrian business. There is no more reason in the poem for believing that the absent one will literally roam than for believing that this absent one will literally run.

Although Walton assigns this poem to the occasion of Donne's trip to France with Sir Robert Drury in 1611, the apocryphal nature of Walton's story is sufficiently indicated by the fact that it does not appear until the 1675 version of his *Life of Donne*. This dating would, at the least, make "A Valediction: Forbidding Mourning" extremely late for the songs and sonnets. Nevertheless, were the poem occasioned by Donne's preparation to travel to France in 1611, reading it as spoken by a woman would still be appropriate, since Donne prepared for this trip by sending his wife and children to stay with relatives on the Isle of Wight several months before he was himself able to embark. In addition, a general knowledge of how poets work suggests that a lyric inspired by a specific occasion is sel-

dom in every particular a document congruent with the poet's actual experience. Perhaps the poem finally says that a woman can make a virtue of necessary separation as well as a man can.

## "TWICKHAM GARDEN"

Among the songs and sonnets are a few poems that seem to have been written for patrons. Since Twickenham is the seat of the earls of Bedford, "Twickham Garden" is assumed to have been written for Lucy, countess of Bedford. According to the poem, the garden is a refuge like Eden, but the persona admits that with him the serpent has been let in. He wishes he were instead an aphrodisiac plant or fountain more properly at home in the place. In the last stanza, he seems to become such a fountain, but he is disappointed to discover that all the lovers who visit the garden are false. The poem ends— perhaps rather curiously for a patronage poem—with the obscure paradox that the only true woman is the one whose truth is killing.

## "A NOCTURNAL UPON ST. LUCY'S DAY, BEING THE SHORTEST DAY"

A similar depersonalization characterizes the riddling poem "A Nocturnal upon St. Lucy's Day, Being the Shortest Day." While the ironies of darkness and light and of the changing movement of time (*Lucy* means light, but her day provides less of it than any other) would have recommended the subject to Donne anyway, it must have been an additional stimulus that this astronomically significant day was the saint's day of one of his patrons. Clarence H. Miller, seeing the poem as unique among the songs and sonnets in describing the union with the lady as exclusively sacred without any admixture of the profane, relates the poem to the liturgy for Saint Lucy's Day. In the body of the poem, however, the persona sees himself as the epitaph for light, as every dead thing. Finally, he becomes Saint Lucy's Day itself—for the purpose of providing lovers with a longer nighttime for lust. Despite a certain bitterness or at least coarseness of tone, the poem is usually seen as a lament for the countess's death (1627); the death of Donne's wife, however, has also been suggested, although Anne More has no special association with Saint Lucy and his love for her could not have been exclusively spiritual. Richard E. Hughes has considered the occasion of the poem from a different point of view and usefully suggested that, though commemorating the countess of Bedford, the poem is not an improbably late lyric for the songs and sonnets but a lament from an earlier period for the loss of the countess's friendship. If the tone is considered in the least charitable light, the poem might even be read as an accusation of patronage withdrawn.

### VERSE LETTERS

The familiar letter came into its own as a genre during the seventeenth century, and collections even began to be published. About two hundred of Donne's letters survive. This is a larger number than for any other figure of the English Renaissance except Francis Bacon, and Bacon's correspondence includes many letters written in his official capacity. Because the familiar letter had only begun to surface as a genre, much of the impersonality and formality of earlier letter writing persist in Donne's correspondence. Donne's son was a rather casual editor, and in light of the sometimes general nature of Donne's letters, the date and intended recipient of many remain unknown. One curiosity of this period of epistolary transition is the verse letter. Almost forty of Donne's letters are written in verse. Some of these are true occasional poems datable from internal evidence, but many are of a more general, philosophical nature.

The most famous of the verse letters are "The Storm" and "The Calm," the first certainly and the second probably addressed to Christopher Brooke. Traditionally, shipwrecks and other dangers of the sea are used to illustrate the unpredictability of fortune in men's lives, but, as B. F. Nellist has shown, Donne does not follow this convention; instead, he teaches that frustration and despair are to be accepted as part of man's lot.

### EPITHALAMIA

While many of the verse letters seem to have been exchanged with friends as *jeux d'esprit*, some are attempts to influence patrons. A group of poems clearly written with an eye to patronage are the epithalamia. Among the weddings that Donne celebrated was that of Princess Elizabeth to Frederick V, elector of the palatinate and later briefly king of Bohemia. Donne also celebrated the wedding of the royal favorite Robert Carr, earl of Somerset, to Frances Howard, countess of Essex. Since the countess was shortly afterward convicted of murdering the essayist Sir Thomas Overbury for having stood in the way of her marriage, this epithalamion must later have been something of an embarrassment to Donne. An occasional poem for which no occasion is ascribed is the "Epithalamion Made at Lincoln's Inn." This is the most interesting of the epithalamia to contemporary taste. Its satiric tone, verbal crudities, and scoffing are a pleasant surprise in a genre usually characterized by reverence, even obsequiousness. The problem of what wedding could have been appropriately celebrated with such a poem has been resolved by David Novarr's suggestion that the "Epithalamion Made at Lincoln's Inn" was written for a mock wedding held as part of the law students' midsummer revels.

### MEMORIAL VERSE

Other poems written for patrons are those usually called the epicedes and obsequies. These are eulogies for the dead—elegies in a more modern sense of the term than the one Donne seems to have in mind. Donne was one among the many poets who expressed regret at the death of Prince Henry, the hope of the dynasty.

Also in the general category of memorial verse are the two poems known as *Anniversaries* (*An Anatomy of the World: The First Anniversary* and *Of the Progress of the Soule: The Second Anniversary*), but these two poems are so unlike traditional eulogies as to defy inclusion in the genre. In their search for moments of intense feeling, the Metaphysical poets, with their love of paradox, did not often try to write long poems. Most of the attempts they did make are unsatisfactory or at least puzzling in some fundamental way. The *Anniversaries* are, indeed, primary texts in the study of the difficulties of the long poem in the Metaphysical mode.

Ostensibly written as memorial poems to commemorate Elizabeth Drury, who died as a child of fourteen and whom Donne had never seen, these poems range over a broad canvas of history. "Shee," as the subject of the two poems is called, is eulogized in an extravagant fashion beyond anything in the obsequies. While O. B. Hardison has shown that these poems were not regarded as bizarre or fulsome when originally published, they were the first of Donne's works to lose favor with the passing of time. Indeed, of *An Anatomy of* the World, Ben Jonson objected to Donne himself that "if it had been writ of the Virgin Marie it had been something." Donne's answer is reported to have been that he was describing not Elizabeth Drury specifically but the idea of woman; but this explanation has not been found wholly satisfactory. Many candidates have been suggested for Shee of the *Anniversaries*—from Saint Lucy and Astraea (Goddess of Justice) to the Catholic Church and Christ as Divine *Logos*. Two critics have suggested Queen Elizabeth, but one finds her eulogized and the other sees her as satirized, indicting in a particularly striking way the problematic nature of these difficult, knotty poems.

Hardison and, later, Barbara Kiefer Lewalski, made the case for the poems as part of a tradition of epideictic poetry—poetry of praise. In this tradition, extravagant compliments are the norm rather than the exception, and all of Donne's individual extravagances have precedents. What such a reading leaves out of account is, on one hand, the extraordinary density of the extravagant praise in Donne's *Anniversaries* and, on the other, the presence of satire, not only the possible satire of the heroine but also explicit satire in the exploration of the decay of nature that forms the subject of the poems. Marjorie Hope Nicholson sees the *Anniversaries* as companion poems, the first a lament for the body, the second a meditation on mortality. Louis L. Martz suggests, further, that the *Anniversaries* are structured meditations. Martz sees *An Anatomy of the World* as a mechanical application of Ignatian meditation and *Of the Progress of the Soule* as a more successful organic application. Meditation theory, however, fails to resolve all the interpretive difficulties. Northrop Frye's theory that the poems are Menippean satire and Frank Manley's that they are wisdom literature also leave unresolved difficulties.

Perhaps these interpretive difficulties are fundamentally beyond resolution. Rosalie L. Colie has usefully pointed out that, in the *Anniversaries*, Donne seems not to be trying to bring his disparate materials to a conventional resolution. The poems accept contradictions as part of the flux of life and should be seen within the Renaissance tradition of paradox. Donne is demonstrably a student of paradox in many of his other works. More specifically, Daniel B. Rowland has placed *An*

*Anatomy of the World* in the Mannerist tradition because in it Donne succeeded in creating an unresolved tension. His purpose may be just to raise questions about the relative weight of praise and satire and about the identity of the heroine Shee. Mario Praz goes further—perhaps too far—when he sees all the work of Donne as Mannerist, as illustrative not of wit but of the dialectics of passion; Mannerism does, however, provide a useful description for what modern taste finds a strange combination of materials in the *Anniversaries*.

### "INFINITATI SACRUM"

An even more difficult long poem is an unfinished one called "Infinitati Sacrum." This strange parable of Original Sin adapts Paracelsus's theory of the transmigration of souls to follow through the course of subsequent history the spirit of the apple plucked by Eve. W. A. Murray has seen in this poem the beginnings of a *Paradise Lost* (1667, 1674). While few other readers will want to go so far, most will agree with Murray and with George Williamson that "Infinitati Sacrum" is a preliminary use of the materials and themes treated in the *Anniversaries*.

Donne has been called a poet of religious doubt in contrast to Herbert, a poet of religious assurance; but Herbert has real doubts in the context of his assurance, and the bold demand for salvation in audacious, even shocking language characteristic of the Holy Sonnets suggests, on the contrary, that Donne writes from a deep-seated conviction of election.

### HOLY SONNETS

Louis Martz, Helen Gardner, and others have shown the influence of Ignatian meditation in the Holy Sonnets. Dame Helen, in fact, by restoring the manuscript order, has been able to see in these poems a sequential meditative exercise. The sensuous language, however, suggests not so much the meditative technique of Saint Ignatius of Loyola as the technique of Saint Francis de Sales. In addition, Don M. Ricks has argued cogently that the order of the poems in the Westmorland Manuscript may suggest an Elizabethan sonnet sequence and not a meditative exercise at all.

Holy Sonnet 14 (10 in Dame Helen's numbering), "Batter my heart, three-personed God," has been seen by Arthur L. Clements and others as hieroglyphically illustrating the Trinity in its three-part structure. This poem opens with the striking dramatic immediacy typical of Donne's best lyrics. Using both military and sexual imagery, Donne describes the frightening, ambivalent feelings called up by the thought of giving oneself over to God's power and overwhelming grace. The soul is a town ruled by a usurper whom God's viceroy, Reason, is inadequate to overthrow. The soul is also the beloved of God though betrothed to his enemy and longing for divorce. The resolution of this sonnet turns on a paradoxical sexual image as the persona says that his soul will never be chaste unless God ravishes him. A similar complex of imagery is used, though in a less startling fashion, in Holy Sonnet 2 (1), "As due by many titles I resign."

Holy Sonnet 9 (5), "If poisonous minerals," begins audaciously by accusing God of unfairness in the consequences He has decreed for Original Sin. In the sestet, the persona abruptly realizes that he is unworthy to dispute with God in this way and begs that his tears of guilt might form a river of forgetfulness inducing God to overlook his sins rather than actually forgiving them. Although this poem does not turn on a sexual image, it does contrast the lot of fallen man unfavorably with that of lecherous goats, who have no decree of damnation hanging over them.

Holy Sonnet 18 (2 in Dame Helen's separately numbered group from the Westmorland Manuscript), "Show me, dear Christ, Thy spouse so bright and clear," has some of the most shocking sexual imagery in all of religious literature. Although the tradition of using erotic imagery to describe the soul's relationship with God has a long history, particularly in exegesis of the Song of Songs, that is helpful in understanding the other Holy Sonnets, the imagery here is of a different order. Like Satire 3, the poem is a discussion of the competing claims of the various Christian churches, but it goes well beyond the courtship imagery of the satire when it praises the Anglican Church because, like a promiscuous woman, it makes itself available to all men.

A distinctly separate series of Holy Sonnets is "La Corona." Using paradoxes such as the fact that the Virgin is her Maker's maker, and including extensive allusions to the divine office, this sequence of seven poems on the life of Christ has been called by Martz a rosary of

sonnets, not so much because of the devotional content as because of the interlaced structure: The last line of each poem is repeated as the first line of the next. Although the ingenious patterning renders the sequence less personal than Donne's best religious poetry, within its exquisite compass it does make a beautiful statement of the mysteries of faith.

In "A Hymn to Christ, at the Author's Last Going into Germany," Donne exaggerates the dangers of a Channel crossing to confront his mortality. Then even in the face of death, the persona pictures Christ as a jealous lover to be castigated if he withdraws his love just because it is not reciprocated; yet the persona does call for a bill of divorcement from all his lesser loves. The poem ends with the thought that, just as dark churches (being free of distractions) are best for praying, death is the best refuge from stormy seas.

"Good Friday, 1613: Riding Westward" is a witty paradox built on Ramist dialectic. Forced to make a trip to the West on Good Friday, the persona feels his soul drawn to the East. Although the heavens are ordered for westward motion, he feels a contradiction even as he duplicates their motion because all Christian iconology urges him to return to the East where life began—both human life in Eden and spiritual life with the Crucifixion. He reasons that through sin he has turned his back on the Cross—but only to receive the correction that his sins merit. He hopes such flagellation will so change his appearance that he will again become recognizable to God as made in his own image. Then he will at last be able to turn and face God.

Another divine poem of witty paradox is "A Hymn to God the Father." Punning on "Son/sun" and on his own name, Donne demands that God swear to save him. Having done so, God will at last have Donne. Because of its frankness and its very personal use of puns, this poem is not really a hymn despite its title—although it has been included in hymnals.

The chapter headings of *Devotions upon Emergent Occasions* as laid out in the table of contents should also be included among the divine poems. Joan Webber has made the illuminating discovery that this table of contents is a Latin poem in dactylic hexameters. This is a particularly surprising element of artistry in a work composed in such a short time and under such difficult conditions. Thus even more self-conscious than had been supposed, *Devotions upon Emergent Occasions* can finally be seen as an explication of the Latin poem.

## OTHER MAJOR WORKS

NONFICTION: *Pseudo-Martyr*, 1610; *Ignatius His Conclave*, 1611; *Devotions upon Emergent Occasions*, 1624; *Death's Duell*, 1632; *Juvenilia: Or, Certaine Paradoxes and Problems*, 1633, 1923; *Six Sermons on Several Occasions*, 1634; *LXXX Sermons*, 1640; *Biathanatos*, 1646; *Fifty Sermons*, 1649; *Essayes in Divinity*, 1651; *Letters to Severall Persons of Honour*, 1651; *A Collection of Letters*, 1660; *XXVI Sermons*, 1660.

## BIBLIOGRAPHY

Bloom, Harold, ed. *John Donne and the Metaphysical Poets*. New York: Bloom's Literary Criticism, 2008. A collection of critical analysis of Donne's poetry and that of the other Metaphysical poets.

Carey, John. *John Donne: Life, Mind, and Art*. Rev. ed. Boston: Faber & Faber, 1990. Carey's exposition of the whole range of Donne's poetry is exact and detailed. Its arrangement is thematic rather than biographical, which produces some forceful new appraisals. Includes an index.

Edwards, David L. *John Donne: Man of Flesh and Spirit*. Grand Rapids, Mich.: William B. Eerdmans, 2002. Biography of Donne that looks at how his life influenced his works.

Guibbory, Achsah, ed. *Cambridge Companion to John Donne*. New York: Cambridge, 2006. Covers both criticism and biography. Topics include Donne's political and religious world, his satires, his erotic poems, an explication of his poems, and gender and death in his poetry.

Johnson, Jeffrey. *The Theology of John Donne*. New York: D. S. Brewer, 1999. A portrayal of the religious writings of Donne as the result of a well-founded knowledge of Christian theology and Donne as a full-fledged religious thinker. Includes bibliographic references and an index.

Saunders, Ben. *Desiring Donne: Poetry, Sexuality, Interpretation*. Cambridge, Mass.: Harvard University Press, 2006. An examination of desire and love in the poetry of Donne that examines the seventeenth century perspective on love and desire.

Sherwood, Terry. *Fulfilling the Circle: A Study of John Donne's Thought*. Toronto, Ont.: University of Toronto Press, 1984. Attempts to trace Donne's understanding of the complex interrelationship of body and soul back from his later, more mature work. Theological and psychological perspectives are central. Includes an index.

Stubbs, John. *John Donne: The Reformed Soul*. New York: W. W. Norton, 2007. A readable and scholarly biography of the poet.

Sugg, Richard. *John Donne*. New York: Palgrave Macmillan, 2007. Provides a coherent overview of Donne's life and work and explains the Renaissance world in which he lived.

Targoff, Ramie. *John Donne, Body and Soul*. Chicago: University of Chicago Press, 2008. Targoff explains the seemingly disparate nature of Donne's writings by arguing that Donne's theme was always the union of body and soul.

*Edmund Miller*

---

# MICHAEL DRAYTON

**Born:** Hartshill, Warwickshire, England; 1563
**Died:** London, England; December 23, 1631

## PRINCIPAL POETRY

*The Harmonie of the Church*, 1591
*Idea, the Shepheard's Garland*, 1593
*Peirs Gaveston*, 1593
*Ideas Mirrour*, 1594
*Matilda*, 1594
*Endimion and Phoebe*, 1595 (revised as *The Man in the Moon*, 1606)
*Mortimeriados*, 1596
*The Tragicall Legend of Robert, Duke of Normandy*, 1596
*Englands Heroicall Epistles*, 1597
*The Barrons Wars*, 1603
*The Owle*, 1604

*Poemes Lyrick and Pastorall*, 1606
*The Legend of Great Cromwell*, 1607
*Poly-Olbion*, 1612-1622
*Poems*, 1619
*The Battaile of Agincourt*, 1627
*Elegies upon Sundry Occasions*, 1627
*The Muses Elizium*, 1630
*The Works of Michael Drayton*, 1931-1941 (5
    volumes; J. W. Hebel, Kathleen Tillotson, and
    B. H. Newdigate, editors)

## OTHER LITERARY FORMS

Except for brief prefaces to his books and letters, four of which were published in the *Works* of his friend William Drummond of Hawthornden, Michael Drayton wrote exclusively in verse. Between about 1597 and 1602, he is reputed to have written or collaborated on twenty plays, all of which are lost except *The First Part of the True and Honorable Historie of the Life of Sir John Old-Castle the Good Lord Cobham* (pr. 1599). The titles indicate that these were chronicle history plays.

## ACHIEVEMENTS

According to Francis Meres in 1598, Michael Drayton was "a man of virtuous disposition, honest conversation, and well-governed carriage; which is almost miraculous among good wits in these declining times." His early reputation was as a Spenserian, and as his life went on, friends perceived him as a conservative man increasingly out of sorts with the post-Elizabethan world. Though inevitably overshadowed by major contemporaries such as Edmund Spenser, his fellow-Warwickshirite William Shakespeare, John Donne, and Ben Jonson, he wrote well in virtually every popular literary genre of his day, and in his "heroical epistles" and Horatian odes, he introduced forms which, while not of major importance thereafter in English literature, he practiced with distinction. With reference to his longest work, Charles Lamb called Drayton "that panegyrist of my native earth; who has gone over her soul in his *Poly-Olbion* with the fidelity of a herald, and the painful love of a son." Drayton's odes in praise of English accomplishments, the "Ballad of Agincourt" and "To the Virginian Voyage," remain anthology favorites, as do several poems from *Idea*, one of the finest sonnet sequences in English.

As one of England's first professional poets, Drayton nearly always wrote competently and on occasion superbly, especially in his lyrics. In his best poems, he blends an intense love of his native land with a classicism marked by clarity, decorum, careful attention to form, and—with respect to all passions except his patriotic fervor—calm detachment.

## BIOGRAPHY

Most of the available biographical facts derive from Michael Drayton's own poems and dedications. He was born in northern Warwickshire in 1563 and seems to have been reared and educated in the household of Sir Henry Goodere at Polesworth, not far from his native village of Hartshill. To fulfill his lifelong desire to be a poet, he moved to London at least by 1591, although more likely in the later 1580's. Beyond reasonable doubt the "Idea" of his sonnets honors Sir Henry's daughter Anne. Drayton may have been in love with Anne; around 1595, however, she married a man of her own class, Sir Henry Rainsford. Of Drayton's ever marrying, there is no record. In later years, the poet spent his summers at Clifford Hall, Gloucestershire, the Rainsfords' seat, and he is known to have been treated by Lady Rainsford's physician, John Hall, who was Shakespeare's son-in-law. Although he apparently lived the last forty years of his life in London, Drayton's fondness for rural England and his admiration for the values of the landed gentry were obviously genuine. He is credited with having been on familiar terms with nearly every important literary Englishman of his time. Dying near the end of 1631, he was buried in Westminster Abbey.

## ANALYSIS

In an age when the writing of poetry was an avocation for actors, courtiers, clergymen, and landed gentlemen, Michael Drayton devoted his life to poetry. In a verse epistle to his friend Henry Reynolds, Drayton writes of how, at the age of ten, he beseeched his tutor to make him a poet. Being a man of the Renaissance, the teacher started him on eclogues, first those of "honest Mantuan," a currently popular Italian humanist, then the great Vergil himself, after which Drayton studied the English poets, beginning, of course, with Geoffrey Chaucer and working through to contemporaries such as Shakespeare, Christopher Marlowe, Samuel Daniel, and Jonson (Drayton having of course grown up in the meantime). Both the classics and the native poetical tradition continued to inspire him throughout his long career, and in his most characteristic work he adapts classical models to his own time, place, and language.

To a greater extent, perhaps, than any of his contemporaries, Drayton straddles the sixteenth and seventeenth centuries and raises the question of whether he was more Elizabethan or Jacobean. As he does not fall squarely into the usual categories of Spenserian, Jonsonian, or Metaphysical, his work challenges the usefulness—certainly the inclusiveness—of these categories of English Renaissance poetry. His career may be divided into three stages, the first and last of which are short but enormously energetic and productive, while the long middle stage demonstrates the characteristic development of his art while incidentally furnishing most of the poems for which he has become best known. In the first and, paradoxically, last stages, he is most Elizabethan, or, to use a term popularized by C. S. Lewis in his *English Literature in the Sixteenth Century* (1954), most "golden."

### EARLY PERIOD

His early period begins with the publication in 1591 of a drab religious exercise called *The Harmonie of the Church*, but between 1593 and 1595, he brought out three works which typify and enrich that most remarkable period in English letters: *Idea, the Shepheard's Garland*; *Ideas Mirrour*; and *Endimion and Phoebe*. The first of these demonstrates a young poet's preliminary pastoral, Vergil having worked from the shepherds' dale to epic heights—a program which the ambitious Spenser had already imitated and which many others, including John Milton, would imitate. The poems are eclogues, shepherds' dialogues on love, death, the decline of the world, and poetry itself; they are meant to exercise a poet's versatility in song. Drayton's are not notable, except perhaps for their unusually frequent references to English topography; they do, however, demonstrate that the poet, at thirty, had long since learned his craft.

### IDEAS MIRROUR

*Ideas Mirrour* is a sonnet sequence, not a classical form to be sure, but one associated with the great fourteenth century classicist, Petrarch. Since the posthumous publication of Sir Philip Sidney's *Astrophel and Stella* in 1591, poets had flooded England with sonnets featuring graceful tributes to beautiful ladies with stylized and often classical names such as Celia, Delia, and Diana, along with the laments of versifying suitors frustrated by the very aloofness that attracted them so fatally. Shakespeare's "Dark Lady," it might be noted, is in a number of respects the exception to the rule. *Ideas Mirrour*, fifty-one sonnets long, is conventionally melancholy, sometimes awkward, and regularly sensuous in the well-bred Elizabethan way.

### ENDIMION AND PHOEBE

*Endimion and Phoebe*, in 516 pentameter couplets, is Drayton's contribution to the Ovidian love narrative, a genre that had already generated Shakespeare's *Venus and Adonis* (1593) and Marlowe's *Hero and Leander* (1598). Endimion is a shepherd lad who loves the fair goddess Phoebe at once passionately and chastely; she rewards him by wrapping him in a "fiery mantle" and lofting him to the empyrean, where he is shown a series of splendors both astronomical and divine. The poem is full of rich, smooth-flowing language—not so thoroughly a thing of beauty as John Keats's *Endymion: A Poetic Romance* (1818) but a joy nevertheless.

### MORTIMERIADOS

Myth, pastoral, and love lyrics provided only limited opportunities for another English obsession in the heady years following the defeat of the supposedly invincible Spanish Armada in 1588: the patriotism that rings forth in John of Gaunt's "Methinks I am a prophet new inspired" speech in Shakespeare's *Richard II* (pr. c. 1595-1596) and so many other poems of the 1590's. Thus, 1596 found Drayton issuing *Mortimeriados*, on the political struggles of the reign of Edward II. Drayton was again following the lead of other poets, this time Shakespeare and Daniel (who had published the first four books of his *Civile Warres* in 1595) more than Spenser and Marlowe. *Mortimeriados*, which can be considered the last of the poems of Drayton's early phase, is only one of a series, begun three years earlier in his *Peirs Gaveston* and continuing throughout most of his life, in which he delves into the history, topography, and presumed national virtues of England.

## MIDDLE PERIOD

As the childless Queen Elizabeth grew old, ambitious courtiers moved into position, and as the problem of the succession loomed, England's mood changed. Spenser died in 1599, leaving *The Faerie Queene* (1590, 1596) unfinished and its shadowy heroine, Gloriana, unwed to Prince Arthur. Shakespeare turned increasingly to the writing of tragedy. Drayton's heart remained, as it always would remain, unabashedly Elizabethan. As his art matured, however, he welded his classicism and patriotism in poems of much greater originality.

## ENGLANDS HEROICALL EPISTLES

*Englands Heroicall Epistles* marks a turning point. Of this work can be said what surely cannot be said of anything in Drayton's earlier poems: It is something new in English literature. His classical model, Ovid's *Heroides* (before 8 C.E.; English translation, 1567), had been imitated as far back as Geoffrey Chaucer's *The Legend of Good Women* (1380-1386), but instead of retaining Ovid's subject matter—the plights of a group of legendary and historical women of the ancient world such as Dido, Medea, and Cleopatra—and forgoing Ovid's epistolary form, as had Chaucer, Drayton wrote his poem in the form of letters to and from such women as Eleanor Cobham, Rosamond Clifford, and Alice, countess of Salisbury—that is, women involved in the political history of England, usually as royal wives or mistresses, although in the case of Lady Jane Grey, as the victim of political intrigue.

Drayton's changes are instructive. All the letters of the *Heroides* are purportedly those of the women, mostly complaints by women abandoned by their consorts, with Ovid avoiding monotony through the exercise of his considerable psychological insight. Drayton, who much preferred to build situations involving the interactions of characters, hit upon the idea of an exchange of letters between the man and the woman, with sometimes hers coming first, sometimes his. Notorious royal mistresses such as Rosamond Clifford and Jane Shore had spoken in verse before, but chiefly in the moralizing vein of that stodgy Elizabethan perennial, *A*

*Mirror for Magistrates* (1555, 1559, 1563), in which the ghosts of people fallen from high place appear for the purpose of lugubriously advising and admonishing the reader. Thomas Churchyard ends his account of *Shore's Wife* (1563), for example: "A mirror make of my great overthrow;/ Defy this world and all his wanton ways;/ Beware by me that spent so ill her days." Drayton's Jane, on the other hand, concludes her letter to Edward IV: "thou art become my fate,/ And mak'st me love even in the midst of hate." He refuses to subordinate his lovers to an abstract moral, though, to be sure, he has selected them in the first place as manifestations of the national spirit.

## THE BARRONS WARS

Drayton's professionalism drove him to protracted and extensive revisions, and many of the works of his middle period are reworkings of earlier poems. In *The Barrons Wars*, he turns the rime royal of *Mortimeriados* into ottava rima, explaining that although the former had "harmony," the latter possessed "majesty, perfection, and solidity." Drayton aspired to an epic, but he was no Vergil, and *The Barrons Wars*, though an improvement on *Mortimeriados*, was no *Aeneid* (c. 29-19 B.C.E.; English translation, 1553). In other cases, his critics find his "improvements" made in vain, as in his *Poemes Lyrick and Pastorall*, which surely made his contemporary readers wonder why, twenty-seven years after Spenser's *Shepheardes Calendar* (1579), Drayton insisted on reworking old eclogues. As for his modern readers, they generally prefer *Endimion and Phoebe* to the new version, *The Man in the Moon*.

## ODES

*Poemes Lyrick and Pastorall* is nevertheless important for introducing another of Drayton's successful classical adaptations, his odes. A deservedly obscure poet named John Southern had made a few Pindaric odes in the 1580's, but Drayton is the first Englishman to imitate the Horatian type. After acknowledging in his preface both Pindar's triumphant and Anacreon's amorous odes, Drayton intimates a fondness for the "mixed" odes of Horace. Having written in both the Ovidian and the Vergilian manner, Drayton was now treading in the footsteps of a poet notable for understanding and working within his limitations. In contrast to the high-flying poets, Horace compares himself in an ode to a bee gathering nectar on the banks of the Tiber. Eschewing the heroic and the passionate, he concentrates on such themes as moderation, hospitality, friendship, and the propriety of accepting one's fate. Although Drayton did not easily accept his fate as a leftover Elizabethan in the age of James I, he recognized in the Horatian ode the vehicle for a range of expression that had not found utterance in earlier English poetry. What he suggested in his odes, Jonson and the neoclassicists of the new century would exploit more thoroughly.

For the ode to become a recognizable form in English, Drayton had to find an equivalent of Horace's favorite four-line Alcaic and Sapphic stanzas. He wisely avoided the English imitations of Latin quantitative verse which had so intrigued some of the Elizabethans but had defeated all of them except Thomas Campion in a handful of lyrics. Drayton favored a five- or six-line stanza with short lines and prominent rhymes. Coupled with his usual end-stopped lines, the rhymes not only create an effect entirely different from Horace's but also force Drayton into an unnatural syntax marked by ellipses, inversions, and the omission of transitions. English poets had tended to avoid short lines except in song lyrics, preferring the opposite risk of the hexameter line, which Alexander Pope would later compare to a "wounded snake," and the even longer fourteener. Whether Drayton thought of his odes as singable or not, he knew that short lines and obtrusive rhymes had been used most successfully for satiric and humorous purposes, as in Chaucer's "Tale of Sir Thopas" and John Skelton's *Phyllyp Sparowe* (c. 1508).

Except in a few instances, such as "The Sacrifice to Apollo," where he fell into a too self-consciously Horatian posture, Drayton avoided servility in the ode as he had in *Englands Heroicall Epistles*. In the odes on Agincourt and the peak, in "To the New Year" and "To the Virginian Voyage," the reader senses an early seventeenth century Englishman responding directly to his milieu as Horace had responded to Rome in the first century B.C.E. The similarity between the two poets, less a formal or temperamental likeness than a kind of equivalent spirit grounded in love for land and landscape, kept Drayton from sounding like an "ancient." He did not have to praise Horace's Bandusian fountain

and Caecubian wine, for he had "Buxton's delicious baths" and good "strong ale" to celebrate. The whole "Ode Written on the Peak" is built on the proposition that England is as worthy of an ode as anything in ancient Rome. Drayton's classicism, then, takes the form of an Englishman singing his own island in a diction and rhythm assertively Anglo-Saxon. Before Drayton, Englishmen, uncomfortable with Horace's Epicureanism, had valued chiefly the Horace of the moral *Satires* (35, 30 B.C.E.; English translation, 1567) and *Epistles* (c. 20-15 B.C.E.; English translation, 1567). Having learned from Drayton, the later Cavalier poets achieved (not without some loss of intellectual vigor) the gracefulness and urbanity that Drayton had not caught in their common master's odes.

## POLY-OLBION

Drayton expressed the same patriotic convictions in a much more expansive way in his magnum opus, *Poly-Olbion*, on which he had been working for many years before its initial publication in 1612. His fondness for myth, the countryside, and antiquarian lore come together in this leisurely survey of England and Wales in which the favorite mode of travel is the river. The poem owes something to the researches of an early Tudor antiquarian, John Leland, and to Drayton's learned contemporary, William Camden. If his preoccupation with rivers needs a model, Spenser, whose *Colin Clouts Come Home Againe* (1595), *Prothalamion* (1596), and the now lost *Epithalamion* (1595) all feature rivers, probably is the man.

To assist the reader through his gigantic poem, Drayton employed the services of another learned man, John Selden, who wrote explanatory notes, and an engraver who furnished maps for each section of the poem. Not at all confident that the work would find a ready audience in what he called "this lunatic age," Drayton wrote an introduction excoriating those who would "rather read the fantasies of foreign invention than to see the rarities and history of their own country delivered by a true native muse." Ten years later, having "met with barbarous ignorance and base detraction" in the reception of the first edition, he nevertheless republished the poem with twelve additional sections.

Few readers today negotiate the full *Poly-Olbion*, but it is a pleasant, if sometimes prosaic, journey. Drayton probably did not visit all the localities described in the poem, and it is unlikely that the reader ignorant of his Warwickshire origin could guess it from this poem. It is an interesting section of the poem, however, detailing at length the Forest of Arden, which Shakespeare had used as the setting for much of *As You Like It* (pr. c. 1599-1600). There may be fools in Shakespeare's Arden, but Drayton's is populated by innumerable birds, beasts, hunters, and a happy hermit who has fled "the sottish purblind world." He also traces the several little rivers that flow into the Avon, which he follows past Stratford, though without mentioning Shakespeare. In this poem, Drayton is more interested in the past, and he tells the legend of Guy of Warwick, who is credited with defeating the Danish champion Colbrand and thus turning away the tenth century invasion. Like many historical poems written in late Tudor and early Stuart England, this one shows the transition from the earlier uncritical acceptance of myth and legend to a more skeptical attitude. The legends still have vitality, but the scholars of the seventeenth century—Selden, Francis Bacon, and the earl of Clarendon—cast increasing doubt on their truthfulness and value.

## IDEA

While at work on *Poly-Olbion*, Drayton was also overhauling his sonnets, now titled simply *Idea*. In this work, his tireless revising paid off handsomely, for by 1619, he had added and rewritten forty-three new sonnets to go with twenty early ones, and the sequence had become a masterpiece. By this time, Donne, the first of the great Metaphysical poets, was writing love poems in other forms and reserving the sonnet for religious purposes, while Jonson and his tribe scorned the sonnet and other nonclassical forms altogether. As a poet born in the decade before Donne and Jonson, Drayton had been enough of a working Elizabethan (and enough of a conservative) to prefer building on the accomplishments of that age. In this endeavor, however, he was alone; all the other Elizabethan poets of consequence—Sidney, Marlowe, Shakespeare, Sir Walter Raleigh, Daniel, all the people he might have wished to please, it must have seemed—were dead. Only Drayton worked on, increasingly testy and ill-humored in his prefaces but as devoted as ever to the perfection of poems of a kind that had fallen out of favor.

As far back as Sidney, English sonneteers had presented the lover as a sometimes comic figure. Despite certain resemblances to his creator, Sidney's Astrophel is a character at whom readers are sometimes encouraged to laugh. In *Idea*, Drayton's speaker even seems to laugh at himself. In the splendid Number 61, "Since there's no help, come let us kiss and part," the speaker, after asserting in a matter-of-fact tone and words chiefly of one syllable—the first thirty-three words, in fact, being monosyllables exclusively—that nothing but a complete break makes any sense, that he is willing to "shake hands" on it, reverts in the third quatrain to a sentimental deathbed scene of love personified, and closes with a couplet the irony of which the speaker surely recognizes: "Now if thou would'st, when all have given him over,/ From death to life, thou might'st him yet recover." The lover in these poems knows that love and passion are silly and that their stylized portrayal in language is sillier yet, but he also knows that to reject them outright is to reject life and the art that attempts to portray it. The perspective here is Horatian: a delicate balance, a golden mean, between involvement and detachment. The poet has mastered his form: He writes English sonnets which frequently retain the capacity of the Italian sonnet for a turning point just past the middle as well as a distinct closing couplet that sometimes brings another, unexpected turn.

Drayton's wit is on display in Number 21, about a "witless gallant" who has asked for and received from the speaker a sonnet to send to his own love. The speaker, however, has written it "as fast as e'er my pen could trot"—just the opposite of the correct, painstaking way. The third quatrain reports that the lady "doted on the dolt beyond all measure," the rueful couplet sadly concluding: "Yet by my troth, this fool his love obtains,/ And I lose you, for all my wit and pains." The reader understands that the "gallant's" success was a hollow one; Idea, whose name is Plato's word for that highest type of beauty and goodness, of which all ordinary earthly manifestations are but shadows, is worth the inevitable disappointments.

In Drayton's very Elizabethan sonnets, the reader comes upon many of the witty, argumentative ploys so characteristic of Donne and Jonson. For Drayton, such wit amounted to a perfecting of the now largely abandoned sonnet cycle in which he saw further possibilities for variety within unity, flexibility within firmness. He is not being Metaphysical or neoclassical, only bringing out the latent potential of the earlier poetry, while displaying in the process a wit, irony, and plainness of diction more characteristic of the new poetry that he was supposedly rejecting.

## THE BATTAILE OF AGINCOURT AND ELEGIES UPON SUNDRY OCCASIONS

With the publication of the complete *Poly-Olbion*, Drayton's most elaborate tribute to the native land he had been praising so long, the poet, now entering his sixtieth year, might have been expected to taper off. Instead, he brought out two books composed primarily of previously unpublished poems. The first, named for a long historical poem, *The Battaile of Agincourt* (no improvement on his "ballad" and not to be confused with it), included another Horatian genre, the complimentary verse epistle, one of which was the letter to Henry Reynolds revealing his early desire to be a poet. He may not have been the first in the field, for Donne and Jonson were also writing them, but his *Elegies upon Sundry Occasions*, as he called them, are more carefully adapted to the "occasions," suggesting that his primary aim was communication at once functional, artful, and expressive of genuine feeling. In this aim, he came closer to the spirit of his Roman Master than did other poets of the time, whose style and tone tend to vary little with the occasion and the identity of the recipient.

## SHEPHEARDS SIRENA

Two poems in *The Battaile of Agincourt*, *Shepheards Sirena* and *Nimphidia*, illustrate Drayton's final lyrical stage. *Shepheards Sirena* sings more purely than any of his earlier pastorals. Sirena dwells in the vicinity of the River Trent, here transmuted into a domestic Arcadia. While vestiges of the competitions and complaints of early English pastoral remain, the best part of the poem is its 170 liquid lines in praise of the lady—praise that never slides into the convolutions of Jacobean wit.

## NIMPHIDIA

*Nimphidia* is quite different. It can be classified roughly as mock-heroic. Pigwiggen, in love with Queen Mab, entices her away from King Oberon and chal-

lenges the latter to a duel for the "dear lady's honor." Having secured seconds and gone through all necessary preliminaries, the champions hack briskly away at each other, though, when the contest threatens to get too bloody, Prosorpina administers the Lethe water that makes them forget their enmity entirely. At the end, the King and Queen, as if nothing had happened, are sitting down to a good fairy meal. That the poem has a satirical purpose is indicated by Drayton's name-dropping: Sir Thopas, Pantagruel, and Don Quixote are all mentioned. The poem brims with parodies of heroic clichés. The emphasis, though, is on fun and fantasy in a delicate miniature world made of spiders' legs and butterflies' wings. Its eighty-eight tripping stanzas, rhyming *aaabcccb* (tetrameter except for the *b* lines, which are a syllable shorter with feminine rhymes), "carry the vein of Sir Thopas into the world of Oberon," as Oliver Elton puts it in *Michael Drayton: A Critical Study* (1966).

## THE MUSES ELIZIUM

Drayton's final volume, issued thirty-nine years after his first and only one year before his death, includes three long "divine poems" on Noah, Moses, and David, but it is best remembered for its title poem, *The Muses Elizium*. Elizium, a "paradise on earth" whose name honors the queen who had now been dead twenty-seven years, can be seen as a nostalgic retreat from the realities of a nation now entered on the "Eleven Years' Tyranny" of Charles I. Made up of ten eclogues, or "nymphals," the work is, like *Shepheards Sirena*, almost purely lyrical, full of flowery meadows and crystal springs, with occasional reminders of the prosaic real world.

One of these occurs in the tenth nymphal. Two nymphs discover a "monster" whom the shepherd Corbilus recognizes as an old satyr, refugee from "Felicia," which is the everyday world, now destroyed by "beastly men." After a suitable opportunity to lament the denuding of the forest by crass builders, the satyr is invited to "live in bliss" in Elizium until such time as the true Felicians reclaim the land. Thus, in his old age, Drayton metamorphoses his conservatism, love of the land, displeasure with the world of 1630, and perhaps—if readers take the satyr to represent the author—a disposition toward a bit of humor at his own expense, into a calm, dispassionate poem whose very preface is, for a change, sweet-tempered. In this last stage, Drayton has receded from the Stuart milieu to the extent of cultivating a pure, "irrelevant" art. The attitude is that of an old man, but one who has ceased to rage; the lyric freshness is that of a young poet not yet fully aware of the indifferent children of the earth whom Drayton has not forgotten.

With its delight in plain, shaggy, rural life, *The Muses Elizium* is likely to remind readers of classical pastoral more of Theocritus than of the more polished poet of the Roman Empire, Vergil. The style here is not of the Greek or Roman Golden Ages, but of the Elizabethan. Drayton had outlived his age, but this poem has outlived the seventeenth century strife in the midst of which it seemed so old-fashioned.

OTHER MAJOR WORK

PLAY: *The First Part of the True and Honorable Historie of the Life of Sir John Old-Castle the Good Lord Cobham*, pr. 1599.

BIBLIOGRAPHY

Brink, Jean R. *Michael Drayton Revisited*. Boston: Twayne, 1990. Offers an excellent introduction to Drayton's life and works. The first chapter substantially revises Drayton's biography. The other chapters deal chronologically with each of his major poems, and the concluding chapter discusses Drayton's impact on later writers. Includes chronology, notes, and a useful select bibliography.

Brooks-Davies, Douglas, ed. *Silver Poets of the Sixteenth Century: Wyatt, Surrey, Ralegh, Philip Sidney, Mary Sidney, Michael Drayton, and Sir John Davies*. Rutland, Vt.: Charles E. Tuttle, 1992. Examines work by Drayton and other sixteenth century poets.

Corbett, Margery, and Ronald Lightbown. *The Comely Frontispiece: The Emblematic Title-Page in England, 1550-1660*. London: Routledge & Kegan Paul, 1979. In this collection of essays, the thirteenth chapter is devoted to the unusual frontispiece to Drayton's *Poly-Olbion*, his lengthy poetic description of the geography and history of Great Britain. An interpretation is offered of the engraving of Great Britain as a woman seated on an imperial throne. Beautifully illustrated.

Curran, John E. "The History Never Written: Bards, Druids, and the Problem of Antiquarianism in 'Poly Olbion.'" *Renaissance Quarterly* 51, no. 2 (Summer, 1998): 498-528. A study of the response of Drayton to the rise of antiquarianism as seen in his depictions of bards and druids in this poem.

Galbraith, David. *Architectonics of Imitation in Spenser, Daniel, and Drayton*. Toronto, Ont.: University of Toronto Press, 2000. Galbraith examines Samuel Daniel's *Civile Warres*, Edmund Spenser's *The Faerie Queene*, and Drayton's *Poly-Olbion* (1612-1622) to explore the boundaries between history and poetry.

Harner, James L. *Samuel Daniel and Michael Drayton: A Reference Guide*. Boston: G. K. Hall, 1980. Approximately one-half of this bibliography is devoted to books and articles written about Drayton. The entries are arranged chronologically beginning with the seventeenth century and concluding with the twentieth. The annotations are reliable and extremely useful.

*Robert P. Ellis*

# WILLIAM DRUMMOND OF HAWTHORNDEN

**Born:** Hawthornden, Scotland; December 13, 1585
**Died:** Hawthornden, Scotland; December 4, 1649

PRINCIPAL POETRY

*Teares, on the Death of Moeliades*, 1613
*Poems*, 1616
*Forth Feasting*, 1617
*Flowres of Sion*, 1623
*The Entertainment*, 1633
*To the Exequies*, 1638

OTHER LITERARY FORMS

William Drummond of Hawthornden's only prose work published during his lifetime was *A Midnight's*

*Trance* (1619), a meditation on death. In its revised form, it was appended to *Flowres of Sion* as *A Cypresse Grove*. His *The History of Scotland from the Year 1423 Until the Year 1542*, his longest piece of prose, appeared posthumously in 1655. This volume also included a section of Drummond's letters, a reprinting of *A Cypresse Grove*, and "Memorials of State," a sample of the political pamphlets Drummond had written (but never published) in the two decades preceding his death. The 1711 edition of Drummond's works remains the most complete collection of the prose; in this edition "Irene: Or, A Remonstrance for Concord, Amity, and Love Amongst His Majesty's Subjects," "Skiamachia," and other political pieces first appeared. Here, too, were first published notes on the famous conversations between Drummond and Ben Jonson.

In 1831, David Laing published *Extracts from the Hawthornden Manuscripts*, which includes "A Brief Account of the Hawthornden Manuscripts in the Possession of the Society of Antiquaries of Scotland, with Extracts, Containing Several Unpublished Letters with Poems of William Drummond of Hawthornden" (*Transactions of the Society of Antiquaries of Scotland*, Volume 5). In the second part of that volume, published in 1832, Laing presented the first complete edition of the *Notes by William Drummond, of Conversations with Ben Jonson*. Subsequent editions of Drummond's poetry have included manuscript material, but the prose remains uncollected.

ACHIEVEMENTS

By 1616, William Drummond of Hawthornden was known as the Scottish Petrarch. His first published poem went through three editions within a year, and the 1616 edition of the *Poems* quickly went into a second impression. John Milton read Drummond with approbation, and Milton's nephew, Edward Phillips, Drummond's first editor, in the preface to the 1656 edition of the poetry, called Drummond "a genius the most polite and verdant that ever the Scottish nation produced," adding "that neither Tasso, nor Guarini, nor any of the most neat and refined can challenge to themselves any advantage above him." For Charles Lamb, a century and a half later, "The sweetest names, and which carry a perfume in the mention, are, Kit

Marlowe, Drayton, Drummond of Hawthornden, and Cowley."

What Alexander Pope observed of the last of these "sweet" poets, however—"Who now reads Cowley?"—is also applicable to Drummond. Though he was the first Scottish poet to produce a substantial body of poetry in English and though much of that poetry demonstrates technical virtuosity, Drummond does not command many readers today. In large part, this neglect has resulted from his theory of composition. Jonson warned him "that oft a man's modesty made a fool of his wit." Drummond's poetic modesty led him to translate and adapt the works of others instead of applying himself to invention. His poetry, therefore, while skillful, is rarely original, and, as Samuel Johnson stated, "No man ever became great by imitation." Drummond's skill with language and the details of prosody guarantee him a secure place among the second rank of Renaissance English poets, but his inability or refusal to go beyond such models as Sir Philip Sidney, Pierre de Ronsard, Petrarch, Battista Marino, and Baldassare Castiglione bars him from the first.

His history of the first five Jameses, like his poetry, is stylistically sound but derivative in content. Although much praised by Drummond's contemporaries and reprinted five times, it has not been reissued since 1711. Laing commented more than a century ago in *Archaeológia Scotiá* (Volume 5) that the work is "only of subsidiary importance," and so it remains. *A Cypresse Grove* may have influenced Sir Thomas Browne's *Hydriotaphia: Urne-Buriall* (1658), but along with virtually all Drummond's other prose works, it has fallen into neglect after enjoying a contemporary popularity. For most students of early seventeenth century British literature, Drummond owes his reputation to a prose work, though it is one that he merely transcribed and that was never published in his lifetime. *Notes of Ben Jonson's Conversations with William Drummond of Hawthornden* (1842), a record of Jonson's comments on himself and his contemporaries—and hence an invaluable primary source for literary historians—is the best known of Drummond's writings today. It is perhaps fitting that a man who shunned originality should owe his fame almost entirely to his transcription of the pronouncements of another.

BIOGRAPHY

The eldest son of John Drummond and Susannah Fowler, William Drummond was born on December 13, 1585, at Hawthornden, some seven miles southeast of Edinburgh. In 1590, Drummond's father was appointed gentleman-usher to King James VI; about this time, too, his uncle, William Fowler, became private secretary to Queen Anne. Drummond thus grew up in a court dedicated to literary pursuits. James VI was a poet, and William Fowler translated Petrarch's *Trionfi* (1470; *Tryumphs*, 1565; also known as *Triumphs*, 1962) and composed original verses as well. Such surroundings must have stimulated Drummond's own literary inclinations.

After taking a degree from the University of Edinburgh in July, 1605, Drummond set out for France to study law at Bourges. During the next four years, Drummond maintained a list of his readings: Of the numerous volumes he read, only one concerns jurisprudence—the *Institutiones* (533; *Justinian's Institutes*, 1915) of Justinian. Other volumes deal in part with religion. Although Drummond was hardly a prejudiced sectarian, his poetry reflects a deep religiosity. Most of Drummond's reading at this time was, however, secular; during his years abroad, he familiarized himself with the major works of the Renaissance, both English and Continental, which later served as the models for his own writings.

By the time he returned to Scotland in late 1608, he was intimately acquainted with the best of Spanish, French, Italian, and English literatures. These he not only read but also acquired: An inventory of his library in 1611 includes more than five hundred titles. This inventory suggests again that Drummond's interest in the law was less than overwhelming, for only twenty-four of those books deal with that field.

Fortunately for Drummond, he was not obliged to rely on the law for a living. On August 21, 1610, "about Noone," according to Drummond's "Memorials," his father died, leaving him laird of Hawthornden. Here Drummond remained for the rest of his life, reading and writing "farre from the madding Worldlings hoarse Discords" (Sonnet 43, part 1, *Poems*).

The death of Prince Henry in November, 1612, inspired Drummond's first published work, *Teares, on the Death of Moeliades*. Shortly afterward, perhaps as early as the next year, another volume appeared, consisting of a sonnet sequence in two parts. In the first section, Drummond speaks conventionally of the pains of love, and in the second, he mourns his mistress's death. Although both Dante and Petrarch had written of their dead mistresses, no one in English had yet done so. Drummond boasted that he was "The First in the Isle that did celebrate a mistress dead."

Life seems to have imitated art in this case. Drummond apparently had fallen in love with a Miss Cunningham in 1614 and had become engaged to her. Shortly before their marriage—but after the completion of most of the sonnets in *Poems*—Miss Cunningham died. Except for his abandonment of love poetry for religious verse, Drummond's writings do not reflect this personal tragedy, but he remained unmarried until 1632, and the woman he did marry—Elizabeth Logan—attracted him in part because she reminded him of his first love.

When the former James VI of Scotland, then James I of England, returned to his native land after a fourteen-year absence, Drummond welcomed him with the effusive encomium *Forth Feasting*, in which he imagines the river's rejoicing to receive its monarch. In general, the poem pleased the king, though his courtiers, and even James, questioned one line: "No Guard so sure as Love unto a Crowne" (line 246). The sentiment was hardly original with Drummond, going back to Aristotle's *Politica* (c. 335-323 B.C.E.; *Politics*, 1598). The Stuarts, however, preferred to govern through fear. In his political pamphlets of the 1630's and 1640's Drummond would expand his view, recommending love and mercy to James's successor.

The following year, Scotland received another visitor—the prince of poets, Ben Jonson. Jonson probably came to Scotland in search of literary material, but in late December, 1618, and early January of the next year, he spent several weeks at Hawthornden conversing with Drummond. It is this visit that has kept Drummond's name alive, for Drummond kept careful notes of Jonson's observations. (The original manuscript apparently has not survived, but a transcription by the antiquary Sir Robert Sibbald has preserved Jonson's remarks.) These observations contain much material about Jonson himself as well as about his contemporaries and so are invaluable to the student of the period, offering information not available elsewhere. They also suggest why Drummond and Jonson ceased corresponding within six months of the latter's return to England. Drummond's notes justify his comment that Jonson was "a great lover and praiser of himself, a contemner and Scorner of others."

*Flowres of Sion*, a collection of religious poetry, appeared in 1623; in 1630 Drummond published a revised edition of this work. In the interval between these editions, Drummond's thoughts turned for a time to earthly matters: He apparently sired three illegitimate children, and in 1627, he received a letter patent for sixteen military and naval inventions. There is no evidence that he ever went beyond theorizing about these weapons of destruction, but his very proposals suggest a concern with the Thirty Years' War raging on the Continent. The "madding Worldlings hoarse Discords" could penetrate even secluded Hawthornden. More consonant with the tenor of Drummond's temper, in 1626, he donated a large portion of his library—more than five hundred volumes—to his alma mater.

By 1633, when Charles I visited Edinburgh, Drummond was regarded as the unofficial poet laureate of Scotland. For the royal visit, he wrote *The Entertainment*, a collection of poetry and prose. As in *Forth Feasting*, the praise is lavish. At the same time, just as *Forth Feasting* had advised James I on the proper way to rule, so *The Entertainment* cautions Charles to rule by love rather than by force and to avoid alienating his subjects through the imposition of new taxes or the creation of court favorites.

Unhappily for Charles I and England, Drummond's warnings went unheeded. Instead of attempting to win the love of Scotland, the king alienated the country by attempting to impose Episcopal rites on the Presbyterian kirk. In 1638, Scottish Presbyterians replied with the National League and Covenant to oppose liturgical alterations, and after much negotiation, Charles yielded. "Irene," a work never published during Drummond's lifetime though circulated in manuscript, urged both parties to abandon the quarrel. Drummond criticized the Covenanters for seeking to overthrow the natural order of society by rebelling against the king, but he also warned Charles not to pursue a harsh policy to-

*William Drummond of Hawthornden* (Hulton Archive/Getty Images)

ward his subjects: "The drawing of your sword against them shall be the drawing of it against yourself; instead of triumphs, you shall obtain nothing but sad exequies and mournful funerals."

The struggle did, of course, continue. Though a Royalist, Drummond signed the Covenant in 1639 to escape being "mocked, hissed, plundered, banished hence," as he expressed his plight in one of his late poems. In another unpublished tract, he nevertheless prophesied that civil war would lead to "one who will name himself PROTECTOR of the Liberty of the Kingdom. He shall surcharge the people with greater miseries than ever before they did suffer . . . and in the end shall essay to make himself King." Drummond's Royalist sentiments surfaced again when the Parliamentary leader John Pym died; Drummond's poem on the occasion does not suggest regret:

> When Pime last night descended into Hell,
> Ere hee his coupes of Lethe did carouse,
> What place is this (said hee) I pray mee tell?
> To whom a Divell: This is the lower house.

In addition to composing political tracts urging moderation, Drummond was working on a history of Scotland during the reigns of the first five Jameses. He had begun his research at least as early as 1633, perhaps as an outgrowth of genealogical research he had undertaken for his kinsman John Drummond, second earl of Perth. James I of Scotland, with whom *The History of Scotland from the Year 1423 Until the Year 1542* begins, was the son of Annabella Drummond and so related to the earl. This work, too, shows Drummond's desire for religious toleration and peace. Drummond also wrote "A Speech on Toleration" for one of the privy councillors of James V, urging the monarch to permit religious freedom. Drummond, however, sensed that his calls for moderation would go unheeded; immediately after this speech Drummond notes, "But the King followed not this opinione."

By the time of his death on December 4, 1649, Drummond had witnessed the fulfillment of his direst predictions. He was buried in the church at Lasswade. When he had been near death in 1620, he had written a sonnet to Sir William Alexander, a friend and fellow poet: "I conjure Thee . . ./ To grave this short Remembrance on my Grave./ Heere *Damon* lyes, whose Songes did some-time grace/ The murmuring Eske, may Roses shade the place." In October, 1893, a memorial with this inscription was at last erected over Drummond's grave.

## ANALYSIS

In an undated letter to Arthur Johnston, court physician to Charles I and himself a poet, William Drummond of Hawthornden expressed his theory of poetic composition. Conservative in his literary as in his political philosophy, Drummond objected to the innovations of John Donne and his followers: "What is not like the ancients and conforme to those Rules which hath been agreed unto by all tymes, maye (indeed) be some thing like unto poesie, but it is no more Poesie than a Monster is a Man." Thus, Drummond valued imitation over invention. He would not seek to create new poetic forms or to develop original themes. For Drummond, as for Pope, the aim of poetry was to give fresh expression to old ideas. The result in Drummond's case is a body of work adapted from classical and Renaissance

sources, elegantly phrased and carefully crafted but lacking the emotion and invention that elevate excellent versifying to the level of first-rate poetry.

## TEARES, ON THE DEATH OF MOELIADES

Drummond's first published piece, *Teares, on the Death of Moeliades*, exemplifies the poet's lifelong habits of composition and reveals his skill as a craftsperson and his techniques of adaptation. According to L. E. Kastner in his 1913 edition of Drummond's poetry, the model for this elegy is one for Basilius in Sir Philip Sidney's *Arcadia* (1590, 1593, 1598). Kastner also points out various specific borrowings from Sidney's poem. Thus, Sidney writes, "O Hyacinth let AI be on thee still"; Drummond changes this line only slightly: "O Hyacinthes, for ay your AI keepe still" (line 127). Drummond's lines "Stay Skie thy turning Course, and now become/ A stately Arche, unto the Earth his Tombe" (lines 137-138) echo Sidney's "And well methinks becomes this vaulty sky/ A stately tomb to cover him deceased." Other lines are drawn from *Astrophel and Stella* (1591) and from Sonnet 16 of *Aurora* (1604) by Sir William Alexander. The poem is full of classical allusions, and the consolation, beginning with line 143, suggests Socrates' vision of heaven in Plato's *Phaedōn* (399-390 B.C.E.; *Phaedo*, 1675).

Despite all these borrowings, however, the poem is decidedly Drummond's rather than Sidney's or Alexander's. Drummond has transposed Sidney's lament into iambic pentameter couplets, a verse form which he handles effectively. Aware of the dangers of falling into singsong monotony, Drummond repeatedly alters the position of the caesura; in the first three lines it occurs after the third, sixth, and fourth syllables respectively. He also alters the iamb. The poem begins with a spondee ("O Heavens!"), as do lines 9 and 19; line 23 begins with a trochee. A potentially monotonous emphasis on the rhyme-words is overcome through frequent enjambment: "That (in a Palsey) quakes to finde so soone/ Her Lover set" (lines 33-34); "A Youth more brave, pale Troy with trembling Walles/ Did never see" (lines 61-62).

Another characteristic evident in this poem is Drummond's musicality. Some of his poetry is clearly intended to be sung, and he was a competent lutanist. Here the refrain—apparently original—repeats the liquid *l* and *r* and combines these with the long *e* and *o* sounds to infuse an appropriately watery sound (since the poet is addressing water spirits) as well as a gentle melancholy tone: "Moeliades sweet courtly Nymphes deplore,/ From Thuly to Hydapses pearlie Shore." (Less happily, this refrain reveals Drummond's fondness for inversion, which occasionally renders a line difficult to decipher.)

Even when he borrows, Drummond frequently improves a verse. He turns Sidney's "I never drank of Aganippe well;/ Nor never did in shade of Tempe sit" into "Chaste Maides which haunt fair Aganippe Well,/ And you in Tempes sacred Shade who dwell" (lines 97-98). The long *u* sounds here, coupled with "haunt," do indeed suggest the "doleful Plaints" that the poet is requesting of the nymphs. Again, Sidney's line about the hyacinths is not much altered, but Drummond does pun on the "AI" that the hyacinth supposedly spells. The sky is to serve as a tomb for both Basilius and Moeliades, but Drummond enriches his couplet by introducing the Copernican worldview of a turning rather than a stationary heaven. (Drummond's awareness of the New Science is evident again in *A Cypresse Grove*.)

Drummond's love of natural beauty is evident even as he asks for that beauty to be lessened in mourning: "Delicious *Meades*, whose checkred *Plaine* foorth brings,/ White, golden, azure Flowers, which once were Kings" (lines 121-122); "Queene of the Fields, whose Blush makes blushe the *Morne*,/ Sweet *Rose*" (lines 125-126); "In silver Robe the *Moone*, the *Sunne* in Gold" (line 160). The language is lush, suggesting Edmund Spenser and Sidney. At the same time, the description is general; here is no Romantic nature worship, no minute Wordsworthian observation.

The immortality that Drummond anticipates is decidedly Christian, but it is also Neoplatonic. In *Teares, on the Death of Moeliades* Drummond portrays Heaven as the abode of perfection, where "other sumptuous Towres" excel "our poore Bowres" (lines 171-172), where songs are sweetest, where all is immutable; he describes God as the supreme exemplar of love and beauty, which those on earth can never truly experience. This Platonism, too, recurs throughout Drummond's poetry.

*Teares, on the Death of Moeliades* is a tissue of allusions, adaptations, and direct borrowings of phrases and ideas. Still, the poem as a whole is distinctly Drummond's in its techniques and themes. Hence, when Drummond turned from an elegy to a sonnet sequence, the poetry did not assume very different characteristics. One might be hard pressed to find the author of "The Extasie" in "Death Be Not Proud," but one would have no difficulty in recognizing the author of *Teares, on the Death of Moeliades* in *Poems*, despite their disparate subjects.

### DEATH

*Teares, on the Death of Moeliades* is as characteristic of Drummond in its themes as in its technique. Drummond's last published poem, like his first, deals with death. He boasted of being the first to write a sonnet sequence in English on the death of a mistress, and the only prose piece he published during his lifetime is an extended meditation on death. The early seventeenth century was obsessed with this subject; yet even those who wrote most eloquently on the theme published on other subjects as well. Not so Drummond—even his love poems are full of the imagery of graves, grief, and death. Clearly the subject was congenial to him.

Related to Drummond's love of death is a contempt for this world. This theme, too, is conventional, yet even before Drummond was imitating and adapting poetry, he wrote from France to Sir George Keith (February 12, 1607), "And truly considering all our actions, except those which regard the service and adoration of God Almighty, they are either to be lamented or laughed at." In his lament for the death of Prince Henry, he presents the moral that he will repeat in numerous poems: "O fading Hopes! O short-while-lasting Joy!/ Of Earth-borne Man, which one Houre can destroy!" (lines 9-10). In his elegy on the death of Jane, countess of Perth, he laments that "fairest Things thus soonest have their End" (line 10). Even in *The Entertainment*, a splendid celebration of temporal power and magnificence, Drummond tells Charles I, "On gorgeous rayments, womanising toyes,/ The workes of wormes, and what a Moth destroyes,/ The Maze of fooles, thou shalt no treasure spend,/ Thy charge to immortality shall tend" (iv, 31-34).

## POEMS

Like *Teares, on the Death of Moeliades*, Drummond's *Poems* (divided into two parts) are heavily indebted to Sidney. Where Sidney celebrates Stella, Drummond sings of Auristella. Kastner notes that Sonnet 27 (part 1) is reminiscent of Sidney's Sonnet 74 in *Astrophel and Stella*, and Drummond's Sonnet 5 is reminiscent of Sidney's Sonnet 30. The sequence also reveals Drummond's intimate knowledge of Italian, French, and Spanish models. The very form is of course traditional, though by 1616 the sonnet sequence was a dying, if not a dead, form. Drummond's use of this poetic model is yet another reflection of his desire to copy the best models instead of striking out on his own.

Drummond invariably ends each sonnet with a two-line summary in the manner of the English rather than the Italian form. Otherwise, however, he is flexible in both rhyme scheme and structure. Sonnet 24 (part 1) has a rhyme scheme of *abab baba cdcd ee*. Two sonnets later, one finds *abba cddc effe gg*, and in the very next sonnet the pattern is different still—*abba abba cdcd ee*. Sonnet 31 (part 1) consists of an octet and sestet in the Italian mode (though still with the concluding couplet); Sonnet 16 has three quatrains and a couplet in the English manner.

The lush language and musicality of *Teares, on the Death of Moeliades* are even more fully realized in *Poems*, aided by the use of feminine rhymes not present in the elegy. Song I (part 1) describes a luxuriant landscape. Often rich description appears in conjunction with an unusual word, as in Sonnet 17 (part 1), "The silver Flouds in pearlie Channells flow,/ The late-bare Woods greene Anadeams doe weare" (lines 3-4)—"anadeam" had entered the language only about ten years earlier. A bit later Drummond writes, "With Roses here *Shee* stellified the Ground" (line 7, Sonnet 23, part 1), and he writes of "Phoebus in his Chaire/ Ensaffroning Sea and Aire" (lines 39-40, Song 2, part 1). This love of exotic diction leads him in at least two instances to new coinings; Drummond's is the only use of "deflourish'd" noted by the *Oxford English Dictionary* ("Deflourish'd *Mead* where is your heavenly Hue?"—line 9, Sonnet 45, part 1) and the same authority lists as the first use of "disgarland" his "Thy Lockes disgarland" (line 90, Song 1, part 2). The descriptions, though rich, are nevertheless general; the landscape is merely a luxurious background for the human actions occurring there.

As in *Teares, on the Death of Moeliades*, Drummond repeatedly invokes mythology. In Song 1 (part 1) he invokes Phaeton, Elysian Fields, Venus, Mars, Adonis, and many other mythological figures. His use of mythology is usually conventional. In one instance, though, Drummond does cleverly invert the traditional story. Daphne and Syrinx were both turned into plants to preserve their chastity; Drummond imagines that he sees the process reversed as "three naked Nymphes" emerge from a myrtle (lines 84-86). This reversal of the traditional myths foreshadows a thematic reversal in the poem. Conventionally, the lover praises his mistress's chastity. When Drummond's mistress enters the "Fort of Chastitie," though, he bemoans his fate both asleep and waking.

Such playful invention is all too infrequent in the sonnets, the commonplace lamentations all too frequent. Drummond recognized the artificiality of such writing. In the first of "Galatea's Sonnets," a sequence of five poems that Drummond chose not to publish, a woman rejects Petrarchan conceits:

> I Thinke not love ore thee his wings hath spred,
> Or if that passion hath thy soule opprest,
> Its onlie for some Grecian Mistresse dead,
> Of such old sighs thou dost discharge thy brest.

Occasionally, Drummond can infuse sincerity into those old sighs, as when he regrets his failure to declare his love (Sonnet 23, part 1) or when he praises the green color of his mistress's eyes (Sonnet 18, part 1); neither of these pieces relies on a specific model. Here the emotions are not exaggerated, the incidents quotidian and hence credible. More often, unfortunately, he is willing to tear a passion to tatters. Sonnet 47 (part 1) sounds like a parody from the rude mechanical's *Pyramus and Thisbe* in William Shakespeare's *A Midsummer Night's Dream* (pr. c. 1595-1596): "O Night, clear Night, O darke and gloomie Day!/ O wofull Waking! O Soule-pleasing Sleepe" (lines 1-2). Though this is the most egregious example, there are enough borrowings from Petrarch, Giambattista Marino, Pierre de Ronsard, and others to suggest that Drummond's inspiration for his sonnets was his library rather than Miss Cunningham.

The sonnet sequence ends with a vision corresponding to the dream in Song 1 from part 1. In that earlier song the poet meets his mistress for the first time; in this final song he becomes reconciled to her death. The poem apparently cost Drummond much effort, for among his manuscripts is a fragment of eight lines translated from Passerat, apparently a draft of this piece. Here one can trace the movement from literal translation to adaptation. The eight lines have been expanded to nineteen, the natural setting elaborated, and phrases repeated to heighten the melancholy musicality.

As the poem begins, Drummond's mistress appears to urge him to abandon his grief. Her arguments begin with stoical reflections: "Was shee not mortall borne? (line 45); "Why wouldst thou Here longer wish to bee?" (line 75). With line 93, the argument moves to Platonism, echoing the consolation in *Teares, on the Death of Moeliades*. Whereas *Teares, on the Death of Moeliads* ended with Platonic idealism, however, the song proceeds to a third stage (lines 181-240), explicitly Christian, exhorting the lover to think of heaven's joys rather than earth's sorrows.

### A CYPRESSE GROVE AND FLOWRES OF SION

*A Cypresse Grove*, which Drummond appended to his next collection of poetry, *Flowres of Sion*, retraces these three stages. Indeed, the prose meditation on death is little more than an expansion of the song, with repetitions of phrases as well as ideas. To cite but one example, in the "Song," Drummond writes, "We bee not made for Earth, though here wee come,/ More than the *Embryon* for the Mothers Wombe" (lines 178-179). In *A Cypresse Grove*, these lines become "For though hee bee borne on the Earthe, hee is not borne for the Earth, more than the Embryon for the mothers wombe."

In fact, the entire volume of *Flowres of Sion* stems logically from the "song," elaborating on the Christian message that concludes that piece. In his edition of Drummond's writings, R. H. MacDonald notes that *Flowres of Sion* proceeds through the three stages of the religious meditation: Sonnets 1-6 depict the poetry's memory of the evils of this world, Sonnet 7 through Hymn 3 (which treat Christ's birth, life, and

death) present an understanding of Christ's solution to those evils, and the rest of the poems adore God's love and meditate on the follies of this world.

The poetic techniques by now familiar to the reader of Drummond remain evident here: the love of exotic words (such as "Jubeling cries" in Hymn 2, line 49; the *Oxford English Dictionary* notes only a single fifteenth century use of this word), borrowings from numerous sources, luxurious general description, and virtuosity in the handling of the sonnet or couplet form. The themes, too, are familiar—the love of death, contempt for the things of this world, and Christianity heavily tinged with Neoplatonism. This sonnet cycle mirrors Drummond's earlier one; both progress from despair to hope, from the pains of this world to the joys of the next. Here, however, the emphasis is on the latter rather than the former, so that, paradoxically, the sequence focusing on death is less depressing than the one supposedly treating love.

### THE ENTERTAINMENT

In the last twenty-six years of his life, Drummond published only two occasional pieces, *The Entertainment* in 1633 for King Charles's visit to Edinburgh and, five years later, an elegy on the death of the son of his longtime friend and fellow poet, Sir William Alexander.

The first of these works combines prose and poetry in an elaborate tribute to the king. For the poetic sections, Drummond uses the heroic couplet almost exclusively, an apt choice to celebrate a grand event, and as usual he handles the verse form competently. Only one poem does not employ the couplet, instead containing three lines of six syllables followed by two lines of ten in each of the four verse paragraphs. This metrical pattern suggests the Italian *canzone*, the madrigal, and the dramatic chorus. The language is ornate, abounding in such epithets as "The Acidalian Queene" (Venus) and "Leucadian Sythe-bearing Sire" (Saturn). As these epithets suggest, Drummond again invokes mythological allusions, as Endymion, Saturn, Jove, Mars, Venus, and Mercury address Charles. In choosing these particular deities, together with the Sun and Moon, Drummond implies that the entire universe rejoices at Charles's visit. Each of the gods ends his speech with a refrain: "Thus heavens decree, so have ordain'd the Fates," alternating with "Thus heavens ordaine, so doe decree the Fates." Drummond had effectively used this rhetorical device in *Teares, on the Death of Moeliades*; though the refrain here lacks the melody of the earlier one, the slight variation shows a concern for preventing monotony.

Although the excessive flattery is obligatory, it does not lack a hortatory edge. The king is urged to avoid excessive taxation and the raising up of favorites, to aid learning and the arts, and to rule through love rather than through fear. The political message thus anticipates such pamphlets as "Irene."

### A PASTORALL ELEGIE

*The Entertainment* is largely original, only occasionally hinting at other poets. *A Pastorall Elegie*, on the other hand, is virtually a translation of Castiglione's "Alcon"; Drummond even refers to the dead Sir Antony Alexander as Alcon. The highly artificial pastoral form and the lack of originality suggest that Drummond was writing from a sense of obligation to his old friend; there is even less emotion here than in *Teares, on the Death of Moeliades*. The technique is as sound as ever, but only in one place does Drummond surpass his model. Ostensibly unaware of his friend's death, the poet imagines that "the populous City holds him, amongst Harmes/ Of some fierce *Cyclops*, Circe's stronger Charmes" (lines 183-184). These Homeric allusions, absent in Castiglione's poem, suggest that the youth in fact will not return but rather suffer the fate of Odysseus's companions. These references thus foreshadow the poet's discovery of the youth's fate.

During his lifetime Drummond suppressed almost as much poetry as he published. In general, he was a sound editor; few of the pieces published since his death add anything to his reputation. Occasionally, though, one of the posthumous poems demonstrates wit and imagination too often lacking in Drummond's published works. The quatrain on Pym's death quoted earlier is original and clever. The five sonnets of Galatea, supposedly written in response to verses such as those Drummond composed in the first part of *Poems*, wittily undercut the Petrarchan conventions by pointing out their artificiality and logical absurdity. "The Country Maid," though slightly bawdy, is mythopoeic. Drummond's decision not to publish poems such as these may have been less a judgment on their quality than an indication of the kind of literary reputation he wished to cultivate. Less concerned with originality and mythopoesis than with correctness, imitation, and technical virtuosity, Drummond published those works that embodied his poetic ideals. Working with established forms and themes, he was able to make these his own and to find a unique voice. His models rarely led him astray; he produced few bad poems, much competent verse, and a handful of memorable pieces such as the "Song" that closes the second part of the sonnet cycle of *Poems* or his sonnet to Sir William Alexander on his own illness. What Samuel Johnson said of another reclusive poet, Thomas Gray, may also be said of Drummond at his best: "Had [he] written often thus, it had been vain to blame, and useless to praise him."

### OTHER MAJOR WORKS

NONFICTION: *A Midnight's Trance*, 1619 (as *A Cypresse Grove*, 1623); *The History of Scotland from the Year 1423 Until the Year 1542*, 1655; *Notes of Ben Jonson's Conversations with William Drummond of Hawthornden*, 1842.

MISCELLANEOUS: *The Works of William Drummond of Hawthornden*, 1711 (2 volumes).

### BIBLIOGRAPHY

Cummings, Robert. "Drummond's Forth Feasting: A Panegyric for King James in Scotland." *Seventeenth Century* 2, no. 1 (1987): 1-18. Cummings discusses Drummond's panegyric in relation to its tradition and the situation at the time. This article, though on a rather specialized subject, makes a useful addition to earlier critical approaches that stress the poet's sonnets and other short lyrics.

Fogle, French Rowe. *A Critical Study of William Drummond of Hawthornden*. New York: King's Crown Press of Columbia University, 1952. The most useful book on Drummond for the general reader, this critical account examines the poet's development with biographical background where necessary. One appendix lists Drummond's reading and a second describes and excerpts poems in the Hawthornden manuscript. Fogle does not deal with Drummond's prose works or conversations with Ben Jonson.

Grosse, Edmund. *The Jacobean Poets*. 1894. Reprint. Charleston, S.C.: BiblioBazaar, 2009. This classic work by Grosse describes the Jacobean poets, including Drummond.

Masson, David. *Drummond of Hawthornden*. 1873. Reprint. Whitefish, Mont.: Kessinger, 2008. Masson's book, though out of date in many respects, is the fullest account of the events of Drummond's life. It is also one of the more readily available works on Drummond.

Rae, Thomas Ian. "The Political Attitudes of William Drummond of Hawthornden." In *The Scottish Traditions: Essays in Honour of Ronald Gordon Cant*, edited by G. W. S. Barrow. Edinburgh: Scottish Academic Press, 1974. Analyzes Drummond's political writings, with particular emphasis on "Irene." Rae argues that Drummond based his political opinions on abstract (and largely obsolete) ideas of the order of the universe and of society. He illuminates a monarchist, conservative side of Drummond which, though less familiar than the poetic craftsperson side, helps readers to understand the nostalgic nature of his personality.

Severance, Sibyl Lutz. "'Some Other Figure': The Vision of Change in *Flowres of Sion*, 1623." *Spenser Studies: A Renaissance Poetry Annual* 2 (1981): 217-228. Seeing the *Flowres of Sion* sequence as a whole rather than as a series of separate sonnets, Severance points out the importance of Drummond's idea of change (earthly mutability) versus permanence (eternity). The argument depends on a detailed numerological analysis of the sequence.

Spence, G. "The Theism of William Drummond." *Keats-Shelley Review* 14 (2000): 71-83. An examination of theological questions raised by Drummond's poetry.

Wallerstein, Ruth C. "The Style of Drummond of Hawthornden in Its Relation to His Translations." *PMLA* 48 (1933): 1090-1107. This detailed article examines the most important aspects of Drummond's poetic style against the background of his translations. Though somewhat technical for many readers, it remains the only thorough analysis of the poet's technique to be found in a major journal.

*Joseph Rosenblum*

# JOHN DRYDEN

**Born:** Aldwinkle, Northamptonshire, England;
    August 19, 1631
**Died:** London, England; May 12, 1700

PRINCIPAL POETRY

*Heroic Stanzas*, 1659
*Astraea Redux*, 1660
"To My Lord Chancellor," 1662
*Prologues and Epilogues*, 1664-1700
*Annus Mirabilis*, 1667
*Absalom and Achitophel, Part I*, 1681
*Absalom and Achitophel, Part II*, 1682 (with
    Nahum Tate)
*Mac Flecknoe: Or, A Satyre upon the True-Blew-
    Protestant Poet, T. S.*, 1682
*The Medall: A Satyre Against Sedition*, 1682
*Religio Laici*, 1682
*Threnodia Augustalis*, 1685
*The Hind and the Panther*, 1687
"A Song for St. Cecilia's Day," 1687
*Britannia Rediviva*, 1688
*Eleonora*, 1692
"To My Dear Friend Mr. Congreve," 1694
*Alexander's Feast: Or, The Power of Music, an
    Ode in Honor of St. Cecilia's Day*, 1697
"To My Honour'd Kinsman, John Driden," 1700

OTHER LITERARY FORMS

If one follows the practice of literary historians and assigns John Milton to an earlier age, then John Dryden stands as the greatest literary artist in England between 1660 and 1700, a period sometimes designated the Age of Dryden. In addition to his achievements in poetry, he excelled in drama, translation, and literary criticism. Dryden wrote or coauthored twenty-seven plays over a period of nearly thirty-five years; among them were successfully produced tragedies, heroic plays, tragicomedies, comedies of manners, and operas.

For every verse of original poetry that Dryden wrote, he translated two from another poet. Moreover, he translated two long volumes of prose from French originals—in 1684, Louis Maimbourg's *Histoire de la*

*Ligue* and in 1688, Dominick Bouhours's *La Vie de Saint François Xavier*—and he had a hand in the translation of the version of Plutarch's *Lives* published by Jacob Tonson in 1683. The translations were usually well received, especially the editions of Juvenal and Persius (1693) and of Vergil (1697).

Dryden's literary criticism consists largely of prefaces and dedications published throughout his career and attached to other works, his only critical work published alone being *Of Dramatic Poesie: An Essay* (1668). As a critic, Dryden appears at his best when he evaluates an earlier poet or dramatist (Homer, Vergil, Ovid, Geoffrey Chaucer, William Shakespeare, Ben Johnson, John Fletcher), when he seeks to define a genre, or when he breaks new critical ground, providing, for example, definitions of "wit" or a theory of translation.

## ACHIEVEMENTS

The original English poetry of John Dryden consists of approximately two hundred titles, or about twenty thousand verses. Slow to develop as a poet, he wrote his first significant poem in his twenty-eighth year, yet his poetic energy continued almost unabated until his death forty-one years later. His poetry reflects the diversity of talent that one finds throughout his literary career, and a wide range of didactic and lyric genres are represented. With *Mac Flecknoe* and *Absalom and Achitophel*, Dryden raised English satire to a form of high art, surpassing his contemporaries John Oldham, Samuel Butler, and John Wilmot, earl of Rochester, as they had surpassed their Elizabethan predecessors. He left his impression on the ode and the verse epistle, and his religious poem *Religio Laici* may be considered an early example of the verse essay. In the minor genre represented by prologues and epilogues, he stands alone in English literature, unexcelled in both variety and quality.

Of Dryden's poetic achievement Samuel Johnson wrote in his *Life of Dryden*: "What was said of Rome, adorned by Augustus, may be applied by an easy metaphor to English poetry embellished by Dryden. . . . [H]e found it brick and he left it marble." Johnson's praise applies primarily to Dryden's significant achievements in style and tone, for Dryden perfected the heroic cou-

plet, the rhymed iambic pentameter form that was to remain the dominant meter of English verse for nearly a century. He demonstrated that a stanza form best suited to lucid and graceful aphoristic wit could be varied and supple enough to produce a range of tones. Building on the achievements of his predecessors Edmund Waller and John Denham and drawing on his own wide experience with the couplet in heroic plays, Dryden polished the form that became for him a natural mode of expression. His couplets are usually end-stopped and closed, achieving a complete grammatical unit by the end of the second line. He makes extensive use of colloquial diction to create a rational, almost conversational tone. The lines contain internal pauses that are carefully regulated, and the syntax usually follows that of idiomatic English. To keep tension in the verse, he relies primarily on balance, antithesis, and other schemes of repetition.

Dryden brought to poetry of his age the energy and directness of expression that critics describe as the most masculine of styles. Accustomed to writing soliloquies and moral arguments in the speeches of heroic drama, he incorporated into his poetry extended passages of reasoning in verse that an age that valued reason found appealing. His inclination to choose for his poetry subjects of interest to contemporaries—science, aesthetics, religion, and politics—enhanced the popularity of his work.

Dryden is essentially a poet of urbanity, wit, and reason, perhaps seeking more to persuade readers than to move them. It has justly been pointed out that his poetry lacks emotional depth. He would rather arouse indignation and scorn over what he opposes than create admiration and appreciation for what he defends. The topical and occasional nature of his poetry suggests his preoccupation with issues of interest to his own day, which are of course less interesting to subsequent ages. His imagery and figures of speech are derived from classical literature, art, and society, not from nature. Even so, modern readers still find appealing those qualities that Dryden himself prized—grace and subtlety of style, rational tone, and vigorous and direct expression.

## BIOGRAPHY

John Dryden was the eldest of fourteen children in a landed family of modest means whose sympathies were Puritan on both sides. Little is known of his youth in Northamptonshire, for Dryden, seldom hesitant about his opinions, was reticent about his personal life. At about the age of fifteen, he was enrolled in Westminster School, then under the headmastership of Richard Busby, a school notable for its production of poets and bishops. Having attained at Westminster a thorough grounding in Latin, he proceeded to Cambridge, taking the B.A. degree in 1654. After the death of his father brought him a modest inheritance in the form of rents from family land, he left the university and settled in London. Though little is known of his early years there, he served briefly in Cromwell's government in a minor position and may have worked for the publisher Henry Herringman. He produced an elegy on the death of Cromwell, yet when Charles II ascended the throne, Dryden greeted the new ruler with a congratulatory poem, *Astraea Redux*. After the Restoration, he turned his main interest to drama, collaborating with Sir Robert Howard on one heroic play. He married Lady Elizabeth Howard, Sir Robert's sister, in 1663, a marriage that brought him a generous dowry and eventually three sons in whom he took pride.

Throughout his career, Dryden was no stranger to controversy, whether literary, political, or religious; in fact, he seemed all too eager to seize an occasion to express his views on these subjects. In literature, he challenged Sir Robert Howard's views on drama, Thomas Rymer's on criticism, and Rochester's and Thomas Shadwell's on questions of literary merit and taste. After receiving encouragement from Charles II, he entered the political controversy over succession to the throne with *Absalom and Achitophel*. Later he explained his religious views by attacking Deists, Catholics, and Dissenters in *Religio Laici*; then he shifted his ground and defended Catholicism in *The Hind and the Panther*.

For a variety of reasons, certainly in some measure because of envy, Dryden was the most often assailed among major poets. In an age when almost everyone prized his own wit, Dryden attained eminence without obviously possessing more of that quality than many others. His willingness to plunge into controversy brought him a host of enemies, and his changes of opinions and beliefs—literary, religious, political—

presented an even greater problem. Examining the changes one by one, a biographer or critic can provide a logical explanation for each. This task is perhaps most difficult in literary criticism, however, where Dryden will defend a position with enthusiasm only to abandon it later for another, which he advocates with equal enthusiasm. To his contemporaries, some of his changes coincided with interest, and, rightly or wrongly, he was frequently charged with timeserving.

In 1668, Dryden was appointed poet laureate, a position he held for twenty years, being deprived of it after the Glorious Revolution of 1688. During his term he received a two-hundred-pound annual stipend, which was later increased to three hundred when he became historiographer royal, but this was irregularly paid. His greatest efforts remained with drama until his satire *Mac Flecknoe* and the beginning of the Popish plot in 1678, when he turned his energies to poetic satire.

*John Dryden* (Library of Congress)

When events surrounding the plot posed a threat to the government of Charles II, Dryden wrote vigorously on behalf of the Tory cause, producing satires, translations, and then his religious poems. Initially, he carried the field for the king, but after the fall of James II and the loss of his political cause, he also lost the laureateship and its accompanying pension.

During the final period of his life, 1688-1700, he made a brief return to the theater but devoted most of his considerable energy and talent to translation, achieving success with his patrons and public. Though he had taken unpopular political and religious positions, he experienced no decline in his literary talent; in his final decade, he produced some of his best poems. Shortly before his death on May 12, 1700, he could look back on his century and epitomize the era poetically in *The Secular Masque*. He represented the Stuart Era by Diana (James I), Mars (Charles I and the Civil Wars), and Venus (Charles II).

|            | All, all of a piece throughout;    |
|------------|------------------------------------|
| (to Diana) | Thy Chase had a Beast in View      |
| (to Mars)  | Thy Wars brought nothing about     |
| (to Venus) | Thy Lovers were all untrue;        |
|            | 'Tis well an Old Age is out,       |
|            | And time to begin a New.           |

## ANALYSIS

To a greater degree than those of most other poets, John Dryden's poems are based on real occasions or events, often of a public nature. His imaginative power lies not in creating original or dramatic situations but in endowing actual events with poetic and sometimes mythic significance. When one looks beyond the rich variety of his poetry, Dryden's art is likely to impress the reader most strongly for the following: his intricate craftsmanship and style, his sense of genre, and his reliance on what he termed parallels, analogies used for both structuring and developing his poems. Craft and style are most readily revealed through analysis of selected passages from the poems, but some clarification of genre and the parallels may be useful at the outset.

Though Dryden possessed a keen sense of poetic genre, questions of classification in his poetry are not always easily resolved, for he writes in genres not well defined during his age. A poem may be assigned to one genre on the basis of its theme or purpose (an elegy, for example) and to another on the basis of form (such as an ode). However, almost any poem by Dryden can be placed with assurance in one of the following genres: lyric forms, especially songs and odes; satires; ratiocinative poems; panegyrics praising public figures or celebrating public occasions; verse epistles, usually in praise of living persons; epigrams, epitaphs, and elegies commemorating the dead; and prologues and epilogues.

For his parallels, which often reveal his preoccupation with monarchy and hierarchy, Dryden goes to the Bible, classical antiquity, or history. They provide a mythic framework within which he develops rational positions or ideals, aided by a set of conventional metaphors such as the temple, the tree, or the theater. Dryden's use of parallels and conventional metaphors indicates his essentially conservative cast of mind, especially about human nature and political affairs.

## POLARITIES AND OPPOSITES

The parallels also afford an opportunity for Dryden's favorite mode of thought—that of polarities or opposites. He delights in presenting contrasting viewpoints and then either defending one as an ideal or steering between them in a show of moderation. Normally such polarities or dichotomies contribute to a rational tone, enabling Dryden to ingratiate himself with the reader, as in his "Prologue to *Aureng-Zebe*" (1675). He contemplates retirement from the stage and contrasts his own plays with those of Shakespeare and his younger contemporaries such as William Wycherley:

> As with the greater Dead he dares not strive,
> He wou'd not match his Verse with those who live:
> Let him retire, betwix't two Ages cast,
> The first of this, and hindmost of the last.

The reader accepts the tone of humility, even though he realizes that it is not entirely ingenuous.

## ANNUS MIRABILIS

Dryden's earliest poems are usually occasional pieces and panegyrics that reveal to some extent a debt to so-called Metaphysical poetry and to Abraham Cowley, an influence he soon rejected for a style more regular and lucid. However, as late as 1667, in *Annus Mirabilis*, a long poem on the London plague and fire and the Dutch war, Dryden still retained some tendency toward Metaphysical conceits. It is notable too that *Annus Mirabilis* employs the four-line heroic stanza from Sir William Davenant's poem *Gondibert* (1651), which Dryden had used earlier in the elegy on Cromwell. Perhaps a more reliable index to his poetic development during the 1660's is represented by *Prologues and Epilogues*, which he began publishing in 1664.

### PROLOGUES AND EPILOGUES

During the Restoration, prologues and epilogues became normal complements to dramatic works. Over nearly four decades, Dryden wrote more than a hundred of them, not only for his own plays but also for those of other dramatists. They employ straightforward, colloquial diction and syntax, and they are normally written in heroic couplets. In his early examples in this genre, Dryden follows established convention by having the poems appeal for the indulgence of the audience and a favorable reception of the play. Later he adapts the poems to varied subjects and purposes, some having little to do with drama. He writes prologues to introduce special performances at unaccustomed sites, such as Oxford, or to greet an eminent person in the audience (a duke or duchess, perhaps), or to mark some theater occasion, such as the opening of a new playhouse. In some of the poems, he reflects on the poor taste of the audience; in others, he explains principles of literary criticism. He may take his audience into his confidence and impart his own personal plans. At times, as in the "Prologue to *The Duke of Guise*" (1684), he outlines his views on political questions, explaining how events chronicled in the play resemble those then current. In more than a few, he titillates the audience with sexual humor, allusion, and innuendo. For all their variety, the poems evidence throughout some of Dryden's most characteristic poetic qualities—directness, clarity, colloquial tone, wit, and adaptability.

### MAC FLECKNOE

Neither the occasion nor the time of Dryden's first satire, *Mac Flecknoe*, a mock-heroic attack on a rival playwright, Thomas Shadwell, is known with certainty. Dryden selects the demise of the poetaster Richard Flecknoe (d. 1678) as the basis of his poem—a mock coronation, in which Flecknoe, dubbed the reigning prince of dullness, chooses Shadwell as his successor. This situation permits scintillating literary inversion; the kingdom of letters, Augustan Rome, and the seriousness of succession to the throne all provide contrasting analogy and allusion. The poem satirizes not only Shadwell but also bad taste in art. Establishing a polarity between true and false wit, Dryden creates by implication an aesthetic ideal.

In the first section of the poem, Flecknoe arrives at his decision regarding a successor. The poem then describes the festivities preceding Shadwell's coronation and the coronation itself, followed by the long oration and fall of Flecknoe. The opening lines invite the reader to assume that selecting a successor to the throne of dullness is serious business:

> All human things are subject to decay,
> And, when Fate summons, Monarchs must obey.
> This Flecknoe found, who, like Augustus, young
> Was call'd to Empire, and had govern'd long;
> In Prose and Verse, was own'd, without dispute
> Through all the Realms of *Nonsense*, absolute.

The sober aphorism in the opening lines, followed by comparison with Augustus, creates a tone of solemnity, to be overturned by the mockery of "Realms of *Nonsense*." As Flecknoe selects Shadwell, he catalogs a series of personal attributes praiseworthy in a dunce, usually deriving from the plays of Shadwell. However, Dryden does not refrain from personal satire directed at Shadwell's size, perhaps because Shadwell himself had used his corpulent appearance as a basis for his resemblance to Ben Jonson:

> Besides his goodly Fabrick fills the eyes,
> And seems design'd for thoughtless Majesty:
> Thoughtless as Monarch Oakes that shade the plain,
> And, spread in solemn state, supinely reign.

Another satiric maneuver is to separate poets into two camps, with Shadwell relegated to the company of dullards. An example occurs when Flecknoe describes the site of the coronation:

> Great Fletcher never treads in Buskins here,
> Nor greater Jonson dare in Socks appear.
> But gentle Simkin just reception finds
> Amidst this Monument of vanish't Minds.

The polarity of artists includes such figures as Ben Jonson, John Fletcher, Sir Charles Sedley, and Sir George Etherege at one end; and John Ogleby, Thomas Heywood, John Shirley, Thomas Dekker, and Richard Flecknoe at the other.

As there is a difference between true and false writing, there is also a hierarchy of forms or genres. Flecknoe admonishes Shadwell to abandon the drama and turn to those poems developed through what Dryden's age considered false wit: pattern poems, anagrams, acrostics, and ballads—works appropriate to his dull wit. In *Mac Flecknoe*, Dryden generally maintains a tone of exuberant good humor and mirth, seldom resorting to lampoon. The poem does, however, illustrate the problem of topicality, since many of its allusions are now obscure and others are altogether lost. Still, as Dryden explores the kingdoms of sense and nonsense, he clearly demonstrates his reliance on parallels and polarities.

### SATIRIC POEMS

Dryden's three later satiric poems—*Absalom and Achitophel, Part I, The Medal*, and *Absalom and Achitophel, Part II* (with Nahum Tate)—concern the struggle of the Whigs to alter the succession in England by excluding James, duke of York, the King's brother, and giving the right of succession to James, duke of Monmouth, the king's illegitimate son. This enterprise was ably led by the earl of Shaftesbury (Achitophel), though he could not prevail against the determined opposition of the king. Charles II (David) understood that permitting Parliament to change the established succession would alter the form of monarchy from a royal one, in which the king normally followed law and established tradition but could exercise extraordinary powers in times of crisis, to a constitutional monarchy in which the king's power became subject to parliamentary restrictions. Dryden's objective in the poem is to persuade readers to support the king in the conflict.

### ABSALOM AND ACHITOPHEL

Thus in *Absalom and Achitophel*, Dryden (then poet laureate) employed his pen in the king's behalf—according to anecdote, at the king's own suggestion. He makes use of the biblical rebellion against David by his son Absalom, at the instigation of Achitophel (II Samuel 13-18), a parallel familiar to his audience.

Dryden freely adds characters and alters the biblical parallel to make it apply to English political leaders and institutions, pointing out that although the biblical account ends with the death of Absalom, he hopes that a peaceful resolution with Monmouth remains possible.

The satire of *Absalom and Achitophel* differs somewhat from that of *Mac Flecknoe*. Although Dryden believed satire to be a form of heroic or epic poetry, implying some narrative content, he had maintained a tone of ironic mockery and fine raillery throughout *Mac Flecknoe*. *Absalom and Achitophel* represents a mixed or Varronian kind of satire, perhaps owing something to Juvenal as well as to Marcus Terentius Varro. The satiric elements are confined chiefly to the first section of the poem, in which Dryden discredits the Whig opponents of the king. Instead of implying an ideal, as satire normally does, Dryden explains it directly in a passage that has come to be regarded as an essay on government (vv. 723-810). Finally, Dryden praises the supporters of the king individually and has the king appear in his own person at the poem's end, showing David (Charles II) facing his opponents with firmness and moderation.

In addition to the biblical parallel, Dryden makes effective use of characters, a technique that owes something to classical satirists but more to the character writers of the seventeenth century. A "character" in Dryden is a passage, sometimes satiric, sometimes serious, delineating a person and creating a unified impression. Though Dryden includes both satiric and complimentary characters, the satiric ones—Achitophel (Shaftesbury), Zimri (Buckingham), Shimei (Slingsby Bethel), and Corah (Titus Oates)—are the most memorable. In his character of Zimri (vv. 543-568), Dryden portrays the duke of Buckingham as foolishly inconsistent: "A man so various, that he seem'd to be/ Not one, but all Mankind's Epitome." In his perversity, Zimri is made to reflect a kind of frenetic energy:

> Stiff in opinions, always in the wrong;
> Was everything by starts, and nothing long;
> But in the course of one revolving Moon,
> Was Chymist, Fidler, States-Man, and Buffoon.

Such an indiscriminate course indicates that Zimri's judgment about human beings and political institutions cannot be trusted, as the character goes on to suggest. The character becomes a major means of discrediting the king's chief opponents, yet it also permits Dryden to praise the king's loyal supporters.

### RELIGIO LAICI

For his religious poem, *Religio Laici*, Dryden assigns no genre, giving as the subtitle "A Poem." In a lengthy preface, he finds precedent for his work in the epistles of Horace. It is often called a ratiocinative poem, but it closely resembles the genre in English poetry designated "verse essay." It surveys a definite subject, presents a variety of positions, explores their bases, provides reasoned analysis, and gives the poet's personal positions. *Religio Laici* surveys religious movements in England during Dryden's day and rejects all except the established church, supporting the official view that the Church of England represents a *via media*—a middle way—avoiding the extremes of the Deists, Catholics, and Dissenters. Dryden upholds biblical authority against the Deists, citing reasons for belief in scriptural authority and arguing that the religious principles advocated by the Deists were first brought to humans by revelation, not innate understanding, as Deists believed, for otherwise the Greeks and Romans would have discovered them. As the Deist relies too heavily on humankind's reason, the Catholic relies too heavily on tradition and the argument of infallibility, while the Protestant errs in the extreme in another direction, relying excessively on private interpretation of the Scriptures, an extreme that leads to disorder in society.

Dryden's conclusion indicates both his moderation and his intensely conservative outlook. Essential points of faith are few and plain. Since people believe more than is necessary, they should seek guidance from reliable ancient theologians on disputed points. If that does not provide adequate enlightenment, they can either leave the matter unsettled or restrain further speculation and inquiry in the interest of public peace and order.

### "TO THE MEMORY OF MR. OLDHAM"

"To the Memory of Mr. Oldham" (1684), a poem that demonstrates the efficacy of heroic couplets for a serious theme, may be Dryden's finest elegy. John Oldham, a younger poet, had attained success with his satires against the Jesuits and had died young. Dryden pays tribute to a fellow satirist with whom he can identify. The opening lines establish the basic tone: "Farewell, too little, and too lately known,/ Whom I began to think and call my own." The classical simplicity of "farewell," the weight and seriousness of the long vowels and semivowels, and the balance within the lines ("too little and too lately" and "think and call") establish a serious, even tone that Dryden can vary, yet preserve. In a second part of the poem, he stresses the youth of Oldham and his early achievement, acknowledging its imperfection. The tone of unqualified praise has altered, but balance and tonal consistency remain. Dryden next demonstrates his exquisite sense of poetic sound when he turns to the defects of Oldham's poetry, choosing to downplay them: "But Satyr needs not those, and Wit will shine/ Through the harsh cadence of a rugged line." The cadence in the second line sounds harsher because it follows a perfectly balanced line. After further downplaying of the importance of a good ear in the insipid passage, "Maturing time/ But mellow what we write to the dull sweets of Rime," Dryden returns to the balanced and rational tone:

> Once more, hail and farewell; farewell thou young,
> But ah too short, Marcellus of our Tongue;
> Thy Brows with Ivy, and with Laurels bound;
> But Fate and gloomy Night encompass thee around.

Allusion to Marcellus enables Dryden to draw the parallel to Augustan Rome, where the nephew who might have succeeded Augustus dies young. Thus, the kingdom of civilized letters in Dryden's age resembles the finest earlier civilization. The balance within the verse ("Ivy and Laurels," "Fate and gloomy Night") ends the poem in a tone of serious, subdued expression of loss.

### ODES

As one would expect, in the ode Dryden abandons the heroic couplet for a more complicated stanza and metrical pattern. His odes are occasional poems either on the death of someone, as in "Threnodia Augustalis," on the death of Charles II, or "To the Pious Memory of the Accomplished Young Lady Mrs. Anne Killigrew," or commemoration of an occasion, as in his two odes for Saint Cecilia's Day, written ten years apart (1687 and 1697), both commemorating the patron saint of music. They share a common theme, the power of music to influence people's emotions or passions. In the first "A Song for St. Cecilia's Day," Dryden employs the traditional association of instruments with particular human passions and develops his theme, "What Passion cannot Musick raise and quell," in a kind of linear fashion, the trumpet instilling courage and valor, the flute arousing love, the violin, jealousy, and the organ influencing devotion. Inclusion of the organ enables Dryden to allude to Saint Cecilia, who is said to have invented that instrument. According to legend, while playing on her invention she drew an angel to earth, the harmony having caused him to mistake earth for heaven. In a concluding grand chorus, Dryden sees music, an element of the creation, as also befitting the end of creation:

> So, when the last and dreadful hour
> This crumbling Pageant shall devour,
> The Trumpet shall be heard on high,
> The Dead shall live, the Living die,
> And Musick shall untune the sky.

## ALEXANDER'S FEAST

*Alexander's Feast*, the second Saint Cecilia ode, is constructed according to a more ambitious plan, for Dryden imagines Alexander celebrating his victory over the Persian king Darius, listening to the music of Timotheus, which has sufficient power to move a hero of Alexander's greatness. The shifts are abrupt, as in the Pindaric ode, yet Dryden preserves the Horatian structure with a regular development of emotional response, as Timotheus causes the monarch to experience a sense of deification, a desire for pleasure, pity for the fallen Darius, and then love. No sooner has Alexander indulged his pleasure than Timotheus, in another strain, incites him to revenge, and the king seizes a torch to set the Persian city aflame. At the poem's end, Dryden compares Cecilia and Timotheus. In this ode, Dryden achieves a remarkably complex, forceful, and energetic movement, and he lends dramatic strength to the familiar theme by creating a dramatic parallel that involves historical characters. Although the ode attains a kind of Pindaric exuberance, Dryden nevertheless follows a regular, linear organization.

## HORATIAN VERSE EPISTLES

One of Dryden's principal poetic forms is the Horatian verse epistle, a type of poetry he wrote over a period of nearly forty years. The genre permits a poet to address an individual, speaking in his own person, and revealing as much or as little about himself as he wishes. Dryden's epistles are usually poems of praise, though wit may sometimes be the chief purpose. Two of his final epistles, "To My Dear Friend Mr. Congreve" and "To My Honour'd Kinsman, John Driden" (a poem addressed to his cousin, who then served in Parliament), are among his most memorable. Dryden's reliance on kingdoms and monarchies comes to the fore in each—the state in the epistle to his kinsman and the kingdom of letters in the poem to the dramatist William Congreve.

A favorite device of Dryden's is to set up polarities between differing ages and make comparisons, as he does in his "Epigram on Milton": "Three Poets in three distant ages born/ Greece, Italy, and England did adorn." The contrasts constitute a witty means of expressing praise, an art that Dryden had mastered in both verse and prose—being as skilled in panegyric as he was in satire.

In "To My Dear Friend Mr Congreve," the colloquial tone of the opening line belies a more serious theme and purpose: "Well then; the promis'd hour is come at last;/ The present Age of Wit obscures the past." Speaking of the wits of his time, Dryden acknowledges that, owing to a deficiency of genius, they have not equaled the achievements of Shakespeare and Jonson, and thus, metaphorically, "The second Temple was not like the first." Having introduced his metaphor of the temple, Dryden exploits it by alluding to another age and comparing Congreve to the Roman architect Vitruvius. Dryden goes on to praise Congreve's specific abilities as a dramatist, comparing him with Jonson, Fletcher, George Etherege, Thomas Southerne, and Wycherley, and, in a further allusion to Rome, with Scipio, for achieving greatness in youth.

Becoming more personal, Dryden shifts the parallel to the kingdom of poetry and, specifically, to his own tenure as poet laureate:

O that your Brows by Lawrel had sustain'd,
Well had I been Depos'd, if You had reign'd!
The Father had descended for the Son;
For only You are lineal to the Throne.

It was a great irony in Dryden's life that the poet he had made successor to the throne of dullness in *Mac Flecknoe*, Thomas Shadwell, had succeeded instead to the laureateship. The poem concludes with Dryden speaking of his own departure from the stage and asking the young Congreve to treat his memory kindly, a request that Congreve, to his credit, fulfilled by editing Dryden's plays and writing a personal testimony and memoir favorable to the older poet. The poem is vintage Dryden, displaying the polarities between ages, the temple metaphor, the Roman allusions, and, above all, the monarchical metaphor involving successions, coronations, and reigns.

## OTHER MAJOR WORKS

PLAYS: *The Wild Gallant*, pr. 1663; *The Indian Queen*, pr. 1664 (with Sir Robert Howard); *The Rival Ladies*, pr., pb. 1664; *The Indian Emperor: Or, The Conquest of Mexico by the Spaniards*, pr. 1665; *Secret Love: Or, The Maiden Queen*, pr. 1667; *Sir Martin Mar-All: Or, The Feign'd Innocence*, pr. 1667 (with William Cavendish, duke of Newcastle; adaptation of Molière's *L'Étourdi*); *The Tempest: Or, The Enchanted Island*, pr. 1667 (with Sir William Davenant; adaptation of William Shakespeare's play); *An Evening's Love: Or, The Mock Astrologer*, pr. 1668 (adaptation of Thomas Corneille's *Le Feint Astrologue*); *Tyrannic Love: Or, The Royal Martyr*, pr. 1669; *The Conquest of Granada by the Spaniards, Part I*, pr. 1670; *The Conquest of Granada by the Spaniards, Part II*, pr. 1671; *The Assignation: Or, Love in a Nunnery*, pr. 1672; *Marriage à la Mode*, pr. 1672; *Amboyna: Or, The Cruelties of the Dutch to the English Merchants*, pr., pb. 1673; *Aureng-Zebe*, pr. 1675; *All for Love: Or, The World Well Lost*, pr. 1677; *The State of Innocence, and Fall of Man*, pb. 1677 (libretto; adaptation of John Milton's *Paradise Lost*); *The Kind Keeper: Or, Mr. Limberham*, pr. 1678; *Oedipus*, pr. 1678 (with Nathaniel Lee); *Troilus and Cressida: Or, Truth Found Too Late*, pr., pb. 1679; *The Spanish Friar: Or, The Double Discovery*, pr. 1680; *The Duke of Guise*, pr. 1682 (with Lee); *Albion and Albanius*, pr., pb. 1685 (libretto; music by Louis Grabu); *Don Sebastian, King of Portugal*, pr. 1689; *Amphitryon: Or, The Two Socia's*, pr., pb. 1690; *King Arthur: Or, The British Worthy*, pr., pb. 1691 (libretto; music by Henry Purcell); *Cleomenes, the Spartan Hero*, pr., pb. 1692; *Love Triumphant: Or, Nature Will Prevail*, pr., pb. 1694; *The Secular Masque*, pr., pb. 1700 (masque); *Dramatick Works*, 1717; *The Works of John Dryden*, 1808 (18 volumes).

NONFICTION: "A Defence of *An Essay of Dramatic Poesy*," 1668; *Of Dramatic Poesie: An Essay*, 1668; "Preface to *An Evening's Love: Or, The Mock Astrologer*," 1671; "Of Heroic Plays: An Essay," 1672; "The Author's Apology for Heroic Poetry and Poetic License," 1677; "Preface to *All for Love*," 1678; "The Grounds of Criticism in Tragedy," 1679; "Preface to *Sylvae*," 1685; "Dedication of *Examen Poeticum*," 1693; *A Discourse Concerning the Original and Progress of Satire*, 1693; "A Parallel of Poetry and Painting," 1695; "Dedication of the *Aeneis*," 1697; "Preface to *Fables Ancient and Modern*," 1700; "Heads of an Answer to Rymer," 1711.

TRANSLATIONS: *Ovid's Epistles*, 1680; *The History of the League*, 1684 (of Louis Maimbourg's *Histoire de la Ligue*); *The Life of St. Francis Xavier*, 1688 (of Dominique Bouhours' *La Vie de Saint François Xavier*); *The Satires of Juvenal and Persius*, 1693; *The Works of Vergil*, 1697.

## BIBLIOGRAPHY

Archer, John Michael. *Old Worlds: Egypt, Southwest Asia, India, and Russia in Early Modern English Writing*. Stanford, Calif.: Stanford University Press, 2001. Contains a scholarly examination of Dryden's *Aureng-Zebe*, along with Shakespeare's *Antony and Cleopatra* and the works of John Milton. Bibliography and index.

Bywaters, David. *Dryden in Revolutionary England*. Berkeley: University of California Press, 1991. Describes the rhetorical stages by which Dryden, in his published works between 1687 and 1700, sought to define contemporary politics and to stake out for himself a tenable place within them. The volume attempts to situate these works in political and literary contexts familiar to Dryden and his readers. The study reveals much about the relationship between Dryden's politics, polemics, and art. Contains an epilogue and extensive notes.

Gelber, Michael Werth. *The Just and the Lively: The Literary Criticism of John Dryden*. New York: Manchester University Press, 1999. Gelber provides a complete study of Dryden's criticism. Through a detailed reading of each of Dryden's essays, the book explains and illustrates the unity and the development of his thought.

Green, Susan, and Steven N. Zwicker, eds. *John Dryden: A Tercentenary Miscellany*. San Marino, Calif.: Huntington Library, 2001. This collection of essays attempts to look at the scope of Dryden's work in its social and political context.

Hammond, Paul. *John Dryden: A Literary Life*. New York: St. Martin's Press, 1991. This study of Dryden's life examines the texts that he produced and the relationship of these texts to the society they reflect. The work consists of chapters on different aspects of Dryden's works. They are arranged approximately chronologically to suggest the shape of his career and to explore his own developing sense of his role as the premier writer of Restoration England, both dominating and detached from the world in which he moved. Includes select bibliography and extensive notes.

Hammond, Paul, and David Hopkins, eds. *John Dryden: Tercentenary Essays*. New York: Oxford University Press, 2000. A collection of twelve essays that place Dryden in the context of his time and suggest a more elevated place for him in literary history.

Lewis, Jayne, and Maximillian E. Novak, eds. *Enchanted Ground: Reimagining John Dryden*. Buffalo, N.Y.: University of Toronto Press, 2004. These essays provide critical analysis of Dryden from new perspectives.

Miner, Earl. *Dryden's Poetry*. Bloomington: Indiana University Press, 1967. A combination of the scholarly and the critical, this authoritative study deals extensively with all the major long poems, the lyric poetry, and the fables. Both Dryden's ideas and his figures are extensively analyzed. Contains a bibliography and an index.

Rawson, Claude, and Aaron Santesso, eds. *John Dryden (1631-1700): His Politics, His Plays, and His Poets*. Newark: University of Delaware Press, 2004. Essays deal with Dryden's drama, his politics, and his poems, among other subjects.

Winn, James Anderson. *John Dryden and His World*. New Haven, Conn.: Yale University Press, 1987. This lengthy work is a fresh attempt to transport its reader to Dryden's time. It examines the man, his work, and the world in which he lived. Considers the subtle relations linking this world's religious beliefs, its political alliances, and the literary styles it favored. Views Dryden's work as a product of his particular historical situation. Includes illustrations and appendixes on Dryden's family history.

Zwicker, Steven N. *Politics and Language in Dryden's Poetry*. Princeton, N.J.: Princeton University Press, 1984. A scholarly work that traces, historically and analytically, Dryden's poetic strategies in dealing with his poetic views. Includes an index.

*Stanley Archer*

---

# WILLIAM DUNBAR

**Born:** Lothian, Scotland; c. 1460
**Died:** Scotland(?); c. 1525

PRINCIPAL POETRY

"The Thrissill and the Rois," 1503
"The Dance of the Sevin Deidly Synnis," c. 1503-1508
"The Goldyn Targe," c. 1508
"Lament for the Makaris," c. 1508
"The Tretis of the Tua Mariit Wemen and the Wedo," c. 1508
*The Poems of William Dunbar*, 1884-1893 (John Small, editor)
*The Poems of William Dunbar*, 1892-1894 (Jakob Schipper, editor)
*The Poems of William Dunbar*, 1932 (W. MacKay Mackenzie, editor)
*Poems*, 1958 (James Kinsley, editor)

*The Poems of William Dunbar*, 1979 (Kinsley, editor)

*The Poems of William Dunbar*, 1998 (Priscilla Bawcutt, editor)

*William Dunbar: The Complete Works*, 2004 (John Conlee, editor)

## OTHER LITERARY FORMS

There is no evidence that William Dunbar wrote in any genre other than short poetry.

## ACHIEVEMENTS

William Dunbar has traditionally been grouped with Robert Henryson, Gavin Douglas, Sir David Lyndsay, and James I of Scotland, author of *The Kingis Quair* (1423-1424; *The King's Choir*), as a "Scottish Chaucerian," because he often used Geoffrey Chaucer's metrical forms and poetic conventions. He may also be considered a Chaucerian in the sense that he and his contemporaries, both in England and Scotland, acknowledged a large debt to Chaucer, the "flower of rhetoricians," who, they believed, raised the English language to a status equal to that of Latin and French, where it could be used for both philosophy and literature. Thus, the Chaucerians felt that one of their important duties was to consolidate this new status by practicing a highly ornate rhetoric, and Dunbar's rhetoric was as self-consciously artful as anyone's. At the same time, however, Dunbar was never a slavish imitator of the great English poet. Indeed, there are more than a few differences between them. Whereas Chaucer was an accomplished storyteller, Dunbar wrote mainly short lyrical poems. Whereas Chaucer was a sensitive creator of literary characters, Dunbar's interests lay elsewhere, and so his characters are never as fully developed. Finally, although Chaucer wrote warm human comedy, the tone of his work is quite different from that of Dunbar's raucous grotesqueries.

One of Dunbar's most noticeable poetic qualities is his professionalism, for he took his job as *makar*, the Scots term for "poet," very seriously. Like his fellow Scots poets, Dunbar had a highly developed sense of the different kinds of poetry that were possible, and thus he cultivated several different poetic forms and levels of language, each of which was chosen expressly to fit differing situations. He was much more a poetic virtuoso than were his contemporaries to the south, and in his small corpus one finds everything from the lowest scatological abuse to the most ornate high-minded panegyric. Furthermore, Dunbar had a gift for picking the correct meter, which he chose from a very extensive repertoire. Finally, Dunbar composed easily on at least three different levels of language: In his eldritch or bawdy poems, he used a very exaggerated Scots voice; in his moral poetry, he used a more normal speaking voice; and in his courtly or panegyric poems, he used a highly literate, aureate voice.

While his lyrical variety looks forward to the Renaissance, Dunbar is more often seen as coming at the end of the long medieval poetic tradition, for his work is usually rooted in traditional forms and themes. Moreover, though his poems may be called lyrical because of their short length and strong musical quality, they are not the products of personal emotion recollected in tranquillity. Dunbar was always a public poet; one never sees him in literary undress. Indeed, Dunbar's interests did not lie with presenting philosophical or moral concepts; still less was he interested in exploring his own emotional depths. He was interested, rather, in presenting traditional materials in highly finished packages. Following medieval thought on poetics, he considered himself primarily a rhetorician, and he wanted his poetry either to explode like colorful and noisy fireworks or to sit "enamelled," "gilded," and "refined," like a delicate piece of china, a precise and static work of art. In short, Dunbar was more concerned with language than with content, and for this reason, his poetry has been called a poetry of surface effects. Commenting on Dunbar's unbounded vitality, C. S. Lewis once remarked: "If you like half-tones and nuances you will not enjoy Dunbar; he will deafen you."

## BIOGRAPHY

How much one claims to know about the life of William Dunbar depends on how much one is willing to trust the claims to be found in his poems, for very little external evidence remains. From Dunbar's poetry, for example, John W. Baxter in his book *William Dunbar: A Biographical Study* (1952) surmises that the poet was descended from the noble house of Dunbar, the earls of which were both powerful and controversial figures in the history of Scotland. Descendants of a Northumbrian earl, Cospatrick, they more than once sided with the English in quarrels between the two countries. In 1402, for example, Henry Dunbar, earl of March, piqued over losses in a personal controversy with the earl of Douglas, aided King Henry IV of England at the Battle of Homildon Hill, thus earning his family the enmity of James I of Scotland, who stripped the clan of most of its lands. If Dunbar had noble blood, then he belonged to a family whose fortunes had fallen considerably.

However that may be, in many of his poems, Dunbar does speak distastefully of the lower classes and of social climbers. In "To the King" ("Schir, yit remember as befoir"), the poet calls himself a "gentill goishalk." This may be significant since the birds of prey were often associated with the nobility in medieval poetry, as, for example, in Chaucer's *Parlement of Foules* (1380). Furthermore, in the same poem, Dunbar complains that while still a youth he was thought headed for a bishopric, but upon achieving maturity he stated, "A sempill vicar I can not be." In short, the tone of many of his poems seems to be that of a frustrated aristocrat.

Dunbar appears to have had a good education, and here again there is much speculation as to exactly where he received it. It was customary for Scottish students of the time to study on the Continent, especially at the University of Paris, but there is absolutely no evidence that Dunbar ever studied there. Again, though Dunbar wrote a poem on Oxford, it is doubtful that he ever attended that university. Rather, it is likely that he wrote his poem while visiting Oxford in 1501, when he helped to arrange James IV's marriage to Margaret Tudor, the daughter of Henry VII of England. Records of St. Andrew's University in Scotland show that a William Dunbar, probably the poet, received a bachelor of arts degree there in 1477 and his licentiate in 1479.

Evidently not independently wealthy, Dunbar chose a vocation in the church and was ordained a priest later in life. The accounts of the Lord High Treasurer of Scotland show that he was given a sum of four pounds eighteen shillings in 1504 as a gift for his first Mass. Moreover, Dunbar spent most of his life waiting for a benefice—a grant of land and a parish from which he could make his living. One of Dunbar's poems, "How Dunbar Was Desired to be a Friar," has led some to speculate that the poet spent part of his early life as a traveling Franciscan novice. In the poem, a devil in the guise of Saint Francis appears to Dunbar in a dream, exhorting him to take up the Franciscan habit. Dunbar, however, will have none of it, and he retorts that, if he must take a religious habit, he will take that of a bishop, for he has read in "holy legends" that more bishops than friars have become saints. Moreover—and this is the tantalizing part—he claims to have already worn the Franciscan habit all over England and France, to have preached openly, and also to have picked up "many a trick and wile" of the friars, who are "always ready to beguile men." Now, however, those days are long past, says the poet, and he is content to live a more honest life. Whether this poem is a reliable autobiographical document or merely an antifraternal jape cannot be determined.

That Dunbar moved in the aristocratic circles of the court of James IV can be determined. Beginning in 1500, Dunbar was awarded an annual pension of ten pounds per year from the king until he should receive a benefice worth at least forty pounds annually. In 1507, this amount was raised to twenty pounds per year, and in 1510, the poet was awarded a very substantial increase to eighty pounds annually. As a rough measure of what these sums were worth, Baxter reports that, when he was receiving a pension of ten pounds, Dunbar was on the same level as the king's steward and clerk of accounts. When he received a pension of twenty pounds, Dunbar was raised above all other members of the royal household except the keeper of the king's silver vessels. His pension of eighty pounds raised the poet above even the principal of King's College, Hector Boece. Thus, despite Dunbar's frequent complaints to the contrary, he was well appreciated and rewarded by King James.

From these generous pensions and from his occasional court poetry such as "To Princess Margaret" and "The Ballade of Barnard Stewart Lord of Aubigny," one can infer that Dunbar held the position of unofficial poet laureate. Indeed, when the printing press was finally introduced into Scotland in 1507 by Walter

Chepman and Andrew Myllar, Dunbar's poems were among the first writings to be printed.

Entries for Dunbar in the royal records cease in 1513. In June of that year, Henry VIII invaded France, and James IV, responding to calls for help from his old French allies, advanced southward with his armies into England. He met the English at Flodden on September 9, but, although his soldiers fought bravely, he was defeated. Most of the great houses of Scotland lost men in that battle, and the king himself was also killed. In its aftermath, Edinburgh fortified itself against an invasion, but Henry VIII decided not to follow up his victory: The new Scottish king, James V, was the son of Henry's own sister, Margaret, and he thus hoped for better relationships with Scotland. Nevertheless, the defeat was disastrous for the country, and it later led to continuous civil strife.

Dunbar was probably too old to have been among the troops at Flodden, but what became of him after that date is unknown. Did he perhaps finally find his long-awaited benefice, or was his pension simply cut off because of Scotland's financial difficulties? The question is further complicated by the fact that the Treasurer's records are often missing for the years between 1513 and 1529.

One poem, "Quhen the Gouvernour past in Fraunce," is often cited as proof that Dunbar continued to write after 1513, since it refers to the visit to Scotland, from 1515 to 1517, of John Stewart, duke of Albany, for the purpose of restoring order to the kingdom. Although the poem is ascribed to Dunbar in an important manuscript, however, Dunbar's editor James Kinsley has deleted it from the poet's corpus, partly because "little else that is attributed to him is as clumsy and undistinguished as this." Since many scholars agree with Kinsley, one can safely say that Dunbar seems to have stopped writing about this time. In any case, in 1530 another Scottish poet, Lyndsay, noted in his "Testament of the Papyngo" that Dunbar had died. If Lyndsay listed the poets in the order of their death, then Dunbar died before 1522, for that is when Douglas, the next poet mentioned, died.

ANALYSIS

Because William Dunbar wrote in his native Scots dialect, it is often difficult for modern English speakers to understand his poetry. Middle Scots, the language of the Scottish Lowlanders, was a development from the northern dialects of Middle English. Its rival, the Gaelic tongue spoken by the Highlanders, is a Celtic language related to Welsh, Irish, and Breton. Although his own Scots shows the influence of Gaelic, Dunbar often spoke scornfully of the Celtic tongue, as, for example, when he insulted Walter Kennedy, a Highlander, in "The Flyting of Dunbar and Kennedy."

Nevertheless, Scots did borrow many words from Gaelic, some of which, such as "canny," "dour," and "bairn," have been taken over into standard English. The Middle Scots dialect can be easily recognized by its diction, by certain grammatical forms, and also by certain peculiarities in spelling and pronunciation. For example, Scots used "qu" or "quh" in place of "wh" in such words as "quhat" (what), "quhilk" (which), and "quhen" (when). The dialect also retained the Old English "a" where it had been replaced by a more rounded vowel in the South: "stane" (stone) and "hale" (whole) are good examples. Also, the northern dialects preferred the plosive consonants "g" and "k" where the southerners adopted the softer "y" and "ch" sounds; thus one finds "kirk" for "church," "mikel" for "much," and "yaf" for "gave." These are only the most noteworthy of many dialectical peculiarities, but they will be of some help when one first encounters Dunbar's poetry.

Nowhere is Dunbar's ability with language more evident than in his "The Goldyn Targe." Although he draws heavily on medieval allegorical traditions, Dunbar here is less interested in the message of the love allegory than in the language with which it is conveyed. Furthermore, this display of poetic virtuosity must have been appreciated in his own day, for "The Goldyn Targe" was one of the six poems of Dunbar printed by Chepman and Myllar in 1507, and it was later singled out by Lyndsay in his "Testament of the Papyngo" to prove that Dunbar "language had at large."

### "THE GOLDYN TARGE"

"The Goldyn Targe" can be placed in the tradition of *Le Roman de la rose* (thirteenth century; *The Romance of the Rose*, partial translation, c. 1370; complete translation, 1900), a long narrative poem written sometime in the thirteenth century by the poets Guillaume de Lorris and Jean de Meung. All the action of the French poem takes place in a dream; the characters are all personifications; and even the settings carry allegorical meanings: The idealized garden represents the life at court, and the rose-plot symbolizes the mind of a young lady. *The Romance of the Rose* was thus a psychological exposition of courtly love.

Although there is some disagreement as to whether courtly love was ever actually practiced or whether it was simply a literary convention, the idea sprang up in the eleventh century in the songs of the French troubadours. Chrétien de Troyes's Lancelot and Guinevere are perhaps the best known courtly lovers, though others such as Tristan and Iseult or Chaucer's *Troilus and Criseyde* (1382) could also be cited. The behavior of the lovers was highly codified in this system, with the woman holding the ascendancy. For his part, the man was to be humble, discreet, and courteous, complying with each whim of his mistress. How does one fall in love, and what are its results? Poems such as "The Goldyn Targe" attempted to explain the process through allegory.

Walking through an idealized garden on a fresh May morning, the narrator of "The Goldyn Targe" soon tires, falls asleep, and has a marvelous dream. He spies a beautiful ship laden with a hundred gods and goddesses from antiquity led by Nature and Venus. They are a merry group, dressed entirely in green, a color symbolic of youth, freshness, and vigor. When the Dreamer tries to get a better look at them, however, he is suddenly caught by Venus, who for no apparent reason orders her "troops" to attack him. The attacking platoons are made up of personified feminine qualities such as Beauty, Delight, and Fine Appearance.

The Dreamer is protected from this onslaught for a time by Reason, wielding his golden shield and successfully repelling all the missiles shot by the attackers. Reason is overcome, however, by Presence, who sneaks up and throws a blinding powder into the eyes of the warrior. Thus, Reason is defeated, and the Dreamer is soon enslaved by Venus. The effect of the victory is short-lived, however, for the goddesses and their partners depart as quickly as they came, leaving the Dreamer in a state of despair. A final trumpet blast from the ship wakens the Dreamer, who again finds himself back in the idealized countryside. The poem

closes with a panegyric to Chaucer, John Gower, and John Lydgate, and with an envoy in which Dunbar sends his "lytill quair [book]" forth into the world, where it must be obedient to all.

The use of the panegyric and the envoy reinforce the fact that Dunbar was thoroughly grounded in medieval poetic conventions. Chaucer, for example, used much the same sort of envoy in *Troilus and Criseyde* (1382). Unlike Chaucer, however, Dunbar was not fundamentally interested in the story, his two-dimensional characters, or the obvious moral that the passions must be controlled by the higher faculty of reason, which, unfortunately, is not always invincible. The poem's greatness, then, necessarily lies in Dunbar's masterful use of language. His smooth iambic pentameter lines are grouped into nine-line stanzas, rhyming *aabaabbab*, the very difficult form which Chaucer first employed in *Anelida and Arcite* (c. 1380). Moreover, though Dunbar could use only two different rhymes per stanza, nowhere did that seem to pose any great difficulties for him.

The highly wrought surface of Dunbar's poem is very clearly seen in his descriptions of the garden. What is created here, in the words of Edmund Reiss (*William Dunbar*, 1979), is "a world combining heaven and earth, one showing nature in idealized, purified, and rarefied splendor." Take, for example, these lines from the second and third stanzas:

> *Anamalit* was the felde wyth all colouris
> The *perly* droppis schake in *silvir* schouris,
>
> . . . . . . . . . . . . . . . . . . . .
>
> The *purpur* hevyn, ourscailit in *silvir* sloppis,
>   [with silver trailing clouds scattered about]
> *Ourgilt* [gilded over] the treis, branchis, lef
>   and barkis. (emphasis added)

Here Dunbar uses aureate terms, together with the recurring images of various gems and precious metals, to create a visionary landscape, reminiscent of Paradise in the Middle English *Pearl* (c. 1400). This is obviously not a personally experienced nature like that of the Romantic poets; Dunbar's nature is founded in the tradition of the *locus amoenus*, an idealized pastoral setting, the characteristics of which had already become standardized in late antiquity.

The word "aureate," signifying a highly wrought style and elevated diction, was coined by the English Chaucerian Lydgate, who borrowed many obscure terms from Latin for the sake of sonority and, hence, for dignifying his subject matter. Whereas Lydgate used his aureate terms basically for religious poetry, Dunbar went well beyond his predecessor and used aureate diction in other types of poems. The use of "artificial" words fit well into medieval poetic theory, and it was not until the nineteenth century, when William Wordsworth began to attack "poetic diction," that "aureate" came to have pejorative connotations.

### "THE TRETIS OF THE TUA MARIIT WEMEN AND THE WEDO"

It is a steep descent from the elevated tone and subject matter of "The Goldyn Targe" to the rowdy burlesque of "The Tretis of the Tua Mariit Wemen and the Wedo," though the level of Dunbar's conscious artistry nowhere flags in the latter piece. The poem, written in 530 lines of alliterative verse, begins delicately in the courtly love tradition, but after the first 40 lines the reader finds himself thrown into a crude display of female candor, where, in Kinsley's words, "Ideal beauty is exposed as the whited sepulchre of lust and greed."

Walking forth on a midsummer's night, the poet discovers a beautiful little garden, wherein are three courtly ladies, described in the typically idealized way: They all have beautiful blond hair, white skin, fine features, rich clothing, and jeweled adornment. That they wear green mantles—reminiscent, perhaps, of the gods and goddesses of "The Goldyn Targe"—seems an innocent innovation at this point, but as soon as the poet notes that they "wauchtit" [quaffed] their wine, the reader suspects that something is amiss.

While the narrator discreetly hides, one of the three women, the Widow, sets the dialogue in motion with a *demande d'amour*: "Bewrie [reveal], said the wedo, ye woddit wemen ying,/ Quhat mirth ye fand in maryage sen ye war menis wyffis." She also wishes to know if they have had extramarital affairs; if, given the chance, they would choose another husband; and if they believe the marriage bond to be insoluble. These are hardly the questions one would expect from a "chaste widow," and what follows are hardly the timid responses expected from two modest young wives.

The first is married to an old man who, like Januarius in Chaucer's "The Merchant's Tale" (*The Canterbury Tales*, 1387-1400), guards her jealously. The lusty young wife, however, reveals that her husband lacks the sexual vitality to satisfy fully her womanly desires, and she nonchalantly confesses that, if she were allowed, she would change husbands yearly, like the birds. For the time being her only satisfaction comes from the many gifts which her husband must give her before she consents to lovemaking.

Here, and in many other parts of this poem, Dunbar employs the style used in "The Flyting of Dunbar and Kennedy" to capture suitably the disgust of this young woman toward her spouse. In this style, a Gaelic poetic tradition, the poet piles up lists of epithets, uses various types of wordplay, and polishes the surface with obtrusive alliteration and rhyme. Generally employed when two poets publicly attacked each other, this style creates a tone that is a mixture of aggression, absurdity, and play. Dunbar's ingenuity and wit are shown when he incongruously transplants this harsh technique into the delicate context of courtly conversation.

The second wife is unhappy as well. Her young husband, though outwardly a ladies' man, is totally worn out from his earlier promiscuous behavior. Thus, she too, using suitably graphic metaphors, attacks her husband, reducing him from "rake" to "snivelling faker," and the three ladies laugh loudly, making "game amang the grene leiffis," and quaff more of the "sueit wyne." The two young wives, and the reader as well, are thus prepared for the presentation of the central character of the poem, the Widow, who is a literary cousin of Chaucer's Wife of Bath. Like Dame Alice, the Widow is both lecherous and proud of it. She is also outspoken, and she preaches the gospel of pleasure openly to her audience. Unlike Dame Alice, however, the Widow has no warmth or humanity; she is thoroughly calculating and vicious.

She begins her "sermon" with a mock invocation to God to send her "sentence," the medieval code word for an edifying moral. Religious parody was not uncommon in medieval literature, and, though Dunbar was a priest, he clearly was having fun here at the expense of the sacred rites. This parody, however, is slight compared to the poet's "The Dregy of Dunbar Maid to King

James the Fowrth being in Strivilling," where he constructed a mock liturgical Office of the Dead to tease James out of his Lenten retreat.

This unholy preacher, the Widow, had been married twice: first to an old Januarius type, and then to a middle-aged merchant. She recounts all the cruel steps which she took to divest the merchant completely of both his goods and his masculinity. When he finally died, she felt no regrets at all, for then she could begin to play the field in church, at public gatherings, and on pilgrimages. She describes, for example, how her black widow's veil can be used to cover her face while she surveys the crowds of men "To se quhat berne [fellow] is best brand [muscled] or bredest in schulderis." Using the language of courtly love literature, the Widow confesses to being the common property of all her "servants" (lovers) and to being a nymphomaniac who "comforts" them all. As a good preacher, however, she cannot recount a tale without offering her moral as well: The secret of a happy life is guile. Her counsel to the young wives is neatly summed up in the following: "Be dragonis baith and dowis [doves] ay in double forme." Hence her "sentence" is as neatly packaged as proverbial wisdom, and the end of her tale is similarly furnished with religious terminology: "This is the legeand of my lif, thought Latyne it be nane." The reference here is to saints' lives, a very popular form of literature in her day, even among the laity.

Dunbar resumes the high style of courtly literature as the three women retire, having passed the night in drunken camaraderie. The coming of the new day is as pleasantly described as if the narrator had just witnessed the first tryst of Troilus and Criseyde, but he ends the poem with a final ironic question: "Quhilk wald ye waill [choose] to your wif gif ye suld wed one?"

The characters in "The Tretis of the Tua Mariit Wemen and the Wedo" are so outrageous that one wonders whether the poem could ever be considered serious antifeminist satire. Perhaps Dunbar's intention lay no further than to produce belly laughs from his audience, especially the women. The poem does, however, show Dunbar's skill in blending various medieval traditions: the tradition of the courtly love narrative, the tradition of the eavesdropping narrator, the antifemin-

ist tradition, and the French tradition of *la chanson de la mal mariée* (the song of the unhappy wife).

**ANGLO-SAXON ALLITERATION**

Not only did Dunbar revive traditional themes, but he also revived, for one of the last times, a very ancient poetic device, the Anglo-Saxon alliterative line used by the poet of *Beowulf* (c. 1000) and his contemporaries. This type of poetic line construction was based not on syllable count and not on metrical feet but on the principle of alliteration. The theory was fairly complex, but basically each verse was constructed from two half-lines, separated by a caesura, each having two, or perhaps three, stressed syllables. Ordinarily the first three stressed syllables per line were alliterated. Thus, Dunbar's "Bewfie, said the wédo/ ye wóddit wémen ying," more than fulfills the requirements, actually adding an unnecessary fourth alliterated syllable. In practice, however, the alliterative line could vary widely in the total number of syllables and in the pattern of stressed alliterations. Moreover, rhyme was normally not used at all as a poetic device.

As Anglo-Saxon evolved into Middle English, chiefly owing to the effects of the Norman Invasion in 1066, alliterative poetry seemed to die out. The French tradition of decasyllabic rhyming verse came to be favored in England; Chaucer, for example, was highly influenced by just such Continental models. His character the Parson, however, does comment on the older verse form in the prologue to his sermon: "But trusteth well, I am a Southern man,/ I kan nat geeste [tell a tale] 'rum, ram, ruf,' by lettre." Nevertheless, there were those in the northwest of England, Chaucer's contemporaries, who could indeed "rum, ram, ruf," and thus English letters experienced an "alliterative revival" in such works as *Sir Gawain and the Green Knight* (c. 1400) and *The Vision of William, Concerning Piers the Plowman* (c. 1362, A Text; c. 1377, B Text; c. 1393, C Text; also known as *Piers Plowman*). Dunbar's work, coming as it does roughly one hundred years after these works, attests not only to a sort of poetic conservatism in Scotland, but also to Dunbar's poetic vigor, which enabled him to revive the old form so successfully.

**"THE DANCE OF THE SEVIN DEIDLY SYNNIS"**

Another traditional form which Dunbar used with imagination was the tail-rhymed stanza, commonly employed by long-winded medieval romancers and parodied by Chaucer in his "The Tale of Sir Thopas" (*The Canterbury Tales*). The pattern called for four-beat rhyming couplets separated by three-beat lines in the following manner: *aabccb* (or, if a twelve-line stanza was desired, *aabccbddbeeb*). Dunbar's "The Dance of the Sevin Deidly Synnis," part 1 of "Fasternes Evening in Hell," is composed of nine twelve-line stanzas with two additional six-line stanzas interspersed. They form another dream poem, like "The Goldyn Targe," but a strange one. The dream takes place on Fasternes Evening, the last day of the carnival before Lent. During this time the public celebrations included colorful pageants, filled with allegorical figures. Baxter notes that one must place the poem in just such a context, imagining the poet reacting to a group of revelers, costumed to represent sins, devils, fairies, and the like, dancing wildly under torchlight in the streets. Dunbar's poem captures them forever in their frenzy.

Indeed, Dunbar's portrait of the Seven Deadly Sins—Pride, Anger, Envy, Greed, Sloth, Lechery, and Gluttony—is probably the most lively of all the many such medieval portraits. In the poem, the Dreamer sees "Mahoun" (Satan) give orders for a dance in Hell, to which the personified vices immediately respond. The context explains why Dunbar's portraits are fairly realistic, and also why, perhaps, Dunbar took the opportunity to poke fun at his Highland foes. In the last stanza, Mahoun orders a Highland pageant to add some additional music to the festivities. Their Gaelic clatter, however, is too much even for Mahoun, who banishes them to the "depest pit of hell."

### "LAMENT FOR THE MAKARIS"

An artistic cousin of the "The Dance of the Sevin Deidly Synnis" is perhaps the *danse macabre*, another medieval commonplace. In painting and in verse, this motif shows the skeletons of people of all social classes dancing together as equals—in death. Dunbar takes up this theme in his poem "Lament for the Makaris," which Kinsley calls "one of the great elegiac expressions of a melancholy age." No longer the brazen poet of "The Tretis of the Tua Mariit Wemen and the Wedo" nor the frenetic poet of "The Dance of the Sevin Deidly Synnis," Dunbar here is saddened, pensive, and grave.

The poem is written in twenty-five stanzas of two tetrameter couplets each, a form which in Old French was called the *kyrielle*. The last line of each stanza is a Latin quotation from the Office of the Dead, "*Timor mortis conturbat me*" (the fear of death alarms me), a refrain that was often heard in an age of frequent war, great poverty, and the Black Plague. Lydgate, for example, used the same refrain in the poem entitled "*Timor Mortis Conturbat Me*," and it was probably Dunbar's model. Dunbar's poem, however, is much more compact and understated, and, as Gregory Kratzmann notes in *Anglo-Scottish Literary Relations, 1430-1550* (1980), these very qualities help give the poem the rhythm of a sober death dance.

The movement of the poem is from the universal to the particular. It begins with the sublunary principle that "Our plesance heir is all vane glory,/ This fals warld is bot transitory"; continues through a catalog of the various classes and professions, noting especially the deaths of his fellow poets; and concludes with the realization that his own death must be close at hand. By including the catalog of his fellow poets, Dunbar particularizes, and thus makes more poignant, this melancholy poetic form.

Dunbar's creativity, shown very well in "Lament for the Makaris," is manifest throughout his works; he seems always able to reinvest older poetic forms with new vigor. He is a poet of high energy, but not of inchoate effusions, for his power is always tightly controlled, each enameled word fitting carefully into a well-wrought framework. Variety is also a characteristic of Dunbar's work. His poetry always has a musical quality to it, for he was a master versifier with an extremely varied repertoire of patterns at his command. Even so, one might be forgiven for clinging to an image of Dunbar composing only his most energetic pieces, since, like his personified Deadly Sins, he seems always ready, in a literary sense, to "kast up gamountis [gambols] in the skyis."

BIBLIOGRAPHY

Bawcutt, Priscilla. *Dunbar the Makar*. New York: Oxford University Press, 1992. A comprehensive critical study of Dunbar's works. Includes a bibliography and an index.

_____. "William Dunbar and Gavin Douglas." In

*The History of Scottish Literature: Origins to 1660* (*Medieval and Renaissance*), edited by R. D. S. Jack and Cairns Craig. Vol. 1. Aberdeen: Aberdeen University Press, 1988. Demonstrates the poet's debt to his Scottish predecessors. Notes the differences between Dunbar and Douglas, who were similar in terms of the lengths of their works, the subjects about which they wrote, and the total works they composed. Includes notes and works for further reading and lists primary and secondary sources.

Baxter, J. W. *William Dunbar: A Biographical Study.* 1952. Reprint. St. Clair Shores, Mich.: Scholarly Press, 1971. Perhaps the seminal introductory volume of commentary on Dunbar, this work traces the poet's life and comments on his poems. Each of its sixteen chapters is highlighted by additional notes. This volume contains six appendixes that range from Dunbar's textual sources to examinations of poems believed to be composed by Dunbar. Contains an extensive bibliography of primary and secondary sources and two indexes. The first index refers to individual poems in the volume; the second is a general index.

Davidoff, Judith M. "William Dunbar's Framing Fiction Poems." In *Beginning Well.* Cranbury, N.J.: Associated University Presses, 1988. In this interesting and novel chapter, Dunbar's parodies of traditional literary forms are discussed. Of particular importance is the demonstration of Dunbar's proficiency in handling traditional literary patterns in "The Goldyn Targe" and the observation that Dunbar comically turns old conventions to original uses.

Kramer, Johanna. "'Falsett No Feit Hes': A Proverb in William Dunbar's 'In Vice Most Vicius He Excellis.'" *English Studies* 89, no. 3 (June, 2008): 263. Presents a profile of Dunbar and examines one of his works.

Mapstone, Sally, ed. *William Dunbar, "the Nobill Poyet": Essays in Honour of Priscilla Bawcutt.* East Linton, East Lothian, Scotland: Tuckwell, 2001. A collection of essays on Dunbar collected in honor of Bawcutt, an expert on the poet.

Reiss, Edmund. "The Ironic Art of William Dunbar." In *Fifteenth Century Studies*, edited by Robert F. Yeager. Hamden, Conn.: Archon Books, 1984. While this study is brief, it offers insight concerning the eclectic nature of Dunbar's poems. These variations are introduced and distinguished in short order; the result is a precise compendium for further study. The work's extensive notes provide a good starting point for anyone interested in Dunbar.

_____. *William Dunbar.* Boston: Twayne, 1979. One of Twayne's English Authors series. The six chapters in this important work are devoted to the various stages and writing styles in the literary career of Dunbar. The work traces his growth from court poet to Christian moralist and to writer of love poems and offers precise explication of many of his works. Contains a brief chronology of important dates and events in Dunbar's life, thorough notes and references, a short select bibliography that lists primary and secondary sources (including general studies, bibliographies, books, and articles), and a thorough index.

Scott, Tom. *Dunbar: A Critical Exposition of the Poems.* 1966. Reprint. Westport, Conn.: Greenwood Press, 1977. Perhaps the definitive critical work on the poems of Dunbar. This study concentrates on the sociocultural milieu of Dunbar. Its primary importance is its value as a contextual approach to the works of Dunbar.

Strong, David. "Supra-Natural Creation in Dunbar's 'The Goldyn Targe.'" *Philological Quarterly* 82, no. 2 (Spring, 2003): 149-67. Strong finds in this work a philosophy that "praises nature's ability to connect the human with the divine."

*Gregory M. Sadlek*

# LAWRENCE DURRELL

**Born:** Julundur, India; February 27, 1912
**Died:** Sommières, France; November 7, 1990
**Also known as:** Charles Norden; Gaffer Peeslake

PRINCIPAL POETRY

*Quaint Fragment: Poems Written Between the Ages of Sixteen and Nineteen*, 1931
*Ten Poems*, 1932
*Bromo Bombastes*, 1933
*Transition*, 1934
*Proems: An Anthology of Poems*, 1938 (with others)
*A Private Country*, 1943
*Cities, Plains, and People*, 1946
*On Seeming to Presume*, 1948
*Deus Loci*, 1950
*Private Drafts*, 1955
*The Tree of Idleness, and Other Poems*, 1955
*Selected Poems*, 1956
*Collected Poems*, 1960
*Penguin Modern Poets One*, 1962 (with Elizabeth Jennings and R. S. Thomas)
*Beccafico = Le Becfigue*, 1963 (English; includes French translation by F. J. Temple)
*Selected Poems, 1935-1963*, 1964
*The Ikons, and Other Poems*, 1966
*The Red Limbo Lingo: A Poetry Notebook for 1968-1970*, 1971
*On the Suchness of the Old Boy*, 1972
*Vega, and Other Poems*, 1973
*Collected Poems, 1931-1974*, 1980
*Too Far to Hear the Singing*, 2005 (Francoise Hestman Durrell, editor)

OTHER LITERARY FORMS

Lawrence Durrell (DUR-uhl) wrote novels, plays, travel books, humorous sketches, and poetry. The differences in genre, however, cannot obscure his fundamental and single identity as a poet. He is best known for his novels, especially *The Alexandria Quartet* (1962) and *The Avignon Quintet* (1992). Any reader of these works will recognize the same hand at work in

Durrell's poems. The beauty of language, the exotic settings, and the subtle treatment of the themes of love, death, and time are elements common to all of Durrell's work. In addition, the novels are rife with interpolated poetry. The characters not only speak poetically, but also quote at length from Greek, Egyptian, French, and English poets. Some have questioned this plethora of verse as unrealistic; others insist that Durrell's use of language and interpolated poetry represents a more intense reality, not a fantasy.

Durrell's poetic drama has inevitably enjoyed less attention than his novels, but it provides an excellent showcase for his skill at characterization and his poetic gifts. Durrell himself considered several passages from *Sappho* (pr. 1950) good enough to include in his *Collected Poems*, and most readers would agree. A later play, *Acte* (pr. 1964), shows that his drama does not rely entirely on the author's magnificent command of English: It was first performed in German, three years before its publication.

Ultimately, Durrell was a word artist, a poet. All genres had for him their particular virtues, and he brought to them all a poetic impulse that no change in form could disrupt.

ACHIEVEMENTS

Lawrence Durrell's accomplishments in prose overshadowed his work in verse. Most readers will turn to the *Collected Poems* only after having read *The Alexandria Quartet*, or perhaps one of the travel books. Durrell won no major awards for poetry, despite his consistent excellence from the 1940's on. His name rarely appears on the lists of major English poets of the twentieth century.

All this notwithstanding, Durrell's achievement as a poet is sound and his eventual recognition assured. His success in other genres left him well-off financially and under no pressure; he could write poetry as he pleased, with no fear of disappointing expectant readers and no burden of leadership. Precisely because Durrell made his formidable reputation as a novelist, he could approach his poetry as an alternative. This does not imply that he merely dabbled—on the contrary, every poem shows the mark of craft and diligence—but rather that the wealth of material afforded by his diverse experience and wide-ranging mind could find its expression in pure poetry. He was free to write only those poems that his good judgment told him to write.

Neither rigidly traditional nor wildly experimental, Durrell's poems represent the subtle innovations of a consummate and independent artist. In this respect, they are reminiscent of the work of Wallace Stevens. Like Stevens, Durrell balanced the demands of tradition and the modern psyche, creating poems that the eye and the mind can follow, but that the soul does not reject as obsolete. Some of them compare favorably with the best of the twentieth century and will someday be read for their own merits, not merely for their connection with the famous novels by the same author.

### BIOGRAPHY

Born in India, Lawrence George Durrell led a wandering life that profoundly influenced all his work. His formal education was adequate but limited; ironically, he could never gain admission to Cambridge, which

*Lawrence Durrell* (©Rosemarie Clausen)

may have motivated his half-jesting claim that he became a writer "by sheer ineptitude." In any event, he managed to acquire an astonishing fund of knowledge, becoming competent as a painter, a jazz pianist, a race-car driver, a teacher, and a diplomat. In his turbulent career, he lived and worked in London, Paris, Cairo, Belgrade, Beirut, Athens, Cyprus, Argentina, and Provence. Naturally enough, he also became an accomplished linguist, particularly in Greek. Many of the places mentioned above are familiar to readers as settings of his novels or travel books; they are also prominent in his poems.

Durrell's personal life was no less an odyssey than his career. Married three times, he went through two divorces and became a widower in 1967. His friendships proved more lasting, in particular his evolving relationship with Henry Miller. Beginning as Miller's disciple and admirer, Durrell virtually turned the tables. Even so, the two remained close and mutually stimulating friends, as evidenced by *Lawrence Durrell and Henry Miller: A Private Correspondence* (1963).

After many years of working at odd jobs, teaching, and representing his country in various diplomatic posts, Durrell settled in Provence in 1957 and devoted his full time to writing. Always a rapid worker—he completed the monumental *The Alexandria Quartet* in less than a year of actual writing time—he published many novels, dramas, and collections of poetry from the 1960's to the 1980's. By the late 1970's, his wanderlust seemed cured; he stirred only reluctantly. In his late seclusion, Durrell was perhaps like Prospero, from William Shakespeare's *The Tempest* (pr. 1611), a favorite character of his—he worked his magic and recalled his life at court. Both his poems and his prose reveal the fruits of an extraordinary life at many Mediterranean "courts." Durrell died in Sommières, France, in 1990.

### ANALYSIS

Lawrence Durrell's poetry has many rare qualities. His multifaceted life gave him a breadth of vision and a balance of mind that, in combination with his natural gifts and hard work, enabled him to produce a body of poetry remarkable for its beauty, richness, and integrity. His poems afford a glimpse into the changeless world of the Mediterranean, and into the ever-changing lives of the people who live there. However, the poems never become mere travelogues; part of Durrell's integrity lies in his adherence to the central purpose of poetry: to illuminate the human experience. He remains faithful to that goal throughout "the wooing and seduction of form."

Reading Durrell's poetry for the first time, a discerning reader might be reminded of T. S. Eliot, echoed in Durrell's sparse but effective rhymes, his facility in finding the mot juste, and some of his astonishing single lines, and think of "The Love Song of J. Alfred Prufrock" (1915) and *The Waste Land* (1922). Reflecting further, the first-time reader would perceive that both Durrell and Eliot are philosophical poets, and that their work shows their common preoccupation with the Western tradition and certain of its key philosophical issues.

Truly discerning readers, however, will conclude that the resemblance ends there. For all his superficial likeness to Eliot, Durrell has a distinctive voice as a poet. The hypothetical discerning reader might well end up thinking of Durrell as a curious mixture of the qualities of Eliot, D. H. Lawrence, and Gerard Manley Hopkins, but even that remarkable formulation would not cover all the facts. Durrell is unique; he is the Anglo-Indian poet of the Mediterranean, craftsperson, and thinker at once.

In an interview printed in the Autumn-Winter issue of *Paris Review* for 1959-1960, Durrell reveals his guiding principle as a poet: "Poetry is form, and the wooing and seduction of form is the whole game." His poems seem rather traditional in their construction; a glance at the printed page reveals few typographical eccentricities. A careful reading, however, will turn up subtle variations in meter, line-length, and rhyme. Durrell worked hard and successfully at wooing and seducing form. He altered form almost imperceptibly, so that a sonnet by Durrell does not seem quite a sonnet. One re-counts lines and syllables and finally admits that the poem is a sonnet, but an odd one. Simply put, Durrell wrested the form away from tradition and made it his own. This victory makes possible—by no means inevitable—the success of the poem.

## "A SOLILOQUY OF HAMLET" AND "STYLE"

An example of this phenomenon is the second of the fourteen poems in "A Soliloquy of Hamlet." The poet has already indicated that the fourteen poems are to be regarded as sonnets. The student of the form, however, will demur because of the lack of rhyme and the arrangement into couplets. On intensive reading, he will be compelled to concede that there is a six/eight structure, the usual arrangement of a sonnet *à rebours*—in short, that his beloved sonnet form has been seduced.

Durrell offers an intriguing, if somewhat deceptive, insight into his art in a poem entitled "Style." The poet strives for "Something like the sea;/ Unlabored momentum of water;/ But going somewhere. . . ." Subsequently, he wishes to write "the wind that slits/ Forests from end to end." Finally, he rejects sea and wind for a third alternative:

> But neither is yet
> Fine enough for the line I hunt.
> The dry long blade of the
> Sword-grass might suit me
> Better: an assassin of polish.

The choice is never really made, of course: Durrell can write in all these manners and many more. The poem serves more to convey a sense of his unending struggle for perfection, in his verse and in his prose, than to issue any artistic manifesto.

In this struggle for perfection, Durrell differed from other writers only in his relative success. Other differences are easier to define and more important to the understanding of his poetry. Here it helps to refer to his prose work. Any reader of the novels and travel books knows Durrell's powers of description, his subtlety in handling love relationships between his characters, and his flair for transforming the mundane into the magical. As a poet, he displays the same talents in a different medium.

### THE IMPORTANCE OF PLACE

As mentioned above, Durrell was the Anglo-Indian poet of the Mediterranean. The phrase is perhaps a trifle awkward, but to omit any element would be to misrepresent the poet. As an Anglo-Indian, he enjoyed at once the benefits of an English education and a childhood in the East. He also suffered, virtually from birth, the plight of the exile, the person without a country. England was alien; English was not. Durrell's work depends on the English literary tradition, even though he could not bear the thought of living in Great Britain. He found a series of homes on the shores of the Mediterranean: Greece, Lebanon, Cyprus, Egypt, France. The Mediterranean is the sine qua non of his work; nowhere else could he have found such "cities, plains, and people." Thus, every element in the description is vital, because Durrell's birthplace, education, and later environment together help to account for the unique nature of his poetry.

### "The Anecdotes"

The importance of place in Durrell's poetry is nowhere more evident than in "The Anecdotes," a series of brief lyrics with subtitles such as "In Cairo," "At Rhodes," and "In Patmos." Durrell has an unsurpassed genius for evoking the peculiar atmosphere of locale, and he makes good use of the imagination-stirring names of Mediterranean cities. "The Anecdotes" concern people and emotions, but the geography helps the reader to understand both.

In the third poem, "At Rhodes," Durrell suggests the languorous beauty of Rhodes by way of a few deft images. The memory of the boats in the harbor, the antics of two Greek children, and the town, "thrown as on a screen of watered silk," becomes a compact poem: "twelve sad lines against the dark." The lines express nostalgia for Rhodes through a few well-chosen emblems of the city, suggesting a lovely tranquillity that the poet now lacks. The personal association—Durrell missed Rhodes sorely during his tour of duty in Egypt—becomes a theme.

The sense of place in the poems generally does have an importance beyond mere exotic appeal. The countries, the cities, even the streets and cafés that Durrell mentions have associations with specific moods and memories. Sometimes the connection is obscure; more often, Durrell selects his images so skillfully that the reader shares the mood without quite knowing why. In the best examples, the poet achieves Eliot's ideal, the "objective correlative."

The fourteenth anecdote, "In Beirut," has the reader sighing with the melancholy of "after twenty years another meeting," though Durrell gives few details of the people involved or of their stories. Beirut takes on the withered nature of the old friends, "flesh murky as old horn,/ Hands dry now as seabiscuit." Even without specific background, the contrast between "breathless harbours north of Tenedos" in April and "in Tunis, winter coming on" is evident. Durrell's beloved Greece comes to represent life and youth; the cities of Asia and North Africa connote aging and death.

### "Mareotis"

One of the best examples of Durrell's artistry in this regard is "Mareotis." The reader need not know beforehand that Mareotis is a salt marsh outside Alexandria; Durrell makes it clear enough, even as he draws the parallel between the atmosphere of the marsh and the climate of his soul. The wind of the place, "Not subtle, not confiding, touches once again,/ The melancholy elbow cheek and paper." The odd blend of discontent and self-knowledge matches the nature of the salt marsh. It misses the changes of spring, remaining the same, just as the poet does. Durrell has performed a sleight of hand, first alluding to a place, then subtly sketching its nature, and ultimately using the finished image to make his poetic point.

### "Cities, Plains, and People"

It must be noted that Durrell's reliance on images of place sometimes renders his poetry difficult to understand. Most readers know next to nothing of the world the poet inhabits, beyond a few clichés. In the novels, he overcomes this problem masterfully by means of long descriptions. In the poems, lacking this resource, he depends on a few striking images. This may account in part for the greater popularity of the fiction. To Durrell's credit, relatively few of his poems are seriously marred by his esoteric geography.

In "Cities, Plains, and People," one of his major poems, Durrell approaches overwhelming questions in the course of a poetic autobiography. He begins under the shadow of the Himalayas, "in idleness," an innocent tyke to whom "Sex was small,/ Death was small. . . ." Both have become very large for the poet as he has grown, but the early years in British India stand as the time before the Fall. There in the mountains, only "nine marches" from inscrutable Lhasa, the boy grows up. He does not, however, go to Tibet:

But he for whom steel and running water
Were roads, went westward only
To the prudish cliffs and the sad green home
Of Pudding Island o'er the Victorian foam

The growing artist finds himself repelled and attracted by Europe; though he knows that "London/ Could only be a promise-giving kingdom," there are always "Dante and Homer/ To impress the lame and awkward newcomer." Impressed in both senses of the word, the Anglo-Indian struggles against the insidious examples of Saint Bede, Saint Augustine, and Saint Jerome, those deniers of the flesh, and mourns the dismal reality, "The potential passion hidden, Wordsworth/ In the desiccated bodies of postmistresses." The associations of place here serve to advance the story and to present the thought of the developing poet.

Durrell goes on to discover the escape hatch, the magic of Prospero's island. Here the literal and the fictive landscapes merge. William Shakespeare and the earthly Mediterranean both have a part in the choice, an eclectic mixture of the best of the British literary tradition and the best of the poet's several homes. The conflict is by no means resolved, but the two great forces have at least acknowledged each other. The Englishman born in India has found something worth having from Pudding Island.

The journey continues because the poet has found only a working arrangement, not an ultimate answer. He still has much to learn of those great matters that the child considered insignificant. He learns much of sex. It becomes "a lesser sort of speech, and the members doors." It is versatile, serving as a means of salvation both spiritual—"man might botch his way/ To God via Valéry, Gide or Rabelais"—the physical: "savage Chatterleys of the new romance/ Get carried off in sex, the ambulance." That Durrell can debunk in one stanza what he affirms so powerfully elsewhere implies not inconsistency but rather an appreciation of the complexity of the matter. The youth has lost his innocence and has also gone beyond a naïve faith in a simple solution. Sex may be an answer but not a simple answer.

Durrell goes on to probe beyond knowledge, "in the dark field of sensibility." As in the novels, he comes to no rigid conclusion. At the end of *The Alexandria Quartet*, Darley sits down to write; "Cities, Plains, and People" ends with an analogous image:

For Prospero remains the evergreen
Cell by the margin of the sea and land,
Who many cities, plains, and people saw
Yet by his open door
In sunlight fell asleep
One summer with the Apple in his hand.

Between Durrell the poet and Durrell the novelist there lies only the difference in genre: The artist and the resolution are the same. Prospero remains, latent with magic—the magic to bring order and beauty to the chaotic world of cities, plains, and people. Darley on his island off the coast of Egypt and the poet somewhere in the Aegean represent Durrell/Prospero, perhaps the key image of his work.

### "PROFFER THE LOAVES OF PAIN"

Durrell's repertoire is by no means limited to extended philosophical ruminations, nor his imagery to geographical references. He has estimable gifts as a lyric poet, which he demonstrates throughout his work. One particularly fine example, "Proffer the Loaves of Pain," shows Durrell's technical wizardry in the manipulation of rhyme. The four stanzas run the gamut of the seasons, echoing sadly: "they shall not meet." The first three stanzas feature half-rhymes: "quantum/ autumn," "saunter/winter," and "roamer/summer." This tantalizing soundplay gives the true rhyme of the conclusion, "ring/spring," a finality not inherent in the words of the stanza. The poem dodges and ducks until the last inexorable rhyme destroys the last hope—in spring, ironically enough.

The poem distinguishes itself in other ways as well. The economy of language requires close attention on the part of the reader, for the clues are subtle. For example, the poet employs the word "this" to modify the seasons in the first two stanzas. Summer and spring, however, serve as objects of the preposition "in." The specific negation of the first half of the poem becomes a chilling "nevermore" in the last two stanzas, by the simple device of a change in grammar.

### "THE DEATH OF GENERAL UNCEBUNKE"

Durrell's melancholy wit and his fascination with the ever-lurking mystery of death come together in

"The Death of General Uncebunke: A Biography in Little," which he labels "Not satire but an exercise in ironic compassion." The biography encompasses not only the general, a Victorian empire builder, but also the dowager Aunt Prudence. Despite the earlier gibes at "Pudding Island," the poet holds true to his word: The poem expresses no contempt for Uncebunke, even if the reader cannot stifle a chuckle or two at the man who "wrote a will in hexameters." Rather, Durrell transmutes the potentially absurd details of the old campaigner's life into symbols of his death. He rides horses, fords rivers, and crosses into Tartary, and the poet invests these adventures with a new and final significance.

Durrell's sentiment is noble and restrained, but his handling of language and form in the poem deserves even more attention. The fourteen "carols" begin in three fashions. Four start with the words "My uncle sleeps in the image of death"; five begin "My uncle has gone beyond astronomy"; the remainder open with references to Aunt Prudence. Thus, the poet achieves at once a compelling repetition and movement; the lines referring to the uncle maintain the elegiac tone, while the stanzas devoted to Prudence reinforce the sense of gradual decay.

A number of phonetic tricks bolster the ironic character of the poem and add to the reader's grasp of the characters. Of the uncle, for example, Durrell says: "he like a faultless liner, finer never took air." The sound play recalls Gerard Manley Hopkins, although the good Jesuit would probably not have indulged in the irony. Aunt Prudence prays earnestly and ridiculously: "Thy will be done in Baden Baden./ In Ouchy, Lord, and in Vichy." By one of his own favorite ploys, here in a new guise, Durrell uses references of place to provoke a response.

Finally, Durrell tosses off one memorable line after another, each in itself worth an ode. Uncebunke in his dotage lives on a country estate, "devoted to the polo-pony, mesmerized by stamps." Aunt Prudence putters about, "feeding the parrot, pensive over a croquet-hoop." The horses in the stable "champ, stamp, yawn, paw in the straw." One suspects that Hopkins—or any other modern poet, for that matter—would have taken pride in such verses.

## "BALLAD OF THE OEDIPUS COMPLEX"

To all his other virtues as a poet, Durrell adds a lively and whimsical sense of humor. Though the prevailing literary prejudices of the twentieth century keep most readers from appraising humorous verse at its full worth, no one who has suffered the slings and arrows of outrageous Freudians will read the "Ballad of the Oedipus Complex" unmoved. Besides poking fun at overworked psychological truisms, Durrell shows a fine English sense of fair play, plunging his own face into a custard pie:

> I tried to strangle it one day
> While sitting in the Lido
> But it got up and tickled me
> And now I'm all libido.

This ability to snicker at his own literary obsessions betokens a fine sensibility in Durrell, as well as a sense of humor so often lacking in his contemporaries.

## OTHER MAJOR WORKS

LONG FICTION: *Pied Piper of Lovers*, 1935; *Panic Spring*, 1937 (as Charles Norden); *The Black Book*, 1938; *Cefalû*, 1947 (republished as *The Dark Labyrinth*, 1958); *Justine*, 1957; *Balthazar*, 1958; *Mountolive*, 1958; *Clea*, 1960; *The Alexandria Quartet*, 1962 (includes previous 4 novels); *Tunc*, 1968; *Nunquam*, 1970; *Monsieur: Or, The Prince of Darkness*, 1974; *Livia: Or, Buried Alive*, 1978; *Constance: Or, Solitary Practices*, 1981; *Sebastian: Or, Ruling Passions*, 1983; *Quinx: Or, The Ripper's Tale*, 1985; *The Avignon Quintet*, 1992 (includes previous 5 novels).

SHORT FICTION: *Esprit de Corps: Sketches from Diplomatic Life*, 1957; *Stiff Upper Lip: Life Among the Diplomats*, 1958; *Sauve Qui Peut*, 1966; *The Best of Antrobus*, 1974; *Antrobus Complete*, 1985.

PLAYS: *Sappho*, pr. 1950; *An Irish Faustus*, pb. 1963; *Acte*, pr. 1964.

NONFICTION: *Prospero's Cell*, 1945; *A Landmark Gone*, 1949; *A Key to Modern British Poetry*, 1952; *Reflections on a Marine Venus*, 1953; *Bitter Lemons*, 1957; *Art and Outrage*, 1959; *Lawrence Durrell and Henry Miller: A Private Correspondence*, 1963 (George Wickes, editor); *Spirit of Place: Letters and Essays on Travel*, 1969 (Alan G. Thomas, editor); *The*

*Big Supposer: Dialogues with Marc Alyn/Lawrence Durrell*, 1973; *Sicilian Carousel*, 1977; *The Greek Islands*, 1978; *Literary Lifelines: The Richard Aldington-Lawrence Durrell Correspondence*, 1981; *The Durrell-Miller Letters, 1935-1980*, 1988; *Caesar's Vast Ghost: A Portrait of Provence*, 1990; *Lawrence Durrell: Conversations*, 1998 (Earl G. Ingersoll, editor); *The Lawrence Durrell Travel Reader*, 2004 (Clint Willis, editor).

TRANSLATIONS: *Six Poems from the Greek of Sekilianos and Seferis*, 1946 (of Eleni Sekilianos and George Seferis); *The King of Asine, and Other Poems*, 1948 (of Seferis); *The Curious History of Pope Joan*, 1954 (of Emmanuel Royidis's biography, revised as *Pope Joan*, 1960).

CHILDREN'S LITERATURE: *White Eagles over Serbia*, 1957.

## BIBLIOGRAPHY

Bengal, Michael H., ed. *On Miracle Ground: Essays on the Fiction of Lawrence Durrell*. Lewisburg, Pa.: Bucknell University Press, 1990. Limited to Durrell's major fiction, these essays reflect the variety of critical responses the novels elicited "from metafiction to close textual analysis to deconstruction to reader response theory." "Overture" by Durrell gives his own understanding of the forces that shaped him. Contains a useful bibliography of secondary sources.

Bowker, Gordon. *Through the Dark Labyrinth: A Biography of Lawrence Durrell*. New York: St. Martin's Press, 1997. Bowker reveals Durrell to be a complex man beset at times by incredibly painful circumstances that he was somehow able to transmute into his fiction.

Durrell, Gerald. *My Family and Other Animals*. 1956. Reprint. New York: Penguin, 2000. This memoir by Durrell's youngest brother, a naturalist, covers the time the family lived in Corfu before World War II. Although hardly complete as a strict biography, this book, along with *Fauna and Family* (1978) offers an interesting and amusing picture of Lawrence Durrell and his literary circle.

Fraser, George S. *Lawrence Durrell*. London: Longman, 1970. A perceptive pamphlet-length study of Durrell's major literary output up to 1970. Contains a select bibliography.

Herbrechter, Stefan. *Lawrence Durrell: Postmodernism and the Ethics of Alterity*. Atlanta: Rodopi, 1999. An investigation of the notions of alterity that underlie the work of Durrell and postmodernist theory.

Kersnowski, Frank, ed. *Into the Labyrinth: Essays Concerning the Art of Lawrence Durrell*. Rochester, N.Y.: University of Rochester Press, 1991. This collection of critical essays and biographical reminiscences contains essays on all forms of Durrell's writing and painting. The reproduction of art by Durrell and the chronology of his life provide information not readily available elsewhere.

MacNiven, Ian. *Lawrence Durrell: A Biography*. London: Faber and Faber, 1998. Written with Durrell's cooperation. MacNiven had extraordinary access to both his subject and his papers (including notebooks and letters). His interviews with Durrell's friends and lovers are integrated into a probing look at the sources of his writing. Includes illustrations, chronology, family tree, and notes.

Morrison, Ray. *A Smile in His Mind's Eye: A Study of the Early Works of Lawrence Durrell*. Buffalo, N.Y.: University of Toronto Press, 2005. Morrison, a friend of Durrell, analyzes his early works, including the poetry, seeing in them a connection to the later works.

Vander Closter, Susan. *Joyce Cary and Lawrence Durrell: A Reference Guide*. Boston: G. K. Hall, 1985. This annotated bibliography of secondary material is essential to anyone writing about Durrell. Reviews, essays, and critical studies from 1937 to 1983 are listed chronologically. The first half of the book concerns Joyce Cary, and the second half concerns Durrell.

Weigel, John A. *Lawrence Durrell*. Rev. ed. Boston: Twayne, 1989. This revision of the 1965 study provides a clear overview of Durrell's life and writing. The discussion of individual works is useful for students approaching Durrell for the first time. Although Durrell's poetry, drama, and criticism are discussed, the study focuses on the novels.

*Philip Krummrich*

# *E*

## T. S. ELIOT

**Born:** St. Louis, Missouri; September 26, 1888
**Died:** London, England; January 4, 1965

PRINCIPAL POETRY

"The Love Song of J. Alfred Prufrock," 1915
*Prufrock and Other Observations*, 1917
*Poems*, 1919
*Ara Vos Prec*, 1920
*The Waste Land*, 1922
*Poems, 1909-1925*, 1925
*Ash Wednesday*, 1930
*Triumphal March*, 1931
*Sweeney Agonistes*, 1932
*Words for Music*, 1934
*Collected Poems, 1909-1935*, 1936
*Old Possum's Book of Practical Cats*, 1939
*Four Quartets*, 1943
*The Cultivation of Christmas Trees*, 1954
*Collected Poems, 1909-1962*, 1963
*Poems Written in Early Youth*, 1967
*The Complete Poems and Plays*, 1969

OTHER LITERARY FORMS

When T. S. Eliot startled the poetic world with the publication of *Prufrock and Other Observations* in 1917, he was already on his way to becoming a prolific, formidable, and renowned literary critic of extraordinary originality and depth. Between 1916 and 1920, for example, he contributed almost one hundred essays and reviews to several journals, some of which he helped edit. Although his most enduring and famous criticism (except for his superb work on Dante) is contained in such essays as "Hamlet and His Problems" and "Tradition and the Individual Talent" (*The Sacred Wood*, 1920), he published thirty books and pamphlets and scores of essays, many of which remain uncollected. Chief among his other volumes of prose are

*Homage to John Dryden* (1924), *Shakespeare and the Stoicism of Seneca* (1927), *For Lancelot Andrewes* (1928), the celebrated *Dante* (1929), *Selected Essays* (1932, 1950), *The Use of Poetry and the Use of Criticism: Studies in the Relation of Criticism to Poetry in England* (1933), *After Strange Gods: A Primer of Modern Heresy* (1934), *Essays Ancient and Modern* (1936), *Poetry and Drama* (1951), and *On Poetry and Poets* (1957). From its inception in 1922 until its last issue in 1939, Eliot was editor of *The Criterion* and an important contributor to that and other journals concerned with literary, cultural, political, and religious matters.

Eliot came to drama later than to poetry and criticism, though the seeds of drama are clearly in his early poetry, and the drama occupied much of his criticism. His dramatic writing ranges from religious pageant-plays in verse, *The Rock: A Pageant Play* (pr., pb. 1934) and *Murder in the Cathedral* (pr., pb. 1935), to quite diverse efforts such as *The Family Reunion* (pr., pb. 1939), *The Cocktail Party* (pr. 1949), *The Confidential Clerk* (pr. 1953), and *The Elder Statesman* (pr. 1958). All his dramatic work has as one of its objects the restoration of poetic drama to the popular theater.

The record of Eliot's achievement is by no means complete. Many of his essays are available only in the journals in which they were published, and his notebooks have not been fully mined. *The Letters of T. S. Eliot: Volume I, 1898-1922*, edited by Valerie Eliot, his second wife, was published in 1988. The letters exemplify Eliot's characteristic civility, and they give glimpses of his occasional insecurities as a young American determined to succeed in England on England's terms. Eliot's thousand or so letters to Emily Hale have not been published; they are in the Princeton University Library and may be made public after January 1, 2020. Valerie Eliot has edited and published *The Waste Land: A Facsimile and Transcript of the Original Drafts Including the Annotations of Ezra Pound* (1971) and Eliot's *Poems Written in Early Youth*. Several of Eliot's manuscripts are in the Berg Collection of the New York Public Library and in the Hayward Collection at King's College, Cambridge.

ACHIEVEMENTS

T. S. Eliot's achievements are such that he became the premier poet of his own generation and enlivened literary criticism by contributing such phrases as "objective correlative," "dissociation of sensibility," and "impersonal" poetry. He greatly helped to foster a resurgence of interest in Dante, in the Metaphysical poets of the seventeenth century, and in Elizabethan and Jacobean drama at a time when such a resurgence was needed. He also provided a strong critical and poetic voice that chided the Victorian and Edwardian poets while furnishing a new poetry that served as a practical criticism of theirs.

The one title he preferred, and the one by which he is best and justly remembered, is "poet." His poetry is not, on first acquaintance, easy; and it may not be so on second or third acquaintance. He is, as he said of his own favorite writer, Dante, "a poet to whom one grows up over a lifetime." His poetic originality, called into question in his early days by those who charged him with plagiarism, lies in the careful crafting and arrangement of lines and phrases, the introduction of literary, historical, and cultural allusions, and the elaboration of image and symbol in highly charged and often dramatic language that both describes and presents a personal emotion or experience and generalizes it. Eliot's careful husbanding of words, phrases, images, and symbols results in a recurrence of those elements and a continuity of subject matter from his juvenilia through his first and second masterpieces ("The Love Song of J. Alfred Prufrock" and *The Waste Land*) to his last (*Four Quartets*). The themes of his greater poems, as of his lesser ones, involve identity, sexuality, the nature of love, religious belief (or its absence), and the telling of a tale/writing of a poem in language adequate to the emotion or state that the telling/writing seeks to express.

It is a short step from the dramatic situations of Eliot's early and middle poetry, situations that owe something to the poetry of Robert Browning, more to John Donne and the Elizabethan and Jacobean dramatists, and most to the Symbolist poetry of Jules Laforgue. One of Eliot's chief aspirations and limited achievements countered the thrust of modern drama since Henrik Ibsen (the Nō drama of William Butler Yeats excepted): Eliot was dedicated to the revivification of verse drama in the twentieth century. He succeeded in doing this, to some extent, in *The Rock*, more so in *Murder in the Cathedral*, and less so in *The Family Reunion* and subsequent plays. Although his account of the martyrdom of Thomas à Becket clearly inspired Jean Anouilh's *Becket* (pr. 1959), Eliot's attempt to revive the poetic drama amounted to a false start, perhaps attributable in part to the highly poetic but undramatic and static nature of his plays.

Eliot's achievements have led at least one critic to state that in the area of humane letters the larger part of the twentieth century may be called the Age of Eliot. Eliotatry aside, there is some merit in the remark. No stranger to prizes and awards, Eliot may have valued, and needed, the *Dial* Award of 1922 for *The Waste Land*. In the course of his long career he received doctoral degrees (*honoris causa*) from a score of British, European, and American universities; was Clark Lecturer at Trinity College, Cambridge (1926), and Charles Eliot Norton Professor of Poetry at Harvard University (1932-1933); and won the Hanseatic Goethe Prize (1954), the Dante Gold Medal (Florence, 1959), the Emerson-Thoreau Medal (American Academy of Arts and Sciences, 1959), and the U.S. Medal of Freedom (1964). In 1948, he achieved a dual distinction: Not only was he awarded the British Order of Merit, but he also won the Nobel Prize in Literature for, he surmised, "the entire corpus."

In another sense, Eliot's continuing achievement may be measured by the extent to which innumerable students, teachers, and researchers have surrendered to him. Each year several books or portions of books, as well as numerous essays, swell the number of works about him, his thought, and his writing; they stand as monuments to his still-unfolding mind and meaning. A legend in his own time, he remains one today.

BIOGRAPHY

To see Thomas Stearns Eliot's end in his beginning is to recall that Andrew Eliot (1627-1704) emigrated from East Coker, Somerset, to Beverly, Massachusetts, in a century that his twentieth century scion would explore and reexplore in poetry and criticism for most of his life. Eliot's grandfather, the Reverend William Greenleaf Eliot, forsook his native New England and

*T. S. Eliot* (©The Nobel Foundation)

went with missionary zeal to the outpost of St. Louis, Missiouri, in 1834. There he founded the (first) Unitarian church of the Messiah and later founded Washington University (originally, Eliot Seminary), where he became chancellor (1870-1887). In the year after William Eliot's death, on September 25, 1888, Thomas Stearns Eliot, the seventh child of a second son, was born to Henry and Charlotte (Stearns) Eliot. Like the Eliots, the American Stearns family hailed from seventeenth century Massachusetts: Members of both families had done what they considered the right thing in the Salem witch trials, Andrew Eliot as a juror, a Stearns as a judge. Eliot's schooling at Smith Academy was punctuated by summers in New England, chiefly at Gloucester and Rockport, Massachusetts (on Cape Ann), not far from the Dry Salvages. After a year at Milton Academy, Eliot matriculated at Harvard College, where he received a B.A. degree (1909) and pursued graduate

studies (1910-1914), completing but not defending a doctoral dissertation on the philosophy of F. H. Bradley (published, 1964).

During the years 1910 to 1917, Eliot visited Paris and Germany (1910-1911) and studied at the Sorbonne; back in Cambridge (1911-1914), he studied philosophy (with Bertrand Russell), Sanskrit, and Pali, along with other subjects, and received a fellowship stipend to study at Marburg, Germany, in 1914—an award that he promptly transferred to Merton College, Oxford, at the onset of World War I. On September 22, 1914, Eliot met Ezra Pound; it was an event that marked the forging of a spiritual bond that endured for the rest of Eliot's life. Since much has been made of Pound's influence on Eliot's poetry, especially *The Waste Land*, it may be useful to recall Pound's statement that Eliot had "trained himself *and* modernized himself *on his own*." It was largely through Pound's influence, however, that the poems of *Prufrock and Other Observations* were first published in American and English periodicals.

Eliot's marriage to Vivien Haigh-Wood, on June 26, 1915, was followed by brief periods of teaching (High Wycombe Grammar School, Highgate School) and lecturing (Oxford University Extension Lectures, 1915-1917). In March, 1917, Eliot secured a post in the Colonial and Foreign Department of Lloyd's Bank, London, where he worked continuously, except for three months' leave for reasons of health in the autumn of 1921, until he joined the publishing firm of Faber and Gwynn (later Faber and Faber) in 1925. His marriage lasted until Vivien's death in 1947, although she and Eliot were officially separated (by letter) in 1933, and thereafter, according to written accounts, they met again only once, and briefly (at one of Eliot's lectures). Several critics have seen the extremely unhappy marriage as fundamental to some of his poems.

Eliot's literary activity between 1916 and 1922 was prodigious: It was the time of his numerous essays and reviews for *The Egoist, The Dial*, the *Athanaeum*, the *Times Literary Supplement*, and many other journals, of *Prufrock and Other Observations*, *Ara Vos Prec*, *Poems*, and his masterpiece, *The Waste Land*. That work would catapult him to a prominence attained by no other poet of the twentieth century. In 1922, he assumed the editorship of *The Criterion*. In 1927, Eliot experienced a sea-change: First, he became a communicant in the Church of England (June 29); then he became a British subject (November). In 1928, a statement in *For Lancelot Andrewes* characterized his newly adopted perspectives: "The general point of view may be described as classicist in literature, royalist in politics, and Anglo-Catholic in religion." The formulation is one that should be approached with caution. Although accurate in some respects and misleading in others, it does help to explain the many turnings in the road from "The Hollow Men" (1925) through the Ariel poems to *Ash Wednesday*.

Before returning from his post as Norton Professor of Poetry at Harvard (1932-1933), Eliot obtained a legal separation from his wife (to whom he had dedicated *Ash Wednesday*) and lectured at the University of Virginia on Christian apologetics, a subject of increasing interest for him. His poetry of the 1930's centered on verse drama and on such disparate efforts as "Five Finger Exercises," "Triumphal March," and *Old Possum's Book of Practical Cats*, but the poetic highlights of the decade are *Ash Wednesday*, *Murder in the Cathedral*, and his best poem of those years, "Burnt Norton."

The first of the poems later to comprise *Four Quartets*, "Burnt Norton" was followed by "East Coker" (1940), "The Dry Salvages" (1941), and "Little Gidding" (1942). In the years following the publication of *Four Quartets*, Eliot wrote little poetry, but he kept on writing verse drama and began to enjoy generous recognition of his work; notably, he received the Nobel Prize in Literature in 1948, a year after the death of Vivien. His marriage to Valerie Fletcher (January 10, 1957) marked another of the many turning points of his life—this time a turn for the better in a happy marriage. Eliot truly became, in the 1940's, 1950's, and 1960's, the elder statesman of letters. His position in the history of modern poetry became unassailable.

Eliot died on January 4, 1965, survived by his wife, Valerie. His ashes were interred in the parish church at East Coker, Somerset, the church of his English ancestors, and a memorial was placed in the Poets' Corner, Westminister Abbey.

ANALYSIS

One useful approach to T. S. Eliot's poetry is to examine voices and fragments as they announce and illustrate themes. In the concluding section of *The Waste Land*, one of Eliot's speakers provides a key to that poem, to Eliot's poetry generally, and to the theory and practice of poetic composition that marked his career as a writer: "These fragments I have shored against my ruins." These fragments consist mainly of highly allusive phrases and quotations, of intricately wrought verbal symbols, of lines of direct simplicity and complex opacity, of passages of sheer beauty and crabbed commonality fixed in formulated phrases, arranged and rearranged until, in the best of the poetry, one finds the complete consort dancing together. On first coming to Eliot's poetry, especially to "The Love Song of J. Alfred Prufrock" or *The Waste Land*, the reader's usual (and perfectly acceptable) reaction is one of bewilderment, excitement, and, at best, an appreciation of the poetic statements that does not necessarily involve an understanding of precisely what is said, the conditions under which it is said, the full nature of the speaker, or his or her aims, intentions, or situation.

The fragments owe much to Eliot's youthful experience in St. Louis, summers on the New England coast, his Harvard education, his visits to Paris and Munich, and the Oxford and London years. Furthermore, they stem from his lifelong immersion in Dante and the Bible and from his omnivorous reading. He was particularly drawn to French Symbolist poetry (especially Laforgue), the Elizabethan and Jacobean playwrights, especially John Webster, Cyril Tourneur, Christopher Marlowe, and William Shakespeare, and Donne and the other Metaphysical poets. To come to Eliot's poetry with such a literary background is to see the phrases of other writers whom Eliot admired take on new and sometimes surprising meanings. To read Eliot's work without such a background may mean that the reader will miss both the larger and the particular allusions, but still the reader may grasp possible meanings of individual poems. The unwary reader may be carried along on the surface of the poem or find himself in sympathy with an expressed emotion without clearly knowing what is at issue. All readers should have recourse to those works to which Eliot seems to allude so that they may proceed the more intelligently with the poem at hand. The fragments that Eliot quotes or alludes to are the necessary baggage of the intelligent reader, *impedimenta* that include much of the Western European tradition and elements from Middle and Far Eastern culture.

In many respects, Eliot the poet became not unlike Joseph Conrad's Mr. Kurtz or, indeed, Marlow: He became "A Voice," an "invisible poet" (Hugh Kenner's phrase) who speaks. The voice or voices in the poems are usually those that repeat formulas embedded in literary, cultural, and religious traditions—uncertain voices that often betray their speakers' lack of self-knowledge or clear identity; they may be voices (especially in the Ariel poems) whose certitudes are affirmed only as they speak them (word becomes act) and which may be truly chimerical. The voices speaking the fragments, even the unified voice of *Four Quartets*, are the voices of humanity (though often a special order of humanity) seeking, as they turn over the fragments and seek the sense of sounds, to understand, explain, and identify themselves in terms of the past, present, and future. The voices, desiderative, expectant, seek in the expression of a word or words to communicate themselves to other communicants (the reader) and to educate those communicants in the mystery of a common life, the implications of action or inaction, the generalizable elements of a particular experience or emotion.

Long before his Paris year (1910-1911), Eliot had read Arthur Symons's *The Symbolist Movement in Literature* (1899) and had come under the sway of French Symbolist poetry. He had published some undergraduate poetry (phrases of which he used in later poems) and had begun two major poems, "Portrait of a Lady" and "The Love Song of J. Alfred Prufrock." He completed the latter at Munich (1911) but it remained in manuscript until Ezra Pound persuaded Harriet Monroe to publish it in *Poetry* (1915); it then formed the nucleus for Eliot's first volume of poetry, *Prufrock and Other Observations*, in which he may justly be said to have inaugurated modern poetry in English. It is with "The Love Song of J. Alfred Prufrock," the first masterpiece of an apprentice, that a just appreciation of Eliot's oeuvre should begin.

## "The Love Song of J. Alfred Prufrock"

Like "Portrait of a Lady" and most of his poetry prior to *Four Quartets*, "The Love Song of J. Alfred Prufrock" is a dramatic, if static, monologue. It is heavily influenced by Jules Laforgue's poetic technique in that it presents an interior landscape of atomized consciousness. The male narrator (the voice) worries about the possibility of an erotic encounter as he worries and puzzles over his own identity, his too conscious sense of self, his meaning and place in a surreal and menacing universe of his own devising, and his observations (objective and subjective genitive, as James Joyce phrased it) while he confides to a reader (who is called on to become part of Prufrock's divided self) the fragmented perceptions of himself and his situation. Prufrock does not, however, arrive at any conclusions about the encounter or about his own identity and meaning.

The epigraph (Dante, *Inferno*, 27) provides a key to the incongruous "love song" of an impossible lover and sets the reader squarely in Hell listening to a reluctant speaker (who cannot say what he means) who will confide in the auditor/reader as Guido did in the character Dante, "without fear or infamy," without fear that the secret will be revealed on earth (will become the subject of "observations"), particularly in the hearing of the perplexing women who "come and go" in the troublesome room or of the desirable but distant and somewhat fearsome recumbent woman. It is possible to exclude the "reader" as the addressee of this poem and to read it as an interior dialogue between "self" and "soul": Such a reading would heighten to a clinical level the disorder of identity that is sensed in Prufrock's divided self.

The voice that addresses the reader in scraps of experience remembered and fearfully anticipated and in fragments of historical- and self-consciousness does so in response to a question, presumably posed by the reader in a Dantesque role. As Hugh Kenner aptly points out, the reader enters a "zone of consciousness" in the poem, not a verifiable or constant "realistic" setting. Prufrock is not a "real" character who tells a logical or temporally sequential story. Indeed, the reader participates in the unfolding narrative by hearing and deciding what is part of the world of recognizable experience and what is intrinsic to a fragmented, disjointed, disordered, diseased consciousness that speaks familiarly ("you and I") of a shared boredom of social rounds and obligations, of the terror of rejection, and (the greater Prufrockian terror) of acceptance and surrender in sexual contact—all of which contribute to a sense of cognitive and emotional paralysis for which Prufrock finds a disordered "objective correlative" in the "sky/ Like a patient etherised upon a table."

The literary fragments in the poem include the central situational analogue in the *Inferno*, the Polonian self-caricature, and grotesque visions of Saint John the Baptist and Lazarus returned from the dead. None of the characters in the fragments belong to the realm of the living and all represent an inability "to say just what I mean."

### "GERONTION"

"Gerontion" (1919) carries on the pattern of monologue that Eliot established in "The Love Song of J. Alfred Prufrock" and "Portrait of a Lady." Here Eliot presents another voice speaking, besides words of his own devising, words from the Bible, William Shakespeare, Cyril Torneur, Thomas Middleton, Ben Jonson, and George Chapman. He intended "Gerontion" to be a prolegomenon to *The Waste Land*, and as such it is more than adequate: It deals with concerns and embodies themes common to the longer poem: themes such as aridity, the inadequacies of the common experience of sexuality and love, history's "contrived corridors," the function of memory, the Christian economy of salvation, and the attempts of consciousness to order disparate experiences and make them comprehensible. Structurally, both works are collages that use allusive language to make human history manageable; technically, they both employ a stream of consciousness tentatively centered in the centrifugal thoughts of a "dry brain in a dry season."

Gerontion and the foreign figures who flit through the Inferno and Purgatorio of his memory are figures of desolation who have reaped the whirlwind of their own personal histories and of history generally. The characters, from Mr. Silvero to Mrs. Cammel, represent some of the dry thoughts that Gerontion houses. They typify one major difficulty that the poem presents: the tension between the past, the past remembered in the present, and the present—the past dominating the present and vitiating it as memory mixes with desire in a futile nostalgia that prevents the narrator from acting (reaching conclusion). This temporal tension is at the poem's core and is resolved only in the poem's emphasis on the act of remembering. Once again, as in "The Love Song of J. Alfred Prufrock" and *The Waste Land*, the self-conscious voices utter personal and historical fragments that illuminate consciousness speaking. The point of remembering these fragments is to identify a fundamental problem of meaning that attaches to peripheral love (of art, for example) and to *love* (possibly of the poem's addressee), its meaning in personal and general historical context, and the relationship of those meanings to the meaning of the death for which Gerontion waits and the possibility of another kind of life hereafter.

### THE WASTE LAND

The transition from "Gerontion" to *The Waste Land*, in which Gerontion is transformed into Tiresias, is a movement from considerable opacity to relative clarity, though the later poem is indeed perplexing. In 1953, Eliot wrote that he did not look forward with pleasure either to literary oblivion or to a time when his works would be read only by a few graduate students in "Middle Anglo-American, 42B." Together with "The Love Song of J. Alfred Prufrock" and *Four Quartets*, *The Waste Land* ensures that neither of those ends is probable. Eliot stunned all, and outraged some, of the literary world in 1922 with the publication (in *The Criterion* and *The Dial*) of *The Waste Land*, a work that has engendered more commentaries, interpretations, and discussions than any other poem of the twentieth century. Structurally, the work is a series of five poems that constitute one poem; parts of it were written and rewritten over the course of at least seven years, with editorial help for the final version from Ezra Pound. When he published it in book form, Eliot added more than fifty notes to the poem, some of which are not helpful and some of which emphasize the importance of vegetation ceremonies and direct the reader to Sir James Frazer's *The Golden Bough* (1890-1915) and to Jessie L. Weston's work on the Grail legend, *From Ritual to Romance* (1920).

The wealth of literary fragments, clues, and allusions to other works, the inclusion of foreign words and phrases and of arcane material, may produce some bafflement and has inspired numerous exegetical tracts. It is of primary importance not to treat the poem as a highly sophisticated double-cross; instead, one should, before beginning a search for sources and analogues, surrender to it as an emotional, intellectual, puzzling, and disquieting poem. It is only in allowing for the experience of communicable and precisely incommunicable emotion that the poem can work as a poem rather than as an occasion for the exercise of literary archeology.

Eliot wrote (note to 1.218), "Tiresias, although a mere spectator and not indeed a 'character,' is yet the most important personage in the poem, uniting all the rest. . . . What Tiresias *sees*, in fact, is the substance of the poem." One may, on Eliot's authority, read the poem as an account of Tiresias's observations as he guides the reader through his own memory to various locations in *The Waste Land* as seen or remembered on a journey that is both in and out of time. Thus, many elements fall into place as Tiresias subsumes all the characters or speakers in a multilayered, cyclical ritual of death and rebirth. Alternatively, one may read the poem as a series of fragmented monologues, in the manner of "The Love Song of J. Alfred Prufrock," so that Tiresias's becomes only one among many voices. So to read it is to find Eliot's note somewhat misleading.

Assuming that this is a Symbolist poem, perhaps the Symbolist poem of the twentieth century, the historical and cultural dimensions that many critics have so ably attributed to it (as being a poem about the disillusionment of a particular generation, about the 1920's, about London, and so on) recede. So, too, do the ubiquitous anthropological considerations of barren land, infertility, initiation rites, and the death of gods. Both sets of data may, then, be treated as "objective correlatives" for emotions that the poet seeks to express. What remain as underlying themes are sexual disorder (basic to the Grail and to vegetation myths), the lack of and need for religious belief (accented negatively by the presence of Madam Sosostris and positively in "The Fire Sermon" and "What the Thunder Said"), and the process of poetic composition (fragments "shored against

my ruins"). These may be seen as elaborations in *The Waste Land* of themes present in "Portrait of a Lady," "The Love Song of J. Alfred Prufrock," "The Hippopotamus" (1917), and "Gerontion"; they are themes that also relate directly to Eliot's lessons from Dante's *La vita nuova* (c. 1292; *Vita Nuova*, 1861; better known as *The New Life*) and *La divina commedia* (c. 1320, 3 volumes; *The Divine Comedy*, 1802).

The diverse interpretations of what the poem is about have obvious implications for how one values the fragments of which it is composed and, to return to the question of voice, how one identifies the speaker and the burden of his speech. If, for example, one assumes that the blind, androgynous Tiresias speaks in many voices and does so with foreknowledge of all, one may conclude that the work stands as a monument to the disillusionment not of one generation but of many. One may also find that the slight progress of the Fisher King from the dull canal behind the gashouse (part 3) to the shore (part 5) has slight significance and that the question about setting his lands in order is, like shoring fragments against ruins, all that can be done before capitulating to the inevitable continuation of a condition in which the land will remain waste. Tiresias has, after all, foreseen this, too. If one assumes a multiplicity of voices, however, beginning with Marie, the Hyacinth Girl (or, in the epigraph, with the Sibyl's complaint and the voice speaking of it), and ending with the Fisher King, the Thunder, and a new voice (or many voices) speaking in the poem's last lines, one has a quite different experience of the poem. In the second reading, one treats the work as a series of soliloquies or monologues all mixing memory with quite different desires, all commenting on various meanings (or lack of meaning) or love, and all concerned with hope or its opposite, hope negated in self-irony, hope centered on the release from individual prisons, hope tempered by trepidations attendant on the "awful daring of a moment's surrender," and, possibly, hope that the Fisher King has finally thrown off accidia by asking himself the one needful question.

In either reading, how one treats the speaker and the meaning of the fragments raises other questions that drive one back into the poem, and each new reading raises new questions. There is no doubt that sexual disorder is a dominant theme, that the disorder concerns the dissociation of appetitive action from the intellectual and emotional aspects that would make the action human and not merely a reflex action, and that the symptoms of disorder are common to such characters as the typist, Mr. Eugenides, Mrs. Porter, Elizabeth I, Tiresias, Philomel, and the Fisher King. Add to this the abiding sense of death and its meaning, and the spiritual teachings of Buddhism and the mystery religions (Christianity among them), and new complexities emerge, as do new questions that only the Thunder can answer.

The poem's last verse paragraph displays little overt coherence once the Fisher King asks his question, but it does nevertheless offer a direct key to understanding the poem. That the Fisher King has traversed the arid plains, has put them behind him and now may have some power to set his kingdom in order, provides a sense of closure. In the next line (1. 427), London Bridge, crossed by so many who had been undone by death in the unreal City (part 1), is falling down: This action will end the procession of dead commuters; in the nursery rhyme there is no adequate means to rebuild the bridge permanently. The next line is from Dante, who is a source for many of the attitudes, emotions, and possibly the situational contexts of many of the poem's speakers: Here Arnaut Daniel, suffering in Purgatory for sins of lust, leaps back into the refining fire of his own accord; this may be seen as a gloss on the "Fire Sermon" and as a cure for the various forms of lust in the entire poem. There follow lines from "Pervigilium Veneris," a reference to Philomela (echoes of parts 2 and 3) and from Gérard de Nerval's "El desdichado." This last may have metapoetical implications for the authorial Eliot and may also recall another quest for rightful inheritance—in Sir Walter Scott's novel *Ivanhoe* (1819). In "These fragments I have shored against my ruins" (1. 430), "these fragments" are the preceding 429 lines, the immediately preceding seven lines, the fragmented speeches, the fragments of poetic and religious traditions, and the fragments of verses composed over many years to form the poem itself. The reference to Thomas Kyd's *The Spanish Tragedy* (pr. c. 1585, 1. 431), in which Hieronymo proposes to "fit" a play using fragments of poetry in several languages (tongues) could, as Bernard Bergonzi indicates, comment di-

rectly on *The Waste Land* itself. The penultimate line repeats the Thunder's statements, giving them more point; and the final lines translated by Eliot as equivalent to "The Peace which passeth understanding."

What do these keys unlock? Surely they suggest what a reader should know of European and Eastern literary, cultural, and religious traditions to grasp some of the poem's meanings. They may also serve to help the reader see, to paraphrase Eliot, the end in the beginning and the beginning in the end. Having come to the end of the poem, one must be prepared to read it anew from the beginning. Bernard Bergonzi, following C. K. Stead's analysis of the pattern and meaning of *Four Quartets*, provides an invaluable guide to the significance of each of the poem's five sections. "The Burial of the Dead" concerns movement in time (seasons, change, reluctant birth); "A Game of Chess" reveals patent dissatisfaction with worldly experience; "The Fire Sermon" leads through purgation in the world and a divesting of the soul of love for created things; "Death by Water" is a brief lyric containing a warning and an invocation; "What the Thunder Said" deals with the issues of spiritual health and artistic wholeness. To read the work as a poem about the artist's concern for artistic wholeness allied to spiritual health offers extraordinary and suggestive possibilities for revaluing it and the poetry that preceded it.

### "THE HOLLOW MEN"

"The Hollow Men" has often been read as a poem written at the nadir of the poet's emotional life, a depressing and depressed poem. This may be a correct reading; it may also be, however much it is favored by scores of writers who seek autobiographical confessions in Eliot's poetry, wide of the mark. The poem seems, indeed, to have been composed from fragments discarded from earlier drafts of *The Waste Land*. Again, voice and fragment should guide the wary reader. The epigraph, from Joseph Conrad's *Heart of Darkness* (1902), should put the reader on guard: The speech is that of an African worker reporting the death of Mr. Kurtz to Conrad's narrator-once-removed, Marlow, whose account is passed on to the reader by one who heard him tell the tale. The reader is, like the hollow men, at several removes from anything like experience at firsthand; and several emotional layers separate

Conrad's reader from Kurtz: Eliot adds another emotional layer of separation but strikes a responsive note of limited sympathy in his readers who have read Conrad. This is only one small reflection of the ways in which *Heart of Darkness* stands in relation to this poem and, by extension, to *The Waste Land* and its "preface," "Gerontion."

This poem, like earlier poems and the later *Ash Wednesday*, is obsessed with death. One of Dante's dead, a "hollow man" (*Inferno*, 3) who lived, without blame and without praise, a life of accidia, addresses the reader in self-explanation and communal confession. Two other major sources inform the poem and quicken the sense of death: the history of the Gunpowder Plot and the Elizabethan dramatic account of assassination found in Shakespeare's *Julius Caesar* (pr. c. 1599-1600, in which the phrase "hollow men" occurs). The reader is clearly in the presence of the dead, just as Dante's Pilgrim listened to the hollow men, who were neither for Jehovah nor against him, in the Hell of their own making. Like the addressee of *Heart of Darkness*, the reader hears, perhaps seated in a club chair, a story of Marlow telling a tale prompted by his observation that his present location (seated on a yawl on the Thames) was once one of the dark places of the earth (and may still be so). In each case, the reader/addressee is told a story of darkness, a story of the Shadow, a story of failure and, ultimately, of inconsequence, a story told to pass the time.

### ASH WEDNESDAY

In *Ash Wednesday*, so named for the first day of Lent, a day for the turnings of Christian metanoia, Dante's mysticism and its correlative tension between flesh and spirit are elaborated. The situation of which the voice speaks, a conversion that is not without difficulty and contention, is told not in logical, sequential narrative but in a disciplined Symbolist dream. Here, for example, the Lady subsumes many ladies (the rejected one of blesséd face, Beatrice, Theologia, Ecclesia) and Eliot's earlier expressions of dehumanization (such as the classic "ragged claws" of "The Love Song of J. Alfred Prufrock") now become expressions of Christian humility. Unquestionably influenced by Eliot's own turning to the Anglican Church in 1928, this poem, together with the Ariel poems, represents poetic pilgrimages of hope that do not necessarily find resolution of the tensions between flesh and spirit but that indicate possibilities for subliminal resolution in transcendence.

### FOUR QUARTETS

The assured masterpiece of his poetic maturity, *Four Quartets* is more immediately accessible than Eliot's early and middle work. The poems that comprise it, like his earlier poetry, grew incrementally from "Burnt Norton," which sprang from lines discarded from *Murder in the Cathedral*, to "Little Gidding," with "East Coker" and "The Dry Salvages" intervening. Unlike his earlier poetry, the poems of *Four Quartets* lack a dramatic character who speaks; instead, they are in the lyric tradition of direct poetic speech in which the speaker has a constant voice that may well be the poet's own. Unfortunately, the speaker sometimes assumes the hortatory voice of the preacher. This shift in poetic style, away from masks and personae, is a new element in Eliot's verse.

Each of the poems adopts a musical and frequently iterative pattern, as if the reader is meant to hear the instrumental conversations endemic to musical quartets. In reading these poems, one is frequently reminded of Walter Pater's dictum that "all art continually aspires to the condition of music." The poems are set pieces in the eighteenth century tradition of verse inspired by a visit to a specific place. Taken together, they constitute some of Eliot's most beautiful (and, in places, most banal) poetry, as the lyricist adopts a consistent poetic voice that muses on the process of cognition and composition.

The essential structure of these poems, filled as they are with local references dear to Eliot, follows the five-part structure of *The Waste Land*. C. K. Stead admirably analyzes the fivefold structure of each of the sections of *Four Quartets* as follows: the movement of time, in which brief moments of eternity are caught; worldly experience, leading only to dissatisfaction; purgation in the world, divesting the soul of love of created things; a lyric prayer for, or affirmation of the need of, intercession; and the problems of attaining artistic wholeness which become analogues for, and merge into, the problems of achieving spiritual health.

The poems of *Four Quartets* in some way negate, by their affirmations, the fragmented, disparate, and "unreal" elements in Eliot's earliest poems, but on the whole, they present a synthesis of Eliot's poetic concerns and his varied statements about the problems and business of being a poet. They stand not at the end of his artistic career but at the summit of his career as a poet whose later work, in both bulk and intensity, is minimal. *Four Quartets* constitutes a compendium of the themes that Eliot pursued from his earliest days as a poet, but with the decided difference that sex has become part of love, belief has been ratified, and the world has become flesh again. The fire and the rose are one.

### OTHER MAJOR WORKS

PLAYS: *Sweeney Agonistes*, pb. 1932 (fragment); *The Rock: A Pageant Play*, pr., pb. 1934; *Murder in the Cathedral*, pr., pb. 1935; *The Family Reunion*, pr., pb. 1939; *The Cocktail Party*, pr. 1949; *The Confidential Clerk*, pr. 1953; *The Elder Statesman*, pr. 1958; *Collected Plays*, 1962.

NONFICTION: *Ezra Pound: His Metric and Poetry*, 1917; *The Sacred Wood*, 1920; *Homage to John Dryden*, 1924; *Shakespeare and the Stoicism of Seneca*, 1927; *For Lancelot Andrewes*, 1928; *Dante*, 1929; *Charles Whibley: A Memoir*, 1931; *Thoughts After Lambeth*, 1931; *John Dryden: The Poet, the Dramatist, the Critic*, 1932; *Selected Essays*, 1932, 1950; *The Use of Poetry and the Use of Criticism: Studies in the Relation of Criticism to Poetry in England*, 1933; *After Strange Gods: A Primer of Modern Heresy*, 1934; *Elizabethan Essays*, 1934; *Essays Ancient and Modern*, 1936; *The Idea of a Christian Society*, 1939; *The Classics and the Man of Letters*, 1942; *The Music of Poetry*, 1942; *Notes Toward the Definition of Culture*, 1948; *Poetry and Drama*, 1951; *The Three Voices of Poetry*, 1953; *Religious Drama: Medieval and Modern*, 1954; *The Literature of Politics*, 1955; *The Frontiers of Criticism*, 1956; *On Poetry and Poets*, 1957; *Knowledge and Experience in the Philosophy of F. H. Bradley*, 1964; *To Criticize the Critic*, 1965; *The Letters of T. S. Eliot: Volume I, 1898-1922*, 1988.

### BIBLIOGRAPHY

Childs, Donald J. *From Philosophy to Poetry: T. S. Eliot's Study of Knowledge and Experience*. London: Athalone Press, 2001. Childs analyzes Eliot's literary works with emphasis on how he expressed his philosophy through his poetry. Bibliography and index.

Cooper, John Xiros. *The Cambridge Introduction to T. S. Eliot*. New York: Cambridge University Press, 2006. Provides an introduction to Eliot's life and works. Looks at the influence of the British and American intellectual climate on Eliot and discusses controversies.

Donoghue, Denis. *Words Alone: The Poet, T. S. Eliot*. New Haven, Conn.: Yale University Press, 2000. A wide-ranging critical examination in the form of an intellectual memoir, and an illuminating account of Donoghue's engagement with the works of Eliot. Includes bibliographical references and index.

Ellis, Steve. *T. S. Eliot: A Guide for the Perplexed*. New York: Continuum, 2009. A critical examination of Eliot's poetry, including early works, *The Waste Land*, and the *Four Quartets*.

Gordon, Lyndall. *T. S. Eliot: An Imperfect Life*. New York: Norton, 1999. In this exhaustive biography, Gordon assiduously tracks down Eliot's correspondence and manuscripts to address the issue of Eliot's anti-Semitism and misogyny. Gordon reinforces her thesis that Eliot's poetic output should be interpreted as a coherent spiritual biography.

Habib, Rafey. *The Early T. S. Eliot and Western Philosophy*. New York: Cambridge University Press, 1999. A look at the philosophical beliefs held by Eliot and how they found their way into his literary works. Bibliography and index.

Moody, A. David, ed. *The Cambridge Companion to T. S. Eliot*. New York: Cambridge University Press, 1994. A comprehensive reference work dedicated to Eliot's life, work, and times. Bibliography and index.

Raine, Craig. *T. S. Eliot*. New York: Oxford University Press, 2006. Prizewinning poet Raine examines Eliot's life and poetry. He argues that Eliot's work can be seen as a unified whole, centering on the theme of the buried life. Provides extended analysis of *The Waste Land* and *Four Quartets*.

Riquelme, John Paul, ed. *T. S. Eliot*. Pasadena, Calif.: Salem Press, 2009. Fourteen essays examine the poetry, plays, criticism, and life of Eliot.

Schuchard, Ronald. *Eliot's Dark Angel: Intersections*

*of Life and Art*. New York: Oxford University Press, 1999. A critical study demonstrating how Eliot's personal voice works through the sordid, the bawdy, the blasphemous, and the horrific to create a unique moral world. Schuchard works against conventional attitudes toward Eliot's intellectual and spiritual development by showing how early and consistently his classical and religious sensibility manifests itself in his poetry and criticism.

*John J. Conlon*

# WILLIAM EMPSON

**Born:** Yokefleet, Howden, England; September 27, 1906
**Died:** London, England; April 15, 1984

PRINCIPAL POETRY
*Poems*, 1935
*The Gathering Storm*, 1940
*Collected Poems of William Empson*, 1949, 1961
*The Complete Poems of William Empson*, 2000
    (John Haffender, editor)

OTHER LITERARY FORMS

William Empson, better known for his criticism than for his poetry, is both famous and notorious for his doctrine of poetic ambiguity. Empson has argued that all good poetry is characterized by ambiguity, by uncertainties and tensions that are sometimes planned, sometimes fortuitous, frequently demanding variant interpretations. As a Cambridge undergraduate, Empson worked with I. A. Richards, whose pioneering "scientific" approach to literature, *Principles of Literary Criticism* (1924), inspired his protégé to judge poetry by its success in exploiting linguistic and semantic possibilities, rather than by concentrating on its affective powers. Indeed, Empson sees "tension" or unresolved conflict as the formative principle of poetry.

Growing out of his work at Cambridge with Richards, as well as his familiarity with *A Survey of Modernist Poetry* by Robert Graves and Laura Riding (1922),

Empson's *Seven Types of Ambiguity: A Study of Its Effects on English Verse* (1930, 1947) is a systematic and elaborate argument for close textual analysis of the semantic indeterminacy that is inherent in language. This remarkable study, which has remained Empson's most influential and celebrated work, demonstrates how various shifting and equivocal denotative and connotative meanings both illuminate and complicate the experience of a poem. Empson conceded, however, that there is a good deal to be said for avoiding ambiguity. Observing that unequivocal, straightforward, prosaic, expository expression certainly leads "to results more direct, more communicable," he warns poets never to be ambiguous "without proper occasion," especially never to exploit plurisignification merely for decorative effect.

Such a brilliant critical work as *Seven Types of Ambiguity* appears even more impressive when one considers that it was an effort by an undergraduate not yet twenty-four years old. Accused of pedantry for his doctrinaire insistence on "scientific" classifications, Empson appears to have anticipated this response, for he explains first that ambiguity in his "extended sense" means whatever he wants it to mean. For the less flexible reader, however, he defines ambiguity as that which "gives room for alternative reactions to the same piece of language." He feels that such categories as his are justified because they provide a "useful set of distinctions" for the critical reader of poetry by both heightening his consciousness of nuance and involving him actively in the process of careful exegesis to determine what the poem means. One may be convinced by Empson's argument for such painstaking *explication du texte*, or may heatedly oppose it, but one cannot ignore it.

Thus Empson takes his place, along with T. S. Eliot and his mentor Richards, as an English exponent of what would come to be known as the New Criticism, that formal and objective position that limits itself to the autonomous context of the work itself, rejecting any historical or biographical concern with either the poem or its creator. Though more open-minded in practice, especially in the glosses and notes that he appended to his own poetry, Empson still stressed the "disassociation of sensibility." He thus aligned himself with the New Critics in opposition to the Romantics and his contemporary neo-Romantics.

Five years after the appearance of *Seven Types of Ambiguity*, Empson continued to extend his concept of essential linguistic complexity, publishing *Some Versions of Pastoral* (1935), a somewhat misleading title for a more mature development of his critical method of verbal analysis. In this series of difficult yet controlled essays (entitled *English Pastoral Poetry* when it was published in the United States in 1938), Empson illustrates his theories with entire works rather than with excerpts, approaching a sophisticated Gestaltic position. Seeing the pastoral as the artificial cult of simplicity ("the process of putting the complex into the simple"), rather than as a conventional genre of poems about rustic life, he demonstrates a sociological bias in choosing his examples, claiming that he is trying to demonstrate how "the social ideas" resulting from such a literary inversion "have been used in English literature."

Empson's third major critical work is *The Structure of Complex Words* (1951), another collection of essays in which he moves away from the traditional aesthetic values of literature, seeing instead expressions of cultural and societal interest—no doubt a reaction to shifts in attitudes around him. Though still concerned with a creative artist's particular brand of linguistic complexity, the publication of this ambitious and learned work seemed to coincide with Empson's ceasing to write poetry, provoking speculation that he had found the satisfaction in criticism that he was unable to achieve in his verse. Ten years later, in 1961, another major work of criticism appeared, *Milton's God*, and a revision followed in 1965. Nothing innovative or brilliantly perceptive is evident here. His best later criticism continued to appear in the form of individual journal essays. Posthumous collections of his critical essays include *Essays on Shakespeare* (1986) and *Argufying: Essays on Literature and Culture* (1987).

As an undergraduate at Cambridge, Empson not only formulated his theory of poetic ambiguity but also edited and contributed to several literary publications, writing poetry and reviews of books, films, and theater productions. He even wrote a play, *Three Stories* (pr. 1927), now lost, in which he acted in a campus production. His lively talents have also been demonstrated in recordings of his poems. It is on *Seven Types of Ambiguity*, however, that Empson's critical reputation rests.

*William Empson* (Hulton Archive/Getty Images)

Its intellectual gusto, engaging wit, jauntiness of tone, and provocative thesis all reflect the brilliant Cambridge undergraduate who would subsequently influence contemporary poetry and its appreciation to a remarkable degree.

ACHIEVEMENTS

To many, William Empson will always be the author of one book and recognized as the legendary "ambiguity man"; indeed, his poetry is often completely overlooked when he is identified only as "a British literary critic." However, he wrote far more than the four critical volumes that established and expanded his analytical theory of linguistic complexity.

After publishing early poems in Cambridge undergraduate magazines, in 1935, he collected what he had written into his first slim annotated volume, *Poems*, all but ten of which were from his Cambridge days. Among the young poets breaking new ground in En-

gland in the 1930's, Empson would prove less successful than his contemporaries, for his style revealed that
his work was so "difficult," so eccentrically brilliant,
that general acclaim beyond academic circles was improbable. Certainly Empson himself knew that his
verses would not suit popular taste.

In 1940, after returning to England from teaching
positions in the Far East, Empson published his second
collection of twenty-one poems, the ostensibly topical
*The Gathering Storm*, including only ten poems that
were previously unpublished. In his view, the work "is
all about politics, saying we're going to have this second world war and we mustn't get too frightened about
it," when in fact all the poems do not reflect the threatening world crisis then provoking contemporary public
anxiety. Demonstrating a static clarity not evident in the
first volume of verse, the new poems revealed not so
much the elegance of a clever and precocious undergraduate as a less-concentrated profundity growing out
of personal pain and conviction, and the volume drew
public attention. Winston Churchill, in fact, appropriated the title for a volume of his history of World War II.

In the 1950's, Empson found himself the somewhat
surprised paragon of what was then seen by some as the
goal of poetic expression, a curious and ironic position
for one who had given up writing poetry almost a decade earlier. Those who now venerated him, calling
themselves collectively the Movement, were part of a
loosely organized highbrow English reactionary group
opposing both the apocalyptic, extreme neo-Romantic
work best exemplified by the spectacularly sensual
Dylan Thomas and that of the Symbolist tradition and
of the Imagists. Members of the Movement were attracted by Empson's urbane wit and control, his penchant not for emotional excess but for "argufying in poetry." In an illuminating article appearing in 1963,
Empson declares that without recognizing the fact, he
must have had "strong feelings" about John Donne for
a long time, not for his being Metaphysical but because
of his "argufying," a desirable and dynamic process
that Empson saw as both mental and muscular and also
as a revolt against Symbolism.

John Wain, one of the best-known members of the
Movement, seeing Empson as the heir to Eliot, called
attention to Empson's poetic work, which exemplified

this rhetorical stance, in his 1950 essay "Ambiguous
Gifts," which would have a profound formative impact
in fashionable academic circles. Empson's functional
and concrete imagery, especially that suggesting scientific ideas, as Wain saw it, is most effective when it
forms a series of intellectually ingenious conceits, much
in the manner employed by the Metaphysical poet John
Donne, and in this characteristic, Empson's work found
its greatest strength. In deprecating current "romantic
scribblers" and their adverse influence on literary taste,
Wain wondered if Empson could be appreciated by the
general public, his cerebral gifts being beyond their
scope. Nevertheless, just as the shrine is not liable for
the acts of the pilgrims, Empson could not be held responsible for his vocal and encomiastic disciples who,
incidentally, soon generally repudiated him and moved
elsewhere for stylistic inspiration.

Perhaps as a result of interest in Empson stirred up
by enthusiastic Movement members forced to use the
1949 American edition of the *Collected Poems*, an English edition appeared in 1955, but by that time much of
the fervid excitement for his work had died down. This
volume brought together all but a few of those poems
that Empson chose to publish, including the three poems he wrote during World War II. Again he provided
extensive notes at the end and even included an explanatory "Note on Notes." He published no new poems
since this volume appeared. In fact, his poems total
only sixty-three.

## Biography

A Yorkshireman of the landed gentry by birth, William Empson, separated from his four older brothers
and sisters by four years, spent his early childhood at
Yokefleet, a remote village. He began his education
at Folkestone Preparatory School, then entered Winchester College as a scholar in 1920, where he was an
active debater. He went up in 1925 to Magdalene College, Cambridge, on a mathematics scholarship. After
passing several levels of degree examinations in mathematics, he shifted his interest to literature and read under the tutelage of the renowned professor I. A. Richards. Before taking his degree with highest honors in
English in 1929, Empson was caught up in the interdis-
ciplinary intellectual fervor then at high pitch in Cam-

bridge and made a name for himself in this heady atmosphere. Excitement grew from individual involvement in widely diverse disciplines, and C. P. Snow, the physicist who would later explore the status of the "two cultures," was then actively involved in the Cambridge life, where at that time the gap between literature and science was slight.

Obviously there was much for Empson to ponder and discuss after both Gertrude Stein and T. S. Eliot lectured at Cambridge in 1926, the latter on the Metaphysical poets, a universally recognized influence on Empson's poetry. In 1927, the undergraduate's first poem was published, and those that followed in his *annus mirabilis* of 1928 reflected the "difficult" mode of the early Andrew Marvell and John Donne as well as that of Eliot. Empson, then, owed much of his success as an undergraduate not only to his natural intellectual gifts but also to the stimulating and congenial atmosphere of Cambridge in the late 1920's.

After the publication in 1930 of his undergraduate thesis as *Seven Types of Ambiguity*, Empson accepted a teaching position from 1931 to 1934 as professor of English literature at Buneika Daigaku University in Tokyo, having been recommended for the post by his tutor Richards. In 1937, after a return to England, he accepted another position in Asia; by this time, he had published his first collection of poetry and his second volume of criticism. His new teaching assignment was on the English faculty of the Beijing National University, but those were the uneasy years of the Sino-Japanese War, and for two years Empson followed academic refugees on the Great March across China in retreat from the invading Japanese forces, teaching from memory, constantly in peril, yet still writing poetry. Forced to return to London on "indefinite wartime leave" during the years of World War II, he served as a writer of propaganda and as Chinese broadcaster for the British Broadcasting Corporation from 1941 to 1946 and published his second collection of poems, many of them the result of his Far East experiences.

During this period in his native country, he married and assumed responsibility for a family. In 1947, he took his wife and two sons to Beijing where he returned to his teaching post, again, however, facing unsettling conditions in China, now under the regime of Mao Zedong. By 1953, he felt the need to settle his family in England and accepted a post as professor of English literature at Sheffield University, where he remained until his retirement in 1971. His involvement with advocates of the New Criticism brought him to the United States on several occasions during his active teaching career, for he always enjoyed traveling. He lived in active retirement in the London suburb of Hampstead until his death on April 15, 1984.

ANALYSIS

William Empson, assessing the inherent relationship between theory and performance, observed in *Seven Types of Ambiguity* that "the methods I have been describing are very useful to critics, but certainly they leave a poet in a difficult position." In his own case, the dilemma is compounded, as even the inexperienced reader naturally seeks to find in Empson's poetic works exemplification of his personal critical doctrine. Without question, Empson's ideas about ambiguity and the tensions generated by contradictions in poetry point directly to the core of what might be a meaning of his "specialized kind" of poetry.

One way to approach Empson's canon might be to note varying degrees of complexity, exemplification of possible multiple meanings discoverable in the poetry. Indeed, his puzzling knotted lines and verses ("my clotted kind of poetry," as Empson himself describes it) prompted the poet to furnish annotative notes with his published collections, admitting, however, that "the better poems tend to require fewer notes." Such finely wrought poetic works reflect Empson's recognition that he "grew up in the height of the vogue for the seventeenth century poet Donne," and that when he started as a poet, he "thought it would be very nice to write beautiful things like the poet Donne," recalling that he began composition by "trying to think of an interesting puzzle."

This familiarity with the Metaphysical poets would seem to illuminate Empson's work—sophisticated, scientific analyses of intensely personal and impassioned emotional states; fantastic, audacious, extremely extended conceits; intellectual, witty, and often unconventional diction—all exploited to unite feeling with thought, to attempt communication of restless, unreasonable expectation beyond reasonable limits. Such taut, controlled technique generally reflects a profound sense of life's difficulties and contradictions, what Empson described as a "conflict which is raging in the mind of the writer but hasn't been solved."

Empson's idea of poetry as the expression of an unresolved conflict ("Verse likes despair," he observes in "Success"), opposing forces seeking some form of equilibrium, is reflected throughout his characteristically argumentative work. One of his most quoted beliefs is that "life involves maintaining oneself between contradictions that can't be solved by analysis." Here his affinity with the American poet and New Critic John Crowe Ransom comes sharply into focus; a line in Ransom's "The Equilibrists" (1927), "Leave me now, and never let us meet" describes the equally unresolved torture of the unfulfilled lovers also seeking a tentative balance in Empson's "Aubade" (1937): "It seemed the best thing to be up and go."

Empson's attempt to reconcile opposing forces may have led to his fascination with Buddhism. Such a philosophical acceptance of human suffering as a way of apprehending reality so appealed to Empson that he put together "The Faces of Buddha," a collection of articles written in Japan and China; the manuscript, however, is regrettably lost. In "Missing Dates" (1937), the despairing refrain of the poem laments that despite humanity's efforts "the waste remains, the waste remains and kills." Whether the ambiguous key word here denotes emptiness, exhaustion, loss, or prodigality, its reality is fatal; nirvana is unattainable. Furthermore, in his published collections of poetry, Empson chose for an epigraph Buddha's "Fire Sermon," recognizing, as did Eliot, that modern humanity shares a universal dilemma.

### EARLY POEMS

An awareness of contradictions, of ideas and emotions held in tension, characterizes Empson's work from the beginning. An early poem that appeared in an undergraduate Cambridge literary journal, "Value Is in Activity," is a recondite, sardonic statement of the ultimate futility of people's attempt to determine their fate, revealing the poet's sense of the relationship between the macroscopic and individual instance. Here man is a "juggler" endlessly tossing rotting apples, exhibited in a "circus" that is the world. Because of his unceasing activity, he cannot eat the Edenic fruit, which is, in any case, worthless, both maggot-filled and sterile ("Dwarf seeds unravelled" by a blighting frost). However, man cannot be idle, though knowing full well the ultimate waste of his frenetic activities and the futility of his situation. Thus Empson challenges people to question what gives value to their actions; he does not, however, rationalize or philosophize.

Bafflement is also in the conclusion of "Plenum and Vacuum," its title suggesting antithetical states of existence. In a particularly characteristic "clotted style," the three stanzas have seven compound hyphenated words, which abound in ambiguities, and use typically Empsonian scientific imagery that reflects the teeming world of Cambridge. However, any exegetic effort ultimately rests on acceptance of the axiom in stanza 3 that "Matter includes what must matter enclose," describing both the ontological statement and the poem itself.

Another important undergraduate poem is "High Dive," in which the subject again recognizes "value in activity," knows that he must "dive" into life ("the enclosed bathing-pool") rather than spend his time in neurotic contemplation, must join those who "tear him down" into a society both "menacing" and "assuring." Empson ominously and admonishingly cites the disastrous dives or falls of Lucifer and Jezebel, however, and the poem ends in desperate recognition that the pool's water is ultimately a vortex that will destroy the diver.

In "To an Old Lady," a tribute to his mother, Empson uses the classic Metaphysical image of the compass to praise her style and confidence; she is not to be pitied, for she is "certain of her pole," not "wasted" as some might presume. Empson concludes the poem with an astronomical conceit pointing up the paradox of proximity and distance between a mother and her son: "Strange that she too should be inaccessible,/ Who shares my son."

One of the most beautiful and Donne-like of Empson's university poems is "Camping Out"; poet Richard Eberhart called it "a brain-tickler which exercised many hours of drawing-room discussion in Cambridge, and withheld its ultimate ambiguous secret for years." Here as the man is watching a desired young woman go about her usual activities (the poem opens with "And now she cleans her teeth into the lake"), he realizes that only in his imagination can any amorous consummation occur.

## RHYME AND METER

At this point it should be noted that despite his startling exploitation of a number of devices of Metaphysical poetry, in many ways Empson's poetics are quite conservative. Criticizing *vers libre*, he declares in his poetic creed, "I am in favor of rhyme and metre"; and he particularly favors terza rima, a three-line stanza, usually in iambic pentameter, rhyming *aba, bcb, cdc,* and so on. An outstanding example of such an interlocked rhyme scheme is "Arachne," one of Empson's most critically acclaimed early poems. Here the ubiquitous muddling young man, as Empson put it, "being afraid of girl, as usual," walks "Twixt devil and deep sea," in precarious existential tension that illustrates Buddha's extremes, "between void and void," balancing like a spider on a filmy cobweb that "is at a breath destroyed." Like Andrew Marvell's lover arguing with his coy mistress, however, the man warns the reluctant threatening woman of the reciprocal dangers of imbalance, that "Male spiders must not be too early slain."

## "THIS LAST PAIN"

"This Last Pain" is invariably included in selections of Empson's best poetry. The speaker appears to be working out a means to survive, a rational acceptance of limitations both as a person and as a poet. Here Empson's total opposition to Victorian certitude and sophistry is set down without equivocation. If Robert Browning optimistically observed that "There's many a crown for who can reach," the characteristically pessimistic yet courageous Empson counters such a sanguine challenge with his belief that the damned "know the bliss with which they were not crowned." Browning proclaimed that "A man's reach should exceed his grasp,/ Or what's a heaven for?" but Empson doggedly holds that only on earth "Is all, of heaven or hell."

Even though humans might pry into the possible bliss of the soul, "may know her happiness by eye to hole," yet they are eternally denied its enjoyment. As Empson stated in his notes to "This Last Pain," "the idea of the poem is that human nature can conceive divine states which it cannot attain." Knowing this, both humans and the poet must nevertheless preserve the ontological fiction of "those large dreams by which men long live well," feigning belief and imagining that which "could not possibly be true,/ And learn a style

from a despair." In the final analysis, as Empson developed earlier in "Value Is in Activity" and "High Dive," activity is better than passivity, and even self-deception and pretense are preferable to nothing, imagination being among the gods' "ambiguous gifts."

## "BACCHUS"

In the laconically entitled "Note on Local Flora," Empson first alludes to Bacchus, that "laughing god" that would be the focus of his personal favorite and most ambitious and complex poem, "Bacchus," a work begun in Japan in 1933 and not finished until 1939 in China. Published in various fragments and first appearing in completed form in 1946, the poem assumes that the reader is familiar with the mythological details of the god's birth. Bacchus is the son of Zeus and Semele, who had asked that the supreme deity appear to her in all his glory. This was a foolish request, for as the god of lightning his presence was fatal, and she was consumed by fire and turned to ashes, an ambiguous emblem of the price one pays for fulfilling knowledge. Zeus, however, snatched their unborn child from the charred remains and carried it in his body until birth. Thus Bacchus, in the earlier brief poem, would "ripen only" as a result of fire, analogous to the cones of an exotic tree in Kew Gardens—"So Semele desired her deity" just as the tree craves fire. In the later poem, Empson characterizes the young god as "born of a startling answer" to the request of the rash Semele, who ultimately is apotheosized and borne away "robed in fire," for "The god had lit up her despair."

Notes to "Bacchus" fill almost six pages, and Empson informs the reader that "a mythological chemical operation to distil drink is going on for the first four verses." Here, by means of chemical analogy, the poet reiterates his belief that one must find existence between contradictions and explains that he chose the metaphor of drink (and Bacchus, the god of wine, as his image) because of its power to make one "most outgoing and unself-critical," and therefore better able to maintain the precarious fictions essential to emotional equilibrium and survival. This is a familiar Empson theme (he elsewhere observes that "It is not human to feel safely placed"), but here it is developed in complexity, surprising at a time when the poet was ostensibly committed to simplifying his knotted, recondite verse. In the conclusion of "Bacchus," Empson also re-affirms his admiration for those who cope, for those who maintain optimistic fictions in the face of over-powering deterministic forces.

### "AUBADE"

Empson's "Aubade" is curiously conversational, un-usually self-revealing, yet evasive in its details. Obviously about his Japanese experience in the 1930's, it is his only original poem of his years there. When asked its subject, Empson responded enigmatically that it was "about a sexual situation." Far less "clotted" than his previous verse, the poem describes an intensely personal relationship between "two aliens" parted by both the forces of nature ("Hours before dawn we were woken by the quake") and the darkening political situation, from which the European flees homeward, only to encounter "the same war on a stronger toe." As he sadly concludes, "It seemed the best thing to be up and go"; yet he is powerfully and angrily drawn to the opposite course of action. The poem, then, is another evocation of Empson's recognition of the tension inherent in con-tradiction and ambiguity, a poetic antithesis.

### THE GATHERING STORM

Continuing to reflect a change in both style and sub-ject, Empson's collection *The Gathering Storm* in-cluded among its twenty-one poems several that reflect the rising political tensions of the preceding decade: "Reflection from Rochester," with its overt reference to "race of armament"; "Courage Means Running," also in terza rima stanzas, restating Empson's belief that "To take fear as the measure/ May be a measure of self-respect"; and the chatty "Autumn on Nan-Yueh," Emp-son's longest and least difficult poem, a description of his peripatetic adventures in China in 1937. Uncongenial critics saw this calmer despair in his later work as evidence of a loss of nerve, of "rot set in," of hollow-ness, or as smoothly surfaced mannerist verse, without substance or depth of experience. Such opinions, how-ever, may reflect more the critical taste of the times than the quality of Empson's verse.

These later Empson poems appear to have been written with a real audience in mind, not that of the pre-viously idealized intellectual university milieu. They are more centripetal in effect, infused with a deeper warmth, and reflect a moral awareness missing in his earlier, flashier work. The informing intelligence now seems to suggest the acceptance of the limits of the ra-tional mind ("this deep blankness"), and the recogni-tion that destructive personal chaos cannot be ordered by logical process ("talk would . . . go so far aslant"). Instead, a static heroism emerges; a more practical stance in facing life's crises is offered.

Among these poems is "Missing Dates," a villa-nelle, a complex and challenging nineteen-line French verse form aimed at the appearance of spontaneous simplicity. "Missing Dates" is often anthologized and recognized for its intense and sustained pessimistic mood, the refrain being "Slowly the poison the whole blood fills./ The waste remains, the waste remains and kills." As a poet sensing his atrophying powers, see-ing himself "not to have fire," Empson echoes the blight and despair of *The Waste Land* (1922), a sterile land of ambiguous "partial fires," a failed situation when carpe diem should have been the prevailing philosophy.

In "Success," as Empson draws toward his conclud-ing poetic efforts (he felt "how right I was to stop writ-ing"), he asserts that by his marriage "I have mislaid the torment and the fear," and his wife "should be praised for taking them away." If "verse likes despair," and he no longer suffers, then in his new state "Lose is Find." He recognizes that as an artist "I feed on flatness" and may have sacrificed by his new happiness his poetic voice: "All loss haunts us."

A final brief poem, "Let it go," almost casual in tone, is one of only three that he wrote during World War II. In two tercets, rhyming *abc, abc*, Empson recalls his perva-sive concern with "blankness," whether emptiness, dis-interest, barrenness, lack of success, or whatever denota-tive or connotative meaning the word might suggest. In "Ignorance of Death," he admitted that "I feel very blank upon this topic," adding, however, that death "is one [topic] that most people should be prepared to be blank upon." In "Aubade," he "slept, and blank as that I would yet lie." Empson's comment that "Let it go" is "about stopping writing poetry" is not surprising. Each of the three lines in the second stanza is end-stopped; the effect is valedictory. Thus, Empson appears to offer here an alternative to continuing his dialectic of despair: a self-protective posture of blankness in the face of a personal and global "madhouse and the whole thing there."

Empson's memorable lines can be eminently savored, as Eberhart noted, "out of context with their grammatical relation to previous or succeeding lines." Total understanding is both undesirable and impossible in poetry so freighted with ambiguous contradictions. Eliot observed that "True poetry can communicate before it is understood"; in Empson's case, poetry often communicates meaning without comprehension.

Empson's efforts to fuse thinking and feeling urge the reader to accept life for what it is, to maintain sustaining "fictions," and in some way to "build an edifice of form/ For house where phantoms may keep warm" ("This Last Pain"). His forms—his poems as well as his critical essays—explore dialectically the possibilities of making limited connections, both personal and linguistic, and demonstrate by metaphysical means that reconciliation of antinomies in human existence is ultimately futile and that resolution is possible only in art, in the poems themselves.

OTHER MAJOR WORKS

PLAY: *Three Stories*, pr. 1927.

NONFICTION: *Seven Types of Ambiguity: A Study of Its Effects on English Verse*, 1930, 1947; *Some Versions of Pastoral*, 1935 (also known as *English Pastoral Poetry*); *The Structure of Complex Words*, 1951; *Milton's God*, 1961, 1965; *Using Biography*, 1984; *Essays on Shakespeare*, 1986; *Argufying: Essays on Literature and Culture*, 1987; *Faustus and the Censor*, 1987; *Essays on Renaissance Literature*, 1993-1994 (2 volumes); *The Strengths of Shakespeare's Shrew: Essays, Memoirs, and Reviews*, 1996; *Selected Letters of William Empson*, 2006.

EDITED TEXT: *Coleridge's Verse: A Selection*, 1972 (with David Pirie).

MISCELLANEOUS: *The Royal Beasts, and Other Works*, 1986.

BIBLIOGRAPHY

Constable, John, ed. *Critical Essays on William Empson*. Brookfield, Vt.: Ashgate, 1993. A collection of reviews, articles, and excerpts on the work of the poet and critic. Includes bibliographic references.

Fry, Paul H. *William Empson: Prophet Against Sacrifice*. New York: Routledge, 1991. Provides an account of this versatile critic's career and discredits the appropriation of his name by the conflicting parties of deconstruction and politicized cultural criticism. Includes a bibliography and an index.

Gill, Roma, ed. *William Empson: The Man and His Work*. Boston: Routledge & Kegan Paul, 1974. This Empson celebration features contributions by such luminaries as W. H. Auden and I. A. Richards. Some of the pieces specifically take up Empson's poetry. A hefty bibliography is provided.

Haffenden, John. *William Empson: Against the Christians*. New York: Oxford University Press, 2006. The second volume in Haffenden's biography of Empson begins during World War II and looks at Empson's work with the British Broadcasting Corporation, his time in China and the United States, and his life in England. Analyzes *Milton's God*.

_____. *William Empson: Among the Mandarins*. New York: Oxford University Press, 2005. The first volume in a biography of Empson, focusing on his studies in 1930's war-torn China and the impact that Eastern culture had on his own writing.

_____, ed. *The Complete Poems of William Empson*. Gainesville: University Press of Florida, 2001. Not merely a collection of all the poetry, including some discovered after Empson's death, this four-hundred-page book draws on unpublished papers, interviews, readings, and broadcasts to add copious appendices along with a detailed introduction by editor Haffenden. Also includes Empson's own notes, which complement the poems, and an interview with Christopher Ricks.

Leader, Zachary, ed. *The Movement Reconsidered: Essays on Larkin, Amis, Gunn, Davie, and Their Contemporaries*. New York: Oxford University Press, 2009. This collection of essays on members of the Movement includes one on Empson, as well as on Philip Larkin, Kingsley Amis, Thom Gunn, and Donald Davie.

Norris, Christopher. *William Empson and the Philosophy of Literary Criticism*. London: Athlone Press, 1978. Empson was known more for his literary criticism than he was for his poetry. Norris describes how Empson developed and applied his doctrine of poetic ambiguity. Contains bibliographical references and an index.

Sale, Roger. *Modern Heroism: Essays on D. H. Lawrence, William Empson, and J. R. R. Tolkien*. Berkeley: University of California Press, 1973. Sale analyzes these three twentieth century writers in terms of the way they used the theme of courage. Technological changes in the twentieth century shifted the meaning of heroism in literature, and these writers have helped shape a new definition. For advanced students.

Willis, John H. *William Empson*. New York: Columbia University Press, 1969. A brief (forty-five-page) review of the poetry and criticism. Calls attention to Empson's debt to T. S. Eliot and the Metaphysical poets and to his use of images and analogies from mathematics and science. Provides brief explications of many of Empson's significant poems. Contains a bibliography.

*Maryhelen Cleverly Harmon*

---

# SIR GEORGE ETHEREGE

**Born:** Maidenhead(?), England; c. 1635
**Died:** Paris(?), France; c. May 10, 1691

## PRINCIPAL POETRY

*The New Academy of Complements*, 1669
*A Collection of Poems, Written upon Several Occasions*, 1673
*Restoration Carnival*, 1954 (V. De Sola Pinto, editor)
*Poems*, 1963 (James Thorpe, editor)

## OTHER LITERARY FORMS

Sir George Etherege (EHTH-uh-rihj) is primarily known not for his poetry but for his plays. He wrote three comedies, all typical representatives of the risqué wit of Restoration comedy. His first comedy, *The Comical Revenge: Or, Love in a Tub* (pr., pb. 1644), however, tended to rely more heavily on farce and burlesque than on wit for its comic effect. His second comedy, *She Would if She Could*, followed in 1668. The play which firmly established Etherege's reputa-

tion, *The Man of Mode: Or, Sir Fopling Flutter*, appeared in 1676. The play's characters, particularly the rake Dorimant, the comic lover Sir Fopling Flutter, and the witty Harriet, are among the most memorable in Restoration comedy.

## ACHIEVEMENTS

Sir George Etherege's reputation as an accomplished dramatist is, without question, secure. In modern times, however, his poetry has been little noticed. This lack of recognition is puzzling in view of the fact that in his own age Etherege's poetry enjoyed a great deal of popularity. Many of his short lyrics were set to music by the best composers of the time, notably Henry Purcell. James Thorpe, Etherege's modern editor, points out that his poems can be found in fifty contemporary manuscripts and in 150 printed books. In his own time, Etherege was considered as accomplished a poet as the earls of Dorset and Buckingham and Thomas Sedley, Etherege's best friend, all of whom are much more frequently anthologized. His "soft lampoons," as one fellow poet expressed it, were "the best of any man." He was noted especially for his concise expression and confident control of metaphor, and for these reasons, he clearly deserves the attention of the modern reader.

Critics often speak of a particular writer as "a man of his times," and this epithet certainly applies to Etherege. His poems can be best understood and appreciated by viewing them as near-perfect reflections of the age in which he was writing. Restoration tastes, recorded so vividly in the drama of the period, emphasized wit, elegance, and sophistication, qualities which characterize Etherege's poems. If one had to characterize Etherege's poems in one word, the best choice would be "effortless." Like so many of his Restoration contemporaries, particularly his friend Sedley, Etherege mastered an art of stylish ease and naturalness. There are no jagged edges to his poetry, no profound explorations of troublesome personal questions. Instead, the reader encounters traditional, familiar themes, graced by a polished elegance.

## BIOGRAPHY

The details of Sir George Etherege's early life are sketchy. The year of his birth is tentatively identified as 1635, and not much is known of his early youth. Following the production of his first two comedies, Etherege began a sporadic diplomatic career. In 1668, he served as secretary to Sir Daniel Harvey in Turkey but returned to England three years later. Following the production of *The Man of Mode* in 1676, Etherege's life was noteworthy only for numerous drunken brawls and for his fathering a child out of wedlock. Later, he was sent to The Hague by Charles II. In 1680, he was knighted, as rumor would have it after purchasing the title so that he could marry a wealthy widow. In 1685, he was sent to Ratisbon, in what is now West Germany, by James II. His diplomatic career in Ratisbon degenerated into a dissolute life of gambling and more drunken tavern brawling. To his squalor can be added sloth and negligence, since, during his diplomatic career in Ratisbon, Etherege never bothered to learn German, and left his records in chaos for others to sort out. He died in 1691, probably in Paris.

From these biographical facts, it is presumed that Etherege was not an admirable man. What is clear, at least, is that the accounts of trickstering, gaming, drinking, loving, and debauchery found in his plays and in some of his poetry are authoritative. Etherege was truly the embodiment of the "Restoration rake."

ANALYSIS

Of the approximately thirty poems in Sir George Etherege's canon, the majority focus on the game of love, the prominent theme of his comedies. Etherege delights in investigating the wooing, the rejecting, and the successes and failures which characterize the game. In the true spirit of Restoration poetry, however, these investigations are never conducted in a personal mode; Etherege is not interested in examining love philosophically or personally. He is most often objective and detached, sometimes bemused, but never intensely involved in his subject matter. Consequently, his investigations of love appear in conventional, readily recognizable forms: the pastoral dialogue, the carpe diem theme, the "forsaken mistress" theme, and the satire based on standard Horatian and Juvenalian forms. Despite the variety of his forms, Etherege's poetic intent remains constant: to depict the game of love in all its manifestations, joyful or sorrowful, poignant or ludicrous.

"SONGS"

With this theme in mind, perhaps Etherege's most significant poem is one of his "Songs," which appears in his play *She Would if She Could*. In this song, Gatty confesses her love for Courtall. Following her song, Gatty is chided by her sister for her frank admission of affection; her sister feels she should dissemble. In this episode, one can find many of the implicit themes of Etherege's poetry in a nutshell. The rules of the game of love call for pretense rather than a sincere declaration of love. To heed this warning is to play the game successfully.

PASTORAL POEMS

Etherege occasionally wrote in the pastoral mode, loosely following a long tradition of poetry which utilizes the theme of rural bliss in uncluttered, paradisiacal settings. The artificiality of pastoral paradises was congenial to his poetic tastes since he apparently never desired to explore anything of topical, immediate significance. Instead, he preferred the timeless world of the pastoral and its often inherent paradox of unhappiness amid pastoral perfection. In his "Song: Shepherd! Why so dull a lover?" the poet exhorts the passive, lethargic shepherd to "lay your pipe a little by" and spring into action lest a life of loving pass him by. Etherege's other attempts at the pastoral, however, are bittersweet, even tragic.

In his "Song: When Phillis watched her harmless sheep," sung by Aurelia and her lady-in-waiting Letitia in Etherege's play *The Comical Revenge*, the poet opens in a rural paradise where the shepherdess Phillis happily occupies her time keeping guard over her sheep. Trouble brews, however, when "her silly heart did go astray," and her sheep, symbolizing her lost innocence and bliss, scatter. By the poem's end, the rejected Phillis wishes only to die. Thus, Etherege creates a tension between the bliss of rural retirement and the quickness with which such happiness can vanish. His exploitation of this tension is not intended, however, to carry with it any didactic message of the need to free one's life from the tyranny of love's transitoriness. Readers are meant to pity Phillis and to consider that such pain might be inflicted on them, but not necessarily to gird against the caprices of fate.

The identical theme is found in "When first Amintas charmed my heart," sung to Harriet by her lady-in-waiting, Busy, in Etherege's play, *The Man of Mode*.

Again, pastoral bliss is threatened when Amintas steals the shepherdess's heart. In this poem, however, Etherege's message is slightly more allegorically constructed. While the shepherdess dallies with Amintas, a pack of wolves that symbolizes the evils of a lack of responsibility devours her "heedless sheep." The shepherdess, who narrates her own sad tale, views the wolves' attack as a foreshadowing of her own lost happiness with Amintas as she concludes ominously, "And all will now be made a prey." Again, Etherege's message is simply the inevitable transitoriness of happiness.

The themes of these two poems afforded Etherege ample opportunity to use his poetry to expound further on the necessity of protecting oneself and others from love's destructive transitoriness. He felt no urge, however, to moralize. His sole poetic impulse was to examine the game of love from all sides. Only the playing of the game matters—a game at which no one wins.

### CARPE DIEM THEME

Two of Etherege's poems focus specifically on the carpe diem theme, a favorite in the seventeenth century, especially among the Sons of Ben and the Cavalier poets. In "To a Lady, Asking Him How Long He Would Love Her," which, as James Thorpe mentions, was probably influenced by Abraham Cowley's "Inconstancy," the lady Cloris has just asked her lover if he can pledge to her his endless love. The lover gives her the traditional answer that because all life is transitory, he can make no such guarantee. In the spirit of the carpe diem tradition, however, he urges her not to be sad but to anticipate their future bliss together, limited though it may be. This poem is noteworthy because it is one of the few times Etherege ventures forth from his amorality to assert a message of warmth. The poem concludes with the lover addressing his mistress: "Cloris, at worst you'll in the end/ But change your lover for a friend." In his other carpe diem poem, entitled simply "Song," however, his message is typically amoral. In an effort to charm his mistress out of her reticence, he compares her kisses to "those cordials which we give/ To dying men, to make them live." His motive is clear: to bedazzle his mistress into succumbing to his desires.

### LAMENT OF THE SUITOR

Counterbalanced by his two pastoral poems, wherein it is the ladies Cloris and Phillis who suffer love's rejec-

tion, are his poems which center on the laments of suitors, heartlessly spurned by their cold mistresses. Like the ludicrous lover in *The Man of Mode*, Sir Fopling Flutter, who luxuriates in his role as rejected suitor ("I sigh! I sigh!"), Etherege's poetic suitors seemingly enjoy their defeats. In his "Voiture's Urania," an imitation of a sonnet by the French poet Vincent Voiture, the rejected lover virtually revels in his despondency: "I bow beneath her tyranny." There is no trace of a resolve on the lover's part to overcome his defeat, but merely a decadent wish to pine: "Hopeless I languish out my days." The masochistic lover surfaces also in "Silvia," which, as Thorpe points out, was perhaps Etherege's most popular poem. Silvia's heartlessness is traditionally depicted: "With a frown she can kill." The poem is noteworthy, however, for its exercise of irony. With typical Restoration wit, Etherege has written the poem in a bouncy anapestic meter, the sprightliness of which ironically undermines the sadness the lover is expressing. Thus, Etherege's game of love is frequently one in which rejection can serve as an energizing force. An equally accomplished poem is his "Song," artfully constructed in two stanzas, wherein the first stanza depicts the wooing lover as a singing voice, while the second stanza portrays the mistress as a lute who, he hopes, will "tune her strings to love's discourse."

### FEMININE BEAUTY

In his continuing investigation of the game of love, Etherege also wrote two poems in the tradition of praising feminine beauty. "To a Lady Who Fled the Sight of Him," influenced, as Thorpe points out, by a Horatian ode, glorifies the beautiful lady whose natural grace and beauty, like Diana's, are sufficient to ward off lust and sexuality. Etherege's commonplace treatment of this tradition, however, is superseded in his poem "To a Very Young Lady." In this poem, the girl's beauty is compared to the rising sun, and the poet wonders how mortals will be able to view the splendor of her beauty's sun as it reaches its noon. Implicit in his praise of the girl's beauty, however, is the inevitability that her beautiful sunrise and glorious noon will eventually become a fading sunset in which the splendor of her beauty will vanish. As is so often the case with Etherege's poetry, this implicit message is not intended as a moral mandate to discourage the lady from worldly preoccupations. If anything, the poet's intent is to remind her uncharitably and with no small trace of cruelty that at any time an "untimely frost" can decay "early glories."

### MISOGYNIST THEMES

This hint of misogyny, ironically embedded in a poem praising feminine beauty, bursts forth with greater intensity in his "Song: Ladies, though to your conquering eyes," which appears in his play *The Comical Revenge*. In this poem, Etherege steps out of his normally cool, detached tone to deliver an angry message to ladies who enjoy spurning their suitors. He snarls, "Then wrack not lovers with disdain/ Lest love on you revenge their pain." Similarly, in a "Song" that appears in a tavern scene in *The Comical Revenge*, the message is clearly stated that men should stay away from aloof women as they are only good for wasting one's time. Instead, men are instructed to "Make much of every buxom girl/ Which needs but little courting." Finally, in his "Song: To happy youths," which, as Thorpe notes, was patterned after Juvenal's sixth satire, Etherege's misogyny is most evident. He warns youth that happiness can be attained only through avoidance of women. No matter how beautiful the woman, he warns, "The snake's beneath the flower." In these three poems, the game of love has lost its charm for Etherege. Tender flirtation and wanton affection are replaced by crudeness and even cruelty toward the woman. Once again, however, no moral message is intended in the poet's disgust. These dark looks at love merely express a temporary loss of a desire to play the game, not a realization of the emptiness of such pursuits.

An uncharacteristic work among Etherege's love poems is "The Divided Heart," in which the poet is worried that his mistress, Celia, will not always be as faithful as she is now. "The Divided Heart" stands alone stylistically as Etherege's only experiment in the courtly tradition of love poetry. It is written in a consciously elegant, stylized manner, which differs from his usual effortless, easy style. On the opposite end of the spectrum is "The Imperfect Enjoyment," which, as Richard E. Quaintance believes, belongs to a genre initiated by Ovid: A lover, initially frustrated by the reluctance of his mistress, is overjoyed when she suddenly becomes receptive to his sexual advances. At the critical moment, however, he is unable to perform the sex

act, and again he is left to languish in frustration. Not surprisingly, the genre underwent a modest revival during the Restoration. In Etherege's poem, the lover concludes that none of this would have happened if his mistress had been "less fair." Although the poem is not bawdy, the low comedy of the lover's misfortunes is far removed from the lofty, stylized elegance of "The Divided Heart" and is yet another indication of the diversity with which Etherege explores the game of love.

### SATIRIC POETRY

In addition to the many poems in which he investigated the game of love, Etherege tried his hand occasionally at satire. Like his love poems, his satires are not didactic attempts at exposing and reforming the hypocrisies of humankind but merely exercises in light, frivolous ridicule. The fervor with which people can become involved in card games is mocked in his poem "A Song on Basset," and the reader is tempted to wonder whether Alexander Pope had read it prior to his account of the game of ombre in *The Rape of the Lock* (1712, 1714). Etherege also composed four satires on John Sheffield, the earl of Mulgrave, the first and most noteworthy of which is entitled "Ephelia to Bajazet." Bajazet is the earl of Mulgrave, who, according to Thorpe, was so extraordinarily ugly that he verged on the grotesque. To compound the absurdity of the man, he was insufferably vain as well. The forsaken Ephelia mourns her rejection at the hands of her cruel Bajazet. Again, one can detect no reforming impulse in the satire, only ridicule. Etherege leaves the decision up to the reader as to who is the more ludicrous: the grotesque, loathsome Mulgrave or the pitiably absurd forsaken mistress who would lament the loss of such an undesirable scoundrel.

Perhaps his most intriguing satire, "A Prologue Spoken at the Opening of the Duke's New Playhouse," reflects Etherege's concern as a dramatist with the problems of having to pander to the public's taste. In this satire, the speaker is a typical Restoration theater owner who proclaims his delight in catering to the extravagant, even vulgar tastes of his audiences. Much of his defense of his pandering centers on his metaphor comparing a play to a kept woman. Just as the woman demands increasingly ornate surroundings, so also do the play and the theater demand more ostentation to appeal to their audiences. The poem is noteworthy as a reflection of Etherege's concern that the dramatists of the period were being increasingly pressured to construct their plays as vulgar extravaganzas.

In both his love poetry and his satires, Etherege accurately reflects the poetic tastes of the Restoration. His poems are witty, sophisticated, detached—without a trace of personal investment. His investigations of love are sometimes poignant, sometimes comic, sometimes sympathetic, sometimes arrogant. At no point, however, does Etherege allow a moral tone to creep into his poetry. He does not demand that the reader consider the moral responsibilities of love, only the game playing itself. Effortless shaping of his poetry, not didactic content, was Etherege's chief goal, and he accomplished it as successfully as any of his more famous Restoration contemporaries.

## OTHER MAJOR WORKS

PLAYS: *The Comical Revenge: Or, Love in a Tub*, pr., pb. 1664; *She Would if She Could*, pr., pb. 1668; *The Man of Mode: Or, Sir Fopling Flutter*, pr., pb. 1676.

NONFICTION: *The Letterbook of Sir George Etherege*, 1928 (Sybil Rosenfeld, editor); *Letters of Sir George Etherege*, 1973.

MISCELLANEOUS: *The Works of Sir George Etherege: Containing His Plays and Poems*, 1704; *The Works of Sir George Etherege: Plays and Poems*, 1888 (A. W. Verity, editor).

## BIBLIOGRAPHY

Boswell, Eleanore. "Sir George Etherege." *Review of English Studies: A Quarterly Journal of English Literature and the English Language* 7 (1931): 207-209. Offers some new information on Etherege's life, particularly during his diplomatic stay at Ratisbon.

Dobree, Bonamy. "His Excellency Sir George Etherege." In *Essays in Biography, 1680-1726*. 1925. Reprint. Freeport, N.Y.: Books for Libraries Press, 1967. In 1685, Etherege went to Ratisbon, in Bavaria, as James II's envoy, and three years later, he left for Paris after the accession of William and Mary. Dobree does not discuss the plays but provides an amusing account of Etherege's licentious behavior and the eventual diminishment of his powers.

Etherege, George, Sir. *The Poems of Sir George Etherege*. Edited by James Thorpe. Princeton, N.J.: Princeton University Press, 1963. This collection is included in secondary sources because the preface by Thorpe provides some useful insights into Etherege's poetry. Notes that in his own time, Etherege was a poet of consequence, his poems being frequently copied. Thorpe remarks that although Etherege chose conventional themes, he nevertheless gave an edge to them in his poems.

Gill, Pat. *Interpreting Ladies: Women, Wit, and Morality in the Restoration Comedy of Manners*. Athens: University of Georgia Press, 1995. This study of women in Restoration comedies examines Etherege's *The Man of Mode* as well as works by William Wycherley and William Congreve.

Huseboe, Arthur R. *Sir George Etherege*. Boston: Twayne, 1987. A useful volume on Etherege's works, including background information on his life and the times in which he lived. Chapter 5 comments on his poetry and mentions that Etherege's poems were widely known in his time but have lost their popularity. Discusses his love poems, including those that were also songs, and poems of praise.

Kachur, B. A. *Etherege and Wycherley*. New York: Palgrave Macmillan, 2004. Although this work looks at the plays of Etherege and William Wycherley, it focuses on the cultural and historical context, thereby providing information useful to the understanding of Etherege's poetry.

Mann, David D. *A Concordance to the Plays and Poems of Sir George Etherege*. Westport, Conn.: Greenwood Press, 1985. A valuable resource for Restoration scholars. Includes approximately thirty poems written between 1663 and 1688. Discusses Etherege's use of language and allusions in the introduction. Cites Bracher's comments on Etherege as a man with a "shrewd eye for pretense and hypocrisy."

_____. *Sir George Etherege: A Reference Guide*. Boston: G. K. Hall, 1981. This guide to Etherege scholarship is designed to help scholars find their way in Restoration drama. Although it needs to be supplemented with bibliographies of recent work, it is extremely useful for the period it covers.

*Elizabeth J. Bellamy*